THE BFI COMPANION TO THE WESTERN

THE BFI
COMPANION TO THE
WESTERN

— EDITED BY —
EDWARD BUSCOMBE

— FOREWORD BY —
RICHARD SCHICKEL

— CONSULTANT EDITORS —
CHRISTOPHER BROOKEMAN, EDWARD COUNTRYMAN,
CHRISTOPHER FRAYLING, PHIL HARDY

A DA CAPO PAPERBACK

Library of Congress Cataloging-in-Publication Data

BFI companion to the western.
The British Film Institute companion to the western/edited by
Edward Buscombe: foreword by Richard Schickel: consultant editors.
Christopher Brookeman . . . [et al.].
p.   cm. — (A Da Capo paperback)
Reprint. Originally published: The BFI companion to the western.
New York: Atheneum, 1988.
Includes bibliographical references and index.
ISBN 0-306-80440-9
1. Western films—United States—Encyclopedias.
2. Western films—United States—History and criticism.
3. Motion picture producers and directors—United States—
Biography—Encyclopedias.   4. West (U.S.)—Encyclopedias.
I. Buscombe, Edward.   II. British Film Institute.   III. Title.
PN1995.9.W4B45 1991
791.43'6278—dc20   91-7906 CIP

This Da Capo Press paperback edition of
The BFI Companion to the Western is an unabridged republication
of the edition published in London in 1988. It is reprinted by
arrangement with Atheneum Publishers.

Published by Da Capo Press, Inc.
A Subsidiary of Plenum Publishing Corporation
233 Spring Street, New York, N.Y. 10013

Printed in Singapore
by Kim Hup Lee Printing Co. Pte. Ltd.

For Jessie, my own cactus rose

MAPS

CONTENTS

Joanne Dru in John Ford's
Wagon Master (1950)

An ENCYCLOPEDIA of Western movies! I never thought I'd live to see the day. Not so long ago, when the Western seemed the movies' most basic and immutable form, and new ones issued forth almost weekly, the idea of such a book would have been utterly improbable, if only because it would have been out of date before it was through the press. Now that it is actually here, I find myself, frankly, somewhat saddened. For useful and attractive as this volume is, its codification of a great screen tradition can have only one meaning: it is the signpost that marks the end of a long and lovely trail.

Thinking about Westerns I find my mind turning to a novel that prefigured my feelings of this moment, Willa Cather's poignant elegy for the land and the people of her youth, *A Lost Lady*. In it, a young man named Niel Herbert functions as the author's surrogate. They shared the same background; they were raised in the last decades of the 19th century in a small town on Nebraska's High Plains 'buried in wheat and corn' as she put it, and dominated, too, by the spirit, and the memories, of the parents and grandparents who had pioneered this good and bountiful land. They shared something else too: a sense that the era of the 'road-making West' was 'already gone ... and nothing could ever bring it back.' She insisted Niel remember it and bear witness to its glories: 'The taste and smell and song of it, the visions these men had seen in the air and followed, – these he had caught in a kind of afterglow in their own faces, – and this would always be his.' Obviously, she felt everyone should emulate him.

Many would. Many more than this great writer could possibly imagine. For moving as that passage is, its emotions are a trifle premature. Absorbed in a hard and lonely task, that of redeeming the American westering experience for a serious literature not much interested in the subject, Willa Cather was unaware that her need to recall and preserve frontier values was widely shared by her contemporaries; unaware that the aura that was so precious to her was not as evanescent as she feared, and unaware, since she disliked movies, of what that new medium was doing to capture and amplify the West's 'afterglow'. But, ironically, by 1923, when she published the plangent passage we have just read, the entire world was beginning to possess it. And be possessed by it.

Some good luck was at work here. The gathering power of urbanization and industrialization focused the attention of the generations that came of age around the turn of the century – including even those who knew nothing at first hand about the West – on the landscapes and values these forces threatened. From 1893, when Frederick Jackson Turner, the historian, published his seminal essay on the significance of the frontier in shaping the American mind and spirit, until the United States entered World War I, anxiety about these matters was central to the nation's consciousness. Whether they were expanding the national park system to preserve a few corners of untamed wilderness for future reference, or romanticizing 'the vanishing American' (the Indian), or simply attending a Wild West Show or making *The Great Train Robbery* the movies' first hit, Americans continually demonstrated that they knew what they were losing and would do whatever they could to arrest the process.

The movies' founding fathers, naturally, were of these generations. Many who emerged as the great Western stars, directors and writers were actually raised in the region they would devote their careers to celebrating. It was easy for them to discern the obvious affinity between the new medium and the Old West. Its vistas called out irresistibly to the camera; everything about the exploration and settlement of the frontier had, in their eyes, the epic air and mythic potential the movies needed – and could so easily accommodate.

We know, of course, that one of the reasons Los Angeles emerged, around 1910, as the movie capital was the easy access it provided to suitable locations for the most popular genre of the moment, the Western. In those pre-metropolitan days it was, moreover, in spirit a real western town, the last railhead on the Santa Fe line. Ranching was still one of California's major industries, and Los Angeles was always full of genuine cowboys who had driven their herds to market there or had simply come to town to spend their pay. Raoul Walsh, a director who had been a cowhand in his youth, would recall that one of his first movie jobs was rounding up stray cowboys after the saloons closed, helping them on their horses and, before dawn, leading them across the hills to Western locations in the San Fernando Valley. (One wonders if, possibly, they clip-clopped past a young emigrant to the valley, John Wayne, on his way to school.)

Thus did authenticity and marvellous riding become available for a dollar a day and a box lunch. If, generally speaking, it was not good for the movies – and movie people – that their chief production centre was established so far from the nation's cultural centres, it was a fine thing for the Western. Everyone did not establish the kind of mystical affinity with the region and its myths that William S. Hart did. ('These hills were mine, and had been mine since my birth,' this sometime travelling player in melodramas grandly proclaimed, though he was actually born in New York.) But for almost everyone working in Westerns, at whatever level, the passing of the frontier and its values was not a subject for idle nostalgia; it was a matter they had anxiously internalized. And it was the most natural and vital subject they could imagine taking up. As late as 1959, when he was making *Rio Bravo*, Howard Hawks would request 'some of that Charlie Russell light' from his cameraman; Hawks had known the great western painter, who spent his late years in Los Angeles, and he had owned some of his paintings. He knew exactly what he was talking about, exactly what he wanted.

So it was. So it had always been. There was no place in America where the 'afterglow' of the pioneering West shone more brightly, no place where the manner and speech, the lore and legend of the Old West could more easily be summoned, no place where its myths more powerfully resonated than in Los Angeles, California in the first half of this century. As a result a form that was narratively as highly stylized as any other movie genre was grounded in a felt reality (and a felt morality, too) that more exotically imagined and situated Hollywood products could not duplicate.

Whatever scenic grandeur it offered, whatever terrors raw nature, raw savagery or the raw greed of the bad men imposed upon its protagonists, the Western was in the final analysis a chaste and homey form, in which quite ordinary and unpretentious people were seen to be doing what we in the audience were also trying to do – building homes and businesses and communities, preserving traditional individualistic values in hard circumstances. This was, of course, John Ford's great theme. He instinctively understood that we did not much want to see contemporary social realism about these subjects, but that the Western could comfortably and engagingly transform them, by placing them in settings that granted them heroic scale and in a context where, since everyone wore a six-shooter, complex moral conflicts could be plausibly resolved in clear, clean violent action.

Another way of putting this is that for most Americans in the first half of this century the typical Western tale was placed at just the right distance from us. It was not too near, not too far, not too quotidian, not too exotic. When I was a boy in the 1940s I sometimes silently shared a porch glider with a handsome and erect old man – clear blue eyes, a great white handlebar moustache. I could never bring myself to speak to him, for he was a retired army officer who, in his youth, had done this awesome thing: he had participated in the pursuit of Geronimo. His sister, who kept house for him, told about seeing the renegade chieftain in captivity. She mentioned the cruel length of his fingernails. People like them, who formed living links between our past and the fictions that helped keep it vivid, were among us until just a moment ago. When the last of them began to pass on, an occurrence implicitly proclaimed by the End-of-the-West Westerns of the 1960s, it became clear that the Western was not as universal or as timeless thematically as its makers or its audience or its first critics and scholars had believed.

It is easy enough to analyze and imitate the comparatively simple fictional foundations on which most Westerns were built, easier still to ape the highly conventionalized visual and verbal mannerisms of the form. Every once in a while a young film-maker still does so. But the work always turns out to be either a conscious (*Silverado*) or an unconscious (*Heaven's Gate*) parody, teaching us a surprising thing: that the Western is (or was) a very fragile form, uniquely dependent upon first-hand knowledge and living memory for its vitality, dependent too on an unspoken conspiracy between the older movie-makers and the older movie audiences to keep alive, if I may borrow another phrase from Willa Cather, 'the precious, the incommunicable past'. Memory, of course, is art's essential ingredient; when it is not present, authenticity is also absent and we are left, at best, with artfulness – and artiness.

Let us, then, propose this paradox: that its very fragility proves that the Western – while it lived the humblest, most familiar and therefore the most easily dismissed movie genre – may actually have been the medium's highest form, depending more fully on genuine experience, authentic recall, than any other for its power. Now that we are bereft of those shaping, creative forces, Americans in particular are bereft as well of an incalculably useful aspect of our past. 'The taste and smell and song of it' no longer reach us in powerfully affecting form. Nor the visions that once shimmered on the western air. Now we must look them up in reference books. And Willa Cather's long-ago elegy strikes us with full force.

CONTRIBUTORS

BA Blaine Allan
MA Manuel Alvarado
CB Christopher Brookeman
CBO Christine Bold
CBU Clive Bush
EB Edward Buscombe
JB John Belton
EC Edward Countryman
JC John Clum
PC Pam Cook
RC Richard Collins
JD Jerome Delamater
PD Phillip Drummond
CF Christopher Frayling
DG Dennis Giles
DGI Denis Gifford
JG Jane Gaines
MG Mick Gidley
BH Brian Henderson
JH John Hawkridge
PH Phil Hardy
DK Diane Koszarski
HL Hartmut Lutz
JL Jack Lodge
TM Tony Mechele
TMI Tom Milne
KN Kim Newman
JP Julian Petley
JPI Jim Pines
MP Martin Pumphrey
TP Tim Pulleine
LQ Leonard Quart
DR Don Ranvaud
TR Tom Ryall
PS Peter Stanfield
RS Richard Slotkin
PT Paul Taylor
ST Stephen Tatum
TV Tise Vahimagi
CW Christopher Wicking
DW David Wilson
GW Graham Webb
JW Jon Whyte
PW Paul Willemen

All unsigned contributions are by the Editor

THE WESTERN is the major genre of the world's major national cinema. Since *The Great Train Robbery* in 1903 more than 7,000 cinema Westerns have been made in the USA, and since the late 1940s several thousand episodes of Western series have appeared on television. And the Western has never been an exclusively American phenomenon. From the earliest years Westerns have been hugely popular in Europe and elsewhere in the world; so much so that several hundred have been made outside the United States in the past quarter of a century.

Nor can the Western be confined to the cinema. By the end of the 19th century a huge corpus of material on the West had accumulated: books of fiction, of history and travel, paintings and sculptures, drawings and photographs and other artifacts. On these the early Western film drew for its raw material and its inspiration, and in the 20th century the flood of literary and visual matter has continued unabated.

Both the volume of this body of work and its imaginative richness compel our attention, yet the enduring vitality and centrality of the Western within the popular culture of our time has still not received its due. Compared to the output of scholarly literature on Arthurian legend or the Homeric epic, the respect paid to the Western is pitifully slight.

Doubtless the sheer proliferation of the genre is a daunting obstacle to exploration. Just as the early settlers in North America hugged the coastline, keeping to their small parcels of domesticated territory, so the written history of the Western has been confined mostly to well-trodden paths. The same small number of films selected from the great hinterland of the genre's past are recirculated over and over again in books and in television and cinema screenings.

No single volume can set out to excavate the Western in its entirety and redeem this neglect. *The BFI Companion to the Western* has two main aims. In the first place, it presents a panoramic history of the cinematic Western which, if it cannot record every feature, tries to encompass more than just the peaks made familiar in earlier histories. It recognizes the contribution not only of directors and stars, but of cameramen, scriptwriters, bit-part players; not only of

the justly famous but of such half-forgotten figures as Francis Ford (brother of the great John), or the silent star and director Nell Shipman. It traces continuities between the silent period and what came after, and acknowledges the crucial role of the B-Western in underpinning the economics of Hollywood. And, unusually for a work of reference, it views television as an extension of the movies.

From this perspective, the focus is on the Western as *cinema*. The Western's narrative structure and motifs are seen to derive less from any real world than from the economic and artistic imperatives of Hollywood, each film finding its plausibility and terms of reference in the audience's previous experience of the genre. This is the thrust of Part I of the book, a short history which traces the development of the Western from the beginning of the 20th century to its most recent achievements.

But from another viewpoint the Western can be seen as a form of *cultural expression*, its characteristic themes and field of reference the product of a long history, in which the real actions of individuals were transformed by the work of scores of writers, artists, ideologues and entrepreneurs into a myth with its roots deep in American society. The second purpose of *The BFI Companion to the Western* is to act as a comprehensive guide to the myth's foundations. Part II takes the form of a dictionary of people, places, events and ideas which have made their mark on the Western. It accords as much attention to the work of the imagination as to historical realities. Fenimore Cooper's Natty Bumppo never existed, but he is as important to the world of the Western as Wyatt Earp, who did. Natty, moreover, was in part based on the real-life figure of Daniel Boone, whereas the cinematic image of Wyatt Earp derives from biographies that are as much works of fiction as of fact. And yet, the legend of Earp has its own imaginative truth which survives our knowledge of his actual character; while the Daniel Boone who is the basis of Natty Bumppo was in turn partly a creation of fanciful biographers. All of which goes to show that we cannot understand the Western just by separating fact from fiction; we need to trace the processes whereby reality imparts credibility to myth, and myth charges reality with imaginative power.

Thus the substantial essays on subjects of particular importance such as Indians, or violence, or the significance of the railroad in Western films, are not chiefly concerned with narrower questions of historical accuracy (though they are never cavalier with the facts), but rather with the resonances which historical facts acquire within films. Thus more space is devoted to the question, why is violence so central in the Western, than to the (more easily answered) one, was there in fact as much violence in the West as in the Western?

Not that the Western is all weighty historical themes. Part II also indexes actions such as taking a bath or rolling a cigarette, plot-devices like the feud or the quest for revenge, and stereotypical characters like the old-timer; each is seen as a nugget of cultural significance sedimented within the strata of the genre, no less important than landscape or historical events in establishing that solidity and authenticity and flavour which allow the audience the pleasure of recognizing the genre.

Part III refocuses on specific films, comprising entries on three hundred selected Westerns. At the end of the day, what makes the Western genre hold our attention is the extraordinary number of good films it contains. Inevitably, limitations of space prevented the inclusion of an entry on every film of importance. The three hundred selected represent, in the Editor's judgement, those which most merit our continued attention for both artistic and historical reasons. If the selection is found to be contentious, the defence must be that any other list would be equally so, and it is hoped that at least there is some consistency in the prejudices revealed.

Part IV consists of entries on those film-makers who left the Western a more considerable thing than they found it. Again, pressures on space were acute. The final selection, though inevitably influenced by personal preferences and critical fashion, is a considered attempt at a balance between stars and character actors, directors and other technicians, and between the silent and sound periods. (The silent Western, it must be admitted, suffers particularly badly from the pressures of space in Part III.)

Part V of the book is the only one which tries to be complete. It contains an entry on every Western television series and every made-for-TV Western. Reference works on the cinema usually ignore television, on the grounds that the two media are separate (and, by implication, unequal). Though we cannot claim to have granted television equal space, we have tried to point to the essential continuity between the cinematic and television Western, in terms of both personnel and content.

NOTE TO THE READER

In compiling filmographies the net has been thrown wide to include most borderline cases. Thus contemporary Westerns such as *Hud*, musicals such as *Oklahoma!* and hybrids such as *Westworld* all find a place. All films are given their original title. Where the American or British title differs from the original a cross-reference can be found in the index, though alternative titles which are particularly well known are given for those films which have entries in Part III. The date given for a film is the year when it was copyrighted, registered or reviewed by the appropriate censorship authority. Dates may sometimes differ from those in other reference books, but we are following the standard practice of the British Film Institute as outlined in the National Film Archive's *Catalogue of Stills, Posters and Designs*. In Part II the filmographies which follow some entries (e.g. Davy Crockett) and which list the films in which historical or fictional characters appear contain not only titles but basic credits. This has led to some duplication, but is surely preferable to displacing such information to the end of the book and obliging the reader to keep a finger permanently stuck in an index. In general an oblique (/) is used to separate successive pieces of information; it does not indicate alternatives. In Part II films are listed in the form: actor playing the role (where appropriate) / title / date / production company / director / leading players. All the film lists in Part II are complete unless otherwise stated. When the title of a film appears in the text followed only by an oblique and a date (*The Searchers*/1956) this signals that there is a separate entry for this film in Part III, and therefore no further credits are given. Cross-references to other entries in Part II are indicated by an asterisk. A list of cross-references of topics and persons entered under another heading (e.g. Hopalong Cassidy under Clarence Edward Mulford) will be found in the Appendix. All films and televi-

sion shows listed in Parts III and V are in colour unless stated otherwise. In the filmographies in Part IV the credits given are for work in the role initially stated in the entry, unless indicated otherwise. Thus Charles Marquis Warren is listed as 'director'. Those films for which he also wrote the script are preceded by (*sc*); those films for which he wrote the script but did not direct are preceded by (*sc only*). The lists which appear in entries for novelists are of films based on their books. Only if an entry is preceded by (*sc*) have they also written the script. Square brackets indicate the original title of a novel on which a film is based. The novel sources of many films are listed under the entry **Sources** in Part II. All the filmographies in Part IV give a complete list of Westerns on which the subject worked, except that apprentice-work (for example as assistant director) is not usually included. Dates given in filmographies in Part IV for television work (e.g. *Gunsmoke*/55) are the year of a first appearance in a series. It proved impossible to list dates of television credits in Part II, though the dates of all television shows can be found in Part V.

ABBREVIATIONS are as follows: AA Allied Artists; COL Columbia; FOX 20th Century-Fox (Fox before 1936); Fr France; GB Great Britain; It Italy; Mex Mexico; MGM Metro-Goldwyn-Mayer; MON Monogram; PAR Paramount; PRC Producers Releasing Corporation; REP Republic; RKO Radio-Keith-Orpheum; Sp Spain; U Universal; UA United Artists; WB Warner Bros.; WG West Germany; *act* actor; *c* cinematographer; *ch* choreography; *cr* created by; *d* director; *ep* episodes; *lp* leading players; *m* music composed by; *md* musical director; *p* producer; *s* (*sc* in Part IV) scriptwriter; *st* story by.

EVEN MORE THAN most books, a work of reference builds upon the work of others. Without those whose labours are recorded in the bibliography there would have been no foundations. My more immediate and personal debt is to my fellow contributors, who are named individually elsewhere. I am also grateful to the four consultant editors on the *Companion*, Chris Brookeman, Ed Countryman, Chris Frayling and Phil Hardy, not only for their signed and visible contributions but for their advice, suggestions and, especially, their enthusiasm. I

doubt if they knew how much that meant. The initial conception for this *Companion* came from the Head of BFI Publishing, Geoffrey Nowell-Smith, who also managed to find the resources which made it possible. Other colleagues in BFI Publishing, especially Roma Gibson, John Smoker and David Wilson, were generous with their time and expertise. The contribution to the book made by John Gibbs was far greater than his title of designer could possibly suggest. A debt of a very different kind I owe to those people who fired and fed my enthusiasm for the Western at a formative period in my life. Those Sunday afternoons I spent with Richard Jacques in the Gaiety and the Embassy in the mid-1960s were a golden age. In 1967 I was a student at the BFI Summer School at St Andrews. The subject of study was the Western and the teachers were Paddy Whannel, Alan Lovell, Jim Kitses, Colin McArthur, Victor Perkins and Peter Wollen. It was a crucial turning point for me, though at the time it felt like two weeks of sheer indulgence. Some of the named contributors must be singled out for special mention. Tise Vahimagi not only took care of the entire television section. He also, with his colleague in BFI Stills, Markku Salmi, rode point along the trail, alerting me to the many ambushes that lie in wait for the unwary filmographer. If the book still contains some maverick entries Tise and Markku cannot be held responsible. Tony Mechele provided invaluable information and advice. Jack Lodge spent many hours checking filmographies; much of whatever has been achieved in terms of accuracy is due to him. Mick Gidley and Christine Bold also provided important assistance, Other BFI colleagues who have contributed beyond the call of duty, or just taken an interest, include David Meeker, Peter Seward, Jim Adams, and staff in the viewing service of the National Film Archive, in the BFI Library and in the BFI Stills, Posters and Designs Department. Mary Corliss of the Museum of Modern Art and Chris Horak of George Eastman House were also invaluable sources of illustrations. Christine Vincent was a tireless picture researcher. Thanks also to Ray & Corinne Burrows for the maps. Bob Baker and Robin McCron helped with information. Laura Morris, editor at André Deutsch, was unfailingly cheerful whatever the difficulties, and always found a solution. Many thanks to Manuel Alvarado, for never once insisting I change the subject. Above all, my undying gratitude to Sarah Boston, for everything else. EB

PART I

THE WESTERN:
A SHORT HISTORY

THE WESTERN is a world of its own; a world more fully-rounded, solid and extensive, perhaps, than any other in fiction; to many more real than any but the one we actually inhabit. It is a world instantly evoked in a host of images and phrases: the good guys and the bad guys, cowboys and Indians, riding off into the sunset. An intimate knowledge of the ways of the Western has spread, during the century or so since it was invented, through all countries and cultures. From Timbuctoo to Tokyo, from Montevideo to Manchester, the figure of a man in a ten-gallon hat is recognizable to all.

The explanation for the astonishing popularity of the Western can be contained in one word: Hollywood. Other countries have had their own myths and heroes: the samurai, King Arthur, El Cid. None of them has been realized in such detail or disseminated to so many people as the Western. Though the cinema did not invent him, the cowboy has galloped through the imagination of the world because American films and American television have, for the past seventy years, saturated the world market. This economic domination, and the huge volume of production that it sustained, have permitted the basic elements of the Western, Hollywood's most popular genre, to be elaborated in literally thousands of variations, distributed into virtually every country of the world.

The resultant richness of the Western's frame of reference has allowed other forms of popular culture and commodity production to feed off it. The Western myth has overflowed its origins in visual and written narrative and fertilized popular music, fashion, children's toys, advertising, and even our everyday speech. When we say an organization has too many chiefs and not enough Indians, when a television programme makes a round-up of the news, when we have a show-down with somebody or our plans don't pan out, we draw on a shared memory sedimented by the consumption of countless Western stories.

Even those who would never call themselves devotees know that the typical Westerner's diet is bacon and beans and his preferred drink coffee or whiskey. In such an elaborately coded universe any departure from the norm is likely to be significant. Wine instead of whiskey probably means we're in Mexico, or in an Italian Western. When in *The Man from Laramie* James Stewart is offered a cup of tea his expression speaks volumes.

No other genre in the cinema delineates so precisely the details of everyday life. Other genres may have appropriate styles of dress: uniforms for war films, togas and helmets for epics. The Western is remarkable for the consistency and rigour with which costumes are assigned to particular roles. Contrary to caricature, the good guys have never been restricted to white hats and the bad guys to black (only those who have never seen Hopalong Cassidy can believe that). But it remains true that a character in a black frock coat, bootlace tie and embroidered waistcoat will be likely to carry a deck of cards about him. As for the cowboy himself, the basic outfit of wide-brimmed hat, jeans and boots has remained constant, despite the subtle but significant variations which modulate between the authentic historical costume and the dictates of contemporary fashion. Nor is dress any less codified for women. The respectable married woman may, it seems, wear one sort of costume and one only: a dress of some sturdy material, typically in a check pattern, buttoned up to the neck, close-fitting round the waist and with a full skirt. The more this costume is deviated from, the further from respectability does its wearer stray.

Consider too the different forms of transport. Supreme is the horse. The horse confers dignity and status. To go on foot is an unthinkable humiliation. To ride a mule or donkey is either to suffer indignity or to be a Mexican (in the Western, despite recent concessions to ethnic sensitivities, much the same thing). Only women, men over a certain age or dudes ride in buggies. When the horse begins to give way to the train, the West is changing. When, as at the beginning of Sam Peckinpah's *Ride the High Country*, it gives way to the car or motorbike the West is fast disappearing. A change in the means of transport, then, marks one of the limits of the genre.

The Western is not merely a milieu or a way of life, but another world, or at least another country. As such it has its own language: its own vocabulary, syntax and accent. Even an English ear can distinguish the difference; not merely the scores of words, many derived from Spanish, which are specific to the Western (buckaroo, chaps, remuda, lasso), but forms of expression. When Henry Fonda in *My Darling Clementine* is asked to dance he replies, 'I'd admire to, ma'am.' In any film other than a Western such a phrase would surely mark him as a hick. Whole sentences from the Western have become common currency: 'A man's gotta do what a man's gotta do.' As for accent and intonation, if there is no adequate way in print to convey the peculiarities of Western speech, we all know a drawl when we hear one.

A SENSE OF PLACE   Yet however successfully it may create the illusion of a self-sustaining world, the Western film has its origins in a specific historical experience and in the wide variety of cultural responses to it. Ever since the discovery of America by Europeans in 1492, those who encountered this strange new land have been trying to make sense of it through factual accounts, imaginative literature, visual representations and other forms of discourse. The first accounts of the West are travellers' tales, written for a European audience eager to hear of the marvels discovered in this 'new world'. From the time of Columbus, America was a source of exotic descriptions of wondrous landscapes, animals and people, and of events both terrifying and inspiring. By the beginning of the 19th century the American 'West' had taken on a character of its own as its location had shifted, first out across the Appalachians and then beyond into that vast area west of the Mississippi, opened up to exploration by the United States through the

Louisiana Purchase in 1803. The exploits of explorers such as Lewis and Clark, Zebulon Pike, John Frémont and John Wesley Powell were written up and disseminated to armchair travellers in the east and in Europe. As the hardships and dangers associated with journeying through the interior of North America became more manageable, scores of writers, celebrated and obscure, rushed into print with their impressions. Several of these, including George Frederick Ruxton, Washington Irving, Francis Parkman and Mark Twain, directly influenced the popular image of what the West was like. Ruxton helped create the figure of the mountain man, Irving and Parkman captured something of the vastness and wildness of the Great Plains before settlers arrived, and Mark Twain produced an unforgettable portrait of the mining frontier in Nevada.

As the very name 'Western' indicates, one of the ways in which we most readily identify a Western film is through its setting. It seems safe to say that a large part of the Western's appeal, especially to easterners and non-Americans, derives from the exotic beauty of the wide open spaces of the plains, mountains and deserts of the trans-Mississippi West. Though very few Westerns have dealt with the actual exploits of explorers or travellers, the evocation of the spirit of place, that sense of the West as a distinctive and special environment which they first articulated, can scarcely be over-estimated as an attraction of Western films. Think, for example, how many contain a place name in their title: *Colorado Territory*, *Rio Bravo*, *North to Alaska*. This is just as true of the B-Western, which we might suppose would operate in a fantasy no-man's-land in which specific geographical reference is subordinate to plot and action. To take an arbitrary example, between 1936 and 1943 the Republic studio made 51 films in their Three Mesquiteers series. Of these, 17 make an explicit reference in their title to a particular locality: the Rockies twice, the Black Hills, Santa Fe twice, the Red River, Texas three times, Wyoming, Kansas, Oklahoma, the Pecos, Sonora, the Cherokee Trail, the Cimarron, the Rio Grande.

What is evoked is of course an imaginative rather than an actual geography. The B-Western with its budget restrictions could rarely afford to shoot in the locations the titles invoked. Even in bigger-budget films authenticity is by no means always observed. The real physical locations in which John Ford's Westerns are shot are often hundreds of miles from where the drama is set. Nevertheless, geographical allusion would appear to constitute one of the parameters of the genre. Westerns must be set in the West.

Attempts by critics to pin down the geographical limits of the genre, however, fail to understand the subtlety of the relation between actual and imaginative geography. Philip French in his book *Westerns* defines the limits as 'west of the Mississippi, south of the 49th Parallel and north of the Rio Grande'. This surely will not do. Many films set outside the trans-Mississippi West still fall within the genre. Mexico and the far north are legitimate settings. Both physically and culturally Mexico can be seen as an extension of Arizona, New Mexico and Texas, while Canada is a northern continuation of the Rockies and plains. It would be an odd definition of the Western which excluded *The Far Country* (set in the Yukon) or *The Wild Bunch* (set mostly in Mexico). *Drums Along the Mohawk* and *Northwest Passage* are notable Westerns set east of the Mississippi. Then there is the Florida Western, dealing with the wars against the Seminole. And what of Hopalong Cassidy, who journeyed as far as China and Arabia? The West of the imagination is grounded in real geography, but not confined by it.

THE GROWTH OF NARRATIVE

The Western is no mere travelogue. From the beginning the West was not just a physical location, however exotic or fascinating. It was also a space where things happened. The very first stories told about the West take the form of captivity narratives. These tales of kidnap by Indians, at first based upon actual experiences but increasingly fictionalized, dramatize the deep-seated racial and sexual fears of the whites confronted with the unknown occupants of a strange land. The first such story was recounted by the Spaniard Cabeza de Vaca in 1542 and tells of his capture by Indians in Texas. Under the Puritans in New England during the 17th and 18th centuries the captivity narrative was developed into something of an art form and continued in the 19th century in both fictional and (more or less) factual versions. It surfaces early in the Western film (for example in *The Indian Vestal*, a Selig production from 1911), and is at the heart of one of the greatest of all Westerns, *The Searchers*.

In the 19th century the American novel, by this time the dominant narrative form, began to concern itself with the West. Though he did not write the first novel on a Western subject, James Fenimore Cooper was undoubtedly the most influential novelist of the West in the first half of the century. His series of Leatherstocking Tales, beginning with *The Pioneers* in 1823, defined a major theme. The figure of Natty Bumppo, poised between the savage but free life of the woods and the refined but constricted society of the settlements, not only established the scout as a popular Western character but also expressed a fundamental tension in the American attitude to the wilderness, by turns compelling and malign. Cooper's other major creation, the Indian Chingachgook, dramatized the figure of the noble savage already given currency in the writings of Rousseau and other Europeans. The German novelist Karl May was to follow in Cooper's footsteps; his Winnetou is an Apache version of the Mohican Chingachgook.

Later in the century other novelists explored the fictional possibilities of a variety of Western milieux. Charles King based his stories on life in the army outposts on the frontier. Helen Hunt Jackson used the novel for propaganda purposes, writing *Ramona* in 1884 to protest about the treatment of the Indians. Bret Harte in his stories of the Californian mining frontier established a gallery of types such as the gambler and the good-hearted whore who would later be taken up enthusiastically in Western films. Then at the turn of the century Owen Wister wrote *The Virginian*, which did more than any other work to establish the cowboy as a central (eventually *the* central) figure on the Western scene.

THE WESTERN AND HISTORY

Other novelists writing early in the 20th century, like Hamlin Garland and Willa Cather, took as their subjects the lives of ordinary people in the West, such as the farmers of Nebraska and South Dakota. The Western film was largely to ignore the kind of material which Cather explored. At the centre of the Western as it evolved in the cinema, and at the centre of the popular fiction which was its immediate predecessor, was physical action: the violent confrontation between men and nature or, even more crucially, between savage or outlaw and the representative of advancing civilization. Some critics, such as John Cawelti, have therefore seen Cooper's exploration of the theme of the frontier as the essential core of the Western, which is 'set at a certain moment in the development of American civilization, namely at the point when savagery and lawlessness are in decline before the advancing wave of law and order, but are still strong enough to pose a local and momentarily significant challenge.' Cawelti perhaps underestimates the extent to which the Western depends on a fruitful tension *between* wildness and civilization, rather than recording the victory of one over the other. But he is right to stress the importance of the conflict. His description of what lies at the heart of the Western clearly has much in common with the theories of the most influential historian of the West, Frederick Jackson Turner, who argued that the peculiar character of American society could be explained by the existence of the frontier, defined precisely as the point at which savagery meets civilization.

The influence of other concepts of nineteenth-century history and politics, such as the doctrine of Manifest Destiny or the protest of the Populist movement, can also be charted in the Western. For example, Peter Wollen has uncovered in John Ford's films an antinomy between the West viewed as a garden or as a desert. These conceptions were traced back to their roots in nineteenth-century economic geography by Henry Nash Smith in his book *Virgin Land*. In his critical study *Horizons West* Jim Kitses sets out a whole series of oppositions which he finds operating in the ideology of the Western. Fundamental is the clash between the Wilderness and Civilization. From this derives a series of structuring tensions: between the individual and the community, between nature and culture, freedom and restriction, agrarianism and industrialism. All are physically separated by the frontier between the West and the East. These differences may be manifested in conflicts between gunfighters and townspeople, between ranchers and farmers, Indians and settlers, outlaws and sheriffs. But such are the complexities and richness of the material that the precise placing of any group or individual within these oppositions can never be pre-determined. Indians may well signify savagery; but sometimes they stand for what is positive in the idea of 'nature'. Outlaws may be hostile to civilization; but Jesse James often represents the struggle of agrarian values against encroaching industrialization.

POPULAR FICTION AND BIOGRAPHY

Yet, important though these insights are, we cannot reduce the Western to a series of statements about the meaning of history. It is, in its narrative structures and visual aesthetics, more than that. And sometimes rather less. Cawelti's phrase 'at a certain moment in the development of American civilization' is a rather highfalutin description of, say, *False Paradise*, a Hopalong Cassidy outing from 1948 in which Hoppy helps an elderly butterfly collector and his daughter hold on to their silver mine against the machinations of a crooked banker.

A major source for such stories and characters, so typical of the B-Western, was a far more popular kind of fiction than that written by Cooper. The hundreds of dime novels turned out by publishers such as Beadle and Adams in the last third of the 19th century entrenched as heroes of the popular imagination the scout, the cowboy and the outlaw. In volume after volume intrepid and dashing frontiersmen took on hordes of painted savages or masked outlaws and defeated them single-handed, while beautiful young women swooned in admiration at their feet. In the dime novel especially we can find the roots of the simple and elemental conflict between individual goodness and villainy, and the impulse towards physical action and adventure, that form the basis of the B-Western.

The larger-than-life characters and sensational situations of the dime novel

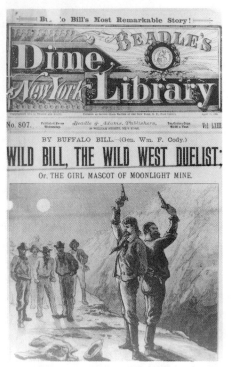

A Buffalo Bill dime novel, 1894

had their origins largely in the fevered imaginations of hack writers. Yet there was a connection, albeit often tenuous, with reality. Some of the heroes of the dime novel, such as Wild Bill Hickok, Buffalo Bill and Jesse James, did in fact exist, even if they performed in reality very few of the exploits attributed to them. Popular biographies of such celebrities made a distinctive contribution to the corpus of Western material. The nineteenth-century historian Thomas Carlyle notoriously remarked that 'history is the biography of great men.' Many of the major actors on the scene of westward expansion, such as General Custer, wrote their memoirs, in which they were only too willing to play up their role in deciding the course of history. Buffalo Bill famously remarked, as if to echo Cawelti's description of the central opposition within the Western: 'I stood between civilization and savagery most all my early days.' Biographies of Daniel Boone, Davy Crockett and Kit Carson played an important part in popularizing a view of the West as a land peopled by extravagantly heroic characters. Some of this material, such as the outrageously fanciful Davy Crockett Almanacs of the 1840s, is indistinguishable from fiction, and John Cawelti's description of the function of the hero in the Western can equally well apply to the role envisaged, by both biographer and subject, for some of the real-life personalities discovered on the frontier: 'The situation must involve a hero who possesses some of the urge towards violence as well as the skills, heroism and personal honor ascribed to the wilderness way of life, and it must place this hero in a position where he becomes involved with or committed to the agents and values of civilization.'

In the course of the 19th century a variety of forms of popular expression such as biography, cheap fiction and drama begin to distil out from an amorphous and heterogeneous mass of material something we can identify as 'the Western'. In this evolving genre, the quintessential Western character is defined as the man of action, the hero brave in the face of physical danger. Popular stage melodrama also made a contribution to the growth of a distinctive Western repertoire. Frank H. Murdoch's play, *Davy Crockett*, first produced in 1872, was hugely successful. *The Great Train Robbery* had been a stage play before becoming one of the very first film Westerns in 1903. The legitimate theatre, in fact, fed straight into the cinema. The greatest Western movie star of the pre-1920 era, William S. Hart, had appeared in 1905 in the stage play *The Squaw Man*, which became in 1914 one of the first feature-length Westerns. Before beginning his movie career Hart also played in the stage version of *The Virginian* in 1907, taking over the lead role from Dustin Farnum, who likewise went on to become a star of Western films.

THE WESTERN AS SPECTACULAR

Of course it is not only a particular kind of hero or story which characterizes the Western film. At the heart of its appeal is not just narrative but spectacle. It's the sight of a chase on horseback, of an Indian attack on the wagon train or a gunfight which thrills the spectator. The huge success of *The Great Train Robbery* was surely based in the main on its non-stop spectacular action, the train hold-up and final shoot-out, filmed in convincing locations. Visual spectacle was one of the mainstays of nineteenth-century theatre. Plays, many of them set in the West, provided scenes of large-scale action which included horse-riding, gunfights, fires and even train crashes. The Western in the cinema could provide the same, only more so.

William Frederick 'Buffalo Bill' Cody also began his show-business career on the stage, and his 'Wild West', a circus-style entertainment which drew on many aspects of Western life and legend, may be seen as a combination of dime novel and stage spectacle. The show celebrated the accomplishments of the cowboy, such as roping and riding skills and fancy shooting. It exhibited real live Indians and buffalo. And it contained embryonic narratives such as an Indian attack on the Deadwood Stage, episodes which came closer than ever before to the cinematic Western. In a parallel development, rodeo, gathering popular appeal at the end of the century, also played its part in packaging the riding and roping skills of the cowboy into a form of commercial entertainment.

Visual media made their own contribution to a public image of the West. Photography was ideal for conveying the splendours of the western landscape and for portraiture. It was also the most important technical progenitor of the cinema, though its direct influence on the early Western film was limited by the relatively slow speed of the first negative plates and by the cumbersome nature of the equipment. As a result photography, though invaluable as a record of how the West looked, was inferior to painting as a medium in which to portray the exciting scenes of action which were at the centre of the film Western's early and sustained popularity. Until the last third of the 19th century, most paintings of the West had aimed at producing an accurate record of the country and its inhabitants, both indigenous and immigrant. Artists like George Catlin and Seth Eastman specialized in ethnographic studies, portraits, landscapes and pastoral scenes. Then, with the growth of the means of mass reproduction, especially chromolithography, and the success of large-circulation magazines such as *Harper's Weekly*, came a new demand for stirring scenes of action and adventure. Thanks to artists such as Frederic Remington, painting reinforced the tendency in popular literature and drama towards making the Western synonymous with exciting narrative.

Thus out of the myriad of experiences, thoughts and imaginings produced by the incursions of the whites into the wilderness there had been fashioned, by the time the cinema was ready to be born, a repertoire of available forms and formats. Anyone who chose to speak about the West found themselves directed along well-defined channels. Certain images or ideas were readily available. Others, not worked over in any of the forms outlined above, were literally unimaginable. To give an obvious but important example, two main concepts of the Indians had become current by the end of the 19th century. According to one, they were noble savages, at an earlier stage of material development than the whites, but still innocent of the corruptions which civilization brings. In the other view, Indians were viewed as inherently inhuman, and so uncivilizable; they were a threat which had to be eradicated. A third concept was theoretically possible: that Native Americans (an unthinkable phrase for the time) had a civilization of their own, one which was, albeit technologically backward, not inferior to white civilization, just different. But this was an idea which could not be fitted into the mental framework of the age.

If some ways of thinking and some forms of experience were excluded by the dominant discourses of the period, there was nevertheless by 1900 a huge array of material, richly evocative, on which Western narratives could draw. A whole gallery of types and situations had been created, with their various possibilities for development into the heroic figures which stories of the West seemed to demand: explorers, mountain men, pathfinders, Indians, scouts, miners, soldiers, outlaws, gamblers, farmers and many more. Of course the primitive Western film could not instantly avail itself of all the possibilities contained in the plethora which literary, dramatic and visual media had developed. It was to be some time, for example, before the full possibilities of the Western landscape were realized. Certain established characters, such as Davy Crockett, were to prove less central to the movie Western than more recent inventions such as the cowboy. The reasons for such shifts in emphasis are never easy to determine, but some of them result from the internal dynamics of the movie Western itself and from the institutional pressures of the film industry. To these we must now turn.

THE BIRTH OF THE WESTERN

Histories of the cinema usually cite *The Great Train Robbery*, directed by Edwin S. Porter for the Edison Company in 1903, as the first Western film ever made. But it depends what we mean by a film. From 1894 onwards Thomas Edison produced a considerable amount of documentary footage showing scenes of Western life. Some of this material, made for projection in the Kinetoscope, featured Buffalo Bill Cody and his Wild West. There were also Indian scenes, shots of cowboys at work and scenic views. Two films made by the Edison Company in 1898 are probably the first to make the crucial leap from the

The Great Train Robbery (1903)

actuality film, which dominated in the very early years of the cinema, to the drama film which succeeded it and upon which Hollywood was to be founded. In the first, entitled *Poker at Dawson City*, four people are sitting round a table playing cards and cheating. A fight breaks out. This is, however minimally, a narrative. And though only the film's title anchors it firmly to a Western setting, card-playing and fistfights were to prove recurrent motifs in the Western.

The other title from 1898 is very similar but somewhat better known. In *Cripple Creek Bar-room* people are drinking in a bar. When they get drunk the barmaid throws them out. As with *Poker at Dawson City*, it is the title which does most to establish the location. (Cripple Creek was the biggest gold strike in Colorado. Mining began in 1890 and peaked in 1901, and the Edison film is therefore contemporary with the scene it represents.) But the costumes also make a gesture towards a distinctively Western style. One or two of the hats show a cowboy influence and one character is dressed in top hat, white shirt and black coat, the traditional garb of the gambler.

There is no denying that *The Great Train Robbery* is a major advance on such productions. It has genuine outdoor locations (though not authentically Western ones – it was shot on the Delaware and Lackawanna Railroad in New Jersey). Its narrative is far more developed. It incorporates into its ten minutes running time many of the motifs which were to become familiar to cinema audiences the world over: train robbery itself (raised to an art by the James gang in the 1870s and soon to become a perennial in Western films), some fisticuffs, a chase on horseback, a scene of a dude being forced to dance at gunpoint, and the final shootout. All that is lacking is for the cyphers who carry out the action to be developed into characters.

THE WESTERN MOVES WEST

Essanay trademark

The Great Train Robbery was probably not the first developed Western narrative in the cinema. That distinction may be held by *Kit Carson*, produced by the American Mutoscope and Biograph company in September 1903. *The Great Train Robbery* was not copyrighted until December 1903. But it is much the most important as an influence on the subsequent development of the genre. It was immensely successful and led to a rash of imitations, such as *The Bold Bank Robbery* and *The Hold-up of the Rocky Mountain Express*. Companies like Essanay, Selig, Biograph, Edison, Lubin, Vitagraph and Kalem vied with each other to exploit the rich vein that had been opened up. At first the pictures continued to be shot in the east, as *The Great Train Robbery* had been; American film producers had not yet made the move out to California which was to transform the industry. Then from about 1907 there was a spectacular expansion in the exhibition side of the film business. The owners of movie theatres were crying out for product. The American industry, still beset by the patent wars which followed Edison's attempt to monopolize production, could not supply the demand, and large numbers of foreign films had to be imported. Robert Anderson has argued that the development of the Western into a fully-fledged film genre was the result of a perception by American producers that if they were to fight back they would need not just improved organization but a product which was distinctive and which could not be easily imitated by the Europeans.

In January 1907 the Selig-Polyscope Company of Chicago sent a film troupe on location out west. They shot a number of films with titles such as *The Girl from Montana* which emphasized both local colour, particularly scenery, and action. Their success led to a further expedition in the summer of 1907 to shoot more films. The first of these to be released, *Western Justice*, was warmly praised in the trade press for its stunning backgrounds and its 'marvelously stirring and sensational chase'. The next year both Selig and Essanay were filming in Colorado. The popularity of these authentically Western productions led to a spate of imitations made in the east. But these were derided in the trade press, which was by now firmly of the opinion that 'cowboys, Indians and Mexicans must be seen in proper scenic backgrounds to convey any impression of reality.'

The arrival in California in late 1909 of the Bison company marked the consolidation of the trend towards authentic locations. Bison soon became the major producer of Westerns. By 1910 the Western had become the first truly cinematic genre and the first distinctively American contribution to the new art form; as *Moving Picture World* put it, the Western was the 'foundation' of American dramatic narrative. So popular had the Western become that in 1910 21 per cent of all American pictures made (213 out of 1001) were Westerns, a percentage which, as we shall see, was to remain remarkably consistent over the years. Indeed, so plentiful had the supply become that in 1911 a writer in the trade journal *Nickelodeon* was moved to protest that Westerns were 'a gold mine that had been worked to the limit.' Such predictions of the genre's imminent demise were to be repeated at regular intervals over the years. In a review of a William S. Hart Western in 1918 the *New York Times* complained: 'that kind of photoplay has been done almost to death.' In 1929 *Photoplay* pronounced, after Lindbergh had flown the Atlantic: 'Lindbergh has put the cowboy into the discard as a type of national hero. The Western novel and motion picture heroes have slunk away into the brush, never to return.'

BRONCHO BILLY ANDERSON

The fledgling genre proved sturdier than jaundiced industry observers allowed. In 1910 it was given a fresh impetus by the emergence of the first Western film star. Gilbert M. Anderson (originally Max Aronson) had played a part (possibly several parts) in *The Great Train Robbery*. In 1907 he formed a partnership with George K. Spoor and the new company was named Essanay after the initials of their last names. Appropriately for a producer of Westerns, the company's trademark was an Indian in feathered head-dress. Anderson made a number of Westerns for his company in Colorado and eventually settled in Niles, California. It was here in 1910 that he made a film based on a story by Peter B. Kyne called 'Broncho Billy and the Baby'. So successful was this film, *Broncho Billy's Redemption*, that Anderson was henceforth known by the name of the character he played.

Significantly, the first Western star based his character on the image of the cowboy. Broncho Billy usually wears a highly elaborate outfit which includes sheepskin chaps, leather gauntlets, twin pistols in holsters, a large neckerchief and a wide-brimmed hat; his garb derives, however distantly, from the costume of the trail herders of the southern plains. His manner around women is gauche but gallant, around men pugnacious. Anderson, with his bulbous nose and bulky figure, was an unlikely hero. But his geniality and awkward good nature shone through and endeared him to the public. The character he played was that of the Good Badman. Broncho Billy was often an outlaw, as in the initial story, but never hesitated to sacrifice himself if a woman or child was in distress.

Of course Broncho Billy isn't a real cowpuncher. What he owes to the traditional image of the cowboy, besides his costume, is a certain simplicity of character, an underlying honesty and a relish for action. And, of crucial importance dramatically, he shares the cowboy's free and easy life-style, which makes him always available for adventure. Even if getting the girl might seem to tie him down (at the end of *Shooting Mad* we leave him pushing a pram down the street), he is invariably footloose again at the start of the next picture. In the person of Broncho Billy the Western was from its earliest days alert to the advantage of series production based on a character not tied by institutional, professional or domestic constraints. The cowboy as rolling stone was of all

Broncho Billy Anderson in Broncho Billy's Double Escape *(1914)*

possible Western heroes (soldier, trapper, emigrant, miner, etc.) the best adapted to the endless repetition with a difference on which the Western, particularly the B-Western, is founded.

Broncho Billy was not the only character to appear regularly at this time. In France an actor called Joë Hamman made a number of appearances as 'Arizona Bill' in 1911 and 1912 in such films as *Les Diables rouges* and *Aux Mains des brigands*. A character called Young Wild West, who originated in *Wild West Weekly* magazine, appeared in half a dozen films produced by the Nestor company in 1912. But for the crucial formative years up until 1913 Broncho Billy was by far the most coherent and attractive character on the Western screen, as well as, with nearly 300 films, the one who appeared most often. Broncho Billy established a type which others had to follow even while they worked their variations on it.

By 1920 Anderson's career as a Western star was over. The Western had grown, both in length (one of the first Western features, DeMille's *The Squaw Man*, was made in 1914) and in emotional stature. More serious or at least more self-conscious artists like William S. Hart and D.W. Griffith had taken the form beyond the childlike naivety of Broncho Billy. But Anderson's part in establishing the Western's popularity through the creation of its first recognized persona can hardly be over-estimated.

INDIANS IN THE EARLY WESTERN

The other major figure besides the cowboy during the first ten years of the Western is the Indian (thus justifying the popular term 'cowboys and Indians' as a synonym for the Western). As well as stories of conflict between Indians and whites there are a surprising number of films which deal with Indian life, if not exactly on its own terms then without the intervention of white characters. *Indian Justice*, a Path film of 1911, and *A Squaw's Love*, a Biograph film of the same year directed by D.W. Griffith, are both stories of Indian love affairs. *Hiawatha* was filmed by the Imp company in 1910 and Longfellow's poem was doubtless a major source for this theme.

Those who assume that the Western hero traditionally preferred horses to women may be unprepared for the frequency with which romantic love turns the mechanism of the plot in these early films. The theme of miscegenation is especially common; predictably love between the races is usually doomed. In *Back to the Prairie*, a Pathé film of 1911, Red Fox falls in love with the daughter of a white man he has rescued. His suit is rejected by the girl's father and, disillusioned, he returns to his own people. Love across the racial border is not always unsuccessful. In *Flaming Arrow* (1913, Bison 101), White Eagle, the son of a white prospector and an Indian woman, falls in love with a colonel's daughter from the neighbouring fort. After he saves her from an Indian attack, the final close-up shows the white girl and White Eagle together. But the more usual outcome is found in *Ramona*, the best known of the early films on this theme. The first version of Helen Hunt Jackson's novel was made by D.W. Griffith for Biograph in 1910. Allessandro, the Indian hero, runs away with his Spanish sweetheart. Eventually he is shot by hostile whites and she is left to grieve by his graveside.

Not all these early films are concerned with cowboys or Indians. No less than thirty-seven films from the period 1908-16 have 'Mexican' as the first word in the title; almost invariably characters from south of the border are villains, often referred to in the most unflattering terms, as in D.W. Griffith's *The Greaser's Gauntlet* (1908). There are stories about miners, lumberjacks and emigrants in wagon trains. There are films about real-life characters such as Kit Carson or Daniel Boone, and many set in the far Northwest or Mexico. Films about the Civil War, many with Western elements, almost constituted a genre on their own.

BISON 101

If the appeal of the cowboy owed much to Broncho Billy, the popularity of Indians in films was doubtless the result of their exotic appearance and the opportunity they provided for exciting scenes of battle. A more direct cause of the frequency of Indians on the screen was that one company, the aptly named Bison, specialized in them. At first Bison had, like other companies, made its Westerns in the east. In 1910, recognizing that authentic locations were becoming essential, Fred Balshofer, the chief director, decided to take the company west. He found an ideal spot at Santa Ynez canyon, near Santa Monica, California and the company took a long lease on a spread of eighteen thousand acres dotted with orange groves and vineyards.

By a happy chance at that time on a tour of the California beach resorts was the Miller Brothers 101 Ranch Wild West show. Based in Oklahoma, on a huge tract of land with its own rodeo arena, the 101 Ranch comprised dozens of real cowboys and Indians, herds of buffalo and cattle, stagecoaches, tepees and other paraphernalia invaluable in the production of Western films. Bison contracted with the Miller brothers for the use of the entire outfit, and overnight Bison 101, as it was renamed, found itself tooled up to become a manufacturer of Westerns on an industrial scale. The company built a permanent wooden fort, which can be seen in such pictures as *At Old Fort Dearborn* (1913). Then, having laid in a stock of Indians, Bison went into the production of Indian pictures with a vengeance.

The investment paid off. In 1912 an English trade journal, *The Bioscope*, wrote: 'The latest 101 Bison is as good as any others which have gone before ... there are ... horses and oxen literally by the dozen, and a splendidly managed explosion, which is the result of something more than threepence-halfpenny worth of gunpowder – the limit of expenditure which so many producers appear to set themselves in arranging similar scenes. The Bison Company's Indians are always

Bison 101 trademark

W.S. Hart (l.), Thomas Ince (centre) and the Inceville Sioux

splendid fellows to behold and, what is more, they always look what they are supposed to be.'

At the same time as it acquired the 101 Ranch, Bison also hired a new director, Thomas Ince. Ince's real genius was as an organizer and supervisor. He also had a considerable talent for self-promotion, which led him to claim credit for the direction of others' films and for the original decision to contract with the 101 Ranch. But Ince's actual achievements were substantial enough. He initiated the practice of making a detailed shooting script which specified every item of décor and costume, every shot and movement. This kind of pre-planning, eventually to become standard industry practice, saved greatly on time and money and streamlined production at the Santa Ynez location, which soon became popularly known as Inceville.

Bison now not only had the best resources for making Westerns; it was also of all companies the best equipped to maximize its potential. But the Ince regime there was shortlived. The New York Motion Picture Company, the parent of Bison 101, was soon absorbed into Carl Laemmle's Universal. Laemmle moved production units into Inceville to make his own Westerns under the 101-Bison brand name, while Ince built a new studio in Culver City. Inceville fell into disuse in the early 1920s, after Universal had consolidated production at their huge new studio built on the old Taylor Ranch five miles north of Hollywood. These new facilities were formally opened on 15 March 1915 in the presence of, among others, Buffalo Bill Cody. Universal City, like Inceville, boasted permanent Western sets, and to this day visitors to Hollywood who take the Universal Studio tour can see whole streets of standing sets for a Western township. Universal's level of investment in Western personnel and suitable real estate (it also owned a ranch in the San Fernando Valley) ensured that it remained the largest producer of Westerns throughout the 1920s.

D. W. GRIFFITH

'Authentic Indian Customs' in a
D.W. Griffith Western

The only man making Westerns in the early days which could rival in sheer scale and in dramatic verve those emanating from Inceville was D.W. Griffith. Of the 571 films made by Griffith's studio, Biograph, between July 1908 and November 1912 74 were, on a broad definition, Westerns. Though the Biograph studios were in New York, from 1910 Griffith regularly took his company to California for the winter. Thus one of Griffith's most successful Westerns, *The Last Drop of Water* (1911), benefits greatly from being shot in what is recognizably a Californian desert. The story concerns two rivals for the love of the heroine, played by Blanche Sweet. She marries the weaker of the two, and his fondness for liquor causes their marriage to deteriorate. A year later the couple and the disappointed suitor join a wagon train of settlers going west. Indians attack them in the desert when they are running out of water. The suitor, still in love with Blanche Sweet, nobly volunteers to go in search of the nearest waterhole. The husband eventually finds him nearly dying of thirst. At first the husband jeers at him, but then redeems himself by giving up his last drop of water before expiring. The suitor revives and fetches the cavalry, who arrive in the nick of time, in the usual manner of a Griffith cliff-hanger ending.

The scenes of the wagon train wending its way through the desert are on an impressive scale. Like Ince's films for Bison, Griffith's Westerns offered higher production values and an emphasis on visual spectacle. This undoubtedly gave a further boost to the genre's popularity. Griffith redefined the possibilities of the genre, grafting on an 'epic' dimension which was to bear fruit later in *The Covered Wagon* and *The Iron Horse*, and which increased the Western's prestige. The Western proved the ideal vehicle for Griffith's skill in creating narrative tension through cross-cutting and also gave full rein to his ability to wring emotion from the audience by placing innocent young women in jeopardy. In his most elaborate early Western, *The Battle of Elderbush Gulch* (1913), Mae Marsh and Lillian Gish play two young sisters who come out west to live. The local Indians go on the warpath and attack the town. A huge battle ensues, directed with all Griffith's customary élan. At the end of the picture it seems as if the Indians must break through into the cabin in which the girls have taken refuge (in an early example of what would become a stock device, one of the women inside is told to save the last bullet for herself). Then at the last moment the cavalry arrive and the Indians are routed.

It may seem strange that the director of *Ramona* or *A Squaw's Love*, with their individually realized and sympathetic Indian characters, could also make a film like *The Battle of Elderbush Gulch* which portrays the Indians as a horde of screaming savages. But the Western has always spoken with a forked tongue, now willing to treat Indians as characters in the drama, now lumping them together en masse as an alien threat. Even in the 1970s, after an unprecedented wave of 'pro-Indian' pictures, a film such as *Ulzana's Raid*, apparently sympathetic to the Apache, rubs its audience's noses in details of Indian torture. That a deep-seated racism has been responsible for the reduction of the Indian to a faceless 'Other' is scarcely in doubt. But we should not underestimate the more immediate requirements of dramaturgy. Both the Western's inheritance from the popular culture of the 19th century and the early success of those films which stressed action and spectacle created the expectation that conflict would be resolved through physical struggle. How could the hero be brave unless there were danger? The plot required a threat, and what better than Indians? Hostility arising from racial difference was an attractively simple trigger for violence, requiring no very complex explanation of motivations.

WILLIAM S. HART

Several Indian actors found interesting and rewarding employment in the early Western, but no Indian ever became a star. Broncho Billy's successor was not William Eagleshirt (prominent among the Inceville Sioux) but another Ince employee, William S. Hart. Though born in New York, Hart was brought up in the Midwest at a time when it was still frontier country, and his entry into pictures was directly motivated by a desire to make Westerns which were more realistic than the ones he saw on the screen. Hart had achieved moderate success as a stage actor. In 1913 he renewed his acquaintance with Thomas Ince, his room-mate when they had toured together in a play. Ince put Hart to work making a couple of features and a succession of two-reelers in the first year or so. The pictures were highly successful, though Ince managed to keep this from Hart for a time, paying him only $125 a week for both acting and directing. When Ince moved to Triangle he took Hart with him and then to Famous Players-Lasky in 1917, where at $150,000 per picture Hart was at last paid in proportion to the sums his pictures earned. (For the equivalent sum in the 1980s we should multiply by at least ten.)

Hart's screen persona has something in common with Broncho Billy. Though he sometimes appears as a prospector or Mountie, he is usually in the costume of a cowboy. Frequently, as in one of his best known films, *Hell's Hinges* (1916), he is the Good Badman, still essentially a cowboy figure, one who has strayed outside the law and who may be reformed by the love of a woman he fears is too good for him. Like Broncho Billy he is ill at ease with women, though in place of Billy's comic bashfulness Hart displays a painfully rigid aloofness. But if Hart owed something to what had gone before, he greatly deepened and enriched the genre. To his roles he brought a moral intensity which, even viewed some seventy years later, retains much of its power. Hart was unsurpassed at communicating, merely through the expression on his face, implacable hatred of wrongdoers or unshakeable resolve to pursue vengeance. Perhaps among Westerners only Randolph Scott was ever to rival Hart in the ability to suggest a soul ennobled by suffering.

Hart also brought to the Western an emphasis, since commonplace, on the

William S. Hart in
Tumbleweeds *(1925)*

hero as loner. He rarely has partners or family. At the same time he introduced the subject that has since become so frequent as to constitute for some the heart of the genre: the frontier town torn between lawlessness and the desire of the decent folk to build a community. However stiff with Victorian melodrama they appear now, Hart's Westerns are always about something. And there is a certain honest austerity in the visual style. Though Hart's world as a whole is no less than any other an artistic construction of a certain *idea* of the West, his frontier towns, evoked in all their drabness and lack of refinement, compare realistically with photographs of actual Western streets.

TOM MIX

Hart's career was at its zenith around 1920. His decline was swift; after 1921 he made only a further three films. *Tumbleweeds*, his last, was completed in 1925. Long before then Hart had been replaced as the number one Western star by a new and totally different kind of hero. Tom Mix had begun working in pictures when he was employed by the Selig-Polyscope Company to handle the horses for its documentary *Ranch Life in the Great Southwest*, made in 1909. Mix also appeared in the film, and went on over the next eight years to make nearly a hundred one- and two-reelers for Selig. But his career really blossomed when in 1917 he moved to Fox. The films he made in the next decade changed the course of the history of the Western.

Mix, like Anderson and Hart before him, based his persona and costume on that of the cowboy – the footloose knight of the plains. His success ensured that henceforth there was no possibility of any other type dominating. Not that the cowboy excluded all others; in the 1920s there were films about mountain men and scouts, soldiers, miners and outlaws; and films about the great Northwest, often based on the novels of Jack London, James Oliver Curwood or Rex Beach, constituted a sub-genre on their own. But it was the cowboy who held centre-stage, until in the 1950s the cowboy proper shaded into the gunfighter.

If Tom Mix followed Hart in being a cowboy, his conception of his role could

Tom Mix (with Mickey Rooney) in My Pal the King (1932)

not have been more different. Where Hart had aimed for moral intensity and realism, Mix aspired only to entertainment. His films were a carefully concocted mélange of stunts, comedy, fistfights, chases and above all glamour. As the 1920s progressed Tom Mix's costumes became ever more elaborate, leaving behind the last vestiges of the authenticity which Hart had claimed, and taking off into a realm of pure fantasy. Frequently the action took place in a contemporary setting, with Tom on his horse Tony chasing cars and even planes. The world of Tom Mix's West was a never-never land; one film is actually set in Ruritania. The stern Victorian morality of Hart's Westerns was left far behind. In Tom Mix the Jazz Age found its ideal Western star.

Mix's films were undeniably enjoyable. The stunt work, much of it performed by Mix himself, was excellent; fights on top of trains were a speciality. The films were usually made on location, often at spectacular sites such as the Grand Canyon. The hero's personality was engaging but uncomplicated: brave, gallant, resourceful. He rarely actually killed anyone. In *The Great K & A Train Robbery* Tom swims underwater to enter the cave where the villains are hiding. He surfaces (still wearing his hat!) and finds them plotting. He places his hat over a frog, which swims away and distracts the gang. Catching them off-guard, Tom then engages them, about a dozen in all, in a huge fistfight and captures the lot.

No less fantastic than any of the plots in his films was the biography that Mix constructed for himself over the years. At various times he asserted that he had charged up San Juan Hill with Teddy Roosevelt, fought in China and the Philippines, joined up with the Boers to fight the British and campaigned against Diaz in Mexico. None of this was true. Though he had joined the army he never saw active service and eventually deserted. More relevant to his film career was the time he spent with the Miller Brothers 101 Ranch, the same outfit which was later to be hired by Thomas Ince. Mix's experience with Wild West shows turned him into an excellent rider, with the result that his films relied greatly on feats of horsemanship (which Hart's never had).

Hoot Gibson

STARS OF THE 1920S

Buck Jones

Tim McCoy

At the close of his career (his last film, *The Miracle Rider*, was made in 1935), Mix returned to his beginnings and toured with the Sam B. Dill Circus. Many other Western stars of the period also had their roots in the world of the circus and Wild West show, where they acquired the traditional skills of the cowboy: riding, roping, shooting. Art Acord, Buck Jones, Hoot Gibson, Ken Maynard, Jack Hoxie, Tim McCoy and William Boyd all at some time appeared live in the arena, and some, like Tom Mix and Ken Maynard, moved back and forth between film work and touring. Maynard had in fact appeared with Pawnee Bill's show in 1920; Pawnee Bill had of course previously been in partnership with Buffalo Bill himself, so the continuity between the Western film and its origins was strong. Ultimately this tradition, the commercialization of the cowboy, was to prove far more influential on the film Western than the world of the legitimate theatre as represented by William S. Hart.

Though Mix was undeniably the brightest Western star of the age, the 1920s were distinguished by a galaxy of Western talent. Besides William S. Hart and Tom Mix, the most active stars of the period were Harry Carey, Jack Holt, Art Acord, Hoot Gibson, Buck Jones, Tim McCoy, Fred Thomson, Ken Maynard. As Appendix, Chart 1 shows, all except Art Acord (dead of cyanide poisoning in a Mexican hotel room in 1931) and Fred Thomson (who died of pneumonia in 1928) proved astonishingly durable and were still playing lead roles in 1940.

All provided a mixture of riding, fighting, comedy and drama. Ken Maynard was the most conspicuously flamboyant, taking even further the emphasis of the Tom Mix pictures on daring feats of horsemanship. Fred Thomson too had glamour; the most handsome of the Western stars of the period, he combined effective stunt action with a strong moral line (as befitted a former preacher). Hoot Gibson, by contrast, relied to a great extent on genial comedy with the minimum of action (he never carried a gun). Buck Jones, though not above humorous interludes, often attained considerable intensity in such roles as Joaquin Murieta in *The Avenger* (1932). Harry Carey, more actor than cowboy, had begun making one-reel Westerns with Griffith at Biograph and had gone on to stardom in a Western series for Universal, many of them directed by John Ford. Carey frequently played a character called Cheyenne Harry, who had in him something of the Good Badman first portrayed by Broncho Billy and W.S. Hart. Carey also shared something of their homespun looks; he could never have been a matinee idol. Art Acord and Jack Holt, in contrast to Carey, had both been cowboys originally and their Western series, though extremely popular at the time, were perhaps the least sophisticated of all the major Western stars of the 20s.

The one who stands out from the rest is Tim McCoy, who took himself a little more seriously. McCoy had run away from home to be a cowboy after being intoxicated by the excitements of a Wild West show. In Wyoming he became skilled with cattle and horses and an expert on the local Arapaho Indians, to the extent that he was called in as advisor for *The Covered Wagon* in 1923. In his prestige series of Westerns for MGM in the late 20s and in his Columbia films of the early 30s he tried hard, within the constraints of the formula, for a degree of historical authenticity and thematic substance. In *End of the Trail* (1932) McCoy plays an army officer sympathetic to the Arapaho (he had also been an advisor on *The Vanishing American*, one of the most pro-Indian features of the 1920s). The

Ken Maynard

film was shot entirely on location at the Arapaho reservation in Wyoming and its Indian scenes were sufficiently convincing for them to be cannibalized in subsequent films. In the continual oscillation within the Western between attempts to ground fiction in history and the desire to escape into the realms of fantasy, Tim McCoy is one of the few stars of the B-Western who incline decisively to the former.

Not that historical references are uncommon in the B-Western. *In Old Oklahoma* (otherwise known as *War of the Wildcats*), a typical Republic picture from 1943, is about the oil industry in Oklahoma at the turn of the century. In the course of the narrative it transpires that the hero, played by John Wayne, has been in the army in Cuba during the Spanish-American War. Frustrated in his attempt to secure leases to drill for oil, he goes to Washington to appeal to the President, who of course turns out to be none other than Teddy Roosevelt. Since the Wayne character had taken part in the charge up San Juan Hill led by Teddy, the President greets him with open arms, grants the leases and makes a speech about the pioneering spirit being 'the essence of America'.

THE EPIC WESTERN IN THE 20S

On the whole, it is true, major historical themes such as the building of railroads are more common in large-scale Westerns, for the obvious reason that they tend to require money. The biggest films of the 20s and 30s, *The Covered Wagon*, *The Iron Horse*, *The Big Trail*, *Cimarron*, *The Plainsman*, *Wells Fargo*, *Union Pacific*, all base themselves in some way on actual events. Yet although the first Western epic, *The Covered Wagon*, produced in 1923, was intended to be as different as possible from the series Western of the day starring Tom Mix and others, it did not wholly abandon the narrative structures and character stereotypes which had become so popular. It had fights and Indian attacks, chases and a final shoot-out, of a sort. But it also had seriousness and a weighty theme. It told the story of an emigrant train going west just after the gold strike in California in

The Covered Wagon (1923)

1848. At the climactic moment of the film the emigrants split between those who opt for the gold diggings and quick money, and those who decide to go to Oregon to settle the land.

What *The Covered Wagon* had above all was scope and scale. Following the success of Cecil B. DeMille's feature-length Western *The Squaw Man* in 1914, William S. Hart had begun making feature-length pictures. By 1917, when John Ford made his first five-reel Western, *Straight Shooting*, features were common enough. But *The Covered Wagon* went further. It was ten reels long when originally released and at $782,000 (about $8 million at 1988 prices) it was far and away the most expensive Western to date. Its big set-pieces, such as the crossing of the river by 400 wagons, a buffalo hunt and the Indian attack on the wagon train, were more spectacular than anything yet seen. If James Cruze now appears a rather pedestrian director, the location work, the most elaborate of its time, is still impressive. The Western at last had stature.

The success of *The Covered Wagon* led, as usual in Hollywood, to imitations. Historians have claimed that as a direct result of *The Covered Wagon*'s popularity with both critics and audiences the production of Westerns increased overall. William K. Everson and George N. Fenin, for example, write in *The Western from Silents to the Seventies*: 'Only fifty Westerns were made in 1923, but the success of James Cruze's film was such that the following year saw the number had almost tripled. Until the elimination of B-Westerns in the Mid-Fifties, the annual Western output never fell below that figure again, and usually exceeded it.'

It's not clear from what sources these figures are drawn. A calculation based on *The American Film Institute Catalog of Motion Pictures Produced in the United States: Feature Films, 1921-1930* shows a rise in the total number of Westerns produced, from 98 in 1923 to 173 in 1924 (see Appendix, Table 1). But 1923 had itself been a slack year compared to 1922, which had seen 145 Westerns made. What is true is that 1925 saw the highest number in the whole period 1921-69, 227 in all. (For the record, as Table 1 shows, the number of Westerns made in

Cecil B. DeMille (seated l.) on location for
The Squaw Man *(1914)*

John Wayne, Marguerite Churchill in
The Big Trail

any one year never in fact reached 150 after 1926, and for much of the 30s did not reach three figures.) But if this increase in 1925 was a direct response to *The Covered Wagon*, how to explain the two-year delay? What may be more significant is a marked increase from 1923 onwards in the number of Westerns over six reels in length, that is in longer, and presumably bigger-budgeted, films. (The figures for Westerns over six reels during the early 20s are: 1922, 4; 1923, 13; 1924, 12; 1925, 26; 1926, 11.) What does seem possible, then, is that *The Covered Wagon* led to an increase in the number of longer, more expensive Westerns.

Of the big Westerns which followed in the wake of *The Covered Wagon*, John Ford's *The Iron Horse*, made for Fox in 1924 with a similarly epic theme of advancement across the continent, is the best known, and deservedly. It is the summation of Ford's achievement in the Western up to that point, and he was to make only one more (*Three Bad Men*, 1926) before *Stagecoach* in 1939. Paramount, who had produced *The Covered Wagon*, followed up with another large-scale drama. This was *North of 36*, based, like *The Covered Wagon*, on a novel by Emerson Hough. If not on quite the same scale as the earlier film (its budget was $350,000, less than half that of *The Covered Wagon*, though still substantial), it too had some spectacular scenes, such as a river crossing by a herd of four thousand cattle.

Most of the epic Westerns of the 1920s are about trail-blazing and conquering new territory, a theme continued into the 1930s with *The Big Trail* and *Cimarron*. James Cruze attempted another big Western in 1925, *Pony Express*, and William S. Hart felt obliged to give an epic dimension to his last film, *Tumbleweeds*, which includes some impressive footage of the Oklahoma land rush. But productions on this scale were very much the exception. The history of the Western in the 1920s was, as it has always been, largely the history (admittedly not always told) of those films which were cranked out year after year to a traditional pattern. As Table 4 (Appendix) shows, between 1926 and 1967, apart from a brief period in the early 30s, Westerns consistently formed around a quarter of all feature films made in Hollywood. This one genre, with its highly formulaic content and steady market, can be seen as the absolute bedrock of Hollywood, the foundation upon which its glittering palaces were erected.

THE AUDIENCE FOR THE WESTERN

The phenomenal success of Tom Mix (by 1925 he was earning $17,000 a week) decisively affected the future course of the Western film, not only through the introduction of a new kind of hero but also in its consequence for the organization of the industry. It showed that there was a ready and dependable market for films that placed action and excitement over complexities of character and theme. Hart's films were made, one assumes, for the general audience that most films were made for. But with the advent of Tom Mix and his imitators and successors there was a shift towards a specialized audience. The absence of killing, and the fact that in his films Tom did not drink, smoke or cuss, made them particularly suitable for juveniles. Tom Mix leads in a straight line to Gene Autry, the most popular cowboy star of the late 1930s and early 40s. Autry it was who codified the behaviour of the Western star into a list of the Ten Cowboy Commandments, which would ensure that his films were fit for youthful consumption. In Gene Autry's world the cowboy hero: 1) Never takes unfair advantage. 2) Never goes back on his word. 3) Always tells the truth. 4) Is always gentle to old people, children and animals. 5) Is never racially or religiously intolerant. 6) Always helps people in distress. 7) Never smokes or drinks. 8) Is always clean in thought, word, deed and personal grooming. 9) Respects women and the nation's laws. 10) Is a patriot (above all).

In 1933 Ralston Purina, a St Louis cereal company, began sponsoring a radio show for children featuring Tom Mix. In turn Buck Jones advertised Grape Nuts and Roy Rogers Quaker Oats to a generation of youthful admirers. Of course an audience of children alone could not have sustained Tom Mix's huge success. As the mass production of Westerns, following on where Tom Mix had blazed the trail, became an increasingly specialized business, the evidence of booking patterns and exhibitors' reports in trade journals such as *Motion Picture Herald* suggests that the audience for this kind of Western was increasingly segregated not just by age but by geographical location. The series Western, of which Mix was the first great exponent, was as time went on sold primarily to theatres in rural areas and in small towns.

Hard information about the audiences for Hollywood films is difficult to come by. With the exception of box-office returns, a notoriously unreliable source of data, Hollywood did virtually no market research during the years of its supremacy as the major purveyor of entertainment to the American people. What little we do know comes from the work of independent sociologists. As early as 1916 a study of schoolchildren in Iowa City by Ray Leroy Short showed that Westerns became less popular as children got older. Research on the kinds of film preferred by audiences in rural New England in 1926 found that Westerns were the most popular of all. A more thoroughgoing study in the same year of 10,000 Chicago schoolchildren discovered that pre-teenage children preferred Westerns most, that boys liked them more than girls, and that with older children Westerns were supplanted in popularity by adventure and comedy films for boys, and romance films for girls.

In a rare piece of research financed by the film industry in the early 1940s, performed for RKO by a group led by George Gallup, the Western came low on the scale of popularity with adults generally, and extremely low with women. The categorization of films in such polls can be problematic. Westerns, after all, may also be comedies, they may contain romance, they may even be musicals. This difficulty of definition was pointed out by one of the pioneers of communications research, Paul Lazarsfeld, in research published in 1947. Nevertheless, Lazarsfeld was able to conclude that preferences for certain subjects did conform to a pattern. For example, Westerns were more popular outside urban areas: 'People want mainly to hear about themselves. In all preference studies we find a strong element of projection.... Westerns are most popular in the Rocky Mountains.'

CATEGORY	MALE	FEMALE
Musicals	35	48
Light comedy	35	42
Serious drama	23	42
Excitement, adventure	39	25
Slapstick comedy	43	18
Army, navy, aviation	40	23
Detective, mystery	36	24
Romance, marriage	9	32
Westerns	16	7

Movie preferences (%) by sex

THE SERIES WESTERN

The special appeal of Westerns to a certain segment of the audience undoubtedly helps explain the bifurcation in production between so-called A-Westerns and B-Westerns. The phenomenon of the series and later of the B-Western deserves more attention than most serious critics have given it. Just as, so far as we can tell, its audience was fairly specific, children and men in the more rural areas being heavy consumers, so too it constituted, up to a point, a self-contained entity within the world of Hollywood film production.

Until the early 1930s we cannot really speak of A- and B-features. Before then

Gene Autry

all Westerns had to make their own way in the market on equal terms with other productions, and all films of feature length would play on their own, accompanied only by one or more shorts. It was the effect of the Depression, with a dramatic decline in box-office receipts, which led in the mid-1930s to the introduction of the double-feature as a novel attraction. This opened an opportunity for the production of films, many produced by small independent companies, which were expressly designed for the bottom or 'B' half of a double bill. Something of a boom in B-Westerns followed, with production by independents leaping from 26 in 1933 to 59 in 1934 and 106 in 1935 (see Table 4, Appendix).

A great many of these B-Westerns were made according to a series format. Westerns were not the only kinds of films made in series, but they were easily the most numerous. In the series Western Hollywood got as close as it could to the production methods of Detroit. The films were, in so far as the necessity for a minimum of novelty permitted, virtually identical. Each one was conceived as part of a package of films, all with the same star and with uniform production values, story-lines, running times and so on. A knowledgeable audience would know exactly what to expect. Narrative expectations were standardized: there would be a fistfight within the first few minutes, a chase soon after and, inevitably, a shoot-out at the end. Plots were usually motivated by some straightforward villainy which could be exposed and decisively defeated by the hero. Even such novelty as the films did possess was sometimes only relative to the audience's ability to recall previous films, for not only did the series Western endlessly recycle plots in a succession of remakes of past successes; it was also common for footage to be reused. Costly scenes of Indian attacks or stampedes would re-appear, more or less happily satisfying the demands of continuity, in subsequent productions.

Series Westerns were planned for production on an assembly-line basis in groups of half a dozen or more, and marketed accordingly in an arrangement known as block-booking. That is, exhibitors were expected to buy not a selected Ken Maynard or Hoot Gibson film, but the whole season's output. An indication of how standardized and predictable the business end had become was that films at the bottom half of a double bill were usually booked not on the basis of a percentage of box-office receipts, as A-features were, but on a flat rate of perhaps $25 or $30 dollars per play-off. If the product was uniform, then so must be the return, and buyer and seller could agree on a fixed price before the film was shown. Most of the pictures produced by the small independent studios were sold on the states' rights system. Instead of running their own costly nationwide network of distribution exchanges, as the major studios did, the independents sold their product off to regional distributors who would act for several small producers at once.

The stars adapted to the system and became more highly specialized. True, Broncho Billy Anderson and William S. Hart had made very few films which were not Westerns. But Tom Mix scarcely ever ventured outside the genre; when he did, with *Dick Turpin*, the film was unpopular with his fans. So closely were the stars identified with their screen persona that by the time of Gene Autry all pretence was abandoned of any distinction between the man and the role. On screen Autry played a character whose name was simply 'Gene Autry'.

This may have taken a tendency to an extreme, but from the 1930s it became a common practice to identify an actor with a role and build a series round him. Thus William Boyd began appearing as Hopalong Cassidy in 1935 and thenceforth never played anyone else. Similarly Charles Starrett's series as the Durango Kid, beginning in 1945, continued with half a dozen or more pictures every year until 1952. A further indication of how the series Western was to an extent a self-contained domain within Hollywood is the fact that from 1936 on, the trade journal *Motion Picture Herald* listed Western stars separately in its annual Top Ten Money-Making Stars poll, in which exhibitors were asked to list the actors whose pictures were the biggest box-office draws. (Buck Jones topped the first poll, but from 1937 it was Gene Autry every year until he was succeeded by Roy Rogers in 1943. Rogers stayed at the top until 1954, by which time series Westerns were no longer being made.)

Studios also specialized. Some designated their Westerns under brand-name titles; thus Universal in the 1920s had its 'Blue Streak Westerns'. We have already seen how Bison, by investing in the Miller 101 Ranch, became overnight the major producer of Westerns in the early 1910s. In the 1920s Universal had its own ranch in the San Fernando Valley in California, which included bunkhouses for the cowboys and an Indian village complete with genuine inhabitants. At that time Universal, with stars like Harry Carey, Jack Hoxie, Art Acord and Hoot Gibson, and Fox with Tom Mix and Buck Jones, were overwhelmingly the biggest producers of Westerns among the Hollywood majors. In the 1930s Universal cut back considerably and, after Tom Mix had moved on, Fox's production declined too. Columbia on the other hand stepped up production, and so did Paramount when they launched Hopalong Cassidy in 1935. (See Table 2, Appendix.) By contrast Warner Bros. were never whole-hearted about Westerns. Their big stars of the 30s and 40s, such as James Cagney, Humphrey Bogart or Bette Davis, were never at home on the range. MGM, after their brief Tim McCoy series in the late 1920s, produced no other series Westerns at all; doubtless the hick associations of the Western ran counter to the studio's sophisticated, metropolitan image.

Though, as Table 2 shows, for a time in the 20s over half of Universal's films were Westerns, the major studios did not normally rely on a single genre to this extent. The so-called 'independent' studios, on the other hand, were all overwhelmingly dependent on the Western. As Table 3 (Appendix) shows, during the five years 1941-5 (despite the war, a not untypical period for Hollywood) the independents produced a total of 645 feature films, of which 313 were Westerns. During this same period, though the eight major studios were supplying between a half and a third of all Westerns made, this level of production represented at most 15 per cent of their total feature output.

As Table 4 (Appendix) demonstrates, the proportion of Westerns within the total production of feature films in Hollywood did not change substantially between the mid-1920s and the late 1950s, apart from a brief hiccup in the early 30s as a result of the introduction of sound and the disruptions caused in the industry by the Depression. Although the majors were not so heavily committed as the independents, Westerns continued for over forty years to comprise between a fifth and a quarter of all films made in Hollywood (and it will be remembered that the proportion was similar even as far back as 1910, though exact calculations are difficult for the period before 1920). This is an astonishingly high proportion for one kind of film. What we have to remember, though, is that all but a few of these Westerns were small-scale productions. Indeed, as Table 5 (Appendix) reveals, big-budget or so-called A-feature Westerns, the kind which might star Gary Cooper or Tyrone Power and which were a monopoly of the major studios, were a rarity. Of the 1,336 Westerns made by all producers between 1930 and 1941, only 66, or a mere 5 per cent, could be classified as A-features.

BUDGETS · The budgets of the series or B-Western had to be kept low, since returns were limited. But there could be considerable variation, all the same. The major studios generally spent more than the independents. In *The Filming of the West* Jon Tuska gives several examples of such budgets. In the 1920s Paramount were spending on average $110,000 each on their series Westerns. Tom Mix's budgets when he moved to Universal in the 1930s were of a similar order. Ken Maynard's budgets for his series with First National starting in 1926 were $75,000 per picture. Somewhat lower down the scale came Buck Jones, who in the 1930s was having to make do on budgets of $25,000 per picture at Columbia (admittedly the poorest of the majors at that time); this financed a shooting schedule of between two and three weeks. The Buck Jones films might average 10,000 play-offs at a flat rate of $25, and so gross $250,000. Out of this sum had to come many overheads in addition to direct production costs, but quite a bit must have been left over for profit. Tim McCoy's budgets at the same studio in the early 30s were slimmer at around $15-20,000. Even this was relative luxury compared with the series of Lone Star Westerns John Wayne made for Monogram in the mid-30s. Budgets were around $5,000 for a shooting schedule of three days.

As an example of how these low budgets were spent, Tuska cites *Prairie Rustlers*, a PRC release of 1945 starring Buster Crabbe. The budget was set at $22,500 and the picture finally came in at $23,304.12 for six days shooting. Buster Crabbe himself got $3,000, his sidekick in the film, Al St John, got $1,000 and the rest of the cast divided just $827 dollars between them. Fred Myton received $1,000 for the screenplay, director Sam Newfield was paid $1,250 and producer Sig Neufeld got $1,200. The sets cost $1,442.50. (To relate 1945 costs to today's prices we should multiply by about seven.)

Republic's total budget for the 1943-4 season gives an idea of how the biggest of the independents carefully graded its budgets to specific types of film. (The break-down demonstrates that production at this level did not start with an idea which was then costed at an appropriate level. Instead, the budget came first and the story and everything else were designed to fit it.) The total production budget was $16 million. Out of this there were to be 32 regular features (not all Westerns) at an average cost of $304,687 each, totalling $9.75 million. Then there was $2.8 million for eight Roy Rogers musical extravaganzas, average cost $350,000. There was a further $2 million for a programme of 24 miscellaneous Westerns starring such as Allan Lane, Bill Elliott and Sunset Carson. The average cost of these would be $83,333. Finally there would be four serials at an average cost of $362,500, $1.45 million in all.

In 1950 Republic financed John Ford's *Rio Grande*. This was one of Republic's rare 'Premiere' category pictures, and for a thirty-two day shooting schedule the total budget was $1,214,899 (production costs rose 60% between 1940 and 1949). In their book *Kings of the Bs* Todd McCarthy and Charles Flynn break

	$
Story	25,450
Staff	214,225
Cast, bits & extras	318,433
Set construction & maintenance	51,384
Set operations	12,699
Set dressing & props	38,993
Wardrobe	27,145
Make-up & hairdressing	7,315
Lighting	8,986
Camera	15,071
Sound	13,683
Music	47,572
Livestock, wranglers, trainers	49,601
Transportation	56,166
Location	68,474
Special effects	12,040
Process & stock shots	227
Film stock	5,595
Laboratory	6,178
Titles & opticals	1,950
Film editing	12,400
Tests	1,500
Non-production salaries & expenses	219,811
TOTAL	1,214,898

this down as shown in the table.

How do these figures compare with the budgets for major studio A-feature Westerns? Direct comparisons between films made in different years are difficult because of inflation. But by any account one of the most expensive Westerns ever made was *Duel in the Sun* (1946), which cost $6 million. At first sight this would appear to be dwarfed by the $35 million reputed to have been spent on *Heaven's Gate* (1980), yet if we muliply by seven to allow for inflation between 1946 and 1980, then the later film does not seem so outrageously expensive after all.

Taking a film of undoubted 'A' quality but more modestly budgeted, we can cite *Red River* (1947), which cost just over $3 million. Of this, $1 million was spent on the two months of location work near the town of Elgin, Arizona. Specialized locations for Westerns existed. In 1940 Columbia had built Old Tucson, twelve miles from the modern Tucson, for its epic *Arizona*. Since then dozens of films and TV shows have been filmed there, including Howard Hawks' *Rio Bravo* and *El Dorado*, though the site is now mainly a tourist attraction. But for *Red River* Hawks preferred a fresh location capable of accommodating the 9,000 head of cattle used in the cattle drive. Even so, several outdoors scenes were shot back in Hollywood, on a huge set 110 x 120 feet. Twenty tons of sand and rocks were imported from Arizona to recreate a desert exterior, at a cost of $20,000 (very nearly as much as the entire budget for PRC's *Prairie Rustlers*). At $150,000 the costumes alone for *Red River* would have paid for a couple of Republic's Sunset Carson Westerns.

The contrast between the resources available to the major studios for their A-features and the meagre outlay possible on Poverty Row suggests that the two worlds were far distant from each other. Many critics of the Western treat them as such, as do aficionados of the B-Western, who regard it as the only pure form of the genre. In their view, stars of A-Westerns such as Gary Cooper should not really be counted as true Western stars because they appeared in other kinds of films as well, thereby diluting the purity of their generic commitment. Nor, it is claimed, did people move from A-Westerns to B-Westerns or back again. John Wayne is cited as the unique example of a star who worked extensively at both the top and bottom ends of the ladder. Everyone else, it is claimed, was rigorously specialized.

But *Red River*, though costing perhaps a hundred times as much as many series Westerns, is evidence that the gulf was never as wide as all that. Besides John Wayne, Montgomery Clift and Walter Brennan the cast includes several actors identified with the series Western: Harry Carey and his son Harry Carey Jr., Noah Beery Jr., Hal Taliaferro (also known as Wally Wales). John Ford too, who had begun by directing Harry Carey at Universal, frequently employed veterans who had once had their own Western series: Tom Tyler in *She Wore a Yellow Ribbon*, Hoot Gibson in *The Horse Soldiers*, Buddy Roosevelt in *The Man Who Shot Liberty Valance*, George O'Brien in *Cheyenne Autumn*.

And yet in many respects the B-Western *was* a world within a world, industrially speaking. Experts on the B-Western (and to be an expert you must have seen literally hundreds of such films) insist that the B-Western took nothing from its supposed superiors. Logic argues that this may well be the case, if only because the B-Western, having a secure market, could afford to remain largely autonomous and self-perpetuating. The A-Western on the other hand was always more of a risk financially; production was more erratic since each film had to sell itself on its merits. For this reason the A-Western was more susceptible to changes of fashion, more influenced by developments in other kinds of films and in Hollywood generally.

THE 30S: CHANGES IN THE INDUSTRY   The 30s has the reputation of being a poor decade for the Western, but production statistics show that this is an over-simplification. Certainly, as Table 5 (Appendix) shows, there was a slump in A-Westerns in the middle of the decade, and a falling off in production of Westerns generally both at the beginning of the decade and again during the middle. Cause and effect cannot be assigned with certainty, but it seems reasonable to attribute the slump in 1930 and 1931 to the introduction of sound. The second dip in numbers can most easily be explained as the result of tightening belts in Hollywood, as the deepening Depression began to bite into theatre attendances. From 1935 the growth of the double-bill increased demand for cheap fillers which the B-Western was ideally placed to fill. The consolidation of several small companies under the umbrella of Republic stabilized this side of the industry, with the result that the production of Westerns by independents jumped from 59 in 1934 to 106 in 1935.

The Western has rarely been at the forefront of stylistic innovation in Hollywood. On the other hand it has generally been in the vanguard of technical advance. One of the first feature films to be shot in two-strip Technicolor was Paramount's *Wanderer of the Wasteland* in 1924. *The Trail of the Lonesome Pine* (1936) was the first picture to be shot on location in the new three-colour Technicolor process. Two big-budget Westerns at the beginning of the 30s, *The Big Trail* and *Billy the Kid*, were made in experimental wide-screen processes, and later when Hollywood was to move more decisively towards wide screens

A Universal Studios Western set

with CinemaScope, Westerns such as *River of No Return* were again among the first films to use the new technology. In the 1960s two Westerns, *Custer of the West* and *How the West Was Won*, were shot in the Cinerama process. When 3-D became a vogue in the mid-50s, Westerns such as *Hondo* and *The Charge at Feather River* seized the opportunity to unleash a shower of projectiles at their audiences.

Sound was to prove a less tractable technology at first. Westerns had always been known for their location work. As we have seen, one of the reasons why production companies moved to California in the early years of the century was in order to exploit the advantage which genuine Western scenery could bring. But the early sound equipment was studio-bound. It required cameras to be heavily insulated so that the noise of their movement would not register on the recording apparatus. This inhibited the transport of the equipment to distant locations, or at least rendered it less mobile.

In addition, sound equipment required a heavy financial outlay. This was at first beyond the capacity of the small companies responsible for a large proportion of Western production. And the small movie theatres in rural neighbourhoods which provided many of the outlets for Westerns also found it hard to lay their hands on the necessary cash to wire for sound. The natural response was to cut back on production while waiting to see what would happen. Eventually, of course, when it became clear that the change-over to sound was complete and irreversible, both producers and exhibitors had to follow suit or go out of business, and production revived.

The second half of the 30s proved in retrospect to be the golden age of the B-Western, which, in addition to meeting a new demand on the bottom half of double-bills, discovered a novel attraction in the form of the singing cowboy. Gene Autry wasn't the first Westerner to warble, but he was the most successful. Beginning with *In Old Santa Fe* in 1934 Autry, accompanied by his guitar and his horse Champion, had strolled amiably through more than ninety films by 1953. For the purist it's hard to see what Autry's films have in common with *The Covered Wagon*; can the term 'Western' really cover two things so dissimilar? But the line from Tom Mix is clear enough if we look at Autry's costume or the scrubbed-clean morality of his films.

There can be no simple explanation of why so few A-Westerns should have been produced in the middle years of the 30s, since the scarcity continued until well after the industry had adjusted to sound. Critics are fond of attributing such shifts in taste to the *zeitgeist*. The 30s, beset as they were with problems as pressing as the relentless growth of unemployment and the rise of fascism, simply could not find time for the Western, which however much or little it attempted to ground itself in history was always more or less escapist. In other areas of artistic production, goes the argument, the 30s were as realistic and documentary a decade as you could wish for; small wonder that Westerns were out of fashion. But such an explanation doesn't stand up if we look at the rest of Hollywood's output during this period, which, a few gritty exercises in realism from Warner Bros. apart, can scarcely qualify as socially concerned. The 30s, after all, were the great age of the Busby Berkeley musical and the screwball comedy. Nor does the argument convince if we look at the Western as a whole, since in the B-Western production boomed, and moved even further away from reality with delirious fantasies such as *Phantom Empire*, in which the singing cowboy is grafted on to the science fiction movie and Gene Autry battles with the denizens of a strange subterranean civilization. If the audience for 'A' pictures was affected by the sober climate of the times, why not that for the B-Western too?

A more plausible reason for the small number of A-Westerns can be found in the box-office returns of the Westerns which were made at the start of the decade. Fox's *The Big Trail* (1930), which was intended to launch John Wayne as a star, did badly, condemning Wayne to Poverty Row for the rest of the decade. RKO's ambitious *Cimarron* (1930) cost $1,433,000 and despite winning an Academy Award for best picture (the only Western ever to do so), it lost some $565,000. Such costly disasters must surely have made the industry think twice about investing heavily in the Western.

Eventually things picked up; not solely, as the legend has it, because of the success of *Stagecoach* in 1939, though that undoubtedly helped. More successful financially and just as influential was Fox's *Jesse James* (1939). Its popularity led not only to a sequel the next year (*The Return of Frank James*) but to a rush of outlaw biographies, including *When the Daltons Rode* (1940), *Bad Men of Missouri* (1941) – about the Younger gang – *Belle Starr* (1941) and *Billy the Kid* (1941), as well as Republic's attempt to cash in by starring Roy Rogers in *Jesse James at Bay* (1941). Other important factors in the renewal of the A-Western were Warners' discovery in Errol Flynn of a star who looked good in period costume and Cecil B. DeMille's rediscovery of the genre he had first entered with *The Squaw Man* in 1914. DeMille's second remake of *The Squaw Man* in 1931 had not been a financial success. But commencing in 1936 with *The Plainsman* he made three Westerns in quick succession, following up with *Union Pacific* (1939) and *North West Mounted Police* (1940). All did well at the box office, helping to re-establish the genre as a major attraction.

THE 40s: RESURGENCE OF THE A-WESTERN

The 1940s proved to be the most decisive decade in the history of the Western. Everything that happened to the genre in the 20s and 30s is in a sense contained within its origins with Broncho Billy, William S. Hart and Tom Mix. But in the 40s the Western set out in new directions. *Stagecoach* and *Union Pacific* are still in their way films of innocence, no less than the fantasies of Gene Autry. Two films of the early 1940s represent a break with the origins of the genre. Howard Hughes' notorious production of *The Outlaw*, begun in 1940, is generally credited with introducing sex into the Western. Broncho Billy, Hart and Mix all got their girl at the end, but their feelings were never less than wholesome. In *The Outlaw* there is a salaciousness that is quite new. If the publicity campaign was more single-minded about sex than the film itself ('What are the two reasons for Jane Russell's rise to stardom?' demanded a poster on which her bosom was prominently displayed), the scene in which she hastily marries the wounded Billy the Kid (Jack Buetel) before jumping into bed with him to keep him warm certainly represented a departure from the tradition of chivalrous romance.

The second film to point in a new direction is *The Ox-Bow Incident* (1942). Before this the hero had always been certain of his moral rectitude in a universe where right and wrong were clearly separated and right was sure of ultimate triumph. In *The Ox-Bow Incident* lynching (which previously, in *The Virginian*, was treated as an unpleasant duty which had to be faced if justice were to be achieved) becomes symptomatic of a community which is rotten inside. Those who perpetrate the crime are driven by a variety of motives, but a desire for justice is not prominent. Though Henry Fonda is ultimately the mouthpiece for decency the film has, properly speaking, no hero and the darkness of its moral universe is unrelieved by the light of any shining armour. *The Ox-Bow Incident* introduces into the Western both a bleak view of the frontier and a complexity in the delineation of character which would lead critics to observe that the Western had 'grown up' since it was now 'about' something. The film is therefore the harbinger of two related tendencies. One is towards the Western which rehearses a 'social' theme. *High Noon*, coming early in the next decade, is probably the best known example of this kind, though the town-taming Western, which contains a social theme in embryo, had renewed its popularity around the turn of the decade with *Frontier Marshal* (1939), *Dodge City* (1939) and *Tombstone, the Town Too Tough to Die* (1942). The second tendency is towards a deepening of character motivation, and in particular the ascription of villainy to more diverse and complicated motivations than a simple greed for money.

The 'adult' or 'social' or 'psychological' Western did not of course replace overnight what went before. In 1943 the decidedly uncomplicated Roy Rogers replaced the equally serene Gene Autry as the top money-making Western star and he was to remain so for the next eleven years. But the trends that had been started gathered pace as the 40s progressed. In 1946 *Duel in the Sun* picked up the torch of sexual desire which *The Outlaw* had lit. In 1947 came Raoul Walsh's

Poster for The Outlaw *(1940)*

Pursued, which went a great deal further down the road of complicating psychology with its Freudian case-history plot. Freudian overtones were also present in the cycle of films centred on the powerfully authoritarian figure of a cattle baron; *Duel in the Sun* is a key film here too.

Why at this point in its history the Western should have developed in this way is not easy to say. The explanation that the new Western was a sign of the times is no more convincing of the 40s than of the 30s. Just because the 40s were, in the conventional account, gloomy years (the atom bomb and the cold war following hard upon the horrors of World War II), there is no particular reason why the Western should follow suit. The B-Western went cheerfully on its way. Nor did other genres always reflect the prevailing angst. The 40s are also the heyday of the MGM musical.

All the same, there is a definite, if not all-encompassing, movement in Hollywood cinema at this time towards a bleaker, even more cynical, view of the world, and also a renewed interest in psychology. This is manifested in the rise of film noir (which dates from the start of the 40s); in *Citizen Kane* (a trendsetting film if ever there was one); and in the prevalence of abnormal psychological states as character motivation in such genres as the melodrama. These influences made their way into the A-Western. That the B-Western was minimally influenced by such developments only demonstrates how self-contained it was.

THE 50S: THE BEGINNING OF THE END?

The 1950s continued what the 40s had begun. As society changed its notions of what was acceptable in the field of sexual activity, so the Western allowed in themes and ideas which had previously been taboo. In 1959 came *Warlock*, which in its portrayal of the relationship between Henry Fonda and Anthony Quinn came closer than anything seen before to suggestions of homosexuality. Two years later, in *The Last Sunset*, the plot turns on the possibility of Kirk Douglas' incest with his daughter.

Not everyone welcomed the new kind of Western. Some film-makers attempted to go their own way without conceding anything to fashion. It's well known that Howard Hawks intended *Rio Bravo* (1958) as a somewhat belated rebuff to the social criticism of *High Noon* (1952), pouring scorn on the notion that any sheriff worth his salt would want help from amateurs. In *Fort Apache* (1948), though John Ford admits the possibility that Henry Fonda as the Custer-figure Colonel Thursday may have acted rashly, this is not allowed to damage the potent myth of the thin blue line.

Some eminent critics also protested. Robert Warshow in his essay on the Western hero written in 1954 attacked recent films for departing from the original purity of the form. *The Gunfighter* (1950) and *High Noon* are accused of distracting us from the central figure of the hero by their insistence on detailing (in what Warshow regards as a fairly humdrum way) the social fabric of the towns where the action happens. Warshow is also suspicious of what he sees as a tendency towards aestheticism in such films as *Shane* (1952). This is similar to the objection by André Bazin, writing just a year later than Warshow in 1955. Bazin identifies something he calls the 'sur-Western', which is 'a Western that would be ashamed to be just itself, and looks for some additional interest to justify its existence – an aesthetic, sociological, moral, psychological, political or erotic interest, in short some quality extrinsic to the genre and which is supposed to enrich it.' As an example he too gives *Shane*, which he feels is too self-consciously at work on the creation of a myth and which he sees as a possible indication of decadence.

Yet the 1950s were also a time of renewal. In 1950 came *Broken Arrow*, a landmark in the Western's treatment of the Indian. As we have seen, the early years of the century saw a number of films which were sympathetic to the

Indian's cause and which even placed the Indian centre-stage. This did not last. With the dubious exception of the Lone Ranger's faithful Tonto, there are no Indians as series heroes in the B-Western and very few in the A-Western between 1920 and 1950. *Broken Arrow* may now be seen as something less than the perfectly liberal movie it was once taken for. No one except the conventional villains out for money is held responsible for the Indians' plight, and the Indian girl with whom the hero (James Stewart) falls in love has to die lest miscegenation become something he and we have to live with. But the film did open up a space in which the Indian might be something more than a faceless screaming savage.

TELEVISION In 1954 Republic released its final series Western, *Phantom Stallion*, and in September of the same year came what is generally regarded as the last B-Western made as part of a series, Allied Artists' *Two Guns and a Badge*. The writing had been on the wall for some time before that. In 1948 William Boyd had sold his Hopalong Cassidy pictures to television, and from 1950 onwards Hollywood released large numbers of films to what was, in effect, the competition. At first the target audience was almost exclusively children. Gene Autry was also an early entrant into television production, with no less than four series in the late 1940s (*Range Rider*, *Buffalo Bill Jr.*, *Annie Oakley* and *The Adventures of Champion*) offered as syndicated features for local stations. Another television series which began in 1948 was *The Lone Ranger*, which had originated in radio and then spun off into other media such as films, newspaper strips and comic books, as well as exploiting the market for children's toys, games and clothing.

For a time the networks held back on producing Westerns for primetime viewing. But by the mid-1950s it was clear that there was a sizeable audience for shows that appealed to adults. In 1955 ABC launched *The Life and Legend of Wyatt Earp*, starring Hugh O'Brian, and *Cheyenne* with Clint Walker. CBS began with *Gunsmoke*, which for several years had been a successful radio show. NBC were slower to find a really successful series, but in 1957 came up with *Wagon Train*, starring Ward Bond, one of the longest running of all television Westerns. Other successful shows of the late 50s included *Maverick*, which made the career of James Garner, and *Have Gun, Will Travel*, with Richard Boone as the elegant mercenary Paladin. Within two years the Western had carried all before it. By the 1957-8 season Westerns completely dominated the ratings. *Gunsmoke* was at number 1, *Tales of Wells Fargo* with Dale Robertson at number 3, *Have Gun, Will Travel* at number 4, *The Life and Legend of Wyatt Earp* at number 6. By 1958-9 six of the top seven shows were Westerns.

Douglas Brode has identified three distinct types of television Western. First came the historical hero, as in *The Life and Legend of Wyatt Earp*, *Bat Masterson*, or *Jim Bowie*. Then there was a vogue for a roving fictional hero, as in *Cheyenne*, *Bronco* or *Have Gun, Will Travel*. Third was the show built around a fictional hero in a fixed locale, such as *Lawman* or *Gunsmoke*. To this Michael Barson adds the show based on a family unit, of which the prime example would be *Bonanza*, which began in the 1959-60 season and continued until 1973. The first colour television Western, *Bonanza*, was astonishingly successful and was outlasted only by *Gunsmoke*.

In fact, as Barson admits, the television Western differed little from its

Gunsmoke: *(l. to r.) James Arness, Milburn Stone, Amanda Blake, Ken Curtis, (seated) Burt Reynolds*

cinematic ancestor. Television drew on the same materials, with series about railroads, outlaws, Indians, the army, about marshals, cowboys, gunmen and settlers. There were even parodies (*Maverick* and *The Wild, Wild West*). Nor was the television Western much different from other kinds of television show in the dramatic formulae it employed. As Barson describes it:

'A Western was likely to draw its conflicts from the range of human drama found across the spectrum of ancient myths up to and including contemporary issues. A father unable to communicate with his son; a mob unwilling to tolerate different kinds of people and beliefs; a wife who no longer loves her husband; a boy, eager to be recognized as a man; an outsider, eager to become part of a community – any one of these story premises might one week be the basis for an episode of a Western, the next the basis for a cop show, a family drama, or an episode of *Star Trek*.'

This is not to say that the television Western lacked originality or artistry, even within the cramped confines of what were, at the beginning, merely half-hour shows. These stories had been the stock in trade of Hollywood for forty years before television picked them up. That hadn't prevented those in Hollywood who had it in them from making good pictures. The television Western didn't lack for talent. It threw up many good actors; among them Steve McQueen from *Wanted: Dead or Alive*, James Garner from *Maverick*, Clint Eastwood from *Rawhide*. And two Western series, *The Rifleman* and *The Westerner*, provided the training ground for the last great director of the Hollywood Western, Sam Peckinpah.

The boom period of the late 1950s didn't last. As the 1960s wore on innovation seemed to wear out and few new successful Western shows were introduced. *Rawhide* had begun in 1959 and reached the list of the top 25 shows for the season 1959-60, but no other Westerns achieved real success in the ratings until *The Virginian* in 1963. By the beginning of the 1970s, as Table 6 (Appendix) shows, the television Western had gone into a steep decline, moderated but not reversed by the 'Middle-Western' *Little House on the Prairie*, which, beginning in 1974, hit number 1 in the ratings by the end of the decade and lasted until 1983.

What brought about the decline in the television Western was not so much a fall in popularity as changes in the means whereby television produced a profile of its audience. Up to the end of the 60s aggregates had been all that mattered: the number of people overall who were watching a show. But then at the beginning of the 1970s arose a new method of audience research known as demographics, which measured not just totals but the numbers of viewers of different social groups within the aggregate. The networks soon discovered that though Westerns were generally popular, they were much more popular with juveniles and among the rural and less well-off part of the population than with the urban and more middle-class audience. Westerns on television were finding an audience very similar to that which B-Westerns had traditionally found in the movie theatres. But since television needed to sell advertising time, not programmes, it soon realized that it could do better with shows which appealed to the more affluent. Suddenly, in the 1971-2 season, there was a pitch for what would now be called the 'yuppie' audience; Westerns, assumed to be for hicks, were out. *The Virginian*, it would appear, was just one of these casualties of demographics.

As the B-Western declined under the influence of television there was renewed activity in a type of film that hovered somewhere between the A- and B-feature. This was less expensive than the full-scale all-star Western, with a cast sometimes of second-rank stars, sometimes of first-rank stars who were aging a little or seeking independence from their studios. Such films, often referred to as co-features (neither top or bottom billing but sharing with a film of equal status), showed considerable vitality and staying power during the long-drawn-out decline of the genre from its position of dominance. Examples of such productions would be the films which James Stewart made with Anthony Mann, starting with *Winchester '73* in 1950, or those in which the talents of Randolph Scott, Budd Boetticher, Harry Joe Brown and Burt Kennedy combined to bring about such minor masterpieces as *The Tall T* and *Comanche Station*.

Despite this, by the end of the 50s the fall-off in production was there for all to see. Not only had the independents collapsed (Republic had ceased production in 1958); the majors too seemed to be losing interest. In 1953 92 Westerns had been made in Hollywood. Ten years later this had sunk to a mere 11. True, production of all kinds of films in Hollywood was in decline; but Westerns sank faster. As a percentage of all films made they went from 27 per cent in 1953 to a mere 9 per cent in 1963. Where once much of the financial stability of the industry had rested on Westerns, now Hollywood seemed to continue making them only out of habit and nostalgia.

THE 1960s: THE INTERNATIONAL WESTERN

Yet if there was by 1960 a drastic decline in the number of Westerns being made, the new decade was to see the genre once again revitalized, this time from an unexpected source. One film right at the start of the 1960s was to prove especially significant in the light of what was to come. *The Magnificent Seven* was based on *The Seven Samurai*, a Japanese film directed by Akira Kurosawa. It demonstrated that however American might be its origins, the Western was by now a truly international form. If a Western could be made from a Japanese movie, with the plot virtually unchanged, then the genre belonged to anybody. As if to prove the point, *The Magnificent Seven*, only moderately successful in America, went on to do huge business in Europe. Ever since World War I the European market had been important to Hollywood. Now, with the uncertainties of the domestic market, it became a good deal more than that. And soon the unthinkable would happen; Europe would itself become a centre for the production as well as the consumption of Westerns.

In 1962 the Germans had pointed the way with *Der Schatz im Silbersee* (*The Treasure of Silver Lake*), the first of the Winnetou films based on the Karl May novels. Its financial success showed that there was an audience for Westerns made in Europe. The Germans had imported Lex Barker, a former Tarzan, to play Old Shatterhand, Winnetou's Aryan friend. Two years later Sergio Leone brought over a minor television star, Clint Eastwood, to play in *Per un pugno di dollari* (*A Fistful of Dollars*), based on another Kurosawa film, *Yojimbo*, and a boom was under way.

The Magnificent Seven also gave a boost to a theme which was to become one of the mainstays of the 60s, that of the small professional élite hired to do a specialist job. Elements of such a theme had long been present in the Western (and indeed in the crime film and war film), and perhaps it had always been embryonic in the figure of the hero whose gunfighting skills secure his triumph

The Magnificent Seven (1960): (l. to r.)
Yul Brynner, Steve McQueen, Horst
Buchholz, Charles Bronson, Robert Vaughn,
Brad Dexter, James Coburn

over evil. But in the 60s the Western hero seemed finally to lose touch with his origins in the cowboy and, retaining only the traditional cowboy costume, become a gunfighter pure and simple. As such he also became a mercenary, hiring out to the highest bidder. The tension between the amorality of the cash nexus and the hero's own loyalties or scruples became the basis for the drama.

The distance between this and the fully-fledged cynicism which was to characterize the Italian Western is perhaps not so great. Cynicism, or something approaching it, had already entered the American Western at least as early as 1954 with Robert Aldrich's *Vera Cruz*, in which a couple of adventurers (Gary Cooper and Burt Lancaster) sell their services below the border. The scene in which they demonstrate their shooting prowess to the Emperor Maximilian is a blueprint for all the show-offs in the Spaghetti Western.

There is rather more continuity between the Hollywood Western and the Italian Western than is usually allowed. The Italians not only imported actors – including, significantly, Eli Wallach, who had made a name for himself as the bandit chief in *The Magnificent Seven* and was to play The Ugly in Sergio Leone's *Il buono, il brutto, il cattivo* (*The Good, the Bad and the Ugly*). They took certain attitudes and themes which had already emerged and pushed them further. The mercenary (and his cousin the bounty hunter) is one of the key characters in the Italian Western, where any motivation but self-interest is regarded with suspicion. Most notoriously, Italian directors displayed a fascination with the violence which was inherent in the dramatic tensions the Western had traditionally explored. One can see in *The Magnificent Seven* a tendency towards the aestheticizing of violence, celebrating the balletic beauty of a gunfight. This was developed by the Italians into a fully-fledged obsession, taken to extremes of parodic excess in which hordes of extras described extravagant parabolas as they fell beneath a hail of bullets. When the supercharged violence of the Italian Western was imported back to Hollywood in such films as *The Wild Bunch* (1969) there was an outcry from critics, eager to make facile connections between what was happening on the screen and the rising tide of crime on the streets of America's cities.

1964, the year of *Per un pugno di dollari*, was also the year which saw *Cheyenne Autumn* and *A Distant Trumpet*, the last Westerns of two great veterans, John Ford and Raoul Walsh. Hollywood productions held steady during the rest of the 60s at about 20 a year, but the old confidence was gone. There no longer seemed any certainty about what kind of Westerns to make. As the 60s gave way to the 70s Hollywood searched, with increasing desperation, for new constituents to replace those who had deserted the traditional Western.

There were, inevitably, imitations of Spaghetti Westerns. Some were feeble, such as *El Condor* (1970), starring Lee Van Cleef, the actor who, after playing innumerable heavies in quality pictures such as *High Noon*, *Ride Lonesome* and *The Man Who Shot Liberty Valance*, had become a star in Italy. Some, such as *Hang 'Em High*, starring Clint Eastwood, who used his Italian success as a springboard to even greater fame in the Hollywood Western, were interesting hybrids. Many of the Italian Westerns were set in Mexico, partly because

Clint Eastwood as the Man with No Name in Per un pugno di dollari *(A Fistful of Dollars) (1964)*

locations in Italy or elsewhere in Europe could be made to stand in for south of the border, partly because that way Latin characters could be privileged at the expense of Anglo-Saxons. The Americans soon followed suit, shooting many of their 1960s Westerns in southern Spain, where the landscape approximated to Mexico and the costs were much lower than Hollywood.

The racial balance of the Western in fact changed markedly by the end of the 60s. Besides more frequent and more dignified Mexican characters, there were, if only occasionally, substantial roles for black actors, as in *The Scalphunters* (1967), in which Ossie Davis took his opportunity well. With *Cheyenne Autumn* John Ford had made a serious, if still compromised, attempt to set the record straight about how the Indians had been treated. Two films in 1970 went further towards closing the gap between the Western's caricature of the Indian and historical reality. *Soldier Blue* tried to shock with explicit depiction of carnage, rape and mutilation in its account of the infamous Sand Creek Massacre. *Little Big Man* attempted to communicate some of the attraction and strangeness of an alien culture. Since there was no such thing as a Native American film industry it was inevitable that Indians would still be seen through white eyes, but the 'me heapum big chief' stereotype had become unusable.

Women, on the other hand, another disadvantaged group in the traditional Western, did not find their role much improved. The Italian Western had virtually ignored them, and although a few films such as *Hannie Caulder* and *Cat Ballou* provided meaty roles for Hollywood female stars, the Western could find no plausible way in which to grant women equal screen time. In part this was doubtless the result of a scarcity of role models in the history of the West (Calamity Jane and Belle Starr notwithstanding). But it had more to do with the fact that the central dramatic conflict in the genre invariably involved a trial of physical prowess. Hollywood could not in its heart believe in women taking up arms; especially in a genre which was, however notionally, set in the age of the crinoline.

The withering away of the traditional audience for the Western had led by the 1970s to a free-for-all, where in order to find a market everything was tried at least once. There were Westerns for children, for blacks and hippies, for liberals and conservatives. There were softcore and hardcore Westerns, science-fiction Westerns and Western allegories about Vietnam. There were ecological and ethnographic Westerns, and plenty of parodies just in case anyone thought Hollywood still took the Western seriously. There were British Westerns shot in Spain, American Westerns shot in Israel, German Westerns shot in Yugoslavia. There was more violence, more sex, more violent sex. The history of the West was ransacked to find new stories or, failing that, a new twist to old stories. Everybody who had ever been anybody, Jesse James and Billy the Kid, Wyatt Earp and General Custer, was debunked.

There were good Westerns, too. Peckinpah was active, as were Burt Kennedy, Monte Hellman, Clint Eastwood, Sergio Leone. Two themes in particular proved fruitful. The first took familiar Western characters or events and tried to tell the story with a little more realism. In *Will Penny* (1967), for example, we are shown the economic hardship and loneliness of a cowboy's life. *The Culpepper Cattle Co.* (1972) is another disenchanted look at the emotional and physical deprivations of a life spent driving cattle. At its extremes, in such examples of the so-called 'mud and rags' school as *The Great Northfield Minnesota Raid* (1972), this approach seemed in danger of romanticizing squalor.

A different variant of the romantic appeared in another popular theme of the 60s and 70s. Sam Peckinpah had set the trend in 1962. His film *Ride the High Country* (*Guns in the Afternoon* in Britain) was about the end of the West, a look back to the moment when motor cars, Chinese restaurants and 'the steady businessman' had conspired to sweep away the era of rugged individualism. This theme can be traced back at least as far as *The Gunfighter*, made in 1950. Its hero (played by Gregory Peck) is tired of his wandering, lonely life, which he feels is appropriate neither to his advancing years nor to the changing life of the frontier, with its new schools and churches. He wants to settle down and raise a family. But his reputation attracts a succession of youths ambitious to achieve fame by beating him to the draw, and one of them proves the impossibility of his dream. In the 1960s the idea of the hero who cannot settle down, who is unable to adjust to change, or perhaps even to society itself, became almost commonplace, and Peckinpah was to return to it obsessively. Two other films of 1962, *Lonely Are the Brave* and *The Man Who Shot Liberty Valance*, also in their very different ways lamented the passing of the Old West. In Peckinpah's work and in other films on the same theme such as *The Good Guys and the Bad Guys* (1969), *Monte Walsh* (1970) and *The Shootist* (1976) the aging cowboy or gunfighter is seen as symptomatic of the decline of the West itself, often signalled by the incursion of modern inventions such as the motor car.

This was not nearly such a novel theme as the film-makers seemed to think. Back in the 1830s the painter George Catlin had lamented the imminent demise of the distinctive Plains Indian culture. At the end of the century Frederic Remington was saddened by the inevitable destruction by the encroaching farmers of the free and open life of the plains. Stephen Crane's story 'The Bride Comes to Yellow Sky', published in 1898, is an elegy for the rowdy excitements of a frontier town. Indeed, it seemed as though at the very moment of its creation the West was suffused with a rosy tinge of nostalgia. But if it was an old theme it was a good one; though perhaps, as Pauline Kael remarked, it wasn't so much the West that was growing old as the Western stars themselves. With Randolph Scott (b. 1903), Joel McCrea (b. 1905), Henry Fonda (b. 1905), John Wayne (b. 1907) and James Stewart (b. 1908) all entering their sixties and few younger stars coming along to play their roles, old age was by the 1960s not so much a theme selected by film-makers as forced upon them.

THE END OF THE WESTERN?   Despite new themes and new talents it was apparent that the Western was running out of steam. Hollywood no longer depended on this one genre the way it had. Not only had the Western ceased to be central; the constant searching for new angles showed that it no longer had a centre. The conventional wisdom now is that the Western was killed off overnight by the monumental extravagance of Michael Cimino's *Heaven's Gate* (1980). This must be an over-simplification. There have been Westerns since then, some of them successful. But both the huge cost of *Heaven's Gate* and its almost total failure at the box office seem to have convinced Hollywood executives that the Western was a bad risk.

Even so, the Western was clearly in trouble long before 1980. It's easy enough to find reasons why, though harder to know what weight to give them. In the first place, Hollywood itself was in trouble; had been, perhaps, as early as 1948, when the 'Paramount decision' of the Supreme Court forced the divorce of the studios from their captive markets, the chains of theatres which they owned. Once the audience began to be seriously eroded by television and other alternative entertainments the studios had to search for new formulas. Something as traditional as the Western was bound to be at a disadvantage. Other genres such as the crime film, the horror film and the science-fiction film were rejuvenated. They appeared to offer excitements that were either more realistic or more fantastic than the Western, but in any case were different. The Western had always offered violence as the solution to the threat of lawlessness, but in a ritualized form, removed from everyday reality by the distance of time and place. Now the crime film shifted its premises, and invaded the Western's territory. In the gangster films of the 1930s crime had been a specialized activity, reserved to criminals, who by and large left the ordinary citizen undisturbed. Then in the 1960s the city became the frontier, and the savages – the muggers and the rapists – were already inside the gates. Don Siegel's *Coogan's Bluff*, made in 1968, made this shift explicit, as an Arizona sheriff pursues his quarry through the streets of New York. The casting of Clint Eastwood, the last great totem pole of the Western, in this contemporary role appeared to authenticate the transference of the Western's traditional themes to the crime film, and Eastwood's subsequent career as the policeman Dirty Harry confirmed it.

A more immediate explanation of the Western's decline may lie in demographics. As is well enough known, many of the changes Hollywood has undergone since the beginning of the 60s have been led by a fundamental shift in the constitution of the audience. Overwhelmingly now the cinema audience is a youthful, even teenage one, especially in America. It was always likely that the Western would suffer in such a situation. Although from time to time the Western had tried to hitch itself to the wagon of youth, flirting with the juvenile delinquent theme in films such as *The True Story of Jesse James* (1957), or building up the baby-faced Audie Murphy into a Western star, it had always been a genre dominated by maturity and experience, nowhere better symbolized than in the recurrent motif of the shooting lesson in which gun lore is imparted by the wise to the not always willing. Once the stars themselves began to change unmistakably from mature to old, with few youthful replacements apart from Eastwood (and even Eastwood was 37 by the time *Per un pugno di dollari* was released in America), the genre began to lose its grip on the youth audience. BBC Audience Research Department figures from 1965 confirm this. Asked to name their preferred type of film, respondents in the 16-19 age group replied 24 per cent for horror films, 29 per cent for science fiction and only 16 per cent for Westerns. The corresponding figures for the 20-29 age group were 3, 13 and 25 per cent.

And yet many elements of the culture of the Western maintain their appeal. Western clothes remain in fashion, not only in the heartland of the western states where stetsons, jeans and high-heeled boots are still everyday wear, but with young people around the world. 'Country and Western' music is more popular than ever. Advertising copywriters still assume familiarity with the world of the Western; a recent hoarding for a bank proclaims it as 'The loan arranger. And pronto.' If the Western was truly a despised or forgotten form nothing would disappear more quickly than such knowing references.

More significantly, in the field of serious literature the Western myth retains its power, enriching the work of writers as diverse as Larry McMurtry and

Thomas McGuane. While novels of the order of *Lonesome Dove* and *Something to Be Desired* can still be written about the West, who can say the Western is dead? Perhaps we too readily import into our discussions inappropriate biological metaphors. The Western is likened to a tree, with its roots in the soil of American history, its trunk the central structuring opposition of savagery and civilization, its branches the thematic variations of cattlemen vs. farmers, cavalry vs. Indians, and so forth. Each season new films appear, like new leaves. The sturdy sapling grows to maturity, but eventually it must wither and die. It is an appealing conceit, but perhaps a misleading one. The history of Hollywood production is best understood not through metaphors of organic growth, but in terms of economic cycles, of boom and slump. As we have seen, the Western was declared exhausted as long ago as 1911; in the late 1930s the major studios appeared to have almost given up on Westerns. So far the genre has always managed to renew itself. Despite changes in the audience its underlying appeal may still be strong enough for a new cycle to emerge. No one can say with confidence that this will happen, still less what kind of spark might rekindle Hollywood's enthusiasm. Only one thing is sure in the cinema: fashions change. The Western may surprise us yet.

REFERENCES
In addition to other books listed in the general bibliography, the following works have been particularly helpful in the writing of this introduction.

Les Adams and Buck Rainey, *Shoot Em Ups* (New Rochelle, New York: Arlington House, 1980)

Robert Anderson, 'The Role of the Western Film Genre in Industry Competition 1907-1911', *Journal of the University Film Association* XXXI, 2 (Spring 1979)

Michael Barson, 'The TV Western', in Brian G. Rose (ed.), *TV Genres* (Westport, Conn.: Greenwood Press, 1985)

André Bazin, 'The Western, or the American film *par excellence*' and 'The Evolution of the Western', in Hugh Gray (ed.), *What Is Cinema?* vol. II (Berkeley and Los Angeles: University of California Press, 1971)

Douglas Brode, 'They Went Thataway', *Television Quarterly*, Summer 1982

Kevin Brownlow, *The War, the West and the Wilderness* (London: Secker and Warburg, 1979)

John Cawelti, *The Six-Gun Mystique* (Bowling Green: Bowling Green University Popular Press, 1971)

William K. Everson, *A Pictorial History of the Western Film* (Secaucus, N.J.: Citadel Press, 1969)

George N. Fenin and William K. Everson, *The Western from Silents to the Seventies* (New York: Penguin, 1977)

Christopher Frayling, *Spaghetti Westerns* (London: Routledge and Kegan Paul, 1981)

Philip French, *Westerns: Aspects of a Movie Genre* (London: Secker and Warburg, rev. ed. 1977)

Phil Hardy, *The Western* (London: Aurum Press, 1983)

Garth S. Jowett, 'Giving Them What They Want: Movie Audience Research Before 1950', in Bruce A. Austin (ed.), *Current Research in Film: Audiences, Economics and Law* vol.I (Norwood, N.J.: Ablex, 1985)

Jim Kitses, *Horizons West* (London: Secker and Warburg, 1969)

Todd McCarthy and Charles Flynn (eds.), *Kings of the Bs* (New York: E.P. Dutton, 1975)

William R. Meyer, *The Making of the Great Westerns* (New Rochelle, New York: Arlington House, 1979) (contains the budget for *Red River*)

Don Miller, *Hollywood Corral* (New York: Popular Library, 1976)

Henry Nash Smith, *Virgin Land* (Cambridge, Mass.: Harvard University Press, 1950)

Peter Stanfield, 'The Western 1909-14: A Cast of Villains', *Film History* I, 2 (1987)

Jon Tuska, *The Filming of the West* (Garden City, New York: Doubleday & Co., 1976) (contains much information on B-Westerns, including budgets)

Jon Tuska, *The American West in Film* (Westport, Conn.: Greenwood Press, 1985)

Robert Warshow, *The Immediate Experience* (Garden City, New York: Anchor Books, 1964)

PART II

THE WESTERN:
A CULTURAL AND HISTORICAL DICTIONARY

A

Abilene · The prototype of all the cow towns that flourished briefly in Kansas at the end of the Civil War, drily described by Robert Dykstra in his study *The Cattle Towns* as 'technically speaking, an interior market facility situated at the juncture of railroad and Texas cattle trail where drovers sold their livestock to buyers.' Abilene opened for business in 1867. Joseph *McCoy, the cattle dealer responsible for developing the town, wrote that he originally found it 'a very small, dead place consisting of about one dozen log huts, low, small rude affairs, four-fifths of which were covered with dirt for roofing.' By 1871, the town's busiest year, it boasted eleven saloons, including the celebrated Alamo, together with dance-halls and brothels. In this year 190,000 cattle were sold in the town. It is in Abilene that Montgomery Clift arrives with his herd in *Red River*/1947 (on 14 August 1865, the film records, which would make them two years early). Wild Bill *Hickok was marshal there for eight months in 1871. As the railroad continued to advance west, Abilene lost business to other towns down the line and in 1872 its chief hotel, the Drovers Cottage, was dismantled and moved to Ellsworth.

Adams, Andy (1859-1935) · Author. *Log of a Cowboy* (1903), Adams' best known work of fiction, draws directly on his experiences driving cattle up from Texas during the 1880s. Its documentary impulse, though not without its own kind of romanticism, was intended to counter the melodrama inherent in other cowboy fiction. Adams' other novels, such as *The Outlet* (1905) and *Reed*

Anthony (1907), are also about the cattle trade.

Adams, Grizzly (1812-60) · A mountain man who specialized in catching bears, Adams set up a menagerie in California in the 1850s. In 1860 Adams and his bears were invited to join Phineas *Barnum's circus in a parade down Broadway. His exploits were later embroidered in dime novels. He is ripely personified by John Huston in *The Life and Times of Judge Roy Bean*/1972.
Television · Dan Haggerty/*The Life and Times of Grizzly Adams* · Dan Haggerty/ *The Capture of Grizzly Adams*

Agriculture · The American West is immensely rich in minerals. But its greatest treasure is its soil and the driving force of development has been that soil's exploitation. The real history of much of the West is consequently the history of its agriculture.

As a subject, agriculture does not loom large in Westerns. A few films celebrate the coming of the small farmers. Many more, especially at the B-level, scorn the 'sod busters' and 'nesters' for their destruction of the cowboy's way of life. *Oklahoma!*/1955 valiantly tries to do both, proclaiming that 'the farmer and the cowboy should be friends.' But by and large, agriculture is as unimportant to the filmic West as the exploits of Billy the Kid are to most serious historians. Farmers and their ways exist, if at all, as mere background, which is not really surprising. For cowboys and farmers alike, the reality of life was hard drudgery. The task of both was the production of food-stuffs for the market. But cowboys were exotic and did it on the move, whereas farmers were prosaically static.

One of the longest-lasting tensions in American public culture posits a gulf between agrarianism and commerce. Here, the argument runs, is the pre-20th century American equivalent of Europe's class struggles, with city folk and corporations on one side and the tillers of the soil on the other. This antinomy between virtuous husbandry and corrupting trade has deep roots, and in the 19th century it seemed often to explain reality, especially the reality of railroads whose basic policy was to gouge their farming customers rather than to serve them.

Historians of American agriculture have indeed found evidence that many farming people organized their lives around other values than the simple desire for gain. From the beginning, staple, market-oriented production was the basis of the southern plantation economy, but in New England and the middle colonies and even in the southern backcountry another way developed. People acquired land to safeguard their families' security, not to speculate in market value. They grew mixed crops for the sake of their own independence, rather than single commodities for high prices. To this extent, *Drums Along the Mohawk*/1939 and *Shane*/ 1952 are correct in their implicit assertion that what small pioneer farmers sought to create was a way of life. *Shane* and *Heaven's Gate*/1980 are equally correct to assert a conflict between that way of life and the goals of people who operated on a larger scale.

None the less, the dominant fact of American agriculture in the era of transcontinental expansion was a market place that embraced the whole world. Frank *Norris's novel *The Octopus* (1901) turns on the traditional tension between the producers of agricultural goods and the manipulators of their value. But his 'farmers' are California wheat growers who produce on a vast scale, and they are fully in touch with market movements as far away as Liverpool. The settlement of the West led to the production of wheat, corn, beef, pork, wool, fruit and mutton in colossal quantities, for the sake of profit. The people who produced them cannot be described as peasants.

Some parts of the West have been small-farmer country from their first settlement. In the 1840s migrants from the forested areas of the east became aware that the Willamette Valley of Oregon (the setting of *Canyon Passage*) offered conditions much like the ones they knew. So, leapfrogging across the Great Plains and the Rocky Mountains, they settled there. Not for decades would Oregon be linked by railroad to California and thus to eastern markets. But people settled rapidly enough for it to acquire statehood as early as 1859. Small-farm economies likewise developed in southern Illinois, in parts of Wisconsin and among the Mormons of the Great Salt Lake Basin.

All of these people tried to recreate the way of life that they and their ancestors had known, but most of the West was unlike 'back east'. The Mormons were among the first to discover this and confront head-on the most severe environmental challenge that the West presented: the absence of water. West of the 98th meridian, which cuts through the eastern Dakotas, central Nebraska, Kansas, Oklahoma and Texas, rainfall is too unreliable for cropping and neither ground nor stream water is enough for general irrigation. The Mormons were the first settlers west of that line, other than on the well-watered Pacific Coast, and they quickly realized that they would have to deal with water in a new way.

In the east, as in England, water was legally a private resource and the use of a stream was the privilege of the owners of its banks. With heavy rainfall and ample flow, that presented no problem. But diverting or even using water from a western river can mean disaster for everyone downstream. Mormon agriculture became possible because the Latter-Day Saints agreed that water had to be treated as a public resource. The survival of their small-farmer individualism depended on their willingness and ability to act as a community. Such problems would be difficult for a Western to treat, but *Wagon Master*/1950 does stress the communal spirit of its Mormon migrants, and *The Ballad of*

Cable Hogue/1970 turns on the absolute importance of water in a parched environment.

For both geographical and social reasons, most western agriculture did not develop on a small-farming basis. Even on the well-watered prairies of the central Mississippi Valley (Indiana, Illinois, Iowa and Missouri), speculators and would-be estate builders took advantage of public land policy to build up vast holdings. In some cases they worked the land with tenants and hired labour. Others, such as the 'Hoosier Cattle Kings' of Indiana, used it to pasture enormous herds. Some of these holdings were in excess of 100,000 acres.

The greatest break with the small-farm tradition was the 'bonanza' farming of the Red River Valley, in the Dakotas, Minnesota and Manitoba. The 'valley' is broad, flat and immensely fertile. Settlement began about 1870, and from the beginning the land was owned in vast units. By 1884 one such establishment contained 33,000 acres and reportedly produced 230,000 bushels of wheat. Such farms were necessarily fully mechanized. As historian Gilbert Fite shows (*The Farmer's Frontier*, 1966), one farm might have as early as the end of its second year of operation as many as '26 breaking plows, 40 plows for turning the broken soil, 21 seeders, 60 harrows, 30 self-binding harvesters, and five steam-powered threshers'. Agriculture in California developed in much the same way; in 1872 the wheat crop of the largest California farm was 1,440,000 bushels, grown in fields as much as 17 miles long.

The prairies, the Great Plains, the intramontane desert and the California interior all presented conditions that forced technological innovation. Because the prairies were unwooded, the earliest whites were slow to

Currier and Ives lithograph: 'The Pioneers: Home on the Western Front' (1867)

appreciate their fertility. On the plains the productive capacity of the rich black soil is limited only by the aridity of the climate, but to work it at all, irrigation and 'dry farming' proved necessary. Even to the east of the 98th meridian the seemingly simple task of breaking the original grass covering proved immensely difficult. Farmers were forced rapidly to abandon the traditional peasant notion that the best way to do things was the way things had always been done.

But innovation was not enough. Though immense gains could be made, the road to them was not easy and few people ever completed the journey. A homesteader had no prospect at all of becoming a bonanza farmer, and all new settlers had to confront great physical difficulties. The lack of wood on the open lands forced people to live in sod houses, made of the native turf. The only source of artificial warmth was 'buffalo chips', or dried dung. Winter blizzards, summer droughts and plagues of insects all brought devastation. Once the turf was broken, the land itself became liable to erosion. Small wonder that many emigrants returned east with slogans like 'In God We Trusted, In Kansas We Busted' emblazoned on their wagons.

A pioneer family in front of their sod house

Animals formed as important a part of the West's production as grain. Cattle were not the only or even the most important animals raised. In 1890 the American hog population stood at 63 million animals, 17 million of them west of a line from Texas to the Dakotas. That represented almost half the number of cattle in the same region. Nebraska, Kansas and Texas all had more hogs than any of the Mountain or Pacific states had cattle and in the same region there were 38 million sheep by 1900, a number far in excess of the cattle population.

Many Westerns have addressed these points. In *The Man Who Shot Liberty Valance*/1962 the link between the coming of the railroad and the flowering of the desert is clear. But the train that figures in the first and last shots is a smoke-belching monster, the epitome of *The Machine in the Garden* discussed by historian Leo Marx (1964). In *Shane* hogs provide important symbols of domesticity. The plot of *Joe Kidd* turns on conflict between a land-engrosser and Mexicans, for whom sheep-herding is a way of life. The post-Civil War small farmers of the Missouri uplands who figure in *The Great Northfield Minnesota Raid*/1972 are losers, not winners in the American race for success, and they turn to banditry in order to express their anger and improve their conditions.

In one sense, the agricultural history of America is an enormous success story. The Mississippi Valley can still feed a large proportion of the world's population. California's production of grain, fruit and vegetables remains enormous. But in another sense it is a story written in human suffering and failure, from 'busted' emigrants returning east, through 'Okies' fleeing the dust bowls in the 1930s, to migrant California labourers seeking unionization and Iowa farmers trying to stave off the bank in our own time. The bleakness of *The Grapes of Wrath* is as much a reflection of the reality of farmers' lives as the sunny optimism of *Drums Along the Mohawk*. EC
Canyon Passage/1946/U/d Jacques Tourneur/*lp* Dana Andrews, Brian Donlevy, Susan Hayward · *Joe Kidd*/1972/ U/d John Sturges/*lp* Clint Eastwood, Robert Duvall

Alamo · Spanish mission and fortress in San Antonio, Texas, occupied in February 1836 by Colonel William Travis and 187 Texans and others on the outbreak of the revolt against Mexico. After a thirteen-day siege by General Antonio Lopez de Santa Anna and

ALASKA AND THE CANADIAN NORTHWEST

Crockett killed at the Alamo (woodcut, 1837)

his army of five thousand, the fortress was taken on 6 March 1836 and all inside perished, including Davy *Crockett and Jim *Bowie. Texans cried 'Remember the Alamo' as they went into subsequent battles against the Mexicans, who were defeated within two months. The ruined fort, a potent symbol of a defeat that was turned into a victory, is now preserved as a national shrine.
The Immortal Alamo/1911/Méliès · *The Siege and Fall of the Alamo*/1913/Siege of the Alamo Motion Picture Co · *The Fall of the Alamo*/1914/The State of Texas/*lp* Ray Myers · *Martyrs of the Alamo*/1915/ Keystone-Triangle/*d* Christy Cabanne/*lp* Sam De Grasse · *Davy Crockett at the Fall of the Alamo*/1926/Sunset/*d* Robert N.

Bradbury/*lp* Cullen Landis · *Heroes of the Alamo*/1937/Sunset/*d* Harry Fraser/*lp* Lane Chandler · *The Man from the Alamo*/1953 · *The Last Command*/1955/REP/*d* Frank Lloyd/*lp* Sterling Hayden, Arthur Hunnicutt · *The First Texan*/1956/AA/*d* Byron Haskin/*lp* Joel McCrea · *The Alamo*/1960/Batjac/*d* John Wayne/*lp* John Wayne, Richard Widmark, Laurence Harvey
Television · *Davy Crockett* · *The Alamo: 13 Days to Glory*

Alaska · Though not part of the American West until 1867, when it was sold to the United States by Russia for $7 million, Alaska provides the venue for scores of Hollywood films. Since almost invariably they are films of action and adventure, set in a recognizably frontier environment, they may legitimately be considered 'northern Westerns'. For these films, Hollywood drew extensively on the work of three writers: Rex *Beach, Jack *London and James Oliver *Curwood. Spectacular mountain scenery and harsh climatic conditions form the location for the stories, but it is gold which usually triggers the plots. Traces had been found in Alaska in the 1880s, but it was the strike on the Klondike in Canada in 1896 which stimulated widespread prospecting and led to the discoveries at Nome and Fairbanks.

Allen, Henry Wilson (b 1912) · Novelist under the pen names of Will Henry and Clay Fisher. Allen began writing Western fiction after nine years at MGM in the shorts department. His novels, some based on historical characters, often take a disenchanted view of the West and especially of the treatment of the Indians.
Santa Fe Passage/1955/REP/*d* William Witney/*lp* John Payne, Faith Domergue · *The Tall Men*/1955 · *Pillars of the Sky* [*To Follow A Flag*]/1956/U/*d* George Marshall/*lp* Jeff Chandler · *Yellowstone Kelly*/1959/WB/*d* Gordon Douglas/*lp* Clint Walker · *Journey to Shiloh*/1967/U/*d* William Hale/*lp* James Caan · *McKenna's Gold*/1968/COL/*d* J. Lee Thompson/*lp* Gregory Peck, Omar Sharif · *Young Billy Young* [*Who Rides With Wyatt*]/1969

Allison, Clay (1840-87) · Gunfighter. Born in Tennessee, Allison fought on the Confederate side in the Civil War, then became a cowboy and rancher, principally in New Mexico. He killed at least four people in gunfights and participated in several lynchings. Legend says he ran up against Bat Masterson and Wyatt Earp in Dodge City, but if so the encounters were inconclusive. Allison died by falling off a wagon drunk.
Television · Jack Kelly/*Cheyenne* · Marc Alaimo/*No Man's Land*

Ambush · Is there always something dishonourable about an ambush? It goes against the cowboy's code of facing up to an opponent in the open street. 'Bushwhacker' is a term of abuse in any Westerner's vocabulary. But the popularity of the ambush as a motif among film-makers no doubt owes much to its purely cinematic possibilities. Louis Simonci in *Le Western* (Paris: 10/18, 1966) has noted how well the cinema is equipped to portray a carefully laid ambush, regulating with precision the difference between what the audience can see and what the characters are aware of. As he notes, there is also the ambush that is a surprise to characters and audience alike. Following Alfred Hitchcock's well-known distinction, we might define this as the difference between suspense and surprise. There are good examples in two Peckinpah films. At the end of *Ride the High Country*/1962 Joel McCrea approaches a farmhouse. We are made dramatically aware, as he is not, that the evil Hammond family (contemptuously dis-

missed as 'dry-gulching Southern trash' once their trick is revealed) are lying in wait. In *Major Dundee*/1964 Charlton Heston is enjoying a moment of relaxation with Senta Berger beside a shady pool. He and the audience are simultaneously surprised when an arrow thuds into his thigh.

Apache · The various peoples of the plains (Sioux, Cheyenne, Comanche, etc.) and the Apache are the only distinctive Indian cultures to feature consistently in the Western. The Apache warrior is instantly recognizable from his shoulder-length, unbraided hair, cloth headband, breech clout and leggings. Long contact with the Spanish influenced Apache culture and in Westerns Apache women usually appear in Spanish-style blouses and skirts.

Some very few Westerns, such as *Broken Arrow*/1950 (about the Apache leader *Cochise) and *Apache*/1954, have attempted to humanize the traditional image of the Apache. In the latter, the hero (Burt Lancaster) tries to raise crops and a family while carrying on a one-man war against the army. More usually even such films as the later *Ulzana's Raid*/1972, which intends a sympathetic portrayal, represent the Apache as incurably warlike, implacably cruel and essentially unknowable: the quintessence of that savagery against which civilization must defend itself. The origins of such a characterization predate the Western and are to be found in the virtually unceasing hostilities between the Apache and Spanish colonists dating back to the 17th century. In this history the Apache undoubtedly received at least as much violence as they gave. Yet though films such as *Duel at Diablo* and *Chato's Land* represent the Apache as more sinned against than sinning, still they go out of their way to depict Apache tortures.

Westerns rarely bother with the finer ethnic and cultural distinctions among the indigenous peoples represented. This can be particularly misleading where the Apache are concerned, since there were so many different groups, some of them going under a variety of names. A broad categorization may be helpful. The Apache are divided into six distinct groups, linguistically related but, in the 19th century, varied in their social habits. Some combined hunting with farming and lived in wickiups, made of brush and covered with skins. Some (for example the Kiowa-Apache) lived mainly on the buffalo like other plains tribes and constructed hide tepees. Of the six groups, the Lipan, who inhabited west Texas, are

Jorge Luke as the Apache scout Ke-Ni-Tay in Ulzana's Raid

now effectively extinct. The Western Apache occupied central Arizona. In 1875 they were defeated by General George Crook and moved to the San Carlos reservation. The Chiricahua occupied eastern Arizona and western New Mexico. They were subdivided into Eastern (otherwise known as Warm Springs, Ojo Caliente or Mimbrenos), Central and Southern bands and are now the best known because of their outstanding nineteenth-century leaders: of the Eastern Chiricahua, *Mangas Coloradas and *Victorio; of the Central, Cochise; of the Southern, *Geronimo and *Chato. The Southern Chiricahua under Geronimo were the last of the Apaches to be defeated, by General Nelson *Miles in 1886. The Mescalero Apache, extending from New Mexico into Texas, were rounded up and placed on a reservation in 1873. The Jicarilla Apaches' territory stretched from northern New Mexico into Colorado and parts of Kansas. The sixth group, the Kiowa-Apache, are linguistically allied to the Apache but their history has been essentially that of the Kiowa.
Duel at Diablo/1965/UA/*d* Ralph Nelson/*lp* James Garner, Sidney Poitier · *Chato's Land*/1971/Scimitar/*d* Michael Winner/*lp* Charles Bronson, Jack Palance

Arizona · First reached by the Spanish in the 1530s, Arizona remained under Spanish, then Mexican, control until the war between Mexico and the United States of 1846-8. After the war most of Arizona, as part of New Mexico Territory, was ceded to the US. The Gadsden Purchase of 1853 extended Arizona south of the Gila River to its present border with Mexico. It became a separate territory in 1863 and a state of the Union in 1912. By 1880 Arizona still had only 40,000 white inhabitants (one to every three square miles), mostly engaged in ranching and mining. But its characteristic desert landscape, decorated with organ-pipe cactus, and stories of *Tombstone, outlawry and the Apache wars have been a constant source of inspiration for the Western. Arizona was also the location for many of the bitter *feuds and range wars that have provided such fertile material for the literary and cinematic Western. Phil Hardy's encyclopedia *The Western* records 32 films in the sound period whose title begins with 'Arizona', which suggests the state is second only to Texas as a popular setting.

Army · In *Rio Grande*/1950 Colonel Yorke (John Wayne) has a warning for his son about the army: 'Put out of your mind any romantic ideas that it's a way of glory. It's a life of suffering and hardship.' In the Western there are few things more romantic than the sufferings, heroically endured, of the thin blue line standing between savagery and civilization. And in the West it was often a very thin line indeed. After the Civil War, which saw the army grow vastly, Congress moved to cut its size, until by 1874 it had been reduced to a paper strength of 27,000 men, of whom perhaps only 19,000 could actually be deployed; and not all of these were stationed in the West.

The post-Civil War army was organized into ten cavalry regiments, five artillery and twenty-five infantry regiments. Cavalry regiments numbered twelve companies (or troops) each, infantry regiments ten companies. Regiments were commanded by a colonel. Each company was commanded by a captain. Company strength might be anywhere between fifty and a hundred men, but the average size of a cavalry company in 1881 was fifty-eight.

Unlike the volunteer regiments of the Civil War, regular regiments had no associations with particular localities. Thus the cavalry regiments were simply numbered 1 to 10. Pay was low – a mere $13 a month for privates in the 1870s – and conditions were bad. Food consisted of little but bacon, beans, hardtack and coffee. Regulation clothing was inadequate for the extremes of heat and cold suffered on the frontier. Training was minimal and equipment often poor (for example, the army persisted with the single-shot *Springfield rifle until well into the 1880s, long after civilians and some Indians had acquired the *Winchester

repeater). Discipline was harsh and disease was rife. Between 1866 and 1868 the 7th Cavalry lost 36 men killed by Indians, 6 drowned, 2 missing in action and 51 dead of cholera. (In all, total army casualties in engagements with Indians between 1866 and 1891 were 932 killed and 1061 wounded.) During the 1880s the army had one man in every 25 hospitalized for alcoholism – and these, presumably, were only the most serious cases. One third of all the men recruited between 1867 and 1891 deserted.

Not surprisingly the army was often outmanoeuvred and outfought by the Indians who were its primary adversaries. The classic image of the cavalry charge, popularized in the paintings of Frederic *Remington and since repeated in countless films, did on occasion occur. But the Indians rarely obliged with a full-scale battle, preferring instead to adopt guerrilla tactics. The cavalry were not always mobile enough to get near the Indians. Army horses were not adapted to foraging like Indian ponies. In consequence, cumbersome supply trains of oats and hay had to accompany cavalry in the field. Nor were the horses able to sustain long campaigns. Though horses could outdistance the foot-soldier over the first few days, the infantry, covering twenty miles a day, could usually outlast the cavalry after a week, and so infantry were frequently used in campaigns against Indians.

Such awkward facts do not fit the cinema's conception. D.W. Griffith established early the convention of the cavalry to the rescue, memorably in *The Battle at Elderbush Gulch*/

1913, and John Ford in *Stagecoach*/1939 fixed it forever in the public's mind. In the late 19th century the novels of the former cavalry captain Charles *King helped to popularize stories about life in the army forts of the West, and introduced the Irish soldier into Western fiction. But it is Ford who is mainly to be credited with creating the dominant conception of the army in the Western. Ford's army is a specifically American construction: democratic, multicultural, even, in *Sergeant Rutledge*/1960, multi-racial. In Ford's idealized army barriers of class, nationality and political ideology are largely dissolved. Defeated Confederates and Irish immigrants are united in a truly national army. The sons of ordinary NCOs (like Michael O'Rourke in *Fort Apache*/1948) may become officers and marry the Colonel's daughter. In the same way that Teddy *Roosevelt's Rough Riders had forged eastern college boys and western cowboys into a unified force to fight the Spanish in Cuba, so the Fordian army forgets its differences in the common cause of battle against the one foe who is unassimilable, the original American.

If the heroism of the cavalry charge may be traced back to Remington, so too may be Ford's deliberate refusal of the vaingloriousness of other military traditions. The troopers in Remington's paintings are weary and dusty, the uniforms battered. Ford's Westerns are conceived in a similar spirit. *Rio Grande* ends as it began, with a cavalry column returning to the fort wounded and bedraggled, despite victory. In Ford's army

Frederic Remington, 'A Cavalryman's Breakfast on the Plains' (c.1890)

Westerns glory belongs most truly to those who do not flaunt it. Only at the moment of his death against hopeless odds does Colonel Thursday in *Fort Apache* achieve the heroic stature he had sought in victory.

Although Thursday is ultimately redeemed, much of what he stands for is pilloried in the film. The stiffness of his bearing is indicative of the hidebound conventionalism which his West Point training has taught him. By contrast with his textbook learning, Captain Yorke (John Wayne) represents first-hand experience. Ford's ideal is a rough and ready army whose competence is based not upon the drill manual but upon a whole way of life, the way of the West.

Thursday stands for the East, and by implication perhaps for European values. This is certainly what is at stake in *They Died with their Boots On*/1941. Errol Flynn as Custer arrives at West Point in a fancy uniform of his own design and announces that his model is Murat, Napoleon's famous general. But then Custer proves his true worth by achieving 'even lower marks' in his final exams than Ulysses S. Grant, and by the end of the film he has rejected the eastern capitalists who try to buy his support, swapped his plumes for buckskin and espoused the virtues of the West. His wife takes up the Indians' cause, and the Englishman in his regiment (the one who has taught him his favourite marching tune of 'Garry Owen') remarks in the midst of battle that 'the real Americans are on the other side of the ridge with feathers in their hair.' Though the notion of Custer as an 'Indian-lover' is inherently implausible, if he is to remain the hero he has to slough off the snobbery which would see them as unworthy opponents for a gentleman.

The rejection of the European military tradition is a thread that runs through many army Westerns. It surfaces in all those films where a *German (i.e. 'Prussian') advisor appears, and in the implicit ridicule of the overdressed French chasseurs in *Major Dundee*/1964. By contrast America can retain its self-image of an anti-imperialist power, its army popularly constituted, not the mercenaries of an autocracy, and devoted to policing its own frontiers, not to foreign adventures.

Like Ford's cavalry trilogy, *Major Dundee* also attempts to stitch up the rent between North and South. In an early scene the command of northern troops and parolled Confederate prisoners leaves the fort in pursuit of the Apache. The northerners sing 'The Battle Hymn of the Republic', the southerners sing 'Dixie'. In reply the small body of muleskinners and scouts, who represent neither North nor South but West, strike up 'My Darling Clementine'. The West is the great unifier, above divisive ideologies.

Westerns have frequently been critical of aspects of military operations. The figure of the martinet, obstinately refusing to listen to those with actual experience of Indian fighting, and often based more or less directly on Custer, occurs not only in *Fort Apache* but in *The Last Frontier*/1955 and in *The Glory Guys*/1965. But not until the beginning of the 1970s did Hollywod feel able to criticize the military's role as such, rather than its aberrant executives. *Soldier Blue*/1970 and *Little Big Man*/1970 both accuse the army of performing not a police action but a kind of internal imperialism designed to reduce the Indians to the status of conquered peoples, and even, through genocidal attacks, to annihilate them altogether. Under the influence of the Vietnam War the Western became suffused with a tide of anti-militarism unequalled, ironically, since the period in which the films are set, the decade following the Civil War, in which war-weariness forced the reduction of the army to a tiny fraction of what it had been in 1865.

Artists and illustrators · When Sir Walter Ralegh tried to establish colonies in North America in the late 16th century, he was accompanied by the watercolourist, John White. White's representations of the Indian peoples he encountered, their villages, games and feasts, helped to develop the image of America as a carefree garden of Eden. White's drawings were engraved by Theodor de Bry and as illustrations in such books as *A Briefe and True Report of the New Found Land of Virginia* became part of the propaganda campaign to lure investors and would-be emigrants. Jacques Le Moyne, an artist who accompanied a French Huguenot exploration of Florida in 1564, helped to imprint a very different propaganda image of America's inhabitants. In the service of a militant and missionary Christianity, De Moyne depicted Indians as sadistic torturers and scalpers of their enemies. These two contradictory iconographies and mythologies continued to influence the look of the American landscape and its original inhabitants as depicted by later artists and illustrators.

When Hollywood took over as the domi-

The Garden of Eden: watercolour by John White (c.1585)

nant purveyor of images of the American West, artists and illustrators like Frederic *Remington and Charles *Russell had already constructed that action-packed presentation of a Wild West frontier that was directly to influence Hollywood. Remington's dynamic canvases, such as 'Cavalry Charge on the Southern Plains' (1907) in which United States troopers with pistols cocked at the ready gallop against the enemy, or his 'Downing the Nigh Leader' (1903; see Plate 18) in which a mounted Indian at full gallop spears a lead horse of a stagecoach under attack, became standard action sequences in the Western film. Russell is best known for his pictures of cowboys in action, busting broncos, roping wayward steers, or branding cattle (Plate 21). Both artists see the West as full of dramatic incident, an arena for the display of warrior courage and physical skill.

Other schools and genres of painting, such as those that romanticized an unspoiled Nature, were available to the early makers of Western films, but they were simply too static. Although the Hollywood Western hero often moves through stunningly picturesque landscapes, he rarely gives vent to Wordsworthian rhapsodies on the beauties of the natural world, nor does he see sermons in stones. He is more likely to be locked in a deadly contest for survival against Nature, outlaws or Indians.

Prior to Remington, many artists began to specialize in scenes of frontier life after the opening up of the trans-Mississippi West in the early 19th century. As the United States entered its urban and industrial phase, a market for images of a primitive frontier world developed in the more metropolitan East. Many of these artists moved out of their eastern studios and went west to the plains. Among the first to do so was George *Catlin. Beginning in 1832, he devoted most of his life to the recording of the Indian way of life, from the Missouri to the Southwest, and later among the Seminoles in the Southeast. He produced almost 500 paintings, both portraits of individual Indians and scenes of Indian life and culture. His portraits of Indian chiefs are remarkable for their ethnographic detail and the way he acknowledges them as important personages, awarded equal status with Boston merchants or Presidents. Catlin also acknowledged the richness and diversity of the Indians' culture, from their complex religious practices to their warrior codes and skill as buffalo hunters. He captured all these activities on his canvases, in which the full range of Plains Indian pursuits are displayed in action. He developed the buffalo hunt (Plate 2), from the initial tracking to the stampede, from the spearing of the single buffalo on horseback to the hunt in the snow on foot, into an iconography used by many later artists and which reached a wide audience when reproduced as Currier and Ives prints.

Catlin used his canvases to publicize the cause of the Indian in Washington. He wanted to persuade the Congress to protect and insulate Indian lands and culture from the dubious blessings of white Christian civilization. In his own words, he wanted the Indians 'preserved in their pristine beauty and wildness, in a magnificent park, where the world could see for ages to come, the native Indian in his classic attire, galloping his wild horse, with sinewy bow, and shield and lance, amid the fleeting herds of elks and buffaloes.' Ironically, Catlin helped to bring this dream into reality, but not as he intended. Beginning in 1837, Catlin exhibited his paintings as an Indian Gallery, often accompanied by some live Indians who would dance and chant hunting and war songs. This, possibly the first version of the Wild West Show, was successfully toured as a mixture of instruction and commercial entertainment to New York, London and Paris. Another part of Catlin's legacy was to imprint on the world's imagination as the only real Indian the image of the feather-bonneted Plains Indian, mounted on horseback and living in a conical-shaped tepee. In reality the culture of the Plains Indian was only one example of the complex cultural systems created by the original Americans, which range from the urban civilizations of the Aztecs to the hunting culture of the Eskimos. Catlin's brand of liberal paternalism had little influence on the Washington makers of Indian policy, who as resistance to white invasion of the Plains area grew among such tribes as the Sioux began to develop a policy of deliberate extermination and control on reservations.

The reports of government expeditions were another major source of documenta-tion and iconography of the West. The instructions given to Samuel Seymour, who with Titian Peale was an official artist on the 1818-19 expedition across the Plains to the Rockies made by Major Stephen Long, summarize the way the West was mythically constructed according to the prevailing aesthetic conventions of the picturesque and sublime. Seymour had to: 'furnish sketches of landscapes, wherever we meet with any distinguished for their beauty and grandeur. He will also paint miniature likenesses, or portraits, if required, of distinguished Indians, and exhibit groups of savages engaged in celebrating their festivals, or sitting in council.'

Wealthy individuals also made grand tours of the West with artists in tow. Karl *Bodmer was hired by a prince of Saxony, Maximilian of Wied Neuwied, to make a visual record of his journeys into the West in the 1830s. The results, published in 1839-41 as *Reise in das Innere Nord-Amerika in den Jahren 1832 bis 1834*, took the form of 82 copperplate engravings that accompanied the text as a separate volume of illustrations. These scenes of Mandan Indian dances (Plate 4), Blackfoot burial grounds and an attack by Assiniboines and Crees on a smaller band of Blackfoot, represent one of the highpoints in the ethnographic realism that was a hallmark of natural history illustrations of this era. On his return to Europe Bodmer collaborated with Jean François Millet in producing a series of prints of dramatic border warfare on the American plains.

Alfred Jacob *Miller was working as a New Orleans portrait painter when he was invited by a Scottish aristocrat, Captain William Stewart, to accompany him on a trip in 1837 to the Rockies to record the scene at the fur-trappers' annual rendezvous. Miller's romantic depictions of the mountain men, their Indian wives, their wild ways and Byronic looks, helped to fix the Rocky Mountain fur trade era as an important part of the legend of the Wild West.

A whole school of painters developed to meet the growing fascination with the picturesque sights of a vanishing frontier. Seth *Eastman developed a wide repertoire of special western effects (Plate 1). His ethnographic drawings of Indian life were used to illustrate the US Government's authorized publication on the North American Indian, Henry Schoolcraft's mammoth *Historical and Statistical Information Respecting the History, Condition, and Prospects of the Indian Tribes of the United States* (1851-7). But

The Indian as savage: Natchez Indians with a prisoner ready for execution, drawing by Du Pratz in Louisiana (1718-34)

Eastman also produced racist melodramatic depictions of Indian violence, as in his most famous and popular picture of an Indian exulting in triumph after completing a scalping, called 'The Death Whoop'.

Charles Bird King (1785-1862) is best known for his series of portraits depicting members of the Indian delegation that visited Washington in 1821. These formed the nucleus of the National Indian Portrait Gallery, which was burned in the Smithsonian Institution fire of 1865. Like Catlin, John Mix Stanley (1814-72) experimented with different forms of display for his North American Indian Gallery of over 150 paintings. He eventually developed a moving panorama. With Stanley narrating as the great canvas unrolled, the viewer was visually escorted across the American continent. The experience was mystic and restful, a mood invariably found in Stanley's landscapes which, unlike Catlin's and Remington's, concentrated on a more tranquil presentation of the western scene, highlighting peaceful Indian encampments and dreamy lookouts. This contradictory mixture of a belief in progress and nostalgia for a romantic vanishing frontier world is caught by a Washington newspaper account of a performance of Stanley's panorama, 'Western Wilds', at the National Theatre in 1854. The newspaper stresses the importance of the show for members of Congress, 'as the panorama shows the nature of the country through which the Northern Railroad route to the Pacific is destined to pass.' Some years later one of the most assertive allegories of *Manifest Destiny was installed as a permanent mural painting in the Capitol building. In 'Westward the Course of Empire Takes its Way' by Emanuel *Leutze (Plate 8) a party of indomitable pioneers surmounts all obstacles in the way of their triumphant conquest of the American continent. This kind of heroic narrative is representative of the dominant shaping ideology that influenced most painters of the American West in the 19th century. There was also an opportunity to display sentimental regret for a lost world of pastoral innocence. Within this over-arching structure, individual artists could examine particular historical phases of the onward western movement of people.

In a series of paintings he began in 1845, George Caleb *Bingham memorialized a frontier society of river-boat men and fur traders in the Midwest. His pictures of fur trappers gliding along the Missouri river, and of boatmen dancing or playing cards on board, touched a nostalgic chord in eastern drawing rooms, making him into one of the first successful western artists. He then captured the rough and ready, populist political culture of frontier society in a series of pictures of elections, which were engraved by European craftsmen and became best sellers. Bingham also painted one of the most rhetorical treatments of the foundation mythology of the West. In his painting 'Daniel Boone Escorting Settlers Through The Cumberland Gap' (1851-2) Boone is seen as a latter-day Moses leading the chosen people through the wilderness to the promised land. (For illustration see Daniel *Boone.)

Another phase of the westward movement that attracted its own school of

Charles Russell, drawing for the first illustrated edition of Owen Wister's The Virginian *(1911)*

artists was the gold rush in California. The brothers Nahl, Charles (1818-78) and Hugo (1820-89), created a violent, bawdy vision of opportunist mining communities, reflected in such Westerns as Ride the High Country/ 1962. Their images were used to illustrate the mining stories and sketches that were much in demand by newspapers and magazines.

In stark contrast to the busy, robust canvases of the Nahls were the artists who celebrated a vision of a towering natural wilderness in landscapes painted after the Civil War. This group, which included Albert *Bierstadt and Thomas *Moran, has been dubbed the 'Rocky Mountain school'. Many of their canvases use the Rockies as a backdrop for radiant evocations of the sublime, Turneresque majesty of an unspoiled Nature showing little trace of human habitation. Peter H. Hassrick describes these paintings' place in the mythology of the West as follows: 'Most of the "grand" style landscapes were painted in full focus so that details of foreground and distance could be identified with equal clarity. This practice allowed the paintings to be viewed with opera glasses, thus effecting a sense of on-the-spot observation and allying the experience very closely with that of theatre. Accordingly, the major works of Bierstadt were as much popular entertainment as works of art. The "wild" in Bierstadt's Wild West expositions was the wilderness – its grandeur and its sublimity.' (Plates 10-12)

This vogue for the pleasures of unspoiled but vanishing landscape and the fast-disappearing Indian was too static and sentimental for the growing nationalist spirit of American society, which wanted a more manly, Empire-building mode to serve its expansionist aims after the Civil War. Remington's images of hard-riding cavalrymen chimed in with this mood.

After the Civil War, which had provided the American public with a daily diet of drama and military heroics, the American military turned to its unfinished business in the West, the conquest of the Plains Indians warriors. Theodor R. Davis (1840-1910), who had provided the new mass circulation magazines like Harper's Weekly (founded 1857) with a steady stream of Civil War illustrations, now provided dramatic sketches from the Indian Wars, which were to last until 1890. Illustrators like Davis and Remington depicted either real events or versions of history as it was being mythically constructed. A good example of this myth-making tendency is the visual treatment of

George Catlin, 'A Crow Chief on Horseback'

Custer's Last Stand. Several paintings were made of this traumatic event, many of which were reproduced as *chromolithographs, the new form of cheap illustration that could be hung on the walls of American homes and saloons. Over 150,000 lithographic versions of the painting of Custer's Last Stand by Cassily Adams were distributed to a sensation-seeking public (Plate 14). Remington's version, entitled 'The Last Stand' appeared in *Harper's Weekly* in 1891. In this, the central figure in the beleaguered group of cavalrymen is not Custer but a bearded and buck-skinned old-timer. The role of such iconographic treatment was to turn defeat into an heroic redeeming myth of Empire-building bravery and sacrifice. It is exactly this process that John Ford examines in *Fort Apache*/1948.

John Ford is on record as having tried to project a Remington look into his Westerns. In conversation with Peter Bogdanovich, Ford remarked: 'I like *She Wore a Yellow Ribbon*. I tried to copy the Remington style there – you can't copy him one hundred percent – but at least I tried to get in his color and movement, and I think I succeeded partly.' CB

Atchison, Topeka and Santa Fe Railroad · The major transcontinental railroad of the Southwest, remembered in the title of a song written by Harry Warren and Johnny Mercer for *The Harvey Girls*/1945. (It was on the route of the 'Santa Fe' that Fred *Harvey established his famous restaurants.) Starting out from Topeka in Kansas along the route of the old Santa Fe Trail in 1868, the railroad eventually reached Los Angeles in 1885. It then built eastwards to Chicago, until by 1890 it ran for 9,000 miles, at the time the longest railroad in the world. In 1878 the 'Santa Fe' was involved in a 'war' with the Denver and Rio Grande line over the use of certain passes through the Rocky Mountains. To protect its workmen the 'Santa Fe' hired a bunch of gunmen, among them Bat Masterson and Doc Holliday.

Australia · The similarities between Australia's nineteenth-century frontier and the American West are alluded to in Butch Cassidy's desire to move there at the end of *Butch Cassidy and the Sundance Kid*/1969. The sentiment is echoed by the father of the contemporary hero of *Junior Bonner*/1972, who longs for the way things used to be and, he assumes, still are Down Under. Besides versions of the legend of Ned Kelly (the nearest thing to Jesse James outside the American West), Australia has inspired a number of films on frontier themes, such as *Robbery Under Arms*, which features cattle rustling, a stage hold-up, a bank robbery and a gold rush town. A more recent 'frontier' film was *The Man from Snowy River*. From time to time, with an eye on the local box office, Hollywood made its own Westerns in Australia, often with titles like *The Kangaroo Kid*. In *Montana* Errol Flynn, playing his actual nationality for once, is an Australian sheep farmer in conflict with cattle ranchers. Ealing Studios attempted a British/Australian version of the Western with *The Overlanders*, about a cattle drive through the outback.

The Overlanders/1946/GB/d Harry Watt/*lp* Chips Rafferty · *Montana*/1949/WB/d Ray Enright/*lp* Errol Flynn, Alexis Smith · *The Kangaroo Kid*/1950/Allied Australian/d Lesley Selander/*lp* Jock Mahoney, Douglass Dumbrille · *Robbery Under Arms*/1957/GB/d Jack Lee/*lp* Peter Finch, David McCallum · *The Man from Snowy River*/1983/FOX/d George Miller/*lp* Kirk Douglas, Jack Thompson

B

Bankers · If the Western as a whole may be said to have a political ideology, that ideology is *Populism. And in the demonology of Populism the banker is Old Nick himself. In the 19th century, as now, the centres of financial power were in the east, and so hostility towards concentrations of capital was bound up with regional chauvinism. Consequently in the Western the banker is almost invariably a figure of scorn. *Stagecoach*/1939 provides one of the best-known examples, in which Henry Gatewood, the banker played by Berton Churchill, is an out-and-out crook. The banker played by Raymond Burr in *A Man Alone*/1955 is no better, nor are the bankers in *The Parson of Panamint*, *4 for Texas* and *Invitation to a Gunfighter*/1964.

The Parson of Panamint/1941/PAR/d William McGann/*lp* Charlie Ruggles · *4 for Texas*/1963/WB/d Robert Aldrich/*lp* Frank Sinatra, Dean Martin, Anita Ekberg, Ursula Andress

Bank robbery · In the crime film the elaborately staged bank robbery, executed with military precision, is a familiar set-piece. In the Western, long on bravado and short on organization, the best-remembered bank robberies are those which go wrong, such as the chaotic debacle at the start of *The True Story of Jesse James*/1957. The various versions of this raid, on the First National Bank of Northfield, Minnesota by the James gang (who committed the first bank robbery in the West in 1866), would in themselves make a study in cinematic styles. But in its deft combination of humour and tension few bank robbery scenes approach the opening of *One-Eyed Jacks*/1960. Marlon Brando sits on the counter of a bank, his gun in one hand and a banana in the other. As Karl Malden urges him to hurry before the Federales arrive, he strolls over to a matron he has observed craftily secreting a ring inside her purse and roguishly scolds her for deceitfulness.

Barbed wire · Patented in 1874 by Joseph Glidden of Illinois, barbed wire transformed agriculture on the plains. It provided a cheap means for the homesteader to fence in crops against the depredations of free-roaming cattle and also allowed improvements in breeding by segregating strains from each other. Its introduction was not without resistance. Outbreaks of fence-cutting occurred when those accustomed to an open range found their way barred or when big ranchers attempted to fence in the public domain.

Barbed wire samples from a catalogue (1880)

In Westerns barbed wire usually stands for the onward march of modern technology (at best a mixed blessing) and triggers the conflict between farmers and the ranchers who cling to the open range. For Kirk Douglas in *Man Without a Star*/1955, who bears the scars of the wire, it at first symbolizes the passing of the West, though by the end of the film he is supporting the small farmers who are using it to protect their land from over-grazing by cattle baron Jeanne Crain. Douglas is again called on to demonstrate his hostility to wire in *Lonely Are the Brave*/1962. In *The First Traveling Saleslady*/1956/RKO/d Arthur Lubin, barbed wire is one of the new-fangled ideas, along with feminism and automobiles, which Ginger Rogers hopes to introduce into Texas.

Henry Fonda at the barber's in My Darling Clementine

Barbers · In *The Log of a Cowboy* Andy *Adams recounts how, within an hour of arriving in Dodge City after several weeks on the trail, 'every mother's son [was] reflecting the art of the barber, while John Officer had his blond mustaches blackened, waxed, and curled like a French dancing master.' But the frequent scenes in barber shops in Westerns do more than nod towards documentary authenticity. In *My Darling Clementine*/1946 Henry Fonda's haircut and shave in the Bon Ton Tonsorial Parlor is the beginning of the civilizing process that takes place in him and Tombstone. In *Gunfight at the O.K. Corral*/1956 it's not the Wyatt Earp character but Doc Holliday who's being barbered. This time a trim seems to represent slickness more than civilization, though Kirk Douglas as Doc nicely resists the implied critique by taking a manly swig from the bottle of after-shave. By tradition barbers themselves are an unheroic bunch: sometimes (ironically) bald, usually cowardly, as in *Dodge City*/1939, *Santa Fe Trail*/1940, *Western Union*/1941, *The Gunfighter*/1950 and *High Plains Drifter*/1972. In both *The Westerner*/1940 and *High Noon*/1952 the town barber doubles as the *undertaker.

Barnum, Phineas Taylor (1810-91) · Showman. Barnum's circus began in 1871 and in 1881 he began his association with James A. Bailey, forming Barnum & Bailey's Greatest Show on Earth. Barnum was one of the first to realize the show-business potential of the West, anticipating some of the attractions of Buffalo Bill *Cody's Wild West. He displayed groups of Iowa Indians at his Ameri-

can Museum in New York in the 1840s, as well as organizing a buffalo hunt in Hoboken, New Jersey in 1843. In 1860 Barnum arranged for Grizzly *Adams' California Menagerie to visit New York; in a parade down Broadway Adams rode one grizzly bear while leading two more on chains.

Bass, Sam (1851-78) · Outlaw. Bass robbed stagecoaches in Deadwood and trains and banks in Texas until shot down by Texas Rangers in the middle of a robbery. Though raised to semi-mythical status by the popular 'Ballad of Sam Bass', he never achieved the first rank among outlaws in the movies. Nestor Paiva/*Badman's Territory*/1946/RKO/d Tim Whelan/lp Randolph Scott · Howard Duff/*Calamity Jane and Sam Bass*/1949/U/d George Sherman/lp Yvonne De Carlo · William Bishop/*The Texas Rangers*/1951/COL/d Phil Karlson/lp George Montgomery · Leonard Penn/*Outlaw Women*/1952/Lippert/d Sam Newfield, Ron Ormond/lp Marie Windsor · Rex Marlow/*Deadwood '76*/1965/Fairway International/d James Landis/lp Arch Hall Jr. · Cliff Alexander/*Ride a Wild Stud*/1969/Vega International/d Revilo Ekard/lp Hale Williams

Television · Chuck Connors/*Tales of Wells Fargo* · Kelly Thordsen/*Maverick* · Alan Hale/*Colt .45* · Jack Chaplain/*The Outlaws*

Baths · Since Cecil B. DeMille first put a girl in a tub, Hollywood has delighted in the bath scene. What distinguishes the Western from other genres is the frequency with which *men* take a bath. The thematic resonances are clear: bathing is part of the process of initiation into civilization; in the West, as elsewhere in the 19th century, cleanliness is next to godliness. But since there is a doubt as to whether manliness is compatible with either, some bathers compromise by keeping their hats on, or at least smoke a cigar, like Dale Robertson in *Dakota Incident*, Burt Lancaster in *The Hallelujah Trail*, Burt Reynolds in *Sam Whiskey*, Lee Marvin in *The Spikes Gang* or Clint Eastwood in *High Plains Drifter*/1972. Some even, like Eli Wallach in *Il buono, il brutto, il cattivo*/1966, keep a gun under the bath water.

In the 'realist' *Will Penny*/1967 we're given some useful information about hygiene in the West when the aging cowboy played by Charlton Heston proudly claims to take a bath eight or nine times a year. But if in practice bathing was infrequent, the (male) bathing scene is a major narrative motif. An

Taking a bath – Jason Robards, Stella Stevens in The Ballad of Cable Hogue

incomplete list would include:
Return of the Cisco Kid/1939/FOX/*d* Herbert I. Leeds/*lp* Warner Baxter · *Dodge City*/1939 · *Kit Carson*/1940/UA/*d* George B. Seitz/*lp* Jon Hall · *In Old Oklahoma*/1943/REP/*d* Albert S. Rogell/*lp* John Wayne · *Across the Wide Missouri*/1950 · *Dakota Incident*/1956/REP/*d* Lewis R. Foster · *The Searchers*/1956 · *The King and Four Queens*/1956 · *Forty Guns*/1957 · *Cowboy*/1958 · *Lonely Are the Brave*/1962 · *The Hallelujah Trail*/1964/UA/*d* John Sturges · *The Rounders*/1964/MGM/*d* Burt Kennedy/*lp* Glenn Ford, Henry Fonda · *Cat Ballou*/1965 · *El Dorado*/1966 · *100 Rifles*/1968 · *Sam Whiskey*/1969/UA/*d* Arnold Laven · *Monte Walsh*/1970 · *A Man Called Horse*/1970 · *Little Big Man*/1970 · *The Hired Hand*/1971 · *Big Jake*/1971/Batjac/*d* George Sherman/*lp* John Wayne, Richard Boone · *The Spikes Gang*/1974/UA/*d* Richard Fleischer · *The Missouri Breaks*/1976

Beach, Rex (1877-1949) · Writer. Abandoning his law studies, Beach joined the gold rush to Alaska in 1898. His first novel, *The Spoilers* (1905), was based on his own experiences in the gold-fields, and despite fiction set in other parts of the world Beach, like Jack *London and James Oliver *Curwood, was always to be identified with stories of the Far North.
The Spoilers was filmed five times: 1914/Selig/*d* Colin Campbell/*lp* William Farnum · 1923/Goldwyn/*d* Lambert Hillyer/*lp* Milton Sills · 1930/PAR/*d* Edwin Carewe/*lp* Gary Cooper · 1942/U/*d* Ray Enright/*lp* Marlene Dietrich, Randolph

Scott, John Wayne · 1955/U/*d* Jesse Hibbs/*lp* Jeff Chandler, Rory Calhoun · Other Western or Northwestern novels filmed include: *Winds of Chance*/1925/First National/*d* Frank Lloyd/*lp* Anna Q. Nilsson, Ben Lyon · *The Barrier*/1926/MGM/*d* George Hill/*lp* Norman Kerry, Lionel Barrymore · *The Michigan Kid*/1928/U/*d* Irvin Willat/*lp* Renée Adorée · *The Silver Horde*/1930/RKO/*d* George Archainbaud/*lp* Evelyn Brent, Joel McCrea · (Beach also wrote some original filmscripts)

Bean, Judge Roy (1825?-1903) · Justice of the peace. After time spent as a Confederate irregular, Bean settled himself in the wilds of west Texas between the Pecos and Rio Grande rivers. He ran a saloon, at first in Vinegaroon, later in a place he called Langtry after the actress Lillie Langtry, with whom he had a life-long obsession. From his saloon Bean, styling himself 'the law west of the Pecos', administered an eccentric but effective justice. Many stories, probably apocryphal, are told, such as that Bean, finding a dead man with forty dollars and a gun on him, fined the corpse an identical sum for carrying a concealed weapon. Though Bean had no training or legal status his bizarre regime was tolerated by the Texas Rangers since it assured peace of a kind. Lillie Langtry finally visited the town named for her ten months after Bean's death.

Bean has been memorably played twice. First was Walter Brennan in *The Westerner*/1940, in a performance which portrayed the Judge as a tyrannical if colourful despot. Thirty years later Paul Newman in *The Life and Times of Judge Roy Bean*/1972 interprets the eccentricity as an indicator that Bean has

survived beyond his time, from frontier days to a more sober and humdrum age.
Also Harry Carey (Bean-type character)/*The Law West of the Pecos*/1938/RKO/*d* Glenn Tryon/*lp* Tim Holt, Ward Bond · Victor Jory/*A Time for Dying*/1969 · (The role of Gannon (John McIntire) in *The Far Country*/1954 clearly owes much to Bean)
Television · Edgar Buchanan/*The Adventures of Judge Roy Bean* · Peter Whitney/*Death Valley Days* · Frank Ferguson/*Sugarfoot*

Beckwourth, Jim [James Pierson] (1800?-1866?) · Mountain man. Beckwourth's mother was a slave in Virginia, and he was the first black on the frontier to become famous. In 1824 he joined William Ashley's fur-trapping expedition to the Rockies and was a companion of Jedediah Smith. In 1828 he was adopted into the Crow Indian tribe. He lived with them for six years, marrying a series of Indian women. Later he was a guide in California during the gold rush, was in Colorado during the Pike's Peak gold rush in 1858 and, as a scout for Colonel Chivington, played a part in the Sand Creek Massacre of the *Cheyenne, though his actual role is disputed. He probably died while visiting the Crow in 1866. In 1854 Thomas D. Bonner interviewed him and published *The Life and Adventures of James P. Beckwourth, Mountaineer, Scout, Pioneer and Chief of the Crow Nation*, which made Beckwourth a celebrity. Despite the production of several Westerns with black characters in the 1970s, Beckwourth's career has been ignored. He is played by Jack Oakie (though not as a black) in *Tomahawk*/1950/U/*d* George Sherman/*lp* Van Heflin.

Judge Roy Bean presiding at the trial of a horse thief in 1900

Bierstadt, Albert (1830-1902) · Painter. Born in Germany and trained in Dusseldorf, the home of German Romantic painting, Bierstadt found fame in the 1860s with his grandiose landscape paintings of the West. From the late 1850s he made several tours of the Rockies and other spectacular landscapes, and his monumental depictions of epic mountain vistas helped to fix in the public's mind a certain image of the West: noble, unspoilt, morally uplifting. Bierstadt's models were European; of the Rockies he wrote: 'as seen from the plains they resemble very much the Bernese Alps; they are of granite formation, the same as the Swiss mountains ... the colours are like those of Italy.' People, if they figure at all in Bierstadt's paintings, are usually dwarfed by the majesty of mountains and waterfalls, though in 'The Oregon Trail' (1869) the grandeur of the sky and the peaks of the Rockies lend dignity and historical portent to the emigrants. (See Plates 10,11)

Billy the Kid (1859?-81) · Outlaw, aka William Bonney, Henry McCarty, William Antrim. There has probably been more tedious argument about the facts of Billy the Kid's life than about anything else in the West. The consensus now is that his real name was Henry McCarty, that he was born in New York, and that he killed his first man at the age of seventeen. He was employed as a cowhand by John *Tunstall on his ranch in Lincoln County, New Mexico. In February 1878 during the so-called *Lincoln County War between Tunstall and his associates and a rival group of ranchers led by Lawrence Murphy, Tunstall was murdered, with Billy a helpless onlooker.

In the next few months Billy and others pursued revenge. Two of Tunstall's murderers were killed, and then Sheriff Brady, a supporter of the Murphy faction. In July there was a full-scale shoot-out in Lincoln between the two groups, in the course of which Alexander McSween, an associate of Tunstall, was killed inside his blazing house. Billy escaped. The next year the new Governor of the Territory, Lew Wallace (author of Ben Hur), offered Billy an amnesty. But, tired of waiting for his promised pardon and failing to get the wages he felt he was owed from John *Chisum, Tunstall's former ally, Billy took to rustling. The new sheriff of Lincoln County, Pat *Garrett, was ordered to bring in the Kid. He captured him at the end of 1880 and the Kid was convicted of the murder of Sheriff Brady. Before he could be hanged he killed two of his guards and

William H. Bonney or Billy the Kid

escaped. Garrett set out after him again and on 14 July 1881 at Fort Sumner in a darkened bedroom shot him dead without warning.

Like some other outlaws in the West, Billy the Kid was being written up as a celebrity even before the end of his short life. (In a scene in *The Left Handed Gun*/1957 Paul Newman sits trying to read reports of his exploits.) But he was not originally a hero. Stephen Tatum's study *Inventing Billy the Kid* traces the legend through its many versions. The first 'biography' of the Kid appeared in the year of his death and like most of the dime novels which followed in the 1880s it portrays Billy as a vicious killer. This was, not surprisingly, the line pursued in Pat Garrett's own account, *The Authentic Life of Billy the Kid* (1882). Not until Walter Noble *Burns' *The Saga of Billy the Kid* (1926) did the figure of the innocent forced into killing by cruel circumstances become the dominant interpretation.

This is certainly the one followed by the movies, dating from the first full-scale screen version, King Vidor's *Billy the Kid*/1930. More recently he has been portrayed by Paul Newman as a martyred illiterate desperately struggling for love and justice, while in *Pat Garrett and Billy the Kid*/1973 Kris Kristofferson articulates an embryo class-consciousness, despising Garrett for throwing in his lot with the big landowners. (The role played first by Bob Steele, then by Buster Crabbe in PRC's Billy the Kid series

listed below has virtually nothing to do with the historical personage, though the character of the innocent forced outside the law by events beyond his control was a staple of the series Western. After *Blazing Frontier* PRC renamed the character Billy Carson when parents' groups complained about children identifying with an outlaw.)
Tefft Johnson/*Billy the Kid*/1911/Vitagraph/d Larry Trimble · *Billy the Bandit*/1916/U/d John Steppling · Johnny Mack Brown/*Billy the Kid*/1930 · Roy Rogers/*Billy the Kid Returns*/1938/REP/d Joseph Kane/lp Smiley Burnette · Bob Steele/*Billy the Kid Outlawed*/1940/PRC/d Sam Newfield/lp Al St John · Bob Steele/*Billy the Kid in Texas*/1940/PRC/d Sam Newfield/lp Al St John · Bob Steele/*Billy the Kid's Gun Justice*/1940/PRC/d Sam Newfield/lp Al St John · Jack Buetel/*The Outlaw*/1940 · Bob Steele/*Billy the Kid in Santa Fe*/1941/PRC/d Sam Newfield/lp Al St John · Bob Steele/*Billy the Kid's Fighting Pals*/1941/PRC/d Sam Newfield/lp Al St John · Bob Steele/*Billy the Kid's Range Law*/1941/PRC/d Sam Newfield/lp Al St John · Robert Taylor/*Billy the Kid*/1941/MGM/d David Miller/lp Brian Donlevy · Buster Crabbe/*Billy the Kid Wanted*/1941/PRC/d Sam Newfield/lp Al St John · Buster Crabbe/*Billy the Kid's Roundup*/1941/PRC/d Sam Newfield/lp Al St John · Buster Crabbe/*Billy the Kid's Smoking Guns*/1942/PRC/d Sam Newfield/lp Al St John · Buster Crabbe/*Billy the Kid Trapped*/1942/PRC/d Sam Newfield/lp Al St John · Buster Crabbe/*Law and Order*/1942/PRC/d Sherman Scott (Sam Newfield)/lp Al St John · Buster Crabbe/*The Mysterious Rider*/1942/PRC/d Sam Newfield/lp Al St John · Buster Crabbe/*The Sheriff of Sage Valley*/1942/PRC/d Sherman Scott (Sam Newfield)/lp Al St John · Buster Crabbe/*The Kid Rides Again*/1942/PRC/d Sherman Scott (Sam Newfield)/lp Al St John · George DeMain/*West of Tombstone*/1942/COL/d Howard Bretherton/lp Charles Starrett · Buster Crabbe/*The Fugitive of the Plains*/1943/PRC/d Sam Newfield/lp Al St John · Buster Crabbe/*Western Cyclone*/1943/PRC/d Sam Newfield/lp Al St John · Buster Crabbe/*The Renegade*/1943/PRC/d Sam Newfield/lp Al St John · Buster Crabbe/*Cattle Stampede*/1943/PRC/d Sam Newfield/lp Al St John · Buster Crabbe/*Blazing Frontier*/1943/PRC/d Sam Newfield/lp Al St John · Dean White/*Return of the Bad Men*/1948/RKO/d Ray Enright/lp Randolph Scott · Lash LaRue/*Son of Billy the Kid*/1949/Screen Guild/d Ray Taylor/

lp Al St John · Audie Murphy/*The Kid from Texas*/1949/u/*d* Kurt Neumann/*lp* Gale Storm · Don Barry/*I Shot Billy the Kid*/1950/Lippert/*d* William Berke/*lp* Robert Lowery · Tyler MacDuff/*The Boy from Oklahoma*/1953/wb/*d* Michael Curtiz/*lp* Will Rogers Jr. · Scott Brady/*The Law vs. Billy the Kid*/1954/col/*d* William Castle/*lp* Betta St John · Nick Adams/*Strange Lady in Town*/1955/wb/*d* Mervyn LeRoy/*lp* Greer Garson, Dana Andrews · Anthony Dexter/*The Parson and the Outlaw*/1957/col/*d* Oliver Drake/*lp* Marie Windsor · Paul Newman/*The Left Handed Gun*/1957 · Jack Taylor/*Fuera de la ley*/1962/Sp/*d* León Klimovsky · Gaston Sands/*A Bullet for Billy the Kid*/1963/Mex/*d* Rafael Baledon/*lp* Steve Brodie · Johnny Ginger/*The Outlaws Is Coming*/1964/col/*d* Norman Maurer/*lp* The Three Stooges · Chuck Courtney/*Billy the Kid vs. Dracula*/1965/Circle/*d* William Beaudine/*lp* John Carradine · Peter Lee Lawrence/*El hombre que matao Billy el niño*/1967/Sp, It/*d* Julio Buchs/*lp* Fausto Tozzi · Geoffrey Deuel/*Chisum*/1970/wb/*d* Andrew V. McLaglen/*lp* John Wayne, Forrest Tucker · Jean-Pierre Léaud/*Une aventure de Billy the Kid*/1971/Fr/*d* Luc Moullet · Dean Stockwell/*The Last Movie*/1971 · Michael J. Pollard/*Dirty Little Billy*/1972/wrg/*d* Stan Dragoti/*lp* Lee Purcell · Kris Kristofferson/*Pat Garrett and Billy the Kid*/1973
Television · Ray Stricklyn/*Cheyenne* · Joel Grey/*Maverick* · Robert Conrad/*Colt .45* · Robert Vaughn/*Tales of Wells Fargo* · Dennis Hopper/*Sugarfoot* · Stephen Joyce/*Bronco* · Richard Bakalyan/*The Deputy* · Clu Gulager/*The Tall Man* · Andrew Prine/*The Great Adventure* · Glenn Whitrow/*Bret Maverick*

Bingham, George Caleb (1811-79) · Painter. Brought up in the Midwest, Bingham had early success with his pictures of relaxed and peaceful scenes on the Missouri River. 'Fur Traders Descending the Missouri' (1845) combines a mood of idyllic repose with a feel for hazy distances. Bingham also painted some lively scenes of electioneering in Missouri in the days before the Kansas-Nebraska Act of 1854 raised the temperature of the slavery issue and made peaceful campaigning a thing of the past. His pictures show frontier democracy in action, open and robust (even in its disreputable drunkenness). But his 'Emigration of Daniel *Boone' (1851) sacrifices some of his attractive earlier informality in the cause of epic seriousness.

Black Bart (1830-1917?) · Outlaw. Nickname of Charles E. Boles, who single-handed and with an empty shotgun held up twenty-eight Wells, Fargo stages in California between 1875 and 1882. He liked to leave poems at the scene of the crime, one of which read:

'I've labored long and hard for bread,
For honor and for riches
But on my corns too long you've tred,
You fine-haired sons of bitches.'
Captured after he had left behind a handkerchief with a tell-tale laundry mark, he was sent to jail. Released in 1888 he vanished for ever, though one report said he died in New York in 1917.
Black Bart/1948/u/*d* George Sherman/*lp* Yvonne De Carlo, Dan Duryea, retains some elements of the true story of the outlaw. Also *Westward Ho*/1935/rep/*d* Robert N. Bradbury/*lp* John Wayne · *The Ride to Hangman's Tree*/1966/u/*d* Alan Rafkin/*lp* James Farentino

Blackfoot · A people of the Algonquian linguistic family occupying an area stretching from present-day Montana up across the Canadian border into Alberta and Saskatchewan. They divided into three groups: the Bloods, the Piegans and the Siksika (the latter meaning black-foot, possibly deriving from a practice of dying their moccasins black). From the time that a Blackfoot was killed by a member of the *Lewis and Clark expedition there was hostility between the Blackfoot and whites. Their fearsome reputation as fighters is variously drawn upon in *Across the Wide Missouri*/1950, *The Big Sky*/1952, *The Naked Spur*/1952 and in Vardis *Fisher's novel *Mountain Man* (1965), the source of *Jeremiah Johnson*/1972.

George Caleb Bingham, 'Fur Traders Descending the Missouri' (1845)

Deadwood in the Black Hills (c.1880)

Black Hills · Located mainly in South Dakota, the Black Hills were sacred to the Sioux and guaranteed to them under a treaty signed at Fort Laramie in 1868. But in 1874 General *Custer led an expedition into the hills and declared that gold existed there. The inrush of miners led directly to the war in which Custer was to lose his life. The subsequent defeat of the Sioux in the campaign following the Battle of the *Little Big Horn opened the way for the miners, and Deadwood, in the northern Black Hills, became a boom town. Among noted Deadwood residents were Wild Bill *Hickok (who was shot in the back there in 1876), the fictitious *Deadwood Dick, and *Calamity Jane, in which part Doris Day in the film of the same name sings 'The Black Hills of Dakota'.

Blacks · The Western is not a genre that one normally associates with images of black people. The American frontier that it mythologizes is quintessentially white Anglo-Saxon Protestant male, encompassing a repertoire of situations and motifs that are rooted in specifically white American experiences and interests. The historical period in which most Westerns are set witnessed the Civil War, as well as the westward migration of hundreds of thousands of black people following Emancipation in 1863. In other words, it is likely that black-white relations played some part, if probably only a marginal one, in the for-

mation of American frontier culture in the late 19th century. Yet these historical themes have not played any role in the evolution of the genre. Thus the contemporary crisis around slavery and abolition, or the relations between white settlers (many of whom migrated from the slave-owning South) and black migrants, for example, is simply avoided in the films. Even stories set in locations like Kansas and Missouri, historically sites of intense intersectional strife during the Civil War period, glide over these relevant social and political issues, whereby characters' identities as 'rebel' supporters or pro-Yankee are subsumed in more broadly defined generic archetypes.

Similarly, the 'Negro cowboy' does not figure prominently in the popular imagery of the Wild West. Most of the first black cowboys were in fact slaves, bought by slave-owning ranchers who ran cattle in Texas. Although they represented a very small minority, compared to the proportion of blacks on the plantations in the South, black cowboys nevertheless constituted a visible part of the ranching milieu in certain areas, breaking horses and handling longhorns alongside white cattle crews. Evidently, it was not uncommon to see all-black cattle crews in some parts of Texas, and there were even a small number of free blacks who owned ranches before the Civil War. Black cowboys were also involved in fighting Indians and were hired as scouts for the cavalry. The establishment of 'Negro

regiments' in the US Cavalry provided another means by which blacks contributed to the expansion of the western frontier – for example, between 1870 and 1890 fourteen Congressional Medals of Honor were awarded to black soldiers for bravery in the Indian Wars. John Ford's *Sergeant Rutledge*/1960 was the first serious attempt to incorporate this history into the mainstream Western.

The history of black representations in the Western can be divided into three brief periods. The first includes the series of Black Westerns made during the period of so-called 'race' movies in America, from the 1900s to the late 1940s. This was followed by a second cycle in the 1960s, when a number of mainstream Westerns began to experiment with civil rights or race relations motifs. Finally, there was the cycle of 'blaxploitation' Westerns made during the Hollywood black exploitation boom in the 1970s. Some of the films adopt what is clearly a deliberate strategy aimed at counter-balancing the Eurocentricity of the Western, whereas others simply mimic the more popular conventions of the genre. But overall the films represent notable attempts by both mainstream and independent, white and black producers to incorporate black-related themes and imagery into the established Western form. Of course, none of the films really challenge the conventions in any fundamental sense; what they do instead is manipulate narrative devices in order to articulate themes which are otherwise alien to the genre.

Until their demise in the late 1940s, the production of 'race' movies provided a kind of alternative cinema, where conventional motifs could be reversed in order to appeal specifically to black audiences. Independently produced by black- and white-controlled companies, with financing from the black bourgeoisie and white backers, these low-budget all-black films were shown in big city ghetto movie houses in the North, in segregated theatres in the South, and in other local black venues including church halls and schools. Some of the films dealt seriously with the experience of black life in America, or tensions within the black community itself, but the majority were geared mainly to entertainment. Indeed, 'race' movies tended to draw heavily on established mainstream forms, the two most popular of which were the gangster film and the Western.

One of the earliest Black Westerns (if not the first), *The Trooper of Troop K* (1916), depicted the exploits of the black cavalry against the Mexican Carranzista army at the Battle of Carrizal in June 1916. The film was produced by the Lincoln Motion Picture Company, one of the first 'race' movie production companies, run by the black actor Noble Johnson (who also appeared in mainstream silent and sound films) and his brother, George. In *Trooper*, Noble plays the 'shiftless Negro' who becomes the redeemed hero, a role which reverses the popular racial stereotype into a more positive figure. The film was well received by black audiences, and is particularly interesting both as a prototype black historical Western, and as an early (black-produced) social conscious-ness film which tries to counter the prolife-ration of racist imagery in mainstream silent film representations of blacks.

Most 'race' Westerns were less socially motivated, however, and tended towards escapism or, at best, simplistic motifs pro-jecting black versions of white cowboy heroes and situations. Bill Pickett, a well-known black rodeo star during the early 1900s, featured in two early black cowboy adventures, *The Crimson Skull* (1921) and *The Bull-Dogger* (1922), in which he was seen performing feats of heroism and honour. Pickett had been a member of the renowned Miller Brothers' 101 Ranch in Oklahoma, which was famous for its big rodeos in the States and Europe, and had worked with Tom Mix and Will Rogers before they became movie stars. His unique style of bull-dogging (the art of wrestling a steer by the horns) evidently led many people to believe that he had invented the sport! Like Mix and Rogers, Pickett successfully trans-ferred his cowboy rodeo skills to the movie screen, though his screen popularity was confined to the segregated milieu of 'race' movies.

In 1939 and 1940, Jed Buell's Hollywood Productions, a white-owned independent company, produced a series of musical Westerns which further enhanced the popularity of 'race' movies among black audiences. The star of the films, Herb Jeffries (aka Herbert Jeffrey) – billed as 'Black America's first singing cowboy in the movies' – was the immaculately dressed archetypal cowboy hero, complete with obligatory white hat, shining pair of pearl-handled revolvers, white horse called 'Star-dust' and trusty sidekick named 'Dusty'. The films were clear imitations of Hollywood Westerns of the period, not only in their choice of hero – Jeffries' singing cowboy was very much in the Gene Autry/

Tex Ritter vein – but also in their highly derivative stories and plot devices. Of course the films were made on considerably cheaper budgets, and they looked it.

For example, *The Bronze Buckeroo* had the usual bar-room brawl, but lacked Hollywood's deft sense of choreographed mayhem. On the other hand, and perhaps uniquely, the film did include two musical poker games in a saloon, with a cowboy performing a solo dance! Chase sequences were also a much-used device, often inter-spersed with moments of comic relief, as in *Harlem Rides the Range* (1939), which told a story of struggle over radium deposits. The commercial viability of these all-black musical Westerns is perhaps best reflected in the reports about Jed Buell's first black Western, *Harlem on the Prairie* (aka *Bad Man from Harlem*) (1937), which probably cost a lot less than $10,000 to produce, but is said to have grossed over $50,000 during its first year of distribution.

Significantly, 'race' Westerns – indeed, 'race' movies generally – often employed the racial stereotypes found in mainstream films, such as the eye-rolling, necrophobic Negro. Moreover, Herb Jeffries represented the archetypal light-skinned black hero, and would be pitted against darker-skinned heavies and comic figures. Even the romantic element in the films conformed to this colour caste convention, whereby the hero would eventually win the light-complexioned heroine. Some critics have argued that such romanticized figures as the black singing cowboy represented essen-tially middle-class heroes, which 'race' movies promoted as an ideal for the black masses. This argument is supported by the significance placed on colour caste and class in the films.

Whereas the early independent black Westerns attempted to appropriate main-stream conventions, for largely entertain-ment purposes, the ethically liberal Hollywood Westerns of the 1960s incor-porated black-related themes into typical (i.e. traditionally white) Western situations, which then became metaphors for inter-racial relations in contemporary America. These thematic shifts within mainstream film representations were in response to the radically changing political climate of the 60s, which was experiencing the full impact of the black civil rights movement and its struggle for social integration and equality. However, the incorporation of these new political values into the Western was not an altogether smooth process, as clearly seen in

Bill Pickett, champion bulldogger (c.1910)

Sergeant Rutledge, a structurally uneasy film, but nonetheless one of the most interesting 'liberal' Westerns of the period.

John Ford could not be described as a liberal director, but he came very close to that when he made *Sergeant Rutledge*, a race-relations drama that embodies the spirit of racial equality and human dignity. Char-acteristic of Hollywood racial motifs of the period, the eponymous central character (played by Woody Strode) is presented as the powerless victim of bigotry, whose only hope for social justice lies in the tenacious support of his white commanding officer (the epitome of liberal humanism), although by the end of the film Rutledge emerges as a noble, almost heroic figure.

But this pro-black image has to be seen in the context of the film's overall shape, which shows clear signs of fracture in the myth-ology of the American frontier West. The romanticized image of the West, which Ford brilliantly conveyed in several Western classics, is simply absent in this film or, rather, it is reversed. Thus, the US Cavalry (especially the leadership) – the traditional symbol of frontier conquest and authority – now appears morally bankrupt and lacking in any sense of purpose. Even the military tribunal that tries Rutledge lacks decorum, reflecting a community that has lost its sense of control. The backdrop for the film's racial theme is an untypical, degenerating frontier culture, where traditional values seem no longer to have ideological force.

Several 1960s Westerns address racial issues by inflecting the typical situation of a group of men from different backgrounds, who come together for some reason, but whose sense of solidarity or purpose is constantly threatened by interpersonal tensions. The inclusion of a black member in the group provides the focus for race-related themes; but the eruption of racial prejudice – which is usually identified with a particular character rather than articulated by the whole group – represents only one among a range of potentially disruptive forces which threaten group cohesion. Indeed, it is never the decisive factor which leads to (say) the violent dissolution of the group. In *The Professionals*/1966, this interracial Western motif is in fact understated, with an unproblematized black character (Woody Strode again) integrated fully into the all-white male situation.

A more complex working out of this theme is found in *Major Dundee*/1964, where the black member of the group (Brock Peters) is a racially significant figure, and racial tension an important aspect of the group dynamics. The cavalry regiment on which this Western is centred comprises a motley collection of 'good' and 'bad' individuals, whose impulse to destroy each other is held uneasily in check. The complexity of the narrative, and therefore the positioning of race within it, derives mainly from the film's problematic hero, Dundee, whose obsessed leadership provides the means through which the regiment is able to suppress its innate self-destructiveness and eventually reach its objective. One historian of the Western has suggested that a relationship can be drawn between the conflicts presented in the film and those underlying the formation of America as a nation. This reading aptly places *Major Dundee* in the context of the political climate of 60s America.

The 60s was a key period for the racialization of the Western, and other Hollywood genres as well. Of course, the films were about white characters' problems, with black characters or race-related themes as important elements in the narrative. But apart from the Western adventures featuring the former football star Jim Brown (as, for example, *100 Rifles*/1968), Hollywood showed no interest in presenting black versions of white Western heroes, for example, nor in producing films which would appeal primarily to black audiences. (This development was to come in the 1970s, when the political and economic climate had changed

considerably.) Nevertheless, the liberalizing effect of the 'social consciousness' Westerns of the early- and mid-1960s opened the way for greater use of racial understatement in popular films. Thus by the end of the decade it was possible for black characters to appear in a wide range of generic situations and social contexts, without necessarily signalling a film's concern with 'social problem' themes.

Although this trend continued into the 1970s, the emergence of black exploitation films in Hollywood during the first half of the decade led to the proliferation of aggressively black-oriented themes and images in popular films, some of which touched on serious social and political issues. In some respects this was a kind of 70s reincarnation of the earlier 'race' movie era, except of course that now the films were supported by the mainstream industry in their financing and exhibition. The main preoccupation during this so-called blaxploitation period was the projection of black super-heroes and, more broadly, the creation of black-oriented movie mythologies that would supplant – for blacks – the cultural dominance of white imagery. Several black character types emerged which were specific to this movement, such as the street hustler in gangster films, and the Wild West black cowboy hero.

Blaxploitation Westerns attempted to

recast the popular image of the West in black terms, drawing partly on significant historical themes, and partly on established conventions of the genre. But in general the films were geared to entertainment rather than social comment, and thus tended to exploit the more commercial aspects of the Western adventure motif. This caused anxiety among some black rights leaders and social commentators, who regretted the passing of the previous decade's sense of social consciousness.

However, the Hollywood liberal tradition was kept alive with Sidney Poitier's directorial début, *Buck and the Preacher* (1971), which had more in common with the social consciousness values of the 60s than with the black exploitation trend of the 70s. The film dramatized a hitherto neglected area of American history – the migration of ex-slaves to the West following the collapse of the Confederacy, and the activities of white bounty hunters hired to force them back into unofficial slavery on the southern plantations. The effectiveness with which this theme was developed enabled the film to achieve a relevance which only white mainstream Westerns had displayed. Moreover, the film was clearly rooted in the Hollywood tradition of the wagon-train epic, and this enhanced its identification with the Western genre.

Buck and the Preacher was the only blax-

Constance Towers, Woody Strode in Sergeant Rutledge

ploitation-period Western that seriously attempted to rework generic conventions from within; that is, with careful regard for the conventions, as opposed to deploying adventure plot devices for sheer excitement. In that sense, it is unmistakably a Western in the full Hollywood sense; its narrative is constructed round a series of set-pieces which play out a number of strictly generic conventions with occasional black inflections. An extreme example is the status of the Indians, who are presented as non-threatening in relation to the blacks. In a particularly revealing scene, Buck (Poitier) invokes solidarity between Indians and blacks, on the grounds that they share a common oppressor. But it is a mark of the film's integrity that this theme is not romanticized or exaggerated: the Indian chief responds by pointing out the contradictions inherent in the black American experience, such as the fact that black people joined with whites to fight the Indians.

The series of Western adventures featuring ex-pro-football star Fred Williamson proved popular with audiences, largely because of Williamson's cultivatedly macho persona, which fitted in neatly with the blaxploitation notion of black super-hero. In *The Legend of Nigger Charley* (1972), he plays the eponymous hero who escapes from slavery and takes up gunfighting in the Wild West. Like its sequel, *The Soul of Nigger Charley* (1973), it is basically a formula picture that relies heavily on action scenes, chase sequences and comic relief from the hero's dependable sidekick (played by D'Urville Martin). But the controversy over their titles helped both films to succeed at the box office.

The general failure of blaxploitation Westerns to experiment with the conventions, and to go beyond adventure motifs, is highlighted in another Williamson vehicle, *Boss Nigger* (aka *Black Bounty Killer* (1974), which is so preoccupied with following the exploits of the film's two protagonists that it neglects the interesting theme of the black sheriff ridding the white town of outlaws. This inability to develop narratives beyond the exigency of exploitation motifs is not a peculiarity of blaxploitation films alone, of course, but it is nonetheless significant in this context. Not surprisingly, therefore, the more interesting interventions tended to happen in non-blaxploitation mainstream Westerns like Mel Brooks' interracial Western parody, *Blazing Saddles*/1974. The blaxploitation era died suddenly in the mid-1970s, after only about five years. There-

after, a kind of reaction set in, prompted in part by Hollywood's economic recovery; by the 1980s black-related themes and imagery of any significance had more or less receded once again into the background, and the Western had ceased to be a relevant arena for contemporary black representations. JPI
The Crimson Skull/1921/Norman Productions/*lp* Anita Bush, Bill Pickett · *The Bull-Dogger*/1922/Norman Productions/*lp* Bill Pickett · *Harlem on the Prairie*/1937/Associated/*d* Sam Newfield/*lp* Herbert Jeffries · *The Bronze Buckaroo*/1939/Hollywood Productions/*d* Richard Kahn/*lp* Herbert Jeffries · *Harlem Rides the Range*/1939/Hollywood Productions/*d* Richard Kahn/*lp* Herbert Jeffries · *Buck and the Preacher*/1971/E&R/*d* Sidney Poitier/*lp* Sidney Poitier, Harry Belafonte · *The Legend of Nigger Charley*/1972/Spangler & Sons/*d* Martin Goldman/*lp* Fred Williamson, D'Urville Martin · *The Soul of Nigger Charley*/1973/PAR/*d* Larry G. Spangler/*lp* Fred Williamson, D'Urville Martin · *Boss Nigger*/1974/Boss Productions/*d* Jack Arnold/*lp* Fred Williamson, D'Urville Martin

Bodmer, Karl (1809-93) · Painter. Swiss-born and trained in Paris, Bodmer was appointed illustrator on the scientific expedition to the upper Missouri organized by Prince Maximilian of Wied Neuwied in

1833. Travelling into present-day North Dakota and Montana, the party wintered at Fort Clark among the Hidatsa and Mandan Indians. The latter were to be all but exterminated by smallpox only four years later and Bodmer's pictures are an invaluable record of a lost culture. Bodmer returned with Maximilian to Europe and never revisited America. A book of his paintings, among the very first of the trans-Mississippi West, was produced as a supplement to Maximilian's account of his expedition, published in German, French and English between 1839 and 1843. Though the purpose of the Prince's journey was primarily scientific, Bodmer's pictures are motivated as much by the tourist's eye for the exotic, an impulse later artists were to capitalize on. (See Plate 4)

Boone, Daniel (1734-1820) · Frontiersman. Boone became a national, indeed international figure during his own lifetime through his role in pioneering the settlement of Kentucky. After his first attempt in 1773 was beaten off by Indians, he led a second party through the Cumberland Gap along the so-called Wilderness Road. On the Kentucky River he helped build Fortress Boonesboro. In 1778 he was captured by Shawnee Indians, but managed to escape after three months and defended the fort against a combined force of British and Indians. But the lands which Boone claimed

George Caleb Bingham, 'Daniel Boone Escorting Settlers through the Cumberland Gap' (1851-2)

for himself in Kentucky he lost through improper registry. In later life he took his family further and further west, ending his days in Missouri.

Boone was the first fully-fledged Western hero, and his contribution to westward expansion was written up as early as 1784 in *The Discovery, Settlement and Present State of Kentucke* by John Filson. An epic poem, *The Adventures of Daniel Boone*, by his nephew Daniel Bryan appeared in 1813, and Byron wrote an extended tribute to him in *Don Juan* (1819):

'Simple, serene, the antipodes of shame,
Which hate nor envy e'er could tinge with wrong;
An active hermit, even in age the child
Of Nature, or the Man of Ross run wild.'

The book which really established him as a major figure of legend was Timothy *Flint's *The Life and Adventures of Daniel Boone, The First Settler of Kentucky* (1833). As Henry Nash Smith shows in *Virgin Land*, Boone became a curiously ambivalent figure. He could symbolize the urge to settle the wilderness; alternatively he could embody the spirit of solitude, resenting the encroachments of civilization. It is primarily as the Pathfinder that he was absorbed into the popular imagination, but his status in the cinema has never matched his historical reputation.

Daniel Boone, or Pioneer Days in America/1907/Edison · *Daniel Boone's Bravery*/1911/Kalem · *Life of Daniel Boone*/1912/Republic · Jack Mower/*In the Days of Daniel Boone*/1923/U/d Frank Messinger · Roy Stewart/*Daniel Boone through the Wilderness*/1926/Sunset/d Robert N. Bradbury · Buffalo Bill Jr./*The Miracle Rider*/1935/Mascot/d Armand Schaefer, B. Reeves Eason/lp Tom Mix · George O'Brien/*Daniel Boone*/1936/RKO/d David Howard/lp John Carradine · Bill Elliott/*The Return of Daniel Boone*/1941/COL/d Lambert Hillyer/lp Dub Taylor · David Bruce/*Young Daniel Boone*/1950/MON/d Reginald LeBorg/lp Kristine Miller · Bruce Bennett/*Daniel Boone, Trail Blazer*/1956/REP/d Albert C. Gannaway, Ismael Rodriguez/lp Lon Chaney Jr.
Television · Peter Graves/*The Great Adventure* · Dewey Martin/*Daniel Boone* · Fess Parker/*Daniel Boone* · Rick Moses/*Young Dan'l Boone*

Border · The Western's most eloquent study of the difference a border can make is *The Wonderful Country*/1959, based on the novel by Tom *Lea, in which the hero is

Robert Mitchum south of the border in The Wonderful Country

forced to choose between two civilizations, the American and the Mexican. Usually the border signifies not so much a change of politics or culture as simply the end of legal jurisdiction, as in *The Far Country*/1954, when James Stewart crosses from Alaska into the Yukon to escape the clutches of John McIntire. Jack Nicholson in *Goin' South*/1978 is outraged when the legal convention is disregarded. He has crossed the river into Mexico and believing himself safe turns to mock his pursuers. They simply chase after him and drag him back to Texas.

Bounty hunter · 'Where life had no value, death sometimes had its price. That is why the bounty killers appeared.' So intones the opening of *Per qualche dollaro in più*/1965. In the cynical world of Sergio Leone the bounty hunter is in his element; hunting down people for money is a game to be enjoyed. In Hollywood Westerns he is more often the outsider, feared and despised by others, mistrusting his own motives, which are as often as not based on revenge rather than greed. In *Ride Lonesome*/1959 it is enough that Karen Steele *thinks* Randolph Scott to be a bounty hunter for her to treat him with contempt. Anthony Mann directed two compelling studies of the type, played by James Stewart in *The Naked Spur*/1952 and Henry Fonda in *The Tin Star*/1957. Other memorably troubled bounty hunters include Glenn Ford in *Santee*/1972 and Randolph Scott in *The Bounty Hunter*/1954/WB/d André de Toth/lp Marie Windsor.

Bower, B[ertha] M[uzzy] (1871-1940) · Author whose work became popular with Hollywood in the teens and 20s. Bower's first Western novel, *Chip of the Flying-U*, a more folksy ranch novel than Owen *Wister's near-contemporaneous *The Virginian*, was an instant success when it appeared in magazine format in 1904. Charles *Russell, reputedly the prototype for Chip, illustrated the hardback edition. Bowers herself wrote the script for the first Hollywood version in 1914, as a result of which experience several of her later stories feature film-making.
Chip of the Flying-U/1914/Selig/d Colin Campbell/lp Tom Mix · remade as *The Galloping Devil*/1920/Canyon Pictures/d Nate Watt/lp Franklyn Farnum · *Chip of the Flying-U*/1926/U/d Lynn Reynolds/lp Hoot Gibson · remade 1939/U/d Ralph Staub/lp Johnny Mack Brown · *Shotgun Jones*/1914/Selig/d Colin Campbell/lp Wheeler Oakman · *Lonesome Trail*/1914/Selig/d Colin Campbell/lp Wheeler Oakman · *The Reveller*/1914/Selig/d Colin Campbell/lp Wheeler Oakman · *The Up-Hill Climb*/1914/Selig/d Colin Campbell/lp Wheeler Oakman · *When the Cook Fell Ill*/1914/Selig/d Colin Campbell/lp Wheeler Oakman · *How Weary Went Wooing*/1915/Selig/d Tom Mix/lp Tom Mix · *North of 53*/1917/FOX/d William Taylor/lp Dustin Farnum · *The Wolverine*/1921/Associated/d William Bertram/lp Helen Gibson · *Taming of the West*/1925/U/d Arthur Rosson/lp Hoot Gibson · *Riding Thunder*/1925/U/d Clifford Smith/lp Jack Hoxie · *Flying U Ranch*/1927/FBO/d

Robert De Lacy/*lp* Tom Tyler · *Points West*/1929/U/*d* Arthur Rosson/*lp* Hoot Gibson · *King of the Rodeo*/1929/U/*d* Henry MacRae/*lp* Hoot Gibson

Bowie, James (1795-1836) · Frontiersman. Credited with the invention of the double-edged knife named for him, Jim Bowie was born in Georgia, Kentucky or Tennessee according to different sources. He moved to Texas, and became a Mexican citizen while Texas was still part of Mexico. In 1830 he enlisted in the Texas Rangers and fought against the Indians. When the Texans rebelled in 1835 Bowie joined them. His small volunteer force eventually found itself at the *Alamo, where along with regular Texas troops it was overcome by a superior Mexican force and Bowie was killed.

The cinema has usually portrayed Bowie as a hard-drinking, rumbustious fighter, though Alan Ladd preferred a more self-contained characterization in *The Iron Mistress*.

Alfred Paget/*Martyrs of the Alamo*/1915/Keystone-Triangle/*d* Christy Cabanne/*lp* Sam De Grasse · Bob Fleming/*Davy Crockett at the Fall of the Alamo*/1926/Sunset/*d* Robert N. Bradbury/*lp* Cullen Landis · Rex Lease/*Heroes of the Alamo*/1936/Sunset/*d* Harry Fraser/*lp* Lane Chandler · Hal Taliaferro/*The Painted Stallion*/1937/REP/*d* William Witney, Ray Taylor, Alan James/*lp* Hoot Gibson, Ray Corrigan · Robert Armstrong/*Man of Conquest*/1939/REP/*d* George Nichols Jr./*lp* Richard Dix, Joan Fontaine · MacDonald Carey/*Comanche Territory*/1950/U/*d* George Sherman/*lp* Maureen O'Hara · Alan Ladd, *The Iron Mistress*/1952/WB/*d* Gordon Douglas/*lp* Virginia Mayo · Stuart Randall/*The Man from the Alamo*/1953 · Sterling Hayden/*The Last Command*/1955/REP/*d* Frank Lloyd/*lp* J. Carrol Naish · Jeff Morrow/*The First Texan*/1956/AA/*d* Byron Haskin/*lp* Joel McCrea · Richard Widmark/*The Alamo*/1960/Batjac/*d* John Wayne/*lp* John Wayne, Laurence Harvey Television · Scott Forbes/*The Adventures of Jim Bowie* · Kenneth Tobey/*Davy Crockett* · Michael Beck/*Houston: The Legend of Texas* · James Arness/*The Alamo: 13 Days to Glory*

Brady, Matthew (1822?-96) · Photographer. By 1860 Brady had already secured his own place in history by the diligence with which he had photographed notable Americans of his time. With the exception of William Henry Harrison (who died one month after

Matthew Brady, photograph of the battle of Gettysburg (1863)

being elected) he photographed every American President from John Quincy Adams to William McKinley. Of the one hundred or so known photographs of Abraham *Lincoln thirty-five are by Brady. He also photographed explorers such as John *Frémont, soldiers such as Winfield *Scott, and naturalists such as John James Audubon. But it is as a photographer of the Civil War that he is best known. He was present at the first major battle, Bull Run, as well as at Antietam and Gettysburg. The cumbersome equipment of the day and the slow exposure speeds made photographing action impossible, except at very long distance. But Brady's pictures of armies before the fight, and most memorably of the dead lying on the field of battle, were the first war pictures to make a major impact on the American public.

Brand, Max (1892-1944) · Author. Pen name for the hugely prolific Frederick Faust, many of whose pulp Western novels were turned into films. Despite a life-long ambition to be a serious poet, Faust achieved recognition only for the potboilers that poured from his pen. He wrote over 300 Western novels and stories, as well as many other works, including the popular Dr Kildare series. He also worked in Hollywood during the late 1930s. His Westerns show little interest in historical or geographical realities and are mainly fantasies about super-heroes. Although Faust suffered from a serious heart complaint, he insisted on becoming a war correspondent in World

War II and was killed in Italy. In his lifetime he published more than twenty-five million words.

His best known Western is *Destry Rides Again*, published in 1930 and filmed as *Destry Rides Again*/1932/U/*d* Ben Stoloff/*lp* Tom Mix · *Destry Rides Again*/1939 (in which the unassuming character played by James Stewart bears no resemblance to the hero of Faust's book) · *Destry*/1954/U/*d* George Marshall/*lp* Audie Murphy · Several Tom Mix silent films were based on his stories, including *The Untamed*/1920/FOX/*d* Emmett Flynn · remade as *Fair Warning*/1930/FOX/*d* Alfred Werker/*lp* George O'Brien · *The Night Horseman*/1921/FOX/*d* Lynn Reynolds · *Trailin'*/1921/FOX/*d* Lynn Reynolds · remade as *A Holy Terror*/1931/FOX/*d* Irving Cummings/*lp* George O'Brien · *Just Tony*/1922/FOX/*d* Lynn Reynolds · *Mile-a-Minute Romeo*/1923/FOX/*d* Lambert Hillyer · *The Best Bad Man*/1925/FOX/*d* John Blystone. Other Western films: *The Adopted Son*/1917/Metro/*d* Charles Brabin/*lp* Francis X. Bushman · *Lawless Love*/1918/FOX/*d* Robert Thornby/*lp* Jewel Carmen · *Three Who Paid*/1923/FOX/*d* Colin Campbell/*lp* Dustin Farnum · *The Gunfighter*/1923/FOX/*d* Lynn Reynolds/*lp* William Farnum · *Against All Odds*/1924/FOX/*d* Edmund Mortimer/*lp* Buck Jones · *The Flying Horseman*/1926/FOX/*d* Orville Dull/*lp* Buck Jones · *The Cavalier*/1928/Tiffany/*d* Irvin Willat/*lp* Richard Talmadge · *The Valley of Vanishing Men*/1942/COL/*d* Spencer G. Bennet/*lp* Bill Elliott · *The Desperadoes*/1943/COL/*d* Charles Vidor/*lp* Randolph

Scott, Glenn Ford · *Rainbow Over Texas*/1946/REP/d Frank McDonald/*lp* Roy Rogers · *Singing Guns*/1950/REP/d R. G. Springsteen/*lp* Walter Brennan · *My Brother the Outlaw*/1951/UA/d Elliott Nugent/*lp* Mickey Rooney · *Branded*/1950/PAR/d Rudolph Maté/*lp* Alan Ladd, Charles Bickford · *The Hired Gun*/1957/MGM/d Ray Nazarro/*lp* Rory Calhoun
Television · *Destry*

Branding · Before *barbed wire fencing was introduced, branding was a necessary means of identifying the ownership of cattle left to roam free on the open range. Marks, usually in the form of letters or numbers, were burnt into the animal's hide. Wandering unbranded cattle were known as 'mavericks', after the Texas lawyer Samuel Maverick (1803-70), who was believed to be the first to mark strays in this way, and became the property of the first person to set a brand on them. The Red River D brand is a motif running through *Red River*/1947; at the end of the film Dunston (John Wayne) adds an M to it for Matthew (Montgomery Clift). In Buster Keaton's satire on the macho Western hero, *Go West*, Buster is too sensitive to burn a brand on to his favourite cow and shaves it on instead.

Bridger, Jim (1804-81) · The most famous of the mountain men, Jim Bridger epitomized the unlettered but supremely knowledgeable trapper, scout and guide. He worked first for William Ashley in the Rocky Mountain fur trade, later for Jedediah Smith, and was a partner in the Rocky Mountain Fur Company. In 1843, with Louis Vasquez, he built Fort Bridger, in present-day Wyoming, an important station on the Oregon Trail. Bridger's knowledge of the geography of the West was second to none (he was probably the first white man to see the Great Salt Lake). He was in demand as a guide for military and scientific expeditions, such as Colonel Johnson's in the Mormon War of 1857-8, and assisted the surveys for the Union Pacific railroad. Many of the reports of these expeditions wrote up Bridger's contribution, so that he became well enough known for Ned *Buntline to put him into dime novels.
Jim Bridger's Indian Bride/1910/Kalem · Tully Marshall/*The Covered Wagon*/1923 · Nelson McDowell/*Kit Carson*/PAR/1928/d Alfred Werker/*lp* Fred Thomson · Raymond Hatton/*Kit Carson*/1940/UA/d George B. Seitz/*lp* Jon Hall · Van Heflin/*Tomahawk*/1950/U/d George Sherman/*lp*

Yvonne De Carlo · Porter Hall/*The Pony Express*/1952/PAR/d Jerry Hopper/*lp* Charlton Heston, Rhonda Fleming · Dennis Morgan/*The Gun That Won the West*/1955/COL/d William Castle/*lp* Richard Denning
Television · James Wainwright/*Bridger* · Jack Kruschen/*The Incredible Rocky Mountain Race* · Reb Brown/*Centennial*

Jim Bridger

Brocius, Curly Bill (?-1882?) · Gunfighter. Aka William Graham, Brocius was an associate of the *Clantons and in 1880 while Virgil Earp was deputy marshal of *Tombstone Brocius shot the marshal there. Brocius probably took part in the murder of Morgan Earp in 1881 and Wyatt *Earp claimed to have killed him in revenge, though this is doubtful.
Joe Sawyer/*Frontier Marshal*/1939 · Edgar Buchanan/*Tombstone, the Town Too Tough to Die*/1942/PAR/d William McGann/*lp* Richard Dix, Victor Jory · Jon Voight/*Hour of the Gun*/1967
Television · William Phipps/*The Life and Legend of Wyatt Earp*

Brown, John (1800-59) · The best known of the abolitionists who attempted in the 1850s to win Kansas for the anti-slavery cause. Brown was in large measure responsible for keeping feelings at fever pitch, and inevitably they boiled over into violence, earning the state its nickname of 'Bleeding Kansas' and ensuring that when the Civil War came it would be contested with special bitterness

in the Midwest. In 1859 Brown led an attack on a federal arsenal at Harper's Ferry in Virginia. It failed and he was promptly hanged by the Virginia authorities, thereby ensuring his martyrdom.

Most Westerns set in the Civil War period lean towards sympathy with the South, but the film which contains the most substantial portrayal of John Brown, *Santa Fe Trail*/1940, goes further than most. Raymond Massey plays Brown as a vindictive zealot who deserves everything he gets. Also Raymond Massey/*Seven Angry Men*/1955/AA/d Charles Marquis Warren/*lp* Jeffrey Hunter, Debra Paget · Royal Dano/*Skin Game*/1971/WB/d Paul Bogart/*lp* James Garner, Lou Gossett

Buffalo · The American buffalo, more correctly the bison (*bos bison americanus*), once covered the plains of the United States and Canada. Their numbers at the beginning of the 19th century have been estimated at between 40 and 60 million. The economy of the Indians of the region was almost entirely dependent on them; buffalo provided not just meat and clothing but hides for tents, sinews for thread, bones and horns for tools, 'chips' (dried dung) for fuel. The hunting and eventually the destruction of the herds by whites began in earnest in the 1870s, when cheap railroad transportation developed the market in the east for hides. Huge numbers were slaughtered. From just one county of Montana 180,000 hides were shipped in 1882. By 1884 the boom was over, the herds reduced to a fraction of what they had been; only bones were left, to be freighted east for fertilizer. And with the passing of the buffalo went the nomadic way of life of the Plains Indians, who were reduced to dependence on government hand-outs in the reservations. In 1874 General Phil *Sheridan was so pleased with the buffalo hunters' achievement he recommended they be given medals: 'These men have

Stewart Granger shooting buffalo in The Last Hunt

Ned Buntline (l.) on stage with Bill Cody and Texas Jack Omohundro (c.1875)

done more in the last two years, and will do more in the next year, to settle the vexed Indian question than the entire regular army has done in the last thirty years.'

Scenes of Indians hunting buffalo were almost obligatory in the repertoire of painters of the West; *Catlin, *Miller, *Bodmer, *Russell and *Remington all produced pictures on this theme. Only rarely has the cinema taken the slaughter of the buffalo as a subject, though Paramount twice filmed Zane Grey's *The Thundering Herd*, in 1925 and 1933. One of the very few films to do justice to the topic is Richard Brooks' *The Last Hunt*/1955. Robert Taylor plays a pathological Indian-hater for whom each buffalo shot means one less Indian, a sentiment echoed by John Wayne in *The Searchers*/1956.

Buntline, Ned (1823-86) · Author. Pen name

of Edward Zane Carroll Judson, an early dime novelist and the man in part responsible for the creation of Buffalo Bill *Cody. According to Don Russell's authoritative *The Lives and Legends of Buffalo Bill*, Buntline did not invent his hero's name and he only wrote four novels about him (compared to the scores written by others). Nevertheless, after their meeting in Nebraska on 24 July 1869 Buntline did set about writing a story, *Buffalo Bill, the King of Border Men*, which was published in December of that year. This story was turned into a play and Buffalo Bill saw it on his first visit to New York in 1872. The publicity surrounding Bill's visit inspired Buntline to write a new play in which the hero would play himself. *The Scouts of the Prairie* was allegedly written by Buntline in four hours, and Buffalo Bill, along with his fellow scout Texas Jack *Omohundro, first appeared in it in Chicago

on 16 December 1872.

The Chicago *Times* critic was not impressed: 'On the whole it is not probable that Chicago will ever look upon the like again. Such a combination of incongruous drama, execrable acting, renowned performers, mixed audience, intolerable stench, scalping, blood and thunder is not likely to be vouchsafed to a city for a second time – even Chicago.' But the play was a huge success, and from that moment the future of the West as America's major source of popular drama and entertainment was assured.

Buntline had comparatively little to do with Buffalo Bill's later career, but his name has come to be synonymous with the dime novel. In *Cattle Annie and Little Britches*/1980/UA/d Lamont Johnson, Burt Lancaster as Bill Doolin is excited to read about his own adventures in a Buntline novel, while in *Buffalo Bill and the Indians*/1976 Lancaster plays Buntline himself.
Also: Dick Elliott/*Annie Oakley*/1935/RKO/d George Stevens/*lp* Barbara Stanwyck · Thomas Mitchell, *Buffalo Bill*/1944
Television · Lloyd Corrigan/*The Life and Legend of Wyatt Earp*

Burnett, W[illiam] R[iley] (1899-1982) · Novelist and scriptwriter. Burnett is better known as a hard-boiled crime novelist (*Little Caesar*, *The Asphalt Jungle*, *High Sierra*). His Westerns have a similar flavour and are frequently concerned with the law and criminals. Burnett's novel *Saint Johnson* (1930), a fictional treatment of the Wyatt Earp story, was four times filmed: as *Law and Order*/1932 · *Wild West Days*/1937/U/d Ford Beebe, Cliff Smith/*lp* Johnny Mack Brown · *Law and Order*/1940/U/d Ray Taylor/*lp* Johnny Mack Brown · *Law and Order*/1953/U/d Nathan Juran/*lp* Ronald Reagan, Dorothy Malone.
Also (*novel only*) *Dark Command*/1940/REP/d Raoul Walsh/*lp* John Wayne, Walter Pidgeon · (*co-st, co-sc*) *San Antonio*/1946/WB/d David Butler/*lp* Errol Flynn, Alexis Smith · (*st, sc*) *Belle Starr's Daughter*/1948/FOX/d Lesley Selander/*lp* George Montgomery · (*st only*) *Yellow Sky*/1948; (*novel only* [*High Sierra*]) *Colorado Territory*/1949 · (*novel only* [*Adobe Walls*]) *Arrowhead*/1953/PAR/d Charles Marquis Warren/*lp* Charlton Heston, Jack Palance · (*novel only*) *The Badlanders*/1958/MGM/d Delmer Daves/*lp* Alan Ladd · (*st, sc*) *Sergeants 3*/1961/UA/d John Sturges/*lp* Frank Sinatra, Dean Martin

Burns, Walter Noble (1872-1932) · Newspaperman whose biographies of famous
Westerners contributed substantially to
their mythification. His book *The Saga of
Billy the Kid* (1926) formed the basis of King
Vidor's *Billy the Kid*/1930 and the remake of
the same title, 1941/MGM/d David Butler/lp
Robert Taylor, Brian Donlevy. Burns' book
about the legendary bandit and revolutionary Joaquin *Murieta, *The Robin Hood
of El Dorado* (1932), was filmed under that
title by William Wellman in 1936. Burns
also wrote a book entitled *Tombstone* (1927),
which was a major factor in establishing the
legend of Wyatt *Earp.

C

Calamity Jane (1852-1903) · Sobriquet of
Martha Jane Cannary, frontierswoman. Her
origins are as obscure as the reason for her
nickname, but she is known to have been in
*Virginia City, Montana from 1865 and
moved to the *Black Hills in Dakota in 1875,
soon after gold was discovered. She often
wore men's clothes and had a reputation for
hard drinking and swearing. This has led
some women, curiously perhaps, to claim
her for feminism. That she was ever romantically involved with Wild Bill *Hickok is
almost certainly untrue, though she did
form a relationship with a Clinton Burke, by
whom she may have had a daughter.
Towards the end of her life she appeared on
stage as 'Calamity Jane, the Famous Woman
Scout of the Wild West', though it seems
likely her relationship to the army was not
that of scout but of occasional camp fol-
lower, i.e. prostitute.

Her fictional image was far more influential on her appearances in the Western film
than was her real life. From the 1880s
Calamity Jane, 'nobbily attired in male garb'
as one description has it, was a popular
character in dime novels written by Edward
L. Wheeler and is usually in love with
another of Wheeler's creations, the wholly
fictitious *Deadwood Dick. None of the less
glamorous facts of her actual career has been
allowed to inhibit the screen image of Calamity; in the most memorable portrayal, that
by Doris Day in *Calamity Jane*/1953, her
buckskins are fetchingly feminine and her
love for Wild Bill is ultimately requited.
Ethel Grey Terry/*Wild Bill Hickok*/1923/
PAR/d Clifford C. Smith/lp William S.
Hart · Louise Dresser/*Caught*/1931/PAR/d
Edward Sloman/lp Richard Arlen · Helen
Gibson/*Custer's Last Stand*/1936/Stage &
Screen/d Elmer Clifton/lp Rex Lease · Jean

Calamity Jane

Arthur/*The Plainsman*/1936 · Marin Sais/
Deadwood Dick/1940/COL/d James W.
Horne/lp Don Douglas · Sally Payne/
Young Bill Hickok/1940/REP/d Joseph
Kane/lp Roy Rogers · Frances Farmer/
Badlands of Dakota/1941/U/d Alfred E.
Green/lp Robert Stack, Richard Dix · Jane
Russell/*The Paleface*/1948/PAR/d Norman
Z. McLeod/lp Bob Hope · Yvonne De
Carlo/*Calamity Jane and Sam Bass*/1949/U/
d George Sherman/lp Howard Duff ·
Evelyn Ankers/*The Texan Meets Calamity
Jane*/1950/COL/d Ande Lamb · Doris Day/
Calamity Jane/1953 · Judi Meredith/*The
Raiders*/1964/U/d Herschel Daugherty/ lp
Brian Keith, Robert Culp · Gloria
Milland/*Aventuras del oeste*/1964/It, WG,
Sp/d J.L. Romero Marchent/lp Rick Van
Nutter · Abby Dalton/*The Plainsman*/
1966/PAR/d David Lowell Rich/lp Don
Murray, Guy Stockwell
Television · Fay Spain/*Death Valley Days* ·
Dody Heath/*Colt .45* · Stephanie Powers/
Bonanza · Kim Darby/*This Was the West
That Was* · Jane Alexander/*Calamity Jane*

California · Ruled first by Spain and then,
after 1821, by Mexico, California was ceded
to the United States on 2 February 1848 as a
result of the Mexican War. At that time the
non-Indian population amounted to only
7,000 people. The discovery of gold nine
days earlier was to bring in 200,000 more
within the next three years. The drama of the

gold rush by the 'forty-niners' provided
plentiful material for writers such as Bret
*Harte, whose stories were the basis of many
early Westerns. But, with occasional exceptions such as *Gold Is Where You Find It*, *Paint
Your Wagon*, *Ride the High Country*/1962 and
the recent *Pale Rider*/1985, the mining frontier of California did not prove to be such a
fertile source for later Westerns. An
occasional film such as *One-Eyed Jacks*/1960
has exploited the distinctive landscape of
California. Mostly Hollywood chose to concentrate on 'Old California', the period
before incorporation into the United States.
Films such as *The Man from Monterey*, *The
Californian* and *In Old California*, together
with the many dramatizations of Zorro, are
set in a world of dashing caballeros, flashing
blades, dark-eyed señoritas and strumming
guitars.
The Man from Monterey/1933/WB/d Mack
V. Wright/lp John Wayne · *The
Californian*/1937/FOX/d Gus Meins/lp
Ricardo Cortez · *Gold Is Where You Find
It*/1938/WB/d Michael Curtiz/lp George
Brent, Olivia De Havilland · *In Old
California*/1942/REP/d William McGann/lp
John Wayne · *Paint Your Wagon*/1969/PAR/
d Joshua Logan/lp Clint Eastwood, Lee
Marvin

Canada · In 1953 Colin Low made one of
Canada's most distinguished movies. A
short (12 minute), minimally edited black-
and-white film made of simple yet strong
cinematographic elements, *Corral* features a
more-or-less Marlboro Man (the bona fide
thing, no costumed model) in the abstracted
landscape of hill, sky, cloud and mountain
background near Waterton Lakes National
Park. From a herd of corralled range-wild
horses the cowboy selects the one he wants,
saddles and mounts it, then rides out into
the freedom of the open range. Although –
or because – it fails to fit a Hollywood
pattern, *Corral*, located somewhere between
love lyric and home movie, is the most
Canadian of Westerns.

At least four types of Canadian Western
can be distinguished: Hollywood Westerns
filmed in Canada which use the landscape
incidentally; Hollywood Westerns which
pretend to be of Canadian stories (usually
seen through American eyes); Canadian
Westerns (company, story, film crew and
actors mostly Canadian), and Canadian
documentaries on Western subjects.

The first category includes several mature
Westerns filmed in the 1960s and 70s:
Arthur Penn's *Little Big Man*/1970, Robert

Altman's *McCabe & Mrs. Miller*/1971 and *Buffalo Bill and the Indians or Sitting Bull's History Lesson*/1976. Filmed on the Stoney Indian Reserve between Banff and Calgary, *Little Big Man* and *Buffalo Bill* used the backdrop of the Rockies, like earlier, less sublime stories such as *The Alaskan* (1924) or the Robert Mitchum-Marilyn Monroe vehicle, *River of No Return*/1954.

The Hollywood Canadian Western, most problematic of these categories, includes several hundred, mostly forgettable, *Mountie and Yukon films, burlesques of northern and Yukon history like *The Far Country*/1954 and *Death Hunt* (1981), and travesties of western Canadian history such as *Canadian Pacific* (1949) and *Saskatchewan* (1954).

In the third category a few fictional Canadian Westerns have attained distinction, notably *The Grey Fox*/1982, a National Film Board of Canada settler saga *The Drylanders* (1962) and the post-oater melancholy romance *Paperback Hero* (1973). Most fictional Canadian Westerns, films like *Alien Thunder* (1973) (renamed *Dan Candy's Law*) and *The Rainbow Boys* (1970) embarrassed the people associated with them more than they illuminated any sense of history or revelled in entertainment values.

In a country noted for its documentary traditions it is unsurprising that its most distinguished and distinctive Westerns representing the meagre fourth category are two National Film Board shorts, *Corral* and Darrold Black's refined, quiet, and humanely gentle *Cowboy* (1986).

In *Hollywood's Canada* (1975) Pierre Berton, a popular Canadian journalist-historian, assaults lengthily and accurately the misrepresentation, exaggeration and myopia of American films made on Canadian topics. The Americans have cast their eyes longingly upon Canada's spectacular scenery, but they have ignored the realities of the history they have chosen to portray. Because Hollywood reflects and has created popular American beliefs and because it has imposed a fallacious image on Canada, its northern neighbour, most Americans believe the ingredients of any Canadian story are forest, mountains and snow. Only native peoples, the Indians and the Inuit, live here, under the benevolent eyes of ubiquitous Mounties.

Canadian historical experience differs from American experience in nearly every respect. For example, when the fur trader Henry Kelsey ventured to the Canadian prairie west in 1690, calling it 'the inland country of good report' in his verse journal, the English colonists of the Atlantic seaboard still huddled by its shore. More than a century passed before Americans began exploring the Far West. The Hudson's Bay and North-West fur companies relied upon the friendship and economic co-operation of western Canada's Indian peoples for their trade purposes. No need to engage in battles with native peoples developed in a region where providing steel implements and bartering them for furs had already co-opted them, a historical trait quite at odds with the American experience. In 1870 the Hudson's Bay Company sold its domain, Rupert's Land, to the new Dominion of Canada, and the first phase of the only major western hostility erupted in the *Riel Rebellion. Canada created the North-West Mounted Police to control that skirmish, and in fact the rule of law preceded nearly all other settlement in western Canada. Building the Canadian Pacific Railway may have been epic in scale, but it is a Canadian saga: overcoming landscape and contending with elements of nature rather than with hostile peoples.

The history and the mythology of the two Wests, then, are as disparate as the experiences of two expanding nations sharing one continent can be. Commercial movie companies were never engaged in teaching history, we know, but it would be a rare American film-maker who would realize that no lawless towns sprang up in Canada, and

no wars erupted between sheep-herders and ranchers. Gold-miners in the Klondike, most of them Americans, discovered the North-West Mounted Police had reached Dawson City before them. No vigilante squads or posses ever pursued rustlers or badmen. In Canada one seeks in vain the mythology sustaining films like *The Gunfighter*/1950, *Gunfight at the O.K. Corral*/1956 or *Little Big Man*.

These differences have not inhibited Hollywood companies. Headlong they impose their ideas of 'how things were' on the Canadian West. *The Far Country*, which misrepresents the history of the 1898 Canadian gold rush, is typical. Filmed in the Canadian Rockies, it shuns the equally beautiful but more remote Yukon border region where its story occurs. Ignoring the law-abiding, if rough-hewn, society that developed in Dawson City, the film has James Stewart as a marshal who will stand alone against the bad guys. The Mounties who were there would never have allowed it. Since most people who bear hand guns in Canada are runaway Americans – and since the Mounties would have taken Stewart's arms away at the border – we cannot tell where *The Far Country* takes place. (Several American writers believe the Klondike was in Alaska, and not much in *The Far Country* can dissuade them from their errors.)

Arthur Penn's *Little Big Man*, based on Thomas Berger's fine novel of the same name, and starring Dan George, Dustin

Filming The Valley of Silent Men *(1922) on Tunnel Mountain near Banff, Canada: (l. to r.) Lew Borzage, Chester Lyons, Cyril Gardner, Edward Fenz Jr., Alma Rubens, Frank Borzage*

Hoffman and Faye Dunaway, attempts to locate a genocide theme in the fable and be a parable concerning the war in Vietnam. Though one can applaud the director's and the writers' intent, they sadly neglected the play around mythology which is the *raison d'être* of the story. Much of the film was bittersweet comedy, but a decade and a half later its quest for meaning makes it a period piece. The Stoney Indians, however, portray the Cheyenne well, and the film gave Canadian Indian actor Chief Dan George international exposure and fame. His Old Lodge Skins is the most dignified and gracious Indian to appear in any Western and, unusual for any film Indian, he shows an elegant sense of humour.

Robert Altman's *McCabe & Mrs. Miller*, despite its Elizabetho-American revenge plot, retrospectively becomes the most mythically interesting Canadian movie, a Canadian movie regardless of its nominal setting in a Pacific Coast No-Name City. Bred from the lyrical songs of Leonard Cohen, the Canadian poet, the film capitalized remarkably on an event that occurred during shooting near Vancouver, B.C. A fortuitous storm dumped a metre or so of traffic-snarling snow on the city and on the film's location, a typical Altman single set construction. Rather than holing up in hotels for the duration of the storm, Altman and his cast and crew reached their location and continued shooting through the three days of blizzard, giving us in the process those indelible scenes of the dying Warren Beatty struggling through snowdrifts. Readers familiar with Warren Tallman's essay on Canadian literature, 'Wolf Against the Snow', recognize the transmutations which occur in the ultimate scenes in the movie which magically transform it into a Canadian film, almost as if the film asserted its Canadian source in Mr Cohen's songs.

The Drylanders, a National Film Board of Canada feature-length film, starring Frances Hyland, about settlers struggling with the elements and landscape in the period of the Great War, provides an interesting comparison to *McCabe & Mrs. Miller* because its blizzard sequence has no reality compared to Altman's. Often moving, despite its shortcomings, *The Drylanders* evokes a western Canadian past as no other film does, one that depicts the trials of settlement two generations ago. It never found an audience, and, shot in black and white, it is rarely seen.

Canadians have been even more enamoured of their railways than have Americans. The story of the making of the Canadian Pacific Railway has been filmed several times. *Canadian Pacific* starred Randolph Scott as Tom Andrews, a manqué American in Canadian guise, six-shooters slung on his hips, eventually roped by a good woman (Jane Wyatt) with whom he settles down. A friendly corporate ally in the CPR – which owned the hotels in which the crews stayed during filming, and the track which was the scene of the action – undoubtedly helped the choice of topic. The CPR is one of the longest railways in the world, but the stories typically concentrate on getting the tracks through the mountains, which are but a difficult fraction of the entirety. Not till the CBC made a television mini-series from Pierre Berton's two-volume history in the mid-1970s was the story told with any integrity.

Phillip Borsos' *The Grey Fox* is the one true-to-genre Canadian subject matter Western made in Canada by Canadians (which may be why Pauline Kael has said 'it isn't exactly a Western', though her point is about its landscape). If Canada's only train robber be the anomalous Bill Miner, a runaway American at that, so be it. Ex-Hollywood stunt man Richard Farnsworth appropriately and ingenuously plays the role. Canadian actress Jackie Burroughs plays the feminist Kate Flynn, and her portrait is among the most interesting of women in any Western. The film reflects several developments which followed the flourishing of Canadian patriotism during the centennial of Confederation in 1967, among them the growth of thematic history parks in which old buildings gather together like Conestogas to stand united against the raids of urban renewal and suburban sprawl, and the desire to create an indigenous feature film industry. Like Fil Fraser's *Marie-Anne* (1977), a fur trade era drama filmed in Fort Edmonton, *The Grey Fox* was filmed in several of British Columbia's history parks, and every still-functioning steam locomotive and item of early twentieth-century rolling stock in the province was called into use.

The Grey Fox is most interesting in its play of cinematic irony, for a showing of *The Great Train Robbery* early in the film suggests that the film industry spurred the myth and the actuality of holding up trains. Film imitates life imitating film, as Bill Miner, the mortal who first spake the immortal phrase 'Hands Up!', falls upon hard times, viz Canada, and makes ends meet only by going back to what he knows well: holding up trains can't be much different from stagecoaches. In another of Canada's great traditions, he fails; the baggage car he breaks into

contains nothing more valuable than a shipment of liver pills. Canadians like both their heroes and their villains to fail.

In 1986 the National Film Board returned to the life of the rangeman in a documentary film called simply *Cowboy*. Like *Corral*, made three decades earlier, it stresses dignity in labour, resourcefulness in working with animals, and the harmony which can exist between people and the land in which they choose to live. Unlike the silent cowboy in *Corral*, the cowpuncher in the later film provides the soundtrack, in which we hear the straightforward, deliberate speech of a man whose pleasure in what he is doing is immeasurable. The film stresses the rhythm of seasons and the rewards of performing a job in tune with landscape, proving – since it has to be proved once a generation – that Canadians can make excellent films about the West when they elect to make them out of their own perceptions. JW

The Alaskan/1924/Famous Players-Lasky/d Herbert Brenon/lp Thomas Meighan · *Canadian Pacific*/1949/FOX/d Edwin L. Marin/lp Randolph Scott, Jane Wyatt · *Saskatchewan*/1954/U/d Raoul Walsh/lp Alan Ladd, Shelley Winters · *The Drylanders*/1962/National Film Board of Canada/d Donald Haldane/lp Frances Hyland, James Douglas · *The Rainbow Boys*/1973/Potterton Productions/d Gerald Potterton/lp Donald Pleasence, Kate Reid · *Alien Thunder*/1973/Onyx/d Claude Fournier/lp Donald Sutherland, Chief Dan George · *Marie-Anne*/1977/Motion Picture Corp. of Alberta/d R. Martin Walters/lp Andrée Pelletier, John Juliana · *Death Hunt*/1981/Golden Harvest/d Peter Hunt/lp Charles Bronson, Lee Marvin

Captain Jack (c.1840-73) · Chief of the Modoc Indians in northern California. At first Keintpoos (his Modoc name) was friendly towards whites. He was only persuaded to fight after the government tried to confine the Modocs together with the Klamath Indians on a reservation in Oregon. During the ensuing Modoc War (1872-3) a small group of Modocs several times defeated superior forces of troops, as well as killing General Canby, sent to negotiate. Eventually Captain Jack was betrayed by some of his own people, captured and hanged on 3 October 1873.
Charles Bronson/*Drum Beat*/1954

Captivity narratives · The theme of Indian captivity is one of the most common in the Western. Merely to cite *The Searchers*/1956,

A nineteenth-century captivity narrative

Two Rode Together/1961, *Northwest Passage*/1940, *Major Dundee*/1964, *Little Big Man*/1970, *Run of the Arrow*/1957, *Soldier Blue*/1970 and *A Man Called Horse*/1970 is evidence enough of its power. The mere suggestion of captivity can be enough to give large meaning to a single shot. When in *Stagecoach*/1939 the gambler Hatfield (John Carradine) puts his gun at the head of Lucy Mallory (Louise Platt), no explanation is necessary: he is going to save her from what the Indians will do when they capture the coach and its party.

The theme's conventions are familiar. If the captive is a woman she can expect the Indians to defile her and it is better for her to die (*Drums Along the Mohawk*/1939, *The Searchers*, *Stagecoach*, *Little Big Man*, *Northwest Passage*). If they do capture her she is shamed, to the point that her place must be with the Indians henceforth (*The Searchers*, *Two Rode Together*). She may be stripped of the codes that define white womanhood, turning into a loud-mouthed hoyden (*Northwest Passage*, *Soldier Blue*, *Little Big Man*). A male captive will be tortured and can expect to live only if he proves that he can survive

the worst the Indians can do (*Run of the Arrow*, *A Man Called Horse*). Children will lose their white ways and become Indians in all but colour (*Little Big Man*, *Major Dundee*, *Two Rode Together*).

Captivity narratives form, in fact, the oldest distinctively American literary genre. As Richard Slotkin has demonstrated (*Regeneration Through Violence*, 1973), that genre first took form in seventeenth-century New England. During King Philip's War (1676) and the endless Anglo-French-Indian wars that followed it, literally hundreds of English people of both sexes fell into the hands of their enemies. An astonishingly large number of them chose either to become Indians or to accept French Catholic ways (see James Axtell, *The Invasion Within*, 1986, and Slotkin) and the ones who did return found themselves permanently changed as a result of their experiences. Here is the historical basis from which the literary genre and the filmic sub-genre developed.

The archetypal statement was Mary Rowlandson's account of her capture during King Philip's War. She published her tale in 1682, and it remained an American best-seller for more than a century afterwards. Rowlandson's captivity was short, for she was quickly ransomed. Her literary achievement was to describe not just her physical sufferings but also her inward transformation. Each of the 'removes' into which she divides her story separates her more fully from her own culture, both in distance and in consciousness. She gradually adapts to Indian ways, and the moment of crisis comes when she finds herself not only able to eat their food but positively relishing it. By

partaking of the 'sacraments of the wilderness' she has discovered the Indian in herself. When she finally returns to her own people she finds that at night 'when all are fast about me, and no eye open, but his who ever waketh, my thoughts are upon things past,' for 'now it is other Wayes with me.'

Rowlandson gives not the slightest hint that she suffered any sexual molestation, and in fact rape was extremely uncommon among the Indians of the eastern woodlands. Captured white women did take Indian men voluntarily, just as captive white men took Indian women, but forced intercourse was not part of their experience. In the aftermath of the Revolution, however, a prurient sexual interest became an ever-stronger theme in captivity imagery. John Vanderlyn's 1803 painting of 'The Death of Jane McCrea', based on an incident that occurred in Vermont in 1777, shows the victim being attacked by two Indian men. One of her breasts is fully exposed and the men's exaggerated musculature contrasts strikingly with her weakness. The whole image is powerfully sexual. The patriotic poet Joel Barlow made much the same point when, describing the same incident, he wrote:
'Her kerchief torn betrays the globes of snow,
That heave responsive to her weight of woe.'

As Clive Bush demonstrates (*The Dream of Reason*, 1977), this interest in cross-racial sexuality became a powerful theme in nineteenth-century captivity accounts. As such, it served a major ideological function. The post-revolutionary era was the time when white America accelerated its push westward; it was also the time of the triumph

John Vanderlyn, 'Death of Jane McCrea'
(1803)

Paulette Goddard in jeopardy in
Unconquered

of genteel sexual repression within middle-class culture. Depicting frontier warfare in terms of Indian sexual aggression served to make the Indians, who in reality were the victims, into the authors of their own justified destruction. Whatever fate they got, they deserved.

Western films have explored almost all the complexities of the captivity theme. King Vidor's *Northwest Passage* is unashamedly racist. Its whole project is to justify the carnage wreaked on a sleeping village by white Rangers under Major Robert Rogers (Spencer Tracy). Based on historical accounts that the real Rogers recorded in his journals, the film traces the Rangers' journey up the Champlain Valley of New York to the St Francis River, where the Indians' village lay. Throughout the journey Rogers harangues his followers on the evils their foes have wrought, their sexual defilement of white women and the torture of white men. Rogers calls forth witnesses to describe what happened to their own kin who had fallen into Indian hands. The intended result is to identify the audience completely with the Rangers as they launch their dawn attack, in which none is spared. The Rangers discover two white women captives. One, old and grey, is delighted to see them. The other, young and blonde, takes the Indians' side, condemns the slaughter, and is subdued only by the threat of violence.

The younger woman is not intended to be sympathetic; she is portrayed as uncouth, indeed as unsexed by her experience. Nonetheless, she reaches both backwards to the captivity theme's origins and forward to the use that later, less hostile film-makers would make of it. By forcefully articulating the Indians' case within the framework of codes established by her blondness and youth, she at least partially undermines the justification of the raid that the Rangers have just inflicted. Demonstrably, 'now it is other Wayes' with her, just as it was with the historical Mary Rowlandson. This minor figure directly foreshadows the major characters of Debbie Edwards (Natalie Wood) in *The Searchers* and Cresta Mary Belle Lee (Candice Bergen) in *Soldier Blue*.

The Searchers is two films in one. Its central character is Ethan Edwards (John Wayne), uncle of Debbie and frustrated lover of her mother (Dorothy Jordan). In that sense, its subject is the classic problem of the European novel: the politics of the family. The answer to the question posed by the credit music – 'What makes a man to wander?' – lies in the impossible tensions that arise when Ethan comes to his brother and his sister-in-law's home. But in narrative terms Ethan's wandering is for the sake of recovering Debbie, taken captive in a raid that destroys the rest of her family. During his five-year journey, Ethan's purpose shifts: instead of rescuing the girl he will kill her. She has reached maturity and has been 'living with a buck'; in the words of another character, her death is what her own mother 'would have wanted'. The brief sequence in which soldiers allow Ethan to question demented female captives whom they have rescued underscores the point.

But Debbie herself has other ideas. The casting of Natalie Wood encodes her as a sympathetic character, and she puts the case for the Indians and the captives who have gone over to them. When she first confronts Ethan and his sidekick, her adopted cousin Marty (Jeffrey Hunter), she is bearing a staff from which the scalp of Marty's own mother dangles. Her first lines are spoken in Comanche, and when she breaks into English it is to tell her 'rescuers' that the Indians are 'my people'. The film's greatest narrative weakness is the simultaneous changes of mind which allow her to go with Ethan and Marty when they return with a party bent on destruction and which permit Ethan to rescue her instead of killing her. Because her return is voluntary, her stance toward her rescuers is different from that of Vidor's unnamed captive. But she makes much the same case, and she does it in terms that are less calculated to undermine her own presentation.

Cresta Mary Belle Lee in *Soldier Blue* can be seen as a synthesis of these two earlier figures. Like Vidor's captive she combines the codes of blondness and youth with those of vulgarity and loudmouthed disrespect for white men's ways. But like Debbie she is presented in a sympathetic way. She has no illusions: she has had a Cheyenne lover; when Kiowas nearly capture her again she expects them to rape and kill her; she sees the carnage when a Cheyenne party ambushes the cavalry unit bringing her back to civilization. But her only reason for leaving the Cheyenne is that she is not an Indian and cannot become one. She wholly accepts the justice of their case. Moreover, unlike the hapless soldier Honus Gant (Peter Strauss) in whose company she finds herself, she knows enough of Indian ways to survive in the wilderness.

In a very real way Gant becomes her captive and learns from her what she has learned from the Indians themselves. Slowly she strips Honus of his uniform, his beliefs, and finally of his inhibitions, and the whole narrative bears a striking resemblance to the tale that Mary Rowlandson told almost three centuries before. As with Rowlandson, the moment of transformation comes when Honus can eat the meat of the wilderness, in this case snake. Cresta has cooked it for him and, in Rowlandson's words, he now finds that he has 'never tasted pleasanter meat'. His eating it marks his recovery both from a wound he has suffered (from a fellow white) and, in a larger sense, from the delusions that have brought him to kill Indians at all. Now he can see the carnage that men like him wreak, and he finally joins Cresta on the Indians' side.

In *Little Big Man* the captive is Jack Crabb (Dustin Hoffman), who falls into the Indians' hands at the age of ten and spends the film moving back and forth between two cultures. His oscillations are picaresque, not heroic, and he can never fully commit himself to the Indians' side. As Custer (Richard Mulligan) puts it after Jack has bungled an attempt to assassinate him, Jack is 'no Cheyenne brave'.

Twice Jack finds that women who were important to him have been captured too. The first, in the opening sequence, is his sister Caroline (Carol Androsky), who is astonished when the Indians do not rape her. The second is his Swedish wife Olga (Kelly Jean Peters). Utterly submissive to Jack in white society, she becomes a tyrant to the Indian husband she takes in her captivity. Jack himself becomes Little Big Man, raids with the Cheyenne against Indian and white enemies, marries an Indian woman, takes on her husbandless sisters at her behest, and ultimately helps lure Custer to his justified destruction. Unlike Honus Gant, or Mary Rowlandson, Jack has no trouble with Indian food.

The most important function of Jack/Little Big Man's wandering is to draw the contrast between a white culture that deserves condemnation and an Indian culture that ought not to have been destroyed. Everything in the white world is hollow: family life, religion, patriotism, commerce and heroics. The preacher's wife who adopts Jack and whom he idolizes reappears as a whore; her husband is a sadistic glutton; Custer begins as a vainglorious fool and ends as a madman; a salesman with whom Jack takes up is a mere swindler; Wild Bill Hickok appears as a trigger-happy paranoid. But in the world of the Cheyenne there is honesty. The creed of the swindler is that the stars above 'twinkle in a void'; the creed of the Cheyenne, as enunciated by their chief Old Lodge Skins (Chief Dan George), is that the whole world is alive.

Soldier Blue and Little Big Man are able to make their pro-Indian statements precisely because of the longevity and the power of the captivity theme in American culture. From the beginning, captivity narratives offered a vehicle for entering the Indians' world, rather than simply one for entertaining or horrifying or titillating. At its most limited, the captivity theme offered a justification for the destruction of Indians that white America was going to wreak in any case. But it has always offered much more, as practitioners from Mary Rowlandson to Ralph Nelson have demonstrated. EC

Cars · Cars, buses and even aeroplanes appear from time to time in Western B-features, where the setting is often, if somewhat imprecisely, contemporary. In the 1960s an increasing number of films dealt self-consciously with 'the end of the West'. A motor car on the screen became a kind of visual shorthand for the encroachment of modern civilization, as for example in The Good Guys and the Bad Guys/1969. Sam Peckinpah, who made this theme his own, includes cars in Ride the High Country/1962, The Wild Bunch/1969 and The Ballad of Cable Hogue/1970. Something of the same effect is achieved by Butch's pushbike in Butch Cassidy and the Sundance Kid/1969. (The first crossing of the West on a bicycle was achieved in 1884, a feat which surely marked as definitively as anything the passing of the frontier.)

Kit Carson in 1868

Carson, Kit [Christopher Houston] (1809-68) · Frontiersman. One of the key figures in the exploration of the West, Carson was even more important to the development of a West of the imagination. In the late 1820s and 30s Carson was a fur trapper in the Rockies. Then by chance in 1842 he met John *Frémont, who was preparing his first western expedition. Carson was engaged as guide and travelled with Frémont on three separate explorations. The last of these, in 1845-6, was to California, where he became involved in the Mexican War, helping guide General Stephen Watts Kearny's force from New Mexico to California. The accounts published at the time of

Frémont's exploits gave full weight to Carson's contribution and were the beginning of his fame. In the 1850s, having married a Mexican woman (he had two Indian wives previously), he took up ranching. Then at the start of the Civil War Carson was commissioned a colonel in the Union Army and led expeditions against the Mescalero Apache and then the *Navaho, whom he obliged to surrender at Canyon de Chelly in 1864.

Carson was one of those Westerners who literally became a legend in their own lifetimes. His considerable real achievements were embroidered in a way that reportedly embarrassed him (as when he found a book dealing with his exploits among the plunder taken by some Apaches from a wagon train). The mountain man or scout as fictional hero first appears in Timothy *Flint's The Shoshonee Valley (1830), as a development of Fenimore *Cooper's Leatherstocking. Carson's exploits with Frémont seemed to suit him ideally for the role and his first appearance in fiction is in The Prairie Flower (1849) by Emerson Bennett. Carson's first major role is in Kit Carson, the Prince of the Gold Hunters (1849) by Charles Averill. In 1858 appeared a full-scale biography by DeWitt C. Peters, entitled The Life and Adventures of Kit Carson, the Nestor of the Rocky Mountains, from Facts Narrated by Himself. This carefully presented the image of Carson which has come to dominate, that of the genteel, upright hero who never touched liquor nor uttered a profane word. Two further biographies further embellished his character, one by Charles Burdett in 1862, another by John S.C. Abbott in 1873. From then on his place

General Mapache's car in The Wild Bunch

Fred Thomson, Dorothy Janis in Kit Carson

in the pantheon of Western heroes was secure: he is, as a Beadle dime novel, *The Fighting Trapper, or, Kit Carson to the Rescue* (1879), has it, simply 'the most renowned Indian fighter the world ever produced.' Yet in the cinema Carson, like other mountain men, never equalled the popularity he attained in books and comics, and his appearances were largely confined to Poverty Row, in which locale the B-Western star named after him, Sunset 'Kit' Carson, flourished.

Kit Carson/1903/American Mutoscope and Biograph · *The Pioneers*/1903/American Mutoscope and Biograph · *Kit Carson*/1910/Bison · *Kit Carson on the Santa Fe Trail*/1910/Kalem · Hobart Bosworth/*Kit Carson's Wooing*/1911/Selig/d Frank Boggs/lp Tom Mix · Jack Perrin/*The Santa Fe Trail*/1923/Arrow/d Robert Dillon, Ashton Dearholt · Guy Oliver/*The Covered Wagon*/1923 · Guy Oliver/*The Vanishing American*/1925 · Jack Mower/*Kit Carson Over the Great Divide*/1925/Sunset/d Frank S. Mattison · Fred Warren/*California*/1927/MGM/d W.S. Van Dyke/lp Tim McCoy · Fred Thomson/*Kit Carson*/1928/PAR/d Alfred Werker · Johnny Mack Brown/*Fighting With Kit Carson*/1933/Mascot/d Armand Schaefer, Colbert Clark/lp Noah Beery · Harry Carey/*Sutter's Gold*/1936 · Sammy McKim/*The Painted Stallion*/1937/REP/d William Witney, Ray Taylor, Alan James/lp Hoot Gibson · Wild Bill Elliott/*Overland With Kit Carson*/1939/COL/d Sam Nelson, Norman Deming · Jon Hall/*Kit Carson*/1940/UA/d George B. Seitz/lp Dana Andrews, Ward Bond · Robert Wilke/*Trail of Kit Carson*/1945/REP/d Lesley Selander/lp Allan Lane · Dean Smith/*Seven Alone*/1974/Doty-Dayton/d Earl Bellamy/lp Dewey Martin

Television · Bill Williams/*The Adventures of Kit Carson* · Channing Pollock/*The Great Adventure* · Ben Murphy/*Bridger* · William Berger/*Tex e il signore degli abissi* · Rip Torn/*Dream West*

Cartoons · Among the earliest cartoon characters to go west were Mutt and Jess in *Subbing for Tom Mix* (1919) and Felix the Cat getting entangled in a Western shoot-out in *Eats Are West* (1925). Seemingly inexhaustible mileage has been extracted down the years from the Lone Ranger and the Pony Express by such stalwarts as Porky Pig, Woody Woodpecker, Mighty Mouse and good ol' Huckleberry Hound. Among the Lone Ranger parodies are a 37-episode series

for television in 1966 and, most memorably, Hugh Harman's *The Lonesome Stranger* (1940), featuring a squat, bizarre-looking hero who rids the town of three Mexican desperados.

Cartoon director Tex Avery (a Texan, no less) had a penchant for cowboy parodies and, when teamed with storyman Henry ('Heck') *Allen, a Western novelist, no holds were barred. Every B-Western cliché was put through the wringer, culminating in a Stone Age Western narrated by Tex Ritter which exposes the legend of *The First Bad Man* (1955), with a posse astride dinosaurs in full pursuit of the loin-clothed villain.

Bugs Bunny went west more often than most, usually pitting his wits against a short-tempered, flame-mustachioed bad guy named Yosemite Sam. The creation of director Fritz Freleng, Sam was loosely based on Red Skelton's radio character Deadeye, though closer sources say Sam's explosive temper was a direct characterization of Freleng himself. As time progressed Sam was seen in other professions such as a pirate, an Arab, a Roman legionary and even an invader from another planet, but always as the bombastic bad guy who lets his audience know how much he 'Hates That Rabbit!'

Walt Disney also has his fair share of Western settings, from Mickey Mouse donning chaps and stetson in *Two-Gun Mickey* (1934) to homebody Donald Duck emerging as one of the *Three Caballeros* in the live action-animation feature of 1944. One of the highlights of Disney's 1948 feature *Melody Time* was the appearance of Pecos Bill. This Western yarn, boldly exaggerated by the storyteller, Roy Rogers, told the tale of a Texan brought up by coyotes to become a rough and ready cowpoke who could lasso cyclones and shoot the stars from the sky, until a woman arrives and makes a sap out of him – much to his horse's chagrin.

Animation's answer to the 'horse opera' was to create a cowboy who *was* a horse, which Hanna-Barbera did in 1959 with *Quick-Draw McGraw*, a bungling equine sheriff complete with stetson and six-shooters and aided by his Mexican sidekick, a donkey.

Children have occasionally featured in Western Cartoons. Disney's *A Cowboy Needs a Horse* (1956) depicted a child's dream of becoming a Western hero. Bob Cannon's classic *Willie the Kid* (1952) is the most original, with Willie and his chums playing cowboys as the clever visuals turn his suburban backyard into the prairie, his home into a ranch and the kids into a collection of

Western characters, including the inevitable bad guy and Mexican sidekick.

In 1964 TV cowboy Dale Robertson put all his money, his voice and himself (in live-action) into a curious Western feature cartoon entitled *The Man from Button Willow*. Intended as the pilot for a TV series which never came to be, the film features the voices of Robertson and Edgar Buchanan, with the singing voice of Howard Keel, and tells the tale of Justin Eagle, a government secret agent, and his fight against lawlessness in a small Texas town.

The Europeans have produced their share of Western spoofs. Dusan Vukotic's *Cowboy Jimmie* is a prime example, showing the local tough sweeping the floor with our hero. Czech animator Jiri Trnka's award-winning *The Song of the Prairie* (1949) involves every Western cliché, from the singing hero on a white horse to the dastardly villain abducting the heroine – all done with puppets. 1971 saw the transition from comic strip to screen of Goscinny and Morris' *Lucky Luke* – truly the epitome of a Western hero, clean-living and temperate (though he does smoke), and a thorough gentleman with the ladies.

There are many more, too humorous to mention, but with the likes of Daffy Duck, Tom and Jerry and the Pink Panther in action we may rest assured that the West will be a safer place – for cartoon characters, that is. GW

Cassidy, Butch (1867-1908?) · Outlaw, born Robert Leroy Parker of Mormon parents in Utah. Parker took his surname from another outlaw, Mike Cassidy; 'Butch' came from his short time spent working in a butcher's shop. By 1889 he was already robbing banks in Colorado; in 1894 he was imprisoned in Wyoming for rustling. Two years later on his release he formed his notorious gang, the Wild Bunch, sometimes known as the 'Hole-in-the-Wall gang' after a place in northern Wyoming used for a hide-out. Together with Harry Longbaugh, the Sundance Kid (1861-1908?), Black Jack *Ketchum and others, the gang robbed banks and trains in the mountain states. By 1901 they had provoked the attention of the *Pinkertons, and Butch and Sundance decided to leave for South America. Their activities there are shrouded in obscurity, but the consensus is that they were shot to death by Bolivian troops following a bank robbery. The date is variously given as 1908, 1909 or 1911. Some have claimed they survived the shoot-out and that Butch Cassidy actually died in

The Wild Bunch: (l.) Harry Longbaugh 'The Sundance Kid' (r.) 'Butch' Cassidy

Spokane, Washington, in 1937, but this seems unlikely.

In early film portrayals Butch and the Sundance Kid oscillated between the villainous (*The Maverick Queen*) and the comical (*Cat Ballou*). The glamour accorded the pair by Paul Newman and Robert Redford is a late accretion.

Arthur Kennedy (Sundance)/*Cheyenne*/1947/WB/d Raoul Walsh/*lp* Dennis Morgan, Jane Wyman · Robert Ryan (Sundance)/*Return of the Bad Men*/1948/RKO/d Ray Enright/*lp* Randolph Scott · John Doucette (Butch), Ian MacDonald (Sundance)/*The Texas Rangers*/1951/COL/d Phil Karlson/*lp* George Montgomery · Gene Evans (Butch), William Bishop (Sundance)/*Wyoming Renegades*/1954/COL/d Fred F. Sears/*lp* Phil Carey, Martha Hyer · Howard Petrie (Butch), Scott Brady (Sundance)/*The Maverick Queen*/1956/REP/d Joseph Kane/*lp* Barbara Stanwyck, Barry Sullivan · Neville Brand (Butch), Alan Hale Jr. (Sundance)/*The Three Outlaws*/1956/Associate Film Releasing Corp./d Sam Newfield · Neville Brand (Butch), Russell Johnson (Sundance)/*Badman's Country*/1958/WB/d Fred F. Sears/*lp* George Montgomery, Buster Crabbe · Arthur Hunnicutt (Butch)/*Cat Ballou*/1965 · Tex Gates (Butch)/*Ride a Wild Stud*/1969/Vega International/d Revilo Ekard/*lp* Hale Williams · Paul Newman (Butch), Robert Redford (Sundance)/*Butch Cassidy and the Sundance Kid*/1969 · William Katt (Butch), Tom Berenger (Sundance)/*Butch*

and Sundance, the Early Days/1979/FOX/d Richard Lester

Television · Steve Brodie/*Bronco* · John Crawford (Butch), John Davis Chandler (Sundance)/*Return of the Gunfighter* · Also Elizabeth Montgomery as Sundance's girlfriend, Etta Place, in *Mrs. Sundance* · Katharine Ross as Etta Place in *Wanted: The Sundance Woman*

Cather, Willa (1873-1947) · Novelist. Cather was brought up in Nebraska, where several of her novels are set. *O Pioneers!* (1913) deals with the experiences of first-generation European immigrants on the plains as they try to scratch a living in the harsh environment. The milieu of *My Antonia* (1918) is similar. *Death Comes for the Archbishop* (1927) is a fictionalized life of a 19th-century Catholic bishop in New Mexico. Cather's novels movingly portray the lives of Westerners, but they lack the drama of violent action and confrontation which would make them true Westerns, and though Warner Bros. twice filmed her novel *A Lost Lady*, in 1925 and in 1934, it is not primarily about the West.

Catlin, George (1796-1872) · Painter. Catlin was not the first to paint Indians, but he was the first artist to dedicate himself to the subject and to bring to it an ethnographic impulse. Embarking on the steamboat *Yellowstone* on its maiden voyage up the Missouri in 1832, he made hundreds of paintings of the tribes he met. A second trip

in 1834 to Indian Territory, where he spent time with the Comanche, provided further material. Many of his pictures were portraits or depictions of hunting and religious customs; he largely avoided the battle scenes so beloved of later artists. To these paintings Catlin added collections of artefacts and some of his live subjects – Sioux, Fox and Sauk Indians – in costume, and from 1839 exhibited the whole as a kind of travelling museum, both in the States and in Europe. William Goetzmann has called this the very first Wild West Show. Its significance for the Western can hardly be over-estimated. Catlin was the first to popularize on a international scale the image of Indians as mounted warriors with plumed headdresses, living in conical shaped tepees and chasing buffalo across the plains. So dominant did this picture become that other possible images of Indian life became overshadowed. In 1841 he produced his major work, the two-volume *Notes to the Manners, Customs and Condition of the North American Indians*, illustrated by himself. Catlin was a self-taught artist and his pictures have all the force and much of the awkwardness of the genuine primitive. His writings are often eloquent on the nobility and precariousness of Indian culture, which he saw as already in the 1840s threatened with extinction:

'The tribes of the red men of North America, as a nation of human beings, are on their wane;... (to use their own very beautiful figure) "they are fast travelling to the shades of their fathers, towards the setting sun"; ... the traveller who would see these people in their native simplicity and beauty, must needs be hastily on his way to the prairies and Rocky Mountains, or he will see them only as they are now seen on the frontiers, as a basket of dead game – harassed, chased, bleeding and dead; with their plumage and colours despoiled' (See Plate 2)

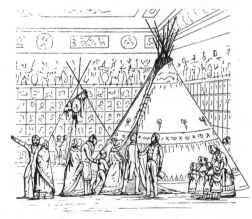

Catlin's Indian Gallery in the Louvre

Cattle · Successive phases of the history of the West might well be told in terms of its animals. First the *horse transformed the culture of the plains Indians. The beaver brought the first white men into the Far West. Eventually the whites killed off the *buffalo, thus destroying the way of life of the Indians. Then came the cattle.

Though cattle have been raised in America since the 16th century, the history relevant to Western films begins in Texas in the aftermath of the Civil War. The millions of head, mostly the distinctive Longhorn breed, that had been running wild on public lands in Texas found no market in the economically depressed South, where prices were as low as $4 a head. But in eastern markets the price was ten times that. The problem was transport. Texans solved this by initiating cattle drives up the *Chisholm and other trails to the newly established railheads in Kansas. In the four years 1867-71 1.5 million head moved up the Chisholm trail alone. Trails were also extended into Colorado and Montana to take cattle to the mining areas. From the 1870s cattle-raising spread on to the northern plains and by the 1880s was booming in Wyoming and Montana, where millions of acres of public land were freely available. This was the heyday of *cattle barons such as Alexander Swan. Rapid expansion also led to those disputes over land and water rights and between farmers and cattlemen which have provided the Western with such a plentiful supply of plots. The disastrous winter of 1886-7 decimated the herds, with the result that the 1890s saw a period of consolidation, improving the quality of the cattle by introducing such breeds as Herefords and protecting stock with fencing. Cattle drives and the open range were things of the past.

Westerns set in the Kansas cow towns are too numerous to mention, but films based on the experience of a cattle-drive are not so common as its place in Western mythology would suggest. Among the best examples are *The Texans*, *Red River*/1947, *The Tall Men*/1955, *Cowboy*/1958, *The Culpepper Cattle Co.*/1972. Among television shows, *Rawhide* is the best remembered. The cattle themselves, usually just background, are foregrounded in a small number of films whose plots centre on improving the breed: *The Untamed Breed*, *The Longhorn*, *The Rare Breed*.

The Texans/1938/PAR/*d* James Hogan/*lp* Joan Bennett, Randolph Scott · *The Untamed Breed*/1948/COL/*d* Charles Lamont/*lp* Sonny Tufts · *The Longhorn*/1951/MON/*d* Lewis Collins/*lp* Bill Elliott · *The Rare Breed*/1965/U/*d* Andrew V. McLaglen/*lp* James Stewart, Maureen O'Hara

Cattle baron · A cycle of films beginning in the late 1940s centred on a patriarchal cattle baron, powerful and usually tyrannical, in conflict with small ranchers and farmers and often with his own family too. These films provided meaty roles for some of Hollywood's best actors, including Lionel Barrymore in *Duel in the Sun*/1946; Spencer Tracy in *The Sea of Grass*/1946/MGM/*d* Elia Kazan/*lp* Katharine Hepburn; John Wayne in *Red River*/1947; Walter Huston in *The Furies*/1950; Emile Meyer in *Shane*/1952; Spencer Tracy again in *Broken Lance*/1954; Edward G. Robinson in *The Violent Men*/1954/COL/*d* Rudolph Maté; Donald Crisp in *The Man from Laramie*/1955; Rock Hudson in *Giant*/1956, and Charles Bickford in *The Big Country*/1958.

Doubtless this cycle owes much to Hollywood's fascination during this period, and not only in the Western, with the family melodrama and Freudian psychology. But there were plenty of real-life models for these characters. Readily available capital (much of it coming from Britain), free land and growing markets in the east produced a boom in the cattle business on the high plains during the 1880s and huge profits for the most successful. Alexander Swan (1831-1905) launched the Swan Land and Cattle Company in 1883. He became a major figure in public life in Wyoming, helping to build the opera house in Cheyenne, until over-ambition and the devastating blizzards of 1886-7 wiped out his assets. Another important figure in Wyoming was John Clay (1851-1934), a Scotsman who was President of the Wyoming Stock Growers Association at the time of the *Johnson County War. In Texas Richard King (1824-85), a former riverboat captain, amassed 1.27 million acres on which he kept 40,000 cattle and 6,000 horses. Two real-life cattle barons who appear in films are John *Chisum and Shanghai *Pierce.

Cemetery · The original Boot Hill was in Dodge City. Whether the town cemetery was really so called because of the number of its occupants who died with their boots on, or whether this is a later embroidery, is now unclear. But the term stuck and other frontier towns also had their Boot Hills.

Something of the shifting sensibilities of the Western over a twenty-year period can be traced in a comparison of three sequences

Clark Gable, Robert Ryan, Jane Russell driving cattle in The Tall Men

set in a cemetery. In a poetic scene in *She Wore a Yellow Ribbon*/1949 John Wayne communes with his dead wife as he sits by her grave the night before his retirement from the army. (Not the least of the things that make the Wayne character in *The Searchers*/1956 such an outsider is that he never has time for a funeral.) In *Ride the High Country*/1962 R. G. Armstrong also kneels by his wife's grave. He appears to be praying until a zoom in reveals the bullet-hole in his face: the evil Hammond family have violated the sanctity of the little cemetery. In the openly cynical *Il buono, il brutto, il cattivo*/1966 the joke on the three seekers after the gold is that it is hidden inside one of the thousands of graves in a vast Civil War cemetery; but which one?

Central Pacific Railroad · The company which built the western half of the first transcontinental railroad. It ran from Sacramento, California to Promontory Point, Utah, where it was joined with the Union Pacific on 10 May 1869. Construction was supervised by Charles Crocker, who imported large numbers of *Chinese as labourers. Collis P. *Huntington organized the financing and Leland *Stanford handled the necessary political liaisons. The crossing of the Sierra Nevada, much of it in winter,

was a notable engineering feat, but the railroad's finances were shaky and eventually it came under the control of the Southern Pacific.

Chato (1860?-1934) · A Southern Chiricahua Apache who made a bid for leadership of the Eastern Chiricahua Apache following the death of *Victorio. After a series of raids in 1882 he was forced to surrender and was taken to the San Carlos reservation. He then became an army scout, and when *Geronimo escaped the reservation in 1885 Chato was instrumental in his capture. After many years on the Mescalero reservation he was killed in an automobile accident.

Eugene Iglesias/*Taza, Son of Cochise*/1953 · George Keynes/*Apache Warrior*/1957/FOX/ d Elmo Williams/*lp* Keith Larsen, Jim Davis · John Hoyt ('Chata')/*Duel at Diablo*/1965/UA/d Ralph Nelson/*lp* James Garner, Sidney Poitier · Woody Strode/ *Shalako*/1968/Kingston/d Edward Dmytryk/*lp* Sean Connery, Brigitte Bardot · Henry Silva ('Chatto')/*The Animals*/1970/ XYZ Productions/d Ron Joy/*lp* Keenan Wynn, Michele Carey · Charles Bronson/ *Chato's Land*/1971/UA/d Michael Winner/ *lp* Jack Palance

Television · Ricardo Montalban/*Gunsmoke* · Cal Bellini/*Go West, Young Girl*

C.E. Watkins, 'Construction of Secrettown trestle in the Sierra Nevada on the C.P.R.R.'

Chato

Cherokee Strip · Part of *Oklahoma, initially Indian Territory, and reserved to the Cherokee until the US government opened it up to settlement at the end of the 19th century. Different areas of Oklahoma were settled at different times. In each case homesteaders were kept off the land by the army and 'Sooners' who attempted to jump the gun were removed. Then at a given signal settlers raced to stake out their claims. In the first Oklahoma land rush in 1889 the town of Guthrie was built in a day. The rush of 1893 was the biggest, with 100,000 people involved. The beginning of the rush, with the lines of wagons waiting for the countdown before racing headlong for the best land, is a scene several times enacted on film, though not always located in Oklahoma. Films include: *Tumbleweeds*/1925 · *Three Bad Men*/1926/FOX/d John Ford/lp George O'Brien, J. Farrell MacDonald · *Cimarron*/1930 · *Oklahoma Frontier*/1939/U/d Ford Beebe/lp Johnny Mack Brown · *The Oklahoma Kid*/1939 · *Return of the Bad Men*/1948/RKO/d Ray Enright/lp Randolph Scott, Robert Ryan · *Cimarron*/1960 The series Western *Cherokee Strip*/1937/WB/d Noel Smith/lp Dick Foran has stock footage from earlier films for the land rush sequences.

Cheyenne · Of all the Indian nations to suffer at the hands of the whites, the Cheyenne and their close allies the Arapaho possibly had the worst experience. Up until the 1860s both the northern Cheyenne, living in Wyoming, and the southern Cheyenne, based in eastern Colorado, had only limited contact with whites. But in 1864 took place the infamous massacre of the southern Cheyenne at Sand Creek in Colorado by a force of Colorado volunteers led by Colonel John Chivington (1821-94), a Methodist minister who had obtained a commission in the Union Army during the Civil War and was known as 'The Fighting Parson'. Chivington had announced before the engagement he wanted no prisoners taken. In the ensuing 'battle' some two hundred Cheyenne were killed, about two-thirds of them women and children. After the fight troops toured the battlefield killing the wounded and scalping and sexually mutilating the bodies. *Soldier Blue*/1970 tries hard, perhaps too hard, to capture the horror of this event.

In 1867 some Cheyenne signed a peace treaty with the whites at Medicine Lodge Creek. But others, led by Woqini – known to the whites as Roman Nose – fought on. In

The land rush in Cimarron (1960)

September 1868 a group of Cheyenne surrounded Major George Forsyth's command at Beecher's Island in Colorado. Roman Nose believed himself protected from harm by the power of his eagle-feathered war bonnet. Persuaded to join the fight before he had properly purified himself after breaking a ritual taboo, he was shot dead early in the action.

Assigned a reservation in Indian Territory, the southern Cheyenne continued to resist. In November 1868 a village on the *Washita was destroyed by Custer's 7th Cavalry. Even then the southern Cheyenne were not decisively defeated until the Red River War of 1874-5. The northern Cheyenne had by now thrown in their lot with the Sioux and assisted at the Battle of the *Little Big Horn in 1876. Defeated in the army's subsequent campaign, they were sent to a reservation in Indian Territory, but in 1878 the harsh conditions they found there led three hundred under Chief Dull Knife to break out and trek north. Cold and hunger forced them ultimately to surrender in Nebraska and they were eventually moved to a reservation in Montana.

This latter episode forms the subject of Mari *Sandoz's book *Cheyenne Autumn* and the film which John Ford based on it. Another film sympathetic to the Cheyenne cause and which contains a powerful dramatization of the Battle of the Washita is *Little Big Man*/1970.

Chinese · Not the least of John Wayne's eccentricities in *True Grit*/1969 is that he has a Chinese landlord. By 1880 there were 105,000 Chinese in America, the great majority living in the urban areas of California and other western states. Most had arrived not as settlers with families but as single male labourers working in mining and railroad construction. Prejudice against them was often violent, resulting in riots and lynchings. Twenty Chinese were murdered by a mob in Los Angeles in 1871, and at least fifty in Rock Springs, Wyoming in 1885. Hostility found legal expression when free entry for Chinese was prevented after the passing of the Chinese Exclusion Act of 1882. Given the importance of their contribution, particularly to the construction of the *Central Pacific railroad, the Chinese are under-represented in the Western, though their role is at least noticed in *The Iron Horse*/1924, *Duel in the Sun*/1946 and *Blazing Saddles*/1974. The TV series *Kung Fu* was an attempt to graft Chinese martial arts on to the Western.

Chisholm, Jesse (1805-68) · Frontier trader. Half-Cherokee, Chisholm was an interpreter and guide for the government in Indian Territory. After the Civil War he cut a trail from his trading post in Kansas south to the Red River. This trail was subsequently used by cowboys driving cattle up from Texas to the Kansas railheads, initially at *Abilene, and was named after Chisholm. Two of many films telling the story of a cattle-drive up the Chisholm Trail are *The Texans*/1938/PAR/d James Hogan/lp Joan Bennett, Randolph Scott and *Red River*/1947.

Chisum, John (1824-84) · Cattle king. Initially active in Texas, in 1867 Chisum moved to New Mexico and built up a vast cattle ranch. He became involved in the *Lincoln County War, on the side of John *Tunstall. Though he never carried a gun, Chisum appears to have had few scruples. Some of his business deals were less than ethical and in 1877 he ordered his men to murder a large number of Mescaleros he suspected of stealing his cattle.

Such uncomfortable facts are ignored when Chisum is played with his usual rowdy expansiveness by John Wayne in *Chisum*/1970/WB/d Andrew V. McLaglen/lp Forrest Tucker, Ben Johnson. Also played by Barry Sullivan in *Pat Garrett and Billy the Kid*/1973, though his scenes did not survive editing.

Chromolithography · First introduced to America in the 1840s, this new printing process permitted the mass reproduction of colour prints for posters, advertising and wall hangings in places of public entertainment such as saloons and hotels. In the remaining years of the century literally millions of prints were produced, with Western subjects among the most popular. Firms such as Currier & Ives (founded 1834) had thousands of different subjects in their catalogues. Prints were offered wholesale to travelling agents and advertised as especially suitable for 'Smoking Rooms, Hotels, Bar and Billiard Rooms, Stable offices, etc.' Favourites among the Western prints were idealized general views (a train crossing the prairie, entitled 'Westward the Course of Empire Takes its Way') and dramatic action scenes (trappers threatened by Indians above the legend 'A Dangerous Neighborhood'). The paintings of celebrated artists such as Albert *Bierstadt and pictures of such momentous events as *Custer's Last Stand could be made readily and cheaply available, at a time when photography was still struggling towards the techniques of mass reproduction, with colour not arriving till the 20th century. Chromolithography was thus the dominant technology whereby the 19th century obtained its visual image of the West. (See Plates 5, 7, 14)

Church · Together with a school and a courthouse, the existence of a church is a sure sign that a town has reached respectability (a saloon, a blacksmith's and a livery stable merely indicating economic viability). The half-built church to which Wyatt Earp escorts his Clementine in *My Darling Clementine*/1946 is the most thematically

Currier and Ives lithograph: 'The Prairie Hunter – One Rubbed Out' (1852)

In Old Arizona: *Warner Baxter (l.) as the Cisco Kid*

resonant of all the churches in Westerns. In another Ford picture, *Rio Grande*/1950, the church is a place of refuge from savage Indians. But respectability has its negative side. In *High Noon*/1952 it's in the church that Gary Cooper as the marshal learns of the townspeople's spinelessness.

The Cisco Kid · Character created by O. *Henry, originally in his story 'The Caballero's Way' (1904), and made into a popular screen character by Warner Baxter in *In Old Arizona*. Baxter's interpretation was not the first but was far the most important and laid the groundwork for others. He portrays the Kid as a charming rogue and ladies' man whose wits get him out of the tight corners which his weaknesses have got him into. *In Old Arizona* provided an alternative to the stereotype of the treacherous, cringing 'greaser' which had hitherto been the rule, and started a trend for south-of-the-border Westerns. It was also the first all-talking Western.

The Caballero's Way/1914/Societé Française · *The Border Terror*/1919/U/ *d* Harry Harvey · Warner Baxter/*In Old Arizona*/1929 · Warner Baxter/*The Cisco Kid*/1931/FOX/*d* Irving Cummings/ *lp* Edmund Lowe · Warner Baxter/*The Return of the Cisco Kid*/1939/FOX/*d* Herbert Leeds/*lp* Lynn Bari, Cesar Romero · Cesar Romero/*The Cisco Kid and the Lady*/1940/ FOX/*d* Herbert Leeds/*lp* George Montgomery · Cesar Romero/*Viva Cisco Kid*/1940/FOX/*d* Norman Foster/*lp* Jean Rogers · Cesar Romero/*Lucky Cisco Kid*/ 1940/FOX/*d* H. Bruce Humberstone/ *lp* Dana Andrews · Cesar Romero/*The Gay Caballero*/1940/FOX/*d* Otto Brower · Cesar Romero/*Romance of the Rio Grande*/1941/ FOX/*d* Herbert Leeds/*lp* Lynne Roberts · Cesar Romero/*Ride On Vaquero*/1941/FOX/ *d* Herbert Leeds/*lp* Mary Beth Hughes · Duncan Renaldo/*The Cisco Kid Returns*/ 1945/MON/*d* John P. McCarthy · Duncan Renaldo/*In Old New Mexico*/1945/MON/ *d* Phil Rosen · Duncan Renaldo/*South of the Rio Grande*/1945/MON/*d* Lambert Hillyer · Gilbert Roland/*The Gay Cavalier*/1946/ MON/*d* William Nigh · Gilbert Roland/ *South of Monterey*/1946/MON/*d* William Nigh · Gilbert Roland/*Beauty and the Bandit*/1946/MON/*d* William Nigh · Gilbert Roland/*Riding the California Trail*/1947/ MON/*d* William Nigh · Gilbert Roland/ *Robin Hood of Monterey*/1947/MON/ *d* Christy Cabanne · Gilbert Roland/*King of the Bandits*/1947/MON/*d* Christy Cabanne · Duncan Renaldo/*The Valiant Hombre*/ 1948/UA/*d* Wallace Fox · Duncan Renaldo/*The Gay Amigo*/1948/UA/ *d* Wallace Fox · Duncan Renaldo/*The Daring Caballero*/1949/UA/*d* Wallace Fox · Duncan Renaldo/*Satan's Cradle*/1949/UA/ *d* Ford Beebe · Duncan Renaldo/*The Girl from San Lorenzo*/1950/UA/*d* Derwin Abrahams
Television · Duncan Renaldo/*The Cisco Kid*

Cities · The town is central to the Western. Though in practice usually little more than a hamlet, with saloon, livery stable, general store, and maybe a bank, blacksmith's and even a hotel, it is an oasis of humanity in the empty wastes of the West. By contrast the city is outside the Western, beyond its borders and essentially alien. This is despite the fact that a significant proportion of the

Burying the Confederate soldier in She Wore a Yellow Ribbon

population of the West lived in cities. San Francisco had 36,000 people by 1852. By 1860 Chicago, on the fringe of the West, had a population of 100,000. Denver, which did not even exist till 1858, was up to 100,000 by 1890. But for the inhabitants of the Western, the metropolis is everything the West is not. The barber in *My Darling Clementine*/1946 may be proud to tell Wyatt Earp his pomade comes all the way from Kansas City, Kansas, but in general the city comes off second best. In *Oklahoma!*/1955 we're informed that 'Everything's up to date in Kansas City/ They've gone about as far as they can go', but that doesn't make it preferable to the open range. In *Calamity Jane*/1953 Calamity, who has just blown in from the Windy City (i.e. Chicago), is certain that 'We've got more life in Deadwood City/Than the whole of Illinois'.

Civil War · The Civil War is the great prism of nineteenth-century American history. Its coming was traumatic, proof to the world that the great republican experiment had failed. Its conduct was devastating, for this was the first 'total' war of the modern era. Its consequences were enormous: the destruction of slavery; the triumph of the national government over the separate states; the victory of the Republicans as the party of industrial capitalist expansion; the forced

modernization of a hitherto backward south; the bitter disappointment of ex-slaves at finding themselves legally free but by no means equal. Its memory lingers: in romantic visions of the 'lost cause'; in mock skirmishes by amateur soldiers in blue and gray; in the die-hard racism of the Ku Klux Klan; in the tragic image of Abraham Lincoln; in the knowledge that John Brown's soul does go marching on.

The fundamental issue at stake was the conflict of two civilizations. One was based on free labour. It was rapidly industrializing. Its cities were swelling to enormous size. It was on a path that would make it the foremost power in the world. An increasing number of its people were convinced that their struggle with the South was a moral crusade, pitting civilization as it ought to be against the powers of darkness. Some of the most convinced were blind to the inequalities of their own world. The other side, though it had factories and cities of its own, was based on slavery and was essentially backward. Effectively, it was an economic colony of the first, and its leaders knew that Lincoln's election to the presidency in 1860 signified their political subordination as well. By 1860 most southern whites had come to believe that they were in a struggle for survival and that to defend the property rights of the small minority who were

Charlton Heston with the Union flag in Major Dundee

slaveholders was to defend their own way of life.

Just as the war focused the issues of the century, so did the West focus the issues of the war. On the surface the great political question was slavery's expansion, not its existence. The Missouri Compromise in 1820; the independence of Texas from Mexico in 1836; its annexation by the United States in 1845; the 'Great Compromise' that admitted California as a free state in 1850; the Kansas-Nebraska controversy in 1854; John Brown's anti-slavery raiding in Kansas in 1856 and the Supreme Court's pro-slavery decision in the case of Dred Scott v. Sanford in 1857: all of these turned on the question of slavery on the expanding frontier.

The Civil War also defines the beginning of the 'classic' historical era that Westerns portray. The great majority are set sometime between the war's end in 1865 and the 'official' end of the frontier twenty-five years later. In many films the era provides no more than a vague Western 'pastness', as in the work of Budd Boetticher. But in many others the war is a touchstone. And film after film refers to it in ways that both articulate and mask the issues from which the war emerged.

Very few Westerns deal with the war itself. The most important are *They Died with their Boots On*/1941, *The Horse Soldiers*/1959 and *Major Dundee*/1964. The first is a romanticized biography of George Armstrong Custer. Of necessity it shows his meteoric rise during the war from a junior post to a generalship, but it says nothing at all about the occasion for his heroics. The only blacks in it are waiters and servants, and their subordination to whites is never questioned. (Another film in which Custer appears, *Santa Fe Trail*/1940, presents a venomous portrait of John Brown and his role in the build-up to the Civil War.)

The Horse Soldiers is perhaps not a Western at all, since it deals with fighting in the settled plantation South. But it has a great deal in common with John Ford's earlier 'cavalry' trilogy, including the presence of John Wayne. *The Horse Soldiers* comes closer than *They Died with their Boots On* to the issues of the war: it does show plantation life and blacks who are enslaved. But it subordinates the tension between freedom and slavery to personal tensions centred on the Wayne character.

The war figures strongly in much of Ford's other work, but only in one film, *The Searchers*/1956, does it generate unresolvable tensions. Ethan Edwards (John Wayne) is an unreconstructed ex-rebel. He will not swear to the State of Texas because he has already sworn 'to the Confederate States of America'. He scorns 'Yankees' and their ways. But whether his bitterness reflects his own loss of slaves, or the mere fact that the Confederacy surrendered, or simply his tormented soul is never said. The film's 'Texicans' are westerners, not southerners.

In the three films that make up Ford's cavalry trilogy the war is a distant background. Its whole function is to emphasize that in the cavalry social tensions could be forgotten and the past buried. In both *Fort Apache*/1948 and *She Wore a Yellow Ribbon*/1949 Ford presents sergeants who had been Confederate officers, and in the latter a mere private is a former Confederate general. When the trooper dies his blue-coated comrades bury him with a home-made Confederate battle flag. It is the strongest possible sign that the bitterness is over and that only the heroic memories remain. In *Rio Grande*/1950 that bitterness had been strong enough to destroy the marriage of Colonel Kirby Yorke (John Wayne), who had married a southern woman (Maureen O'Hara). But the film ends with the two people, and by implication the two sections, reunited.

Shane/1952, which owes an enormous amount to Ford, uses the war to much the same effect. Its means is Torrey (Elisha Cook Jr.), a dirt farmer from Alabama who has migrated to the unspecified valley where the film is set. Torrey is a caricature of 'southern honour'; one of his neighbours pokes fun at him by playing 'Dixie'. The taunt that leads him to his death slurs the honour of General 'Stonewall' Jackson. Torrey serves much the same function as southerners in Ford's cavalry films. The South has lost honourably, and its fight was a sign of its own dignity, not of its commitment to a system of racial oppression.

Sam Peckinpah's *Major Dundee* is the work of a radical social critic, not of a nostalgic visionary. Set in the last months of the war, it uses the familiar Fordian material: a cavalry unit made up of unionists and beaten Confederates must unite against a common enemy, the Apache. But there is no pretence that the South was going down in defence of a gracious way of life. Peckinpah's southerners are degenerate racist trash, 'rednecked peckerwoods'. His one southern gentleman (Richard Harris) is in fact an Irish immigrant who has been cashiered from the US Army. When the unit rides out Peckinpah turns the parade into a battle of marching songs: 'Dixie', 'The Battle Hymn of the Republic', and (from the unit's civilian members) 'My Darling Clementine'.

In Samuel Fuller's *Run of the Arrow* an

ex-Confederate named O'Meara (Rod Steiger) is captured by the Sioux, survives the ordeal to which they subject him, and decides to join them. But ultimately he finds he cannot, and with his Indian wife (Sarita Montiel) he returns to white society. Like Ford, Fuller gives no indication that race relations underlie the war. But like Peckinpah he offers no pretence either that the war was gallant or that it could easily be forgotten. When O'Meara returns home after the surrender (at which he almost kills General Grant), his travelling companion loudly sings defiance to the North. O'Meara's people are poor whites, but unlike Peckinpah's poor southerners they are not trash. Olive Carey, cast as O'Meara's mother, brings a tragic dignity to her performance, shared by the bit players who surround her. She and they have much in common with the poor rebel dirt farmers of Missouri, whose Civil War experience forms the background to both *The Great Northfield Minnesota Raid*/1972 and *The Outlaw Josey Wales*/1976.

Missouri was admitted to the Union as a slave state in 1820, in the first of the series of compromises between North and South that eventually led to the war. Its people were southern migrants, and it became a staging point for the southern side in the bitter Kansas warfare of 1854-6. But Missouri never developed a plantation economy or a planter class, and it stayed in the Union when the slave states further south seceded in 1860 and 1861. During the war it was the scene of guerrilla fighting, not of pitched battles between well-drilled armies.

Missouri's poor whites were backward, virtually peasants, and for them the war was a confrontation with forces set on dragging them into modernity. It was from this context that historical outlaws like Jesse and Frank *James and the *Younger brothers emerged. As the historian Eric Hobsbawm observes (*Primitive Rebels*, 1959 and *Bandits*, 1969), these men must be understood not simply as thieves and not just as defenders of slavery. They fought, during and after the war, to protect themselves and their communities against a modernization that they did not want.

The Outlaw Josey Wales is wholly fictional, but it makes precisely that point. Wales (Clint Eastwood) becomes a southern guerrilla only when northern irregulars attack his dirt farm and destroy his family. Like Ford's Ethan Edwards and Fuller's O'Meara, Wales refuses to surrender when it ought to be all over. Instead, pursued by bounty-hunting northerners, he flees into Indian country, picking up a surrogate mixed-race family as he goes. Eventually he and his pursuers do resolve the issue, but it is out of exhaustion rather than as the result of any renewed patriotism.

Philip Kaufman's *The Great Northfield Minnesota Raid* pushes this theme of post Civil War 'social banditry' further. It places Jesse James (Robert Duvall) and Cole Younger (Cliff Robertson) firmly within a community of small, backward farmers. Their culture is oral, as Younger's endless story-telling shows. It is primitive and superstitious, a point demonstrated both by Jesse's trances and by the chanting 'yarb' (herb) woman on whom they call for medical help. The bandits enjoy the open support of their own people, who applaud and shelter them. Banditry and the ordinary way of life of these farmers are both out of place in a world of railroads, detectives, banks, baseball games, steam calliopes and corruptible state legislatures. The bandits are still fighting their own civil war when they stage, and bungle, the bank raid from which the film takes its title.

No Western directly confronts the problem of the Civil War; perhaps none could. Ford's 'black' cavalry film *Sergeant Rutledge*/1960 comments on the genre as much as on American history when it speaks to the limits of the freedom the ex-slaves had. More surprisingly, no Western really deals adequately with the place of the West in the war's coming. On the surface what happened in 'bleeding Kansas' seems to offer fertile material, but with the possible exception of the contentious *Santa Fe Trail*/1940 it is largely unexploited, whether by direct reconstruction or in fictionalized form. EC

Clanton family · The Clantons had been established as ranchers and rustlers around *Tombstone for some time before Wyatt *Earp and his brothers arrived. The feud between the two families, which culminated at the O.K. Corral, was a struggle for political and economic supremacy in the area. 'Old Man' (N.H.) Clanton died some time before the fight took place (though survives to participate in some film versions). The youngest son, Billy (b 1862) was killed at the O.K. Corral. Ike survived the encounter but was shot by a sheriff in 1887. The other son, Phineas, was not present at the fight.
Victor Jory (Ike)/*Tombstone, the Town Too Tough to Die*/1942/PAR/d William McGann/lp Richard Dix, Kent Taylor · Walter Brennan (Old Man Clanton), John Ireland (Billy), Grant Withers (Ike), Fred Libby (Phin)/*My Darling Clementine*/1946 · Bill Bishop/*Gun Belt*/1953/UA/d Ray Nazzaro/lp George Montgomery · Lyle Bettger (Ike), Dennis Hopper (Billy)/*Gunfight at the O.K. Corral*/1956 · Gerald Milton/*Toughest Gun in Tombstone*/1957/UA/d Earl Bellamy/lp George Montgomery · Robert Ryan (Ike), Walter Gregg (Billy)/*Hour of the Gun*/1967 · James Craig/*Arizona Bushwhackers*/1967/PAR/d Lesley Selander/lp Howard Keel, John Ireland · Mike Whitney (Ike), Bruce M. Fisher (Billy)/*Doc*/1971
Television · Trevor Bardette (Old Man Clanton) /*The Life and Legend of Wyatt Earp* · Charles E. Fredericks/*The Deputy* · Charles Benton (Ike), Tom Assalone (Billy)/*I Married Wyatt Earp*

Clark, Walter van Tilburg (1909-71) · Novelist and short story writer, brought up in Nevada, where most of his writing is set. His first novel, *The Ox-Bow Incident*, was published in 1940 and is a powerfully written account of the hysteria which leads to a lynching and of its consequences. It made a memorable film in 1942. Clark's second book, *The City of Trembling Leaves* (1945), though set in Nevada, does not qualify as a Western. His third novel, *The Track of the Cat* (1949), is a philosophical study of evil couched in a story about the hunting of a panther. This was filmed in 1954, directed, like *The Ox-Bow Incident*, by William Wellman. 'The Ox-Bow Incident' was remade as an episode in *The 20th Century-Fox Hour* on television in 1955.

Clum, John P. (1851-1932) · Indian Agent at the San Carlos Apache reservation 1874-7, where he kept the army at arm's length and experimented with using Apache scouts to police the reservation. In 1876 Clum took twenty Apache to Washington, where he intended to exhibit them in a show, but the venture failed. He resigned from the Indian Service over the issue of whether reservations should be controlled by the military or by civilians. From 1880 he was the publisher of the *Tombstone Epitaph*, in which he wrote editorials against the activities of the *Clantons and sided with Wyatt *Earp. Audie Murphy/*Walk the Proud Land*/1956/U/d Jesse Hibbs/lp Anne Bancroft · Larry Gates/*Hour of the Gun*/1967 · Dan Greenberg/*Doc*/1971
Television · Stacy Harris/*The Life and Legend of Wyatt Earp*

John P. Clum with the Apaches Diablo and Eskiminzin in 1875

Cochise (1824?-74) · A leader of the Chirica-hua Apache. Cochise's impressive stature (he was over six feet), and the fact that he only began to fight the United States in 1860, after the army had falsely accused him of kidnapping and had killed some of his relatives, fitted him for the role of 'good Indian' in which the cinema cast him. Certainly his military achievements were impressive. Together with his father-in-law *Mangas Coloradas (who was killed in 1863) Cochise held the army at bay and wrought widespread destruction in the Southwest during and after the Civil War. He was finally induced to surrender by Tom Jeffords in 1872. Jeffords (1832-1914) was a scout who had befriended Cochise. He became Indian agent at the Chiricahua reservation where Cochise spent his last years. The story of this relationship is told in *Broken Arrow/*

1950, in which Jeffords is played by James Stewart.

Antonio Moreno/*Valley of the Sun*/1942/ RKO/*d* George Marshall/*lp* Lucille Ball, Dean Jagger · Miguel Inclan/*Fort Apache*/ 1948 · Jeff Chandler/*Broken Arrow*/1950 · Chief Yowlachie/*The Last Outpost*/1951/ PAR/*d* Lewis R. Foster/*lp* Ronald Reagan, Rhonda Fleming · Jeff Chandler/*The Battle at Apache Pass*/1952/U/*d* George Sherman/ *lp* John Lund · John Hodiak/*Conquest of Cochise*/1953/COL/*d* William Castle/*lp* Robert Stack · Jeff Chandler/*Taza, Son of Cochise*/1953 · Michael Keep/*40 Guns to Apache Pass*/1966/COL/*d* William Witney/ *lp* Audie Murphy

Television · Michael Ansara/*Broken Arrow* · Ricardo Montalban/*Broken Arrow* (pilot) · Jeff Morrow/*Bonanza* · Paul Fix/*The High Chaparral*

Cody, Buffalo Bill [William Frederick] (1846-1917) · Scout and showman. The key figure in the process whereby the historical West was transformed into 'the Western', for it was above all in the person of Buffalo Bill that the raw metal of experience was converted into the currency of show business. His beginnings were little different from dozens of other army scouts on the frontier, though colourful enough: *Pony Express rider (at the age of fourteen), friend of Wild Bill *Hickok, stagecoach driver, buffalo hunter (hence the name) and scout for, among others, General *Custer. On 24 July 1869 Cody was introduced to the dime novelist Ned *Buntline, a meeting which changed his life. Though Cody was already well enough known in the West, Buntline set him on course for national, then international, fame with the first of the four dime novels he wrote about him, *Buffalo Bill, King of the Border Men*. Buffalo Bill took his first trip east in 1872 (he was born in Iowa) and saw a stage production of this novel in New York. Buntline persuaded the scout to appear as himself in a new play, *The Scouts of the Prairie*, which opened in Chicago on 16 December 1872. As Cody's biographer, Don Russell, has said, that night witnessed the birth of the Western.

For the next ten years Cody spent his winters on the stage and his summers back in the West, escorting celebrities or scouting for the army. He was in the field in the summer of 1876 in the campaign that saw the defeat of Custer, and it was in this campaign, on 17 July 1876, that he killed and scalped the Indian chief Yellow Hand, an incident later much celebrated in dime novels as 'the first scalp for Custer'. Buffalo Bill's Wild West (he never actually called it a Wild West Show) began in 1883, and for the next thirty years Cody toured with his company in a production that featured a combination of speciality acts and crypto-narrative material. Thus there were sharp shooters like Annie *Oakley, cowboys like Buck *Taylor doing rodeo-type roping and riding, set pieces such as an Indian attack on the Deadwood Stage or an emigrant train, and dramatizations of the ride of the Pony Express and Custer's Last Stand. Later versions of the spectacle incorporated Teddy *Roosevelt's charge up San Juan Hill in the Spanish-American War and even scenes from the Boxer Rebellion in China. (See Plate 16)

e.e. cummings' epitaph is an evocative picture of Cody's stage presence in his heyday:

Buffalo Bill's
defunct
    who used to
      ride a watersmooth-silver
           stallion
and break onetwothreefourfive pigeons-
justlikethat
                      Jesus

he was a handsome man
          and what i want to know is
how do you like your blueeyed boy
Mister Death

Buffalo Bill's Wild West was phenomenally successful, though Cody, not a great
financial manager, had a hard job keeping
hold of the money. There were foreign tours
and performances in front of European
royalty. And all the time a stream of writings
kept the persona of Buffalo Bill before the
public. In 1879 he published an autobiography, *The Life of Hon. William F. Cody,
Known as Buffalo Bill*, which was not too
unreliable. But from the mid-1870s there
had appeared a series of highly fanciful
stories about his exploits. In all some 557
separate dime novels were written about
him, only four by Ned Buntline but 121 by
Prentiss *Ingraham, who wrote 23 in 1896
alone. In 1890, during the troubles over the
Ghost Dance, Buffalo Bill offered his services
to General Nelson *Miles; *Sitting Bull,
who was caught up in these events, had for
one season toured with the show. But before
Cody could get to see him Sitting Bull was
killed. Later that year came the Massacre of
*Wounded Knee, in which some 150 Sioux,
including women and children, were killed
by troops of the 7th Cavalry.

In 1913 Cody made a film of these events,
which also managed to include his fight with
Yellow Hand. Kevin Brownlow in *The War,
the West and the Wilderness* recounts how
Nelson Miles himself appeared in it,
together with impressive numbers of
soldiers and Indians. The film, *The Indian
Wars*, has unfortunately been lost, but some
Edison Kinetoscope footage of Buffalo Bill's
company taken in 1894 does survive.
The following films featured Buffalo Bill
in person: *Buffalo Bill and Escort*/1897/
Edison · *Parade of Buffalo Bill's Wild West
Show*/1898/Edison · *Buffalo Bill's Wild
West Parade*/1902/American Mutoscope
and Biograph · *Buffalo Bill's Wild West
and Pawnee Bill's Far East*/1910/Buffalo Bill
and Pawnee Bill Film Co. · *The Life of
Buffalo Bill*/1910/Buffalo Bill and Pawnee
Bill Film Co./d Paul Panzer · *The Indian
Wars*/1913/Essanay and Colonel W.F.
Cody Historical Pictures/d Theodore
Wharton · *Sitting Bull – the Hostile Sioux
Indian Chief*/1914/American Rotograph ·
Patsy of the Circus/1915/Bison/d Henry
MacRae · *The Adventures of Buffalo Bill*/
1917/Essanay

Cinema portraits of Buffalo Bill have
mostly taken him at face value, producing
the filmic equivalent of dime novels. Only
very recently, as in *Buffalo Bill and the
Indians*, has an attempt been made to dig
deeper into the most famous Westerner of
all.

Art Acord/*In the Days of Buffalo Bill*/1922/
U/d Edward Laemmle · George Waggner/
The Iron Horse/1924 · John Fox Jr./*The
Pony Express*/1925/PAR/d James Cruze ·
Jack Hoxie/*The Last Frontier*/1926/PDC/d
George B. Seitz/lp J. Farrell MacDonald ·
Edmund Cobb/*Fighting with Buffalo Bill*/
1926/U/d Ray Taylor · Roy Stewart/*Buffalo
Bill on the U.P. Trail*/1926/Sunset/d Frank
S. Mattison · Duke R. Lee/*Buffalo Bill's
Last Fight*/1927/MGM/d John W. Noble ·
William Fairbanks/*Wyoming*/1928/MGM/d
W.S. Van Dyke · Tim McCoy/*The Indians
Are Coming*/1930/U/d Henry MacRae ·
Tom Tyler/*Battling with Buffalo Bill*/1931/
U/d Ray Taylor/lp Rex Bell · Douglas
Dumbrille/*The World Changes*/1933/WB/d
Mervyn LeRoy/lp Paul Muni, Mary Astor
· Earl Dwire/*The Miracle Rider*/1935/
Mascot/d Armand Schaefer/lp Tom Mix ·
Moroni Olsen/*Annie Oakley*/1935/RKO/d
George Stevens/lp Barbara Stanwyck ·
James Ellison/*The Plainsman*/1936 · Ted
Adams/*Custer's Last Stand*/1936/Stage &
Screen/d Elmer Clifton/lp Rex Lease,
William Farnum · Carlyle Moore/*Outlaw
Express*/1938/U/d George Waggner · John
Rutherford/*Flaming Frontiers*/1938/U/d Ray
Taylor, Alan James · Roy Rogers/*Young
Buffalo Bill*/1940/REP/d Joseph Kane/lp

Buffalo Bill Cody (c.1895)

TOP: *Jack Hoxie as Buffalo Bill in* The Last Frontier
BOTTOM: *Louis Calhern, Edward Arnold, J. Carrol Naish in* Annie Get Your Gun.

George Hayes · Bob Baker/*Overland Mail*/1942/U/d Ford Beebe, John Rawlins · Joel McCrea/*Buffalo Bill*/1944 · Richard Arlen/*Buffalo Bill Rides Again*/1946/Screen Guild/d Bernard B. Ray/*lp* Jennifer Holt · Monte Hale/*Law of the Golden West*/1949/REP/d Philip Ford · Louis Calhern/*Annie Get Your Gun*/1950 · Dickie Moore/*Cody of the Pony Express*/1950/COL/d Spencer G. Bennet/*lp* Jock O'Mahoney · Tex Cooper/*King of the Bullwhip*/1951/Western Adventure/d Ron Ormond/*lp* Lash LaRue · Clayton Moore/*Buffalo Bill in Tomahawk Territory*/1952/UA/d Bernard B. Ray/*lp* Chief Thundercloud · Charlton Heston/*Pony Express*/1952/PAR/d Jerry Hopper/*lp* Rhonda Fleming · Marshall Reed/*Riding

with Buffalo Bill*/1954/COL/d Spencer G. Bennet/*lp* Rick Vallin · Malcolm Atterbury/*Badman's Country*/1958/WB/d Fred F. Sears/*lp* George Montgomery, Buster Crabbe · James McMullan/*The Raiders*/1964/U/d Herschel Daugherty/*lp* Brian Keith, Robert Culp · Rick van Nutter/*Aventuras del Oeste*/1964/It, WG, Sp/d J.L. Romero Marchent/*lp* Elga Sommerfeuld · Gordon Scott/*Buffalo Bill l'eroe del west*/1963/It, WG, Fr/d Mario Costa/*lp* Jan Hendriks · Guy Stockwell/*The Plainsman*/1966/U/d David Lowell Rich/*lp* Don Murray · Michel Piccoli/*Touche pas la femme blanche*/1973/Fr, It/d Marco Ferreri · Paul Newman/*Buffalo Bill and the Indians or Sitting Bull's History Lesson*/1976 · Ted Flicker/*The Legend of the Lone Ranger*/1981/ITC/d William A. Fraker/*lp* Klinton Spilsbury · Brian Dennehey/*Annie Oakley*/1985/Platypus/d Michael Lindsay-Hogg/*lp* Jamie Lee Curtis Television · Britt Lomond/*Colt .45* · Matt Clark/*This Is the West That Was* · Buff Brady/*The Last Ride of the Dalton Gang* · R.L. Tolbert/*The Legend of the Golden Gun* · Ken Kercheval/*Calamity Jane*

Colonial period · The historical core of the Western genre is white America's conquest of its continent, and that process took almost three centuries to complete. It began in 1607, with the first successful English beachhead at Jamestown, Virginia. It concluded ('officially' at least) in 1890, when the Bureau of the Census announced that the frontier was closed. For its first century and three quarters the conquest was painfully slow; at the beginning of the Revolution European settlement reached only a few hundred miles inland. But during its last century it went forward with amazing speed.

In a sense, the whole process was one of colonization. In the colonial period itself, which lasted until independence, Britain's North American provinces were economically, culturally and politically dependent on their European metropolis. For more than a century afterwards, the states and territories of the expanding interior and of the south were effectively colonies of the industrial northeast. The classic questions of the Western – expansion, cultural contact, racial war, economic development, community formation – were being posed from the very beginning.

But the early period, from original colonization to independence, has been of negligible interest to film-makers. Perhaps only two films set before 1800, *Drums Along the

Mohawk*/1939 and *Northwest Passage*/1940, would count as major Westerns. Why should the colonial period have been so neglected? On the surface it seems to have much to recommend it. One of the standard themes in the Western is the awesome power wielded by hostile Indians who threaten a timorous, fragile white community. 'Custer is dead.... Another such defeat and it will be a hundred years before another wagon train dares to cross the plains,' intones the opening voice-over in *She Wore a Yellow Ribbon*/1949. Yet by 1876, the year of Little Big Horn, white America had become a full-blown industrial-urban civilization, with a population in the tens of millions. By then the Indians numbered in the mere thousands, and their cause was doomed. The real historical points at which militant Indians might have triumphed in a way that made a difference came far earlier, with the Virginia 'massacres' of 1622 and 1644, with King Philip's War in New England in 1676 and, just possibly, with Pontiac's midwestern 'conspiracy' of 1763. Yet none of these has provided significant material for film-makers.

Any explanation must be speculative, but a number of factors seem to be involved. At the most elementary level there is iconography, especially costume. Though women's clothing has changed drastically since the late 19th century, Western-style men's wear has not. The clothing itself is thus a sign system, not just in the good guys/white hats tradition but in the sense of providing a means of identification between male characters and male viewers. But a story set earlier must necessarily be a costume drama. What women wear is much the same as in a Western set later. But men's knee breeches and tricorn hats distance the audience, rather than providing identification.

Second comes the problem of international politics. One of the most basic premises of the Western is its bi-polar, either-or mode of explanation. This itself is an old American way; the history of 'structuring oppositions' in American thought reaches back to New England Puritanism, as Perry Miller showed long ago (*The New England Mind*, 2 vols., 1939, 1951). But the reality of colonial life was too complex ever to be explained in bi-polar terms. International rivalry among the English, the Dutch and the French, inter-colonial struggles for land titles and for political control, religious and class conflict among whites, a growing black presence: all of these prevented it. So did a tangled pattern of Indian-white relations that turned on sophisticated diplomacy and delicate balances of power rather than on a simple opposition between civilization and savagery.

Third comes the actual pattern of colonial development, which followed no single path. In New England the long-term process led from a utopian effort to create a static, communal, Christian agrarian paradise to a recognition that commerce and competition were inescapable. In the south commerce and competition were present from the beginning, and the result was a nightmare of violence and exploitation. When the nightmare ended, its fruit was slave-based plantation society. The 'Middle Colonies' (New York, New Jersey, Pennsylvania and Delaware) developed through the interplay of land patterns that are best described as neo-feudal, and patterns of exchange that were explicitly commercial.

None of these can be reconciled easily to the image of a 'fee-simple empire' of small-farmer individualism which, ideologically at least, was the centrepiece of American public policy after independence. None of them fits at all with the intense individualism that is inherent in the mythology of the frontier hero, be it Leatherstocking or General Custer. Such all-pervasive individualism is difficult to reconcile with the essentially non-individualistic ethos of much of colonial America, whatever form that ethos took. Among Westerns the cavalry sub-genre does provide a means to discuss societies in which individualism is not the primary value. But among major non-cavalry Westerns only the idiosyncratic *Duel in the Sun*/1946 comes close to articulating a non-individualistic social vision. It is, of course, set nowhere near the colonial period.

For the specialist historian, early America is vibrant with conflict, ambiguity and life. It seems, as well, to be an era populated by heroes and demigods: Captain John Smith being rescued by Pocahontas; the stern John Winthrop, first governor of Massachusetts; Benjamin Franklin, pulling himself to world fame from his obscure Boston birth; John Adams who (in Esmond Wright's words) 'carried his rectitude like a banner and ... stopped now and then to salute it'; Thomas Jefferson, writing the Declaration of Independence; Washington himself, beyond all human reproach. Even the villains are unambiguous. Buffs and specialists still argue about Custer. But what would be the point of dispute about Benedict Arnold, the

Spencer Tracy in Northwest Passage

(r.) Henry Fonda, Claudette Colbert in Drums Along the Mohawk

brilliant revolutionary general who went over to the British and tried to take West Point and a captured George Washington with him? The colonials seem too good or, in rare instances, too bad to be true. Whatever the specialist may know, their popular image offers only the stuff of hagiography. That is yet another reason why so few film-makers have bothered with them and their time.

Northwest Passage offers a perfect example of the problem. The film is derived from

Kenneth *Roberts's novel of the same title (1937). Roberts, in turn, drew his book from the journals of Major Robert Rogers who, played by Spencer Tracy, is the film's protagonist. The historical Rogers was more than a killer and a self-publicist: he was also an amateur playwright, author of *Ponteach*, the first American drama on an 'Indian' theme. But he was no paragon and after the exploits that the film chronicles he sank into alcoholism. Eventually he became a loyalist during the American Revolution. In the film, however, Rogers appears as a super-man, powerful enough to overcome the weaker wills of his soldiers and all the obstacles that nature can place in his way.

The film's point-of-view character is Langdon Towne (Robert Young), a would-be 'American artist' who intends to immortalize Rogers. Loosely based on such real eighteenth-century artists as Benjamin West, John Singleton Copley and John Trumbull, the character speaks to another dimension of the problem: the achievement of such artists themselves. Art historians agree that they were the originators of the genre of modern-dress history painting that spread through the Atlantic world during the age of the American and French Revolutions. West's 'Death of General Wolfe' (1770) was a manifesto, a statement that history of world importance was being made in the American wilderness. As such, it addressed concerns that would be central in the Western. But the painting genre that it launched remained, for the most part, at the level of the purely heroic, with not the slightest hint of moral or historical ambiguity.

That same lack of ambiguity permeates the two major 'colonial' Westerns. Both *Northwest Passage* and *Drums Along the Mohawk* centre on the conflict of whites and Indians; in both, the conflict is one of natural forces that must collide. In both the reasons for the collision are psycho-sexual rather than social and economic. In both, the Indians are presented as aggressors, and their defeat is an unqualified good.

Both films accomplish this against a 'real' historical background that is vastly more complex, and *Northwest Passage*, at least, does hint at the complexities. Its opening sequences, set in Portsmouth, New Hampshire, comment quickly on the intersection of family life and economic production in pre-industrial society, on the decay of Puritanism's moral power, and on the arrogance of British imperial officials. Later the film briefly introduces Sir William Johnson, the redoubtable 'Mohawk baronet' who created both a neo-feudal world and a workable Indian policy on New York's colonial frontier. Johnson, in fact, was the architect of the world of *Drums Along the Mohawk*. But unlike the novels by Walter D. *Edmonds and Kenneth Roberts from which they are respectively drawn, neither *Drums* nor *Northwest Passage* proves able to deal with a society that was divided on class as well as racial lines. EC

Colter, John (1775-1813) · Mountain man. A member of *Lewis and Clark's expedition and then a trapper in the Rockies. In 1808 he was captured by Blackfoot Indians, who offered him the chance to run for his life. With 500 warriors in pursuit Colter made his dash for safety. He managed to outrun them all, killing the last pursuer with the Indian's own weapon. Washington *Irving gives an account in *Astoria*, his history of the fur trade, and several Westerns contain variations on this episode, including *John Colter's Escape*/1912/Selig/lp Bessie Eyton, Herbert Rawlinson · *Drums Along the Mohawk*/1939 · *Across the Wide Missouri*/1950 · *Run of the Arrow*/1957 · *The Mountain Men*/1979/COL/d Richard Lang/lp Charlton Heston, Brian Keith.

Colt revolver · Samuel Colt (1814-62) first patented a hand-gun with a cylinder revolving about a single barrel in 1836. Financial problems and technical difficulties prevented mass production of a successful model until the late 1840s. The California gold rush of 1849 boosted sales and during the Civil War Colt's armoury produced over 300,000 revolvers, mostly of the .36 calibre Navy Model of 1851 and the .44 calibre Army Model of 1860. All these earlier versions were fired by percussion caps, the ammunition being loose powder and ball or paper cartridges; not until 1873 was the metallic cartridge introduced, for the .45 calibre New Model Army or 'Peacemaker' type. (This basic design, when modified to take the same cartridge as the .44 Winchester rifle, was known as the 'Frontier' model). This gun, the most famous of all those used in the West, was first a single action repeater; that is, the hammer was cocked by the hand for each shot. In the later double-action model (after 1877) the action of the trigger first cocks the piece, then releases the hammer to fire it. BACKGROUND: *Colt revolver (Springfield model 1888)*

Comanche · Originally from the mountainous north (they are of the same language group as the Shoshone of Montana), the Comanche moved out on to the southern plains in the late 17th century. The acquisition of horses allowed them to range freely over vast areas of the Southwest, where they came into continual conflict with other Indian peoples and with Mexicans and Texans, and gained a reputation for horsemanship and belligerence. Warfare on the Texas border between whites and Comanches was particularly bitter, with

massacres on both sides. Twice the Comanche were involved in battles at Adobe Walls in the Texas Panhandle. In the first, in 1864, they were beaten off by Kit *Carson and his troops. On the second occasion, in 1874, a group of buffalo hunters which included Bat *Masterson held out against seven hundred warriors. The Red River War (1874-5) conducted by the army under General Phil *Sheridan destroyed Comanche resistance and forced them onto a reservation in Oklahoma, where one of their leaders was *Quanah Parker.

When the Comanche appear they are invariably threatening, memorably in two John Ford Westerns, *The Searchers*/1956 and *Two Rode Together*/1961, in *Comanche Station*/1959 and in *The Outlaw Josey Wales*/1976.

George Catlin, 'Comanche Warrior'

Comancheros · Originally traders in New Mexico who were permitted by the Spanish authorities to deal with the Comanches and other southern tribes. When the Southwest came under the control of the United States such traders were increasingly regarded as renegades who sold the Indians guns and whiskey in return for stolen cattle. This is certainly John Wayne's view in *The Comancheros*/1961. Clint Eastwood encounters some particularly brutish Comancheros in *The Outlaw Josey Wales*/1976.

Comics · The editor of *Pluck*, a popular 'penny dreadful' for British boys, had an exciting announcement for his young readers on 29 November 1913. 'This week you have, my chums, the first of the grand new series of tales from cinematograph films that I am going to present to you.' And the first of *Pluck*'s weekly 'Tales from the Cinema' was a

Western, *Blood Will Tell*, anonymously adapted from the Universal picture and illustrated by G.M. Dodshon. Actors were not named, but the hero was Buffalo Bill. Westerns figured strongly in the films selected for fictionalization, and the rise of the cowboy film star can be seen on the front cover of *Pluck* no. 562, dated 7 August 1915: a portrait of 'popular Tom Mix' in *The Stagecoach Driver*. By now the fictionalizers themselves were credited too: 'Written specially from the great Selig Western Drama by Lewis Carlton'.

Story versions of favourite films proved so attractive to young British film fans that on 13 December 1919 the publishers of *Pluck* expanded the idea into a complete film fiction weekly and launched no. 1 of *Boy's Cinema*, a 28-page twopenny that ran for 21 years. In that time many B-Westerns were fictionalized. The dominance of the Western is evident in that first issue. Not only is the cover given over to William S. Hart, featured as no. 1 of a series of 'Life Stories of Screen Heroes', but the leading film adaptation is *The Sheriff's Son*, starring Charles Ray, and a Grand Free Art Plate of Tom Mix is given away with every copy.

Film Fun, following hot on the heels of *Boy's Cinema* (no. 1 was dated 17 January 1920), was the first comic to concentrate on strip cartoons of cinema stars, but it was not until 1933 that an adventure strip was introduced among the cast of comedians. And the star of the first ever serial strip to be built round a film hero was Buck Jones, 'by permission of Columbia Pictures'. Instead of adapting an actual film, Frederick Cordwell, editor of *Film Fun*, opted for an original story entitled 'Rogues of the Rockies', billing it as 'Our Thrilling New Picture-Serial of Pluck, Peril and Adventure'. To illustrate the script, Cordwell chose J.H. Valda, a veteran illustrator from the boys' story-papers. When Buck's contract expired, it was Valda who continued the two-page, ten-picture tradition with another top B-Western hero, Tim McCoy, in 1934.

The popularity of Western strips in *Film Fun* inspired Cordwell to devise a new comic which would concentrate entirely on strip adaptations of current movies, and so no. 1 of *Film Picture Stories* went on sale on 16 July 1934. This historic issue – it was the first all-adventure strip comic ever – featured four films in strip form and, of course, one was a Western. This was *The Fighting Code*, starring Buck Jones, and the illustrator was another veteran, Joseph Walker. Although the comic was not a success and ran for only

A British Western comic of the 1930s

30 weeks, it preserves in pictorial format a body of B-movies which otherwise would be lost to us. Westerns featured included Randolph Scott in *Man of the Forest*, Bob Steele in *The Galloping Romeo*, Rex Bell in *Rainbow Ranch*, Tom Tyler in *Riding Thru*, and Ken Maynard in *Honor of the Range*. Artists included Valda, Walker, Harry Lane, George W. Wakenfield and Serge Drigin.

The back page of the tabloid penny comics had, by the 30s, become the traditional province of adventure serial strips. In

1936 the editor of a group of these comics, Stanley Gooch, conceived the idea of substituting popular film stars for the fictional heroes who had hitherto featured in these serials. Thus it was that Tim McCoy galloped on to the back page of *Funny Wonder*, Gary Cooper arrived on the back of *The Jester*, and Ken Maynard rode on to the two-colour back page of *Tip Top*.

Editor Gooch obviously knew the drawing power of the cowboy hero, for when he launched *Radio Fun* in 1938 he included the decidedly non-wireless personality Tom Keene in his pictorial programme. In 1939 he replaced Keene with the biggest Western hero of the day, William Boyd in his role of Hopalong Cassidy, as illustrated by C. E. Montford. Hoppy had previously appeared in no fewer than three strips based on the Paramount films *Hills of Wyoming*, *Borderland* and *North of the Rio Grande*, in the otherwise all-story weekly, *Modern Boy* (1937). The artist was the ubiquitous J.H. Valda.

It was the veteran comic *Film Fun* which led the way in the postwar Western boom. No. 1,532, dated 28 May 1949, brought action back to its traditionally comical strips with a pictorial adaptation of Monogram's *Valley of Fear*, which for four weeks ranged across its centre-spread. The star was Johnny Mack Brown. From then on it was one Western a month, the series including Gregory Peck in *Yellow Sky*, Wayne Morris in *The Younger Brothers*, John Wayne in *The Fighting Kentuckian*, and Ronald Reagan in *Law and Order*.

The decline of the traditional comic saw the rise of a new form of comicbook, the pocket-size 'library' with 64 pages of picture strips. The first ever was called *Cowboy Comics* (May 1960), and the first ever hero was – Buck Jones. DGi

[In America, scores of Western comics flourished during the 1940s and 50s, the golden age of the comicbook. There were comics based on movie stars; some major (John Wayne), and many minor (Tim Holt, Gabby Hayes, Lash LaRue). Comics seemed to exist in a kind of time warp. Thus Buck Jones comics were still being published as late as 1951 (Jones had died in 1942) and Tom Mix as late as 1953 (Mix had his fatal car crash in 1940). There were comics based on Western characters, both real (Buffalo Bill, Kit Carson, Annie Oakley, Butch Cassidy – as early as 1951) and fictional (The Cisco Kid, Zorro, Hopalong Cassidy). Comics were spun off from radio and TV series (*Gunsmoke*, *Wagon Train*, *The Lone Ranger*, *Laramie*). Individual Western movies were turned into comics (in 1965 not only *Rio Conchos* but also *Cheyenne Autumn*). And there were Western variations on the 'True Romance' type of comic; for example in 1949 *Western Love* ('romance with all the fury of a blazing six-gun').]

Cooper, James Fenimore (1789-1851) · Novelist. Views may differ as to Cooper's true literary merits (Mark *Twain delivered a punishing attack on him in 'Fenimore

Cooper's Literary Offences'), but that he is the father of Western fiction there can be no doubt. He did not invent the idea of the West or the figure of the frontiersman, but what he found he deepened and crafted into a form that was to have a widespread and lasting influence.

Cooper's greatest creation is the figure of Natty Bumppo, also known variously in the five novels about him as Hawk-eye, Deerslayer and Pathfinder. Based in part on Daniel *Boone, Natty is a hunter who exists metaphorically as well as actually on the frontier. His life is lived on the line that separates the whites from the Indians, in this case the Iroquois. Suspicious of the constrictions of civilization, Natty yet cannot totally renounce it in favour of the woods, for this would be to risk lapsing into the primitive barbarism of their inhabitants. But the Indians in the novels are split too, between

The Last of the Mohicans (1920)

the Mohicans who are the allies of the Americans, and the evil Hurons. Natty's friend Chingachgook is the prototype of the noble savage: strong, chivalrous, wise.

Natty Bumppo first appeared in *The Pioneers*, published in 1823 and set in what were then the wilds of upper New York State. Cooper returned to the character in four more novels. The next to be published, *The Last of the Mohicans* (1826), is chronologically the second in the series. *The Prairie* (1827) is chronologically the last; Natty, like

Daniel Boone, has been driven ever further west by encroaching settlements and finally dies way out on the plains. *The Pathfinder* (1840) deals with events which come after *The Last of the Mohicans* and before *The Pioneers*. The last book to be published, *The Deerslayer* (1841), is chronologically the start of the series, dealing with Natty's initiation into manhood.

Cooper's conception of the frontiersman, straddling two ways of life, too wild for society, too white to go completely native, found its way, albeit coarsened, into innumerable other fictions: dramas, dime novels and, eventually, the cinema.
The Deerslayer/1913/Vitagraph/d Hal Reid, Larry Trimble/lp Hal Reid, Wallace Reid · *The Last of the Mohicans*/1920/Associated Exhibitors/d Maurice Tourneur/ lp Wallace Beery · *The Last of the Mohicans*/ 1932/Mascot/d B. Reeves Eason, Ford Beebe/lp Harry Carey · *The Last of the Mohicans*/1936/UA/d George B. Seitz/ lp Randolph Scott · *The Pioneers*/1941/MON/ d Al Herman/lp Tex Ritter · *Deerslayer*/ 1943/REP/d Lew Landers/lp Larry Parks, Yvonne De Carlo · *The Last of the Redmen*/1947/COL/d George Sherman/lp Jon Hall · *The Prairie*/1947/Zenith/d Frank Wisbar/lp Alan Baxter · *The Iroquois Trail*/ 1950/Edward Small/d Phil Karlson/lp George Montgomery · *The Pathfinder*/ 1952/COL/d Sidney Salkow/lp George

Montgomery, Jay Silverheels · *The Deerslayer*/1957/FOX/*d* Kurt Neumann/*lp* Lex Barker, Forrest Tucker
Television · *Hawkeye and the Last of the Mohicans* · *The Last of the Mohicans*/71 · *The Last of the Mohicans*/77 · *The Deerslayer*
(There have also been a number of films based somewhat loosely on Cooper's characters, including *Leatherstocking*/1909/Biograph/*d* D.W. Griffith · two films called *The Last of the Mohicans* in 1911 · a German film entitled *Lederstrumpf* in 1920 · *Leatherstocking*/1924/Pathé/*d* George B. Seitz · *Der letzte Mohikaner*/1965/WG, It, Sp/*d* Harald Reinl · *Chingachgook – Die grosse Schlange*/1967/WG/*d* Richard Groschopp/*lp* Rolf Romer)

Cortez, Gregorio (1875-1916) · Mexican folk hero, the subject of the 'Corrido de Gregorio Cortez', which tells how in 1901 in Karnes County, Texas, Cortez was compelled to kill the sheriff who was unjustly trying to arrest him. Cortez managed to elude the posse sent after him for several days and 400 miles, but was eventually captured and tried. Acquitted of murdering the first sheriff, he was sentenced to life imprisonment for the killing of another sheriff while on the run. Not until 1913 was he granted a pardon, and his case became a *cause célèbre* among Mexican people. These events are the subject of *The Ballad of Gregorio Cortez*/1982/USA, Mex/*d* Robert M. Young/*lp* Edward James Olmos.

Costume · Costume conventions in the Western evidence a commitment to keeping a toe-hold in historical reality while enlarging upon it and inventing around it. Leather chaps, for instance, were worn by the original cattleherder, who would have needed this trouser reinforcement protection from the *chaparro prieto* or thorny bush. The movie cowpuncher, exhibiting the full variety of this item of clothing, was seen in both closed and open-legged chaps made in the full range of materials – from the short-haired calf-, goat- or wolf-skin, to the long-haired angora sheepskin, to fringed cowhide. In the 'real West' the mode in chaps was linked to regions. The longer-haired, wide bat-wing chap served its extra protective function in the Northwest, while the shorter-haired and stove-pipe shape evolved in the Southwest. But if Broncho Billy Anderson or William S. Hart were more often outfitted in the winged chap, it was not for reasons of geographical authenticity but

Linen dusters in Pale Rider

Marlon Brando, 'the antithesis of Western asceticism' in The Missouri Breaks

because of the flamboyance of this style, which suggests why chaps later came to be associated with dudes. The relative fanciness of the movie cowboy also has to do with his source in the Wild West Show entertainer, whose wardrobe was an eclectic mix of the showiest range gear – hence the chaps decorated with large silver conchos or fur trim, the fringed and beaded jacket, the fringed cuffed glove, and the pearl-buttoned plaid shirt with piping and embroidery seen especially in the 1930s B-Westerns. It was the cowboy showman and not the 1870s range rider who wore an ornate belt buckle and the John B. Stetson deeper crown and narrower rimmed-hat, which was introduced into the motion picture costume lexicon via Wild West star Buffalo Bill *Cody.

The costume of the silent star Tom Mix and his descendants, Hopalong Cassidy and the singing cowboys Gene Autry and Roy Rogers, as it drew on earlier popular entertainment, adhered to a derived code and was thus two steps removed from the 'real West'. Periodically, however, in an effort to renew Hollywood's lease on realism, creative personnel would raid the historical records for fresh signs of western authenticity. Costumers cite Howard Hawks' *Red River*/1947 as a turning point in the renewed commitment to costume realism. Although *Red River* is rich in the detail of everyday life on the cattle drive, the only significant article of clothing it adds to the Western mythic repertoire is the rubber slicker, which, if made to historical specifications, not only was slit up the back to facilitate riding, but was fitted with a triangular piece between the two sides to cover this divide. Further historical research turned up the linen duster or frock coat adapted from the Civil War medical coat, which appeared on the Ward Bond character in *The Searchers*/1956, and later surfaced occasionally in the bloodier and grittier pictures of the 60s and 70s such as *The Wild Bunch*/1969. The slicker becomes stylized as worn by the James and Younger brothers in *The Long Riders*/1980 (Plate 26) and the seven identically dressed deputies in *Pale Rider*/1985.

Hollywood also reconstructed the mythic image of the Wild West by adapting and re-shuffling costume pieces, so that, for instance, the common 'dog' or 'mule ear' boot, with its scruffy connotations, shows up on the farmer or the miner but never on a hero. The hero wears the basic side-seam boot with pre-1877 style high heel and pointed toe if he is to be romanticized and

the square sensible toe if he is to be de-mythologized. The fringed buckskin jacket taken from the Indian style has undergone considerable modification as motion picture cowboy gear and finally as a mass-produced Western wear standard. The modern shorter-fringed version erases the functionality of the original, in which the long, tough fringe pieces doubled as handy ties, facilitated water drainage and sometimes, it was said, worked to 'shoo off' flies. This long-fringed jacket makes an appearance on Lee Clayton, the Marlon Brando character in *Missouri Breaks*/1976, who satirizes the costuming aberrations often used to mark the anti-social eccentricity of the bounty hunter. Clayton, who wears a sombrero, a Chinese straw coolie hat and a pink polk bonnet, but never once the basic broad-rimmed, high-crowned wool, is the antithesis of Western asceticism.

The ideal Westerner usually had one outfit of clothes which he slept in and rarely changed. If he stripped, which was seldom, he was still covered in his long underwear. The prickliness of the one-piece long john suggests the vulnerability and sensitivity of the untoughened white flesh beneath, which no western woman would ever touch. Male sexuality in the Western is deflected to the hip and the heel, where the lethal concentration of steel and leather held in check the possibility that the male body might turn into pure spectacle. As Steve Neale has suggested, the sadism and masochism which characterize the Western 'disqualify' the male body as an erotic object. But banning the representation of male sexuality requires a peculiar relation between all male bodies in the Western, as one body monitors, measures and obliterates another. Western individualism is the variable in this stalking pattern, which has its visual equivalent in each man's refined and perfected mode of wearing weapons on his body. Narrative expectations are thus worked out through costuming, which efficiently establishes a character as a type who wears one or two guns in holsters at the side or in the centre of his waist, slings gun belts over his shoulder in Mexican bandolero style (single- or double-crossed in front), carries a knife in his boot, or conceals a second pistol in his

Changing styles in hats; Bob Hope and Roy Rogers in Son of Paleface *(1952) – Glenn Ford in* The Fastest Gun Alive *(1956) – and Clint Eastwood in* Hang 'Em High *(1968)*

pocket and a third tucked into the same belt he uses to hold up his pants.

The double function of the cowboy's clothes and gear corresponds with classical narrative film economy, as each item serves dual purposes necessitated by the survival economy of the lone rider. The gun often becomes a splint, the belt a whip, the neckerchief a protective mask, and the hat a dipper or a decoy. One of the oldest Western movie tricks is based on the metonymic effectiveness of the cowboy's bedroll or hat which stands in for his body, taking the beating or stopping the bullet for him. The Western costume also served the ends of the narrative by enhancing the star appeal of the actor and by contributing to the illusion of continuity and chronology. Using mineral oil to simulate sweat, the costume department would produce three different hats for before, during and after the ride, anticipating the probability that the order of the shoot would not correspond with the order of the story. The effect of time, trouble and everyday wear was produced on cotton trail clothes by means of sandpaper, fuller's earth and blow torches. For a single picture, John Wayne might have as many as eight identical shirts ready for any out-of-continuity take, each worn, torn, and tattered by degree. Wayne's trademark, the dark flannel shield or placket-front shirt with its buttoned panel creating the illusion of a fortified chest, carried over the military and authoritarian connotations associated with his star persona. The taller hat and the tighter-fitting pant leg elongated and enlarged all the Western heroes, but the costuming illusion was most essential to Alan Ladd, who wore five-inch leather insteps in his boot.

The Western worked out its indifference and its commitment to a real historical American West through costume devices, but with this same iconography the genre also made its gesture toward the contemporary period. In the 40s, Western men wore padding in their jackets and shirts, following the vogue at the time. Sergio Leone's trilogy with Clint Eastwood echoes the 'hippie' look of the 1960s in Eastwood's 'laid back' serape and in the exaggerated bell bottom trousers of the Mexican villains. But women's fashions in the Western are even more tied to trends, which often resulted in an improbable period hybrid, as, for instance, Jane Greer's strapless wasp-waisted net evening gown with bustle in the 1948 *Station West* (designed by RKO's Renie), or Angie Dickinson's late-1950s pillbox hat and suit featuring the fashionable short

jacket, as seen in *Rio Bravo*/1958. The bustle, fashionable around 1885, was recruited into the mythic West anywhere from 1860 to 1890, and, like the ruffled garter, the fishnet stocking, the ostrich feather boa and the black lace corset, it signified the incongruousness of Woman, either dangerous or comic in a rough masculine world. The ludicrousness of the Dodge City residents' effort to defend themselves against starving Indians in *Cheyenne Autumn*/1964 is epitomized in the one 'casualty' of the battle: a prostitute's red silk skirt. The skirtless woman rides home pantaloon-side up in the

John Wayne's placket-front shirt in The Sons of Katie Elder

lap of Wyatt Earp. Indicative of the serious threat posed by marriage in the Western, the woman's wardrobe item least often seen is the bridal gown. When the woman wears it, as in *Shane*/1952 and *Ride the High Country*/1962, it is an unsettling prelude to a brawl, a murder or a massacre. JG
Station West/1948/RKO/d Sidney Lanfield/lp Dick Powell, Jane Greer

Cowboy · The heyday of the cowboy was a brief one; in less than a generation from the start of the great cattle-drives over the plains, the cowboy as we know him in the cinema had reverted to a mere ranch-hand. In the years immediately following the Civil War, the presence of large numbers of cattle on the open plains of Texas, and the absence of any market for them in the south, encouraged men to drive herds hundreds of miles

up the *Chisholm and other trails as far as Kansas. This was the location of the nearest railroad tracks, which could transport the live animals to Chicago, from where, using new techniques of refrigeration, the meat could be taken on to consumers in the east.

The first cattle were shipped from *Abilene in 1867. As the railroad extended west, other towns sprang up as shipping points: Ellsworth from 1871, *Wichita from 1872, *Dodge City from 1876. Trails were opened to the northern plains of Wyoming and Montana, to stock their newly emergent ranching industry and to supply beef to the Indians reservations now that the buffalo were gone. Somewhere between 6 and 9 million cattle were driven out of Texas between 1867 and 1886. Perhaps 25,000 men made the trip north, and altogether there were around 50,000 cowboys at work during the height of the cattle boom.

First-hand accounts, such as Andy *Adams' *Log of a Cowboy*, make it clear that the cowboy's life held little glamour. On the trail sleep was short, food was bad and there was the ever-present danger of stampede. River crossings were also hazardous; several major rivers, including the Brazos, Trinity, Red, Washita, Canadian, Cimarron and Arkansas, flowed east across the path of the herd. Pay was poor; cowboys earned about $30 a month for the trip, which normally took between two and three months to Kansas, and nearer six to Montana. After a day or two of excitement in town at the end of the trail, it was back to Texas for the winter. Since far less men were required to mind the cattle on the open range than to drive them up the trail, many of the men were laid off once the drive was over. Edward Aveling, Karl Marx's son-in-law, who visited America in 1887, wrote that 'Out in the fabled West, the life of the "free" cowboy is as much that of a slave as is the life of his Eastern brother, the Massachusetts mill-hand.' In 1883 cowboys in Texas went on strike for higher wages, though they were unsuccessful. The aura of 'freedom' which has surrounded the cowboy's existence derives in part from his job insecurity (thus many cowboys did literally wander the West in search of work), and from the mobility experienced on the trail – though here the cowboy was really no more free than a modern truck-driver.

Those who owned the cows could make a lot of money. One calculation in 1884 showed that three thousand cattle needed nine men and a cook to move them, and that their pay ($30 for the hands, $100 for the trail boss), together with provisions, would cost $500 a month. Cattle that were worth $11-14 a head in Texas could be sold for $20-24 in Abilene. The profit on each cow might therefore be $10, or $30,000 for the herd, for expenses of only $1,000-1,500. Despite the hazards along the trail, losses apparently averaged only 16 per 1,000. (In *Red River*/1947 John Wayne offers his fellow ranchers only $2 a head when he takes their cattle north. His losses on the trail are heavy; only 8,200 left from 10,000 when they get to Abilene. But since they sell at $21 a head, profits are even higher than average.)

By the 1890s the days of the trail drive and the open range were over. The railroad reached Fort Worth in 1876, which meant cattle could be shipped directly from the south, and in any case the development of agriculture and hostility to the splenic fever borne by Texas cattle produced increasing resistance to the herds by farmers in Kansas. (Hence – despite all the pious hopes in *Oklahoma!*/1955 that 'the farmer and the cowboy should be friends' – the feuds between cowboys and 'sodbusters' which form the theme of many Westerns, including, most famously, *Shane*/1952.) The great blizzard of 1886-7 wrought havoc with the herds on the High Plains, and hastened the introduction of *barbed wire fencing, which made it easier to care for cattle in winter by restricting their movements, and permitted controlled breeding to improve stock. Of course ranch-hands were still needed, and they might call themselves cowboys, but the days of the wide-open range, which only thirty years previously had stretched from the Gulf of Mexico to the Canadian border, were gone for ever.

Yet even before the cowboy was eclipsed he had started to become an object of fantasy. Already by 1887 an English visitor to the West could write that:

'The cowboy has at the present time become a personage: nay, more, he is rapidly becoming a mythical one. Distance is doing for him what lapse of time did for the heroes of antiquity. His admirers are investing him with all manner of romantic qualities; they descant upon his manifold virtues and his pardonable weaknesses as if he were a demigod.... Meantime, the true character of the cowboy has been obscured, his genuine qualities are lost in fantastic tales of impossible daring and skill, of daring equitations and unexampled endurance.'

Some details of how this process of mythification took place remain obscure. No real-life working cowboy ever achieved the

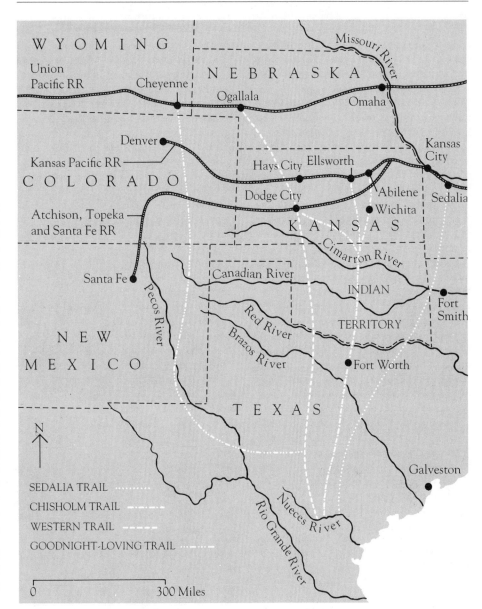

PRINCIPAL CATTLE TRAILS AFTER 1865

lasting fame of some other Western types. The mountain man, the scout, the Indian, the soldier, the lawman or the outlaw may be represented by Kit Carson, Buffalo Bill, Sitting Bull, General Custer, Wyatt Earp or Jesse James. But which historical figure stands for the cowboy? The myth, we may assume, required some historical reality on which to build. But we have only a limited knowledge of what that reality was, and still less of the precise steps by which and through whom it was transformed into something else.

The circumstances of a cowboy's life did not encourage the production of written

records. Some were nevertheless forthcoming. In *Forty Years on the Frontier*, Granville Stuart wrote about the cowboys he had employed on his Montana ranch in the 1880s. He describes their distinctive costume:

'They wore the best clothes they could buy and took great pride in their personal appearance and in their trappings. The men of our outfit used to pay $25 a pair for made-to-order riding boots when the best store boots in Helena were $10 a pair. Their trappings consisted of a fine saddle, silver mounted bridle, pearl-handled six-shooter, latest model cartridge belt with silver buckle, silver spurs, a fancy quirt with silver mountings, a fine riata sometimes made of rawhide, a pair of leather chaps and a fancy hatband often made from the dressed skin of a diamond rattlesnake. They wore expensive stiff-brimmed light felt hats with brilliantly colored handkerchiefs knotted about their necks, light colored shirts and exquisitely fitted high-heeled riding boots.'

This costume may have had its origins in practical requirements (high-heeled boots to keep the foot in the stirrup, chaps to protect the legs against thorns, the handkerchief to keep out dust), but its potential as the exotic regalia of an elite caste is obvious. In other ways too, the cowboy's lifestyle offered up opportunities to myth. The Kansas cowtowns in which the cowboys were paid off at the end of the trail acquired an early reputation for rowdiness. In 1882 readers of *Frank Leslie's* magazine were told that 'When off duty cowboys are a terror in the way they manifest their exuberance of spirits.... They practise a kind of guerrilla warfare during their brief and infrequent holidays in the towns.' Artists such as Rufus Zogbaum, Frederic *Remington and Charles *Russell helped build up this image of violent anarchy. (The reality has of course been hugely exaggerated; during the whole period of the cattle boom the yearly average homicide rate in the Kansas cow towns was only 1.5. Bat Masterson, Wild Bill Hickok and Wyatt Earp between them killed only three men in Kansas.)

Probably the first actual cowboy to lend a hand in the production of the myth was Texas Jack *Omohundro, who had been on a cattle-drive to Kansas before, in 1872, appearing in Chicago with Buffalo Bill in Ned *Buntline's play *The Scouts of the Prairie.* Texas Jack was made a hero of dime novels both by Buntline and by Prentiss *Ingraham. However, his image appears to have been nearer to that of the scout, like Buffalo Bill, than to a true cowboy. Another of Cody's associates, Buck *Taylor, better deserves the title of the first famous cowboy. He had worked on Cody's ranch in Nebraska before he began appearing in Buffalo Bill's Wild West in 1884, billed as 'King of the Cow-Boys'. Taylor and others such as Bronco Bill Bullock and Johnny Baker, the Cowboy Kid, performed a variety of more or less authentic cowboy feats such as bronc riding, steer roping, and trick riding stunts like picking up handkerchiefs from the ground while riding at full speed.

Ingraham soon put Cody's new discovery into dime novels. *Buck Taylor, King of the Cowboys,* appeared in 1887, published by Beadle. In it Taylor does little actual cowboying; instead, he joins the Texas Rangers and is captured by Comanches. This was to prove the pattern, in popular fiction at least: cowboys are presented not as men whose job is to tend cows, but as a class of daring adventurers, footloose and fancy-free.

Ingraham obviously felt that some enhancement of the cowboy's image was necessary. The term 'cowboy' itself, according to Charles Webber, writing in 1854, had originally been used in Texas of men:

'who drove in the cattle of the Mexican rancheros of the Rio Grande border, either by stealth, or after plundering or murdering the herdsman! They were, in short, considered as banditti before the Revolution, and have been properly considered so since. This term "cowboy" was even then – and still more emphatically later – one name for many crimes; since those engaged in it were mostly outlaws....'

In 1881 in a message to Congress President Chester A. Arthur had denounced a band of 'armed desperadoes known as "Cowboys"' who were creating a nuisance in Arizona. John Clay, the Scotsman who was president of the Wyoming Stock Growers Association, wrote that 'the chief obstacle on the range at that time was the cowboys, who were mostly illiterate, uncivilized; who drank and thieved and misbranded cattle....'

And so in *The Cowboy Clan; or, The Tigress of Texas. A Romance of Buck Taylor and his Boys in Buckskin* (1891), Prentiss Ingraham puts into Buck's mouth a general defence of the cowboy's reputation. Protesting that cowboys are 'noble in their treatment of a friend or a fallen foe', the hero goes on: 'We lead a wild life, get hard knocks ... and the settling of a difficulty is an appeal to revolver or knife; but after all we are not as black as we are painted.'

Ingraham's attempt to rehabilitate the cowboy had been anticipated by Theodore *Roosevelt, who in 1888 wrote in *Ranch Life and the Hunting Trail* that cowboys were:

'as hardy and self-reliant as any men who ever breathed – with bronzed, set faces, and keen eyes that look all the world in the face without flinching.... Except while on ... sprees they are quiet, rather self-contained men, perfectly frank and simple.'

It was Roosevelt too who first struck the note of self-righteousness combined with a bravado teetering on the brink of fascist arrogance which has characterized some cinema cowboys:

'There is a high regard for truthfulness and keeping one's word, intense contempt for any kind of hypocrisy, and a hearty dislike of

John C.H. Grabill, 'Mounted Cowboy' (c. 1887)

a man who shirks his work.... The cowboy will not submit tamely to an insult ... nor has he an overwrought fear of shedding blood. He possesses, in fact, few of the emasculated, milk-and-water moralities admired by pseudo-philanthropists, but he does possess, to a very high degree, the stern, manly qualities that are invaluable to a nation.'

It was Roosevelt's friend Owen *Wister who did most to propel the cowboy to the front of the parade of popular heroes. *The Virginian*, published in 1902, was an instant success. Like the cowboys of the dime novels, Wister's hero does little in the way of cow-punching. But in providing him with Southern ancestry, Wister endows him with the gentility necessary if a hero is to rise above the limitations of the dime novel.

Wister's novel fed both the popular imagination, being disseminated in stage and then film versions, and the more serious kind of fiction. Among the important writers of cowboy novels have been Eugene Manlove *Rhodes and Emerson *Hough. In another vein, in addition to Andy Adams there have been a few significant cowboy autobiographers, such as Charlie *Siringo and Will *James.

As far as the cinema is concerned, the most intriguing question is: why should the cowboy, of all the available kinds of West-ern hero, come to be so utterly dominant that the term 'cowboy film' has become synonymous with Western? Part I of this book, in the course of a brief history of the Western on film, has argued for the crucial influence of such early stars as Broncho Billy Anderson, William S. Hart and Tom Mix, who all adopted a cowboy persona. Other factors may have helped to elevate the cowboy to his pre-eminent role. Firstly, the freedom which, however romantically, was associated with the nomadic life of the cattle-drive up the trail from Texas had both a powerful emotional appeal in itself, and was ideally suited to the cinema's requirement for constantly renewable narrative structures. If cowboys were always on the move, their presence in any particular location needed only minimal explanation, and their supposedly free-wheeling occupation permitted them to ride off on adventures at a moment's notice; especially since they were apparently unencumbered by family ties or the constraints of other social institutions. The soldier is subjected to army discipline, the miner must guard his claim, the farmer his crops. The cowboy in reality tended his herd; but in the myth he is free. His much-vaunted individualism, though doubtless the channel through which a deep-seated national fantasy has been expressed, ought also to be seen in relation to Hollywood's need for a hero who retains the minimal necessary plausibility of an occupation, while not having to work at it (the number of Hollywood cowboys who are actually seen to herd cows being small).

Secondly, the cowboy had style. Early accounts pay special attention to his costume. By contrast, apart from the soldier's uniform and the mountain man's suit of animal skins, few occupations out west had a distinctive appearance. The cowboy also had a gun, however little in practice he may have used it. The mountain man and soldier were also armed as a matter of routine; but the cowboy weapon par excellence was the hand-gun, the Colt or other revolver. One reason, surely, why the cowboy reigns supreme in the cinema's primary genre of violence, the Western, is that because his gun is attached to his body, in the way that the mountain man's Kentucky rifle was not, it becomes more truly a part of his nature. The gun is for the cowboy the physical, corporal expression of his moral nature, his 'code'. This means that in the cinema 'action' (i.e. violence) can be guaranteed; sooner or later in the narrative the hero must show himself for what he is; then he will shoot.

Finally, the cowboy also rides a horse. The horse is as much a part of him as his gun. This not only permits the mobility necessary to perform his trail-driving functions; it guarantees the physical movement which is in part the appeal of popular cinema. The original Western hero, the pathfinder drawn by Fenimore *Cooper from such models as Daniel *Boone, was always likely to prove, in both senses, too pedestrian for the cinema as he trudged through the woods on foot. The horse, by contrast, the perfect transport for the free-roaming individual (only lesser mortals ride in wagons), made the cowboy a subject second to none for a cinema of the outdoors.

Crane, Stephen (1871-1900) · Writer and journalist. Crane died young, his tuberculosis worsening after he had reported the Spanish-American War. His most famous novel, *The Red Badge of Courage*, published in 1895, is a story of the Civil War and only marginally a Western, though it made a memorable film. But Crane wrote several Western stories, including 'A Man and Some Others', 'The Blue Hotel' and 'The Bride Comes to Yellow Sky', the last forming half, with Joseph Conrad's *The Secret Sharer*, of the two-part film *Face to Face*. As

Frederic Remington, 'Painting the Town Red' (1888)

one critic has remarked, Crane's stories were producing a subtle, ironic critique of the Western almost before the form had solidified into a genre. In 'The Bride Comes to Yellow Sky', first published in 1898, the stock situation of a showdown between a newly married sheriff and a gunfighter (prefiguring *High Noon*/1952) enables Crane to say with affectionate humour almost all the things about the incompatibility of West and East, legend and reality, wildness and domesticity that Ford or Peckinpah would later build their films on.
The Red Badge of Courage/1951/MGM/d John Huston/lp Audie Murphy · remade for television 1974 · *Face to Face*/1952/ RKO/d Bretaigne Windust/lp Robert Preston, Marjorie Steele

Crazy Horse (c.1841-77) · Leader of the Oglala branch of the Teton Sioux. Crazy Horse (or Tashunca-uitco) was an inspiring military leader who took part in many of the major battles on the plains in the post-Civil War period, including the Fetterman Massacre (1866) and the Wagon-Box Fight (1867). When the army ordered all Indians into reservations during the gold rush in the *Black Hills, Crazy Horse was one of those who refused. His mixed force of Sioux and Cheyenne imposed heavy losses on General Crook at the Battle of the Rosebud, 17 June 1876. A week later Crazy Horse combined with the warriors of *Sitting Bull and Chief *Gall to defeat *Custer at the *Little Big Horn. The next year Crazy Horse surrendered. After rumours that he planned to escape the reservation and restart hostilities he was arrested and taken to Fort Robinson. He resisted being locked in a cell and was bayoneted in the ensuing mêlée.
High Eagle/*Custer's Last Stand*/1936/Stage & Screen/d Elmer Clifton/lp Rex Lease, William Farnum · Anthony Quinn/*They Died with their Boots On*/1941 · Chief Thundercloud/*Buffalo Bill*/1944 · Iron Eyes Cody/*Sitting Bull*/1954/UA/d Sidney Salkow/lp Dale Robertson, J. Carrol Naish · Victor Mature/*Chief Crazy Horse*/1955/U/ d George Sherman/lp John Lund, Ray Danton · Murray Alper/*The Outlaws Is Coming*/1964/COL/d Norman Maurer/lp The Three Stooges · Iron Eyes Cody/*The Great Sioux Massacre*/1965/COL/d Sidney Salkow/lp Joseph Cotten, Phil Carey · Will Sampson/*The White Buffalo*/1977/ Dino de Laurentiis/d J. Lee Thompson/lp Charles Bronson, Kim Novak
Television · George Keymas/*Stories of the Century* · Michael Pate/*Branded* · Michael

Dante/*Custer* · Mike Mazurki/*The Incredible Rocky Mountain Race*

Crockett, Davy (1786-1836) · Frontiersman and politician. More than with most Western heroes, the actual achievements of Crockett are almost buried beneath the encrustations of myth. Much of his career was spent drifting around the frontier in Tennessee. He saw some action in Andrew *Jackson's campaign against the Creek Indians, but missed the major battles. After serving in the Tennessee state legislature he was elected to Congress in 1827. Defeated in 1835, he set out to explore Texas, got caught up in its war with Mexico and met his death at the *Alamo on 6 March 1836.

To further his political career he had collaborated in 1834 with Thomas Chilton on a fanciful autobiography, *A Narrative of the Life of David Crockett, of the State of Tennessee*. His fame spread rapidly and in 1835 appeared the first of a series of almanacs containing apocryphal stories of Crockett's hunting and military exploits. The distinctive contribution of the Crockett persona to the Western is the tall tale, which if he did not invent Crockett certainly popularized as a characteristic form of Western humour. In the almanacs Crockett wrestles bare-handed with panthers and bears and not only scalps Indians but eats them too. Tall tales are placed in the mouth of a Crockett-like figure in Emerson Bennett's *The Prairie Flower* (1849) and are common in later dime novels in which Crockett appears. The frontiersman was also a popular figure on the nineteenth-century stage. Frank Murdoch's play *Davy Crockett, or Be Sure You're Right, Then Go Ahead* opened in 1872 and was a favourite until Frank Mayo, who played Crockett, died in 1896.

In the 20th century Crockett's fame has far outstripped that of comparable frontier characters such as Mike Fink (1770-1823), the Mississippi boatman and mountain man who was also a folk hero; though, as with Kit Carson, Crockett's appearances in the movies are not as frequent as in other media. In the 50s two Disney films created a craze for coonskin caps, which raised the wholesale price of raccoon tails by two thousand per cent. (It is very doubtful whether Crockett ever wore such an item.) A million records of the theme song for *Davy Crockett, King of the Wild Frontier* were sold.
Charles K. French/*Davy Crockett – In Hearts United*/1909/Bison/d Fred Balshofer

James Hackett in the role of Nimrod Wildfire in the play Lion of the West *(1831), a version of the Davy Crockett myth*

Page from a Davy Crockett Almanac (1846)

· Hobart Bosworth/*Davy Crockett*/1910/ Selig/d Frank Boggs · W.E. Browning/ *Davy Crockett Up-to-Date*/1915/Superba/lp Rolinda Bainbridge · A. D. Sears/*Martyrs of the Alamo*/1915/Keystone-Triangle/d Christy Cabanne/lp Walter Long · Dustin Farnum/*Davy Crockett*/1916/Pallas/d William D. Taylor/lp Winifred Kingston ·

Cullen Landis/*Davy Crockett at the Fall of the Alamo*/1926/Sunset/*d* Robert N. Bradbury · Jack Perrin/*The Painted Stallion*/1937/REP/*d* William Witney, Ray Taylor, Alan James/*lp* Hoot Gibson, Sammy McKim · Lane Chandler/*Heroes of the Alamo*/1937/Sunset/*d* Harry Fraser/*lp* Rex Lease · Robert Barrat/*Man of Conquest*/1939/REP/*d* George Nichols Jr./*lp* Richard Dix, Joan Fontaine · George Montgomery/*Davy Crockett, Indian Scout*/1950/UA/*d* Lew Landers/*lp* Ellen Drew · Trevor Bardette/*The Man from the Alamo*/1953 · Arthur Hunnicutt/*The Last Command*/1955/REP/*d* Frank Lloyd/*lp* Sterling Hayden, Ernest Borgnine · James Griffith/*The First Texan*/1956/AA/*d* Byron Haskin/*lp* Joel McCrea · Fess Parker/*Alias Jesse James*/1959/Hope Enterprises/*d* Norman McLeod/*lp* Bob Hope, Rhonda Fleming · John Wayne/*The Alamo*/1960/Batjac/*d* John Wayne/*lp* Richard Widmark, Laurence Harvey, Richard Boone · Also Bill Elliott as *The Son of Davy Crockett*/1941/COL/*d* Lambert Hillyer/*lp* Dub Taylor

Television · Fess Parker/*Davy Crockett* · Brian Keith/*The Alamo: 13 Days to Glory*

Cross-genre films · So rich is the visual repertoire of the Western that other genres have frequently borrowed its trappings. Thus Hollywood found in the early 1930s, the heyday of the gangster film, that in films such as *Gun Smoke* and *Cross Fire* a gangster plot could be given a novel twist if the action was extended on to the range. A couple of years later science fiction was dressed in Western garb in *The Phantom Empire* and *Ghost Patrol*. The end of the 1950s saw a brief vogue for horror films in a Western setting, beginning with *Curse of the Undead*, followed by *Billy the Kid vs. Dracula* and *Jesse James Meets Frankenstein's Daughter*. More recently there have been renewed attempts to marry science fiction to the Western in *Westworld*, *Timerider* and *Outland*, all of which attempt a more complex relation between generic elements of plot and setting. Comedy too often relies on mixing genres. *Blazing Saddles*/1974 literally breaks through the boundary separating one genre from another as the Western bursts through into the musical shooting on the next sound stage. The *locus classicus* of cross-genre remains the two Raoul Walsh films of the 1940s, *High Sierra* (1941) and *Colorado Territory*/1949. The first is unmistakeably a film noir, the second a Western; but the plots and characters are remarkably similar, thus calling into question whether narrative structure can be a defining characteristic of the genre.

Gun Smoke/1931/PAR/*d* Edward Sloman/*lp* Richard Arlen, William Boyd · *Cross Fire*/1933/RKO/*d* Otto Brower/*lp* Tom Keene · *The Phantom Empire*/1935/Mascot/*d* Otto Brower, B. Reeves Eason/*lp* Gene Autry · *Ghost Patrol*/1936/Puritan/*d* Sam Newfield/*lp* Tim McCoy · *Curse of the Undead*/1959/U/*d* Edward Dein/*lp* Eric Fleming · *Billy the Kid vs. Dracula*/1965/Circle/*d* William Beaudine/*lp* John Carradine · *Jesse James Meets Frankenstein's Daughter*/1965/Circle/*d* William Beaudine/*lp* John Lupton · *Westworld*/1973 · *Outland*/1981/Ladd Company/*d* Peter Hyams/*lp* Sean Connery · *Timerider*/1983/Jensen-Farley Pictures/*d* William Dear/*lp* Fred Ward, Belinda Bauer

Curtis, Edward Sheriff (1868-1952) · Photographer. In 1895, after much landscape work, Curtis began to focus on Indians, funding his field work from the profits of his successful Seattle portrait studio. In 1906 the millionaire J. Pierpont Morgan agreed to help finance Curtis to produce the most complete single record of Native American life: *The North American Indian*, twenty volumes of illustrated text and twenty portfolios of photogravures, with a Foreword by Theodore *Roosevelt. The work was published between 1907 and 1930 and for it Curtis produced over forty thousand images of some eighty separate tribes – many of which, like the Pima or the Northwest Coast peoples, differed greatly from the stereotype of the Plains Indian and rarely if ever appeared in Westerns. Curtis made movie footage of Indian ceremonies as early as 1904, and used it, together with music and lantern slides, in an elaborate 'picture-opera' in 1911. In 1914 he completed *In the Land of the Headhunters*, a dramatic feature-length film reconstruction of the lives of the Kwakiutl of British Columbia. Curtis was also employed intermittently as a still or movie cameraman on such Cecil B. DeMille pictures as *The Ten Commandments* (1923) and *The Plainsman*/1936. MG

Curwood, James Oliver (1879-1927) · Writer. Curwood was one of the few Western writers whose fame placed his name above the title of a film. He became virtually synonymous with stories of the Far North in which handsome, morally upright Mounties pursued their man. His work, which now seems excessively romantic and dated, forms the basis of numerous films of the teens and

Gene Autry battles it out with Muranians in Phantom Empire

Edward Curtis, 'The Wedding Party – Qagyhuhl Indians'

20s, and of many Poverty Row pictures of the 30s and 40s, as well as occasional bigger productions.

Films include: *God's Country and the Woman*/1916/Vitagraph/*d* Rollin S. Sturgeon/*lp* William Duncan · remade as *God's Country and the Law*/1921/Arrow/*d* Sidney Olcott/*lp* Fred C. Jones · remade as *God's Country and the Woman*/1936/WB/*d* William Keighley/*lp* George Brent · *Back to God's Country*/1919/First National/*d* David M. Hartford/*lp* Nell Shipman · remade 1927/U/*d* Irvin Willat/*lp* Renée Adorée · remade 1953/U/*d* Joseph Pevney/*lp* Rock Hudson, Steve Cochran · *The River's End*/1920/First National/*d* Marshall Neilan/*lp* Charles Bickford · remade 1930/WB/*d* Michael Curtiz/*lp* Charles Bickford, ZaSu Pitts · remade 1940/WB/*d* Ray Enright/*lp* Dennis Morgan · *The Golden Snare*/1921/First National/*d* David M. Hartford/*lp* Lewis Stone, Wallace Beery · *Valley of Silent Men*/1922/PAR/*d* Frank Borzage/*lp* Lew Cody · *The Alaskan*/1924/PAR/*d* Herbert Brenon/*lp* Thomas Meighan · *Steele of the Royal Mounted*/1925/Vitagraph/*d* David Smith/*lp* Bert Lytell · *The Ancient Highway*/1925/PAR/*d* Irvin Willat/*lp* Jack Holt · *The Flaming Forest*/1926/MGM/*d* Reginald Barker/*lp* Renée Adorée · *Prisoners of the Storm*/1926/U/*d* Lynn Reynolds/*lp* House Peters · *The Country Beyond*/1936/FOX/*d* Eugene Ford/*lp* Rochelle Hudson · *Call of the Yukon*/1938/REP/*d* B. Reeves Eason/*lp* Richard Arlen · *The Wolf Hunters*/1949/MON/*d* Budd Boetticher/*lp* Kirby Grant · *Call of the Klondike*/1950/MON/*d* Frank McDonald/*lp* Kirby Grant
Television · *Saturday Roundup*

Custer, George Armstrong (1839-76) · The most famous, or notorious, soldier in the history of the West. After a stormy career at West Point Custer had a highly successful Civil War, distinguishing himself at Gettysburg and ending the war as the army's youngest major-general. He was then assigned to the 7th Cavalry, which was engaged in a series of campaigns against the plains Indians. Court-martialled and suspended from duty for a year for harsh treatment of his troops, Custer was reinstated in time to lead his regiment at the so-called Battle of the *Washita in present-day Oklahoma. There on 27 November 1868, with the band playing Custer's favourite tune 'Garry Owen', the 7th Cavalry charged through heavy snow against a sleeping Cheyenne village. More than a hundred men, women

General Custer (l.) posing with Grand Duke Alexis of Russia (c.1872)

Custer's Last Stand: Dustin Farnum in Flaming Frontier

Custer's Last Stand: Errol Flynn in They Died with their Boots On

and children were massacred.

In 1874 the regiment was transferred to Dakota, after the discovery of gold in the *Black Hills, an area reserved to the Sioux by treaty, had led to an influx of miners and consequent Indian retaliation. A full-scale campaign against the Indians of the northern plains developed. The 7th Cavalry found themselves in Montana pursuing a large

force of Sioux and Cheyenne. Here, in the valley of the *Little Big Horn on 25 June 1876, Custer's battalion, which he had foolishly allowed to become detached from the rest of his command, was surrounded and destroyed, with the loss of the commander and 200 other men.

On his death Custer was hailed as a hero and his 'Last Stand' became the subject of many adulatory paintings. Later historical writing has revised this view, emphasizing his recklessness, arrogance and mania for publicity. (Custer prided himself on his dandified appearance – he liked to pose for photographs – and in 1874, at the age of only thirty-five, he published his autobiography, *My Life on the Plains*.) His image in films has undergone a similar change. We have had the dashing hero as represented by Ronald Reagan and Errol Flynn (in the latter case, not without a hint of instability), and the unyielding martinet portrayed by Henry Fonda in *Fort Apache* (the story of Custer in everything but name). *7th Cavalry*, directed by Joseph H. Lewis in 1956, is a halfway house; Randolph Scott is an army officer who is a friend of Custer (who does not appear in the film) and defends his reputation after the massacre, yet the evidence of Custer's arrogance and incompetence presented by Scott's fellow-officers is all but overwhelming. Custer's reputation could hardly be expected to survive the wave of anti-militarism which followed the Vietnam war in the late 1960s. By the time we get to *Little Big Man* in 1970 the only way to make sense of Custer is to portray him in the grip of a deep psychosis. (See Plate 14)
Custer's Last Stand (On the Little Big Horn)/1909/Selig/*d* Frank Boggs/*lp* Hobart

Bosworth, Tom Mix · *On the Little Big Horn*/1910/Nestor · *Custer's Last Stand*/1910/Chicago Film · Francis Ford/*Custer's Last Raid*/1912/Bison/*d* Francis Ford/*lp* William Eagleshirt · *The Big Horn Massacre*/1913/Kalem/*d* William H. West/*lp* Marin Sais, Jack Hoxie · *Campaigning with Custer*/1913/Bison · *Custer's Last Scout*/1915/Bison/*d* Henry McRae/*lp* William Clifford · Dwight Crittenden/*Bob Hampton of Placer*/1921/First National/*d* Marshall Neilan/*lp* James Kirkwood · Dustin Farnum/*The Flaming Frontier*/1926/U/*d* Edward Sedgwick/*lp* Hoot Gibson · John Beck/*General Custer at the Little Big Horn*/1926/Sunset/*d* Harry L. Fraser/*lp* Roy Stewart · *Spoilers of the West*/1927/MGM/*d* W.S. Van Dyke/*lp* Tim McCoy · William Desmond/*The Last Frontier*/1932/RKO/*d* Spencer Bennet/*lp* Lon Chaney Jr. · Clay Clement/*The World Changes*/1933/WB/*d* Mervyn LeRoy/*lp* Paul Muni, Mary Astor · Frank McGlynn Jr./*Custer's Last Stand*/1936/Weiss-Mintz/*d* Elmer Clifton/*lp* Rex Lease, William Farnum · John Miljan/*The Plainsman*/1936 · Roy Barcroft/*The Oregon Trail*/1939/U/*d* Ford Beebe, Saul A. Goodkind/*lp* Johnny Mack Brown · Paul Kelly/*Wyoming*/1940/MGM/*d* Richard Thorpe/*lp* Wallace Beery · Ronald Reagan/*Santa Fe Trail*/1940 · Addison Richards/*Badlands of Dakota*/1941/U/*d* Alfred E. Green/*lp* Robert Stack, Richard Dix · Errol Flynn/*They Died with their Boots On*/1941 · Henry Fonda (in a Custer-type role)/*Fort Apache*/1948 · James Millican/*Warpath*/1951/PAR/*d* Byron Haskin/*lp* Edmond O'Brien, Dean Jagger · Sheb Wooley/*Bugles in the Afternoon*/1951/WB/*d* Roy Rowland/*lp* Ray Milland, Hugh Marlowe · Douglas Kennedy/*Sitting Bull*/1954/UA/*d* Sidney Salkow/*lp* Dale Robertson, J. Carrol Naish · Britt Lomond/*Tonka*/1958/Buena Vista/*d* Lewis Foster/*lp* Sal Mineo, Phil Carey · Andrew Duggan (in a Custer-type role)/*The Glory Guys*/1965 · Phil Carey/*The Great Sioux Massacre*/1965/COL/*d* Sidney Salkow/*lp* Joseph Cotten · Leslie Neilsen/*The Plainsman*/1966/U/*d* David Lowell/*lp* Don Murray, Guy Stockwell · Robert Shaw/*Custer of the West*/1966/Cinerama/*d* Robert Siodmak/*lp* Mary Ure, Jeffrey Hunter · Richard Mulligan/*Little Big Man*/1970 · Marcello Mastroianni/*Touche pas la femme blanche*/1973/Fr/*d* Marco Ferreri/*lp* Catherine Deneuve, Michel Piccoli · Lincoln Tate/*The Legend of the Lone Ranger*/1981/ITC/*d* William A. Fraker/*lp* Klinton Spilsbury

Television · Whit Bissel/*Cheyenne* · Barry Atwater/*Cheyenne* · Robert Lansing/*Branded* · Wayne Maunder/*Custer* · James Olsen/*The Court Martial of George Armstrong Custer* · Keir Dullea/*The Legend of the Golden Gun*

D

Dalton gang · Outlaws. Like the James and Younger gangs before them, the Daltons were a product of the turbulence of the Kansas-Missouri border in the post-Civil War period, though in the movies the Daltons lack the class of these other outlaw bands, never quite rising above the level of the B-feature. After their older brother Frank was killed while serving as a peace officer, Grattan (1865-92), Robert (1870-92)

The Dalton gang after the raid on Coffeyville

and Emmett (1871-1937) also took up as lawmen, but soon found horse-stealing more profitable. With a gang which included Bill *Doolin, the Dalton brothers then graduated to train and bank hold-ups in Kansas and Oklahoma in 1892. Near the end of that year they planned a double bank raid at Coffeyville, Kansas, but their arrival was expected and the gang was cut to pieces. Grat and Bob were killed; Emmett was captured and imprisoned. A fourth brother, Bill (1866-95), later also took up outlawry and joined the new Bill Doolin gang (Doolin had

missed the Coffeyville raid). He was shot by a posse while hiding at his home.

When Emmett came out of jail in 1907 he became a crusader for penal reform. He also made some motion pictures which were intended to give a realistic portrayal of the West. *The Last Stand of the Dalton Boys* (1912) portrays the brothers' careers. Presumably it was successful since according to Kevin Brownlow, whose book *The War, the West and the Wilderness* has a chapter on Emmett Dalton, someone took the trouble to make a fake version of it in 1914. Emmett Dalton then remade his film, more ambitiously, as *Beyond the Law*/1918/Southern Feature Films, in which he appeared not only as himself but as his brothers too. Emmett claimed the film 'depicts something real and typical of western life.' He further contributed to his fame by appearing in Pawnee Bill *Lillie's live Wild West show.

Later screen versions of the Daltons' story were part of the vogue for tales of outlawry set off by the success of *Jesse James*/1939. They are usually sympathetic; as with the accounts of the James and Younger gangs, the rapacity of the railroads and northern carpetbaggers is blamed for the brothers' descent into crime.

Brian Donlevy (Grat), Broderick Crawford (Bob), Stuart Erwin (Ben), Frank Albertson (Emmett)/*When the Daltons*

Rode/1940/U/*d* George Marshall/*lp*
Randolph Scott, Kay Francis · *In Old
Oklahoma*/1943/REP/*d* Albert S. Rogell/*lp*
John Wayne · Alan Curtis (Emmett), Kent
Taylor (Bob), Lon Chaney Jr. (Grat),
Noah Beery Jr. (Ben)/*The Daltons Ride
Again*/1945/U/*d* Ray Taylor/*lp* Thomas
Gomez · Steve Brodie (Bob), Phil Warren
(Grat), William Moss (Bill)/*Badman's
Territory*/1946/RKO/*d* Tim Whelan/*lp*
Randolph Scott · Lex Barker (Emmett),
Walter Reed (Bob), Michael Harvey
(Grat)/*Return of the Bad Men*/1948/RKO/*d*
Ray Enright/*lp* Randolph Scott · Robert
Lowery (Bob)/*The Dalton Gang*/1949/
Lippert/*d* Ford Beebe/*lp* Don Barry · *The
Daltons' Women*/1950/PRC/*d* Thomas
Carr/*lp* Lash LaRue, Al St John · Tony
Curtis ('Kit' Dalton)/*Kansas Raiders*/1950/
U/*d* Ray Enright/*lp* Audie Murphy, Brian
Donlevy · Noah Beery Jr. (Bob), Palmer
Lee (Grat), Rand Brooks (Emmett),
William Reynolds (Will)/*The Cimarron
Kid*/1951/U/*d* Budd Boetticher/*lp* Audie
Murphy · Scott Brady (Bob), Ray Teal
(Emmett)/*Montana Belle*/1951/RKO/*d* Allan
Dwan/*lp* Jane Russell, George Brent ·
James Griffith (Bob), William Tannen
(Emmett), John Cliff (Grat), Bill Phipps
(Bill)/*Jesse James vs. the Daltons*/1953/COL/*d*
William Castle/*lp* Brett King · Merry
Anders, Lisa Davis, Penny Edwards, Sue
George/*The Dalton Girls*/1957/Bel-Air/*d*
Reginald Le Borg · *The Dalton That Got
Away*/1960/Jimmy Salvador/*lp* Michael
Connors · Joe Bolton (Bob)/*The Outlaws
Is Coming*/1964/COL/*d* Norman Maurer/*lp*
The Three Stooges · Scott Glenn (Bill)/
Cattle Annie and Little Britches/1980/UA/*d*
Lamont Johnson/*lp* Burt Lancaster, Rod
Steiger
Television · Jim Davis, Forrest Tucker/
Death Valley Days · Myron Healey, Fess
Parker, Robert Bray/*Stories of the Century* ·
Robert Lansing, Larry Pennell/*The
Outlaws* · Robert Conrad (Bob), Richard
Jaeckel (Grat), Tim Matheson (Emmett)/
The Last Day · Cliff Potts (Bob), Larry
Wilcox (Emmett), Randy Quaid (Grat),
Mills Watson (Bill), Don Collier (Frank)/
The Last Ride of the Dalton Gang · Jesse
Vint (Bob), Alan Vint (Grat)/*Belle Starr*

Dancing · In musical Westerns like *Seven
Brides for Seven Brothers*/1954 dance is a
spectacle in itself. But no one uses dance to
such powerful thematic effect as John Ford.
In *My Darling Clementine*/1946 Wyatt Earp's
waltzing of Clementine on the floor of the
half-built church in the middle of the desert

is a triumph of civilization over the wilderness. In *The Searchers*/1956 and *Two Rode
Together*/1961 the interruption of a dance
signals the social disorder which is caused by
racial hostility. When Clint Eastwood uses a
dance at the end of *The Outlaw Josey Wales*/
1976 in order to knit together his strange
little community, the Fordian association is
irresistible; as indeed it is when the farmers
dance to the tune of 'I'm leaving Cheyenne'
in *Shane*/1952, or the immigrants dance on
roller skates in *Heaven's Gate*/1980.

Deadwood Dick · A dime novel hero,
created by Edward L. Wheeler in the 1880s
in such literary productions as *Deadwood
Dick's Protégée; or, Baby Bess, the Girl Gold
Miner. A Tale of Pistol Pocket* (1887). His
character, manly and dashing, contributed
to the prototype on which the literary
representation of Buffalo Bill was founded.
He is frequently the consort of Calamity
Jane.

Dentists · Three dentists have made a
notable contribution to the Western. Doc
*Holliday abandoned dentistry for gam-
bling, drinking and dry desert air. Zane
*Grey made the switch from dentistry to
literature. And Bob Hope, as Painless Potter,
gives up his profession for the toothsome
Jane Russell in *The Paleface*/1948/PAR/*d*
Norman Z. McLeod.

Derringer · A compact, single-shot pistol of
large bore with a short barrel and distinctive
bird's head handle, originally designed by
Henry Deringer (*sic*) of Philadelphia (1786-
1868), though later also produced by the
*Colt and Remington companies. As a
weapon small enough to be concealed, its
possession is, in Westerns, considered
appropriate only to gamblers, women and
those who don't fight fair. This is exemplified in a routine Western such as *Texas
Lady*/1955/RKO/*d* Tim Whelan/*lp* Claudette
Colbert, in which gambler Barry Sullivan
shoots the local gunfighter with a Derringer
which has the added refinement of a spring-
holster. The gun achieved notoriety when
John Wilkes Booth used one to assassinate
Abraham Lincoln.

Desert · Henry Nash Smith's magisterial
book *Virgin Land* (1950) traces the history of
the antinomy of desert and garden which
governed so much nineteenth-century
thinking about the West. (This antinomy is
both symbolized and transcended, in the
way that Claude Lévi-Strauss says myth

*A double-barrelled Derringer made by the
Remington Company*

*John Wayne presents Vera Miles with a
cactus rose in* The Man Who Shot Liberty
Valance

manages contradictions, by the delicate
image which Ford employs in *The Man Who
Shot Liberty Valance*/1962, that of the cactus
rose.) Originating in the early 1800s, the
notion that everything west of the Mississippi was the Great American Desert proved
extraordinarily resistant to empirical evidence. It was only finally abandoned when
promoters, including railroad companies,
discovered an interest in declaring the entire
West to be ideal for agriculture. In the last
quarter of the 19th century, painters such as
Thomas *Moran and photographers such as
Timothy *O'Sullivan revealed just how
spectacular desert scenery could be.

In the cinema, desert landscapes have
proved as popular with film-makers as ver-
dant ones, at least as far back as D.W.
Griffith's *The Last Drop of Water*/1911. The
deserts of Arizona, Nevada and California,
conveniently adjacent to Hollywood, are

still largely untouched, and so, unlike the present-day prairie, allow the film-maker an untramelled view.

Diaz, Porfirio (1830-1915) · Mexican dictator who served with *Juárez in the war against *Maximilian. He became effective ruler of Mexico in 1876 and remained in power until overthrown in 1911 in the events which ushered in the turbulent and proto-revolutionary period of *Villa and *Zapata.
Carlos Rivas/*The Undefeated*/1969/FOX/d
Andrew V. McLaglen/*lp* John Wayne, Rock Hudson

Dime novels · While factual information about the American frontier and West is offered in frontier literature prior to the Civil War, a mythic vision comes to dominate as the male adventurer immerses himself in a wilderness experience and learns – if in the receptive state of mind best exemplified by *Cooper's Natty Bumppo – moral truths which renew his resolve, strengthen his social duty and clarify his conscience. With the important exception of Cooper's Leatherstocking Tales, however, frontier literature on the eve of the Civil War does not question or test the values and attitudes associated with mainstream American culture's faith in *Manifest Destiny. Rather, as one contemporary observer complained, frontier literature degenerated into 'tomahawks and wigwams, sharp-shooting and hard fights, log cabins, rough speech, daredevil boldness, bear-hunting and cornhusking, prairie flowers, bandits, lynch-law and no-law-at-all miscellaneously mixed into 25 cents novels.' Whatever the accuracy of this observer's catalogue, there is no doubt regarding the appropriateness of his complaint: except for Emerson Bennett's *The Prairie Flower* (1849), the most popular literature about the West published in the later part of the 19th century appeared in the various dime novel or pulp magazine formats (newspaper, or 5" x 7" pamphlet of 100 pages, or 8" x 12" magazine of 16 to 32 pages).

Inexpensive serial fiction designed for a growing mass audience was a staple of the publishing industry in the United States prior to Beadle and Adams's publication in 1860 of the first dime novel – Ann Stephens' *Malaeska: The Indian Wife of the White Hunter* – but with the invention of the steam rotary press and the development of improved marketing and distributing techniques the dime novel achieved tremendous popular success. Edward *Ellis' *Seth Jones: or*

An early Beadle dime novel

the Captives of the Frontier (1860), for instance, eventually sold, sources estimate, more than 600,000 copies. Containing between thirty and fifty thousand words, the dime novels varied in price (5¢ to 25¢), were often reprinted with different titles and, while designed for the juvenile and working-class audience, were read by nearly all segments of American society. The major publishers (Beadle and Adams, Frank Tousey, Street and Smith) at one point were publishing nearly one hundred different series of novels devoted to such adventurous types as pirates, desert brigands and urban detectives, and fully three-quarters of the titles published in these series featured Western types such as the backwoodsman, scout, plainsman, outlaw and cowboy.

As a material cultural artefact the dime novel, like printed matter in general, does not figure prominently in Western films. There are of course exceptions, since one of the Western's infrequent concerns in the last couple of decades has been with the role of the press in distorting history or in fashioning legendary reputations. One thinks here of *The Man Who Shot Liberty Valance*/1962, *Buffalo Bill and the Indians or Sitting Bull's History Lesson*/1976 or of the scene in *The Left Handed Gun*/1957 when the jailed Billy the Kid (Paul Newman) reads dime novels about his sensational life. Nevertheless, the dime novel's importance to the Western lies more in how its action-adventure narrative pattern, its characterization of frontier types and its use of the

western landscape created a West of the imagination that influenced the film genre's form, style and content.

As Daryl Jones and other students of the dime novel have noted, the western setting prior to 1875 was used paradoxically to affirm both utilitarian and primitivist views of nature. The gleaning of an unused nature's spoils by pioneer settlers was in novel after novel viewed as both a moral and patriotic obligation, one whose fulfilment forecasted the nation's greatness. On the other hand, accolades to the sublime beauty of an unexploited wilderness were voiced in several novels. Characteristically, dime novels resolved the conflict of visions in the manner of Ellis' *Seth Jones*. Here a Daniel Boone- or Natty Bumppo-like figure leads a band of settlers into a landscape clearing destined to be a pastoral utopia and yet surrounded by a sublime wilderness landscape. The transformation of the landscape into an agrarian utopia affirmed a benevolent historical process; the continuing presence of an untouched landscape on the horizon served to assuage any anxieties felt over the exploitation of the land and the dispossessing of the native people's title to it. Further, the settlers themselves were shown to be regenerated through hard work and sacrifice, by living in a frontier community ideally situated between the city and the raw wilderness, where individual freedom and equality coexisted with social harmony. This utopian pastoral vision reappears in numerous later B-Westerns and is, essentially, the vision parodied by Mel Brooks's *Blazing Saddles*/1974.

In dime novels published after 1875 the western landscape is portrayed more as a killing ground, a badlands whose openness and desolation serve as a visual allegory for the hero's perilous journey either to rescue a young woman, a companion, a gold shipment or payroll – or to capture a badman or gang of thieves. The rock-strewn landscapes, massive geological formations, dry river-beds and lonely trails harbouring outlaws and renegades function in these later dime novels to highlight the human actors struggling in the foreground for control of the region's bounty – and future. Thus, whereas early dime novels focused on the settlers' triumph over both nature and Indians, later ones emphasize both the social problems (gambling; political corruption; blackmail; theft; land hunger) besetting newly established frontier towns or mining camps and the actions taken to resolve them, as in the various Deadwood Dick stories in which the hero rids the landscape of corrupt politicians, greedy land barons and treacherous law officers.

Within the western setting two types of heroes, both of whom function as agents of civilization, dominate the early dime novels. The violent, crude Indian-hater who descends from Robert M. Bird's *Nick of the Woods* (1837) and is a fixture in such Westerns as *The Searchers*/1956 represents one type. However, the more prominent hero descends from Cooper's Natty Bumppo. Seth Jones, for instance, is one of nature's noblemen yet, like Natty, is an irascible, eccentric and older backwoodsman who speaks in dialect and serves as a guide to pioneers. What is interesting is how the dime novel formula evolved so that such an adventure figure could appear also as a romantic lead. In what would later become a convention in Western films of the 1930s and 1940s, in dime novels such as *Old King Brady and Billy the Kid* (1890) a younger, more genteel hero named Harry Ringwood gallops across the sagebrush in pursuit of a dastardly Kid, aided by the mature wisdom of Old King Brady, the experienced man of the western woods or prairie. Further, the capable western hero would occasionally be given a sidekick in the Gabby Hayes or Al St John mould who would bear the comic burden of the story and speak in dialect, thus again allowing the westerner to attain a more heroic and romantic status.

Eventually, in the last two decades of the century, dime novelists like Prentiss *Ingraham portrayed such historical figures as Kit *Carson, Davy *Crockett and Buffalo Bill *Cody as characters who synthesized the westerner's wilderness freedom, wit and survival skills with the easterner's gentlemanly traits. Such a transformation, one that we later see clearly represented in Gary Cooper's portrayal of the Virginian in 1929, is in part an aesthetic consequence conditioned by the novel's need to streamline its form, to shift from the motif of the manly, handsome hero disguised as venerable, buckskin-clad patriarch in order to accomplish his tasks. Yet it seems equally clear that this familiar type of Western hero – whose survival depends not upon wealth, name, formal education or connections but upon his native intelligence and physical abilities – was popular and became an integral part of the Western formula for two reasons: because his actions reaffirmed faith in the power of the individual to affect change; and because his rising status reaffirmed faith in a society whose class structure was not yet rigidly set. Further, because of the influence of William Cody's Wild West, dime novelists also intensified the hero's theatrical style by dwelling on his flashy attire and his courtly bearing during such chivalric exploits as rescuing young women from danger or fighting gun duels in the open street.

The early dime novel hero was involved in initiation stories which combined both adventure and romance in plots featuring the good guys' violent actions to aid society's westward advance. After 1875, however, dime novel plots typically focus on the western landscape as an arena for the hero's individual actions to abolish economic and/or sexual oppression. In either case, the complexities inherent in Fenimore Cooper's questioning – but not, to be sure, undermining – the westward-moving course of empire are reduced in the dime novel to a simple opposition of clearly-defined good and evil forces. Instead of moving further westward or lamenting the loss of wilderness freedoms, the dime novel hero acts single-mindedly as a purifying force purging a fledgling frontier community of its evil (however that is defined), just as William S. Hart's character will act in the classic *Hell's Hinges*/1916. While the conflict between good and evil ultimately requires violence, the hero's code – what in fact will become the sanitized cowboy code promoted by Gene Autry and Roy Rogers – is aligned with the community's interests and does not represent an anarchical threat to their wholesome middle-class existence. The hero is neither so totally pure as to refrain from a violent response to those threatening his code (although, as in *The Iliad*, suspense is occasionally created by delaying the hero's aggressive response), nor so totally depraved as to become obsessed with power (and it is often offered to him). Instead, he defines the classic western protagonist whose departure from society, ritual testing at the hand of nature, triumph over a deadly adversary and return to the community regenerated by his action resolve in fantasy the anxieties and preoccupations of the reading or viewing audience.

The service this fantasy performed for late nineteenth-century reading audiences witnessing the transformation of the United States into an urban-industrial state with imperialist ambitions is obvious. What is not so obvious perhaps is how the popularity of the dime novel's western adventures transformed what was heretofore children's literature into a *boy's* literature advocating daring, courage, and flamboyant physicality. And, in the process, the dime novel also provided the basic format (chase-pursuit-capture), the conventional plot conflicts (civilization versus savagery), the allegorical use of setting and the conventional, albeit prejudicial, racial iconography (of Irish, Jews, Indians and Mexicans) that appear in classic Western films before 1960. The Western hero's magical appearance against the landscape or sky; the tenderfoot and sidekick; the helpless role assigned to women; the use of the vernacular – these and other motifs familiar to us from countless popular Westerns become integral parts of the dime novel's highly imaginative portrait of the West.

The point to be made in conclusion, however, is that the dime novels' devotion to adventure and spectacle and to an unreflective, action-oriented hero does not function to intensify the hero's shifting mental state, his interior life as he confronts the hard facts of survival, as he negotiates the boundaries or discovers the problematic relationships between self and society, between race and race, between male and female and between civil law and moral justice. Instead, whatever interest we can glean from the dime novel and its Western film and television offspring results rather from the suspense surrounding *how* the hero will survive – not *whether* he will survive, and certainly not whether he himself wonders about the certainty of his convictions. Given this perspective on the film genre provided by the dime novel, then, we can better locate the power of such later 'adult' Westerns as, say, *High Noon*/1952 or the under-rated *Garden of Evil* (1954). In these examples of the 'best' Westerns those pivotal, fleeting moments when the hero pauses to consider why the pattern of action is unfolding in just this way come into view. That is to say, during such moments the Western confronts the luminous questions inherent in, but only occasionally developed by, its dime novel antecedents: just why is it that Fate works to choose the strong to defend the good and the weak; that Evil, however defined, triumphs only in the short run; that one must often choose between loyalty to friendship and defence of justice. What happens, then, is that such Westerns leave the genre's dime-novel-inspired stress on self-sufficient, certain actions done spontaneously and suggest instead that even the pristine, open landscape and stereotyped characters of the Western are seen occasionally as through a glass darkly, and that the

hero must act not only out of a true sense of self but also out of his best self. That one's true self is not necessarily one's best self occasions in the Western a sense of wonder as well as a sense of beauty. ST
For further reference see the works by Daryl Jones and Richard Slotkin cited in the general bibliography · *Garden of Evil/ 1954/FOX/d* Henry Hathaway/*lp* Gary Cooper, Susan Hayward

Doctors · So persistent is the stereotype of the drunken doctor in the Western that its origins surely predate the genre. Thomas Mitchell in *Stagecoach/*1939 provides the definitive portrayal. The scene where he sobers up to attend a woman patient is repeated in *My Darling Clementine/*1946, with Victor Mature as the more tragically drunken Doc Holliday. In *The Man Who Shot Liberty Valance/*1962 Ken Murray appears as another drunken doctor. He calls for whiskey, ostensibly for the patient, and swigs it himself. This gag, old at the time, was good enough for James Stewart to use again in *Cheyenne Autumn/*1964 when, as Wyatt Earp, he is about to operate on the cowboy he has just shot in the foot. Curiously, the same joke appears in *Billy the Kid vs. Dracula*. Here the whiskey-swigging doctor is played by Olive Carey. Since she and her co-star in the picture, John Carradine, were both members of the Ford stock company, one suspects a Fordian influence. But Ford

had no monopoly on drunken doctors. Gabby Hayes has a go in *Dark Command*; the role is dusted down and recycled fifteen years later in *Great Day in the Morning/*1956 and another fifteen years after that in *Support Your Local Gunfighter/*1971. Of course doctors don't have to be drunk or comic. Altogether more worthy medics are John McIntire in *The Tin Star/*1957, Gary Cooper in *The Hanging Tree/*1959 and William Holden in *The Horse Soldiers/*1959.
*Dark Command/*1940/REP/*d* Raoul Walsh/ *lp* John Wayne, Claire Trevor · *Billy the Kid vs. Dracula/*1965/Circle/*d* William Beaudine

Dodge City · The most celebrated of all the Kansas cow towns. Situated on the *Atchison, Topeka and Santa Fe railroad, Dodge first boomed as a centre of the trade in buffalo hides, millions of which were shipped east in the early 1870s. By 1876 most of the buffalo were gone and Dodge began shipping cattle instead. Its heyday lasted barely ten years. Opposition to the cattle trade by local farmers had a more dampening effect than the phalanxes of reforming spinsters who troop through the movies. The huge herds from Texas trampled local crops and carried splenic fever, endemic in the south; eventually they were discouraged by fences and quarantine legislation.

Dodge City may for a time have been as lively as its reputation suggests (it was repor-

ted in 1879 that for a mere 700 residents the town boasted fourteen saloons, two dance-halls and forty-seven prostitutes). But it probably owes its pre-eminence to the fact that several of the most charismatic figures in the history of the West spent time there. Bat *Masterson was sheriff 1877-80 and for part of this period Wyatt *Earp served as assistant marshal. Both were members of the so-called Dodge City Gang, which controlled local politics and the liquor, gambling and prostitution trades. When another member, the gambler Luke *Short, got into trouble with reformers in 1883 he sent for his friends Masterson, Earp and Doc *Holliday to help him in what became known as the Dodge City War, though in truth not a shot was fired. *Dodge City/*1939 is the most wholehearted celebration of the legend, though its characters have fictional names.

Donner party · The single most horrific episode in the history of the West. The Donner party of emigrants, some eighty-seven men, women and children, left Independence, Missouri in April 1846, heading for California and led by George and Jacob Donner. Delays and arguments along the route, plus a fateful decision to take an imperfectly surveyed short-cut, meant that the party did not begin their climb over the Sierra Nevada till the end of October. That year the winter storms came early; one night it snowed heavily, the passes were blocked and the Donner party snowed in at Truckee (now Donner) Lake.

By December it was clear someone had to go for help if the whole party was not to die of hunger, so fifteen of their number (five women and ten men, including their two Indian guides) set off. They had taken a mere six days' food for a journey that, as a result of violent storms, was to take a whole month. Soon people began to die along the trail; their companions, now literally starving to death, decided there was no alternative but to eat them. The two Indians refused to touch human flesh so were shot and themselves eaten. Eventually seven of the original fifteen reached help. But it was February before rescuers could get to those still trapped in the mountains and when they did it was to discover that they too had been driven to cannibalism. Of the original party of eighty-nine, only forty-five survived the ordeal. The full story is told in George R. Stewart, *Ordeal by Hunger* (New York: Houghton Mifflin, 1960). The only attempt to put these events on screen is, surprisingly in view of the horrors of the tale, a television

Dodge City in the 1880s

production, *Donner Pass: The Road to Survival*.

Doolin, Bill (1858-96) · Outlaw. A member of the *Dalton gang who set up in business for himself when they were destroyed in the Coffeyville raid in 1892. 'The Oklahombres', as Doolin's gang called itself, committed a number of bank and train robberies in Oklahoma before Doolin was captured by sheriff Bill *Tilghman. He escaped but was eventually killed by a posse.
Robert Armstrong/*Return of the Bad Men*/1948/RKO/d Ray Enright/lp Randolph Scott · Randolph Scott/*The Doolins of Oklahoma*/1949/COL/d Gordon Douglas/lp George Macready, John Ireland · Burt Lancaster/*Cattle Annie and Little Britches*/1980/UA/d Lamont Johnson/lp Rod Steiger · Frenchy LeBoyd/*Ride a Wild Stud*/1969/Vega International/d Revilo Ekard/lp Hale Williams
Television · Bo Hopkins/*The Last Ride of the Dalton Gang*

Dragged by a horse · One of the most dangerous stunts in the cinema, in which a rider falls from a horse and is then dragged along behind with one foot caught in the stirrup. The stuntman wears a close-fitting jacket, from which a wire goes down the trouser leg and on to the horse's stirrup, thus reducing strain on ankles and hips. Nevertheless the danger to the head remains considerable.

As Jean Wagner remarks in *Le Western* (Paris: 10/18, 1966), given how much the Western has invested in the noble partnership of rider and mount there's a particular indignity in a man being dragged along behind a horse. Thus the action often occurs when the high and mighty are brought low or as part of a hero's humiliation. Wagner's example is James Stewart in *The Man from Laramie*/1955, but it happens also to Lionel Barrymore in *Duel in the Sun*/1946, Richard Rust in *Comanche Station*/1959, Richard Boone and company in *Rio Conchos*/1964, Jason Robards in *Comes a Horseman*/1978 and to one of Clint Eastwood's opponents in *Pale Rider*/1985. There's a typically Sam Peckinpah variation in *The Wild Bunch*/1969, where Angel is dragged along behind a car filled with whores and jeering soldiers.

Drama · The American theatre found a strong indigenous voice only when it stopped relying wholly on productions of European plays and discovered the frontier as subject-matter. For most of the 19th century, the frontier came to the stage via its literary manifestations: the story of western drama, therefore, follows in large part the story of western fiction. Through its emphases and physical conventions, however, melodrama was a formative influence on Western films.

As with other developments in the Western, James Fenimore *Cooper's Leatherstocking Tales (1823-41) played an important role, being adapted for the stage frequently from the 1820s onwards. It was one of Cooper's imitators, however, who gave western drama its greatest boost. In 1837, Robert Montgomery Bird published *Nick of the Woods*, a novel written partly in imitation and partly in refutation of Cooper's work. The main figure, Nathan Slaughter or 'the Jibbenainosay', is a sensationalized version of Natty Bumppo, Cooper's frontier hero caught between two races and two times. Nathan is much more spectacularly divided, spending half his waking hours as a gentle Quaker woodsman and the other half as a savage Indian killer. The Indians in Bird's novel are unregenerately evil, designed to give the lie to Cooper's 'noble savage'. This explosive concoction was adapted by Louisa Medina Hamblin in 1838, under the title *The Jibbenainosay*, and became the most successful American melodrama of the first half of the 19th century. Its emphasis on exciting action, breathtaking rescues and blood-curling combat also set the tone for a generation of western plays. Depending largely on dime novel material, western drama flourished throughout the century, making prominent the heroic frontiersman, the eccentric sidekick and the villainous red man, who survive into the modern period as movie stereotypes.

Later in the 19th century, the fiction of Bret *Harte was adapted for the stage, adding sentimentality and romanticism to the exciting action of dime novel adaptations. Following Harte's lead, western melodrama took the mining camp as one of its settings and featured the altruistic prostitute and the chivalrous badman as proofs of human goodness on the frontier. The effect of romanticism is evident in Frank Hitchcock Murdoch's *Davy Crockett; or, Be Sure You're Right, Then Go Ahead*, a very popular melodrama from 1872 to 1896. In 1830,

Dragged by a horse: The Glory Guys

*Crockett had served as the model for the comic eccentric in James K. Paulding's *Lion of the West*; in 1872, at the hands of Murdoch and actor Frank Mayo, Crockett appeared as the knightly hero, quoting Walter Scott's 'Young Lochinvar' and carrying off his victimized sweetheart to the sanctity of a church wedding.

As the 19th century ended, two more western types were added to the repertoire. Glamorous outlaws like *Deadwood Dick, Jesse *James and *Billy the Kid, highly popular in the later dime novels, also took centre-stage in the melodrama. Heroic, romantic cowboys were also borrowed from best-selling fiction, particularly from Owen *Wister's *The Virginian* (1902), which was first dramatized in 1904. One final, crucial figure of this period was David Belasco, as both author and director of melodrama. He heightened the visual impact of the theatre with mobile panoramas and skilful lighting effects. When in 1905 Belasco staged his *Girl of the Golden West* (later made into an opera by Puccini), he showed that western drama could be effectively independent of novels and that it could profit from ingenious *mise en scène*. Both lessons were remembered by film-makers when they began to edge out popular theatre in the early 1900s, and Belasco's play was to be filmed four times.

Despite the dependence of popular melodrama on literary material, the theatre made its own distinctive contribution by the immediacy with which it mythologized history. The case is seen most clearly with Buffalo Bill. Bill *Cody was brought east by the publicist Ned *Buntline in 1872, to star in Buntline's hurriedly composed play, *The Scouts of the Prairie*. The play proved the primacy of spectacle in melodrama: despite the incoherence of the script, the crowds were delighted to witness Buffalo Bill's sheer presence. The interpenetration of theatre and history was demonstrated in 1876, when Cody interrupted his acting to participate in the Indian wars out west. While there, he dressed in one of his stage costumes to fight Yellow Hand, a battle which ended in Cody scalping the Indian chief; on his return to New York, this event immediately became the centrepiece of his newest play *The Red Right Hand; or, Buffalo Bill's First Scalp for Custer* (by the actor J.V. Arlington). As Richard Slotkin has pointed out, Cody conducted an actual killing according to melodramatic conventions approved by eastern audiences, then heightened the realism of his fictional performances by re-enacting the same deed. Thus was history

Poster for Buffalo Bill's first stage appearance in 1872

infiltrated by theatre: the physicality and immediacy of the theatre could elide fictional and factual West more thoroughly than the written word ever could.

The immediate descendants of popular western drama were the *Wild West shows – most notably, Buffalo Bill's Wild West, beginning in 1883 – which thrived on the proven popularity of violent spectacles and clearly opposed combatants. In turn, the Wild West shows and the surviving melodramas fed into the silent films, which adopted much of the theatricality of melodrama, with its stress on physical heroics and mechanical effects. Initially, the film industry also used scripts from the popular theatre, many of them stage versions of novels. Later, with the coming of sound, movies developed away from those formulas but continued to revolve around types – like the cowboy, the outlaw and the comic sidekick – whom the melodrama had first presented in the flesh. It is by this rather tortuous route that a connection can be made between the nineteenth-century stage, the Western and contemporary drama. Sam Shepard's *True West* (1981) derives its irony and energy from references to filmic conventions; nevertheless, the stereotypes and tableaux which it parodies ultimately owe their existence, however unknowingly, to those early productions of Hamblin and Buntline and Belasco. CBO

The Girl of the Golden West/1915/Lasky/d Cecil B. DeMille/lp Mabel Van Buren, House Peters · remade 1923/First National/d Edwin Carewe/lp Sylvia Breamer, J. Warren Kerrigan · remade 1930/First National/lp Francis Dillon/lp Ann Harding, James Rennie · remade 1938/MGM/d Robert Z. Leonard/lp Jeanette MacDonald, Nelson Eddy

Drinking · Two of the earliest movie narratives on a Western subject, Edison's *Cripple Creek Bar-room* (1892) and *The Great Train Robbery*/1903, contain scenes set in a saloon. The close association between the West and drinking goes back a lot further than that. Indeed, it must sometimes have seemed as if the entire West floated on a tide of liquor. In 1853 California received shipments of '20,000 barrels of whiskey; 400 barrels of rum; 9,000 casks, hogsheads and pipes, 13,000 barrels, 2,600 kegs and 6,000 cases of brandy; 34,000 casks and hogsheads, 13,000 barrels and 23,000 cases and boxes of beer; and 5,000 pipes and casks, 6,000 barrels, 5,000 kegs, 8,000 cases and 1,600 packages of "unspecified liquors".' (J.S. Holliday, *The World Rushed In*) All this for a population of about 250,000. In 1880 Leadville, Colorado, boasted 249 saloons for around 15,000 inhabitants, and in 1890 San Francisco had a licensed bar for every 96 inhabitants.

In the Western drinking is mostly confined to the A-feature. The heroes of B-Westerns, mindful of their youthful audience, rarely sip anything stronger than sarsaparilla (a kind of root beer). What kind of drink is taken is rigidly codified. Beer may be more thirst-quenching, but whiskey is the drink for men. When Kenneth More walks into the saloon in *The Sheriff of Fractured Jaw*/1958 he is curtly informed, 'Mister, we got whisky and we got water. We don't serve water.'

In John Ford's films drinking is usually life-enhancing, the occasion of some of his richest comedy in those scenes where Victor McLaglen or Edmond O'Brien is allowed to have his fling. In *The Man Who Shot Liberty Valance*/1962 O'Brien as the alcoholic newspaperman Dutton Peabody is told the bar is closed for the elections. He pleads for a drink, to no avail. He tries one final, to him clinching, argument: 'Give me a beer. A beer's not drinking.'

Ford's own brother Francis made something of a career out of playing amiable drunks. Only rarely, as with the drinking of Doc Holliday (Victor Mature) in *My Darling Clementine*/1946, does Ford allow it to become a serious issue. Rivalling Mature for the best-acted alcoholic in the Western is Dean Martin in *Rio Bravo*/1958. The role was repeated, but played more for laughs, by Robert Mitchum in Howard Hawks' next Western, *El Dorado*/1966.

Dude ranch · In western parlance, a dude is anyone who comes west just for fun. The first commercial dude ranch, where visitors could watch and, if they wished, participate in such ranching business as round-ups and branding, was founded by Howard Eaton in Dakota Territory in 1881. As communications improved and tourism developed, the number of dude ranches grew, and the Dude Ranchers' Association was formed in 1926. The business was big enough by 1935 for the University of Montana to offer a degree in 'recreational ranching'.

Dude ranches were a popular setting for B-Westerns of the 1930s and 40s, especially comedies and singing cowboy films; for example, *The Cowboy Millionaire* and *Cowboy from Brooklyn*. In *Ride 'Em Cowboy* the dude ranch visited by Abbott and Cos-

tello comes complete with a black dance group and a swimming pool full of bathing beauties.
The Cowboy Millionaire/1935/FOX/d Edward F. Cline/lp George O'Brien, Evalyn Bostock · *Cowboy from Brooklyn*/1938/WB/d Lloyd Bacon/lp Dick Powell, Pat O'Brien, Ronald Reagan · *Ride 'Em Cowboy*/1941/U/d Arthur Lubin/lp Bud Abbott, Lou Costello, Dick Foran

Duel · That differences out west were actually settled by a ritual face-to-face armed encounter in the street may be doubted. Robert Dykstra in *The Cattle Towns* calculates that in the heyday of *Dodge City, *Abilene and other Kansas towns there was an average of only 1.5 homicides a year, and in these only a third of those victims who were killed by gunfire managed to shoot back. But by the end of the century the formal duel had become a fixed convention. Frederic *Remington's picture 'A Fight in the Street' illustrated Teddy *Roosevelt's *Ranch Life and the Hunting Trail*, published in 1896. Owen *Wister's *The Virginian* appeared in 1902. The gunfight between the hero and Trampas which resolves Wister's novel was undoubtedly in large part responsible for establishing the duel as *the* way to end a cowboy narrative, even down to the threat by Trampas to the Virginian to get out of town by sunset. Neither the self-conscious elegiacs at the end of Sam Peckinpah's *Ride the High Country*/1962 and *The Wild Bunch*/1969 nor the parodic excesses which conclude Sergio Leone's films have drained the dramatic potential from the duel, still in place at the end of *Pale Rider*/1985.

Dynamite · Invented in 1867 by Alfred Nobel (after whom the prizes are named) and first employed in the West in mining operations, dynamite is used to great effect by John Wayne in *Rio Bravo*/1958 to winkle out his opponents. By the 1970s spectacular explosions had become just another gimmick, especially in Italian Westerns such as *Il buono, il brutto, il cattivo*/1966 and in Hollywood films influenced by them, like *Two Mules for Sister Sara*/1969 and *High Plains Drifter*/1972.

James Coburn as the IRA dynamiter in Giù la testa

E

Earp, Wyatt (1848-1929) · Lawman. The most famous member of a family which also included James (1841-1926), Virgil (1843-1906), Morgan (1851-82), Warren (1855-1900). That Wyatt Earp's life did not fully justify his status as one of the greatest heroes of the West must by now be well enough known. The facts are simple enough. After some years as a teamster, gambler and buffalo hunter, Wyatt arrived in *Wichita in

Frederic Remington, 'A Fight in the Street' (*from Theodore Roosevelt,* Ranch Life and the Hunting-Trail, *1888*)

Wyatt Earp

1874, where his brother James was a bartender and James' wife ran a brothel. Wyatt was hired as a policeman. In 1876 he joined the police force in *Dodge City and was made assistant marshal in 1878. It was during this period that he made friends with Luke *Short, Doc *Holliday, Bat *Masterson and the people who controlled the gambling and prostitution business in town, the 'Dodge City Gang'. His actual achievements in Dodge City were unremarkable.

In 1879 Wyatt moved to *Tombstone, Arizona, where Virgil was deputy United States marshal. Wyatt soon became deputy sheriff of Pima County. Morgan and James arrived too and the brothers formed a close association with the local business community, including John *Clum. In October 1880 Marshal Fred White was shot; Wyatt arrested Curly Bill *Brocius for the crime and Virgil became town marshal. This episode sparked off a feud between the Earps and local cowboys, who resented attempts to prevent rowdiness in town and rustling outside it. 'Old Man' *Clanton and his sons Ike, Phin and Billy were the leaders of this group. Things came to a head in a gunfight at the O.K. Corral on 26 October 1881, in which Wyatt, Morgan, Virgil and Doc Holliday met Ike and Billy Clanton and Frank and Tom McLaury. The McLaurys and Billy were killed. Afterwards there was considerable controversy over whether the Clantons had really intended to fight, and Virgil was dismissed from office. Two months later he was shot and wounded in ambush and in March 1882 Morgan was killed. Wyatt avenged him by shooting dead Frank Stilwell and Florentino Cruz, whom he suspected of Morgan's murder.

After this Wyatt reverted to his earlier career of gambler, drifting from one goldmining town to another. At various times he was in Cripple Creek, Colorado, in Alaska and Nevada. The end of his life was spent in Hollywood. He became friends with William S. Hart, Tom Mix and John Ford, who claimed that in My Darling Clementine/1946 he shot the gunfight at the O.K. corral just the way Earp said it happened. (This could hardly be the case since Old Man Clanton, killed in the fight in Ford's film, actually died several months before.)

Despite his eventful life, it was not until the publication of two books, one just before his death, one shortly after, that Wyatt Earp became a hero. Walter Noble *Burns' Tombstone (1927) and Stuart *Lake's Wyatt Earp: Frontier Marshal (1931), the latter written with Earp's assistance, created

from this not particularly promising material the legend of the fearless town tamer, the bringer of law and order. Much of Lake's book is pure fabrication, including the story of the 'Buntline Special'. This was a Colt with a barrel a foot long, supposedly presented to Earp by Ned *Buntline, the dime novelist, and used by Earp to knock troublemakers on the head.

That such a fanciful figure should be created was an inevitable result of the dynamics of the Western myth. That it should have been Wyatt Earp who was chosen for elevation to the position is largely an accident of his living long enough to be in the right place at the right time. In the cinema he has yet to undergo the thorough debunking which other plaster saints have received. Only James Stewart's portrayal, significantly played entirely for laughs, and to a lesser extent those by James Garner and Harris Yulin have chipped away at the monument. But, one might riposte, with a portrait as beautiful as that by Henry Fonda in My Darling Clementine/1946, who wants true? (In the following list, (f) indicates that the character, though based on Earp, has a fictional name): Walter Huston (f)/Law and Order/1932 · George O'Brien (f)/Frontier Marshal/1934/FOX/d Lew Seiler/lp Ward Bond · Randolph Scott/Frontier Marshal/1939 · Errol Flynn (f)/Dodge City/1939 · Johnny Mack Brown (f)/Law and Order/1940/U/d Ray Taylor/lp Fuzzy Knight · Richard Dix/Tombstone, the Town Too Tough to Die/1942/PAR/d William McGann/lp Victor Jory · Henry Fonda/My Darling Clementine/1946 · Will Geer/Winchester '73/1950 · Ronald Reagan/Law and Order/1953/U/d Nathan Juran/lp Dorothy Malone · James Millican/Gun Belt/1953/UA/d Ray Nazarro/lp George Montgomery · Rory Calhoun (f)/Powder River/1953/FOX/d Louis King/lp Cameron Mitchell · Bruce Cowling/Masterson of Kansas/1954/COL/d William Castle/lp George Montgomery · Joel McCrea/Wichita/1955 · Burt Lancaster/Gunfight at the O.K. Corral/1956 · Barry Sullivan (f)/Forty Guns/1957 · Buster Crabbe/Badman's Country/1958/WB/d Fred F. Sears/lp George Montgomery · Hugh O'Brian/Alias Jesse James/1959/Hope Enterprises/d Norman McLeod/lp Bob Hope, Rhonda Fleming · James Stewart/Cheyenne Autumn/1964 · Guy Madison/Jennie Lees ha una nuova pistola/1964/It/d Tullio Demichelli · Bill Camfield/The Outlaws Is Coming/1964/COL/d Norman Maurer/lp The Three Stooges · James

Garner/Hour of the Gun/1967 · Harris Yulin/Doc/1971
Television · Hugh O'Brian/The Life and Legend of Wyatt Earp · Med Flory/Maverick · Bruce Boxleitner/I Married Wyatt Earp

Eastman, Seth (1809-75) · Painter. An army officer who served in Minnesota, Texas and in the Seminole War, Eastman was also a careful observer of Indian life whose paintings have a strong ethnographic impulse. He illustrated several books written by his wife Mary, including Dakotah: Life and Legends of the Sioux (1849), often thought to be the inspiration for Longfellow's Hiawatha. Eastman was selected to illustrate The Indian Tribes of the United States (1851-7) by Henry Schoolcraft (1793-1864), generally accounted the first major work of American ethnology. In the 1860s Eastman was commissioned to do a series of paintings of Indian life for the US Capitol. (See Plate 1)

Edmonds, Walter D. (b 1903) · Author. Edmonds' career seems the essence of an American establishment life. Born in upstate New York, he was educated at Harvard, which eventually awarded him an honorary doctorate and membership of its Board of Overseers. A prolific historical novelist, his main source of influence on the Western film was Drums Along the Mohawk, which he published in 1936 and which John Ford filmed in 1939. His twofold achievement in the book was to fictionalize lightly a very well researched account of the American Revolution in western New York and to tell the story from the viewpoint of an ordinary couple. Ford's film is quite another matter. Edmonds' other historical novels are Chad Hanna (1940), The Matchlock Gun (1941), In the Hands of the Senecas (1947). EC

Elder, Kate (?-1881?) · Prostitute and friend of Doc *Holliday, otherwise known as Big-nose Kate or Kate Fisher. This last is the name used in Gunfight at the O.K. Corral/1956, in which Jo Van Fleet gives a powerful portrayal of a woman too intelligent to be fooled by Doc's charm, too weak to break away from it. Faye Dunaway in Doc/1971 gives the part rather more glamour. The Sons of Katie Elder/1965/PAR/d Henry Hathaway/lp John Wayne, Dean Martin, has little to do with the historical character.
Also: Geraldine Chaplin/Verflucht dies Amerika/1973/WG/d Volker Vogeler

Ellis, Edward S. (1840-1916) · Author of

Emigrants on the trail at the foot of the Rockies

Seth Jones; or, The Captives of the Frontier (1860), no. 8 of Beadle's original series of dime novels and one of the most famous and successful. It eventually sold over 400,000 copies. The hero is a Leatherstocking-type who eventually proves to be a well-bred young gentleman in disguise. Ellis wrote dime novels for Beadle for the next thirty years.

Emigrants · In 1843 Horace *Greeley, usually assumed to be an unrestrained enthusiast for westward migration, attempted to warn off a party setting out for Oregon by writing an article in the *Daily Tribune*. He protested that the attempt to cross the West by a land route wore 'an aspect of insanity'; such were the dangers of the terrain, climate and hostile Indians, he asserted, 'we do not believe nine-tenths of them will ever reach the Columbia alive.'

Yet already several hundred had made the trip by wagon, spurred on by boosters who wished to see Oregon settled by Americans, thus solving *de facto* the dispute with Britain over ownership. And between 1840 and 1870, by which time the railroad linked east and west, anything between a quarter and half a million people took the overland trail, at first to Oregon and then, after gold was discovered in 1848, to California. In addition, 40,000 Mormons migrated to the area around Salt Lake City.

Most emigrants followed a route that began at one of the towns on the Missouri River such as Independence, St Joseph or Council Bluffs. From there they proceeded up the Platte River to Fort Laramie and then, via South Pass, over the continental divide. Up to this point the going was relatively easy. At Fort Bridger the trail divided, the northern route going to Oregon, the southern to California. On both the terrain grew much rougher. Those bound for Oregon followed a tortuous track along the Snake River, then across 150 miles of semi-desert and the Blue Mountains, up which wagons had to be manhandled with ropes and pulleys.

The route to California went south till it struck the Humboldt River, which it followed until the river expired in the Nevada desert. There then followed a fifty-mile journey across a waterless waste before the climb up the precipitous Sierra Nevada and down to the Sacramento Valley.

In all the journey to either destination was about 2,000 miles. In their slow-moving Conestoga wagons, or prairie schooners, drawn by oxen or mules, most emigrant parties averaged between 15 and 20 miles a day. Beginning in May, as soon as the prairie was firm enough for the wagons, they could hope to arrive in September. But many misfortunes could intervene and cause settlers to slip behind schedule. The consequences of this could be serious. If the wagons failed to get across the Sierra Nevada before the winter snows set in, the settlers could become completely marooned. This is what happened in 1846 to the unfortunate *Donner party, with disastrous results.

Despite the publication of guides and much free advice in the newspapers, emigrants were not always well prepared. Often wagons were hopelessly overloaded; eventually the trail became littered with the debris which had been thrown away to lighten the load. In *The Plains Across* John D. Unruh records, besides blacksmith's anvils, cooking stoves and huge piles of excess food abandoned, 'an iron safe, a gothic bookcase, law and medical books – even a diving bell and accompanying apparatus.' Conversely, many travellers were ill-provisioned and had to beg or buy food along the way. Short-cuts promoted by unscrupulous owners of ferry boats or trading posts along the 'quicker' route often proved fatal to those whose sense of western geography was sketchy.

The dangers from Indians, which loom so large in fictional accounts, were in reality less significant than other threats. Unruh calculates that about 10,000 people died on the trail in the period 1840-60. Of these most were killed by disease, especially cholera. Considerable numbers died in shooting accidents with the huge arsenal of weapons the emigrants took along. Some 300 died by drowning in rivers (in an area originally designated 'The Great American Desert'). Compared to this, only 362, less than 4 per cent of the total casualties, died from Indian action. Most of these fatalities occurred west of the Rockies, where, contrary to stereotype, the Indians were more hostile than on the plains. Although, as in the popular image, Indian attacks on a circle of besieged wagons did occasionally happen, most engagements took the form of short skirmishes or ambushes on individuals. According to Unruh the settlers gave more than they got, killing a total of 426 Indians along the trail by 1860.

The overland migration of the 1840s and 1850s is one of the pivotal events in the story of western expansion. It caught the imagination of contemporary writers, artists and general public. (See Plate 10.) The emigrants themselves perceived that they were taking part in one of the great historical movements of peoples. Nearly 800 diaries and letters describing their experiences have been preserved.

One might suppose the story of a wagon train to be ideally suited to the cinema. The ideology of going west to till the land and construct an American community fits ideally into the Western; as the opening titles to *The Covered Wagon*/1923 have it: 'The blood of America is the blood of pioneers, the blood of lion-hearted men and women who carved a splendid civilization out of an uncharted wilderness.' The structure of a journey is also tailor-made for narrative, providing a ready-made beginning, middle and end.

In fact only a small number of film-makers have explored this potential. D.W. Griffith was one of the first, and *The Last Drop of Water*/1911 makes the most of its desert location, as the wagon train is attacked by Indians and its water runs out. W.S. Hart's *Wagon Tracks* (1919) stars Hart as a

buckskin-clad guide leading a wagon train and searching among its members for the murderers of his brother. Four years later came *The Covered Wagon*/1923, the first truly epic Western and a huge success. Yet though other film-makers immediately attempted to imitate its size and scope, they chose not the wagon train but the building of the railroad or the cattle-drive as their setting. Not until Raoul Walsh's *The Big Trail*/1930 was there another big picture about emigrants. Shot in a special widescreen process, the film contains exciting sequences of wagons crossing rivers and being lowered down cliffs. But it failed with the public.

The next important emigrant picture, John Ford's *Wagon Master*/1950, came twenty years later. Ford mixes the standard ingredients of crossing rivers, Indian attacks and running out of water with his usual finesse, and although his wagon train of Mormons are driven by a powerful vision of the promised land, he gives the picture a pleasingly intimate feeling.

Anthony Mann's *Bend of the River*/1951 is more overtly ideological. It reaches back to the climactic moment of *The Covered Wagon*, when the settlers have to decide whether they will continue on to Oregon and become farmers, or divert to the newly discovered goldfields of California. In *Bend of the River* the hero (James Stewart) has to decide whether to remain loyal to the hard-pressed emigrants he has joined along the road to Oregon, or to give in to the miners who are prepared to offer a fortune for his food supplies. Needless to say, the agrarian ideal wins out.

Of all the films based on the emigrants' experience, *The Way West* is the most firmly rooted in historical accounts. A.B. *Guthrie's novel of the same title works into its story a host of details of life along the trail, and the film reproduces them. The wagons are pulled by oxen and mules, not horses. The emigrants carve their names on the famous Chimney Rock. Clocks and peach-trees are thrown out of the wagons to lighten the load across the mountains. Unfortunately the film's leaden pace precludes its being the epic that was all too obviously intended.

In the 1950s the episodic potential of the emigrant party was put to good use in the long-running TV series *Wagon Train*. The pioneers' slow progress towards their destination (which could be almost indefinitely postponed) gave time for an almost limitless number of stories, and the notional presence of a hundred or more emigrants occasioned

a plentiful supply of situations. Not the least of the format's advantages was that the mixture of sexes and generations in the wagon train permitted the kinds of story ideally suited to the family audience television sought. If others tamed the Wild West, *Wagon Train* domesticated it.
Wagon Tracks/1919/PAR/*d* Lambert Hillyer/*lp* W.S. Hart, Jane Novak · *The Way West*/1967/UA/*d* Andrew V. McLaglen/*lp* Kirk Douglas, Robert Mitchum, Richard Widmark

English · There's something about the English that is inherently un-Western; or at least the cinema makes them so. Often they are figures of fun, like Charles Laughton in *Ruggles of Red Gap*/1935, Kenneth More in *The Sheriff of Fractured Jaw*/1958 or Arthur Askey in *Ramsbottom Rides Again*. As frequently they are aristocrats who adapt with difficulty if at all to a rougher and more democratic way of life, as for example in *Shalako* or *McKenna's Gold*. Honourable exceptions are the Englishman who teaches Custer 'Garry Owen' in *They Died with their Boots On*/1941 and Richard Harris in *A Man Called Horse*/1970 (as an aristocrat-turned-Sioux who gives the phrase 'noble savage' a new twist). But even these are just passing through; not being settlers, like the Irish or the Swedes in John Ford's films, they never get to be fully at home in the West.

Despite this, the English (more precisely, the British) soon developed an appetite for the Western. Edward *Ellis' dime novel *Seth Jones* was published in England in 1861. Even

From an unidentified English Western (c.1910)

Charles Laughton as the Englishman in Arizona in Ruggles of Red Gap

before that Britain had developed its own best-selling Western novelist in the form of Mayne Reid (1818-83), an Irishman whose first Western novel was *The Scalp Hunters* (1851). The prolific pulp novelist J.T. Edson, born in Derbyshire in 1928, continues the tradition of the British Western. Though little is known about them, some Western films were made in England in the early years of the century.
Ramsbottom Rides Again/1956/GB/d John Baxter/lp Arthur Askey, Sidney James · *Shalako*/1968/Kingston Films/d Edward Dmytryk/lp Sean Connery, Brigitte Bardot · *McKenna's Gold*/1968/COL/d J. Lee Thompson/lp Gregory Peck, Omar Sharif

Europeans · Shortly before he died, John Ford was asked by fellow director Burt Kennedy whether he had seen any of the European Westerns which were flooding onto the American market. Ford's answer was short and predictable: 'You're kidding!' When the Italian and German Westerns were first released internationally, from 1966 onwards, most English and American critics tended to react in much the same way – inventing the terms 'Spaghetti Western' and 'Sauerkraut Western' in the process as a way of associating the European films with popular, touristic, stereotypes of eating habits in the old world.

The arrival of the first Italian Westerns – made by Sergio Leone, Sergio Corbucci and Sergio Sollima, or rather 'Bob Robertson',

'Stanley Corbett' and 'Simon Sterling' – on the international scene, following hot on the heels of a series of West German Westerns derived from the late nineteenth-century novels of Karl *May, forced these critics to articulate a basic assumption which had seldom been made so explicit before – that 'the Western' really belonged to a folk culture rather than an entrepreneurial culture; a folk culture which may have contained some Biblical, medieval and European motifs, but which, in the end, was essentially American in character. David McGillivray of *Films and Filming*, for example, wrote that: 'In the American Western, we are accustomed, however imperfectly, to a sense of poetry – from John Ford via Martin Ritt to Andrew V. McLaglen – bred by an ingrained tradition. In the European Western, this tradition is non-existent, so that all the films produced in this genre are nothing more than cold-blooded attempts at sterile emulation.' Leslie Halliwell was content to categorize Spaghettis as 'savage Westerns on the American pattern', while Philip French at that time thought that a list of the most important Italian Westerns up to 1971 read 'like a brochure for a season in hell'.

In a series of magazine articles Sergio Leone, the director of the four best-known Italian Westerns, challenged John Ford's casual 'you're kidding' – in particular, Ford's underlying belief that the 'sense of poetry' of the Hollywood Western bore some mystical relationship with the Ameri-

can historical experience (rather than a more pragmatic relationship with the changing tastes of American cinema-going audiences): 'Several great Western directors come from Europe: Ford is Irish; Zinnemann, Austrian; Lang, German; Wyler and Tourneur, French.... I really don't see why an Italian should not be included in the group.' 'The man of the West bore no resemblance to the man described and celebrated by Hollywood directors, screenwriters, cinéastes. The whiter than white redresser of wrongs did not exist, any more than the bandit leader without any scruples or the always warlike Indian. One could say that all the characters they present to us come from the same mould: the incorruptible sheriff; the romantic judge; the glamorous brothelkeeper; the cruel bandit; the naive girl from the east and so on. And the women – those inevitable women! All these moulds are mixed together, before the happy ending, to produce a kind of cruel puritan fairy-tale. It is the Far West reinterpreted by Frankenstein and Disneyland...'

But Leone's defence of the European Western as a distinctively old world critique of 'the American cinema par excellence' (and specifically of the 1950s adult Western – before the days of Sam Peckinpah's Wagnerian fantasies, Robert Altman's group therapy Western *McCabe & Mrs. Miller*/1971 and Michael Cimino's *Heaven's Gate*/1980, or *Novecento* meets *C'era una volta il west*/1968, all of which were made possible at one level by the popularity of the Italian Westerns in America) went unnoticed: so Papa Ford's view became orthodoxy. It was generally considered that *any* Westerns which were not made in Hollywood, using American desert locations and based on American literature or history, had by definition to be rootless parodies. The fact that countless horse operas – some with the emphasis on the horse, some on the opera – had been produced in France, Italy, Germany, the Soviet Union and Japan ever since the days of *The Great Train Robbery*/1903 was quietly forgotten. Gaston Méliès (brother of Georges) had been among the first, with a series of one-reelers shot in Chicago and Texas between 1909 and 1911 for the Star Film Company. Joë Hamman had appeared as 'Arizona Bill' in a series of twenty French Westerns (filmed in the Camargue and the suburbs of Paris) between 1907 and 1913: they competed in European amusement arcades with the products of Denmark's Great Western Film Company, and were later to be satirized in Jean Renoir's *Le Crime de Monsieur Lange*. In 1913, three years after Puccini completed the first horse opera worthy of the name, *The Girl of the Golden West*, Vincenzo Leone (Sergio's father) had directed the first Italian Western, *The Indian Vamp*, on location· near Turin, with the silent star Bice Valerian (Sergio's mother) as the raunchy Indian maiden of the title. In the inter-war years, Germany had produced *The Last of the Mohicans* (with Bela Lugosi, in a pre-Dracula incarnation, as Uncas), Luis Trenker's *Der Kaiser von Kalifornien* (a distinctly 'Aryan' version of the same *Sutter's Gold* story which the Soviet director Sergei Eisenstein had recently tried to set up in Hollywood), and a superstar to rival William S. Hart (or 'Rio Jim' as he was known in Europe) in the person of Hans Albers, the *Übermensch* hero of *Sergeant Berry* and *Wasser für Canitoga*. During World War II Carl Koch (assisted by his wife, the animator Lotte Reiniger) had directed the first full-length Cinecittà Western – *Una signora dell'ovest*, with Michel Simon as a grizzled old prospector, Valentina Cortese as a good-time girl and Rossano Brazzi as a rich cattle baron: even in 1942, Koch had been criticized for not 'setting his film amongst our own Italian cattlemen, the *buteri*, and transferring the action to a more realistic setting.' If we add to all these the Akira Kurosawa samurai films of the 1950s and early 1960s (which demonstrated, said Kurosawa, how much he had learned 'from the grammar of the American Western', and ◂which were immensely popular in Europe), as well as such oddballs as Walsh's *The Sheriff of Fractured Jaw*/1958 (a sort of shoot-out at Saville Row), it is clear that the non-American Western film had a long-standing, if not a particularly distinguished, pedigree by the time the 'Spaghettis' first started attracting international attention. And it certainly had a huge audience. When A. C. Lyles produced a series of low-budget Westerns in the mid-1960s, which brought together as many survivors from the B-Western era as could still struggle on to a horse, he discovered that the films made over twice as much money in Europe as they did on the home market, and often turned magically from B- into A-features in the process. There were regular B-Western conventions in most of the capital cities of Europe. If Hollywood wasn't producing the kinds of Western the delegates wanted, then someone else would have to.

Isolated examples of the European Western could safely be ignored by the critics: *four hundred* Spaghettis, hard on the trail of a whole tribe of West German contributions, with identifiable rules all of their own, could not – especially when they started to attract co-production money from American subsidiaries in Europe. So when, in 1962-5, studios in Japan, West Germany and Italy began to produce Westerns in which the hero much prefers to survive than to behave like 'the last gentleman', with musical scores which sounded like a deafening mixture of Puccini, Rodrigo and Duane Eddy recorded in a bathroom, it occurred to some critics that the Axis was at last taking its revenge on the culture of the invading GIs....

Of the many European films which were released in the mid-1960s, the Italian versions tended to subscribe to a Hobbesian vision of the West (where 'life had no value, but death, sometimes, had its price'), while the West German versions represented a kind of dime-novel adaptation of Rousseau (where the fine, upstanding Apache warrior teamed up with the flower of romantic German manhood). Both traditions had their literary origins in the 18th century: their *literary* pedigree was in fact far more substantial than their *cinematic* pedigree. In 1772, for example, the Abbé Raynal invited the Academy of Lyon to discuss the vexed question 'Was the discovery of America a blessing or a curse for mankind?' and donated a substantial sum of money as a prize for the best essay. The contestants were fairly evenly divided between those who thought that America would become the 'cradle of progress' and those who thought its savagery made even Europe look civilized. These rival views of America were to find their visual equivalents in the work of European artists who depicted the forests and rivers of 'the new golden land'. They entered the world of European *popular* culture – through novels, pamphlets, engravings and what today we would call 'comics' – following the publication of Fenimore *Cooper's Leatherstocking Tales.

Cooper's works – and especially *The Last of the Mohicans* (1826), *The Pathfinder* (1840) and *The Deerslayer* (1841) – were phenomenally successful in Europe, where they were (remarkably) marketed as 'accurate portrayals' and at the same time as natural successors to the symbolic myths of Europe, which were becoming increasingly remote from everyday experience in industrial cities. They led to countless home-grown spin-offs, in which English public schoolboys, German craftsmen, French traders and Scandinavian ministers pitted their wits against the hostile wilderness and the (sometimes) hostile Indians. Even Goethe planned to write a novel about the West in 1827, and encouraged other writers to experiment with the form. One of the best-known novelists of this phase in the European Western was Charles Sealsfield (born Karl Postl in Austria), who had spent some time on the Louisiana frontier in the 1820s. His first novel (of six), published in Germany in 1833, was called *Tokeah or The White Rose*, and it told of the unsuccessful struggle of the Cherokee chief Tokeah to protect his ancestral lands from greedy 'Yankees' under Andrew Jackson. The book's avowed purpose was to 'transfer the freshly pulsating blood of the Transatlantic Republic into the senile veins ·of the Old World', and to recount the epic conflict between Nature and Materialism.

The second phase was stimulated by the success of Robert Montgomery Bird's *Nick of the Woods: A Story of Kentucky* (1837), with its appropriately named hero Nathan Slaughter, who spent the entire book torturing and killing Indians to avenge the massacre of his family. Gustave Aimard (born Olivier Gloux in Paris) was the best-known exponent, with novels such as *The Trappers of Arkansas* and *The Pirates of the Prairies* (published in the late 1850s). Aimard had lived 'among the Indians' along the Mexican-American border, and claimed to set the adventures of his serial heroes – 'Loyal Heart', an Indian fighter with two enormous bloodhounds as inseparable companions; and Valentine Guillois, rescuer of damsels in distress who never uttered a word 'which would prove offence to the most delicate mind' – in a world '*which he has seen*'. In Britain, 'Captain' Mayne Reid, who had enlisted with American troops in the Mexican War, produced over seventy Western novels with titles such as *The Rifle Rangers* (1850) and *The Scalp Hunters* (1851). According to Ray Allen Billington (who has chronicled the European literary image of the American frontier in *Land of Savagery, Land of Promise*), *The Scalp Hunters* is so gruesome that 'simply to count the number of scalps lifted ... would test the capacity of a computer.' It was Mayne Reid who first developed the character of the lone Westerner with a mysterious past, the noble gunfighter. Other British contributions included the children's novels of R. M. Ballantyne (who had been a clerk with the Hudson's Bay Company for six years) – such as *The Wild Man of the West* and *The Red Man's Revenge* – and Western adventures by G. A. Henty, including *In the Heart of the*

Rockies (1895), whose schoolboy hero prides himself on the fact that through his veins runs 'a large share of the restless spirit of enterprise that has been the main factor in making the Anglo-Saxons the dominant race of the world.'

But by far the most significant – and substantial – writer of European Western novels in the 19th century was Karl May. Like the others, he claimed that he lived among the Apache warriors about whom he wrote: the difference was that he never visited America in his youth, since he was in fact doing time in Zwickau prison (for impersonating a police lieutenant), where he became prison librarian and seems to have read the works of Fenimore Cooper as well as German travellers' tales about life in the West. By the time of his release in the early 1870s, publishing houses were competing for the rights to print his tales of Winnetou the Warrior and his German companions Old Shatterhand, Old Firehand, Old Surehand and Old Wabble. The young hero of *Winnetou I* (whose name is Karl) is christened 'Old Shatterhand' on account of his ability to 'knock out bruisers with one blow': after learning the ways of *der Wildwest* from Mr Henry, a gunsmith, and Sam Hawkens, another German immigrant who has become 'one of the most famous hunters and scouts between the Mississippi and the Rocky Mountains'. Shatterhand eventually gets to meet Winnetou, a fine specimen of Mescalero Apache manhood: 'He held a book in his hand. On the cover of the book, in large golden letters, was the word "Hiawatha". This Indian, this son of a people that many call "wild", could, apparently, not only read, but possessed a mind and taste for culture. Longfellow's famous poem, in the hand of an Apache Indian...!'

Having established that they share the same literary tastes, Shatterhand and Winnetou take on Santer ('a Yankee villain with a sneaky look about him') and his gang in a distinctly Teutonic variation on Leslie A. Fiedler's 'myth of the two good companions in the wilderness'. Other members of the tribe may speak the Apache language (about which May appears to have known a great deal), but Winnetou and his Chief Intschu-tschuna usually talk in High German, with a tendency to end their long speeches on the portentous line 'Howgh. Ich habe gesprochen' – at which the other Apache warriors animatedly reply 'Uff Uff.' In a later book, *Winnetou III*, Winnetou dies after saving Shatterhand's life; as Karl sings the Ave Maria, the dying warrior whispers 'Scharlih,

I believe in the Saviour. Winnetou is a Christian. Farewell.' This strange blend of mysticism, Indian lore, ecology and Christian fellowship – the favoured reading of Albert Einstein, George Grosz and Adolf Hitler – has kept Karl May's Western novels in print from the 1890s right up to the present day. The success in the early 1960s of several West German Winnetou films led directly to the 'Spaghetti Western' boom.

If Winnetou harks back to the German popularity of Fenimore Cooper, and to countless polemics about 'the noble savage', the Spaghettis hark back to the *Nick of the Woods* phase, when the European Western stopped preaching and started to get violent. Both share an 'old world' detachment from 'Yankee know-how' – the one moral, the other cynical. Of the two traditions, the German has had the longer literary life, while the Italian has had the more profound impact on the Western film since the late 1960s. John Wayne's valedictory film, *The Shootist*/1976, was produced by Dino de Laurentiis. No kidding. CF

Der Kaiser von Kalifornien/1936/Tobis/d Luis Trenker/lp Luis Trenker, Viktoria von Ballasko · *Sergeant Berry*/1938/Tobis/d Herbert Selpin/lp Hans Albers, Roni von Bukovics · *Wasser für Canitoga*/1939/ Bavaria-Filmkunst/d Herbert Selpin/lp Hans Albers, Charlotte Susa · *Una signora dell'ovest*/1942/Scalera/d Carlo Koch/lp Michel Simon, Isa Pola

Evarts, Hal G[eorge] (1887-1934) · Author who enjoyed considerable popularity in the 1920s. Several of his novels are based on historical events; *Tumbleweeds* (1923), which was to become the last film of William S. Hart, is set in the *Cherokee Strip at the time of the land rush.

The Silent Call [*The Cross Pull*]/1921/First National/d Lawrence Trimble/lp Strongheart (dog) · *Tumbleweeds*/1925 · *The Santa Fe Trail* [*Spanish Acres*]/1930/ PAR/d Otto Brower, Edwin H. Knopf/lp Richard Arlen · *The Big Trail*/1930

Exploration · The dynamics of westward expansion, or that part of it most relevant to the Western film, were settled in 1803 when, in the largest real estate deal in history, President Jefferson purchased Louisiana from the French. This acquisition of 800,000 square miles doubled the existing area of the United States. Jefferson had already planned an exploration of this far western territory to be led by Captains Meriwether *Lewis and William Clark, which now became a map-

ping out of American possessions. Jefferson's instructions to Lewis and Clark were: 'to explore the Missouri river, and such principal stream of it, as, by its course and communication with the waters of the Pacific Ocean ... may offer the most direct and practicable water communication across this continent for the purposes of commerce.' The President's brief to the expedition also included instructions to make records of the soil and topography of the lands they passed through, and to note the languages, traditions, monuments and possessions of the peoples they encountered.

Lewis and Clark started up the Missouri River on 14 May 1804 with 17 regular soldiers, 11 enlisted men, an interpreter and Clark's black servant York. Later while wintering in Fort Mandan at the mouth of the Knife river, two others joined the party, the trapper Toussaint Charbonneau and his Shoshone wife *Sacajawea, who was to prove an invaluable aid in their encounters with the Indian peoples they met. In Paramount's wildly inaccurate version of the expedition, *The Far Horizons* (1954), Clark, played by Charlton Heston, falls in love with Sacajawea, causing a rift between the leaders. In reality, after a certain amount of desertion and flogging at the beginning, the expedition held together well. During their journeys by river and overland, Lewis and Clark covered a total distance of 7,689 miles, making the westward journey together. On the return journey they split into two parties, rejoining one another at the junction of the Yellowstone and Missouri rivers. They reached St Louis on 23 September 1806.

A number of government-sponsored expeditions followed on the heels of Lewis and Clark. Two of them, one led by Zebulon Pike (1779-1813), another by Stephen Long (1784-1864), hold a contradictory status in the history of American exploration, in that they both helped to generate and to propagate the myth of the 'Great American Desert' lying athwart the westward advance of the American people. Pike, Long and others before them had clung to the notion that most of the area between the Mississippi and the Rocky Mountains was an arid, uninhabitable wasteland. Pike declared that 'these vast plains of the western hemisphere may become in time as celebrated as the sandy deserts of Africa.' It was not until the 1860s that later travellers, scientists and railroad promoters succeeded in exploding this particular myth.

The first Americans to make a living out of the Far West that Lewis and Clark had

PRINCIPAL EXPLORATIONS 1539–1828

CANADA

Lewis and
Clarke
1804–6

La Salle
1681–2

Mississippi River

Jedediah
Smith
1826–8

Coronado
1539–42

De Soto and
Moscoso
1539–43

MEXICO

0   500 Miles

traversed were the fur trappers or *mountain men, who swarmed into the Rockies in the 1820s and 30s. A by-product of their trapping was a fund of geographical knowledge that was to prove of inestimable value in later phases in the opening up of the West. The most important figures in this context were Jedediah Smith, Peter Skene Ogden and Joseph Reddeford Walker, who pioneered the trails through the Rocky Mountains to California and Oregon. Their knowledge provided the foundations for the trails that the overland wagon trains of the 1840s and 1850s, and later the railroads of the 1860s, would use to transport emigrants from the east.

Although the exploration of the trans-Mississippi West was at times a haphazard affair, with trails being discovered and rediscovered by Indians, Spanish, French, English and American explorers, eventually the tradition of federally sponsored enterprise established by Lewis and Clark became the dominant one, particularly through the

exploits of the flamboyant J.C. *Frémont in the years 1839-46. Frémont fitted perfectly the role of romantic incarnation of the ideology of *Manifest Destiny and was a protégé of the leading advocate of westward expansion, Senator Thomas Hart Benton of Missouri. In terms of actual discovery historians are not impressed by Frémont's activities. William Goetzmann argues that Frémont 'located no new pass or any route to Oregon', and Frémont's peak was not the highest in the Rockies, as he claimed. However, his highly colourful accounts of his journeys were best sellers and did more to glamorize the idea of the West than the actual discoveries of the mountain men, some of whom, like Kit *Carson, accompanied Frémont on his expeditions.

All this American activity in the Far West, which included Jacob Astor's fur trappers, the prospectors and immigrants, represented the first wedge of eventual American sovereignty over the whole region. Texas was annexed in 1845, Oregon was ceded in

1846, California in 1848 and the Gadsden Purchase completed in 1853. The United States had now become a transcontinental world power between the 49th and 37th parallels.

After the Civil War a host of government-sponsored topographical and railroad surveys, often supported by the new medium of photography, began to fill in the details of the American lands in the West. Yet the explorer has never attracted the attention that the soldier or cowboy has commanded in the Western film. The idea of penetrating into unknown, possibly hostile, territory for the first time is often a basic premise in the Western film. But because he has not been seen as a bringer of community or law to the West, the trail-blazer has remained an element in the historical narrative of the West without ever being central to Hollywood mythology. CB
The Far Horizons/1954/PAR/d Rudolph Maté/lp Fred MacMurray, Charlton Heston, Donna Reed

F

Family · Archetypally, as in *Shane*/1952, the Western hero is a loner. Where the gangster hero displays an unhealthy obsession with family relations ('Made it, Ma, top of the world'), the Western hero is more usually unencumbered. Of course there are exceptions. Burt Lancaster as the hero of *Apache*/1954 fights for his wife and child; in *The Unforgiven*/1959 he fights for his mother, brothers and sister, and in *Gunfight at the O.K. Corral*/1956 he fights side by side with the other brothers in the Earp family. Clans such as the Earps, the Daltons and the Youngers are not uncommon; they afford solidarity. It's wives and children that tie you down, as Van Heflin finds when he wants to be a hero in *3:10 to Yuma*/1957. In *The True Story of Jesse James*/1957 Jesse's wife Zee calls him, with an irony only she is unaware of, 'just a man who loves his family'.

Farny, Henry (1847-1916) · Painter. Born in France but brought up in Cincinnati, Farny first went west in 1881. The experience encouraged him to become a painter of Indians. As well as making sketches on his various trips west he took photographs and collected artefacts in order to ensure the authenticity of the pictures he painted in his studio. He did many illustrations for popular magazines in the 1880s, including *Harper's Weekly*. What is probably his best-known painting, 'The Song of the Talking Wire' (1904) is replicated in a shot from *How the West Was Won*/1962. His work was highly praised by Theodore Roosevelt and

Henry Farny, 'The Song of the Talking Wire' (1904)

Ulysses S. Grant, whom he once introduced to Sitting Bull.

Ferber, Edna (1885-1968) · Middlebrow author of short stories, plays and novels. Four of Ferber's novels are set in the West, presenting an epic panorama of westward expansion, frequently with strong female characters. *Cimarron* (1930) is located in Oklahoma, beginning with the land rush and continuing up to the discovery of oil. *Great Son* (1945) takes place in Washington State, *Giant* (1952) in Texas and *Ice Palace* (1958) in Alaska. Three of these have been turned into monumental, sometimes top-heavy films: *Cimarron*/1930 · *Giant*/1956 · *Cimarron*/1960 · *Ice Palace*/1960/WB/*d* Vincent Sherman/*lp* Richard Burton, Robert Ryan.

Feud · The classic feud in the form of a long-running dispute between families is hardly exclusive to the Western; after all, Shakespeare used it in *Romeo and Juliet*. Stories of feuding families set in the backwoods of Kentucky are plentiful in early Hollywood cinema. But the feud is certainly a common motif in the Western, both in popular literature by writers such as Zane *Grey and Ernest *Haycox and in the cinema. A real-life conflict which provided the prototype for much Western fiction was the Graham-Tewksbury feud. It began in 1886 in Pleasant Valley, Arizona in a dispute between two families, the Grahams and the Tewksburys, both small ranchers. The Grahams moved to an alliance with the larger cattle-owning interests in the region and this provoked the Tewksburys into bringing sheep into the valley. A shepherd was murdered; later in 1887 some other men on the side of the Grahams were killed. Retaliation followed until by 1892, after a series of ambushes by each side, over twenty men had been killed and only one member of the families originally involved, Ed Tewksbury, was left alive. Zane Grey's twice-filmed novel *To the Last Man* (1922) draws on these events.

Fighting Indians at night · In *Bullet for a Badman* Darren McGavin reminds Audie Murphy of how when they were in the Texas Rangers they were told Comanche didn't attack at night, and then they did. Yet even as late as *Billy Two Hats*, made in 1973, this piece of folklore has still not been abandoned. In *The Charge at Feather River*/1953 someone explains that Indians fear if they're killed at night it will be dark in the happy hunting ground. James Stewart in *Winchester '73*/1950 has a slightly different theory; Indians believe, he explains, that if it's dark the Great Spirit won't be able to find their souls. In *The Law and Jake Wade*/1958 Robert Taylor is more discriminating: 'Apaches don't attack at night, but they're the only ones who don't. These are Comanches.'

Hollywood never resolved its confusion on this subject, though whether such statements about Indian behaviour have any basis in fact is doubtless beside the point. One doesn't look to the Western for correct ethnography. What is certain is that those Indians who do attack at night, in *Red River*/1947 or *Distant Drums*/1951 or *Bend of the River*/1951, have apparently never heard the theories, even though in the contemporaneous *The Big Sky*/1952 Arthur Hunnicutt can be heard expounding them all over again to anyone who will listen.
Bullet for a Badman/1964/U/*d* R. G. Springsteen/*lp* Audie Murphy, Darren McGavin · *Billy Two Hats*/1973/UA/*d* Ted Kotcheff/*lp* Gregory Peck, Desi Arnaz Jr.

Fisher, Vardis (1895-1968) · Author. Fisher wrote several impressively researched and stylishly written novels based on episodes in the history of the West. *Children of God* (1939) deals with the Mormons. *City of Illusion* (1941) is set in *Virginia City, Nevada during the silver rush. *The Mothers: An American Saga of Courage* (1943) is about the disastrous *Donner expedition. *Tale of Valor* is the story of the *Lewis and Clark exploration. Fisher's last novel was *Mountain Man* (1965) and is based on legends around the life of 'Liver-Eating' *Johnson. It was filmed as *Jeremiah Johnson*/1972.

Fistfights · Though a gun may be needed to resolve the issue at the end of the picture, a fistfight is the most physical way of demonstrating the hero's courage and manliness. In *Between Men*, a W.S. Hart film from 1915, Hart as the Western hero has outwitted the fraudulent schemes of the eastern stockbroker villain. But he still needs to give him a physical beating to prove his point. Forty years later in *The Big Country*/1958 Gregory Peck as an Easterner proves he is a real man in a stand-up fight with Charlton Heston. In the B-Western a fistfight in the first reel was virtually obligatory. One of the best-known set-piece fistfights comes in Rex *Beach's *The Spoilers*. In the 1942 version John Wayne and Randolph Scott begin their fight upstairs, crash over the banisters, wreck the saloon and end up in the street, still punching. The rules of a fistfight, not always adhered to, are spelt out by the Rev. Samuel Clayton (Ward Bond) in *The Searchers*/1956: 'No bitin' or gougin' and no kickin' either.' The comic fight has been a popular variation; see John Ford's films *passim*, but especially *She Wore a Yellow Ribbon*/1949, in which a beatific smile spreads across Victor McLaglen's face as successive waves of opponents are launched against him. *Dodge City*/1939, *Across the Wide Missouri*/1950 and *North to Alaska*/1960 also have elaborately staged comic brawls. And though ladies shouldn't fight, Marlene Dietrich and Una Merkel have a famous set-to in *Destry Rides Again*/1939.
Between Men/1915/Triangle/*d* William S. Hart/*lp* William S. Hart, House Peters ·
The Spoilers/1942/U/*d* Ray Enright/*lp* John Wayne, Randolph Scott, Marlene Dietrich

Five Civilized Tribes · The name given to the confederacy of Indian nations formed in 1843 between the Cherokee, Creek, Choctaw, Chickasaw and *Seminole. All of these peoples originally lived east of the Mississippi in Alabama, Georgia, Mississippi and Florida. From the beginning of the 19th century some of them, especially the Creek and Cherokee, developed a relatively advanced agricultural economy, and the Cherokee had become literate in their own language during the 1820s. But pressure by the whites for them to evacuate their lands grew rapidly after the election of Andrew *Jackson to the Presidency in 1828. The Creek were forced to migrate to Indian Territory during 1834-5. In 1839 the Cherokee were marched west by soldiers; many

died along what became known as 'the trail of tears'. By the 1840s the removal was complete.

The Five Civilized Tribes made persistent attempts to set up their own independent government in the lands assigned them. But their case was not helped by their decision to support the Confederate side in the Civil War (some members of the Tribes owned negro slaves) and at the end of the war much of the Indians' land was taken from them. Towards the end of the century most of the rest of Indian Territory was opened up for white settlement and in 1907 it was incorporated into the new state of *Oklahoma.

Chief Dan George in *The Outlaw Josey Wales*/1976 has a wry comment on how the whites have treated the unwarlike Cherokee: 'They call us civilized because we're easy to sneak up on.'

Flint, Timothy (1780-1840) · Author who has some claim to have written the first work of Western fiction. *Francis Berrian, or, The Mexican Patriot* (1826), in its story of an upright Anglo-American in conflict with a treacherous Mexican for the love of a beautiful Spanish maiden, set the pattern for many later works. Another Flint novel, *The Shoshonee Valley* (1830), was the first to take mountain men as its theme. Flint's biographical memoir of Daniel *Boone (1833) played an important part in building up the legend of the frontiersman.

Food · The novelist Edna *Ferber claims in *Cimarron* that the West was founded on canned tomatoes. It's not surprising, then, that when they come to describe the cuisine on view in Westerns the French authors of *Le Western* (Paris: 10/18, 1966) can barely conceal a shudder. 'The lack of originality in the menus and dishes is compensated for by the almost total lack of culinary taste among cowboys, farmers and soldiers,' remarks Bertrand Tavernier severely. There is, it must be admitted, not a great deal of exaggeration in Roger Tailleur's recipe for how to prepare coffee out west: 'Take a pound of coffee, add water, boil for half an hour. Throw in a horseshoe; if it sinks add more coffee.' Certainly the repertoire is limited. The restaurant where James Stewart works in *The Man Who Shot Liberty Valance*/1962 appears to serve two items only, steak and deep-dish apple pie. Nowhere in the cinematic Western is there any equivalent to the sumptuous meals that the hero of Vardis *Fisher's novel *Mountain Man* prepares for himself in the wilds. Directors of Westerns

are less interested in the food itself, more in the opportunity a meal provides for the exploration of dramatic tensions. Social animosities are revealed as the travellers sit down to eat in *Stagecoach*/1939; in *Shane*/1952 and *3:10 to Yuma*/1957 small boys gaze in awe at the strangers invited to the family meal table. In Budd Boetticher's Westerns the repeated exchange of cups of coffee around the camp fire becomes a visual equivalent to the verbal exchanges as the characters play out their games of shifting allegiances.

Ford, Bob (1861-92) · Outlaw. Remembered as, in the words of the popular ballad, 'the dirty little coward/who shot poor Mr Howard', i.e. Jesse *James. Ford and his brother Charlie were members of the James gang. Having done a deal with the Governor of Missouri over reward money, Bob Ford shot Jesse in the back at his house in St Joseph on 3 April 1882. For this and a previous killing he was pardoned and went on tour with a stage version of his deed. Charlie shot himself in 1886. Bob was shot in the saloon he ran in Colorado. Besides appearing in the various films about Jesse James, Bob Ford (played by John Ireland) was given a whole film to himself in Sam Fuller's *I Shot Jesse James*/1948.

Frémont, John (1813-90) · Explorer, soldier, politician. Frémont's fame, in his own time and subsequently, rests on his achievements as an explorer, on his flamboyant personality and on his wife's literary efforts in promoting his reputation. He never really attained the military glory or political success he several times sought.

In 1838 he was commissioned in the United States Corps of Topographical Engineers; after two journeys in the West with the noted French scientist Nicollet, Frémont was ordered in 1841 to survey the Platte River. This he did, continuing as far as South Pass and into the Wind River Mountains. On his next expedition, guided like the first by Kit *Carson, Frémont explored the Great Basin between the Rockies and the Sierra Nevada. In 1847 his third expedition had reached California when hostilities broke out between the Mexican authorities and American settlers there. Frémont's battalion helped to secure California when war was declared between Mexico and the United States. Frémont made two further expeditions, to survey the route for a railroad to the Pacific. The publication of the narratives of his travels, in the writing of which Frémont was greatly helped by his wife Jessie, the daughter of the influential senator Thomas Hart Benton, made him famous. In 1856 he stood as Presidential candidate for the newly formed Republican party, but lost to James Buchanan. During the Civil War he was put in command of the Department of the West, but was not a success. He was soon relieved of his command and resigned from the army. Though later a Governor of Arizona (1878-81), Frémont was not a success at this either. Everything of note in his life was achieved by the age of 40.

Arthur Hotaling/*Kit Carson over the Great Divide*/1925/Sunset/*d* Frank S. Mattison/*lp* Jack Mower · Dana Andrews/*Kit Carson*/ 1940/UA/*d* George B. Seitz/*lp* Jon Hall Television · Richard Chamberlain/*Dream West*

French · The major role played by the French in the discovery, exploration and development of the West is scarcely reflected in the Western. This may result from the fact that very few Westerns deal with the early period of exploration, when the French exercised their major influence. In a few films about the fur trade and the mountain men the French get a chance: *Hudson's Bay*, *Across the Wide Missouri*/1950, *The Big Sky*/ 1952. In *Invitation to a Gunfighter*/1964 Yul Brynner plays a French-speaking Creole who insists at the point of a gun on having his name (Jules Gaspard D'Estaing) pronounced correctly.

Yet though the French may be underrepresented in the Western, they have excelled in their devotion to it. Such was its popularity with French audiences in the period before World War I that Pathé and other French companies produced their own brands. Joë Hamman (1885-1974) was one of the stars, playing a character called Arizona Bill. Jean Renoir alludes affectionately to this French craze for Westerns in the character of 'Arizona Jim' in *Le Crime de M. Lange* (1936).

French critics were among the first to treat the Western with respect. André Bazin's essays 'Le western ou le cinéma américain par excellence' and 'Evolution du western', written in the 1950s, were highly influential both in France and elsewhere. J-L. Rieupeyrout's book *La Grande aventure du western* (1964) remains one of the most detailed histories written. A collective effort, *Le Western*, published in the 10-18 series in 1966, was, in its combination of filmographic information, historical perspective and fascination with stylistic motifs, one of the

inspirations behind the present volume. Jean-Louis Leutrat's book, entitled (once again) *Le Western* (1973), brings to bear, in a highly productive fashion, some of the ideas which cinema studies has borrowed from formalism and structuralism.

Hudson's Bay/1941/FOX/*d* Irving Pichel/*lp* Paul Muni, Gene Tierney

Frontier · The frontier is the central organizing concept for understanding the history of American expansion. Some historians have even argued that it provides the most powerful tool for understanding America itself. The technical definition that the Federal government used for the frontier in the 19th century is simple: land was in the frontier stage when the census showed that it had a population of fewer than two persons per square mile. According to that criterion, the age of the frontier (or, to put it another way, the age of the land that was free for the taking) came to an end about 1890. But far more is involved in the notion of the American frontier than simple population density.

Cultural historians such as Henry Nash Smith (*Virgin Land*, 1950) and Richard Slotkin (*Regeneration Through Violence*, 1973 and *The Fatal Environment*, 1985) have demonstrated that from the beginning of settlement the frontier generated a distinctive ideology and even a distinctive mythology. Among that mythology's creators were such disparate figures as Mary Rowlandson, the seventeenth-century Massachusetts woman who originated the captivity narrative as a literary genre; Cotton Mather, the minister and writer who raised the captivity theme to the level of mythopoeic thought; James Fenimore *Cooper, whose Leatherstocking Tales created a literary archetype; and George Armstrong *Custer, without question foremost of the West's many astute self-publicists. But pride of place in terms of shaping understanding of what the frontier was and what it meant must go to the historian Frederick Jackson Turner (1861-1932). The paper that he gave in 1893 on 'The Significance of the Frontier in American History' must still rank as the single most important piece of writing ever produced about the American past. Though few academic historians would now wholly accept the 'Turner thesis', they still debate it hotly. Moreover, its influence is clearly present in the work of such film-makers as John Ford (*Drums Along the Mohawk*/1939), George Stevens (*Shane*/1952), Sam Peckinpah (*Ride the High Country*/1962), William Fraker (*Monte Walsh*/1970) and Don Siegel

(*The Shootist*/1976).

Turner's paper was no simple, dispassionate scholarly discussion. To his professional colleagues at the American Historical Association's convention Turner was arguing that the West needed to be taken seriously. He was issuing a manifesto for a new field, comparable to the manifestos of black and feminist historians in more recent times. To the larger world Turner was arguing that the closing of the frontier provided an explanation for America's *fin-de-siècle* economic and political crisis. Future presidents Theodore *Roosevelt and Woodrow Wilson, both historical scholars in their own right, paid close attention to what Turner said.

Turner's central point was that the phenomenon of a moving frontier explained American uniqueness. Strongly influenced by the Italian economist Achille Loria, who, in turn, was influenced by Marx, Turner maintained that it provided, in effect, a source of free capital. This was, in the words of Fulmer Mood, 'the material cause, the fundamental economic factor' in American history. Thanks to the moving frontier, the nineteenth-century American landscape had presented a geographical cross-section of the whole of human history. 'Stand at the Cumberland Gap,' Turner wrote, 'and watch the procession of civilization, marching single file.... Stand at South Pass in the Rockies a century later and see the same procession with wider intervals between.' From this all else sprang. The distinctive American national character was the result of the stripping away of the European veneer as whites encountered raw nature. American democracy itself was the product of the frontier. 'It was *western* New York that forced an extension of suffrage in ... that State in 1821.... The rise of democracy as an effective force in the nation came in with western preponderance under [Presidents Andrew] Jackson and William Henry Harrison, and it meant the triumph of the frontier.'

Though the frontier explained individualism in Turner's eyes, he did not structure his argument in terms of the free individual. Instead, he wrote about large, conflicting social forces, determined by the relationship of many individuals to the productive possibilities that the West offered. The many frontiers – of trappers, traders, miners, cattlemen, farmers – represented different social formations, and as one succeeded another it was by a process of conflict. Moreover, the end of the frontier, as announced in 1890, posed the problem of a future in which the historic wellspring of democracy and individualism had run dry. The 'safety valve' of free land was gone, and with it the possibility of a continuous re-creation of society. The discontented could no longer find (in Lee Benson's words) 'unoccupied land' which could 'be culti-vated and possessed without capital'. The future that loomed was not one in which social problems could be escaped. It was one in which the internal tensions of an urban, industrial society would have to work them-selves out.

There are many reasons why historians no longer accept Turner's thesis in its entirety. One is its failure to confront the historic agony of American race relations. For Turner the Indians' only function was to get out of the way, and the presence of a huge black minority was a mere sideshow. A second reason is the failure of Turner's imagery completely to describe reality. Though the Census Bureau announced the frontier's 'closing' in 1890, in the sense that a line could no longer be drawn to separate the zone of settlement from the wilderness, there was still a great deal of 'free' land available until into the 20th century. Con-versely, the urban unrest and labour vio-lence that so preoccupied the mind of middle-class America in Turner's day began well before 1890. The 'closing' of the fron-tier could not possibly explain it. Turner's most famous image, of the frontier rolling implacably westward, fails as well. The reality was that the zone of settlement expanded not only from the east but from western cores, including northern California after the Gold Rush of 1849, Oregon's Willamette Valley and the Mormon Zion in the Utah desert.

The notion of one 'stage' of development mechanically giving way to the next as the frontier moves on also falls down. The idea of a cattle kingdom yielding to a farmers' republic may hold for the Illinois and Indiana prairies. But it never applied to Minnesota or the intra-montane desert or the Pacific Coast. Finally, the frontier could produce a society based on inequality as easily as one based on democracy. The historian Paul Wallace Gates has demon-strated how great estates were built in the upper Mississippi Valley. He has also shown how railroads and land-grant universities and speculators all used the government's land policy to create a society far removed from the Jeffersonian goal of one built on small freeholders. In the South, the moving frontier meant the expansion of slavery; in *Uncle Tom's Cabin* (1852) Harriet Beecher Stowe used the figure of a frontier farmer – Simon Legree – to represent the worst of the slave system.

But Turner was undoubtedly correct in two major respects. One was to conceive American history in social rather than heroic-individualistic terms. The other was to understand the enormous challenge that the western environment posed. The fron-tier thesis has found filmic expression in two separate respects. One is the awareness of some film-makers that the West's history is a tale of social development and conflict. The other is their concern, especially in the 1960s and the 1970s, with the problems that the 'end of the West' posed. *Shane* provides a splendid example of the first. *Monte Walsh* and practically all the Westerns of Sam Peckinpah speak to the second. In these films (and they are not the only ones), one can see a sharp historical consciousness, as opposed to the vague, undefined 'pastness' of such other 'quality' films as *Rio Bravo*/ 1958, *True Grit*/1969, *She Wore a Yellow Ribbon*/1949, *Johnny Guitar*/1954 or *High Plains Drifter*/1972. That is not even to mention the essential a-historicity of most B-westerns and television series.

Shane, like such films as *The Man Who Shot Liberty Valance*/1962 and *Heaven's Gate*/ 1980, is constructed in Turnerian terms. The action takes place as the pastoral stage of development is reaching its limits and is about to give way to the stage of small farming. For George Stevens, as for Turner, the movement is progressive, to be applauded. *Shane*'s cattlemen are essentially a force of nature, like the cattle they herd. As such, they are surrogates for the Indians (though it should be noted that they are also surrogates for rapacious capitalism). They form an all-male, violent society, unable to reproduce itself. The film's sodbusters are the force of civilization, and their triumph will bring a world of families, churches, schools and law. In the centre of the film, Stevens creates a moonlight debate between spokesman for each side, and each puts his case eloquently. There is no question as to which side the film endorses. But in this sequence, at least, the conflict is one of historical stages, not simply one of good and evil.

Monte Walsh speaks to the same problem, which is not at all surprising given that Jack Schaefer wrote the novels from which both films are derived. Again, the cattle frontier is passing, and unlike *Shane*, which has no specific setting in time or place, the informed viewer knows when. It is just after the great blizzard of 1885, when the herds of the high plains were decimated. But now the cow-boy's life is giving way to corporate capi-talism, not to small farmers and their families. The 'Consolidated Cattle Corpor-ation' is buying up ranches and closing them to suit its own needs. The problem that faces the film's cowboys is not farmers taking over the range. It is structural unemployment, that not only drives them off it but makes it impossible for them to find any other way to live. Few Westerns come so close to a genuinely class-based perspective.

But others do address the problem of the West's end. *The Man Who Shot Liberty Valance* speaks to the human price exacted by the ending of frontier social conditions. *Ride the High Country*, *The Wild Bunch*/1969 and *The Ballad of Cable Hogue*/1970 are all set in the post-frontier world of the early 20th century. In all of them that world (full of banks, Chinese restaurants, corporations and machines) has no place for sturdy individuals who have lived beyond their day. As Pike Bishop (William Holden) puts it in *The Wild Bunch*, their need is to recognize that their own 'days are closing fast'.

Frederick Jackson Turner developed his understanding of the frontier's significance against the background of two different problems that faced his own time: the West's need to assert that what had hap-pened in it was historically important, and American society's need to face the prob-lems posed by a new (as Turner saw it) historical conjuncture. A historical era was ending, and Turner knew it. The emergence in Westerns of the theme of the 'end of the West' came as another era, the short-lived 'American century' of world supremacy, was coming to its own end. As Philip French has suggested, Westerns provided a power-ful means for American society to comment on itself during the decades of its world triumph. The 'end of the West' as a theme, the effective end of the Western as a popular genre, and the end of American supremacy as a historical development seem to be more than coincidentally related. EC

Fur trade · The hunting or trapping of fur-bearing animals and the exchange of their skins and pelts were among the first economic activities of Europeans in North America. As early as 1535 the Frenchman Jacques Cartier on his first expedition to Canada had obtained some furs from Indians in the St Lawrence region. With the founding of Quebec in 1608, the French began a vigorous pursuit of the fur trade that led their bands of trappers into the Great Lakes and along the Mississippi river. There they came into conflict with the British, who had found that furs obtained from the Indians were a highly lucrative commodity. As well as pushing into the Appalachians from Virginia and the Carolinas, the British launched another fur trade venture in the far north when the *Hudson's Bay Company was chartered in 1670. It was to become the greatest fur trading corporation of North America.

The first American challenge to the European trappers and traders was mounted in the early part of the 19th century after President Jefferson's acquisition of lands across the Mississippi, known as the *Louisiana Purchase. American fur gatherers pushed westward from the Kentucky and Ohio country across the Mississippi into the vast Louisiana territory and the Rockies. The early route of the fur men was up the Missouri River in keelboats, a mode of transport that Howard Hawks in *The Big Sky*/1952 conceived as being as epic as the covered wagon or railroad. Although the trapper prided himself on his individualism as a man alone in the wilderness, he came increasingly under the control of firms like the American Fur Company, established in 1808 by John Jacob Astor (1763-1848).

The control of the trapper over his destiny was further curtailed by a mode of organization known as the rendezvous system, established by William Ashley in 1825. The trapper or *mountain man would spend the winter working up to his waist in the fast-running streams that abounded in the Rocky Mountains. Here he laid his traps and caught the beaver. He could team up with other trappers, living in camps which offered some protection from hostile Indians. In the summer he would take his pelts to a predetermined meeting place at the foot of the Rockies known as the 'rendezvous'. Here he would meet the supply party of traders from St Louis who would buy his pelts and sell him supplies for the rest of the year. The rendezvous period was also a chance to live it up for a while and epic bouts of drinking and general hell-raising became part of the folklore of the mountain man, along with his single-handed struggles with mountain bears and bands of Indians. In reality the trapper was in part a victim, whose labour was exploited by traders like Astor, who made fortunes out of the sale of fur as fashionable hats and trimmings. The heyday of the Rocky Mountain fur trade lasted until the 1840s, when a declining demand for his single commodity (fashion began to dictate silk not beaver for hats) forced the trapper to adapt. Some tried farming in Oregon but often found that the pioneer communities turned against them, their Indian wives and children. Others became scouts for the army or guides to the emigrant wagon trains. Their important role as explorers and trailblazers for American interests, particularly in establishing a challenge to British designs on Oregon, has never exerted the imaginative power of their hell-raising legend as wild frontiersmen. Their role in the Hollywood Western has been relatively marginal, though the figure of the trapper or hunter was present at the birth of the fictional Western hero. With moccasins on his feet, a coon-skin or beaver cap on his head and in a buckskin tunic fringed with tassels, he moved heroically through the pages of Fenimore *Cooper's Leatherstocking novels in the form of Natty Bumppo. CB

G

Gall (c.1840-94) · A chief of the Hunkpapa Sioux. Originally named Pizi, his later name derives, in one account, from his attempt as a starving child to eat an animal's gall bladder; in another from his mean streak. Gall resisted the army's attempt to herd all Indians on to reservations after 1868. He was a close associate of *Sitting Bull and one of those principally responsible for the victory at the *Little Big Horn. He surrendered in 1880 and later became a judge of the Indian Court at the Standing Rock reservation. John Russell/*Yellowstone Kelly*/1959/WB/*d* Gordon Douglas/*lp* Clint Walker

Gambling · 'Is this a game of chance?' enquires a tyro poker player of W.C. Fields in *My Little Chickadee*. 'Not the way I play it,' Fields retorts. Gambling may have been the West's most popular pastime, but in the Western its dramatic potential derives from its association with criminality. As Bernard Eisenschitz says in *Le Western* (Paris: 10/18, 1966), the gambler 'introduces into a heroic cinema the possibilities of the anti-hero, the attraction of vice and corruption, presented under the fascinating cover of the seducer.' This aura of seductive corruption may derive in part from the fact that both poker and faro originated not in the WASP areas of the States but in Catholic, French-speaking New Orleans.

If there is usually a doubt about the honesty of gamblers, they are not usually given the benefit of it, which is why even a sheriff as venal as Guthrie McCabe (James Stewart) in *Two Rode Together*/1961 can peremptorily order a couple of them out of town. Of course the gambler can redeem himself, as do Stephen McNally in *Apache*

Marlene Dietrich's gambling saloon in Rancho Notorious

Playing faro in a saloon in Leadville, Colorado (c.1899)

Drums, Robert Young in *The Half-Breed*, Barry Sullivan in *Texas Lady* and Stuart Whitman in *The Comancheros*/1961. But the fancy waistcoat and bootlace tie will not immediately gain him respect as a real man; he has to earn the title. Even Doc Holliday is treated with suspicion by Wyatt Earp for most of *Gunfight at the O.K. Corral*/1956.

Gambling has been part of the Western from the start. There is a card game in *Poker at Dawson City*, an Edison film of 1898, and plenty of gambling in the films of Broncho Billy Anderson. It's a common motif in the Westerns of W.S. Hart. Both the character and appearance of the gambler have remained remarkably stable. The gamblers in the stories of Bret *Harte, who was largely responsible for introducing the type into western fiction, are cool but courteous, especially to ladies, and fastidious about their clothes, just like John Carradine in *Stagecoach*/1939. A perfect example of the stereotype is Wendell Corey in *The Furies*/1950. He wears a bootlace tie and long coat, rides not on horseback but in a rig, carries a *Derringer and is a consummate ladies man. The most engaging gambler in the Western is undoubtedly Bret Maverick, played by James Garner in the TV series *Maverick* and its sequels. In *Silverado*/1985 the stock character of the gambler who keeps a Derringer up his sleeve is still going strong. Two films of the 1960s, *A Big Hand for the Little Lady* and *5 Card Stud*, based their entire plots on a game of poker.

My Little Chickadee/1940/U/d Edward Cline/*lp* Mae West, W.C. Fields · *Apache Drums*/1950/U/d Hugo Fregonese/*lp* Stephen McNally, Coleen Gray · *The Half-Breed*/1952/RKO/d Stuart Gilmore/*lp* Robert Young, Jack Buetel · *Texas Lady*/1955/RKO/d Tim Whelan/*lp* Claudette Colbert, Barry Sullivan · *A Big Hand for the Little Lady*/1966/WB/d Fielder Cook/*lp* Henry Fonda, Joanne Woodward, Jason Robards · *5 Card Stud*/1968/PAR/d Henry Hathaway/*lp* Dean Martin, Robert Mitchum

Garrett, Pat[rick Floyd] (1850-1908) · Lawman. For the rest of his life, after he shot *Billy the Kid at Fort Sumner, New Mexico, on 14 July 1881, Pat Garrett was known for that one thing only. Elected sheriff of Lincoln County to bring order in the aftermath of the *Lincoln County War, Garrett got little thanks for what he had done and was not renominated for office. To justify his action he wrote a book with a journalist friend, *The Authentic Life of Billy the Kid*

Pat Garrett

(1882). After periods as a Texas Ranger and customs officer Garrett tried ranching. As the result of a feud over property he was shot in the back while urinating on a country road in New Mexico, though who actually killed him is uncertain. Since almost all films about Billy the Kid have made the Kid a hero, Garrett's pursuit of him has been viewed with, at best, mixed feelings.

Wallace Beery/*Billy the Kid*/1930 · Wade Boteler/*Billy the Kid Returns*/1938/REP/d Joseph Kane/*lp* Roy Rogers · Thomas Mitchell/*The Outlaw*/1940 · Brian Donlevy (as Jim Sherwood = Garrett)/*Billy the Kid*/1941/MGM/d David Miller/*lp* Robert Taylor · Charles Bickford/*Four Faces West*/1948/UA/d Alfred E. Green/*lp* Joel McCrea · Dean White/*Return of the Bad Men*/1948/

RKO/d Ray Enright/*lp* Randolph Scott · Frank Wilcox/*The Kid from Texas*/1949/U/d Kurt Neumann/*lp* Audie Murphy · Robert Lowery/*I Shot Billy the Kid*/1950/Lippert/d William Berke/*lp* Don Barry · James Griffith/*The Law vs. Billy the Kid*/1954/COL/d William Castle/*lp* Scott Brady · James Craig/*Last of the Desperados*/1955/Associated/d Sam Newfield · John Dehner/*The Left Handed Gun*/1957 · George Montgomery/*Badman's Country*/1958/WB/d Fred F. Sears/*lp* Buster Crabbe, Neville Brand · Fausto Tozzi/*El hombre que matao Billy el niño*/1967/Sp/d Julio Buchs/*lp* Peter Lee Lawrence · Glenn Corbett/*Chisum*/1970/WB/d Andrew V. McLaglen/*lp* John Wayne · Rod Cameron/*The Last Movie*/1971 · James Coburn/*Pat Garrett and Billy the Kid*/1973 · Rod Cameron/*Die letzten Zwei vom Rio Bravo*/1964/WG, It, Sp/d Mario Caiano
Television · Rhodes Reason/*Bronco* · Barry Sullivan/*The Tall Man*

Gatling gun · Designed in 1861 by Richard Gatling (1818-1903), the Gatling gun was a crank-operated weapon with several barrels revolving around a central shaft for rapid firing; in other words, a kind of early machine gun. It was adopted by the US Army in 1866. Numerous refinements brought its fire-power up to 3,000 rounds a minute by 1911. Gatling himself perceived how symptomatic his invention was of the modern world: 'It bears the same relation to other firearms that McCormack's Reaper does to the sickle, or the sewing machine to the common needle.' (Quoted in John Ellis, *The Social History of the Machine Gun*.) In the Western its possession provides a decisive technological advantage. The incidence of Gatling guns in films increased with the advent of Italian Westerns and the boost they gave to novel weaponry of all kinds. Films in which the Gatling gun appears include: *The Siege at Red River*/1953/FOX/d Rudolph Maté/*lp* Van Johnson, Joanne Dru · *Indio Black, sai che ti dico: sei un gran figlio di...*/1970/It/d Frank Kramer/*lp* Yul Brynner · *Something Big*/1971/Cinema Center/d Andrew V. McLaglen/*lp* Dean Martin, Brian Keith · *Rooster Cogburn*/1975/U/d Stuart Millar/*lp* John Wayne, Katharine Hepburn · *The Gatling Gun*/1971/Western International/d Robert Gordon/*lp* Guy Stockwell, Woody Strode

Geography · The area between the Mississippi and the Pacific divides broadly into three distinct kinds of terrain: the plains, the mountains and the deserts. The Western employs all three as a setting, though not in equal proportion. Few Westerns use the actual landscape of the plains, possibly because the plains today, unlike the mountains and deserts, have been changed in appearance by the operations of agriculture. Mile upon mile of geometrically arranged cornfields do not present the aspect of Kansas which a film set in 1867 requires.

The question of the precise geographical locations of Westerns is an intriguing one. A count was made of all titles listed in Phil Hardy's encyclopedia, *The Western* (1983), which referred to a specific locality, including states (*Colorado Territory*/1949), towns (*The Man from Laramie*/1955) and other features of natural or human geography (*Across the Wide Missouri*/1950). In addition, films with known specific locations were added to the figures (thus *My Darling Clementine*/1946 takes place in Tombstone, Arizona; *Duel in the Sun*/1946 is set in Texas).

The resultant statistics can only be a rough guide. But they indicate a pronounced geographical imbalance in the location of the Western film. The figures are as follows (note that they apply only to the sound period):

Arizona	83
California	82
Canada (inc. Alaska & Yukon)	62
Colorado	27
Dakota (North and South)	21
Idaho	3
Kansas	34
Missouri	12
Montana	16
Nebraska	3
Nevada	21
New Mexico	44
Oklahoma	44
Oregon	9
South of the Border	68
Texas	198
Utah	10
Wyoming	58

Texas looms as proportionately large in the Western as it does in actuality. The figure would be even higher if we were to include films about the Texas Rangers or

Westerns with 'Lone Star' in the title. Perhaps more surpising than the dominance of Texas is the extent to which the Southwest (Arizona and New Mexico) far outweighs in importance the Northwest: Oregon and Idaho figure modestly, the state of Washington not at all. However, a high proportion of those films set in the Southwest are located in two places only: Tombstone (Arizona) and Santa Fe (New Mexico). Most of the Westerns set in California, one of the largest and now most populous states, take place in 'Old California'; that is, California before it became part of the United States. 'South of the Border' is a deliberately vague category, because it includes not only films which are unequivocally set in Mexico (such as *Vera Cruz*/1954), but many which take place either on or just across the border (such as *The Wonderful Country*/1959). Of those states which technically form part of the eastern-most fringe of the (trans-Mississippi) West, only Missouri (the 'border country', home of the James gang and other bandits) has a significant presence in the Western. Wyoming is a particularly popular location, partly because of the number of films which refer to Cheyenne (the town, not the Indian nation). Finally, Canadians may be offended at the lumping together of Alaska and the Yukon, but in the Western (whatever may have been the reality) they form a homogeneous whole.

Germans · The Germans not only helped in large numbers to settle the West, especially the northern plains; in Karl *May they had a writer who made a major contribution to the invention of the Western. May was not the only German novelist in the 19th century adding to the myth of the West. Both Karl Postl (1793-1864), writing as Charles Sealsfield, and Friedrich Gerstäcker (1816-72) achieved large sales and helped fuel a passion for the West which both encouraged emigration and led to the creation of Wild West clubs in which enthusiasts could play at cowboys and Indians. Over 120 of these clubs were reported in existence as recently as 1970.

An occasional German Western had been made in the 1930s, such as *Der Kaiser von Kalifornien* (1936) and *Sergeant Berry* (1938), starring Hans Albers. Beginning with *Der Schatz im Silbersee* in 1962, a number of German Westerns were made during the 1960s from Karl May's books. Mostly shot in Yugoslavia, their success paved the way for the Italian Western.

In the Hollywood Western the stereotype

of the stiff-necked martinet popularized by Erich von Stroheim and given a new lease of life by World War II is virtually the only role assigned to Germans. This character, usually acting as military adviser to a Mexican general or revolutionary, appears in: *Vera Cruz*/1954 · *Cheyenne Autumn*/1964 · *100 Rifles*/1968 · *The Wild Bunch*/1969 · *Indio Black, sai che ti dico: sei un gran figlio di ...*/1970/It/d Frank Kramer/lp Yul Brynner · *Cannon for Cordoba*/1970/UA/d Paul Wendkos/lp George Peppard, Raf Vallone · *Los amigos*/1972/It/d Paolo Cavara/lp Anthony Quinn, Franco Nero

Geronimo (1829?-1909) · The Mexican name for Goyathlay, leader of the Chiricahua *Apache. At first a noted warrior under *Cochise, Geronimo became virtual chief of the Chiricahua after Cochise's death in 1874. In 1877 he and his band were taken to the San Carlos reservation in Arizona by John *Clum, but in 1881 Geronimo broke out. Persuaded by General Crook to surrender in 1883, he broke out again in 1885 and for a third time in 1886. His final and unconditional surrender was negotiated by General Nelson *Miles in September 1886 after Geronimo had been pursued on both sides of the border by 42 companies of the American army and 4,000 Mexican troops, equipped, as a contemporary account put it, with 'the best military apparatus of modern warfare, including steam, electricity and the heliostat'. Geronimo was sent into exile in Florida, then in Oklahoma, where he was reduced to selling pictures of himself to tourists. He allowed himself to be an exhibit at the St Louis World's Fair in 1904. He was the last Indian leader to surrender to the United States.

In the cinema Geronimo seems to have been played by more real Indians than any other Indian character, though this has not necessarily led to more sympathetic portrayals.
Geronimo's Last Raid/1912/American/d G.P. Hamilton · Chief White Horse/*Stagecoach*/1939 · Chief Thundercloud/*Geronimo!*/1940/PAR/d P.H. Sloane/lp Preston Foster, Ellen Drew · Tom Tyler/*Valley of the Sun*/1942/RKO/d George Marshall/lp Lucille Ball, Dean Jagger · Chief Thundercloud/*I Killed Geronimo*/1950/Schwarz/d John Hoffman/lp James Ellison · Jay Silverheels/*Broken Arrow*/1950 · John War Eagle/*The Last Outpost*/1951/PAR/d Lewis R. Foster/lp Ronald Reagan, Rhonda Fleming · Miguel Inclan/*Indian Uprising*/1951/COL/d Ray Nazarro/lp

George Montgomery · Jay Silverheels/*The Battle at Apache Pass*/1952/U/d George Sherman/lp John Lund, Jeff Chandler · Chief Yowlachie/*Son of Geronimo*/1952/COL/d Spencer G. Bennet/lp Clayton Moore · Ian MacDonald/*Taza, Son of Cochise*/1953 · Monte Blue/*Apache*/1954 · Jay Silverheels/*Walk the Proud Land*/1956/U/d Jesse Hibbs/lp Audie Murphy, Anne Bancroft · Pat Hogan/*Geronimo's Revenge*/1960/d James Neilson, Harry Keller/lp Tom Tryon · Chuck Connors/*Geronimo*/1962/UA/d Arnold Laven/lp Adam West Television · Charles Stevens/*The Adventures of Rin Tin Tin* · Mike Mazurki/*F Troop* · Enrique Lucero/*Mr. Horn*

Ghost town · On one level a ghost town is just a picturesque and convenient location. But ghost towns are usually mining towns, deserted when the seam played out. Thus both their present physical desolation and their past history are, in Philip French's words, 'the objective correlative of the impermanence of American life, a pessimistic feeling about the fragility of American civilization and its problems in putting down roots.' *Yellow Sky*/1948, *The Law and Jake Wade*/1958 and *Man of the West*/1958 all use their ghost town settings to enhance the bleakness of their stories, in which civilization is a thin veneer on the surface of human villainy. Today, ghost towns such as Calico in California and Virginia City in Nevada have been restored and thrive as tourist attractions.

Glass, Hugh (?-1833?) · Mountain man, one of William Ashley's trappers. In 1823 occurred the experience which made Glass a legendary figure. As a member of Andrew Henry's expedition up the Missouri he was attacked and badly mauled by a bear. After five days, John Fitzgerald and Jim *Bridger, the two men ordered to stay with Glass, convinced themselves that he could not live, took his rifle and knife and reported that they had buried him. But after ten days Glass recovered enough to crawl. Sustaining himself on berries, he dragged himself half the length of South Dakota back to safety at Fort Kiowa. Eventually he was able to confront the two who had left him for dead, but took no revenge other than that of surviving to witness their discomfiture.

Glass' experience was the subject of an epic poem by John G. Neihardt, *The Song of Hugh Glass* (1915) and written up as the novel *Lord Grizzly* (1954) by Frederick Manfred. The story was told in *Man in the Wilderness*/1971/WB/d Richard Sarafian/lp Richard Harris, John Huston, though for some reason the hero is called Sam Bass, a very different character.

Goodnight, Charles (1836-1929) Cattleman. After the Civil War Goodnight decided to seek a market for his Texas cattle with the army in New Mexico. Another Texas cattleman, Oliver Loving (1812-67), had already in 1858 made the first recorded cattle-drive north from Texas, all the way to Chicago. In 1866 these two pioneered a trail, known as the Goodnight-Loving Trail, from Fort Belknap, Texas to Fort Sumner, New Mexico. This became one of the major routes for livestock movement in the West. On their third trip Loving was killed by Indians, but Goodnight continued to drive cattle up the trail, working with New Mexico cattlemen such as John *Chisum. Andy *Adams' *Reed Anthony* (1907) is a fictional portrait of Goodnight.

Gould, Jay (1836-92) · Financier, the prototype of the 'robber baron'. Gould's specu-

'The Modern Colossus of (Rail) Roads': William Henry Vanderbilt controls the railroads with the help of C.W. Field and Jay Gould

☜Geronimo (at the wheel) on the 101 Ranch in Oklahoma (c.1905)

lation in railway bonds brought him control of the *Union Pacific Railroad in the early 1870s. Then, having pushed up the price of the stock by raising freight rates, he sold out at a profit. Later Gould bought Kansas Pacific stock and threatened to extend its network to the Pacific, thereby endangering the revenues of the Union Pacific. U.P. then offered him a merger. This raised the value of Gould's Kansas Pacific stock and again he sold out at a profit. Control of other railroads followed, and of the Western Union Telegraph Company, newspapers and other businesses. Small in stature, tubercular and not over-sentimental, Gould's reputation was soon secure in populist mythology, justifiably or not, as a grasping monopolist and heartless manipulator. Every Western with an unsympathetic big business character owes something to Jay Gould.

Grant, Ulysses S[impson] (1822-85) · 18th President of the United States 1869-77. Though he served in the Mexican War and later in California and Oregon, it is not for his actual achievements in relation to the West that Grant deserves mention. Rather, it's that since he was President at the time a lot of Westerns are set, his bearded, stocky

figure makes an occasional appearance, usually on the end of a fat cigar. Joseph Crehan, who appears as Grant in *Union Pacific*/1939, practically had a monopoly on the character, playing him over fifty times, though not all those films are Westerns. He also appears as Grant in *They Died with their Boots On*/1941.
Also: Walter Rogers/*The Flaming Frontier*/1926/u/d Edward Sedgwick/lp Hoot Gibson · Stan Jones/*The Horse Soldiers*/1959 · Henry Morgan/*How the West Was Won*/1962 · Jason Robards/*The Legend of the Lone Ranger*/1981/itc/d William A. Fraker/lp Klinton Spilsbury
Television · Paul Birch/*The Adventures of Rin Tin Rin* · William Bryany/*Branded* · Roy Engel/*The Wild, Wild West* · James Gregory/*The Wild, Wild West* · Richard Dysart/*The Court Martial of George Armstrong Custer*

Greeley, Horace (1811-72) · Newspaperman. Founder of the New York *Tribune* in 1841, Greeley was an enthusiastic promoter of the West and in particular of the homestead idea, which he believed would syphon off surplus labour from the east and so prevent social unrest. In 1859 he made a trip

to California and published an account, *An Overland Journey from New York to San Francisco* (1860). If he probably did not originate the phrase 'Go West, young man, and grow up with the country,' which Henry Nash Smith dates as early as 1837, he certainly popularized it.

Grey, Zane (1872-1939) · Author. Probably the most popular writer of Western fiction ever and certainly the most frequently adapted by the cinema, Grey is more impressive as a phenomenon than as a writer. It is hard to believe now that *Riders of the Purple Sage*, with its quaint attempts at western dialect and its juvenile morality, has sold more than two million copies since it was published in 1912. Some of his seventy-eight books deal with aspects of the historical West; thus *The Thundering Herd* (1925) is about the slaughter of the buffalo, *The U.P. Trail* (1918) about the coming of the railroad, and *Western Union* (1939) about building the transcontinental telegraph. But all Grey's novels are essentially adolescent fantasies set in a never-never land of romance and adventure.

Whatever their literary merits, Zane Grey novels were made and remade into

Ulysses S. Grant in 1864

A Zane Grey adaptation of the 1930s

Hollywood films until well into the 1940s (and many of his books continue in print seventy or more years after their first appearance). He was one of the few writers whose name appeared above the title of films as a selling point. His huge popularity made him irresistible to Hollywood. And the fact that his work was so formulaic made it ideal material for the series Westerns which Fox and Paramount endlessly spun out.

The publicity value of Grey's name was such that producers sometimes played fast and loose with his work, attaching Zane Grey titles to new plots or switching the titles of his books around. Compiling an accurate filmography is therefore difficult. *Desert Gold*/1919/PAR/d T. Hayes Hunter/lp E.K. Lincoln, Russell Simpson · remade 1926/PAR/d George B. Seitz/lp Neil Hamilton · remade 1936/PAR/d James Hogan/lp Robert Cummings · *Riders of the Purple Sage*/1918/FOX/d Frank Lloyd/lp William Farnum · remade 1925/FOX/d Lynn Reynolds/lp Tom Mix · remade 1931/FOX/d Hamilton MacFadden/lp George O'Brien · remade 1941/FOX/d James Tinling/lp George Montgomery · *The Light of Western Stars*/1918/Sherman-United/d Charles Swickard/lp Dustin Farnum · remade 1925/PAR/d William K. Howard/lp Jack Holt · remade 1930/PAR/d Otto Brower, Edwin H. Knopf/lp Richard Arlen, Victor Jory · remade 1940/PAR/d Lesley Selander/lp Russell Hayden · *The Rainbow Trail*/1918/FOX/d Frank Lloyd/lp William Farnum · remade 1925/FOX/d Lynn Reynolds/lp Tom Mix · remade 1931/FOX/d David Howard/lp George O'Brien · *The Border Legion*/1919/ Goldwyn/d T. Hayes Hunter/lp Hobart Bosworth · remade 1924/PAR/d William K. Howard/lp Antonio Moreno · remade 1930/PAR/d Otto Brower, Edwin H. Knopf/lp Richard Arlen, Jack Holt · remade as *The Last Round-Up*/1934/PAR/d Henry Hathaway/lp Randolph Scott · remade as *The Border Legion*/1940/REP/d Joseph Kane/lp Roy Rogers · *The Last of the Duanes*/1919/FOX/d J. Gordon Edwards/lp William Farnum · remade 1924/FOX/d Lynn Reynolds/lp Tom Mix · remade 1930/FOX/d Alfred Werker/lp George O'Brien · remade 1941/FOX/d James Tinling/lp George Montgomery · *The Lone Star Ranger*/1919/FOX/d J. Gordon Edwards/lp William Farnum · remade 1923/FOX/d Lambert Hillyer/lp Tom Mix · remade 1929/FOX/d A.F. Erickson/lp George O'Brien · remade 1941/FOX/d James Tinling/lp John

Kimbrough · *The U.P. Trail*/1919/ Hodkinson/d Jack Conway/lp Roy Stewart · *Riders of the Dawn* [*The Desert of Wheat*]/ 1920/Hodkinson/d Hugh Ryan Conway/lp Roy Stewart · *Man of the Forest*/1921/PAR/ d Benjamin B. Hampton/lp Carl Gantvoort · remade 1926/PAR/d John Waters/lp Jack Holt · remade 1933/PAR/d Henry Hathaway/lp Randolph Scott, Harry Carey · *The Mysterious Rider*/1921/ PAR/d Benjamin B. Hampton/lp Jack Holt · remade 1927/PAR/d John Waters/lp Jack Holt · remade 1933/PAR/d Fred Allen/lp Kent Taylor · remade 1938/PAR/d Lesley Selander/lp Russell Hayden · *Golden Dreams*/1922/Goldwyn/d Benjamin B. Hampton/lp Rose Dione · *The Last Trail*/ 1921/FOX/d Emmett J. Flynn/lp Maurice Flynn · remade 1927/FOX/d Lewis Seiler/lp Tom Mix · remade 1933/FOX/d James Tinling/lp George O'Brien, Claire Trevor · *When Romance Rides* [*Wildfire*]/1922/ Goldwyn/d Eliot Howe, Charles O. Rush, Jean Hersholt/lp Claire Adams · remade as *Red Canyon*/1948/U/d George Sherman/lp Howard Duff · *To the Last Man*/1923/PAR/ d Victor Fleming/lp Richard Dix · remade 1933/PAR/d Henry Hathaway/lp Randolph Scott · *Call of the Canyon*/1923/PAR/d Victor Fleming/lp Richard Dix · remade 1942/REP/d Joseph Santley/lp Gene Autry · *Heritage of the Desert*/1924/PAR/d Irvin Willat/lp Bebe Daniels · remade 1932/PAR/ d Henry Hathaway/lp Randolph Scott · remade 1939/PAR/d Lesley Selander/lp Donald Woods · *Wanderer of the Wasteland*/1924/PAR/d Irvin Willat/lp Jack Holt · remade 1935/PAR/d Otho Lovering/ lp Buster Crabbe · remade 1945/RKO/d Edward Killy, Wallace Grissell/lp James Warren · *Code of the West*/1925/PAR/d William K. Howard/lp Owen Moore · remade as *Home on the Range*/1934/PAR/d Arthur Jacobson/lp Randolph Scott · remade as *Code of the West*/1947/RKO/d William Berke/lp James Warren · *The Thundering Herd*/1925/PAR/d William K. Howard/lp Jack Holt · remade 1933/PAR/d Henry Hathaway/lp Randolph Scott · *The Vanishing American*/1925/PAR/d George B. Seitz/lp Richard Dix · remade 1955/REP/d Joseph Kane/lp Scott Brady · *Wild Horse Mesa*/1925/PAR/d George B. Seitz/lp Jack Holt · remade 1932/PAR/d Henry Hathaway/lp Randolph Scott · remade 1947/RKO/d Wallace Grissell/lp Tim Holt · *Forlorn River*/1926/PAR/d John Waters/lp Jack Holt · remade 1937/PAR/d Charles Barton/lp Buster Crabbe · *Born to the West*/1926/PAR/d John Waters/lp Jack Holt

· remade 1938/PAR/d Charles Barton/lp John Wayne, Johnny Mack Brown · *Lightning*/1927/Tiffany/d James C. McKay/ lp Jobyna Ralston · *Nevada*/1927/PAR/d John Waters/lp Gary Cooper · remade 1935/PAR/d Charles Barton/lp Buster Crabbe · remade 1944/RKO/d Edward Killy/lp Robert Mitchum · *Open Range*/ 1927/PAR/d Clifford Smith/lp Lane Chandler · *Drums of the Desert* [*Captives of the Desert*]/1927/PAR/d John Waters/lp Warner Baxter · *Avalanche*/1928/PAR/d Otto Brower/lp Jack Holt · *The Water Hole* [*Lost Pueblo*]/1928/PAR/d F. Richard Jones/lp Jack Holt · *Under the Tonto Rim*/ 1928/PAR/d Herman Raymaker/lp Richard Arlen · remade 1933/PAR/d Henry Hathaway/lp Stuart Erwin · remade 1947/ RKO/d Lew Landers/lp Tim Holt · *The Vanishing Pioneer*/1928/PAR/d John Waters/lp Jack Holt · remade as *The Rocky Mountain Mystery*/1935/PAR/d Charles Barton/lp Randolph Scott · *Stairs of Sand*/ 1929/PAR/d Otto Brower/lp Wallace Beery · remade as *Arizona Mahoney*/1936/PAR/d James Hogan/lp Robert Cummings · *Sunset Pass*/1929/PAR/d Otto Brower/lp Jack Holt · remade 1933/PAR/d Henry Hathaway/lp Randolph Scott · remade 1946/RKO/d William Berke/lp James Warren · *Fighting Caravans*/1931/PAR/d Otto Brower, David Burton/lp Gary Cooper · remade as *Wagon Wheels*/1934/PAR/d Charles Barton/ lp Randolph Scott · *Golden West*/1932/ FOX/d David Howard/lp George O'Brien · *Robbers' Roost*/1932/FOX/d Louis King/lp George O'Brien · remade 1955/UA/d Sidney Salkow/lp George Montgomery · *Smoke Lightning* [*Canyon Walls*]/1933/FOX/d David Howard/lp George O'Brien · *Life in the Raw*/1933/FOX/d Louis King/lp George O'Brien · *The Dude Ranger*/1934/FOX/d Edward Cline/lp George O'Brien · *West of the Pecos*/1935/RKO/d Phil Rosen/lp Richard Dix · remade 1945/RKO/d Edward Killy/lp Robert Mitchum · *Thunder Mountain*/1935/FOX/d David Howard/lp George O'Brien · remade 1947/RKO/d Lew Landers/lp Tim Holt · *Drift Fence*/1936/ PAR/d Otho Lovering/lp Buster Crabbe · *The End of the Trail* [*Outlaws of Paloose*]/ 1938/COL/d Erle C. Kenton/lp Jack Holt · *Arizona Raiders* [*Raiders of Spanish Peaks*]/ 1936/PAR/d James Hogan/lp Buster Crabbe · *Roll Along Cowboy*/1937/FOX/d Gus Meins/lp Smith Ballew · *Thunder Trail* [*Arizona Ames*]/1937/PAR/d Charles Barton/ lp Gilbert Roland · *Knights of the Range*/ 1940/PAR/d Lesley Selander/lp Russell Hayden · *Western Union*/1941 · *Gunfighters*

[*Twin Sombreros*]/1947/COL/d George Waggner/lp Randolph Scott · *The Maverick Queen*/1956/REP/d Joseph Kane/lp Barbara Stanwyck · Zane Grey also wrote a comic strip, *King of the Royal Mounted*, and based on this are: *King of the Royal Mounted*/1936/FOX/d Howard Bretherton/ lp Robert Kent · *King of the Royal Mounted*/1940/REP/d William Witney, John English/lp Allan Lane · *King of the Mounties*/1942/REP/d William Witney/lp Allan Lane
Television · *Dick Powell's Zane Grey Theatre*

Gunfighters · Every Western hero is in a sense a gunfighter; a conflict with firearms is the almost invariable conclusion to a Western film. If the modern Western may be said to begin with *Wister's *The Virginian*, so does the ritual of the gunfight, though his description is perfunctory:
'A wind seemed to blow the sleeve off his arm, and he replied to it, and saw Trampas pitch forward. He saw Trampas raise his arm from the ground and fall again, and lie there this time still. A little smoke was rising from the pistol on the ground, and he looked at his own, and saw the smoke flowing upward out of it.
"I expect that's all," he said aloud.'

The outlaw, who lives by the gun, has been a major figure in the Western since the earliest days; in *The Gun Fighter* (1917) William S. Hart plays Cliff Hudspeth, the gunfighter of the title, who is the leader of a band of Arizona outlaws. Since then Billy the Kid, Jesse James and fictional outlaws without number have shot their way across the screen. Henry King's *The Gunfighter*/ 1950 marked a significant development, a fresh look at the psychology of the man who makes his living by violence. Jimmy Ringo is tired of killing and wants to settle down; but his very presence incites the violence he wishes to renounce.

Though not every protagonist is a gunfighter by trade, increasingly the Western has concerned itself not just with outlaws but with professionals who hire out to the highest bidder. Portraits of gunfighters have explored the incompatibility between their trade and the values of civilized society. In *Shane*/1952 Alan Ladd's skills with a gun, honed to a peak of almost aesthetic perfection, prove necessary to the preservation of the farmers' rights, but ultimately he has no place in their community. In a key scene in *The Magnificent Seven*/1960 the band of hired guns debate the advantages of their chosen calling. On the plus side, no respon-

sibilities, no ties, no enemies (– 'alive'); against that, no family, no friends, no prospects.

As the 60s progressed the professional gunfighter became an increasingly central figure in the Western. The more untenable his position in society became, the more he despised its comfortable complacency. If the professionals in Hawks' *Rio Bravo*/1958 and *El Dorado*/1966 do not quite disdain the honest civilians, they do not need their help either. In such films as *Invitation to a Gunfighter*/1964 the gunfighter is the catalyst who brings to the surface the community's venality and hypocrisy. In the Italian Western the hired guns have become bleakly existential figures in a landscape almost devoid of human society.

The paradox which the Western sees as lying at the heart of the gunfighter's condition, that society needs his unique skills yet hates him for reminding it of that need, finds its logical conclusion in *The Shootist*/1976. The legendary gunfighter J .B. Books (John Wayne) is dying of cancer. In a climactic suicidal shoot-out he simultaneously rids the town of its villains and of the embarrassment of his own presence.
The Gun Fighter/1917/Triangle/d William S. Hart

Guns · As Eric Mottram has said, 'Guns are historically part of human rights in America.' That is, the question of the right of the citizen to bear arms has historically been linked to the issue of individual freedom – however puzzling, or downright unacceptable, that may be to Europeans and even to many Americans. The centrality of guns in the Western is not merely a formal convention. The gun symbolizes the individual's right to self-protection in a society where the law is unreliable or absent altogether. Only when the town-taming sheriff has established his rule can he forbid the carrying of weapons.

The Western is unthinkable without the gun. In turn, many have argued that the pervasiveness of a 'gun culture' within American society derives ultimately from the Western; that the anachronistic continuation into contemporary urban life of the frontier mentality is the main cause of America's appalling crime rate.

A more limited but still suggestive connection between guns and the development of American society can be traced in the history of weapons technology. Most of the major innovations during the 19th century were American. Eli Whitney (1765-1826),

the inventor of the cotton gin, effectively demonstrated the virtues of mass production when he began at the end of the 18th century to manufacture muskets from standardized interchangeable parts. Using this technique, his company produced huge numbers of revolvers and rifles during the Civil War. Samuel *Colt had perfected the first practical revolver in the early 1840s. (It was successfully tested by the Texas Rangers against the Comanche in 1844.) In 1860 Smith and Wesson patented a rim-fire metallic cartridge, which enormously improved the ease and rapidity of fire of small-arms. Richard *Gatling produced the first effective machine gun in 1861. Subsequent advances in machine gun technology, by Maxim, Browning and Lewis, were all American.

A particular combination of factors stimulated these advances. The Civil War produced major leaps forward in weaponry. The frontier created a steady civilian demand for cheap, reliable hand-guns and rifles. Above all, the acute labour shortage in nineteenth-century America, coupled with the absence of the skilled artisans who hand-crafted guns in Europe, gave a powerful impetus to the machine tool industry. Americans were forced to mechanize, and encouraged to believe that the machine and progess were synonymous, that technology could solve all social problems. There is a special irony in the combination within the Western of a traditional ideology of self-reliant individualism which is, paradoxically, dependent on the gun, a piece of technology which was one of the earliest flowers of the industrialized collectivism of the machine age.

Guthrie, A[lfred] B[ertram] (b 1901) · Author. A newspaperman who was brought up in Montana, Guthrie has produced several extensively researched and carefully written novels. His first major Western novel was *The Big Sky* (1947), about the mountain men of the 1830s. *The Way West* (1949) deals with a wagon train of emigrants crossing to Oregon. It won the Pulitzer Prize. *These Thousand Hills* (1956) is a cattle-ranching story. Other novels set in the West include *Arfive* (1970), *The Last Valley* (1975) and *Fair Land, Fair Land* (1982), a sequel to *The Way West*.
The Big Sky/1952 · *These Thousand Hills*/ 1958 · *The Way West*/1967/UA/d Andrew V. McLaglen/lp Kirk Douglas, Robert Mitchum, Richard Widmark · Guthrie also worked in Hollywood on the scripts of *Shane*/1952 and *The Kentuckian*/1955

TWO OF THE EARLIEST painters to depict the West were Seth Eastman and George Catlin, who from the 1830s and 1840s both displayed an ethnographic interest in the everyday life of the Indians. Yet almost simultaneously Alfred Miller and Karl Bodmer showed an eye for the exotic and picturesque. The possibilities of the wilderness landscape were first developed by the Hudson River School, with Thomas Cole one of its best known disciples. By the 1860s Albert Bierstadt had achieved fame with his spectacular paintings of western lakes and mountains, executed on an heroic scale. In a calmer style Worthington Whittredge and Jules Tavernier exploited the wide open spaces of the plains. Thomas Moran continued in the Bierstadt vein until the end of the century, with huge canvases of such landmarks as the Grand Canyon and Yellowstone Park.

1
Seth Eastman
'Spearing Fish in Winter', c. 1868
31 × 44ins, oil on canvas
Architect of the Capitol

As a subject for painting, the West had always offered not just superb vistas but exciting incident. Karl Wimar's picture of an Indian attack is an early example. By the last quarter of the 19th century Frederic Remington, Charles Schreyvogel and Charles Russell had raised the depiction of dramatic action to new heights of realism. Popular prints and posters of the day, illustrating such famous events as Custer's Last Stand or the entertainments of Buffalo Bill, reinforced the view of the West as a land of conflict and daring. A more self-conscious vision comes in the popular prints produced by Currier and Ives, which offered to the public western scenes rich in ideological significance. Emanuel Leutze's painting for the Congress, 'Westward the Course of Empire Takes its Way', performs the same function in a more sophisticated manner.

The rise of the Taos School early in the 20th century brought the wheel full circle. Ignoring landscape and narrative excitements, Joseph Sharp's painting of Indian ritual returns to an interest in the traditional Indian way of life.

2
George Catlin
'Buffalo Hunting', n.d.
16 × 21ins, oil on canvas
Enron Art Foundation, Joslyn Art Museum,
Omaha, Nebraska

3
Alfred J. Miller
'Fort Laramie', c. 1837
9 × 12ins watercolor touched with gouache
Public Archives of Canada

4
Karl Bodmer
'Bison Dance of the Mandan Indians in front
of their Medicine Lodge', n.d.
Lithograph
Thomas Gilcrease Institute of American
History and Art, Tulsa, Oklahoma

5
Currier and Ives
'The Rocky Mountains/Emigrants Crossing
the Plains', 1866
Lithograph
Museum of the City of New York

6
Thomas Cole
'Scene from "The Last of the Mohicans",
Cora Kneeling at the Feet of Tamenund',
1827, 25 × 35ins, oil on canvas
Wadsworth Atheneum, Hartford, Connecticut

7
Currier and Ives
'Across the Continent/Westward the Course
of Empire Takes its Way', 1868
Lithograph
Museum of the City of New York

9
Karl Wimar
'The Attack on an Emigrant Train', 1856
55 × 79ins, oil on canvas
University of Michigan Museum of Art

8
Emanuel Leutze
'Westward the Course of Empire Takes its
Way', 1859
30 × 40ins, oil
Architect of the Capitol

10
Albert Bierstadt
'The Oregon Trail', 1869
31 × 49ins, oil on canvas
The Butler Institute of American Art,
Youngstown, Ohio

Colour plate

11
Albert Bierstadt
'The Rocky Mountains, Lander's Peak', 1863
73 × 121ins, oil on canvas
The Metropolitan Museum of Art, Rogers
Fund, 1907

12
Thomas Moran
'The Grand Canyon of the Yellowstone',
1893, 96 × 185ins, oil on canvas
National Museum of American Art,
Smithsonian Institution

13
Worthington Wittredge
'Crossing the Ford, Platte River', 1870
40 × 68ins, oil on canvas
Frick Art Reference Library, New York

14
Otto Becker
'Custer's Last Fight', 1896
32 × 42ins, lithograph after a painting by
Cassilly Adams, printed by Milwaukee Litho-
graphic & Engraving Co.
The Century Association

15
Jules Tavernier
'Indian Camp at Dawn', c. 1875
24 × 34ins, oil on canvas

Thomas Gilcrease Institute of American
History and Art, Tulsa, Oklahoma

16
Poster for Buffalo Bill's Wild West,
'Buffalo Bill to the Rescue'
Buffalo Bill Historical Center, Cody,
Wyoming

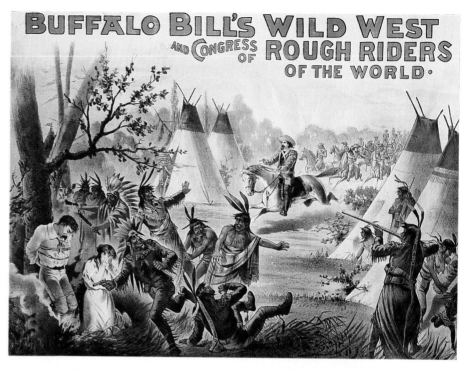

17
Frederic Remington
'A Dash for the Timber', 1889
48 × 84ins, oil on canvas
Amon Carter Museum of Western Art,
Fort Worth, Texas

18
Frederic Remington
'Downing the Nigh Leader', 1907
30 × 50ins, oil
Museum of Western Art, Denver, Colorado

19
Frederic Remington
'The Scout: Friends or Enemies?', c. 1890
27 × 40ins, oil on canvas
Sterling and Francine Clark Art Institute,
Williamstown, Massachusetts

20
Charles Schreyvogel
'Breaking Through the Line', c. 1895
39 × 52ins, oil on canvas
Thomas Gilcrease Institute of American
History and Art, Tulsa, Oklahoma

21
Charles Russell
'In Without Knocking', 1909
20 × 30ins, oil on canvas
Amon Carter Museum of Western Art,
Fort Worth, Texas

22
Joseph H. Sharp
'Prayer to the Spirit of the Buffalo', 1910
29 × 39ins, oil on canvas
The Rockwell Museum, Corning, New York

H

Half-breed · Racial difference is often more important than sexual difference as a motor for Western plots, and the half-breed provides the perfect opportunity to explore the clash of cultures. According to Kevin Brownlow in *The War, the West and the Wilderness* early portrayals were frequently racist and the first sympathetic portrayal of a half-breed did not come until Allan Dwan's *The Half-Breed*, made in 1916, which starred Douglas Fairbanks in the title role. In fact, there is a 'good' half-breed in *Flaming Arrow* (Bison, 1913); typically his goodness consists in helping the whites against the Indians. John Ford's *The Iron Horse*/1924 reverts to a half-breed villain. As Hollywood slowly revised its racial attitudes, the representation of the half-breed often became more liberal than that of the full-blooded Indian, as if the deliberate creation of a character who crosses the racial divide forced film-makers to think beyond their usual stereotypes. This would certainly be true of the characters played by Robert Wagner in *Broken Lance*/1954, Jeffrey Hunter in *The Searchers*/1956, Richard Widmark in *The Last Wagon*/1956, Jack Buetel in *The Half-Breed*, Elvis Presley in *Flaming Star*/1960, Tom Laughlin in *Billy Jack* and Desi Arnaz Jr. in *Billy Two Hats*. But Jennifer Jones as Pearl in *Duel in the Sun*/1946 doesn't escape from the clichés about the sexuality of the non-white races.
The Half-Breed/1952/RKO/*d* Stuart Gilmore/*lp* Robert Young, Jack Buetel · *Billy Jack*/1971/WB/*d* Tom Laughlin/*lp* Tom Laughlin, Dolores Taylor · *Billy Two Hats*/1973/UA/*d* Ted Kotcheff/*lp* Gregory Peck, Desi Arnaz Jr.

Hamilton, Donald [Bengtson] (b 1916) · Author. Hamilton's first Western novel, *Smoke Valley* (1954), was filmed as *The Violent Men*/1954/COL/*d* Rudolph Maté/*lp* Edward G. Robinson, Barbara Stanwyck. Its hero has something in common with the hero of *The Big Country*/1958, filmed from Hamilton's novel of the same title. Both are reluctantly drawn into other men's fights; in the latter, Gregory Peck plays the sea captain who comes to Texas to marry his fiancée and becomes involved in a feud. Hamilton's other Western novels are *Mad River* (1956), *The Man from Santa Clara* (1960) and *Texas Fever* (1960).

Hanging · In *Westerns* Philip French writes: 'Certain crude movies of the Fifties which

Two men hanged at Helena, Montana, 27 April 1870

A hanging in True Grit

most critics roundly condemned – *The Hangman* (1959) and *Good Day for a Hanging* (1959) – led to the multiple legal executions shown in *Hang 'Em High, Bandolero!* and *True Grit*. The executions in *True Grit* might be explained away as the presentation of the true facts of frontier life and even their brutalizing effects on the young, and intermittently in that picture there is a vein of black humour which informs the opening section of *Bandolero!*, in which James Stewart poses as a public hangman to free his brother's gang, and turns the notion of gallows humour into rope-and-timber reality. There is, however, in both films a morbid streak which colours the whole of *Hang 'Em High*, where the central

relationship is between a law enforcement officer and a self-righteous "hanging judge" based on the celebrated Isaac Charles *Parker of Arkansas Territory, a personal appointee of President Grant. John Huston's *The Life and Times of Judge Roy Bean* (1972) also exploits the darkly comic aspects of hanging, to dubious effect. There are undoubtedly reflections of the time here, but whichever way one cares to look at the matter, the Western – for all its constant preaching against lynch law – remains firmly committed to capital punishment. One could argue that for it to be otherwise would be a gross falsification of history. It is at such moments that one recalls a Western of a more conventionally liberal cast, Raoul Walsh's *The Tall Men* (1955), which opens with Clark Gable and Cameron Mitchell riding towards a corpse hanging from a tree: "Looks like we're near civilization," says Gable.'
The Tall Men/1955 · *Good Day for a Hanging*/1958/COL/*d* Nathan Juran/*lp* Fred MacMurray, Robert Vaughn · *The Hangman*/1959/PAR/*d* Michael Curtiz/*lp* Robert Taylor, Fess Parker · *Hang 'Em High*/1968 · *Bandolero!*/1968 · *True Grit*/1969 · *The Life and Times of Judge Roy Bean*/1972

Hardin, John Wesley (1853-1895) · Gunfighter. The son of a Methodist preacher (hence his middle name), Hardin is variously credited with the killing of forty-four, twenty or merely eleven men. He was born in Texas and grew up during the lawless post-Civil War period. Few if any of Hardin's killings were committed for profit; many of the early ones were related to the feuds and hatreds arising from the turbulent politics of Reconstruction (the first man he murdered was an ex-slave). As a result he was something of a hero to the anti-Reconstruction faction.

Hardin worked for a time as a cowboy, driving cattle up the *Chisholm Trail to *Abilene, where in 1871 he had a brief, though bloodless, confrontation with Wild Bill *Hickok. Hardin's habit of getting into drunken fights and killing his opponent brought him to the notice of the *Texas Rangers and he fled to Florida, where he was eventually captured in 1877. He spent the next fourteen years in jail learning to be a lawyer, but he had few clients on his release. In his ample leisure time in the last months of his life he composed his autobiography, *The Life of John Wesley Hardin as Written by Himself*. He had reverted to robbery and heavy drinking by the time he was shot in the back in 1895 while playing dice in a saloon.

While the cinema has ignored other more colourful Texas gunmen, such as John King Fisher (1854-84) (who wore silk shirts and tiger-skin chaps), Hardin, racist and drunk, has been portrayed as a hero. Rock Hudson portrays him as a victim of unkind circumstances. In Bob Dylan's 1968 album *John Wesley Harding* (sic), he becomes a Robin Hood figure who 'was always known to lend a helping hand'.
John Dehner/*The Texas Rangers*/1951/COL/ d Phil Karlson/lp George Montgomery, Gale Storm · Rock Hudson/*The Lawless Breed*/1952 · Jack Elam/*Dirty Dingus Magee*/1970/MGM/d Burt Kennedy/lp Frank Sinatra, George Kennedy
Television · Richard Webb/*Stories of the Century* · Scott Marlowe/*Bronco*

Harte, [Francis] Bret (1836-1902) · Author. Born in New York, Harte went to California in 1854, where he found work as a typesetter and occasional writer on a newspaper in San Francisco. His literary career took off in 1868 when he became editor of *Overland Monthly*. In this periodical he published the stories of the California gold camps which were to make him famous: 'The Luck of Roaring Camp', 'Tennessee's Partner', 'The Outcasts of Poker Flat' and others. In 1878 Harte went to Europe as a consular official. His literary reputation gradually subsided and he never returned to the United States.

Harte's stories, with their strong plots, sharply etched characters – gamblers, prostitutes, stagecoach drivers – and tendency towards the sentimental, attracted many early film-makers. Only the irony with which Harte punctured pretension and prudery was not so easily translated to the screen. Harte must be given much of the credit for establishing certain types as part of the stock repertoire of the Western. John Ford's *Stagecoach*/1939 is supposed to owe much to Maupassant's story 'Boule de suif', but its dramatis personae could mostly have come straight from Bret Harte. And long before Ford in *3 Godfathers*/1948, Harte discovered in 'The Luck of Roaring Camp' the effect to be obtained by confronting rough frontier types with a new-born baby.
The Luck of Roaring Camp/1909/Edison/d Edwin S. Porter/lp Barney Sherry, Mary Fuller · remade 1917/Edison/d Floyd France/lp Ivan Christy, Eugene Field · remade 1937/MON/d I. Willat/lp Owen Davis Jr. · *Ononko's Vow*/1910/Edison/d Edwin S. Porter/lp Mary Fuller · *In the*

Aisles of the Wild/1912/Biograph/d D.W. Griffith · *Salomy Jane*/1914/Alco/d Paul Armstrong · remade 1923/PAR/d George Melford/lp Jacqueline Logan · *The Half-Breed* ['In the Craquinez Woods']/1916/ Triangle/d Allan Dwan/lp Douglas Fairbanks · *M'liss*/1915/World/d O.A.C. Lund/lp Barbara Tennant, Howard Esterbrook · remade 1918/PAR/d Marshall Neilan/lp Mary Pickford · remade as *The Girl Who Ran Wild*/1922/U/d Rupert Julian/lp Gladys Walton · remade as *The Man from Red Gulch*/1925/PDC/d Edmund Mortimer/lp Harry Carey · *The Outcasts of Poker Flat*/1919/U/d John Ford/lp Harry Carey · remade 1937/RKO/d Christy Cabanne/lp Preston Foster, Van Heflin · remade 1952/FOX/d Joseph M. Newman/lp Dale Robertson, Anne Baxter · *Fighting Cressy*/1919/Pathé/d Robert T. Thornby/lp Blanche Sweet, Russell Simpson · *Tennessee's Partner*/1916/Lasky/d George Melford/lp Fannie Ward, Jack Dean · remade as *The Flaming Forties* /1924/PDC/d Tom Forman/lp Harry Carey · remade as *Tennessee's Partner*/1954/RKO/d Allan Dwan/lp John Payne, Ronald Reagan · *The Golden Princess*/1925/PAR/d Clarence Badger/lp Betty Bronson · *Taking A Chance*/1929/FOX/d Norman Z. McLeod/lp Rex Bell
Television · *California Gold Rush*

Harvey, Fred (1866-1928) · Entrepreneur. Harvey opened his first restaurant on the *Atchison, Topeka and Santa Fe railroad in 1876. By 1883 he had seventeen establishments and the business was still growing. Good food in pleasant surroundings served by smartly uniformed waitresses was a major advance of civilization over the pitiful facilities offered by the way-stations along the stagecoach routes. The waitresses proved so popular that Harvey introduced a clause in their contract requiring them to forfeit half their wages if they married during their first

John Hodiak, Judy Garland in The Harvey Girls

year of employment. Songs and poems were written in their honour:
'I have viewed the noblest shrines in Italy And gazed upon the richest mosques in Turkey-
But the fairest of all sights, it seems to me, Was the Harvey girl I saw in Albuquerque.'
The business is celebrated, with better lyrics, in *The Harvey Girls*/1945.

Haycox, Ernest (1899-1950) · Author. One of the most prolific and successful writers of Western pulp fiction. Most of his novels and stories were originally published in magazines, both in pulps and in slicks such as *Colliers* and *Saturday Evening Post*. Though always working within the conventions of the formula Western, Haycox's best writing can achieve considerable intensity and his heroes are often thoughtfully concerned with moral dilemmas, not just men of action. Haycox's skilled use of the formula influenced other practitioners such as Luke *Short and Frank *Gruber. At the time of his early death Haycox was attempting in a novel about settlers, *The Earthbreakers* (published posthumously in 1952), to get beyond formula into a deeper statement on the significance of westward expansion.
Union Pacific [*Trouble Shooter*]/1939 · *Stagecoach* ['Stage to Lordsburg']/1939 · remade 1966/FOX/d Gordon Douglas/lp Ann-Margret, Alex Cord · *Apache Trail* ['Stage Station']/1942/MGM/d Richard Thorpe/lp Lloyd Nolan, Donna Reed · remade as *Apache War Smoke*/1952/MGM/d Harold Kress/lp Gilbert Roland · *Sundown Jim*/1942/FOX/d James Tinling/lp John Kimbrough · *Abilene Town* [*Trail Town*]/ 1946/UA/d Edwin L. Marin/lp Randolph Scott · *Canyon Passage*/1946/U/d Jacques Tourneur/lp Brian Donlevy, Susan Hayward · *Montana*/1949/WB/d Ray Enright/lp Errol Flynn · *Man in the Saddle*/1951 · *Bugles in the Afternoon*/1951/ WB/d Ray Rowland/lp Ray Milland
Television · *Stagecoach*

Henry, O. (1862-1910) · Pen name of William Sydney Porter. While a young man Porter was accused of embezzlement. On the run in British Honduras he made the acquaintance of Al *Jennings, the train robber and future film actor, and travelled through South America with him. When he returned to the States Porter was imprisoned for five years, but on his release established himself as a short story writer. His stories reveal no great literary style but are slickly plotted, with almost invariably a twist at the end. Many of the stories in his collection *Heart of the West* (1904) are set in Texas. O. Henry's most famous Western creation was the *Cisco Kid.

Also: *The Texan*/1930/PAR/d John Cromwell/lp Gary Cooper · remade as *The Llano Kid*/1939/PAR/d Edward Venturini/ lp Tito Guizar · *Black Eagle*/1948/COL/d Robert Gordon/lp William Bishop · 'The Ransom of Red Cloud', episode in *O. Henry's Full House*/1952/FOX/d Howard Hawks/lp Fred Allen, Oscar Levant

Hickok, Wild Bill [James Butler] (1837-76) · Scout and lawman. Hickok is one of the few figures whose reputation as a gunfighter, albeit embellished by legend, had a secure basis in fact. He was a good shot, he probably killed at least seven men, and the man who got him had to shoot him in the back. At first a stagecoach and wagon driver, then an army scout, Hickok derived his initial fame from an interview with Colonel George Ward Nichols published in *Harper's New Monthly Magazine* in 1867. In it he told about his fight with the Dave McCanles gang at Rock Creek, Nebraska on 12 July 1861. Hickok, who was prone to exaggeration, inflated the number of men killed from three to ten. Nichols also published Hickok's version of his fight with Dave Tutt in Springfield, Missouri on 21 July 1865. After the Civil War he became a marshal, in Hays City, Kansas and then in April 1871 in *Abilene.

His appearance was striking. His long flowing locks, picturesque buckskin clothes and stylish way of wearing his six-guns with the butts thrust forward, all made him good material as a hero. He was first featured in a dime novel, *Wild Bill, the Indian Slayer*, in 1867. In 1873 Hickok appeared with Buffalo Bill *Cody in the play *The Scouts of the Plains*, but his dramatic career was brief. Cody sacked him for rashly shooting too close to the actors playing the Indians and giving them powder burns. Despite the legend, it seems unlikely that he was ever romantically involved with *Calamity Jane, but in March 1876 Hickok married a Mrs Thatcher. Five months later he was dead, shot in the back during a poker game in Deadwood by Jack McCall on 2 August 1876.

As William K. Everson has remarked, Hickok's status in the movies declined sadly after the noble figures portrayed by William S. Hart in the 20s and Gary Cooper in the 30s. By 1953 Hickok had moved all the way from hero to villain, in *Jack McCall Desperado*. By the time of *Little Big Man*/1970 he

Wild Bill Hickok (second from l.) on stage with Ned Buntline, Buffalo Bill, Texas Jack Omohundro and another (1874)

has been reduced to a jumpy neurotic with a hang-dog expression. The series of B-Westerns starring Bill Elliott, like the TV series of the 50s, relate to the historical character of Hickok through the use of the name only.

The Pioneer Peacemaker/1913/Hugh McDonald Co. ('two episodes in the life of Wild Bill Hickok') · William S. Hart/ *Wild Bill Hickok*/1923/PAR/d Clifford Smith · John Padjan/*The Iron Horse*/1924 · J. Farrell MacDonald/*The Last Frontier* 1926/PDC/d George B. Seitz/lp Jack Hoxie · Yakima Canutt/*The Last Frontier*/1932/ RKO/d Spencer G. Bennet/lp Lon Chaney Jr. · Gary Cooper/*The Plainsman*/1936 · George Houston/*Frontier Scout*/1938/Fine Arts-Grand National/d Sam Newfield/lp Al St John · Gordon (Bill) Elliott/*The Great Adventures of Wild Bill Hickok*/1938/ COL/d Mack V. Wright, Sam Nelson/lp Monte Blue · Bill Elliott/*The Return of Wild Bill*/1940/COL/d Joseph H. Lewis/lp Luana Walters · Bill Elliott/*Prairie Schooners*/1940/COL/d Sam Nelson · Bill Elliott/*Beyond the Sacramento*/1940/COL/d Lambert Hillyer · Bill Elliott/*Wildcat of Tucson*/1940/COL/d Lambert Hillyer · Roy Rogers/*Young Bill Hickok*/1940/REP/d Joseph Kane/lp George Hayes · Lane Chandler/*Deadwood Dick*/1940/COL/d James W. Horne/lp Don Douglas · Bill Elliott/*Across the Sierras*/1941/COL/d D. Ross Lederman · Bill Elliott/*North from the

Lone Star*/1941/COL/d Lambert Hillyer · Bill Elliott/*King of Dodge City*/1941/COL/d Lambert Hillyer/lp Tex Ritter · Bill Elliott/ *Hands Across the Rockies*/1941/COL/d Lambert Hillyer · Bill Elliott/*Roaring Frontiers*/1941/COL/d Lambert Hillyer · Bill Elliott/*Lone Star Vigilantes*/1942/COL/d Wallace Fox/lp Tex Ritter · Bill Elliott/ *The Devil's Trail*/1942/COL/d Lambert Hillyer/lp Tex Ritter · Richard Dix/*The Badlands of Dakota*/1941/U/d Alfred E. Green/lp Robert Stack · Bruce Cabot/*Wild Bill Hickok Rides*/1942/WB/d Ray Enright/lp Constance Bennett, Ward Bond · Reed Hadley/*Dallas*/1950/WB/d Stuart Heisler/lp Gary Cooper, Ruth Roman · Robert Anderson/*The Lawless Breed*/1952 · Douglas Kennedy/*Jack McCall Desperado*/ 1952/COL/d Sidney Salkow/lp George Montgomery · Forrest Tucker/*Pony Express*/1952/PAR/d Jerry Hopper/lp Charlton Heston, Rhonda Fleming · Ewing Brown/*Son of the Renegade*/1953/UA/ d Reg Brown/lp John Carpenter · Howard Keel/*Calamity Jane*/1953 · Tom Brown/*I Killed Wild Bill Hickok*/1956/Wheeler/d Richard Talmadge/lp John Forbes · Robert Culp/*The Raiders*/1964/U/d Herschel Daugherty/lp Brian Keith · Adrian Hoven/ *Aventuras del oeste*/1964/It, WG, Sp/d J. L. Romero Marchent/lp Rick van Nutter · Paul Shannon/*The Outlaws Is Coming*/ 1964/COL/d Norman Maurer/lp The Three Stooges · Robert Dix/*Deadwood '76*/1965/

Fairway International/d James Landis/lp
Arch Hall · Don Murray/The Plainsman/
1966/U/d David Lowell/lp Guy Stockwell ·
Jeff Corey/Little Big Man/1970 · Charles
Bronson/The White Buffalo/1977/Dino de
Laurentiis/d J. Lee Thompson/lp Jack
Warden, Kim Novak · Richard
Farnsworth/The Legend of the Lone Ranger/
1981/ITC/d William A. Fraker/lp Klinton
Spilsbury
Television · Guy Madison/The Adventures
of Wild Bill Hickok · Rhodes Reason/Death
Valley Days · Jack Cassidy/Bronco ·
Charles Cooper/Bronco · Lloyd Bridges/
The Great Adventure · Ben Murphy/This
Was the West that Was · L.Q. Jones/Wild
Times · Frederick Forrest/Calamity Jane

Historians · The writing of the history of the
West and the filming of it have been very
different enterprises. A measure of the
difference can be seen in the standard textbook, Ray Allen Billington's Westward
Expansion (4th ed., 1974). The book is
comprehensive, based on enormous
research and reading, and it contains hardly
a mention of most of the figures and events
that are familiar to viewers of Westerns.
Billington has no space in his 800 pages for
Billy the Kid, or John Chisum, or the
Lincoln County or Johnson County range
wars. He has none for Jesse James or Wyatt
Earp or Pat Garrett. Even George Armstrong Custer receives only three short
entries. Among familiar icons the Indians
alone fare better, for Billington does mention Geronimo, Crazy Horse, Red Cloud
and Satanta, and he has three entries for
Sitting Bull.

Serious historians of the West can be
divided into several categories. First, in the
19th century, came the celebrants, bent on
telling the heroic story of white America's
conquest of its land and determined to tell it
in terms of the deeds of great men. The
foremost was Francis *Parkman, whose
study of France and England in North
America (8 vols., 1865-92) still counts as one
of the major achievements of American
historical writing. Parkman's prose was eloquent, and his sense of powerful individuals
was compelling. Most of what he produced
is set in the 18th century, but he also wrote
The Oregon Trail (1849), a first-hand account
of his own western adventures. Few historians would now follow Parkman's romantic
and nationalist lead, but one who did was
Theodore *Roosevelt, President of both the
United States (1901-09) and the American
Historical Association (1912). Among other

studies, Roosevelt was author of The Winning of the West (6 vols., 1889-96).
Roosevelt's title and his purpose found an
echo in How the West Was Won/1962.

Since the late 19th century most historians have abjured the path of Parkman and
Roosevelt. Instead, they have concentrated
on three main approaches. First, both chronologically and in terms of his impact on the
writing of American history, came the work
of Frederick Jackson Turner. In 1893, when
he was a young assistant professor, Turner
delivered his epochal paper on 'The Significance of the Frontier in American History'
to the Chicago convention of the American
Historical Association. Turner's paper was
an attempt to make sense of the whole of
American history in terms of the westward
movement. Turner wrote it not in terms of
great individuals, bringing to reality what
they wanted to achieve, but in terms of
anonymous social forces.

Based at the University of Wisconsin and
later at Harvard, Turner had an enormous
impact on the writing of American history.
Among the most distinguished of his heirs
have been Frederick Merk, who succeeded
him at Harvard, Paul Wallace Gates, who
spent his long career at Cornell, Billington,
of Northwestern and later of the Huntington
Library, and Walter Prescott Webb, of the
University of Texas.

For all these historians, the West was an
arena of social conflict rather than one of
heroic individualism. Merk traced the interplay of Manifest Destiny and Mission in
American History (1963). Gates, in many
books, considered the land policy of the
United States, showing starkly the unequal
basis on which the land was handed out.
Billington wrote a sprawling textbook that
he put through many editions, a work of
scholarship in its own right. Webb's account
of The Great Plains (1931) demonstrates the
difficulties that faced the people who tried to
settle the central region of the continent.

Anyone interested in what really happened in the West must still confront these
writers. But filming 'social forces' and
abstract theses is much less easy than writing
about them, and one must look hard to find
evidence of their impact on film. Shane/1952
and The Man Who Shot Liberty Valance/1962
make attempts, but the Western that comes
closest is the much-reviled Heaven's Gate/
1980. Michael Cimino's film is set against
the background of the events in Johnson
County, Wyoming, about 1890. Whatever
the historical facts really were, Heaven's Gate
poses the problem in social terms, not

individualistic ones. Shane uses the same
events as background for a story in which a
few towering figures could act out a whole
community's problems. But in Heaven's
Gate what counts is numbers and organization, not virtue and heroism.

In the mid-20th century a different theme
began to appear, as cultural historians
turned to the image of the West in 'the
American mind'. This new group looked to
the West as a place where mythology helped
to create national unity, rather than as one
where social forces worked out their conflicts. The pioneering study was Henry Nash
Smith's Virgin Land (1950). Nash used the
methods of literary criticism and dealt with
such major writers as James Fenimore
Cooper and Walt Whitman. But his prime
concern was with the sub-literature of the
19th century. Taking *dime novels seriously, he probed them for their images of
heroism. He looked at speeches by politicians and at autobiographies of frontier
heroes and at the writers whom Nathaniel
Hawthorne dismissed as 'scribbling
women'. Turner himself became a figure in
Smith's text, for the one historian read the
other's work as part of nineteenth-century
America's effort to make sense of itself.

Teaching first at the University of Minnesota and later at the University of California,
Berkeley, Smith established a powerful professional presence. Among important
writers stimulated by Virgin Land have been
Leo Marx of Amherst College (The Machine
in the Garden, 1964), Arthur K. Moore of the
University of Kentucky (The Frontier Mind,
1957) and the Englishman Clive Bush of the
University of Warwick (The Dream of
Reason, 1977). Perhaps Smith's most notable
successor has been Richard Slotkin of Wesleyan University, who is producing a multi-
volume study of frontier mythology in
American history (to date: Regeneration
Through Violence (1973) and The Fatal
Environment (1985)). Unlike Smith, though
like Bush, Slotkin is interested in the social
production of mythology and in the social
interests it serves. Both historians acknowledge the influence that Marxism has had on
them. In that sense, they work toward a
synthesis of Smith, with his concern for
consciousness, and Turner, whose own debt
to Marx was considerable, if indirect.

The problems that Turner and his heirs
explored lurk beneath the Western genre;
the questions that interest Smith, Leo Marx,
Bush and Slotkin run through it. What
Smith has to say in Part III of Virgin Land,
where he explores the notion that the West

constituted the 'garden of the world', is vital to an understanding of most of the work of John Ford. Bush's interest in visual imagery can sensitize the serious film-watcher to film-makers' use of the landscape in virtually every case where location work has meant going outside the environs of Los Angeles. The argument that Leo Marx develops gives depth to the opening and closing sequences of *The Man Who Shot Liberty Valance*, as well as to such films as *Last Train from Gun Hill*/1958, *3:10 to Yuma*/1957 and virtually all the work of Sam Peckinpah. Slotkin's project is not complete and he hints at a direct treatment of film in his next volume. As matters stand, his first book is vital to reading any film that deals with Indian captivity. His second presents by far the best discussion of the image of General Custer.

The third and most recent tendency has led to a radical revaluation of the whole process of contact between Indians and whites. It began with Dee Brown's immensely popular *Bury My Heart at Wounded Knee* (1972), subtitled *An Indian History of the West*. Brown's book was written much in the spirit of such films as *Soldier Blue*/1970 and *Little Big Man*/1970, with which it was roughly contemporaneous. It was a tale of blood and gore, written from the 'Indian' rather than the white point of view.

More recent pro-Indian historians have developed their point with rather more subtlety. One of the foremost is Jack D. Forbes of the University of California, Davis, who himself is a Native American. Forbes' writings began with *The Indian in America's Past* (1964). The most original and compelling 'Indian' account of the events of the 19th century is the massive two-volume *People of the Sacred Mountain* (1979) by Peter John Powell. Powell is an Episcopalian (Anglican) priest and an honorary chief of the Cheyenne nation. His book is built on tribal recollections and it is written wholly within a nineteenth-century Cheyenne conceptual framework. The book includes full-colour reproductions of drawings that Cheyenne artists did during the Plains Wars, and it is a stunning achievement.

But the most stimulating revaluation of Indian-white contact has come from historians interested in the colonial period. The pioneer was Francis Jennings of the Newberry Library, whose *The Invasion of America* (1975) is an impassioned but scholarly discussion of 'Indians, Colonialism and the Cant of Conquest'. More recently, Jennings has explored *The Ambiguous Iroquois*

Empire (1985). James Axtell's *The Invasion Within* (1986) is the first book in a multi-volume series intended to be a reply to Parkman. In Axtell's pages, as in Jennings's, Indians emerge as historical agents who had a hand in shaping their own futures, rather than as mere victims, condemned by fate to die or to get out of the way. The same is true in the work of such younger historians as Neil Salisbury (*Manitou and Providence*, 1982), Calvin Martin (*Keepers of the Game*, 1978) and William Cronon (*Changes in the Land*, 1983).

All of these scholars have worked against the background of a dramatic re-estimate of the actual numbers of Native Americans. For generations, academics and the general public alike have accepted that in numerical terms the Indians never amounted to much, perhaps one million at first contact in all of the modern United States and Canada. But current thinking holds that in 1492 there were roughly ten times that number and that the population of the whole hemisphere approached one hundred million. The great dying that ensued was the result not of white malevolence but of the Indians' lack of natural immunity to a whole range of European diseases. Since they had never been exposed to such illnesses as diphtheria, smallpox, measles, influenza and chicken pox, their bodies had never had the chance to develop antibodies. The 'green field' epidemics that resulted were the worst demographic disaster in history, including even the Black Death. Some scholars estimate that the native population fell by a factor of nine in ten by 1600. To use Jennings's phrase, what America offered to the invaders was 'widowed' rather than 'virgin' land.

Little of the recent historical writing has had any impact on the Western. Virtually the only major film to try seriously to give the perspective of people who had never seen a European is *The Savage Innocents* (1960), which is set among Eskimos and predates all these more recent books. Like Powell's *People of the Sacred Mountain*, *The Savage Innocents* presumes nothing derived from European culture.

But the current revaluation of Indian history is a late fruit of the same cultural conjuncture that produced the 'pro-Indian' Westerns of the early 1970s. For all the achievement of *Soldier Blue* and *Little Big Man*, they remain within a framework much like the one used by Dee Brown. If historically conscious film-makers ever return to the Indian theme and want to do more than

just reverse the traditional white point of view, they will have to take account of this generation of historians. EC

Holliday, Doc [John Henry] (1852-87) · Gambler and gunman. Born in Georgia, Holliday trained as a dentist. Tuberculosis forced him to seek the drier air of the West, where he soon abandoned dentistry for poker and faro. Holliday drifted round many of the boom towns of the West: Denver, Cheyenne, Deadwood and in 1877 *Dodge City, where he became friends with Wyatt *Earp. According to some accounts

Doc Holliday

he saved Earp's life by disarming a rowdy cowboy. In Dodge City he also met Kate *Elder, whom he may have married. In 1880 he followed Earp to *Tombstone, where he took part in the gunfight at the O.K. Corral, in which he was slightly wounded. Afterwards he assisted Wyatt Earp in gaining revenge on the killers of his brother Morgan. In 1883 Holliday, together with Earp and Bat *Masterson, was in Dodge City to help Luke *Short during the Dodge City War. His tuberculosis and alcoholism finally got the better of him in 1887.

Doc Holliday's screen image has been dominated by his cough, his drinking and the quick temper and icy nerve which apparently made him dangerous to deal with. Victor Mature's performance is the most complex, portraying Holliday as that rarity in the Western, an intellectual.
Harry Carey/*Law and Order*/1932 · Harvey Clark/*Law for Tombstone*/1937/U/d Charles

Jones, B. Reeves Eason/*lp* Buck Jones ·
Cesar Romero/*Frontier Marshal*/1939 ·
Walter Huston/*The Outlaw*/1940 · Kent
Taylor/*Tombstone, the Town Too Tough to
Die*/1942/PAR/*d* William McGann/*lp*
Richard Dix · Victor Mature/*My Darling
Clementine*/1946 · Chubby Johnson (as
Denver = Doc Holliday)/*Law and Order*/
1953/U/*d* Nathan Duran/*lp* Ronald Reagan
· James Griffith/*Masterson of Kansas*/1954/
COL/*d* William Castle/*lp* George
Montgomery · Kirk Douglas/*Gunfight at
the O.K. Corral*/1956 · Arthur Kennedy/
Cheyenne Autumn/1964 · Jason Robards/
Hour of the Gun/1967 · Stacy Keach/*Doc*/
1971 · William Berger/*Verflucht dies
Amerika*/1973/WG/*d* Volker Vogeler
Television · Douglas Fowley/*The Life and
Legend of Wyatt Earp* · Myron Healey/*The
Life and Legend of Wyatt Earp* · Dewey
Martin/*Dick Powell's Zane Grey Theatre* ·
Adam West/*Colt .45* · Adam West/
Sugarfoot · Gerald Mohr/*Maverick* · Peter
Breck/*Maverick* · Martin Landau/*Tales of
Wells Fargo* · Adam West/*Lawman* ·
Christopher Dark/*Bonanza* · Jack Kelly/
The High Chaparral · Dennis Hopper/*Wild
Times* · Jeffrey De Munn/*I Married Wyatt
Earp*

Hollywood · The most engaging attempt to
capture both the charm and the tawdriness
of the world of the Hollywood Western is
Hearts of the West/1975, in which Jeff Bridges
plays an aspiring writer who becomes a
stuntman in silent Westerns. Previous to
this Hollywood had taken several not very
acerbic looks at the business of putting the
West on screen, mostly in B- and series
Westerns.
Examples include: *Scarlet River*/1933/RKO/*d*
Otto Brower/*lp* Tom Keene · *The Thrill
Hunter*/1933/COL/*d* George Seitz/*lp* Buck
Jones · *Hollywood Round-up*/1937/COL/*d*
Ewing Scott/*lp* Buck Jones · *Shooting High*/
1940/FOX/*d* Alfred E. Green/*lp* Gene
Autry · *The Cowboy and the Blonde*/1941/
FOX/*d* Ray McCarey/*lp* George
Montgomery · *Sons of Adventure*/1948/REP/
d Yakima Canutt/*lp* Ross Hayden ·
Callaway Went Thataway/1951/MGM/*d*
Melvin Frank, Norman Panama/*lp* Fred
MacMurray, Howard Keel, Dorothy
McGuire · *Slim Carter*/1957/U/*d* Richard
Bartlett/*lp* Jock Mahoney, Julie Adams

Horgan, Paul (b 1903) · Novelist, military
librarian and archivist whose works have
been mainly centred on New Mexico and
include *Main Line West* (1936), *Lamp on the
Plains* (1937) and *Great River* (1954), a history of the Rio Grande. *A Distant Trumpet*
was published in 1960 and is a long, ambitious novel tracing the career of a young and
idealistic cavalry lieutenant during the
Apache wars. Filmed in 1964, it was the last
work to be directed by Raoul Walsh.

Horn, Tom (1860-1903) · Scout. After
working at a variety of occupations such as
miner and stagecoach driver, Horn became
an army scout with Al *Sieber and assisted
in the final surrender of *Geronimo in 1886.
He was a rodeo cowboy and deputy sheriff in
Arizona and in 1890 he joined the *Pinkerton Agency. In 1894 Horn hired out to the
Wyoming Stock Growers Association to
track down and kill rustlers, though he
seems not to have been directly involved in
the *Johnson County War. In 1902 he was
arrested and hanged on a charge of shooting
down a fourteen-year-old boy by mistake for
a sheepman he had been hired to kill. The
major evidence against him was a 'confession', made when he was drunk and which
he later denied. Though Horn undoubtedly
did kill people, there is considerable doubt
that he committed the murder he was
hanged for.
George Montgomery/*Dakota Lil*/1949/FOX/
d Lesley Selander/*lp* Marie Windsor, Rod
Cameron · Steve McQueen/*Tom Horn*/
1980
Television · David Carradine/*Mr. Horn*

Tom Horn

Horses · Rudyard Kipling might have been
talking about the Western when he wrote:
'Four things greater than all things are, –
Women and Horses and Power and War.'
The horse is central not only to the Western
but to the whole culture of the West. The
image of the Indian on horseback is so
familiar that it is possible to forget that
horses were a late acquisition of the indigenous peoples of North America. Only when
the Spanish arrived at the end of the 15th
century was the horse introduced on to the
continent. Gradually the use of the horse
spread north from Mexico until by the
middle of the 18th century all the plains
peoples had adapted to a horse-based
culture.
The effect of the change from walking to
riding must have been dramatic. Hunting,
especially of the buffalo, was transformed
and the scope for warfare enormously
broadened. Rapidly the Cheyenne, the
Comanche and others evolved the distinctive mounted culture which was to capture
the imagination of writers and painters from
the beginning of the 19th century and has
occupied such a central position in the
cinema. By contrast, the peoples of the east
such as the Iroquois, whom the horse had
scarcely reached before their subjugation by
the whites, never (*pace* James Fenimore
Cooper) matched the plains Indians in imaginative appeal.
Because the use of horses in America
originated with the Spanish, most of the
accoutrements and vocabulary are Spanish
too. Mustang and bronco, chaps and lariat
derive from both the speech and the working
practices of the vacqueros (anglicized as
buckaroos), who first learned the use of the
horse in cattle-raising. Their methods were
adopted wholesale by the cowboys of the
1880s who, together with the plains Indians,
did most to establish the horse as an indispensable element in our image of the West.
This image has its own history. Until the
middle of the 1880s a galloping horse was
conventionally represented in painting with
both its front and rear legs stretched full out.
We can find examples in the work of George
*Catlin and Alfred Jacob *Miller, two of the
earliest artists to paint the plains Indians. In
the 1870s Eadweard *Muybridge began to
perform some photographic experiments
for the railroad magnate Leland *Stanford.
He produced a series of high-speed photographs of Stanford's horse (named, aptly in
the present context, Occident). These
revealed what the eye could not see unaided,
that the movements of a horse in full flight

were quite different from how they were conventionally represented in painting. In 1887 Muybridge published the results of his studies in a large work entitled *Animal Locomotion*.

Artists were immediately impressed. In Europe the French painter of battle scenes, Messonier, modified his picture of Napoleon entitled 'Friedland 1807' in order to make the horses more realistic. In pictures of the West, where the horse was already a central icon, the transformation was rapid. Frederic *Remington, on his way to becoming the most celebrated painter of Western subjects and who chose as his epitaph 'He knew the horse', was reported to have 'foresworn conventions and to [have] accepted the statement of the camera as his guide in the future.' The new, improved method of depicting the horse undoubtedly added an extra dimension of realism to paintings of the West, just at the time that the West as a subject of entertainment was enormously increasing in popularity.

In a machine he called the Zoopraxiscope Muybridge later combined his still photographs into a reproduction of movement which anticipated the basic effect of a motion picture projector. He thus ensured that the movements of the horse and the invention of the cinema were to be intimately connected. So inseparable from the Western film are horses that a film without them could scarcely qualify as a Western at all. Conversely, several films set in the 20th century, outside the normal temporal bounds of the Western, still retain a feel of the genre in part by virtue of the mere presence of horses. One thinks, for example, of *Lonely Are the Brave*/1962 or *Comes A Horseman*/1978, *Giant*/1956 or *The Misfits*/1961. (In the last the ultimate crime is committed, that of killing horses for meat, and dogfood at that.) In the B-Western, too, horses are often major signifiers, confirming, despite the presence of cars or planes or gangsters, that we are still in a Western world.

Once the production of Westerns became a major part of the film industry, Hollywood found that it needed specialists in the handling of horses and genuine cowboys were in demand. *Rodeo and circus stars were hired to display their skills, and *stunts with horses, performed by experts such as Yakima Canutt, became a feature of Westerns.

Scenes of breaking in horses were part of the genre even before the cinema; there are examples in the paintings of both Frederic Remington and Charles *Russell. In a West-

Frederic Remington, 'Bronco Busters Saddling' (from Theodore Roosevelt, Ranch Life and The Hunting-Trail, *1888)*

The Misfits

Ken Maynard performing

BELOW: *Eadweard Muybridge's experiments, published 1887*

ern narrative, of course, such scenes rarely exist simply as spectacle; usually they reveal character as well. In *The Unforgiven*/1959 John Saxon as the part-Indian Portugal has a way with unbroken horses the white men can only envy. In *Major Dundee*/1964 the antics of Dundee's troops as they attempt to master their mounts prior to setting off after the Apache demonstrates graphically how under-prepared they are. In *Western Union*/1941 the foppish Robert Young shows his mettle when he masters the wild horse some pranksters have set him on. Gregory Peck, the eastern dude in *The Big Country*/1958, spoils the fun by declining to do the same, but we know he's not really a coward and that he will eventually tame the unruly steed.

The loss of a horse is the biggest threat to the hero's chances of survival in hostile country; but worse than that, it is an affront to his dignity. The word chivalry comes ultimately from 'cheval', the French for horse; ill-treatment of a horse is an infallible sign of a bad character. When in *Bite the Bullet* a boastful young man punches his horse on the jaw, he is severely chastised by Gene Hackman and James Coburn; though in the downbeat *Cowboy*/1958 Glenn Ford takes a more disenchanted view ('Do you know a horse has a brain just about the size of a walnut?'). The heroes of Western series personified their horses, giving them names and in some cases virtually co-star status. William S. Hart was probably the first to name his horse (Fritz) in the credits of a film, but it was Ken Maynard who made the most of equine entertainment. Scenes were written into the scripts of his series for First National in the mid-1920s calling for his horse Tarzan to dance, play dead, nod his head to answer questions, jump off cliffs, drag Ken to safety or push him into the arms of the leading lady.

Virtually every B-Western and series star had his regular partner, a truly stable relationship. Pairings included: Tony with Tom Mix; Mutt with Hoot Gibson; White Eagle and Silver with Buck Jones; Silver King with Fred Thomson; Mike with George O'Brien; Midnight with Tim McCoy; Duke with John Wayne; Baron with Tom Tyler; Scout with Jack Hoxie; Champion with Gene Autry; Trigger with Roy Rogers; King with Bill Cody; Rebel with Reb Russell; Falcon with Buster Crabbe; White Flash with Tex Ritter; Topper with William Boyd (Hopalong Cassidy); Sonny and Thunder with Wild Bill Elliott; Black Jack and Feather with Allan Lane; Starlight with Jack Perrin; Cyclone with Don Barry; Silver with Sunset

Carson; Silver Bullet with Whip Wilson; Koko with Rex Allen; Shamrock with Bob Livingstone; Rush with Lash LaRue; Silver with the Lone Ranger; Knight with Rod Cameron; Lightning and Duke with Tim Holt. Roy Rogers' Trigger died at the ripe old age of twenty-eight; he now resides, stuffed, at the Roy Rogers Museum in Apple Valley, California.

In *Butch Cassidy and the Sundance Kid*/1969 a bicycle salesman announces, 'The horse is dead.' That's how we know the heroes' days are numbered.

Hough, Emerson (1857-1923) · Author. Hough died the year his most famous novel, *The Covered Wagon* (1922), became a highly successful film. His first book, *The Story of the Cowboy*, published in 1897, was a history. In 1900 he published his first novel, *The Girl at the Halfway House*, a vivid picture of the cattleman's frontier. Hough's importance to the Western was that to the tale of stirring action he added a romantic love story. Hollywood, which had already found this to be a winning combination, took to Hough's work with enthusiasm. *The Covered Wagon* established the story of a wagon train on the Oregon trail as a standard narrative. Hough also helped make the trail-driving story one of the staples of the genre. His novel *North of 36*, three times filmed, follows a herd of cattle up the *Chisholm Trail. This time Hough had to work harder than in *The Covered Wagon* to find a plausible reason for the presence of a woman, and when the book appeared in 1923 he was criticized for glamorizing the cowboy's life.
The Sagebrusher/1920/Hodkinson/d Edward Sloman/lp Roy Stewart, Marguerite de la Motte · *The Covered Wagon*/1923 · *The Man Next Door*/1923/Vitagraph/d Victor Schertzinger/lp David Torrence · *Way of a Man*/1924/Pathé/d George B. Seitz/lp Allene Ray · *North of 36*/1924/PAR/d Irvin Willat/lp Jack Holt · remade as *The Conquering Horde*/1931/PAR/d Edward Sloman/lp Richard Arlen · remade as *The Texans*/1938/PAR/d James Horgan/lp Randolph Scott, Joan Bennett

Houston, Sam (1793-1863) · Soldier and statesman. In his early years Governor of Tennessee and a political associate of Andrew *Jackson, Houston settled in Texas in 1832. When the Texans revolted against Mexican rule Houston was made commander of the army and, after the heroic defeat at the *Alamo, won a decisive victory against Santa Anna at San Jacinto. Houston then

became the first president of the new Republic of Texas in 1836 and was later Governor after Texas joined the Union. His anti-secessionist views led him to refuse to take the oath to the Confederacy in 1861 and he was replaced.
Tom Wilson/*Martyrs of the Alamo*/1915/Keystone-Triangle/d Christy Cabanne/lp Sam De Grasse · William Farnum/*The Conqueror*/1917/FOX/d Raoul Walsh/lp Jewel Carmen · Ed Piel/*Heroes of the Alamo*/1937/Sunset/d Harry Fraser/lp Rex Lease · Richard Dix/*Man of Conquest*/1939/REP/d George Nichols Jr./lp Joan Fontaine · William Farnum/*Men of Texas*/1942/U/d Ray Enright/lp Robert Stack, Broderick Crawford · Moroni Olsen/*Lone Star*/1951/MGM/d Vincent Sherman/lp Clark Gable, Ava Gardner · Howard Negley/*The Man from the Alamo*/1953 · Hugh Sanders/*The Last Command*/1955/REP/d Frank Lloyd/lp Sterling Hayden, Arthur Hunnicutt · Joel McCrea/*The First Texan*/1956/AA/d Byron Haskin/lp Felicia Farr · Richard Boone/*The Alamo*/1960/Batjac/d John Wayne/lp John Wayne, Richard Widmark, Laurence Harvey Television · Robert Culp/*The Great Adventure* · Sam Elliott/*Houston: The Legend of Texas* · Lorne Greene/*The Alamo: 13 Days to Glory* · Sam Houston's son, Temple, who became a lawyer, was the basis for *Temple Houston*

Hudson's Bay Company · Hudson's Bay was discovered by the English navigator Henry Hudson in 1610. After the efforts of such as Pierre Radisson had demonstrated the potential of central Canada as a source of valuable furs, the Hudson's Bay Company was granted its charter by Charles II in 1670 and given a monopoly on the fur trade in Rupert's Land, comprising one third of present-day Canada. The Hudson's Bay Company ruled supreme in Canada and Oregon until the 1820s, when American companies, including those of John Jacob Astor and William Ashley, began to compete in the Rocky Mountains, where no agreed boundary existed between British territory and the United States until 1846. Eventually the Hudson's Bay Company relinquished to the Canadian government its administrative control over its land, but it continues to trade to this day.

In *Hudson's Bay*/1940/FOX/d Irving Pichel/lp Paul Muni, Gene Tierney, Muni plays Pierre Radisson with a thick French accent and thinly disguised anti-British sentiments. Television · *Tomahawk*

Hudson River School · The artists commonly designated under this description were the first to develop an authentically American school of landscape painting. By the middle of the century their work had helped to educate the American public into a taste for both sublime and spectacular representations of the great outdoors. Their painting derived its inspiration not from European models but from the beauties of the Hudson River Valley and the Catskill Mountains in New York State. Even in the 1840s, this was hardly frontier country, but it was, in comparison to European landscapes, wild and largely untrammelled by civilization. Thomas Cole (1801-48) was among the first to devote himself to the scenery of the Hudson, transforming it into daring vistas, some of which he produced as illustrations of scenes from the novels of Fenimore *Cooper. Asher Durand (1796-1886), with typical new-world optimism, viewed nature as inherently good and its contemplation as morally uplifting. The paintings of Frederick Church (1826-1900) were on an altogether grander scale. Though he painted Niagara Falls, it was in South America that he found subjects that truly gave scope to his ambitions. By contrast John Frederick Kensett (1816-72), who became one of the most popular painters of his time, produced landscapes and seascapes full of the ordered serenity that many city-dwellers preferred to find in nature. (See Plate 6)

Huerta, Victoriano (1854-1916) · Mexican general. When in 1911 President *Diaz was forced out of office by *Zapata and *Villa and *Madero became President, he in turn faced revolts and only the troops of Huerta kept him in power. Two years later Huerta suddenly changed sides. Madero was deposed and murdered and Huerta became President. But Villa, Zapata and others refused to recognize his regime and in July 1914 he was made to resign. Photographs of Huerta show him as the epitome of the modern military technocrat, with sunglasses adding just a touch of Rommel-style glamour. In the movies he's the ruthless villain, in contrast to the romantic Villa.
Frank Silvera/*Viva Zapata!*/1952 · Herbert Lom/*Villa Rides*/1968

Humour · Most students of American humour adopt an evolutionary perspective, arguing that America's national humour evolved from European sources in response to the new world's different environmental,

General Huerta in 1912

can humour functioned not only as entertainment but also as a way of parodying various Utopian dreams about America and of exorcizing the hardships of daily life, particularly the raw life of the unsettled wilderness. Still, distinct comic modes should be recognized. In the hands of the Connecticut Wits, for instance, a genteel humour focusing on amiable eccentrics was basically intent on unmasking folly and pretence within a framework of satisfaction with the institutional *status quo*; in the hands of the humorists of the Old Southwest between the 1830s and the 1860s, however, an earthy, more aggressive and – ultimately – more subversive satirical humour emerged, one exalting individual cunning and emphasizing a universe dominated by chance and force.

The background to the rise of southwestern humour includes the work of storytellers, folk journalists and hack-writers who transformed such historical figures as Mike Fink and Davy Crockett into comic demigods whose exploits and sayings filled jokebooks, newspapers, magazines and almanacs in the 1820s and 1830s. Along with this athletic, boastful, unlettered frontier type, the confidence-man/trickster figure was popularized by sketches in such influential periodicals as the New York-based *Spirit of the Times* and in *Georgia Scenes* (1835) by A.B. Longstreet, in *Sut Lovingood's Yarns* (collected 1867) by George Washington Harris, in *Some Adventures of Simon Suggs* (1845) by Johnson Jones Hooper, and in *Mysteries of the Backwoods* (1846) by Thomas Bangs Thorpe. As several critics have noted, this intensely masculine humour arising from gambling, horseracing, hunting, sexual escapades, camp meetings and wrestling matches paradoxically provided both an outlet for southern and western regional pride and a confirmation of a northeastern genteel culture's negative opinion of Jacksonian men-on-the-make. In its basic pattern the vernacular hero is seen either bilking dispossessed women, blacks, Indians and other poor whites (thus confirming northeastern stereotypes), or duping figures of authority such as preachers, teachers, politicians and city-slickers (thus demonstrating the local hero's prowess). Such a double view of a Sut Lovingood or Simon Suggs is often reinforced formally when the vernacular hero's narrative is framed by a genteel narrator's typically condescending remarks. The humour of this school of writers thus can be quite complex, since a particular story could be criticizing the

social, political and economic conditions. The emergence of American humour is thus variously traced to an oral tradition responding to the extravagant claims made by promotional tracts and travel narratives, to the aphorisms and *tall tales fostered by the exigencies of the frontier experience, to the political satire of the revolutionary period, and even to the folk-journalism and comic lecturers' performances in the Jacksonian era. However its origins are explained, American humour's distinctive characteristics were moulded together by 1830 and, as numerous critics then and now have observed, provided tangible proof of the United States' cultural independence and its emerging national character.

Conditioned by responses to the continent's vast physical landscape, by the population's rapid mobility, by the medium of folk journalism (which promoted the anecdote, wisecrack, aphorism, and sketch) and by the anxieties resulting from the population's democratic freedoms, humour flourished in antebellum America as different ethnic groups, regional types and social classes juxtaposed and the resulting incongruities exploited for comic effects. In oral narratives, on stage or in the pages of the periodical press and the book, American humour prior to the Western's advent was characterized by its exaggeration

and irreverence, its use of localized settings and characters, its reliance on idiomatic speech, and its often grotesque imagery. By 1830 comic characters based on such regional types as the shrewd Yankee or the Ring-tailed Roarer of the frontier were well-known via tales and legends associated with such figures as Major Jack Downing, Mike Fink and Davy *Crockett. At the same time the confrontation of an unlettered, poker-faced, rural 'philosopher' and a pretentious dude or city-slicker had become a stock narrative motif, one perhaps best exemplified in the encounter between Brom Bones and Ichabod Crane in Washington *Irving's 'The Legend of Sleepy Hollow', or the verbal exchanges between Fenimore *Cooper's Natty Bumppo and Obed Battius in *The Prairie* (the motif is of course later exploited in the films of Will Rogers, Henry Fonda and Gary Cooper). We can consider as a classic example of this type of American humour the masterful opening section of Thomas Bangs Thorpe's 'The Big Bear of Arkansas', in which Jim Doggett of Shirt-tail Bend, Arkansas, spins tall tales about planting and hunting in Arkansas that enthral, dupe and ridicule the various Hoosiers, Suckers, and Yankees aboard a steamboat on the Mississippi River.

Through its hyperbole and sceptical debunking of authority, antebellum Ameri-

rogue or confusing him with a hero, siding with the narrator or ridiculing him as a pompous prig – or, as in some of Longstreet's stories, poking fun at the illiterate hero, the literate narrator, *and* the human object of the hero's chicanery.

The contrast between the aggressive boaster and his reserved respondent, the inventive play with language and the stretching of factual content (political, geographical, historical, etc.) so that the gullible listener is the butt of the humour, of course characterize the humour of Mark *Twain in such productions as 'The Celebrated Jumping Frog of Calaveras County' and the semi-autobiographical account of his western travels, *Roughing It*. In the latter text, Mark Twain's comic genius at creating situations showing the disparity between the illusions fostered by inherited traditions and the realities of daily experience extends the tall tale as a device of comic exaggeration. Here the tenderfoot narrator adventuring in a new territory converts the failure of his quest – he repeatedly goes through the same disillusionment as a result of his failure to learn from his experiences – into a series of episodic tales pointing out, as James Cox has said, that in a world full of lies the only truth is the tall tale which openly advertises its falsehood.

Mark Twain's importance to American humour lies in his originality in writing hoaxes, burlesques, sketches, stories, satires, travel books and monologues over the course of fifty years. In his experiments with narrative voices he fashioned an oral-sounding prose and eliminated the frame technique separating the genteel and vernacular narrators. He mastered the deadpan delivery and the ironic understatement and skilfully created the American character who refuses to be impressed when expected to be by the evidence of European or eastern cultural achievements. While his comic achievement reigns supreme in the late 19th century, Mark Twain's interest in the often bizarre features of the western landscape, in vernacular frontier characters and in the comic juxtaposition of the genteel and the unwashed was shared by other comic journalists and lecturers of the era. George Horatio Derby ('John Phoenix'), Charles Farrar Browne ('Artemus Ward') and William Wright ('Dan DeQuille') wrote and lectured on life in the West, like Mark Twain capitalizing on grotesque exaggerations, the unexpected conflation of the trivial and the grand, deadpan assertions of truthfulness about absolutely fantastic

events, and burlesques about scientific expeditions and geological surveys in the West.

Tall tales about life in the West continued to circulate after the Civil War, and the local colour writings of Alfred Henry Lewis, Andy *Adams and Owen *Wister reveal the exaggeration, irreverence, and respect for vernacular language and stories drawn from everyday life which characterized American humour of the pre-20th century. Wister's *The Virginian* (1902) – containing a tale-telling contest between Trampas and the Virginian and a practical joke switching babies' blankets in a nursery (this drawn from one of Derby's actual pranks of fifty years earlier) – utilizes both the clever hero and the man with 'horse sense' humorous traditions. Nevertheless, there was a shift between about 1895 and World War I, from a predominantly rural humour to a more urbane humour associated with the republic of letters, one that continues the more genial tradition represented by Irving, Holmes and the Connecticut Wits. This shift was fuelled, of course, by the transformation of the nation into an urban-industrial state and the rise of the mass media's importance in transmitting a 'federal' culture rather than a local one. The erosion of interest in local colour was furthered by changes in taste, as defenders of genteel humour such as John Kendrick Bangs of *Harper's Magazine* derided the slang, vulgarity, lewdness and violence of popular frontier humour. And it seems clear, given the anxieties over American identity during this period of mass immigration, that many observers believed the purpose of humour was to promote national unity – to portray the reconciliation of ideological and ethnic differences – rather than either to accentuate them or to subvert established cultural authorities.

While the 'black' comedy present in nineteenth-century southwestern humour occasionally appears in the film Western – one thinks here of scenes from *McCabe & Mrs. Miller*/1971 – the Western's humour tends to domesticate any subversive tendencies. The lovable, eccentric frontier character speaking in dialect; the wisecrack or practical joke; the garrulous teller of tales; the unlettered innocent who outwits city-slickers and corrupt businessmen – these characteristics of American humour are all present in the Western. Gabby Hayes and Walter Brennan update Natty Bumppo's role as foil to the romantic lead; McCabe's remark that 'if a frog had wings he wouldn't bump his ass so much' reminds us of the

Western's reliance on the aphorism or wisecrack; Jeremiah Johnson's initiation into the life of the mountain man plays on the kind of humour we see in Mark Twain's *Roughing It*. We can consider the deadpan humour of *My Darling Clementine*/1946 as well, as in the scene where Earp (Henry Fonda) inquires of the ancient bartender Mac (J. Farrell MacDonald) whether he has ever been in love. 'No sir, been a bartender all my life,' replies Mac. These humorous conventions function in the Western to ease tensions between individuals and groups, to provide dramatic irony, and to offer more relaxed interludes between the plot's action episodes. This is certainly the case in the popular singing Westerns and the 'trio' Westerns of the 1930s, and even the parodies of the classical Western's conventions – *Along Came Jones* (1945); *The Paleface* (1948); *Butch Cassidy and the Sundance Kid*/1969 – are indulgent and playful rather than satirical. Given the Western's roots in the romance pattern of heroic adventure and its thematic concern with violence, race relations and justice, perhaps it is not surprising that the rogue-Sut Lovingood type is more likely to be a 'sidewinder' than a comic sidekick whose antics are in the service of a strong, self-reliant hero ultimately loyal to society's values. ST

Along Came Jones/1945/UA/d Stuart Heisler/lp Gary Cooper, Loretta Young (Further Reading: Walter Blair and Hamlin Hill, *America's Humor* (1978) · William Bedford Clark and W. Craig Turner, *Critical Essays on American Humor* (1984) · Constance Rourke, *American Humor* (1931) · Jesse Bier, *The Rise and Fall of American Humor* (1968) · Jennette Tandy, *Crackerbox Philosophers in American Humor and Satire* (1925) · Hennig Cohen and William B. Dillingham (eds.), *Humor of the Old Southwest* (1964) · James M. Cox, *Mark Twain: The Fate of Humor* (1966))

Huntington, Collis Potter (1821-1900) · Railroad magnate, largely responsible for the construction of the *Central Pacific and Southern Pacific railroads. Shrewd, tight-fisted, with not an ounce of spare sentiment, Huntington was, together with Jay *Gould, the archetypal grasping railroad capitalist whom the populists loved to hate. His Southern Pacific was nicknamed the 'Octopus' in Frank *Norris' famous novel of that name.
Charles Newton ('Cottis P. Harrington')/ *The Iron Horse*/1924

I

Indian Agent · In *Fort Apache*/1948 the corrupt Indian agent Meacham is caught red-handed with the guns and whiskey he intends selling to the Indians. When Meacham protests he has a licence, John Wayne as Captain Yorke retorts that he has been given it by 'the Indian Ring, the dirtiest, most corrupt political group in our history.' Corruption among those responsible for dealing with Indians on the reservations was indeed one of the major scandals of the 19th century. The appointment of Indian agents licensed to trade and charged with the disbursement of federal funds was an important channel of patronage for unscrupulous Washington politicans, and the agents once appointed had few checks on their opportunities to profiteer. A short-lived experiment under the Grant administration in 1869 saw religious leaders appointed as agents (hence the Quakers on the reservation in *Cheyenne Autumn*/1964), but the policy was soon undermined by those who gained advantage from the old system.

That stock figure of the Western, the corrupt Indian agent, therefore has a basis in history. Noah Beery plays the part in *The Vanishing American*/1925 and the role reappears in *She Wore a Yellow Ribbon*/1949, as well as in dozens of B-Westerns such as *The Law West of Tombstone* and *Indian Agent*. In *Ulzana's Raid*/1972 Burt Lancaster accuses the agent of giving short weight on the beef he supplies to the Indians. Not all were corrupt; a different calibre of Indian agent was John *Clum. If the stereotype persisted, this may owe less to historical truth, and more to Hollywood's preference for individual villainy over complex social conditions as the cause of such events as Indian wars.

The Law West of Tombstone/1938/RKO/d Glenn Tryon/lp Harry Carey, Tim Holt · *Indian Agent*/1948/RKO/d Lesley Selander/ lp Tim Holt, Noah Beery Jr.

Indians/Native Americans · Next to the cowboy, the American Indian is the most prominent figure in the Western. Unlike the cowboy hero, however, he (or she) is seldom seen as an individual human being. Instead there is the stereotype of 'the Indian', as either an immovably stoic and noble savage or a ferociously bloodthirsty red devil. Between these extremes there is a human blank. Literally, 'stereotypes' are solid forms from which identical copies are drawn – 'if you've seen one you've seen them all.' Stereotypes of racial groups make no allowance for individuality and have a tendency to harden into racial prejudice, thus serving to uphold existing racial hierarchies and forms of racist oppression. This is reflected in most Westerns. Instead of portraying believable Native Americans, individual members of the many ethnic and cultural groups indigenous to the Americas, they tend to show ready-made and easily recognized images of painted and befeathered 'savages'. But, even with a wig, bandanna and war club, a white actor like Chuck Connors impersonating an Indian war leader in *Geronimo* (1962) reveals more about Euro-American attitudes towards Apaches and Indians in general than about that member of the Bedonkhoe band, Goyathlay, known as '*Geronimo', who surrendered to US Army General Nelson *Miles a hundred years ago on 4 September 1886.

From the beginning Europeans have perceived Native Americans according to their own political and economic needs. Around the year 1000 Vikings from Greenland and Iceland met Native Americans in 'Vinland' and described them as 'small and treacherous-looking' – and killed them. Five hundred years later Columbus found them gentle and physically strong – and helped enslave them. New England Puritans in the 17th century saw them as devil-worshippers or even children of Satan – and massacred them with the help of divine providence. Throughout Native American-white history, as Francis Jennings puts it, the myth of 'an Indian Menace' was 'the boomerang effect of the European Menace to the Indians'.

At the same time, those people in Europe who were economically and emotionally less directly involved tended to idealize Native American life. Indians were seen as Arcadians, as survivors of the Golden Age, and French Romanticism turned them into Noble Savages, these positive stereotypes being used to criticize the corruption of European societies. As a general rule, whites farthest removed from the frontier were the most likely to idealize Native Americans, whereas those closest in contact (and conflict) with Indians (geographically, socially, historically) were the most likely to describe them negatively.

Out of the French and British colonial wars, fought with Native allies, developed the first American literary genre, the *captivity narrative. This soon developed into fictional gothic tales and frontier romances like James Fenimore *Cooper's Leatherstocking Tales. In Cooper's *The Last of the Mohicans*, filmed three times between 1920 and 1936, both stereotypes co-exist: the blood-drinking, lecherous, fiendish Magua contrasts with Uncas, last of his 'dying race', too noble to be true and doomed to die. And there is also the stereotypical 'red-white' male couple, the frontiersman Natty Bumppo and his loyal, stoic Indian friend

Noble savages: 'Danse de mariage chez les Canadiens'
(18th century, artist unknown)

Not-so-typical Indians of the Pacific Northwest: Edward Curtis,
'Masked Dancers, Qagyuhl Indians'

Chingachgook, a noble savage about to become a 'good Indian', i.e. an acculturated 'domesticated' servant to white expansionism and law-and-order ideology, like the Lone Ranger's Tonto. Even at the height of *Manifest Destiny ideology in the second half of the 19th century, when crude social Darwinism and biological racism culminated in 'new' negative stereotypes of dumb and innately inferior Indians, the good-bad dichotomy persisted.

Just as bi-racial male couples have persisted as stock characters, so there have always been frontiersmen who fall in love with Indian 'princesses' of the Pocahontas type (from *The Squaw Man* in 1914, 1918 and 1931 to 'classics' like *Broken Arrow*/ 1950, *Across the Wide Missouri*/1950, *The Big Sky*/1952, *The Last Hunt*/1955, *Run of the Arrow*/1957). Often, they would be killed off by treacherous antagonists before they and the white heroes could trespass against the implicit rules of Indian-white apartheid (as in *Across the Wide Missouri* and *Broken Arrow*). 'Of course' there was nothing wrong with a white hero's temporary concubinage with a 'squaw' (*The Last Hunt*, *The Searchers*/ 1956), but if they persisted in staying together, it had to be away from 'civilization', i.e. in an Indian village (*The Big Sky*) or in the (Californian) West (*Two Rode Together*/1961).

The dominant visual stereotype of the Indian was first provided by George *Catlin and Karl *Bodmer around the middle of the 19th century. Their paintings came to represent all Native Americans, and their image of the mounted, war-bonneted, buffalo-hunting plains warrior came to stand for 'the Indian'. When in the 1870s the Sioux, Cheyenne and other plains tribes offered fierce resistance to dispossession, this added to their fascination for white audiences. Buffalo Bill and other managers of Wild West shows often insisted on showing 'real' Sioux and Cheyenne, who would attack wagon trains and railroads, take captives and scalps, burn and torture and d.nce their 'war dances' in gorgeous outfits. Ever since, mounted and befeathered plains Indians of the Catlin-Bodmer format have remained the most 'typical' Indians, habitually rigged out in, as Ralph and Natasha Friar put it, the 'instant [plains] Indian kit' of war-bonnet, fringed buckskin shirt, breastplate, shield, moccasins, tomahawk, bow and arrow or rifle.

Besides the 'plains Indian kit', Western movies occasionally use the 'instant woodland Indian kit', consisting of 'Mohawk' hairstyle, a lot of warpaint, naked chest and legs, breech-clout (cum bathing trunks) – and no horses. Such simple garb is used in films dealing with the colonial frontier east of the Mississippi – for example in *Pocahontas* (1908), *America* (1924), *The Last of the Mohicans* (1920, 1932, 1936), *Unconquered*/ 1947, *Seminole* (1953), *Mohawk* (1955).

Such rigid codifications cannot, of course, do justice to the multitude of distinct national cultures which existed in America before the whites arrived. Anthropologists count between 300 and 500 distinct nations (tribes, bands, etc.) in North America, divided into about ten larger separate cultural groups and comprising about 10-18 million people before contact. This diversity ranges from whale-hunting and fishing economies with sea-faring vessels in the Northwest, whose people lived in large communal log houses, to desert-dwelling survival experts in the Southwest, living on insects, rodents, seeds and roots in small family units, right next to corn-, beans- and squash-growing horticulturalists such as the Hopi. And there are many others. The 'typical' bison-hunting economy of the mounted plains people, by contrast, was only a short-lived one, because these peoples did not obtain horses until very late in their history (the Kiowa and Shoshone around 1700, the Cheyenne, Arapahoe, Pawnee, Teton Dakota around 1750, the Blackfoot and Cree around 1775). Likewise, the linguistic diversity of Native America is unparalleled in the world – linguists count about 200 mutually unintelligible languages in North America alone, belonging to nine large language stock families. But in Westerns Indians for a long time were reduced to speaking a homogenized and degrading 'Indian garble', a kind of grammatically flawed, childish and verbally extremely limited 'indianlect' of bad English.

While most Westerns treat all Indians as basically alike, some tribes are obviously more 'Indian' than others, and these are generally those who fought the hardest or most successfully against white encroachment, for example the Sioux and the Apache. The defeat of *Custer at the *Little Big Horn by the Sioux, together with their Cheyenne, Arapahoe, Blackfoot and other allies, one week before the nation's first Centennial in 1876 was shocking news, and resulted in over a century of Custer mythmaking, including more than 30 films since 1909. Similarly, the Apache wars in the Southwest from the 1860s to the 1880s, and especially Geronimo's guerrilla raiding, left

deep scars in US military self-esteem and cultural chauvinism. Consequently, the 'belligerence' of the Apaches, the Sioux, the Cheyenne, Comanche, Seminole and other nations who waged extended wars of resistance are shown over and over again, providing *post facto* explanations for Indian wars, glorifying white victories while usually putting the blame on the historical victims.

In *The Only Good Indian* Ralph and Natasha Friar list 81 films which deal with the Sioux and 43 with the Apache. The Comanche (25), Cheyenne (20), Navaho (16), Seminole (15) and Blackfoot (10) follow next. By contrast, the Crow and Pawnee, who were 'friendly' Indians and often served as Army scouts (as did many Apache against their own people), received much less publicity (4 films each). Those who offered no substantial military resistance at all, like the numerous Indian peoples in California, appear only four times altogether on the Friar list – this includes the several versions of *Ramona*, Helen Hunt *Jackson's pro-Indian novel about a victimized half-breed maid among mission Indians. Thus, ideologically, while the general role of Indians in Westerns has been to serve as backdrop and as plot function, the inclusion of certain tribes in preference to others has tended to justify centuries of genocide and continued forms of ethnocide against an indigenous population of which at least 170 distinct ethnic groups are living today, comprising about two million people in Canada and the US (*Harvard Encyclopedia of American Ethnic Groups*, 1980).

The Western as a genre has traditionally celebrated the myth of taming the frontier 'wilderness'. As such it has been able to see the Indian only as the unknown 'other', a part of those forces which threaten the onward march of Euro-American civilization and technological progress. Like rivers, mountains, deserts, wild animals or thunderstorms, Indians were shown to be part of the 'natural givens' of the 'new' continent, threatening white expansionism.

Consequently, the portrayal of Native Americans could scarcely but be unsympathetic, Eurocentric and degrading. The very few exceptions which try to understand the Indian, like *Ramona*, *The Dawn Maker* (1916) or *The Vanishing American*/1925, remain almost negligible drops in a deluge of films showing Indians as anonymous hordes and as dog-eating 'primitives'. Indians pour over the hills to attack peaceful settlers, as in *The Battle at Elderbush Gulch*/1913, and in at least 111 other films between 1909 and 1964

Warner Baxter, Dolores Del Rio in Ramona *(1928)*

Robert Taylor, James Mitchell in Devil's Doorway

Debra Paget, James Stewart, Jeff Chandler, Argentina Brunetti in Broken Arrow

Richard Dix in The Vanishing American

(according to Friar and Friar). Indians attack over and over again: 72 attacks on wagon trains (as in *The Covered Wagon*/1923), 32 attacks on stagecoaches and stations (such as *Stagecoach*/1939), 14 attacks on railroads (*The Iron Horse*/1924), and 45 attacks on forts or blockhouses (*Taza, Son of Cochise*/1953).

If they appear as individuals rather than as an anonymous mass, Indians are most commonly chiefs (81 films listed by Friar and Friar), 'princesses' or chief's daughters (19), 'maidens' (39) or medicine men or women (19). Other recurring Indian stock characters are mute female beasts of burden, misnamed 'squaws', occurring in 22 titles, or over-aggressive males (22), 'good Indians' (renegades, turncoats and converts), or simply drunken Indians, who appear in at least 53 films from *The Call of the Wild* (1908) to *Flap* (1970). By an inherent mechanism most of these types work for their own destruction, either incurring God's, civilization's or the white hero's wrath and vengeance, or falling victim to their own incompetence, sloth, innate aggressiveness or alcoholism. Even the noble savage is part of a dying species, while the good Indian is eager to give up his Indianness and become white, ready to sell out his own culture and people.

In the 1950s, out of feelings of racial guilt, the Western's Indian 'blossomed into a misunderstood, mistreated, sensitive and intelligent human being', according to Rainey and Adams in *Shoot Em Ups*. Indeed, there was a markedly more liberal attitude towards Indians in some Westerns, and films dealing with race-relations and miscegenation abounded for a while, though older stereotypes still persisted, often in the same movie. Two films of the same year,

Devil's Doorway/1950 and *Broken Arrow*/1950, the latter even employing several Native Americans in supporting roles, address issues of Indian dispossession and 'red-white' love affairs, and both establish 'new' patterns. *Devil's Doorway* shows how a returned war veteran and school graduate, Broken Lance, fights against white corruption with the help of a white woman lawyer who loves him. But their love cannot be; he dies melodramatically in his uniform and medals from gunshot wounds given him by white intruders on Shoshone lands. In *Broken Arrow* the love affair between the white hero, Jeffords, and the Apache chief's daughter (Debra Paget) cannot be fulfilled. The Indian bride is killed by white racists. In each case, the inclusion of a white hero/heroine falling in love with an Indian invited the audience's identification and made it easier to accept Indians as human beings – but in each case the Indian partner had to die before a happy ending. In *Across the Wide Missouri*, the Indian wife of a white trapper (of course a chief's daughter) is killed by fellow Blackfoot warriors after giving birth to a mixed-blood child, and in *The Big Sky* the white trapper leaves white society to stay with his Indian wife, again a Blackfoot chief's daughter. For inter-racial couples, there was no future, only death or exile. *Arrowhead* (1953) was a return to old racist clichés. Toriano (Jack Palance), a fictitious Apache war leader and eastern college graduate, wages a hopeless war against the deportation of his people to Florida, and in the final hand-to-hand combat Ed Bannon (Charlton Heston), the white Indian-hater embodying white racism and superiority, breaks Toriano's neck.

Other films of the 50s try to propagate peace and assimilation. Robert Aldrich's

Apache/1954 did so very much against the director's will. Depicting the flight of Massai (Burt Lancaster) from the train deporting him to Florida, back across a 'settled' West to his Apache homeland, Aldrich's film was planned to end with his hero killed by whites. But United Artists insisted on a totally unbelievable happy ending in which Massai, alienated from his culture, turns into a peaceful farmer and family man. Such happy endings in Westerns are necessarily fake and unconvincing, for example in *The Savage* (1952), where the Sioux chief's white son establishes peace between the army and his father's people, or in *Taza, Son of Cochise, White Feather* (1955) or *Cattle Queen of Montana*/1954, which all end with peaceful red-white coexistence. The last film demonstrates the persistence of the dual stereotype even in more liberal Westerns. Besides Barbara Stanwyck and Ronald Reagan, the film also stars Rodd Redwing as its only Native American actor (in a minor role). It is set in Glacier National Park, formerly part of the Blackfoot Reservation in Montana, and it portrays good and bad Blackfoot alike. Nachakos (Anthony Caruso) is both the old-fashioned blood-thirsty red devil and the modern dumb and drunken Indian wrapped into one – hating white settlers, lusting after white women, collaborating with white criminals, drinking their whiskey. His opponent, the chief's son Colorados (Lance Fuller), is noble but colo-nized, having been to university – though still speaking 'garble' – and helps the white heroine to reclaim 'her' land in his tribe's territory, finally even fighting those of his tribe who support Nachakos. At the end of the film, after Nachakos and the white criminals have been 'taken care of', Colo-rados remains an unmatched third man next to the white couple. There is no future for him or his people.

Some films in the 1950s did make a stand. *The Last Hunt* is a scathing attack on geno-cide and Euro-American ecological ruthless-ness, and *Run of the Arrow* deals with the insanities and horrors of all wars, both white and Indian, and with the problems of cross-cultural perceptions – themes taken up again by *Ulzana's Raid*/1972.

John Ford's treatment of Indians in his films is notorious. Though often employing Native American actors in supporting roles, his films generally celebrate the status quo of white supremacy. In *The Searchers* it is acceptable for a white man to sleep with an Indian woman, but a red man loving a white woman – a theme that had been taken up more openly and progressively in *The Van-ishing American* and *Devil's Doorway* – deserves death. In *Two Rode Together* Ford attempts to treat the situation of ethnic trans-culturization in greater detail; a freed white captive of the Comanches is lynched by a white mob after having killed his white step-mother, and the white hero and his half-breed wife remove further west – white society accepts neither red-white couples nor their children. (See also Don Siegel's *Flaming Star*/1960, with Elvis Presley as the half-breed.) *Cheyenne Autumn*/1964, reputedly Ford's 'Apology to the Indians', is a monumental but melodramatic rendering of Mari *Sandoz's superb novel. Instead of following the book Ford included a white Quaker schoolmarm as a 'reliable witness' (?) to accompany the Northern Cheyenne during their flight towards Montana. Again, leading Indian characters are played by white or Mexican-American actors. However, Ford's last Western is quite modern in using episodes from Indian history to reflect and criticize more contemporary events – in this case the genocidal treatment of the Cheyenne by army officer Wessels parallels the genocide of the Nazis.

In the latter half of the 1960s US national self-esteem suffered severe setbacks. Mount-ing black militancy, the horrors of the Vietnam war, student revolt and the hippie movement added momentum to the struggle of racial minorities to end discrimination and stereotyping. White liberals and even film producers discovered parallels between My Lai and massacres committed against Native Americans. Abraham Polonsky's *Tell Them Willie Boy Is Here*/1969 depicts the pursuit of a victimized Paiute offender, tracked down by a white sheriff and his posse, and it may be understood equally well as Polonsky's reaction to having been black-listed during the McCarthy anti-Communist witch-hunts, and as a parable for US imperia-lism, in which, as Dan Georgakas put it, Indians serve as 'stand-ins for Vietnamese, blacks or youth culture'.

Soldier Blue/1970 was heralded by its pro-moters as 'the most brutal and liberating, the most honest American film ever made' (quoted by Wayne Michael Sarf, *God Bless You, Buffalo Bill*, 1983). While it is certainly brutal and bloodily honest in its slow-motion depiction of the carnage at the Sand Creek Massacre (1864), its liberating value seems nil. This story of a white captivity is merely the frame for detailed scenes of killing, and although the title song was written and sung by Cree singer and activist Buffy Sainte-Marie, leading parts were played by white actors. Another political film of 1970, *Flap*, is merely a flop, ridiculing the American Indian movement and Indian alcoholism in a melodrama starring Anthony Quinn as the Navaho Flapping Eagle. By contrast, *A Man Called Horse*/1970, another white captivity story, contains 80 per cent Lakota dialogue and attempts great anthropological accuracy. But basic assumptions are still Eurocentric. The white hero's sado-masochistic test of endurance is copied from George Catlin's depiction of a Mandan ritual. *Akwesasne Notes*, the largest pan-Indian newspaper in the US, commented in May 1971: 'Same old savage stereotype. White actors playing cigar store Indians.' Much of the film was shot on the Rosebud Sioux reservation with the enthusiastic sup-port of its inhabitants, who believed it would be an authentic film about Sioux culture. After the film's release they became the laughing stock of Indian America.

The most famous 'new' Indian film, dis-carding old myths and stereotypes, is *Little Big Man*/1970, based on Thomas Berger's novel. The film does justice to the novel's balance of tragedy and comedy. While debunking Custer as a self-righteous, unher-oic character, whose bravery as a soldier is based on ignorance, it again draws parallels with the Vietnam war – as does *Ulzana's Raid*.

In the US the 'new wave' culminated in 1973 with Marlon Brando's refusal to accept his Academy Award. Native American actress Sacheen Littlefeather, sent to deliver his speech, later starred in *Winterhawk* (1975), another pro-Indian film. With Richard T. Heffron's television film *I Will Fight No More Forever* and Claude Fournier's *Alien Thunder* (1973, Canada), the Indian Western may have found a 'new' subject, i.e. recording the history of America's indige-nous people and their conflict with Euro-civilization, while basing that history on the heroism of famous groups or individuals like the Nez Percé Chief *Joseph or the Cree warrior Almighty Voice.

However, such promising changes do not mean that the old stereotypes have vanished. Rather, the stereotype seems to have expanded, allowing also for the portrayal of more sophisticated and culturally authentic Indians, while retaining much of the old savagism or Tontoism. *The White Buffalo* (1977), for example, uses a superficially authentic Sioux setting and a real Creek Indian actor, Will Sampson, for a wholly unbelievable, sensationalist rehash of *Jaws* in a Western setting. Sampson was the most conspicuous Native American actor of his time, after his success as Chief Bromden in *One Flew Over the Cuckoo's Nest*.

The most controversial recent 'Indian' Western is the TV series *Mystic Warrior*, which also features Will Sampson and is based on Ruth Beebe Hill's 'authentic' Indian saga *Hanta Yo* (1979), a book against which Native American groups and indi-viduals waged such a relentless campaign in the early 1980s that Theodore Wolpers and Warner Bros. found not a single reservation in Canada or the US willing to have the film shot on their territory, and so the film was made in Mexico. Native Americans had learned the lesson of the Rosebud Sioux during the filming of *A Man Called Horse*.

For ideological reasons, the filming of pro-Indian Westerns is perhaps more diffi-cult in the US (and Canada?) than in Europe, and various European Westerns have attempted to portray history from a Native point of view or at least from a perspective sympathetic to their cause. These range from the sentimental, poorly made and soggy West German productions based on Karl *May's Winnetou novels and starring French actor Pierre Brice as Winnetou, the 'apple' Apache (red outside, white inside), to East Germany's DEFA-produced Indian films like *Tecumseh* (1972), *Apachen* (1973) and *Ulzana* (1974), starring Yugoslav actor Gojko Mitic as both the Shawnee and the Apache patriot alike. In Michael Winner's British 'brutalo-Western' *Chato's Land* (1971) Charles Bronson rendered an Apache half-breed as a relentless and cruel avenger, but also a loving and humane husband and father. A Swedish film of 1973, *Nybyggarna*, stands out as the most successful. It treats, among other things, the relationship between newly arrived Swedish settlers in Minnesota and displaced Santee Sioux, showing the so-called Minnesota Uprising (1862) as what it was: the desperate attempt of betrayed and starving Indians to survive, which resulted in the greatest mass execution in US history, the public hangings of 39 Santee insurgents at Mankato on 26 December 1862.

One persistent factor in almost all the Westerns discussed so far is their use of non-Native actors to play the Indian parts. Yet the presence of Native actors is no guarantee that Indians will be represented as people. Geronimo, the famous Apache war leader, was portrayed in films more often than any other Native American individual (16 times); even more than the Sioux chiefs Sitting Bull (14), Crazy Horse (9), Red Cloud (6), or his fellow Apache Cochise (8), Mangas Coloradas (4) and Victorio (3). Geronimo was several times played by Native American actors, in particular by Chief Thundercloud, Jay Silverheels, John War Eagle and Chief Yowlachie. Yet this did not prevent him being characterized as, for the most part, a treacherous villain. Native American actors were for the most part helpless to effect any change in the familiar distortions. Will Rogers, part-Cherokee, is still remembered among Native Americans as one who campaigned throughout his career for an acceptance of Indians as human beings, and similar things are said about Sioux actor John War Eagle. Chief Dan George, who won fame as a supporting actor playing Old Lodge Skins in *Little Big Man*, started his film career too late in life to perform more than a very few good roles before retiring, including *Our Totem Is the Raven*, an Indian-cast story of initiation set in modern Canada. But Will Sampson's career, which went into steep decline after *One Flew*

Over the Cuckoo's Nest, illustrates the inevitable predicament of all Native actors; being forced to accept Hollywood's terms, they have little chance of overcoming the limitations set by the film industry. Without Native American self-determination, without control of resources, of direction, of script-selection and casting, there will be no real Native Americans in the movies. HL
The Call of the Wild/1908/Biograph/d D.W. Griffith/lp Florence Lawrence · *Ramona*/1910/Biograph/d D.W. Griffith/lp Mary Pickford · *Ramona*/1916/Clune/d Donald Crisp/lp Adda Gleason · *Ramona*/1928/UA/d Edwin Carewe/lp Warner Baxter, Dolores Del Rio · *Ramona*/1936/FOX/d Henry King/lp Loretta Young, Don Ameche · *The Squaw Man*/1914/Jesse Lasky/d Cecil B. DeMille/lp Dustin Farnum · *The Squaw Man*/1918/PAR/d Cecil B. DeMille/lp Elliott Dexter · *The Squaw Man*/1931/MGM/d Cecil B. DeMille/lp Warner Baxter · *The Dawn Maker*/1916/Triangle-Kay-Bee/d William S. Hart/lp William S. Hart, Blanche White · *The Last of the Mohicans*/1920/Associated Exhibitors/d Maurice Tourneur/lp Wallace Beery · *The Last of the Mohicans*/1932/Mascot/d B. Reeves Eason, Ford Beebe/lp Harry Carey · *The Last of the Mohicans*/1936/UA/d George B. Seitz/lp Randolph Scott · *America*/1924/UA/d D.W. Griffith/lp Lionel Barrymore · *The Savage*/1952/PAR/d George Marshall/lp Charlton Heston · *Arrowhead*/1953/PAR/d Charles Marquis Warren/lp Charlton Heston, Jack Palance · *Seminole*/1953/U/d Budd Boetticher/lp Rock Hudson · *White Feather*/1955/FOX/d Robert Webb/lp Robert Wagner, Debra Paget · *Mohawk*/1955/d Kurt Neumann/lp Scott Brady, Neville Brand · *Geronimo*/1962/UA/d Arnold Laven/lp Chuck Connors, Kamala Devi · *Flap*/1970/WB/d Carol Reed/lp Anthony Quinn, Shelley Winters · *Chato's Land*/1971/GB/d Michael Winner/lp Charles Bronson, Jack Palance · *Nybyggarna*/1973/Sw/d Jan Troell/lp Max von Sydow, Liv Ullman · *Alien Thunder*/1973/Onyx/d Claude Fournier/lp Donald Sutherland, Chief Dan George · *Winterhawk*/1975/Charles B. Pierce/d Charles B. Pierce/lp Michael Dante, Leif Erickson · *The White Buffalo*/1977/Dino De Laurentiis/d J. Lee Thompson/lp Charles Bronson, Will Sampson

Ingraham, Prentiss (1843-1904) · Prolific dime novelist, author of some six hundred novels. Ingraham is said to have written one

story of 35,000 words in a single day. He is credited by the best authority with 121 Buffalo Bill stories, as well as novels about *Deadwood Dick and other Western heroes. He also wrote plays for Buffalo Bill *Cody and publicity for his Wild West. Not the inventor of the Buffalo Bill legend, but one of its principal perpetrators.
Allan Nichols, *Buffalo Bill and the Indians*/1976

Irish · Though the overwhelming proportion of Irish immigrants to America remained where they landed, in the northeast, the Irish appear early in the Western. There's an Irish army sergeant in Frank Borzage's 1917 picture about the Mounties, *Until They Get Me*. Fifty years later James Coburn plays an IRA explosives expert in *Giù la testa*/1971. As we would expect, the Irish are seen building the railroad in *Union Pacific*/1939. In *Run of the Arrow*/1957 Rod Steiger is an Irish Southerner, like Richard Harris in *Major Dundee*/1964. It's in the work of John Ford that the Irish come into their own, especially in the brawling, drunken but warm-hearted characterizations of Victor McLaglen (Sgt. Mulcahy in *Fort Apache*/1948, Sgt. Quincannon in *She Wore a Yellow Ribbon*/1949 and *Rio Grande*/1950). That the Irish were plentiful in the post-Civil War army is borne out by statistics: they made up twenty per cent of the entire force (Germans were the next most common group). The comment of an officer of the 4th Cavalry on his Irish troops rather goes against the Fordian conception: 'I preferred the Irish; they were more intelligent and resourceful as a rule.'
Until They Get Me/1917/Triangle/d Frank Borzage/lp Jack Curtis

Iroquois · A confederation of Indian peoples originally occupying most of upstate New York and consisting of the Mohawks, the Oneida, the Onondaga, the Cayuga and the Seneca. In the wars against the French in North America the Iroquois generally sided with the British and continued to do so during the American Revolution. This proved to be their undoing; the colonists conducted several successful campaigns against them and after the war they were obliged to relinquish most of their lands. The Iroquois appear in Westerns mainly in dramatizations of the works of Fenimore *Cooper. In his novels the Iroquois (whom he often calls Mingoes) are the brutal and bloodthirsty enemies of civilization. His Indian hero Chingachgook, the noble friend of the whites, is described by Cooper as a Mohican (sometimes written as Mohegan or Mahican). The Mohicans (not to be confused with the Mohawks, listed above as part of the Iroquois confederacy), were loosely allied to the Delaware (Cooper treats them as being the same); both were members of the Algonquian language group. In practice these distinctions usually count for little in the Western, virtually all Indians of the northeast wearing the distinctive shaved haircut with scalp-lock now known, courtesy of the punks, as a 'Mohican'.

Irving, Washington (1783-1859) · Essayist and historian. Though his fame now largely rests on such stories as 'Rip Van Winkle' and 'The Legend of Sleepy Hollow', his writing about the West, pleasant rather than profound, popularized a picturesque view of the characters who inhabited it in the 1830s. *A Tour on the Prairies* (1835) is an account of his own travels, *The Adventures of Captain Bonneville* (1837) a novel about trappers, and *Astoria* (1836) a history of John Jacob Astor's role in the development of the *fur trade.

W.H. Jackson, 'Chalk Creek Canyon' (c.1887)

J

Jackson, Andrew (1767-1845) · 7th President of the United States. Though not a scout or an explorer like Daniel *Boone, in his early years Jackson did as much as anyone to create and popularize the image of the frontiersman. He first sprang to fame when his force of Tennessee volunteers defeated the Creek Indians at the battle of Horseshoe Bend in Alabama in 1814. The next year Jackson routed the British at the battle of New Orleans. When he became President (1829-37) he pursued a vigorously nationalist and expansionist policy involving the forcible removal of large numbers of Indians from their homes in the east to lands west of the Mississippi. Besides his military feats, Jackson was popular with the electorate for his lack of social pretensions (he was sketchily educated), his pugnaciousness (he fought several duels) and his suspicions of banks and taxation: all essential qualities of the frontier 'character' he helped define. *Andrew Jackson*/1913/American/*d* Allan Dwan · Russell Simpson/*The Frontiersman*/1927/MGM/*d* Reginald Barker/*lp* Tim McCoy · Lionel Barrymore/*The Gorgeous Hussy*/1936/MGM/*d* Clarence Brown/*lp* Joan Crawford, Robert Taylor · Hugh Sothern/*The Buccaneer*/1938/PAR/*d* Cecil B. DeMille/*lp* Fredric March · Edward Ellis/

Man of Conquest/1939/REP/*d* George Nichols Jr./*lp* Richard Dix · Brian Donlevy/*The Remarkable Andrew*/1942/PAR/*d* Stuart Heisler/*lp* William Holden · Lionel Barrymore/*Lone Star*/1951/MGM/*d* Vincent Sherman/*lp* Clark Gable, Ava Gardner · Charlton Heston/*The President's Lady*/1952/FOX/*d* Henry Levin/*lp* Susan Hayward · Carl Benton Reed/*The First Texan*/1956/AA/*d* Byron Haskin/*lp* Joel McCrea, Felicia Farr · Charlton Heston/*The Buccaneer*/1958/PAR/*d* Anthony Quinn/*lp* Yul Brynner, Charles Boyer Television · Basil Ruysdael/*Davy Crockett* · John Anderson/*The Great Adventure* · Victor Jory/*The Great Adventure* · John Anderson/*Bridger*

Jackson, Helen Hunt (1830-85) · Writer. In 1881 Jackson published her history *A Century of Dishonor*, an indictment of the American government's relations with the Indians. The book aroused an outcry and Jackson further popularized the Indians' cause with her best-selling novel *Ramona* (1884). It tells the story of a half-Indian girl who falls in love with a mission Indian in California. Disowned by her parents, the girl elopes with her lover. Though he is later murdered by whites the novel ends happily when Ramona is accepted back by her family.

Ramona/1910/Biograph/*d* D.W. Griffith/*lp* Mary Pickford, Henry B. Walthall · *Ramona*/1916/Clune/*d* Donald Crisp/*lp* Adda Gleason, Monroe Salisbury · *Ramona*/1928/UA/*d* Edwin Carewe/*lp* Warner Baxter, Dolores Del Rio · *Ramona*/1936/FOX/*d* Henry King/*lp* Loretta Young, Don Ameche · Also Martha Vickers as the daughter of Ramona, *Daughter of the West*/1949/Martin Mooney Productions/*d* Harold Daniels/*lp* Philip Reed

Jackson, William Henry (1843-1942) · Photographer. Jackson's first major series of photographs was made when he accompanied F.V. Hayden's survey expedition of 1870 into Wyoming, where he photographed Washakie, chief of the Shoshone. On Hayden's next expedition Jackson was joined by the artist Thomas *Moran and the two of them were the first to bring back pictures, both photographs and paintings, of the wonders of the Yellowstone region. Jackson became the most celebrated photographer of the western landscape as a result of this and other notable 'firsts', such as his pictures of the cliff dwellings of Mesa Verde and of the Mount of the Holy Cross, Colorado, which Moran later painted. Jackson's views of the West, usually on the heroic

Jesse and Frank James

scale, were disseminated in thousands of tinted postcards distributed by the Detroit Publishing Company, and helped to form and extend a taste for the grandeur which the western landscape was particularly suited to provide.

Jail · Jail can be a place to meet interesting people (in *The Big Sky*/1952, Kirk Douglas finds himself in the same cell as Arthur Hunnicutt, who offers to take him to the Blackfoot country). It's also the negation of the freedom the Western hero craves, a place to break out of. The tradition of busting out of jail begins early, with several Broncho Billy Anderson films; for example *Broncho Billy and the Sheriff's Kid, The Outlaw and the Child, Shooting Mad*. It continues in the B-Westerns of the 1930s; in the all-black but otherwise entirely typical *Harlem Rides the Range* the hero is wrongly imprisoned by the corrupt sheriff and breaks out. Jail functions as a metaphor for modern life in the contemporary Western *Lonely Are the Brave*/1962. Jail-breaking remains a healthy instinct in *Silverado*/1985, which works a new variation on the old problem of how to get the jailer's keys when they have fallen out of reach beyond the bars (the prisoner uses the outstretched leg of the dead jailer to draw them near). Other vari-

ations on this include using a blanket (*The Bravados*) and a chair leg (*One-Eyed Jacks*/ 1960). Films about *Billy the Kid often have a jail-breaking scene; for example *Billy the Kid*/1930, *The Left Handed Gun*/1957, *Pat Garrett and Billy the Kid*/1973. Though the Kid did in fact break out of jail, it must be the sheer force of cinematic tradition rather than history that makes for the inclusion of a jail-break scene in such a marginal Kid film as *Billy the Kid vs. Dracula*.
Harlem Rides the Range/1939/Hollywood Pictures/d Richard Kahn/lp Herbert Jeffrey · *The Bravados*/1958/FOX/d Henry King/lp Gregory Peck, Joan Collins · *Billy the Kid vs. Dracula*/1965/Circle/d William Beaudine/lp Chuck Courtney, John Carradine

James, Jesse [Woodson] (1847-82) Outlaw. With his brother Frank[lin] (1843-1915), Jesse James was the leader of the most celebrated gang of bank and train robbers in American history and, together with a select band such as Kit Carson and Buffalo Bill, was both famous in his own time and a legend after. Sons of a Baptist minister, the James brothers were brought up in Missouri, at the time torn by sectional strife and a crucible of outlawry. In the Civil War they rode with *Quantrill's raiders; when Jesse tried to

surrender at the end of the war he was shot and seriously wounded.

The James gang was born on 13 February 1866 when they robbed a bank at Liberty, Missouri. In the course of the next few years other bank robberies followed and, from 1873, the James brothers, often together with the *Youngers, robbed trains too. This brought the *Pinkertons on their trail. In 1875 detectives surrounded the house of Jesse's mother. A bomb was thrown inside; the explosion tore off Mrs James' arm and killed Jesse's young half-brother. Neither Jesse nor Frank was home at the time. This episode increased public sympathy for the gang, whose popularity was already considerable in areas which had sided with the Confederacy and which viewed railroads as oppressive monopolies, and Yankee ones at that.

Jesse, in fact, was fast turning into a Robin Hood figure; as the 'Ballad of Jesse James' was later to put it:
'Jesse James was a lad who killed many a man
He robbed the Glendale train.
He took from the rich and he gave to the poor,
He'd a hand and a heart and a brain.'
Typical of the stories told about Jesse is the tale of the poor widow whose mortgage is about to be foreclosed. Jesse gives her the money to pay off the banker, then lies in wait until she has done so. As the banker rides away Jesse holds him up and takes the money back again. There is no evidence that the story is true, but the incident is reported in several written accounts and depicted in Nicholas Ray's film *The True Story of Jesse James*/1957.

The first book to celebrate the James' exploits was *Noted Guerrillas, or the Warfare of the Border* (1877), by John Edwards; it was only one of many which took a strongly sympathetic view. It was followed in the 1880s and 1890s by literally hundreds of stories about the James gang in dime novels and magazines.

Things went badly wrong for the gang during an attempted bank robbery at Northfield, Minnesota on 7 September 1876. The townspeople stood and fought; three of the gang were killed and the three Younger brothers, two badly wounded, were captured. Frank and Jesse got away, but had to lie low for some time. By 1879 they had reorganized and were back robbing trains. But now there was a large price on their heads and on 3 April 1882, as he stood on a chair in his house in St Joseph, Missouri, straightening a picture, Jesse was shot in the

Frank James in 1914

back by Bob *Ford, a member of his own gang. Six months later Frank gave himself up to the authorities. He was tried on several different charges, but public sympathy was such that the law could not get a conviction. Frank later dabbled in show business, including for a time running a Wild West show with Cole Younger, and died peacefully in Missouri many years later.

Almost all the vast literature on the James brothers portrays them as authentic American heroes. This is how the cinema has seen them, at least until the 1960s, when it became fashionable to debunk virtually everybody. But they were slow to achieve in the cinema the status they acquired in the literature of the time. In 1908 Essanay made a film entitled *The James Boys in Missouri* and in 1915 Luna produced *The Near Capture of Jesse James*. After this, apart from two cheap productions starring Jesse James' son in the early 1920s and a Fred Thomson vehicle in 1927, the James brothers did not appear on screen until incarnated by Tyrone Power and Henry Fonda in 1939. The great success of this film ensured that Jesse would henceforth become the most popular of all cinematic outlaws.

(Frank James in brackets): *The James Boys in Missouri*/1908/Essanay · *Jesse James Jr.*/*Jesse James Under the Black Flag*/1921/ Mesco Pictures/d Franklin B. Coates/lp Diana Reed · Jesse James Jr./*Jesse James as*

the *Outlaw*/1921/Mesco Pictures/d Franklin B. Coates/lp Diana Reed · Fred Thomson (James Pierce)/*Jesse James*/1927/ PAR/d Lloyd Ingraham/lp Nora Lane · Tyrone Power (Henry Fonda)/*Jesse James*/ 1939 · Don Barry (Michael Worth)/*Days of Jesse James*/1939/REP/d Joseph Kane/lp Roy Rogers · (Henry Fonda)/*The Return of Frank James*/1940 · Roy Rogers/*Jesse James*

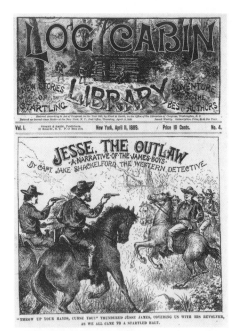

A Jesse James dime novel

at *Bay*/1941/REP/d Joseph Kane/lp George Hayes · Alan Baxter/*Bad Men of Missouri*/ 1941/WB/d Ray Enright/lp Dennis Morgan, Jane Wyman · Rod Cameron/*The Remarkable Andrew*/1942/PAR/d Stuart Heisler/lp William Holden · Don Barry (as Jesse James' son)/*Jesse James Jr.*/1942/REP/d George Sherman/lp Lynn Merrick · Lawrence Tierney (Tom Tyler)/*Badman's Territory*/1946/RKO/d Tim Whelan/lp Randolph Scott · Clayton Moore/*Jesse James Rides Again*/1947/REP/d Fred C. Brannon, Thomas Carr/lp Linda Stirling · Clayton Moore (Steve Darrell)/*Adventures of Frank and Jesse James*/1948/REP/d Fred Brannon, Yakima Canutt · Reed Hadley (Tom Tyler)/*I Shot Jesse James*/1948 · Dale Roberston/*Fighting Man of the Plains*/ 1949/FOX/d Edwin L. Marin/lp Randolph Scott · Keith Richards (Robert Bice)/*The James Brothers of Missouri*/1950/REP/d Fred C. Brannon/lp Robert Bice · (Don Barry)/ *Gunfire*/1950/Lippert/d William Berke/lp Robert Lowery · Audie Murphy (Richard Long)/*Kansas Raiders*/1950/U/d Ray Enright/lp Brian Donlevy · (Reed Hadley)/ *The Return of Jesse James*/1950/Lippert/d Arthur Hilton/lp John Ireland · MacDonald Carey (Wendell Corey)/*The Great Missouri Raid*/1950/PAR/d Gordon Douglas/lp Ward Bond, Edgar Buchanan · Lawrence Tierney (Tom Tyler)/*Best of the Badmen*/1951/RKO/d William D. Russell/lp Robert Ryan, Robert Preston · Ben Cooper (James Brown)/*The Woman They Almost Lynched*/1953/REP/d Allan Dwan/lp Joan Leslie · Willard Parker/*The Great Jesse James Raid*/1953/Lippert/d Reginald Le Borg/lp Barbara Payton · Brett King (as Jesse James' son)/*Jesse James vs. the Daltons*/1954/COL/d William Castle/lp Barbara Lawrence · Don Barry (Jack Buetel)/*Jesse James' Women*/1954/UA/d Don Barry · Robert Wagner (Jeffrey Hunter)/ *The True Story of Jesse James*/1957 · Henry Brandon (Douglas Kennedy)/*Hell's Crossroads*/1957/d Franklin Adreon/lp Steve McNally, Robert Vaughn · Wendell Corey (Jim Davis)/*Alias Jesse James*/1959/ UA/d Norman McLeod/lp Bob Hope, Rhonda Fleming · Ray Stricklyn (Robert Dix)/*Young Jesse James*/1960/FOX/d William Claxton/lp Willard Parker · Wayne Mack/*The Outlaws Is Coming*/ 1964/COL/d Norman Maurer/lp The Three Stooges · John Lupton/*Jesse James Meets Frankenstein's Daughter*/1965/Circle/d William Beaudine/lp Narda Onyx · Audie Murphy/*A Time for Dying*/1969 · (William Fosterwick)/*Ride a Wild Stud*/1969/Vega

Tyrone Power in Jesse James

International/d Revilo Ekard/lp Hale Williams · Robert Duvall (John Pearce)/ *The Great Northfield Minnesota Raid*/1972 · James Keach (Stacy Keach)/*The Long Riders*/1980
Television · Mike Road/*Colt .45* · James Coburn/*Bronco* · Christopher Jones (Allen Case)/*The Legend of Jesse James* · Stuart Margolin/*The Intruders* · Michael Cavanaugh (Gary Combs)/*Belle Starr* · Harris Yulin/*The Last Ride of the Dalton Gang* · Kris Kristofferson (Johnny Cash)/ *The Last Days of Frank and Jesse James*

James, Will (1892-1942) · Novelist and illustrator. James' best known book is *Smoky* (1926), a story about a horse written for children. Other novels include *The Drifting Cowboy* (1925), *Cow Country* (1926) and *The Three Mustangeers* (1933). In 1930 James published *The Lone Cowboy*, which he claimed was an autobiographical account of his early years. Some of what the book relates is true, including his time in prison for cattle rustling and a spell in the army breaking horses. But James' account of his origins is a fantasy. Instead of being orphaned and brought up by an old trapper in Montana, as the book recounts, James was born Ernest Dufault of French-Canadian parents in Quebec and left home at fifteen. The book is nevertheless eloquent both about horses and about the freedom which goes hand in hand with the cowboy's rootlessness.
Smoky/1933/FOX/d Eugene Ford/lp Victor Jory · *The Lone Cowboy*/1933/PAR/d Paul Sloane/lp Jackie Cooper · *Smoky*/1946/FOX/d Louis King/lp Fred MacMurray, Anne Baxter · *Smoky*/1966/FOX/d George Sherman/lp Fess Parker, Katy Jurado · *Shoot Out* [*The Lone Cowboy*]/1971/U/d Henry Hathaway/lp Gregory Peck

Jefferson, Thomas (1743-1826) · 3rd President of the United States (1801-9). His importance in the development of the West is twofold. Firstly, Jefferson believed that true democracy was dependent on a social system based on the small farmer. This philosophy led eventually to the policy of settling the public lands in small lots, enshrined in the Homestead Act. Secondly, Jefferson believed in the United States' right to expand westward, even into land under the sovereignty of other powers. It was under Jefferson's presidency that the *Louisiana Purchase was made from France. He was directly involved in the despatching of *Lewis and Clark to explore the Northwest as far as the Pacific.

Jefferson lived too early to feature in many Westerns, though his name is sometimes invoked in the hushed and reverent tones employed by Woody Strode in the schoolroom scene in *The Man Who Shot Liberty Valance*/1962.
Allan Cavan/*Old Louisiana*/1937/Crescent/ d I.V. Willat/lp Tom Keene · Herbert Hayes/*The Far Horizons*/1954/PAR/d Rudolph Maté/lp Fred MacMurray, Charlton Heston

Jennings, Al (1864-1961) · Bank robber. As an outlaw his accomplishments were minor, but on coming out of jail in 1907 he was by chance given the opportunity to take part in a film reconstruction of a bank raid he had carried out in Oklahoma. *The Bank Robbery* (1908) also featured Sheriff Bill *Tilghman playing himself. As described by Kevin Brownlow in *The War, the West and the Wilderness*, the film's utter lack of artistry lends it conviction as a portrait of the banality of a small-town robbery. Jennings went on to appear in another film in 1908, *The Wolf Hunt*, and later found work as a technical adviser and bit-part player in several Hollywood productions.
These include *Beating Back*/1914/ Thanhouser/d Carroll Fleming · (technical adviser) *Jordan Is a Hard Road*/1915/Fine Arts-Triangle/d Allan Dwan/lp Dorothy Gish, Owen Moore · *Lady of the Dugout*/ 1918/Ernest Shipman/d W.S. Van Dyke/lp Frank Jennings · *Bond of Blood*/1919/d William Bertram · *Fighting Fury*/1924/U/d Clifford Smith/lp Jack Hoxie · *The Demon*/ 1926/U/d Clifford Smith/lp Jack Hoxie · *The Ridin' Rascal*/1926/U/d Clifford Smith/ lp Art Acord · *The Border Sheriff*/1926/U/d Robert N. Bradbury/lp Jack Hoxie · *Loco Luck*/1927/U/d Clifford Smith/lp Art Acord · *The Land of Missing Men*/1930/

Tiffany/d J. P. McCarthy/lp Bob Steele · *Song of the Gringo*/1936/Grand National/d John P. McCarthy/lp Tex Ritter · Dan Duryea plays the outlaw in *Al Jennings of Oklahoma*/1951/COL/d Ray Nazarro/lp Gale Storm

Johnson County War · Resentment against rustlers and settlers by the cattle kings who formed the Wyoming Stock Growers' Association came to a head in 1892. In previous years some exemplary lynchings had been carried out. One victim was Ella Watson (1862?-88), otherwise known as Cattle Kate, a prostitute who accepted rustled cattle in exchange for her services. Now the big stock owners determined to teach the local people a lesson. Gunmen were recruited and a party of forty-six, calling themselves the Regulators, set off by train from Cheyenne for Johnson County, some 250 miles northwest, where the centre of the rustling was thought to be. A list had been prepared of the principal suspects, who were to be eliminated. Some killings were carried out. A cowboy named Nathan Champion (1857-92) was besieged along with his friend Nick Ray at the KC Ranch. Though Ray was shot early on, Champion held out all day until the house was set on fire. As he ran into the open he was cut down in a hail of bullets. By this time the local people had risen up against the invaders in a posse two hundred strong and surrounded them. The Regulators eventually had to be extricated by the cavalry. In spite of the outrage they provoked and the murders that had been committed, none of those involved was ever brought to trial.

The incident has remained prominent in the history of the West as the most dramatic encounter between big ranchers and small farmers, a struggle that has some of the classical hallmarks of class conflict. *Heaven's Gate*/1980 (in which Isabelle Huppert plays Cattle Kate and Christopher Walken is Nate Champion) is the most recent and ambitious account of these incidents, though many films, including *Shane*/1952, draw indirectly on them.

Johnson, Dorothy [Marie] (1905-84) · Writer. Her first collection of short stories was *Indian Country*, published in 1953. This was followed by another, *The Hanging Tree* (1957). Several of her stories are about whites living among Indians and work subtle variations on the Indian *captivity narrative. She also wrote western history, some of it for children, and two novels, *Buffalo Woman*

(1977) and *All the Buffalo Returning* (1979).
The Hanging Tree/1959 · *The Man Who Shot Liberty Valance*/1962 · *A Man Called Horse*/1970 · *Return of a Man Called Horse*/1976/UA/d Irving Kershner/lp Richard Harris

Television · *Wagon Train* ('A Man Called Horse')

Johnson, 'Liver-eating' (1823?-1900) · John Johnson was a mountain man who got his nickname from his vow of vengeance against the Crow Indians, who murdered his Flathead wife in 1847. He is reputed to have killed over two hundred Crows, though whether he ate their livers as he threatened is not established. Vardis *Fisher's novel *Mountain Man* (1965) is a fictionalized version of Johnson's story and formed the basis for the film *Jeremiah Johnson*/1972.

Joseph, Chief (1840-1904) · Leader of the Nez Percé. His father, a convert to Christianity, was known as Old Chief Joseph. When gold was discovered on their lands in the Wallowa valley in Oregon the Nez Percé were ordered by the US government to a reservation in Idaho. Chief Joseph, hitherto more a political than a military leader, decided to fight. This led to the Nez Percé War of 1877. Joseph led his people on an epic march 1,000 miles long, fighting a rearguard action all the way. They were caught by the army on the Canadian border and, exhausted and starving, surrendered. The Nez Percé were sent to a reservation in Oklahoma and then eventually to Washington Territory. Chief Joseph's struggle, though ignored by the cinema, is one of the most famous episodes in the history of White-Indian relations. His final words on surrendering are among the most-often quoted by any Indian leader: 'From where the sun now stands I will fight no more forever.'

Television · Ned Romero/*I Will Fight No More Forever*

Juárez, Benito (1806-72) · Statesman. Juárez was chief minister of Mexico from 1855 to 1857, when his reforms provoked a civil war. Juárez eventually re-established his position, but his action in suspending repayment of foreign debts gave the French an excuse to invade the country and put *Maximilian on the throne. Eventually, with some help from the USA, the French were obliged to withdraw, Maximilian was shot and Juárez became President until his death. The most notable film portrayal of Juárez is

Chief Joseph

by Paul Muni in Warners' *Juarez* (1939), but this is not a Western, more a cross between a Warners social problem film and a costume drama. The Maximilian episode forms part of the background for several Westerns, notably *Major Dundee*/1964.

K

Kane, Paul (1810-71) · The first important painter of the Canadian West. Brought up in York (later to become Toronto), he travelled abroad and in London in the early 1840s he viewed George *Catlin's exhibition of Indian pictures and artefacts. Returning to Canada he journeyed across the country as far as British Columbia with the assistance of the Hudson's Bay Company. Once back in the east he produced a series of over 100 large canvases, many of them portraits of Indians and ethnographic studies in the mode of Catlin. Kane later published in London an illustrated account of his travels, *Wanderings of an Artist Among the Indians of North America* (1859).

Paul Kane, 'Medicine Mask Dance'

Kansas · The overwhelming majority of the Westerns set in Kansas take place in its famous cow towns, notably *Dodge City and *Abilene. But there is another Kansas connection. The agitation during the 1850s over whether Kansas should be a slave or free state frequently broke out into violence, some of it caused by the activities of John *Brown. During this period the territory acquired the name of 'Bleeding Kansas'. When the Civil War began, a body of irregulars was formed by 'Doc' Charles Jennison to harry the Confederate side. But under the guise of fighting for the north these guerrillas, nicknamed 'Jayhawkers', were more interested in pillage and looting. The Jayhawkers were in fact the northern equivalent of the notorious *Quantrill's Raiders, who operated out of the neighbouring state of Missouri. In December 1861 the Jayhawkers sacked Independence, Missouri, an action which was answered by the infamous raid on Lawrence, Kansas by Quantrill's Raiders in August 1863. The Jayhawkers were eventually disbanded, but re-formed as the Red Legs and continued to mount raids against Confederate areas.

This history forms the background for a number of films, especially those depicting the careers of famous outlaws such as the *James and *Younger gangs. The raid on Lawrence, Kansas is depicted in *Kansas Raiders*/1950/U/d Ray Enright/lp Audie Murphy, Brian Donlevy.

Kelly, Yellowstone [Luther Sage] (1849-c.1920) · Army scout named after the region in Wyoming with which he was chiefly associated and which became a national park in 1872. Kelly was appointed chief of scouts by General Nelson *Miles in the aftermath of the Custer defeat, and later Teddy *Roosevelt made him Indian agent at the San Carlos reservation in Arizona.

Clint Walker/*Yellowstone Kelly*/1959/WB/d Gordon Douglas

Ketchum, Black Jack (1866-1901) · Outlaw. A member in the 1890s of the Hole-in-the-Wall gang led by Butch *Cassidy. Wounded in an attempted train robbery in New Mexico, Ketchum was captured and hanged.

Howard Duff/*Blackjack Ketchum, Desperado*/1956/COL/d Earl Bellamy/lp Victor Jory

Television · Rhodes Reason/*Frontier Doctor* · Michael DeLano/*Desperate Women*

King, Charles (1844-1933) · Author of

John Ford's version of 3 Godfathers *(1948)*

romantic fiction, much of it set in the West, who saw service on the plains with the 5th Cavalry. King published a score of novels between 1883 and 1909 with titles such as *The Deserter* (1887), *An Army Portia* (1893) and *An Apache Princess* (1903). Frequently set on an army fort during an Indian campaign, his novels combine military action with a love story and may be seen as the distant ancestors of John Ford's cavalry trilogy.

Knives · 'Whatever the provocation I could never use a knife,' remarks a gossiping lady in Alfred Hitchcock's *Blackmail* (1929), and some such feeling seems to exist in the Western too, where knives lack the respectable status of fists or guns. And yet there are heroes who favour a blade. For example, John Wayne in *The Big Trail*/1930, Kirk Douglas (as Doc *Holliday) in *Gunfight at the O.K. Corral*/1956, James Coburn in *The Magnificent Seven*/1960, James Caan in *El Dorado*/1966 and Alan Ladd (as Jim *Bowie) in *The Iron Mistress*/1952/WB/d Gordon Douglas/lp Virginia Mayo.

Kyne, Peter B[ernard] (1880-1957) · Author whose influence on the development of the Western film was out of all proportion to his literary merit. Kyne's story 'Broncho Billy and the Baby', which appeared in *The Saturday Evening Post* in 1910, was bought by G. M. Anderson and formed the basis for his 'Broncho Billy' character. Kyne later wrote up this story as a novel entitled *Three Godfathers* (1913), which was several times filmed. In the 20s and 30s Kyne became one of the few authors whose name alone, placed above the title, could help sell a picture. He wrote stories for, or in some cases merely lent his name to, many Westerns in the 1920s and 1930s.

Three Godfathers/1916/U/d Edward J. Le Saint/lp Harry Carey · remade as *Marked Men*/1920/U/d John Ford/lp Harry Carey · remade as *Hell's Heroes*/1929/U/d William Wyler/lp Charles Bickford · remade as *Three Godfathers*/1936/MGM/d Richard Boleslawski/lp Walter Brennan, Lewis Stone · *3 Godfathers*/1948 · remade for TV as *The Godchild* · Other films include *Red Courage*/1921/U/d B. Reeves Eason/lp Hoot Gibson · *The Beautiful Gambler*/1921/U/d William Worthington/lp Jack Mower · *War Paint*/1926/MGM/d W.S. Van Dyke/lp Tim McCoy · *California*/1927/MGM/d W.S. Van Dyke/lp Tim McCoy · *Galloping Fury*/1927/U/d B. Reeves Eason/lp Hoot Gibson · *A Hero on Horseback*/1927/U/d Del Andrews/lp Hoot Gibson · *The Rawhide Kid*/1928/U/d Del Andrews/lp Hoot Gibson · *Tide of Empire*/1929/MGM/d Allan Dwan/lp Renée Adorée, George Duryea · *Flaming Guns*/1932/U/d Arthur Rosson/lp Tom Mix · Kyne's story 'The Parson of Panamint' was filmed as *The Parson of Panamint*/1916/PAR/d William Desmond Taylor/lp Dustin Farnum · *While Satan Sleeps*/1922/PAR/d Joseph Henabery/lp Jack Holt · *The Parson of Panamint*/1941/PAR/d William McGann/lp Charles Ruggles

L

Lake, Stuart (1889-1964) · Author. Lake's biography *Wyatt Earp: Frontier Marshal* was based partly on his conversations with *Earp, whom he had met in Los Angeles when the latter was enjoying his retirement. It was published in 1931, two years after Earp's death. The book glossed over many unsavoury aspects of his career and some of it was pure fiction (for example, Lake simply invented the story of the Buntline Special,

the long-barrelled Colt supposedly presented to the marshal by Ned *Buntline, the famous dime novelist). Nevertheless the book was largely responsible for Earp's elevation to the status of hero and was the basis for three film versions of Earp's life: *Frontier Marshal* (1934), *Frontier Marshal*/1939, *My Darling Clementine*/1946. Lake also provided the original stories for *Wells Fargo*, *The Westerner*/1940, *Winchester '73*/1950 and *Powder River*.
Frontier Marshal/1934/FOX/d Lew Seiler/lp George O'Brien · *Wells Fargo*/1937/PAR/d Frank Lloyd/lp Joel McCrea, Frances Dee · *Powder River*/1953/FOX/d Louis King/lp Rory Calhoun, Cameron Mitchell

L'Amour, Louis (b 1908) · Author, the best known of contemporary Western fiction writers. L'Amour's Western novels number over seventy and consistently remain in print. His total world sales have been put at more than fifty million copies. In 1984 he was awarded the Presidential Medal of Freedom by Ronald Reagan. L'Amour's formula never varies; tough, uncomplicated heroes and plenty of action (i.e. violence) but little sex appear to keep his huge public happy. Hollywood has found him a fruitful source of raw material, though some of the films of his work, for example *Hondo* and *Heller in Pink Tights*, have been considerably altered from the original novels.
Hondo/1953 · *Four Guns to the Border*/1954/U/d Richard Carlson/lp Rory Calhoun, Walter Brennan · *Treasure of Ruby Hills*/1955/AA/d Frank McDonald/lp Zachary Scott, Lee Van Cleef · *Stranger on Horseback*/1954 · *Blackjack Ketchum, Desperado*/1956/COL/d Earl Bellamy/lp Howard Duff, Victor Jory · *The Burning Hills*/1956/WB/d Stuart Heisler/lp Tab Hunter, Natalie Wood · *Utah Blaine*/1957/COL/d Fred F. Sears/lp Rory Calhoun, Ray Teal · *The Tall Stranger*/1957/AA/d Thomas Carr/lp Joel McCrea, Virginia Mayo · *Apache Territory*/1958/COL/d Ray Nazarro/lp Rory Calhoun, John Dehner · *Guns of the Timberland*/1959/WB/d Robert D. Webb/lp Alan Ladd, Jeanne Crain · *Heller in Pink Tights* [*Heller With a Gun*]/1960 · *Taggart*/1964/U/d R.G. Springsteen/lp Tony Young, Dan Duryea · *Kid Rodelo*/1965/Trident/d Richard Carlson/lp Don Murray, Janet Leigh · *Shalako*/1968/Dimitri de Grunwald Production/d Edward Dmytryk/lp Sean Connery, Brigitte Bardot · *Catlow*/1971/MGM/d Sam Wanamaker/lp Yul Brynner
Television · *Hondo* · *The Sacketts* · Louis

L'Amour's 'The Shadow Riders' · The Quick and the Dead

Land policy · One of the most common structuring elements in the Western is the opposition between the open, undeveloped range and the small enclosed landholding. Sometimes (as in *The Ballad of Cable Hogue*/ 1970) it is framed in terms of the wilderness versus the garden; sometimes (*Drums Along the Mohawk*/1939) it is a matter of Indians versus whites. In some films (*Shane*/1952, *Heaven's Gate*/1980) the problem is ranchers versus settlers; in others (*The Searchers*/ 1956) it is the lone individual versus the ties of family. The theme's constant presence reflects a fundamental problem in the West's history: how and for whose benefit the vast amount of land that the United States acquired would be distributed.

On the surface there seems to be no problem. The Homestead Act, adopted in 1862, provided that any citizen, or alien who intended to become a citizen, could receive 160 acres of public land in return for minimal fees. If he or she (the act allowed the privilege to both sexes) made 'improvements' and stayed on the land for five years the government would grant a permanent title. Here, it seems, is the social realization of Thomas Jefferson's famous dictum that 'those who labor in the earth are the chosen people of God'. Here, too, is the legal cornerstone of the 'fee-simple empire' of democratic small property holders that makes up the American heartland.

But as Paul Wallace Gates, the foremost historian of American land policy, observed long ago, the Homestead Act operated within an incongruous land system. That it brought real benefit to large numbers of people is undeniable, as Gilbert Fite demonstrates in *The Farmer's Frontier* (1966). Between 1863 and 1880, 136,842 farms were acquired under the act in Minnesota, the Dakotas, Nebraska and Kansas. That was well over half of all the farms created in the region during those years. But many obstacles stood in the way of the would-be homesteader. Some were inevitable: the cost of transportation, fencing, seed, farm equipment, breaking the ground, housing and initial supplies. Others were social, as much the results of public policy as the Homestead Act itself.

From the beginning the European invaders of America were unable to make up their minds about how to use the land they were seizing. Some of the earliest New England Puritans treated it as the basis for community rather than for individualism. Many a father of a large colonial family acquired as much as he could, but it was not simply insatiable greed. Instead, his goal was to guarantee that his many children would enjoy the material basis for families of their own. But from New York to the Carolinas, other colonials set out to engross the land on a colossal scale. To take just one example, New York's Livingston family parlayed a royal grant that was intended to total only 6,000 acres into a holding of 160,000 acres by simple boundary fraud.

Independence brought with it an enormous public treasure. This was the vast expanse of land that lay west of the original thirteen states and east of the Mississippi, that Britain ceded when it made peace in 1783. The seven decades of expansion that followed multiplied that treasure several-fold, as the *Louisiana purchase (1803), the Florida purchase (1819), the annexation of Texas (1845), the Mexican cession (1846), the splitting of the Pacific Northwest between America and Britain (1846) and the Gadsden purchase along the Mexican border (1853) produced the present-day shape of the continental United States. All that remained to acquire among the present fifty states were *Alaska (purchased from Russia in 1867) and Hawaii (annexed in 1898 after a 'revolution' by Americans against its Polynesian queen). But the republic's rulers proved no more successful than the colonials at working out a single coherent policy for disposing of the public land. The central problem remained: would it be the basis for community, or would it be a source of revenue for the government and of speculative gain for the people who acquired it?

The initial federal land policy was set by the Northwest Ordinance of 1785. This established the grid pattern of six mile-square 'townships' and mile-square 'sections' that anyone who overflies the Midwest can still see. The act provided that half the townships would be sold whole and the other half in individual sections, at $1 per acre. The combination of a rigid surveying pattern and of sale in large plots for a relatively high price made Congress's choice clear: it would use the land to benefit the public coffers and the few who had the money to buy in quantity.

The passage of the Homestead Act eight decades later was the culmination of a long process of whittling away at this initial decision. By 1820 it was possible to buy a small farm for only $100. But at the same time both the separate states and the federal government were following policies that led to the creation of great estates, rivalling those of colonial New York and Virginia. By the mid-19th century a farmer on the central prairies was as likely to be a tenant on somebody else's land as the owner of his own. The Ellsworth family, headed by a political figure and major office-holder, acquired 110,328 acres in Indiana and Illinois. The family of Solomon Sturges gained 173,000 acres and the Buckinghams won 103,000. Thirty-four others there gained holdings in the thousands and tens of thousands of acres. It was much the same elsewhere in the central Mississippi Valley, and after the Civil War the Red River Valley of Minnesota and the Dakotas was divided into 'bonanza farms' of similar dimensions. The baronial 'Spanish Bit' in *Duel in the Sun*/1946 has as much basis in historical reality as the small farms of *Shane*.

More was involved, however, than simple speculation and large-scale estate building. The settlement of the West could not have proceeded without the 'internal improvements' of canals, roads and railroads. In some instances – New York's Erie Canal provides the best example – governments built the facilities themselves, using bonds, taxes and toll revenues for finance. But beginning with the Illinois Central Railroad, constructed in the mid-19th century, a different pattern emerged. The government would encourage private capitalists to organize the building by deeding over large amounts of land, which could be sold to provide the necessary finance.

The classic pattern was represented in the grant that financed the *Union Pacific and *Central Pacific companies, which together built the first transcontinental line. The same session of Congress that passed the Homestead Act gave the companies a grant of twenty square miles for each mile of track laid in the territories and ten square miles for each mile laid in the states. Some later ventures received twice as much. As Fred A. Shannon observes in *The Farmer's Last Frontier* (1945), the total given to the railroad companies was 183,000,000 acres, 'an area larger than the State of Texas, or nearly a tenth that of all the United States'. The land was granted in a checkerboard pattern of alternating squares on each side of the right of way. Land in the squares not granted was held back 'until the railroads received their full shares'. So was a great deal of land outside the strip of grants, with the effect that a would-be homesteader might have to settle as much as sixty miles from the railroad line that offered the only practicable means to market crops. Not until 1887 was the public land that lay closer to the lines opened for settlement.

In the period after the Civil War the government passed other land laws, and they proved just as ambiguous. The Timber Culture Act of 1873, the Desert Land Act of 1887 and the Timber and Stone Act of 1878 were the most important. The first offered a homesteader 160 more acres in return for planting trees on a portion of it. The second was nominally for the benefit of small purchasers who would irrigate the desert section by section, but its real effect was to open non-arable desert land to large-scale operators. The third allowed the sale of western timberland for $2.50 per acre, which, in Shannon's words, was 'less than the value of one log from one tree where it stood as yet unfelled.'

Perhaps curiously, the one issue that the government never directly faced was open-range herding on the high plains. West of a line that approximates the 98th meridian, aridity makes conventional farming practically impossible. It happened, however, that a succession of extremely wet years followed one another in the late 1870s and the early 1880s, coinciding with attempts by small farmers to penetrate the region. The short-term result was a fixed but false belief that rain would 'follow the plough'. But it did not, and the longer-term result was America's first dust bowl.

Hence the value of the high plains would lie in their pasturing capacity, save where irrigation was possible. A sensible solution might have been the one adopted in New Zealand and Australia, where the government retains title and leases the land to stockgrowers. But instead, the American government continued to dispose of the land piecemeal in units far too small for effective use, while the railroads sold it for what the market would bear. The net result was immense fraud. Cowboys 'homesteaded' and took out land under the other acts for their employers. They would 'improve' it by bringing in a house on wheels or one that measured in inches rather than feet. They would 'irrigate' it by pouring out a bucket of water. Then, title assured, they could sell it to the big operator who was actually paying the costs. Moreover, after *barbed wire became available, big operators and small did not hesitate to fence off public land without any hint of a title. The Illegal Fencing Act of 1885 was intended to stop the practice, but 'as late as 1908, a number of illegal enclosures were still to be found.'

To speak, then, as if there were a single 'land policy' is to miss the reality. The basic premise throughout the 19th century was that it was the government's duty to transfer the land from public to private hands. But 'private hands' meant anything from a homesteader living in a sod house on his isolated 'quarter-section' to a railroad corporation with holdings larger than many a sovereign nation.

Perhaps the most spectacular and historically accurate filmic treatment of the land question comes in two films that deal with the Oklahoma land rush of 1890: the silent *Tumbleweeds*/1925, and *Cimarron*/1960. The historical reality was that the federal government decided (yet another time) to throw open to settlement land that had been reserved for the Indians. The excuse was a combination of the Indians 'not needing it' and of the sudden realization that it was fertile after all. To ensure fairness to all non-Indian comers, the government distributed the land by allowing a race for it. The result was one of the most spectacular competitions in American history, and William S. Hart and Anthony Mann, who made the respective films, caught the events perfectly. EC

Landscape ·

Lois Wilson: Death Valley fills you with terror, doesn't it?
Tom Mix: It's all in how you look at it, I guess. I kinda like it myself. (*Rider of Death Valley*, 1932)

In any society the representation of landscape involves the entire values of the culture, from its technology of representation to its psychology and politics. The American landscape as presented in the Western is no exception. Yet perhaps more than in most cultures the actual landscape in the Western hovers between being and nothingness. It is there and not there at the same time. In a visit to the museum at Versailles Theodore *Roosevelt, Rough Rider and Conservationist, declared, 'I do not greatly care for the representation of landscapes which, in effect, I see whenever I ride or walk. I wish the "light that never was on land or sea" in the pictures I am to live with.'[1] Frederick Jackson Turner, theorist of the frontier, turned his own 'light that never was' on a West variously characterized as 'open', progressing from primitive to civilized, a state of mind and urbanite fantasy. The Western film-maker, too, was in a strangely landless state of mind. He worked 'on location' – that

A sod house somewhere in western Kansas

is, neither in it nor permanently part of it. The 'it' had to be invented in the cutting room after being transformed by prop personnel, the very light filtered (Ford's roofed sets), the sequences interspersed with painted scenes, the very points of view transformed by horizon shots, pit shots, tracking shots. The 'West' was technically perceived where human eye never was. That eye was all-knowing also and it could persuade an audience it was theirs: 'You have seen the Jack Ford pictures,' said cameraman L. William O'Connell about *Sundown* (1924), the story of the last great cattle-drive, 'where he opens up on an Indian sitting on his horse, on a high cliff overlooking a valley. If you was observant, that was a common sight during the day's travel.'[2]

The connection between impression and code here assumes the persuasive order of mimesis, but it was far more than that as Ford deployed distance, middle-ground and close-up in the service of theme and narrative. Realism became a strategy and the directors were grateful for any help. Like Ford himself, the critics rush to remind us of the arbitrary fall of snow on Monument Valley in *Stagecoach*/1939, or the desert storm in *She Wore a Yellow Ribbon*/1949 which got Winton C. Hoch an Academy Award for cinematography. The weather was an empirical relief in the construction of an imaginative landscape. Stubborn detail, generalized effects, symbolic routes through symbolic terrain, the 'shot' of a landscape which always represented another landscape together with the camera which always lied are the essence of the landscape of the Western. As the oxen slid into the water at the second attempt in *The Covered Wagon*/

1923 and as the 3, 5 and 6 inch lenses with their apertures set at 5.6 focused on infinity, the lake on the Baker ranch became the Platte, the historians fumed that bull-trains never swam rivers with neck yokes on and the world received an imperishable vision of the Western landscape; dark cattle heads moved across still waters (the Platte was a great deal more turbulent), the line setting at an angle to the dark shore, the hills rose behind, and the light that never was filled two-thirds of the frame, setting off the immaculate billowing white coverings of the line of prairie schooners.[3]

Dedicated to Roosevelt, the same film showed that famous moment where the wagons split north and south for California and Oregon: the movement in the landscape predetermined by the abstract geometrical calculations of the navigator. The moment has the quality of the sacred. The rhetoric of the critics, too, when they describe other aspects of the Western's landscape encompasses just this quality. Monument Valley becomes an 'inferno' through which 'heroes' pass, 'reborn' of their 'transcendent purposes'.[4] The 'desert,' said Walter Prescott Webb in *The Great Plains*, has 'contributed a mysticism and spiritual quality which have found expression in the lofty and simple teachings of Jesus and Mohammed, both of whom lived in a region so like the Great Plains that the similarities have often been pointed out.' Typically this domain of the sacred is juxaposed with the worldly, *theatrical* space of the familiar 'town' set. In *High Noon*/1952, the hero begins his walk down *the* street, past blacksmith, general store owner, the banker out for a stroll, and comes to rest in the saloon. The tension between

the 'wilderness' and the community coded by business signs constitutes a double world which creates, in the words of Hoaram Astre (*Univers du Western*), the essential 'dramaturgie westernienne'.

The drive was for location without location, to render the sacred palpable. Martin Ritt's cameraman in *Hud*/1962, James Wong Howe, put a filter on the lens whenever clouds got in the way: 'the sky photographed very light that way.'[5] When the 'natives' said of the high plateau country, 'There's nothing between here and the North Pole but barbed-wire fence,' he was delighted. 'I needed that real sense of space from the beginning.' That real sense of space was large, abstract and empty, as the titles of many films show: *The Big Trail*/1930, *The Big Sky*/1952, *The Far Country*/1954, *The Big Country*/1958. The landscape was also hostile and morally anarchic: *The Badlanders* (1958), *The Burning Hills* (1956), *Lawless Valley* (1938), *Vengeance Valley* (1951). Specific references are often to whole states: *Arizona*/1940, *Colorado Territory*/1949, *North to Alaska*/1960. Many titles emphasize *movement through* a territory, the view of the imperial patrol and eastern settler (few immigrants recently arrived in America ever went west): *Across the Wide Missouri*/1950, *Along the Great Divide*/1951, and perhaps most tellingly *Crashin' Thru* (1939).

As the American Dream darkened, the landscape increasingly became reduced to binary codes of plains-mountains, claustrophobic interior-open range, pastoral-savage, Main Street-hostile territory, with the emphasis increasingly on the second of the pairs. In Jim Kitses' words, Ford was left with a 'nostalgia for the desert'; Mann's

Snow in Monument Valley in Stagecoach

heroes occupy the above-snow-line world of lonely brutal rocks in the 'name of the furrowed earth'. The elemental structures of Greek tragedy and Christian morality play seem reinforced by the stark doubleness of the landscape. Early conditions for filming meant that a historical 'crisis' of occupying the landscape tended to reproduce the same experience as filming it. Ford cut his way through forest and marsh to 'gain access to the location' in *Drums Along the Mohawk*/ 1939. Film company hospital tents were filled with the 'war wounded' at the end of a day's filming of *They Died with their Boots On*/1941.[6] Filming the West was part of the history of the West. Kevin Brownlow concludes, 'The motion picture not only reconstructed western history – it became an extension of that history.'

The sacred landscape, no less than for Parsifal, turned time into space in the representation of the 'West'. Behind the sacred, however, is always a politics and an ideology. Few cared about what actually happened at *Little Big Horn. From 1919 – that high point of American radicalism and repression – when Ince's *Breed of Men* had American cowboys lassoing a Chicago boss with the help of stockyard workers to save a *one-woman* homestead, to Leone's *C'era una volta il west*/1968, typically condemned as 'a dime novel by Marx',[7] the politics of the Western reinforced social, psychological and sexual conservatism, with the 'land' and 'history' present only as aesthetic colouring. If the 'West' died as history and was reborn as myth around 1891, *fin-de-siècle* American politics played a not insignificant part in the construction of the image. In the historical context of land fraud, farming crisis, appalling frontier social conditions, the economic brutality of the railroads and acts of genocide against native races, the invention of a 'Western landscape' was absolutely required. It was an upper-class, eastern, monied consciousness that identified the 'West' with American nationalism, itself designed to sanction wars against Spain and the Philippines. Image became politics in a new sense. Geopolitics required 'universal' images of 'man' within a 'transcendent' landscape.

The key figure is Theodore Roosevelt, who made a strong impression on the early motion picture. His portrait was part of Paramount's publicity for *The Rough Riders* of 1927. The rough rider was a part of Roosevelt's political image, though the name had been borrowed from Bill Cody's famous show. For the educated Roosevelt

the 'West' was at once an escape from and fulfilment of a complex of cultural values with roots deep in the European past. The aristocratic vision had space for both conservation and hunting.

The roots of the Western's landscape can be traced back to early literary allegories. Spenser's gentlemanly Christian knight begins his epic quest riding on a *plain* (long shot from convenient canyon top). Bunyan's Christian had to cope with the *valley* of the Shadow of Death (Death Valley). Post-Puritan America needed no encouragement toward a sacramental earth in which to fight the good fight. Romanticism with its analogies of falling empire and fallen earth, and nineteenth-century geology with its equation of time and strata, ensured that rock outcrops would be 'monuments' to death and nostalgia. In American literature it was James Fenimore *Cooper who established the Manichean landscape of storm and calm, settlement and wilderness, with characters modified from Scott romance, and enough political and ecological issues developed in a Hobbesian world of either-or power plays to provide any genre with immortal life. Nathaniel Hawthorne developed an analysis of sexual politics coded in wilderness-path-settlement images, and Thoreau's literary trip up Mount Ktaadn pointed the contrast between noble and sacred peaks and deracinated tribes. Few film critics mention the importance of late nineteenth-century naturalism which represented the earth as at the mercy of indifferent 'forces', an intellectual and social consequence of the Death of God and Social Darwinist theories in actual travesty of Darwin's biological theories. As William S. Hart gazed down on the landscape of the over-grazed trail of the cattle trains, he meditated on 'that lawless law, "the survival of the fittest", that disregards all law.'[8] Frank *Norris's railroad octopus in *The Octopus* (1901) represented technological progress as *natural* inside an alternately fecund and barren earth, and in *McTeague* (1899), filmed by Stroheim as *Greed* (1925), the two male protagonists slug it out in the desert in true Western style.

American painters from Thomas Cole to *Bierstadt developed the cultural perception of landscape. Cole depicted 'The Course of Empire' as a five-act tragedy, tied like Ford's canyon peaks to a geological outcrop as an icon of compensatory transcendence (Plate 6). Bierstadt's magnificent western canvases revealed the 'West' as vertical receding spaces bathed in strange light, mediating an old European landscape iconography of the

sublime and the beautiful. They showed the real beauty of the West as conceived in a romantic imagination and offered a sublime prospect of the 'untouched' for the grasping hand of the eastern capitalist patron (Plates 10, 11). In the popular prints Fanny Palmer's well-known *Across the Continent* (1869), the year of the trans-continental railroad link, is an exemplary pre-Western landscape of the Western (Plate 7). The telegraph and railway cut through the plain between settlement and mountain; one side Disneyland civilization, the other the sentimental 'West' of Indians, untouched nature and mountains. The landscape mood was always nostalgic. Furness, the Shakespeare editor, met *Wister, the literary creator of Roosevelt's 'West', and exclaimed, 'Why won't some Kipling save the sage brush for American literature' before it goes 'the way of the Californian forty-niner.'[9] Since George *Catlin, American painters have had the same thought.

Roosevelt's painter friend Frederic *Remington's pictures of the West emphasize surfaces of green and yellow emptiness as if the landscape had yet to come into being (Plates 17-19). In exemplary contrast Thomas *Moran's glorious watercolours of what is now Yellowstone Park (Plate 12) portrayed a love of that extraordinary country not revealed in Remington, a man who, in Wister's words, had stamped the American soldier on the American mind 'with a blow as clean cut as the impress of the American eagle upon our coins in the mint.'[10]

Still photographers also contributed their share of images of the pre-Western West. A. J. Russell, the Union Pacific photographer, photographed wherever the railroad went, the point of view determined by surveyors – destiny on the level. Later Pullman observation cars ensured the 'view' for all. Russell revealed to the world for the first time the Laramie Range. John K. Hillers photographed the Colorado river through the Arizona canyons, giving the first glimpse of what was to become *the* West. Roosevelt took photographers on his own excursions and they established a very recognizable iconography of river bend, cattle on sandbars, mid-day meals, the corral, high noon, captured thieves, Deadwood and so on.[11]

In the hands of a Ford, the many possible ways of representing the actual Western landscape in film aid a powerful *dramatic* complexity. The famous storm in Monument Valley in *She Wore a Yellow Ribbon*, for example, has multiple functions: it heightens the dangerous escape of the sub-lieutenant, emphasizes a moment of general threat, points up the agony of a wounded man inside the wagon, sanctions the drunkeness of a nurse, and alcohol as an anaesthetic, portrays the storminess of a lover's quarrel, and in a final rumble across the canyon makes an ironic reflection on marriage. For the rest the many rich possibilities outlined above are realized only when the skill of the director, the pressures of the times, and an ability to cope with that legacy of the sacred come together. For, in D.H. Lawrence's words, 'there is always a certain slightly devilish resistance in the American landscape, and a certain slightly bitter resistance in the white man's heart.' CBU

REFERENCES
[1] William Davison Johnston, *T.R.: Champion of the Strenuous Life* (New York: Farrar, Straus and Cudahy, 1958) p. 104.
[2] Kevin Brownlow, *The War, the West and the Wilderness* (London: Secker and Warburg, 1979) p. 363.
[3] Brownlow, *The War, the West and the Wilderness*, p. 371.
[4] J. A. Place, *The Western Films of John Ford* (Secaucus, N. J.: The Citadel Press, 1974) p. 36.
[5] Jon Tuska, *The American West in Film* (Westport, Conn.: Greenwood Press, 1985) p. 102.
[6] William R. Meyer, *The Making of the Great Westerns* (New Rochelle, New York: Arlington House Publishers, 1979) pp. 84, 119.
[7] Jay Hyams, *The Life and the Times of the Western Movie* (Bromley, Kent: Columbus Books, 1983) p. 171.
[8] William S. Hart, *My Life East and West* (Boston and New York: Houghton Mifflin Co., 1929) p. 45.
[9] Owen Wister, *Roosevelt: The Story of a Friendship, 1880–1919* (New York: The MacMillan Co., 1930) p. 29.
[10] G. Edward White, 'Roosevelt, Remington, Wister: Consensus and the West,' from *The Eastern Establishment and Western Expansion* (New Haven, Ct.: Yale University Press, 1968), reprinted in Richard A. Maynard, *The American West on Film: Myth and Reality* (Rochelle Park, N.J.: Hayden Book Co. Inc., 1974) p. 46.
[11] James D. Horan, *The Great American West: A Pictorial History from Coronado to the Last Frontier* (New York: Crown Publishers Inc., 1959) p. 214.

Edward Curtis, 'Navajos Ride Through the Canyon de Chelly'

Breed of Men/1919/Artcraft/*d* W.S. Hart, Lambert Hillyer/*lp* W.S. Hart, Seena Owen · *Sundown*/1924/First National/*d* Laurence Trimble, Harry O. Hoyt/*lp* Bessie Love, Roy Stewart · *The Rough Riders*/1927/PAR/*d* Victor Fleming/*lp* Noah Beery, George Bancroft · *The Rider of Death Valley*/1932/U/*d* Albert Rogell/*lp* Tom Mix, Lois Wilson · *Lawless Valley*/1938/RKO/*d* David Howard/*lp* George O'Brien · *Crashin' Thru*/1939/MON/*d* Elmer Clifton/*lp* James Newill · *Vengeance Valley*/1951/MGM/*d* Richard Thorpe/*lp* Burt Lancaster, Robert Walker · *The Burning Hills*/1956/WB/*d* Stuart Heisler/*lp* Tab Hunter, Natalie Wood · *The Badlanders*/1958/MGM/*d* Delmer Daves/*lp* Alan Ladd, Ernest Borgnine

Language · T. J. Ross has argued (in *Focus on the Western*) that the dialogue in most Westerns is anachronistic, more in tune with the time when the film was made than with the period in which it is set. As an example he gives a line from *Forty Guns*/1957: 'Here you are drawing good pay in a good job and you gotta go and rob the mails – you outta go see a head doctor!' Yet there is also dialogue which is deliberately archaic, or at least specific to the genre. This was true even before the Western film talked. The title-cards of Broncho Billy films are full of western dialect like 'hog-tied'. Expressions like 'pard' and 'plumb loco' abound in the early films of Tom Mix. The very titles of Hoot Gibson's films suggest a specifically Western style of speech: *The Smilin' Kid, The Shootin' Fool, Sure Fire, The Shoot 'Em Up Kid.* In the Western ordinary English words can take on specially codified meanings; thus two or three houses together will always be a town, if inhabited by whites. But a conurbation of several hundred tepees will still be only a village. The repertoire of Western expressions is wonderfully parodied by Bob Hope, who in *Son of Paleface*/1952 launches into a richly absurd speech which begins 'I was sashayin' my mavericks...'

Dialect speech as a means of connoting 'Western-ness' dates back at least as far as Fenimore *Cooper, though Mark *Twain is usually given the credit for introducing dialect into respectable American literature, and no doubt the Western owes him a lot too. It has partly repaid its debt by giving to everyday speech such expressions as 'to go on the warpath', after which we 'bury the hatchet'. Words such as 'maverick' or phrases such as being 'stampeded into' something you don't want to do are so common their Western origins may be all but forgotten. Even the word 'cowboy' itself has now acquired a use in non-Western speech, as in 'cowboy builder', while catchphrases such as 'meanwhile back at the ranch' and 'a man's gotta do what a man's gotta do' have become so clichéd that they can now be used only as camp.

Latter-day Saints · The Church of Jesus Christ of Latter-day Saints, more commonly known as the Mormon Church, was founded by Joseph Smith (1805-44) in New York State in 1830. A revision of Christianity, the new religion was based on the Book of Mormon, translated by Smith from ancient texts inscribed on golden plates which he claimed to have received from the angel Moroni. These texts recount the journeys of ancient peoples to the western hemisphere. Mormonism is thus in both its origins and mythology an indigenous American religion.

The Saints, as they called themselves, first attempted to gather in Missouri, but were eventually driven out by mobs which raped, looted and murdered. The Mormons settled next in Illinois at Nauvoo. Here Joseph Smith was arrested and then murdered by a mob which broke into the prison. Brigham Young (1801-77) became leader and decided to remove to the West. In 1847 he set out on an exploratory expedition to the Rocky Mountains and decreed that the Salt Lake valley should be the Mormon sanctuary. With great energy the Mormons set about making the valley fertile and bringing in immigrants both from the States and from Europe.

As a result of the Treaty of Guadalupe Hidalgo in 1848, Utah, where the Mormons had settled, became part of the United States. There was increasing friction with the US government, especially over the issue of polygamy, which the Saints had declared was a tenet of the church. Troops were sent against the Mormons in 1857. During this unrest occurred the Mountain Meadows Massacre, in which a group of non-Mormon ('Gentile') emigrants were wiped out by a combined force of Mormons and Indians. But the threatened war between the Church and the US government was avoided and under Young's firm leadership the Mormons concentrated on developing their economic resources and encouraging new converts, especially in Europe. Yearly migrations to Utah were organized, including parties who crossed the plains on foot with their belongings in handcarts. When the railroad reached Utah in 1869, Young participated in developing branch lines into the territory. Mining, however, was discouraged for a long time, since the sober and industrious Mormons did not wish to import the rowdiness inevitably associated with mining camps. The Mormons kept themselves economically as well as religiously isolated from the rest of the United States, and animosity towards them only began to disappear when the Church renounced polygamy in 1890.

John Ford's *Wagon Master*/1950 is about a group of Mormons crossing the plains. But these Mormons, though they like to pray, are really no different from the other God-fearing emigrants in Ford; the film is disappointingly silent about any religious or marital peculiarities. Wallace Beery, in *Bad Bascomb*/1946/MGM/d S. Sylvan Simon/lp

Margaret O'Brien, is a bank robber hiding out in a Mormon wagon train. Jean Seberg is an improbable Mormon in *Paint Your Wagon*/1969/PAR/d Joshua Logan/lp Lee Marvin, Clint Eastwood. Mormons also put in an appearance in *Lo chiamavano Trinità*/1970. The villain of Zane Grey's novel *Riders of the Purple Sage* is a Mormon, but not in the several film versions. Brigham Young is played by Charles K. French/*Hands Up!*/1926/PAR/d Clarence Badger/lp Raymond Griffith, and by Dean Jagger/*Brigham Young – Frontiersman*/1940.

Lawyers · In *Jesse James*/1939 Henry Hull as a fire-eating newspaper editor thunders: 'If we are ever to have law and order in the West, first thing we gotta do is take out all the lawyers and shoot 'em down like dogs.' This is taking a prejudice to an extreme, but lawyers don't fare well in the Western. Their role so often seems marginal. It's not the lawyer but the sheriff who represents the law, who is the 'lawman' and who stands not only for law but, in a synecdochal relationship, for civilization itself. In *Riders of the Purple Sage*/1925, Warner Oland plays the kind of shyster lawyer more common in crime films. Joseph Cotten as the lawyer son of patriarch Lionel Barrymore in *Duel in the Sun*/1946 is nice but weak. *The Man Who Shot Liberty Valance*/1962 perfectly illustrates the problem of the lawyer as hero. When the chips are down, which in the end they always are in the Western, law books aren't enough. Faced with the brutal Liberty Valance, Stewart as the peaceable lawyer Ransom Stoddard has no option but to pick up a gun. Luckily he's backed up by somebody who knows how to shoot.

Lea, Tom (b 1907) · Texas-born writer and illustrator. Lea's first novel, which he illustrated himself, was *The Brave Bulls* (1949), about bullfighting in Mexico. It was filmed by Robert Rossen in 1951. Lea's masterpiece is *The Wonderful Country* (1952). This is the story of Matthew Brady, a gunfighter, set on the border between Mexico and Texas in the 1880s. The novel is both an exciting Western, peopled with Apaches, bandits and Texas Rangers, and a subtle study of cultural difference. It was memorably filmed as *The Wonderful Country*/1959. Lea also wrote a two-volume history, *The King Ranch* (1957), about the famous Texas ranch.

Leonard, Elmore (b 1925) · Author. Though now much better known for his thrillers, Leonard has also written some

stylish Western fiction. Like his crime stories, Leonard's Westerns are peopled by tough, smart characters not always on the right side of the law but often more morally scrupulous than the respectable citizens. His Western novels are: *The Bounty Hunters* (1954), *The Law at Randado* (1955), *Escape from Five Shadows* (1956), *Last Stand at Saber River* (1957), *Hombre* (1961), *Valdez Is Coming* (1970), *Gunsights* (1979).
The Tall T ['The Hostage']/1956 · *3:10 to Yuma*/1957 · *Hombre*/1966 · *Valdez Is Coming*/1970/UA/d Edwin Sherrin/lp Burt Lancaster · *(sc)* Joe Kidd/1972/U/d John Sturges/lp Clint Eastwood, Robert Duvall
Television · *High Noon Part II* · *Desperado*

Leutze, Emanuel (1816-68) · Painter. Leutze was born in Germany, grew up in America and returned to Germany to live in Dusseldorf until 1851. One picture made him famous: 'Washington Crossing the Delaware'. Leutze first painted it in 1851; the original stayed in Germany (and was destroyed in World War II), but Leutze made a copy, which is now exhibited in a building created especially for the purpose on the banks of the Delaware and is possibly America's most popular picture. On the strength of this success, in 1859 Leutze was commissioned by Congress to paint a mural. The result was 'Westward the Course of Empire Takes its Way', the best-known visual embodiment of the idea of *Manifest Destiny. (See Plate 8)

Lewis, Meriwether (1774-1809) · Explorer. Together with William Clark (1770-1838) and his other companions, Lewis was the first white man to cross the western half of the United States. The expedition was conceived by Thomas *Jefferson when the west of North America was still outside United States frontiers. But by the time Lewis and Clark set off, 14 May 1804, the *Louisiana purchase had been made. With some thirty companions Lewis and Clark made their way up the Missouri River and wintered with the Mandan and Minnetaree Indians in present-day North Dakota. In April 1805 they resumed their journey, accompanied now by the Shoshone woman *Sacagawea, crossed the Rockies and reached the Pacific on 18 November 1805. They passed the winter at the mouth of the Columbia River, then commenced their return the following March and finally arrived at St Louis on 23 September 1806. In the course of their travels they journeyed eight thousand miles, with the loss of only one man, and opened

up the trans-Mississippi West.
Fred MacMurray (Lewis), Charlton
Heston (Clark)/*The Far Horizons*/1954/PAR/
à Rudolph Maté/*lp* Donna Reed
Television · Skip Riley/*The Seekers*

Lillie, Pawnee Bill [Gordon William]
(1860-1942) · Showman. Originally a buffalo
hunter and interpreter for the US government (he was fluent in the Pawnee language,
hence his name), Lillie went into show-
business in 1888 and toured with his own
company. Lillie's was just one of the many
shows that attempted to exploit the popularity of Buffalo Bill *Cody and his Wild
West. For a time after 1911 when Cody was
in financial straits the two shows merged,
and Pawnee Bill made his own appearance in
the dime novel literature supporting the
Buffalo Bill industry.
Edward Arnold/*Annie Get Your Gun*/1950

Lincoln, Abraham (1809-65) · 16th President of the United States. Despite his 'log
cabin' origins and country lawyer image,
Lincoln was not as President much concerned with the West; during the Civil War
the major theatre of conflict was east of the
Mississippi. But Lincoln does make brief,
highly symbolic appearances in a number of
Westerns. Even when absent in the flesh, his
stern expression is often seen looking out
from a picture frame on the wall. John Ford
is particularly fond of Lincoln references. In
Ford's first major Western, *The Iron Horse*/
1924, it is Lincoln who is given credit for the
vision needed to build the railroad across to
the Pacific and so unite the nation. In Ford's
last Western, *Cheyenne Autumn*/1964,
Edward G. Robinson as Secretary Schurz
turns to Lincoln's portrait in his hour of
trouble and asks, 'Old friend, what would
you do?' Charles Laughton's rendition of
Lincoln's Gettysburg Address in *Ruggles of
Red Gap*/1935 is the most memorable film
quotation from the great man.
Films (Westerns only) include: Charles
Edward Bull/*The Iron Horse*/1924 · George
Billings/ *Hands Up!*/1926/PAR/*d* Clarence
Badger/*lp* Raymond Griffith · Frank
McGlynn/*The Plainsman*/1936 · Frank
McGlynn/*Wells Fargo*/1937/PAR/*d* Frank
Lloyd/*lp* Joel McCrea, Frances Dee ·
Victor Kilian/*Virginia City*/1940 ·
Raymond Massey/*How the West Was
Won*/1962

Lincoln County War · A range war that
developed at the end of the 1870s in Lincoln
County, New Mexico, between rival fac-

Pawnee Bill Lillie (l.) and Buffalo Bill Cody (1908)

tions each seeking economic domination.
On the one side was Lawrence Murphy, an
associate of the powerful Santa Fe Ring, a
group who controlled much of the political
and economic life of the area. On the other
was John *Chisum, a cattle baron who was
determined to challenge the Ring's monopoly of local trade and government beef
contracts. Associated with Chisum were
another rancher, John *Tunstall, and a
lawyer, Alexander McSween. When Tunstall was murdered on 18 February 1878 his
supporters and employees, including *Billy
the Kid, embarked on revenge. Further
killings followed, including the murder of
Sheriff Brady by the Kid and the burning
alive of McSween in his house. After the Kid
was shot by Pat *Garrett in 1881 and Chisum
died in 1884, peace returned to the area.

Literature: popular Western fiction
Popular Western fiction has bequeathed to
the cinema both the mechanism of the

endlessly repeatable formula and the audience appetite for it. Popular Westerns can be
recognized by their adherence to a stylized
situation, cast and outcome. Generally, the
action is set somewhere between the 100th
meridian and the Pacific Coastal mountains;
out of the arid climate and high elevation of
that topography came the open-range ranching which boomed between about 1865 and
1900. Within this arena, the focus is on the
confrontation between wilderness and civilization, with the heroic, untutored westerner
trapped between these two forces. In playing
out his role as protector of civilizing immigrants, the hero conventionally executes the
villain (a man often associated with the
corruption of industrialized society) and
marries the heroine (usually an easterner
who carries with her evidence of learning
and culture). The plots which order these
events are so standardized that Frank
Gruber summarized them in seven categories: the railway story, the ranch story, the

cattle empire story, the revenge story, the cavalry versus Indians story, the outlaw story and the marshal or 'law and order' story. Together, setting, characters and plots ritualize elemental conflicts between past and present, adolescence and maturity, individualism and community. The effect is not to enlighten the audience with psychological or social insights but to codify a moment of change in the nation's life. By fulfilling audience expectations, popular fiction reassures readers about the rightness of their worlds, both personal and national.

The history of popular Western fiction, then, is the history of a pattern which developed through time, adapting in small ways to changes in the cultural climate, but never breaking with its original configuration. Despite the thousands of writers of formulaic Westerns, a relatively small number of names can be identified as initiators of distinct phases. Considered sequentially, the productions of these key figures chart the rise and impact of the genre in its written form.

It is generally agreed that the father of Western fiction was James Fenimore *Cooper. When he created his Leatherstocking Tales (1823-41), he encapsulated in a series of adventure stories one conflict at the heart of the nation's development. Modelling his hero, Natty Bumppo, loosely on Daniel *Boone, Cooper placed his frontiersman between two races – red and white – and two times – the receding wilderness of America's past and the encroaching civilization of its present. The central dilemma of each novel is Natty's. While he loves the freedom and individualism offered by the wilderness, his racial associations are with the whites whom, by serving as hunter and guide, he helps inadvertently to despoil and systematize the landscape. Natty has no place in such a society, yet he cannot be an Indian in colour or religion. As the man caught in a paradox, he symbolizes the innocence and freedom which are necessarily lost by America's progression to a modern, industrialized society.

The imaginative power of Cooper's vision was proved by the crowd of imitators who adopted his model. When mass publishing took off in America around 1860 with the invention of the *dime novel, the asssembly-line writers copied Cooper's Leatherstocking Tales more than any other work. Dime novelists imitated Cooper's wilderness setting, his heroic frontiersman, his genteel, helpless easterners and his chase-capture-escape sequence of adventurous action. However, they diluted his theme by using disguise as a device to dodge the issue of the alienated, anachronistic hero. In the hands of the dime novelists, the hero could be both frontiersman (in disguise, skilfully guiding easterners through the wilderness for most of the novel) and genteel easterner (shedding his disguise at the novel's close to marry the aristocratic heroine). The general cosiness of the outcome was reinforced when dime novelists also drew on the sentimentality of Bret *Harte's mining-camp tales.

The key work in the rise of the modern Western appeared in 1902: *The Virginian* by Owen *Wister. In his novel, Wister repeated Cooper's theme once again, but he reworked it in accordance with early 20th century mores and anxieties. In particular, his character relationships and his plot resolution can be understood as a fictional reaction against the view that the Wild West was dying out. In 1893, Frederick Jackson Turner had declared that the frontier was closed; soon the belief spread that the healthy spaces of the open West were being overtaken by the corrupt forces of eastern industrialization.

Wister codified the power struggle between East and West in three major relationships in his novel. First, a tenderfoot easterner comes to Wyoming in the late 19th century, there encountering the Virginian, top ranch-hand and untutored gentleman. Instinctively admiring this new type from the first, the tenderfoot narrator learns both frontier skills and natural wisdom from the Virginian in the course of the novel. The next meeting is more dramatic: Molly Wood, an eastern schoolma'am, comes west to escape the pressures of social and familial expectations. She is initially contemptuous of the Virginian's lack of formal education and etiquette, later fearful of his violent code of conduct in hanging and shooting down malefactors, but finally persuaded of his natural virility, morality and general superiority to herself. The final conflict represents the West's need to clean out its own savage elements before it can be entirely acceptable to easterners. Throughout the novel, the Virginian's primary enemy is Trampas, a renegade cowboy, cattle rustler and murderer; after a series of confrontations between the two, the novel climaxes in a duel in which the Virginian kills Trampas.

Most new and influential in this action was the marriage of the Virginian and Molly. While the Virginian's mixture of gentility and wilderness is similar to Natty's, the heroic cowboy can transcend the paradox of his position in a way that the hunter could not. One major difference is that the Virginian operates in a socialized West, not a savage wilderness: his occupation is part of a chain of industrialization, and it allows him to rise through the occupational ranks from ranch-hand to foreman to rancher to, at the very end of the novel, exploiter of mineral resources. That social and financial mobility in turn enables him to enter the romantic and domestic sphere. For the first time in popular Western literature, the frontier hero marries the eastern heroine.

The resolution in the adventure story is also a fictional resolution of East-West tensions in the modernizing of America. By joining the best of East and West together (and by killing off the unruly face of the frontier), Wister played out the regenerative movement which he, like many of his peers, wished for but doubted would ever occur. There are all kinds of discordant details at the end of the novel which suggest that the author realized the implausibility of his happy ending; nevertheless, the novel's massive popularity (with immediate best-seller status and subsequent sales of over 2 million) suggests that it answered to a longing of the public at large.

Wister's work very soon became the new model for imitation, giving rise to a second cycle of formulation. In the cinema, this cycle was evident in the repeated filming of the novel – in 1914, 1923, 1929 and 1946 – and in the television series which began in 1964. In fiction, the crowd of imitators was led, most famously and most prolifically, by Zane *Grey and Max *Brand, many of whose works in turn were reproduced in scores of silent and sound films. Together, these two authors removed Wister's action from the particular social and political circumstances which it can be seen to reflect. In their version of the formula, melodrama and mythology become the dominant motifs.

Zane Grey began publishing Western fiction in 1903, but it was really with *The Heritage of the Desert* in 1910 that he instituted the emphases that survive throughout his subsequent 50-odd Western novels. His love stories are more central and more sexual than Wister's, and they play out the confrontation between dissolute East and regenerative West more sensationally: many of Grey's heroines experience abduction and the threat of rape; the closest Wister's Molly came to danger was when her stagecoach tipped over in a river. The atmosphere is further charged by Grey's style, with its ornate descriptions of sublime landscapes and its profusion of exclamation marks. But Grey's vision is not mere fantasy, nor is it all incoherent. He uses his character types to comment on modern issues, such as the dangers of Mormonism, the horrors of World War I and the hedonism of the Flappers. Moreover, his melodramatic action is structured according to archetypal story patterns. As well as imagery from pastoral and romance traditions, there are obvious similarities with the mythological pattern of adventure identified by Joseph Campbell in The Hero with a Thousand Faces (1949): many of Grey's gunfighter and cowboy heroes are plunged into an underworld of danger, mystery and violence before returning, cleansed, to the domestic arena. Whatever the ingredients, the result was spectacularly successful, with Grey's sales keeping him high in the best-seller lists for ten years. His popularity clearly affected cinematic fashions too: John Cawelti has shown the similarity between the passionate religiosity of William S. Hart and that of Grey.

Max Brand began writing in 1917 and in many ways he was Grey's successor, retaining his popularity right up to the 1940s. In content, Brand's Westerns are, like Grey's, patterned on classical models and often incorporate references to mythological heroes. But the prose is much leaner than Grey's and the action much less titillating, with Brand eschewing sexual description to concentrate on heroic feats of horsemanship and marksmanship. Without the moralizing on contemporary conditions, Brand's Westerns are both faster paced and more purely escapist than Grey's.

The major difference between the two authors, however, lies in the comparative sizes of their output. Brand's real name was Frederick Faust, and his use of 20 pseudonyms (of which 'Max Brand' was the most famous) epitomized his attitude to his work. He was much more indiscriminately prolific than Grey – tossing off over 300 book-length Westerns – and much more cynical about the limitations of popular writing. He once remarked: 'your bank account need never fail if you follow the rules, and clip carefully along the marked lines. And not so carefully at that.' As well as having a particular view of formula writing, Brand had a particular medium: the pulp magazine. Virtually all his work was published in the pulps before it appeared in book form; thus his output represents a degree of repetition and dis-

semination far outstripping Zane Grey's. More than any of his peers, Brand epitomized the assembly-line production of B-Westerns: in both magazine and on film, the episodes were churned out with just enough variation to keep the audience guessing about the details which would lead to the wholly predictable ending.

By and large, these two authors stamped the features of the genre between the wars. Individual writers did add their own marks. In his Hopalong Cassidy novels, Clarence *Mulford contributed more detailed historical accuracy and more sense of an heroic community than his two peers. Ernest *Haycox added a degree of psychological realism when he created heroes who are more meditative and philosophical than, though just as physically superior as, those of Grey and Brand. The variables, however, are generally grafted on to the formulaic model: they do not disturb its basic pattern of violent action and romantic resolution.

It was after World War II that the really important development occurred, when a new sense of dislocation entered the popular novel. This change was signalled most famously in Jack *Schaefer's Shane (1949; filmed in 1952). If Wister fitted the heroic Westerner into domestic society, Schaefer demonstrated that such a role could not be permanent. Schaefer touched, once again, the root theme established by Cooper, by focusing on the Westerner whose violence simultaneously facilitates the settlement of the untamed frontier and disqualifies the hero from participating in the settlers' society. Most of Schaefer's novels and short stories explore this paradox in terms of open-range ranching. Shane, for example, is the gunfighter who helps a farming family to establish its claim in the face of a bullying rancher who tries to hold on to his expansive territory. The climax of the action – Shane's victory in a gun duel – is familiar from The Virginian, but the elegiac mood is different. When Shane rides off into the sunset, his isolation signifies the dislocation between old and new West and the ultimate alienation of the rugged individual.

Schaefer's work, with its thematic seriousness and its realization that the winning of the West necessarily involved loss, brings the popular Western close to its literary or serious counterpart, showing that the dividing line between the two levels of writing becomes increasingly unclear from this point on. But ultimately Schaefer does stay in the popular camp, because he depends on predictable character types and

stock situations to communicate his message. The hero remains stoically superhuman and the villain completely evil; it is the consequences of their confrontation which are reformulated.

The sense that Schaefer initiated a new phase of the formula rather than a decisive break with it is suggested, too, by the kinds of offshoots which have proliferated in the post-war decades. First, there are those quite subtle authors like Alan *LeMay who convey the same atmosphere of elegy as Schaefer. Then there are the more conventional, adventure-filled novels of Luke *Short and Louis *L'Amour; even their triumphant resolutions pay lip-service to the problems of ethnic minorities and embittered heroes, in line with the atmosphere of social complexity. (L'Amour has also added a veneer of authenticity by injecting a profusion of historical and informational details into his formulaic action, and has thus won the largest Western audience of all time, with sales currently estimated at well over 50 million.) Finally, there are the 'adult Westerns' by the likes of George G. Gilman; these novels take Schaefer's portrait of dislocation and explode it into an orgy of violence and sex. Altogether, these novels – like their cinematic counterparts – echo the cultural unease and insecurity of the post-war world. None of these works explores modern complexities directly; instead, with greater and lesser degrees of sensitivity, they ritualize problems in familiar, cathartic ways.

The final development in the popular genre in fact takes the fictional material beyond its formulaic limits. The latest category has been labelled by Leslie Fiedler in The Return of the Vanishing American (1968) 'the anti-Western Western'. According to Fiedler, the type 'begins by assuming the clichés and stereotypes of all the popular books which precede it, and aims not at redeeming but at exploiting them, bringing the full weight of their accumulated absurdities to bear in every casual quip.' Fiedler's distinction is precise. The anti-Western does not belong to the tradition of serious Western writing, which aims to expose the reality of frontier conditions (a famous example is Wallace Stegner's The Big Rock Candy Mountain, 1943). Instead, anti-Western Westerns stem from a caricatured vision of the West; they need the formula to fuel their parody. E.L. Doctorow's Welcome to Hard Times (1960; filmed in 1966) takes the familiar configuration of villainous outlaw, protective gunfighter and town prostitute, but through the action of gunfights and love scenes Doctorow insists on the absurdity and danger of these stereotypes. In *Midnight Cowboy* (1965; filmed in 1969) James Leo Herlihy exposes the hollowness of the cowboy hero when he plunges one adherent of the myth into the horrors of New York City. In Ishmael Reed's *Yellow Back Radio Broke-Down* (1968) the absurdity goes further: here a 'hoo doo cowboy' is a Satanic actor in a dadaist scene of impossible fantasy and pointless violence. These works can be understood to contain serious implications about various aspects of the human condition, but they are not serious explorations of the frontier West. Again, there are parallels with cinematic developments: these novels, like film spoofs of the order of *Cat Ballou*/ 1965, belong to the popular tradition because they subsist on the caricature, absurdity and repetition embedded in the formula.

In two ways, then, popular Western fiction moves little beyond its early precepts: both in geography and in meaning. The majority of popular Westerns (and anti-Westerns) focus on the open-range ranching of the late 19th century; those which do not nevertheless tend to clothe their characters in the costume which it produced. With these materials, authors create not sheer fantasy but what is often termed a 'morality play': a stylized, polarized version of a historical development. It is difficult to be certain where the fiction set the course for films and where the influence worked in the other direction. Again, two things are clear, however: hundreds of formulaic novels have fed into cinematic output by being filmed: and the fiction set in motion a pattern of development which has reverberated throughout both media. From the beginning, popular Western fiction has revolved around one basic formula, with variations occurring in response to changes in the cultural climate. By adhering to this pattern, popular novels demonstrate both the timeless appeal of the Western formula and its flexibility in registering and encoding its changing social environment. CBO

Literature: serious Western fiction

Coming out of the same topography and literary origins as the popular Western, but developing in a very different direction, is another kind of fiction, usually labelled 'serious' or 'literary' or 'highbrow'. Serious Western fiction is devoted to a vision which is individualistic, unpredictable and historically authentic; that priority is its first distinction from formulaic publications, which operate within a pre-established pattern to gratify audience expectations with ritualistic melodrama. Moreover, the serious writer treats landscape differently from his popular counterpart: the former explores the meanings and problems of the environment, particularly in its effects on human character; the latter simply exploits the landscape as the backdrop to adventurous action.

Nevertheless, popular Western fiction did lead the way in at least two respects. First, both types of literature owe their thematic concerns to the same progenitor – James Fenimore *Cooper – but popular, imitative writers came to the model more quickly and consistently than their more respected colleagues. Also, popular authors determined the specific setting which became central to the American idea of 'the West': the land is bounded by the 100th meridian on the east, the Sierra Nevadas on the west, and north and south by the Canadian and Mexican borders. That delimitation in turn determines which literary authors can be clearly seen to contribute to the genre known as 'the Western'. Willa *Cather, for example, has to be omitted from such a grouping: she is indisputably major as a western author, but because she writes mainly about the midwestern farm rather than the 'Wild West' frontier, her work has not significantly affected the development of the genre as a whole.

Because serious fiction is determinedly individualistic, it is difficult to generalize about the shape of its development. Easiest to see are the contributions of specific novels to cinematic production. One milestone was Walter van Tilburg *Clark's *The Ox-Bow Incident* (1940; filmed in 1942). Clark said that he wrote the novel to rid himself of the subject's formulaic ingredients; the novel attacks the popular Western's easy assumptions about acceptable violence and the nature of frontier justice. Another significant novel was *The Brave Cowboy* (1956) by Edward Abbey (b 1927), filmed as *Lonely Are the Brave* in 1962: an elegiac dramatization of the death of the Old West and the doom of the anachronistic hero. And the 1970 film of *Little Big Man* (1964) by Thomas Berger (b 1924) not only reversed stereotypes about Custer in particular and American mythology in general, but was also the first modern big-budget film to give a major role to an Indian actor.

The significance of these novels, however, does not merely lie in their individual contributions to Western films. They also fit into a larger pattern of literary development independent of, although at times parallel to, cinematic trends. There are three distinguishable periods: the 19th and very early 20th centuries; the period from the 1920s to the 1960s; and the recent decades from, approximately, the mid-1960s.

The first phase includes the rise of the Western theme and scattered reflections on its possibilities. The beginning, again, is Cooper's Leatherstocking cycle (1823-41). Where formulaic fiction adopted Cooper's adventurous action, ritualizing the conflict between wilderness and civilization, serious writers inherited the terms and consequences of that conflict suggested in the more reflective passages in Cooper's work. These writers were influenced by the elegiac vision of Natty Bumppo as the wilderness man threatened by onrushing civilization, and by the sympathy for the Native American implicit in Cooper's portrait of the noble savage.

Later in the 19th century and into the early years of the 20th, these concerns of Cooper's were explored piecemeal by writers not exclusively interested in the West. Early examples were Mark *Twain's *Roughing It* of 1872 and Stephen *Crane's 1898 short stories 'The Bride Comes to Yellow Sky' and 'The Blue Hotel'. In these works, the heroic violence of the West is revealed as a farcical but sometimes fatal delusion which distorts both easterners' and westerners' understanding of the environment. Early in the 20th century, Frank *Norris and Jack *London dramatized the tenets of naturalism and social Darwinism in wilderness settings, thus demonstrating the power of the environment to mould men into savage beasts intent on survival. Mary Austin (1868-1934) was equally concerned with the properties of the western landscape, but her conclusions were very different from those of her male peers. In the sketches which make up *The Land of Little Rain* (1903), Austin tries to harmonize both her perspective and her language with the desert landscape. In large part, she achieves this empathy through her identification with the American Indian, whom she sees in a symbiosis with the land which is foreign to the exploitative white man. She is an early writer to echo the pantheism of Natty Bumppo while avoiding Cooper's sentimental exaggerations. What we see in these writers are foreshadowings of themes, ironies, subjects and techniques which become central to the later western novel. In their attempts to understand the meanings of the wilderness, they act as a bridge between Cooper and the twentieth-century inheritors of his vision.

The first generation of wholeheartedly western novelists included many kinds of writers, but common to them all was a strong identification and intimacy with their regions, both in their choice of home and in their demand for accuracy in literature. From the 1920s to the 1960s a generalized pattern emerges: from an initial emphasis on socio-historical realism and environmental description arise two impetuses: one to replace the stereotypes of popular literature with authentic heroism, and the other to combat fraudulent images by emphasizing the negative, unheroic face of the West.

Harvey Fergusson (1890-1971) is generally identified as the first of the major novelists of the West, in his case mainly the Southwest. From his first novel, *The Blood of the Conquerors* (1921), he set in motion preoccupations which recur repeatedly in the writing of his successors. First, he focused on the landscape. In *Home in the West* (1944) he wrote 'Only the land lasts forever', and there is in his fiction a sense of the setting moulding and affecting the inhabitants' actions. Within this environment, he dramatizes the perennial clash of two cultures: here, the Anglo-American and the Spanish. But the action in Fergusson's fiction insists on the complexity of that confrontation, to the extent that no race has the monopoly on either civilization or wilderness. In *Blood of the Conquerors*, Ramon is a young Spaniard in whose veins runs the blood of pagans, while Julia is an eastern débutante, redolent of metropolitan sophistication; in *Wolf Song* (1927; filmed in 1929), however, the white suitor is a wild mountain man (loosely modelled on Kit Carson) while his Spanish wife is rich, cultivated and protected. The theme is handled in some of its complexity too: in both novels, what look like conventional love stories turn into troubling compromises. In the earlier work, the problems of interracial alliances turn the woman into a promiscuous, dissatisfied socialite, while the man retreats into chauvinistic peasantry; in *Wolf Song*, the marriage is allowed only when the white man converts to Catholicism, convinced not by the vision of the crucified Christ but by the image of his sensual, naked wife. Fergusson eschews melodrama, heroics and even final resolutions to grapple with the complex forces of history, environment and character as they come together in a partly civilized West.

The novelists who came after Fergusson followed his realist prose style and his desire to strip the locale of artificiality. However, these successors also seemed to remain conscious of the popular image of the West, and one result of these combined concerns was a literature which tried to replace the false heroism of the formula with the authentic heroism of real frontiersmen. Perhaps the best-known author of this type is the Pulitzer-Prize winner A.B. *Guthrie Jr. (who also crossed into the popular arena when he wrote the screenplay for the film of *Shane*). In a series of five novels, published between 1947 and 1975, Guthrie fictionalized the westward movement from the mountain men of the 1820s to the post-World War II town. The first of the series, *The Big Sky* (filmed in 1952), establishes theme, character type and authorial attitude. The novel tells the story of Boone Caudill, a mountain man who comes to the job just after the heyday of the beaver trade. Caudill is locked into the same tragic paradox as Natty Bumppo but, like Bumppo, he is clearly heroic in his physical capacities, his wilderness knowledge and his love for the land and certain Indians. True, his career is marked with venereal disease, smallpox, sexual jealousy and at least one stabbing – none of them stereotypical experiences for the Western hero. But the author's suggestion is that Caudill represents the authentic individualism of the Old West, a self-reliance that is not entirely virtuous but is certainly courageous, loyal and heroic. Many well-known novelists seem to agree with this vision: both Vardis *Fisher and Frederick Manfred (b 1912) in his Buckskin Man tales, for example, rewrite legends about the West without denuding them of their heroic implications.

Another kind of response to the myth of the West is exemplified by Wallace Stegner (b 1909), recipient of both the Pulitzer Prize and the National Book Award, particularly in *The Big Rock Candy Mountain* (1943). The novel's main protagonist, Bo Mason, is the recognizable adventurer come west to make his fortune in land, livestock or minerals. He arrives, however, in the early 20th century – just too late for any of the booms – and the novel charts his inevitable decline from optimism to violence, poverty, criminality and suicide. None of the stock events – his marriage to an easterner, his thrashing of enemies or his raising of two sons – works out successfully for him, and the emphasis of the entire novel is on the danger and the fraudulence of the myth of easy opportunities in the West. Perhaps Stegner's most

famous successor is Larry *McMurtry, whose *Horseman, Pass By* (1961; filmed as *Hud* in 1962) dismisses nostalgic notions of the heroic West with a vicious anti-hero who thrives in the modern West. There is a sense, however, in which this determinedly realist strand allows for a latent romanticism. For all their insistence on the unheroic West of the modern world, neither Stegner nor McMurtry clearly demolishes the image of the admirable Old West. This perspective survives even in McMurtry's recent novel *Lonesome Dove* (1985; again a Pulitzer winner) which, despite its publication date, belongs to the earlier tradition. In the novel, three ex-Texas Rangers are involved in a quixotic cattle-drive which proves only that they have outlived the possibilities for heroic action; the implication remains that, in an earlier era, at least two of them had been in the thick of glamorous events.

There is one final important development in this period: the appearance of the Native American voice. Sympathetic, informed portraits of Indians appear regularly in these decades at the hands of white writers like Dorothy *Johnson as well as of the part-Indian Frank Waters (b 1902). The most significant publication, however, was surely *Black Elk Speaks*, the spiritual, visionary autobiography of an Oglala Sioux as recorded by John Neihardt (1881-1973). At its first publication, in 1932, the book won little notice from the general public; once it had been endorsed by Jung, however, it was re-issued in 1961 and soon achieved cult status. The effect on Western writing was revelatory: here was a signal that there was a huge audience for the lyrical viewpoint of the Indian.

By and large, what characterizes the productive period from the early 1920s to the early 60s is a struggle against the already popular formula of superheroes who win their women and participate in wholly justified violence against savages, red and white. As Russell Martin has said, there was an urge 'to by God set the record straight.' The resulting depth and seriousness of the literature began to be paralleled in the cinema after about 1950; in both media, the focus becomes trained on troubled, disappointed characters who have seen the old verities crumbling.

The recent period, from about the mid-1960s to the present, has moved beyond that emphasis in at least one prominent way. Many contemporary writers forego their predecessors' obsession with false stereotypes: instead of constantly reacting against illusory Wests, they treat the modern arena on its own terms. Technically, too, there is a difference: short pieces – novellas and short stories – appear more frequently than ever before. Waning, it would seem, is the impetus of a Guthrie, a Stegner or a McMurtry to create a blockbuster which will sum up the whole Western experience.

As with the previous generation, many of these writers live in the West, clustering in Montana and New Mexico particularly. Many of the Montana residents – Ivan Doig, Norman Maclean, David Quammen, Richard Ford, William Kittredge – have connections with the writing programme at the University of Montana in Missoula. Perhaps because of these associations, these writers continue the close attention to landscape, and they retain interest in the manly rituals of hunting and fishing; however, they also allow previously held distinctions between fantasy and actuality to fade out. Most famous of this group is Thomas *McGuane, who has contributed directly to the cinema with his screenplays for *Rancho Deluxe*/1974, *Tom Horn*/1980 and *The Missouri Breaks*/1976, and whose fiction takes to an extreme many characteristics of his generation.

McGuane's most emphatically Western novels – *Nobody's Angel* (1981) and *Something to be Desired* (1985) – explore the chaos of the modern small town and open country of the mountain West. This is a region thick with missed connections between people and times, an area now penetrated by rich oil men and diminutive Pacific Islanders. At the centre of these novels stumble isolated, lonely men bereft of parents, wives, children, and searching incoherently for some kind of secure order. Into the poignant absurdity of this scene pop relics of a recognizable, fictional West – a grandfather takes down his trousers to audition (successfully) for *Hondo's Last Move*; a tough barroom displays the cover of the dime novel *Deadwood Dick on Deck* – but these stereotypes have no clear meaning in the modern world. Like his peers, McGuane portrays the power of the landscape but eschews epic heroism: in *Nobody's Angel*, Patrick Fitzpatrick 'wanted his heart to seize the ancient hills, the old windmills and stock springs. Now all he seemed to care about were the things that lived and died on a scale of time an ordinary human being could understand.' All this is conveyed in a fragmented prose which symbolizes the fragmentation of the Western self but also delights and surprises with comic genius. McGuane has said 'The

West is a wreck. I'd like to document that without getting totally depressing about it.' That sentiment summarizes the main thrust of new Western writing. Even a novel which defies the formal trends of recent times – *Seven Rivers West* (1986), which is long and historical and by New York resident Edward Hoagland – still retains the dominant mood. The novel charts the western odyssey of an eastern bear-tamer in the 19th century. The hero's maturation takes place in a landscape which is partly fantastical; it is an absurdist frontier which fails to fulfil conventional expectations but proves that true heroism lies in the capacity for human tenderness.

In this new freedom which allows myriad possibilities to the West, the Indian voice, too, has found increased strength. N. Scott Momaday, James Welch and Leslie Marmon Silko, among others, have mixed old and new West, red and white, myth and reality, to convey vividly the heritage and confusion of the modern Indian. While their message about cultural displacement can be bitter, their voices remain more lyrical and their landscapes more sacrosanct than their white peers'. Silko's *Storyteller* (1981) plays with mixed elements particularly creatively, marrying short stories, memories, folk tales and photographs into a rich expression. The work also testifies to a great confidence in the ability of language – especially spoken narrative – to unite the generations.

The literary Western novel, then, has changed and experimented and matured in ways that its popular counterpart has not. Larry McMurtry has declared that 'the effectiveness of the Western as a genre has never depended upon realism', and it is true that the predominantly realist development described here has not influenced or echoed the cinematic genre as closely as the popular tradition has done. Nevertheless, serious Western fiction has facilitated risks and changes in screen production, sometimes through individual novels which led the way for films, sometimes more generally by contributing to an atmosphere of psychological exploration or social concern. Above all, serious fiction at all periods has contributed to the appreciation of the power and meaning of the western landscape. From the lyricism of Guthrie to the factual realism of McMurtry to the animism of Silko, authors have helped to enrich the visual articulation of the Western film. CBO

Little Big Horn · Battle fought on 25 June 1876 on the Little Big Horn River in Montana between a combined force of Sioux and

Cheyenne and the 7th Cavalry commanded by General *Custer. Custer's troops were part of a large column conducting a campaign against the Indians, but Custer's command had become detached from the rest. When it was reported that they were facing a huge concentration of Indians, possibly as many as four thousand warriors, Custer refused to believe his scouts and decided to attack. He then split his own force of some 700 men into three, and led one group in a direct assault. Custer and all the men under his direct command were killed in this action; 212 bodies were later buried. In addition one of the other two sections of the 7th Cavalry lost 47 dead in a related action. Since there were no survivors among Custer's troop and Indian accounts were only gathered much later, we cannot be sure exactly how the battle ended. But Custer, standing with drawn sword in the centre of his men, who have dismounted and formed a circle, soon became an iconic figure represented in millions of lithographic prints, and this image has fed directly into the cinema. (See Plate 14)

London, Jack (1876-1916) · Author. Born in San Francisco, Jack London had from early days a struggle to support himself. Hardship and observation made him a convinced socialist. Hoping to get enough money to help his mother and pay for his education, he joined the gold rush to the Klondike in 1898. This experience provided the material for the adventure stories of the north which London helped to establish as virtually an autonomous sub-division of the Western genre. London's heroes are often supermen, sometimes with unpleasantly

Clark Gable in Jack London's Call of the Wild

racist tinges, and his Social Darwinism often comes close to a glorification of sheer brute force; but all his books show genuine sympathy for the weak and unfortunate. *The Son of the Wolf* (1900) was his first collection of stories. Two of his most famous novels set in the north take as their heroes dogs who struggle both against a harsh and pitiless nature and against wicked men: *Call of the Wild* (1903) was a huge success; *White Fang* followed in 1906. Like Ernest Hemingway, to whom Marcus Cunliffe has perceptively compared him, Jack London committed suicide.

The Call of the Wild/1908/Biograph/*d* D.W. Griffith/*lp* Florence Lawrence · remade 1923/Pathé/*d* Fred Jackman · remade 1935/FOX/*d* William A. Wellman/*lp* Clark Gable, Loretta Young · remade 1972/It/*d* Ken Annakin/*lp* Charlton Heston, Michele Mercier · *Two Men of the Desert*/1913/Biograph/*d* D.W. Griffith/*lp* Harry Carey · *The Mohican's Daughter*/1922/American Releasing Corp./*d* S.E.V. Taylor/*lp* Nancy Deaver · *The Son of the Wolf*/1922/Robertson Cole/*d* Norman Dawn/*lp* Wheeler Oakman · *White Fang*/1925/FBO/*d* Larry Trimble/*lp* Theodore von Eltz · remade 1936/FOX/*d* David Butler/*lp* Michael Whalen, Slim Summerville · remade as *Zanna bianca*/1974/It/*d* Lucio Fulci/*lp* Franco Nero, Virna Lisi · *Stormy Waters*/1928/Tiffany/*d* Edgar Louis/*lp* Eve Southern · *Smoke Bellew*/1929/First Division/*d* Scott Dunlap/*lp* Conway Tearle · *Wolf Call*/1939/MON/*d* George Waggner/*lp* John Carroll · *Queen of the Yukon*/1940/MON/*d* Phil Rosen/*lp* Charles Bickford · *North to the Klondike*/1942/U/*d* Erle C. Kenton/*lp* Broderick Crawford · *Alaska*/1944/MON/*d* George Archainbaud/*lp* Kent Taylor

Television · *Call of the Wild* · *Jack London's Tales of the Klondike*

The Lone Ranger · One of the few Western stories to have been equally popular on radio and television and in the movies. *The Lone Ranger* began as a radio show in 1930, created by George W. Trendle and Fran Striker, and lasted for twenty years. The central character is a Texas Ranger whose troop is lured into an ambush and wiped out by the Butch Cavendish gang. John Reid, the sole survivor, is nursed back to health by an Indian, Tonto. He vows revenge and adopts a masked disguise. He and Tonto, who refers to the Ranger as 'kemo sabe' ('trusty scout') ride the West righting wrongs, the Lone Ranger on his horse Silver (hence his famous cry 'Hi-yo Silver, away!').

Rossini's 'William Tell Overture', used to introduce the show, rapidly became the best known piece of classical music in the West. In 1938 Republic produced a movie serial in fifteen episodes, with Chief Thundercloud as Tonto and five actors playing characters who may be the masked Lone Ranger (eventually Lee Powell proves to be the real one). The next year Republic followed up with *The Lone Ranger Rides Again*, with Robert Livingstone as the eponymous hero and Chief Thundercloud again playing Tonto. In 1949 ABC began the television version, with Clayton Moore as The Lone Ranger and Jay Silverheels as Tonto. These two also played in the third movie version, which Warner Bros. called simply *The Lone Ranger* (1956). This was highly successful and in 1958 United Artists released *The Lone Ranger and the Lost City of Gold*, with the same two actors in the lead roles. A less successful attempt to revive the character was *The Legend of the Lone Ranger* (1981), with

Klinton Spilsbury as The Lone Ranger and Michael Horse as Tonto.

Louisiana purchase · The most significant land deal in the history of the United States. America paid $15 million under a treaty dated 30 April 1803 for all the land which France laid claim to between Canada and the Gulf of Mexico, an area which effectively doubled the size of the United States. Though now this seems an unbelievably good bargain, hindsight also shows that Talleyrand in negotiating for the French was probably only getting the best price for a transfer of ownership which had become inevitable. France under Napoleon was preoccupied with Europe; American emigrants were pouring into the Mississippi valley anyway; and the agreement ensured that at least the British would not have it. But it showed the Americans what could be done and set a pattern for later deals with the Russians over *Alaska and with the Mexicans in the Southwest.

Lynching · Historically, lynching was practised on a wider scale in the South than in the West, and the term itself originates during the Revolution in the punishment handed out to collaborators with the British by Charles Lynch, a Virginia planter. But there were periodic outbreaks of vigilantism in the West (notably in San Francisco in the 1850s and in *Virginia City, Montana in the 1860s) and these produced their share of lynchings. The various film versions of *The Virginian*, as well as Owen *Wister's original novel, are rare examples of the approval of lynching; in this case the dramatic conflict is between the Virginian's loyalty to his friend and the need to punish rustlers. Generally Westerns take a strongly anti-lynching position in which

Tonto and the Lone Ranger sign up

Henry Fonda, Paul Burns, Frank Conroy in The Ox-Bow Incident

TERRITORIAL EXPANSION OF THE UNITED STATES IN THE 19TH CENTURY

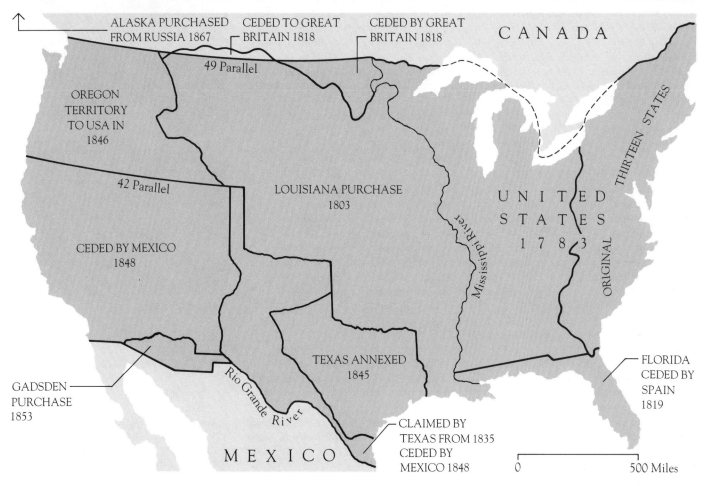

ALASKA PURCHASED FROM RUSSIA 1867

CEDED TO GREAT BRITAIN 1818

CEDED BY GREAT BRITAIN 1818

CANADA

49 Parallel

OREGON TERRITORY TO USA IN 1846

42 Parallel

LOUISIANA PURCHASE 1803

Mississippi River

UNITED STATES 1783

THIRTEEN STATES

ORIGINAL

CEDED BY MEXICO 1848

TEXAS ANNEXED 1845

FLORIDA CEDED BY SPAIN 1819

GADSDEN PURCHASE 1853

Rio Grande River

CLAIMED BY TEXAS FROM 1835 CEDED BY MEXICO 1848

MEXICO

0   500 Miles

the drama arises from the conflict between mob hysteria and the forces of reason and the law, often represented by a lone individual. The definitive anti-lynching Western is *The Ox-Bow Incident*/1942; other films with powerful lynching scenes include *Johnny Guitar*/1954, *The Tin Star*/1957, *The Unforgiven*/1959, *Two Rode Together*/1961.

M

McCoy, Joseph (1837-1915) · The entrepreneur most responsible for establishing *Abilene as the first major cattle town and for laying out the *Chisholm Trail to that point. In 1874 he wrote *Historic Sketches of the Cattle Trade of the West and Southwest*, which presents his views of the cattle business and cowboys. He is not always complimentary: 'It is idle to deny the fact that the wild, reckless conduct of the cow-boys while drunk ... [has] brought the personnel of the Texan cattle trade into great disrepute, and filled many graves with victims, bad men and

good men, at Abilene, Newton, Wichita and Ellsworth. But by far the larger portion of those killed are of that class that can be spared without detriment to the good morals and respectability of humanity.' McCoy is sometimes, though not incontrovertibly, identified as the initial referent of the phrase 'the real McCoy'.

McCulley, Johnston (1883-1958) · Fiction writer. McCulley worked in Hollywood in the 1930s and supplied original stories for some low-budget Westerns as well as working on other screenplays. He is known principally for his creation of Zorro, a kind of swashbuckling Robin Hood of Old California.
Zorro was first played in the cinema, with great panache, by Douglas Fairbanks in *The Mark of Zorro*/1920/UA/d Fred Niblo · Then: Douglas Fairbanks/*Don Q, Son of Zorro*/1925/UA/d Donald Crisp · Robert Livingstone/*The Bold Caballero*/1936/REP/d Wells Root · John Carroll/*Zorro Rides*

Again/1937/REP/d William Witney, John English · Reed Hadley/*Zorro's Fighting Legion*/1939/REP/d William Witney, John English · Tyrone Power/*The Mark of Zorro*/1940 · Linda Stirling/*Zorro's Black Whip*/1944/REP/d Spencer Bennet, Wallace

Basil Rathbone and Tyrone Power in The Mark of Zorro

Grissell · George Turner/*Son of Zorro*/
1947/REP/*d* Spencer Bennet, Fred C.
Brannon · Clayton Moore/*Ghost of Zorro*/
1949/REP/*d* Fred C. Brannon. In the 50s
and 60s Zorro was adopted into the pulp
cinema of Europe and Mexico. Apart
from television, he didn't find his way
back to Hollywood until the camped-up
Zorro the Gay Blade/1981/Melvin Simon/*d*
Peter Medak/*lp* George Hamilton, Lauren
Hutton
Television · *Zorro*/57 · *Zorro*/60 · *Zorro and
Son* · *The Mark of Zorro*

MacDonald, William Colt (1891-1968)
Author. MacDonald worked at Columbia in
the 30s, writing scripts for their Tim McCoy
series, but is best known as the creator of the
Three Mesquiteers (Tucson Smith, Lullaby
Joslin, Stony Brooke), who first appeared in
a novel, *Law of the Forty-Fives*, in 1933. The
Three Mesquiteers are cowboy pals who
ride the range righting wrongs and doing nice
folks a good turn.

MacDonald's novel was filmed two years
later as *Law of the .45s*/1935/First Division/*d*
John P. McCarthy, with Guinn 'Big Boy'
Williams as Tucson, Al St John as Stony;
there was no Lullaby. Then followed *Powdersmoke Range*/1935/RKO/*d* Wallace Fox,
with Harry Carey as Tucson, Hoot Gibson
as Stony and Guinn Williams as Lullaby
Joslin. In 1936 Republic embarked on their
long-running series; initially Ray Corrigan
played Tucson, Bob Livingstone Stony and
Syd Saylor was Lullaby. Other actors who
appeared as one or other of the Mesquiteers
were Max Terhune, John Wayne, Raymond
Hatton, Duncan Renaldo, Bob Steele, Rufe
Davis, Tom Tyler and Jimmy Dodd. The
series was highly successful and set a fashion
for series Westerns with a triad of heroes, as
for example with Republic's own Rough
Riders series.
The full list of Republic's Three
Mesquiteers films is: *The Three*

*Guinn Williams, Hoot Gibson, Harry Carey
in* Powdersmoke Range

Mesquiteers/*Ghost Town Gold*/*Roarin' Lead*/
1936 · *Riders of the Whistling Skull*/*Hit the
Saddle*/*Gunsmoke Ranch*/*Come On Cowboys*/
Range Defenders/*Heart of the Rockies*/*Trigger
Trio*/*Wild Horse Rodeo*/1937 · *Purple
Vigilantes*/*Call of the Mesquiteers*/*Outlaws
of Sonora*/*Riders of the Black Hills*/*Heroes of
the Hills*/*Pals of the Saddle*/*Overland Stage
Raiders*/*Santa Fe Stampede*/*Red River Range*/
1938 · *Night Riders*/*Three Texas Steers*/
Wyoming Outlaw/*New Frontier*/*Kansas
Terrors*/*Cowboys from Texas*/1939 · *Heroes of
the Saddle*/*Pioneers of the West*/*Covered
Wagon Days*/*Rocky Mountain Rangers*/
Oklahoma Renegades/*Under Texas Skies*/
Trail Blazers/*Lone Star Raiders*/1940
Prairie Pioneers/*Pals of the Pecos*/
Saddlemates/*Gangs of Sonora*/*Outlaws of the
Cherokee Trail*/*Gauchos of El Dorado*/*West
of Cimarron*/1941 · *Code of the Outlaw*/
Raiders of the Range/*Westward Ho!*/*Phantom
Plainsman*/*Shadows on the Sage*/*Valley of
Hunted Men*/1942 · *Thundering Trails*/
Blocked Trail/*Santa Fe Scouts*/*Riders of the
Rio Grande*/1943

McMurtry, Larry (b 1936) · Novelist. All
the films which have been made from
McMurtry's books with a western setting
take place in the contemporary period.
Unusually for the Western, sexual
relationships, often unorthodox, are central
to McMurtry's stories. McMurtry's most
recent novel, *Lonesome Dove* (1985), is his
masterpiece. Traditional in form but powerfully written, it is an epic story of a cattle-
drive from Texas to Montana in the 1880s
and places McMurtry in the forefront of
present-day writers about the West.
Hud [*Horseman, Pass By*]/1962 · *The Last
Picture Show*/1971/COL/*d* Peter
Bogdanovitch/*lp* Ben Johnson, Cybill
Shepherd · *Lovin' Molly* [*Leaving
Cheyenne*]/1974/COL/*d* Sidney Lumet/*lp*
Anthony Perkins, Beau Bridges

Madero, Francisco (1873-1913) · Mexican
politician. A well-meaning liberal, Madero
was installed as President after the autocrat
*Diaz had been forced out. Madero insti-
tuted some political reforms; but the
popular leaders who had put him in office,
such as *Villa and *Zapata, wanted more
radical economic changes that would
improve the lives of the peasants. Eventually
Madero was deserted by his strong man
*Huerta, then arrested and murdered. In
films such as *Viva Villa!*/1934 his role is
usually to demonstrate that meaning well is
not enough.

Francisco Madero (seated) in 1911

Henry B. Walthall/*Viva Villa!*/1934 ·
Harold Gordon/*Viva Zapata!*/1952 ·
Alexander Knox/*Villa Rides*/1968

Mangas Coloradas (1795?-1863) · Leader of
the eastern Chiricahua Apache. His name
means 'Red Sleeves'. During the 1840s and
1850s Mangas Coloradas, together with his
son-in-law *Cochise, waged unremitting war
against the Mexicans. When, as a result of
the Civil War, the United States army
withdrew from Arizona, Mangas extended
his operations to include the Anglos. He was
wounded when Union troops attacked him
at the Battle of Apache Pass in July 1862 and
the following year was captured. There are
conflicting reports of his death, but the most
reliable is that he was shot while trying to
resist soldiers who were torturing him with
red-hot bayonets.
Abel Fernandez/*Fort Yuma*/1955/Bel-Air/*d*
Lesley Selander/*lp* Peter Graves, Joan
Taylor · Lex Barker/*War Drums*/1956/Bel-
Air/*d* Reginald LeBorg/*lp* Ben Johnson ·
Charles Horvath/*Gunmen from Laredo*/
1958/COL/*d* Wallace MacDonald/*lp* Robert
Knapp, Jana Davi · Ross Martin/*Geronimo*/
1962/UA/*d* Arnold Laven/*lp* Chuck
Connors

Manifest Destiny · The phrase was first
coined in 1845 by John L. O'Sullivan, but
the ideas it expresses go back further, at least
as far as Benjamin Franklin (1706-90).
O'Sullivan wrote of 'our manifest destiny to

overspread the continent allotted by Providence for the free development of our yearly multiplying millions.' The dramatic expansion of the United States in the 19th century, first with the *Louisiana purchase, then in the 1840s with the rapid acquisition of Texas, Oregon, California and vast areas of the Southwest, seemed to contradict the country's anti-imperialist origins. Expansion needed a justification and in the doctrine of Manifest Destiny it found one. It combined a belief that such expansion was divinely ordained, with confidence in the superior virtue of the American system (slavery notwithstanding) and a good deal of geopolitical realpolitik.

There are strong reasons for supposing that the expansion would have happened whatever justification was proposed. The European powers that stood in the way were impotent or preoccupied, the original inhabitants ultimately defenceless, and the push of population growth and the pull of free land all but irresistible.

Masculinity · On the surface Westerns seem to give, in the unassailable masculinity of their heroes, a wholly unambiguous statement of what men should and should not do. Repeatedly that masculinity is identified as the only source of stability in a frontier world where the clash of savagery and civilization threatens cultural and social order. Characteristically what defines it, puts it beyond question, is not sexual prowess or brute strength, good looks or smooth talk but the ability to be 'tough', and it is here, right at the point where there seems least reason for doubt, that difficulties begin. The male toughness that distinguishes Western heroes generates contradictory social attitudes.[1] Combining the capacity to control people and situations, determination of will, 'coolness', resourcefulness and stoicism, 'tough' is a quality at once admirable and potentially antisocial, a quality that can and does distinguish both heroes and villains. That paradox has indelibly marked the genre's history.

The observation that Western heroes regularly combine the characteristics of outlaw and saviour is not new. Critical discussions of that duality, however, have focused too often on narrative resolutions and obscured the gender confusions it embraces. Critics like Kitses, Cawelti and McArthur, for example, who have defined the Western as centrally concerned with the epic struggle between Civilization and the Wilderness, have portrayed the genre as

functioning (like myth or ritual) to *resolve* conflicts between key values in American culture. And Will Wright, though he draws attention to the difficult relationships between the genre's outsider heroes and the societies with which they unwillingly become involved, makes the question of the hero's *reintegration* into society the basis for distinguishing between the formulas around which he constructs his historical account.[2] The emphasis is misleading. Whether Western heroes end up 'inside' or 'outside' society, whether they ride out or settle down, cannot hide the fact that the conflict between male toughness and social order has embedded unresolvable tensions in the Western's representations of masculinity.

Villains rather than heroes make the point most clearly. Customarily they display a toughness that equals and proves the hero's own. There are exceptions. Non-white villains, Mexicans and Indians (the racism is seldom covert) usually gain strength from numbers; urban villains, bankers and entrepreneurs pay others to be tough. But with formulaic regularity the hero and the villain he must defeat share specialist (combat) skills and knowledge. Often too they share similar experiences; they will be old friends or have old scores to settle. In villains, however, assertiveness and individualism are transformed into selfishness, greed, violent aggression and dishonesty. Villains abuse women and animals, oppress the weak, are motivated by unredeemed self-interest and irrational obsessions. Their toughness is unrestrained by the internal checks that make Western heroes seem ultimately, in narrative terms, to affirm, as Theodore *Roosevelt in 1899 said of the cowboy, 'the stern, manly qualities that are invaluable to a nation'.[3]

Much footage has been spent demonstrating the restraint Western heroes place on their desires. It is true the very earliest silent films revelled in the sheer badness of the kind of cowboy villain who fills the opening and closing frames of Edwin Porter's *The Great Train Robbery*/1903; but once Westerns began to take shape around stars like Broncho Billy Anderson and W.S. Hart, the attempt to mask the antisocial dimensions of male toughness became a source of the genre's most familiar narrative moments. When examined, those moments – the refusal to draw first, the gentlemanly kindnesses, the glass of milk or soda pop in the saloon – reveal an ideal of masculinity founded on fundamental contradictions. Heroes must be *both* dominant and deferen-

tial, gentle and violent, self-contained yet sensitive, practical yet idealistic, individualist but conformist, rational but intuitive, peace-loving yet ready to fight without 'quitting' when honour demands. They must bridge, that is, not simply the division between savagery and civilization but the anxiously guarded (ambiguously experienced) frontier between the two worlds usually coded as masculine and feminine.

On the face of it, this might seem to imply that Westerns propose a code of behaviour that transcends gender. Certainly *High Noon*/1952 is not unusual in making Marshal Kane's ex-lover his equal in toughness and knowledge of the world, nor in saving him through the intervention of his new (Quaker) wife. In fact, however, the genre makes an absolute and value-laden division between the masculine and feminine spheres. While it links masculinity with activity, mobility, adventure, emotional restraint and public power, it associates femininity with passivity, softness, romance and domestic containment. This involves more than the simple question of how female characters behave. While the essential qualities of womanhood that tie women to domesticity are nostalgically honoured in Westerns, femininity as a social force is represented as a threat to masculine independence and as the negative against which individual masculinities are tested.

Defenceless and incompetent men are marked with implicitly feminine characteristics – are shown as committed to romance or willing to expose emotions, as over-idealistic or passive. Domesticity and serving others (as in *The Man Who Shot Liberty Valance*/1962) are conditions a man must rise above if he is to achieve hero status. Conversely women who show strength are viewed positively only if they have unassailably womanly qualities. They must be associated with motherhood and family like the pioneer woman, or demonstrate the emotional commitment of the faithful wife or lover. Signalling incompleteness and inability, femininity requires male action and creates plot motivation or interrupts male fun (with grudging clumsiness in Howard Hawks' *Red River*/1947, for example) to create plot endings. It makes women a symbol of the cultural values men must defend but identifies them at the same time with the encroachments of civilization, clocks and complexity into the mythical (natural) male world of conflict. 'We're not here for romance, son,' growls the aging Randolph Scott in *Ride the High Country*/1962.

Inevitably the attempt to mark acceptable limits to masculine toughness – to 'feminize' masculinity – exposes contradictions. Though these are often 'resolved' at the end of the narrative, they remain irreducibly part of the experience, and indeed often surface quite overtly at the narrative level. *The Searchers*/1956 nicely illustrates the point. It is a film composed around comparable and contrasting characters who offer the spectator different, valid masculinities to consider. From the opening song ('What makes a man to wander, to turn his back on home?') and the film's opening shot (that watches from within the enclosed frame of the homestead as Ethan, the outlaw, Confederate and bank robber approaches across the dry open Texas landscape), home and wilderness, marriage and not-marriage, masculine and feminine spheres are established as narrative polarities. Lodged securely, not uncritically, in the homesteaders' domesticated world, the camera seeks as the narrative unfolds both to map the contours of Ethan's unbending masculinity ('Don't believe in surrender. I still got my sabre') *and* to find a way of affirming the social stability that masculinity quite obviously threatens. It does this through the constellation of characters and interlocking short narratives that surround and define Ethan.

Thus Ethan's unswerving pursuit of the Indians who killed his brother's family and kidnapped the young Debbie is positively highlighted by the weakness of some of the homesteaders (not the women) who want to give up the struggle to build their farms. His practical ability contrasts with the inexperience of the young Martin and the ineffectiveness of Brad, the romantic young lover, who dies in an hysterical attack on the Indian camp. At the same time, Ethan's limitations – the negative implications of his implacable determination – are made clear by the presence of the muscular preacher and Texas Ranger, the Reverend Captain Clayton, representative of law, order and social cohesion, who shares Ethan's courage but has an exuberance and love of society that he lacks. Finally it is through Martin, torn between riding with Ethan or marrying and staying at home, that the unacceptable extremism of Ethan's pursuit of revenge becomes clear. By contrast with Martin (who is surrounded in turn by his own constellation of alternative masculinities – Charlie, the childish singing cowboy, the over-emotional Brad, the ridiculous cavalry messenger) – Ethan ultimately becomes identified both with the urban villain, the

trader he kills and strips without remorse, and the Indians he hunts. Scar, the Indian chief, has had members of his family killed by whites. A mirror image of Ethan, he too seeks revenge, and it is his scalp that Ethan takes in a final gesture of negative identification.

The film can thus be read as a debate over gender that circles around the question of how far masculinity can survive contact with the feminine sphere of home, romance, family and marriage, and how far femininity can survive in the wilderness. Unable in the end to answer its own questions, it splits its commitment between Martin who marries into and Ethan who remains outside the homesteaders' settlement. Yet while the film questions the spectator's identification with the ego ideal represented by Ethan, it never accords the representatives of 'home' his heroic qualities. Gesturing towards a world of solitary males in which there is no place for femininity and relationships between men are merely tenuous, Ethan is the focus of narrative and visual attention. It is his departure not Martin's marriage that ends (without closing) the film.

Looking at men

Westerns have always implied that relationships between men are more satisfying or at least more worthy of narrative attention than relationships between men and women. Indeed, army, cattle-drive, outlaw band and buddy Westerns often create male societies where masculinity has simply taken over female functions and made women redundant. In such situations even the suggestion of homoerotic desire has necessarily to be rendered unthinkable.

Stephen Neale has argued convincingly that the repression of homoeroticism is a facet of all mainstream cinema. Where it is acceptable to make a (naked) woman's body the object of an erotic gaze (a character's or the spectator's), it is taboo to do the same with the male body. Since power over looking is culturally coded as masculine (as opposed to the feminine activity of being looked at), such manoeuvres dangerously acknowledge forbidden desires and feminize the male body being looked at. Neale's suggestion is that, seeking to disavow homoeroticism, representations of the male body in mainstream cinema oscillate anxiously between the image of the male 'as a source of identification' (the male as ego ideal) and as a 'source of contemplation' (offering possible erotic pleasure).[4] This has particular relevance to the Western, where looking is

consistently marked as an act of masculine control. Whether surveying a landscape, spotting the tremor of a curtain that warns of a hidden gunman or reading tracks and signs, the hero's look affirms his power and, by camera positioning or editing, invites the spectator's identification. Conversely, the act of looking *at* the hero, who after all is a focus of narrative attention, is approached with the utmost circumspection.

The display of the male body in Westerns, for example, is surrounded by complex patterns of evasion. Both dressing and nakedness present problems. There are historical and subgenre differences here. The exuberant dress and athleticism of some of the silent Western stars (Tom Mix for example, but not W.S. Hart) overtly make the male body an object of visual pleasure in ways that imply either, as Joan Mellen has suggested, less anxiety about masculinity or, more probably, less rigidly fixed notions about visual coding and gendered audiences.[5] Dandyism, too, is a distinctive element both in the singing Western and in such series Westerns as the Lone Ranger. By the 1930s however, any significant attention to bodily display in mainstream Westerns (beyond neatness and selected character touches) marks a male character as a villain, city slicker or weakling. The sympathetic treatment of the gambler and gunfighter for whom dandyism is an identifying feature, in the 1950s and 1960s (Gregory Peck in *The Gunfighter*/1950 for example) exploits and inflects rather than denies the code.

The taboo on male nakedness in the Western (challenged unsuccessfully by *A Man Called Horse*/1970) is a whole subject in itself. Indians and (sometimes) villains are seen decently naked, the hero almost never and then for clearly defined reasons like taking a bath (with hat) or sleeping (with trousers at least). Significantly it is combat that creates excuses for exposing the male body. Thus hand to hand fighting serves not only to demonstrate the hero can fight without technology but also allows him to remove (some of) his clothing. Similarly beating, torture and wounding can be converted into opportunities for male exposure. Fetishizing of the male body is carefully masked. Fragmented close-ups of males are used sparingly and then only for explicit purposes – to express emotions otherwise silenced by male reserve, for example. Alternatively when contemplation *is* invited, the spectator's gaze is strongly mediated. Thus, as Stephen Neale has pointed out, in Sergio Leone's shoot-outs the spectator is not allowed to look directly at the fetishized male images on the screen but forced to experience them through the heavily edited interaction and animosity of the combatants.

The clash between homophobic anxieties and the creation of an unassailably masculine hero on whom the other characters and the male spectator must inevitably look is nicely illustrated in *Shane*/1952, a film that has been variously read as a 1950s classic concerned with social conflict and the problem of violence, and as a self-conscious reworking of America's Western foundation myths. Fair as they are, those readings do little to account for the ambiguous eroticism that surrounds the figure of Alan Ladd.

Looking is established as a form of control in the opening shot, that invites the spectator to follow Shane as he rides down into the valley where the action will take place. The point is confirmed when, in their first encounter, Shane says to the boy Joey, 'You were watching me. I like a man who watches things going around. Means he'll make his mark someday.' That exchange (a neat statement of the power of the phallic gaze) is preceded by a fast edited sequence in which all three members of the Starrett family watch the stranger as he rides up. Throughout what follows, Shane remains the object of attention but from then on the spectator's gaze passes solely through Mrs Starrett and Joey. Mirroring as it does the first-person narrative of Jack Schaefer's novel, the film seems to intend that the spectator identify primarily with the boy. Consistently Shane is viewed from below, from the boy's angle of vision. The presence of Mrs Starrett, however, makes this increasingly ambiguous. At points the spectator views Shane (with Joey) as an object of identification, at others (with Mrs Starrett, whose interest is registered in a series of looks) as an object of heterosexual erotic desire. For the male spectator the two positions become unsettlingly interchangable. In two key scenes, Mrs Starrett and Joey are positioned together as they watch Shane – once as he stands in the rain framed by the window through which they and the spectator look, and once as they crouch together beneath the saloon door watching him fight.

This confusion of the filmic and cultural conventions of the look has repercussions elsewhere in the narrative. Once he is marked as a possible object of erotic contemplation, Shane ceases to be looked at directly by Joe Starrett despite their growing friendship – something that requires some virtuoso bashful acting and lowered eyebrows from Van Heflin. Rather, their affection for each other is expressed through fighting – first with Nature (the tree stump), then with their enemies and finally with each other. My suggestion here is *not* that the relationship between the two men is covertly homosexual, though the film certainly sets ambiguities in motion. (Joey's fascination with guns, for example, invests Shane's gun with quite obviously phallic implications – something all too familiar in the Western.) The point I do want to make is that the collision between two different kinds of looking caused by the way Shane's masculinity is displayed poses a threat to the film's otherwise strenuous efforts to affirm a heterosexual social order based on the family, the clear division of masculine and feminine spheres and the idea of a stable community. The film's attempts to render homoerotic desire unthinkable (inadvertently?) bring to light how fundamentally homophobic anxieties structure its representations of masculinity and male relationships. Speculatively, one might suggest it is homophobia rather than the rejection of violence that requires Shane's final wounding and exclusion from the valley. MP

REFERENCES
[1.] See Rupert Wilkinson, *American Tough* (Westport, Conn.: Greenwood Press, 1984).
[2.] J. G. Cawelti, *The Six-Gun Mystique* (Bowling Green: Bowling Green University Press, 1971); Jim Kitses, *Horizons West* (London: Thames and Hudson, 1969); Colin McArthur, 'The Roots of the Western', *Cinema*, October 1969, No. 4; Will Wright, *Six Guns and Society* (Berkeley: University of California Press, 1975).
[3.] Quoted in William Savage Jr., *The Cowboy Hero* (Norman: University of Oklahoma Press, 1979) p. 96.
[4.] Stephen Neale, 'Masculinity as Spectacle', *Screen* vol. 24, no. 6, 1983.
[5.] Joan Mellen, *Big Bad Wolves* (London: Elm Tree Books, 1977).

Bat Masterson

Masterson, Bat [Bartholomew] (1853-1921) · Lawman. Like his friend Wyatt *Earp, Bat Masterson was a buffalo hunter for a time, and took part in the Battle of Adobe Walls, 27 July 1874, between hunters and a band of Comanche and Kiowa led by *Quanah Parker. In 1876 he moved to *Dodge City, where the following year he became deputy sheriff and then sheriff of the county. It was an eventful time. Masterson's brother Ed, town marshal, was killed in a gunfight, Bat chased train robbers and other outlaws and in September 1878 pursued a band of Cheyenne led by Dull Knife (an event commemorated in the farcical Dodge City episode of John Ford's *Cheyenne Autumn*/1964, though Bat Masterson does not appear in the film). He was closely involved with the 'Gang', the group who controlled the business life of Dodge City. In 1879 he was voted out of office. He went to *Tombstone for a time with Wyatt Earp, and in 1883 he was sent for, along with Earp and Doc *Holliday, by Luke *Short to support him in the so-called Dodge City War.

From then until the end of the century Masterson made his living gambling, mostly in Colorado. He then moved to New York City, where he was briefly made a deputy federal marshal by Theodore *Roosevelt. He spent the last few years of his life as a newspaperman (some of the films in which he appears, such as *Trail Street*, allude to his journalistic ambitions). He composed some sketches of fellow Western celebrities and became a drama critic and sports reporter on the New York *Morning Telegraph*. Among

Alan Ladd, Van Heflin in Shane

his contributions was a review of William S. Hart's performance as the desperado Dan Stark in the Western melodrama *The Barrier*. The story goes that Masterson died of a heart attack at his desk and on it were found these words: 'There are many in this old world of ours who hold that things break about even for us. I have observed, for example, that we all get about the same amount of ice. The rich get it in the summer and the poor get it in the winter.' Photographs show him as dapper, often wearing a derby as in the brief glimpse we get of him in *Gunfight at the O.K. Corral*/1956.

Jack Gardner/*Wild Bill Hickok*/1923/PAR/d Clifford S. Smith/lp William S. Hart · Albert Dekker/*The Woman of the Town*/1943/d George Archainbaud/lp Claire Trevor · Randolph Scott/*Trail Street*/1947/RKO/d Ray Enright/lp Robert Ryan, Steve Brodie · Monte Hale/*Prince of the Plains*/1949/REP/d Philip Ford · Steve Darrell/*Winchester '73*/1950 · George Montgomery/*Masterson of Kansas*/1954/COL/d William Castle/lp Nancy Gates · Keith Larsen/*Wichita*/1955 · Kenneth Tobey/*Gunfight at the O.K. Corral*/1956 · Gregory Walcott/*Badman's Country*/1958/WB/d Fred F. Sears/lp George Montgomery, Buster Crabbe · Joel McCrea/*The Gunfight at Dodge City*/1958/UA/d Joseph M. Newman/lp John McIntire · Ed T. McDonnell/*The Outlaws Is Coming*/1964/COL/d Norman Maurer/lp The Three Stooges
Television · Mason Alan Dinehart III/*The Life and Legend of Wyatt Earp* · Gene Barry/*Bat Masterson*

Maximilian (1832-67) · Ferdinand Maximilian Joseph was the brother of Emperor Francis Joseph of Austria. In 1863 he was persuaded to accept the crown of the Catholic empire which Napoleon III of France was seeking to establish in Mexico. When, under American pressure, the French withdrew their troops the ill-fated venture fell apart. Maximilian fell into the hands of *Juárez, who had him shot. This adventure explains the presence of French troops in fancy uniforms in *Vera Cruz*/1954; *Major Dundee*/1964; *The Undefeated*/1969/FOX/d Andrew V. McLaglen/lp John Wayne, Rock Hudson; *Two Mules for Sister Sara*/1969.

Some of these events are recounted in *The Eagle and the Hawk*/1950/PAR/d Lewis Foster/lp John Payne. Maximilian is played by George Macready in *Vera Cruz*; also by Brian Aherne in *Juarez*/1939/WB/d William Dieterle/lp Paul Muni.

Maxwell Land Grant · In the 1870s a dispute broke out in New Mexico between the interests which controlled the Maxwell Land Company, named after Lucien Maxwell (1818-75), and a mixed group of miners, small ranchers and others. The latter were opposed to the influence of the so-called Santa Fe Ring, a group of moneyed men who administered the company's vast land holdings. In 1875 this dispute erupted into the Colfax County War, in which a number of people on both sides were murdered. The Texas gunfighter Clay *Allison helped lynch one and shot another of the two men who had murdered the local Methodist minister for attacking the Ring. Maxwell's father-in-law had originally been awarded the land by the Mexican government in 1841. The dispute thus offers a historical precedent for the stories of disputes over Spanish land grants in *The Baron of Arizona*/1950 and numerous B-Westerns such as *Arizona Territory*/1942/REP/d George Sherman/lp Don Barry, Al St John. The episode is also the background to the feuds and range wars that provide the stories for scores of other Westerns.

May, Karl (1842-1912) · German writer. Born in great poverty, May trained to be a teacher, but was jailed for fraud. While in prison he began to write, at first the cheapest kind of fiction, then from 1887 until 1900

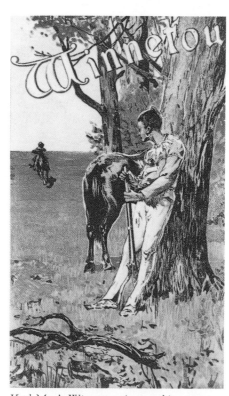

Karl May's Winnetou *(1900 ed.)*

more ambitious adventure novels, of which some twenty were set in the American West. Among the most popular were *Winnetou* (1893), *Der Schatz im Silbersee* (1894) and *Old Surehand* (1894-6). The books about Winnetou, the Apache warrior, and his companion Shatterhand, the fair-haired German-born hero, were influential on a whole generation of Germans, including, apparently, Adolf Hitler. May appears to have been considerably influenced by Fenimore *Cooper, and Winnetou is a noble savage in the tradition of Chingachgook. But unlike Natty Bumppo, Shatterhand (whose real name is Karl) is a cultivated gentleman, proficient in anthropology, zoology and other sciences, besides having 'an extraordinarily robust body'.

May did not visit the United States until after these books had been written, but he claimed that the adventures related in them were based on his own experiences. Revelations of this deception and of his criminal record produced in May a nervous collapse, though it did not ultimately affect his popularity. Over 26 million copies of his books have been sold worldwide. In the 1960s, for the first time, May's books were filmed, mostly on location in Yugoslavia by West Germans. The success of these films, as Christopher Frayling has said, 'created a commercial context which made the Italian Westerns possible.'

Der Schatz im Silbersee/1962/WG/d Harald Reinl/lp Lex Barker, Pierre Brice · *Winnetou*/1964/WG/d Harald Reinl/lp Lex Barker, Pierre Brice · *Winnetou II*/1964/WG/d Harald Reinl/lp Lex Barker, Pierre Brice · *Unter Geiern*/1964/WG/d Alfred Vohrer/lp Stewart Granger, Pierre Brice · *Shatterhand*/1964/WG/d Hugo Fregonese/lp Lex Barker, Pierre Brice · *Winnetou III*/1965/WG/d Harald Reinl/lp Lex Barker, Pierre Brice · *Winnetou und sein Freund Old Firehand*/1966/WG/d Alfred Vohrer/lp Rod Cameron, Pierre Brice · *Winnetou und das Halbblut Apanatschi*/1967/d Harald Philipp/lp Lex Barker, Pierre Brice · *Winnetou und Old Shatterhand im Tal der Toten*/1968/WG/d Harald Reinl/lp Lex Barker, Pierre Brice

Mexico · At the end of *¡Three Amigos!* (1987), a patchwork parody of Cisco Kid movies, *The Magnificent Seven*/1960, Sam Peckinpah and Spaghetti Westerns, one of the heroes, Lucky Day (Steve Martin), turns to a young Mexican girl whose village he has just saved from the vicious bandit El Guapo and delivers the traditional fadeout line: 'I'll come back one day.' She pauses, and asks 'Why?' Looking around at the squalor, the dust and the desert, Lucky Day can't think of a single reason. Nor can his amigos Dusty Bottoms (Chevy Chase) and Ned Nederlander (Martin Short). Together, in their glitzy *caballero* outfits, they ride off into the sunset without looking back.

It was a good question. For, ever since the earliest silent Westerns (to which *¡Three Amigos!* also refers, in its scattershot way), Hollywood has had a love-hate relationship with the people and the landscape 'south of the border, down Mexico way'. Mexico has been presented as a place of escape, a refuge; a noisy, exotic alternative; a place for seeking lost ideals; and – its most characteristic role – as a breeding ground for vicious (and apparently unmotivated) bandits. When Gene Autry sang 'South of the Border' in 1939, he was referring to a fictional Latin American country called Palermo: but, fictional or not, it was still a sandpit for the 'Anglo' hero to play in. Before World War I, the relationship was mostly hate. The Mexican heavy in *Broncho Billy's Redemption* (1910) is given money to buy essential medicine for a dying man, but instead steals the money and tears up the prescription. In *The Cowboy's Baby* (1910), the Mexican throws the hero's child into a river. By the time of *Broncho Billy and the Greaser* (1914) and *The Greaser's Revenge* (1914), it went without saying that the Mexican was 'an evil halfbreed' and that (unlike WASP villains) he rather enjoyed it as well. Only after protests from successive Mexican governments (and even threats of a boycott) did the word 'greaser' disappear from movie titles. But the stereotype remained – as unavoidable as the presentation of Mexican women *either* as 'spitfires' (the 'Yonkee Peeg' school of acting, according to Puerta Rican actress Rita Moreno) *or* competition, in the form of the dark lady, for the likes of *My Darling Clementine*/1946.

The first major sound Western, *In Old Arizona*/1929, introduced an all-talking and all-serenading Cisco Kid, dressed up to the nines and behaving like a Latinized Robin Hood (unlike O. Henry's original story), a characterization which made it fashionable for Hollywood stars such as Tyrone Power to play Zorro and *The Captain from Castile*. The Cisco Kid (always accompanied by his buffoonish sidekick Pancho, the one who says 'let's went') was to be played in a long-running series of films by Warner Baxter, Cesar Romero (the archetypal Latin hero, born in New York City) and, after

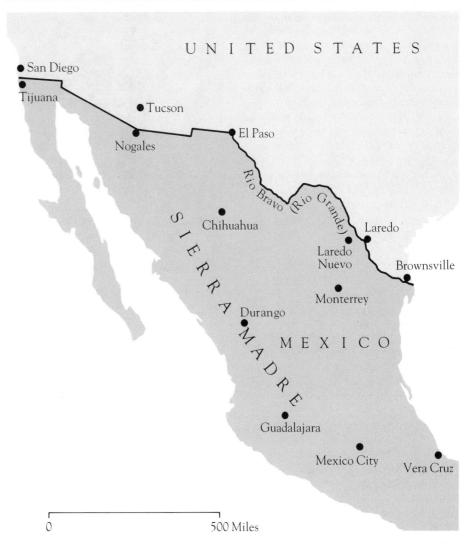

MEXICO

0 ———————————— 500 Miles

Raoul Walsh (r.) in The Greaser *(1915)*

Romero left to join the US Navy, by Duncan Renaldo. On television, Renaldo was joined by Leo Carrillo as Pancho: Carrillo had made his name in *Girl of the Rio* (1932), in which he played the oil-rich playboy Señor Tostado (meaning toast), whose behaviour as 'the best *caballero* in all Mexico' was *so* corrupt that the Mexican chargé d'affaires in Washington requested that the film be banned outright. But at least the Mexican-as-swashbuckler had introduced another stereotype to the Western – the Spanish nobleman who leads a double-life as protector of the wretched of the earth, and thus implicitly questions the need for bloody revolutions. Strangely, though, even when 'Latin lovers' were all the rage, it was very rare for Mexicans to play them: Ramon Novarro, for example, who *was* born in Durango, played Ben Hur, Rupert of Hentzau and a South Seas chieftain – but although his publicity handouts claimed that 'the imperial blood of the Aztecs flows through the heart of Novarro', and although he was quoted in 1923 as saying 'women must be wooed long and ardently, preferably under balconies', he very rarely played a Latin American character. Instead, they tended to be played by 'Ricardo Cortez' (real name Jacob Kranz, from Budapest).

Nevertheless, 'Mexico' was becoming more and more associated with 'exotic' – a tendency which peaked during Hollywood's 'good neighbor policy' during World War II. What the 'good neighbor committee' under Nelson Rockefeller had requested was a new symbol expressing the close relationship between 'the Latin nations' and the United States: 'we need to create "Pan-Americana", a noble female figure, bearing a torch and a cross, subtly suggesting both the Virgin Mary and the Goddess of Liberty'.

What they got instead was Walt Disney's *The Three Caballeros* (1944), which featured Joe Carioca, a brightly coloured Brazilian parrot in a boater who came on like a streetwise version of Carmen Miranda, and squawked things like 'you keel my head'. During the title number, Carioca introduced a bemused Donald Duck to the third caballero – a Mexican chicken in a sombrero and a pink Cisco Kid outfit firing his two guns in all directions while yelling 'hi caramba' ('What means hi caramba?' asks Joe; 'I don't know,' replies the highly strung chicken). The 'three happy chappies in snappy serapes' then proceed to whistle at a curvaceous 'Latin baby' who dances for them.

In *The Treasure of the Sierra Madre* (1948), Mexico (and it really *was* Mexico this time) is still exotic, but for the bunch of American outcasts who want to strike it rich there, it comes to represent both random violence (the cantinas, the desert, the vicious bandits, led by Alfonso Bedoya, who machete Humphrey Bogart to death – as he expected all along), and spiritual renewal (the village which accepts Walter Huston as its leader, once he has proved his worth to the *peons*). This dualism was to find its way, most spectacularly, into the films of Sam Peckinpah, from *The Wild Bunch*/1969 to *Bring Me the Head of Alfredo Garcia* (1974).

But, in the history of the Western, the image of Mexico which has had the most profound (and long-lasting) impact is that of the barren land where social revolutions take place. This image hasn't exactly been historical; rather, it has provided a suitable

Wallace Beery in Viva Villa!

backdrop for footloose American heroes to discover for themselves that 'a man's gotta do what a man's gotta do.'

During the Mexican Revolution of 1911-19, Hollywood film-makers saw the events south of the border as a great opportunity to capture some real-life action footage. Pancho Villa, no less, signed a contract with the Mutual Film Corporation for $25,000, which permitted Mutual's cameramen exclusive coverage of his battles: in return for the money (urgently needed to buy arms), Villa agreed to fight as far as possible during the hours of daylight, and to delay his cavalry charges until the cumbersome cameras were set up. This footage eventually became *War in Mexico* (1913). He also permitted Mutual to make a feature, *Life of Villa*, in 1915 (with Raoul Walsh playing him as a young man, and directing the second unit). But it was John Reed's book *Insurgent Mexico* (1914), rather than the action footage, which made the most impact on the Hollywood Western – although some of that footage did turn up in *Viva Villa!*/1934, with Wallace Beery's face superimposed upon it, and with a title-card saying 'hate thundered out of the cactus fields'. One passage of *Insurgent Mexico* in particular seems to have struck a chord. It describes Pancho Villa receiving a medal for devotion to the Revolution, at the splendid Governor's Palace in Chihuahua City, March 1914: 'Villa entered the aisle between the rigid lines of soldiers, walking a little pigeon-toed, in the fashion of a horseman, hands in his trouser pockets. He seemed slightly embarrassed.... "There is no word to speak," he said. "All I can say is my heart is all to you." Then he sat down, spitting violently on the floor.'

This passsage (which goes into great detail about the contrast between the ornate sur-

roundings and Villa's informal reaction to them) is one of the centrepieces of John Reed's book, and it was to become the *point d'appui* for most Hollywood films about the Revolution. In *Viva Villa!* Wallace Beery plays him as a scruffy, ruthless bandit with a heart of gold; in *The Treasure of Pancho Villa* (1955) Villa works with unscrupulous bank-robbers and gun-runners, but somehow (the fact is never explained) inspires the love that asks no questions; in *Villa Rides*/1968, he is randy and impulsive (there is a running gag about his many marriages), with a disregard for all types of red tape – and a preference for followers like Rodolfo Fierro (Charles Bronson), who gets a kick out of executing 300 prisoners in one session, pausing only to lubricate a badly bruised trigger finger. In all these films, and many more besides, the image of the colourful 'primitive rebel' is set against that of a taciturn, detached American observer, who becomes increasingly (though sometimes reluctantly) loyal to the rebel as the story progresses. In *Viva Villa!* the American is supposed to be John Reed himself, and one of the central scenes of the film shows how uncomfortable the bandit feels at a banquet in the grand setting of the Presidential Palace: watched by all the dignitaries, the dirty, unshaven Villa sits on an ornate desk and proceeds to take his boot off in order to massage his foot. In *The Treasure of Pancho Villa*, the American is a black-clad mercenary (Rory Calhoun) – armed with a prized machine-gun which he has christened 'La Cucaracha' – who robs banks and trains apparently on behalf of Villa, but in fact out of loyalty for his friend Gilbert Roland, and who is finally persuaded by a schoolteacher in sympathy with the Revolution (Shelley Winters) to donate all his treasure to the cause of the *peons*.

In *Bandido*/1956, the American is a cynical arms dealer (Robert Mitchum), an outsider who becomes increasingly impressed by the commitment of the revolutionaries, led by Gilbert Roland. In *Villa!* (1958), the American journalist is played, in characteristically wholesome style, by Brian Keith (while Villa himself is played by a real live Mexican – a unique occasion in Hollywood history). In *The Wild Bunch*, the well-meaning chaos of the Revolution (represented by a brief appearance of the Villistas, and by the character of Angel, an idealist) is contrasted with the cool efficiency of Pike Bishop's gang: the American bunch are, however, sufficiently impressed by Angel's commitment to his local (colourful) peasant community to put aside for him a box of arms and ammunition (provided he sacrifices his cut of the proceeds). Before the final curtain, four of the Americans wipe out a large, faceless army of nasty Mexicans, partly to honour Angel's memory, partly because they do not like German armaments experts and partly because they want to go down fighting ('Why not?'). And in *Villa Rides* (co-scripted by Peckinpah), the American is a footloose aviator (Robert Mitchum again – the part seems to suit his image as an outsider without a cause) who teams up with Villa.

Other adventure films dealing with revolution and bandit warfare in Mexico have also featured sophisticated American mercenaries, soldiers of fortune or 'observers', whose function is to intervene (with their superior fire-power or expertise) when the going gets rough. In *Vera Cruz*/1954 (which is set during an earlier period of Mexican history, when Juárez was mounting a republican rebellion against the emperor Maximilian), the standard conflict in the genre between the lure of the dollars and the attractions of commitment is represented, uncharacteristically, by *two* Americans – one (Burt Lancaster) an unscrupulous but lovable gunman, the other (Gary Cooper) a Southern gentleman. These two heroes are easily identifiable; the Juaristas, by contrast, appear in their hundreds as an undifferentiated mass – their function being simply to help us decide which of the gringos we like best. Of *The Magnificent Seven* , only one of the seven turns out to be mercenary to the core – the rest offer their versatile services free of charge to the poor villagers who are being terrorized by a local warlord. 'You *come back ... why?*' In *The Professionals*/1966 the heroes also realize that there is more to life than the almighty dollar, when they refuse to shoot it out with the Mexicans on behalf of their employer, an Eastern businessman. Again, the specialists are prepared to offer their services to the Mexicans, even if it means working at a loss or challenging their ethic of professionalism. But though the message may be more sympathetically presented than in *The Magnificent Seven*, the 'hidden' theme of paternalism is as strong as ever.

John Wayne's *The Alamo* (1960) had been one of the few films of this type in which neither cash *nor* sympathy with the Mexicans came into it – the prime motivation throughout was straightforward lone star patriotism, expressed as the urge to kick the dictatorial greasers out of Texas and in so doing demonstrate to the world 'that the

spark of freedom might blaze into a roaring flame'. This was, of course, set at a time well before the Revolution – like the opening sequence of *Red River*/1947, where Tom Dunson shoots one of Don Diego's outriders, to prove his point that the grazing land north of the Rio Grande now belongs to *him*.

Two Mules for Sister Sara/1969 is more characteristic, when it contrasts the cool efficiency of the mercenary with the well-intentioned but amateurish commitment of the Juarista captain. Eastwood can even blow up a bridge when he's had too much to drink: it is clear that the Mexicans are incapable of doing it for themselves when sober.

In short, John Reed's famous description of the scene in Chihuahua City could quite easily have been slipped into most Hollywood accounts of revolution and bandit warfare in Mexico. The passage contains all the staple ingredients: the American 'outsider' watching Villa's boorish behaviour from a distance, at the same time being impressed by the man's personal charisma; the contrast between the revolutionary bureaucracy and the grass-roots 'primitive rebel', the issues of the Revolution symbolized by the *personalities* of the main protagonists; 'exotic' local colour – the mules, the crucifixes, the cactus, the sombreros, the fiestas and the machismo in peacetime; the horses, the armoured cars and the flying machines, the machetes and machine-guns, the deserts and the barbed wire in wartime – a prime function of which is to provide a series of spectacular backdrops; and so on. By emphasizing this aspect of *Insurgent Mexico* to the exclusion of all others (including Reed's own position *vis-à-vis* the Revolution), the directors and writers of these 'Western-Mexican' adventures may have been attempting to create a generic figure (the 'outsider') with whom audiences could identify, or implicitly stressing the role of 'invisible' dollar imperialism during the period when the movies were released. Either way, it usually came over as if a series of action-packed films about the Soviet Revolution were telling the story of an American journalist's developing friendship with one of the 'army of the unfed' (who is tempted to join the Red Army) during the civil war of 1918, *and* paying lip service to the notion that the apparently chaotic events described (perhaps a train robbery, perhaps the blowing up of a palace) really 'shook the world'.

Even in the late 1960s, when the number

of Hollywood adventure films set in Mexico significantly increased (partly as a result of the good fortune of some Spaghetti Westerns on the American market), the narratives of the most successful ones seldom made *explicit* reference to the parallel with contemporary events (for example, in southeast Asia): instead, scriptwriters spiced the traditional formula with extra ingredients such as a lot of blood (after all, both portable machine-guns *and* barbed wire had been invented by 1911) and new-look stars with new-look images (Clint Eastwood or Charles Bronson as opposed to Robert Mitchum or Rory Calhoun). Ironically, since the Spaghetti Westerns were being castigated for their 'gratuitous violence' at that time, it was the Italians who attempted to make the Mexican Revolution *mean* something. Films such as *Quien sabe?*/1966, *Il mercenario*/1968, *Vamos a matar, compañeros* (1970) and *Giù la testa*/ 1971 explored the events of 1911-19 from the perspective of Frantz Fanon's writings about revolution in the emerging nations. Where Hollywood was concerned, it was a case (in Jenni Calder's phrase) of 'chili con carnage'. Mexico (or Spain) simply provided colourful exteriors, cheap extras and a fashionably 'Third World' ambiance – it had become ideologically unsound to slaughter Native Americans, so now it was the turn of Mexicans, in their hundreds. In the final sequence of *Butch Cassidy and the Sundance Kid*/1969, our two heroes take on the entire Bolivian army. When informed that the 'Bolivia' of the film looked nothing like the Bolivia of real life, director George Roy Hill replied, 'Well, it does now.'

The one great exception to this 'Western-Mexican' formula was *Viva Zapata!*/1952, which has as its main theme the distinction between a harmless rebel ('a man of individual conscience', in Kazan's words) and a harmful revolutionary (who can say 'I'm a friend to no one – to nothing except logic. This is a time for killing!'). In order to make Zapata seem more like a 'man of individual conscience' (Actors' Studio variety), scriptwriter John Steinbeck presents him as an illiterate peasant on a white horse (he was, in fact, a literate tenant-farmer) and sets him against a 'Communist' intellectual, a semi-alcoholic brother Eufemio (played by Anthony Quinn, who *is* part-Mexican) and a sincere liberal politician, Madero. As a matter of historical fact, however, the intellectuals played little part in framing Zapatista policy, Eufemio was not a heavy drinker at that time, and Madero betrayed Zapata on several occasions. This should not, of course, matter very much – were it not for Steinbeck and Kazan's insistence that they did not in any significant way falsify the historical record. In *Viva Zapata!*, the concerns of the Mexican Revolution become the concerns of the middle American cinema-going public of 1952: 'Liberty – not a word, but a man sitting safely in front of his house in the evening.' And Marlon Brando is at his most charismatic when he tells the *peons* that 'there's no leader but yourselves'.

Originally Kazan had wanted to shoot *Viva Zapata!* in Mexico, and so he submitted the script to the head of the Mexican film technician's union, Gabriel Figueroa. It was Figueroa who had photographed Ford's *The Fugitive* and all of Buñuel's Mexican films. But Kazan was not impressed with him ('He loved very corny effects like large crowds carrying candles') and Figueroa was even less impressed with the script. As Kazan was to recall: 'He read the script and his whole face changed. He demanded certain changes; he said he couldn't work on the picture unless certain things were different. Furthermore, he would oppose its being made in Mexico unless we made those changes, and we told him to go to hell. The conversation ended abruptly and we said we are going to shoot it somewhere else.... We left Mexico the next morning.' Actually, the official Mexican criticisms of the script were largely about historical inaccuracies (some of which have been mentioned above). But for Steinbeck and Kazan the meeting had really been about a hidden agenda. For, as Kazan later explained, 'John said "I smell the party line." I smelled it too.' The trouble with attempting to break the formula was that it *might* lead to serious thoughts about the Mexican Revolution. CF
The Treasure of Pancho Villa/1955/RKO/d George Sherman/lp Rory Calhoun, Shelley Winters · *The Alamo*/1960/Batjac/d John Wayne/lp John Wayne, Richard Widmark, Laurence Harvey · *Vamos a matar, compañeros*/1970/It/d Sergio Corbucci/lp Franco Nero, Jack Palance · *¡Three Amigos!*/1987/Orion/d John Landis/lp Chevy Chase, Steve Martin, Martin Short

Miles, Nelson Appleton (1839-1925) Soldier. One of the few really successful Indian fighters the United States army produced in the second half of the 19th century. Miles had been a clerk in a crockery store before the Civil War and to the end of his career had no great opinion of those who had been to West Point. By the end of the

war he was a major-general. He was then posted to the frontier and took part in the Red River War (1874-5) against the Kiowa, Comanche and Cheyenne. He was prominent in the campaign against the Sioux that followed their defeat of *Custer in 1876, and in 1877 he was responsible for forcing Chief *Joseph of the Nez Percé to surrender. In 1886 Miles replaced General George Crook in Arizona and was given the job of bringing in *Geronimo. This he achieved by using highly mobile troops and modern communications, but he was forced to negotiate rather than gain the unconditional surrender he wanted. Geronimo was sent into exile in Florida (and so were the Chiricahua who had remained on the reservation and the Apache scouts who had worked for the army). Miles was also in command during the troubles associated with the Ghost Dance, though not responsible for the massacre at *Wounded Knee in 1890. He led the troops against the strikers in the Pullman strike in 1894 and was commander of the army during the Spanish-American War. A man of ruthless ambition, vain and quarrelsome, he was undeniably effective.
John Litel/*Comanche*/1955/UA/d George Sherman/lp Dana Andrews
Television · Stafford Morgan/*Mr. Horn*

Miller, Alfred Jacob (1810-74) · Painter. Trained in Paris, Miller was a portrait painter in New Orleans when by chance he met William Drummond Stewart, a Scotsman who needed an artist to record a hunting trip he proposed. Accordingly in 1837 Miller accompanied Stewart into Wyoming and eventually over into Oregon Territory, where the party joined the fur trappers' rendezvous on the Green River. On this, his only trip to the West, Miller made a large number of watercolours, some of which he later worked up as oils for Stewart's castle in Scotland. He was the only artist to record the era of the mountain men and the first to get deep into the Rockies. His pictures, souvenirs for his wealthy patron, are romantic idealizations of a world scarcely yet touched by civilization, his Indians noble savages living in Arcadian bliss. Only a very small proportion of Miller's work was publicly known in his lifetime. Bernard De Voto's history of the mountain men, *Across the Wide Missouri* (1947), comments extensively on the Stewart expedition and Miller's part in it. In William Wellman's film of the same title, made in 1950 and based very loosely on the book, there is a painter who appears briefly and is presu-

mably Miller, though his character, nationality and name have been changed into a comical Scot called Gowie. (See Plate 3)

Mining · 'Where there's gold there's stealing, and where there's stealing there's killing,' says an inhabitant of Dawson City in *The Far Country*/1954. This has been the consensus view in the Western, which has had little good to say about gold-mining.

In some ways this is surprising, given the importance of mining in the economic and social history of the West. Gold was discovered on John *Sutter's ranch on 24 January 1848. Up to that time the total non-Indian population of California was no more than 7,000. By the end of the next year the population had been swollen by 89,000 forty-niners; 42,000 of these had come across land, 41,000 by sea (either round the Horn or across the Panama isthmus); the remainder were Mexicans from Sonora.

Much has been written about this unique episode in American history, but nowhere have the forty-niners been better eulogized than in Mark *Twain's classic *Roughing It* (1872):

'It was a splendid population – for all the slow, sleepy, sluggish-brained sloths stayed at home – you never find that sort of people among pioneers – you cannot build pioneers out of that sort of material. It was that population that gave to California a name for getting up astounding enterprises and rushing them through with a magnificent dash and daring and a recklessness of cost or consequences, which she bears unto this day.... But they were rough in those times! They fairly reveled in gold, whiskey, fights, and fandangoes, and were unspeakably happy. The honest miner raked from a hundred to a thousand dollars out of his claim a day, and what with the gambling dens and the other entertainments, he hadn't a cent the next morning, if he had any sort of luck.'

Though some didn't stay and few found riches, the long-term effects on the West were considerable. By the end of the century $1,300 million of gold had been taken out of the ground in California alone. And mining called forth other industries: logging, food production, transport. Had there been no gold in California the transcontinental railroad might have happened a decade or more later, and taken the route to Oregon instead.

Later gold and silver rushes in the West were less spectacular, but played their part in opening up the country, and many found their own place in Western mythology. In

THE MINING FRONTIER 1848–1900

1859 came the first Colorado gold rush, to the Pike's Peak area. The same year saw the discovery of the fabulous Comstock lode, at what was to become *Virginia City, Nevada. In the 1860s the mining boom moved north into Idaho and then into Montana, where there was a particularly promising strike at Last Chance Gulch, later renamed Helena. Two discoveries in 1876 were important. At Leadville, ten thousand feet up in the Rockies in Colorado, vast reserves of silver enabled the town to grow rapidly to over 15,000 inhabitants. By 1879 it boasted 10 stores, 4 banks, 31 restaurants, 4 churches, 120 saloons, 19 beer halls and 118 gambling houses. The legendary silver king H.A.W. Tabor built an opera house for 'Baby Doll', his wife, to sing in.

Also in 1876 came the gold rush into the *Black Hills of Dakota. Soon Deadwood was booming, despite the eruption of the Indian troubles which led to the defeat of *Custer at the battle of the *Little Big Horn.

Two years later silver was discovered at *Tombstone in Arizona, a spot equally famous in the annals of the Western, though it was a short-lived boom. Reputedly 'too tough to die', the town had tottered into old age by the 1890s.

There was one further major strike in Colorado, at Cripple Creek in 1890, before the centre of interest shifted north. In 1896 a big strike in Canada, on the Klondike River

John C.H. Grabill, 'Panning in Dakota' (1889)

in the Yukon, drew thousands of miners to Dawson City, some up the Yukon through Alaska, others by foot across the Chilkoot and White Horse passes just north of Skagway. The Canadian mining frontier differed from the situation in the States. A legal and administrative structure was already in place, enforced by the North West Mounted Police, who also checked all incoming miners at the frontier to ensure they had sufficient supplies to support themselves in the harsh conditions. As a result the lawlessness endemic on the American frontier was largely avoided.

By the end of the century Dawson too was nearly played out, but gold discoveries in Alaska, at Nome in 1898 and Fairbanks in 1903, enabled the boom in the mining of precious metals to survive into the 20th century. By this time the search for base metals such as copper and for oil had become of more economic significance, if less appealing to the imagination.

Mining and the search for gold inspired a plentiful literature. Besides *Roughing It*, which despite its encomium to the fortyniners is mostly about Virginia City, Nevada, there are the stories of Bret *Harte, set in the mining camps of the Sierras. Later the lust for gold which led men into the 'frozen north' became the foundation for the novels and stories of Rex *Beach, James Oliver *Curwood and Jack *London. Yet gold fever never really caught on in the Western film. This is surprising; not only because gold was one of the main spurs to westward expansion, but also because the mining camp would appear to offer plenty of colour and drama to the film-maker. The gambling dens and saloons, the dance-halls and brothels of Virginia City or Leadville certainly rivalled anything that Dodge City or Abilene had to offer. Yet for every Western set in a mining camp there are scores about cattle towns.

In the very early days of the Western this imbalance is not so marked. Many films were based on the works of the writers cited above, and many others, such as *Broncho Billy and the Claim Jumpers* (1915), spun stories out of mining. But in the 1920s the rise to dominance of the cowboy combined with an ideology which found its most influential expression in *The Covered Wagon*/1923. As a result the miner, though not totally excluded from the repertoire of the Western, became a far less popular hero.

The crucial moment in the narrative of *The Covered Wagon* comes when the wagon train of emigrants, journeying across the plains to the rich farming land of Oregon, learns of the discovery of gold in California. Although some are determined to pursue their original goal, others decide to light out for the diggings. In a heavily symbolic shot the wagon train divides in two, and those going south to California abandon their ploughs by the side of the trail.

This view, that mining and farming represent mutually exclusive choices (and that, by implication, mining is the less noble alternative) was to recur frequently in later films. In *Bend of the River*/1951 the hero (James Stewart) accompanies a band of settlers who will plant apple trees in the wilderness. The villain (Arthur Kennedy) is willing to sacrifice them (and the future of the country) to his own greed, by selling the food he has promised the settlers to a group of miners.

The opposition between farming and mining is no less explicit in *River of No Return*/1954. At the beginning of the film Marilyn Monroe is involved with a two-bit gambler who wins a claim in a card game. When the gambler deserts her she is befriended by Robert Mitchum, a farmer. Though forced temporarily to abandon his land by marauding Indians, Mitchum, who has a son, represents permanence and the future; by contrast the gambler and the mining camp stand for nothing but a transitory shiftlessness.

The Far Country also holds out an agrarian ideal. James Stewart plays a cowboy who joins the gold rush to Dawson City. His initial plan is simply to drive his herd of cattle to the diggings and sell them. From the profits he and his partner (Walter Brennan) intend to buy a ranch in Utah. Against Stewart's better judgment they do eventually pan for gold and the money they make leads to Brennan's death. As Jay C. Flippen says, gold 'does something to you – it drives a man crazy.'

Mining appears to be incompatible with the dominant ideal of the Western, that civilization advances through the settlement of the land. The mining camp was, of course, inherently transient; no lode, however rich, could last for ever, even though some towns founded on mining, such as Denver, eventually transcended their origins. The mining town is also in the mythology of the Western inherently hostile to the family, on which civilization equally depends. If there are women present at all, they are not the kind who raise children. (The absence of women has a firm basis in fact; in 1850 women formed only 8 per cent of the population of

California.) Furthermore, the mining frontier is an urban frontier; however impermanent, mining towns often grew rapidly to a considerable size, leapfrogging over the stages of development undergone by the agricultural frontier. Towns such as Virginia City or Leadville are difficult to reconcile with the predominantly rural or small town community which is the Western's ideal.

This incompatibility between mining and the Western's vision of an ideal community is surely the explanation of the curious fact that though Tombstone owed its entire existence to silver mining, there is not a single mention of it in *My Darling Clementine*/1946. Instead, Wyatt Earp is presented as a cowboy (which he never was) who will make the town safe for the church-going farmers who apparently comprise the population.

Perhaps the most powerful portrayal of a mining camp in any Western is that in *Ride the High Country*/1962. In Peckinpah's vision Coarse Gold, in the California Sierras, is a 'sinkhole of depravity', marked by drunkenness, sexual vice and the breakdown of law and order and civilized values. Even the miners' court, extolled by some writers as the expression of a native Anglo-Saxon gift for democracy, offers little protection to the virtuous. Admittedly this time farming, as represented by the heroine's bigoted father, offers no very enticing alternative.

As the 19th century wore on mining techniques improved. At first in California it was mostly placer mining, as the forty-niners

searched for gold on or near the surface, using water to sluice away impurities. In Virginia City, Nevada the ore had to be quarried, the 'hard rock miners' tunnelling into the mountainside. The gold or silver was then extracted by crushing or by using a variety of chemical techniques or smelting. As the easier deposits became exhausted new techniques were devised, including the use of cyanide to refine the ore. Deeper mines and more expensive processes required larger amounts of capital. Mining became increasingly dominated by large companies, and as a consequence the workers organized. At Cripple Creek in the 1890s the Western Federation of Miners led a strike against the employers, which ended in violence and much bitterness.

Clint Eastwood's *Pale Rider*/1985 reflects these tensions in its struggle between the individualist small-scale miners the hero befriends (and whom he exhorts to stand together) and the large, arrogant mining company which is attempting to force them off their claims. The big company compounds its offence by the ecological damage it causes through the practice of hydraulic mining, using high-pressure jets of water to force ore out of the hillside and in the process rendering the land useless for any other purpose. Compared to vandalism on such a scale, those who are merely grubbing with a pickaxe can (at last) seem positively virtuous; and yet a doubt remains about the acceptability of mining, so that their spokesman feels the need to announce: 'Gold ain't

Currier and Ives lithograph: 'Gold Mining in California' (1871)

what we're about. I came out here to raise a family.'

Montez, Lola (1818-61) · Born in Limerick, Ireland (real name Marie Gilbert), Montez found fame in Europe as an actress and dancer, and notoriety as the mistress of Franz Liszt, Alexandre Dumas and Ludwig I of Bavaria. In 1853 she arrived in San Francisco and at first was a sensation. In her dance *La Tarantula* she would pretend to be attacked by a spider hidden on her person and would attempt to find it. But her acting ability was limited and even her erotic dancing eventually palled. She left San Francisco after a month. Various comebacks failed and she left the West for good in 1856. Max Ophuls' great film *Lola Montez* (1955) omits her experiences in the American West, but some Westerns do not.
Rebecca Wassem/*Wells Fargo*/1937/PAR/d Frank Lloyd/lp Joel McCrea, Frances Dee · Yvonne De Carlo/*Black Bart*/1948/U/d George Sherman/lp Dan Duryea

Monument Valley · Situated in a remote area on the border between Arizona and Utah, Monument Valley covers 1,500 square miles and is part of the Navaho Reservation. Its huge red sandstone outcrops rising over 1,000 feet from the valley floor create a uniquely American landscape and must instantly evoke in any enthusiast of the Western the name of John Ford. The first film Ford shot in Monument Valley was *Stagecoach*/1939. The others were *My Dar-*ling *Clementine*/1946, *Fort Apache*/1948, *3 Godfathers*/1948, *She Wore a Yellow Ribbon*/1949, *Wagon Master*/1950, *Rio Grande*/1950, *The Searchers*/1956, *Sergeant Rutledge*/1960, *Cheyenne Autumn*/1964.

The Vanishing American/1925 used the location before Ford, though since *Stagecoach* other film-makers have generally avoided it, possibly not wishing to be accused of plagiarism. Other films shot there include *Billy the Kid*/1941/MGM/d David Miller/lp Robert Taylor · *C'era una volta il west*/1968; *The Legend of the Lone Ranger*/1981/ITC/d William A. Fraker/lp Klinton Spilsbury, Jason Robards.

Moran, Thomas (1837-1926) · Painter. Born in England but brought up in Philadelphia, Moran returned to England in his twenties and was much impressed with the painting of J.M.W. Turner. Moran sprang to fame in the early 1870s with his pictures of the Yellowstone, which he had visited with F.V. Hayden's expedition and in the company of the photographer W.H. *Jackson. The pictures the two brought back played a vital role in convincing Congress to designate the Yellowstone as the first national park. Moran next accompanied John Wesley *Powell in his epic exploration down the Colorado and through the Grand Canyon in 1873. Moran's huge canvases of this and other scenic wonders such as Yosemite made him one of the most successful painters of the period. Through magazines such as *Scribner's* his work achieved wide currency, establishing a public taste for grandeur and sublimity in views of the western landscape. That his paintings were intended to communicate a specific idea of the West rather than a mere record of reality, he himself acknowledged: 'I place no value upon literal transcripts from Nature. My general scope is not realistic; all my tendencies are towards idealization.' (See Plate 12)

Mountain men · Henry Nash Smith in *Virgin Land* identifies the mountain man as the second generation Western hero, following after the pathfinders such as Daniel *Boone and Fenimore *Cooper's Leatherstocking. Whereas these earlier heroes have an ambiguous relation to civilization, half in it, half beyond it, the mountain man is an entirely free spirit, often viewed as little more civilized than the Indians he moves among.

Among the mountain men whose exploits caught the popular imagination and who appear in the cinema are Jim *Bridger, Jim *Beckwourth, Kit *Carson, Hugh *Glass and John *Colter. Many others, equally important to history, have so far escaped notice by Hollywood. Among those who deserve an honourable mention are:

Jedediah Smith (1799-1831), in 1824 the first white man to go west through South Pass, a route through the Rockies which became of major importance for emigration to California and Oregon. In 1826 he began his greatest expedition, via the Great Salt

Lola Montez

Monument Valley in Stagecoach

Lake, along the Colorado, across the Mojave Desert and on to the Californian coast near present-day Los Angeles. Smith and his party were the first white men to reach California overland from the east. On the way back Smith crossed the Sierra Nevada, again the first white man to do so. Ten days after arriving at the trappers' rendezvous for 1827, at Bear Lake in northern Utah, Smith was off again, retracing his steps to California. This time his party was attacked by Mojave Indians and ten were killed. Eventually Smith reached California, only to be interned by the Mexican authorities on suspicion of spying. On his release he led his men north up the coast into Oregon; along the route there was another massacre, by Umpqua Indians, and only Smith and three others survived from the eighteen who had set out. He was killed by Comanche Indians on the Santa Fe trail.

René Auguste Chouteau (1749-1829), who helped found St Louis and who began trading with the Osage Indians in the 1780s. His half-brother Jean Pierre (1758-1849) was the father of Auguste Pierre Chouteau (1786-1838), who came to dominate the fur trade of the Southwest, and Pierre Chouteau (1789-1865), who was a major figure in the Missouri fur trade.

William Sublette (1799-1845), eldest of five brothers, who accompanied Jedediah Smith through South Pass in 1824 and two years later joined with Smith in buying out the fur trapping firm of William Ashley. In 1832 he was wounded in the famous Battle of Pierre's Hole, when a group of mountain men were besieged by Gros Ventre Indians. His brother Milton (1801-37) was also at Pierre's Hole, married a Shoshone woman and became a partner in the Rocky Mountain Fur Company. A third brother, Andrew (1808?-53), also at Pierre's Hole, worked for his brother William, fought in the Mexican War and was killed by a grizzly. The fourth brother, Pinckney (1812?-28), was killed in

the Blackfoot country. The youngest of the five brothers, Solomon (1816?-57), travelled and traded in the Southwest and Oregon and worked for a time with Joseph Walker. When he and his wife died in 1857 and their child soon after, the dynasty died with them.

Joseph Reddeford Walker (1798-1876), who was already an experienced explorer when he was made guide for Captain Benjamin Bonneville's party, which left the 1833 trappers' rendezvous on the Green River in Wyoming bound for California. Walker led them to the Great Salt Lake, then down the Humboldt River to the Humboldt Sink and across the Sierra Nevada to California, where they were probably the first white men to see the wonders of Yosemite Valley. Walker later guided emigrant trains to California and took John *Frémont there in 1845.

Old Bill Williams (1787-1849), who spent ten years living with the Osage Indians before becoming a trapper. He was a member of Joseph Walker's expedition to California in 1833. Later he was a guide for Frémont's third expedition and afterwards went to live with the Ute Indians. In 1848 he was wounded in a fight with some Utes he had deceived over a pack of furs. He was then a guide for Frémont's foolhardy expedition of 1848-9 which in the middle of winter attempted to find a route for a railroad across the Rockies. Eleven men froze to death and Williams was killed by the Utes, who doubtless remembered his earlier deception.

The first fictional representation of the mountain man is in *The Shoshonee Valley* by Timothy *Flint, published in 1830. Other fictional accounts followed in the 1840s, some of them drawing on George *Ruxton's memoirs of his travels in the West, *Adventures in Mexico* (1847) and *Life in the Far West* (1849). Eventually the mountain man, often incarnated as Kit Carson, found his way into the dime novel. Kit Carson continued into

the 20th century as a hero of popular fiction and comic books. The mountain man or trapper has also been a subject of more serious literature; for example Harvey Fergusson's *Wolf Song* (1927), A.B. *Guthrie Jr.'s *The Big Sky* (1947) and *The Way West* (1949), Forrester Blake's *Johnny Christmas* (1948), Frederick Manfred's *Lord Grizzly* (1954), Vardis *Fisher's *Mountain Man* (1965). But apart from the films made from these novels, such as *Wolf Song*, *The Big Sky*/1952, *The Way West* and *Jeremiah Johnson*/1972, plus some low-budget features about Kit Carson and rarities such as *Across the Wide Missouri*/1950, the mountain man has been overshadowed in the cinema by such late arrivals as the cowboy, the soldier and the lawman. In the 1970s there was a brief vogue for 'wilderness' pictures, family entertainments set in the great outdoors with titles such as *Mountain Family Robinson*. Though these films are not really Westerns, part of their appeal lies in the exploitation of western mountain scenery and of the idea of self-sufficiency in the wilderness which the mountain man epitomizes.

Wolf Song/1929/PAR/d Victor Fleming/lp Gary Cooper, Lupe Velez · *The Way West*/1967/UA/d Andrew V. McLaglen/lp Kirk Douglas, Robert Mitchum, Richard Widmark

Mounties · More precisely the North West Mounted Police, formed by the Canadian authorities in 1873 as a force under civilian control which would bring law to the unsettled areas of north and west Canada. The impetus behind their creation was the Cypress Hills Massacre which brought to a head trouble between Indians and whiskey traders on the plains. The force originally numbered only 300 men, and even by 1910 there were only 600. Their distinctive red jackets were copied from the British Army. In 1920 the force became the Royal Canadian Mounted Police.

The distinctive Mountie myth, that of the lone representative of authority who by dogged persistence eventually gets his man, was an early entry into the Western, as for example in *Sergeant Byrne of the N.W.M.P.*/1912/Selig/d Colin Campbell/lp Thomas Santschi, Eugenie Besserer, and *Until They Get Me*/1917/Triangle/d Frank Borzage/lp Jack Curtis, in which the hero spends seven years pursuing a fugitive from justice. Broncho Billy Anderson produced *Andy of the Royal Mounted* for Essanay in 1915 and stories of the Mounties were popular in the 1920s, the American Film Institute catalogue

Alfred Jacob Miller, 'Joseph Reddeford Walker and his Squaw'

Robert Redford as a mountain man in Jeremiah Johnson

listing 78 such films between 1921 and 1930.

Many Western series stars had a go at Mountie stories, including Tim McCoy, Buck Jones, Tom Mix and Tom Tyler. Kermit Maynard starred in a Mountie series for Ambassador Pictures, beginning with *The Fighting Trooper*/1934/Ambassador/*d* Ray Taylor/*lp* Barbara Worth. Another series was based on Renfrew of the Royal Mounted, created by Laurie York Erskine; James Newill starred and the films were produced by Grand National, then Monogram. Many of the Mountie stories were billed as by James Oliver *Curwood, whose name was virtually synonymous with northern locations, though often nothing of Curwood's but his name was used. Other Mountie films include *Rose-Marie*/1928/MGM/*d* Lucien Hubbard/*lp* Joan Crawford, James Murray · remade 1936/ MGM/*d* W.S. Van Dyke/*lp* Jeanette MacDonald, Nelson Eddy · remade 1954/ MGM/*d* Mervyn LeRoy/*lp* Ann Blyth, Howard Keel · *O'Malley of the Mounted*/ 1936/FOX/*d* David Howard/*lp* George O'Brien · *North West Mounted Police*/1940/ PAR/*d* Cecil B. DeMille/*lp* Gary Cooper, Preston Foster · *The Wild North*/1951/ MGM/*d* Andrew Marton/*lp* Stewart Granger, Cyd Charisse · *Saskatchewan*/ 1954/U/*d* Raoul Walsh/*lp* Alan Ladd, Shelley Winters · *The Canadians*/1961/ FOX/*d* Burt Kennedy/*lp* Robert Ryan, John Dehner

Mulford, Clarence Edward (1883-1956) · Author of Western fiction and creator of Hopalong Cassidy and other characters associated with the Bar 20 ranch. Cassidy, originally known as Bill, first appeared in 1907 in the book *Bar 20*. Mulford featured the character in a series of novels till 1941. In the books Hopalong got his name from a bullet wound that made him limp, but the impediment did not long survive in the film versions. The first Hopalong Cassidy film appeared as *Hop-A-Long Cassidy*/1935/PAR/*d* Howard Bretherton. (The hyphens were soon dropped.) William Boyd played the lead part in this and all 66 subsequent Hopalong Cassidy films. (For a list see William Boyd, Part IV.) 41 Hoppy films were produced at Paramount before William Boyd and his producer Harry Sherman moved to United Artists for the remaining 25 films. Four later Hopalong Cassidy books were written by Louis L'Amour under the name Tex Burns.

The budgets for the films were high by Western series standards. Boyd, who was already white-haired and nearly forty when the series began, lent the films dignity. Contrary to the literary original, the Hoppy of the films neither drank nor smoked nor cussed and parents approved the moral tone. Comic relief was initially provided by Gabby Hayes. In the late 40s Boyd acquired the television rights to his films and then on the crest of a new wave of popularity made a television series, *Hopalong Cassidy*. There was also a radio show; comic books, records and merchandizing deals followed.

A non-Hopalong Cassidy film based on a Mulford novel is *The Deadwood Coach*/ 1925/FOX/*d* Lynn Reynolds/*lp* Tom Mix.

Murieta, Joaquin (c.1830-53 or c.1878) · Legendary Californian bandit and/or revolutionary. Very little is known for certain about Murieta (or possibly Murrieta), but he is generally supposed to have been a Mexican from Sonora who was attracted to the gold-fields of California in the late 1840s. Many of the miners were Mexicans and the object of racist attacks by those from the States. Murieta gathered together a band of men and began a series of raids in the early 1850s which the Mexicans regarded as justifiable guerrilla retaliation. In 1853 the California Rangers thought they had executed Murieta but some reports have him still alive in the 1870s. Certainly by then his legend was flourishing and in the 1880s he was the hero of such lurid accounts as *Joaquin, The Terrible, The True History of the Three Bitter Blows That Changed an Honest Man to a Merciless Demon*.
Buck Jones/*The Avenger*/1931/COL/*d* Roy William Neill/*lp* Dorothy Revier · Warner Baxter/*The Robin Hood of El Dorado*/1936 · Carlos Thompson/*El ultimo rebelde*/1961/ Mex/*d* Miguel Contreras Torres/*lp* Rodolfo Acosta · Valentin De Vargas/*The Firebrand*/1962/FOX/*d* Maury Dexter · Jeffrey Hunter/*Joaquin Murrieta*/1964/Pro-Artis Iberica/*d* George Sherman

Television · Ricardo Montalban/*Desperate Mission* · Victor Mohica/*California Gold Rush*

Music · The Western has had a decisive influence on the development of American popular music of the 20th century. The singing cowboy movies of the 30s and 40s both widened the audience for country music and had a profound effect on its development, making cowboy attire and themes an integral part of country music (for a while the music was even called 'Country and Western'). It is a (largely romantic) legacy that remains to this day, seen on both the sleeves of country (and since the 70s many rock) albums and heard on the records they contain, and one that has had both positive and limiting effects on country music.

The frontier was not only a place where people sang the traditional songs the American immigrants had brought with them from Europe. Frontier occupations, such as lumbering, trapping and the search for gold, brought forth a rich new body of folk songs which were among the first American songs, American both in origin (if only through the process of adaptation) and in subject. Uniquely American amongst these occupations was that of the cowboy, who herded the cattle along the trails to the northern beef markets in the years after the Civil War. As well as singing traditional songs (such as the Irish ballad 'Brennan on the Moor') and hymns, they sang about their specific concerns. Occasionally accompanied by fiddle and jews harp, but definitely not by the guitar (an instrument that did not become popular in America until after 1900), they sang about their work. These songs, which included 'Old Paint', 'The Chisholm Trail' and 'The Colorado Trail' – perhaps the most beautiful cowboy ballad of all – were sung (and hummed) for relaxation as they rode the trail (hence the large number of verses

William Boyd (l.) as Hopalong Cassidy, with Gabby Hayes in Hopalong Rides Again *(1937)*

Arthur Rothstein, 'Singing at Roundup, Quarter Circle U Ranch, Montana' (1939)

some of the songs have) and to calm the cattle (hence the soothing quality of many of them). In a different, gentler way, they offer romantic descriptions of the cowboys' life similar to those written by European travellers and the dime novelists.

With the passing of the cowboy, his songs were incorporated into the larger body of American folk songs. In the 1920s there was a revival of interest in cowboy songs amongst country performers from the Southwest. At the same time performers like Jimmie Rogers did much to 'Westernize' hillbilly music, as country music was then called. But it was Gene Autry who did most to complete the process of romanticizing the cowboy within the country music tradition and make country music an integral part of the Western. A farm boy – despite the legend that later grew around him, he had no cowboy connections – with a soft nasal vocal style modelled on Rogers, by the early 30s Autry began describing himself as possessing a 'Western' and cowboy background rather than a rural one. Autry was already a successful singer and radio personality before he sought work in the series Westerns then in vogue in Hollywood – his 1931 recording of 'That Silver Haired Daddy of Mine' sold over a million copies. With the advent of sound, music had become a central element in other genres besides the musical. Impressed by Autry's success, especially with his large radio following in the American heartlands, the prime audience for the series Westerns, Nat Levine of Mascot Pictures brought Autry to Hollywood. (As the owner of The American Record Company, to which Autry was contracted, Herbert Yates, head of Republic Pictures – soon to swallow up Mascot – must also have known of Autry.) Levine first featured him warbling in support of Ken Maynard (who has the distinction of being the first cowboy star to sing on screen) in *In Old Sante Fe* (1934) and then starred him in the twelve-chapter serial *Phantom Empire*.

A bizarre mixture of science fiction and the Western, *Phantom Empire* starred Autry as himself, a cowboy with a radio show that was regularly broadcast from his ranch and on which he sang in between dealing with assorted Muranians (members of a subterranean civilization located below Autry's land) and gangsters seeking valuable radium deposits. Both this and Autry's first starring feature, *Tumbling Tumbleweeds* (1935), the title song of which gave him another million-selling record, were enormously successful and launched the singing cowboy as a central

element of the series Western. Quickly Dick Foran, Roy Rogers, Tex Ritter, Eddie Dean, Monte Hale, Rex Allen, Jimmy Wakely and others were saddled up and pressed into service, their heads thrown back in song as they rode to the defence of damsels in distress, brought low by claim jumpers, bandits, gangsters, crooked lawyers and the like.

All were derivative of Autry but significantly none matched him in his commitment to singing rather than fighting his way out of a hole. A classic example of this is *Mexicali Rose* (1939), in which outlaw Noah Beery's hobby is collecting Gene Autry records and Autry wins Beery's affections by singing to him, in fact by continuing (complete with orchestral backing) the song Beery is playing on his phonograph when the record is inadvertently broken. This air of unreality, in which Autry became a knight in shining armour keeping the peace of a mythical range (and one full of anachronisms), precisely reflected the relationship of the music Autry sang to the traditions of country music of the time. Just as the films had little relationship to the West of memory, let alone reality, so Autry's music once he took to the screen had little in common with country music. Indeed, despite his huge influence on the development of country music, most of his subsequent record successes came in the pop charts.

With most singing cowboys, the music they sang similarly bore little relationship to country music. Dick Foran, for example, was a one-time opera singer. However, a few important country stars did further their careers through appearances in series Westerns. Apart from Tex Ritter, the most significant of these were Bob Wills (who with his Western Swing band, the Texas Playboys, co-starred in several films with Charles Starrett), Spade Cooley and Jimmy Wakely.

Interestingly, though the sub-genre could easily be manipulated to incorporate the likes of R&B star Louis Jordan (*Look Out Sister*, 1949) or band leader Vaughan Monroe (*Toughest Man in Arizona*, 1952), the singing cowboys had virtually no effect on the A-Western. When Roy Rogers attempted a move to A-Westerns with *Dark Command* (1940), he left his guitar and songs behind. However, events outside influenced B-Westerns. Thus, in the wake of the Broadway production of *Oklahoma!* in 1943, Rogers' Republic outings were restyled in imitation of the Broadway show. Then, in the late 40s, they were transformed into

decidedly bloody action-oriented films, with lengthy fistfights in Trucolor, a direct reflection of the general drift to greater 'realism' apparent throughout Hollywood productions of the period.

Of all the stars of singing Westerns, probably the most influential on the A-Western were The Sons of the Pioneers and Tex Ritter. The Sons of the Pioneers, the group that Roy Rogers founded and which subsequently supported him in numerous outings, were featured in several mainstream films (notably John Ford's *Rio Grande*/1950) and for many their sweet harmony singing was the definition of cowboy balladry. Furthermore Bob Nolan, the group's leader, wrote many of the classic Western songs, including 'Tumbling Tumbleweeds' and 'Cool Water'. Ritter's low-budget Westerns (made for Grand National, Monogram and PRC) were decidedly inferior to those of Autry and Rogers. Nonetheless, Ritter was far more influential beyond the small world of the series Western than either Autry or Rogers. Ritter's series Westerns were merely part of his long career, which included a string of successful records in the 40s (including 'There's a New Moon Over My Shoulder', 'Rye Whiskey' and the original version of 'Deck of Cards') and a surprise return to Western fame when he sang the theme song to *High Noon*/1952. Ritter went on to sing the themes to *The Marshal's Daughter* (1953) and *Wichita*/1955, and henceforth most major Westerns would have a theme song. Many of Autry's earlier films had been constructed around and had drawn their titles from songs (for example *Mexicali Rose*, *South of the Border*) but in the late 40s and 50s Hollywood discovered that as well as songs helping promote films, films could also help sell records, and the studios instructed their composers accordingly. The culmination was *Blazing Saddles*/1974, proof that a parody Western needs a parody theme song. Hence 'Blazing Saddles', sung by Frankie Laine, who earlier had had a million seller with his version of 'High Noon', probably the best remembered Western theme song.

Also in the 1950s, The Kingston Trio's successful recording of 'Tom Dooley' (1958) inspired *The Legend of Tom Dooley* (1959). And when Marty Robbins (a country performer who claims Gene Autry and his films as a prime influence) turned to films, he naturally made Westerns (including *The Badge of Marshal Brennan*, 1958 and *Buffalo Gun*, 1961, which also starred country singer Webb Pierce). Similarly, Robbins' highly successful series of 'gunfighter' ballads, such as 'El Paso' (1959) and 'Big Iron' (1960), owed more to Westerns and the popular images of the cowboy they offered than to the cowboy ballads of the 19th century.

Robbins' flirtation with the Western is revealing of the long dependence of country music on Western imagery and motifs. This enduring relationship has lasted some 50 years. Even now, both low-budget films featuring country performers (*Uphill All the Way*, 1985) and bigger budget ones (for example the films of Willie Nelson) still tend to be Westerns.

Outside America, this relationship between sound and image has been equally strong. In the early 60s the German Westerns which appeared in the wake of *Der Schatz im Silbersee* (1962) were accompanied by a revival of interest in all things Western, including comics and Western-inspired pop songs ('Der Wind der Prairie'). Similarly, Ennio Morricone's instantly recognizable scores were a central element in the popularity of the Italian Westerns that followed upon the Winnetou series. PH

In Old Santa Fe/1934/Mascot/d David Howard/lp Ken Maynard, George Hayes, Gene Autry · *Phantom Empire*/1934/Mascot/d Otto Brower, B. Reeves Eason/lp Gene Autry · *Tumbling Tumbleweeds*/1935/REP/d Joseph Kane/lp Gene Autry, Smiley Burnette · *Mexicali Rose*/1939/REP/d George Sherman/lp Gene Autry, Smiley Burnette · *South of the Border*/1939/REP/d George Sherman/lp Gene Autry, Smiley Burnette · *Dark Command*/1940/REP/d Raoul Walsh/lp John Wayne, Claire Trevor, Roy Rogers · *Look Out Sister*/1949/Ascot/d Bud Pollard/lp Louis Jordan · *Toughest Man in Arizona*/1952/REP/d R.G. Springsteen/lp Vaughn Monroe, Joan Leslie · *The Marshal's Daughter*/1953/UA/d William Berke/lp Hoot Gibson, Laurie Anders · *The Badge of Marshal Brennan*/1957/AA/d Albert C. Gannaway/lp Jim Davis, Arleen Whelan · *The Legend of Tom Dooley*/1959/COL/d Ted Post/lp Michael Landon, Jo Morrow · *Buffalo Gun*/1961/Globe/d Albert C. Gannaway/lp Webb Pierce, Marty Robbins · *Der Schatz im Silbersee*/1962/WG/d Harald Reinl/lp Lex Barker, Pierre Brice · *Uphill All the Way*/1985/Melroy-Guardian/d Frank Dobbs/lp Burl Ives, Roy Clark, Glen Campbell

Muybridge, Eadweard (1830–1904) · Photographer. Basing himself in San Francisco in the 1860s, Muybridge produced a series of pictures of Yosemite which rivalled those of C. E. *Watkins and which made his name. But he is better known today for the experiments he began in 1872 at the request of the railroad magnate Leland *Stanford. The object was to demonstrate through photography the precise movements of a *horse in motion. After many difficulties Muybridge was successful in 1878, proving conclusively that the conventional artistic portrayal of a galloping horse was wrong. (See *Horses for an illustration.) Muybridge's experiments had two effects on the Western. Firstly, the development of his Zoopraxiscope was a step along the road that led to the cinema. Secondly, his photographs influenced contemporary artists, among them Frederic *Remington, and introduced a powerful new realism into the depiction of the horse in Western art.

N

Navaho · Linguistically and culturally related to the Apache, the Navaho moved into the Southwest from the plains in the 16th century. They practised agriculture and stockraising and lived in hogans, houses of earth and sticks. In the 18th century they came into increasing conflict with their neighbours, both whites and Pueblo Indians such as the Zuni and Hopi. Once Arizona and New Mexico became part of the United States in 1848 the Navaho became a problem for the American army. There were numerous clashes up until 1863, when Kit *Carson led a punitive expedition which killed hundreds of Navaho and destroyed their homes and livestock. After this the Navaho signed a treaty and were given reservation areas in northern Arizona and New Mexico. The Navaho were perhaps fortunate in that their land in the high desert was never coveted by whites and today they are the largest grouping of Native Americans, numbering over 100,000. Included in the Navaho reservation is *Monument Valley, and the Navaho made frequent appearances (usually as Apaches or Comanches) in the films that John Ford shot there.

Newspapers · In the early 1850s San Francisco had no less than twelve daily newspapers and throughout California over a thousand people were occupied in journalism. Newspapers rose up throughout the West almost as rapidly as the towns which supported them. *Dodge City, with a population of around 2,000 in the mid-1880s, supported three papers, the *Times*, the *Globe* and the *Democrat*. Each vied with the others to sing the praises of Dodge over its rivals for the Texas cattle trade such as Ellsworth or *Abilene. (Bat *Masterson, sheriff of Dodge City in the late 1870s, had ambitions to be a newspaperman himself and ended his days as sports editor of the New York *Morning Telegraph*.)

It is to these local newspapers that we owe a good deal of what we know about outlaws, lawmen and other inhabitants of the West. Yet the mere existence of a newspaper tends to suggest that civilization is on its way in and that the days of the old West are numbered. This is certainly the implication of the scene in *Butch Cassidy and the Sundance Kid*/1969 in which Butch and the Kid sit reading clippings about their exploits.

Whatever their actual historical role, in the town-taming Western newspapers almost invariably stand for the forces of progress, for the growth of community and the benefits of law and order. For this reason it is less surprising than it might otherwise seem that newspaper owners and editors in Westerns often turn out to be women. It is, after all, the presence of women which usually indicates a town has taken the first step on the ladder of respectability. Thus in *Dodge City*/1939 and *Carson City*/1951 we see women slaving over the hot metal type. So too in *Badman's Territory* and *Texas Lady*, and in *Jesse James*/1939 even Jesse's future wife Zee is discovered at work in the newspaper office of her uncle. In Edna *Ferber's *Cimarron*, though it is a man who founds the town newspaper, it is his wife who ends up running it. Her mission is to raise the level of consciousness in town to the point where civic responsibility will prevail over the entrenched forces of vested interests.

But in the Western right rarely wins without might. The moral authority of the press is not enough to win the day; the women need a man to back them up. Similarly in *Fort Worth*: Randolph Scott attempts to exchange his guns for the power of a newspaper as a means of combating the ambitions of the local big landowner, but he eventually has to take up arms again.

If the message is ultimately the same in *The Man Who Shot Liberty Valance*/1962, it is less straightforwardly put. The drunken newspaper editor Dutton Peabody (Edmond O'Brien) is scarcely a knight in shining armour, but he stands, albeit unsteadily, alongside what is decent in the town of Shinbone. Along with the law, the schoolroom and the small entrepreneur, he represents community against savagery. When he is brutally beaten and his printing

LEFT: *Women typesetters on the Kansas Workman* RIGHT: *Roscoe Ates and Estelle Taylor in the newspaper office in* Cimarron *(1930)*

press smashed by Liberty Valance, it is clear that the pen is not mightier than the sword. Force must be met with force. But things are more ambiguous than they appear. Valance is not defeated in a fair fight. A trick makes it seem so, but in fact he has been shot by a third party, Tom Doniphon (John Wayne). What complicates the film's view of the press is that when the truth emerges in the framing narrative around the story, the press then offers its complicity in the preservation of the deceit. It is the newspaperman interviewing James Stewart who says, 'This is the West, sir. When the legend becomes fact print the legend.'

The exact meaning of this oft-quoted utterance becomes less clear the more we reflect upon it, but one thing is certain: the press no longer stands for the truth in all its shining innocence. From this position it is perhaps not so far as it might seem to Ford's last Western, *Cheyenne Autumn*/1964. As the Cheyenne get nearer to Dodge City we see the press at one moment hysterically exaggerating the number of Indians on the loose and the next deciding, with a cynicism Fleet Street could hardly better, that more copies can be sold by running a campaign to support them.
Badman's Territory/1946/RKO/*d* Tim Whelan/*lp* Randolph Scott, Ann Richards · *Fort Worth*/1951/WB/*d* Edwin L. Marin/*lp* Randolph Scott · *Texas Lady*/1955/RKO/*d* Tim Whelan/*lp* Claudette Colbert, Barry Sullivan

Norris, [Benjamin] Frank[lin] (1870-1902) · Novelist whose early death prevented the completion of his ambitious trilogy 'The Wheat'. The first volume, *The Octopus* (1901), is a powerful story of the conflict between the railroads (in effect, the Southern Pacific) and the big landowners of

southern California. If not in every respect a Western, it articulates some typical Western themes such as the rapacity of the railroads and the arrogance of land barons. It was filmed as *The Octopus*/1915/Selig/*d* Thomas Santschi/*lp* Thomas Santschi, Lillian Hayward. The second volume in the trilogy, about grain speculators in Chicago and entitled *The Pit* (1903), formed the basis of D.W. Griffith's *A Corner in Wheat* (1909). An earlier Norris novel, *McTeague* (1899), which has its climactic scene in Death Valley, California, was filmed as *Desert Gold* (1914) and then became Erich von Stroheim's *Greed* (1923).

O

Oakley, Annie (1860-1926) · Stage name of Phoebe Ann Moses, the trick-shooting sensation of Buffalo Bill's Wild West. Born in Ohio, she never was in the West except on tour but came to typify the all-action Western heroine. 'Little Sure Shot', as she was known, joined Buffalo Bill *Cody in 1885 and her exploits brought her huge success. She could shoot cigarettes out of men's mouths, fire backwards using mirrors and once broke 943 out of 1,000 glass balls thrown in the air, using a .22 rifle. She also appeared with Pawnee Bill *Lillie and in stage plays and became a heroine of comic books.
Barbara Stanwyck/*Annie Oakley*/1935/RKO/*d* George Stevens/*lp* Preston Foster, Melvyn Douglas · Betty Hutton/*Annie Get Your Gun*/1950 · Gail Davis/*Alias Jesse James*/1959/Hope Enterprises/*d* Norman McLeod/*lp* Bob Hope, Rhonda Fleming · Nancy Kovack/*The Outlaws Is Coming*/1964/COL/*d* Norman Maurer/*lp* The Three Stooges · Angela Douglas/*Carry On Cowboy*/1965/GB/*d* Gerald Thomas/*lp* Sid

James, Kenneth Williams · Geraldine Chaplin/*Buffalo Bill and the Indians*/1976 · Jamie Lee Curtis/*Annie Oakley*/1985/Platypus/*d* Michael Lindsay Hogg/*lp* Brian Dennehey
Television · Gail Davis/*Annie Oakley*

Oddities · Any attempt at a neat definition of the Western in terms of historical setting (the 19th century) or geographical location (the trans-Mississippi United States) runs slap up against the fact that in practice almost anything goes. Phil Hardy's plot description of *Hawaiian Buckaroo* in his encyclopedia *The Western* begins: 'Set in Hawaii, it features singing cowboy [Smith] Ballew and his side-kick [Benny] Burt starting a pineapple plantation...' *King of the Mounties* has Allan Lane as a Mountie in World War II. The enemy are 'agents of Germany, Japan and Italy helping to prepare for an Axis invasion of Canada by bombing it from an undetectable plane. An inventor who comes up with a new kind of plane detector is killed, leaving Lane to protect the detector and rescue the inventor's daughter...' The Western, in fact, is capable of almost any mutation. In *The Phantom Empire* Gene Autry plays a singing cowboy who runs a radio station. As Hardy describes it: 'A gang of crooks covet his radium mine and, while being pursued by Autry, they stumble upon the entrance to Murania, an underground civilization far in advance of ours but riven by similar tensions which are exacerbated by exposure to mankind.' The titles of *Billy the Kid vs. Dracula* and *Jesse James Meets Frankenstein's Daughter* speak for themselves. So does *Hard on the Trail*, one of a number of pornographic Westerns made in the 1970s. And so, perhaps, does *Harlem Rides the Range*, a B-Western with an all-black cast. Actually, after the first five

Annie Oakley in 1898

minutes this isn't really odd at all, even for a white audience, since apart from the casting it's a highly conventional film. So in one sense is *The Terror of Tiny Town*, with its plot of a villain inciting two families into a feud so as to take over their land. But since the film is played by a cast of 60 midgets at whose attempts to look big and tough we are expected to be amused it's not only odd but distasteful.

The Terror of Tiny Town

The Phantom Empire/1934/Mascot/*d* Otto Brower, B. Reeves Eason/*lp* Gene Autry · *Hawaiian Buckaroo*/1938/FOX/*d* Ray Taylor/*lp* Smith Ballew · *The Terror of Tiny Town*/1938/COL/*d* Sam Newfield/*lp* Billy Curtis · *Harlem Rides the Range*/1939/Hollywood Pictures/*d* Richard Kahn/*lp* Herbert Jeffrey · *King of the Mounties*/1942/REP/*d* William Witney/*lp* Allan Lane · *Billy the Kid vs. Dracula*/1965/Circle/*d* William Beaudine/*lp* Chuck Courtney, John Carradine · *Jesse James Meets Frankenstein's Daughter*/1965/Circle/*d* William Beaudine/*lp* John Lupton · *Hard on the Trail*/1971/Brentwood International/*d* Greg Corarito/*lp* Lash LaRue, Donna Bradley

Oil · Though there was oil production in California from the 1860s, until 1900 western states contributed only a small proportion of America's total output. In the first ten years of the 20th century huge oilfields were discovered in Texas, Louisiana, Oklahoma and California. By 1911 almost three-quarters of national oil production originated in the West and today virtually all of it comes from the trans-Mississippi states. As its nickname of 'black gold' suggests, oil can occupy the same place in popular mythology as the precious metals which first formed the basis of the West's mineral wealth. It motivates the same kinds of dramatic conflicts, based on jealousy and greed, the arrogance of wealth and power, and skulduggery of all kinds. *Terror in a Texas Town*/1958 uses the familiar plot of the rich man trying to force small farmers off their land, in this case because he knows there's oil underneath. James Dean's discovery of oil on his small plot of land in *Giant*/1956 allows him to stand up against the imperious Rock Hudson, who, like Jason Robards in *Comes a Horseman*/1978, refuses to allow oil exploration on his cattle range. In *Cimarron*/1931 and /1960 the discovery of oil transforms the frontier economy. Like gold, oil is rarely seen as an unmixed blessing. In *Broken Lance*/1954 it is the black sheep of a ranching family (Richard Widmark) who wants to sell off land to an oil company and who tries to cheat Robert Wagner out of his inheritance. The association between oil, wealth and the West continues as strong as ever on contemporary television, in the Texas setting of *Dallas* and the Colorado locale of *Dynasty*.

Oklahoma · The land now covered by the state of Oklahoma was originally called simply 'Indian Territory'. In the 1830s it was designated as the permanent home for the *Five Civilized Tribes, removed from their homes in the southeast. In the course of the 19th century more and more tribes were ousted from their original lands, until by 1885 over fifty different Indian peoples had been forcibly resettled in Indian Territory. By this time white settlers were putting pressure on the government to open this land up for homesteading, and groups of 'Sooners' as they were called continually attempted to move illegally on to what were still Indian lands. Eventually the government gave way and a number of 'runs' were organized, in which the first homesteaders to arrive on the spot and stake a claim took the land. The most famous of these was the race for the *Cherokee Strip.

In the 1890s Oklahoma was the theatre of operations for the *Dalton gang.

Three large-scale Westerns which, in different ways, celebrate the state rather than simply set their action there are the two versions of *Cimarron*/1931 and /1960, and the musical *Oklahoma!*/1955. As the title song of the latter puts it confidently:
'We know we belong to the land
And the land we belong to is grand.'

Old-timer · In the Western, youth is often an object of ridicule; old age laughs at itself. The comic old man is a conception as old as drama, but in the Western it has been raised to the status of an institution. Only in the Western did a whole troop of actors make a living specializing in this one part; indeed the Western devised, in the phrase 'old-timer', its own term for the role. Though the precise proportions of garrulity and cantankerousness varied, memorable performances were produced by Walter Brennan, Jay C. Flippen, Francis Ford, Will Geer, George 'Gabby' Hayes, Arthur Hunnicutt, Chubby Johnson, Russell Simpson, Al St John. A variation was worked by Chief Dan George, who in such films as *Little Big Man*/1970 and *The Outlaw Josey Wales*/1976 played a comic Indian old-timer. Not that age is always funny, as Walter Brennan himself showed as the malevolent elder Clanton in *My Darling Clementine*/1946.

Olsen, T[heodore] V[ictor] (b 1932) · Author of a score or more Western novels, some under the pseudonym Joshua Stark. Two have been filmed. *The Stalking Moon*/1968 is about a white woman rescued from Indian captivity together with her half-Indian son. The boy's father attempts to take him back again. Olsen's novel *Arrow in the Sun* (1969), which also has a heroine who has been captured by Indians, was filmed as *Soldier Blue*/1970. The novel is set in the period following the defeat of *Custer in 1876 and contains no massacre of Indians by whites, but the film, apparently in order to point up contemporary parallels with events in Vietnam, concludes with the Sand Creek Massacre of the *Cheyenne in 1864.

Omohundro, Texas Jack (1846-80) · Army scout and friend of Buffalo Bill *Cody. Texas Jack appeared as himself in 1872 in the play *The Scouts of the Plains* which Ned *Buntline wrote for Buffalo Bill. He had worked as a cowboy in Texas, and was therefore in all likelihood the first actual cowboy ever to appear before the public, though since his role on stage was as a scout he was not, as some have claimed, the first cowboy star (a distinction which more properly belongs to Buck *Taylor). Texas Jack also appeared in several dime novels such as *Texas Jack, the Prairie Rattler*, and briefly formed his own theatrical company. (See *Buntline for illustration.)

Openings · 'Everybody knows' that a Western opens with a long shot of one or more riders in a landscape. For once, the commonplace observation is accurate. The great majority of Westerns actually do begin in this way, instantly establishing the sense of place and the suggestion of movement so important to the genre. Variations work upon the audience's expectations, giving a sense of strangeness or shock; thus at the beginning of *The Left Handed Gun*/1957 we see Paul Newman as Billy the Kid actually walking, carrying his saddle. Both *Wagon Master*/1950 (directed by John Ford, the master of the long shot) and *The True Story of Jesse James*/1957 open with a series of midshots of a hold-up in progress. Sergio Leone has cunningly exploited the conventional opening. The first shot proper of *Per un pugno di dollari*/1964 is a close-up of the ground and horses' hooves. *Per qualche dollaro in più*/1965 reverts to tradition and shows a tiny figure on horseback in a huge landscape – who is then shot off his horse. In *Il buono, il brutto, il cattivo*/1966 Leone opens with a long shot of a rocky landscape, and then in the same shot a face comes across the frame in an extreme close-up.

The convention is well enough established to hold even for a film such as *Rio Bravo*/1958, which is hardly aware of the outdoors at all yet begins with an establishing shot of a landscape with cactus, or for a director such as Sam Fuller who, though often given to shock effects, begins *Forty Guns*/1957 with an extreme long shot of open country with a wagon driving along a trail. Sometimes it is not a rider but a train which appears in the distance, as in *The Man Who Shot Liberty Valance*/1962. In Westerns with a contemporary setting, for example *Hud*/1962, it may be a car.

To ascertain exactly when the stylistic convention first appeared would need very detailed research, but it is certainly well established by the time of William S. Hart's *Hell's Hinges*/1916, which after a brief prologue in the east starts the action proper with a cut to a long shot of a stagecoach moving along a road. *Straight Shooting*, directed by John Ford in 1917, opens with a long shot of cattle coming towards the camera. In *The Covered Wagon*/1923, after some initial exposition the story properly begins with a long-shot of the wagons moving west. And in the latest Clint Eastwood Western, *Pale Rider*/1985, the tradition is upheld, as a group of riders in long-shot come down out of the mountains.

O'Sullivan, Timothy (1840-82) · Photographer. O'Sullivan photographed the Civil War and afterwards was hired by the geologist Clarence King to take pictures for a government survey of Nevada in 1867. O'Sullivan photographed the Humboldt Sink and the Truckee River, as well as Virginia City, where he took pictures down the Comstock mine. In 1871 he joined another survey, led by George Wheeler, which journeyed up the Colorado River. O'Sullivan thus became the first to photograph the Grand Canyon and on a later survey was among the first to photograph the Canyon de Chelly. His images of the harsh mountains, deserts and canyons of the Southwest anticipate the feel for landscape of such Western directors as Ford and Boetticher.

P

Parker, Isaac Charles (1838-96) · Judge. Appointed by President Grant in 1875 to clean up the Western District centred on Fort Smith, which also had jurisdiction over the lawless Indian Territory, Parker proceeded to hang 88 people over the next twenty years. Whether or not Parker deserved his later reputation for sadism, he lived on as the model of a 'hanging judge'. At the beginning of a routine Western such as *The Dragoon Wells Massacre*/1957/AA/d Harold Schuster/lp Barry Sullivan, Dennis O'Keefe, we are informed that some prisoners are being delivered to Judge Parker. We need be told no more to know what fate is in store for them.
James Westerfield/*True Grit*/1969 · John McIntire/*Rooster Cogburn*/1975/U/d Stuart

Timothy O'Sullivan, photograph of his darkroom taken on the King Survey, Sand Springs, Nevada (1867)

Millar/*lp* John Wayne, Katharine Hepburn · A hanging judge based on the prototype of Parker appears in *Hang 'Em High*/1968 Television · Dale Robertson/*The Last Ride of the Dalton Gang*

Parkman, Francis (1823-93) · Author. Parkman's travels on the Great Plains in 1846, recounted in his book *The Oregon Trail* (1849), were intended to provide a prologue to *France and England in North America*, his vast history in eight volumes of the struggles of France and Britain for supremacy on the North American continent, begun in 1851 and concluded in 1892. In the event it was *The Oregon Trail* which achieved both popularity and status as a classic of nineteenth-century travel literature. Parkman was one of the first and most gifted writers to put into words the romance of adventures in the wide open spaces of the prairie. There he encountered the Plains Indians at the height of their power and the fur trappers in their heyday.

Parodies · There's a tendency to assume that when a genre begins to parody itself decadence has set in. In fact *The Great Train Robbery* was itself subject to parody, and Douglas Fairbanks was poking fun at Westerns before the end of World War I. Most of Hollywood's comic stars had a go at a Western parody, including Charlie Chaplin (*The Gold Rush*), Buster Keaton (*Go West*), Jack Benny (*Buck Benny Rides Again*), Joe E. Brown (*Shut My Big Mouth*), W.C. Fields (*My Little Chickadee*), The Marx Brothers (*Go West*), Laurel and Hardy (*Way Out West*/1937), Abbott and Costello (*Ride 'Em Cowboy*), Bob Hope (*The Paleface* and *Son of Paleface*/1952), Dean Martin and Jerry Lewis (*Pardners*), The Three Stooges (*The Outlaws Is Coming*). Through virtually all these parodies runs a single thread. This is the comic contrast between the demands which the code of the West places on the courage of those who would be men, and the comedian's own cowardice. This theme is also the basis of most of the humour in such otherwise widely varied films as *Lonesome Cowboys*/1968, *Support Your Local Sheriff!*, *Carry On Cowboy* and *Blazing Saddles*/1974. Parody, in order to find its target, must lock on to the mechanism which makes its subject tick. In seizing on the figure of the macho hero it reveals what, at least in the popular mind, constitutes the heart of the Western. *The Gold Rush*/1925/UA/*d* Charlie Chaplin · *Go West*/1925/MGM/*d* Buster Keaton · *Buck Benny Rides Again*/1940/PAR/*d* Mark

Laurel and Hardy in Way Out West

Sandrich · *Go West*/1940/MGM/*d* Edward Buzzell/*lp* The Marx Brothers · *Shut My Big Mouth*/1942/COL/*d* Charles Barton · *My Little Chickadee*/1940/U/*d* Edward Cline · *Ride 'Em Cowboy*/1942/U/*d* Arthur Lubin · *The Paleface*/1948/PAR/*d* Norman Z. McLeod · *Pardners*/1956/PAR/*d* Norman Taurog · *The Outlaws Is Coming*/1964/COL/*d* Norman Maurer · *Support Your Local Sheriff!*/1968/UA/*d* Burt Kennedy/*lp* James Garner, Joan Hackett · *Carry On Cowboy*/1965/GB/*d* Gerald Thomas/*lp* Sid James

Photography · It may have been a mere coincidence of chronology that most of the era of massive and rapid American expansion into the trans-Mississippi West after the Civil War took place within the era of photography, but it is not an accident that so many aspects of this phenomenon came before a camera lens. Most of the principal agents of westward movement – whether government explorers, army surveyors and fort builders, the manufacturers of wagons for the Oregon and other trails, the great railroads which connected the centres of population, or the ranchers who initially settled the intervening acres – employed photographers to record their activities. Eventually, of course, professional photographers themselves, as individual entrepreneurs, began to set up shop in the new towns of the region, and finally amateur photography became possible.

Photography was intimately part and parcel of a colonizing movement and inevitably it reflected the expropriating and exploitative ideology which underwrote westward expansion. However, as is well-known, despite the often jingoistic utterances of American political leaders, the fundamentally imperialistic aspect of the movement into the West tended to be downplayed, with the emphasis of overt expression falling instead on the range of democratic opportunities for

ordinary white folk which were undoubtedly opened up by such expansion, and on the strength required to impose civilization and the rule of law in such a vast and initially alien territory.

Photography, like the Western, represented this complex of assumptions. Not surprisingly, therefore, its subjects overlap with the traditional settings and situations of the Western film. Andrew J. Russell was an official photographer for the *Union Pacific Railroad and took numerous views not only of bridges, tunnels, water towers and steep inclines, but also, together with others, photographed the celebrations at Promontory Point, Utah, when the transcontinental track was joined in May 1869. Laton Huffman made hundreds of images of cattle ranch and range life on the northern plains just as, after the turn of the century, F.M. Steele did on the southern plains. Will Soule, who was employed by the army to document the building of Fort Sill in Indian Territory, made numerous Indian portraits in his makeshift studio as well as a depiction of two cavalrymen inspecting a scalped white man found dead on the baked earth of the plains in 1868. W. H. Illingworth accompanied *Custer on his expedition into the *Black Hills in 1874, when he photographed the line of wagons and troops entering this land sacred to the Sioux in an incursion which helped to trigger the fateful Battle of the *Little Big Horn two years later. Some photographers, notably Edward S. *Curtis, but also amateurs like A. C. Vroman, dedicated themselves almost exclusively to the coverage of American Indians. Camillus S. Fly, a photographic entrepreneur in Tombstone, Arizona, photographed both the captured Apache leader Geronimo and many famous – and infamous – lawmen and outlaws, such as Wyatt Earp and Bat Masterson. Often a town photographer like Fly would be called in to take 'mug shots' of the arrested desperados – though sometimes such men had earlier visited the studio of their own volition. Businessmen photographers also participated in the boosting of towns, recording their growth from early campground-like settlement to the development of wood-fronted stores and plank side-walks; perhaps the most dramatic series of such pictures was that made by Alexander Forbes at the opening up of Guthrie, Oklahoma, at the time of the celebrated race for land claims in the *Cherokee Strip in April 1889.

Photographers like these also, of course, trained their cameras on to the forms of the land itself, its seemingly endless prairies, its strange buttes and other rock formations, its mountains, valleys and dry river beds. Eadweard *Muybridge – who was ultimately more significant for his success in photographing the movements of horses and humans in series in an anticipation of the motion picture itself – was also well known as a photographer of immense landscapes. William Henry *Jackson, who worked for various government agencies, for the railroads and as a freelance, made literally thousands of studies of landmark sites. His 'North from Berthoud Pass' (1874), with its lone figure seemingly about to move off into the (visually) unknown, is a definitive romantic evocation of the westering experience.

Such views, along with those of Timothy *O'Sullivan, who had earlier photographed the Civil War battlefields for photographic entrepreneur Matthew *Brady and who created numerous images while employed by government geological survey parties, were probably the most significant of all. Often O'Sullivan's pictures present the Great Plains with an emphasis on openness and aridity, and the semi-desert with the inhospitable aspect most prominent, so that the viewer is made aware, almost in a tactile sense, of extremes of climate. Certainly the viewer is made to see the isolation of any white settlements depicted and must gauge their tenuous links with 'civilization'. Above

W.H. Illingworth, photograph of General Custer's expedition in the Black Hills, Castle Creek Valley (1874)

all else, the viewer becomes critically conscious of a sense of staggering space. These are renderings of grandeur *and* harshness.

Such a vision was shared to some extent by landscape painters of the West – Albert *Bierstadt, for instance, or Thomas *Moran – but later painters like Frederic *Remington became more interested in offering moments of action or the illusion of stories in miniature: an Indian watching the wagon train or the stagecoach at speed. During the heyday of Jackson and O'Sullivan photography was not at its best in the rendering of action and its duotone nature brought out more uncompromisingly than painting could the abstract qualities of land forms. The very stillness of these photographs gives the impression that careful photographers habitually represented the West as a series of awesome arenas, arenas fit for severe, even ultimate, conflicts.

It may be claimed that in this and other respects Western photographers of the 19th and early 20th centuries both recorded aspects of the West and helped to create an idea of it, almost an iconography of it, that has retained its potency, especially as replicated in the Western film. This is *not* to say, of course, that there were invariably direct links between Western photographs and film – though there were some. Studio research departments seem to have had recourse to archival photographs for set designs, landscape settings and costumes. Sometimes the photographers themselves moved into films: Curtis, for instance, both made a documentary feature of his own in 1914 and was a cameraman for Cecil B. DeMille's *The Plainsman*/1936, working with Indians who had reconstructed battle scenes for his own still camera thirty years earlier. Usually, however, in the early years the connections were oblique, circumstantial, and only partly conscious – and, therefore, perhaps all the more pervasive.

The following three links will illustrate the point. First, it has been observed that the movie Western included visual motifs from paintings by such artists as Remington in an amalgam with plot elements from Western dime novels and melodramatic plays and aspects of spectacle from Wild West shows. What is less often recognized is that Remington himself worked from photographs. He used his own Kodak snaps as the groundwork for paintings and illustrations, he based other pictures on the work of such figures as Laton Huffman and, of course, he relied crucially on Muybridge's studies of horses in motion for such subjects as troops

of cavalry racing for shelter from pursuing Indians.

Second, photographs of the West were not seen by most people – unless as stereocards – in direct photographic form; rather, they first permeated the culture reproduced as woodcuts and other kinds of engraving in the illustrated journals of the time. Soule's image of a scalped man mentioned above, for example, appeared as a woodcut in *Harper's Weekly*. This means that, in the formative years, photographic images of the West were inflected by the preconceptions held by engravers and enjoyed a similar status to actual engravings. That is, they contributed, willy nilly, to the limitation – indeed, the standardization – of representation of the West.

Third, this process was accelerated by the fact that in several respects visual representations of the West in painting, film and photography developed concurrently in the early years of Western movies. Erwin Smith, for instance, perhaps the most prolific photographer of cowboy life, did the bulk of his work after 1905 and several of his most evocative photographs were firmly based on paintings, often famous ones. In turn, a number of major figures in the development of the Western, such as Dustin Farnum and William S. Hart, consulted Smith and his files for visual information on cowboy paraphernalia; also, since Smith's pictures were used as cover illustrations for almost fifty years by *The Cattleman*, a cowboy journal much circulated in the Western states, his vision was widely disseminated. Concurrent development of the principal media of representation – and reciprocity between them – led, in other words, to a reinforcement of appropriate views of the West.

The sheer profligacy of photography and the increasing ease of reprography of its images meant that, even more than painting, photography was a repository of such views. Typical would be Jackson's image from below of a train atop an apparently insubstantial, thin-legged bridge on the Colorado Central Railway; Huffman's depiction of a log-built ranch; Smith's hill-top vantage of thousands of Texas longhorns being driven to the railhead; Curtis' profile of a plains war party descending a steep slope; John Swartz' Fort Worth studio group portrait of Butch *Cassidy, the Sundance Kid and three of their cronies; Arundel C. Hull's gruesome rendition of a hanged man, dead at the hands of vigilantes in the lawless Laramie of 1868; and Solomon Butcher's portrait of a pioneer family posed outside their sod-roofed

Nebraska home.

John Ford was prepared to record an indebtedness to Frederic Remington in the making of his cavalry Westerns and there are reproductions of Remington and Charles M. *Russell paintings in the credit sequences of such later movies as *The Last Hunt*/1955 and *Monte Walsh*/1970. However, despite this continuing appeal of paintings, more often than not the makers of 'revisionist' Westerns, perhaps partly through their efforts to get out from under Ford, so to speak, had greater recourse to photographic imagery. While in fact, as has been implied already, photographs were just as much *representations* of the West as other forms of imagery, they have frequently been treated as if they were actual fragments of reality itself. That is, the desire to get back to history as it actually was often becomes, in visual terms, an attempt to present things as they look in old photographs. Thus *The Red Badge of Courage* (1951) owes much to Civil War photographs by Brady, O'Sullivan and others. *Butch Cassidy and the Sundance Kid*/1969 opens with a series of sepia studio stills of the protagonists (probably inspired by images like Swartz's) before breaking into vivid colour for the action itself, implying that the film proper constitutes a kind of animation of the past itself. Even as baroque a film-maker as Sergio Leone looked to archival photographic prints for costumes and objects in his Westerns, and in *Il buono,*

il brutto, il cattivo/1966, Brady the photographer figures as a character in the movie.

Photographers seem to have appeared only rarely in the gallery of the Western's characters, and then usually in the context of an examination of the Western itself – or, at least, of myths and ideas of the West. For instance, the off-beat Canadian Western, *The Grey Fox*/1982, with its incorporation of movie footage from *The Great Train Robbery*/1903 and other reflexive devices, includes a sensitive portrait of an independent woman photographer. She takes pictures of unspoilt landscapes on the one hand and of labour disputes on the other (which in itself constitutes a kind of commentary on white expropriation) *and* becomes the lover of the film's protagonist, an outlaw who is already, as is often said in Westerns, a legend in his own lifetime. Similarly, *Butch and Sundance: The Early Days* (1979), even more obviously a re-examination of a Western myth, features a photographer who is after the likenesses of the young heroes themselves. And *Buffalo Bill and the Indians or Sitting Bull's History Lesson*/1976, Robert Altman's highly knowing film (it even has a pun on the Wild West show as an effort to 'Codyfy' the West) implicitly and explicitly includes photography among the targets of its burlesque. In fact the movie is not so much primarily about Buffalo Bill Cody – or Sitting Bull – as it is a debunking of the Wild West show, dime novels and other representations of the

Erwin E. Smith, 'Frank Smith watering his horse, Cross-B Ranch, New Mexico' (c.1910)

heroic West. In assembling the cast of the show for a group portrait, one of the characters says, 'A hundred years from now this picture will still be in existence. This is the way people will remember you,' and it is such reasoning that leads Sitting Bull (an obvious representative of the victims of western appropriation in all its forms) to demand from Cody the retention of his legal control of his own photographs. As it happens, due to the sudden arrival of a messenger with the news that the President is on his way to visit the show, the photograph is never taken. However, at the very end of the film, the still image under the credits is precisely the group portrait that might have been; it does, and does not, exist. This playfulness offers an insight into the special position of photographs – and certainly, of western photographs: they give such a powerful illusion of reality, seemingly the light itself of eighty or a hundred years ago, and yet we also *know*, simultaneously, that we cannot always believe all that we see in a photograph. MG

Butch and Sundance: the Early Days/1979/ FOX/d Richard Lester/lp William Katt, Tom Berenger, Jeff Corey · (For further illustrations see entries on individual photographers and on *Agriculture, Butch *Cassidy, *Cowboys, *Railroads.)

Pierce, Shanghai [Abel Head] (1834-1900) · Texas rancher who built up a huge cattle empire and a personal reputation to go with it in the years following the Civil War and who is credited with introducing the Brahman breed to America. According to reliable testimony Pierce never carried a gun, except during his celebrated feud with Colonel Miller of the 101 Ranch. Charlie *Siringo worked for him and wrote about Pierce in his book *A Texas Cowboy* (1885). As played

Andrew J. Russell, 'Temporary and permanent bridge and Citadel Rock, Green River, Wyoming' (1867)

by Ted De Corsia in *Gunfight at the O.K. Corral*/1956 Pierce is somewhat rumbustious (he lets his cowboys have fun breaking up a church social) but ultimately has the good sense not to cross Wyatt Earp.

Pinkerton Detective Agency · Founded by Allan Pinkerton (1819-84), a Scotsman, the Pinkertons became the most significant non-governmental organized force against crime. After the Civil War, during which Pinkerton helped organize the Union's secret service, the agency became notorious for its strike-breaking activities, notably in the 'Molly Maguires' dispute of 1874-5 and later in both railroad and mining strikes in the West. Its popularity with the public, never high, sank to a new low as a result of an attack on the *James gang in 1875. A bomb was thrown into a cabin where the James boys were mistakenly believed to be hiding. It killed the James' eight-year-old half-brother and tore the arm off their mother. Pinkerton men make occasional appearances in film biographies of badmen, pursuing, besides the James brothers, Sam Bass, the Younger gang and the Wild Bunch. In *Jesse James*/1939 and *The True Story of Jesse James*/1957 the agency's name is changed to Remington.

Pinkerton trade-mark

Playbill · The Western is the only cinematic genre to have its own typeface. The modern Playbill was developed from a variety of nineteenth-century faces such as French Antique and Italian, originally cut in wood. Its distinctive characteristic is that the serifs are heavier than the main strokes. As the name Playbill suggests, such faces were employed in the 19th century for theatrical posters and other public announcements. Playbill has come to be associated with the Western and the West in general, possibly as a result of its use in the 'Wanted' posters of the period. It can be seen in the opening titles of many of John Ford's films, as well as scores of others.

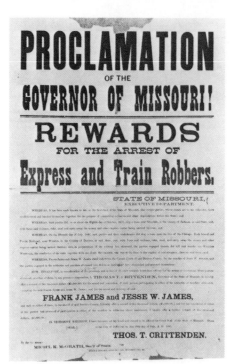

Wanted poster for the James brothers (3rd and 6th lines set in Playbill)

Plots · Frank Gruber, an experienced writer of Westerns, believed there were only seven basic plots. The first is the cavalry and Indians story. Second is the Union Pacific or Pony Express theme, 'where you are fighting the elements of nature to build a business or some other big project.' Then there's the homesteaders story, the conflict between cattlemen and farmers. There's the dedicated lawman story and also the story 'humanizing or glorifying some outlaw'. Next is 'the revenge theme', and then the empire story, which has 'the builder of a ranch or a way of life threatened with decline because of an outside threat or maybe a weak second generation.'

This leaves a few films unaccounted for. Where would *The Covered Wagon*/1923 fit in? And the 'revenge theme' is surely a category of a different kind, not specific to the Western. Another historian who has produced a taxonomy of Western stories is William K. Everson. In *A Pictorial History of the Western Film* he separates out from plots what he calls 'themes', examples of which would be 'the wagon train or cattle herd trek or the building of a railroad'. He then identifies twelve different plot variations. The first is the one about the hero cleaning up a town in the grip of crooked saloon owners or whatever. Second is the cattle baron greedy for power. Then there are the three reasons why the villain may want to get

settlers off their land: he wants to control the water rights; gold or other minerals have been discovered; or the railroad is coming through. In the sixth kind of plot a lawman joins an outlaw band in order to defeat it. Next is the 'Reconstruction' Western, with carpetbaggers and outlaws terrorizing the country. In the eighth type of plot someone, usually a crooked Indian agent, is stirring up the Indians. Another plot has a hero who has been framed and is trying to clear his name. Tenth comes the range war, eleventh the problems of running a stage line or other enterprise, and lastly the hero's search for the murderer of his father.

Everson's breakdown is based in large part on the B-Western, where character motivation is unambiguous and the world divides neatly into goodies and baddies. His focus on villainy as the motor of the plot works well enough to produce a typology of this kind of film. But it simply doesn't cover enough Westerns. Could a film like *The Unforgiven*/1959, where the racial conflict on which the plot turns is not villainy of the kind he describes, be assigned to any of Everson's categories?

John Tuska in *The American West in Film* also finds seven basic narratives:
1) The Pioneer Achievement story. This includes the construction of railroads and building up a cattle empire.
2) Picaresque Wanderers and Searchers. This can mean just looking for someone or something, or it can be combined with revenge.
3) The Ranch story or Town story, involving conflicts between settlers and cattlemen, etc.
4) The Justice/Revenge theme.
5) The Indian story. (In Tuska's view this is mainly the anti-Indian story.)
6) The Outlaw story, usually about a man who is unjustly forced outside the law.
7) The Lawman story, in which justice is imposed.

Tuska then argues that all seven plot types can be reduced to a single basic situation: 'There is a conflict in the community. The hero eventually decides to take part in the conflict and his involvement precipitates the death-struggle between himself and one or more villains.'

Tuska's attempt at identifying a Western ur-narrative is nothing if not bold, and it is possible with a bit of push and shove to fit a good many Westerns into some such schema. Unfortunately for his argument, there are plenty of examples which resist it. Do Butch Cassidy and the Sundance Kid (in the Newman and Redford version) choose the community? In many Italian Westerns it is difficult to identify a community at all. In fact the idea of the reluctant hero who eventually sides with the community sounds suspiciously like an abstraction from *Shane*/ 1952, a film so often, because of its 'classic' status, the source of rash generalizations about what the Western essentially is.

Plummer, Henry (c.1837-64) · Robber. Apparently a plausible and charming man, in 1862 Plummer got himself elected sheriff of Bannack in the gold-mining area of Montana. During a two-year period he and his gang, calling themselves The Innocents, robbed and murdered over one hundred people. Eventually local citizens formed a vigilante band and tracked down and hanged twenty of the gang, including Plummer himself. Plummer supplies the historical origin, if one is needed, for the character of the outwardly honest sheriff who is an undercover criminal; a figure familiar from such B-Westerns as *Black Hills Express*/1943/REP/d John English/*lp* Don Barry. Zane Grey's *The Border Legion* (1916), several times filmed, is based on Plummer's career.

Pontiac's Rebellion (1763-5) · Pontiac was a leader of the Ottawa Indians, who inhabited eastern Michigan in the second half of the 18th century. During the wars between the French and the British the Ottawa sided with the French. Lord Amherst's harsh policies towards the Indians provoked unrest in 1762 and in May of the following year Pontiac led an attack against Fort Detroit, resulting in a siege that lasted until October. Although Fort Detroit was not taken, several other forts were and the British were forced back in the West. But support for the rebellion gradually faded away and the tribes eventually made peace. Pontiac was murdered by an Illinois Indian in 1769. Major Robert Rogers, the soldier who is the hero of King Vidor's *Northwest Passage*/1940, based on the novel by Kenneth *Roberts, wrote a play, *Ponteach, or the Savages of America* (1766), claimed to be the first American play about Indians, though it was never produced. In it Pontiac emerges, in Richard Slotkin's words, as 'a kind of Arthurian figure ... a symbolic distillation of actual or potential American virtues.'
Some of the events of Pontiac's Rebellion are recounted in *The Conspiracy of Pontiac*/ 1910/Kalem/d Sidney Olcott · *Winners of the Wilderness*/1926/MGM/d W. S. Van Dyke/*lp* Tim McCoy, Joan Crawford, with Chief Big Tree as Pontiac ·

Unconquered/1947 · *The Battles of Chief Pontiac*/1952/Realart/d Felix Feist/*lp* Lex Barker, with Lon Chaney as Pontiac

Pony Express · Despite its fame, a short-lived and financially unsuccessful attempt to set up a regular fast mail service across the West. The Pony Express was inaugurated on 3 April 1860 by the firm of Russell, Majors and Waddell, who hoped to win the government mail contract away from the more southerly route followed by the stage-coaches of the Butterfield Overland Mail. Way stations were established every ten miles on the route between St Joseph, Missouri and Sacramento, California and the service took thirteen days. Its fate was sealed by the transcontinental telegraph, which was already under construction when the Pony Express began. The telegraph was completed on 24 October 1861 and the Pony Express abandoned two days later.

Undoubtedly the fame of the Pony Express owes much more to its best-known rider than to any intrinsic importance in the venture. Buffalo Bill *Cody was a rider at the age of fourteen and the Pony Express regularly featured as one of the acts of his Wild West show. In the cinema, the short life of the Pony Express has not prevented the myth of the venture from being exploited to the full. At the beginning of *She Wore a Yellow Ribbon*/1949 Pony Express riders are shown carrying the news of Custer's death, which occurred some fifteen years after the service was abandoned.

The subject was one of the most popular in the early Western, appearing as early as 1907, when Kalem produced *The Pony Express*, and in 1909 Edwin S. Porter made a film for Edison with the same title. Two years later the Nestor company also produced *The Pony Express*. Selig made *Saved by the Pony Express* in 1911 and Kalem followed with *The Pony Express Girl* in 1912. Many Western stars were attracted to the subject, including Broncho Billy Anderson, Tom Mix, Harry Carey, Hoot Gibson, Tim McCoy, Buck Jones, Roy Rogers, Bill Elliott and Gene Autry.

Populism · Populism was both a political philosophy and the creed of a party. The philosophy may doubtless be traced back beyond the 19th century, but Populism as an organized movement came into being during the last two decades before 1900. It originated as a response on the part of the agricultural regions of the United States (that is, primarily of the South and the

West) to the dominance which industrial capitalism and those who controlled it had come to assume over the affairs of the nation. Worsening economic conditions for farmers towards the end of the century helped fuel resentment against those they saw as responsible for their plight; especially the banks, railroads and other elements of big business. While falling some way short of socialism (though it did call for the nationalization of the means of transport and communication), Populism for a time articulated a kind of class as well as regional consciousness. The Populist candidate, General Weaver, did well enough in the Presidential election of 1892 to suggest that a third party could break the mould of the two-party system. In 1896, when William Jennings Bryan became the Democratic candidate for president, it seemed as though the Populists could dictate the platform of a major party. But Bryan had become obsessed by the issue of the free coinage of silver, a monetarist panacea which had become a plank of Populist economic policy. At the Democratic convention he made his speech containing the famous phrase: 'You shall not press down upon the brow of labor this crown of thorns, you shall not crucify mankind upon a cross of gold.' This may sound like a plea to put human values above economics but in fact it was a call for the currency to be based on silver instead of gold, on the grounds that this would produce freer credit and help the western states (who also produced all the silver). In the event William McKinley defeated Bryan in the election, which proved to be a watershed. Gradually the Populist thrust diminished.

In a sense, perhaps, the Western genre is inherently populist, in that it values the experience of the West over that of the East. More specifically, we may discern some trace of populist sentiment in any film with a conflict between small farmers and big land-owners, or which presents unsympathetically a banker or a businessman or which touches on the unscrupulousness of the railroad magnates. By this token *Shane*/1952 and *Heaven's Gate*/1980, *Stagecoach*/1939, *Jesse James*/1939 and *C'era una volta il west*/ 1968 all draw on the politics of Populism.

Posse · 'Who *are* those guys?' Butch Cassidy wonders, gazing back at the body of horsemen who keep on coming after him and Sundance. The answer is, to judge from most of the posses who appear in Westerns: a group at best incompetent, at worst as criminal as those they are chasing. Despite all the talk of law and order, when a few are pursued by the many the Western seems instinctively to side with the underdog. Rarely is the posse (from the Latin *posse comitatus*, meaning 'a force of the county') worthy of its task. When not simply a lynch mob, as in *The Ox-Bow Incident*/1942 or *Johnny Guitar*/1954, they turn out to be more interested in the loot than in justice; as in *The Last Posse* or *Bullet for a Badman*. This is taken to its logical extreme in *Posse*/1975, in which Bruce Dern turns his pursuers into a replacement for the gang they have destroyed.

The Last Posse/1953/COL/d Alfred Werker/ *lp* Broderick Crawford, John Derek, Charles Bickford · *Bullet for a Badman*/ 1964/U/d R. G. Springsteen/*lp* Audie Murphy, Darren McGavin

Powell, John Wesley (1834-1902) · Explorer and scientist. Powell lost part of his right arm at the Battle of Shiloh but became a self-taught scientist and explorer. His major expedition in 1869 was the navigation of the turbulent waters of the Colorado River, including the passage of the Grand Canyon. Powell and his party, in four small boats, journeyed a thousand miles in three months. Powell later became head of the United States Geological Survey and a major advocate of conservationist policies in the West.

A Disney film with John Beal as John Wesley Powell centres on the journey down the Colorado: *Ten Who Dared*/1960/Buena Vista/d William Beaudine/*lp* Brian Keith.

Prostitution · The tart with a heart has been as appealing a stereotype in the Western as in any other kind of popular fiction. She makes an early appearance in the stories of Bret *Harte, from where it is a short jump to the dance-halls and gambling dens of W.S. Hart's films, which are well peopled with the 'soiled doves' of Victorian melodrama. Until the 1960s prostitutes had to be referred to under some such euphemism as 'saloon girl'; once the last vestiges of the Hays Code had been swept away Hollywood was freed from such hypocrisies. Suddenly every Western town contained, beside its bank, jail, saloon and livery stable, a brothel too. Not all of them were as opulent and wholesome as the one James Stewart inherits in *The Cheyenne Social Club*; though few were as realistically sordid as the one at the back of Kate's saloon in *Ride the High Country*/1962.

Prostitution, which was rife on a frontier where men invariably outnumbered women, could have had little about it that was glamorous. Why then the succession of sympathetic whores who parade through the Western of the 70s? Possibly, besides expressing the fantasies of (male) filmmakers, they reflect the difficulty of finding other interesting and plausible roles for women in a male-dominated genre. Among those who made the most of their opportunity once the prostitute was allowed to 'come out' are Claudia Cardinale in *C'era una volta il west*/1968, Shirley MacLaine in *Two Mules for Sister Sara*/1969, Stella Stevens in *The Ballad of Cable Hogue*/1970, Jeanne Moreau in *Monte Walsh*/1970, Faye Dunaway in *Little Big Man*/1970, Julie Christie in *McCabe & Mrs. Miller*/1971 and Isabelle Huppert in *Heaven's Gate*/1980.

The Cheyenne Social Club/1970/National General/d Gene Kelly/*lp* James Stewart, Henry Fonda

Q

Quanah Parker (c.1845-1911) · Comanche chief, the son of a white captive mother and Indian father and the leader of those Comanches who refused to retreat to the reservation after the Medicine Lodge Treaty of 1867. He led his band against a group of buffalo hunters at the Battle of Adobe Walls in 1874, but the following year surrendered to the army. Once settled on the reservation he adapted to the political structure and worked to get the best deal when the government wished to negotiate away Indian land rights in 1892. Culturally he was a conservative, refusing assimilation, and is regarded as the founder of the peyote religion or Native American Church.

John War Eagle/*They Rode West*/1954/COL/ d Phil Karlson/*lp* Robert Francis, Donna Reed · Kent Smith/*Comanche*/1955/UA/d George Sherman/*lp* Dana Andrews · Henry Brandon/*Two Rode Together*/1961

Quantrill, William Clark (1837-65) · Guerrilla leader. The principal figure in the bitter and bloody border wars in Kansas and Missouri before and during the Civil War. Quantrill organized a band of irregulars which harried Union forces and anti-slavery civilians. On the northern side an equivalent band, named the Jayhawkers and led by Charles Jennison, skirmished against the Confederates. Jennison was so brutal in his attacks against civilians that in 1862 he was removed from command and the Jayhaw-

kers redeployed east of the Mississippi. Another irregular Northern force, known as the 'Red Legs' and led by George Hoyt, re-emerged in 1863.

Quantrill's Raiders were eventually commissioned into the regular Confederate army. On 21 August 1863 Captain Quantrill, as he now was, led his men in the infamous attack on Lawrence, Kansas in which 150 civilians were massacred. Quantrill himself was fatally wounded in Kentucky in May 1865, but he left as a legacy a band of young men, trained in guerrilla warfare and embittered by defeat. Among them were the *James brothers and the *Youngers.

In the movies Quantrill himself (sometimes called Quantrell or Cantrell) poses a problem. Westerns usually side with the South; yet to make the bloodthirsty Quantrill a heroic figure would strain the bounds of poetic licence. The usual solution is to play down Quantrill's political motivations and present him as driven by purely selfish ambition, thus leaving intact the credentials of the Southern cause he fought for.

Quantrell's Son/1914/Vitagraph/d Robert T. Thornby · Walter Pidgeon/*Dark Command*/1940/REP/d Raoul Walsh/*lp* John Wayne, Claire Trevor · Ray Corrigan/ *Renegade Girl*/1946/Screen Guild/d William Berke/*lp* Alan Curtis · Brian Donlevy/*Kansas Raiders*/1950/U/d Ray Enright/*lp* Audie Murphy · John Ireland/ *Red Mountain*/1951/PAR/d William Dieterle/*lp* Alan Ladd, Lizabeth Scott · Reed Hadley/*Kansas Pacific*/1953/AA/d Ray Nazzaro/*lp* Sterling Hayden · Brian Donlevy/*The Woman They Almost Lynched*/ 1953/REP/d Allan Dwan/*lp* Joan Leslie, John Lund · Leo Gordon/*Quantrill's Raiders*/1958/AA/d Edward Bernds/*lp* Steve Cochran · Emile Meyer/*Young Jesse James*/ 1960/FOX/d William Claxton/*lp* Ray Stricklyn · Fred Graham/*Arizona Raiders*/ 1965/Admiral/d William Witney/*lp* Audie Murphy, Buster Crabbe · Bill Ferrill/*Ride a Wild Stud*/1969/Vega International/d Revilo Ekard/*lp* Hale Williams
Television · Bruce Bennett/*Stories of the Century* · Peter Whitney/*The Legend of Jesse James* · Robert Davi/*Legend of the Golden Gun*

R

Radio · One of the first Western series on the radio began in 1930 and featured a character who was to become one of the most famous fictional cowboys. *The Lone*

Quanah Parker sitting next to a portrait of his mother (c.1891)

ern series in 1949. *Riders of the Range*, based on the comic strip in *The Eagle*, featured the adventures of Jeff Arnold, an easy-going young cowboy, played by Paul Carpenter. In the early 1960s the BBC decided to try a run of the radio version of *Gunsmoke*, with William Conrad as Matt Dillon. Though popular, this was the last Western series on British radio. Radio Westerns include:

The Lone Ranger (1930)
Death Valley Days (1930)
The Tom Mix Straightshooters (1933)
Renfrew of the Mounted (1936) *lp* House Jameson
Hoofbeats (1937) *lp* Buck Jones
The Johnny Mack Brown Show (1939)
Sergeant Preston (1939)
Gene Autry's Melody Ranch (1940)
The Cisco Kid (1942)
Red Ryder (1942)
Death Valley Sheriff (1944)
The Roy Rogers Show (1944)
Destiny's Trails (1945) *lp* Stacy Harris
Sky King (1946)
Hawk, Durango (1946) *lp* Elliott Lewis
Hawk, Larabee (1947) *lp* Barton Yarborough
The Adventures of Champion (1949) *lp* Gene Autry
Hopalong Cassidy (1949) *lp* William Boyd
Curly Bradley, the Singing Marshal (1950) *lp* Curly Bradley
Tales of the Texas Rangers (1950) *lp* Joel McCrea
Wild Bill Hickok (1952) *lp* Guy Madison
Frontier Town (1952) *lp* Jeff Chandler
The Six Shooter (1953) *lp* James Stewart
Gunsmoke (1954) *lp* William Conrad
Fort Laramie (1955) *lp* Raymond Burr
Frontier Gentleman (1958) *lp* John Dehner
Have Gun, Will Travel (1958) *lp* John Dehner
(Variety shows have been excluded unless they starred movie actors.) TM

Railroads · It is no surprise that the first true Western, *The Great Train Robbery*/1903, should have been a railroad picture. Trains provided the inspiration for dozens of plays, ballads and dime novels in the last quarter of the 19th century. In the theatre startlingly realistic effects were achieved as smoking engines careered across the stage and bandits blew up mail cars with explosives. In *The Fast Mail*, produced in 1899, two trains chased one another across the stage. Buffalo Bill added the robbery of a Union Pacific train to the programme of his *Wild West show. And *The Great Train Robbery* was itself a play before it became a film.

America's love affair with the railroad had begun as soon as the first passenger train

Ranger, created by Fran Striker and George W. Trendle, continued its stories of the mysterious masked rider and his faithful Indian companion Tonto for over twenty years. Many of the top Western stars of the 30s and 40s appeared on the radio. Some, like Gene Autry, Roy Rogers and Johnny Mack Brown, played in variety shows, others such as Buck Jones, Joel McCrea and James Stewart appeared in drama series. With the end of the B-Western in the early 1950s and the rise of the TV Western, the radio era ended, although for a time radio shows were turned into TV series. Occasio-

nally the two ran side by side, even with the same actor in both, as for example with *The Adventures of Wild Bill Hickok* and *Hopalong Cassidy*. In the case of *Have Gun, Will Travel* the reverse happened, with a radio version produced as a result of the TV series' success.

Only a few of these radio shows crossed the Atlantic to Britain, and these were mainly played on the commercial station Radio Luxemburg. Among these were *Steve Larabee* in 1952, followed by *Hopalong Cassidy*, with William Boyd. *Western Trail*, in 1959, was the last of the Luxemburg Westerns. BBC radio had produced its own West-

MAJOR WESTERN RAILROADS BY 1900

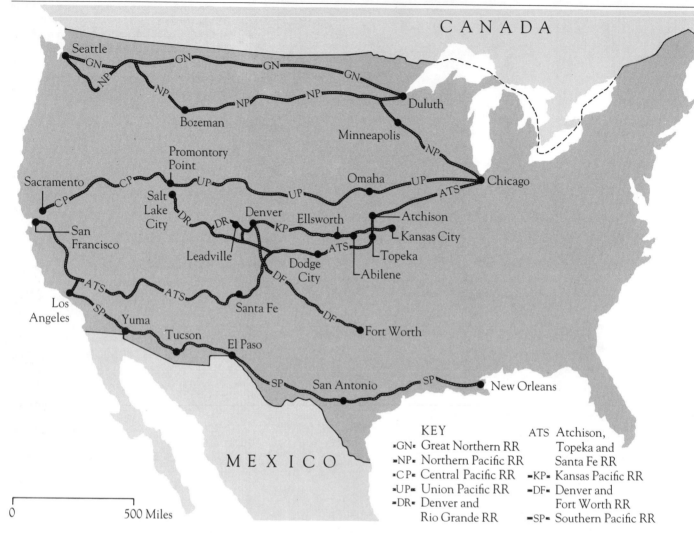

KEY
- **GN** Great Northern RR
- **NP** Northern Pacific RR
- **CP** Central Pacific RR
- **UP** Union Pacific RR
- **DR** Denver and Rio Grande RR
- **ATS** Atchison, Topeka and Santa Fe RR
- **KP** Kansas Pacific RR
- **DF** Denver and Fort Worth RR
- **SP** Southern Pacific RR

0   500 Miles

entered service, in Charleston, South Carolina in 1831. Visionaries such as Asa Whitney (1797-1872) were soon calling for a railroad to link the Atlantic with the Pacific. After years of argument about the best route to follow, Abraham Lincoln signed the Pacific Railroad Act in July 1862. It provided for a start to be made at each end by two separate companies, the *Union Pacific, originating in Omaha, Nebraska, and the *Central Pacific, which started in Sacramento, California.

Construction was to be financed by a system of loans and land grants. The Government lent the companies $16,000 a mile across the plains, $32,000 in the Great Basin area and $48,000 over the mountains. In addition it granted alternate sections of land ten miles square on either side of the track. This land could be sold to settlers and so help finance the enterprise.

Progress at first was slow, because of the difficulty of raising capital at a time when the Civil War promised entrepreneurs quicker profits elsewhere. The war also meant shortages of materials and labour. Even when the financing problems were solved the hostility of much of the terrain was a severe challenge to the engineering techniques of the time. The Central Pacific had first to tackle the Sierras, which required dozens of tunnels and bridges. A scarcity of labour obliged the contractors to experiment with *Chinese workers, despite the violent prejudices against them at the time. So effective were they that more were imported from mainland China.

On the Union Pacific side the largest single group of workers were the Irish. Though the country to be traversed was at first flat or gently rolling plains, the logistical problems were immense. Everything had to

be hauled hundreds of miles from the east, including the ties (or sleepers), since the few poor trees of the area were useless for this purpose. The weather was often atrocious, and there was the constant threat of Indian attack, though actual encounters were fewer than fiction suggests.

Towns such as Ogallala and Julesberg, Laramie and Cheyenne mushroomed as the railroad passed through, though many fell back into obscurity once the construction crews passed by. Many of the facilities which the track-layers required, including those for recreation, were housed in a temporary town of tents and shacks, known as 'hell on wheels', which could be packed up and re-erected as the line moved on.

At last, nearly seven years after the enterprise had begun, the Union Pacific and Central Pacific tracks were joined, at Promontory Point, Utah, on 10 May 1869. Leland

*Stanford, the Governor of California and one of the directors of the Central Pacific, helped drive in the last ceremonial golden spikes, assisted by Thomas Durant for the U.P. Within twenty years the total amount of track laid west of the Mississippi had risen to 72,000 miles. The Southern Pacific completed a transcontinental link in 1883, and the Northern Pacific in the same year. Two years later came the *Atchison, Topeka and Santa Fe. In order to get them built Congress had been obliged to make land grants to the companies totalling 181 million acres, more than three times the size of Utah. The only railroad to be built without such grants, the Great Northern, was completed in 1893.

Despite these huge public subsidies – and in part because of them – the finances of the railroads were in constant turmoil. Speculators such as Jay *Gould were attracted to railroads not by the prospect of profits from running a passenger and freight service, but by the riches promised by the exploitation of the land grant and by manipulating the price of company stock. The most notorious railroad scandal of the era involved the Credit Mobilier, a company set up by the Union Pacific to carry out the construction of its track. It was revealed that the directors of U.P. contracted with Credit Mobilier at a price well above what the latter needed to spend on laying the track. The difference was pocketed by the directors, leaving the dividends of ordinary shareholders depressed by the artificially high price paid for construction.

Railroad companies were also heavily involved in the graft which became endemic in the so-called Gilded Age. Congressmen by the dozen were suborned in order to pass legislation favourable to the companies. Suspicion reached all the way up to President Grant, and James Garfield, a future President, received gifts of Union Pacific stock.

Despite the financial skulduggery, the railroad had initially been equated with progress, and even with the democratic impulse itself. The statesman Daniel Webster had declared that it would 'equalize the condition of men'. But as popular experience of railroads grew, hostility arose, especially in the West. The monopolistic power which each company exercised in the country through which it ran led to accusations of high-handedness and profiteering. In the 1870s the Granger movement, an association dedicated to the economic and social advancement of farmers, managed to push through several western legislatures laws regulating freight rates and in other

Trains in Buffalo Bill's Wild West (poster, 1907)

ways curbing the power of the railroads. Far from the railroad bringing prosperity and progress to all, it was charged, 'the history of the present railroad monopoly is a history of repeated injuries and oppressions, all having in direct object the establishment of an absolute tyranny over all the people of these States.' The *Populist party continued this struggle into the 1890s, and by the end of the century Frank *Norris could write in *The Octopus*, his novel about the Southern Pacific, of 'the terror of steel and steam with a single eye, cyclopean, red, shooting from

Andrew J. Russell, 'Iron trussed span, Weber Canyon, Utah, 1869'

Andrew J. Russell, 'East and West Shaking Hands, 10 May 1869'

horizon to horizon ... the symbol of a vast power, huge, terrible, flinging the echo of its thunder over all the reaches of the valley, leaving blood and destruction in its path, the leviathan with tentacles of steel clutching into the soil, the soulless force, the ironhearted power, the monster, the colossus, the octopus.'

In the Western the symbolic significance of the railroad has described a similar trajectory. Of course not all films make trains into symbols. Often the train or the *station itself functions merely as a particularly satisfying décor around which to focus the story, as in *High Noon*/1952 or *3:10 to Yuma*/1957. Those early films which take a positive view of the place of the railroad within the history of the West often make an epic out of its construction against heroic odds. The first of these is *The Iron Horse*/1924. The scope of Ford's film is vast, beginning with Lincoln's early experiences in Springfield (his endorsement of the project rendering it above criticism), and encompassing the Chinese and the Irish, battles against Indians, driving cattle up from Texas to feed the crews, appearances by Buffalo Bill and Wild Bill Hickok and much else besides. For Ford the railroad symbolizes the unity of the nation, the 'buckle in the girdle of America', as the hero puts it. The villains of the film are not the crooked financiers of the railroad itself, but merely some local land speculators trying to ensure the track passes through their holdings.

Cecil B. DeMille's *Union Pacific*/1939 ends, like Ford's film, with the ceremony at Promontory Point. This time the villain is a Chicago speculator who has bought stock in the rival Central Pacific and will make money if the eventual link-up point is

further east than Ogden (because the C.P. will get bigger land grants for laying more track). He therefore attempts to disrupt the U.P. construction programme by employing gamblers and whiskey sellers to distract the predominantly Irish workforce. In De-Mille's film the enterprise of building the railroad has three purposes. It will provide work for unemployed soldiers, and help boost trade (thus the film displays the economic preoccupations of the Depression, when it was made); and it will unite the country in the wake of a divisive Civil War.

A scene at the start of the contemporaneous *Dodge City*/1939 features a race between a train and a stagecoach. Aboard the train is Colonel Grenville Dodge (an army officer who became the Union Pacific's chief engineer). When the train has won the race he exclaims, 'Gentlemen, that's a symbol of America's future. Iron men and iron horses – you can't beat 'em.' Once in Dodge City (named after him on the spot at the instigation of Errol Flynn), Dodge makes a speech about the blessings of civilization, in which key words such as 'home', 'church' and 'school' ring out like bells.

This enthusiasm in the Western for the railroad as the bringer of progress continued into the next two decades. In *Duel in the Sun*/1946 it is the civilized and gentle lawyer Jesse (Joseph Cotten) who favours its arrival, while his father, a bullying and backward-looking cattle baron (Lionel Barrymore), refuses to allow it on his land. Similarly, in *Johnny Guitar*/1954 it is the local land-owners, led by Mercedes McCambridge, who attempt to prevent the railroad coming to town, because it will encourage immigration from the east. 'Dirt farmers, is that what you want?' she screams at Joan Craw-

ford, who has built her saloon as a speculation on the railroad's arrival.

In *Carson City*/1951 Randolph Scott is a railroad engineer given the job of constructing a route from Virginia City to Carson City. Some of the townspeople don't want it, fearful that the railroad will bring in the wrong sort of people. But Scott brushes these misgivings aside, remarking that there are bound to be growing pains in the march of progress. The actual technology of track-laying is powerfully presented in scenes of steam-driven drills biting through solid rock.

Yet well before this an alternative view of the railroad company had emerged in the Western. Beginning with *Jesse James*/1939, practically every film which attempted to deal with the historical facts surrounding the life of the West's most famous outlaw incorporated the anti-railroad feeling embedded in the Jesse *James legend. Railroads are legitimate targets, since they are viewed as monopolies dedicated to the oppression of the farmer, and Yankee ones at that. As the opening titles to *Jesse James* put it: 'The advance of the railroads was, in some cases, predatory and unscrupulous. Whole communities found themselves victimized by an ever-growing ogre – the Iron Horse.'

This view becomes an even more explicit and central theme in some Westerns of the 1960s and 1970s. In *The Professionals*/1966 a railroad magnate hires the heroes to rescue his wife from captivity. They oblige him to surrender his wife again when they discover she would prefer to stay with her bandit captor. The values of the railroad baron and of corporate capitalism are contrasted with the sense of honour and loyalty and the

The ceremony at Promontory Point in The Iron Horse

The ceremony at Promontory Point in Union Pacific

independence of spirit which the heroes, free agents to a man, display.

A similar contrast, though expressed in a more light-hearted manner, informs *Butch Cassidy and the Sundance Kid*/1969, as the pair hold up trains and lead the pursuing Pinkertons a merry dance around the West. In the same year *The Wild Bunch*/1969 painted an altogether more bitter contrast between its noble but doomed heroes and the dregs of society who have been hired by the railroad to hunt them down. By now the railroad represents not merely a soulless and oppressive monopoly; it has come to symbolize all the forces which threaten to bring about the end of the West.

The summation of this perspective on the railroad is Leone's *C'era una volta il west*/1968, which sets out systematically to deconstruct *The Iron Horse* (as well as, in its opening sequence, providing an amusing parody of *High Noon*). The villain of the film is Morton (Gabriele Ferzetti), the consumptive capitalist whose dream is to spread his railroad over the whole of the West and who sits like a diseased spider at the heart of his network. Henry Fonda, Fordian hero *par excellence*, is Frank, the mercenary hired by Morton (whose name surely carries an echo of death) to execute those who stand in the way of his ambitions. Leone's target is not merely the arrogant power of monopoly, but capitalism itself and even the very idea of technological progress.

Raine, William MacLeod (1871-1954) · Author. Raine produced over seventy Western novels and achieved great popularity both in Britain and America during the 1910s and 20s with his solidly constructed stories of upright heroes defending the besieged virtue of wilting heroines. Courage is the most highly prized quality; in *The Fighting Edge* (1922) the young hero is shamed by a moment of cowardice but through an effort of will nerves himself to confront a bully in a final showdown. Raine's novels formed the basis of some Tom Mix and Buck Jones Westerns, including: *Fighting for Gold*/1919/FOX/*d* Edward J. LeSaint/*lp* Tom Mix · *Hands Off*/1921/FOX/*d* George Marshall/*lp* Tom Mix · *The Big Town Roundup*/1921/FOX/*d* Lynn Reynolds/*lp* Tom Mix · *The Desert's Price*/1925/FOX/*d* W.S. Van Dyke/*lp* Buck Jones · *A Man Four-Square*/1926/FOX/*d* R. William Neill/*lp* Buck Jones

Rape · Although rape may be the act round which the plot sometimes pivots, Westerns don't examine the experience, or the consequences except in one respect: rape is the occasion for the outraged to seek revenge. Until very recently this was invariably the task of the man; as in *Rancho Notorious*/1952, *The Bravados*, *Last Train from Gun Hill*/1958, *The Magnificent Seven Ride!* In what some might see as a feminist variation, Raquel Welch seeks her own revenge in *Hannie Caulder*/1971. The erosion of censorship in the 1960s led, predictably, not to a deeper exploration of the theme of sexual aggression, merely to more graphic gratification of the (male) spectator's voyeurism, as in the rape of Charles Bronson's wife in *Chato's Land*.

Rape is also what is ultimately at stake in the Indian *captivity narrative; to be raped by Indians is indeed the 'fate worse than death' which the Victorians could not bring themselves to name. The Western established early the convention whereby the woman saves the last bullet for herself; it's used by D. W. Griffith in *The Battle at Elderbush Gulch*/1913. In *Stagecoach*/1939 John Carradine is just about to administer the last bullet to the army officer's wife when he is shot. In *Winchester '73*/1950, when the Indians attack Shelley Winters doesn't have to be told; 'I know about the last bullet,' she says as James Stewart hands her the gun. *The Bravados*/1958/FOX/*d* Henry King/*lp* Gregory Peck, Joan Collins · *Chato's Land*/1971/GB/*d* Michael Winner/*lp* Charles Bronson, Jack Palance · *The Magnificent Seven Ride!*/1972/UA/*d* George McCowan/*lp* Lee Van Cleef, Stephanie Powers

Red Cloud (Makhpiya-Luta) (1822-1909) · A leader of the Oglala branch of the Teton Sioux. In 1866 the United States army attempted to open the Bozeman trail, which crossed the Sioux hunting preserve and led from Julesberg, Colorado, through the Powder River country to the goldfields at Virginia City, Montana. Red Cloud led the Indians' resistance in what became known as Red Cloud's War (1866-8). Forts along the trail were besieged and Red Cloud, a fierce fighter and skilled tactician, was responsible for the action which wiped out Lieutenant-Colonel William Fetterman and eighty of his men near Fort Phil Kearny on 21 December 1866. As a result the army were forced to abandon their forts and close the trail. In 1871 Red Cloud retired with some of the Sioux to the agency in Nebraska which the government had created in his name. He took no further part in hostilities between the US government and the Sioux, and this lost him much of his popularity with those who continued to oppose the whites. He nevertheless remained clearsighted about what had been done to his people, as in his famously succinct summary of the whites' behaviour: 'They made us many promises, more than I can remember, but they never kept but one. They promised to take our land, and they took it.'

Red Cloud (1880)

Len Haynes/*Warrior Gap*/1925/Davis/*d* Alvin J. Neitz/*lp* Ben Wilson, Neta Gerber · Chief Big Tree/*Spoilers of the West*/1927/MGM/*d* W.S. Van Dyke/*lp* Tim McCoy · Chief White Eagle/*End of the Trail*/1932/COL/*d* D. Ross Lederman/*lp* Tim McCoy · John War Eagle/*Tomahawk*/1950/U/*d* George Sherman/*lp* Van Heflin · Jay Silverheels/*Jack McCall Desperado*/1952/COL/*d* Sidney Salkow/*lp* George Montgomery · John War Eagle/*The Great Sioux Uprising*/1953/U/*d* Lloyd Bacon/*lp* Jeff Chandler, Faith Domergue · Robert Bice/*The Gun That Won the West*/1955/COL/*d* William Castle/*lp* Dennis Morgan, Paula Raymond · Morris Ankrum/*Chief Crazy Horse*/1955/U/*d* George Sherman/*lp* Victor Mature · Eduard Franz/*The Indian Fighter*/1955 · Manuel Donde/*The Last Frontier*/1955 · Frank de Kova/*Run of the Arrow*/1957 · Eddie Little Sky/*Revolt at Fort Laramie*/1957/Bel-Air/*d* Lesley Selander/*lp* John Dehner
Television · Ned Romero/*Peter Lundy and the Medicine Hat Stallion*

Religion · The Western has been almost entirely a secular genre. In Owen *Wister's *The Virginian* a fundamentalist preacher who visits the ranch is ridiculed by the Virginian, who then expounds his own, much vaguer, religion: '"As for salvation I have got this far: somebody," he swept an arm at the sunset and the mountains, "must have made all that, I know."' With the exception of a few curiosities such as *The Persuader* (1957), which sparked off a small cycle of films made specifically for the midwest Bible Belt, religion as a theme has occupied a minor role. On the other hand there have been priests and parsons in plenty, since the man of the cloth offers rich dramatic opportunities in a world as full of sin as the Western.

In the main they fall into three categories. The first is akin to an Old Testament prophet, preaching woe and damnation and frequently meting out vengeance with the gun. Such is R. G. Armstrong in *Major Dundee*/1964, a role building on his portrayal of the religious zealot in *Ride the High Country*/1962 and reprised in *Pat Garrett and Billy the Kid*/1973. Frequently such characters are tinged with madness, as Robert Mitchum in *5 Card Stud*, Jack Palance in *The Desperados*, Joseph Wiseman in *The Unforgiven*/1959 and Donald Pleasence in *Will Penny*/1967. The latest in this tradition, not deranged but touched with supernatural powers, is Clint Eastwood in *Pale Rider*/1985.

The second category is that of the religious hypocrite. Often it's lechery that contrasts with professed piousness, as with David Warner in *The Ballad of Cable Hogue*/1970, John Carradine in *Five Bloody Graves* and Faye Dunaway (wife of the Rev. Pendrake) in *Little Big Man*/1970. Sometimes it's simple greed. Thus the unctuous Meacham (Grant Withers) in *Fort Apache*/1948 keeps the whiskey he sells to Indians inside a crate marked 'Bibles'. The anti-clericalism common in the Italian Western greatly increased the incidence of holy hypocrites; see, for example, the gluttonous priest in *Giù la testa*/1971.

These first two kinds of characters are usually subsidiary to the main action. The third often takes centre-stage. This is the man who is torn between his vocation as a man of God, and therefore of peace, and the seeming impossibility in the West of adopting a consistent pacifism. This paradox of the gun-slinging or fist-swinging parson appears in *The Disciple*, in which William S. Hart plays Jim Houston, the 'Shootin' Iron

Parson', and is the basis for the drama of *The Parson of Panamint*, *Stars in My Crown* and *Heaven with a Gun*.

It's an indication of how unproblematic religion generally is for John Ford that the contradiction expressed in the title of the Reverend Captain Clayton (Ward Bond) in *The Searchers*/1956 should simply be taken in his stride. So, too, the Mormons of *Wagon Master*/1950 manifest a serenely untroubled confidence in their religion (never in fact discussed). Perhaps the secret of Ford's sunny attitude towards religion lies precisely in his (Catholic?) refusal of the dark, sin-obsessed Old Testament world, an attitude perfectly expressed by Russell Simpson in *My Darling Clementine*/1946: 'I've read the good book from cover to cover and back again and I ain't nairy found one word agin dancin'.' All the more strange that Ford should have directed a version of Graham Greene's *The Power and the Glory*. *The Disciple*/1915/Triangle/d William S. Hart/lp William S. Hart, Dorothy Dalton · *The Parson of Panamint*/1941/PAR/d William McGann/lp Charlie Ruggles, Ellen Drew · *Stars in My Crown*/1949/MGM/d Jacques Tourneur/lp Joel McCrea, Ellen Drew · *The Persuader*/1957/AA/d Dick Ross/lp William Talman, James Craig · *Heaven with a Gun*/1969/MGM/d Lee H. Katzin/lp Glenn Ford, Carolyn Jones · *5 Card Stud*/1968/PAR/d Henry Hathaway/lp Dean Martin, Robert Mitchum · *The Desperados*/1969/COL/d Henry Levin/lp Vince Edwards, Jack Palance · *Five Bloody Graves*/1969/Dix International/d Al Adamson/lp Robert Dix, Scott Brady

Remakes · People who don't like Westerns often say they're all the same. The fact that remakes have been from the beginning common practice in the industry gives some slight credence to this charge. Thus Cecil B. DeMille made three versions of *The Squaw Man* (in 1914, 1918 and 1931), and before being filmed it was already a successful stage

Randolph Scott, Marlene Dietrich, John Wayne in the 1942 version of The Spoilers

play by Edwin Milton Royle (in which W.S. Hart had starred). *The Virginian* was also frequently repeated. Hart starred in the stage version of the best-selling novel by Owen *Wister before it was first brought to the screen in 1914 by Cecil B. DeMille. It was then remade in 1923, 1929 and 1946 before finally (?) being turned into a TV series running from 1962-70. Other notable remakes include *The Spoilers* from Rex *Beach's novel, filmed in 1914, 1923, 1930, 1942 and 1955, and Max *Brand's *Destry Rides Again*, filmed in 1932, 1939 and 1954 and the basis for a TV series in 1964. Many of Zane *Grey's novels were filmed several times. In the 1930s in particular it was common for the stars of series Westerns to remake their films with only a brief space between the two versions. Thus, as Phil Hardy notes, Buck Jones' film *The Fighting Ranger* (1934) is a remake of his own *Border Law* (1931). A high degree of repetition is built into the Western by the fact that so many films are based, albeit loosely, on history. Thus the various versions of the *Billy the Kid story are also in a sense remakes. Sequels such as *Return of the Seven*, *Guns of the Magnificent Seven* and *The Magnificent Seven Ride!* are another way in which the industry has sought security at the box office by combining repetition with variation.

The Squaw Man/1914/Jesse Lasky/d Cecil B. DeMille/lp Dustin Farnum · remade 1918/PAR/d Cecil B. DeMille/lp Elliott Dexter, Jack Holt · remade 1931/MGM/d Cecil B. DeMille/lp Warner Baxter, Lupe Velez · *Border Law*/1931/COL/d Louis King/lp Buck Jones · *The Fighting Ranger*/1934/COL/d George B. Seitz/lp Buck Jones, Dorothy Revier · *Return of the Seven*/1966/UA/d Burt Kennedy/lp Yul Brynner · *Guns of the Magnificent Seven*/1968/UA/d Paul Wendkos/lp George Kennedy · *The Magnificent Seven Ride!*/1972/UA/d George McCowan/lp Lee Van Cleef · For filmographies of *The Virginian*, *The Spoilers*, *Destry Rides Again*, see entries on Owen Wister, Rex Beach, Max Brand

Remington, Frederic Sackrider (1861-1909) · Painter, the most famous of all those who drew and painted the West. After dropping out of Yale, Remington took a trip to Montana at the age of twenty and decided to devote himself to a visual record of the West he felt was already passing away. After a time as an unsuccessful saloon owner and sheep rancher in Kansas, Remington had his first picture published by *Harper's Weekly* in

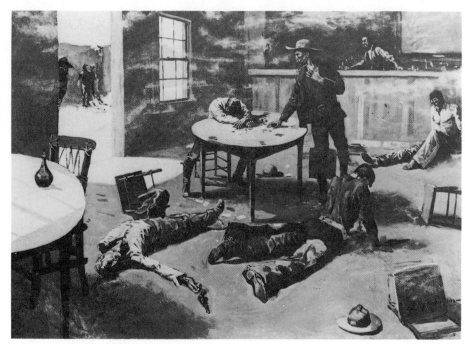

Frederic Remington, 'A Misdeal' (1897)

1886. The same year he toured army outposts in the Southwest and observed General Crook's campaign against Geronimo. Remington's pictures of this for *Harper's* and *Outing* magazines brought him further commissions. He rapidly became one of America's most sought-after illustrators, doing hundreds of pictures for the most popular magazines of the day as well as for books by Theodore *Roosevelt and Owen *Wister. In 1898 during the Spanish-American War he was a war correspondent in Cuba for William Randolph Hearst.

Remington was also an accomplished writer. He published collections of his stories in *Pony Tracks* (1895) and *Crooked Trails* (1898). Increasingly his work was coloured by nostalgia, a sense that the West he loved was doomed to pass away. In 1905 he wrote: 'I knew the railroad was coming. I saw men already swarming into the land. I knew the derby hat, the smoking chimneys, the cordbinder and the thirty-day note were upon us in a restless surge. I knew the wild riders and the vacant land were about to vanish for ever, and the more I considered the subject, the bigger the forever loomed.' His only novel, *John Ermine of the Yellowstone* (1902), about a white boy raised by Indians who becomes an army scout, contains much similar feeling.

Though he produced striking pictures of cowboys and of Indian life, the subject Remington returned to time and again was the United States cavalry and its operations against the Indians, particularly in the Southwest. Remington wanted his epitaph to read 'He knew the horse' and indeed his pictures of horses at the gallop are remarkable for their energy. Remington derived added realism from his study of the photographs of Eadweard *Muybridge. But it is always the human drama, often expressed in the form of an incipient narrative, that is at the centre of his pictures. Unlike most painters of the West, he seems to have been relatively indifferent to the possibilities of the landscape. Remington was one of those mainly responsible for defining, by the end of the 19th century, an idea of the West whose centre was the scene of violent conflict. (See Plates 17, 18, 19)
John Ermine of the Yellowstone/1917/U/d Francis Ford/*lp* Francis Ford, Mae Gaston

Reno gang · Outlaws. The Reno brothers, John, Frank, Simeon and William, committed the first train robbery in the United States on 6 October 1866 near Seymour, Indiana. If this was not technically in the West, those which followed, in Iowa and Missouri, were. John was captured and given forty years in jail; later the Pinkertons arrested the rest of the gang but were unable to prevent them being lynched by vigilantes in New Albany, Indiana in 1868.
Forrest Tucker (Frank), J. Carrol Naish (Sim), Myron Healey (John)/*Rage at Dawn*/1955/RKO/d Tim Whelan/*lp* Randolph Scott · *Johnny Reno*/1965/A. C.

Lyles/*d* R. G. Springsteen/*lp* Dana Andrews, Jane Russell

Revenge · The Western can hardly be credited with inventing the revenge plot; indeed Jacobean drama is virtually founded on it. But revenge as a motive has been more common at certain periods in the Western than at others. In his book *Sixguns and Society* Will Wright finds that vengeance plots proliferated in the 1950s and 1960s, in films such as *Winchester '73*/1950, *The Man from Laramie*/1955, *One-Eyed Jacks*/1960, *Nevada Smith* (1965). Wright sees the revenge plot as a later variation on the classical plot. In the classical plot the hero, who begins outside society, is drawn into it because society is threatened and cannot defend itself without the aid of a strong man. In the revenge plot the hero is forced to leave society in order to pursue his revenge. The villains are still anti-social, but more of a threat to the hero than to society at large, which is now more securely established. In pursuing his revenge he is in conflict with the values of society, which would prefer him to renounce private violence. The revenge plot therefore points to an increasing incompatibility between the hero and society. This becomes overt in the next development, that of the 'professional' plot, in which the heroes are pursuing their own goals and are largely independent of society. Somewhat controversially, Wright relates these developments to changes in American society, as it moves away from an individualistic, market-oriented structure towards a managed economy and the emergence of élites.
Nevada Smith/1965/Avco/*d* Henry Hathaway/*lp* Steve McQueen, Karl Malden

Rhodes, Eugene Manlove (1869-1934) · Writer, most of whose novels and short stories were set in New Mexico, where he had worked as a cowboy. He wrote eight novels in all: *Good Men and True* (1910), *Bransford in Arcadia, or The Little Eohippus* (1914), *West Is West* (1917), *Stepsons of Light* (1921), *Copper Streak Trail* (1922), *The Trusty Knaves* (1933), *Beyond the Desert* (1934) and *The Proud Sheriff* (1935). Of his many short stories, the best known is 'Pasó Por Aquí', about an outlaw on the run who sacrifices his freedom to help the victims of an epidemic. Rhodes' villains are, in the populist tradition, land speculators and bankers. His heroes are ennobled by a Western code of honour which Rhodes' best writing raises to a rare poetic intensity.

Films include: *West Is West*/1920/U/*d* Val Paul/*lp* Harry Carey · *The Wallop* ['The Desire of the Moth']/1921/U/*d* John Ford/*lp* Harry Carey · *Sure Fire* [*Bransford in Arcadia, or The Little Eohippus*]/1921/U/*d* John Ford/*lp* Hoot Gibson · *Good Men and True*/1922/FBO/*d* Val Paul/*lp* Harry Carey · *Four Faces West* ['Pasó Por Aquí']/1948/UA/*d* Alfred E. Green/*lp* Joel McCrea, Charles Bickford

Richter, Conrad (1890-1968) · Author. Most of Richter's fiction has been set in the West. His best known novel is *The Sea of Grass* (1937), a story of conflict between a cattle baron and the nesters he tries to keep off the land. The book is written in a self-consciously poetic style which can at times appear pompous, though it won him much critical acclaim. Richter's other novels set on the frontier are his trilogy about the Ohio valley, *The Trees* (1940), *The Fields* (1946) and the Pulitzer Prize-winning *The Town* (1950); two stories set in the Southwest, *Tacey Cromwell* (1942) and *The Lady* (1957), and two novels about Indians, *The Light in the Forest* (1953) and *A Country of Strangers* (1966).
The Sea of Grass/1946/MGM/*d* Elia Kazan/*lp* Spencer Tracy, Katharine Hepburn, Melvyn Douglas · *The Light in the Forest*/1958/Buena Vista/*d* Herschel Daugherty/*lp* Fess Parker, Wendell Corey
Television · *The Awakening Land*

Riel, Louis (1844-85) · Canadian political leader. In 1869 the Hudson's Bay Company was preparing to hand over jurisdiction of Rupert's Land to the Canadian government. Around the Red River area of present-day Manitoba the métis (people of mixed Indian and white, usually French, descent) saw in the change of administration a threat to their way of life and to their rights over their land. Riel became their leader and led the resistance. There was some violence and Riel himself was banished from Canada for five years. In 1884 trouble broke out again as the métis, who had moved west into Saskatchewan and were hunters as well as farmers, were threatened by encroaching white settlement. Riel returned from his exile to lead what became known as the Northwest Rebellion. When Riel's men defeated a force of Mounties at Duck Lake soldiers were sent in and Riel captured. After a legal debate about his sanity (he had been in and out of mental hospitals) he was hanged 16 November 1885. This ended the last resistance to agricultural settlement in the Canadian

West, but did nothing for the future of relations between English-speaking Canadians and those of French descent, to whom Riel remains a hero. A highly unreliable account of the rebellion occurs in *North West Mounted Police*/1940/PAR/*d* Cecil B. DeMille/*lp* Gary Cooper, Preston Foster. A more sober account is *Riel*/1985/CBC – Green River Pictures/*d* George Bloomfield/*lp* Raymond Cloutier, Christopher Plummer.

Ringo, Johnny (1844?-82) · Gunfighter. Sometimes it seems as if every other character in a Western is called Ringo. Not much about this Ringo is known for certain, but he was involved with the *Clanton gang around *Tombstone and had a confrontation there with Doc *Holliday in January 1882. Later that year he was found dead, presumably a suicide. John Ireland plays him in *Gunfight at the O.K. Corral*/1956 minus his habit of quoting Greek, which Ringo as an educated man was apparently prone to do.
Also: George Montgomery/*Gun Belt*/1953/UA/*d* Ray Nazzaro · Richard Boone/*City of Bad Men*/1953/FOX/*d* Harmon Jones/*lp* Dale Robertson, Jeanne Crain · Jim Davies/*Toughest Gun in Tombstone*/1957/UA/*d* Earl Bellamy/*lp* George Montgomery · Hal Fryar/*The Outlaws Is Coming*/1964/COL/*d* Norman Maurer/*lp* The Three Stooges · Fred Dennis/*Doc*/1971
Television · Britt Lomond/*The Life and Legend of Wyatt Earp* · Norman Alden/*The Life and Legend of Wyatt Earp* · Don Durant/*Johnny Ringo* · Henry Brandon/*The Deputy* · Robert Viharo/*The High Chaparral*

Roberts, Kenneth (1885-1957) · Author. Roberts was a major figure in American letters during the second quarter of this century. Throughout his literary career he had two major aims: accurate description of events and situations, and unashamed elitism. *Northwest Passage*, which he published in 1937, is his major contribution to the Western, thanks to King Vidor's filming of the first part of the novel three years later. Set in the mid-18th century, the film is totally anti-Indian, but it nonetheless prefigures much of *Soldier Blue*/1970. It is based on historical events, but about the film Roberts, who never minced words in private, was 'characteristically sulfurous because of its inaccuracies'. It was remade as a television series in 1958. EC

Rodeo · Like the movies, rodeo has made entertainment (and money) out of the

Bull-riding in J W Coop

cowboy. Its origins are obscure. As with many cowboy terms, the word itself comes from the Spanish, 'rodear' meaning to encircle, or round up. Rodeos presumably began, like other sports, as an amateur competition, probably by cowboys amusing themselves on completion of the biennial round-up. During the 1880s and 1890s Buffalo Bill *Cody and other showmen began introducing into their programme such cowboy skills as roping steers and bronco riding.

What is distinctive about the rodeo is that it is performed competitively, for cash prizes. By the end of the century yearly festivals such as the Cheyenne Frontier Days were organizing rodeo events within the context of a variety of western-style exhibitions. Rodeo was brought east in 1916, when the New York Stampede was held in Brooklyn. During the 1920s the sport became hugely popular and evolved into its present form, with five main events. These are bareback horse riding, saddle bronc riding, steer wrestling (or bulldogging), bull riding and calf roping. Other events such as team roping competitions may be added. Since the early 1900s there have been women's events such as barrel racing, a horse race around a tightly twisting course, though the other events on the circuit are closed to women.

Riding unbroken horses, with saddle or without, was a skill which had a clear relation to the everyday work of a cowboy, and so did roping cattle (necessary in order to brand them). But the other two events were included simply for their entertainment value. Riding a huge Brahma bull weighing over a ton added the element of danger which attracted crowds. Bulldogging was popularized in the early 1900s by the Miller 101 Ranch from Oklahoma, and especially by its black cowboy star Bill Pickett. Pickett would leap from his horse on to a running steer, grabbing a horn in each hand. Twisting the animal's neck until its nose came up he would bite its lip, forcing it to a halt. Then he would fall to one side, pulling the steer down to the ground. Only the lip-biting has been omitted from the modern version of this event.

As rodeo evolved the rules became codified into a complicated system of points based on the time taken to perform an event and the degree of style achieved. Competitors, whose only reward was prize money, would travel huge distances in the course of a year as they moved around the circuit, from the Mexican border up into Canada, and from New England to California. Rodeo, more than most professional sports, has cultivated a showbiz image, and to add to its popularity it incorporated elements from the circus and Wild West show. Clowns were employed to keep the audience amused between events or to distract the attention of a bull which had thrown its rider. And there were feats of equestrianism, such as 'Roman riding', in which a performer would ride a pair of horses standing up, one foot on each. (This trick is demonstrated by Ben Johnson in *Rio Grande*/1950.)

In the 1930s the sport became increasingly professionalized. In 1936, to ensure fair competition and honest promoters, rodeo performers organized themselves into a body called the Cowboy's Turtle Association (so called because 'A turtle never gets anywhere if he doesn't stick his neck out'). This became the Rodeo Cowboys' Association in 1945 and is the body which now controls rodeo in its professional form. Rodeo remains one of the biggest spectator sports in the USA. In addition to the thousands of amateur competitions, some even for children, several thousand professional rodeo performers compete in over 500 rodeos every year for prize money of around $15 million. The top money winners then meet in the National Finals Rodeo, which has recently moved, in what has been seen as a symbolic development, from the cattle country of Oklahoma City to the showbiz mecca of Las Vegas. Opposition by animal rights groups to the cruel means sometimes employed to make the horses buck has not so far threatened the sport's success.

The Hollywood Western has had a continuing but somewhat indirect relation to rodeo. There has been a more direct input into the movies through rodeo's cousin, the Wild West show. Both Tom Mix and Buck Jones were employed by the Miller 101 Ranch before making films. Many other series and B-Western stars came out of such live entertainments and some of them went back into them when their movie contracts ended. Bill Pickett made a low-budget Western, *The Bull-Dogger*, for a Florida-based company in 1923, but with a few notable exceptions, such as Ben Johnson, rodeo stars have not generally taken the road to Hollywood. This might suggest that rodeo is after all more sport than showbiz and that the qualifications for success in the one don't necessarily have any relevance to the other.

Perhaps, too, rodeo performers haven't cared for the image which Hollywood has thrust upon them. A consistent pattern runs through most of the films which Hollywood has devoted to the rodeo cowboy. The contemporary setting seems inevitably to lead to a contrast between the modern world and the old-fashioned cowboy. If this contrast is by no means always to the disadvantage of the cowboy, the modern world being often inhabited by hucksters and worse, it nevertheless seems as though the cowboy can only be at best an anachronism, a living but fading symbol of the values of the old West.

This would be bad enough, but to the accusation of being out of date is added the charge of emotional inadequacy. Rodeo cowboys, at least in the movies, are only good with horses. With human beings, especially females, they are hesitant, inarticulate, suspicious, unreliable. The implication is that their itinerant lifestyle, the general shiftlessness of their profession, disqualifies them from forming adult relationships.

This isn't true in every case. It wouldn't apply to *The Cowboy and the Lady*, in which Gary Cooper successfully upholds western values against eastern, like any true cowboy. But in Budd Boetticher's *Bronco Buster* Scott Brady is an egocentric show-off. Nicholas Ray's *The Lusty Men*/1952 presented its hero, Robert Mitchum, as a tragic figure desperately trying to make something of his life, but too late. In *The Misfits*/1961 Montgomery Clift is a washed-up rodeo cowboy pathetically living a fantasy that he will get back to the arena. The image of the rodeo cowboy as essentially a loser is one that the movies returned to time and again, notably in a group of four films made in the early 1970s. Steve McQueen in *Junior Bonner*/1972 wants to settle down, only to find his home has been sold by his hustler of a brother. Cliff Robertson in *J W Coop*/1971, James Coburn in *The Honkers* (1971) and Richard Widmark in *When the Legends Die* (1972) all, in their individual ways, are men without a future because they are living a fantasy whose roots are in the past.
The Cowboy and the Lady/1938/Goldwyn/*d* Henry C. Potter/*lp* Gary Cooper, Merle Oberon · *Bronco Buster*/1951/U/*d* Budd Boetticher/*lp* John Lund, Scott Brady · *The Honkers*/1971/UA/*d* Steve Ihnat/*lp* James Coburn, Lois Nettleton, Slim Pickens · *When the Legends Die*/1972/ Sagaponack/*d* Stuart Millar/*lp* Richard Widmark, Frederic Forrest

Rogers, Will[iam Penn Adair] (1879-1935) · Entertainer. Rogers, who was part-Cherokee, was brought up on a ranch in what was then Indian Territory. From 1902 he toured with circuses and Wild West shows, performing a riding and trick-roping act. He appeared in some silent films, including the 1922 short *The Ropin' Fool* and *Doubling for Romeo*/1921/Goldwyn/*d* Clarence Badger, a satire on Hollywood Westerns. There were other shorts on the same theme, including a skit on *The Covered*

Will Rogers (1906)

Wagon called *Two Wagons – Both Covered* (1924). Increasingly, it was verbal comedy that was at the centre of his act and he moved into vaudeville and then into talking pictures and radio, where his ready wit, folksy philosophy and southwestern drawl made him one of the most loved figures of the Depression years and a key figure in the development of the cowboy as a truly national hero. Before his early death in a plane crash in Alaska he starred in over a dozen films, including three with John Ford (*Doctor Bull, Judge Priest, Steamboat 'Round the Bend*). None of these, surprisingly, are Westerns. Some glimpses of Rogers' stage act are in the screen biography, *The Story of Will Rogers*/1952/WB/d Michael Curtiz/lp Will Rogers Jr., Jane Wyman.

Roosevelt, Theodore (1858-1919) · 26th President of the United States. Roosevelt's experiences on his ranch in Dakota in the mid-1880s convinced him that the strenuous, manly life of the cowboy was not only a good cure for the physical and emotional troubles he had experienced but a firm moral basis for the country as a whole. His exploits (knocking down a bully, tracking robbers, shooting game) followed in the tradition of the pioneers he admired and described in his mammoth history, *The Winning of the West* (1889-96). He wrote about his own experiences in *Ranch Life and the Hunting Trail* (1888), illustrated by his friend Frederic *Remington.

Roosevelt was Assistant Secretary of the Navy when the Spanish-American War broke out in 1898. He resigned to form a regiment he called the Rough Riders, many of whom were drawn from the West. The name derived from Buffalo Bill's 'Wild West and Congress of Rough Riders of the World', to give *Cody's show its full title. Buffalo Bill later repaid the compliment by

incorporating into his programme the battle of San Juan Hill, which Teddy was popularly, though inaccurately, supposed to have won by leading a mounted charge against the Spanish (in fact the terrain was unsuited to mounted troops). To cement the connection with the West, at a ceremony to mark the disbanding of the regiment Teddy was presented with a Frederic Remington bronze, 'The Bronco Buster'.

Roosevelt's exploits with the Rough Riders, which Remington and others celebrated in heroic paintings, made him a national hero and governor of New York. (In *Bite the Bullet*/1975/COL/d Richard Brooks/lp Candice Bergen, James Coburn, the character played by Gene Hackman relates the story of San Juan Hill while drinking a toast to Teddy.) Roosevelt became Vice-President under McKinley in the election of 1900 and President on McKinley's assassination the following year.

Through his writings, his personal example and his friendship with other popularizers of the frontier experience such as Remington and Owen *Wister, Roosevelt infused into the popular view of the West a kind of moral, if at times adolescent, earnestness and energy. He also gave the West the political and intellectual prestige it previously lacked.

Portrayals of Roosevelt in a Western context include Hobart Bosworth/*Up San Juan Hill*/1910/Selig/d Frank Boggs/lp Thomas Santschi, Tom Mix · E. J. Radcliffe/*Sundown*/1924/First National/d Laurence Trimble, Harry O. Hoyt/lp Bessie Love · Frank Hopper/*The Rough Riders*/1927/PAR/d Victor Fleming/lp Noah Beery, George Bancroft · Erle C. Kenton/*End of the Trail*/1938/COL/d Erle C. Kenton/lp Jack Holt · Sidney Blackmer/*In Old Oklahoma*/1943/REP/d Albert S. Rogell/lp John Wayne · Sidney Blackmer/

Buffalo Bill/1944 · John Alexander/*Fancy Pants*/1950/PAR/d George Marshall/lp Bob Hope, Lucille Ball · Edward Cassidy/*The First Traveling Saleslady*/1956/RKO/d Arthur Lubin/lp Ginger Rogers, Carol Channing · Karl Swensen/*Brighty of the Grand Canyon*/1966/Stephen F. Booth Productions/d N. Foster/lp Joseph Cotten Television · Peter Breck/*Sugarfoot* · Karl Swensen/*The Virginian* · David Doyle/ *Wild and Wooly*

Russell, Charles Marion (1864-1926) · Painter. Russell and Frederic *Remington are the best-known painters of Western subjects. Born in St Louis, Russell went to Montana at the age of sixteen and worked as a cowboy. In 1888 he spent six months living with the Blackfoot. By this time he had started to have his pictures published in magazines such as *Harper's Weekly*, but it was not until he married Nancy Cooper in 1896 that, as a result of her energetic promotion, his pictures began to sell readily and he took to painting as a career. Though he continued to live in Montana, Russell became increasingly well known in the east. After 1919 he and his wife regularly spent part of each winter in California. Here Russell became friends with several members of the movie colony. William S. Hart, Douglas Fairbanks, Noah Beery, Harry Carey and Will Rogers all bought pictures from him.

Many of his early paintings are of cowboy subjects and record the scenes of dramatic action that were so popular in the magazines of the day. Later he turned to historical subjects and paintings of Indians, combining a romantic sense of composition with meticulous attention to details of costume. (See Plate 21)

'Night of the Wrangler' was the pilot episode of a 1961 TV series *Russell*/d Arthur Hiller/s Borden Chase/lp Fess Parker.

Frederic Remington, 'Charge of the Rough Riders up San Juan Hill'

Teddy Roosevelt being presented with Remington's 'The Bronco Buster' as the Rough Riders disband

Ruxton, George Augustus Frederick (1821-48) · Born in England, Ruxton was one of the 19th century's most energetic travellers. In 1843 at the age of twenty-two, inspired by the novels of Fenimore *Cooper, he set out with an Indian as guide through upper New York and Ontario. In 1846 he began an expedition from the south of Mexico up through the Rockies and on to the Plains. His narrative of this, *Adventures in Mexico and the Rocky Mountains 1846-7*, was followed in 1849 by *Life in the Far West*, a fictional but realistic account of mountain men which set the pattern for much later writing on this subject.

S

Sacajawea (c.1790-1812) · Shoshone woman who became the guide and interpreter of *Lewis and Clark on their expedition to the Pacific 1804-6. Sacajawea had been captured by the Hidatsa Indians and then sold to Toussaint Charbonneau, a French-Canadian, who married her. When Charbonneau was hired by Lewis and Clark, they insisted Sacajawea come too. She carried her new-born son on her back. When the expedition reached the Rockies Sacajawea persuaded her people, the Shoshone, to let Lewis and Clark have the horses they sorely needed. Most authorities are persuaded she died on the Missouri in 1812, but some accounts claim she survived on a reservation in Wyoming till 1884. The journals of Lewis and Clark helped to make her into one of the very few acknowledged Indian heroines.
Donna Reed/*The Far Horizons*/1954/PAR/d Rudolph Maté/lp Fred MacMurray, Charlton Heston

Sandoz, Mari (1896-1966) · Novelist and historian, brought up in Nebraska. Her Western novels include *The Tom-Walker* (1947), the saga of three generations of a family in the post-Civil War West; *Miss Morissa: Doctor of the Gold Trail* (1955), about a young woman doctor on the frontier; *The Horsecatcher* (1957), a novel for juvenile readers about a young Cheyenne boy who wants to tame wild horses. Sandoz is better known for historical works such as *Old Jules* (1935), her biography *Crazy Horse: The Strange Man of the Oglalas* (1942) and *Cheyenne Autumn* (1953), the powerfully told story of the Cheyenne's attempt in 1878 to flee from Oklahoma back to their homeland on the Yellowstone, filmed by John Ford in 1964.

Scalping · Historians have argued about whether scalping as a custom of war was indigenous to North America or introduced by whites. The consensus is that while some tribes in the east were already scalping their enemies before the 16th century, the practice became more widely disseminated by the actions of the British and French, who encouraged inter-tribal warfare for their own purposes and introduced a bounty on the scalps of their enemies. As a result, by the 19th century scalping, greatly facilitated by the white man's sharp steel knives, had spread to the Plains tribes. It was never taken up by the Navaho and Apache, although bounties on Apache scalps were still being paid by the authorities late in the 19th century.

Whatever the facts, in the popular mind scalping has remained a savage and typically Indian practice. Fenimore *Cooper's Leatherstocking did not condone it among whites. When whites do resort to scalping it therefore has a shock effect. In *The Big Sky*/1952 the young Indian-hater (Dewey Martin) carries around the scalp of a Blackfoot he thinks killed his father; when he learns to know the Indians as people, he burns it. Telly Savalas' gang of renegade whites in *The Scalphunters* are the scum of the frontier, hunting Kiowa scalps for money. One of the most chilling moments in *The Searchers*/1956 comes when Ethan scalps Scar, the Comanche chief, thus confirming how far he is himself beyond the pale of civilized behaviour. And when some Texas cowboys throw a Cheyenne scalp on the bar of the saloon in Dodge City in *Cheyenne Autumn*/1964 the apparently easy-going Wyatt Earp (James Stewart) is moved to anger.
The Scalphunters/1967/UA/d Sydney Pollack/lp Burt Lancaster, Ossie Davis, Telly Savalas

Schaefer, Jack (b 1907) · Author. *Shane*, published in 1949, established Schaefer's reputation as one of the best post-war writers of Westerns. Its story of the gunfighter who is drawn into the struggle of homesteaders against a cattle baron has the power of an archetype. Schaefer wrote it in an admirably simple and economical style. *Monte Walsh* (1963), an even better achievement, is a contrast. Its loosely episodic story, recounting incidents in the lives of a couple of cowboys, is held together by Schaefer's relaxed humour and gentle nostalgia. His other novels are *First Blood* (1953), *The Canyon* (1953 – in which the protagonist is a

Cheyenne), *Company of Cowards* (1957), which is set in the Civil War, and *Mavericks* (1967). Schaefer has also written three volumes of short stories: *The Big Range* (1953), *The Pioneers* (1954) and *The Kean Land and other stories* (1959).
Shane/1952 · *The Silver Whip [First Blood]*/1953/FOX/d Harmon Jones/lp Dale Robertson, Rory Calhoun · *Tribute to a Badman ['Jeremy Rodock']*/1955 · *Trooper Hook*/1957/UA/d Charles Marquis Warren/lp Joel McCrea, Barbara Stanwyck · *Advance to the Rear [Company of Cowards]*/1963/MGM/d George Marshall/lp Glenn Ford, Melvyn Douglas · *Monte Walsh*/1970
Television · *Shane*

Schoolteachers · 'She was a schoolteacher, you know,' remarks John Qualen of his wife, Olive Carey, after she's taken the jug away and ordered the men off to bed in *The Searchers*/1956. It's a schoolteacher who domesticates the Virginian in Owen *Wister's novel, and in *The Vanishing American*/1925 a pretty teacher wins the Indian hero over to white society with the gift of a New Testament. Along with the church, the school is a sure sign of a leap from wilderness to civilization. That's certainly the significance of the other schoolteachers in John Ford Westerns: Cathy Downs in *My Darling Clementine*/1946, James Stewart (temporarily) in *The Man Who Shot Liberty Valance*/1962, Carroll Baker in *Cheyenne Autumn*/1964. A similar symbolic weight is carried by the schoolteacher in *The Gunfighter*/1950. She's what Jimmy Ringo (Gregory Peck) wants to settle down to and can't. Teacher Jean Simmons is a civilizing influence in *The Big Country*/1958, though Katharine Hepburn as the feisty schoolmarm in *Rooster Cogburn* fails to entirely persuade John Wayne away from uncouth habits. By contrast, Etta Place (Katharine Ross) abandons the classroom and throws in her lot with the outlaws in *Butch Cassidy and the Sundance Kid*/1969. What gets taught doesn't come out of books when Mae West takes class in *My Little Chickadee* or when Betty Grable hides out as a schoolmistress in *The Beautiful Blonde from Bashful Bend*/1949.
My Little Chickadee/1940/U/d Edward Cline/lp Mae West, W.C. Fields · *Rooster Cogburn*/1975/U/d Stuart Millar/lp John Wayne, Katharine Hepburn

Schreyvogel, Charles (1861-1912) · Painter. In his early days, unable to afford a trip to the West, Schreyvogel practised his art by drawing the Indians in Buffalo Bill's Wild West. In 1893 he did finally travel, to the Ute reservation in Colorado, and brought back sketches, Indian artefacts and costumes. These he worked up into large paintings in his studio in Hoboken, New Jersey. At first he could sell nothing, but Schreyvogel became famous overnight after winning a prize at the National Academy of Design in 1900 with a picture entitled 'My Bunkie', depicting a cavalryman rescuing a comrade whose horse has been shot. (An identical incident occurs in John Ford's *Rio Grande*/ 1950.) Schreyvogel specialized in scenes of conflict between Indians and the army and after Frederic *Remington's death was the best known painter of the West. His large-scale canvases, highly dramatic, even cinematic, were made available to the public in platinum prints and in half-tone reproductions in book form. (See Plate 20)

Scots · A Scotsman, Alexander Mackenzie, was the first white man to complete a crossing of the North American continent to the Pacific when he journeyed through Canada to reach Puget Sound in 1793, and in the 19th century Scots were also highly active south of the 49th Parallel, particularly in the *cattle industry. Scots in the Western generally fare better than the *English. Billy the Kid's mentor, John *Tunstall, in fact an Englishman, is played as a kindly Scot in *The Left Handed Gun*/1957. Despite some routine jokes about meanness, the Scots of the Italian comedy Western *Sette pistole per i Mac Gregor* come out of it well. In *Billy Two Hats* the hero, Gregory Peck, is a Scot (as indeed is the author of the script, Alan Sharp). The problems Peck has with the accent show, perhaps, why Hollywood used Scots sparingly. American actors seem to find an Irish accent so much easier.
Sette pistole per i Mac Gregor/1966/It/d Franco Giraldi/lp Robert Woods · *Billy Two Hats*/1973/UA/d Ted Kotcheff/lp Gregory Peck, Desi Arnaz Jr.

Scott, Winfield (1786-1866) · Soldier. Scott fought in the *Seminole War and in 1839 was in charge of the removal of the Cherokee to Indian Territory along the so-called Trail of Tears. In 1841 he became commanding general of the US army. In 1847 during the Mexican War Scott landed a large force at Veracruz, took the town and moved inland towards Mexico City, which he captured on 14 September 1847, effectively ending the war. A large and able man, fond of fancy uniforms (which earned him the nickname

Charles Schreyvogel, 'My Bunkie' (1900)

Old Fuss and Feathers) he is presumably the original of General Quait in Paul *Horgan's *A Distant Trumpet*. He is portrayed as a jovial but astute gourmet by Sydney Greenstreet in *They Died with their Boots On*/1941.

Scout · The figure of the scout is an attractive one. Of the army but not exactly in it, he moves between the world of the regimented soldiers and their Indian quarry, often having charge of the friendly Indians the army has employed. This closeness to the Indian can place him in conflict with his commanders, whose pride and pigheadedness will not allow them to accept his advice. The prototype of all scouts, on whom much of the mythology was based, is of course Buffalo Bill *Cody. Al *Seiber is another original, in a different mode. Some of the more memorable fictional scouts have been played by James Coburn in *Major Dundee*/1964, Gregory Peck in *The Stalking Moon*/1968, Burt Lancaster in *Ulzana's Raid*/ 1972.

Seminole · Strictly speaking, perhaps, the two wars (1816-18, 1835-43) against the Seminole, one of the *Five Civilized Tribes, are too early and too far southeast to form material for Westerns. But it would be an over-restrictive definition which excluded *Distant Drums*/1951 or *Seminole*. The first war, in which the American troops were led by Andrew *Jackson, was inconclusive. In the second, a war of attrition in the swamps,

the American troops were led by General Zachary *Taylor. He built a series of forts which enabled him to gain ground systematically, though with considerable loss of life. But the Seminole were never comprehensively defeated and eventually a cash offer was made to persuade them to leave Florida for the Indian Territory.

Several very early Westerns such as *The Seminole's Trust*/1910/Kalem and *The Seminole's Sacrifice*/1911/Selig draw on these events. In fact the Kalem company seemed particularly drawn to the subject, producing *The Seminole's Vengeance or the Slave Catchers of Florida* in 1909 and *The Seminole Half-Breed* in 1910. The most important leader of the Seminole during the second war was Osceola (c.1800-38), who was popularly believed to have died of grief after being betrayed to the whites and captured. Films about Osceola include: *The Indian's Revenge, or Osceola, the Last of the Seminole*/1906/Vitagraph · *Seminole*/1953/ U/d Budd Boetticher/lp Rock Hudson, with Anthony Quinn as Osceola · *Naked in the Sun*/1957/AA/d John Hugh, with James Craig as Osceola · See also *Seminole Uprising*/1954/AA/d Earl Bellamy/lp George Montgomery

Serials · The cinema did not of course invent the serial, the continuous narrative in weekly or monthly instalments with a cliff-hanging end to each segment. Dickens' novels were originally published in this way.

But once cinema-going had become established as a regular habit, the production of serials was a logical development. Many of the very first film serials such as *The Hazards of Helen* and *The Perils of Pauline*, both dating from 1914, contained Western elements in their settings and plots, and once the first true Western serial, *Liberty*, had been completed in 1916 Westerns came to be the largest single genre produced in the serial format. The seemingly endless possibilities the Western offered for fights and stunts of all kinds made it well adapted to the frenzied action the serial required. But in order to increase the elements of suspense and mystery upon which serials also necessarily relied, the Western was frequently combined with elements more commonly associated with other genres, such as masked heroes (as in *The Lone Ranger*), or villains whose identity is uncovered only in the last reel.

Serial production was highly specialized. Three studios, Universal, Pathé and Mascot, were the best known producers in the silent period. Mascot eventually evolved into Republic, who, together with Universal and Columbia, were the major producers in the sound period. Production values were invariably low and a great many later serials relied on recycled footage from earlier days. But they kept their popularity until the decline in the regularity of cinema-going in the 1950s meant the serial ceased to be viable. Columbia's Western *Blazing the Overland Trail* (1956) was the last serial to be made for cinema viewing. Though television seized on the serial format, which in soap operas continues popular to this day, television Westerns were made as series, not serials.

NOTABLE WESTERN SERIALS INCLUDE:
Liberty/1916/U/d Jacques Jaccard, Henry MacRae/lp Jack Holt, Eddie Polo
In the Days of Buffalo Bill/1922/U/d Ed Laemmle/lp Art Acord
The Oregon Trail/1923/U/d Ed Laemmle/lp Art Acord
Riders of the Plains/1924/Arrow/d Jacques Jaccard/lp Jack Perrin
Fighting with Buffalo Bill/1926/U/d Ray

Taylor/lp Wallace MacDonald
The Indians Are Coming/1930/U/d Henry MacRae/lp Tim McCoy
Battling with Buffalo Bill/1931/U/d Ray Taylor/lp Tom Tyler, Rex Bell
The Vanishing Legion/1931/Mascot/d B. Reeves Eason/lp Harry Carey
The Last Frontier/1932/RKO/d Spencer Bennet/lp Lon Chaney Jr.
The Law of the Wild/1934/Mascot/d Armand Schaefer, B. Reeves Eason/lp Rin Tin Tin Jr., Bob Custer
The Red Rider/1934/U/d Louis Friedlander/lp Buck Jones
Phantom Empire/1934/Mascot/d Otto Brower, B. Reeves Eason/lp Gene Autry
The Miracle Rider/1935/Mascot/d Armand Schaefer, B. Reeves Eason/lp Tom Mix
The Roaring West/1935/U/d Ray Taylor/lp Buck Jones
Custer's Last Stand/1936/Stage and Screen/d Elmer Clifton/lp Rex Lease, William Farnum
The Phantom Rider/1936/U/d Ray Taylor/lp Buck Jones
The Painted Stallion/1937/REP/d William Witney, Ray Taylor/lp Ray Corrigan, Hoot Gibson
The Great Adventures of Wild Bill Hickok/1938/COL/d Mack V. Wright, Sam Nelson/lp Bill Elliott
The Lone Ranger/1938/REP/d William Witney, John English/lp Lee Powell, Chief Thundercloud
The Lone Ranger Rides Again/1939/REP/d William Witney, John English/lp Bob Livingston, Chief Thundercloud
Overland with Kit Carson/1939/COL/d Sam Nelson, Norman Deming/lp Bill Elliott
Zorro's Fighting Legion/1939/REP/d William Witney, John English/lp Reed Hadley
Adventures of Red Ryder/1940/REP/d William Witney, John English/lp Don 'Red' Barry
King of the Royal Mounted/1940/REP/d William Witney, John English/lp Allan Lane
The Valley of Vanishing Men/1942/COL/d Spencer Bennet/lp Bill Elliott
Jesse James Rides Again/1947/REP/d Fred Brannon, Thomas Carr/lp Clayton Moore

Blazing the Overland Trail/1956/COL/d Spencer Bennet/lp Dennis Moore

Series · During the 1930s and 1940s the B-Western searched continuously for stability of production in what was, at the lower end of the market, always a precarious business. The creation of long-running series (some of which ran to over fifty separate films) seemed to guarantee distributors and audiences a product which, if it lacked novelty, had a reassuring dependability. Some series were based on a fictional or, loosely, an historical character, some on the work of a single writer and some on the personality of a star. And so Fox spun off a *Cisco Kid series from *In Old Arizona* (not in itself a B-feature) and Paramount had Hopalong Cassidy, in addition to seemingly endless remakes of Zane *Grey stories. PRC had its *Billy the Kid series, and Columbia a Wild Bill *Hickok series and Charles Starrett's Durango Kid Series. Republic had great success with singing cowboys such as Gene Autry and Roy Rogers, in films patterned on a rigid formula. Following the popularity of Republic's Three Mesquiteers, based on stories by William Colt *MacDonald, other studios made series with a trio of heroes; for example, Monogram's Range Busters series.

Sharps rifle · The gun favoured by buffalo hunters for its long range and heavy bullet. Designed by Christian Sharps (1811-74), it was a single-shot .45 calibre weapon in which the breechblock was lowered for loading by pulling down the trigger guard. The gun was produced in both carbine and rifle models. It's a Sharps rifle that brings down Gregory Peck at the range of a mile or so in *Billy Two Hats*, and with which Burt Lancaster holds off his pursuers in *Valdez Is Coming*; Fabio Testi wreaks devastation with a Sharps at the end of *China 9 Liberty 37*.
Billy Two Hats/1973/UA/d Ted Kotcheff/lp Gregory Peck, Desi Arnaz Jr. · *Valdez Is Coming*/1970/UA/d Edwin Sherrin/lp Burt Lancaster · *China 9 Liberty 37*/1978/Lorimar/d Monte Hellman/lp Warren Oates, Fabio Testi

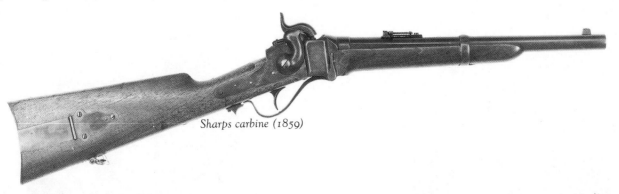

Sharps carbine (1859)

Sheep · Though by the end of the 19th century sheep rearing was economically as important as cattle raising, the shepherd never achieved any significant place in the folklore of the West. Sheep only appear in the Western in the context of the *feuds between cattlemen and sheep-herders. These feuds, the best known of which was the Pleasant Valley War or Graham-Tewksbury Feud in Arizona, beginning in 1887, were ostensibly caused by cattlemen's belief that sheep destroyed the pasture for cattle. But undoubtedly much of the Anglo-Saxon prejudice against sheep derived from the fact that sheep had first been introduced into North America by the Spanish and sheep-herding was traditionally an occupation of Spanish-speaking natives of the Southwest or of Indian peoples such as the Navaho. The dislike of sheep thus carried class and racist overtones, interestingly explored in *Joe Kidd*, though not in earlier films about sheep wars such as *Montana*, *The Sheepman*/1958 or *Heaven With a Gun*.
Montana/1949/WB/d Ray Enright/lp Errol Flynn, Alexis Smith · *Heaven With a Gun*/1968/MGM/d Lee H. Katzin/lp Glenn Ford, Carolyn Jones · *Joe Kidd*/1972/U/d John Sturges/lp Clint Eastwood, Robert Duvall

Sheridan, Philip Henry (1831-88) · Soldier. After a distinguished record in the Union Army during the Civil War, Sheridan was made military commander of Texas and Louisiana. So harsh was his rule that President Johnson had to remove him and Sheridan was let loose on the Indians as commander of the Division of the Missouri,

which comprised the departments of Dakota, Missouri, the Platte and Texas. Sheridan gave *Custer the orders which resulted in the massacre of the *Washita and energetically campaigned against the Apache and the Sioux. The saying, 'The only good Indian is a dead Indian', is supposed to derive from Sheridan's statement, 'The only good Indians I ever saw were dead', though Sheridan can scarcely be credited with originating the sentiment. He became commander of the army in 1883.
Frank Campeau/*Abraham Lincoln*/1930/UA/ d D.W. Griffith/lp Walter Huston · Ernie Adams/*Union Pacific*/1939 · David Bruce/ *Santa Fe Trail*/1940 · John Litel/*They Died with their Boots On*/1941 · J. Carrol Naish/ *Rio Grande*/1950 · Lawrence Tierney/ *Custer of the West*/1966/Cinerama/d Robert Siodmak/lp Robert Shaw
Television · Laurence Dobkin/*Cheyenne* · Laurence Dobkin/*The Rifleman* · Paul Fix/ *Tales of Wells Fargo* · Gary Merrill/*Hondo* · Nicholas Coster/*The Court Martial of George Armstrong Custer*

Sheriffs and marshals · Though the plots of some films turn on them, the conflicts in jurisdiction between sheriffs and marshals are not always easy to grasp. Briefly, the marshal, or more properly federal marshal, was an officer of the district court (which in the West might cover a very wide area) and appointed directly by presidential authority. The marshals and their deputies issued subpoenas, executed writs and apprehended those wanted by the courts for offences, especially federal offences such as robbery of the mails. Sheriffs, on the other hand, were appointed by the particular community they served, the county, and functioned as a local police force, keeping the peace within the area of their jurisdiction. To confuse the picture slightly, towns sometimes appointed their own marshals. Thus Wyatt Earp, who had been assistant marshal of Dodge City, was in 1880 made deputy sheriff of Pima County, in which was located the town of Tombstone. But he was never marshal of Tombstone. His brother Virgil, on the other hand, who was initially a deputy federal marshal based in Tombstone, did become town marshal there in 1881.

Sherman, William Tecumseh (1820-91) · Soldier. Sherman had a highly successful Civil War, though his notorious March to the Sea through Georgia in 1864, during which he burned out the civilian population, did not endear him to the South. From 1866 till 1869, when he was made commander of the army, he was in charge of the Division of the Missouri, which embraced the whole of the plains. He pursued a hard-line policy and favoured transferring responsibility for the Indians from the Bureau of Indian Affairs to the War Department. The army would then confine Indians to reservations and severely punish those who resisted. As commander he continued this policy from Washington until his retirement in 1883.
Richard Cutting/*The Horse Soldiers*/1959 · John Wayne/*How the West Was Won*/1962 Television · John Wayne/*Wagon Train* · J. D. Cannon/*The Court Martial of George Armstrong Custer*

Shooting lesson · Of all the common motifs in the Western, the scene in which the hero passes on his knowledge of the gun is perhaps that which most obviously binds the genre into a system of patriarchal authority. Usually the recipient of the lesson is a young boy or youth, as in *Shane*/1952, *River of No Return*/1954, *Man Without a Star*/1955 ('Get it out fast and put it away slow,' advises Kirk Douglas), *Great Day in the Morning*/1955, *The Tin Star*/1957, *Nevada Smith*. Sometimes it is a woman (*Rachel and the Stranger*, *Hannie Caulder*/ 1971) or someone in an equally inferior position, such as the Mexican peasants in

General Philip Sheridan

General William T. Sherman (1865)

Anthony Perkins (l.) learns shooting from Henry Fonda in The Tin Star

Robert Taylor gives instruction in Westward the Women

The Magnificent Seven/1960. Robert Taylor in *Westward the Women*/1951 initiates an entire party of emigrant women. In parodies this relationship is reversed. Thus in *Little Big Man*/1970 Jack (Dustin Hoffman) is shown how to shoot by his sister, and in *The Sheriff of Fractured Jaw*/1958 Kenneth More as the Englishman out west is given a shooting lesson by Jayne Mansfield.
Rachel and the Stranger/1947/RKO/*d* Norman Foster/*lp* Loretta Young, William Holden, Robert Mitchum · *Nevada Smith*/1965/Avco/*d* Henry Hathaway/*lp* Steve McQueen, Karl Malden

Short, Luke (1854-93) · Gambler and member of the so-called *Dodge City 'Gang'*, a loose association of gamblers and saloon-keepers active in local politics. Short, noted in true gambler style for his snappy dress, was a friend of Bat *Masterson and Wyatt *Earp and followed them from Dodge City to *Tombstone in 1881. There he killed a man and was advised to return to Dodge City. A power shift in the town politics of Dodge resulted in a reform faction being elected and Short's saloon was prosecuted for prostitution. Short then sent for his friends, including Doc *Holliday, Earp and Masterson. Their arrival led to a confrontation which became known as the 'Dodge City War', though in fact not a shot was fired.

Short, Luke (1908-75) · Pen name of Frederick Dilley Glidden (who apparently only heard about the real Luke *Short after he had chosen his name). Short was a prolific novelist whose books became very popular with Hollywood in the late 1940s and 50s. He wrote over fifty Western novels, most of which were serialized first in newspapers or journals such as the *Saturday Evening Post* and *Colliers*. Short's novels rely on the traditional virtues of popular Western fiction: strong plots with plenty of action and suspense, sharply etched characters and a serviceable, not over-literary style. Such qualities facilitated adaptation.
Ramrod/1947 · *Coroner Creek*/1948/COL/*d* Ray Enright/*lp* Randolph Scott · *Albuquerque* [*Dead Freight for Piute*]/1948/ PAR/*d* Ray Enright/*lp* Randolph Scott · *Station West*/1948/RKO/*d* Sidney Lanfield/*lp* Dick Powell, Jane Greer · *Blood on the Moon*/1948 · *Ambush*/1949/MGM/*d* Sam Wood/*lp* Robert Taylor, Arlene Dahl · *Vengeance Valley*/1950/MGM/*d* Richard Thorpe/*lp* Burt Lancaster, Robert Walker · *Silver City* [*High Vermillion*]/1951/PAR/*d* Byron Haskin/*lp* Edmond O'Brien, Yvonne De Carlo · *Ride the Man Down*/ 1952/REP/*d* Joseph Kane/*lp* Brian Donlevy · *Hell's Outpost*/1954/REP/*d* Joseph Kane/*lp* Rod Cameron · *The Hangman*/1959/PAR/*d* Michael Curtiz/*lp* Robert Taylor, Fess Parker

Shotgun · Despite the obvious fact that at close range a shotgun would be a more effective weapon than most, is there something illegitimate about it as a weapon in the Western? The use of buckshot by Gil Westrum (Randolph Scott) in his shooting booth in *Ride the High Country*/1962 is the first sign of his corruption. Both Doc Holliday (Kirk Douglas) in *Gunfight at the O.K. Corral*/1956 and Mississippi (James Caan) in *El Dorado*/ 1966 employ a shotgun. But each also favours a knife, an even more dubious weapon, and, worst of all, is fond of cards. It's true that Mr Potts (James Coburn), the most admirable character in *Major Dundee*/ 1964, also carries a shotgun; but then he only has one arm.

Sieber, Al (1844-1907) · Civil War veteran and chief of scouts for the army at the San Carlos Indian Reservation 1870-90. Grey-haired and tough (he was reputed to have survived twenty-nine wounds from gun and arrow), Sieber was active in the hunt for *Geronimo and his Apache scouts were highly effective trackers. Tom *Horn described him as 'the greatest and best man I ever knew.' In *Apache*/1954 John McIntire plays him as a grizzled old grouch with a heart of gold, contemptuous of government policies towards Indians.
Also Charlton Heston (as 'Ed Bannon')/ *Arrowhead*/1953/PAR/*d* Charles Marquis Warren/*lp* Jack Palance
Television · Richard Widmark/*Mr. Horn*

Sioux · The best known of all the indigenous peoples with whom the whites came into conflict in the 19th century. The name Sioux is a French abbreviation of an Ojibwa word *nadowe-is-iw*, meaning 'snake' or 'enemy'. The Sioux most commonly referred to themselves as 'Dakota', meaning 'allies'. By 1800 the Sioux had divided into three main groups, called by the whites Santee, Yankton and Teton. The Santee lived as settled farmers in fixed villages in present-day Minnesota. Peaceful at first, they were gradually compressed by white settlers into reservations, where corrupt administration provoked violence. In the Minnesota Uprising of 1862 the Santee killed over seven hundred whites. After the uprising was harshly suppressed most of the Santee were expelled to reservations in Nebraska or the Dakotas.

The Yankton Sioux for the most part took more readily to agriculture and settled on reservations in South Dakota. The Teton Sioux comprised seven separate sub-groups: Oglala, Brulé, Sans-Arc, Two Kettle, Minneconjou, Hunkpapa and Blackfoot (not to be confused with the Algonquian-speaking Blackfoot living on the upper Missouri and Saskatchewan rivers). It was upon the Teton Sioux that the archetype of the Plains Indian came to be based: the feather-bonneted, buffalo-hunting mounted warrior. Nomadic, with a loose political organization based on small extended-family bands and a culture dominated by mystical religion and the rituals of warfare, the Teton Sioux roamed over much of present-day South Dakota, Wyoming and Montana. In the mid-1860s war broke out with the whites along the Bozeman trail. The Sioux, under the Oglala chief *Red Cloud, forced the closure of the trail after inflicting severe losses on the whites, including the Fetterman massacre in which eighty soldiers from Fort Phil Kearny were wiped out. A treaty in 1868 secured a fragile peace until the discovery of gold in the *Black Hills of Dakota brought an influx of prospectors into lands sacred to the Sioux and promised to them by treaty. This led to a war in which the Teton Sioux under the Oglala *Crazy Horse and the Hunkpapa *Sitting Bull, together with the Cheyenne, defeated General *Custer at the *Little Big Horn. But their triumph was short-lived and by the spring of 1877 most had surrendered and been forced onto reservations. The Sioux did not easily adapt to the settled agricultural existence the whites wished to impose on them and in the late 1880s a cult known as the Ghost Dance religion, which promised the restoration of their former power, spread rapidly. The army was sent by a nervous government to guard against any uprising. At *Wounded Knee in South Dakota in 1890 nearly one hundred and fifty Sioux men, women and children were massacred by soldiers, the last major outbreak of violence between whites and Native Americans.

Siringo, Charlie (1855-1928) · Texas-born cowboy who began his career working for Shanghai *Pierce. In 1885 he published his autobiography, *A Texas Cowboy, or, Fifteen Years on the Hurricane Deck of a Spanish Cow Pony*. It was a huge success and did much to build up the public fascination with cowboys. In the 1890s Siringo joined the *Pinkerton detective agency, helping them break strikes in Idaho and also pursue the Wild

Bunch. His later works include *The Cowboy Detective* (1912), about his time with the Pinkertons, and *A History of Billy the Kid* (1920).
William Berger/*Faccia a faccia*/1967/It/d Sergio Sollima/lp Gian Maria Volonté, Tomas Milian
Television · L. Q. Jones/*Mrs. Sundance* · Steve Forrest/*Wanted: The Sundance Woman*

Sitting Bull (Tatanka Iyotake) (c.1831-90) · The best known of all the Indians of the West. Sitting Bull was a chief of the Hunkpapa group of the Teton *Sioux and a greatly respected mystic. He first fought against the whites in the aftermath of the Minnesota Uprising of 1862, which had initially involved the Santee Sioux. Sitting Bull consistently urged resistance to white aggression, even after 1868 when a sizeable portion of the Teton Sioux agreed to make peace in return for a large reservation in the *Black Hills of Dakota. Sitting Bull eventually became chief of all the Teton Sioux and when gold was discovered in the Black Hills in 1874 and the whites swarmed in, he refused government orders to gather on the reservation. In the spring of 1876 the army was sent out and great numbers of Sioux, Cheyenne and Arapaho rallied to Sitting Bull. At the ensuing Battle of the *Little Big Horn he remained in camp fasting and

praying, as was fitting to his position (in a vision he had foreseen the defeat of *Custer). In the aftermath of the battle and the subsequent retaliation Sitting Bull retreated to Canada, but was eventually forced south again and surrendered on 19 July 1881. He was confined to a reservation, but in 1885 he toured briefly with Buffalo Bill's *Wild West, bearing with dignity what must have been a somewhat humiliating experience. In 1890 when the Ghost Dance swept the plains, Indian agent James McLaughlin feared that Sitting Bull might re-emerge as a leader. Indian police were sent to arrest him. In the ensuing struggle Sitting Bull was shot dead.
Sitting Bull, the Hostile Sioux Chief/1914/ American Rotograph · Noble Johnson/ *Hands Up!*/1926/PAR/d Clarence Badger/lp Raymond Griffith · Noble Johnson/ *Flaming Frontier*/1926/U/d Edward Sedgwick/lp Hoot Gibson, Dustin Farnum · Chief Yowlachie/*Sitting Bull at the Spirit Lake Massacre*/1927/Sunset/d Robert N. Bradbury · Chief Thunderbird/*Annie Oakley*/1935/RKO/d George Stevens/lp Barbara Stanwyck, Preston Foster · Howling Wolf/*Custer's Last Stand*/1936/ Stage and Screen/d Elmer Clifton/lp Rex Lease, William Farnum · J. Carroll Naish/ *Annie Get Your Gun*/1950 · Michael Granger/*Fort Vengeance*/1953/AA/d Lesley Selander/lp James Craig · J. Carrol Naish/

George Catlin, 'Sioux Women Dressing Hides'

Sitting Bull with Buffalo Bill (1885)

Sitting Bull/1954/UA/d Sidney Salkow/*lp* Dale Robertson, Iron Eyes Cody · John War Eagle/*Tonka*/1958/Buena Vista/d Lewis Foster/*lp* Sal Mineo, Phil Carey · Michael Pate/*The Great Sioux Massacre*/1965/COL/d Sidney Salkow/*lp* Joseph Cotten, Phil Carey · Alain Cuny/*Touche pas la femme blanche*/1973/Fr/d Marco Ferreri/*lp* Marcello Mastroianni, Catherine Deneuve · Frank Kaquitts/*Buffalo Bill and the Indians*/1976 · Nick Ramus/*Annie Oakley*/1985/Platypus/d Michael Lindsay-Hogg/*lp* Jamie Lee Curtis Television · Frank De Kova/*Cheyenne* · Francis McDonald/*Cheyenne* · Anthony Caruso/*The Great Adventure* · Felix Locher/*Branded*

Slade, Jack [Joseph] (1824-64) · Ruffian. Slade was a superintendent for the Central Overland, California and Pike's Peak Express Company, but alcoholism got him the sack and he moved to *Virginia City, Montana, where he tried ranching. There his rowdyism so exasperated the miners, who were in the middle of a bout of vigilantism, that they hanged him. Mark Twain gives a highly coloured account of Slade in *Roughing It* (1872).
George Bancroft/*Pony Express*/1925/PAR/d James Cruze/*lp* Ricardo Cortez, Betty Compson · Duke R. Lee/*Son of the Golden West*/1928/FBO/d Eugene Ford/*lp* Tom Mix · Mark Stevens/*Jack Slade*/1953/AA/d Harold Schuster/*lp* Dorothy Malone · John Ericson/*The Return of Jack Slade*/1955/AA/d Harold Schuster/*lp* Mari Blanchard

Smoke signals · Ernest *Haycox's story 'Stage to Lordsburg', on which John Ford's *Stagecoach*/1939 is based, begins: 'This was one of those years in the Territory when Apache smoke signals spiraled up from the stony mountain summits and many a ranch house lay as a square of blackened ashes on the ground....' An extension of Indian sign language, the communications system of the technology-less, and the lingua franca of the plains from which the US Army developed semaphore, smoke signals can be more frightening than the actual appearance of the Indians they foreshadow. Fear of the Other and the unknown feeds on this simultaneous presence and absence in *River of No Return*/1954; *The Last Wagon*/1956; *Comanche Station*/1959.

Smoking · 'If there's one thing thet brands a tenderfoot, it's the way he rolls a cigarette,' drawls a character in Zane Grey's *Western Union*. Ideally it should be done with one hand while on horseback. It's one of the signs of how low alcoholism has brought Dean Martin in *Rio Bravo*/1958 that he can no longer manage to roll a smoke. As far back as 1915 in *Between Men* W. S. Hart, temporarily in New York and wearing a lounge suit, shows himself a true man of the West by striking a match on his thumb (a typically macho action wonderfully improved upon by Stan Laurel in the parody *Way Out West*/1937, when he strikes a light from his thumb without benefit of match at all). Clint Eastwood's career since he first appeared in Italian Westerns is an example of what a cigar can do for a man, though perhaps few would go as far in their opinion as Johnny Guitar: 'Well, when you boil it all down, what does a man really need? – just a smoke and a cup of coffee.' The best known smoking cowboy of all is the anonymous Marlboro Man, first used by Philip Morris in 1954 to sell its novel filter cigarettes by giving a masculine image to a product originally designed for women.

Sources in novels of selected Westerns · The following list, arranged in order of film titles, gives the authors of the original novels or stories on which the films have been based. Authors marked * are given a separate entry in Part II or Part IV.
Abilene Town (1946): Ernest *Haycox
Advance to the Rear (1963): Jack *Schaefer
Albuquerque (1948): Luke *Short
Along Came Jones (1945): Alan *LeMay
Ambush (1949): Luke *Short
Apache/1954: Paul *Wellman
Apache Drums (1950): Harry *Brown
Apache Territory (1958): Louis *L'Amour
Arrowhead (1953): W.R. *Burnett
Backlash (1956): Frank *Gruber
The Badlanders (1958): W.R. *Burnett
Belle Starr's Daughter (1948): W.R. *Burnett
The Big Country/1958: Donald *Hamilton
The Big Land (1957): Frank *Gruber
The Big Sky/1952: A.B. *Guthrie
The Big Trail/1930: Hal G. *Evarts
Billy the Kid/1930: Walter Nobel *Burns
Blackjack Ketchum, Desperado (1956): Louis *L'Amour
Blood on the Moon/1948: Luke *Short
The Border Legion (1919, etc.): Zane *Grey
Branded (1950): Max *Brand
Broken Arrow/1950: Elliott Arnold (b 1912. Based on *Blood Brother*, 1947)
Bugles in the Afternoon (1951): Ernest *Haycox
Bullet for a Badman (1964): Marvin H. Albert

The Burning Hills (1956): Louis *L'Amour
Call of the Wild (1908, etc.): Jack *London
Canyon Passage (1946): Ernest *Haycox
Catlow (1971): Louis *L'Amour
Cheyenne Autumn/1964: Mari *Sandoz
Chip of the Flying-U (1914, etc.): B.M. *Bower
Cimarron/1930/1960: Edna *Ferber
The Cisco Kid (1931): O. *Henry
Colorado Territory/1949: W.R. *Burnett
The Comancheros/1961: Paul *Wellman
Coroner Creek (1948): Luke *Short
The Covered Wagon/1923: Emerson *Hough
Dark Command (1940): W.R. *Burnett
The Deerslayer (1957): James Fenimore *Cooper
The Desperadoes (1943): Max *Brand
Destry Rides Again/1939: Max *Brand
A Distant Trumpet/1964: Paul *Horgan
Drums Along the Mohawk/1939: Walter *Edmonds
Duel at Diablo (1965): Marvin H. Albert
Duel in the Sun/1946: Niven *Busch
El Dorado/1966: Harry *Brown
Flaming Star/1960: Clair *Huffaker
Four Faces West (1948): Eugene Manlove *Rhodes
Friendly Persuasion (1956): Jessamyn West (b 1902. Based on *The Friendly Persuasion*, 1945. Jessamyn West collaborated on the screenplay of *Friendly Persuasion* and on the screenplay of *The Big Country*/1958)
Frontier Marshal/1939: Stuart *Lake
The Furies/1950: Niven *Busch
Giant/1956: Edna *Ferber
God's Country and the Woman (1936): James Oliver *Curwood
The Great Missouri Raid (1950): Frank *Gruber
Guns of the Timberland (1959): Louis *L'Amour
The Hanging Tree/1959: Dorothy *Johnson
The Hangman (1959): Luke *Short
Heller in Pink Tights/1960: Louis *L'Amour
Hell's Outpost (1954): Luke *Short
Heritage of the Desert (1924, etc.): Zane *Grey
The Hired Gun (1957): Max *Brand
Hombre/1966: Elmore *Leonard
Hondo/1953: Louis *L'Amour
Hop-A-Long Cassidy (1935): Clarence *Mulford
Hud/1962: Larry *McMurtry
In Old Arizona/1929: O. *Henry
The Iron Mistress (1952): Paul *Wellman
Jeremiah Johnson/1972: Vardis *Fisher
Joe Kidd (1972): Elmore *Leonard
Journey to Shiloh (1967): Henry Wilson *Allen
Jubal/1956: Paul *Wellman
The Kansan (1943): Frank *Gruber

The Last of the Mohicans (1936): James Fenimore *Cooper

The Last Picture Show (1971): Larry *McMurtry

The Last Trail (1921, etc.): Zane *Grey

The Law and Jake Wade/1958: Marvin H. Albert

The Lawless Valley (1938): W.C. *Tuttle

Law and Order (1932, etc.): W.R. *Burnett

The Light in the Forest (1958): Conrad *Richter

The Light of Western Stars (1918, etc.): Zane *Grey

Little Big Man/1970: Thomas Berger (b 1924. *Little Big Man* was published in 1964)

The Lone Star Ranger (1919, etc.): Zane *Grey

Lonely Are the Brave/1962: Edward Abbey (b 1927. Based on *The Brave Cowboy*, published in 1956)

Lovin' Molly (1973): Larry *McMurtry

McKenna's Gold (1968): Henry Wilson *Allen

A Man Called Horse/1970: Dorothy *Johnson

Man in the Saddle/1951: Ernest *Haycox

The Man Who Shot Liberty Valance/1962: Dorothy *Johnson

The Mark of Zorro/1940: Johnston *McCulley

The Maverick Queen (1956): Zane *Grey

Montana (1949): Ernest *Haycox

Monte Walsh/1970: Jack *Schaefer

My Brother the Outlaw (1951): Max *Brand

My Darling Clementine/1946: Stuart *Lake

The Mysterious Rider (1921, etc.): Zane *Grey

North of 36 (1924): Emerson *Hough

Northwest Passage/1940: Kenneth *Roberts

The Oregon Trail (1945): Frank *Gruber

The Outcasts of Poker Flat (1919, etc.): Bret *Harte

The Ox-Bow Incident/1942: Walter van Tilburg *Clark

The Pathfinder (1952): James Fenimore *Cooper

Pillars of the Sky (1956): Henry Wilson *Allen

The Pioneers (1941): James Fenimore *Cooper

Posse from Hell (1961): Clair *Huffaker

Powder River (1953): Stuart *Lake

The Prairie (1947): James Fenimore *Cooper

Quincannon, Frontier Scout (1956): Will Cook (1922-64)

Ramona (1910, etc.): Helen Hunt *Jackson

Ramrod/1947: Luke *Short

The Red Rider (1934): W.C. *Tuttle

Red River/1948: Borden *Chase

Riders of the Purple Sage (1925, etc.): Zane *Grey

Ride the Man Down (1952): Luke *Short

Rio Conchos/1964: Clair *Huffaker

The Robin Hood of El Dorado/1936: Walter Noble *Burns

Santa Fe Passage (1955): Henry Wilson *Allen

The Santa Fe Trail (1930): Hal G. *Evarts

The Sea of Grass (1947): Conrad *Richter

The Searchers/1956: Alan *LeMay

Sergeants 3 (1961): W.R. *Burnett

Seven Ways from Sundown (1960): Clair *Huffaker

Shalako (1968): Louis *L'Amour

Shane/1952: Jack *Schaefer

The Shepherd of the Hills (1927, etc.): Harold Bell *Wright

The Shootist/1976: Glendon *Swarthout

Shoot Out (1971): Will *James

Silver City (1951): Luke *Short

The Silver Whip (1953): Jack *Schaefer

Smoky (1933, etc.): Will *James

Soldier Blue/1970: T. V. *Olsen

The Spoilers (1914, etc.): Rex *Beach

Stagecoach/1939: Ernest *Haycox

The Stalking Moon/1968: T. V. *Olsen

Station West (1948): Luke *Short

Stranger on Horseback/1954: Louis *L'Amour

The Sundowners (1949): Alan *LeMay

The Tall Men/1955: Henry Wilson *Allen

The Tall Stranger (1957): Louis *L'Amour

The Tall T/1956: Elmore *Leonard

Tennessee's Partner (1954): Bret *Harte

Tension at Table Rock (1956): Frank *Gruber

The Texan (1930): O. *Henry

The Texans (1938): Emerson *Hough

These Thousand Hills/1958: A.B. *Guthrie

They Came to Cordura (1959): Glendon *Swarthout

3 Godfathers/1948: Peter B. *Kyne

The Three Mesquiteers (1936): William Colt *MacDonald

3:10 to Yuma/1957: Elmore *Leonard

The Thundering Herd (1925, etc.): Zane *Grey

To the Last Man (1923, etc.): Zane *Grey

Track of the Cat/1954: Walter van Tilburg *Clark

Tribute to a Badman/1955: Jack *Schaefer

Trooper Hook (1957): Jack *Schaefer

True Grit/1969: Charles Portis (b 1933)

Two Rode Together/1961: Will Cook (1922-64)

Tumbleweeds/1925: Hal G. *Evarts

Under the Tonto Rim (1928, etc.): Zane *Grey

The Unforgiven/1959: Alan *LeMay

Union Pacific/1939: Ernest *Haycox

Utah Blaine (1957): Louis *L'Amour

Valdez Is Coming (1970): Elmore *Leonard

The Valley of Vanishing Men (1943): Max *Brand

The Vanishing American/1925: Zane *Grey

Vengeance Valley (1950): Luke *Short

The Violent Men (1954): Donald *Hamilton

The Virginian/1929: Owen *Wister

Warlock/1959: Oakley Hall (b 1920. *Warlock*, his first Western novel, was published in 1958)

Warpath (1951): Frank *Gruber

The Way West (1967): A.B. *Guthrie

Welcome to Hard Times/1966: E.L. Doctorow (b 1931)

Western Union/1941: Zane *Grey

Whispering Smith (1916, etc.): Frank *Spearman

White Fang (1925, etc.): Jack *London

Wild Horse Mesa (1932, etc.): Zane *Grey

Winnetou (1964): Karl *May

The Winning of Barbara Worth (1926): Harold Bell *Wright

The Wolf Hunters (1949): James Oliver *Curwood

The Wonderful Country/1959: Tom *Lea

Yellow Sky/1948: W.R. *Burnett

Yellowstone Kelly (1959): Henry Wilson *Allen

Young Billy Young (1969): Henry Wilson *Allen

Yukon Gold (1952): James Oliver *Curwood

Spearman, Frank (1859-1937) · Author whose most famous character, Whispering Smith, a western railroad detective, first appeared in a novel of that name in 1906. *Whispering Smith*/1916/Mutual/d J. P. McGowan/lp Helen Holmes · *Whispering Smith*/1926/PDC/d George Melford · *Whispering Smith Rides*/1927/U/d Ray Taylor/lp Wallace MacDonald · *Whispering Smith Speaks*/1935/FOX/d David Howard/lp George O'Brien · *Whispering Smith*/1949/PAR/d Leslie Fenton/lp Alan Ladd, Robert Preston · (*Whispering Smith Hits London*, an RKO film of 1951, removed the character from the Western into a contemporary crime setting.) Television · *Whispering Smith*

Sports · On 7 June 1763 during *Pontiac's Rebellion a group of Ojibwa were playing lacrosse beneath the walls of Fort Mackinac. Under the guise of rushing in after a ball, they suddenly turned on the British garrison and sacked the fort. Westerns don't usually run much to ball games; sports if any will be more like the shooting competition in *Winchester '73*/1950. But in *Jeremiah Johnson*/1972 the Flathead Indians play a kind of hockey. In *Cattle Annie and Little Britches*, *Ulzana's Raid*/1972, *Posse*/1975 and *Heaven's Gate*/1980 there are games of baseball, which

A sporting interlude in Buffalo Bill's Wild West: Indians playing table tennis

appear to function rather like the motor cars that appear in Peckinpah Westerns, as signs of 'progress'. Cole Younger (Cliff Robertson) in *The Great Northfield Minnesota Raid*/1972 has the last word on this. As they ride up to town he and his gang see a baseball game in progress. 'It's the new national pastime,' he is told. 'Our national pastime is shooting and always will be,' says Cole, blowing the ball away with his shotgun.
Cattle Annie and Little Britches/1980/UA/*d* Lamont Johnson/*lp* Burt Lancaster, Rod Steiger

Springfield rifle · Manufactured at the government armoury at Springfield, Massachusetts, the muzzle-loading .58 calibre Springfield rifle was produced in vast quantities for the Union forces during the Civil War. After the war these weapons were converted to breechloaders with a so-called 'trap-door' mechanism in which , the breechblock was raised to allow for the insertion of a fresh cartridge. The Springfield was standard issue for the army during the Indian wars of the 1870s and 1880s. Its disadvantage was that it was a single-shot weapon, but it was cheap and reliable. As well as being the weapon that engenders the denouement of *Springfield Rifle*/1952 it was also *The Gun That Won the West*/1955/COL/*d* William Castle/*lp* Denis Morgan.

Stanford, Leland (1824-93) · One of the 'Big Four' (along with Charles Crocker, Mark Hopkins and Collis P. *Huntington) who built the *Central Pacific and Southern Pacific Railroads. It was Stanford who on 10 May 1869 at Ogden, Utah, drove in the Central Pacific's ceremonial spike linking it with the *Union Pacific to complete the first transcontinental railroad. Stanford also sponsored the experiments in high-speed photography conducted by Eadweard *Muybridge which contributed towards the invention of the cinema.
Guy Usher/*Union Pacific*/1939
Television · R. G. Armstrong/*The Last Ride of the Dalton Gang*

Starr, Belle (1848-89) · Outlaw. Born Myra Belle Shirley, she was brought up in Missouri during the troubled era of the border wars. Her first lover was Cole *Younger, who probably fathered her daughter Pearl. Soon after Belle had a second child, Edward, by Jim Reed, another outlaw. When Reed was killed she organized her own band of outlaws in Indian Territory and took up with a Cherokee, Sam Starr, whose name she adopted. In 1883 they were both sentenced to a year's jail for horse stealing by Isaac *Parker, the notorious hanging judge. Other lovers and more banditry followed before Belle was shot in the back by an unknown assassin. Lurid newspaper and dime novel accounts raised her to celebrity status after her death, emphasizing both the frequency with which she changed lovers and the reckless bravery with which, dressed in velvet skirt and plumed hat, she played the part of a 'bandit queen'.
Betty Compson/*Court-Martial*/1928/COL/*d* George B. Seitz/*lp* Jack Holt · Gene Tierney/*Belle Starr*/1941/FOX/*d* Irving Cummings/*lp* Randolph Scott, Dana Andrews · Isabell Jewell/*Badman's Territory*/1946/RKO/*d* Tim Whelan/*lp* Randolph Scott · Isabell Jewell/*Belle Starr's Daughter*/1948/FOX/*d* Lesley Selander/*lp* George Montgomery · Jane Russell/*Montana Belle*/1951/RKO/*d* Allan Dwan/*lp* George Brent, Forrest Tucker · Merry Anders/*Young Jesse James*/1960/FOX/*d* William Claxton/*lp* Robert Stricklyn · Sally Starr/*The Outlaws Is Coming*/1964/COL/*d* Norman Maurer/*lp* The Three Stooges · Elsa Martinelli/*Il mio corpo per un poker*/1967/It/*d* Nathan Wich · Pat Quinn/*Zachariah*/1970/ABC/*d* George Englund/*lp* John Rubinstein · Pamela Reed/*The Long Riders*/1980 · (Keith Larsen plays the title role in *Son of Belle Starr*/1953/AA/*d* Frank McDonald/*lp* Dona Drake)
Television · Carole Matthews/*Death Valley Days* · Marie Windsor/*Stories of the Century* · Jean Willes/*Maverick* · Elizabeth Montgomery/*Belle Starr*

Belle Starr (1889)

Springfield rifle (1888)

ACCESSION TO STATEHOOD

States and territories · Constitutionally, the United States is a federal republic, not a unitary one. That means that the fifty separate states are 'independent' entities. Unlike the counties of Britain or the *départements* of France, their boundaries and their legal existence cannot be altered by action of the federal government. Each has its own written constitution which, like the Federal Constitution, is nominally the supreme expression of the political will of its particular citizens. Each has a political structure which mimics the one in Washington, with executive, legislative and judicial branches. Each state, regardless of its population, elects two members of the United States Senate, and each chooses at least one member of the House of Representatives, with increasing numbers according to population.

This arrangement reflects the fact that the original thirteen states existed before the Republic itself. During the period between independence (1776) and the adoption of the

Federal Constitution (1787-8) their relationship to one another bore many of the characteristics of a treaty organization, rather than of sub-entities of a single nation. Vestiges of that still linger, in the equal representation of all states in the Senate and in the legal doctrine that each separate state is 'sovereign'.

The Republic's expansion from the original thirteen states to the present fifty has taken place, for the most part, according to the provisions of the 'Northwest Ordinances' of 1784 and 1787. These acts, adopted by the Confederation Congress that preceded the present government, were intended to organize the western lands that had been ceded by Britain when it recognized American independence in 1783. Congress acquired the responsibility to do so when the original states finally agreed to yield their conflicting claims to land west of the Appalachians.

The Act of 1784 was the brainchild of Thomas *Jefferson. It proposed to solve

America's new-found colonial problem by creating ten new states, bearing names like Chersonesus, Assenisipia and Polypotamia. Jefferson's pen, usually facile, had failed him, but the idea proved good. In its final form the 1784 Ordinance provided for the temporary government of western 'territories', whose people would eventually gain the right to establish their own state constitutions and to petition for admission to the Union 'on an equal footing with the original states'. The Ordinance of 1787 changed some details, and forbade slavery north of the Ohio.

The principle that was established in 1784 governed the admission of new states down to the entry of Alaska (1959) and Hawaii (1961). As finally worked out, the progress to statehood was to follow three stages. Until a region reached a population of 5,000 it would be an 'unorganized territory', with its government in the hands of a judge appointed by the central government. From that point until it reached a population of

60,000 it would be an 'organized territory'. Its people would have the right to elect their own legislature, together with a non-voting delegate to Congress, but they would be subject to a governor appointed, like the judge who previously had ruled them, from afar. Then they could seek statehood.

Only to a small extent, however, does the political process of acquiring statehood figure in Westerns. The Billy the Kid films, especially *The Left Handed Gun*/1957 and *Pat Garrett and Billy the Kid*/1973, make some play of the fact that General Lew Wallace (author of *Ben Hur*) was governor of New Mexico during the Kid's time of notoriety, when territorial politics were in a state of turmoil. In *The Man Who Shot Liberty Valance*/1962 John Ford makes much of a convention that will decide between seeking statehood and remaining as a territory. At issue is the question of progress, which statehood will bring but which remaining in territorial status will thwart. Under a territorial administration, the film implies (without, perhaps, making it altogether clear), the big landowners, who have the ear of Washington, will continue to dominate. Statehood, however, will bring full democracy; the small farmers and traders can make their voices heard locally. But the real purpose of the sequence is to allow Ford to indulge his taste for folksy populism at the expense of the long-winded politicians who argue on each side.

In political terms the progress from territory to state status was at the heart of America's organization of its western empire. But in filmic terms it is a relatively minor motif, often 'present' as background information but rarely treated as a major problem in its own right. EC

Station · The train station suggests the wider symbolic possibilities of the railroad, a tiny outpost connected by a thin steel link to civilization. In a trio of 1950s Westerns the station functions more formally as the *mise en scène* for tense dramas measured against the ticking clock as a deadline inexorably approaches: *High Noon*/1952, *3:10 to Yuma*/1957, *Last Train from Gun Hill*/1958. It's a fitting location, since it was the needs of the nineteenth-century railroad system which ushered in accurate time-keeping and the standardization of time across continents.

Steamboats · The classic paddle-steamer type of riverboat had its heyday on the Mississippi during the 1850s; after that the development of the railroad, first in the east,

then after the Civil War in the West, led to a sharp decline in river traffic. In the Western the steamboat signals the opulence, perhaps even the decadence, of the South as contrasted with the rugged West – a fitting location for the brocade waistcoat of the gambler and the décolletage of the expensive women who are not perhaps quite ladies; as for example in *4 for Texas*/1963/WB/d Robert Aldrich/lp Frank Sinatra, Dean Martin, Anita Ekberg, Ursula Andress.

Stunts · In *Dark Command*, in one of the most famous stunts in the Western, Yakima Canutt and Cliff Lyons, doubling for John Wayne and Gabby Hayes, drive a wagon and team of horses over the edge of a cliff into a lake. Movie companies had realized early on that the star system necessitated the employment of doubles for the dangerous stunts popular in action pictures. An injury to a stunt man was inconvenient; an injury to a star was expensive, possibly ruinous, because of time lost waiting for a recovery. Some Western stars prided themselves on their ability to perform their own stunts (Tom Mix was especially proficient, and Ken Maynard was an extremely accomplished horseman), but as demand grew for more and more spectacular jumps and falls the job was increasingly given to specialists.

Since the most popular stunts in West-

erns involved horses, stunt men were recruited from among working cowboys and rodeo performers. Techniques were perfected for performing a number of standardized routines. There was the 'transfer' in which a rider drew alongside a moving train or stagecoach and jumped from his horse on to the vehicle. Canutt was particularly skilled at this manoeuvre, embellishing it into a complicated routine such as the one he performs in *Sunset in Eldorado*. Having transferred from his horse to a stagecoach, he fights the villain and is knocked down between the galloping horses. As the coach passes over him he grabs an axle, pulls himself up on to the back of the coach and resumes his fight. The whole stunt is performed in a single take, without the cuts that would permit cheating.

Other standard stunts included the cliff leap on horseback. Since a horse could not be trained to throw itself from a great height (horse-sense?) a chute was constructed. The horse and rider were dropped on to it by a trap and because the chute was greased both slid down and over the edge of the cliff. This stunt is performed in *Jesse James*/1939 and repeated in *The True Story of Jesse James*/1957.

Falls of various kinds have been in demand by Western directors from the earliest days. One method is to dig a pit,

Yakima Canutt making a transfer

cover it and ride the unsuspecting horse into it. A more complicated method is known as the 'running W'. Wires are fixed to hobbles on the horse's legs, usually to all four. The wires are then gathered through a ring, coiled up on the ground and attached to a strong anchor point. The wires are long enough to allow the horse space to break into a gallop before the wires are fully extended. When the horse reaches the point where the slack is taken up the wires tighten and the horse is brought crashing to the ground, at a pre-ordained position just in front of the camera.

This method produced spectacular falls at a great risk of injury to the horse. As the result of bad publicity in the late 1930s, especially when large numbers of horses were killed making *The Charge of the Light Brigade* in 1936, the American Humane Association intervened and the 'running W' was banned. This put the emphasis on training horses to fall rather than forcing them. Stunt artists also explored new ways of falling off horses while leaving the horse standing. One effective method uses a harness worn under the clothing. One end of a wire is attached to the harness, the other end to a fixed point. The horseman rides past and then, rather in the manner of the 'running W', the wire draws tight, pulling him off the horse. (See also *Dragged by a horse.)
Dark Command/1940/REP/d Raoul Walsh/lp John Wayne, Claire Trevor, Walter Pidgeon · *Sunset in El Dorado*/1945/REP/d John McDonald/lp Roy Rogers, George Hayes

Sutter, John (1803-80) · Sutter arrived in California from Switzerland in 1839 and was granted a large area of land in the Sacramento valley by the Mexican authorities. This he developed into a prosperous ranch on which he built Sutter's Fort, a impressive adobe structure which became an important trading centre. On 24 January 1848 one of his workmen discovered gold in the American River on Sutter's property. Nine days later, before the news had properly got out, Mexico ceded California to the United States. The secret of Sutter's gold could not be kept for long and the gold rush was on. His employees deserted him for the diggings, his land was invaded by miners and his livestock and crops destroyed. Not till 1864 did he get recompense from the state of California.

As Christopher Frayling has shown in *Spaghetti Westerns*, the story of Sutter is full of symbolic resonance, some of which is brought out in the various attempts at a screen version. In 1930 Sergei Eisenstein planned a film for Paramount based on Blaise Cendrars' novel about Sutter, *L'Or* (1925), but it was never made. In 1936 the Nazi film industry produced its own version of Sutter's story, *Der Kaiser von Kalifornien* (*The Emperor of California*). At the same time came Paramount's version, *Sutter's Gold*.
Charles Brinley/*California in '49*/1924/Arrow/d Jacques Jaccard/lp Edmund Cobb · Luis Trenker/*Der Kaiser von Kalifornien*/1936/Tobis/d Luis Trenker/lp Viktoria von Ballasko · Edward Arnold/*Sutter's Gold*/1936
Television · Royal Dano/*Donner Pass: The Road to Survival* · John Dehner/*California Gold Rush*

Swarthout, Glendon (b 1918) · Author. Swarthout's novel *They Came to Cordura* (1958) is set in 1916 at the time of General Pershing's abortive 'punitive' expedition against Pancho Villa. Written in a lean and sinewy prose, it tells the story of an officer escorting back to base through hostile country a group of men who are to be given awards for bravery. This was filmed as *They Came to Cordura*/1959/COL/d Robert Rossen/lp Gary Cooper, Rita Hayworth. Swarthout has written several other Western novels, but the only other one to be filmed is *The Shootist*, published in 1975 and filmed the next year, with John Wayne in a part specially written for him, that of the aging gunfighter dying of cancer. Swarthout also supplied the story basis for *7th Cavalry*/1956/COL/d Joseph H. Lewis/lp Randolph Scott.

Swedes · 'Swedes in this country, they keep popping up like jack-rabbits,' says the bigshot in *Terror in a Texas Town*/1958. In fact there's only Sterling Hayden and his father, though it proves enough. They do keep popping up in John Ford films, though, and played by John Qualen, as in *The Searchers*/1956 and *The Man Who Shot Liberty Valance*/1962. There's a comic Swede in *The Big Trail*/1930, a Swedish farmer in *Shane*/1952, a Swedish gunsmith in *El Dorado*/1966, and in *The Beautiful Blonde from Bashful Bend*/1949 there's a Swedish marshal with a funny accent who sounds like the original for the Swedish chef in *The Muppet Show*. On a more serious note, in the early 70s Jan Troell directed a pair of films, *Utvandrana* (*The Emigrants*) (1970) and *Nybyggarna* (*The New Land*) (1973), about Swedish settlers in nineteenth-century Minnesota.

T

Tall tales · A distinctive type of western humour much favoured by mountain men and Mark *Twain. It appears only rarely in the Western film, though to some effect when told by a consummate actor; such as James Stewart in *Destry Rides Again*/1939 and in *How the West Was Won*/1962, or Henry Fonda in *The Cheyenne Social Club*. Arthur Hunnicutt tells a tall tale in *The Big Sky*/1952, about how he'd sewn a man's ear back on when it had been torn off by a bear. The trouble was, he'd sewn it on backwards, which made the man angry because every time he heard a rattlesnake he turned the wrong way about.
The Cheyenne Social Club/1970/National-General/d Gene Kelly/lp James Stewart, Henry Fonda

Taos School · The Taos Society of Artists, founded in 1912, originally had six members: Joseph Sharp (1859-1953), Bert Phillips (1868-1956), Oscar Berninghaus (1874-1952), Ernest Blumenschein (1874-1960), Eanger Irving Couse (1866-1936) and W. Herbert Dunton (1878-1936). Basing themselves at Taos in New Mexico this group, later augmented by others, devoted itself to producing an authentically American art based on the colours and shapes of the landscape of the Southwest and on Indian life. Many of their paintings have a pronounced ethnographic impulse, depicting Indian ceremonies or the work of potters and weavers. (See Plate 22)

Tavernier, Jules (1844-89) · Painter. In 1873 Tavernier, together with a fellow Frenchman Paul Frenzeny, was sent by *Harper's Weekly* on a tour from New York to San Francisco. The pair sketched the cattle trade in Wichita, the Indian Sun Dance in Nebraska, sod houses on the Kansas plain, mining in Colorado, Mormons in Utah and the Chinese in San Francisco. Over the next two or three years their pictures appeared regularly in the magazine, representative of the mass of material about the West which appeared in popular publications in the last quarter of the century. Tavernier also painted some evocative western landscapes. (See Plate 15)

Taylor, Buck (1857-1924) · The first true cowboy hero, in fact as well as fiction. Taylor worked with cattle from an early age, was taken on by Buffalo Bill *Cody at his Nebraska ranch and toured with his original

Buck Taylor (c.1890)

Wild West show. Taylor also appeared in the first dime novel about a cowboy, *Buck Taylor, King of the Cowboys*, published in 1887 and written by Prentiss *Ingraham. In a later work, *Buck Taylor, The Saddle King* (1891), anticipating the sartorial effects of Tom Mix, he appeared 'dressed in somewhat gaudy attire, wore a watch and chain, diamond pin in his black scarf, representing a miniature spur, and upon the small finger of his right hand there was a ring, the design being a horseshoe of rubies. About his broad-brimmed, dove-colored sombrero was coiled a miniature lariat, so that the spur, horseshoe and lasso designated his calling.'
Fred N. Larsen/*Buffalo Bill and the Indians*/1976

Taylor, Zachary (1784-1850) · Soldier and 12th President of the US. Taylor saw service in the War of 1812 and in the *Seminole Wars. But his main claim to fame came later. In 1846 Taylor led his troops into the disputed area between the Nueces and Rio Grande rivers in Texas. When Mexican troops attacked war was declared. Taylor fought several successful battles, including Buena Vista, at which Santa Anna was defeated. Within two years the war was over, with Mexico defeated, and the United States had acquired vast new territories from Texas to the Pacific. Taylor was a hero and was elected President in 1848, but died of cholera while in office.

Allan Cavan/*Rebellion*/1936/Crescent/*d* Lynn Shores/*lp* Tom Keene · Robert Barrat/*Distant Drums*/1951

Telegraph · In 1860 Congress passed a bill authorizing a subsidy of $40,000 a year for ten years to pay for the construction of a transcontinental telegraph wire. The telegraph, for which Samuel Morse (1791-1872) received a patent in 1844, already connected Omaha, Nebraska to the east, and the Western Union Telegraph Company began construction up the Platte along the emigrant trail to South Pass. Despite the logistical problems of transporting thousands of poles across the treeless prairie the wire from the east was joined with one from California in Salt Lake City on 24 October 1861. These events form the background to *The Telegraph Trail*/1933/WB/*d* Tenny Wright/*lp* John Wayne, Yakima Canutt, and the more considerable *Western Union*/1941, based on the Zane Grey novel of the same title.

Texas · General Phil *Sheridan, who had first-hand experience, once famously remarked that if he owned hell and Texas he'd live in hell and rent out Texas. Such a disenchanted view has not been shared by Western film-makers, for whom Texas has been the most popular geographical point of reference. Phil Hardy in his encyclopedia *The Western* lists 46 films of the sound period whose titles begin with the word Texas and there are scores more with Texas in the title somewhere, not to mention *Dallas, Fort Worth, San Antonio*, etc. To some extent this may reflect no more than the sheer size of the place, Texas being the largest of the contiguous states (Alaska is twice as big), and over five times the size of England. But more importantly, Texas is the origin and still the centre of the distinctive cowboy culture that came to dominate the popular idea of the West.

Texas was under Spanish and then Mexican rule until the 1830s, when the large numbers of English-speaking colonists rebelled. Although defeated at the battle of the *Alamo in March 1836, the Anglos under the command of Sam *Houston turned the tables on the Mexican general Santa Anna at San Jacinto the next month. Texas was then an independent republic until 1845, when by mutual consent it became part of the United States. This led to war with Mexico, but a victory for the US in 1848 secured the status of Texas. During the Civil War Texas sided with the Confederacy despite the opposition of Sam Houston, its

Governor until deposed. The period after the Civil War was difficult. The economy was depressed. Low prices for livestock led to the cattle-drives north to the railheads in Kansas in search of better markets. During Reconstruction the zeal of radicals and the rapaciousness of northern carpetbaggers led to the alienation of many Texans from government. Consequently an atmosphere of lawlessness thrived in which outlaws and gunmen such as John Wesley *Hardin and John King Fisher flourished. Gradually the *Texas Rangers restored order, though much of their energies were directed against the Comanche.

Cattle continued to be a major business in Texas in the 1870s. The Texas and Pacific railroad arrived in Dallas in 1873 and Fort Worth in 1876, turning both into boom towns, and signalling the end of the trail drives north. Agriculture continued to dominate until the discovery of vast oilfields in 1901 led to the state's transformation to its present-day predominantly industrial and urban economy. Yet the image of Texas, as soap operas like *Dallas* confirm, continues to be that of a frontier society.

Films set in Texas are too numerous to review. Curiously, some of the best known are among the longest Westerns ever made, as though the size of the state calls up in the film-maker a corresponding urge to sprawl. Thus *Giant*/1956 is 197 mins; *The Alamo* is 192 mins; *The Big Country*/1958 163 mins; *Duel in the Sun*/1946 138 mins.
The Alamo/1960/Batjac/*d* John Wayne/*lp* John Wayne, Richard Widmark, Laurence Harvey

Texas Rangers · It was the early Texas colonist Stephen Austin who first organized a permanent body of armed men to conduct campaigns against the Indians. The Rangers were more formally constituted in 1835, immediately prior to the war which brought Texas its independence. During the war and after they played a major role in fighting against both Indians and Mexicans. The Rangers were an irregular body, furnishing their own horses and weapons, wearing no uniform and submitting only to what discipline they chose. They were reorganized during the lawless period following the Civil War and from then until the end of the century they brought to justice a number of outlaws such as Sam *Bass and John Wesley *Hardin. The Rangers still operate as a small élite force of criminal investigators. The dozens of B-features about Texas Rangers pay little attention to history and merely

draw on an evocative name. But King Vidor's *The Texas Rangers* claims to be based on documentary records. Sam Bass and the Sundance Kid (whom the Rangers also pursued) appear in the 1951 version.
The Texas Rangers/1936/PAR/*d* King Vidor/*lp* Fred MacMurray, Jack Oakie · *The Texas Rangers*/1951/COL/*d* Phil Karlson/*lp* George Montgomery

Theatre · The theatre counts for culture, even refinement, in the various versions of the Judge Roy Bean story, in which Bean's obsession with the elegant Lillie Langtry is the counterpoint to his administration of rough justice. This apart, the theatrical performances we actually see in the Western tend to be made fun of when they are not treated with outright hostility. It's as though the West can't afford to take the East's culture at its own valuation. This is certainly true of the thespians (it seems the right word) in John Ford's *My Darling Clementine*/1946 and *Wagon Master*/1950, where Alan Mowbray is wonderfully Dickensian in his seedy pretentiousness. (In *My Darling Clementine* when Walter Brennan hears the word Shakespeare he literally does reach for his gun.) The hamminess of Victorian theatre is again joyfully seized on in *Calamity Jane*/1953. What's so pleasing about *Heller in Pink Tights*/1960 is that director George Cukor has great fun at the expense of theatrical tawdriness, yet moves us with Anthony Quinn's dignity in rising above it.

Tilghman, William (1854-1924) · Lawman. After a wild youth, in which he was arrested for horse-stealing though not convicted, Tilghman, or 'Uncle Billy' as he became known, served as marshal of *Dodge City 1884-6. When Oklahoma was opened up in 1889 Tilghman took part in the land rush, but soon reverted to marshalling in the new territory. He was sent, along with Chris Madsen and Heck Thomas (the three were known as the 'Oklahoma Guardsmen'), to capture Bill *Doolin and his gang, and Tilghman, single-handed, caught him at Eureka Springs, Arkansas in 1896. In 1908 he appeared in *The Bank Robbery*, a film describing the exploits of Al *Jennings, whom Tilghman had once pursued. In 1915 Tilghman himself directed a movie entitled *The Passing of the Oklahoma Outlaws*, which detailed the capture of the Doolin and Jennings gangs and featured actual participants such as Tilghman's fellow marshal Chris Madsen. For several years Tilghman toured theatres with his film and his collec-

tion of six-guns.
Rod Steiger/*Cattle Annie and Little Britches*/1980/UA/*d* Lamont Johnson/*lp* Burt Lancaster

Titles · Alain Bony writes in *Le Western*, edited by Jean-Louis Leutrat (Paris: Armand Colin, 1973):
'One of the most notable characteristics of Western titles is that they are almost always recognizable as such. Purely psychological titles, such as *The Misfits*, are very rare. Usually titles evoke the world of the Western, that is when they do not suggest an entire sequence of events.
a) *People*
Often the title mentions the name of the principal person in the film, alone or associated with other terms which determine it as belonging to the genre. Some names, especially those of famous outlaws or historical people, do not need to be more precisely characterized (Billy the Kid, Jesse James, Geronimo, Sitting Bull, Buffalo Bill, Davy Crockett, etc.). Others are identified by rudimentary psychological descriptions corresponding to a loose typology of the genre ("lucky", "evil", etc.), or by a mention of physical, social or professional stereotyped characteristics, or by a place of origin preceding or following the name (*Nevada Smith*, *Al Jennings of Oklahoma*). But it's a person's function which counts more than their name, hence the frequency in titles of roles designated by such terms as outlaw, gunfighter, rider, and especially cowboy, sheriff, etc., and also the number of explicitly narrative functions such as "bad man". Moreover, anonymity in a title is not without significance. All those titles beginning "The man who..." or "The man from..." refer to that other stereotype of the Western, the stranger, the man who comes from somewhere else.
b) *Place names*
First there are the places famous in the history of the West: Abilene, Santa Fe, Tombstone; and western states: from California to Arkansas, from Texas to Montana. Also some other areas such as the badlands (of South Dakota) and the Texas Panhandle. And then there are all those combinations possible with terms such as creek, gulch, rio, mesa, the names of Indian lands or expressions relating to geographical characteristics of the West such as mountains, canyons, prairie.
c) *Specific references*
Many titles use terms or expressions deriving from particularly evocative sour-

ces: terms of Spanish and especially Mexican origin; flora and fauna of the West; Indian words which for the most part escape translation (squaw, tomahawk, tepee, etc.); and above all three of the richest sources: everything relating to horses and the equestrian arts, to weapons and their use, and to cards and the activities of gamblers. The extreme technicality of such references makes it impossible to begin an inventory. But they do supply the clue to certain mysterious titles; for example, *One-Eyed Jacks*, a reference to cards (of the four Jacks, two are seen only in profile and hence only one eye is visible, whence comes the title, applied to those individuals who, lacking in frankness, hide their real thoughts...).
d) *The syntax of titles*
When it doesn't refer simply to a person or a place, a title describes an action or summarizes a story. People, as we have seen, are presented in a dynamic fashion, by means of their role or their temperament or their origin. But this latent action becomes explicit in those titles which are complete sentences, as in *I Killed Wild Bill Hickok* or *It Happened in Hollywood*, or in those titles which take a more traditional form but which do contain a complete phrase, such as *The Man Who Shot Liberty Valance*, or titles of the type *When the Redskins Rode*. Action is present, in the form of a geographical displacement, in all those titles which indicate a direction: *Across the Badlands*, *Along the Oregon Trail*, *Below the Border*, *Beyond the Pecos*, *Crossing the American Prairie*, *Down Texas Way*, *West of Tombstone*, *North of the Rio Grande*, *Westbound*; also in *Escape from Fort Bravo*, *The Man from Laramie*, or in *The Overlanders*, etc. Violent action, obvious in "fight", "kill", "shoot", is also evident in titles which put people in jeopardy, such as *Jesse James vs. the Daltons*, or in notices such as *Have Gun, Will Travel* or *Wanted...*

After exoticism, a feature of almost all titles, and then movement and violence, it's the endurance of the West and the indestructibility of its heroes and myths which mark out the formula, as in *The Unconquered*, *The Undefeated*, *The Unforgiven*; or those periodic reappearances (*The Return of Jack Slade*, *Lightning Carson Rides Again*), that eternal return which wipes away nostalgia for what has passed (*When the Daltons Rode*, *The Days of Jesse James*) so that the Western can be what it has always been: a saga living still in the evocative sound of its titles, even in the macabre alliterations of *Deadwood Dick* or *Tombstone, the Town Too Tough to Die*.'

Tombstone · In films Tombstone is usually represented as a cattle town, but its prosperity was founded entirely on mining. Silver was discovered in 1877 and for ten years Tombstone was booming. Curly Bill *Brocius, Doc *Holliday, Johnny *Ringo, Luke *Short and Wyatt *Earp are some of the famous or notorious names associated with the town, whose most celebrated event was the gunfight at the O.K. Corral on 26 October 1881. By the mid-1890s mining had become sporadic; today Tombstone exists solely as a tourist attraction.

Torture · Ray Allen Billington in his study of European images of the American frontier, *Land of Savagery, Land of Promise*, has compiled a little catalogue of Indian tortures drawn from the febrile brains of nineteenth-century novelists:

'Captives were nailed to trees to be consumed by animals, skinned alive, roasted over slow fires, buried in the arms of an already dead comrade, their flesh sliced off and eaten as they watched, sulfur matches lighted between their fingers, wooden splinters thrust under their nails, their faces coated with honey to lure bees that would sting them to death, molten gold poured into their mouths (a favorite means of disposing of miners), thongs slipped through gashed skin and used to suspend the sufferer, eyes plucked from their heads and the sockets filled with live coals.'

Needless to say, in these novels torture, like *scalping, is assumed to be a practice performed exclusively by Indians on whites. The same assumption has prevailed in the cinema; but, inhibited by the power of the visual image, more closely policed by the censors, and with an audience perhaps more humane, perhaps more squeamish than the Victorians, film-makers have more often suggested torture than shown it. In *The Plainsman*/1936 Indians are briefly shown to torture Wild Bill Hickok (Gary Cooper) by suspending him over a fire. Thirty years later, despite the 'realism' generally supposed to have invaded the Western in the 1960s, we get more or less the same thing, with not much more detail, in *Major Dundee*/1964.

Train robbery · The first train robbery in America was committed by the *Reno gang in Indiana in 1866, and the technique of robbing trains was perfected by the *James gang, who robbed their first train near Council Bluffs, Iowa, on 21 July 1873. They soon worked out a standard procedure

(faithfully described in *Jesse James*/1939 and *The True Story of Jesse James*/1957): flag down the train at a lonely spot, separate the express car from the passenger cars in order to minimize interference, loot the safe, escape on horseback. This they followed successfully in train robberies in Missouri and Kansas. Later noted train robbers included the *Dalton gang, the Wild Bunch and Sam *Bass. By 1890 the *frontier may have been closed, at least according to Frederick Jackson Turner; but it has been calculated that in the 1890s there were 261 train robberies in America, in the course of which 88 people were killed. This makes *The Great Train Robbery*/1903 no less contemporary in its reference than the gangster movies of the 1930s.

Henry Fonda (centre, with gun) robs a train in The Return of Frank James

Transport · The most palpable fact about the West is its size. The Great Plains alone cover an area equal to Great Britain, Ireland, France, Germany, Denmark, Holland, Belgium, Austria, Italy, Spain, Portugal and one-fifth of European Russia. The distance between Chicago and San Francisco is equivalent to that between London and Moscow. Texas alone is more than five times the size of England.

Small wonder, then, that space and movement are such important constituents of the Western. If the films can be divided into those structured by a journey and those which are static, even in the latter there is usually a sense of distance outside, of isolating space. In a world so physically vast, transport becomes of prime importance.

Two of the major forms of transport in the Western, the *horse and the *railroad, are dealt with separately. Of other forms, the wagon was the most important economically. The most famous wagon route across the west was the Central Overland Road. Beginning at the Missouri River, it stretched 200 miles along the Platte to Fort Kearny, in

present-day Nebraska, and, still following the Platte, on to the Rockies. These it crossed via South Pass. Soon after this it branched, one road going northwest along the Snake River and through further mountain ranges to Oregon, the other southwest across the Nevada desert and the Sierra Nevada to California.

The word 'road' may give a misleading impression. The route along much of the way was no better than a track, and in many places not even that. But from the 1840s, after the United States had acquired California and other areas of the West from Mexico, improvements were constantly being made. The myth of the hardy and independent pioneer, spurred on by rugged individualism, blazing his own trail west, dies hard. In fact both the army and the Department of the Interior were heavily involved in a western roads programme. Army topographers surveyed for better routes and in parts constructed them. In the 1850s and 1860s the government, through mail contracts and land grants, was to be closely involved with the establishment of stagecoach lines and railroads.

Despite improvements, travel in the heavy wagons, including the classic Conestoga wagon familiarly associated with the emigrants, remained slow. Wagons were generally pulled by mules, which were hardier than horses and ate less, or by oxen, which could in emergency themselves be eaten (the taboo against eating horses seems to have been as strong in actuality as it is in the Western film). Wagon trains might travel only 15 miles a day, making for a three- or four-month trip to California.

In the period after the California gold rush freighting became a highly organized business. Though in some limited areas river transport by *steamboat could carry heavy goods, wagons were in most areas the only means. In 1853 William Waddell and William Russell secured a government contract to transport military supplies down the Santa Fe Trail into New Mexico. The next year the pair were joined by Alexander Majors and formed the firm of Russell, Majors and Waddell, which for the next few years was the most famous company in western transport. By 1858 it was employing four thousand men. Its fame was enhanced when in 1860 it began the celebrated, though brief, *Pony Express service.

In 1857 Congress decided, since there appeared to be no immediate prospect of a railroad across to the Pacific, that a transcontinental stagecoach line should be estab-

WAGON ROADS AND STAGE LINES

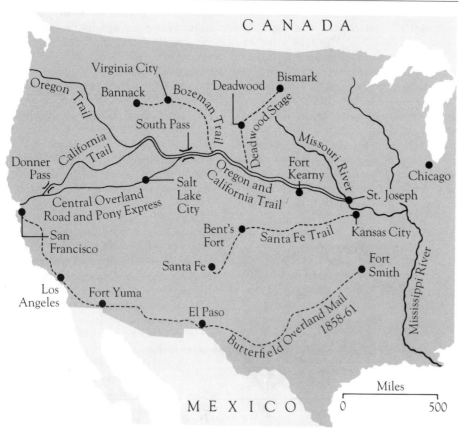

Wells, Fargo stage, Virginia City, Montana

lished. This was in effect subsidized through the award of a contract to carry mail. The successful bidder for the contract was John Butterfield (1801-69), whose Overland Mail Company inaugurated a twice-weekly mail and passenger service, beginning on 16 September 1858. Butterfield's stagecoaches followed a southerly course, known from its shape as the 'oxbow' route, from Fort Smith, Arkansas through Texas, New Mexico and Arizona, to Los Angeles and San Francisco. This route had to be abandoned at the start of the Civil War and a new, central one established. From 1864 the Overland Mail plied a route west of Salt Lake City to California. East of Salt Lake City, as far as St Joseph, Missouri, the mails were carried by another company, the Overland Stage Line, organized by Ben Holladay (1819-87). It's an Overland Stage Line coach in which the passengers are travelling in *Stagecoach*/1939.

Butterfield (who appears, played by Robert Emhardt, in *3:10 to Yuma*/1957) had got into financial difficulties and he had been replaced as president of the Overland Mail in 1860. Holladay, on the other hand, soon became known as 'the stagecoach king' as he gained control of other stagecoach lines, including the Central Overland California and Pike's Peak Express Company, and also of Russell, Majors and Waddell. But in 1866 Holladay was himself bought out by the firm of Wells, Fargo and Company.

Henry Wells (1805-78) and William Fargo (1818-81) had formed their firm in 1852, originally to transport freight to and from California. The company also acted as a bank, accepting deposits of gold from miners. Wells, Fargo were soon operating stagecoaches too; they had a financial interest in Butterfield's Overland Mail from the start, and when they acquired Holladay's interests they were in effective control of the entire stagecoach and express business in the West. The completion of the transcontinental railroad in 1869 forced the company to modify their business, but they remained pre-eminent in the field of express and security services. (*Wells Fargo*/1937/PAR/*d* Frank Lloyd/*lp* Joel McCrea is a heavily fictionalized story of the company's early days.)

The stagecoach remained the major form of publicly available transport in the West until supplanted by the railroad, and in some areas this was not until towards the end of the century. The most popular model was the Concord coach, the type almost invariably seen in the Western. It was of sturdy construction, its oval-shaped body suspended on heavy leather straps which allowed it to roll rather than bounce. Coaches were often highly decorated; Holladay's Overland Stage Company favoured vermilion for the coach body, yellow for the running gear, russet for the curtains. Landscape pictures were often painted on the doors. Nine passengers could be accommodated inside, with another two on top. The trip from the Missouri to California, some 2,000 miles, would take around twenty days.

The hazards routinely encountered in the cinema, though of course exaggerated, were real enough. During the Civil War period especially, Indian attacks were a serious problem for wagons and stagecoaches along the Central Overland Road, while Wells, Fargo recorded 313 robberies of its stagecoaches in California alone during the period 1870-84, 27 of them by the notorious *Black Bart. It is probable, though, that more passengers were injured by accidents than by attack, especially on the dangerous mountain roads. Despite this, the dominant sensation must have been tedium, as the stage or wagon trundled across the seemingly endless wilderness; but if the cinema can suggest tedium, it can hardly afford to communicate what it feels like.

Tunstall, John Henry (1853-78) · An Englishman and rancher in Lincoln, New Mexico. Tunstall was the employer of *Billy the Kid and his murder by a posse precipitated the *Lincoln County War. In films he is generally portrayed as a peaceable, Christian man whose influence is the only thing holding Billy back from resuming his career as a killer. In King Vidor's *Billy the Kid*/1930 he's called Tunston and played by Wyndham Standing. The name is changed to Eric Keating when he's played by Ian Hunter in *Billy the Kid* (1941). In *The Kid from Texas* he's called Roger Jameson and played by Shepperd Strudwick. He's played by Colin Keith-Johnston in *The Left Handed Gun*/1957 as a saintly Scotsman who teaches Billy to read the Bible. In *Chisum* Tunstall is played by Patric Knowles, and we know he's a good man because he smokes a pipe. *Billy the Kid*/1941/MGM/*d* David Miller/*lp* Robert Taylor · *The Kid from Texas*/1949/U/*d* Kurt Neumann/*lp* Audie Murphy · *Chisum*/1970/WB/*d* Andrew V. McLaglen/*lp* John Wayne

Tuttle, W[ilbur] C[oleman] (1883-1969) · Pulp fiction writer, many of whose stories were first published as magazine serials. Tuttle's books, beginning with *Reddy Brant, His Adventures* in 1920, appeared at the rate of over one a year for nearly fifty years. Many have a range detective as a hero and Tuttle's novels usually have plenty of humour. They formed the basis for several low-budget films of the 20s and 30s. Films include *The Man with the Punch*/1922/U/*d* Ernst Laemmle/*lp* Hoot Gibson · *The Border Sheriff* ['Straight Shooting']/1926/U/*d* Robert N. Bradbury/*lp* Jack Hoxie · *The Fighting Peacemaker*/1926/U/*d* Clifford Smith/*lp* Jack Hoxie · *The Wild Horse Stampede*/1926/U/*d* Albert Rogell/*lp* Jack Hoxie · *Rocky Rhodes*/1934/U/*d* Al Raboch/*lp* Buck Jones · *The Red Rider*/1934/U/*d* Lew Landers/*lp* Buck Jones · *The Lawless Valley*/1938/RKO/*d* David Howard/*lp* George O'Brien. One of Tuttle's stories, 'Sir Peegan Passes', was filmed as *Man in the Rough*/1928/FBO/*d* Wallace Fox/*lp* Bob Steele · remade as *The Cheyenne Kid*/1933/RKO/*d* Robert Hill/*lp* Tom Keene · remade as *The Fargo Kid*/1940/RKO/*d* Edward Killy/*lp* Tim Holt

Twain, Mark (1835-1910) · Pen name of Samuel Langhorne Clemens. Perhaps Mark Twain is not primarily a western writer. The books for which he is best known, *The Adventures of Tom Sawyer* (1876) and *The Adventures of Huckleberry Finn* (1884) are set in the Mississippi valley of his boyhood, which even then was hardly the frontier. However, the frontier and the wilderness beyond it are ever-present in Huck Finn's imagination and the urge to 'light out for the territories' is as fundamental as in any Western.

Twain became a writer after going to Nevada in 1861 to work for his brother, who had become a secretary to the territorial governor. Following some unsuccessful prospecting Twain became a reporter in *Virginia City, Nevada. In 1864 he went to California, where he met and later collaborated with Bret *Harte. Twain's famous story 'The Celebrated Jumping Frog of Calaveras County' was written during his time in San Francisco and is a classic example of the western *'tall tale'. After travels in Hawaii and the Mediterranean he settled in Connecticut for the rest of his life. In 1872 he produced *Roughing It*, a narrative of his experiences journeying across the plains and the Rockies, which has strong claims to being the most entertaining book about the West ever written.
Television · Dabbs Greer/*Laramie* · Howard Duff/*Bonanza* · Ken Howard/*Bonanza* · William Challee/*Bonanza* · Christopher Connelly/*The Incredible Rocky Mountain Race* · Walker Edmonston/*Mark Twain's America*

U

Undertaker · Death in the Western is attended with due solemnity; those who don't respect the dead are themselves despised. The rituals of death – funeral processions, the burial itself, the reading over the grave – are invested with a weight of meaning. (By contrast, though gangster films also make much of funerals, however lavish their obsequies they confer no dignity on the dead.) Only *in extremis* may the rituals be dispensed with; thus in *The Last Wagon*/1956 Richard Widmark has great difficulty in persuading his charges to leave their dead companions unburied even though they are on the run from Apaches. Despite this solemnity, the appearance of the undertaker is often treated as an occasion for Dickensian humour. In *The Westerner*/1940 the undertaker, a comic little man who doubles as town barber, measures Gary Cooper for his coffin even before Walter Brennan (as Judge Roy Bean) has delivered his verdict.

Union Pacific · The company which built the eastern half of the first transcontinental railroad. Track laying began on the western bank of the Missouri River at Omaha, Nebraska on 2 December 1863, and the Union Pacific joined up with the *Central Pacific at Promontory Point, Utah on 10 May 1869. Despite being awarded large government land grants the Union Pacific was never adequately financed, and before long accusations of corruption emerged in the Credit Mobilier scandal of 1873. The Union Pacific was unable to build the wider network of feeder lines that might have given it financial security and in 1893 it went bankrupt and had to be rescued by Edward Harriman. Some sense of the endless financial machinations that marked the railroad's history survives amid the heroics of Cecil B. DeMille's *Union Pacific*/1939. See also the TV series *Union Pacific*.

V

Victorio (1809?-80) · Chief of the Mimbreno or Warm Springs Apache. Associated in the 1850s with *Geronimo and then with *Mangas Coloradas, Victorio agreed in 1865 to settle with his people on the Ojo Caliente (or Warm Springs) reservation in New Mexico. But in 1877 the US government forcibly removed them to the inhospitable San Carlos reservation in Arizona. Victorio and a group took off to Chihuahua in Mexico, fighting and pillaging. For two years Victorio's skills as a military strategist kept him out of reach, but on 14 October 1880 he and his force were surrounded and wiped out.

Michael Pate/*Hondo*/1953 · Larry Chance/ *Fort Bowie*/1957/UA/d Howard W. Koch/*lp* Ben Johnson · Dan Kemp/*Cry Blood Apache*/1970/Golden Eagle–Goldstone/d Jack Starrett/*lp* Jody McCrea, Joel McCrea Television · Michael Pate/*Hondo* · Greg Suke/*September Gun*

Villa, Pancho (1878-1923) · Mexican bandit and revolutionary, usually portrayed in the cinema as a good-hearted but simple-minded and politically naive peasant. In 1910, despite having promised to relinquish power and hold elections, the Mexican president *Diaz imprisoned the liberal candidate Francisco *Madero. This led to uprisings by the peasants, one of whose leaders was Villa. Diaz was forced to resign and Madero was elected president. But he was reluctant to institute radical reforms and there were further revolts, put down by General Victoriano *Huerta and Pancho Villa. Villa was accompanied on this campaign by the American journalist John Reed, whose account, *Insurgent Mexico*, pictured Villa as a Mexican Robin Hood. In 1913 Huerta suddenly switched sides. Madero was arrested and shot 'while trying to escape'. Huerta made himself president, but Villa and Emiliano *Zapata refused to acknowledge him. Huerta was forced out and the forces of Villa

Pancho Villa (3rd from r.) with his troops (1911)

and Zapata occupied Mexico City.

But now they were in dispute with the forces of Venustiano Carranza, a former comrade and supporter of Madero. In October 1915 the USA recognized Carranza as president. Villa in disgust led a guerrilla raid on Columbus, New Mexico. In retaliation President Woodrow Wilson ordered General Pershing to undertake a 'punitive' expedition and pursue Villa into Mexico. Villa eluded Pershing, but eventually was persuaded to retire from public life. In 1923 he was assassinated when gunmen shot up his car.

Wallace Beery's performance in *Viva Villa!*/1934, though it contains some elements of truth in its acknowledgment of Villa's illiteracy and political naivety, relies overmuch on the concept of a lovable rogue, but at least Villa is centre-frame. In *Villa!* (1958) and in *Villa Rides*/1968 it's the American gun-runners who are at the centre of the story, despite the casting in the latter of Yul Brynner as Villa.

Also: Raoul Walsh/*The Life of General Villa*/1912/Mutual/d Christy Cabanne · Domingo Soler/*Let's Go With Pancho Villa*/1936/Mex/d Fernando de Fuentes · Maurice Black/*Under Strange Flags*/1937/ Crescent/d I.V. Willat/*lp* Tom Keene · Leo Carrillo/*Pancho Villa Returns*/1950/ Mex/d Miguel Contreras Torres · Alan Reed/*Viva Zapata!*/1952 · Rodolfo Hoyos/ *Villa!*/1958/FOX/d James B. Clark/*lp* Brian Keith, Cesar Romero · Pedro Armendariz/ *Así era Pancho Villa*/1958/Mex/d Ismael Rodrigues · Pedro Armendariz/*Pancho Villa y la Valentina*/1958/Mex/d Ismael Rodrigues · Eraclio Zepeda/*Reed: Insurgent Mexico*/1971/Mex/d Paul Leduc · Telly Savalas/*Pancho Villa*/1971/Sp/d Eugenio Martin/*lp* Clint Walker, Chuck Connors Television · Hector Elizondo/*Wanted: The Sundance Woman*

Violence · Violence is central to the Western, and the forms it takes are as various as the different story-types that make up the genre. One could make some fairly clear and useful formal distinctions between subtypes of the Western by distinguishing the special images, ideological rationales, compositions and narrative structures particular to each. The cavalry Western has its Indian massacre or charge into battle, the gunfighter or town-tamer movie its climactic shoot-out in the street, the outlaw movie its disastrous last robbery or assassination, the romantic Western its bullet-riddled rescue scene. When we are told that a certain film is a Western, we confidently expect that it will have a certain geographical and temporal setting, visualized in predictable ways; that whatever its plot line, the violence of nature and of men will be an essential part of its landscape; and that it will probably reach its moral and emotional climax in a singular act of violence.

The centrality of violence in the Western is of more than formal significance. One of the guiding assumptions in the movie depiction of Western violence has been the belief that the frontier was an especially violent environment; and that frontier environments have played a dominant role in shaping American institutions and national character. Although statistical studies have proved time and again that (after 1850) only a small minority of Americans ever went to the frontier – and that the West, as a region, was far less violent than the cities of the Northeast or certain counties in the South – popular myth continues to assert that the frontier was pre-eminently the realm of violence. Similarly, both journalistic and official surveys of the causes of American violence persist in asserting that the present rate of violent crime and domestic bloodshed derives in significant measure from America's frontier origins.

From both a formal and a mythological perspective, the *climactic* act of violence in the Western is obviously of the greatest significance, since it is the crisis towards which the energy of the story is directed. However, the normative quality of Western violence is best suggested by its appearance as something ordinary and predictable, an aspect of folklore, as natural as clear skies and sagebrush. This normative quality of Western violence appears most clearly in the 'bar-room brawl' scene, which has a long history as a convention or icon of the Western. Elaborately choreographed, stereotypical and even stylized in its stages and movements, the 'brawl' serves the Western's larger themes in a variety of ways – usually by providing a more-or-less comic variation on the film's dominant themes. Two cases suggestive of the range of possibilities are the brawls in *Dodge City*/1939 and *Shane*/1952. The former is clearly intended to provide comic relief, whereas the latter is needed to vindicate Shane from an accusation of cowardice and establish the brotherhood of Shane and the farmer Joe Starrett. But both present their violence in a way that is as comic as it is brutal; both deploy the same exaggerated fisticuffs and bashings with chairs and bottles. Both stage the brawl in a building which is architecturally divided between the male-dominated space of the saloon and a 'female' space: in *Shane*, the general store; in *Dodge City*, the meeting-room of the Pure Prairie League (temperance union). In both cases the women are represented as opposed to both liquor and male violence; in both the men vindicate themselves by moving away from the female/temperance room and into the male/saloon world of the brawl. In *Dodge City* the world of references surrounding the brawl (Civil War animosities, trail-drive customs, temperance iconography) establish the notion that saloon brawls have the authenticity of folklore; by the time of *Shane*

the convention is so well established that it needs no such framing to evoke audience expectations – the movie convention itself has become folkloric.

Violence has become a primary formal element in Western movies, but its centrality in the genre derives from sources that are pre-cinematic. The subjects, themes, character types and story forms we associate with the Western are derived from perhaps the oldest of American myths, the 'Myth of the Frontier' – a body of literature, folklore, historiography and polemics produced over a period of three centuries by the settlement-promoters, ideologists, historical romance-writers, dime novelists, melodramatists, historians, journalists and Wild West show entrepreneurs. (See Richard Slotkin, *Regeneration Through Violence*, 1973 and *The Fatal Environment*, 1985.) By the beginning of the 20th century this myth had become one of the central tropes of American ideology and cultural production (at both the élite and the popular levels). The myth of the frontier used westward expansion as a metaphor, expressing in a single dramatic image or fable all the essential elements of America's rapid rise from impoverished colony to industrial world-power.

The Frontier Myth celebrated the conquest and subjugation of a natural wilderness by entrepreneurial individualists, who took heroic risks and so achieved windfall profits and explosive growth at prodigious speeds. There is an implicit violence in the speed with which nature on the frontier is converted into the basis of material progress: the hunting of beasts and the felling of trees reflect the violent and swift transformation of life and character associated with America's highly mobile, growth-oriented, individual-centred political economy. But there was also from the beginning a primary and explicit scenario of violence, necessary to both the historical development of the frontier and to its mythic representation, which was directed against the Native Americans. The Anglo-American colonies grew by displacing the Natives in favour of white colonists and (until 1865) Afro-American slaves. As a result, the Indian war became a characteristic episode of each phase of westward expansion; and the conflict of cultural and racial antagonists became the central dramatic structure of the Frontier Myth. Settler/Indian conflicts were the archetype of frontier conflicts, and provided the symbolic reference points for describing and evaluating other kinds of conflict, such as those between different

generations or classes of settlers.

The effect of the myth was therefore to represent the western frontier as the symbolic 'cutting edge' of American civilization and progress; and as a place in which extreme opposites of value and culture meet, inevitably clash, and pursue their conflict to extreme ends.

By the time movies were invented, the stories that constituted the Frontier Myth had acquired vast popularity in a wide range of cultural productions. The category of 'Western' was in that sense ready-made, and when narrative films began to be produced in commercial quantities scenarists tended to exploit existing properties and formulae.

Of all the ideological elements of the myth, violence translates most effectively to the screen. A few effective images of struggle, connected by editing techniques that emphasize the speed and violence and precarious balance of the actors, make more impact in less time than a page of action-writing by *Cooper or Owen *Wister, or even Louis *L'Amour. In the Frontier Myth, violence was an ideological necessity; in film, the obvious power and appeal of visualized mayhem gave violent scenes a special appeal; and over time and usage, violence became a formal as well as an ideological necessity of Western movies.

Since both form and ideology require that the essential conflicts be resolved in a violent confrontation, it may be said that the irreducible core of the Western story-line is to provide a rationalizing framework which will explain and perhaps justify a spectacular act of violence. Since violence and force are aspects of politics and social control, when the movie-maker provides a motive and scenario for Western violence some of the basic ideological concerns of the society are engaged. When is social or individual violence justified by necessity? Is it a necessary evil or positive good? Who are its legitimate targets? By posing and answering the question in the terms of Western movies, the artist accepts the limits and imperatives of the genre's special ethical or ideological vocabulary.

These concerns are both immediate and historical: immediate, because the rationales of social violence are part of contemporary existence; and historical, because the central premise of the Western is that it is about the American past, and specifically about the origins of American democracy. In the Western movie we see a re-enactment of the forming of a primitive social compact, the explicit making of that mythic exchange of freedom for protected liberty that lies behind the Declaration of Independence and the Constitution. But the Western portrays violent force as the essential element in the social contract. Without the heroic exertion of force, savage, anarchic or regressive forces will engulf the settler community. And although this exercise of force is represented as checked by symbols of social peace or non-violence (generally embodied in women), the Western narrative makes it clear that moral suasion without violent force to back it is incapable of achieving its civilizing ends – is foolish at best, and at worst a species of complicity with evil.

To be justifiable, the violence must be redemptive: it must produce a transformation in human affairs that is clearly 'progressive' in some sense (which will be established by the movie). Redemption can take various forms, singly or in combination, along a spectrum that would run from the purely individual redemption of the violent hero, to the redemption of some other individual whom the hero rescues, to the implied redemption of society through the violent removal of some dark threat to its further progress: the Indian, the outlaw, the tyrannical land baron or corporation, the lingering power of older forms of proprietorship, culture and technology.

The moral tension at the heart of the Western's violence comes from the opposition between purely individualistic or self-ish motives, and motives which are (in effect) the expression through an individual of social or community values and needs. The Western hero, as he appears in those films which established the tradition of the genre, acts consciously or unconsciously for the good of the community; and his triumph suggests that the canons of American communal solidarity rest not merely on some form of law, but on the natural inclinations of self-willed individualities.

The mythic tradition provided film-maker and hero with ready-made devices for expressing the hero's affinity with social values. The most elemental symbol for such values has been the White Woman, in whose name and for whose sake the hero fights the Indians or the outlaws, circumvents the crooked banker or politician. The phrase 'to make this town safe for women and children to walk the streets ...' is one of the most familiar clichés of Western dialogue. The roots of this symbol go right back to the origins of the Frontier Myth in the *captivity narratives of the seventeenth-century Puritan colonists. The treatment of

women (and children) is the moral litmus-test of the Western: we identify villains by their mistreatment of women, their making of widows and orphans instead of whole families; and identify heroes or 'good guys' by the respect even the roughest will show a woman.

The power of this female symbolism runs with great consistency right up to the mid-1960s, and is not entirely absent in later films. In *Dodge City* this symbolic language is developed in a traditional way. The hero (played by Errol Flynn) is at first too independent and self-concerned to take a hand in cleaning up Dodge City. But when the criminals kill the child of an already-widowed mother, he takes up the badge, serves the community, and earns the love and approval of a good woman. *High Noon*/1952 acquires great ironic power by its deliberate inversion of this standard scenario: it begins where *Dodge City* ends, and shows how the moral cowardice of the citizens undoes the bond between hero and community, throwing the town-taming Marshal back on a code of individual integrity. Yet even in this dark and often cynical film, the redemptive woman preserves her role and iconic power: the Marshal's Quaker wife is the only character who moves from an ethic of passivity to active support of the hero and his idea that force is the only answer to certain kinds of evil; and although the Marshal rejects both the town and the badge at the end of the movie, the climactic scene has him rescue his wife from the villain, who (in very traditional iconography) is using her as a shield. Though all other symbols of community morality are discredited in *High Noon*, the 'white woman' retains her status.

So well-established is this convention that small variations in its usage can produce powerful resonances. In the classic outlaw movie *Jesse James*/1939 the hero's degeneration from populist Robin Hood to professional criminal is registered in the responses of his wife: when he is outlawed by an unjust society, she marries him despite the stigma; when he becomes a 'mad wolf', this appears first in his mistreatment of her; when she rejects him, he has hit his moral low point, and when she takes him back he approaches redemption.

The values women represent often militate against violence in principle. One of the perennial conflicts of the genre pits a 'female' insistence on social peace and Christian forgiveness against a 'male' determination that pride, honour or practical

necessity will require 'stern measures'. This sexual polarization of the moral politics of the genre has pre-movie sources: it is central to Owen Wister's *The Virginian* (1902), and appears in Cooper's *The Deerslayer* (1841). Although female complaints about violent heroics are a cliché of the genre, the Western movie has handled this ideological complex with a great deal of variety and moral acuity.

Since the hero is the instrument of violence, he is in a sense tainted by the disease he comes to eradicate. It has been an essential trait of the frontier hero, from Cooper's Leatherstocking to Clint Eastwood's *Pale Rider*/1985, that his character includes within it a strong element of the dark force he fights to expel. Cooper's hero was a white man who was raised by Indians, who had an Indian consciousness; and it is this that makes him the most effective eliminator of Indians. However, this characteristic also makes him ideologically unacceptable as a potential husband for a 'white woman'. This ideological pattern is an essential structure in Western movies, which traditionally is envisioned in the hero's riding over the horizon at the film's end, leaving romance behind, as in *My Darling Clementine*/1946 and *Shane*. In Westerns made after 1950 – where the hero is often one who has himself been an outlaw, a gunfighter or a semi-savage Indian hater – his redemption of the community may not be perfected until he himself has been eliminated, through the sacrifice of his life (*The Wild Bunch*/1969), or through self-exile, like John Wayne's Ethan Edwards in *The Searchers*/1956, or the gunfighters in *The Magnificent Seven*/1960.

An alternative ending unites the wild hero and the civilized woman in a marriage that is meant to symbolize the reconciliation of their different value systems. The literary model here is Wister's *The Virginian*; and examples of this kind of 'happy' ending abound in movies. However, the centrality of male violence in resolving the crisis of Western narratives usually makes this 'marriage' an unequal one. While the female critique of male violence is given nominal sanction in the marriage, far more weight is given to the woman's moral acquiescence in the male principle that justice and law can only be established through violence.

For example, in William S. Hart's *Hell's Hinges*/1916 the hero is a 'good badman', whose soul is saved by the presence of a 'good woman', an eastern preacher's sister; but Blaze Tracey's redemption is ratified not by his conversion of the townsfolk, but by his apocalyptic single-handed destruction of the town, revenging the town's abuse of the preacher and his saintly sibling. In *Rio Grande*/1950 the cavalry Colonel who knows how to fight the Apache must overcome the linked resistance of his antimilitary anti-war wife and a 'soft' set of bureaucrats in Washington, even if he has to violate the law to do so. In *High Noon* the Marshal is able to defeat the criminals because his Quaker wife abandons her moral pacifism to join her husband, and to kill a man herself. In each instance, the heroic critique of 'female' moralism outweighs the female critique of violence.

So far, the ethics of Western violence coincide with the imperatives of entrepreneurial ideology which are the core of the political-economic mythology of the United States. However, the Western deflects, masks or denies the validity of economic self-interest – 'greed' – which is the motivating principle of that ideology. In this Westerns perform the classic function of cultural myth, offering a vehicle in which the culture can both affirm its values and express its doubts and ambivalences.

Stated in its simplest terms, it is generally the case that in Westerns the violence of men is seen as a thing too precious and significant to be given for money. Like a woman's favours and affections, the Western man's gift for violence may be freely given for honour or love, for the protection of the weak or the achievement of progress, but is corrupted when given for money. The simplest kinds of Westerns present this complex issue as a direct opposition of chivalric to fiscal motives: the hero is a knightly cowboy, of no apparent means; the villain a selfish and greedy rich man who is after the heroine's land. The B-Westerns of the 1930s reduced this to a formula through constant repetition: the heroes of series like *The Three Mesquiteers* will come by chance on people in difficulty, and their code will not let them go about their business without helping.

John Ford's *Stagecoach*/1939 offers a microcosm of society in which the mix of motives is carefully represented: the crooked banker absconding with the deposits represents capitalist greed in caricature; at the opposite extreme the Ringo Kid is on a quest to redeem his honour in justified revenge, and this chivalric figure (who treats all women with a naive but courtly courtesy) has been reduced to a commodity by the banker and his kind – he has 'a price on his head'. Between the banker and Ringo Kid, the other characters represent a spectrum of relations to money and honour. Two of them – Dallas and the Sheriff – stand on a point of balance between the two codes, and both 'save' themselves by identifying with Ringo and against the commercial values of their society: the Sheriff lets Ringo escape, and Dallas gives up prostitution for love of the Kid. But the Kid himself finds regeneration of spirit and fortune only by achieving revenge through violence – gentleness to woman is the outward sign of his chivalry, but its essence is still the violent quest.

It is possible to build an extremely good Western around the simplest version of this opposition of values, as the success of *Shane* and *Pale Rider* attest. However, most of the more interesting Westerns play complex variations on the opposition of fiscal and chivalric motives for violence. Perhaps the most basic and pervasive of these variations is the fable of heroic redemption, in which a hero (and/or heroine) begins as someone immersed in the values and practices of the cash nexus, and through the course of the adventure becomes more chivalric. In *My Darling Clementine*, Wyatt Earp at first refuses the town's request that he become its marshal because his concern is bound up with his family and his cattle business. Only when his brother is killed and the cattle stolen does Earp take the marshal's job, and begin to acquire a sense that bonds of affection and mutual support must grow beyond those of the clan.

The silent Westerns of William S. Hart typically show the hero as an outlaw or gambling man, whose illicit activities are an exaggeration of capitalist values and practices; but the touch of a 'good woman' evokes the chivalric element in the 'good badman', producing something akin to a religious conversion – in *Hell's Hinges* the hero is literally converted, and becomes the agent of a violent biblical doom on the Western Sodom in which he once thrived. In *Jesse James* the pattern is reversed: as Jesse becomes absorbed in his success as a robber, his original chivalric motives are attenuated, and he loses the moral sanction of his wife's support.

This pattern is very persuasive, because it begins 'where we are', acknowledging the power of money in our lives; and then evokes and invites us to imaginatively act out our queasiness about greed and selfishness, and our affection for other, perhaps older values. After 1950, this theme became perhaps the most prominent of Western story-types, particularly marked in the numerous movies made about gunfighters and ex-outlaws who come to the aid of helpless or oppressed citizens. These heroes are represented as craftsmen and professionals, who have accepted money values as determinants of the value and purpose of their work. The movie presents them in a situation that calls these values into question, and evokes in them the precapitalist values of honour, paternity and love, giving them new and better reasons for the violence that is in any case their calling. The scale of the problem may be small and intimate, or large in social resonance. In *The Naked Spur*/1952, for example, the choice between love and cash values is presented in purely personal terms; in the numerous Westerns made about American gunfighters helping Mexican peasants against their oppressors (*Vera Cruz*/1954, *The Magnificent Seven*, *The Professionals*/1966, *The Wild Bunch*) the choice has the largest kind of political and social resonance.

In these films, the heroes' initial devotion to cash values and professionalism is an essential part of their heroism, because it marks them as realists, men able to get along in the world as it is. When a professional gunfighter chooses an idealistic and 'impractical' course of action, his choice emphasizes the power of the ideal in whose name he acts, and also suggests that idealism may not be so 'impractical' as we believe: with a little courage and technical know-how, we may be able to effect ideal ends by pragmatic means. This is a powerful trope in the American democratic ideology. John Ford uses this suggestion to powerful effect in *Two Rode Together*/1961, a darkly ironic movie in which sentimental idealism proves to be the source of social cruelty and hypocrisy, while the hero's almost religious devotion to pure cash values seems to give him a grounding in reality that in the end shows him to be more humane.

The *formal* evolution of scenes of violence is in some ways independent of developments in the ideology of social violence. As the goal towards which the film narrative moves, the act of violence became a natural focus for creative energy and the play of artistic and technical variation. Over time, this focus has tended to bring the act of violence forward as a scene good and necessary in and of itself: as a climax whose *aesthetic* necessity and power become an acceptable substitute for the moral and ideological plot-rationales that originally provided the scene's motivation and justification.

Perhaps the best example of this tendency

is the evolution of the outlaw/gunfighter theme from 1939 to 1970. In Henry King's *Jesse James* the subject was a historical figure, a social bandit who figured in folklore and popular culture as a real-life American Robin Hood. In 1950 King made a significant formal variation on the outlaw theme, *The Gunfighter*/1950. The opening titles and suggestions within the dialogue indicate clearly that this hero's past is not unlike that of Jesse James. But the actual social basis of his initial rebellion is invisible, abstracted into dialogue and gesture; what we see is a man who has professionalized himself by exaggerating one of the outlaw's formal attributes: his speed and accuracy with a gun. This single fatal skill becomes a stylized and concise substitute for all the social and psychological complexity of the outlaw's motivation. Later versions of the gunfighter figure carry the process of stylization even further, so that the gunfighters appear to us as if they had no past at all, and hence lack the normal social or psychological motivation of ordinary men. Shane is an early version of the type; Clint Eastwood's 'Man With No Name' is perhaps its quintessence – all marks of a human identity or history have been dissolved in a figure who is pure skill and pure present-ness.

This identification of the hero with 'pure' violence – violence whose motive is professional and abstract rather than socially or personally specific – is accompanied by a necessary shift in the ideology of heroism. Violence which lacked clear social justification had been the traditional code-sign of the badman or the savage. Although the gunfighter typically moves in the direction of socially justified violence, his native element is violence *per se*, or violence for pay (which is traditionally the worst of motives). When the gunfighter shows himself to be morally as well as professionally 'good', he suggests a revaluation of those motives which have been regarded with moral disdain: perhaps killing for money and honing the art of murder are valid preparations for moral heroism. If that is true, perhaps the traditional virtues lauded by earlier Westerns, and embodied in the Christian and peace-loving virtues of white women, are to be taken as only nominally valid, or dismissed as hypocritical or incompetent. From *The Gunfighter* to *The Wild Bunch* it is easy to trace a line of Westerns which work towards the reversal of traditional Western roles and ideologies: women cease to function as supreme embodiments of Christian and social values, and become objects of

Gregory Peck in The Gunfighter

William Holden is shot in The Wild Bunch

sexual aggression or violence – the women in *The Wild Bunch* are whores or betrayers for the most part, and the heroes kill them or use them as shields (both hallmarks of traditional villains).

This stylization of heroic character was matched in the transformation of the scene of climactic violence. To increase the power and impact of scenes which, through repetition, must tend to become cliché, moviemakers developed techniques for representing violence more 'realistically' and/or shockingly. The death of a badman in a Western of the 30s or 40s involves a facial grimace, a clutch at the abdomen, and a slow crumple to earth. A steady movement in the direction of literalism has taken us to the present point, in which a killing will seem comically inauthentic without a burst of blood, a violent backward hurl of the body which is transformed with terrible speed into an awkwardly dumped laundry-sack of bones.

This has two kinds of effect. One is to demystify the evasions of screen violence by showing the reality of death and pain; the other is to glamorize the spectacle of violence, giving it an elaborate choreography through the use of sophisticated editing techniques and rhythms, the mixture of

slow- and regular motion, etc. to create an exciting and appealing aesthetic form.

The formal emphasis on virtuoso gunplay reinforces the idea that skill and firepower might be things good and beautiful in themselves – a set of values that were drawn directly from the political culture of the Cold War and especially the Vietnam War, where they defined the style and technique of combat and operational thinking. It may not be coincidence that Westerns fell out of favour with both film-makers and audiences in the early 1970s, just as this formal over-development of violence reached its peak. Yet disgust with graphic violence (often linked to disgust with the Vietnam War) has, surely, little to do with the demise of the genre. If anything, the role of graphic movie violence has grown in power and popularity through the re-emergence of traditional genres like the horror movie and the urban crime movie, through hyper-violent variations on the traditional war movie, and in the new sub-genre of 'slasher' movies. Indeed, it might be said that the Western imposed too many limitations on the formal elaboration of pure violence – limitations native to the genre. For one thing, the Western cannot escape its specific historical associations, and these impose clear limits on firepower and technique. But I would also argue that the Western as a genre has been linked for so long to a specific set of traditional ideological structures that there are real limits to the movie-maker's freedom of abstraction and formal play. Ironic reversals of traditional roles work only if the tradition itself is still understood and accepted as a reference point. If one wishes simply to make a movie in which violent acts are the formal and moral centre; and to dissolve all the moral, motivational, and ideological references native to the Western in purely formal inventions; and to dispense with all the specific historical references and limitations that belong to the Western – then there is really no reason at all to make your movie as a *Western*. RS

Virginia City, Montana · Not to be confused with its sister city in Nevada, after which it was named, Virginia City, Montana was based on gold mining and sprang up in 1863. Its first year was plagued by a gang of bandits who robbed and killed over a hundred miners, until vigilantes hanged Henry *Plummer, the sheriff and leader of the outlaws. By 1870 the gold was played out.

Virginia City, Nevada · As the Errol Flynn

vehicle *Virginia City*/1940 has it, 'Home of the fabulous Comstock mines. The richest and roughest town on the face of the earth.' It mushroomed in the summer of 1859 when silver was discovered. At its height the city boasted a Millionaire's Row of mansions, an opera house and five newspapers, on one of which Mark Twain worked in 1862. In 1867 alone the Comstock lode produced $16½ million worth of precious metals. But by the end of the 1870s decline set in as the silver petered out.

W

Washita, Battle of · An attack by General *Custer and the 7th Cavalry against a sleeping Cheyenne village on the Washita River in present-day Oklahoma on 27 November 1868. General Phil *Sheridan had ordered a winter campaign to force the Cheyenne and Arapaho on to the reservations. Custer's troops charged in at dawn with the band playing 'Garry Owen'. The village Custer attacked was that of Black Kettle and was actually situated on reservation land. Black Kettle was killed in the fight, together with about 100 other Indians and 21 soldiers. This incident forms one of the most memorable scenes in *Little Big Man*/1970.

Watkins, Carleton E. (1829-1916) · Photographer. Watkins was especially famed for his pictures of Yosemite, which he first photographed in 1861. These were the earliest pictures of any of the natural wonders of the West. His vast landscapes, taken with a specially built 18-by-22 inch camera, were influential in creating a taste for the spectacular and the sublime. He was a friend of Collis P. *Huntington, the railroad magnate, and did some pictures of the Southern Pacific Railroad route from California to Tombstone.

Weapons, concealed and ingenious · The gangster movie ruse of a machine-gun in a violin case is appropriated by the Western in *The Fastest Guitar Alive*, in which Roy Orbison has a rifle in his guitar case. Similar subterfuges include rifles inside crates of Bibles in *Great Day in the Morning*/1955, a man disguised as a priest who has a gun inside a cut-out Bible in *Cat Ballou*/1965, and in *Son of Paleface*/1952 Roy Rogers, anticipating Orbison, keeps his gun inside his guitar. A gun in your hat or your boot or better still hidden in a bag of buried money is such an old trick it's surprising Richard Widmark should fall for it in *The Law and Jake Wade*/1958. Ingenious weapons, apart from occasional instances such as Sterling Hayden's harpoon in *Terror in a Texas Town*/1958, only fully came into their own with the rise of the Italian Western, which saw the wholesale importation of all kinds of weapons, ranging from cannons and Gatling guns to the miniature armoury Lee Van Cleef carries around in *Per qualche dollaro in più*/1965.
The Fastest Guitar Alive/1967/MGM/d Michael Moore/lp Roy Orbison, Sammy Jackson

Wellman, Paul I[selin] (1898-1966) · Novelist and historian. Like much Western fiction that has been adapted for the cinema, Wellman's novels display strong plots, with plenty of action and sexual tension, not overburdened with felicities of literary style. Several of his novels, such as *Bronco Apache* (1936), are sympathetic to the Indians, who are the subject of his historical study, *Death on Horseback* (1947). *The Iron Mistress* (1951) is a fictional biography of Jim *Bowie.
The Iron Mistress/1952/WB/d Gordon Douglas/lp Alan Ladd, Virginia Mayo · *Apache* [*Bronco Apache*]/1954 · *Jubal* [*Jubal Coop*]/1956 · *The Comancheros*/1961

Welsh · There was a persistent theory in the 19th century that the Mandan Indians, who lived along the upper Missouri and whose skins were lighter coloured than their neighbours, were the descendants of a band of ancient Welsh immigrants led by Prince Madoc. This fantasy apart, the Welsh have never held a secure place in the mythology of the Western. But in *Apache Drums* Arthur Shields gives a memorable performance as a Welsh preacher. When the townspeople are attacked by Indians and take refuge in the church, he maintains morale with a spirited rendering of 'Men of Harlech'.
Apache Drums/1950/U/d Hugo Fregonese/lp Stephen McNally, Coleen Gray

Whip · Like the knife the whip is a dubious weapon, often used by bullies: Lee Marvin in *The Man Who Shot Liberty Valance*/1962, Ted de Corsia in *Showdown at Abilene* and Clint Eastwood's assailants in *High Plains Drifter*/1972. If the whip-wielding Spencer Tracy in *Broken Lance*/1954 isn't a bully, he's certainly an oppressive authoritarian. It may be employed as an instrument of humiliation, as by Walter Matthau in *The Kentuckian*/1955 or Karl Malden in *One-Eyed Jacks*/1960, or even as self-humiliation, as when Kirk Douglas orders his servant to whip him in *The Way West*. Yet when wielded by Zorro the whip is a legitimate weapon, signalling not brutality but the exoticism of Old California. Doubtless it was in the hope of borrowing some of this exoticism that B-Western actors chose to name themselves Whip Wilson and Lash LaRue. But none of these manifestations carries the sado-masochistic charge of Barbara Stanwyck in *Forty Guns*/1957, playing a haughty ranch-boss whom the film's theme song describes as 'the high-riding woman with the whip'.
Showdown at Abilene/1956/U/d Charles

Sterling Hayden with his harpoon in Terror in a Texas Town

Marlon Brando whipped by Karl Malden in One-Eyed Jacks

Carlton E. Watkins, 'Yosemite Valley' (*1886*)

Haas/*lp* Jock Mahoney, Martha Hyer ·
The Way West/1967/UA/*d* Andrew V.
McLaglen/*lp* Kirk Douglas, Robert
Mitchum, Richard Widmark

Whittredge, Thomas Worthington (1820-1910) · Artist. After briefly working as a sign painter in Cincinnati, Whittredge spent ten years abroad, mainly in Dusseldorf and Italy. On his return he took up landscape painting and became a member of the *Hudson River School. In 1866 he accompanied General John Pope on his expedition across the plains to the Rockies and back via Santa Fe. He made a second expedition west in 1870 and this inspired him to paint the western landscape. For Whittredge the distant, flat, endlessly receding horizon was its most remarkable feature; his mood is usually quiet, the calm before the storm unleashed by later, more melodramatic painters. (See Plate 13)

Wichita · After *Dodge City and *Abilene the best known of the Kansas cow towns. The railroad arrived in 1872, thus allowing Wichita a brief moment of glory as the most dynamic centre of the cattle trade. But if Wyatt *Earp had not been a peace officer there in 1875 the town might have been no more celebrated in the cinema than other Kansas cow towns such as Hays City or Newton, once equally bustling.

Wilder, Laura Ingalls (1867-1957) Author. Brought up in Wisconsin and Dakota, Wilder published her first book, *Little House in the Big Woods*, in 1932. This became the beginning of a sequence which eventually comprised *Little House on the Prairie* (1935), *On the Banks of Plum Creek* (1937), *By the Shores of Silver Lake* (1939), *The Long Winter* (1940), *Little Town on the Prairie* (1941), *These Happy Golden Years* (1943) and *The First Four Years* (published posthumously in 1971). The sequence is semi-autobiographical, recounting from the point of view of a young girl the daily lives of a homesteading family on the northern plains. It became a popular television series.
Television · *Little House on the Prairie* · *The Little House Years* · *Little House: A New Beginning* · *Little House: Bless All the Dear Children* · *Little House: The Last Farewell*

The Wild West show · Described by Don Russell in *Wild West: A History of Wild West Shows* (1970) as 'an exhibition illustrating scenes and events characteristic of the American Far West frontier', the Wild West show enjoyed its heyday from the 1880s until World War I and is indissolubly associated with the name of William F. 'Buffalo Bill' *Cody, who launched his 'Wild West' in 1883. It grew out of a whole range of influences, including the equestrian displays of the classical circus, the contests and games that the mountain men and Indians shared at their annual saturnalia during rendezvous, the Western stage melodramas in which Buffalo Bill and others starred, and the various professional skills of the cowboy such as roping steers and breaking horses.

William Goetzmann in *Exploration and Empire* (1966) argues that the opening of George *Catlin's Indian Gallery at the Stuyvesant Institute on Broadway in 1837, when Ioway chief Keokuk and an assembly of Sioux and Fox Indians performed war dances and shot arrows, marks the beginning. Henry Nash Smith in *Virgin Land* (1950) argues for a later date: 'In 1882 the citizens of North Platte, Nebraska, decided to organize a big Fourth of July celebration, an "Old Glory blowout", that would resemble what we know as a rodeo. Cody, who was already a famous theatrical figure and had bought a ranch in the vicinity, was appointed Grand Marshal. Thus was the Wild West show born. Since North Platte was in cattle country, the roping and riding and shooting contests dominated the celebration and determined the character of the show which Cody took on the road next year. His brightest cowboy star was Buck *Taylor, who could ride the worst bucking horse, throw a steer by the horns or tail, and pick up a neckerchief from the ground at full speed.'

Buffalo Bill's first full-scale version of the 'Wild West' (he didn't like the term show, feeling that it lacked dignity) took place at the Omaha Fair Grounds on 19 May 1883. The event was billed as 'the Wild West, Hon W.F. Cody and Dr. W.F. Carver's Rocky Mountain and Prairie Exhibition'. It included an attack on the Deadwood Stage, the Pony Express, 'Cowboys' Fun', shooting and races. The closing spectacle was 'A Grand Hunt on the Plains', with buffalo, elk, deer, mountain sheep, wild horses and long-horns (Plate 16).

The commercial exploitation of the Wild West by characters who had themselves participated in its historical creation is the characteristic feature of Buffalo Bill's career. In 1876, while acting as chief scout for Colonel Merrit's 5th Cavalry, he partici-pated in a skirmish at War Bonnet Creek and killed and scalped a Cheyenne named Yellow Hand. The picture of Cody waving aloft what he dramatized as 'the first scalp for Custer' was featured on the covers of Buffalo Bill dime novels and Wild West programmes for years to come. *Custer's Last Stand was incorporated into the Wild West format, as was the story of *Wounded Knee. *Sitting Bull joined the show in 1884 and *Geronimo is believed to have played the circuit in 1906. Clearly the Wild West show was taking its ideological cues from the creed of *Manifest Destiny. In 1899 the Charge at San Juan Hill by Teddy *Roosevelt and his Rough Riders during the Spanish-American war replaced Custer's Last Fight in the programme.

The narrative format was never rigid. Train robberies and the simulated hanging of horse thieves proved popular additions. Certain conventions were maintained. Annie *Oakley, dubbed 'Little Sure Shot' by Sitting Bull, and who joined the circuit in 1885, invariably appeared as the second act. The growing popularity of the spectacle in America was to be almost immediately repeated in Europe. In 1887 in London during a royal command performance the Deadwood Coach, driven by Buffalo Bill, carried four kings and the Prince of Wales. During the 1890 tour of Italy when the show played in the Roman amphitheatre of Diocletian at Verona, a Wild West delegation was blessed by Pope Leo XIII.

Buffalo Bill's was not the only Wild West in town. 1888 saw the birth of another show destined for the big-time: Pawnee Bill's Historical Wild West Exhibition and Indian Encampment. Gordon W. *Lillie (Pawnee Bill) had been an interpreter for the Pawnee Indians in the original Cody and Carver Wild West of 1883. As early as 1843, another circus impresario, P.T. *Barnum, had organized an exhibition of yearling buffalo in Boston. In 1887 Adam Forepaugh added 'Custer's Last Rally' to the '4-Paws Wild West' that was one feature of his circus. Another important show was the Miller Brothers' 101 Ranch Wild West show (later to play a major part in early Western films). Even Frank *James tried to cash in on his part in the story of the Wild West with a short-lived show in 1903. Alongside the big-budget shows were a host of small operators who were active in the early years of the 20th century at county fairs and carnivals.

The outbreak of World War I saw the end of the heyday of the Wild West show;

Buffalo Bill died on 10 January 1917. There were attempts to revive the formula in the 30s. Tom Mix, who like Will Rogers had moved into Hollywood from the world of rodeos and Wild West shows, put together the Tom Mix Circus and Wild West that ran for three seasons from 1935. Timothy J. McCoy's show, entitled Colonel Tim McCoy's Real Wild West and Rough Riders of the World, had a month's run in 1938.

The action-packed spectacles of the Wild West show clearly provided an iconography and narrative line for the Hollywood Western. They also provided a melodramatic version of the frontier spirit of America, a foundation myth that was re-enacted, as a Wild West show, as part of the open-air entertainment at the opening of the 1984 Los Angeles Olympics. Once again, for the benefit of the millions watching on television, the West was won. CB

RIGHT: *Tim McCoy's Wild West show*
BELOW: *Buffalo Bill Cody in the arena (1906)*

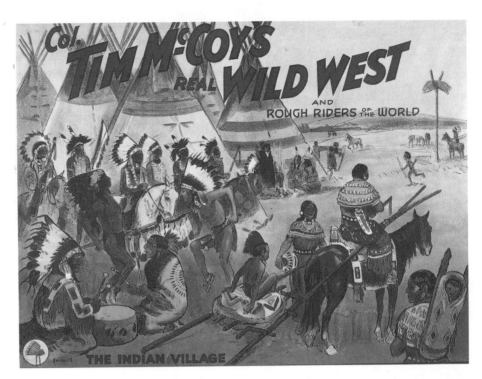

Wimar, Karl (1828-62) · Painter. Born in Germany, Wimar emigrated to St Louis at the age of fifteen. After helping to paint a massive panorama of the Mississippi which was exhibited in New Orleans, he went to Dusseldorf to study. On his return to America he made a journey up the Missouri in 1858, which furnished material for a succession of Western pictures, many of which focus on the dramatic narrative incident then becoming popular. He was one of the first, for example, to paint Indians attacking a wagon train, in 1856. Wimar helped found the Academy of Western Art in St Louis, which put the production of paintings of western subject matter on an institutionalized footing. (See Plate 9)

Winchester rifle · Along with the *Colt revolver, the most famous gun of the West. In 1858 Oliver Winchester (1810-80), an arms manufacturer of New Haven, Connecticut, employed Benjamin Tyler Henry (1821-98) to design a repeating rifle. The Henry rifle had a magazine capacity of 15 rounds and specially designed metal-cased ammunition. It was recharged by pulling the trigger guard lever downwards in a quick and easy action. The Henry rifle became a popular weapon. In 1866 Winchester reorganized his company as the Winchester Repeating Arms Company and produced a new version of the Henry rifle called the Winchester Model 1866. A further refined model became the famous Winchester '73 rifle, which carried 15 .44 calibre cartridges in its magazine. *Winchester '73*/1950 spins its story round a particularly fine example ('one in a thousand') of this gun. In 1878 the Colt company brought out a new model of its Peacemaker revolver adapted to take the same .44 cartridge as the Winchester.

Wister, Owen (1860-1938) · Novelist. Wister's novel *The Virginian*, an instant success on its publication in 1902, did more than any other work of fiction to establish a certain conception of the cowboy hero: laconic yet chivalrous and manly; slow to anger yet politely menacing when provoked. This particular combination of manner and moral character is perfectly expressed in the book's most famous remark, the Virginian's reply to an insult: 'When you call me that, smile.' Wister's first book, stories entitled *Red Men and White* (1896), appeared after a summer spent in Wyoming to improve his health before going to Harvard to study law. He continued to visit the West for the next ten years or so, and other fiction followed: *Lin McLean*/(1898), *The Jimmyjohn Boss* (1900), *Members of the Family* (1911), *When West Was West* (1928). Wister's friendship with Theodore *Roosevelt and Frederic *Remington served to crystallize a certain eastern establishment view of the West which stressed its morally bracing, character-forming properties.
A Western Romance/1910/Edison/d Edwin S. Porter/lp J. Barney Sherry · *The Virginian*/1914/PAR/d Cecil B. DeMille/lp Dustin Farnum · *A Woman's Fool* [*Lin McLean*] 1918/d John Ford/lp Harry Carey · *The Virginian*/1923/Preferred Pictures/d Tom Forman/lp Kenneth Harlan, Florence Vidor · *The Virginian*/1929 · *The Virginian*/1946/PAR/d Stuart Gilmore/lp Joel McCrea, Brian Donlevy
Television · *The Virginian*

Women · Recently, the American West has once again become disputed territory. Historians have turned their attention to women's participation in the westward trek and have discovered, to no great surprise, that their real contribution was far more extensive and diverse than traditional histories and literature have led us to believe.[1] When it comes to movies, the picture is much the same: the impoverished range of female stereotypes on offer (mother, school-teacher, prostitute, saloon girl, rancher, Indian squaw, bandit) never matches up to

Gary Cooper (l.) in The Virginian *(1929)*

Women branding on the Rio Grande ranch, Colorado (1894)

Winchester model 1873

reality. In the epic battle between heroes to tame the wilderness, the heroines who fought to change the course of history (the suffragettes, farmers, professional women) fare badly – even the maligned American Indian has been afforded the dubious luxury of liberal reassessment.

It's tempting to put this down, as many critics have,[2] to the male oedipal bias of the Western, a narrative based on a masculine quest for sexual and national identity which marginalizes women. Fruitful though this approach may be, it has not really come to terms with the dual, contradictory role of women. On the one hand she is peripheral (Budd Boetticher: 'What counts is what the heroine provokes, or rather what she represents. She is the one ... who makes him act the way he does. In herself the woman has not the slightest importance.'). On the other hand she is central (Anthony Mann: 'In fact, a woman is always added to the story because without a woman the Western wouldn't work.'). By the same token, the demand for more realistic images of women does not account for the fact that what lingers in the memory, refusing to be dismissed, is a series of extraordinary heroines, from Mae West's Klondike Annie and Doris Day's Calamity Jane, to Joan Crawford's Vienna and Barbara Stanwyck's Jessica Drummond. The search for realism is perhaps rather self-defeating in a genre which is more concerned with myth than historical accuracy. It might be more illuminating to shuffle the deck (bearing in mind that female card-sharps in the Western are few and far between) and see what permutations emerge.

Following Henry Nash Smith, the frontier has often been seen in symbolic terms as a boundary or barrier between opposing ideas: the Garden/Wilderness dichotomy translating into Culture/Nature, and so on. This formulation has both a relationship to actual events (the breaking down of the barrier between East and West under pressure from eastern expansion), and also a link with psychic and social reality (the loss of boundaries of sexual difference, as eastern 'feminine' values came into contact with the 'masculine' Wild West). Not surprisingly, then, many Westerns work away at the problem of re-establishing sexual boundaries: it's unusual for the woman who starts out wearing pants, carrying a gun and riding a horse to be still doing so at the end of the movie. Suitably re-clad in dress or skirt, she prepares to take her place in the family, leaving adventure to the men.

Of course, the hero's destiny is also circumscribed: rather than remain a nomad, he has to become civilized and participate in building a new society inside rather than outside the law. In both cases, the rehabilitation can be ambivalent, but the results are different. Over and over again, the woman relinquishes her desire to be active and independent, ceding power to the hero and accepting secondary status as mother figure, educator and social mediator. If she is allowed to be active, it is in the hero's cause rather than her own; in High Noon/1952 the young Quaker wife puts aside her pacifist principles to support her husband's heroic stand.

This pattern is remarkably consistent, but the most interesting Westerns explore its inherent tensions. Stagecoach/1939, directed by John Ford, whose reverence for motherhood and family is legendary, produced some significant reverberations: the East/West conflict is centred on two women, the respectable Lucy Mallory and the prostitute Dallas, and is played out at the point of life and death as the stagecoach and its motley group of passengers come under attack from savage Apaches. The hope for future civilization (revolving around who is a 'good mother': Mrs Mallory, who gives birth during the journey, or Dallas) lies not with the effete, class-conscious visitors from the East, but with the westerners, who in spite of their 'illegality' have an instinctive compassion and sense of right and wrong. Dallas herself, reviled by the snobbish easterners, is presented as a more 'natural' mother than Lucy Mallory: shots of her cradling Lucy's baby while the stage is under attack are quite transgressive, since prostitutes are outside the family and the law. It's true that the resolution is entirely conventional: Dallas is the civilizing force that brings the outlaw Ringo back into society. Nevertheless, she remains an ambiguous figure, half prostitute, half wife, partly because of the positive value attached by Ford to renegades and social outcasts.

Similar tensions are worked through in My Darling Clementine/1946, where East meets West in the confrontation between schoolteacher Clementine and westerner Wyatt Earp. Clementine is a civilizing influence on Earp, but he makes the passage from Nature to Culture unwillingly, as though resisting the colonizing impetus of the East; and while the wild saloon girl Chihuahua is banished from the scene, her memory lurks in the shadows as a reminder of what civilization represses.

Male ambivalence towards home and family is also at the centre of The Lusty Men/1952, but here Louise Merritt's resistance to the virile, itinerant world of the rodeo to which her husband Wes becomes attached is given a positive critical force. Jeff, Wes's friend, wants to quit that world, and is attracted to Louise; tragically, he is unable to escape either the rodeo's competitive ethos or the male alliances on which it is based. The film's focus on its heroes' crisis of identity paradoxically allows space in the masculine Western scenario for Louise's own problems with her wife/mother role.

A mother who resists her secondary status is Ma Callum in Pursued/1947, a film noirish Western which approaches its subject in an unusually introspective way. The hero, Jeb, is prevented from achieving proper manhood by Ma Callum's refusal to give him essential knowledge about his past. Only when she tells him the truth, in effect relinquishing the control she has guarded so jealously, can he pass into adult masculinity. Simultaneously powerful and powerless, mothers in the Western do indeed reflect the two sides of the Mann/Boetticher coin.

If the good mother represents the feminine ideal in the Western, what then of the 'bad girls', the law-breakers against which the ideal is measured? These shady ladies threaten to upset the applecart by challenging men on their own ground; adventurers all, they demand equal status and refuse to take second place, at first, anyway; they wear pants and brandish guns, own land, property and business, demand sexual independence. It's true that this is usually only temporary – if the tomboy has not abandoned her transvestite garb for the arms of the hero by the end of the movie, then she comes to a sticky end. (In Arizona/1940, Phoebe Titus' independence is revealed as masquerade and she cedes the struggle to laconic westerner Peter Hunsey.) Nevertheless, the passage to femininity is not always smooth; the bad girl's vacillation between tomboy and wife, with its attendant cross-dressing games, offers some interesting possibilities.

Calamity Jane/1953 contains some extraordinary gender confusions which its somewhat arbitrary double wedding finale does not entirely iron out. Calamity's feminization is not quite complete – at the end of the movie she is back in buckskins as gun-toting guard of the Deadwood Stage, while her marriage to hero Wild Bill Hickok is haunted by the spectre of the scene in which, for the slightest of narrative excuses, he dresses as an Indian squaw. The combination of a comedy-of-errors with the utopian structure of the musical and Western conventions enables an egalitarian fantasy (one which the traditional Western mobilizes in order to undermine) to prevail.[3] In a different way, Marlon Brando's dressing up as a pioneer woman in The Missouri Breaks/1976 also brings to the surface some of the unspoken contradictions in the Western's privileging of masculine desires.

Both these films exploit and expose a potential perversity at the heart of the genre, its regressive drive to elude the law of the father, to play forbidden games. The tomboy offers a different sort of erotic pleasure from the mother, one focused on her bottom, and which provokes the desire of the hero to spank her. This sexual tussle, usually played for laughs, is a kind of parody of the father/daughter, father/mother power relations which will eventually put the tomboy in her place. In Dodge City/1939, Errol Flynn offers to spank Olivia De Havilland when she has the temerity to want to work on the town newspaper and contribute actively to the town's political development. Their rough and tumble is a playful prelude to a more serious confrontation, apparently a reversal of roles, in which De Havilland lays out for Flynn the moral necessity of his defending the burgeoning community against the villain. De Havilland's passage to mother figure is played out against two other feminine stereotypes, seen as less than ideal: the saloon girl, who sides with the villain, and the comically ineffectual, repressive temperance league women. The heroine's successful putting aside of her tomboy identity brings the errant hero back into society, and so ushers in progress.

There are women whose status as good or bad Western heroines is less easily defined, sisters to the femmes fatales of film noir. These duplicitous creatures often inhabit revenge Westerns, which focus on the hero's obsessive drive to seek out and kill his alter ego for a crime committed against his family. The woman takes on a sphinx-like quality: she both represents, and holds the key to, the enigma he must resolve. In Winchester '73/1950 the neurotic hero, Lin McAdam, is matched by an ambivalent heroine, Lola Manners, who may or may not be a prostitute, may or may not be complicit with villain Waco Johnnie Dean, but is indirectly responsible for the latter's death at the hands of McAdam. Her ambivalent status is maintained until the end: as she and McAdam embrace, his long-time buddy High Spade looks on with a quizzical expression as if to question his friend's judgement.

Occasionally, the duplicitous heroine takes on a more sympathetic, tragic hue. In Fritz Lang's extraordinary Brechtian Western, Rancho Notorious/1952, the hero Vern's obsession with avenging the death of his wife turns him into a ruthless, inhuman monster whose sadistic attitude towards the woman, Altar Keane, whom he believes holds the secret to his wife's murder, turns out to be an error of judgement with dire consequences. Believing Altar to be complicit with the murderer, Vern realizes his mistake too late, after Altar dies saving his buddy Frenchy's life. Partly because of distancing techniques used in image, sound and narrative, this is one of a few Westerns in which the over-riding male perspective is brought into question: Altar is explicitly seen as a victim of Vern's need to project on to an external image his own violent, destructive urges. In Rancho Notorious, women are finally evacuated from the scene completely, as Vern and Frenchy ride off together.

Hannie Caulder/1971 puts its heroine in the vengeful hero's place. Hannie sets out to avenge her own rape and her husband's murder, acquiring sharp-shooter skills and much-abbreviated masculine garb (a hat, boots and man-with-no-name-style poncho, but no pants). In spite of an obvious intention to titillate, Hannie Caulder also manages to produce some interesting reflections on male heroism. Hannie learns from her mentor (who later dies – no easy romantic transition here) the practical and emotional skills required to be a westerner. No room for compassion or love – Hannie must stand alone in the wilderness. She succeeds in killing the villains, satisfying justice, and at the end she is not returned immediately to home and family. But in an elegiac conclusion, she comes face to face with a mysterious man in black who has haunted her progress, and whose presence is a reminder of a final boundary Hannie can never cross. For women can never really be heroes in the Western: that would mean the end of the genre.

The Western is haunted by the fear of miscegenation, the myth of the rapacious Indian bent on capturing and breeding with white women. When white women mate with Indians, the results are generally catastrophic: the woman is seen to be contaminated by the primitive (polygamous) laws of the wilderness and henceforth unfit for monogamous family life. It's different when a civilized white man mates with an Indian woman. Surprisingly, perhaps, Indian women are often quite positively portrayed as noble, brave, intelligent and self-sacrificing. But this is merely a variation on the mother figure, whose function is to smooth the way for the male transition to maturity. In The Big Sky/1952, Teal Eye enables the relationship between Jim and Boone to move beyond the latently homosexual to a mature friendship, also allowing the younger Boone to overcome his hatred of Indians, while in Run of the Arrow/1957 Yellow Moccasin supports O'Meara through his crisis of national identity, even to the extent of giving up her Sioux nationhood to return with him to the States when the crisis is over.

Sometimes, however, the race/sex/nation conflict is less easily resolved. Ethan Edwards, the hero of The Searchers/1956, is a classic westerner. Solitary, asexual and taciturn, he is driven to seek out and destroy his alter ego, the Comanche chief Scar, epitome of the primitive sexuality Ethan's culture represses. Ethan and his quest are imbued with epic overtones: nevertheless, his rescue of his niece Debbie from Scar's clutches is seen as a highly ambiguous act on a par with Scar's original act of abduction, since Debbie makes it clear she wants to remain with the Indians. Debbie's refusal to see herself as a victim, or to accept a position as object of exchange between the two cultures, doesn't affect her final destiny; but it does allow a criticism of Ethan's racist puritan code to surface, a criticism not entirely erased by the elegiac overtones of the hero's final act of walking out alone into the desert. Five years later, in Two Rode Together/1961, Ford's criticism becomes more explicit. Marshal McCabe (James Stewart) rejects the racist attitudes of cavalry and white settlers by leaving for California with Elena, a kidnapped white girl turned Indian squaw.

King Vidor's magnificently melodramatic Duel in the Sun /1946 unusually focuses on a woman's crisis of identity. Its racially ambiguous heroine, Pearl Chavez (daughter of a white father and Mexican Indian mother) vacillates between two lovers (the 'good' brother Jesse, epitome of civilized eastern values, and the 'bad' brother Lewt, barbaric and brutal), who represent the struggle within herself between good and evil, wife and tomboy. Pearl is unable to accept her feminine role as Jesse's wife and pursues her transgressive desire for Lewt. On one level, the struggle is between the 'primitive' Indian and 'civilized' white in Pearl – her inability to control her sexual desire is partly responsible for her death. But melodrama's characteristic focus on female desire turns the normal moral order on its head: the forces of civilization become forces of repression which lead precisely to the excess which brings about Pearl and Lewt's deaths. Pearl Chavez's tragedy is that of all the Western's tomboys, writ large.

One reason for the Western's decline could be its resistance to the impact of social change. One attempt to capitalize on an emerging women's movement was *The Ballad of Josie* (1967), a comedy Western starring Doris Day as Josie Minick, the wife of a violent alcoholic in nineteenth-century Wyoming territory, forced to become an independent woman after his death. After a succession of menial jobs, she uses her savings to set up a sheep farm in what has traditionally been cattle country, provoking a range war. The film attempts a blending of contemporary feminist issues (wife-battering, child custody, job discrimination) with historical material like prostitution and women's suffrage, set against the characteristic trajectory of the Western heroine from tomboy to wife; but the feminist influence sits uneasily with the Western narrative.

Perhaps the nearest Hollywood has come to a feminist Western, *Johnny Guitar*/1954, predates the modern women's movement by more than a decade and does not deal directly with social issues at all. Set in a timeless desert wasteland with only the most perfunctory signs of civilization in evidence, *Johnny Guitar* is overtly presented as myth. Vienna, the film's extraordinary heroine and one of the most compelling female images the Western has produced, has often been seen as a feminist ideal, a woman who survives on equal terms with men (though reservations have been expressed about the misogynist representation of Vienna's opponent, Emma Small, and the disappointing shoot-out between the two women).[4] Vienna is certainly unusual: a powerful combination of several Western heroines in one (a gunslinger, a musician and a successful entrepreneur who outwits everyone by buying up land to capitalize on the coming of the railroad, she is sexually independent but also mother to the disillusioned Johnny and the Dancin' Kid's gang). Feminine in her white dress, masculine in black shooting gear, she moves between tomboy and mother figure with ease, demonstrating and maintaining a level of control allowed to very few women. But the film's feminism goes deeper than this, extending to a criticism of the Western's male values. Destructive masculine drives have gone out of

Joan Crawford with Sterling Hayden in Johnny Guitar

Wooden Indian in Blazing Saddles

control, creating a world dominated by death, betrayal and revenge. Emma Small is complicit in this process, while Vienna keeps a distance, speaking out against moral disintegration, expressing perhaps director Nicholas Ray's own disillusionment with the US in the grip of McCarthyism. It is in this light, rather than as a failure of her positive qualities, that Vienna's half-hearted shoot-out with Emma Small can be seen. Vienna has had enough of death and revenge; she and Johnny leave the ranchers, bankers and outlaws to their own devices. At the end of *Johnny Guitar*, still in pants, still more than equal to any man, having successfully resisted all attempts to bring her down, Vienna bids farewell to the Western.

PC

REFERENCES
[1] Sandra L. Myres, *Westering Women and the Frontier Experience 1800–1915* (Albuquerque: University of New Mexico Press, 1982). Julie Roy Jeffrey, *Frontier Women: The Trans-Mississippi West* (New York: Hill and Wang, 1979).
[2] For example John Cawelti, *The Six-Gun Mystique* (Bowling Green: Bowling Green Popular Press, 1971).
[3] Mandy Merck, 'Travesty on the Old Frontier' in *Move Over Misconceptions: Doris Day Reappraised* (London: British Film Institute, 1980).
[4] Jacqueline Levitin, 'The Western: any good roles for feminists?', *Film Reader* no. 5, 1982.

The Ballad of Josie/1967/U/d Andrew V. McLaglen/lp Doris Day, Peter Graves, George Kennedy

Wooden Indian · By tradition the carved and painted wooden Indian stands outside a cigar store like the striped pole outside a barber shop. Its presence in a film may be

inert, part of the décor as in *Union Pacific*/1939, or, as in the comedy *Support Your Local Gunfighter*/1971, it may be just another Western cliché. But it's more likely to be the occasion of a joke. In *Calamity Jane*/1953 Doris Day as the unsophisticated heroine wide-eyed in Chicago mistakes a wooden Indian for a real one, an error also made by Carol Channing in *The First Traveling Saleslady*. In *Son of Paleface*/1952 Bob Hope refines the gag. He strikes a match on a wooden Indian, then later, mistaking a real Indian for a wooden one, tries to strike a match on him too.

The First Traveling Saleslady/1956/RKO/d Arthur Lubin/lp Ginger Rogers, Carol Channing

World War II · The B-Western did its bit during World War II. From 1942 until the end of the war its heroes regularly fought with Nazis and unmasked Japanese spies. Most of the plots involved sabotage or attempts by foreign agents to secure supplies of strategic materials. Though the action usually took place inside the United States, in *Texas to Bataan* the Range Busters got as far as the Philippines in pursuit of the Japanese. As with so many other things Western, William S. Hart had shown the way in a World War I short called *A Bullet for Berlin*. Asleep beside his horse Fritz, Hart dreams of going to Berlin, where he shoots up the Kaiser. He then wakes up and rushes off to buy war bonds.

Mounties vs. the Japs
in King of the Mounties

Memorable World War II titles include:
King of the Mounties/1942/REP/d William
Witney/lp Allan Lane (Mounties against
Axis spies) · *The Valley of Hunted Men*/
1942/REP/d John English/lp Bob Steele,
Tom Tyler, Jimmie Dodd (the Three
Mesquiteers against Nazi spies) · *Cowboy
Commandos*/1943/MON/d S. Roy Luby/lp
Ray Corrigan, Dennis Moore, Max
Terhune (the Range Busters against Nazi
saboteurs) · *Wild Horse Rustlers*/1943/PRC/d
Sam Newfield/lp Bob Livingstone, Al St
John (the Lone Rider against Nazi
saboteurs) · *Texas to Bataan*/1942/MON/d
Robert Tansey/lp John King, Max
Terhune

Wounded Knee, Massacre of · The ignoble
end to the Indian wars of the plains. In 1890
there appeared among the Sioux and other

Big Foot lying dead in the snow after
Wounded Knee

tribes a new religious rite known as the
Ghost Dance. It was propagated by
Wovoka, a Paiute who had had a vision
promising that if the Indians danced the
Ghost Dance the whites would disappear
and the Indians' lands would be restored to
them. Nervousness about this movement led
the army to bring troops into the Pine Ridge
Reservation in South Dakota. Only a week
before the Wounded Knee incident *Sitting
Bull had been killed when Indian police tried
to arrest him. Then on 29 December 1890
the 7th Cavalry under Colonel James Forsyth surrounded a band of Minneconjou
Sioux at Wounded Knee Creek. While the
troops were disarming the Indians fighting
broke out. The army opened fire with its
Hotchkiss guns. 146 Indians were killed
(including over 60 women and children).
The army lost 25 killed, mostly by its own
fire. The event has since become a symbol of
white aggression towards the original inhabitants of America, especially since the
popular success of Dee Brown's history,
Bury My Heart at Wounded Knee (1970).

Wounds · Death is serious, but wounds can
be funny. In *The Beautiful Blonde from Bashful Bend*/1949 Betty Grable can't stop shooting people in the behind. When Ward Bond
as the Rev. Captain Clayton is wounded in
the same spot in *The Searchers*/1956 it's his
dignity that is hurt most. The joke is good
enough to be used again in *Major Dundee*/
1964 and in *Big Jake* six years after that. John
Ford has fun with a foot-wound in *Cheyenne
Autumn*/1964, when Wyatt Earp (James Stewart) takes charge of the operation. Howard
Hawks also relishes medical humour. In *The
Big Sky*/1952 there are lots of laughs when
Kirk Douglas has his finger amputated. (This
scene was apparently originally intended for
John Wayne in *Red River*/1948, but he
refused it.) And there's a delicious moment
in *El Dorado*/1966 when the doc goes off
leaving Robert Mitchum with his own finger
stuck in a hole in his side like the little Dutch
boy plugging the dyke.

But a wound in the arm is no laughing
matter when it stops you shooting. One of
the classic instances is in *One-Eyed Jacks*/
1960, in which Marlon Brando practises for
long hours beside the sea shore to get his
broken gun-hand working again. In *Showdown at Abilene* Jock Mahoney has suffered a
wound which has left him psychologically
rather than physically incapacitated. At the
end of the film he manages to fire his gun and
becomes a whole man again. In his films with
Anthony Mann James Stewart sustains more

than his share of wounds. In both *The Far
Country*/1954 and *The Man from Laramie*/
1955 he's hurt in the hand. In the former he
slowly nurses himself back to health. In the
latter he makes a mysteriously rapid
recovery.

The most blatantly sexual treatment of a
wound in the Western is when Montgomery
Clift sucks the poison from the arrow
wound in Joanne Dru's shoulder in *Red
River*/1947.
Showdown at Abilene/1956/U/d Charles
Haas/lp Jock Mahoney, Martha Hyer · *Big
Jake*/1971/Batjac/d George Sherman/lp
John Wayne, Richard Boone, Maureen
O'Hara

Wright, Harold Bell (1872-1944) · Author.
A preacher whose stolidly written Western
novels contain copious amounts of sermo-
nizing, though this was filtered out by
Hollywood in its several successful versions
of his works. In 1919 Wright himself wrote,
produced and directed a film of his first
Western novel, *The Shepherd of the Hills*,
starring Harry Lonsdale. It was remade twice
under this title: 1927/First National/d Albert
Rogell/lp Alec B. Francis · 1941/PAR/d Henry
Hathaway/lp John Wayne.
Other films: *When a Man's a Man*/1924/
First National/d Edward Cline/lp John
Bowers · remade 1935/FOX/d Edward
Cline/lp George O'Brien · *The Winning of
Barbara Worth*/1926/UA/d Henry King/lp
Vilma Banky, Ronald Colman · *The Mine
with the Iron Door*/1924/UA/d Sam
Wood/lp Pat O'Malley · remade 1936/
COL/d David Howard/lp Richard Arlen ·
Wild Brian Kent/1936/FOX/d Howard
Bretherton/lp Ralph Bellamy · *Western
Gold*/1937/FOX/d Howard Bretherton/lp
Smith Ballew · *It Happened Out West*/
1937/FOX/d Howard Bretherton/lp Paul
Kelly · *Secret Valley*/1937/FOX/d Howard
Bretherton/lp Richard Arlen

Younger brothers · Outlaws. There were
four Younger brothers: Cole (1844-1916),
John (1846-74), James (1850-1902), Robert
(1853-89). Brought up in Missouri amid the
hatred and violence that marked the border
in the pre-Civil War years, the four
brothers, like the *James and *Dalton gangs,
turned outlaw when the war ended. Cole and
James had ridden with *Quantrill, and Cole
had taken part in the notorious raid on
Lawrence, Kansas. By 1866 they had had
plenty of practice with the gun and in that

Cole Younger and Jim Younger after capture at Northfield, Minn. 1876

year Cole joined Jesse James in the first of his bank robberies, at Liberty, Missouri. In 1868 Jim Younger followed Cole and by 1872 John and Bob were also members of the James-Younger gang, as it became known. Cole, meanwhile, had become involved with Belle *Starr, who had a child by him in 1867. In 1874 John was shot dead in a confrontation with *Pinkerton detectives, but the rest of the gang continued their raids on trains and banks. The fame of the Youngers began to spread with the publication in 1875 of *The Guerrillas of the West; or the Life, Character and Daring Exploits of the Younger*

Brothers by Augustus Appler. This work, like others after it, was generally sympathetic to the Youngers, seeing their crimes as a justifiable response to the iniquities visited on the defeated South by the hated Yankees.

The end of the Youngers' career came on 7 September 1876 when they, the James brothers and three others tried to rob a bank in Northfield, Minnesota. The people of the town turned on them. In the battle that followed two of the gang were shot dead, Jim Younger's jaw was partly shot away and Bob's elbow smashed. Jesse James decided he and his brother Frank could not afford to be encumbered by the wounded and they made their escape. Cole stayed with his brothers and all three were eventually captured and sentenced to life imprisonment. Bob died in jail of tuberculosis, but in 1901 Cole and Jim were paroled. Jim's health and spirit were broken and he committed suicide the next year. Cole took a job selling tombstones and then organized a touring Wild West show with Frank James. In 1903 he published his autobiography, *The Story of Cole Younger, by Himself*.

In the cinema, as in his life, Cole Younger never quite emerged out of the shadow of his more famous associate, Jesse James, and the films in which the Youngers appear without the James have been less impressive than the ones in which they have a supporting role. Glenn Strange (Cole)/*Days of Jesse James*/1939/REP/d Joseph Kane/lp Roy Rogers, Don Barry · Dennis Morgan (Cole), Wayne Morris (Bob), Arthur Kennedy (Jim)/*Bad Men of Missouri*/1941/WB/d Ray Enright/lp Jane Wyman · Steve Brodie (Cole), Richard Powers (Jim), Robert Bray (John)/*Return of the Bad Men*/1948/RKO/d Ray Enright/lp Randolph Scott, Robert Ryan · Wayne Morris (Cole), Bruce Bennett (Jim), James Brown (Bob), Robert Hutton (John)/*The Younger Brothers*/1948/WB/d Edwin L. Marin/lp Alan Hale, Tom Tyler · James Best (Cole), Dewey Martin/*Kansas Raiders*/1950/U/d Ray Enright/lp Audie Murphy, Brian Donlevy · Bruce Bennett (Cole), Bill Williams (Jim)/*The Great Missouri Raid*/1950/PAR/d Gordon Douglas/lp Wendell Corey, MacDonald Carey · Jack Buetel (Bob), Bruce Cabot (Cole), Bob Wilke (Jim), John Cliff (John)/*Best of the Badmen*/1951/RKO/d William D. Russell/lp Robert Ryan · Jim Davis (Cole)/*The Woman They Almost Lynched*/1953/REP/d Allan Dwan/lp John Lund, Joan Leslie · Sam Keller (Cole)/*Jesse James' Women*/1954/UA/d Donald Barry/lp Don Barry, Jack Buetel · Barry

Sullivan (impersonating 'Jeff Younger', Cole's nephew)/*The Maverick Queen*/1956/REP/d Joseph Kane/lp Barbara Stanwyck · Alan Hale (Cole), Biff Elliot (Jim), Anthony Ray (Bob)/*The True Story of Jesse James*/1957 · Myron Healy (Cole)/*Hell's Crossroads*/1957/REP/d Franklin Adreon/lp Steve McNally, Robert Vaughn · Frank Lovejoy (Cole)/*Cole Younger, Gunfighter*/1958/AA/d R.G. Springsteen/lp James Best · Willard Parker (Cole)/*Young Jesse James*/1960/FOX/d William Claxton/lp Robert Stricklyn · Bruce Sedley (Cole)/*The Outlaws Is Coming*/1964/COL/d Norman Maurer/lp The Three Stooges · Cliff Robertson (Cole), Matt Clark (Bob), Luke Askew (Jim)/*The Great Northfield Minnesota Raid*/1972 · David Carradine (Cole), Keith Carradine (Jim), Robert Carradine (Bob), Kevin Brophy (John)/*The Long Riders*/1980
Television · Phil Carey (Cole)/*Cheyenne* · Gregory Walcott (Cole)/*Maverick* · John Milford (Cole), Tim McIntire (Bob)/*The Legend of Jesse James* · Gene Evans (Cole), Zalman King (Bob)/*The Intruders* · Cliff Potts (Cole)/*Belle Starr*

Young man · The old-timer is usually a source of humour; the young man is often the butt. In the 1950s, as Hollywood discovered the youth market, there was a short-lived move towards Westerns with younger heroes, providing roles for Tab Hunter, Robert Wagner, Audie Murphy and others. But more common were youths of a mean disposition with something to prove; 'juvenile delinquents', in the language of the day. Skip Homeier may have started the trend in *The Gunfighter*/1950, and he went on to specialize in the part. Even nice boys had to be brought down a peg. In *The Searchers*/1956, not content with having Jeffrey Hunter spend the whole film being humbled by John Wayne, at the end John Ford brings in Wayne's own son Pat and humiliates him too. Similarly in *Ride the High Country*/1962 two old veterans of the trail, Randolph Scott and Joel McCrea, vie with each other to teach their young companion (Ronald Starr) who's boss. In several of the films which Budd Boetticher made with Randolph Scott, including *The Tall T*/1956, *Ride Lonesome*/1959 and *Comanche Station*/1959, callow youths learn hard lessons, sometimes too late.

In Howard Hawks' Westerns a succession of young men engage in a battle of wits and sometimes fists with the older hero before being accepted into the inner circle of the

Hawksian élite. Robin Wood in his book *Howard Hawks* (London: BFI, 1981) finds a particular significance in this: 'One also notes the procession of young men (particularly in Hawks' later work) who have the appearance of gay male icons and whose role invariably involves a close intimacy with the hero, carrying the constant (if constantly submerged) impression of being an alternative to the woman: Montgomery Clift in *Red River*, Dewey Martin in *The Big Sky* ..., Ricky Nelson in *Rio Bravo*, James Caan in *El Dorado*.'

Z

Zapata, Emiliano (1879-1919) · Mexican revolutionary. Like his comrade Pancho *Villa, Zapata first took up arms against the dictator *Diaz in 1910 only to be disappointed with the political timidity of the new president Francisco *Madero, who would do nothing about land reform, the only issue that had meaning for the peasants. After Madero was murdered in 1913 by his treacherous general *Huerta, Zapata and Villa fought in concert with another of Madero's supporters, Venustiano Carranza, and Huerta was deposed. But again Zapata was disappointed. Carranza, who eventually came to power with the support of the United States, wanted merely a political, not an economic, solution to the problems of the people. In 1919 Zapata was lured to a meeting with an agent of Carranza and assassinated.

Apart from Marlon Brando's charismatic performance in *Viva Zapata!*/1952, Zapata has been only a minor figure in the American cinema. Whereas there are several films about Villa, who gets a walk-on part in *Viva Zapata*, Zapata scarcely ever appears in the other films made about the Mexican revolution of the years 1910-20. Villa's fame was greater, especially in America. This was in part because the American journalist John Reed made a hero out of Villa in his book *Insurgent Mexico*. Villa also became well known to the American public as a result of the expedition mounted against him by General Pershing in 1916.
Also Tony Davis/*Guns of the Magnificent Seven*/1968/UA/d Paul Wendkos/lp George Kennedy, James Whitmore

Villa and Zapata (centre) with their followers in the National Palace, 6 December 1914

PART III

A

Across the Wide Missouri · Wellman's elegiac tale about the destruction of the mountain men's way of life was based on Bernard De Voto's historical account, published in 1947, of the adventures of Flint Mitchell, who controlled trade with the Blackfoot in the Rocky Mountains in the 1820s. Flint (Gable) incarnates the spirit of pioneer America, as the trader and adventurer able to live with all ethnic groups and married to an Indian maiden, Kamiah (Marques). Their idyllic life is disrupted by the ruthless expansion of white civilization, i.e. trade, triggering a lethal but doomed retaliation by the Indians. Kamiah is killed and the lonely hero tries to postpone the day he will have to send their son to school, taking him back into the mountains. Shot on location in Colorado, the film alternates between explosions of raw, often destructive energy and intensely lyrical celebration of the majestic landscapes of woods and mountains. MGM savagely cut the picture after it was previewed, adding a voice-over narration by Howard Keel and destroying its epic rhythm, while attenuating the bitter undertones of one of Wellman's finest achievements. PW
1950/78 min/MGM/*p* Robert Sisk/
d William A. Wellman/*s* Talbot Jennings/
c William C. Mellor/*m* David Raksin/
lp Clark Gable, Ricardo Montalban, Adolphe Menjou, Maria Elena Marques, John Hodiak, J. Carrol Naish, Jack Holt

Along the Great Divide · A psychological Western in the tradition of his earlier *Pursued*, Walsh's *Along the Great Divide* transforms the cross-country trek of Marshal Ken Merrick (Douglas) with prisoner Pop Keith (Brennan), an admitted cattle rustler who is also accused of murder, into an oedipal odyssey. After rescuing his prisoner from a lynch mob led by Rodin, father of the victim, Merrick is beset not only by the hardships of the landscape (desert sandstorms, lack of water) and the ambushes set by the pursuing Rodin, but also by the taunts of Pop Keith, who resembles Merrick's own father, a marshal like himself, who had been lynched years earlier when he refused to surrender a prisoner to a mob. Merrick's obsessive adherence to the letter of the law and attempt to repress his own feelings are repeatedly threatened by the prisoner's daughter (Mayo), who steals his gun while romancing him, by the brother of the victim, whom Merrick arrests for the murder of his deputy, and by another deputy, who mutinies when the water supply is exhausted. Faced with a nightmarish repetition of the past when Keith is convicted, Merrick finally discovers that the victim's brother, jealous of his father's affection for his elder sibling, had killed him. After the killer shoots his own father in an attempt to escape, Merrick guns him down. Oedipal and legal conflicts are resolved in the re-enactment of the past and its rewriting in the present, freeing the hero from the neurotic guilt feelings he has over his own role in his father's death. JB
1951/b & w/88 min/WB/*p* Anthony Veiller/*d* Raoul Walsh/*s* Walter Doniger, Lewis Meltzer/*c* Sid Hickox/*m* David Buttolph/*lp* Kirk Douglas, Virginia Mayo, John Agar, Walter Brennan, Ray Teal

Annie Get Your Gun · Ethel Merman powered her way through over a thousand stage performances of Irving Berlin's hit show about Annie Oakley. Judy Garland was cast for the film version, but suffered a breakdown before she finished. Betty Hutton was then drafted in to play the sharp-shooting star of Buffalo Bill's show. As if this wasn't enough, the film had three directors. Busby Berkeley was replaced by Charles Walters, who eventually gave way to George Sidney. And Frank Morgan died before he could complete his role as Buffalo Bill, Louis Calhern taking over. Despite all this the result was one of MGM's most successful musicals ever. The plot, as with any musical, concerns a love affair, in this case between Annie and the star of the rival Pawnee Bill show (Howard Keel). Among the best-known numbers are 'Doin' What Comes Naturally', 'Anything You Can Do,(I Can Do Better)' and the finale to end all finales, 'There's No Business Like Show Business'. EB
1950/107 min/MGM/*p* Arthur Freed/
d George Sidney/*s* Sidney Sheldon/
c Charles Rosher/*songs* Irving Berlin/
ch Robert Alton/*lp* Betty Hutton, Howard Keel, Edward Arnold, J. Carrol Naish

Apache · As one might expect, Aldrich's contribution to the early 50s pro-Indian cycle is one of the toughest, and for the most part avoids easy liberal sentiments. It is the story of Massai, one of Geronimo's braves, who wages a one-man war against the army until he meets Nalinle (Peters) and begins to turn his thoughts to peace. Particularly striking is Massai's escape from a deportation train: in a series of stunning travelling shots Aldrich shows in the process of formation the garish, mushroom-growth white 'civilization' which will destroy Massai's

people even more effectively than the army's guns. Aldrich wanted to have Massai killed at the end but the studio imposed an unlikely happy ending. As the director put it: 'you make a picture about one thing, the inevitability of Massai's death. His courage is measured against the inevitable. The whole preceding two hours becomes redundant if at the end he just walks away.' James R. Webb went on to write *Cheyenne Autumn*, Aldrich to direct *Ulzana's Raid*, two even bleaker pictures of the Indians' fate. JP
1954/91 min/Linden – UA/p Harold Hecht/d Robert Aldrich/s James R. Webb/c Ernest Laszlo/m David Raksin/lp Burt Lancaster, Jean Peters, John McIntire, Charles Bronson, Monte Blue

Arizona · Ten years after *Cimarron*, Columbia hired Wesley Ruggles, director of the earlier epic, and gave him a budget large enough to produce a Western of equal stature. Unfortunately, this story of the settlement of the state of Arizona plays on the rather plodding character interaction that had flawed Ruggles' first attempt at a large-scale Western, and rather skimps on the spectacle. Considering that the film-makers went to the expense of constructing a minutely detailed replica of old Tucson, which has been preserved by the state as a national monument, the film, outside of a few Civil War sequences, boasts surprisingly little in the way of spectacular action. The development of Arizona is paralleled by the personal story of Phoebe Titus (Arthur), a frontier woman who struggles to keep her freight business going despite hardship, war and outlaws. William Holden, making his Western début in a role intended for Gary Cooper, is her loyal top hand and love interest. KN

Bad Day at Black Rock

1940/b & w/127 min/COL/p/d Wesley Ruggles/s Claude Binyon/c Joseph Walker/m Victor Young/lp Jean Arthur, William Holden, Warren William, Porter Hall, Paul Harvey

B

Bad Company · Like Benton and Newman's other genre pieces, *Bonnie and Clyde* and *There Was a Crooked Man...*, and Benton's own *The Late Show*, *Bad Company* infuses a traditional form with an ironic and decidedly contemporary spirit. This tale of deserters and draft dodgers who set off west to become outlaws is less lightweight and jokey than *Butch Cassidy and the Sundance Kid* but nor is it a 'mud and rags' Western in the style of *The Great Northfield Minnesota Raid*. The film demythologizes without debunking, is eccentric and elegiac by turn, and is concerned both with the reality and the mythology of the West. The comic quirkiness is complemented by a loving concern with period 'feel' and a range of remarkable autumn landscapes captured by Willis' magnificent photography. JP
1972/92 min/Jaffilms – PAR/p Stanley R. Jaffe/d Robert Benton/s Robert Benton, David Newman/c Gordon Willis/m Harvey Schmidt/lp Jeff Bridges, Barry Brown, Jim Davis, David Huddleston

Bad Day at Black Rock · A contemporary Western and very much a product of the Dore Schary 'socially conscious' period at MGM, for whom it was also Spencer Tracy's final feature. Here he plays a one-armed stranger, John Macready, who turns up in the isolated town of Black Rock in the California desert, looking for a local, but Japanese-born, farmer in order to deliver his son's posthumously awarded war medal. When he discovers that the farmer was murdered by the locals at the outbreak of war he determines to track down the culprits and wreak revenge. The film is distinguished not only by its liberalism (evoking an obvious comparison with *High Noon*) but also by Sturges' extremely taut direction, which makes an almost Antonioni-like use of figures in the CinemaScope screen, and by the real sense of menace exuded by the heavies – especially Lee Marvin, in one of his most unpleasant roles. JP
1954/81 min/MGM/p Dore Schary/d John Sturges/s Millard Kaufman/c William C. Mellor/m André Previn/lp Spencer Tracy, Robert Ryan, Ernest Borgnine, Dean Jagger, Walter Brennan, Lee Marvin

The Ballad of Cable Hogue · Very much a companion piece to *The Wild Bunch* in its concern with shrinking frontiers, but this time showing the comic side of the coin as Jason Robards' Cable Hogue, a freebooting prospector robbed and left to die in the desert, is vouchsafed a glimpse of salvation through the miraculous discovery of a waterhole. Cunningly exploited, this brings him a fortune and the love of a good woman in the shape of a cheery prostitute (Stella Stevens); but driven by his thirst for revenge, Hogue is unable to seize his chance to escape a world dying as civilization encroaches, and himself dies grotesquely under the wheels of a motor car. Illuminatingly described by Peckinpah as 'a new version of Sartre's *The Flies* with a touch of Keystone Cops', *The Ballad of Cable Hogue* is indeed about a man who defies God (represented by David Warner's disreputably Luciferian itinerant preacher) and is unable to see that he has been shown the way to Eden. A relaxed, tenderly ironic and very funny film, it is more serious in purpose than its surface allows. TMi
1970/121 min/Phil Feldman Prods – WB/p/d Sam Peckinpah/s John Crawford, Edmund Penney/c Lucien Ballard/m Jerry Goldsmith/lp Jason Robards, Stella Stevens, David Warner, Strother Martin

Bandido · Rather less interesting than Fleischer's other Western, *These Thousand Hills*, and certainly not a patch on his masterpiece, *The Vikings*, *Bandido* is nonetheless amiable enough. Mitchum plays a gun-runner trying to get arms for Mexican rebel leader Roland and tangling with Scott, who is working for the Regulares. He also becomes romantically involved with Scott's wife (Ursula Thiess). Although the action drags somewhat in places and the script's attempts at tongue-in-cheek humour do not really come off, the film is distinguished by its lush setting, excellent photography and some fine playing: in particular the interplay between Mitchum and Thiess, which was considered rather daring in a Western at the time. JP
1956/92 min/Bandido Prods – UA/p Robert L. Jacks/d Richard Fleischer/s Earl Felton/c Ernest Laszlo/m Max Steiner/lp Robert Mitchum, Zachary Scott, Gilbert Roland, Ursula Thiess, Henry Brandon

Bandolero! · McLaglen's intriguing though uneven film offers an uneasy mix of Richard Brooks and John Ford. His work always reverberates with memories of previous films but he nevertheless refuses to cross over into a conscious assumption of film

Dean Martin, James Stewart in Bandolero!

Willie Nelson, Gary Busey in Barbarosa

history, as Monte Hellman or Burt Kennedy have. Instead, McLaglen tends to stage the death of the now aged stars of the 50s. The plot, adapted from Stanley L. Hough's story, tells of a gang of bank robbers led by the brothers Bishop (Martin and Stewart) and chased by Sheriff Johnson (Kennedy) and his posse. The brothers also drag the reluctant Maria (Welch) along as a hostage. Both groups of Yankees are attacked by Mexican bandoleros and the brothers are killed. The Fordian moments come mainly at the beginning: the town festively preparing for a hanging by the smartly dressed hangman who takes pride in his professionalism; the treacherous Pop Chaney (Geer) exasperated by his son's nose-picking habit. A plethora of older Western actors fill out the cast, including Donald 'Red' Barry, Harry Carey Jr., Jock Mahoney and Roy Barcroft. PW
1968/106 min/FOX/p Robert L. Jacks/ d Andrew V. McLaglen/s James Lee Barrett/c William H. Clothier/m Jerry Goldsmith/lp James Stewart, Dean Martin, Raquel Welch, George Kennedy, Will Geer, Denver Pyle

Barbarosa · Distinctly underrated, this rather easeful tall tale of a Tex-Mex border country blood-feud crosses the sure-footed play with outlaw mythology that Schepisi had shown in his Australian saga *The Chant of Jimmie Blacksmith* with the stress on familial loyalties and frictions regularly explored by regionalist screenwriter Wittliff (*Raggedy Man, Honeysuckle Rose, Country*). Gauche farmboy Busey is pursued into the desert by his German immigrant relatives after an accidental shooting, and virtually apprentices himself to Nelson's grizzled wanderer, himself the elusive prey of a murderous vendetta sustained over 30 years by Roland's crippled Spanish patriarch. Tutored in survival tactics by this wily redbeard, Busey also learns both the extent and the functional importance of Nelson's legendary status, and – having seen the man

rising once from his intended grave – decides to maintain the myth of the gringo bogeyman even after his mentor's mortality is finally confirmed. PT
1982/90 min/ITC/p Paul N. Lazarus III/ d Fred Schepisi/s William D. Wittliff/c Ian Baker/m Bruce Smeaton/lp Willie Nelson, Gary Busey, Gilbert Roland, Isela Vega

The Baron of Arizona · Fuller's second film and first Western is very loosely based on a real character, James Addison Reavis, who here works in a land office and over the years forges 'evidence' to prove that his wife is heir to Arizona. Though little known, the film reverberates with themes which dominate Fuller's later work: the misuse of education, the relationship between a child and an older man, the power of obsession, the quest for allegiance and identity, the clash of European and American cultures. For a Western the film contains some remarkably Gothic sequences in the European interlude, but what really distinguishes it is the grandiloquence of Price's megalomaniac vision, matched by Fuller's suitably powerful and idiosyncratic direction. JP
1950/b & w/93 min/Deputy Corp – Lippert/p Carl K. Hittleman/d/s Samuel Fuller/c James Wong Howe/m Paul Dunlap/lp Vincent Price, Ellen Drew, Beulah Bondi, Vladimir Sokoloff, Reed Hadley

Barquero · Douglas incorporated back into the Hollywood Western aspects of the Italian version of the genre, as exemplified by the presence of Van Cleef, the border setting, light-hearted brutality and weirdly staged confrontations with exotic weaponry such as a fortified barge. Van Cleef is the haughty, grizzled ferryman who, aided by a hulking backwoodsman (Tucker) who casually licks the ants from the back of his hand, foils and eventually kills the outlaw Remy (Oates) and his gang as they try to cross the river with their wagonload of loot before the Rurales catch up with them. Oates gives an

exuberant performance as the drug-addicted outlaw, exasperated by the wily tricks played by the two tough old-timers. Douglas tells the unconventional story with an emphatic stylization reminiscent of the cruelly cynical and misogynist approach deployed by a Corbucci or a Sollima, although he lacks their wholehearted commitment to style. PW
1970/114 min/Aubrey Schenck Enterprises – UA/p Hal Klein/d Gordon Douglas/ s George Schenck, William Marks/c Jerry Finnerman/m Dominic Frontiere/lp Lee Van Cleef, Forrest Tucker, Warren Oates, Kerwin Mathews, Mariette Hartley

The Battle at Elderbush Gulch · One of the most successful of all Griffith's Biograph films, it was made on location in San Fernando, California in July 1913. Two young girls and a young married couple (Harron and Gish) with their baby arrive by stagecoach in the 'still unsettled West'. In revenge for the tragic shooting of a chief's son, the Indians attack the town and besiege the cabin in which Gish and the children are hiding – but rescue is at hand in the shape of the cavalry. As with many of Griffith's later Biograph films, suspense is created through the use of parallel action, and there is an impressive use of high-angle shots to show the Indian attack. The film's melodramatic plot makes a sharp distinction in its depiction of whites and Indians. The white settlement is sentimentally portrayed, with a dramatic emphasis on babies, children and puppies, whilst the Indians, eaters of dogs and murderers of children, are shown as wholly savage. JH
1913/b & w/2,021 ft/Biograph/d/s D.W. Griffith/c Billy Bitzer/lp Mae Marsh, Alfred Paget, Charles H. Mailes, Lillian Gish, Robert Harron

The Battle at Elderbush Gulch

Betty Grable (centre) in The Beautiful Blonde from Bashful Bend

The Beautiful Blonde from Bashful Bend ·
Preston Sturges' last Hollywood film is often
regarded as an unsuccessful attempt to rein-
vigorate his waning career, but it merits
attention as a rare parody of the Western's
conventions from the classic period of the
genre. Pin-up star Betty Grable plays Freddie
Jones, a saloon singer with the gun skills of a
traditional Western hero. After accidentally
shooting a judge in the rear during a con-
tretemps with her gambler friend Blackie,
she escapes to Snake City where she is
mistaken for the new schoolteacher. Instead
of the civilization which such an iconographic figure usually brings to the West,
Freddie introduces anarchy and gunplay,
and the comic centrepiece of the film is a
prolonged parody of a Western shoot-out
involving Freddie, the town notables, the
town disreputables and Blackie. The film
ends in chaos as she marries Blackie then
again manages accidently to shoot the unfortunate judge in his sore spot. TR
1949/79 min/FOX/p/d/s Preston Sturges/
c Harry Jackson/m Cyril Mockridge/
lp Betty Grable, Cesar Romero, Rudy
Vallee, Olga San Juan

The Beguiled · One of the high points of
both the Siegel and Eastwood oeuvres, *The
Beguiled*, like others of Eastwood's attempts
to escape from his Man With No Name/
Dirty Harry personae, was a commercial flop
and a critical success. Here he plays a Union
soldier who finds refuge, though eventually
death, in a ladies' seminary. As has been
pointed out, the film both looks back to
Ford's *Seven Women* and forward to Eastwood's *Play Misty For Me*, but the style is
full-blown Southern Gothic larded with all
the atmospherics and sexual tensions of a
Carson McCullers story. A mixture of
psychodrama and Western, *The Beguiled*
invokes throughout its length a sustained,
overt stylization that normally erupts only

occasionally in either Siegel's or Eastwood's
work. If much of the film is reminiscent of
Reflections in a Golden Eye, the climax is
worthy of John Webster. JP
1970/105 min/Malpaso – U/p/d Don
Siegel/s John B. Sherry (aka Albert Maltz),
Grimes Grice (aka Irene Kamp)/c Bruce
Surtees/m Lalo Schifrin/lp Clint
Eastwood, Geraldine Page, Elizabeth
Hartman, Jo Ann Harris, Darleen Carr

Bend of the River (Where the River Bends)
· Reuniting Anthony Mann with James
Stewart and writer Borden Chase, his collaborators on *Winchester '73*, this film has
Stewart as an ex-Missouri raider, now a
reformed character working as guide to a
wagon train heading for farming land in
Oregon. Along the way, he rescues another
such raider (Arthur Kennedy) from summary hanging, and in the upshot confronts
his *alter ego*. At first Kennedy is a loyal
companion, and in an exciting sequence
saves Stewart's life when the two men
ambush a band of marauding Indians. Gradually, though, Kennedy's crooked impulses
come to the fore, and a fast-moving series of
events climaxes with him and Stewart battling it out in the Snake River of the title, with
the settlers' vital provisions at stake; Stewart
ultimately drowns Kennedy, and with him,
his own hidden past. The narrative spring is
tightly coiled, and, as later in *The Man from
Laramie*, Kennedy contributes a persuasive
portrait of corrupt charm. TP
1951/91 min/U/p Aaron Rosenberg/
d Anthony Mann/s Borden Chase/c Irving
Glassberg/m Hans Salter/lp James Stewart,
Arthur Kennedy, Julia Adams, Rock
Hudson, Jay C. Flippen

The Big Country · Jessamyn West, the
author of *Friendly Persuasion* which was
filmed by Wyler in 1956, again collaborated,
uncredited, on this pacifist story that
prompted the critic Bosley Crowther to
remark: 'Peace is a pious precept, but fightin'
is more excitin'.' Two enemy cattlemen
(Bickford and Ives) try to acquire the
property of the schoolteacher (Simmons)
because it has a well. Peck comes to marry
Bickford's daughter (Baker) but falls foul of
the macho foreman (Heston), who eventually wins Baker while Peck settles for the
schoolma'm after he has proved himself a
real man by defeating the ugly brute Connors in a duel. The two patriarchs then also
kill each other, allowing peace to return to
the big, beautifully filmed country. The
film's highlights, apart from Heston's tower-

ing performance, unfailingly come with the
staging of violence: Peck's solitary breaking
of a wild horse, his moonlit fight with
Heston, and the final shoot-out amongst
some giant rocks. This may explain why a
pacifist movie became a smash hit. PW
1958/163 min/Anthony – Worldwide –
UA/co-p Gregory Peck/co-p/d William
Wyler/s James R. Webb, Sy Bartlett,
Robert Wilder/c Franz Planer/m Jerome
Moross/lp Gregory Peck, Charlton
Heston, Charles Bickford, Burl Ives, Jean
Simmons, Carroll Baker, Chuck Connors,

The Big Sky · Like *Red River*, *The Big Sky*
deals with the mastery of the western landscape by entrepreneurial pioneers. The blazing of the Chisholm trail in the former film is
mirrored here by the 1830 keelboat expedition of fur traders and a handful of mountain
men, from St Louis 1,200 miles up the
uncharted Missouri River, through hostile
Sioux and Crow territory, to the Blackfoot
Indian country of Montana. Fashioning a
screenplay from only the first part of A.B.
Guthrie's 1947 novel, Hawks and Dudley
Nichols omit the darker aspects of the novel,
such as the massacre of the men on the
Mandan and the murder of Deakens (Douglas) by Boone (Martin), in favour of a vision
of the West as a setting for the realization of
personal as well as professional
relationships. Hawks celebrates not only the
cooperative nature of the business venture
(all the men have shares in the profits), but
also the growth of an intricate system of
personal interdependency; just as the crew
need the Blackfoot hostage, Teal Eye
(Threatt), to facilitate their trading activities,
so they need one another to guarantee the
success of their mission. From Deakens,
Boone and Zeb (Hunnicutt) to the French-
speaking crew of the *Mandan*, to Teal Eye
and the crazed Indian Poordevil (Worden),
Hawks's characters cross linguistic and cultural boundaries to form a community in
which all but sexual difference dissolves.
Tied together by their common needs, they
constitute a Hawksian ideal – a group
wedded, like Boone and Teal Eye, by both
personal and professional desires. JB
1952/b & w/122 min/Winchester –
RKO/p/d Howard Hawks/s Dudley Nichols/
c Russell Harlan/m Dimitri Tiomkin/
lp Kirk Douglas, Dewey Martin, Elizabeth
Threatt, Arthur Hunnicutt, Hank Worden

The Big Trail · One of several early 30s
experiments with 70mm widescreen processes, *The Big Trail* stands as an odd false

Johnny Mack Brown, *Wallace Beery* in Billy the Kid

Mel Brooks in Blazing Saddles

Walter Brennan (l.), Robert Mitchum (centre) in Blood on the Moon

start for the Western itself and for the genre's biggest star. John Wayne was recommended to director Raoul Walsh by John Ford, and the inexperienced player was given the lead role Walsh had himself intended to play. However, the film and Wayne's vengeance-seeking hero were not popular and the actor retreated to B-movies until Ford summoned him for *Stagecoach*. The film is a would-be epic in the style of *The Covered Wagon* and, while the story of Wayne's search for his father's murderers is not overly compulsive, the background details of the first big wagon train in Oregon territory are persuasively and spectacularly put up on the then-giant screen. Among the set-piece perils Walsh has his settlers triumph over are Indian attacks, blizzards, raging rivers and mountains. Swedish dialect comedian El Brendel provides irritating comic relief in the tradition that would eventually be refined by Walter Brennan and John Qualen. KN
1930/b & w/110 min/FOX/d Raoul Walsh/ s Jack Peabody, Marie Boyle, Florence Postal, Fred Serser/c Lucien Andriot, Arthur Edeson/m Arthur Kay/lp John Wayne, Marguerite Churchill, Ward Bond, Tyrone Power Sr., El Brendel

Billy the Kid · Originally shot in MGM's 70mm Realife Grandeur system to give full value to the New Mexico landscapes, this is a handsome-looking film; particularly impressive is the vast cave where Pat Garrett runs Billy to ground. There's also a piece of brilliantly handled tragi-comedy where Old Stuff (Roscoe Ates) makes a run for water while under fire and is shot. The story is faithful to tradition in the murder of Billy's mentor Tunstall (though here called Tunston), the burning of McSween's house and Billy's break-out from jail. Only the ending is changed, when Garrett inexplicably lets Billy go. The real weakness of the film is in

the performances, especially that of Johnny Mack Brown in his last big picture before Poverty Row. Brown is merely adequate, and that simply isn't enough to generate the intensity of emotion that usually distinguishes a Vidor film. EB
1930/b & w/90 min/MGM/d King Vidor/ s Wanda Tuchock, Laurence Stallings, Charles MacArthur/c Gordon Avil/lp Johnny Mack Brown, Wallace Beery, Kay Johnson, Russell Simpson, Roscoe Ates

Blazing Saddles · Mel Brooks, mining the clichés with gusto, struck box-office gold; by 1983 this had become the top-grossing Western of all time. It starts well, with an over-the-top Frankie Laine theme song and a group of blacks on a railroad construction gang singing 'I get no kicks from champagne'. Much of the humour comes from racial stereotypes: Brooks himself as a Jewish Indian chief, Cleavon Little as the black sheriff hired to demoralize the townsfolk into selling their land to a crooked speculator. Little's role also neatly inverts the sweaty macho image of the West; his saddle is by Gucci and he drinks his whiskey from a wineglass. But after a while the unrelenting pace proves wearisome, and Brooks' much vaunted 'bad taste', as in the scene of cowboys eating beans and farting, no more than schoolboy humour. EB
1974/93 min/Crossbow – WB/p Michael Hertzberg/d Mel Brooks/s Norman Steinberg, Andrew Bergman, Richard Pryor, Alan Uger, Mel Brooks/c Joseph Biroc/m John Morris/lp Gene Wilder, Cleavon Little, Slim Pickens, Mel Brooks

Blood on the Moon · Although Wise is on record as disliking the Western (he made only three) *Blood on the Moon* he describes as his 'first big feature'. It is also an excellent example of his noir-ish 40s work, Musuraca's shadow-filled, threatening images recall-

ing their earlier collaboration on *Curse of the Cat People*. The story of a gunslinger (Mitchum) who is hired by a cattle rustler (Preston) to scare ranch owner Bel Geddes into selling her cattle cheaply but who falls in love with her instead, *Blood on the Moon* is a largely 'indoor' Western. Low-ceilinged sets add to the claustrophobic air (a reminder of Wise's work with Welles) and the film's highlight is a gruelling, brutal and seemingly endless fist-fight between Mitchum and Preston. JP
1948/b & w/87 min/RKO/p Theron Warth/d Robert Wise/s Lillie Hayward/ c Nicholas Musuraca/m Roy Webb/ lp Robert Mitchum, Barbara Bel Geddes, Robert Preston, Walter Brennan, Tom Tyler

Brigham Young – Frontiersman · The tale of the Mormon trek from Illinois to Utah in flight from religious persecution, told with more solemnity than historical accuracy and little of the lyricism which made an intimate epic of the same story in Ford's *Wagon Master*. Lavishly mounted and splendidly shot by Arthur Miller, it has impressive sequences, most notably the lynching of Joseph Smith (Price) which forces the exodus, and the threatened destruction of the first spring crop in Salt Lake City by a plague of locusts, averted (in accordance with Mormon legend) when clouds of seagulls descend in response to Brigham Young's prayer. Despite a deeply etched performance from Jagger in the title role, too much of the film is conventional spectacle, not least Power and Darnell, along for the ride to provide the non-polygamous romantic interest. TMi
1940/b & w/114 min/FOX/p Kenneth MacGowan/d Henry Hathaway/s Lamar Trotti/c Arthur Miller/m Alfred Newman/ lp Dean Jagger, Tyrone Power, Linda Darnell, Brian Donlevy, Vincent Price

Broken Arrow · Along with Mann's under-rated *Devil's Doorway*, *Broken Arrow* was one of the first Westerns to regard the Indians in a sympathetic light. It seems altogether fitting that it was the first Western directed by Delmer Daves, whose contributions to the genre are marked by their straightforward honesty, their respect for history and ordinary people and their human warmth. This story of a Civil War veteran (Stewart) who becomes a scout, goes to live with the Indians and marries an Indian girl (Paget) was originally a Losey project and a first version of the script was written by Albert Maltz, who had collaborated with Daves twice before. Daves drew upon his extensive first-hand knowledge of Indian culture and history to make his moving vindication of the American Indian as convincing as possible. The film's achievements may now seem somewhat limited – Daves was forced to have white performers playing Indian roles, and Paget dies, allowing Stewart to return to white society – but at the time it made a stand against racism. JP
1950/93 min/FOX/*p* Julian Blaustein/
d Delmer Daves/*s* Michael Blankfort/
c Ernest Palmer/*m* Hugo Friedhofer/
lp James Stewart, Jeff Chandler, Debra Paget, Arthur Hunnicutt, Will Geer, Jay Silverheels

Broken Lance · Spencer Tracy is an overbearing cattle baron with three sons by an earlier marriage and one, Robert Wagner, by his current wife, a Comanche. The three older sons, led by Richard Widmark, are ne'er-do-wells, jealous that Wagner is their father's favourite. Tracy starts a feud with some copper miners who are poisoning his water. When the mine is burnt to the ground Widmark ensures that Wagner takes the rap. The film in fact begins with Wagner coming out of jail, effectively dispossessed by his brothers now that Tracy is dead; most of the narrative is then, unusually for a Western, unfolded in flashback. Wagner seems a very 50s hero with his short leather jacket, brilliantined hair and edgy manner, and Widmark is splendid, full of sneers and machinations. When he commits the unpardonable offence of selling off cattle land to an oil company it's only a matter of time before he gets his deserts, though Wagner is spared from committing fratricide when Widmark is shot by an elderly Indian relative. EB
1954/96 min/FOX/*p* Sol C. Siegel/*d* Edward Dmytryk/*s* Richard Murphy/*c* Joseph MacDonald/*m* Leigh Harline/*lp* Spencer Tracy, Robert Wagner, Jean Peters,
Richard Widmark, Katy Jurado, Hugh O'Brian

Bronco Billy · Eastwood's seventh film as a director is also one of his most personal, despite its lightweight appearance. It is also the one in which he most decisively abandons – indeed even parodies – his Man With No Name/Dirty Harry personae. The story of an ex-prisoner and shoe salesman turned proprietor of a Wild West show peopled by misfits and outcasts is virtually Capra-esque in tone, both touching and amusing in equal quantities and in an engagingly dry and understated fashion. A commercial failure and critical success, the film is not in fact that different in terms of its values from Eastwood's more macho efforts. Given his remark that 'what attracted me right away was the idea of a character rejecting all the modern cynicism around him with a positive attitude about his purpose, his life, his self-image as a traditional hero, and his sense of what is important and what is not', it is hard not to see *Bronco Billy*, on one level at least, as a Reagan era fable about the need for community and the restoration of American self-confidence and traditional affirmative values. JP
1980/116 min/WB/*p* Dennis Hackin, Neal Dobrofsky/*d* Clint Eastwood/*s* Dennis Hackin/*c* David Worth/*m* Snuff Garrett, Steve Dorff/*lp* Clint Eastwood, Sondra Locke, Geoffrey Lewis, Scatman Crothers, Bill McKinney

Buchanan Rides Alone · The most playful entry in the series of Randolph Scott vehicles directed by Budd Boetticher and produced by Harry Joe Brown. Scott appears as a cheery independent spirit, who on returning from Mexico gets caught up in a blood feud in the border outpost of Agrytown – owned lock, stock and barrel by the corrupt Agry family – after coming to the aid of a young Mexican bent on avenging his sister's dishonour at the hands of one of the Agry clan. A pell-mell succession of judiciously tongue-in-cheek incidents, including a narrow escape from hanging and an elaborate gun battle all over the town, ends with the villains and most of their adherents defunct and Scott continuing his carefree loner's progress. In an appropriate fade-out line, the tough but basically decent ex-Agry henchman (Craig Stevens), on whose shoulders the mantle of town boss has fallen, surveys the litter of corpses and brusquely instructs a minion to go and get a shovel. TP
1958/77 min/Producers-Actors Corp – COL/*p* Harry Joe Brown/*d* Budd Boetticher/*s* Charles Lang Jr./*c* Lucien Ballard/*lp* Randolph Scott, Craig Stevens, Barry Kelley, Tol Avery

Buffalo Bill · The standard movie biography of Buffalo Bill Cody, which opts to follow Buntline's sanitized and exaggerated version of Cody's career rather than attempt, as Robert Altman's later *Buffalo Bill and the Indians* does, to delve into the gap between the legend and the truth. Joel McCrea is a sturdily handsome, morally irreproachable Buffalo Bill, who earns the respect of Indian chief Anthony Quinn by besting him in hand-to-hand combat and thereafter becomes a champion of the red man's cause. The first half of the film is directed with verve by Wellman – who agreed to do the movie so that he would be given a free hand with *The Ox-Bow Incident* – as Buffalo Bill carves his myth in the West, but the movie sags when its hero goes to Washington to be a lobbyist and finally gets into the circus business. Any ironies implicit in Cody's transformation from 'authentic' frontier hero to cash-in showman are studiously avoided, and biopic clichés like a guest appearance by Sidney Blackmer as Teddy Roosevelt soon become embarrassing. Also in the cast are Maureen O'Hara as the archetypal supportive wife, Linda Darnell as a very unlikely Indian princess and Thomas Mitchell as a blustering Buntline. KN
1944/90 min/FOX/*p* Harry Sherman/
d William A. Wellman/*s* Aeneas MacKenzie, Clements Ripley, Cecile Kramer/*c* Leon Shamroy/*m* David Buttolph/*lp* Joel McCrea, Maureen O'Hara, Thomas Mitchell, Anthony Quinn, Linda Darnell, Edgar Buchanan, Sidney Blackmer

Buffalo Bill and the Indians or Sitting Bull's History Lesson · A suitably sour but dismally over-schematic sideswipe at the abiding values of sham and showbiz fakery inherent in America's self-image, Altman's crudely ironic contribution to the Bicentennial celebrations focuses on the vast gap between matters of record and representation instanced by the travesty of Buffalo Bill Cody's Wild West show. Newman's scout-cum-superstar, surrounded by those who both print the legend and profit by it, unsteadily faces up to doubts and guilt when political prisoner Sitting Bull joins his entourage and demands some authenticity be applied to his act. He finds himself,

however, already prey to audience expectations, and unable to intervene in the systematic denial of justice to the Indian chief and his people. Almost redundantly didactic, the film is perked up solely by the collective charisma of a typically sizeable and starry Altman ensemble cast. PT
1976/123 min/Dino De Laurentiis Corp – Lion's Gate Films/p/d Robert Altman/ s Alan Rudolph, Robert Altman/c Paul Lohmann/m Richard Baskin/lp Paul Newman, Burt Lancaster, Joel Grey, Geraldine Chaplin, Harvey Keitel

Il buono, il brutto, il cattivo (The Good, the Bad and the Ugly) · The third of Leone's 'Dollars' films, which introduces American history into the lives of the bounty hunters in the form of the American Civil War. Each of the main characters is introduced with the appropriate label ('good', 'bad' and 'ugly'), and the picaresque plot leads us to question two of the labels – 'the bad' (played by Lee Van Cleef) remains all bad throughout. Owing as much to Chaplin's *Monsieur Verdoux* as to the American Western, the film aims for a more international audience than the first two (with a budget to match), and introduces a talkative Actors' Studio character in the uproarious form of Eli Wallach (the 'ugly' – Eastwood, of course, is the 'good'). The climax, which takes place in a huge war cemetery, involves a shoot-out between the three of them – to the accompaniment of an all-stops-out 'anthem' by Ennio Morricone. This replaces the traditional main street with a circular arena, and lasts a whole reel. Again, the visual rhetoric is far more important than the episodic story. CF
1966/180 min/PEA – UA/p Alberto Grimaldi/d Sergio Leone/s Age Scarpelli, Luciano Vincenzoni, Sergio Leone/ c Tonino Delli Colli/m Ennio Morricone/ lp Clint Eastwood, Lee Van Cleef, Eli Wallach, Aldo Giuffre, Mario Brega

Butch Cassidy and the Sundance Kid · Not the first filmic portrayal of these two historical characters, but outstandingly the most successful at the box office. Though Newman and Redford are undeniably attractive as Butch and the Kid respectively, much of the film veers from the chic to the merely slick. It's full of the nostalgia for the last days of the West that had become fashionable by the end of the 60s ('The horse is dead,' announces a bicycle salesman), and the frequent use of sepia-tinted sequences and still photographs attempts to supply a

Clint Eastwood, Eli Wallach in Il buono, il brutto, il cattivo

Paul Newman, Robert Redford in Butch Cassidy and the Sundance Kid

historical dimension. But the heart of the film lies in the relationship of the two buddies, preserved for ever in the final freeze-frame. For them the West is a spree. Katharine Ross as Etta Place is required to do little more than look on affectionately. EB
1969/110 min/Campanile – FOX/p John Foreman/d George Roy Hills/s William Goldman/c Conrad Hall/m Burt Bacharach/ lp Paul Newman, Robert Redford, Katharine Ross, Strother Martin

C

Calamity Jane · An engagingly energetic musical which has a lot of fun with sexual stereotypes. Doris Day as Calamity in soiled buckskins continuously tries to gain the attention of Howard Keel as Wild Bill Hickok, who's more interested in his card game. Eventually she changes into a skirt and succeeds, but not before Bill has been humiliated by having to dress up as an Indian squaw after losing a bet. And by the end Calamity's in trousers again, albeit smarter ones. Plenty of good songs by Sammy Fain and Paul Francis Webster, including 'The Deadwood Stage', 'The Black Hills of

Dakota', the million-selling 'Secret Love' and 'Just Blew in from the Windy City', which nicely points up the traditional contrast between eastern sophistication and western vitality. EB
1953/101 min/WB/p William Jacobs/ d David Butler/s James O'Hanlon/c Wilfrid M. Cline/md Ray Heindorf/lp Doris Day, Howard Keel, Allyn McLerie, Phil Carey

Carson City · One of several superior Westerns in which André de Toth directed Randolph Scott. This time Scott is a railroad engineer, first discovered in a saloon on a binge, who is hired to build a track between Virginia City and Carson City, in the gold-mining area of Nevada. Scott stands for the forces of progress, powerfully embodied in the technology of steam-driven drills tunnelling their way through solid rock. The townspeople, with the exception of Lucille Norman as a forward-looking newspaperwoman, are timorous folk, fearful that the railroad will bring undesirable elements. But undesirables are already at work in the person of Raymond Massey. Nicknamed 'The Champagne Bandit' because of his fondness for toasting success in bubbly, Massey is making a good living robbing the stages on which the gold is brought out. He is finally bested by Scott in a splendid fight on a train. EB
1951/87 min/WB/p David Weisbart/ d André de Toth/s Sloan Nibley, Winston Miller/c John Boyle/m David Buttolph/ lp Randolph Scott, Lucille Norman, Raymond Massey, Richard Webb

Cat Ballou · By the mid-1960s parody seemed to be one of the few lines of development left open to the Western. *Cat Ballou* manages to have plenty of fun at the expense

Jane Fonda, Lee Marvin in Cat Ballou

Lance Fuller, Barbara Stanwyck, Chubby Johnson in Cattle Queen of Montana

Henry Fonda in C'era una volta il west

Dolores del Rio, Sal Mineo in Cheyenne Autumn

of the generic clichés while remaining faithful to a traditional narrative. The bad guys, the Wolf City Development Corporation, who are trying to push Cat's father off his land, are defeated in the end. Lee Marvin's wonderful portrait of the aging and drunken gunfighter Kid Sheleen satirizes the conventions through sheer excess (he literally can't hit a barn door) but doesn't subvert the myth; he is, finally, the hero. The film is fashionably knowing about its Western history: Cat Ballou (Jane Fonda) hires the Kid because she's read about him in a dime novel; in a brief appearance Butch Cassidy and the Sundance Kid are worn-out shadows of their former selves; there's a politically-conscious Indian. And there's a modernist touch about the ballad-singers (Nat 'King' Cole and Stubby Kaye) who punctuate the narrative. EB
1965/96 min/Harold Hecht Corp – COL/ p Harold Hecht/d Elliot Silverstein/s Walter Newman, Frank R. Pierson/c Jack Marta/m Frank DeVol/lp Lee Marvin, Jane Fonda, Michael Callan, Arthur Hunnicutt, Jay C. Flippen

Cattle Queen of Montana · An entirely formulaic Western, enlivened by Barbara Stanwyck's strutting feistiness as Sierra Nevada Jones, a pioneer woman struggling to retain her dead father's rangeland despite the presence of Gene Evans as the land-grasping owner of the neighbouring Bear Claw Ranch, and Anthony Caruso as Natchakoa the renegade Indian. As with Stanwyck's other 50s Western heroines (Forty Guns, The Maverick Queen), Sierra Nevada was thought to be a strong enough character for the film to get away with a leading man of rather less star presence and acting ability, in this case Ronald Reagan. The future President's one-dimensional performance as a hired gun working for Evans leaves no doubt

in the audience's mind but that he will be revealed in the last reel to be an upstanding undercover man out to get the goods on the bad guys. Veteran director Dwan and photographer John Alton get the most pictorially out of the outdoor settings. KN
1954/88 min/RKO/p Benedict Bogeaus/ d Allan Dwan/s Robert Blees, Howard Estabrook/c John Alton/m Louis Forbes/ lp Barbara Stanwyck, Ronald Reagan, Gene Evans, Anthony Caruso, Jack Elam

C'era una volta il west (Once Upon a Time in the West) · Leone hoped to introduce his fourth Western by killing his three protagonists from Il buono, il brutto, il cattivo during the credit titles – to show how he was cutting loose from the Cinecittà Western. But by then Clint Eastwood had moved on. This film is structured around a series of 'citations' from classic Hollywood Westerns (High Noon, Shane, The Searchers, Pursued in the first fifteen minutes alone), which were collected by Leone and Bernardo Bertolucci (one of the writers of the original story). In each case, the 'citation' makes us *think* we've seen it all before when we haven't – for the atmosphere, the visual style and the overall operatic quality present the greatest hits in a completely new light. The story – about the struggle over water rights between a widow from New Orleans and a railroad company – has been told a thousand times before, but Leone uses it to collide the stereotypes of the Western with the 'progress' of American history. Leone calls it 'a ballet of the dead', and it's also been called 'an opera in which the arias are not sung, they are *stared*.' Among other things, this means it has the longest credits sequence in the history of the Western. CF
1968/165 min/Rafran – San Marco – PAR/ p Fulvio Morsella/d Sergio Leone/s Sergio Leone, Sergio Donati/c Tonino Delli

Colli/m Ennio Morricone/lp Henry Fonda, Claudia Cardinale, Jason Robards, Charles Bronson, Lionel Stander, Jack Elam, Woody Strode

The Charge at Feather River · With the added attraction of 3-D and stereo sound, this was the most commercially successful Western of its year. Frontiersman Madison leads a detachment of guardhouse volunteers to the rescue of Miles and Westcott, who have been captured by the Indians. Without the eye-catching distractions of objects and bodies flying out of the screen, it is easier to enjoy Douglas' forceful, no-nonsense direction and Marley's pleasing lensing of the landscape. Not up to the standard of the wonderful Rio Conchos, but nonetheless a high point in the uneven canon of Gordon Douglas Westerns. JP
1953/96 min/WB/p David Weisbart/ d Gordon Douglas/s James R. Webb/ c J. Peverell Marley/m Max Steiner/lp Guy Madison, Frank Lovejoy, Helen Westcott, Vera Miles, Dick Wesson

Cheyenne Autumn · John Ford's last Western, a film usually seen as reparation to the Indians for the war crimes committed against them in innumerable films, not only Ford's. Certainly there's a solemnity about the enterprise (based on the book by Mari Sandoz), not much leavened by the banter between Richard Widmark and his troop of cavalry as they pursue the small band of Cheyenne who have fled the harsh conditions of their reservation. Ford's compositions, noble as ever, breathtaking at times, are at moments just *too* stately. His creative use of geography is even more in evidence than usual. After the Cheyenne have been in flight for a good hour of the film we are still patently where we began, in Monument Valley, standing in, somewhat improbably,

for Oklahoma. What redeems the film is the richly cynical episode in Dodge City, with James Stewart as Wyatt Earp and Arthur Kennedy as Doc Holliday insisting that an Indian attack cannot possibly be allowed to interrupt their card game. It's a stroke akin to the porter scene in *Macbeth*. EB
1964/159 min/Ford-Smith Prods – WB/
p Bernard Smith/*d* John Ford/*s* James R. Webb/*c* William H. Clothier/*m* Alex North/*lp* Richard Widmark, Carroll Baker, James Stewart, Arthur Kennedy, Edward G. Robinson, Karl Malden

Cimarron · The first, and thus far only, Western ever to carry off the Academy Award for Best Picture. Predictably, the very qualities which doubtless recommended it to the Oscar voters in 1931 now make it seem like a half-hearted fizzle. Adapted from the best-selling novel by Edna Ferber, the film features a spectacular recreation of the Oklahoma land rush and much incidental detail about the obstacles pioneers Richard Dix and Irene Dunne must overcome, but it

is far more interested in being a family saga and a pageant of American history than it is in being a Western. The story follows Dix and Dunne through the harsh days from 1890 onwards as the territory is opened up and Oklahoma attains its statehood, but also deals with the effects on the family of World War I and the oil boom of the 20s. As in John Huston's *The Life and Times of Judge Roy Bean*, the latter symbolizes the destruction of noble frontier values and the flabbiness of twentieth-century life. With its novelettish emphasis on the stoic forebearance of Dunne when faced with the fecklessness of Dix and the ingratitude of her children, the film is perhaps best considered as a woman's picture out West rather than as a true Western. KN
1930/b & w/131 min/RKO/*p* William Le Baron/*d* Wesley Ruggles/*s* Howard Estabrook/*c* Edward Cronjager/*m* Max Steiner/*lp* Irene Dunne, Richard Dix, Estelle Taylor, Nance O'Neil, Roscoe Ates

Cimarron · This remake of the RKO movie of

1930 was Anthony Mann's last Western, and sadly suffered considerable studio truncation, causing it to be largely disowned by the director. It remains, though, despite the further handicap of some curious casting, a work of much interest. The early sequences of the Oklahoma land rush and its aftermath are realized with great drive and attack, and there is a formal originality about the way that as the territory is settled, the protagonist Yancey Cravat (Glenn Ford) – 'gambler, gunman, lawyer' – is steadily effaced from the dramatic action, finally to die off-screen fighting with British troops in World War I. The external knowledge that this effect is partly due to changes forced on Mann by the front office adds a fitting touch of irony to the film's exploration of the gap between historical forces and individual action. TP
1960/135 min/MGM/*p* Edmund Grainger/ *d* Anthony Mann/*s* Arnold Schulman/ *c* Robert L. Surtees/*m* Franz Waxman/ *lp* Glenn Ford, Maria Schell, Anne Baxter, Russ Tamblyn, Mercedes McCambridge

Cimarron (1930)

Colorado Territory · This is the best version of W.R. Burnett's *High Sierra*, filmed by Walsh himself as a classic gangster picture eight years earlier. McCrea is Wes, the escaped convict who falls for the sensuous Indian girl Colorado (Mayo). Although wanting to go straight, he is dogged by bad luck and agrees to one more train robbery with his former gang. Meeting with nothing but betrayal, the tragic lovers, on the run to Mexico, are hunted down and killed in a bleakly barren rockscape. Walsh eliminated the sentimentality from the original story – in a memorable scene a sheriff strikes a match on a hanged man's boot – and delivered a dark but intensely romantic tale of doomed love in the vein of Ray's *They Live By Night* (1948) or his own *Pursued* (1947). The ending, as the lovers choose to die together amidst the gigantic sun-cracked rocks, McCrea's bullet-ridden body caught in an extraordinary optical zoom as his hand reaches for Mayo's, is one of the finest moments in Walsh's work. PW
1949/b & w/94 min/WB/*p* Anthony Veiller/*d* Raoul Walsh/*s* John Twist, Edmund H. North/*c* Sid Hickox/*m* David Buttolph/*lp* Joel McCrea, Virginia Mayo, Dorothy Malone, Henry Hull

The Comancheros · Curtiz completed this film only a month before his death and as a large-scale, none-too-serious but highly enjoyable action adventure it is in many ways a fitting tribute and climax to his career. Based on a little-known episode in American history, *The Comancheros* pits Texas Ranger Wayne against Confederate renegade Persoff, who is intent on building an empire in Mexico, arming the Indians and sending them against the Union. However, as a film from Wayne's tongue-in-cheek period *The Comancheros* is higher on comedy than drama or history, and the relationship between Wayne and Whitman as a gambler reluctantly drawn into the action has all the characteristics of a long drawn-out poker game. Though occasionally marred by a rather pedestrian academicism *The Comancheros* is for the most part a straightforward open-air Western. The excellent action sequences were directed by Cliff Lyons. JP
1961/107 min/FOX/*p* George Sherman/*d* Michael Curtiz/*s* James Edward Grant, Clair Huffaker/*c* William H. Clothier/*m* Elmer Bernstein/*lp* John Wayne, Stuart Whitman, Ina Balin, Nehemiah Persoff, Lee Marvin

Comanche Station · Cody, an aging loner whose wife was abducted by Indians ten years earlier, rides throughout the West searching for her. Using trinkets and small goods to barter with the Indians, he rescues other women. In this instance he journeys to Lordsburg with Mrs Lowe, whom he has just rescued, and, joined by Ben, an older gunman, and his two companions, Cody vows to fulfil his mission. The gunman, aware of the reward for her return, wants a share of the prize, and knows that pay will be on delivery – dead or alive. Cody's mission is one of honour, but he never lets on that he does so without thought of reward – in spite of the woman's hostility to him as a bounty hunter. In the end Cody and Ben are forced into a showdown and Cody, whose honour is complemented by a 'way with a gun', returns Mrs Lowe to her family. A spare, even austere, film, *Comanche Station* presents the issues of the genre in their most elemental form. JD
1959/73 min/Ranown – COL/*p*/*d* Budd Boetticher/*s* Burt Kennedy/*c* Charles Lawton Jr./*m* Mischa Bakaleinikoff/*lp* Randolph Scott, Nancy Gates, Claude Akins, Skip Homeier

Comes a Horseman · Set in Montana towards the end of World War II, Pakula's film is an intriguing generic hybrid, transposing from its usual urban environment a palpable sense of political paranoia (cf. the same director's *The Parallax View*, *All the President's Men* and *Rollover*) and insinuating it into an almost stock range-war scenario. Fonda and ex-GI Caan are the small ranchers, Robards the empire-rebuilding cattle baron, while Grizzard as the oilman and more anonymous agent of progress is the only character not fixated on idyllic visions of the Western past. The movie is hardly elegiac, though, for all the dignity it affords Farnsworth's aging cowhand and its opening, funeral-scene nod to John Ford. Its more Gothic dynamic actually emanates from the extent to which Robards' attempts to turn back the clock take on a pathological profile, culminating in his resort to a gunfight with the ranchers which is as politically anachronistic as it is apocalyptic. PT
1978/118 min/UA/*p* Gene Kirkwood, Dan Paulson/*d* Alan J. Pakula/*s* Dennis Lynton Clark/*c* Gordon Willis/*m* Michael Small/

Virginia Mayo, Joel McCrea in Colorado Territory

Randolph Scott in Comanche Station

lp James Caan, Jane Fonda, Jason Robards Jr., Richard Farnsworth, George Grizzard

Coogan's Bluff · Eastwood's first film with Siegel playfully and ironically transposes the concerns of the Western to the urban setting of the contemporary crime thriller. Deputy Walt Coogan arrives in New York to bring back an escaped killer, Ringerman. Coogan's appearance brands him as a displaced Westerner, while he in turn resists police red tape. When he abducts Ringerman from hospital and then loses him, he is taken off the case, but via Ringerman's girlfriend Linny Raven he again tracks down his quarry and, after a spectacular citizen's arrest, is allowed to take him back to Arizona. Although the liberal concerns of the probation officer Julie challenge Coogan's machismo, they are shown to be no match for an urban decadence associated with a psychotic version of the 'alternative' youth culture of the later 60s. If Siegel begins by mocking Coogan's 'country' style, he goes on, especially in the final motorcycle chase that re-plays the film's opening man-hunt, to celebrate the individualist skills that place Coogan in instinctual control of the environment, 'natural' or 'urban'. PD
1968/94 min/Malpaso – U/*p*/*d* Don Siegel/ *s* Herman Miller, Dean Riesner, Howard Rodman/*c* Bud Thackery/*m* Lalo Schifrin/ *lp* Clint Eastwood, Lee J. Cobb, Susan Clark, Tisha Sterling, Don Stroud

The Covered Wagon · The first truly epic Western, *The Covered Wagon* works hard to achieve its archetypal status. It was made on a lavish scale, ten reels long, with almost the whole picture shot on location in Utah and Nevada, and cost $782,000, unprecedented for a Western. The set-pieces are impressive: the river crossing by 400 wagons, a buffalo hunt, the Indian attack, wagons marooned in snow. The film is founded on one of the major polarities within the Western myth. It is 1848; the emigrants set out with ploughs and livestock, intending to farm in Oregon. On the way they hear that gold has been discovered in California. Half the party continue on to Oregon, opting for a future of agrarian self-sufficiency. The other half, abandoning their ploughs beside the trail, set out for the gold mines, choosing industrialism and a money-based economy. What, sixty years later, makes parts of the film hard to sit through is the banality of some of the human drama, including a particularly vapid love story. But in 1923 that didn't stop the film becoming one of the biggest grossing of

all silent films. EB
1923/b & w/9,407 ft/PAR/*p*/*d* James Cruze/ *s* Jack Cunningham/*c* Karl Brown/ *m arr* Hugo Riesenfeld/*lp* J. Warren Kerrigan, Lois Wilson, Ernest Torrence, Alan Hale, Tully Marshall

Cowboy · The last of Daves' three Westerns for Columbia starring Glenn Ford, *Cowboy* is based on Frank Harris' *My Reminiscences as a Cowboy*. In line with Daves' preference for the quotidian over the mythological the film sets out to do for cowboys what *Broken Arrow* had done for Indians: 'show them as they really are'. But the trend toward greater realism was fairly general in 50s Westerns and *Cowboy* is better viewed less as a documentary drama than as a straightforward, sturdily constructed tale of apprenticeship in which a young man learns not only a trade and a way of life but also gains insight and self-knowledge – a trajectory typical of Daves' Westerns. For ultimately *Cowboy* is more concerned with Frank's moral evolution than his social background – richly detailed though this is. JP
1958/92 min/Phoenix – COL/*p* Julian Blaustein/*d* Delmer Daves/*s* Edmund H. North/*c* Charles Lawton Jr./*m* George Duning/*lp* Jack Lemmon, Glenn Ford, Brian Donlevy, Anna Kashfi, Dick York

The Cowboys · In a period when *McCabe & Mrs. Miller* explored the moral complexities of the Western, *The Cowboys* endorsed the simple values of property, duty, revenge, and 'a man's gotta do what a man's gotta do.' Preparing to take his herd to market, rancher John Wayne loses all his hired men to the gold rush. He replaces them with a crew of boys, and takes on the charismatic story-teller Roscoe Lee Browne as the cook. He turns down the psychotic ex-convict Bruce Dern for a job on the cattle-drive, but Dern and his cohorts follow their trail. He instigates a fight with Wayne, but the older Westerner thrashes him, and the crazed Dern repays the rancher with a bullet in the back and an extra couple in the legs. After Wayne's death the boys insist on avenging him and retrieving the cattle, and with Browne's help they kill off the rustlers, take the herd to market and buy a stone to mark their symbolic father's grave. Marketed as a large-scale, family picture, it aroused critical dispute over its depiction of violence and its theme of maturation through brutality. BA
1971/128 min/Sanford Productions – WB/ *p*/*d* Mark Rydell/*s* Irving Ravetch, Harriet Frank Jr., William Dale Jennings/

c Robert Surtees/*m* John Williams/*lp* John Wayne, Roscoe Lee Browne, Bruce Dern, Colleen Dewhurst, Slim Pickens

The Culpepper Cattle Co. · 'Cowboying's what you do when you can't do nothin' else,' one of the Culpepper hands tells the youthful hero (Gary Grimes), who has signed up as the outfit's 'Little Mary' (cook's assistant) in a spirit of impressionable romanticism about life on the trail. In common with several other Westerns of the early 70s, this film gestures toward a muddily 'realistic' depiction of frontier existence. More essentially, though, it is a variation on the theme of the adolescent's rite of passage to manhood: Grimes experiences, via the drovers' encounters with rustlers, a ruthless land-baron, and finally a band of Mormon settlers, the difficulty of reconciling moral choice with necessity. The film's detailed richness of characterization and setting is such that the ending, with Grimes rejecting the Mormons' righteous piety yet tossing away his gun in disavowal of violence, smacks not of evasion but of a genuine and satisfying ambiguity. TP
1972/92 min/FOX/*p* Paul A. Helmick/ *d* Dick Richards/*s* Eric Bercovici, Gregory Prentiss/*c* Lawrence Edward Williams, Ralph Woolsey/*m* Tom Scott, Jerry Goldsmith/*lp* Gary Grimes, Billy Green Bush, Luke Askew, Bo Hopkins, Geoffrey Lewis

D

Day of the Evil Gun · Echoing the plot of *The Searchers*, Thorpe's direction evinces an eye for bizarre detail more reminiscent of a Peckinpah movie. Ford is an ex-gunslinger who teams up with rancher Kennedy to search for his wife and children, abducted by the Apaches. Hank Worden's role is here taken by Jagger, talking in rhymed couplets to convince the Indians that he is crazy and to whom simulating madness has become a way of life. As the search proceeds – gloriously shot even though the film was intended for television – they survive capture by the Indians, torture, a cholera-ridden village and a fight with Confederate renegades in a Mormon ghost town. In the process, the rancher discovers he has a taste for killing and when the group returns home with the rescued women, Kennedy challenges Ford to a duel. When the latter refuses to draw, a bystander intervenes; in attempting to prevent a coldblooded murder he shoots Kennedy dead. PW

1968/93 min/MGM/p/d Jerry Thorpe/
s Charles Marquis Warren, Eric Bercovici/
c W. Wallace Kelley/m Jeff Alexander/
lp Glenn Ford, Arthur Kennedy, Dean
Jagger, Paul Fix, Royal Dano, Harry Dean
Stanton

Day of the Outlaw · This magnificent Western is the crowning achievement in the
still under-rated de Toth canon. The story
revolves around the conflict between tough
rancher Ryan and outlaw leader Ives, whose
gang take over an isolated community while
fleeing from the cavalry. The almost tangible
atmosphere of death and hatred recalls *Man
of the West*, but what really distinguishes the
film is its chilling, wintry atmosphere. De
Toth's icy direction, Harlan's fittingly bleak
black and white photography, and the intensity of Ryan and Ives' performances all build
the film towards an unforgettable climax, a
gunfight in a raging blizzard. JP
1959/b & w/96 min/Security Pictures –
UA/p Sidney Harmon/d André de Toth/
s Philip Yordan/c Russell Harlan/
m Alexander Courage/lp Robert Ryan,
Burl Ives, Tina Louise, Nehemiah Persoff,
Jack Lambert

The Deadly Companions · Given the mar-
ginality of female roles in most of Sam
Peckinpah's films, it is unsurprising that the
root of his much-expressed dissatisfaction
with his big-screen directing début was the
power wielded by its strong-willed star,
Maureen O'Hara. Because producer Charles
FitzSimons was O'Hara's brother, Peckinpah was not allowed to shape the actress's
performance as he would have liked, and she
is therefore left to her own devices. However, in all other respects this is a fine,
effective Western, with an oddly assorted
group of desperados accompanying prostitute O'Hara on her trip to a ghost town
where she wants to bury her dead son beside
his father. Brian Keith, with whom Peckinpah had worked on his television series *The
Westerner*, is the half-scalped ex-Union
soldier, seeking both revenge on the psychotic Johnny Reb and card-sharp Turk (Chill
Wills) and a way to become psychologically
whole again. The film is an early demon-
stration of the director's flair for almost
operatic violence – particularly a sequence in
which a band of drunken Indians dressed as
white men whoop it up on the stagecoach
they have robbed – and of the misanthropy
whereby his heroes and villains, crazed and
destructive as they are, are seen to be better
than the hypocritical 'normal' townsfolk

who egg them on to ever more ghastly acts.
KN
1961/90 min/Carousel – Pathé –
American/p Charles FitzSimons/d Sam
Peckinpah/s A.S. Fleischman/c William
H. Clothier/m Marlin Skiles/lp Maureen
O'Hara, Brian Keith, Chill Wills, Steve
Cochran, Strother Martin

Death of a Gunfighter · Frank Patch, an
aging marshal with a reputation for being
trigger-happy, confronts a town that questions his kind of justice. The council members of Cottonwood Springs view Frank as
the past and getting rid of him as progress.
Their concept of progress, however, is one
that willingly sacrifices ethics and integrity
for material good. Frank, who has been
marshal at the same salary for twenty years,
is unwilling to resign, thereby bringing him
into conflict with those whose mercantile
values suggest different approaches to solving problems. One significant shot depicts
the essential conflict: as Lou, the county's
Mexican sheriff, leaves the city hall to persuade Frank to resign, a long shot reveals a
horse tethered to a hitching post, screen left,
while someone polishes a car, screen right.
Progress is necessary in a civilized world but
sacrificing men like Frank Patch questions
that civilization. JD
1969/100 min/U/p Richard E. Lyons/
d Allen Smithee (Robert Totten, Don
Siegel)/s Joseph Calvelli/c Andrew
Jackson/m Oliver Nelson/lp Richard
Widmark, Lena Horne, Carroll
O'Connor, Royal Dano, John Saxon

Decision at Sundown · This is more dour in
tone than most of the Randolph Scott-Budd
Boetticher series. The action unfolds wholly
in the confines of the town of Sundown.
Scott and sidekick Noah Beery arrive and
cast a shadow over the impending wedding
of local bigshot John Carroll when Scott
challenges him to a showdown over Carroll's earlier seduction of his wife. The
situation is developed quite tensely and
eventfully – the town's sheriff is, of course,
in Carroll's pocket – and Carroll, though not
a performer much associated with the genre,
makes a colourful, ambiguously sympathetic, antagonist for the monolithic Scott.
However, the conclusion, with the avenger
recognizing the sterility of his quest – he
learns that his wife was not the paragon he
believed – and abandoning it, is more interesting in conception than satisfying in
dramatic terms. TP
1957/77 min/Producers-Actors Corp –

COL/p Harry Joe Brown/d Budd
Boetticher/s Charles Lang Jr./c Burnett
Guffey/m Heinz Roemheld/lp Randolph
Scott, John Carroll, Karen Steele, Noah
Beery Jr., Andrew Duggan

Destry Rides Again · Max Brand's novel
(1930) was originally adapted for the screen
by Universal in 1932, when Tom Mix starred. Remade in 1939, from a completely new
screenplay, this version was to provide the
first major Western roles for both James
Stewart and Marlene Dietrich. The result
was a Western that, utilizing the very
different screen personae of its stars – the
mild-mannered innocence of Stewart and
the brash sexuality of Dietrich – gently
mocks the genre's conventions. Destry (Stewart) is summoned to Bottleneck to bring
law and order to a town which is being run
from the Last Chance saloon by a crooked
gambler (Donlevy) and his sexually provocative girl (Dietrich). Preferring anecdotes to
gunplay, Destry is not taken seriously by his
adversaries, although his simple charm has a
fatal attraction for Frenchy. Destry has
eventually to strap on his gunbelt, but even
the drama of this final confrontation is
undercut by the intervention of the towns-
women, who win his fight for him. JH
1939/b & w/94 min/U/p Joe Pasternak/
d George Marshall/s Felix Jackson, Henry
Myers, Gertrude Purcell/c Hal Mohr/
songs Frederick Hollander, Frank Loesser/
m Frank Skinner/lp James Stewart,
Marlene Dietrich, Brian Donlevy, Charles
Winninger, Mischa Auer

Devil's Doorway · Made the same year as
Broken Arrow, *Devil's Doorway* shared that
film's pro-Indian sentiments but not its
box-office success. The film is, in fact,
uncompromising in refusing to soften its
story of a Shoshone chief (Robert Taylor),
who having served with distinction in the
Union army returns home to find that the
Homesteading Act has legislated his land
away from him simply because he is an
Indian. His efforts to gain redress are
thwarted by officialdom and vested interests
(the latter represented by Louis Calhern's
cynical, cigar-chewing bigot), and the film
concludes with Taylor and the handful of
Shoshone braves who have fled the reservation to join him being wiped out in a battle
with locals reinforced by a cavalry detachment. Grittily bare settings and lighting
effects which verge on the expressionistic
combine to heighten the film's downbeat air
of moral anger. TP

1950/b & w/83 min/MGM/p Nicholas
Nayfack/d Anthony Mann/s Guy Trosper/
c John Alton/m Daniele Amfitheatrof/
lp Robert Taylor, Paula Raymond, Louis
Calhern, Edgar Buchanan, Marshall
Thompson

Distant Drums · During the Seminole Wars
in Florida in the 1840s Gary Cooper leads an
expedition against a band of gun-runners
who have been supplying the Indians. On
the way back the party are pursued by the
Seminole through the swamps. Cooper is
aloof and embittered, pining for his dead
wife, a Creek princess. Mari Aldon, as a
beautiful captive he has rescued, works on
his frozen feelings during the rare quiet
moments along the trail. Walsh admirably
exploits the colourfully different landscape
inhabited by panthers, alligators and Seminoles in garish head-dresses running through
the dense green undergrowth (it's that rarity,
a Western without horses). Cooper finally
saves the day for his outnumbered force by
defeating the Seminole chief in a splendid
underwater fight in a lagoon. The film is
loosely based on Walsh's war film, *Operation Burma* (1945). EB
1951/101 min/United States Pictures –
WB/p Milton Sperling/d Raoul Walsh/
s Niven Busch, Martin Rackin/c Sid
Hickox/m Max Steiner/lp Gary Cooper,
Mari Aldon, Richard Webb, Ray Teal,
Arthur Hunnicutt

A Distant Trumpet · Raoul Walsh's last
film, a cavalry Western adapted from Paul
Horgan's novel, in which the director
returns to the themes of *They Died with their
Boots On*. It is an index of changing attitudes
to the Indian wars that hero Troy Donahue
gets the Congressional Medal of Honor not
for a military victory but for negotiating a
peace treaty, and refuses to accept it because
of the way his Apache allies have been
mistreated. For the most part, the film is
concerned with wooden Donahue's
attempts to lick the slackers of Fort Delivery
into shape, assist General James Gregory
with his campaigns, and romance married
heroine Suzanne Pleshette (whose officer
husband is thereby condemned to an off-
screen death). Claude Akins fills the old
Arthur Kennedy role of the unscrupulous
businessman, representing the Eastern interests who are perceived to be the cause of the
wars by selling guns to the Apache and
sapping cavalry morale with his travelling
brothel. Max Steiner's trumpet-heavy score
makes up for the colourlessness of the lead

actors by stirring emotions that Donahue
and Pleshette are unable to convey, and
Walsh still has his sure hand with battle
scenes. As a concession to the passing
decades, we not only have camp followers,
unpunished adultery and Indians speaking
in subtitles, but also a few nasty shots of the
Apaches' victims buried in sand or crucified
on wagon wheels. KN
1964/117 min/WB/p William H. Wright/
d Raoul Walsh/s John Twist/c William H.
Clothier/m Max Steiner/lp Troy Donahue,
Diane McBain, Suzanne Pleshette, James
Gregory, Claude Akins

Django · A spin-off from the success of *Per
un pugno di dollari* which pits the wits of the
central character (who travels around with a
coffin containing a machine-gun) against
red-hooded Klansmen *and* wild Mexican
bandidos. He plays both sides off against
each other – in a southwestern town which
looks like a building site outside Madrid –
until the final shoot-out, where he has to face
the Klansmen having lost the use of his
hands. Django seems less like the stylish
'Man with No Name' than an agricultural
labourer on his way home from the fields –
and, perhaps as a result, he became a serial
hero to southern Italian audiences. A manic
film, which was banned outright from
England in the 1960s, but which now has a
substantial cult following. Jamaican Ska
music (and the Jimmy Cliff film *The Harder

They Come*) turned *Django* into a *style*. CF
1966/95 min/BRC — Tecisa/p Manolo
Bolognini/d Sergio Corbucci/s Sergio and
Bruno Corbucci, Franco Rossetti, José G.
Naesso, Piero Vivarelli/c Enzo Barboni/m
Luis Enrique Bacalov/lp Franco Nero,
Loredana Nusciak, Eduardo Fajardo

Doc · A reworking of the famous Tombstone showdown, historically more accurate
than *My Darling Clementine*, less so than
Gunfight at the O.K. Corral, in which an
insistent grubbiness, both physical and
moral, testifies to an attempt to probe the
heart of darkness in the myths of the old
West. The Clanton brothers become semi-
innocent victims, Wyatt Earp a black-
hearted villain, and Doc Holliday a wandering gunslinger haunted by love, the
imminence of death, and some enigmatic
inner quest. The problem is that Perry's
evident lack of interest in the genre leaves his
exploration of it high and dry on the makeshift Spanish locations. Heavy with symbolism, the film emerges as a muddy
contemporary allegory, with Earp (Yulin) as
the opportunistic political manipulator,
Holliday (Keach) as the bystander yearning
to drop out but manoeuvered into adopting
a reactionary stance. TMi
1971/96 min/Frank Perry Films/p/d Frank
Perry/s Pete Hamill/c Gerald Hirschfeld/
m Jimmy Webb/lp Stacy Keach, Faye
Dunaway, Harris Yulin, Mike Witney

Gary Cooper (l.) in Distant Drums

Alan Ladd, Charles Bronson in Drum Beat

Dodge City · A very different film from *Stagecoach*, made the same year, but both can be seen in terms of the renaissance of the A-feature Western, after the doldrums of the 30s. With Curtiz directing and Errol Flynn starring in this lavish Technicolor production, it is not surprising that action and spectacle are to the fore. Opening with an exciting race between a stagecoach and a locomotive, the narrative, through the use of wipes and dissolves, moves rapidly from sequence to sequence, in the process incorporating many of the thematic and iconographic interests of the Western (including cattle-drives, buffalo hunting, gambling halls and Boot Hill). Flynn, with all the swagger of his swashbuckling roles, plays a cattleman who very reluctantly pins on the marshal's badge to bring law and order to Dodge. He eventually achieves this by shooting down the villains from a blazing railway car. At the film's conclusion Flynn and De Havilland set off for Virginia City, another anarchic township in need of cleaning up. The following year Curtiz and Flynn made *Virginia City*. DR 1939/104 min/WB/*p* Robert Lord/ *d* Michael Curtiz/*s* Robert Buckner/*c* Sol Polito/*m* Max Steiner/*lp* Errol Flynn,

Olivia De Havilland, Bruce Cabot, Ann Sheridan, Alan Hale

Dragao da maldade contra o santo guerreiro (Antonio-das-Mortes) · Glauber Rocha drew upon many key elements, myths and motifs from the Western in making *Antonio das Mortes*. Antonio, a hired killer renowned for having tracked and murdered the legendary *cangaceiro* leader Lampiao in the 1930s, is called out of retirement to hunt down and kill a new 'bandit' leader, Coirana. From the Western come both a basic theme of the film – that of bounty hunting – and a number of visual and plot elements: the use of landscape, the bar-room set, the Winchester-style rifle, the corrupt landowner and 'his' law officer (Colonel Horacio and Police Chief Mattos), the hiring of a gang of gunslingers (Mata Vaca and his men). In addition, Rocha avowedly wished in his penultimate scene to 'recapture the spirit of *Ride the High Country*' and the 'image of Randolph Scott and Joel McCrea firing side by side at the end.' The chief interest of the film lies in the constant transformation of these elements to make a political statement about the agrarian and

economic problems of the ravaged wilderness which is the Northeast of Brazil. *Cangaceiros* were political radicals; Antonio changes sides and the film ends with his aiding the black peoples and the peasants of Brazil to overthrow their oppressors. In the final shot he walks away under a Shell oil sign, signifying his return to civilization. MA 1969/95 min/Glauber Rocha – Producoes Cinematograficas Mapa/*p* Glauber Rocha, Claude Antoine Mapa/*d/s* Glauber Rocha/*c* Alfonso Beato/*m* Marlos Nobre, Walter Queiroz, Sergio Ricardo/ *lp* Mauricio do Valle, Lorival Pariz, Odete Lara, Hugo Carvana, Othon Bastos, Joffre Soares

Drum Beat · This tale of settlers vs. Indians on the Oregon-California border and the eventual signing of a peace treaty with the Modoc is a little like *Broken Arrow* in reverse, since the story is told very much from the settlers' point of view. However, Daves' penchant for historical accuracy is very much in evidence here, since he based an important section of the film on the record of an actual trial, and if the film is low on conventional heroics it compensates by an elaborate though never ostentatious *mise en scene*; indeed, Bertrand Tavernier has described it as 'a slow, meditative poem of great visual sumptuousness'. Charles Bronson appears here in his first major role, as the Indian chief Captain Jack. JP

1954/111 min/Jaguar – Ladd Enterprises – WB/*p* Alan Ladd/*d/s* Delmer Daves/*c* J. Peverell Marley/*m* Victor Young/*lp* Alan Ladd, Audrey Dalton, Charles Bronson, Marisa Pavan, Robert Keith

Drums Along the Mohawk · One of John Ford's three major films of 1939, and his first in colour, *Drums Along the Mohawk* was derived from an immensely popular novel by Walter D. Edmonds. Based on prodigious research, the book shows the social complexities of the American Revolution on New York's western frontier, taking the point of view of an ordinary farm couple. Ford's film ignores the social complexities in favour of an account framed in terms of psycho-sexual conflict between Indians and whites. This was by deliberate choice of the executive producer, Darryl F. Zanuck, who set out to 'give a show' about 'a pioneer boy who took a city girl to the Mohawk Valley to live'. Much more than *Stagecoach*, made the same year, *Drums Along the Mohawk* provides the initial statement of many of Ford's later characteristic Western themes and motifs. EC

1939/103 min/FOX/*p* Raymond Griffith/*d* John Ford/*s* Lamar Trotti, Sonya Levien/*c* Bert Glennon, Ray Rennahan/*m* Alfred Newman/*lp* Claudette Colbert, Henry Fonda, Edna May Oliver, John Carradine

Duel in the Sun · Orphaned when her father is condemned for murdering his Indian wife and her lover, Pearl Chavez goes to live with Texan Senator McCanles, his wife and sons. She is attracted by the affectionate charm of Jesse (Cotten) – who is banished for contesting his father's opposition to the railroad – but is eventually overwhelmed by the virile arrogance of Lewton (Peck), from whom she extracts an empty promise of marriage. Lewton guns down her eventual husband-to-be on the eve of the wedding, and escapes into exile. In an ambivalent finale, full of *amour fou*, Pearl accepts, with ambiguous relish, an invitation to join the outlawed Lewton at Squaw's Head Rock, where the two engage in an agonized shoot-out before dying in a final embrace. Told in a gigantic flashback, Selznick's operatic epic – the most lucrative Western ever – is unusual for its relative lack of interest in the external social world; for the sustained emotionalism of its family melodrama; and for its erotic preoccupation, in a masculine genre, with the feminine experience of its racially and sexually ambiguous heroine. PD

1946/138 min/Vanguard – Selznick/*p* David O. Selznick/*d* King Vidor/*s* David O. Selznick/*c* Lee Garmes, Harold Rosson, Ray Rennahan/*m* Dimitri Tiomkin/*lp* Jennifer Jones, Joseph Cotten, Gregory Peck, Lionel Barrymore, Herbert Marshall, Lillian Gish

E

Eagle's Wing · An ironically inconclusive, almost absurdist pursuit movie in which a white stallion, the steed of a dead Comanche chief, becomes the object of an obsessive quest for both greenhorn trapper Sheen and Kiowa brave Waterston. A series of episodic sub-plots involve a procession of emblematic minor characters in the circular chase. A certain straining towards allegorical abstraction is detectable in Briley's script for this British-financed foray into the genre, with the Western wilderness posited as a harshly blank background for the semi-ritual moves and motives of appropriation, possession, re-possession and envy, but Harvey draws much quirky humanity from his fine cast, Williams' images are seductively luxuriant, and the horse itself is as beautiful a corporeal character as it is a symbol. PT

1978/111 min/Eagle's Wing Prods – Rank/*p* Ben Arbeid/*d* Anthony Harvey/*s* John Briley/*c* Billy Williams/*m* Marc Wilkinson/*lp* Martin Sheen, Sam Waterston, Harvey Keitel, Stephane Audran, Caroline Langrishe

El Dorado · Whether or not the classic Western can be said to have died with John Wayne, it nevertheless *aged* with him. From 'sunset' Westerns of the mid-1960s such as *El Dorado* or Peckinpah's Wayne-less *Ride the High Country* (1962), which also deals with aging lawmen and gunfighters, to *The Shootist* (1976), the closing of the frontier, the end of the West and the encroachment of modern times became familiar generic motifs, ideally suited to the somewhat revisionist tastes of contemporary film-makers and to the advancing years of traditional

Jennifer Jones, Gregory Peck in Duel in the Sun

Sam Waterston in Eagle's Wing

icons such as Wayne, McCrea and Scott. If, for Ford and Siegel, Wayne embodies the values of the Old West whose demise is witnessed in films like *The Man Who Shot Liberty Valance*, for Hawks Wayne remains less a symbol of abstract values than a flesh-and-blood force, whose mythic status, detached from any historical context, is rendered purely in terms of moral strength, not symbolic function. The codes of Wayne's Cole Thornton in *El Dorado*, shared by the diverse characters who band together with him and sheriff J.P. Harrah (Mitchum) to thwart the efforts of land-grabber Bart Jason (Asner), are more ethical than professional. At the centre of the film's involved system of personal loyalties and obligations stands Wayne, whose intuitive knowledge of and innate possession of ethical values which are as much Hawksian as Western in origin make him the supreme arbiter of the moral economy which governs the film's tangle of relationships and network of allegiances. JB (Plate 30)
1966/126 min/Laurel – PAR/*p*/*d* Howard Hawks/*s* Leigh Brackett/*c* Harold Rosson/*m* Nelson Riddle/*lp* John Wayne, Robert Mitchum, James Caan, Charlene Holt, Arthur Hunnicutt, Edward Asner

Escape from Fort Bravo · This was Sturges' second Western and the first of a series which established him as a significant, though perhaps not major, figure in the genre in the 50s. The story concerns a group of Confederate soldiers imprisoned in an Arizona fort who escape, are pursued by William Holden's Captain Roper, and then attacked by Mescalero Indians. The story may be a familiar one but what distinguishes it is Sturges' bold and imaginative use of space and his dramatic handling of complex action sequences. Particularly impressive are the Indian attacks, in which geometric groupings of figures look forward both to *Bad Day at Black Rock* and the films of Miklós Jancsó. This was MGM's first film to be lensed specifically for wide-screen projection in an aspect ratio of 1.66 to 1; Sturges rises to the challenge magnificently. JP
1953/98 min/MGM/*p* Nicholas Nayfack/*d* John Sturges/*s* Frank Fenton/*c* Robert Surtees/*m* Jeff Alexander/*lp* William Holden, Eleanor Parker, John Forsythe, William Demarest, John Lupton

F

The Far Country · Of the several collaborations between director Anthony Mann,

screenwriter Borden Chase and star James Stewart, this film achieves the most complete formal clarity. Beginning with Stewart as the epitome of ruthless self-interest, the narrative subjects him to a series of tests as he contrives to run a herd of cattle to the gold-strike town of Dawson and subsequently buys his own gold-mining stake. He is gradually won over to a belief in community values, though it takes the death of his aged partner (Walter Brennan) to commit him fully to the cause; with fitting irony, his conversion is partly achieved through a thirst for revenge. The structural logic of the story might threaten to make the movie schematic, but the danger is easily averted, thanks to the individuality with which life in Dawson is invested, and especially to the Dickensian relish which John McIntire brings to the chief villain, the sinisterly genial 'Mr Gannon'. TP
1954/96 min/U/*p* Aaron Rosenberg/*d* Anthony Mann/*s* Borden Chase/*c* William Daniels/*m* Joseph Gershenson/*lp* James Stewart, Ruth Roman, Walter Brennan, John McIntire, Corinne Calvet, Jay C. Flippen

Flaming Star · One of the very first Westerns to deal seriously with the question of 'miscegenation', *Flaming Star* is also Elvis Presley's best film. Here he plays a half-caste whose loyalties are divided when the Kiowas attack the whites. A late entry into the Indian Western canon, *Flaming Star* is both violent and pessimistic, refusing easy liberal sentiments and conclusions, stressing how deep-seated is prejudice and showing how violence follows inexorably in its wake. The film was originally written for Marlon Brando, and the Barbara Eden role was originally meant for horror star Barbara Steele. JP
1960/101 min/FOX/*p* David Weisbart/*d* Don Siegel/*s* Nunnally Johnson, Clair Huffaker/*c* Charles G. Clarke/*m* Cyril Mockridge/*lp* Elvis Presley, Barbara Eden, John McIntire, Dolores Del Rio, Steve Forrest

Fort Apache · The first of three John Ford films pitting the US Cavalry against Indians in the Southwest, all starring John Wayne. He is here a bachelor captain with deep knowledge of Indian ways, who makes peace with local tribes. An arrogant lieutenant-colonel from the East (Henry Fonda) takes command and brings spit and polish to the fort. Despising Indians and hoping to advance his career, he breaks Wayne's agreement with

Cochise and launches a Custer-like charge that wipes out his entire force. (This superb set-piece is one of many last stands in Ford, who knew that defeat moves viewers more than victory does.) Now the fort's commander, Wayne gives reporters to believe that Fonda died gloriously – the cavalry survives the blunders of its leaders and absorbs them, transformed, into its tradition. Especially memorable is the film's portrait of home and social life at a cavalry post in 1876: the reunions and separations of loved ones; drinking and singing interludes with three Irish sergeants; several dances, including a Grand March at a non-commissioned officers' ball; army wives starting off a newcomer with gifts of simple furniture; a soldier reading the bible alone. A sub-plot in the domestic sphere concerns the romance of Fonda's daughter (Shirley Temple) and the officer son of a sergeant-major (Ward Bond), which is bitterly opposed by Fonda. The latter's death permits both the marriage and the birth of a son, whose full name includes Fonda's, Wayne's and Bond's (Michael Thursday York O'Rourke). He thus reconciles characters living and dead, and assures the continuity of the cavalry. An incompetent remembered as a hero, the cherished realm of family life shown to reproduce military power – Ford's bifocal vision puts myth and truth side by side. BH
1948/b & w/127 min/Argosy – RKO/*p* John Ford, Merian C. Cooper/*d* John Ford/*s* Frank S. Nugent/*c* Archie Stout, William Clothier (2nd unit)/*lp* John Wayne, Henry Fonda, Shirley Temple, John Agar, Ward Bond, George O'Brien, Victor McLaglen, Pedro Armendariz

Forty Guns · Fuller's tale of a 'high-riding woman with a whip', memorably played by Stanwyck, who's brought to heel by a morally superior man, is probably his finest example of cinema as a 'battleground of emotions'. The stylistic excesses of the film, which for an American production appears brutally primitive, have lost nothing of their power despite similarities to later Spaghetti Westerns. This is a film of pure energy, in which there is hardly a moment to catch your breath between the opening crane-shot of a buggy peacefully winding its way through an empty and silent landscape, that becomes transformed into clouds of dust amid the thunderous pounding of horses' hoofs, and the last scene when good-guy Sullivan coolly and dispassionately shoots Stanwyck down, so that he can kill her brother who was using her as a shield. DR

Randolph Scott in Frontier Marshal

1957/b & w/80 min/Globe Enterprises – FOX/*p/d/s* Samuel Fuller/*c* Joseph Biroc/ *m* Harry Sukman/*lp* Barbara Stanwyck, Barry Sullivan, Dean Jagger, Gene Barry, Eve Brent

Frontier Marshal · With his first dramatic entrance from a rooftop, the Wyatt Earp of Allan Dwan's *Frontier Marshal* is invincible. Selflessly, he subordinates his personal interests to the needs of Tombstone and, in contrast to the flawed Doc Holliday, is a model of virtue, honour, and courage. Indeed, he is left alone to finish the gunfight at the O.K. Corral. Although the film provides historical background (an introductory montage of a gold strike, building the town, the migration west, and gunfights with outlaws; references to Eddie Foy, Jennie Lind, Lillie Langtry), like the other Earp films it is essentially a fiction about the taming of a Western community. Earp is humanized as he wins the affections of Sarah Allen away from Doc, and Tombstone, civilized by the marshal's victory at the gunfight, institutionalizes its progress with a savings bank. JD
1939/b & w/71 min/FOX/*p* Sol M. Wurtzel/*d* Allan Dwan/*s* Sam Hellman/ *c* Charles G. Clarke/*m* Samuel Kaylin/ *lp* Randolph Scott, Cesar Romero, Nancy Kelly, John Carradine, Ward Bond

The Furies · In New Mexico Territory in the 1870s Walter Huston is a patriarchal cattle baron with a bust of Napoleon in his study. Barbara Stanwyck is the daughter who is infatuated with him. But Huston bribes Stanwyck's suitor, a fortune-hunting gambler played by Wendell Corey, to desert her. He then proposes to remarry, to a vain and shallow socialite (Judith Anderson). In a fit of jealousy Stanwyck stabs her in the face with a pair of scissors. When, determined to get Mexican squatters off his land, Huston hangs their leader (Gilbert Roland), one of Stanwyck's oldest friends, this is the last straw. Stanwyck and Corey unite, buy up all Huston's credit notes and dispossess him. Based on a novel by Niven Busch, who also wrote *Duel in the Sun*, *The Furies* has much of the earlier work's melodrama and hysteria, overlaid with a fashionable touch of Freu-

Barbara Stanwyck, Wendell Corey in The Furies

dianism. But the effect is oddly schematic, the characters obstinately refusing to come to life amid the studio sets and gloomy lighting. Possibly Anthony Mann's least successful Western. EB
1950/b & w/109 min/PAR/*p* Hal B. Wallis/ *d* Anthony Mann/*s* Charles Schnee/ *c* Victor Milner/*m* Franz Waxman/ *lp* Barbara Stanwyck, Walter Huston, Wendell Corey, Judith Anderson, Gilbert Roland

Fury at Showdown · This is director Gerd Oswald's favourite film and ranks with *A Kiss Before Dying* as his finest achievement. Almost unbelievably, it was shot in five days, and like the work of Edgar Ulmer demonstrates how the most rigorous economy can bring its own rewards. Around the story of gunman John Derek trying to go straight against mounting odds Oswald has fashioned a stark, glacial, almost abstract work. The feeling of doom is all-pervasive, and as in the films of Fritz Lang the characters seem pinned down under the staring eye of the camera, in sets and situations stripped bare to the point of asceticism. JP
1956/b & w/75 min/B.G. Productions – UA/*p* John Beck/*d* Gerd Oswald/*s* Jason James/*c* Joseph LaShelle/*m* Harry Sukman/ *lp* John Derek, John Smith, Nick Adams, Gage Clarke, Carolyn Craig

G

Giant · Epic film version of Edna Ferber's best-selling novel about a wealthy Texas ranching family, the Benedicts. The film centres on the spirited, sophisticated, beautiful Leslie Benedict (Elizabeth Taylor), ambiguous adjustment to a more conservative, vulgar Texas society. However, her conflicts with her stolid husband Bick (Rock Hudson) are just one theme among many. *Giant* also attempts to deal with Anglo discrimination against Mexicans, the resentment of Jett Rink (James Dean) – a sullen ranch-hand turned alcoholic oil millionaire – towards Bick and other members of the moneyed élite, and the transformation of rugged Texas individualism into oil-rich materialism and conformity. *Giant* is a lengthy, liberal soap opera of a film, which is redeemed by the coiled tension and energy of Dean's haunting, nuanced performance and by George Stevens' gift for composing striking images; especially of the desolate grandeur of a Texas landscape which is all infinite sky and prairie. LQ
1956/198 min/Giant Prods – WB/*p* George

Stevens, Henry Ginsberg/*d* George
Stevens/*s* Fred Guiol, Ivan Moffat/
c William C. Mellor/*m* Dimitri Tiomkin/
lp Elizabeth Taylor, Rock Hudson, James
Dean, Mercedes McCambridge, Jane
Withers, Dennis Hopper

**Giù la testa (Duck, You Sucker/A Fistful
of Dynamite)** · Originally to be directed by
Sam Peckinpah, then by Peter Bogdanovich.
Sergio Leone took over this Italian 'post-
Western' (which he had helped to write) at a
late stage. It tells of an IRA man-on-the-run
(James Coburn) and a Mexican bandit (Rod
Steiger) whose paths cross during the Mexican Revolution. Sean wants to free political
prisoners (with the aid of his nitro-glycerine,
or 'holy water'), while Juan just wants to rob
the great bank at Mesa Verde. In the end,
Juan becomes a (reluctant) political hero,
while Sean begins to become cynical about
revolutionary politics. The picaresque story
(which is full of Leone's by-now characteristic stylistic effects) is constructed like a
puzzle, which only a final flashback to
Dublin in 1916 can fully resolve. The punch-
line (that 'revolution means confusion') was
intended to comment both on the 'political'
Spaghetti Westerns of the late 1960s and on
Hollywood's treatment of the Mexican
Revolution (which Leone puts down as 'the
romance of the sombrero'). CF
1971/150 min/Rafran – UA/*p* Fulvio
Morsella/*d* Sergio Leone/*s* Luciano
Vincenzoni, Sergio Donati, Sergio Leone/
c Giuseppe Ruzzolini/*m* Ennio Morricone/
lp Rod Steiger, James Coburn, Romolo
Valli, Maria Monti, Rick Battaglia

The Glory Guys · A large-scale cavalry vs.
Indians story set during the Plains Indians
Wars of the 1870s, which succeeds not so
much for its spectacle of cavalry charges and
epic battle scenes, but rather with its individual skirmishes between the rag-tag soldiers
and the grotesquely-painted hostiles. Often
quite violent and at times cut with the
shock-effect suddenness of a horror film
(particularly during a dense, closely-shot
water hole sequence), Peckinpah's raw and
realistic screenplay of a doomed military
adventure is deprived and diluted by Arnold
Laven's adherence to the stock depiction of
the cavalry Western. However, one of the
brighter sparks of interest is young James
Caan's rough 'n' ready immigrant Irish
trooper, a loud and colourful character that
makes one think of Victor McLaglen's Sgt
Quincannon in his early years. The screenplay is based on the novel *The Dice of God* by

Hoffman Birney. TV
1965/112 min/Bristol Pictures – UA/
p Arnold Laven, Arthur Gardner, Jules
Levy/*d* Arnold Laven/*s* Sam Peckinpah/
c James Wong Howe/*m* Riz Ortolani/
lp Tom Tryon, Harve Presnell, Senta
Berger, James Caan, Slim Pickens

Goin' South · Clearly revelling in the disparity of his roles on this semi-anarchic
Western comedy – subtly orchestrating a
fairy-tale farce from the director's chair
while indulging in a broad performance of
eye-rolling frenzy in front of the cameras –
Nicholson yet makes a coherent joy of his
belated ironic edifice to the drop-out spirit.
His Mexico-bound minor-league outlaw is
seized by a Texan posse, but saved from the
gallows by the application of a bizarre local
ordinance that delivers him over to a
spinster ranch-owner (Steenburgen) in
matrimonial bondage. Several irresistible
challenges arise from this situation: to bed
his distinctly unimpressed bride-cum-boss;
to discover the gold that will keep the ranch
out of railroad hands; and to thwart his old
gang's designs on such riches. After much
bawdy malarkey, Nicholson (now plus
woman and wealth) resumes his southerly
flight. PT (Plate 26)
1978/108 min/PAR/*p* Harry Gittes, Harold
Schneider/*d* Jack Nicholson/*s* John
Herman Shaner, Al Ramus, Charles
Shyer, Alan Mandel/*c* Nestor Almendros/
m Van Dyke Parks, Perry Botkin Jr./
lp Jack Nicholson, Mary Steenburgen,
Christopher Lloyd, John Belushi,
Veronica Cartwright

The Good Guys and the Bad Guys · Made
the same year as *The Wild Bunch*, this movie
treats an ostensibly similar theme – traditional Westerners made anachronistic by
the march of time – but in a vein of cheerful
comedy. Robert Mitchum, veteran marshal
of the sardonically named town of Progress,
is forced into retirement by the go-ahead
mayor (Martin Balsam) over the threat to
civic stability, and his own re-election
chances, posed by the marshal's call for
action to forestall a gang of would-be train
robbers. Mitchum teams up with an old
bandit adversary (George Kennedy), who
has been alienated by the callowness of his
junior partners in crime, and after some wild
action, climaxing in a chase involving a
runaway train and numerous prototype
automobiles, they save the threatened gold
shipment and regain heroic status. Directed
with unforced pace and invention, the film

conveys a spirit not of lampooning the genre
but of humorously celebrating its conven-
tions. TP
1969/90 min/WB/*p* Ronald M. Cohen,
Dennis Shryack/*d* Burt Kennedy/*s* Ronald
M. Cohen, Dennis Shryack/*c* Harry
Stradling Jr./*m* William Lava/*lp* Robert
Mitchum, George Kennedy, Martin
Balsam, David Carradine, Tina Louise

Great Day in the Morning · Tourneur's last
Western, adapted from a novel by Robert
Hardy Andrews, echoes the man-boy
relationship at the centre of his favourite
film, *Stars in My Crown* (1950). In Denver,
just before the Civil War, Owen Pentecost
(Stack) takes under his wing the son of a man
he killed, teaching the boy to shoot knowing
he is likely to become the kid's first victim
when the boy finds out who orphaned him.
This sensitively drawn oedipal story is told
against the background of an action plot in
which Stack gets involved in running a
shipment of gold to the Confederacy,
although his ultimate allegiance is only to his
personal ethical code rather than to a social
cause. The war story and the man-boy tale
never quite mesh, making it a flawed film,
but Tourneur is particularly good at creating
the right atmosphere for his narratives, using
light and colour to convey the sense of a
chilly but sunlit spring morning and at the
same time suggest the complex undertones
and tragic evanescence of the affective bonds
between Stack and the growing boy. PW
1956/92 min/Edmund Grainger Prods –
RKO/*p* Edmund Grainger/*d* Jacques
Tourneur/*s* Lesser Samuels/*c* William
Snyder/*m* Leith Stevens/*lp* Robert Stack,
Virginia Mayo, Ruth Roman, Raymond
Burr, Leo Gordon

The Great K & A Train Robbery · A typical
Tom Mix picture, made during the heyday
of his career at Fox, when he was the most
successful Western star of the age, earning
$17,000 a week. From the opening, when
Tom slides down a rope suspended from a
cliff while bandits shoot at him, the action
never lets up. Immediately he has to ride to
the rescue of a girl in a runaway buggy,
pulling her off the rig in the nick of time.
Happily, she turns out to be the daughter of
the president of the railroad which Tom is
trying to save from the bandits. The president's male secretary is also wooing the girl,
but since he's a cissy ('If he went to college it
was Vassar') he's no match for Tom. With
the help of his faithful horse Tony and a
bewhiskered hobo who turns out to have

been Tom's buddy at Verdun in World War I (!), Tom defeats the entire bandit gang in a final furious fistfight. EB

1926/b & w/4,800 ft/FOX/d Lewis Seiler/s John Stone/c Dan Clark/lp Tom Mix, Dorothy Dwan, William Walling

The Great Northfield Minnesota Raid · Kaufman's first big budget film essays a revisionist mythology, its narrative decentring the James boys, who share the new centre with their cousins the Youngers. Old myths about Jesse are reworked and reversed; his benevolence to the poor widow whose mortgage is foreclosed is enacted, but given a novel twist in her murder by him. Other familiar elements of the James genre lexicon are present: Pinkerton, Jesse's transvestism, and the representation of the James/Younger boys as champions of the southern peasantry against northern industrial and finance capital. Kaufman blows the gaff on the repertoires of rival myths for and against Jesse James, who here is as barmy and crooked as his Minnesotan adversaries. This is a Western after the movies' age of innocence; its self-conscious pillaging of dime novel fiction and Remington palette is deployed to pull the wool from the audience's eyes and tickle their palates for post-Peckinpah cynicism. RC

1972/90 min/Robertson & Associates – U/p Jennings Lang/d/s Philip Kaufman/c Bruce Surtees/m Dave Grusin/lp Cliff Robertson, Robert Duvall, Luke Askew, R.G. Armstrong, Elisha Cook Jr.

The Great Train Robbery · A train is held up, and the mail carriage and passengers are robbed. The robbers make their escape on horseback. Meanwhile, the telegraph operator, who had been bound and gagged, raises the alarm at a 'typical Western dance hall' (Edison catalogue). A posse is raised and the robbers hunted down and killed. Filmed on location in New Jersey and in the Edison studios, this is Porter's most celebrated film, and one of the earliest fictional narratives with a 'Western' setting. The ten-minute narrative is constructed in a series of thirteen 'tableaux' shots (the robbery, the dance hall, etc.), and a medium close-up of the outlaw leader firing point-blank at the audience. Exhibitors could place this latter shot at the beginning or end of the film. The tableaux are all filmed in long shot; consequently individual characters are difficult to discern, and dramatic intensity is achieved not by any variation in the shot lengths, rather by the players' actions and quickened movements within the frame. The film was hugely popular and greatly influential. DR

1903/b & w/740 ft/Edison/d/s/c Edwin S. Porter/lp Broncho Billy Anderson, George Barnes, A.C. Abadie, Mari Murray

The Grey Fox · The feature début of an Australian director, conjured into existence by Canada's expensive desire to build a national cinema. Borsos' film modernizes the Western, showing its hero refining his robbery techniques after seeing *The Great Train Robbery*. Canadian train robbers are of course nicer than the American kind and only rob to escape the drudgery of the lumber mill. Accordingly hero Bill Miner is rewarded by the love of a radical feminist photographer. They deserve each other and the soft focus ending. The Canadian Western idiolect is different from the American, and popular though *The Grey Fox* was in Canada (and well received in the US) it is chiefly interesting as a Canadian hijack of a Hollywood genre. Its niceness, beautiful landscapes and good guy and girl triumphing are far less of a monument to the difference of the Canadian West and Canadian cinema than is the National Film Board's austere first feature, *Drylanders*. RC

1982/91 min/Mercury Pictures/p Peter O'Brian/d Phillip Borsos/s John Hunter/c Frank Tidy/m Michael Conway/lp Richard Farnsworth, Jackie Burroughs, Ken Pogue

Gunfight at the O.K. Corral · This reconstruction of the famous showdown and the myriad events leading up to it was an enormously successful and influential film. It grossed $4.7m in North America alone and paved the way for the Western superproductions of the 60s. In retrospect it seems somewhat over-rated, most memorable for its casting of Lancaster as Wyatt Earp and Douglas as Doc Holliday, and deftly handled staging of the climactic shootout (which lasts six minutes on screen but took 44 hours to film). Technically highly proficient but otherwise curiously flat, *Gunfight at the O.K. Corral* is ultimately less impressive than its much less well known sequel, the bitter *Hour of the Gun*. JP

1956/122 min/PAR/p Hal B. Wallis/d John Sturges/s Leon Uris/c Charles B. Lang Jr./m Dimitri Tiomkin/lp Burt Lancaster, Kirk Douglas, Rhonda Fleming, John Ireland, Jo Van Fleet, Lyle Bettger

Kirk Douglas, Burt Lancaster, DeForrest Kelly, John Hudson in Gunfight at the O.K. Corral

The Gunfighter · The elegiac Western has been central to the genre since the early 1960s and Henry King's 1950 picture must be regarded as its most important precursor. In particular, its distinction derives from Gregory Peck's Jimmy Ringo, the aging gunfighter, which remains the definitive portrait of this now-familiar type. Although the film begins and ends with classic images of a lone rider in a typical Western landscape, the bulk of the action takes place indoors. The bar of the saloon, the marshal's office and the barbershop are the arenas of Ringo's doomed quest for peace and a settled life with a wife and son he has not seen for many years. Inevitably he dies, shot in the back by Skip Homeier's 'squirt', whose penance is to inherit the burden of fame and notoriety which led to Ringo's demise. TR
1950/b & w/84 min/FOX/p Nunnally Johnson/d Henry King/s William Bowers, William Sellers/c Arthur Miller/m Alfred Newman/lp Gregory Peck, Helen Westcott, Millard Mitchell, Karl Malden, Skip Homeier

Gun Fury · Originally shown in 3-D, this is a gutsy attempt by Raoul Walsh to transplant the vein of psychosis he had been mining in his gangster films (particularly *White Heat*) to a Western setting. However, while the casting of James Cagney as charismatic psychopath and Edmond O'Brien as unsympathetic hero in *White Heat* allowed Walsh to delve interestingly into the character of the villain, he is forced here to accord much more screen time to plodding hero Rock Hudson at the expense of flamboyant outlaw boss Phil Carey, a far more intriguing figure. Hudson is a settler heading west with fiancée Donna Reed when she is abducted by Carey's gang (who include such evil stalwarts as Lee Marvin and Neville Brand to play up the noir connection). Although a man of peace, Hudson tracks down the kidnappers and stands up for his ideals in a shoot-out with Carey. KN
1953/83 min/COL/p Lewis J. Rachmil/d Raoul Walsh/s Roy Huggins, Irving Wallace/c Lester H. White/m Mischa Bakaleinikoff/lp Rock Hudson, Donna Reed, Phil Carey, Lee Marvin, Neville Brand, Leo Gordon

H

The Halliday Brand · One of the four major Westerns that closed Lewis' directorial career – and which stand in starkly intelligent and complex contrast to the slew of singing cowboy pictures on which he first learnt his craft – this explicitly Freudian reading of familial and racial conflicts works as an intense and incisive critique of patriarchal law. Bond is the land-owning sheriff with a deep-seated terror of the 'foreign' and the feminine, whose tyranny provokes a humiliatingly retributive rampage from his son, Cotten, who is himself indelibly marked by the same psychological brand. Sexual symbolism abounds in Lewis' characteristically expressionist mounting of an acute script, and the microcosmic political dimension of the movie emphatically disrupts prevalently complacent and conformist notions of the nation-as-family. PT
1957/b & w/78 min/Collier Young Associates – UA/p Collier Young/d Joseph H. Lewis/s George W. George, George S. Slavin/c Ray Rennahan/m Stanley Wilson/lp Ward Bond, Joseph Cotten, Viveca Lindfors, Betsy Blair

Hang 'Em High · This was the American cinema's first major attempt to play the Spaghetti Westerns at their own game, and who better to hire as a star than Eastwood himself? It was produced by his own company, Malpaso, on a budget of $1.6m, which it recovered within ten weeks of opening. Eastwood lobbied successfully for Ted Post, a veteran of *Rawhide*, as director, and also took a hand in directing parts of the film himself. The story of a deputy sheriff (appointed by a hanging judge based on the real-life Judge Parker) who uses his job to track down the nine men who nearly lynched him, *Hang 'Em High* borrows its violence, revenge theme and grimy view of the West from Leone *et al.*, whilst dispensing with the Italians' visual invention and subversiveness and attempting to make Eastwood's No Name persona more acceptable to an American audience. The result, though commercially successful, is uneven. JP
1968/114 min/Leonard Freeman Prods – Malpaso – UA/p Leonard Freeman/d Ted Post/s Leonard Freeman, Mel Goldberg/c Leonard South, Richard Kline/m Dominic Frontiere/lp Clint Eastwood, Inger Stevens, Ed Begley, Pat Hingle, Ben Johnson

The Hanging Tree · This is Daves' most complex and ambitious film and certainly his finest Western. It was also his last. The story of a frontier doctor with a murky past whose arrival at a mountain mining town causes ructions in spite of his good intentions, it is a brooding, romantic, opaque work of great dramatic intensity and breathtaking visual beauty. The film is an almost explicit critique of the Bildungsroman schema that underlies so many Hollywood Westerns and has certain interesting parallels with André Gide's novel *La Symphonie Pastorale* and the 1946 film made from it. Where *The Hanging Tree* really scores, though, is in its style: few Westerns have been as successful in their dramatic use of space. JP
1959/106 min/Baroda – WB/p Martin Jurow, Richard Shepherd/d Delmer Daves/s Wendell Mayes, Halsted Welles/c Ted McCord/m Max Steiner/lp Gary Cooper, Maria Schell, Karl Malden, George C. Scott, Ben Piazza

Rock Hudson, Donna Reed in Gun Fury

Hannie Caulder · With this picture (technically, a British production) Kennedy updated the female gunslinger story (for example, Corman's *The Gunslinger* and *Oklahoma Woman*, both 1956) and anticipated the female revenge-for-rape plot popular in the 80s. Three degenerate bandits on the run (Elam, Martin and Borgnine) rape Hannie (Welch) and kill her husband. Dressed only in a poncho, she sets out to kill the villains. Culp is the bounty hunter who teaches her to shoot and Lee is the unlikely gunsmith who furnishes her with a custom-made weapon. She kills Elam in a brothel, Martin in a perfume store and the knife-throwing Borgnine in a disused prison – with the help of a mysterious gunfighter called the Preacher, a parody version of Eastwood in his Leone Westerns. Kennedy's mixture of send-up and stylization at times lapses into camp, but mostly manages to produce a pleasantly fetishistic performance of the Western-as-play-with-motifs, conveying a fascination with the genre itself, avoiding the extremes of irreverence or aloofness. PW
1971/85 min/Curtwel – Tigon British/ *p* Patrick Curtis/*d* Burt Kennedy/*s* Z.X. Jones (Burt Kennedy, David Haft)/ *c* Edward Scaife/*m* Ken Thorne/*lp* Raquel Welch, Robert Culp, Ernest Borgnine, Jack Elam, Strother Martin, Christopher Lee, Diana Dors

The Harvey Girls · Confirmation that this is more of a musical than a Western comes in the last shot, which shows not the hero riding off on horseback but a happy couple embracing. But before that the film has worked familiar Western territory, exploring the traditional conflict between the wild and the civilized. The wild is a 'saloon' (i.e. bawdy house) run by John Hodiak. On the other side of the street, determined to bring etiquette and good square meals to the West, are the waitresses of the Fred Harvey chain of railroad restaurants, which spread, initially through the Southwest, in the 1870s. The conflict in life-styles is expressed choreographically, the 'immodest' dancing of the saloon girls contrasting with a square dance at the Harvey girls' party, at which the 'genteel' waltz is also introduced to the West. Eventually opposites are reconciled when Hodiak chooses waitress Judy Garland in preference to a saloon girl. Johnny Mercer and Harry Warren won an Oscar for the film's best-known song, 'On the Atchison, Topeka and the Santa Fe'. EB
1945/101 min/MGM/*p* Arthur Freed/ *d* George Sidney/*s* Edmund Beloin, Nathaniel Curtis, Harry Crane, James O'Hanlon, Samson Raphaelson/*c* George Folsey/*ch* Robert Alton/*md* Lennie Hayton/*lp* Judy Garland, Ray Bolger, John Hodiak, Preston Foster, Angela Lansbury, Cyd Charisse

Robert Culp, Raquel Welch in Hannie Caulder

Judy Garland in The Harvey Girls

Heartland · An affecting, miniaturist portrait of the constant rigours and occasional joys of turn-of-the-century pioneer life, and an effective tribute to the real-life 'wilderness woman', Elinore Randall Stewart, on whose papers the script is based, this is a good example of the retrospective docu-drama strain of independent US film-making. Ferrell is the widow who answers Torn's newspaper ad for a housekeeper at his remote Wyoming ranch, and who gradually adapts to both the hostile environment and her employer's (and later husband's) taciturn obstinacy. Deprivation and death (of cattle, of a new baby) are ever-present, but so is spirited determination to build and rebuild a viable life and relationship. The crystalline landscape photography and fine performances are complemented by a script which respects the silences of both resentment and mutual resolve. PT
1979/96 min/Wilderness Women Prods – Filmhaus/*p* Michael Hausman, Beth Ferris/*d* Richard Pearce/*s* Beth Ferris/ *c* Fred Murphy/*m* Charles Gross/ *lp* Conchata Ferrell, Rip Torn, Barry Primus, Lilia Skala, Megan Folsom

Heartland

Hearts of the West (Hollywood Cowboy) ·
A charming celebration of the vitality and
naive values of both the Zane Grey school of
Western literature and the Hollywood
horse-opera's bedrock of Poverty Row programmers. This amiably rambling comedy is
set in the 1930s and concerns the misadventures of aspiring novelist Bridges as he
takes refuge from a pair of pursuing con-men
by joining a Western film crew. With the aid
of aging cowboy extra Griffith, spunky
scriptgirl Danner, and eccentric director
Arkin, Bridges learns the hilarious, hard-
knocks rudiments of screen acting and
stuntmanship, but falls foul of the apparent
theft of his wonderfully clichéd novel,
Hearts of the West, and looks like falling
victim to the violent retribution of the
con-men until Griffith's blank-shooting, costumed gunslinger comes to the approved
last-minute rescue. A cherishably affectionate yet unsentimental evocation of the
'innocent' imagination. PT
1975/103 min/MGM/*p* Tony Bill/*d* Howard
Zieff/*s* Rob Thompson/*c* Mario Tosi/
m Ken Lauber/*lp* Jeff Bridges, Andy
Griffith, Blythe Danner, Alan Arkin

Heaven's Gate · Michael Cimino may go
down in history as The Man Who Killed
The Western, in that this incredibly expensive box-office disaster effectively dissuaded
the studios from investing in Westerns in
the 80s. Pulled from its original release and
pruned from 205 to 149 minutes, *Heaven's
Gate* has been both over-damned and over-
praised, especially since the general availability of two different versions. Its politics
are somewhat simple-minded, with evil
capitalists picking on immigrants in Wyoming and none of the characters emerging with
honour from the Johnson County War of
1892, but it does boast several genuinely
stirring epic sequences – a Harvard gradu-
ation dance and a rollerskating-rink celebration are musical numbers in the grand
Fordian tradition, and the final massacre is a
devastatingly effective application of post-
Vietnam brutality to the Western setting.
Cimino also scores in his depiction of the
ethnic diversity of the West and in his
evocation of the harsh landscape. However,
his central characters – lawman Kris Kristofferson, gunman Christopher Walken and
hooker Isabelle Huppert – are shallow and
uninvolving, going through the motions of a
very trite triangular relationship which has
little to do with the plot, and the film is
stubbornly unable to transfer its sweeping
grasp of the processes of history to any kind

of human drama. Much of the film is
magnificent, but it is nevertheless and at any
of its lengths also an often downright boring
endeavour. KN (Plate 29)
1980/205 min/Partisan Prods – UA/*p* Joann
Carelli/*d*/*s* Michael Cimino/*c* Vilmos
Zsigmond/*m* David Mansfield/*lp* Kris
Kristofferson, Christopher Walken, John
Hurt, Sam Waterston, Isabelle Huppert,
Jeff Bridges, Joseph Cotten, Mickey
Rourke, Brad Dourif

Heller in Pink Tights · Cukor's only Western, gaily weaving the genre conventions
into a characteristically affectionate tribute
to the theatre as a troupe of travelling
players, desperately struggling to make ends
meet, bring European blood-and-thunder to
the violent frontier. The flavour of
nineteenth-century melodrama is entranc-
ingly reconstructed in the stage performances, but the real joy of the film is the skill
with which Cukor combines his disparate
elements: a magical moment, for instance, in
which a band of marauding Indians bedeck
themselves in the colourful finery of silken
dresses, crowns and Roman helmets looted
from the actors in a stagecoach attack;
another when a hunted gunslinger makes his
escape from the theatre during a performance of *Mazeppa*, masquerading in wig,
cloak and on horseback as the hero(ine) of
the play. Hoyningen-Huene's colour effects
are marvellous, and so are the performances.
TMi

1960/100 min/Ponti-Girosi Prods – PAR/
p Carlo Ponti, Marcello Girosi/*d* George
Cukor/*s* Dudley Nichols, Walter
Bernstein/*c* Harold Lipstein/*m* Daniele
Amfitheatrof/*lp* Sophia Loren, Anthony
Quinn, Margaret O'Brien, Steve Forrest,
Ramon Novarro

Hell's Hinges · The most spectacular of the
features made in the three-year active partnership between pioneer producer Thomas
H. Ince and his protégé, William S. Hart.
The script by Ince stalwart C. Gardner
Sullivan contrasts concisely the reformation
of Hart's notorious gunman with the fall of a
young minister, newly arrived in Hell's
Hinges with his sister. Hart is led to grace by
the young woman's trust and simplicity
while the weakling brother is corrupted by
the local saloonkeeper with drink and loose
women. Leading a mob to burn his own
church, the minister is killed, the church
razed, the sister left prostrate. Hart seeks
vengeance on his erstwhile saloon mates,
first corralling the ungodly in the dance hall
as he sets it afire, then driving the wailing
crowd through the flaming streets of the
town. Ince allotted handsome production
values which Hart managed (with aid from
nominal director Charles Swickard) to maximum effect, while delivering one of the most
intense and focused performances of his
career. DK
1916/b & w/5 reels/Triangle/*p* Thomas H.
Ince/*d* Charles Swickard/*s* C. Gardner

Hearts of the West

Sullivan/c Joe August/lp William S. Hart, Clara Williams, Jack Standing, Louise Glaum, Alfred Hollingsworth

High Noon · The newly-married Will Kane stays on as sheriff of Hadleyville on hearing that his old enemy Frank Miller, of whom Kane once purged the town, has been released from prison and will arrive by the noon train to reassemble his gang and seek revenge. At noon, Kane, abandoned by his Quaker bride and spurned by the townsfolk, joins battle alone. Rejoined, however, by Amy, he triumphs, and contemptuously discards his badge before the couple quit town. The film is memorable for its careful illusion of 'real time' suspense, and as a transitional Western whose hero is under threat not only from traditional villains, but from an indifferent society, from which he must escape. Though arguably a pragmatic endorsement of the United States' return to armed conflict in Korea, High Noon, written by the blacklist victim Carl Foreman, is more usually interpreted as a liberal allegory of existential man faced by the horrors of McCarthyism. The film's social critique angered John Wayne, who took part in Howard Hawks' film riposte, Rio Bravo. PD
1952/b & w/85 min/Stanley Kramer Prods – UA/p Stanley Kramer/d Fred Zinnemann/s Carl Foreman/c Floyd Crosby/m Dimitri Tiomken (singer Tex Ritter)/lp Gary Cooper, Grace Kelly, Thomas Mitchell, Katy Jurado, Lloyd Bridges

High Plains Drifter · Extraordinary gothic Western in which Eastwood returns – literally, it seems – from the grave to exact revenge on the townsfolk who once stood by and watched him, their sheriff, whipped to death by a trio of hired gunmen. A weird aura of exorcism hangs over the film as Eastwood drives the character who made him famous, 'The Man with No Name', to his logical conclusion as the angel of death. It is there in the tombstone inscriptions which dedicate the town of Lago to his twin mentors, Leone and Siegel; and it is there in the apocalyptic prelude to revenge which requires the citizens of Lago to make an inferno of their town by painting it red and changing its name to Hell. Eastwood hasn't quite come out from under the Leone influence here, and although powerfully employed, the derivative mannerisms (endless brooding pauses, stylized flashbacks explaining the character's motivation) mark the film as a way station on Eastwood's road to the magisterial narrative authority of The Outlaw Josey Wales. TMI
1972/105 min/Malpaso – U/p Robert Daley/d Clint Eastwood/s Ernest Tidyman/c Bruce Surtees/m Dee Barton/lp Clint Eastwood, Verna Bloom, Marianna Hill, Mitchell Ryan, Jack Ging

High, Wide and Handsome · Probably more important as a contribution to the history of the musical than the Western, this screen original, written by Oscar Hammerstein II with a score by Hammerstein and Jerome Kern, prefigured some of the themes of Rodgers and Hammerstein's later stage musical Oklahoma. But it had the added benefit of director Rouben Mamoulian's knack for stretching the sometimes restrictive genre format by integrating the production numbers into an outdoors story. Set in 1859 in Pennsylvania, the film follows the exploits of oil prospector Randolph Scott as he struggles against various varmints and vested interests out to wreck his business, and tries to keep his marriage to Irene Dunne together despite the tempting presence of saloon singer Dorothy Lamour. The hit songs were 'The Folks Who Live on the Hill' and 'Can I Forget You?', but the score also includes 'Allegheny Al' and 'Will You Marry Me Tomorrow, Maria?'. Although the film sometimes concentrates on romance to the exclusion of more traditional Western pursuits like shooting, fighting and taming the wilderness, amiable villainy is provided by reliables like Alan Hale, Charles Bickford and Akim Tamiroff. KN
1937/b & w/111 min/PAR/p Arthur Hornblow Jr./d Rouben Mamoulian/s Oscar Hammerstein II/c Victor Milner, Theodor Sparkuhl/m Jerome Kern/ch LeRoy Prinz/lp Irene Dunne, Randolph Scott, Dorothy Lamour, Alan Hale, Charles Bickford, Akim Tamiroff

The Hired Hand · Something of the tone of this film, Fonda's directorial début, can be judged by his statement that 'the Western is the Greek drama of America. You can use large symbols and attain a perspective that you lose in a modern "slice of life" picture. For me it was a symphony.' Sharp's script is excellent, as is the cast, but Fonda has tried to inject 'significance' into this simple story

Sophia Loren, Anthony Quinn in Heller in Pink Tights

Gary Cooper in High Noon

of two drifters attempting to settle down to domesticity by indulging in a mass of contrived, self-indulgent and 'arty' effects. Even Zsigmond's superb photography seems strained and Fonda's attempts to adapt the elements of Western mythology to his own ends by adopting a would-be 'epic' style are merely ponderous and pretentious. JP
1971/90 min/Pando–U/p William Hayward/d Peter Fonda/s Alan Sharp/c Vilmos Zsigmond/m Bruce Langhorne/lp Peter Fonda, Warren Oates, Verna Bloom, Robert Pratt, Severn Darden

Hombre · A good deal of the leisurely scene-setting characteristic of Ritt goes into establishing Newman as a white loner brought up by Apaches to believe that civilization is hell. The script (from a novel by Elmore Leonard but carrying strong echoes of *Stagecoach*) then sets up a classically ironical confrontation in which, at first shunned by a party of travellers who think he is an Indian but acclaimed as their guardian angel when bandits threaten, Newman meets the cries of humanitarian disapproval from his flock as he ruthlessly begins to pick off the villains one by one before they are ready for battle. The element of message fortunately takes a back seat as the film gets out into the harshly sunstruck Death Valley locations, the action bowls along agreeably in a fine array of gunfights and tight corners, and the admirable supporting cast (with Boone outstanding as the elephantinely amiable bandit leader) begin to round out vivid characterizations. TMi
1966/111 min/Hombre Prods – FOX/ p Martin Ritt, Irving Ravetch/d Martin Ritt/s Irving Ravetch, Harriet Frank Jr./ c James Wong Howe/m David Rose/lp Paul Newman, Fredric March, Richard Boone, Diane Cilento, Martin Balsam, Barbara Rush

Hondo · An intriguing 3-D Western that finds John Wayne, whose company was involved in the production, beginning to find his feet outside the influence of John Ford (who nevertheless turned up on set to 'help out' Farrow) and developing as a screen character. While Wayne would later (in *The Searchers*) win plaudits for undermining the heroism of his characters by exposing their grim fanaticism, *Hondo* concentrates on a humanizing process whereby the title character – an embittered Indian fighter – is softened and redeemed by a relationship with frontier widow Geraldine Page and her son. The loner throws in his lot with the homesteaders, who are living on the fringes of Indian territory and thus subject to random attacks, and manages not only to find a family but to make his peace with the Apaches. Uniquely, Farrow uses 3-D for psychological reasons – although the film is complete with such gimmicks as flaming arrows shooting into the audience, the visual plan finds Wayne's distinctive figure increasingly removed from sparse landscapes and comfortably accommodated in domestic interiors. Although made three years before Ford's masterpiece, *Hondo* can almost stand as a sequel/counterpoint to *The Searchers*. KN
1953/93 min/Wayne-Fellows Prods – WB/p Robert Fellows/d John Farrow/s James Edward Grant/c Robert Burks, Archie Stout/m Emil Newman, Hugo Friedhofer/ lp John Wayne, Geraldine Page, Ward Bond, Michael Pate, Leo Gordon, James Arness

Horizons West · Texas immediately after the Civil War provides the setting for a confidently handled Western which mixes several traditional themes to unpretentiously exciting effect. Robert Ryan and Rock Hudson are ex-Confederate brothers returning to impoverishment; Ryan's search for quick money leads to his humiliation at the hands of crooked big-shot Raymond Burr; he subsequently throws in with a gang of desperados, becomes their leader, and profitably wages war on Burr and his allies. Hudson, victimized by Burr's faction on the assumption that he is in league with Ryan, assumes the burden of social responsibility to the extent of becoming marshal and seeking to bring his brother to book; Ryan, cornered, declines to come quietly and is gunned down by one of Hudson's deputies. The narrative is invigorated by the splitting of dramatic focus between the brothers, and Ryan cuts a persuasively commanding figure as the anti-hero. TP
1952/81 min/U/p Albert J. Cohen/d Budd Boetticher/s Louis Stevens/c Charles P. Boyle/md Joseph Gershenson/lp Rock Hudson, Robert Ryan, Julia Adams, John McIntire, Raymond Burr, Dennis Weaver

The Horse Soldiers · An under-rated Civil War Western, leisurely and sometimes simplistic, but mostly quintessential Ford in its casual celebration of the movement of men and horses, as Wayne's hard-nosed colonel and Holden's humanitarian doctor debate (and embody) opposing ideologies of war while leading a Union cavalry patrol deep behind Confederate lines on a mission to destroy a vital railway. A concluding scene of battle carnage designed to illustrate the futility of the war was abandoned when stuntman Fred Kennedy died during filming. This undoubtedly leaves the film unbalanced, but paradoxically lends it strength by highlighting another example of moral absurdity: a magnificent sequence in which children from a military academy march cheerfully off to the accompaniment of fife and drum to mount a last-ditch defence of the Confederacy, only to see the battle-scarred Union troops scatter in disarray, unable to cope with the imperatives involved in mowing down a parade of toy soldiers. TMi
1959/119 min/Mirisch – UA/p/s Martin Rackin, John Lee Mahin/d John Ford/c William H. Clothier/m David Buttolph/lp John Wayne, William Holden, Constance Towers, Althea Gibson, Hoot Gibson

Hour of the Gun · This is a sequel to Sturges' *Gunfight at the O.K. Corral* and although not well received at the time of its release is actually more interesting than its predecessor, and far and away the best of the director's mainly disappointing 60s Westerns. Opening with a bang (a reprise of the famous gunfight) it then charts Wyatt Earp's descent from lawman to avenger, a process counterpointed by Doc Holliday's moral development. Sturges' talent for directing action sequences is much in evidence but the film's most interesting aspect is its cool, quiet, measured tone. As in other late 60s Westerns one senses the beginning of the end of an era as the familiar heroes age. JP
1967/100 min/Mirisch – Kappa – UA/ p/d John Sturges/s Edward Anhalt/c Lucien Ballard/m Jerry Goldsmith/lp James Garner, Jason Robards Jr., Robert Ryan, Albert Salmi, Jon Voight

How the West Was Won · A massive would-be epic designed to show off the dramatic possibilities of Cinerama, hitherto used only for travelogues. The three-camera system, projected on to a huge screen, certainly showed to good advantage in the numerous set-pieces such as the buffalo stampede, shooting the rapids and an Indian attack on a wagon train. The film is organized chronologically, with loosely connected episodes tracing most of the high points in the history of the West. We start with a mountain man (James Stewart), and then move back east for some Mark Twain-type scenes on the Erie Canal. Then it's on to 1848, covered wagons and the California

gold rush. The Civil War sequence, with John Wayne as General Sherman, is low-key and intimate, as we would expect from its director, John Ford. After this comes a potted history of communications in the West, with the stagecoach, the Pony Express, the telegraph and the railroad following in quick succession. Then comes the cowboy, and lastly a train robbery, which seems to have little thematic connection but offers an opportunity for some more spectacular effects. As a whole the film is considerably less than the sum of its parts, never building up any head of steam as a narrative, and technologically it proved a dead end. But just occasionally it takes your breath away. EB (Plate 23)
1962/162 min/MGM – Cinerama/p Bernard Smith/d Henry Hathaway ('The Rivers', 'The Plains', 'The Outlaws'), John Ford ('The Civil War'), George Marshall ('The Railroad')/s James R. Webb/c William Daniels, Milton Krasner, Charles B. Lang Jr., Joseph LaShelle/m Alfred Newman/lp Debbie Reynolds, Carroll Baker, Lee J. Cobb, Henry Fonda, Karl Malden, Gregory Peck, George Peppard, Robert Preston, James Stewart, Eli Wallach, John Wayne, Richard Widmark, Walter Brennan, Andy Devine, Spencer Tracy (narrator)

Hud · One of the bleakest of contemporary Westerns. Newman is the embittered and nihilistic Hud who can see nothing of lasting value and purpose in the flat and barren Texas landscape. Douglas plays his father, a man who passionately loves the land and deplores his son's meaningless existence. De Wilde plays Hud's young nephew, uncertain whether to emulate the uncle he idolizes or the grandfather he respects. His indecision is brought to a head when their cattle contract foot-and-mouth disease. Hud would sell the cattle before the authorities can have them condemned, but Douglas won't allow it and the cattle are slaughtered along with the values they had come to represent. When Douglas dies, De Wilde recognizes Hud for the hollow sham that he is and finally leaves the ranch to make his own way. Hud, seemingly unconcerned by all that has happened, is left to reside in isolation over a spiritually and physically dead ranch. PS
1962/b & w/112 min/Salem – Dover – PAR/p Martin Ritt, Irving Ravetch/d Martin Ritt/s Irving Ravetch, Harriet Frank Jr./c James Wong Howe/m Elmer Bernstein/lp Paul Newman, Melvyn Douglas, Patricia Neal, Brandon De Wilde

Paul Newman in Hombre

John Wayne, Geraldine Page in Hondo

Robert Ryan (centre) in Horizons West

James Garner in Hour of the Gun

John Ford directing John Wayne, Constance Towers, William Holden in The Horse Soldiers

Paul Newman, Brandon De Wilde in Hud

I

The Indian Fighter · One of the most interesting early 50s Indian Westerns and a high point in de Toth's fascinating but underrated oeuvre, *The Indian Fighter* has been described by one French critic as 'one of the most beautiful pantheistic poems that the Western has given us, for which I would give all the Fords and Walshs of the period 1940-1955'. And indeed this story of Douglas' attempts to forge a peace treaty with the Sioux, during which he falls for an Indian girl (Martinelli), fairly exudes a full-blown Rousseauesque romanticism. The scenes in which Martinelli bathes naked in a river gave the film a slightly 'risqué' reputation for a time. JP
1955/88 min/Bryna – UA/p William Schorr/d André de Toth/s Frank Davis, Ben Hecht/c Wilfrid M. Cline/m Franz Waxman/lp Kirk Douglas, Elsa Martinelli, Walter Matthau, Lon Chaney Jr., Elisha Cook Jr.

In Old Arizona · The first major talking Western stars Warner Baxter as O. Henry's gentleman outlaw, The Cisco Kid, and Edmund Lowe as the Texas Ranger who continually puts off arresting his friend in order to indulge in the kind of good-natured horseplay director Raoul Walsh perfected in his silent films with Victor McLaglen and Lowe as brawling World War I buddies Quirt and Flagg. Contemporary critics were impressed not so much by the dialogue and performances (although Baxter was the first cowboy to get a Best Actor Oscar) but by Walsh's use of the sounds of the prairie – gunshots, galloping horses' hoofs, stampeding cattle and cowboy ballads like the successful 'My Tonia'. The Cisco Kid, who had begun his career in the early silent cinema (and had been hanged in his screen début) soon slipped from the A-feature range and found himself played by Baxter in the increasingly cheap likes of *The Cisco Kid* and *Return of the Cisco Kid*. KN
1929/b & w/95 min/FOX/d Raoul Walsh, Irving Cummings/s Tom Barry/c Arthur Edeson/lp Warner Baxter, Edmund Lowe, Dorothy Burgess, J. Farrell MacDonald, Tom Santschi

Invitation to a Gunfighter · A Western fable, stressing the venality of bourgeois townsfolk after the manner of such fairytales as *The Pied Piper of Hamelin*. When poor homesteader George Segal barricades himself in the house slimy businessman Pat Hingle has cheated him out of, Hingle and the town elders hire Creole gunslinger Jules Gaspard D'Estaing (Yul Brynner) to bring him in. However, the frenchified killer, besides being particular about how his name is pronounced, makes moral judgements about his employers and decides to chastise the guilty, whereupon Hingle has to appeal to Segal – an embittered reb lately returned from the Civil War – to help him get rid of the octoroon. Brynner uses his exotic appearance very cleverly, and the rather heavy-handed symbolism doesn't get in the way of some tense shoot-outs and stand-offs. KN
1964/92 min/Kramer Co – Larcas – Hermes – UA/p/d Richard Wilson/s Richard Wilson, Elizabeth Wilson/c Joseph MacDonald/m David Raksin/lp Yul Brynner, Janice Rule, Pat Hingle, George Segal, Brad Dexter, Strother Martin

The Iron Horse · Epic may be an overworked term in the cinema, but nothing else will do for Ford's early masterpiece. Not satisfied with merely telling the story of the building of the first transcontinental railroad, completed in 1869, Ford manages to work in a cattle-drive from Texas, the Pony Express, Wild Bill Hickok and Buffalo Bill, not to mention any amount of typical Western motifs such as a comic dentist, a heroic saloon brawl and several Indian attacks (one of which makes exquisite use of a sunlit snowy landscape). All this is preceded by a prologue in Springfield, Illinois, in which Abe Lincoln appears as the spiritual father of the enterprise, willing its completion in order to unite the country. The final scene at Promontory Point, where the Union Pacific is finally joined with the Central Pacific, reproduces in tableau form the scenes recorded by photographers at the time, thus justifying, if little else in this boisterously inventive film does, the claim in the opening titles to be 'accurate and faithful in every particular'. EB
1924/b & w/10,424 ft/FOX/d John Ford/s Charles Kenyon/c George Schneiderman/lp George O'Brien, Madge Bellamy, Judge Charles Edward Bull, William Walling, Fred Kohler, J. Farrell MacDonald

I Shot Jesse James · Sam Fuller's directorial début is uncharacteristic of Jesse James or Fuller movies. It has few Western motifs and its staccato rhythm finds few echoes in Fuller's later ideolect of long takes and magisterial *mise en scène*. Bob Ford is a dishonourable, un-Fulleresque hero who

Kirk Douglas, Elsa Martinelli in The Indian Fighter

George Schneiderman (l.), John Ford (r.) on location for The Iron Horse

kills Jesse to escape outlawry and become respectable enough to marry. But the fratricidal murder (Bob shares Jesse's home and alias of Howard) and denial of love and trust disqualifies Bob from marriage – he is the 'dirty little coward' of the ballad. He accuses his rival for Cynthy: 'You don't love her enough to kill for her.' It's Bob's fate to be proved wrong. Kelly kills him and Bob the protagonist is shown unable to qualify himself for Cynthy's love either by killing or dying for her. A harsh melodrama with a contingent relation to the Western; a curiosity, of interest as Fuller's juvenilia. RC
1949/b & w/81 min/Lippert – Screen Guild Prods/p Carl K. Hittleman/d/s Samuel Fuller/c Ernest Miller/m Albert Glasser/lp Preston Foster, Barbara Britton, John Ireland, Reed Hadley

23

How the West Was Won (1962) took
advantage of its 70mm technology to produce
some spectacular mountain landscapes which
Albert Bierstadt would not have disdained

24

In its depiction of the desert Mackenna's
Gold (1968) drew on a long tradition in the
photography of western landscapes, dating
back to Timothy O'Sullivan, W.H. Jackson
and Edward Curtis

25
In conveying its nostalgic view of the ending of the West, Monte Walsh (1970) consciously invoked the paintings of Remington and Russell

27
The Long Riders (1980), a reworking of the Jesse James story, was an example of the so-called 'mud and rags' school of hyper-realism in the portrayal of the West

26
Shooting a scene from Goin' South (1978), which indicates how much artifice is needed to show the West 'as it really was'

28
Schatz im Silbersee (The Treasure of Silver Lake) (1962) was the first of the West German Winnetou films based on the writings of Karl May. Lex Barker starred as Old Shatterhand

29
Heaven's Gate (1980), the film which
spared no expense and allegedly broke the
Western's back

30
El Dorado (1966). Left to right, James
Caan, John Wayne and Arthur Hunnicutt.
Youth, maturity and age – three generations
of Hawksian male camaraderie (though John
Wayne was actually born the earliest!)

J

The Jayhawkers! · Although it tackles an intriguing and little-explored subject (the bands of raiders operating along the Kansas border before the Civil War) *The Jayhawkers!* largely eschews history and politics (for example the raiders' anti-slavery sentiments are barely mentioned), in favour of a delirious portrait of rampant megalomania and barely suppressed homo-eroticism. The Jayhawkers are led by Luke Darcy (Chandler), who is using them in order to become a Napoleon of the plains. Emotionally cold with women – except for one, who reminds him of his mother – he develops an ambiguous friendship with Mexican War hero Cam Bleeker (Parker), who starts off wanting to revenge himself on Darcy for causing the death of his wife but ends up joining his private army! A heady brew indeed, and quite as strange as it sounds. Panama's direction may lack the élan of the not dissimilar *Rio Conchos* but the interior scenes are especially striking thanks to the fittingly ornate art direction, the exteriors benefit from luxuriant VistaVision photography, and the massed rides of the rampaging Jayhawkers recall Fuller's magnificent *Forty Guns*. JP
1959/100 min/Parkwood – PAR/*p* Norman Panama, Melvin Frank/*d* Melvin Frank/*s* Melvin Frank, Joseph Petracca, Frank Fenton, A.I. Bezzerides/*c* Loyal Griggs/*m* Jerome Moross/*lp* Jeff Chandler, Fess Parker, Nicole Maurey, Henry Silva

Jeremiah Johnson · One of the most interesting and spectacular Westerns of the 70s, this is the story of an ex-soldier who, tired of civilization, decides to become a mountain man and eventually attains near-legendary status. Although it lacks the fascinating historical detail of its sources (*Mountain Man* by Vardis Fisher and *Crow Killer* by Raymond W. Thorp and Robert Bunker) it is by far the most impressive of the entries in the 'wilderness' cycle of the early 70s, though it cannot quite make up its mind whether it is trying to demythologize its hero or precisely the opposite. In the end it works best as a series of picaresque and visually magnificent adventures tracing, as Tom Milne has put it, 'Jeremiah's progress from Candide in the wilderness to skilled and ruthless fighter and beyond again to a kind of pantheistic resignation.' JP
1972/108 min/Sanford Prods – WB/*p* Joe Wizan/*d* Sydney Pollack/*s* John Milius, Edward Anhalt/*c* Andrew Callaghan/*m* John Rubinstein, Tim McIntire/*lp* Robert Redford, Will Geer, Stefan Gierasch, Allyn Ann McLerie

Jesse James · The first film about the James brothers that attempted historical authenticity, with location shooting around Pineville, Missouri – classic James gang territory – and Jesse's granddaughter given research credit. It now appears a fine, if nostalgic, memorial to three-colour cinematography. Henry Fonda gives his first portrayal of Frank and Tyrone Power establishes Jesse as a scion of the Old South. The James boys are established as defenders of the rural arcadia against invading Northern capital embodied in banks and railways. The best scene, to become a staple of the James cycle, has Jesse triumphantly capering along the roof of a moving train in a night robbery. Jane Darwell, best known as Ma Joad, plays the outlaws' mother and her pairing with Fonda as mother and son presents the James and the Joads of *The Grapes of Wrath* as equivalent victims of American capitalist development. Excellent, topped only by Ray's 1957 remake. RC
1939/105 min/FOX/*p* Darryl F. Zanuck/*d* Henry King/*s* Nunnally Johnson/*c* George Barnes, W.H. Greene/*md* Louis Silvers/*lp* Tyrone Power, Henry Fonda, Randolph Scott, John Carradine, Jane Darwell

Johnny Guitar · An extraordinarily baroque, passionate and oneiric film (but nonetheless one that stays firmly within the Western canon and indeed demonstrates the remarkable flexibility of the genre), *Johnny Guitar* revolves around ex-dance hall girl Vienna (Crawford), whose gambling saloon is on land wanted by the railroad and who becomes the victim of mob fever engineered by Bond's tyrannical rancher and McCambridge's sexually frustrated spinster. Dialogue, lighting, sets, direction and the performances of Hayden and Crawford all combine to create an almost overpoweringly lyrical atmosphere, but it should not be forgotten that the film is not simply an expression of hyper-Romantic sensibility, but also a powerful attack on McCarthyism which greatly displeased the censors. JP
1954/110 min/REP/*p* Herbert J. Yates/*d* Nicholas Ray/*s* Philip Yordan/*c* Harry Stradling/*m* Victor Young/*lp* Joan Crawford, Sterling Hayden, Mercedes McCambridge, Scott Brady, Ward Bond

Jubal · After the pompous and over-rated *Broken Arrow*, Delmer Daves turned out a

Glenn Ford, Valerie French in Jubal

string of under-stated, intriguing Westerns. The moody, grim drama of *Jubal* supposedly draws its inspiration from *Othello*, but is much less faithful to its Shakespearean text than the Italian Western *Johnny Hamlet* or the British gangster movie *Joe Macbeth* are to theirs. Glenn Ford is an outcast, rejected by his own mother (who blames him for the death by drowning of his father), taken in by simple-minded but decent rancher Ernest Borgnine. However, while Ford is teaching the Martyish Borgnine how to make love to his wife (Valerie French), whining Iago-type Rod Steiger does his best to make it seem as if French is making up to Ford. While Ford is being forced to gun down his friend, Steiger rapes and beats up French, planning to blame Ford and set the local lynch mob on the outsider. Daves' dusty, realistic West and widescreen landscapes serve as a perfect backdrop for his tightly-wound, heavily fatalistic plot. In the end, French's last words save Ford's life, but he is left with an emotional graveyard after he has taken his revenge on Steiger. KN
1956/101 min/COL/*p* William Fadiman/*d* Delmer Daves/*s* Delmer Daves, Russell S. Hughes/*c* Charles Lawton Jr./*m* David Raksin/*lp* Glenn Ford, Ernest Borgnine, Rod Steiger, Valerie French, Charles Bronson, Jack Elam

Junior Bonner · Transferring the action from the mythic past (*The Wild Bunch*) to the unheroic present in Prescott, Arizona, Peckinpah again tells of a cowboy (McQueen) who finds himself out of date, hanging on to his rodeo past while his home is being bulldozed to make way for the ready-made dwellings of a Home on the Range retirement plan promoted by his wheeling and dealing brother. Since urbanization and industrialization have left homeless the old American values of rugged individualism, incarnated by the brothers' wayward father (Preston), the film has nowhere to go either and fragments into a kaleidoscopic celebration of physical movement itself. Sequences seem built on the alternation of different registers of gesture such as walking, riding, loving, rodeo, fighting, dancing, parading, etc., making it into a quasi-musical dedicated to showing off the male body in action, opposing the 'free' male's range of gestures to the cramped, relentlessly linear movement of machines and the phony joviality of the huckster dressed in constricting show clothes. PW
1972/103 min/ABC Pictures – Wizan Prods – Solar – Cinerama/*p* Joe Wizan/ *d* Sam Peckinpah/*s* Jeb Rosebrook/*c* Lucien Ballard/*m* Jerry Fielding/*lp* Steve McQueen, Robert Preston, Ida Lupino, Joe Don Baker, Ben Johnson

J W Coop · One of the clutch of latter-day Westerns in the 70s using the rodeo as a symbol for the decline of the frontier spirit. Robertson, here making his début as a director, plays a rodeo cowboy who picks up his career after ten years in jail, only to discover that the old ways have become subject to intensive specialization and publicity techniques. His rise to success, capped by a comeuppance that can be seen coming a mile off, makes the film blander than *Junior Bonner* or *When the Legends Die*. But where it scores is in the flow of endearingly offbeat characters who punctuate *J W Coop*'s odyssey in discovery of the brave new world that has grown up in his absence, among them a garrulous hog farmer who runs through an entire thesis on American history as he explains how he beat the system, from Depression through wartime munitions to private enterprise. Such asides hardly add up to a movie, but they do make *J W Coop* an oddball pleasure. TMi
1971/112 min/Robertson & Associates – COL/*p*/*d* Cliff Robertson/*s* Cliff Robertson, Gary Cartwright, Edwin Shrake/*c* Frank Stanley/*m* Don Randi, Louie Shelton/*lp*

Cliff Robertson, Geraldine Page, Cristina Ferrare, R.G. Armstrong, John Crawford

K

The Kentuckian · Burt Lancaster's first attempt at direction is a pleasant, rambling tale of a Kentucky backwoodsman's trek to the promised land of Texas in the 1820s with his small son and their dog. Inclined to progress by fits and starts through a series of picaresque adventures which highlight Lancaster's swashbuckling talents (family feud, tentative romance, whip duel, kidnapping, deadly ambush), the film suffers badly from a lack of overall pace, while the characterizations (with very variable performances revealing Lancaster's inexperience in handling actors) are not nearly incisive enough. Nevertheless, in its rawboned feel for the wide open spaces, and in its artless adherence to the concept of the noble savage as Lancaster's Kentuckian gradually realizes that he isn't cut out for the town life, it at times comes within hailing distance of the rough poetry that infused Ford's vision of the pioneer days. TMi
1955/104 min/James Prods – UA/*p* Harold Hecht/*d* Burt Lancaster/*s* A.B. Guthrie Jr./*c* Ernest Laszlo/*m* Bernard Herrmann/ *lp* Burt Lancaster, Dianne Foster, Walter Matthau, John McIntire, John Carradine

Kid Blue · A wry post-hippie fable that still works superbly as a 'shrunken frontiers' Western, *Kid Blue* sketches the process by which failed outlaw Hopper (first seen leaping on to a train roof with larcenous intent, and promptly falling off) is soon marked too as a failed upright citizen of the Texan town of Dime Box. Harassed by Johnson's sheriff, unable to survive independently or adapt to work in the local factory (which manufactures ashtrays topped with a flag-waving Santa Claus), and unwilling to settle to the divergent romantic ideals either co-worker Oates or the latter's wife (Purcell) would have him share, he is virtually forced back into his outlaw persona. Enlisting a trio of marginalized Comanches in a robbery scheme, he sees one fall to an absurdly dignified death before Johnson's posse, but himself attempts escape on the prototype 'aerocycle' invention of eccentric preacher Boyle. As he falls to earth, a neat reversal of cliché sees the remaining Indians ride to his rescue in the nick of time. PT
1973/100 min/Marvin Schwartz Prods – FOX/*p* Marvin Schwartz/*d* James Frawley/ *s* Edwin Shrake/*c* Billy Williams/*m* John

Rubinstein, Tim McIntire/*lp* Dennis Hopper, Warren Oates, Peter Boyle, Ben Johnson, Lee Purcell

The King and Four Queens · Walsh's delightful picture mischievously sends up Gable's macho image. He is the conman Dan Kehoe, out to grab a gang's loot stashed on a farm inhabited by their four wives and ruled with an iron fist by the wily matriarch Ma McDade (Van Fleet). Gable tries to charm the women into betraying their secret but he is outwitted by Ma and slowly begins to realize that he is the one being used by the females for their own pragmatic and erotic purposes. In the end, Sabrina (Parker) wins the prize and the couple are last seen setting off together, keeping a watchful eye on each other. Walsh pushed the fraught male-female relationship of *The Tall Men* one step further and turned it upside down, having Gable recite passages from Shakespeare while the title ironically puns on the star's Hollywood nickname. Gable's performance as the cockily overconfident conman is timed to perfection, recalling his 30s successes in comedies. Walsh, the incarnation of a masculine cinema, is also revealed as a most astute chronicler of male neuroses. PW
1956/84 min/Russ-Field Corp – Gable Prods – UA/*p* David Hempstead/*d* Raoul Walsh/*s* Margaret Fitts, Richard Alan Simmons/*c* Lucien Ballard/*m* Alex North/ *lp* Clark Gable, Jo Van Fleet, Eleanor Parker, Jean Willes, Barbara Nichols, Jay C. Flippen

L

The Last Drop of Water · One of Griffith's engaging little morality melodramas, described in an introductory title as 'A Story of the Great American Desert'. Jilting Charles West, who loves her, Blanche Sweet marries Joseph Graybill, unaware of his weakness for drink. A year later, all three are with a wagon train heading west which is attacked by Indians. When the two men set out in turn in search of water, Graybill atones for his drunken maltreatment of Sweet by saving West's life at the cost of his own, and the cavalry come to the rescue in the nick of time. Using fixed set-ups throughout, Griffith makes tentative use of cross-cutting during the Indian attack and quest for water, but relies chiefly on beautifully expressive compositions: Sweet proudly erect with a frightened woman clutching her knees as the battle rages behind them, for instance, or Graybill's grave looming in the foreground as the wagon train disappears over the horizon in the last shot. Unlike Thomas Ince in his contemporary Westerns Griffith shows little interest in the Indian as anything other than a savage. TMI 1911/b & w/1,057 ft/Biograph/*p*/*d*/*s* D.W. Griffith/*c* G.W. Bitzer/*lp* Blanche Sweet, Charles West, Joseph Graybill, Christie Miller, Robert Harron

The Last Frontier · Although spoiled by some knockabout comedy capers and possessed of a laughably tacked-on happy ending, *The Last Frontier* is one of the first Westerns to give voice to the feeling that the coming of civilization to the Wild West was a step away from natural values. Victor Mature plays a free-spirited, none-too-presentable trapper who longs to exchange his fringed buckskins for a smart cavalry uniform, and who wins the love of Anne Bancroft by virtue of his heroism during the first skirmishes of the Indian wars. However, Colonel Robert Preston, Bancroft's husband, is a Custer-style martinet and all-round fool whose stubborn attitudes lead to an escalation of the conflict, and who represents the worst that a hypocritical

civilization can import to the rough and tumble Eden of the frontier. Mature is reconciled to the cavalry, and ends the film saluting the flag, but his best friends are not so easily accommodated in the civilized order of things – father-figure James Whitmore getting killed during a needless battle and Indian side-kick Pat Hogan returning to the mountain wilderness. KN
1955/97 min/COL/*p* William Fadiman/*d* Anthony Mann/*s* Philip Yordan, Russell S. Hughes/*c* William C. Mellor/*m* Leigh Harline/*lp* Victor Mature, James Whitmore, Robert Preston, Guy Madison, Anne Bancroft, Pat Hogan

The Last Hunt · This condemnation of the slaughter of the buffalo is perhaps the toughest, most polemical and least compromising of all the pro-Indian 50s Westerns, as one might expect from a film directed by Brooks during Dore Schary's time as head of production at MGM, when 'social consciousness' was the order of the day. In his central character, the Indian-hating hunter Charles Gilson (Taylor), for whom 'one less buffalo means one less Indian', Brooks has painted an unforgettable

picture of racism and pathological machismo. Hardly surprisingly, this bleak and violent film was a commercial disaster, but is one of Brooks' very finest works, in which the message is never allowed to dominate the action and arises naturally from the material. A vitriolic exercise in demythologization, *The Last Hunt* is a meditation not only on violence but on America itself. JP
1955/108 min/MGM/*p* Dore Schary/*d*/*s* Richard Brooks/*c* Russell Harlan/*m* Daniele Amfitheatrof/*lp* Robert Taylor, Stewart Granger, Lloyd Nolan, Debra Paget, Russ Tamblyn

The Last Movie · Made back to back with *Easy Rider* (1969) but two years in the editing, Dennis Hopper's film delivered a fascinating meditation on the powers of cinema and the evils of US imperialism while that country was beginning to reassess its founding myths. But in spite (because?) of its prize at the Venice festival, American critics bitterly refused its lucidity and buried it until its reverential re-release in 1982. Starting with the ending, the film tells of Kansas (Hopper), who stays behind when a Hollywood unit headed by a flamboyant

Burt Lancaster in The Kentuckian

Jo Van Fleet (with rifle) in The King and Four Queens

James Whitmore, Victor Mature, Pat Hogan in The Last Frontier

The Last Movie

director (Fuller) leaves the Peruvian location after the death of a stuntman (Stockwell) playing Billy the Kid. The Peruvians then use the set and whicker effigies of the camera, boom, etc. for a cargo cult of film-making in which the violence is for real, nearly costing Kansas his life as he is forced to 'play' Billy the Kid's death in their production. Crammed with references to Hollywood's mythologies (especially James Dean's death) and movies, Hopper weaves the tragic story about film-as-Real Illusion (i.e. religion) together with stories about contemporary Americans and their brutally callous attitudes towards others. He refuses to glorify his own character as much as he refuses pat solutions to the reality-illusion tensions that irrigate culture in general and cinema in particular. This is one of the very few masterpieces to have come out of Hollywood in the 60s. PW
1971/108 min/Alta-Light Inc – U/p Paul Lewis/d Dennis Hopper/s Stewart Stern/c Laszlo Kovacs/m Kris Kristofferson, John Buck Wilkin, Chabuka Granda, Severn Darden, villagers of Chinchero, Peru/lp Dennis Hopper, Stella Garcia, Julie Adams, Tomas Milian, Don Gordon, Samuel Fuller, Dean Stockwell, Rod Cameron, Kris Kristofferson

The Last Sunset · Charming but unstable gunman Kirk Douglas is pursued across the border to Mexico by marshal Rock Hudson. Here Douglas meets his childhood sweetheart Dorothy Malone and her daughter Carol Lynley, who are about to embark on a cattle-drive to California. Douglas and Hudson join the drive, and en route to the border, where a showdown is to occur, Malone and Hudson fall for each other. So do Douglas and Lynley who, though they do not know it, are actually father and daughter.... Its crepuscular title and incestuous overtones notwithstanding, this is one of the director's least harsh films and, unusually, abounds in outdoor shots. These are much enhanced by Laszlo's lyrical photography and the film contains a number of characteristic *tours de force* – for instance the death of Joseph Cotten, Hudson being swallowed up by a marsh, Lynley's appearance at a Mexican festival and Douglas' flamboyant suicide. JP
1961/112 min/Bryna – U/p Eugene Frenke, Edward Lewis/d Robert Aldrich/s Dalton Trumbo/c Ernest Laszlo/m Ernest Gold/lp Rock Hudson, Kirk Douglas, Dorothy Malone, Joseph Cotten, Carol Lynley, Neville Brand

Kirk Douglas, Rock Hudson in The Last Sunset

Last Train from Gun Hill · Sturges' last Western before *The Magnificent Seven* is clearly indebted to *3:10 to Yuma* in its story of a marshal determined to bring in the man who raped and murdered his wife. Rape was still a fairly new subject for explicit treatment in the Western, and its occurence is all the more unpleasant because of its idyllic woodland setting, its racist overtones (the victim is an Indian) and through being witnessed by the woman's young son. Sturges' direction is as taut as ever, and he is greatly aided by the camerawork of Charles Lang Jr., one of the great outdoor specialists. Particularly impressive here is the dramatic placing of actors in the landscape – very much a Sturges trademark. JP
1958/98 min/Wallis and Hazen – Bryna – PAR/p Hal B. Wallis/d John Sturges/s James Poe/c Charles B. Lang Jr./m Dimitri Tiomkin/lp Kirk Douglas, Anthony Quinn, Earl Holliman, Brian Hutton, Carolyn Jones

The Last Wagon · Although *The Last Wagon* returns obliquely to the Indian theme of *Broken Arrow* its major strengths are as an allegory about survival and as a typically Davesian journey of growing self-knowledge on the part of the central character. This is the trapper Comanche Todd (Widmark), so-called because he grew up with the Indians, who revenges himself on the killers of his Indian wife and children before being captured. On his way to face trial for murder Todd and his captors fall in with a wagon train which is attacked by Indians. Eventually it is Todd who leads them to safety. The overt anti-racist theme co-exists rather uneasily with the conventional representation of the Indians pursuing the wagon train, but where *The Last Wagon* really scores is in the tangibly *physical* fashion in which Todd's spiritual progress is registered, the boldly symbolic use of land-

Richard Widmark, Felicia Farr in The Last Wagon

scape à la Anthony Mann, and the stunning direction of the opening scenes in which Todd's flight from his pursuers is graced by complex crane movements across huge craggy landscapes. JP
1956/99 min/FOX/p William B. Hawks/d Delmer Daves/s James Edward Grant, Delmer Daves, Gwen Bagni Gielgud/c Wilfrid M. Cline/m Lionel Newman/lp Richard Widmark, Felicia Farr, Nick Adams, Timothy Carey, Tommy Rettig

The Law and Jake Wade · One of Sturges' very best Westerns, in which sheriff Taylor saves his one-time friend Widmark from a hanging. The two were once bandits together and Widmark then forces Taylor to help him find the proceeds of a bank robbery which they buried long ago. Laconically scripted, marvellously acted and beautifully photographed, *The Law and Jake Wade* also contains some of Sturges' finest action sequences, climaxing in a brilliantly staged Indian attack on a ghost town, which rival those in *Escape from Fort Bravo* for sheer excitement. JP
1958/86 min/MGM/p William Hawks/d John Sturges/s William Bowers/c Robert Surtees/lp Robert Taylor, Richard Widmark, Patricia Owens, Robert Middleton, Henry Silva

Law and Order · Edward L. Cahn's first and best Western has Walter Huston playing Wyatt Earp by any other name (actually, he's Frame Johnson, commonly known as Saint for his stern rectitude as a lawman) and cleaning up the town of Tombstone with the aid of three relatives (among them Harry Carey as his Doc Holliday). Despite fairly extensive use of stock footage at the beginning, it's a strikingly spare, bleakly downbeat film which hammers home its thesis – that law and order involves a lot of killing – with a savagely ironic sequence in

Walter Huston (centre) in Law and Order

Paul Newman, Wally Cox in The Left Handed Gun

Paul Newman in The Life and Times of Judge Roy Bean

which the new regime is inaugurated by the token hanging of a bumbling farmer (Andy Devine) guilty of an accidental killing. Based on the novel *Saint Johnson* by W.R. Burnett, author of *Little Caesar*, the film draws much of its power, not least in a shoot-out from which only Huston emerges alive, from a transferral to the West of the prevalent image of urban gangsterism. There were routine remakes in 1940 and 1953. TMi
1932/b & w/70 min/U/d Edward L. Cahn/ s John Huston, Tom Reed/c Jackson Rose/lp Walter Huston, Harry Carey, Raymond Hatton, Andy Devine

The Lawless Breed · Veteran Raoul Walsh's direction lays solid narrative foundations for this fictionalized account of the life and times of Texas gunslinger John Wesley Hardin (Rock Hudson). Alienated from his killjoy, Bible-thumping father (John McIntire), Hardin goes in search of excitement, only to kill a man in self-defence in a bar-room brawl, and then (echoes of *The Gunfighter*) progressively to become the prisoner of his reputation. Like Jesse in *The True Story of Jesse James*, he achieves domestic happiness under an assumed name (Julia Adams is the ex-saloon girl who becomes his loving wife), but all too soon the law catches up with him. The movie's fatalistic air is heightened by its construction, unfolding in flashback from the elderly Hardin's release from jail after a long sentence. In a coda, Hardin is able to save his hot-headed son from following in his own footsteps, but the ostensible happy ending is ambiguous to the extent that in the closing images Hardin resembles a spent force. TP
1952/82 min/U/p William Alland/d Raoul Walsh/s Bernard Gordon/c Irving Glassberg/md Joseph Gershenson/lp Rock Hudson, Julia Adams, John McIntire, Mary Castle, Hugh O'Brian, Dennis Weaver, Lee Van Cleef

The Left Handed Gun · In Penn's psychologically oriented version of the legend of Billy the Kid, William Bonney sets out to avenge the murder of cattle-boss Tunstall by Sheriff Brady and his colleagues during the Lincoln County Wars. Billy violates a general amnesty, and his friend Pat Garrett's wedding, with a final slaying, whereupon the outraged Garrett agrees to become sheriff. His sidekicks dead, Billy surrenders and faces hanging, but escapes. In an ambiguous finale, the feverish Billy is killed by Garrett after feinting to draw upon an empty holster. Penn's début feature about youth in revolt has clear roots in 50s family melodrama. Bonney's initially heroic oedipal quest – incorporating strong criticism of corrupt law, and satirizing the parasitism of popular mythologies about the West – spirals into a subjective tragedy. The elaborate human and dramatic interest generated by Newman's increasingly troubled renegade is eventually eclipsed by the film's moral preference for the moderate Garrett as the bearer of a now reformed and socially harmonious legality. PD
1957/b & w/102 min/Haroll – WB/p Fred Coe/d Arthur Penn/s Leslie Stevens/ c J. Peverell Marley/m Alexander Courage/ lp Paul Newman, John Dehner, Hurd Hatfield, Lita Milan

The Life and Times of Judge Roy Bean · After being run out of the outlaw town of Vinegaroon, the robber and rapist Roy Bean (Newman) is left for dead. But Bean returns to take his revenge, and manages to seize control. Under his corrupt regime, the town, renamed Langtry in honour of his womanly ideal, prospers, but also achieves a veneer of respectability that leaves Bean disillusioned. Bean departs, only to return twenty years later, to seek revenge again on a town that is now full of automobiles and oil derricks. In Wyler's version of the Judge

Roy Bean story (*The Westerner*, 1940), Bean is the villain, and the extremes of action are the prerogative of Bean himself. In Huston's 70s version Bean has become the hero, and through a technique that Huston has termed 'fragmented', it is the narrative which seesaws from drama to comedy, from cynicism to romanticism. It is an uneasy mix, a quirky interlude which does for the Western what *Prizzi's Honor* would later do for the gangster film. DR
1972/124 min/Coleytown – First Artists – National General/p John Foreman/d John Huston/s John Milius/c Richard Moore/ m Maurice Jarre/lp Paul Newman, Jacqueline Bisset, Ava Gardner, Stacy Keach, Anthony Perkins

Little Big Man · A mock-epic fresco of the West drawn from Thomas Berger's harshly satirical novel, and contributing mightily to belated popular recognition of America's guilty history of genocide towards its original inhabitants, this exercise in ironic iconoclasm is largely narrated in flashback by Dustin Hoffman's 121-year-old yarn-spinner. A picaresque participant in and witness to the Western myths in-the-making, Hoffman throughout the movie criss-crosses the cultural divide between a corruptly expansionist white society and his adoptive Cheyenne family, with Chief Dan George as his sagacious surrogate father. The movie takes the massacre of the Washita in 1868 as its centrepiece and climaxes with a bitter re-reading of Custer's Last Stand. At the time of filming, George's casting alone was sufficient to signal a new attitude emerging to the (ongoing) 'Indian question'. PT
1970/147 min/Hiller Prods – Stockbridge – Cinema Center/p Stuart Millar/d Arthur Penn/s Calder Willingham/c Harry Stradling Jr./m John Hammond/lp Dustin Hoffman, Faye Dunaway, Chief Dan George, Martin Balsam, Richard Mulligan

Lo chiamavano Trinità (They Call Me Trinity...) · The first fully-fledged slapstick Italian Western, which tells of the adventures of Trinity (Terence Hill) and his sheriff brother (Bud Spencer) among the Mormons. Trinity rides his horse as if it were a Lamborghini, Bambino (Spencer) packs a knockout punch (aided and abetted by his deputy named Jonathan Swift), and together they protect the settlers against the evil Mexican Mescal. The emphasis is on elaborate stunts, on Hill's athletic prowess, and on how many people Spencer can knock over with one punch. The film was a spectacular success in Italy, and launched a series of sequels. By this (late) stage in the Italian Western boom, European audiences apparently wanted to see live-action cartoons, rather than ironic variations on the old Hollywood stories. CF
1970/100 min/West Film/p Italo Zingarelli/ d/s E. B. Clucher (Enzo Barboni)/c Aldo Giordani/m Franco Micalizzi/lp Terence Hill (Mario Girotti), Bud Spencer (Carlo Pedersoli), Farley Granger, Steffen Zacharias

Lonely Are the Brave · In this contemporary Western Douglas plays an itinerant cowboy who gets himself sent to prison in order to break free a friend who has been sentenced for helping illegal immigrants from Mexico. However, his friend prefers to serve out his sentence, so Douglas escapes alone and goes on the run. The film is clearly intended as a statement about American society and its inability to tolerate misfits, but unfortunately it tends to be led astray by its good intentions and cannot resist the temptation to spell things out. This results in

Kirk Douglas in Lonely Are the Brave

frequent lapses into self-consciousness, a certain stridency in the direction, and an unwillingness to let the images speak for themselves. If only writer and director had taken their cues from Matthau and Douglas, whose performances are nicely understated and all the more effective for it. JP
1962/b & w/107 min/Joel – U/p Edward Lewis/d David Miller/s Dalton Trumbo/ c Philip Lathrop/m Jerry Goldsmith/lp Kirk Douglas, Gena Rowlands, Walter Matthau, George Kennedy

Lonesome Cowboys · A rare step outside the Factory confines for Warhol's self-styled superstars, indulging their libidinous fantasies to hilarious effect in a parodic Western that Morrissey's uncredited guiding hand steers perilously close to narrative coherence. Waldon's gang of hunky gay cowboys rides into town, to the delight of Viva and Mead, and to a show of consternation from the transvestite sheriff, and from then on only a shared cultural understanding of Western movie myths and manners underpins the improvised confrontations and couplings. PT
1968/110 min/Factory Films/p/d/s Andy Warhol/c Paul Morrissey/lp Viva, Taylor Mead, Louis Waldon, Tom Hompertz, Joe Dallesandro

The Long Riders · In Hill's episodic, visually poetic version of the Jesse James legend, the brothers of the loosely-knit gang of outlaws are played by actual brothers: Jesse and Frank James by James and Stacy Keach; the Youngers by the Carradines, the Millers by the Quaids. *Riders* firmly places the band of bank and train robbers within the rural folk-culture of post-Civil War Missouri, stressing the tight family relationships which inevitably cause tensions among the gang members, the social rituals of the country people, and the curious mixture of rough exhuberance and formal courtesy of this 'Border' community. Relentlessly pursued by the Pinkerton Agency, fiercely protected by their neighbours and relatives, the gang sporadically robs, dissolves, reunites again, as its members try to pursue private, 'legal' lives in the interim. The spectacular but disastrous Northfield, Minnesota raid, followed by the murder of Jesse by the treacherous Ford brothers, effectively ends the precarious career of the mythical outlaws. DG (Plate 27)
1980/100 min/UA/p Tim Zinnemann/ d Walter Hill/s Bill Bryden, Steven P. Smith, Stacy and James Keach/c Ric

Waite/m Ry Cooder/lp James and Stacy Keach; David, Keith and Robert Carradine; Dennis and Randy Quaid; Christopher and Nicholas Guest; Pamela Reed

The Lusty Men · This was Ray's first Western. Like another fine modern-day Western, Peckinpah's *Junior Bonner*, it is a story of rodeo riders, but also a characteristic Ray work in its concentration on tormented outsiders and misfits, especially, in this case, Robert Mitchum, the ex-rodeo star who desperately wants to settle down but seems fatally unable to do so. Ray's direction here is considerably less flamboyant and vigorous than in his more baroque works, but none the less effective or quintessentially cinematic for that. JP
1952/b & w/113 min/Wald-Krasna Prods – RKO/p Jerry Wald, Norman Krasna/ d Nicholas Ray/s Horace McCoy, David Dortort/c Lee Garmes/m Roy Webb/ lp Susan Hayward, Robert Mitchum, Arthur Kennedy, Arthur Hunnicutt, Lane Chandler

M

McCabe & Mrs. Miller · Robert Altman's film is set in a Northwestern mining town at the turn of the century. McCabe is a blustering, bumbling, small-time gambler who becomes a business partner of and then falls in love with the tougher, more sophisticated Mrs. Miller (Julie Christie), an opium-smoking madame. He dreams of building a city out of the half-completed, mud-inundated frontier settlement, but before his plans can be realized he is killed in a showdown with gunmen sent by an insidious and powerful mining company. *McCabe & Mrs. Miller* is no traditional Western: its hero is a uneducated clod who doesn't wear a gun; bar-room talk is about the shaving of moustaches; both dialogue and action overlap; and there is much improvisation by the actors. At its best, it is a melancholy visual poem filled with rich, warm colours which sides with the losers and dreamers – the inarticulate poetic spirits who are willing to die for their vision. LQ
1971/120 min/WB/p David Foster, Mitchell Brower/d Robert Altman/ s Robert Altman, Brian McKay/c Vilmos Zsigmond/songs Leonard Cohen/lp Warren Beatty, Julie Christie, René Auberjonois, Shelley Duvall

The Magnificent Seven · This was the film that set trends for the Western for the rest of

the 60s and beyond. Its origins in the Japanese classic *The Seven Samurai* (1954) demonstrated the universal appeal of the Western formula; and its huge success in Europe showed in which direction lay the economic rejuvenation of the genre. Its Mexico setting was to prove increasingly popular with both American and Italian producers as the decade progressed. The plot, in which a hand-picked group of professionals carry out a difficult and dangerous task just for money, seemed to strike a more contemporary note than that of the lone gunfighter standing up for what he believes is right. The film was also to be a major stepping stone in the careers of several of its cast; Steve McQueen, Charles Bronson, James Coburn and Eli Wallach, for example, went on to bigger things in the Western and elsewhere. The film is also oddly prophetic of Vietnam. Though professionals, Yul Brynner's band discover a moral purpose as they are called in by the peasants to defend them against local bandits. Having fortified the village and won hearts and minds by feeding the kids, they are then let down by the peasants' lack of fighting spirit. Ultimately, though, what lingers in the mind is style more than substance: the confident swagger of the seven, the slick choreography of the action scenes. EB
1960/138 min/Mirisch – Alpha – UA/p/d John Sturges/s William Roberts/c Charles B. Lang Jr./m Elmer Bernstein/lp Yul Brynner, Eli Wallach, Steve McQueen, Horst Buchholz, James Coburn, Charles Bronson, Robert Vaughn, Brad Dexter

Major Dundee · Despite extensive mutilations by the studio and producer Jerry Bresler, a magnificent Western in which Peckinpah takes up and elaborates the conflict of *Ride the High Country*, where two old comrades find themselves in a situation which revives and tests old loyalties. The opposition here, fuelled by internecine attitudes since the setting is towards the end of the Civil War, is between Charlton Heston's Major Dundee, a Northern martinet currently serving a disciplinary stint as commandant of a camp for Confederate prisoners, and Richard Harris' Captain Tyreen, a flamboyant Southern cavalier who 'volunteers' his fellow-prisoners in a temporary alliance to round up a band of murderously marauding Apaches. Although the subtle ramifications of the collision – Heston, living by the book, finds everything he touches going sour, while Harris, acting on romantic impulses, shows how it should

be done – are run ragged by cuts that are particularly damaging towards the end, the schema is evident enough to lend both depth and power to a vision quite superbly realized in Sam Leavitt's breathtaking images. TMi
1964/134 min/Jerry Bresler Prods – COL/p Jerry Bresler/d Sam Peckinpah/s Harry Julian Fink, Oscar Saul, Sam Peckinpah/c Sam Leavitt/m Daniele Amfitheatrof/lp Charlton Heston, Richard Harris, Jim Hutton, James Coburn, Senta Berger

A Man Alone · Milland's directorial début also remained his best effort in this unfamiliar role. His jaundiced look at the Arizonian citizenry starts with the hero, Wes Steele (Milland), shooting his sick horse in the desert and stumbling upon a robbed stagecoach with six corpses strewn around it. In the nearest town he is suspected of the crime and while hiding in cellars he discovers that the local banker and the sheriff (Bond) are the real villains. Living in the sheriff's basement, Milland enlists the help of the lawman's daughter (Murphy) to vindicate himself, which also involves persuading Bond to mend his corrupt ways. Milland and Murphy eventually settle in the town because they know that any other town is likely to be just as corrupt. After the opening scenes in the desert, the movie settles into a morally as well as physically claustrophobic space with long dialogue-less sequences of Milland skulking in underground areas as he tries to avoid the town's murderous burghers. The script was based on a story by Mort Briskin and the casting of Bond, the icon of Western Moral Law, as a corrupt sheriff is nothing less than inspired. PW
1955/96 min/REP/p Herbert J. Yates/d Ray

Ray Milland in A Man Alone

Milland/s John Tucker Battle/c Lionel Lindon/m Victor Young/lp Ray Milland, Ward Bond, Mary Murphy, Raymond Burr, Lee Van Cleef

A Man Called Horse · A curious film in which Harris plays an English lordling, visiting America to hunt in the 1820s, who is captured by Sioux amused by his blond colouring, and survives thoroughgoing humiliations to win through to leadership of the tribe. Although a fetish is made of authenticity, credibility is severely undermined by the casting of Judith Anderson (the memorable Mrs Danvers of *Rebecca*) to ludicrous effect as a shrewish old Indian crone. Since much of the dialogue is in Sioux but left untranslated, one can't help feeling that the film-makers are less interested in elucidating Indian attitudes than in gloating over the ritual of the Sun Vow, a sadistic endurance test ultimately banned by the US Government. As the aristocrat suffering an identity crisis and achieving self-respect by bravely undergoing the tortures of the Sun Vow, Harris is a further liability in a performance of smug complacency. Fascinating, all the same, for its acceptance (and detailed depiction) of Indian customs as a valid counter-culture. TMi
1970/114 min/Sanford Howard Prods – National General/p Sandy Howard/d Elliot Silverstein/s Jack DeWitt/c Robert Hauser/m Leonard Rosenman/lp Richard Harris, Judith Anderson, Jean Gascon, Manu Tupou, Dub Taylor

The Man from Laramie · A comparatively early and particularly effective use of CinemaScope in the Western, this film deploys both expanses of landscape and movement within the frame to lend physical immediacy to a story that in some underlying aspects is ritualistic. Revenge motivates the drama: James Stewart plays an incognito army officer seeking out the gun-runner whose supply of arms to the Indians has caused his younger brother's death. The guilty party is Arthur Kennedy, deceptively amiable foreman of prominent rancher Donald Crisp. But in tandem with his unmasking, the movie explores, with grandiloquent neoclassical overtones, Stewart's involvement with the dying Crisp, his degenerate son (Alex Nicol), and his stepson (Kennedy), basically decent but corrupted by ambition. An exceptionally powerful sequence depicts Nicol avenging himself on Stewart by shooting him at point-blank range through the hand. The evocative title song contributed

James Stewart in The Man from Laramie

Lee J. Cobb, Gary Cooper, Julie London in Man of the West

to the film's popular success. TP
1955/101 min/COL/*p* William Goetz/
d Anthony Mann/*s* Philip Yordan, Frank
Burt/*c* Charles B. Lang Jr./*m* George
Duning/*lp* James Stewart, Arthur
Kennedy, Alex Nicol, Donald Crisp,
Cathy O'Donnell

The Man from the Alamo · A modestly
scaled picture, but one benefitting from a
story idea which ingeniously embroiders
history, as well as from that unobtrusive
exactitude of mounting and technique which
was a common feature of Universal movies
of this time. The action begins at the siege of
the Alamo, with Glenn Ford as the man
volunteering to leave the garrison to go to
the aid of the defenders' families at a nearby
settlement; the latter, including his own wife
and child, prove to have been massacred by
renegade Texans led by Victor Jory. The
ensuing revenge story is crossed with the
theme of self-vindication: Ford has been
taken for a deserter from the Alamo by
many of the citizens of the nearest town, and
in strong and silent style has declined to
proffer the real explanation. The twin
strands satisfyingly merge, with Ford heroically organizing the evacuation of the town,
the next object of renegade attack, and
bringing Jory to book after an exciting fight
on the edge of a waterfall. TP
1953/79 min/U/*p* Aaron Rosenberg/*d* Budd
Boetticher/*s* Steve Fisher, D. D. Beau-
champ/*c* Russell Metty/*m* Frank Skinner/
lp Glenn Ford, Julia Adams, Chill Wills,
Victor Jory, Hugh O'Brian, Neville Brand

Man in the Saddle · Even when not up to the
standard of the remarkable *Day of the*

Outlaw and *The Indian Fighter*, de Toth's
Westerns are always watchable on account
of his punchy direction and strong sense of
narrative economy. One of a number of
Randolph Scott Westerns which de Toth
directed at this time, this one has big-time
rancher Knox attempting to run small
farmer Scott off the range after marrying
Leslie, Scott's former fiancée. The film
boasts splendid High Sierra scenery,
excellent performances and plenty of rugged
action, including a cattle stampede, a gunfight in a totally darkened saloon, and a
long-drawn-out brawl between Scott and
Russell which recalls the famous punch-up
in *Blood on the Moon*. Lawton's night-time
photography is superb. JP
1951/87 min/Producers-Actors Corp –
COL/*p* Harry Joe Brown/*d* André de Toth/
s Kenneth Gamet/*c* Charles Lawton Jr./
lp Randolph Scott, Joan Leslie, John
Russell, Alexander Knox, Ellen Drew

Man of the West · Made a few years after his
cycle of Westerns with James Stewart,
Anthony Mann's heroically-titled *Man of
the West* stands apart from them in that its
hero (Gary Cooper) is not an obsessed
outcast who must be socialized, but the same
sort of figure a few years later. At the start of
the action he appears to be a mild-mannered
boob thoroughly at home in his small town,
but it transpires that he was once a member
of the killer brood headed by Dock Tobin
(Lee J. Cobb), his uncle and once his father-
figure, and the story concerns the hero's
attempts, when circumstances force him
back into Dock's gang, to retain his ration-
ality. Finally, he can return to civilization, but
only after he has been driven to exterminate

Cobb's entire 'family', partially in order to
purge himself of his evil impulses and partially to avenge the humiliation heaped upon
his travelling companion (Julie London).
The central conflict between 'father' and
'son' (oddly, not undermined by the fact
that Cobb was ten years younger than
Cooper) harks back to the oppositional
twinnings of hero and villain in Mann's
earlier Westerns. Also notable is the brutality of the violence, and the perverse eroticism surrounding London, who is forced by
Jack Lord to strip off her clothes when he
holds a knife to Cooper's neck, an outrage
later avenged when Cooper forces him to
disrobe in front of *her*. This prefigures the
bleak finale in which Cobb rapes London in
order to drive Cooper to finish off the job he
has started by killing the gang members and,
finally, Cobb. The power of the latter's
performance hints that Mann's last, unpro-
duced project, a Western version of *King
Lear*, wasn't as crazy as it sounds. KN
1958/100 min/Ashton Prods – UA/
p Walter M. Mirisch/*d* Anthony Mann/
s Reginald Rose/*c* Ernest Haller/*m* Leigh
Harline/*lp* Gary Cooper, Lee J. Cobb,
Julie London, Jack Lord, Royal Dano,
John Dehner

The Man Who Shot Liberty Valance · The
transition of the West from wilderness to
garden has consequences which are as much
linguistic as historical, marking passage from
the concreteness of the natural world to the
abstractions of the words culture which
supplants it. Associated with intangible
ideals such as chivalry, etiquette, education,
and the law, Ranse Stoddard (Stewart)
enters a world of violence and primal appe-

tite in which the abstract has virtually no institutional base, save the newspaper office of Dutton Peabody (O'Brien), which becomes, in turn, the site of Shinbone's first school. Shinbone's inhabitants cannot understand the abstract values – the Law – to which Stoddard appeals when he is robbed and beaten up by outlaw Liberty Valance (Marvin). Stoddard's role in the community is to help realize that abstraction, presiding over the transition to an order based on conceptual authority rather than brute strength. Valance rips up Stoddard's law books, unaware that the ideas they contain cannot be destroyed. Stoddard ultimately defeats Valance and wins the West through education, 'the basis of law and order'. Teaching Shinbone about Washington and Lincoln, he enables the town to see beyond the present moment, to conceptualize their own position within history and recognize the forces of progress with which they are allied. Yet the triumph of word-culture is attended by great loss. Linguistic facility brings with it the power to lie. Peabody offers, for the price of a jug, to make the cowardly marshal as famous as Buffalo Bill; Starbuckle, the cattlemen's 'mouthpiece', manipulates language, describing Valance as 'an honest citizen'. Stoddard's taming of the West, symbolized in his attainment of the illiterate Hallie (Miles), whom he teaches to read and write, is similarly ambivalent, the outcome of self-sacrifice and loss: Doniphon's (Wayne) demise and Hallie's repression. And in giving Hallie something to read and write about, Senator Stoddard himself lives a lie as 'the man who shot Liberty Valance'. Even the newspaper editor, who refuses to print Ranse's 'confession', acknowledges the power of the lie in word-culture, noting that 'when the legend becomes fact, print the legend.' JB
1962/b & w/122 min/John Ford Prods – PAR/p Willis Goldbeck/d John Ford/ s James Warner Bellah, Willis Goldbeck/ c William H. Clothier/m Cyril Mockridge/ lp John Wayne, James Stewart, Vera Miles, Lee Marvin, Edmond O'Brien, Andy Devine, Woody Strode

Man Without a Star · Amid the tatty 'spectaculars' and trashy melodramas of King Vidor's later career, Man Without a Star is outstanding, and it is perhaps the director's most satisfying contribution to the Western. Drifter Kirk Douglas and sidekick William Campbell arrive at an isolated settlement and are taken on by ruthless rancher Jeanne Crain. Campbell

tries to be like the macho hero he thinks Douglas is, while Douglas subtly educates the kid in non-violence. A subsidiary theme is the closure of the West, with Douglas holding barbed wire in especial contempt for the anti-community values it symbolizes and because he was once, as is shown in a nasty flashback, whipped with the stuff. Vidor's signature is on the film in the teasing eroticism of Douglas' scenes with the unbalanced Crain (who recalls such Vidor heroines as Ruby Gentry and Pearl Chavez in Duel in the Sun), but also in his liberal concern for the community. As a minor footnote, it is worth mentioning that this film depicts the historic moment when indoor plumbing came to the West. In 1968, James Goldstone remade the film faithfully as A Man Called Gannon, with Anthony Franciosa, Michael Sarrazin and Judi West taking over from Douglas, Campbell and Crain. KN
1955/89 min/U/p Aaron Rosenberg/d King Vidor/s Borden Chase, D. D. Beauchamp/ c Russell Metty/md Joseph Gershenson/ lp Kirk Douglas, Jeanne Crain, William Campbell, Claire Trevor, Richard Boone, Jay C. Flippen

The Mark of Zorro · This version of Johnston McCulley's masked caballero adventure gallops madly between genres. Set in the Old California settlement of Los Angeles during the early 1800s, the film enjoys all the traditional swordplay and aesthetics typical of the swashbuckler while at the same time driving its characters through a story of small-town corruption, personal revenge, hold-ups, robbery and furious chases on horseback. Overall the film is closer to Robin Hood than Jesse James, but director Mamoulian brilliantly blends the rapiers and cloaks of Spanish California with the landscape and colourful atmosphere of the 'Old West'. Tyrone Power's Don Diego/Zorro ('a young blade taught the fine and fashionable art of killing') overdoes the foppish part to the point of caricature – and is thus totally at odds with the traditionally tough and masculine Western hero – but the period costumes and manner give him licence to effect a less than heroic cover. Though more active with swordplay than gunplay, this version of the Zorro story is even so closer to Republic's Zorro's Fighting Legion than to the original Fairbanks treatment. TV
1940/b & w/93 min/FOX/p Raymond Griffith/d Rouben Mamoulian/s John Taintor Foote/c Arthur Miller/m Alfred Newman/lp Tyrone Power, Linda Darnell,

Basil Rathbone, Gale Sondergaard

Il mercenario (A Professional Gun) · A Polish mercenary named Sergei Kowalski (Nero) teams up with a Mexican worker Eufemio (Musante), in the hope that he can make some money out of the Mexican Revolution, using Eufemio as a 'front'. Under Kowalski's guidance, Eufemio learns how to become an effective guerrilla fighter, and 'the Polak' gets rich. But, as Eufemio begins to understand what the Revolution is really about, he falls out with the cynical and opportunistic mercenary, and eventually turns him over to the authorities. Meanwhile, both of them cross the path of Curly (Palance), an outrageously camp adventurer. The climax has Eufemio (by now working as a rodeo clown), Curly and Kowalski (who has escaped from prison) meeting in a bullring for the settling of accounts. Curly is shot, his white carnation turning to crimson.... A characteristic story by Franco Solinas is transformed, in the hands of Sergio Corbucci, into a wild fantasy, comic-strip style, about political commitment: Frantz Fanon for beginners with a bizarre sense of humour. Palance in a curly wig has to be seen to be believed. CF
1968/105 min/PEA — Profilms/p Alberto Grimaldi/d Sergio Corbucci/s Sergio Corbucci, Luciano Vincenzoni, Sergio Spina/c Alejandro Ulloa/m Ennio Morricone, Bruno Nicolai/lp Franco Nero, Tony Musante, Jack Palance, Giovanna Ralli, Eduardo Fajardo

Il mio nome è Nessuno (My Name Is Nobody) · 'Supervised' by Sergio Leone, and directed by his assistant Tonino Valerii, this Italian Western has an Italian-style hero (Terence Hill) who hero-worships an American 'national monument' (in the charismatic form of Henry Fonda), and eggs him on to greater and greater feats of daring so that he can 'go down in history'. The climax has Fonda on one side of the railroad tracks and 'one hundred and fifty sons of bitches' (known as the Wild Bunch) on the other. Fonda wins, by shooting at the dynamite which they keep in their saddlebags. Then he has to 'retire' (in a staged duel with Nobody, which is also a parody of C'era una volta il west). This bizarre film interestingly contrasts the Italian and American traditions of the Western, and although Leone called it his 'arrivederci', it was followed by a less successful sequel, Un genio, due compari e un pollo. By this (late) stage in the Spaghetti boom, parodies of Sam Peckinpah were

beginning to appear: his name is written on one of the crosses in the inevitable cemetery sequence of *Il mio nome è Nessuno*, and other references abound. CF
1973/116 min/Rafran – Jacques Leitienne – Alcinter – Rialto/*p* Claudio Mancini/ *d* Tonino Valerii/*s* Ernesto Gastaldi/ *c* Giuseppe Ruzzolini/*m* Ennio Morricone/ *lp* Henry Fonda, 'Terence Hill' (Mario Girotti), Leo Gordon, R.G. Armstrong, Piero Lulli

The Misfits · This was both Gable's and Monroe's last film and is fittingly bleak and valedictory in tone. The 'misfits' in question are wild horses too small for riding but worth money as dogfood. But of course the title also refers to the ill-assorted group of loners and no-hopers who live from rounding them up. Huston said that 'we live in a society where the dogs eat the horses' and *The Misfits* offers up a stark portrait of contemporary America where no new undiscovered frontiers beckon and there is no place for the non-conformist, the outsider and the refugee from industrial society. Where *The Misfits* scores immeasurably over the similarly concerned *Lonely Are the Brave* is in the remarkable intensity of the performances and the delineation of the characters' complex relationships. It remains one of the finest works of all involved. JP
1961/b & w/124 min/Seven Arts – UA/ *p* Frank E. Taylor/*d* John Huston/*s* Arthur Miller/*c* Russell Metty/*m* Alex North/ *lp* Clark Gable, Marilyn Monroe, Montgomery Clift, Thelma Ritter, Eli Wallach

The Missouri Breaks · A gloriously grotesque, folkloric ode to the dangerous eccentricities of the West, this centrepiece to screenwriter McGuane's genre trilogy (flanked by *Rancho DeLuxe* and *Tom Horn*) adds layer after layer of flamboyancy to the cliché configurations of the rancher-rustler-regulator formula, and marshals the perversities of character and context into a coherent comedy of violent absurdity. Nicholson is the leader of a gang of horse thieves who, incognito, buys land from one of his victims, a rancher (McLiam), to use as a relay station for his rustling operation. While he is sidetracked by the pleasurable lure of McLiam's daughter (Lloyd) and a new-found liking for the farming life, his gang are individually picked off by the outrageously quirky regulator, Brando, whose gun has been hired initially by the increasingly deranged McLiam, but is now pursuing its own pro-

Henry Fonda in My Darling Clementine

cess of elimination. A first, inconclusive, confrontation between stalker and prey confirms Brando as a mesmeric presence, but Nicholson eventually reverses their roles with startling finality. Throughout, director Penn's shuffling of ironically unexpected moods of harshness and lyricism is superbly handled, while McGuane's stacking of the movie's deck with jokers is inspired. PT
1976/126 min/EK Prods – UA/*p* Robert M. Sherman/*d* Arthur Penn/*s* Thomas McGuane/*c* Michael Butler/*m* John Williams/*lp* Marlon Brando, Jack Nicholson, Kathleen Lloyd, John McLiam, Harry Dean Stanton

Monte Walsh · One of a number of films of the 60s and 70s to attempt a more authentic portrayal of cowboying. However, Fraker tilts rather more towards the romantic than the authentic in this elegy on the passing of the Old West, as Marvin, at the climax, plays out the greatest of all Western clichés when he faces down the killer of his friend in a dimly lit abattoir. Palance and Marvin are the two middle-aged cowboys who find their world turned upside down when the ranch they work for is sold to a faceless eastern finance corporation. Unemployment becomes rife as the corporations fence in more and more land and those without work find themselves turning to crime. Leisurely comic scenes of bunkhouse life, saloon brawls and the drudgery of ranch work are played out against Remingtonesque landscapes suffused with the orange light of an omnipresent dusk. PS (Plate 25)

1970/108 min/Cinema Center Films – National General/*p* Hal Landers, Bobby Roberts/*d* William A. Fraker/*s* David Zelag Goodman, Lukas Heller/*c* David M. Walsh/*m* John Barry/*lp* Lee Marvin, Jack Palance, Jeanne Moreau, Jim Davis

My Darling Clementine · Perhaps Ford's most poetic Western, a free interpretation of the classic showdown between the Earps and the Clantons, rendered as a microcosm of that historic process whereby, with the serpent of evil at last driven out of Tombstone, the wilderness could become a garden. Starting with the moonlit murder of the youngest Earp brother, and ending with the cleansing dawn of the gunfight at the O.K. Corral, the film is haunted by the romantic imagery of paradise lost and regained. On the one hand, Victor Mature's Luciferian Doc Holliday, struggling to atone for a sullied past; on the other Cathy Downs' Clementine, sweetly determined to create a future for innocence. And between them, the secret heart of the film, the wonderful sequence of the founding of the town's new church and its dedication in a square dance social where Henry Fonda's somberly gauche Wyatt Earp, leading the way with his darling Clementine, hesitantly inaugurates the new era. TMi
1946/b & w/96 min/FOX/*p* Samuel G. Engel/*d* John Ford/*s* Winston Miller, Samuel G. Engel/*c* Joseph MacDonald/ *m* Cyril Mockridge/*lp* Henry Fonda, Linda Darnell, Victor Mature, Cathy Downs, Walter Brennan

N

The Naked Dawn · This was Ulmer's second (and last) Western, the first being the pseudonymously directed *Thunder over Texas*. One of his undoubted masterpieces, it is an intimate chamber Western involving only three characters, a bandit and the young peasant couple with whom he tangles. It is a film of stark simplicity, stripped to essentials and bordering on abstraction. There is little 'action' in the conventional sense, the pace is mostly slow, the landscapes and décor barren, the dialogue mainly philosophizing about the basics of life. Ulmer has likened his films to modern morality plays and the description is nowhere more apt than here, where the rituals of his characters' daily lives are transcribed with a lyricism which turns them into pure poetry, and Ulmer's remarkable *mise en scène* imbues a simple story with profound moral and metaphysical overtones. JP
1954/82 min/U/*p* James O. Radford/
d Edgar G. Ulmer/*s* Nina Schneider,
Herman Schneider/*c* Frederick Gately/
m Herschel Burke Gilbert/*lp* Arthur
Kennedy, Betta St John, Eugene Iglesias

The Naked Spur · Howard Kemp (Stewart), a bounty hunter trying to earn money to buy back land he unfairly lost while away in the Civil War, attempts to bring a wanted man to justice. Confronted by his own values and the greed of the four people with him (Ben, the wanted man; Lina, Ben's girlfriend; Lt. Anderson, a renegade officer escaping from Indians; and Jesse, an old man hired to help Kemp), Kemp makes a mental journey that corresponds to their arduous physical journey through a varied landscape. The film's nature metaphor is especially significant when Kemp, failing at the beginning to climb a bluff in his attempt to capture his prey, succeeds at the end in overcoming a similar obstacle, even though severely wounded. For the other three men the journey reveals only their worst instincts; as a result, they die. By contrast, Kemp, who throughout the film has relived the bitterness of his past, finds solace with Lina and sees the futility of his vengeful pursuit. JD
1952/91 min/MGM/*p* William H. Wright/
d Anthony Mann/*s* Sam Rolfe and Harold
Jack Bloom/*c* William C. Mellor/
m Bronislau Kaper/*lp* James Stewart,
Robert Ryan, Janet Leigh, Ralph Meeker,
Millard Mitchell

North to Alaska · A boisterous semi-comic movie in which John Wayne and Stewart Granger play gold-prospecting partners in 1890s Alaska. The plot revolves partly around the romantic complications which ensue when Granger's mail-order sweetheart (Capucine) falls for Wayne instead, and partly from the machinations of the local crook (Ernie Kovacs, perpetually brandishing a large cigar) in seeking to cheat the heroes out of their strike. Matters culminate happily in the wake of a well-orchestrated brawl all over the town of Nome. Jack Martin Smith's art direction lends the ramshackle community a picturesque individuality, Hathaway's direction is fully up to scratch for command of narrative tempo, and altogether the promise held out by the rousing ballad sung over the opening titles by Johnny Horton is amply sustained. TP
1960/122 min/FOX/*p/d* Henry Hathaway/
s John Lee Mahin, Martin Rackin, Claude
Binyon/*c* Leon Shamroy/*m* Lionel
Newman/*lp* John Wayne, Stewart
Granger, Ernie Kovacs, Capucine, Fabian,
Mickey Shaughnessy

Northwest Passage · This was originally conceived as the first of two films based on Kenneth Roberts' novel about the historical character Robert Rogers – it bears the subtitle *Rogers' Rangers* – the second of which was never made, perhaps because star Spencer Tracy and director King Vidor had a falling-out, and perhaps because the second half of Rogers' career was considerably less heroic than the events documented here (he changed sides and fought for the British during the War of Independence, and died in drunken obscurity and disgrace in exile in England). *Northwest Passage* follows Rogers (Tracy) and his band of hard-bitten rangers as they trek into Canada to help out some settlers who have been under attack by Indians. Vidor makes marvellous use of a landscape which is both beautiful and dangerous, and turns the overcoming of such obstacles as raging torrents into bravura sequences. Less attractive is the highly racist treatment of the Indians, who are seen throughout as sub-human monsters capable of any atrocity. The grim strain which would probably have become more evident in Part Two surfaces in some strikingly brutal massacres and in a twisted sub-plot about a crazed ranger who resorts to cannibalism. Tracy's stalwart heroism is supported by fine, typical performances from Robert Young as the dude map-maker who becomes a man by enduring hardships and Walter Brennan as the ever-complaining whiskery comic sidekick. KN
1940/126 min/MGM/*p* Hunt Stromberg/
d King Vidor/*s* Laurence Stallings, Talbot
Jennings/*c* Sidney Wagner, William V.
Skall/*m* Herbert Stothart/*lp* Spencer
Tracy, Robert Young, Walter Brennan,
Lumsden Hare, Ruth Hussey

O

Oklahoma! · When it was first produced on the stage in 1943, *Oklahoma!* was admired for its dynamic, innovative choreography (by Agnes De Mille) and stylized sets. The score probably contains more well-known tunes than any other stage musical. Between the opening number, 'Oh What a Beautiful Mornin'', and the finale, 'Oklahoma!', are at least a dozen standards such as 'I Cain't Say No', 'People Will Say We're in Love', 'All er Nuthin'' and 'Surrey With the Fringe On Top'. As a Western, its interest lies mainly in how it makes explicit some traditional thematic oppositions, such as those between (eastern) town and (western) country – 'Everything's Up To Date in Kansas City' – and farmers and ranchers ('The Farmer and the Cowman Should Be Friends'). But if the trappings (costumes, scenery, no longer stylized) are Western, the narrative remains quintessentially a musical: boy and girl fall in love, fall out, are reconciled. EB
1955/145 min/Rodgers and Hammerstein
Pictures – Magna – RKO/*p* Arthur
Hornblow Jr./*d* Fred Zinnemann/*s* Sonya
Levien, William Ludwig/*c* Robert Surtees/
m Richard Rodgers/*lyrics* Oscar
Hammerstein II/*lp* Gordon MacRae,
Gloria Grahame, Shirley Jones, Rod
Steiger, Roy Barcroft

The Oklahoma Kid · Given that 1939 – the year of *Stagecoach*, *Jesse James*, *Union Pacific*, *Dodge City* and *Destry Rides Again* – marked the Western's re-emergence from the B-picture and series doldrums into the Hollywood mainstream, Warner Bros. seem to have felt obliged to work over the formula of their successful gangster movies by adding cowboy hats. Here, James Cagney is the white-hatted outlaw who reforms in order to bring the murderers of his crusading father to justice, and Humphrey Bogart is all in black as the leader of a band of claim-jumpers, but the insults they trade sound rather more suited to squabbles about bootlegging on the East Side of New York than to the wide open prairies, and the fast-shooting urban actors are visibly uncomfortable in the saddle. In its plot, *The*

Oklahoma Kid has several parallels to contemporary crime films like *Angels With Dirty Faces* and *The Roaring Twenties*, where Cagney and Bogart played basically the same roles but in more congenial surroundings. As a curiosity, however, the film does have considerable interest, particularly when Cagney ventures jauntily into Gene Autry territory and gives voice to 'I Don't Want to Play in Your Yard'. KN
1939/b & w/85 min/wb/*p* Samuel Bischoff/ *d* Lloyd Bacon/*s* Warren Duff, Robert Buckner, Edward E. Paramore/*c* James Wong Howe/*m* Max Steiner/*lp* James Cagney, Humphrey Bogart, Rosemary Lane, Donald Crisp, Ward Bond

One-Eyed Jacks · The *Heaven's Gate* of its day, with a protracted production history and a first cut running almost five hours. The film, directed by its star, belongs with *Johnny Guitar* and *The Outlaw* in the category of the bizarre. Like *The Outlaw* it is based on the Billy the Kid legend, with Marlon Brando playing Rio, the Kid figure, and Karl Malden as Dad Longworth in the Pat Garrett role. Although the narrative springs from a conventional betrayal and revenge structure, the dramatic and masochistic centrepiece – in which Longworth takes a whip to Rio and crushes his gunhand with a rifle butt – pulls the film away from the generic mainstream. Add to that the oedipal complications of Rio's romance with Longworth's stepdaughter, and the coastal scenery, unusual for the Western, and we are left with a film poised at the edges of the traditional generic boundaries. TR
1960/137 min/Pennebaker – PAR/*p* Frank P. Rosenberg/*d* Marlon Brando/*s* Guy Trosper, Calder Willingham/*c* Charles B. Lang Jr./*m* Hugo Friedhofer/*lp* Marlon Brando, Karl Malden, Pina Pellicer, Katy Jurado, Slim Pickens

100 Rifles · After his downbeat *Will Penny* Gries delivered this modish testimony to the impact of Italian Westerns on Hollywood. The plot, derived from a Robert MacLeod novel, pits sheriff Brown, a mustachioed half-Mexican Reynolds and the pseudo-Yaqui Indian Welch against the Mexican Army, who are advised by a blond, heel-clicking Prussian and a railway tycoon (O'Herlihy). Gries makes a stab at direction by using telescopic lenses to suggest the throbbing power and heat emanating from a locomotive and by having a yellow vintage car to suggest the dawning of the post-horse era, but the film's interest lies elsewhere.

Raquel Welch in 100 Rifles

Notably, there are the scenes in which Welch has her body drenched in water to exploit her image as sex goddess. Even though she is not supposed to be Aryan in the film, her steamy love scenes with Brown must have touched a sensitive nerve in racist Hollywood, because she is killed off at the end of the picture to atone for her wayward sexuality, which is otherwise liberally exploited by this melting-pot movie which took the precaution of making her 'only' an Indian. PW
1968/109 min/Marvin Schwartz Prods – FOX/*p* Marvin Schwartz/*d* Tom Gries/*s* Tom Gries, Clair Huffaker/*c* Cecilio Paniagua/*m* Jerry Goldsmith/*lp* Jim Brown, Raquel Welch, Burt Reynolds, Fernando Lamas, Dan O'Herlihy

Only the Valiant · A tough, rugged but thoughtful cavalry Western in which Peck plays a martinet determined at all costs to hold a mountain pass through which Apaches are trying to force a path to enable them to attack an undermanned garrison. In the process he almost causes his men to mutiny. Douglas makes the very most out of this 'huis clos' situation, the characters are well delineated, and the intelligent script is based on a novel by Charles Marquis Warren, who directed numerous Westerns himself and later worked as executive producer on television's *Gunsmoke* and *Rawhide*. JP
1950/105 min/William Cagney Prods – wb/*p* William Cagney/*d* Gordon Douglas/ *s* Edmund H. North, Harry Brown/*c* Lionel Lindon/*m* Franz Waxman/*lp* Gregory Peck, Barbara Payton, Ward Bond, Gig Young, Lon Chaney Jr.

The Outlaw · André Bazin regarded *The Outlaw* as 'one of the most erotic films ever made' and it is usually Howard Hughes' calculated exploitation of Jane Russell's celebrated physique that dominates discussion of the picture. Though the film's release was delayed due to censorship problems and the

footage which survives does have some memorable moments of erotic suggestion, its centre of interest seems often to lie elsewhere. *The Outlaw* focuses on the jealousies of a small male group – the historical figures of Doc Holliday, Pat Garrett and Billy the Kid – a theme which probably emerged from Howard Hawks' brief involvement and Jules Furthman's script. This tangled triangle does involve Russell (as Rio) but the Doc and Billy, in a game of cards, place more value on a horse. Garrett, enraged at the friendship of these two, finally kills Doc and, in a weird distortion of the historical facts, allows Billy to ride off into the sunset with Rio, while he inscribes the Kid's name on Doc's tombstone. TR
1940/b & w/121 min/Howard Hughes Prods – RKO/*p/d* Howard Hughes/*s* Jules Furthman/*c* Gregg Toland/*md* Victor Young/*lp* Jane Russell, Jack Beutel, Walter Huston, Thomas Mitchell

The Outlaw Josey Wales · One of the best Westerns of the 70s and one of Eastwood's finest films (either as actor or director), this was originally to be directed by its co-scenarist Philip Kaufman, but Eastwood took over soon after shooting commenced, due to a disagreement over the nature of the central character. At the start Eastwood is a peaceable Missouri farmer whose wife and children are suddenly murdered by Unionist guerrillas. He then joins a Confederate gang and exacts revenge on the Unionists till the war ends, when he makes a picaresque journey to Texas, picking up various companions along the way and eventually setting up a commune where, gradually, his thoughts return from killing to farming. A lyrical epic of great scope and grandeur, *The Outlaw Josey Wales* is, for all its violence, a film of reconciliation and considerable tenderness. This aspect is memorably underlined by Surtees' radiantly lyrical landscape photography. JP
1976/134 min/Malpaso – wb/*p* Robert Daley/*d* Clint Eastwood/*s* Phil Kaufman, Sonia Chernus/*c* Bruce Surtees/*m* Jerry Fielding/*lp* Clint Eastwood, Chief Dan George, Sondra Locke, Bill McKinney, John Vernon

The Ox-Bow Incident · A self-important Western that prefigures the 'adult' themes of the genre a decade or so later, but suffers somewhat from a speechifying script by Lamar Trotti (from Walter van Tilburg Clark's novel), particularly in the message-happy finale as hero Henry Fonda shames

Clint Eastwood in Pale Rider

the lynch mob by reading aloud a letter composed by the innocent man they have hanged. The somewhat simplistic story concerns three drifters (Dana Andrews, Anthony Quinn and Francis Ford) who are unjustly accused of cattle rustling, tried by kangaroo court, and lynched. As an indictment of mob rule, it doesn't have the force of contemporary dramas like Fritz Lang's *Fury* or Mervyn LeRoy's *They Won't Forget*, and as a Western, it is hampered by a low budget that forced Wellman to shoot the whole thing in the studio. It does, however, have a fine gallery of film noir-style portraits of the venal townspeople who make up the lynch mob – Frank Conroy as a sham Southern colonel with a family secret, Paul Hurst as a stirrer-up, and Jane Darwell as an inflexible rancher who represents the moral majority long before such a term was thought up. KN
1942/b & w/75 min/FOX/p Lamar Trotti/ d William A. Wellman/s Lamar Trotti/c Arthur Miller/m Cyril Mockridge/ lp Henry Fonda, Dana Andrews, Anthony Quinn, Henry Morgan, Jane Darwell, Frank Conroy, Paul Hurst, Francis Ford

P

Pale Rider · A small community of miners, struggling to work their claims in Carbon Canyon, is constantly harassed by big mine-owner Coy LaHood, until a mysterious stranger on a pale horse comes to their rescue.... At first sight Eastwood's back-from-the-dead hero seems to recall *High Plains Drifter*, but here the lone avenger has been replaced by the saviour of the community in need. As Richard Combs has put it, 'the Leone-like insistence on the venality of all and sundry' has here been replaced by 'a more four-square, traditional Western structure and morality, reminiscent in many details of *Shane* and that self-consciously "classic" liberal-humanist line in the American Western.' *Pale Rider* is directed with considerable imagination and energy, and is much more firmly grounded in American history and pioneer experience than its supernatural predecessor. And as in *The Outlaw Josey Wales*, Surtees' photography captures beautifully the vibrant lyricism of nature in all its various moods. JP
1985/116 min/Malpaso – WB/p Fritz Manes/d Clint Eastwood/s Michael Butler, Dennis Shryack/c Bruce Surtees/m Lennie Niehaus/lp Clint Eastwood, Michael Moriarty, Carrie Snodgrass, Christopher Penn, Richard Dysart

Pat Garrett and Billy the Kid · Peckinpah's farewell to the Western is a film about memory and death. Originally there was a prologue and epilogue detailing the murder of Garrett (James Coburn) many years later; the film then told the story of Billy the Kid (Kris Kristofferson) as recollected by Garrett in flashback. This framing structure along with much else was removed when the studio re-edited Peckinpah's film into the occasionally incoherent version we have

today. (No less than six editors are credited.) Nevertheless, a powerfully elegiac tone survives, not only in the figure of the doomed Billy but in the wistful talk of days gone by which punctuates the frequent scenes of arbitrary and violent death. Garrett tries to get Billy to adjust to the modern world ('It feels like times have changed'), but Billy despises Garrett's accommodation with the money men of the Santa Fe ring in New Mexico, accusing him of having sold out to 'every goddam landowner who's trying to put a fence round this country'. Whether the film as Peckinpah wanted it would have been his masterpiece is hard to say. Evidence both internal and external suggests the director never did make up his mind on what exactly Bob Dylan was doing in the picture, for example. But the scene of Slim Pickens' death is as moving as anything in Peckinpah's work, and that's saying a lot. EB
1973/106 min/MGM/p Gordon Carroll/ d Sam Peckinpah/s Rudolph Wurlitzer/ c John Coquillon/m Bob Dylan/lp James Coburn, Kris Kristofferson, Bob Dylan, Richard Jaeckel, Katy Jurado, Slim Pickens, Chill Wills, Jason Robards, R. G. Armstrong, Jack Elam, Harry Dean Stanton

Per qualche dollaro in più (For a Few Dollars More) · Sequel to *Per un pugno di dollari* which contrasts 'the Man with No Name' from the first film with the taciturn 'Colonel Mortimer' (played by Lee Van Cleef, who was re-discovered in retirement). The story – two bounty hunters with very different styles uneasily team up to hunt the vicious, pot-smoking bandit El Indio – is less important than the flamboyant way in which it is told. The final duel, for example, which involves all three of the main protagonists, is

James Coburn, Kris Kristofferson in Pat Garrett and Billy the Kid

filmed as if it is part of the Liturgy. If the previous film introduced an Italian's vision of the wild Southwest, this one shows what can happen when the script gets shorter and the pauses get longer. The style of Leone's mature films is emerging. CF
1965/130 min/PEA Prods – Constantin – Arturo Gonzales/p Alberto Grimaldi/ d Sergio Leone/s Sergio Leone, Luciano Vincenzoni/c Massimo Dallamano/ m Ennio Morricone/lp Clint Eastwood, Lee Van Cleef, Gian Maria Volontè, Klaus Kinski, Marianne Koch

Per un pugno di dollari (A Fistful of Dollars) · The first of Sergio Leone's Italian Westerns, and the one which launched the genre internationally. Partly derived from Kurosawa's samurai film *Yojimbo*, partly from Dashiell Hammett's novel *Red Harvest*, but most of all from Goldoni's eighteenth-century play *The Servant of Two Masters*, the film also launched Clint Eastwood as a movie star. Its Latin ambiance (family clans, church bell-towers, the rituals of the bullfight), together with its emphasis on how the characters *look* (cigars, ponchos, interesting faces) were superimposed on the visual clichés of the American Western, and the result was to change the history of the form. The music (traditional themes re-arranged for electric guitar and shouting voices) was also influential. CF
1964/100 min/Jolly – Constantin – Ocean – UA/p Arrigo Colombo, Giorgio Papi/ d Sergio Leone/s Sergio Leone, Duccio Tessari/c Jack Dalmas (Massimo Dallamano)/m Dan Savio (Ennio Morricone)/lp Clint Eastwood, 'John Wells' (Gian Maria Volontè), Marianne Koch, Pepe Calvo, Wolfgang Lukschy

The Plainsman · A spectacular Cecil B. DeMille Western centred on some of the legendary historical figures of the West and freely using key historical events from the period after the Civil War. A somewhat didactic opening contrasts Lincoln's vision of the West as a haven of opportunity for men returning from the war with the more mercenary vision of arms suppliers planning to sell rifles to the Indians. Thereafter the film picks up, with Wild Bill Hickok (Gary Cooper), Calamity Jane and a newly-wed Buffalo Bill Cody battling against gunrunners and Indians alike. Hickok's turbulent romance with Jean Arthur's Calamity Jane is contrasted with Cody's settled domestic situation, but Hickok is eventually shot in the back by one of the gun-runners, to join the long list of Western heroes for whom settling down was an impossible option. TR
1936/b & w/110 min/PAR/p/d Cecil B. DeMille/s Waldemar Young, Harold Lamb, Lynn Riggs/c Victor Milner/ m George Antheil/lp Gary Cooper, Jean Arthur, James Ellison, Helen Burgess

Posse · A gently sardonic political Western that trusts its audience to make contemporary connections without undue nudging, and boasts a plot of ingeniously precise irony. Douglas is the US Marshal who decides his power-hungry aspirations to a Senate seat will be perfectly served by the publicity value of his capturing notorious train-robber Dern, and who utilizes a hand-picked super-posse to achieve this end. The functionally militaristic posse are, however, a disruptive threat to the civilian law-and-order of the small Texan town where Dern is incarcerated, and when Dern manages to escape and turn the tables on Douglas by holding him hostage, he exploits their mercenary nature both to replace the loot he'd lost on arrest and to take them on as his new

gang. Leaving, to all intents and purposes, Douglas to a Nixonian disgrace before his chastised electorate. PT
1975/93 min/Bryna – PAR/p/d Kirk Douglas/s Christopher Knopf, William Roberts/c Fred Koenekamp/m Maurice Jarre/lp Kirk Douglas, Bruce Dern, Bo Hopkins, James Stacy, Luke Askew

The Professionals · One of the most financially successful Westerns of the 60s, this is also one of Brooks' finest films, one in which the expression of themes and ideas is, for the most part, successfully integrated into a tightly controlled and vigorous narrative structure. Four mercenaries are hired to rescue a millionaire's wife from a Mexican revolutionary leader who has kidnapped her, only to discover that she does not want to return. Very different in tone from the harsh, bleak *The Last Hunt*, *The Professionals* contains a good deal of toughly self-parodic humour, but at the same time it is a serious and recognizably Brooksian exploration of the theme of conflicting codes of loyalty and the need for a personal ethic. And like Peckinpah was to do a few years later, Brooks also seems to be exploring the gradual disappearance of the Old West and its heroes. Conrad Hall's red desert-scapes are magnificent. JP
1966/123 min/Pax Enterprises – COL/p/d/s Richard Brooks/c Conrad Hall/m Maurice Jarre/lp Burt Lancaster, Lee Marvin, Robert Ryan, Jack Palance, Ralph Bellamy, Claudia Cardinale, Woody Strode

Pursued · Walsh's exquisitely 'noir' masterpiece, set in the 1890s and often wrongly described as the first psychological Western, tells of Jeb (Mitchum), a man pursued by obscure childhood memories involving a fallen woman, Ma Callum (Anderson), a pair of spurred boots and flashes of light. In his doomladen life he has to kill his adoptive brother, causes his foster-mother's hatred and marries his adoptive sister Thorley Callum (Wright) knowing she will try to kill him on their wedding night. The story is told in flashback as the lovers await the attack of the vengeful one-armed lawyer, Grant Callum (Jagger), in the ruins of Jeb's childhood home, the scene of his traumatic memory. With the noose already around his neck, Jeb learns the truth: Ma Callum's sexuality had disrupted the Callum household and he was the symbol of her illegitimate desires. Only when she finally kills the patriarch is the cloud over Jeb's life lifted. The towering rocks of Monument Valley,

Jean Arthur, Gary Cooper in The Plainsman

Kirk Douglas in Posse

Claudia Cardinale, Lee Marvin, Robert Ryan, Woody Strode in The Professionals

Robert Mitchum, Teresa Wright in Pursued

Mitchum's brooding performance and Wong Howe's menacingly shadowy images may have been some of the reasons that prompted Walsh to comment in an interview: 'I love that movie.' PW
1947/b & w/101 min/Hemisphere Films – WB/p Milton Sperling/d Raoul Walsh/ s Niven Busch/c James Wong Howe/m Max Steiner/lp Robert Mitchum, Teresa Wright, Judith Anderson, Dean Jagger, Alan Hale

Q

Quien sabe? (A Bullet for the General) · The Italian Western which launched the series of 'political' Spaghettis – most of which drew direct parallels between the involvement of American 'observers' in the Mexican revolution and the involvement of the CIA in Latin America. This one has Bill Tate, 'the gringo' (Lou Castel), offering assistance to El Chuncho, the bandit-revolutionary (Gian Maria Volonté), while really trying to destabilize the revolution. El Chuncho, meanwhile, is transformed from being a bandit into a believer in 'the cause'. Later examples of a similar theme included *Il mercenario* and *Vamos a matar, compañeros!* CF
1966/135 min/MGM/p Bianco Manini/ d Damiano Damiani/s Salvatore Laurani/ c Toni Secchi/m Luis Enrique Bacalov/ lp Gian Maria Volonté, Lou Castel, Martine Beswick, Klaus Kinski

R

The Raid · In 1951 Fregonese had directed the only Western produced by Val Lewton, *Apache Drums*, and in the unjustly neglected *The Raid* he shows a similar talent for suspense and shadowy *mise en scène*. Taken from Herbert Ravenall Sass's true story *Affair at St Albans*, the film tells the grim story of a group of Confederate soldiers who escape from a Union prison camp and sack a Northern town in revenge for the destruction of its Southern counterparts. Fregonese's direction is rugged, and the long build-up to the climactic scenes of destruction is handled most assuredly and with the maximum accretion of tension. Ballard's photography provides a suitably dark, threatening atmosphere, and the scenes of the sacking of the small town bring home the horrors of war far more effectively than many more elaborate efforts. JP
1954/83 min/Panoramic – FOX/p Robert L. Jacks/d Hugo Fregonese/s Sidney Boehm/ c Lucien Ballard/m Roy Webb/lp Van Heflin, Anne Bancroft, Richard Boone, Lee Marvin, Peter Graves

Ramrod · A dark, savage film and a prime example, alongside *Pursued*, of that anomalous hybrid the 'noir-Western'. The archetypal range war plot of sheep-herders versus cattlemen is given a new lease of life as violence begets violence until neither side is left unbrutalized in the struggle. McCrea plays the decent law-abiding foreman caught between Foster's land-greedy cattle king and Lake's revenge-seeking frontier *femme fatale* – described in the film's publicity as having 'the face of an angel – the soul of a scorpion'. McCrea finally steps outside of the law when Lake, unbeknown to him, arranges to have her own cattle stampeded in order to frame Foster, which leads to the murder of the sheriff and McCrea's subsequent acts of revenge. Learning later that Lake had engineered the whole show from start to finish, the only gesture left to McCrea is to reject her plea for forgiveness and to leave town with Whelan. PS
1947/b & w/94 min/Harry Sherman Pictures – UA/p Harry Sherman/d André de Toth/s Jack Moffitt, Graham Baker, Cecile Kramer/c Russell Harlan/m Adolph Deutsch/lp Veronica Lake, Joel McCrea, Arleen Whelan, Preston Foster

Rancho DeLuxe · A contemporary Western, set in Livingston, Montana, which marks the screenwriting début of novelist McGuane and establishes the template for his later variants, *The Missouri Breaks* and *Tom Horn*. Bridges and his half-Indian buddy Waterston rustle cattle for rent-money or mere kicks, while their favourite herd-owning target, James, becomes exasperated enough to hire Pickens' decrepit and seemingly inactive stock detective to investigate his losses. The rustlers eventually rope in two of James' ranch-hands for a major livestock heist, but one of the latter (Harry Dean Stanton) has also been seduced by Pickens' daughter (Dallas) and an expedient betrayal delivers both cattle and criminals back to James. The plot is, clearly, perfunctory and treated as a near-whimsical subsidiary to a series of sarcastic reflections on the culture-

Jack Elam, Tyrone Power in Rawhide

Joanne Dru, John Wayne in Red River

clash distortions of Old West values in a 1970s landscape, where computer games have begun to invade the saloons and Navajo rugs have become chic status symbols. PT
1974/94 min/EK Corp – UA/*p* Elliott Kastner/*d* Frank Perry/*s* Thomas McGuane/*c* William A. Fraker/*m* Jimmy Buffett/*lp* Jeff Bridges, Sam Waterston, Clifton James, Slim Pickens, Charlene Dallas

Rancho Notorious · The rape and murder which begin *Rancho Notorious* set its hero, Vern Haskell, on a traditional Western journey of revenge. However, as the film progresses the revenge theme recedes somewhat and the film strays from the clear moral universe of the Western into the bleaker pessimistic world of the Lang thriller. The centre of gravity shifts to Altar Keane – a retired saloon girl played by Marlene Dietrich – who runs a hideout for fugitive outlaws. Her faded yet still powerful mystique attracts Haskell, although he has also befriended her longtime lover, Frenchie Fairmont. Haskell's revenge is finally satisfied when the killer is shot by Frenchie, but Altar also dies when she throws herself in front of a bullet meant for him. A notable Lang picture, and a rare Western with flashbacks, *Rancho Notorious* has been called 'Brechtian' for its use of a theme song to comment on the action, and for the unsettling effect of its stylized, studio-bound appearance. TR
1952/89 min/Fidelity Pictures – RKO/
p Howard Welsch/*d* Fritz Lang/*s* Daniel Taradash/*c* Hal Mohr/*m* Emil Newman/
lp Marlene Dietrich, Arthur Kennedy, Mel Ferrer

Rawhide · Hathaway's return to the Western after a successful series of film noir thrillers that included the cynically cruel *Kiss of Death* mixes the two genres with the help of a claustrophobic script by Nichols, the scenarist of Ford's *Stagecoach*. Power, Hayward and her child are trapped in a stagecoach way station by a gang lying in wait for a gold shipment. The villains lay seige to the place but begin killing off each other as the night wears on. The final confrontation is between a fearful Power and a demented Elam, who is eventually despatched by Hayward just as the hero is about to be shot. Hathaway's direction is precise, punctuated by lovingly shot bits of grotesque sadism or insanity, characteristic of his work. Here he engineers an effective sequence in which Elam playfully terrorizes a small baby by putting bullets right next to it. One can imagine Hathaway gleefully directing the planting of small powder charges and exploding them as the crying child crawled around in the sand. PW
1950/b & w/86 min/FOX/*p* Samuel G. Engel/*d* Henry Hathaway/*s* Dudley Nichols/*c* Milton Krasner/*m* Sol Kaplan/
lp Tyrone Power, Susan Hayward, Jack Elam, Hugh Marlowe, Dean Jagger, Edgar Buchanan

Red River · A reworking of *Mutiny on the Bounty*, *Red River* rewrites the conflict between ruthless authority and democratic defiance in the language of the Western. Isolated from the law of the community, such as that of the wagon train and the woman, both of whose 'contracts' he refuses in the opening scene, Dunson (Wayne) creates his own laws, which he then rigidly enforces. This stoic inflexibility, seen as necessary for survival in the Old West, appears arbitrary in the post-war period of Reconstruction and common misfortune to which Dunson's adopted 'son' Matt (Clift) is sensitive. The larger historical transformation of the West from the domain of the pioneering empire builder to that of a community of wage-earning cowboys and small ranchers finds dramatic form in the oedipal conflict between Dunson and Matt, a conflict that is ultimately resolved when Dunson encounters the signs of the new West and retraces his steps to the sense of community he initially abandoned. The recognition of his contractual and emotional bond to and need for others is marked by his addition of an 'M' to the Red River 'D' brand at the end. Unlike Ford, who might view the new West in terms of the toll it has taken upon the old, Hawks reintegrates the old into the new, emphasizing the continuity of historical change over the dialectical oppositions that underlie it. JB
1947/b & w/125 min/Monterey – UA/*p*/*d* Howard Hawks/*s* Borden Chase, Charles Schnee/*c* Russell Harlan/*m* Dimitri Tiomkin/*lp* John Wayne, Montgomery Clift, Joanne Dru, Walter Brennan, John Ireland, Noah Beery Jr., Hank Worden

The Return of Frank James · Fritz Lang observed of the Western that it 'is not only the history of this country, it is what the Saga of the Nibelungen is for the European'. In this, his first Western, the sequel to Fox's *Jesse James*, he emphasizes the mythological rather than the historical. Frank James' well-theorized political analysis (a contemporary reported him as 'hating the so-called protective tariff as a huge monster of political trickery devised by ghouls for the devouring of the poor'), his knowledge of Elizabethan drama and his lunch with Teddy Roosevelt aren't shown. Rather, Lang's

presentation of the mythical revenging brother integrates familiar Western icons – the night train robbery, the trial, the revenge motif – with arresting novelties – Frank ploughing and a theatre show of Jesse's death and the James' banditry. Though neither one of Lang's nor the Jesse James cycle's best films, a rewarding curiosity. RC
1940/92 min/FOX/*p* Darryl F. Zanuck/ *d* Fritz Lang/*s* Sam Hellman/*c* George Barnes, William V. Skall/*m* David Buttolph/*lp* Henry Fonda, Gene Tierney, Jackie Cooper, Henry Hull

Ride in the Whirlwind · Made back to back with the same team's extraordinary *The Shooting* in the Utah desert, this story was devised by Nicholson after reading some old diaries of the period from which he drew the poetic lines and cadences of dialect speech. The plot has two cowboys, Nicholson and Mitchell (in the best performance of his career), become entangled with a group of outlaws chased by vigilantes. The exuberance and casual hospitality offered by the outlaws contrasts starkly with the brutality of the 'citizens', who simply hang whoever they can catch. Eventually, one of the outlaws is killed and the film ends with the echo of the hooves of the survivor's horse galloping away on an endless flight. Although the film conveys more of a social world than its companion piece, its view is unremittingly bleak: the vigilantes represent a brutalized sense of legality while a farmer is shown hacking away at a tree-stump for days on end in mind-numbing but futile activity. Only the outlaws are allowed a sense of aliveness, up to their inevitably violent deaths. Hellman negates the agrarian populism characteristic of most Westerns by showing the pathetic meanness and stultifying drudgery of everyday life, making the drifter with scant regard for legality into a figure who pays for his freedom from everyday emptiness with the brevity of his life. The disillusioned romanticism of Hellman's movies, full of stunted lives and naive idealism, recently earned his work the label of 'existential Westerns'. However, since the films make living itself the only real value, rather than social existence, anarchic nihilism might be a more accurate description of his overwhelmingly intense pictures. PW
1966/82 min/Proteus Films/*p* Jack Nicholson, Monte Hellman/*d* Monte Hellman/*s* Jack Nicholson/*c* Gregory Sandor/*m* Robert Drasnin/*lp* Jack Nicholson, Cameron Mitchell, Millie Perkins, Harry Dean Stanton

Ride Lonesome · Perhaps the simplest of the beautiful series of Westerns Budd Boetticher made with Randolph Scott, usually from scripts by Burt Kennedy, and one of the most impressive B- (more correctly, double feature) movies of the 1950s. An elegant set of plot mechanics is put in motion when lawman Scott and outlaws Pernell Roberts and James Coburn capture young gun James Best. Scott takes an unnaturally long while over the trip into town, because he is really after the kid's brother (Lee Van Cleef), who long ago hanged Scott's wife, while Roberts and Coburn will get an amnesty if they bring in Best. Also along for the ride is Karen Steele, newly widowed and the focus of much sexual tension. The clever inversion of the usual race-against-time theme, whereby the hero is trying to stretch out the quest, allows Boetticher and Kennedy to build up tension by taking things slowly. Scott self-effacingly allows himself to be upstaged by the supporting cast, whose eccentricity plays off against his gnarled heroism. Even Van Cleef is allowed to be likable as the chief killer, vaguely ashamed of the atrocities he committed needlessly when he was a less professional outlaw. Despite the comic charm of much of the campfire conversation, the finale is particularly bleak for Scott. He gets his revenge and symbolically burns down the hanging tree that has been the focus of his obsession, but has been on his revenge mission for so long that he is reluctant to participate in the happy ending enjoyed by Steele, Roberts, Coburn and even Best. KN
1959/73 min/Ranown – COL/*p*/*d* Budd Boetticher/*s* Burt Kennedy/*c* Charles Lawton Jr./*m* Heinz Roemheld/ *lp* Randolph Scott, Karen Steele, Pernell Roberts, James Best, Lee Van Cleef, James Coburn

Ride the High Country (Guns in the Afternoon) · Ex-sheriff Steve Judd takes a job escorting gold from the mountains into town, and is joined by former partner Gil Westrum – now running a sideshow as 'The Oregon Kid' – his youthful sidekick Heck Longtree, and Elsa Knudsen, fleeing the violent hypocrisy of her religious father to join her fiancée Billy Hammond at the mining camp. After a grotesque marriage ceremony in the camp brothel, Elsa has to be rescued from the brutal attentions of the five Hammond brothers. On the return journey, pursued by the Hammonds, Judd foils his partners' attempts to steal the money. In a final successful confrontation with the Ham-

Randolph Scott, Karen Steele in Ride Lonesome

Walter Brennan, John Wayne in Rio Bravo

monds, the escaped Westrum returns to assist, and Judd dies hearing Westrum's promise to complete his mission. Scott's and McCrea's farewell Western is characterized by a nostalgic sense of the passing of the Old West; a preoccupation with the emotionality of male bonding and of the experiential 'gap' between the young and old; and a fearful evocation, in the form of the Hammonds, of these preoccupations transmuted into brutal and perverse forms. PD
1962/98 min/MGM/*p* Richard E. Lyons/ *d* Sam Peckinpah/*s* N. B. Stone Jr./*c* Lucien Ballard/*m* George Bassman/*lp* Randolph Scott, Joel McCrea, Ronald Starr, Mariette Hartley, James Drury

Rio Bravo · Unlike the historically-based, epic plots of Hawks' earlier Westerns, the more lyrical *Rio Bravo* concerns the efforts of Sheriff Chance (Wayne) and his motley crew of deputies (Brennan, Martin and Nelson) to hold, in defiance of the counter-efforts of the prisoner's wealthy brother, a murderer in

jail for four days until the arrival of a US Marshal. Though made partially in reaction against *High Noon*, *Rio Bravo* is problematically non-Western in its plot, which is a hodge-podge of earlier Furthman scenarios such as *Underworld*, *Only Angels Have Wings* and *To Have and Have Not* and which will provide source material, in turn, for John Carpenter's thriller, *Assault on Precinct 13* (1976). Its setting, too, abandons the wide open exteriors of the traditional Western landscape for the claustrophobic interiors of the town's bars, hotel and jail. And unlike the heroic empire builders of Hawks' previous Westerns, *Rio Bravo*'s characters do not so much win the West as maintain it. What makes *Rio Bravo* a Western, albeit a minimalist one, is not so much its background as the iconic presence in the foreground of Wayne and Brennan, whom Hawks sets within the more immediate demands of day-to-day existence in a West that no longer belongs to pioneers but to second-generation professionals, consisting of the freight haulers, hotel keepers, gamblers, hired guns and lawmen who make their livings off its urban landscape. JB
1958/141 min/Armada – WB/*p/d* Howard Hawks/*s* Jules Furthman, Leigh Brackett/ *c* Russell Harlan/*m* Dimitri Tiomkin/*lp* John Wayne, Dean Martin, Ricky Nelson, Angie Dickinson, Walter Brennan

Rio Conchos · Douglas' Westerns are an uneven bunch but this baroque, delirious confection stands out a mile and deserves to be regarded as one of the director's finest achievements. Here O'Brien is an obsessive Confederate Colonel who attempts to continue the Civil War by other means by arming the Apaches and sending them against the Union. Douglas' direction is almost as grandiloquent as O'Brien's megalomaniac dreams: movement and invention abound, violent and picaresque incidents follow one another with demented abandon, and the film's climax – the razing of O'Brien's half-built headquarters – is a veritable Western *Götterdämmerung*. A real oddity, and quite splendid. JP

1964/107 min/FOX/*p* David Weisbart/ *d* Gordon Douglas/*s* Joseph Landon, Clair Huffaker/*c* Joseph MacDonald/*m* Jerry Goldsmith/*lp* Richard Boone, Stuart Whitman, Tony Franciosa, Wende Wagner, Edmond O'Brien

Rio Grande · The last film in Ford's cavalry trilogy, *Rio Grande* literalizes the quasi-metaphorical equation set forth in *Fort Apache* of fort community and family. While both films play the arbitrariness of military codes and the demands of duty off against the 'naturalness' of family, *Rio Grande*, unlike *Fort Apache*, violates more than it observes the law, endorsing an illegal incursion of US troops across the border into Mexico in pursuit of Indians who have taken a wagonful of fort children captive. The estrangement of Yankee colonel Yorke (Wayne) and his Confederate wife (O'Hara), caused by Yorke's devotion to duty during the Civil War, when his troops were ordered to burn down her family plantation, finds symbolic resolution in the post-war West, where Yankee and Confederate fight side by side against a new enemy, and where their son (Jarman), a new trooper under Yorke's command who helps rescue the children, succeeds in reuniting two families – the fort community and his own parents. The West becomes a site not only for the healing of old wounds created by the Civil War, but also for the creation of a new, ideal community which collapses both national, militaristic needs and those of the family. JB
1950/b & w/105 min/Argosy – REP/*p* John Ford, Merian C. Cooper/*d* John Ford/ *s* Kevin McGuinness/*c* Bert Glennon/ *m* Victor Young/*lp* John Wayne, Maureen O'Hara, Ben Johnson, Claude Jarman Jr., Harry Carey Jr., Chill Wills, J. Carrol Naish, Victor McLaglen

Rio Lobo · Cord McNally (Wayne), an ex-Union cavalry officer, joins forces with his former Confederate enemies to catch a traitor who once sold secret information about gold shipments to the enemy and who has since become a Texas carpetbagger.

When Hawks initially sketched out the story, Wayne, sensing its similarity to *Rio Bravo* and *El Dorado*, quipped, 'Do I get to play the drunk this time?' He does, but his drunk is neither the tragically self-destructive deputy with the DTs of *Rio Bravo* nor the slapstick buffoon played by Mitchum in *El Dorado*; Wayne can hold his liquor – and a rifle as well. Wayne's Western hero has loosened considerably over the years, abandoning the self-repressive qualities of his earlier persona (seen in Dunson's abstention from sex), which were necessary for his elevation to the status of mythic hero, and assuming a 'low mimetic' (in Frye's sense of the word) function, lowering himself, often through comedy, to the level of the ordinary world. For Hawks, Wayne and the West itself, constrained by their mythic roles, have to be humanized; they must leave the world of Mount Olympus and Monument Valley for that of men. JB
1970/114 min/Malabar – Cinema Center – National General/*p/d* Howard Hawks/ *s* Burton Wohl, Leigh Brackett/*c* William H. Clothier/*m* Jerry Goldsmith/*lp* John Wayne, Jorge Rivero, Jennifer O'Neill, Jack Elam, Chris Mitchum

River of No Return · Shot in Canada and set somewhere in the great Northwest, this is Otto Preminger's only Western. The Viennese-born Preminger is no more a natural for the Western than is Robert Mitchum for the part of the poor farmer who saves Marilyn Monroe from the clutches of a two-bit gambler, but it works surprisingly well. Preminger's measured, expository style of narrative gives full weight to both protagonists. Mitchum represents the agrarian ideal, but his rather glum demeanour (he has recently been in prison for killing a man) means we don't automatically take his part. We first meet Monroe dressed in red velvet and singing in a gold-mining camp. This is for the Western traditionally the sink of iniquity; yet her innocence disarms even Mitchum's surly self-righteousness. Most of the action takes place aboard a raft as Mitchum and Monroe

Rio Grande

Marilyn Monroe, Rory Calhoun in River of No Return

James Cagney in Run for Cover

(now more appropriately in trousers) brave rapids, Indians and near-starvation. The film was one of the first Westerns shot in CinemaScope, which suits Preminger's preference for developing action within the frame rather than through editing. EB
1954/91 min/FOX/p Stanley Rubin/d Otto Preminger/s Frank Fenton/c Joseph LaShelle/m Cyril J. Mockridge/lp Robert Mitchum, Marilyn Monroe, Rory Calhoun, Tommy Rettig

The Robin Hood of El Dorado · When the first anglo settlers came to California, the hispanic population suffered dispossession and injustice. Most of the comparatively few films on the subject have focused on the romantic figure of Joaquín Murrieta, a peon who, as represented here by Warner Baxter, reacted to the murder of his wife (Margo) by becoming a Zorro-style avenger and terrorizing the land-grabbers. Made by William Wellman in a self-important mood, the film spends much of its time indicting injustices, much as the Henry King *Jesse James* would do, before getting down to the outlaw's heroic exploits. Almost uniquely, and in tune with Hollywood's version of the original Robin Hood, Baxter's campaign of terror is given a political dimension even if it does mean a romantic alliance with a stock heroine of the revolution (Ann Loring). KN
1936/b & w/86 min/MGM/p John W. Considine Jr./d William A. Wellman/ s William A. Wellman, Joseph Calleia, Melvin Levy/c Chester Lyons/m Herbert Stothart/lp Warner Baxter, Ann Loring, Bruce Cabot, J. Carrol Naish, Margo

Ruggles of Red Gap · The third version of this social comedy about a prim and proper English butler, Ruggles (Laughton), who is won in a poker game and brought to the turn-of-the-century American frontier by a yahooing, snorting, nouveau riche rancher, Egbert Floud. The film centres around Ruggles' adjustment to Red Gap, where he is initially treated as an aristocrat because of his manner and accent. After it is revealed that he is a butler, Ruggles decides to dispense with the past and declare his independence. He embraces the democratic world of Red Gap and opens up a restaurant, the Anglo-American Grill. McCarey uses Ruggles' transformation into an American entrepreneur to provide a skilful but complacent homage to American egalitarianism and individualism. In the process he satirizes, in 30s Hollywood style, the pretensions and snobbery of the town's 'civilized' elite. The film's most famous set-piece is Ruggles' eloquent, profoundly-felt recitation of the Gettysburg Address to the awed reaction of a crowd of ten-gallon-hatted ranch-hands. It's a stirring scene, successfully arousing patriotic sentiment from the most sceptical of viewers. LQ
1935/b & w/91 min/PAR/p Arthur Hornblow Jr./d Leo McCarey/s Walter De Leon, Harlan Thompson/c Alfred Gilks/ m Ralph Rainger/lp Charles Laughton, Mary Boland, Charlie Ruggles, Zasu Pitts, Roland Young

Run for Cover · In this story of a young tearaway (Derek) who refuses the advice of a gunfighter-turned-sheriff (Cagney) and turns to a life of crime before meeting a violent end at the hands of his father-figure, Ray explores, in a Western context, the world of the young outsider, an area which he had already made peculiarly his own in *Knock on Any Door* (which also starred Derek) and the better known *Rebel Without a Cause*. Considerably less flamboyant and baroque than *Johnny Guitar*, which it succeeded, it is also rather more kinetic and violent than the almost elegiac *The Lusty Men*. JP
1954/93 min/Pine-Thomas Prods – PAR/ p William H. Pine, William C. Thomas/ d Nicholas Ray/s Winston Miller/c Daniel Fapp/m Howard Jackson/lp James Cagney, Viveca Lindfors, John Derek, Grant Withers, Ernest Borgnine

Run of the Arrow · In Fuller's intricate drama of national and ethnic allegiance and identity, Irish Virginian infantryman O'Meara (Steiger) wounds Yankee Lt Driscoll (Meeker) with the last bullet of the Civil War. The emotionally displaced O'Meara joins the Sioux after surviving the 'run of the arrow' thanks to rescue by Yellow Moccasin, with whom he settles down to find home and nation. He is attached as scout to the project to build Fort Abraham Lincoln, but the liberal commanding officer is killed by Crazy Wolf, whom O'Meara in turn submits to the run, which is violated when the combative Lt Driscoll wounds the Indian. Driscoll assumes command, and relocates the fort. The Sioux wipe out the development, and the captured Driscoll is put out of his misery with O'Meara's souvenir bullet. In an ambiguous ending, O'Meara leaves the Sioux, together with his wife and adopted child, but a caption advises 'The end of this story can only be written by you.' The film's liberal critique of US militarism has not prevented it from asserting a final 'difference' between 'American' and 'Indian' identities. PD
1957/85 min/Globe Enterprises – RKO/ p/d/s Samuel Fuller/c Joseph Biroc/ m Victor Young/lp Rod Steiger, Sarita Montiel, Brian Keith, Ralph Meeker, Charles Bronson

S

Santa Fe Trail · An astonishingly partisan account of events in Kansas leading up to the Civil War, and a film which must go a long way towards undermining Warners' reputation as the most liberal studio of the New Deal era. Flynn is Jeb Stuart, later to become a Confederate hero and first encountered at

West Point, where he condescends mightily to an argumentative northerner arguing for emancipation. He is then posted to Kansas, with his buddy George Custer (Ronald Reagan in a role Flynn himself would play with more dash the following year). Here a bloodthirsty agitator named John Brown (Raymond Massey) keeps stirring up trouble by rescuing from slavery blacks who ought to be perfectly happy as they are. Brown's activities also interfere with the efforts of a tycoon, the father of Flynn's fiancée (De Havilland), who is building a railroad from Leavenworth to Santa Fe (hence the title). Brown's career as a troublemaker is brought to an abrupt halt amidst stirring action at the battle of Harper's Ferry, after which he is summarily hanged. Audiences must have wondered why the Civil War took place after all. EB
1940/b & w/110 min/WB/p Robert Fellows/d Michael Curtiz/s Robert Buckner/c Sol Polito/m Max Steiner/lp Errol Flynn, Olivia De Havilland, Raymond Massey, Ronald Reagan, Alan Hale

Santee · A fine, classically-styled Western which marries the obsessional motif of Boetticher's *Comanche Station* to an almost biblical overview of human endeavour that derives from Peckinpah's *Ride the High Country*. The first half follows relatively conventional lines as an orphaned boy (Michael Burns) swears revenge on a bounty hunter (Glenn Ford) who guns down the outlaw father he had supposed to be a rancher. Predictably switching to hero-worship when he realizes that Ford is driven by an obsessive hatred of outlaws following the murder of his own son ten years earlier, Burns settles happily into a recreated family circle with Ford and his wife (Dana Wynter). At which point, keyed by a resonant exchange between sheriff and bounty hunter ('Isn't that account square by now?' – 'I don't keep the books'), the film's inner tensions screw up a notch, unexpectedly evolving into an inexorable retribution as Ford, belatedly relinquishing his claims to the divine right of revenge, sees it assumed with tragic results by his substitute son. TMi
1972/93 min/Vagabond/p Deno Paoli, Edward Platt/d Gary Nelson/s Brand Bell/c Donald Morgan/m Don Randi/lp Glenn Ford, Michael Burns, Dana Wynter, Jay Silverheels, Harry Townes

The Searchers · Ex-Confederate Ethan Edwards (Wayne) returns to his brother's

Dorothy Jordan, John Wayne, Pippa Scott, Lana Wood, Walter Coy in The Searchers

house on the Texas frontier in 1868. Neither cavalry officer nor community leader, possibly a criminal, he is John Ford's first anti-hero. A suppressed love is implied between Ethan and his brother's wife – unthinkable in earlier Ford – but brother, wife and a son are killed by Comanches, who also abduct their two daughters. The settlers give chase but soon turn back and forget – they lack the sacred cohesion of earlier Ford groups. Joined by Martin Pawley, an orphan with Cherokee blood adopted by the dead couple, Ethan finds the older girl dead and pursues the younger, Debbie, until snow covers the Indians' tracks. When he sets out again, Indian-hating Ethan plans to kill Debbie – she is old enough to have married within the tribe – and Martin follows to stop him. The two wander for five years, posing as traders, until a Mexican takes them to Chief Scar, one of whose wives is Debbie. She wants to stay with her people, Ethan tries to shoot her and Martin intervenes. Ethan is wounded by a Comanche but he and Martin escape, eventually arriving home to find Martin's sweetheart Laurie marrying another man – the rivals fight and the wedding is called off. A cavalry officer reports that Scar is camped nearby – Martin sneaks in alone to save Debbie and kills Scar as the rangers attack. Ethan rides down a terrified Debbie but lifts her up as he did long ago and takes her home. Martin rejoins Laurie but Ethan, for whom there is no one and no home, rides off.

The Searchers' stunning colour and monu-

mental vistas are perhaps the most beautiful in cinema but belong inseparably to its fictional world. Max Steiner's score, among Hollywood's best, is so integral to the action that it's rarely noticed. Wayne maps Ethan so closely to his own gestures that it seems non-acting. A world is created, it lives and breathes, but it's filled with contradictions and unanswered questions. This engages and moves the viewer more than smoothed-over films do. BH
1956/119 min/C.V. Whitney Pictures – WB/p Merian C. Cooper/d John Ford/s Frank S. Nugent/c Winton C. Hoch/m Max Steiner/lp John Wayne, Jeffrey Hunter, Vera Miles, Ward Bond, Natalie Wood, John Qualen, Olive Carey, Henry Brandon, Ken Curtis, Harry Carey Jr., Hank Worden

Sergeant Rutledge · One of Ford's latter-day atonements for his history of racial stereotyping, this has Woody Strode, long-serving Top Sergeant in one of two black cavalry regiments formed during the years of reconstruction after the Civil War, charged with raping and murdering a white girl. With his innocence manifest, the courtroom scenes in which he is defended by his lieutenant (Jeffrey Hunter) are fairly statutory, propped up by awkward injections of comedy and melodrama. But the flashback sequences, involving stirring bursts of cavalry action and Indian fighting as Strode's record is evoked in his defence, are Ford at his best. An unintentional irony underlies the fact that Sergeant Rutledge's heroism is thus established at the expense of the red man, but the film's hero undoubtedly – and magnificently – acquires epic status. As Strode himself commented, 'You never seen a Negro come off a mountain like John Wayne before.' And although the script is inclined to skim the surface of its theme, one superbly gothic sequence – blonde Constance Towers suddenly confronted by Strode in a storm-tossed encounter at a remote way station – accurately pinpoints fear of black sexuality as what the fuss is all about. TMi

1960/111 min/WB/*p* Willis Goldbeck, Patrick Ford/*d* John Ford/*s* James Warner Bellah, Willis Goldbeck/*c* Bert Glennon/ *m* Howard Jackson/*lp* Jeffrey Hunter, Constance Towers, Woody Strode, Willis Bouchey, Billie Burke

Seven Brides for Seven Brothers · The plot is essentially a parable about the civilizing effect of women on the frontier. Seven brothers live like pigs in a hovel in the wilds of Oregon in the 1850s. The eldest (Howard Keel) takes a bride (Jane Powell). Convinced, after initial resistance to her influence, that women have something to offer, the remaining brothers kidnap girls from the village and, by the end of winter, have persuaded them to marry. The number 'Sobbin' Women' (drawing a deliberate parallel with the rape of the Sabine women) is an uncomfortable joke about how when women say no they really mean yes. But the real spirit of the film is all in favour of manners and respect. And the singing and (especially) the dancing are splendid. The choreography in the barn-raising sequence is simply spectacular. 'Goin' Courtin'', 'Bless Your Beautiful Hide' and 'Wonderful, Wonderful Day' are among the more memorable numbers. EB

1954/104 min/MGM/*p* Jack Cummings/

Six brides in Seven Brides for Seven Brothers

d Stanley Donen/*s* Albert Hackett, Frances Goodrich, Dorothy Kingsley/*c* George Folsey/*songs* Gene de Paul, Johnny Mercer/*ch* Michael Kidd/*lp* Howard Keel, Jane Powell, Jeff Richards, Russ Tamblyn, Howard Petrie

Seven Men from Now · The first of the series of extraordinary Westerns directed by Budd Boetticher and starring Randolph Scott, most often written by Burt Kennedy and produced (after this initial entry, which was backed by John Wayne's Batjac company) by Harry Joe Brown for Ranown, the company he owned with Scott. Although *Seven Men from Now* looks a little like a rough sketch for the brilliance that would emerge in later, neater works like *Ride Lonesome*, *The Tall T* and *Comanche Station*, it is by no means an inconsiderable work in itself. Scott plays Ben Stride (the first of a series of grim character names he will bear in the series), a vengeance-obsessed man on the trail of the gang who killed his wife during their robbery of a Wells Fargo station. In the desert while tracking the seven murderers, Stride falls in with an eastern couple secretly transporting a gold shipment, and the group is joined by a pair of outlaws – John Larch and Lee Marvin – who are after the gold. Tensions ride high within the band of travellers, and Scott has to take over the protection of the woman (Gail Russell) when her weak husband is killed, and it all resolves itself with an inevitable gunfight between Scott and the semi-psychotic Marvin. The ending, in which it is suggested the hero will be able to settle down with the woman he has won, is more conventional, less interesting than the tragic/ironic finales of the later films, in which the inflexible Scott character must continue his exile from society even if he has fulfilled his self-imposed mission. KN

1956/78 min/Batjac – WB/*p* Andrew V. McLaglen, Robert E. Morrison/*d* Budd Boetticher/*s* Burt Kennedy/*c* William H. Clothier/*m* Henry Vars/*lp* Randolph Scott, Gail Russell, Lee Marvin, John Larch, Walter Reed, Donald Barry

Shane · Shane is often taken to be a distillation of the whole Western genre, particularly as it was developed by John Ford. But despite its self-consciously mythic qualities, the film has a sophisticated historical content. Though it refers directly to no specific time or place, the film clearly alludes to the Johnson County range war in Wyoming in 1892, an episode that figures more explicitly

Alan Ladd, Brandon De Wilde in Shane

in *Heaven's Gate*. More importantly, *Shane* is built around a sophisticated understanding of the social processes of American history. Its central problem is the shift from one historical stage (pastoralism) to another (small farming), and its core sequence is a moonlight debate (on July 4th) in which spokesmen for the two stages state their case. As a synthesis, *Shane* is virtually self-contained. But it is also riddled with internal tensions, which Clint Eastwood lays bare in his 're-make', *Pale Rider*. EC

1952/118 min/PAR/*p/d* George Stevens/ *s* A.B. Guthrie Jr./*c* Loyal Griggs/*m* Victor Young/*lp* Alan Ladd, Jean Arthur, Van Heflin, Brandon De Wilde, Emile Meyer, Ben Johnson, Jack Palance

The Sheepman · Marshall's nonchalant comedy casts Ford as the tough, cigar-chewing Jakob Lieblich, who is determined to set up as a sheep farmer in Powder Valley's cattle country, ruled by the villainous rancher Nielson, whose tomboyish girlfriend (MacLaine) eventually becomes the hero's accomplice and lover. The tone is set in the opening scenes as Ford coolly orders a glass of milk in the saloon and then matter of factly picks a fight with Jumbo (Shaughnessy), the town bully, in the local eatery: he flicks ash into Jumbo's drink, stirs it with a cigar and stubs it out in Jumbo's plate of food before beating him up, just to establish his credentials as a man not to be trifled with. The final shoot-out on Nielsen's ranch is a professionally staged piece with

some good stuntwork. With this picture Ford began a series of comedies often directed by Marshall (*Imitation General*, *The Gazebo*, *It Started with a Kiss*). Marshall's blend of slapstick and action foreshadowed the more sophisticated and less reverent approach to the genre by Burt Kennedy, who found in James Garner both a more urbane and urban development of Ford's middle-American comedy persona. PW
1958/91 min/MGM/p Edmund Grainger/ d George Marshall/s James Edward Grant, William Bowers/c Robert Bronner/m Jeff Alexander/lp Glenn Ford, Shirley Mac-Laine, Leslie Nielsen, Edgar Buchanan, Mickey Shaughnessy, Slim Pickens

The Sheriff of Fractured Jaw · It's an odd Western indeed which begins with Robert Morley as the lord of an English stately home, and indeed this is that rarity, a British-made Western. Kenneth More is Morley's son, and the heir to the family firm of gunsmiths. In order to drum up business, it's suggested he goes out West: 'There's some frightful female there called Jessie James and she's shooting at everyone.' Cut to a stagecoach going across the plains, with, on top, Sid James as a drunk, in a not-so-dry run for his role as the Rumpole Kid in *Carry On Cowboy* (1966). More, while remaining attached to his bowler hat and brolly, is fascinated with the West, especially with its most attractive citizen, Jayne Mansfield. She, in a neat role-reversal, teaches him to shoot, but hankers for the sophistication of the east. By the end of the film More has conquered the timidity endemic in the heroes of parody Westerns and has domesticated the Wild West, to the extent of training an Indian to serve him tea. EB
1958/103 min/FOX/p Daniel M. Angel/ d Raoul Walsh/s Arthur Dales/c Otto Heller/m Robert Farnon/lp Kenneth More, Jayne Mansfield, Bruce Cabot, Robert Morley, Henry Hull

She Wore a Yellow Ribbon · The second of three John Ford cavalry films with John Wayne, the only one in colour and with a voice-over narration. Its first words – 'Custer is dead' – link it to the fictional massacre in *Fort Apache*. It takes place the same year as that film (1876) but seems much later since Wayne, once more a captain, is now an old man about to retire. His last patrol is 'hamstrung' by two women he must escort to a stagecoach. Hence he can do nothing when he sees Arapaho on the march, arrives too late to save a patrol and

later an outpost from Indian attack, and cannot stop a delivery of rifles to the Indians or their murder, in one case preceded by torture, of the whites who brought them. He leaves two squads to cover his withdrawal and bitterly returns to the fort. The Fordian staging of failure is as usual but it results here in subtle visual narrative. We see a series of effects – an Indian community on the move, wounded men telling of a massacre, an outpost with more wounded and a burning stagecoach – but not the actions that caused them. Wayne is forcibly retired but heads back in civilian clothes to the men he left behind, since joined by a relief troop. He goes to the Indian camp to make peace with the chief but finds that his Indian friend, like himself, has been replaced by young leaders and that it is too late to avoid war. Wayne and his troops run off the tribes' pony herd, however, and thereby prevent conflict. Astounding but true – this kiddie-matinée cavalry film has no Indian-killing! Much less subtle, alas, are the squabbles of Harry Carey Jr., Joanne Dru and John Agar (the most puerile love interest in Ford), the drinking and brawling of Victor McLaglen, and the latter's verbal sparring with Wayne, inspired by the Capt. Flagg–Sgt. Quirt exchanges in Stallings' and Maxwell Anderson's play *What Price Glory?* The film's colour, a homage to the Remington style, is, however, glorious: the earth hues of Monument Valley, the blue and gold uniforms, red sunsets on a desert cemetery and, most famously, the darkly saturated colours of troops, wagons and sky in a thunderstorm. The ostensible theme, as in much postwar Ford, is leadership, the price of which, as in *Fort Apache*, is loneliness and celibacy. Wayne is here a widower whose daughters and wife have died; like many Ford heroes, he talks to her grave. Only the third cavalry film, *Rio Grande*, treats the leader's relationship with a living woman. BH
1949/103 min/Argosy – RKO/p John Ford, Merian C. Cooper/d John Ford/s Frank S. Nugent, Laurence Stallings/c Winton C. Hoch/m Richard Hageman/lp John Wayne, Joanne Dru, John Agar, Ben Johnson, Harry Carey Jr., Victor McLaglen

The Shooting · Roger Corman provided minimal finance ($150,000) for his two protégés, Hellman and Nicholson, to make two Westerns in the Utah desert. After a gruelling seven weeks, they returned with the footage for *The Shooting* and *Ride in the Whirlwind*, the two most extraordinary

Westerns of the 6os. *The Shooting* is an hallucinatory revenge story with Oates as a bounty hunter hired by Perkins to hunt down an unnamed man who turns out to be his twin brother. Like everyone who sees his double, the experience proves fatal for the hero, although Oates' character is more dogged than heroic. On their trek through the desert they are joined by an enigmatic, black-clad gunslinger (Nicholson) and a naive cowpoke (Hutchins). The film reduces social reality to a minimum, the characters lost in time and space, making this the only Beckettian Western on record. Hellman introduces his characters via extreme close-ups (a thigh and a holster for Nicholson, a gloved hand shooting a horse for Perkins) edited so as to produce a complete loss of spatial relationships between the characters. The claustrophobic, dreamlike atmosphere is maintained throughout the film in spite of the vast spaces that serve as the location for the action. The terse lines appear spoken for their rhythmic and tonal qualities rather than as communicative dialogue, suggesting each individual is imprisoned in his or her own isolation which it would be pointless, even dangerous to try and breach. Hellman refuses any idealization and sentimentality as he depicts a barbarically cynical world in which one can only hope to survive for as long as possible. The film was vehemently rejected by both critics and audiences in the US at the time, as was its less austere companion piece. PW
1966/81 min/Santa Clara/p Jack Nicholson, Monte Hellman/d Monte Hellman/s Adrien Joyce/c Gregory Sandor/m Richard Markowitz/lp Jack Nicholson, Warren Oates, Millie Perkins, Will Hutchins

The Shootist · In his farewell movie the dying Wayne plays the cancer-ridden gunfighter J. B. Books, who spends his final week in Carson City, where he prepares a birthday shoot-out that will clear up town and/or save him further pain. Developing a rapport with his landlady Bond Rogers and her son Gillom, he despatches murderous intruders, jockeys with the heartless town marshal, and resists attempts by the press to exploit his presence. In the finale he kills three local hard men, but is killed in turn by the bartender – whom Gillom then shoots with Books' gun, before discarding it with Books' dying approval. The unsuspecting killer walks away as the crowds arrive. This measured narrative, largely limited to the taut pathos of the daily round, features

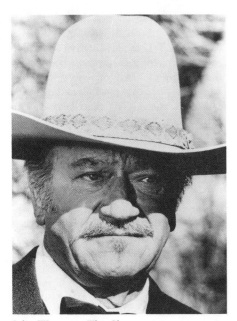

John Wayne in The Shootist

Wayne's most underplayed and poignant role as the honourable gunfighter out of place in the largely cynical modernity of the days following the death of Queen Victoria in January 1901. PD

1976/100 min/Dino de Laurentiis Corp – PAR/*p* M. J. Frankovich, William Self/*d* Don Siegel/*s* Miles Hood Swarthout, Scott Hale/*c* Bruce Surtees/*m* Elmer Bernstein/*lp* John Wayne, Lauren Bacall, Ron Howard, James Stewart, John Carradine

Silverado · A late-entry Western with references to its antecedents, *Silverado* pits four renegade men allied with homesteaders against a cattle rancher and his cohorts. The idealized but ironic town name/film title represents the oppositions of the two groups. The homesteaders want land where they can settle down, farm and raise families. For them Silverado is a communal goal achieved after long travel and hard work. For McKendrick, the boss of the territory, and Cobbs, his sheriff and partner, Silverado is a power base and source of income; outsiders must be destroyed. One of the four, Paden, Cobb's former henchman, is protagonist and moral norm for the film. Initially not wanting to get involved, he ultimately joins the beneficent forces of civilization against corrupt power. Photographed against a background of the town's white church during his shoot-out with Cobbs, Paden remains in Silverado (as sheriff) when his three companions strike out for a further frontier – California. Raising issues of the quality of law and life in the West,

racial prejudice and responsibility for others, *Silverado* employs the gamut of Western icons and conventions to show that in the 80s the genre is wounded but still living. JD

1985/132 min/COL/*p*/*d* Lawrence Kasdan/*s* Mark and Lawrence Kasdan/*c* John Bailey/*m* Bruce Broughton/*lp* Kevin Kline, Brian Dennehy, Scott Glenn, Danny Glover, Linda Hunt, John Cleese

Silver Lode · An ambitious B-Western with a political dimension, as the frenzy of Dan Duryea's lynch mob is made to recall that of Senator McCarthy's witch hunts. John Payne is unjustly accused of murder; only a telegraph message, agonizingly delayed, will allow him to escape the posse and expose the real killer. Although stereotyped as the director who had to fight against every hardship to get his films made– short schedules, pulp screenplays, unsympathetic producers, limited resources – Dwan here seems to have been given a freer hand than usual, and has not only an interesting cast to work with but the excellent cinematography of John Alton. KN

1954/80 min/RKO/*p* Benedict Bogeaus/*d* Allan Dwan/*s* Karen De Wolfe/*c* John Alton/*m* Louis Forbes/*lp* John Payne, Lizabeth Scott, Dan Duryea, Dolores Moran, Emile Meyer, Harry Carey Jr.

Silver River · Set in the context of the development of the mining industry in the post-war West, *Silver River* documents the effect upon western economy of the devaluation of silver when the federal government shifted to a gold standard in the 1870s and 1880s. It's a film about money. During the Civil War, the hero, Union officer Mike McComb (Flynn), sets fire to a payroll wagon in order to prevent its capture by Confederate troops, an action for which he is tried and dishonourably discharged. The innocent hero's earlier, well-intentioned destruction of money is answered later by his selfish accumulation and cynical use of it in an attempt to secure personal power and freedom. McComb's attempts, as empire builder, to impose himself upon the landscape are seen initially in the gambling casino sign with his name on it and culminate in his construction of a castle in the desert. In reply to the architect who objects that his proposed marble mansion is at odds with the rugged terrain, McComb answers, 'I don't intend to blend with the landscape; I intend to fill it.' Compared by his philosophizing conscience, town drunk and lawyer Plato

Beck (Mitchell), to Caesar and King David, McComb can only redeem himself from the European and Old Testament vanities of power and ambition by accommodating himself to the landscape and to the democratic principles its middle-class inhabitants uphold. Losing his wealth in the byzantine economics of the 'Silver Wars', McComb assumes responsibility for the mass unemployment his stock manipulations have created, wins the loyalty of the town's miners, and selflessly leads them to victory over corrupt and selfish men like himself who have gained control over his former empire. JB

1948/b & w/110 min/WB/*p* Owen Crump/*d* Raoul Walsh/*s* Stephen Longstreet, Harriet Frank Jr./*c* Sid Hickox/*m* Max Steiner/*lp* Errol Flynn, Ann Sheridan, Thomas Mitchell, Bruce Bennett

Sledge · The under-rated Morrow's eccentric European Western with Hollywood leading actors offers a grotesquely stylized version of the genre tinged with bitterness, in the manner of Dennis Hopper in *The Last Movie*. Morrow also precedes Coppola's mannerist storytelling style, most evident in *One from the Heart*. The ballad structure of the tale, underscored by a relentlessly recurring song about gold and greed, is reinforced by a shooting style in which composition and camera movement at times seem to take on a life of their own, as in Weaver's death, where his body and the camera circle in opposite directions as he falls from his horse. The plot concerns a gold bullion robbery staged in a nightmarish prison in which one of the demented inmates howls at

James Garner in Sledge

a naked lightbulb the way a wolf howls at the moon. The gang then disintegrates as they cheat and murder each other for the loot. The final hallucinatory sequences are set in an apparently deserted Mexican village where Morrow mixes sexual sadism with surreal anti-clericalism as the wounded Garner straps a crucifix to his broken arm to shoot his accomplices. The movie refuses its characters any sense of heroism, optimism or even hope in this fascinating though flawed mixture of uncompromising ethnography and operatic stylishness. PW
1970/92 min/Dino De Laurentiis Cinematografica/p Dino De Laurentiis/ d Vic Morrow/s Vic Morrow, Frank Kowalsky/c Luigi Kuveiller/m Gianni Ferrio/lp James Garner, Dennis Weaver, John Marley, Claude Akins, Laura Antonelli

Soldier Blue · Like *The Wild Bunch*, *Soldier Blue* is usually remembered for its violence, but is a considerably inferior film. Bergen and Strauss are the sole survivors of a Cheyenne attack and are attempting to reach an army outpost when they become caught up in the events leading to a massacre of the Indians by the Army. The massacre itself is based on those at Sand Creek (1864) and Wounded Knee (1890), and Nelson himself has stated that he intended a parallel with My Lai. Unfortunately these admirable sentiments and the attempt to put the historical

record straight vis-à-vis the Indians are marred by the film itself, which undercuts itself by opening on a slaughter *by* the Indians, and then dissipates much of its force in a soppy, soft-focus idyll. Too often the film lapses into cliché and stridency, and, most importantly, it lacks any real *explanation* for the final massacre, which it turns into a *mere* exercise in bloodletting of the kind it purports to condemn. JP
1970/114 min/Avco-Embassy/p Gabriel Katzka, Harold Loeb/d Ralph Nelson/ s John Gay/c Robert Hauser/m Roy Budd/ lp Candice Bergen, Peter Strauss, Donald Pleasance, Bob Carraway, Jorge Rivero

Son of Paleface · After co-writing the box-office hit *The Paleface* (1948), a parody of Owen Wister's *The Virginian*, and débuting as director on Hope's *The Lemon Drop Kid* (1951), Tashlin was put in charge of this superior sequel in which the Hope-Russell team are strengthened by Roy Rogers and Trigger. Hope is the cowardly, fast-talking and insufferably vain Harvard man, Potter Jr., who arrives in the West to claim his inheritance. He falls for Russell, an outlaw on the run from Government agent Rogers. The plot is merely an excuse to string Hope's one-liners together but Tashlin, an inspired cartoonist responsible for some of Jerry Lewis' best work, matches the comedian's verbal wit with a truly anarchic sense of visual humour that respects neither

the rules of the genre nor those of physical probability, treating live action as if it were animation. Trigger particularly comes in for some irreverent gags. Surprisingly, Tashlin didn't permit himself (or wasn't allowed) to lampoon Russell's image the way he did with Jayne Mansfield a few years later, and the actress emerges as an accomplished comedienne well able to hold her own in the face of the scene-stealing Hope. The movie repeats the hit song of the original, 'Buttons and Bows', and adds a few new numbers, including 'Wing Ding Tonight' and a rendering of 'A Four-Legged Friend' that should have meant the retirement of Trigger and Rogers from the movie business. PW
1952/95 min/Hope Enterprises – PAR/ p Robert L. Welch/d Frank Tashlin/s Frank Tashlin, Robert L. Welch, Joseph Quillan/c Harry J. Wild/m Lyn Murray/ lp Bob Hope, Jane Russell, Roy Rogers, Trigger, Lloyd Corrigan, Iron Eyes Cody

Springfield Rifle · The arrival of the Springfield rifle and the development of counter-espionage techniques by the army are the bases of this Gary Cooper vehicle. In his first film after *High Noon* he plays a Union officer, Major 'Lex' Kearny, who goes underground in order to infiltrate the gang that is stealing Union horses in Colorado and selling them to the Confederacy. De Toth makes particularly effective use of the moving camera and the locations are spectacular; the terse script was based on a story by Sloan Nibley, who wrote many Roy Rogers scripts. Deceitfulness and deviousness were unusual characteristics for a Western hero in the early 50s; when operating under cover Cooper even has to deceive his own wife. Is it too fanciful to suggest that the film relates to the 'end justifies the means' politics peddled by McCarthyism at the time? JP
1952/93 min/WB/p Louis F. Edelman/ d André de Toth/s Charles Marquis Warren, Frank Davis/c Edwin Du Par/m Max Steiner/lp Gary Cooper, Phyllis Thaxter, David Brian, Paul Kelly

The Squaw Man (The White Man) · Originally *The Squaw Man* was a melodramatic stage play by Edwin Milton Royle, first produced in 1905. A heady brew based on racial, sexual, class and national differences, the story concerns James Wynnegate, an Englishman nobleman who comes out west to escape a sexual and financial scandal. In Wyoming he makes an enemy of the rustler Cash Hawkins (a role first played on stage by William S. Hart). Wynnegate marries an

Candice Bergen in Soldier Blue

Roland Young, Warner Baxter, Lupe Velez in The Squaw Man *(1931)*

Indian girl, who in turn kills Hawkins and then commits suicide, thus releasing Wynnegate to marry his English sweetheart, who has arrived with the news that the scandal is now happily resolved. DeMille was so attached to this story that he filmed it three times. His first version is often given credit as the first feature-length Western and the first feature shot in Hollywood. In truth it was neither, but its success did much for the confidence of both genre and town. EB
1914/b & w/6 reels/Lasky/p/d/s Cecil B. DeMille, Oscar C. Apfel/c Alfred Gandolfi/lp Dustin Farnum, Monroe Salisbury, Winifred Kingston, Red Wing, Billy Elmer
1918/b & w/6 reels/Famous Players – Lasky/p/d Cecil B. DeMille/s Beulah Marie Dix/c Alvin Wyckoff/lp Elliott

Dexter, Ann Little, Katherine MacDonald, Jack Holt, Thurston Hall
1931/b & w/106 min/MGM/p/d Cecil B. DeMille/s Lucien Hubbard, Lenore Coffee/c Harold Rosson/m Herbert Stothart/lp Warner Baxter, Lupe Velez, Eleanor Boardman, Paul Cavanagh, Charles Bickford

Stagecoach · *The* official Western classic, John Ford's drama greatly helped revive the fortunes of the A-feature Western after the doldrums of the mid-30s. A whore, a gambler and a drunken doctor, later joined by outlaw the Ringo Kid (John Wayne), travel west in the title conveyance with a dishonest banker, a whiskey drummer and the well-bred wife of a cavalry officer. Social tensions among the passengers – including the arrest of vengeance-bent Ringo – propel the plot as tirelessly as the horses pull the coach. The feared Apaches appear suddenly and attack spectacularly, until the cavalry arrives. The wife, who has given birth with Doc Boone's aid, survives but the gambler dies – his aristocratic values have no place in a democratic West. Ringo kills Luke Plummer and his two brothers (with three bullets) in a shoot-out in Lordsburg. The sheriff looks the other way as Dallas – the whore – and Ringo go off to settle the West. Bracingly modern in all this – Brechtian in fact – is the cheerful coward Buck (Andy Devine), the mannerless stage driver who thinks only

of food. He asks the sheriff, 'Do you think I ought to charge Mrs Mallory's baby half fare?' The exteriors, shot in Monument Valley, transformed the look of the Western forevermore. The interiors at Dry Fork and Apache Wells were innovatively shot with a low-angle camera that required sets with ceilings two years before *Citizen Kane*. The film also made a star of unknown John Wayne, lending the postwar Western its most important player. BH
1939/b & w/97 min/Walter Wanger Prods – UA/p Walter Wanger/d John Ford/s Dudley Nichols/c Bert Glennon/m Richard Hageman, Franke Harling, John Leipold, Leo Shuken, Louis Gruenberg/lp John Wayne, Claire Trevor, Thomas Mitchell, John Carradine, Andy Devine, George Bancroft, Berton Churchill, Louise Platt, Donald Meek

The Stalking Moon · This is Mulligan's only Western, perhaps not surprisingly for a director who has always seemed most at home indoors or in the city. Here Peck plays a cavalry scout retiring from the Army in Arizona to his remote ranch in New Mexico. Reluctantly he agrees to take along a white woman, recently released from Indian captivity, and her young son. Gradually he realizes that they are being pursued by the boy's father, an Apache chief. Mulligan has here reduced a familiar narrative device – the pursuit – to its barest essentials and the film seems to be aspiring to the level of allegory, telling the story of a mythic struggle between pioneer and Indian for the soul of the little half-breed boy. Unfortunately the film is much too talky and static in its first part, and the climactic stalk is confusingly presented, thus robbing it of much of its excitement. JP
1968/109 min/Stalking Moon Co – National General/p Alan J. Pakula/d Robert Mulligan/s Alvin Sargent/c Charles B. Lang Jr./m Fred Karlin/lp Gregory Peck, Eva Marie Saint, Robert Forster, Noland Clay

Stranger on Horseback · Tourneur's best Westerns, like *Stars in My Crown* and *Way of a Gaucho*, exist at the very limits of the genre. Like the former this stars Joel McCrea (who also appears in *Wichita*). Here he plays a circuit judge who arrives in a small western town to find it under the thumb of cattle baron McIntire, a situation which he is determined will not last. McCrea's performance is credible and authoritative, the Mexican locations pleasingly captured in Ansco Color and Tourneur provides sensitive and

Stagecoach

atmospheric direction to match. JP
1954/66 min/Leonard Goldstein Prods –
UA/p Robert Goldstein/d Jacques
Tourneur/s Herb Meadow, Don Martin/
c Ray Rennahan/m Paul Dunlap/lp Joel
McCrea, Miroslava, John McIntire, Kevin
McCarthy, Emile Meyer

Support Your Local Gunfighter · A sequel
to the successful *Support Your Local Sheriff!*,
and a judicious example of the comedy
Western, this film has the considerable
advantage of utilizing personnel with long
and honourable association with the genuine
article. The narrative, involving an itinerant
con-man (James Garner) caught up in a feud
between rival gold-mine owners, is artificial
enough, but it works on its own terms, and is
certainly sufficiently eventful to defy brief
synopsis. The humour is not externally
imposed, but emerges from an instinct for
comic detail in treatment and characterization. Jack Elam is especially engaging as a
slow-witted drunk required by the plot to
pass himself off as a notorious gunman;
needless to say, the object of impersonation,
in the shape of a glowering, bald-wigged
Chuck Connors, subsequently appears on
the scene, bent on upholding his reputation.
An appropriate finishing touch has Elam's
character regaling the audience with the
participants' impending futures, including
the disclosure that he himself was to become
'a big star in Italian Westerns'. TP
1971/92 min/Cherokee – Brigade – UA/
p William Finnegan/d Burt Kennedy/s
James Edward Grant/c Harry Stradling
Jr./m Jack Elliott, Allyn Ferguson/lp James
Garner, Suzanne Pleshette, Jack Elam,
Chuck Connors, Harry Morgan, John
Dehner, Joan Blondell

Sutter's Gold · Based on the life of Johann
August Suter (or Sutter), a European immigrant on whose land the first golden nuggets
were found that precipitated the California
gold rush of '49. The Soviet director Sergei
Eisenstein had first shown interest in Sutter's saga, but the project for Paramount in
1930 never got beyond the script stage.
Instead James Cruze, who had directed the
silent epic *The Covered Wagon*, made it for
Universal. Falsely accused of murder, Sutter
flees to the New World. Entranced by tales
of riches for the taking he embarks on the
perilous journey to the West Coast. In
California he attempts to build a kingdom,
but his affair with a conniving Russian
countess destroys his plans when she per-
suades him to deny his workers a share in the

Ann Sheridan in Take Me to Town

newly found gold. In response they take it all
and Sutter is reduced to near poverty. The
film was a major box-office flop and nearly
bankrupted the studio. DR
1936/b & w/94 min/U/p Edmund
Grainger/d James Cruze/s Jack Kirkland,
Walter Woods, George O'Neal/c George
Robinson/m Franz Waxman/lp Edward
Arnold, Lee Tracy, Binnie Barnes, Harry
Carey, Katherine Alexander

T

Take Me to Town · Sirk described this
lovely, lighthearted Western as 'a little lyrical poem to the American Western past',
but it seems more an affectionate tribute to
the popular roots of nineteenth-century
melodrama. Even the plot of 'the preacher
and the 'dance hall girl' is borrowed from
that tradition and the film culminates in a
bravura set-piece mixing the performance of
an amateur melodrama at a village fete with
the climactic fight between hero and villain
on the edge of a rockface, with the two levels
of the action often occurring within the same
shot. Sheridan is the sassy Vermillion
O'Toole who hides from the law by getting
herself accepted as cook and housekeeper by
the widowed preacher Will Hall (Hayden)
and his three small boys. Sirk's impeccable
sense of timing and direction of actors help
turn this charming tale, derived from the
scenarist's own novel *Flame of Timberline*,
into a delightfully astute look at the narrow-
mindedness and puritanism mixed with
brashness and vitality which irrigate American popular culture at its most characteristic. PW
1953/80 min/U/p Ross Hunter/d Douglas
Sirk/s Richard Morris/c Russell Metty/
m Joseph Gershenson/lp Sterling Hayden,
Ann Sheridan, Larry Gates, Phyllis
Stanley, Philip Reed, Lane Chandler

*Maureen O'Sullivan, Randolph Scott,
Richard Boone in* The Tall T

The Tall Men · The Allinsons (Clark Gable,
Cameron Mitchell), ex-Quantrill guerrillas,
refugees from the defeated Confederacy,
ride north. Their journey is a metaphorical
transit of America, their dilemmas para-
digmatic of the choices faced by the American Everyman at the Frontier. Their
adversary and Gable's rival for Jane Russell
is the Yankee entrepreneur Nathan Stark
(Robert Ryan). Stark and the Allinsons
collaborate on a cattle-drive, in the Western's most important symbol (after the
railway) of corporate endeavour. The drive
survives Indians, Jayhawkers and vigilantes
and Gable saves Russell from suffocation by
Ryan, but however warm the film's resolution of conflict Walsh eschews a cosy
nostalgia: the collaboration of Reb and
Yankee is unstable. The several false resolutions that precede Gable and Russell's
arcadian union in Prairie Dog Creek demonstrate the provisionality of the narrative's
closure, for Stark survives, owns Montana
and as Gable says 'He won't stop there.' RC
1955/121 min/FOX/p William A. Bacher,
William B. Hawks/d Raoul Walsh/
s Sydney Boehm, Frank S. Nugent/c Leo
Tover/m Victor Young/lp Clark Gable,
Jane Russell, Robert Ryan, Cameron
Mitchell

The Tall T · In this second Western directed
by Budd Boetticher from a Burt Kennedy
script – its predecessor was *Seven Men from
Now* – Randolph Scott plays one of the
victims of a stage hold-up by a gang comprising Richard Boone and two vicious under-
lings, Henry Silva and Skip Homeier. The
murder of Scott and his two fellow-
passengers, John Hubbard as a cowardly
businessman and Maureen O'Sullivan as his
wife, is forestalled by Hubbard's attempt to
do a deal with Boone involving ransom
money. A murderous game of bluff and

Rock Hudson in Taza, Son of Cochise

Susan Clark, Robert Redford in Tell Them Willie Boy Is Here

Henry Fonda in There Was a Crooked Man...

double-bluff ensues, with Scott gradually taking command of the situation, and spreading mutual distrust among the bandits. By the aftermath of the climactic showdown between Scott and Boone, only Scott and O'Sullivan remain alive. Following a deceptively leisurely exposition, the narrative is developed with savage concision, and the psychopathic distinctiveness of the villains is played off to particular effect against Scott's reassuring air of laconic decency. TP
1956/77 min/Producers-Actors Corp – COL/*p* Harry Joe Brown/*d* Budd Boetticher/*s* Burt Kennedy/*c* Charles Lawton Jr./*m* Heinz Roemheld/ *lp* Randolph Scott, Richard Boone, Maureen O'Sullivan, Arthur Hunnicutt, Henry Silva, Skip Homeier, John Hubbard

Taza, Son of Cochise · A significant Western by Douglas Sirk (the master of melodrama), and his first film with Rock Hudson, who he later directed in three of his finest films: *Magnificent Obsession*, *Written on the Wind* and *All That Heaven Allows*. Here Hudson, in the title role, strives to see his father's dream of peace between the whites and the Indians succeed, but first he must overcome the obstacles of a cynical US cavalry and a belligerent brother. Cochise, who lives only long enough to pass on his mantle of leadership to Taza, is played by Jeff Chandler; a role he had assumed on two previous occasions. The film was originally released in 3-D. DR
1953/77 min/U/*p* Ross Hunter/*d* Douglas Sirk/*s* George Zuckerman/*c* Russell Metty/*m* Frank Skinner/*lp* Rock Hudson, Barbara Rush, Gregg Palmer, Morris Ankrum

Tell Them Willie Boy Is Here · The blacklisted Polonsky's return to direction is an

intimate and yet laconic drama of race and individualism. Returning to the reservation, Willie is refused permission to marry Lola, whose vengeful father is shot with his own weapon when he stalks the couple to a nocturnal rendezvous. A lengthy chase ensues as the disenchanted Sheriff Cooper pursues the runaways through the Mojave, taking time off to police a visit by President Taft. A member of the posse is killed, and Lola is found dead, shot through the heart. Moving ahead to pursue Willie alone, Cooper kills him in a face-off only to discover that Willie's rifle is empty. A supporting posse tries to rescue Willie's corpse from the funeral pyre ignited by Cooper's Indian helpers. This bleakly romantic film is notable for the emotional subtlety of its critique of white racism; for the restrained intensity of Blake's performance as Willie; and for the intriguing sourness of Redford's sheriff, rendered all the more complex in his troubled relationship with the Reservation Superintendent, Dr Elizabeth Arnold (Susan Clark). PD
1969/98 min/U/*p* Philip A. Waxman/*d*/*s* Abraham Polonsky/*c* Conrad Hall/*m* Dave Grusin/*lp* Robert Redford, Robert Blake, Katharine Ross, Susan Clark

Terror in a Texas Town · Over the years this has acquired a reputation as perhaps the most legendary B-Western of all. The plot, as always in the B-Western, is in outline utterly conventional; the realization is all. The local big-shot, the champagne-guzzling Sebastian Cabot, is trying to force the small farmers off their land, in this case because he's discovered oil on it. One of the farmers, a Swede, attempts resistance. The big-shot orders him killed by his henchman, a marvellously baroque conception named Johnny, a gunfighter who wears black gloves to conceal the fact that his right hand has

been shot off and replaced by a steel claw. Cabot, who understands business, likes to lecture him on how the West is changing and how it's more important to be smart than tough. The gunfighter (Ned Young) knows no other trade. Enter, in a tweed suit and derby hat, Sterling Hayden as the sea-going son of the dead Swedish farmer. Despite being warned off and beaten up, Hayden just keeps on coming and, in the bizarre but effective climax in the main street of town, skewers the gunfighter with a harpoon. EB
1958/b & w/81 min/Seltzer Films – UA/ *p* Frank Seltzer/*d* Joseph H. Lewis/*s* Ben L. Perry/*c* Ray Rennahan/*m* Gerald Fried/ *lp* Sterling Hayden, Sebastian Cabot, Carol Kelly, Victor Millan, Ned Young

There Was a Crooked Man... · A wonderfully cynical Western crossbreed that is part chain-gang melodrama, part comedy of manners, and part satire on moral do-gooders. Douglas, dangerously amiable in steel-rimmed spectacles, is brilliant as the cold-blooded outlaw – gifted with the confidence man's art of winning friends and influencing people – who polishes off a robbery by killing his last surviving accomplice, hiding the loot in a rattlesnake pit, and going happily to jail to await the moment when he can safely collect. There he becomes everybody's favourite person, an inspiration to the inmates and so helpful to Fonda's warden in his reformist zeal that the prison is finally opened, complete with hilarious tea-party entertainments, for inspection by VIPs. At which point Douglas breaks out. The twist in the tail whereby Fonda eventually makes off with the loot comes much too pat; but a script bristling with dry, civilized ironies is given full value by a marvellous supporting cast playing the gallery of fools, knaves and innocents caught up in a veritable holocaust of mayhem and murder. TMi

1970/126 min/WB/*p/d* Joseph L.
Mankiewicz/*s* David Newman, Robert
Benton/*c* Harry Stradling Jr./*m* Charles
Strouse/*lp* Kirk Douglas, Henry Fonda,
Hume Cronyn, Warren Oates, Burgess
Meredith

These Thousand Hills · This is based on A.
B. Guthrie's novel of the same name, the
third in a trilogy which began with his
Pulitzer Prize-winning *The Way West*. A
thoughtful Western, it explores such unfamiliar themes as arrivisme and social ambition in its story of Don Murray, a penniless
young man on the make in the frontier
Northwest who uses and loses his friends on
his way to the top. Although the film is a
little abstract, and even rather unclear at
times, Fleischer manages extremely well for
the most part to integrate his theme within a
good-looking, intelligently scripted, well
acted and occasionally quite spectacular
framework. JP
1958/96 min/FOX/*p* David Weisbart/
d Richard Fleischer/*s* Alfred Hayes/*c*
Charles G. Clarke/*m* Leigh Harline/*lp* Don
Murray, Richard Egan, Lee Remick,
Patricia Owens, Albert Dekker

They Died with their Boots On · Stirring,
romantic and at the same time highly
glamorized biography of George Armstrong
Custer, an irresponsible character who is
projected as a dashing, devil-may-care
soldier impatient with personal triumph and
restless in the pursuit of glory ('the greater
the odds, the greater the glory'). This large-
scale production, perfectly tuned to the
Errol Flynn persona, takes the Custer story
from his enlistment at West Point in 1857
through to his climactic 'last stand' at the
Little Big Horn in 1876. The first half of the
film moves at a stately pace, introducing
various interweaving relationships: this part
draws in some excellent montage sequences
showing Custer gaining recognition through
his reckless Civil War exploits. Once Custer
has been given command of the 7th, following the Civil War, he's seen as a more
serious, conscientious character in his new-
found role as a defender of the Indians'
rights. In fact, the relationship between the
central characters takes on a darker, more
psychological tone. Nevertheless, under the
rousing chorus of the regiment's 'Garry
Owen', the 7th Cavalry battles and hounds
the Sioux into a treaty over the Black Hills,
which Custer promises to keep free of the
encroaching white man. With some deliberate shifting of history Custer and his com-

mand eventually are forced to ride into
Sioux territory and face the combined
fighting forces of the Sioux, Cheyenne 'and
every living tribe between mountains and
great waters'. It's Flynn and Warners first,
Custer and history second, but the final
result is still a fine action brew. TV
1941/b & w/140 min/WB/*p* Hal B. Wallis/
d Raoul Walsh/*s* Wally Kline, Aeneas
MacKenzie/*c* Bert Glennon/*m* Max
Steiner/*lp* Errol Flynn, Olivia De Havilland, Arthur Kennedy, Charley Grapewin,
Gene Lockhart, Anthony Quinn

3 Godfathers · A remake of Ford's favourite
silent Western, *Marked Men* (1919), to
whose star Harry Carey *3 Godfathers* is
dedicated, and whose namesake son it introduces. Three bank robbers escape from
Welcome, Arizona, into the desert, pursued
by Sheriff B. Sweet. They lose water and
horses, and discover an abandoned wagon
where the sheriff's niece – her missing 'tenderfoot' husband having wrecked the local
water supply – gives birth and dies. Godfathers and baby head for New Jerusalem,
pursued all the more vehemently by the
posse, who mistakenly blame them for the
tragedy. Only the hallucinating Robert
Hightower survives the journey, thanks to
the help of a miraculous pair of donkeys
which enable him to deliver the infant to
town on Christmas Day. He receives a
minimum jail sentence, keeps the child, and
once more intrigues the banker's daughter.
The increasing anti-realism of the film,
abetted by some evocative desert cinematography, reworks the story of the Magi with
sentiment and humour, while the masculine
preoccupations of the genre are satirized
in the comic baby-minding sequences. PD
1948/106 min/Argosy – MGM/*p* John Ford,
Merian C. Cooper/*d* John Ford/*s* Laurence
Stallings, Frank S. Nugent/*c* Winton C.
Hoch/*m* Richard Hageman/*lp* John
Wayne, Pedro Armendariz, Harry Carey
Jr., Ward Bond

3:10 to Yuma · Daves' suspense Western,
like the earlier *High Noon*, deals with the
psychological tensions of characters in waiting. A drought-stricken Arizona rancher,
Dan Evans, accepts a commission to escort
outlaw Ben Wade to jail in Yuma. In a drama
which relies as much on the terse flow of
dialogue as on the outer drama of physical
action, tension mounts as, faced by the
Wade gang, small-town self-interest and
cowardice are exposed. Held in the sensual
claustrophobia of a hotel bridal suite, the

charismatic Wade attempts to seduce Evans
with a complex mixture of derision and
material suggestion, in a conscious working
of the Faust myth. After the characteristic
spatial and geographical complexities of the
siege and of the journey to the station, Wade
agrees to join the train with Evans. In a lyric
adumbration of the central metaphors of the
genre, the film, which opened with images of
cracked earth and of outlaws shrouded in
dust, culminates in cloudy images of locomotive vapour and a final shower of rain
which celebrates the garden yet to bloom. PD
1957/b & w/92 min/COL/*p* David Heilweil/
d Delmer Daves/*s* Halsted Welles/
c Charles Lawton Jr./*m* George Duning/
lp Glenn Ford, Van Heflin, Felicia Farr,
Richard Jaeckel

A Time for Dying · After spending the best
part of a decade on *Arruza*, his definitive
bullfighting film, Budd Boetticher came out
of the wilderness and dashed off this film-
out-of-time for producer-star Audie
Murphy, which stands as his last film as a
director. It's a grimly comic little movie
about a young fast gun (Richard Lapp) en
route to an early grave, which must have
appealed to Murphy, the boy war hero who
found peace-time movie stardom so unsatis-
factory that he launched a Mike Hammer-
style crusade against drug pushers and the
Mafia with predictably unheroic results and
who was dead barely two years after this, his
final film. Although Murphy appears as Jesse
James and Victor Jory is flamboyantly insane
as the senile but legendary Judge Roy Bean,
A Time for Dying is more concerned with the
absurd losers who didn't carve names for
themselves on the frontier. Lapp is the
rabbit-like Cass Bunning, and his eventual

Leora Dana, Glenn Ford in 3:10 to Yuma

killer is the equally absurd Billy Pimple (Bob Random), whose no-less-silly real name is William C. Cootes and of whom it is remarked 'he ain't Billy the Kid but he sure wants to be.' KN
1969/90 min/Fipco/p Audie Murphy/d/s Budd Boetticher/c Lucien Ballard/m Harry Betts/lp Richard Lapp, Anne Randall, Bob Random, Victor Jory, Audie Murphy

The Tin Star · Scripted by Dudley Nichols, writer of *Stagecoach*, *The Tin Star* is more centrally built around domestic and community themes than Anthony Mann's other Westerns. The protagonist (Henry Fonda), an ex-lawman embittered by the death of his wife and now a bounty hunter, is a characteristic Mann hero; the process of his regeneration, however, sets him somewhat apart. This comes about through his becoming the initially grudging helpmate to the tyro sheriff (Anthony Perkins) of the small town where he has temporarily fetched up (a figure who represents his younger self), and by his becoming surrogate husband and father to a young widow and her son, in whose home he lodges. After the colour of his previous five Westerns, Mann reverts to black and white, adopting a more formalized visual style which makes bold use of deep focus; particularly striking is the episode in which the buggy belonging to the town doctor (John McIntire) proceeds haltingly along the main street until the citizenry realize with horror that the occupant has been murdered. TP
1957/b & w/93 min/PAR/p William Perlberg, George Seaton/d Anthony Mann/s Dudley Nichols/c Loyal Griggs/m Elmer Bernstein/lp Henry Fonda, Anthony Perkins, Betsy Palmer, Neville Brand, John McIntire, Lee Van Cleef

Tom Horn · A long-gestating project plagued by production difficulties when finally mounted by McQueen's own company, this is a disappointingly prosaic focus on the last two years in the life of Tom Horn – a living legend for his earlier capture of Geronimo, but now hired as a stock detective by Wyoming rancher Farnsworth, and implicitly encouraged to adopt a policy of murderous rough justice on rustlers by the local cattlemen's association. McQueen is left to articulate his own out-of-time status as he resigns himself to negotiating a relationship to his corrupt context, but he can't win, with his very efficiency rendering him a political embarrassment. A frame-up over a boy's shooting and a rigged trial hurry him towards the gallows. Altogether, the film is marked by an overly reticent fatalism rather than the resonant filigree expected of a McGuane script contribution, and perversely it displays greater fidelity to factoid tele-movie formulae than does the William Goldman-scripted long-form television feature *Mr. Horn*, which largely stole its thunder. PT
1980/97 min/Solar – First Artists – WB/p Fred Weintraub/d William Wiard/s Thomas McGuane, Bud Shrake/c John Alonzo/m Ernest Gold/lp Steve McQueen, Linda Evans, Richard Farnsworth, Billy Green Bush, Slim Pickens

Track of the Cat · After the success of his *The High and the Mighty* (1954), John Wayne offered to produce Wellman's next film regardless of its subject matter. He chose a long cherished project to make a colour film in black and white, using a novel by van Tilburg Clark, whose *The Ox-Bow Incident* he had filmed earlier. Set in the 1880s in an isolated, snowbound California farm, the story concerns a warped family ruled by a bigoted mother (Bondi) whose two sons, Hunter and a marvellously edgy Mitchum, are at each other's throats. The claustrophobic family's neuroses are externalized in the shape of a black panther roaming in the woods, obsessively hunted by Mitchum, who also seems to enjoy a deep understanding with a wizened Indian Methuselah (Switzer). Wellman's austerely stylized image of life on the farm offers a salutory corrective to the many idealizations of Californian ruralism, here reduced to a forbidding snowscape. If *Across the Wide Missouri* showed the loss of an edenic America and *Westward the Women* the price people paid to reach their idea of the promised land, this film gives a lucid account of what became of people brutalized by a hard life in inhospitable surroundings. This is one of the most intelligent as well as beautiful Westerns ever filmed. PW
1954/102 min/Batjac – WB/p John Wayne, Robert Fellows/d William A. Wellman/s A. I. Bezzerides/c William H. Clothier/m Roy Webb/lp Robert Mitchum, Tab Hunter, Beulah Bondi, Teresa Wright, Carl 'Alfalfa' Switzer

Tribute to a Bad Man · This was one of Cagney's very few Westerns (his best one being *Run for Cover*) and also represents the Hollywood début of Irene Papas. The title is something of a misnomer, since Cagney is less bad than hard-bitten, a tough rancher

Steve McQueen in Tom Horn

Robert Mitchum in Track of the Cat

who has to enforce his own law on his limitless range in the Colorado Rockies (photographed splendidly by Robert Surtees). He is viewed through the eyes of young Dubbins, an eastern lad who comes to work for him and almost wins Papas away from him. A mixture of rugged actioner and domestic drama, *Tribute to a Bad Man* works well on both levels. The Cagney role was originally intended for Spencer Tracy, but star and director fell out. JP
1955/95 min/MGM/p Sam Zimbalist/d Robert Wise/s Michael Blankfort/c Robert Surtees/m Miklos Rozsa/lp James Cagney, Don Dubbins, Irene Papas, Vic Morrow, Royal Dano

True Grit · One of the most popular Westerns of all time (it grossed nearly $12million in North America alone), *True Grit* won Wayne his first Academy Award and is one of director Hathaway's best Westerns. It tells the story of a young girl (Darby) whose father is murdered by a farmhand and who hires drunken marshal Rooster Cogburn (Wayne) to track down the killer. A hugely enjoyable film, even if quite lightweight, *True Grit* scores on account of Ballard's stunning autumnal photography, its colourfully colloquial script (which owes much to Charles Portis' original novel), a marvellously judged performance from Wayne, and its expert blend of humour, tenderness and excitement. The film spawned a sequel (*Rooster Cogburn*), and the pilot for a proposed television series, but neither was a patch on the original. JP
1969/128 min/Hal B. Wallis Prods – PAR/ *p* Hal B. Wallis/*d* Henry Hathaway/ *s* Marguerite Roberts/*c* Lucien Ballard/ *m* Elmer Bernstein/*lp* John Wayne, Glen Campbell, Kim Darby, Robert Duvall, Dennis Hopper

The True Story of Jesse James (The James Brothers) · Nicholas Ray's superb remake of Henry King's *Jesse James* exemplifies on a psychological, interior level and a social, external level Frederick Jackson Turner's thesis of the frontier as 'a meeting place between savagery and civilization'. It begins with the Northfield raid that ended the James' banditry. Its stunning violence and confusion overarch Jesse's career, the 'key' to which is shown as the oppression visited on the James family and other Southern settlers by Jayhawkers. A marvellous scene follows (unprecedented in other Jesse James films) where opposites are peacefully reconciled as Jesse and his bride are baptized (by John Carradine who played Robert Ford in *Jesse James* and *The Return of Frank James*). The film closes with a return to the Northfield raid from the outlaws' point of view, Jesse's murder by Robert Ford and the ballad of Jesse James. Notwithstanding Ray's judgement that it was 'a very ordinary film', a marvellous movie. RC
1957/92 min/FOX/*p* Herbert B. Swope Jr./ *d* Nicholas Ray/*s* Walter Newman/*c* Joseph MacDonald/*m* Leigh Harline/*lp* Robert Wagner, Jeffrey Hunter, Hope Lange, Agnes Moorehead, John Carradine

Tumbleweeds · A big project combining William S. Hart's personal interest in the Western with the vogue for epics initiated by *The Covered Wagon*, intended as his comeback vehicle after breaking with Paramount in 1923. Set in 1889, the opening of the Cherokee Strip in Oklahoma Territory, Hart's film addressed changing audience tastes by adding a comic sidekick and an 'aw shucks' courtship to his usually sombre style. The land-rush sequence, with so many struggling to stake their claim and Hart outracing all on horseback, is grand spectacle Reeves Eason style, more flamboyant than Hart's typically sober management of the chase. *Tumbleweeds* failed, partly from lacklustre distribution, and Hart rather reluctantly retired. The film's reissue in 1939 with a moving spoken prologue by the star generated new respect for his contributions as a Western interpreter. DK
1925/b & w/7,254 feet/William S. Hart Co – UA/*p* William S. Hart/*d* King Baggot/*s* C. Gardner Sullivan/*c* Joseph August/ *lp* William S. Hart, Barbara Bedford, Lucien Littlefield, Gordon Russell

Two Flags West · Something of a precursor to *Major Dundee*, *Two Flags West* finds Joseph Cotten as the Confederate officer in charge of a group of prisoners-of-war who are detailed to serve under rabid rebel-hater Jeff Chandler in New Mexico, where the Indians are being driven to an uprising by Chandler's murderously unreasonable behaviour. Like *Fort Apache*, the film makes a tentative stab at undermining the Custer myth by presenting the Indian wars as the result of the psychotic behaviour of high-ranking US army officers rather than, as in *They Died with their Boots On*, the side-effects of the unscrupulous speculations of various eastern interests. *Two Flags West* suffers from Chandler's overacting in the key role, and the faintly liberal intentions of Robert Wise lead to a rather muddled tone that is less interesting and affecting than Sam Peckinpah's red-handed treatment of similar material. To add a touch of film noir-style perversion to the film, screenwriter Casey Robinson has the Chandler character unhinged not only by his bigotry but by an uncontrollable, debatably incestuous obsession with sister-in-law Linda Darnell. KN
1950/92 min/FOX/*p* Casey Robinson/ *d* Robert Wise/*s* Casey Robinson/*c* Leon Shamroy/*m* Hugo Friedhofer/*lp* Joseph Cotten, Linda Darnell, Jeff Chandler, Cornel Wilde, Dale Robertson, Arthur Hunnicutt, Jay C. Flippen

Two Mules for Sister Sara · This was Eastwood's second film for Don Siegel and his fourth Western since returning from Italy (if one includes *Coogan's Bluff*). It was based on a story by Budd Boetticher, who had intended to make it into a film with John Wayne and Silvia Pinal. In Siegel's version the female role was originally meant to be played by Elizabeth Taylor but she became unavailable at the last moment. Described by Eastwood as 'kind of *African Queen* gone west', it is the story of Eastwood rescuing a nun (MacLaine) who turns out to be a prostitute. They then join forces to help Mexican revolutionaries overrun a French garrison. Although the action sequences are spectacularly staged the film does not really work: it seems a curious choice of subject for Siegel and the chemistry between Eastwood and MacLaine is wrong. Given the director's remark that 'Eastwood thinks he's leading her around but she's leading him – he's the second mule in the title' the film is perhaps best viewed as a foreshadowing of *The Beguiled*. JP
1969/116 min/Malpaso – Sanen Prods – U/*p* Martin Rackin, Carroll Case/*d* Don Siegel/*s* Albert Maltz/*c* Gabriel Figueroa/*m* Ennio Morricone/*lp* Shirley MacLaine, Clint Eastwood, Manolo Fabregas, Alberto Morin, Armando Silvestre

Two Rode Together · One of Ford's most persistently under-rated films, often dismissed as an inferior rehash of *The Searchers*. The theme is again the rescue and rehabilitation of children captured by Indians, with James Stewart as the cynically corrupt sheriff hired to negotiate the repatriation of a group of children, and Richard Widmark as the idealistic cavalry officer who insists on going along because he is suspicious of double-dealing somewhere along the line. The easy friendship between the two, expressed with wonderful simplicity in a long single-take shot as they sit by a river to talk things over, is used as a kind of watershed in the film: one acts through self-interest, the other through simple humanity, but both eventually have to watch in helpless disgust as the brutalized, alienated children they bring back are rejected by a civilized world governed by greed, hypocrisy and double standards. As a bleakly despairing vision of the darker side of the frontier, *Two Rode Together* is almost Swiftian in its savagery. TMi
1961/109 min/John Ford Prods – Shpetner Prods – COL/*p* Stan Shpetner/*d* John Ford/*s* Frank S. Nugent/*c* Charles Lawton Jr./*m* George Duning/*lp* James Stewart, Richard Widmark, Shirley Jones, Linda Cristal, Andy Devine

U

Ulzana's Raid · Aldrich's dark drama recounts a brutal cat-and-mouse game between the US Cavalry under the idealistic young Lt Debuin and the Apache chief Ulzana, in flight from the reservation. In one ambush, a soldier feels obliged to kill the woman he is escorting, and to commit suicide; her besieged husband is discovered tortured to death, as is a fellow homesteader whose raped wife attempts to drown herself. The killing of Ulzana's son is the prelude to a finale in which McIntosh is fatally wounded and Ulzana is in turn killed by the young Apache army scout, Ke-Ni-Tay. *Ulzana's Raid* provides an interestingly oblique role for its star, Burt Lancaster, as McIntosh. But by focusing on the 'mystery' of the frequently invisible Ulzana, this grim and even gothic narrative makes a paranoid contribution to the genre in its post-liberal, 'Vietnam' death-throes. It is an ideological effect not expunged by the film's eventual sympathy for the crippling tragedy of Ulzana's parental loss. PD
1972/103 min/U/*p* Carter De Haven/ *d* Robert Aldrich/*s* Alan Sharp/*c* Joseph Biroc/*m* Frank De Vol/*lp* Burt Lancaster, Bruce Davison, Jorge Luke, Richard Jaeckel, Joaquin Martinez

Unconquered · Characteristically overblown DeMille epic about the making of America, set in the pre-Revolutionary pioneer days of 1763 and none too subtly designed as an anti-Communist declaration of faith by the Hollywood Right. Howard Da Silva is the dastardly trader stirring up Indian troubles in pursuit of his own villainous ends, Paulette Goddard the downtrodden but beautiful English bondslave on the run from his lecherous clutches, and Gary Cooper the stout-hearted frontiersman who makes the world safe for her. Lushly shot in Technicolor and with an equally fulsome score, it has an aimlessly busy plot in which, aside from the endless Indian-vs.-colonist skirmishes and battles, plentiful innocent titillation is supplied as Goddard suffers torture at the stake, escapes by shooting the rapids, and is even required to take the inevitable DeMille bath. Entertaining in a sluggish sort of way, the film acquires momentary dignity through the unlikely but imposing presence of Boris Karloff, who reputedly spoke his part of an Indian chief in the genuine Senecan tongue. TMi
1947/147 min/PAR/*p*/*d* Cecil B. DeMille/ *s* Charles Bennett, Frederic M. Frank,

John Huston (l.) directs The Unforgiven

Jesse Lasky Jr./*c* Ray Rennahan/*m* Victor Young/*lp* Gary Cooper, Paulette Goddard, Howard Da Silva, Boris Karloff, Cecil Kellaway

The Unforgiven · Based, like *The Searchers*, on an Alan LeMay novel, *The Unforgiven* offers a kind of captivity narrative in reverse. Audrey Hepburn is a Kiowa Indian who has been brought up by Lillian Gish as one of her own children after Hepburn's people have been massacred by whites. But the secret comes out and the family, led by Burt Lancaster as the eldest son, is isolated. The neighbouring whites reject Hepburn, the Kiowa want her back. The Indians attack the lonely ranch, and in a marvellous scene Gish counters the weird and threatening sound of Indian flutes with a spirited rendering on her piano of Beethoven's 'Moonlight Sonata'. The climactic battle is brilliantly staged. But the film is not nearly so liberal as it thinks it is. Though it condemns the racism of the whites, the Indians are not an alternative culture but a totally alien 'other'. Hepburn may in a moment of anger assert her Indian identity by smearing paint on her face, but there's never any real doubt she will choose to stay with her adopted family. EB
1959/125 min/James Prods – UA/*p* James Hill/*d* John Huston/*s* Ben Maddow/*c* Franz Planer/*m* Dimitri Tiomkin/*lp* Burt Lancaster, Audrey Hepburn, Audie Murphy, John Saxon, Charles Bickford, Lillian Gish

Union Pacific · Unwilling to tackle the Western unless the subject matter offered a suitably epic potential, Cecil B. DeMille was

here tempted by the story of the construction of the first transcontinental railroad. Naturally, he conceived this in terms of spectacular disasters and dime novel heroics, and his cast was encouraged to compete with the big-scale action by overdoing everything. Joel McCrea as the two-fisted engineer in charge of the project is his usual heroic self and therefore tends to get lost in the spectacle, but Barbara Stanwyck as a fiery Irish postmistress is more than able to hold her own amid the crashing locomotives and protracted slugfests. The plot, which is reminiscent of the contemporary Western serials, has sneaky Brian Donlevy and boyish Robert Preston in the employ of an unscrupulous senator who wants the railroad stopped and tries again and again to thwart McCrea's efforts through sabotage, treachery and violence. Like all of DeMille's non-Biblical historical epics, this substitutes rampant right-wing patriotism for overwhelming fundamentalist religiosity as leavening for the romance, violence and action. KN
1939/b & w/133 min/PAR/*p*/*d* Cecil B. DeMille/*s* Walter DeLeon, C. Gardner Sullivan, Jesse Lasky Jr./*c* Victor Milner/ *m* John Leipold, Sigmund Krumgold/*lp* Barbara Stanwyck, Joel McCrea, Robert Preston, Brian Donlevy, Akim Tamiroff, Anthony Quinn

V

The Vanishing American · Pleasantly sentimental tale of a Navajo Indian (Richard Dix) who returns after serving valiantly at the front during World War I to find his idyllic way of life, already circumscribed by the advance of white civilization, further threatened by his tribe's forced removal from its lush reservation to arid desert lands. Steadfastly evading the issues, the script contrives to place all the blame on the machinations of one villainously mustachioed, sneeringly corrupt Indian agent (Noah Beery), while an Indian war is avoided because Dix is purportedly loved by a white schoolteacher (Lois Wilson), although he is conveniently killed to allow her to escape miscegenation. Heartfelt performances, allied to some spectacularly beautiful camerawork, over-ride most of these naiveties; but a rather sour taste is still left by a lengthy prologue which explains the disappearance of the Indian in historical terms (a cycle in which stronger tribes defeat the weaker), backed by a quotation from Herbert Spencer on 'the survival of the fittest'. This prologue, unintentionally fascistic in tone, was not reproduced in the otherwise dismally routine 1955 remake. TMi

1925/b & w/9,916 ft/Famous Players-Lasky – PAR/p Adolph Zukor, Jesse L. Lasky/ d George B. Seitz/s Ethel Doherty/c C. Edgar Schoenbaum, Harry Perry/ lp Richard Dix, Lois Wilson, Noah Beery, Malcolm McGregor, Shannon Day

Vera Cruz · As one French critic has put it: 'the release, in quick succession, of *Apache*, *Vera Cruz* and *Kiss Me Deadly* was perhaps the single most exciting cinematic event of the mid-50s. Aldrich seemed to provide the ideal and much-needed link between the old and the new, demonstrating an ability to function within a tradition (the "craftsmanlike" practice of the genres) while at the same time transcending it through *enhancement*, be it lyrical (*Apache*), humorous (*Vera Cruz*) or paroxysmal (*Kiss Me Deadly*).' Certainly it is the element of humour that makes this one of Aldrich's most entertaining and interesting films, and the extremely *cynical* tone of the humour gives it an extraordinarily modern tone (also causing it to be disliked at the time of its release). The story is simple: Lancaster and Cooper are two adventurers in Mexico at the end of the Civil War who try to out double-cross each other over a hoard of gold. Since their main characteristics are greed, treachery and amorality this makes *Vera Cruz* one of the very first Westerns to dispense with the Manichean moralism that had underpinned the genre for so long, thus paving the way for the Italian Westerns and especially those of Sergio Leone (with whom Aldrich worked –

unhappily – on *Sodom and Gomorrah*). JP 1954/94 min/Flora Prods – UA/p James Hill/d Robert Aldrich/s Roland Kibbee, James R. Webb/c Ernest Laszlo/m Hugo Friedhofer/lp Gary Cooper, Burt Lancaster, Denise Darcel, Cesar Romero, Sarita Montiel

Villa Rides · Peckinpah and Towne (author of *Chinatown*) based their script for this Mexican Revolution epic on William Douglas Lansford's biography of Pancho Villa, but in truth this is less a biopic than an action-packed and extremely violent adventure film in which the complex political and historical issues involved get rather short shrift. Robert Mitchum stars as a composite fictional American aviator-adventurer-mercenary who comes to the aid of the revolution being led by Brynner's be-wigged Villa and his sadistic sidekick Fierro (an excellent performance by Charles Bronson). Kulik's direction of the action sequences is forceful enough, but overall the pace is rather too leisurely and the structure too episodic. JP
1968/124 min/PAR/p Ted Richmond/ d Buzz Kulik/s Robert Towne, Sam Peckinpah/c Jack Hildyard/m Maurice Jarre/lp Yul Brynner, Robert Mitchum, Maria Grazia Buccella, Charles Bronson, Robert Viharo

Virginia City · 'We're off to Virginia City,' Flynn and his sidekicks announced at the end of *Dodge City*. This is not, however, a sequel, even though it was made in the following year and by much the same supporting cast and production team. Southern sympathizers in Virginia City have raised $5 million in gold to be smuggled out and delivered to the Confederate forces. Scott is the rebel officer entrusted with getting the gold through. Out to stop him is the Unionist spy Flynn. But when they are both faced by alien aggressors, in the shape of Bogart's marauding Mexicans, they find strength through unity, which leads to a symbolic though rather banal reconciliation when Flynn refuses to hand the captured gold over to his government. Despite the star-studded cast and Civil War setting the film lacks the epic grandeur and sweep of *Dodge City* and is a rather lacklustre affair. PS
1940/b & w/121 min/WB/ass p Robert Fellows/d Michael Curtiz/s Robert Buckner/c Sol Polito/m Max Steiner/ lp Errol Flynn, Randolph Scott, Humphrey Bogart, Miriam Hopkins, Guinn 'Big Boy' Williams

The Virginian · Owen Wister's famous novel was the source of several screen adaptions, but the early sound version, which brought Gary Cooper to prominence as a star, is the best known. Wister's story, in which a man (the Virginian of the title) watches impassively as his best friend is lynched by a posse for cattle rustling, is a radical break with the 'codes of the West', a transgression of Western mythology. When the Virginian (Cooper) falls for Molly, the new schoolteacher (Mary Brian), his old friend Steve (Richard Arlen) starts trailing with the cattle rustler Trampas (Walter Huston). Steve's hanging causes Molly to spurn the Virginian, but they are eventually reconciled, and the Virginian guns Trampas down. Though the film is slow-paced, as were many Westerns adapting to the new sound technology, its use of sound is nevertheless notable, both in the case of Cooper's affected drawl, and in the use of whistle calls between Cooper and Arlen, the ultimate manifestation of which poignantly signals Arlen's death. DR
1929/b & w/90 min/PAR/p Louis D. Lighton/d Victor Fleming/s Howard Estabrook/c J. Roy Hunt/lp Gary Cooper, Walter Huston, Richard Arlen, Mary Brian

Viva Villa! · A major Hollywood production, nominated for Oscars for best picture and script. Although Conway is credited with the direction, Howard Hawks is said to have had a hand in the picture, since it includes his characteristic energetic blend of action and comedy. Wallace Beery stars as the passionate and unpredictable Francisco (Pancho) Villa, as seen through the eyes of a US newspaperman in both the triumphant and the lowest points in his controversial career as Mexican bandit/revolutionary. Beery plays Villa with all the earthy excess attributed to this impetuous historical figure – by turns idealist, killer and clown. The performances by the well-known character actors are equally outstanding in a film which presents Mexican *machismo* in its most aggressive – and sometimes, its most self-pitying – posturings. Both loved and despised, the historical Villa, like Beery, was a showman equal to none; always consciously playing to an audience, he performed his role to the hilt. *Viva Villa!* captures the spirit of Villa, even if it fudges a bit on the facts. DG
1934/b & w/115 min/MGM/p David O. Selznick/d Jack Conway/s Ben Hecht/ c James Wong Howe, Charles G. Clarke/

m Herbert Stothart/*lp* Wallace Beery, Leo Carrillo, Fay Wray, Donald Cook

Viva Zapata! · A 'political' Western based on the career of the martyred Mexican revolutionary, Emiliano Zapata. Kazan directs young 'Method' actor Brando in a potent physical performance in one of the few films which grasps the idealism, opportunism, and the failures of the Mexican Revolution. Steinbeck's script, shot near Cuernavaca, stresses both the necessity of revolt against a corrupt regime and the danger that ambitious leaders will betray the people. Fighting for land reform against the dictator Diaz and so-called 'revolutionary' governments, Zapata briefly grasps the reins of power only to realize, in a dramatic confrontation with the peasants of his home, that he now represents 'the system'. Leaving the capital to resume the fight for justice, he is tricked into ambush, but his horse, Blanco, escapes to the mountains – the unbridled image of freedom. Memorable moments include Brando's confession to his bride that he is illiterate and Quinn's performance as Zapata's passionate brother, Eufemio. DG
1952/b & w/112 min/FOX/*p* Darryl F. Zanuck/*d* Elia Kazan/*s* John Steinbeck/*c* Joseph MacDonald/*m* Alex North/*lp* Marlon Brando, Anthony Quinn, Jean Peters, Joseph Wiseman, Harold Gordon

W

Wagon Master · A film without stars that John Ford made for himself between larger projects – a remake of *Stagecoach* in an Eisensteinian choral mode. As before, society's outcasts journey across country and settle in the West after a rite of passage comprising internal and external dangers. Entire groups are 'invited out of town' this time, not just individuals – the Mormon community, two horsetraders who later turn wagonmasters, and a dubious trio of showpeople. Companions unwelcome to all are murderous, bank-robbing Uncle Shiloh Clegg and his cretinous nephews – they are killed just before the mountain is crossed and the promised land entered. (The Indians in the film are benevolent, however, wanting only to dance with the settlers as they pass through.) What the actors play are less characters in a drama than figures in a pageant – even the romance, between Ben Johnson and Joanne Dru, is seen from a great distance. The best passages indeed contain no dialogue: stark shots of the wagon train

struggling to cross the landscape as the Sons of the Pioneers sing its praises on the soundtrack. BH
1950/b & w/86 min/Argosy – RKO/*p* John Ford, Merian C. Cooper/*d* John Ford/*s* Frank S. Nugent, Patrick Ford/*c* Bert Glennon/*m* Richard Hageman/*lp* Ben Johnson, Harry Carey Jr., Joanne Dru, Ward Bond, Alan Mowbray, Jane Darwell, Russell Simpson, Hank Worden, Charles Kemper

Warlock · A flawed but fascinating film which works a series of variations on the gunfight at the O.K. Corral, with Henry Fonda as a Wyatt Earp-type hired to clean up a town, and Anthony Quinn as his blond-haired, club-footed Doc Holliday. Complications and subtle shifts in allegiance come thick and fast as Dorothy Malone arrives in town seeking revenge for the murder of her lover by either Fonda or Quinn, gradually uncovering the latter's darkly passionate attachment to the friend it is his mission in life to protect; and as Richard Widmark's reformed baddie, earning Fonda's grudging respect as he turns sheriff to protect the town against their protectors, stirs further eddies in the muddy homosexual undercurrents. The atmosphere of rising hysteria, climaxing with Fonda being forced to kill the now berserk Quinn and then gravely staging a Viking funeral for him, sometimes seems rather arbitrarily contrived, with motivations only half-digested by a script valiantly trying to take in proliferating subplots from Oakley Hall's novel. An impressive attempt, nonetheless, to tackle Western mythology in terms of Shakespearean tragedy. TMi
1959/122 min/FOX/*p*/*d* Edward Dmytryk/*s* Robert Alan Aurthur/*c* Joseph MacDonald/*m* Leigh Harline/*lp* Henry Fonda, Richard Widmark, Anthony Quinn, Dorothy Malone

Way of a Gaucho · Peronist Argentina took protective measures against the US, forcing Fox to spend some of its accumulated takings locally. Tourneur was despatched with a crew and cast to bring back an Argentinian Western based on a story by Herbert Childs. Calhoun is Alverde, the fiery gaucho steeped in the dying traditions of cattle ranching on the pampas. He organizes a gang to stop the inroads of agricultural rationalization and big business. Boone is the policeman sent after him. Tourneur uses the pampas to spectacular effect with unusual colour compositions and striking framing. One memo-

Anthony Quinn, Henry Fonda in Warlock

Rory Calhoun in Way of a Gaucho

rable shot shows Calhoun silhouetted as he stands on his horse to extend his field of vision in the empty-looking plains. The movie can be seen as the most outstanding precursor of Peckinpah's work, suggesting Peckinpah absorbed more than just experience when he was dialogue director on the beautiful *Wichita*. PW
1952/91 min/FOX/*p* Philip Dunne/*d* Jacques Tourneur/*s* Philip Dunne/*c* Harry Jackson/*m* Sol Kaplan/*lp* Rory Calhoun, Richard Boone, Gene Tierney, Hugh Marlowe, Everett Sloane, Enrique Chaico, Lidia Campos

Way Out West · Generally considered to be among the most accomplished of Laurel and Hardy's feature-length vehicles. Stan and Ollie play court officers who arrive in the frontier town of Brushwood Gulch to hand over the deeds of a gold mine to an orphan girl, but fall prey to a plot by the grasping saloon boss (James Finlayson, veteran stooge to the two comedians) and his wife to pass off the latter as the heiress. Needless to say, all comes out well in the end, but en route the stars get the chance to give their inimitable rendering of 'Trail of the Lonesome Pine', the record of which was over 40 years later to become a surprise 'top 20' hit in Britain. Very much a comedy Western rather than a spoof, the film gains in comic compression from utilizing the traditional atmospheric props of the musically-oriented B-Western. TP
1936/b & w/65 min/MGM/p Hal Roach/d James Horne/s Jack Jevne, Felix Adler, Charles Rogers, James Parrott/c Art Lloyd, Walter Lundin/m Marvin Hatley/lp Stan Laurel, Oliver Hardy, James Finlayson, Sharon Lynne

Welcome to Hard Times (Killer on a Horse) · Hard Times is an isolated western outpost, where the stage is due in a week – or maybe two – and storms, cold and mud accentuate the difficulty of survival. The satanic man from Bodie predicates the action. Riding in from nowhere, he kills and rapes and leaves the town in flames. Should the town be saved? The store owner leaves, but Blue, the embodiment of civilization, realizes the necessity of finally sticking it out. As Hard Times struggles to rebuild (with the help of an itinerant entrepreneur and nearby mineworkers for customers), Blue, Molly

and a fatherless boy become a parody of a family as Molly awaits the rapist's return and, against Blue's wishes, trains their 'son' to shoot. A particularly bleak and pessimistic image of the West, the film represents a changed attitude from the classics of the genre. The traditional roles are reversed: the hero does shoot the devil when he returns but only because the villain runs out of bullets, whereas the woman is unremitting in her thirst for vengeance. The film ends with hope, however, as a young couple get married, the store owner returns, and the money arrives for the mine to stay open. Hard Times will survive. JD
1966/105 min/MGM/p Max E. Youngstein, David Karr/d/s Burt Kennedy/c Harry Stradling Jr./m Harry Sukman/lp Henry Fonda, Janice Rule, Keenan Wynn, Aldo Ray

Westbound · Set in 1864, this is one of the rare Westerns which sides unequivocally with the Northern cause in the Civil War. Scott is an army officer charged with ensuring that gold from the California mines is shipped safely across to the east. (A monetarist government official explains that the war cannot be financed except on the basis of sound money backed by gold.) Scott sets about organizing the Overland Stage line through Colorado. But Julesberg is controlled by Confederate sympathizers, led by Andrew Duggan, who stop at nothing, even the killing of children, to prevent the stages getting through. At the end of the film Scott has his choice of two women. One is Virginia Mayo, who though in love with Scott has married the rich Duggan while he's been away in the war. The other is Karen Steele, who is married to a farmer who has lost his arm on the Union side in the war. When both their husbands are dead Scott, as a true Westerner, chooses the trouser-wearing farmer's wife over the fancily-dressed lady. Entertaining enough, the film has suffered by comparison with the two masterworks in the Scott-Boetticher canon which follow it, *Ride Lonesome* and *Comanche Station*. EB
1958/72 min/WB/p Henry Blanke/d Budd Boetticher/s Berne Giler/c J. Peverell Marley/m David Buttolph/lp Randolph Scott, Virginia Mayo, Karen Steele, Andrew Duggan, Michael Pate

The Westerner · Wyler and Toland were happier working in the studio than on location, and in *The Westerner* it is the drab interiors that are the site of dramatic emphasis, where dialogue has prominence over

action. Both Brennan and Cooper give subtly comic performances, with Brennan's characterization of Judge Roy Bean a mixture of the callous and the sentimental, a performance which won Brennan an Oscar. Cooper is the drifter who falls into the hands of Bean, who has his own brand of summary frontier justice. There follows a long sequence of beguiling black humour, in which Cooper bargains for his life by pretending to be the possessor of a lock of Lillie Langtry's hair. This fetish establishes a necessary alliance between the two, but it is Bean's obsession with Lillie Langtry that proves to be his undoing. Cooper finally confronts Bean in an empty theatre where Langtry is due to give a performance, and in the gunfight which ensues, Bean is shot down. JH
1940/b & w/100 min/Samuel Goldwyn – UA/p Samuel Goldwyn/d William Wyler/s Jo Swerling, Niven Busch/c Gregg Toland/m Dimitri Tiomkin/lp Gary Cooper, Walter Brennan, Doris Davenport, Chill Wills, Lillian Bond

Western Union · Lang's second Western, about the transcontinental extension of the telegraph system, belongs ostensibly with films such as *Wells Fargo* and *Union Pacific* which highlight the role of technology in the conquest of the West. However, the film's centre of interest is the divided hero, Vance Shaw (Randolph Scott), and his struggle to live down an outlaw past. He gets a job with Western Union despite suspicions about his record but the outfit is constantly threatened by a bunch of renegade confederates led, we eventually learn, by Shaw's brother. The 'Cain and Abel' theme is appropriately concluded with Shaw's death at the hand of his villainous brother after his gun hand has been badly burned in a forest fire. The brother is then shot by Robert Young's deceptively skilled 'dude' and the closing scenes celebrate the westward progress of the telegraph line in the context of a lament for Vance Shaw. TR
1941/93 min/FOX/ass p Harry Joe Brown/d Fritz Lang/s Robert Carson/c Edward Cronjager, Allen M. Davey/m David Buttolph/lp Randolph Scott, Robert Young, Dean Jagger, Virginia Gilmore, Barton MacLane

Westward the Women · Frank Capra's story 'Pioneer Woman' provided his friend Wellman with an ideal pretext to pay tribute to the hard-nosed mothers of America. Shot on location in the Mojave desert, it tells of a

Randolph Scott, Virginia Mayo in Westbound

Walter Brennan, Gary Cooper in The Westerner

Vera Miles, Joel McCrea in Wichita

wagon train of 150 women led by the woman-hating Buck (Taylor) crossing from Chicago to California, braving hunger, disease, Indian attacks (shown characteristically mainly through their results), trekking across the rockies and through the desert. Only a hundred make it to the all-male settlement awaiting the arrival of their mail-order brides. As a reward for having shown themselves to be as tough as men, the women are allowed to choose their mates. Taylor, having tamed the French ball of fire Darcel by beating her up, then consents to marry her. Wellman directed in an uncompromising manner, with harshly lit images and a relentless rhythm, but he also shot the women as heroic figures, from below, as they wearily struggle forward. PW
1951/b & w/118 min/MGM/p Dore Schary/ d William A. Wellman/s Charles Schnee/ c William C. Mellor/m Jeff Alexander/ lp Robert Taylor, John McIntire, Denise Darcel, Hope Emerson, Marilyn Erskine

Westworld · Generically a sci-fi movie, but buoyed by a large helping of Western mythology, Crichton's hi-tech thriller features a holiday theme camp where environmental and robotic simulations allow pleasure-seekers to experience situations from the past: in Roman World, Mediaeval World or Westworld. The latter option is chosen by vacationing businessmen Benjamin and Brolin, who there encounter a black-clad, gunslinging robot (played by a cold-eyed Brynner) in a no-lose face-off. Malfunctions spread throughout the complex, however, with the hitherto servile robots exhibiting signs of self-awareness and survival instinct; and when the tourists next face the gunfighter, Brolin is shot dead, and Benjamin forced to flee for his life from the cybernetic killer. PT
1973/89 min/MGM/p Paul N. Lazarus III/d/s Michael Crichton/c Gene Polito/m Fred

Karlin/lp Richard Benjamin, James Brolin, Yul Brynner, Alan Oppenheimer, Linda Scott

Wichita · Tourneur's modest but spectacular movie with a hit song by Tex Ritter elaborates on the well-worn myth of Wyatt Earp (McCrea), the quiet gunslinger who is elected marshal to clean up the booming trailhead cowtown but then falls foul of the local businessmen who prefer profits to law and order. The movie enacts the contradiction between law and business (Whose Law?) as a conflict between spaces: inside-domestic vs. outside-public, with the town boundaries, doors and windows functioning as the markers guarded by the law but transgressed by economic forces (the cattle trade). These transgressions produce the film's abiding images: a small boy accidentally shot dead as he peeps out of a window, the banker's wife shot through the front door of her house. Peckinpah worked as dialogue director and Stuart Lake, Earp's hagiographer, was technical advisor, which may account for the film's historical inaccuracy: the events depicted resemble what happened in Wichita in 1873, a year before Earp arrived there. The historical hero was a Judge Tucker; Earp 'appropriated' his actions and cast himself as the hero. PW
1955/81 min/AA/p Walter Mirisch/ d Jacques Tourneur/s Daniel B. Ullman/ c Harold Lipstein/m Hans J. Salter/lp Joel McCrea, Vera Miles, Lloyd Bridges, Wallace Ford, Edgar Buchanan, Jack Elam, Robert Wilke

The Wild Bunch · Pursued by bounty hunters into Mexico after an unsuccessful bank raid, Pike Bishop's gang become involved in the civil war between General Mapache and guerrilla forces. Gang member Angel kills his fiancée, now Mapache's moll. He is only rescued when Pike agrees to steal

US army rifles for Mapache, but he is subsequently recaptured and murdered. The gang engage Mapache in a final battle against impossible odds, which wipes out the major protagonists and leaves ex-associate and chief bounty hunter Thornton disconsolately joining the guerrillas. Peckinpah's 'professional' Western explores the group dynamics, and masculine identities, of a series of interlocking military and paramilitary antagonists bent on mutual elimination. This violent scenario is rendered frequently sensual, balletic and surreal through the choreographic use of camera movement, slow motion and Eisensteinian editing. In a world effectively outside society, the politics of civil war are little more than a backdrop for Peckinpah's romantic tragedy of impossible male bonding, for the nihilism of his characters' amoral heroism, and for their futureless preoccupation with the memories and identities of a now superceded West. PD
1969/145 min/WB/p Phil Feldman/d Sam Peckinpah/s Walon Green, Sam Peckinpah/c Lucien Ballard/m Jerry Fielding/lp William Holden, Ernest Borgnine, Robert Ryan, Edmond O'Brien, Warren Oates

Wild Rovers · Blake Edwards' only Western as director, although he had started out in the genre as a tyro producer, scriptwriter and actor with *Panhandle* (1948) and *Stampede* (1949). A conscious attempt to sidestep the myths of the heroic West, it has Holden and O'Neal as a pair of cowboys, tired of their joylessly humdrum lives, who rob a bank and head for Mexico with a vague notion of becoming cattle barons themselves. Hired hands rather than heroic outlaws – and so unprofessional that O'Neal, in a charmingly quaint conceit, takes a tiny puppy along for the ride and has to face the problem of milk to feed it – the pair ramble

along in an engagingly picaresque odyssey sparked by occasional flights of lyricism, like their attempt to rope a wild mustang (celebrated in ecstatic slow motion). Quirkishly funny and oddly affecting, it is played out against a background of complete credibility, even though the myths catch up with the film for a grimly ironic ending in the desert clearly inspired by Stroheim's *Greed*. TMI
1971/132 min/Geoffrey Prods – MGM/ *p* Blake Edwards, Ken Wales/*d/s* Blake Edwards/*c* Philip Lathrop/*m* Jerry Goldsmith/*lp* William Holden, Ryan O'Neal, Karl Malden, Lynn Carlin, Tom Skerritt, Joe Don Baker

Will Penny · Like a number of Westerns made in the late 60s and early 70s (and perhaps reflecting the uncertainty of those years), *Will Penny* offered a revised, if not exactly subversive, perspective on the romantic mythology of the cowboy. Paid off at the end of a cattle-drive, cowpuncher Will Penny (Charlton Heston) is left to fend for himself during the winter and is soon bushwhacked by the marauding preacher Quint (Donald Pleasence) and his sons. He finds salvation in a woman from the east (Joan Hackett), en route to California and using Will's shack as winter quarters. Tom Gries' film largely dispenses with conventional narrative action to construct a portrait of the cowboy as casual labourer, dwarfed by the landscape and vulnerable to its dangers. Illiterate and dirty (he baulks at the suggestion that after months on the trail he might need a bath), Will receives a sentimental education from the woman but finally declines her offer of stability in favour of the comforting anxieties of life as a high plains drifter. DW
1967/108 min/PAR/*p* Fred Engel, Walter Seltzer/*d/s* Tom Gries/*c* Lucien Ballard/ *m* David Raksin/*lp* Charlton Heston, Joan Hackett, Donald Pleasence

Winchester '73 · The film which established Anthony Mann as a Western auteur, and the first of his several collaborations with both James Stewart and writer Borden Chase. Strikingly visualized in high-contrast monochrome, the fast-moving narrative rests on an elemental version of the revenge theme: the hero (Stewart) is bent on tracking down an antagonist (Stephen McNally), who proves to be his brother and the murderer of their father. The prize rifle of the title, which is won by Stewart in a shooting contest at the outset and then stolen from him by McNally, provides a dramatic focus for the

Dan Duryea, James Stewart in Winchester '73

episodic plot. As the rifle passes from hand to hand, the film is able (in a spirit which seems to set a seal on Mann's embrace of the genre) to run a gamut of the movie West: cavalry, Indians, gun-runners, settlers, badmen. The last category memorably comprises not only McNally but his unbalanced partner in crime, a brilliant study in sneering villainy by Dan Duryea. TP
1950/b & w/92 min/U/*p* Aaron Rosenberg/ *d* Anthony Mann/*s* Robert L. Richards, Borden Chase/*c* William Daniels/ *md* Joseph Gershenson/*lp* James Stewart, Dan Duryea, Stephen McNally, Millard Mitchell, John McIntire, Will Geer

The Wonderful Country · Perhaps the best film of editor-turned-director Parrish, in which his modest talents are propped up by Robert Ardrey's thoughtful script and the personal involvement of star Robert Mitchum (whose company produced the film). Mitchum is a hired gun smuggling guns across the Texas-Mexican border who must overcome the physical wounds he sustains falling from his horse and come to some sort of peace with himself. *The Wonderful Country* is, like *Vera Cruz* and many of Sam Peckinpah's films, partially a meditation on the differences between America and Mexico and furthers the Western's use of the Latin country as either the United States' unconscious or its libido. KN
1959/96 min/DRM – UA/*p* Chester Erskine/ *d* Robert Parrish/*s* Robert Ardrey/*c* Floyd Crosby, Alex Phillips/*m* Alex North/*lp* Robert Mitchum, Julie London, Pedro Armendariz, Victor Mendoza, Gary Merrill, Jack Oakie, Albert Dekker

Y

Yellow Sky · A stark, superbly acted film trailing echoes of *Greed* and *The Treasure of the Sierra Madre* in Joe MacDonald's bleakly expressive camerawork, as Gregory Peck's

seven-man outlaw gang, parched and exhausted after evading pursuit in the desert, finally stumble on a ghost town where a half-crazed old prospector (James Barton) and his tomboy daughter (Anne Baxter) are jealously guarding a rich gold strike. The inevitable internecine warfare is beautifully structured as lust for both gold and the girl divides the gang and a band of Indians provides a variable factor in the battle lines. But the real strength of the film is the subtlety with which its script, based on a W.R. Burnett story and weaving a loose variation on *The Tempest*, draws complex resonances from the characters, with Peck's cynicism eroded as much by the Prospero prospector's world-weary wisdom as by the wonder of his Miranda, while the surviving gang members (variously motivated by romanticism, homosexual inclinations and animal loyalty) are gradually alienated by the ferocity of Widmark's greed for gold. TMI
1948/b & w/98 min/FOX/*p* Lamar Trotti/ *d* William A. Wellman/*s* Lamar Trotti/ *c* Joseph MacDonald/*m* Alfred Newman/ *lp* Gregory Peck, Richard Widmark, Anne Baxter, Henry Morgan, James Barton

Young Billy Young · One of Burt Kennedy's most characteristic movies – significantly, he was working from his own screenplay – *Young Billy Young* combines laconic humour, of a sometimes quite broad variety, with a tightly developed revenge narrative. Robert Walker plays a naive young would-be gunslinger who is taken under the paternal wing of a roving stranger (Robert Mitchum). The latter proves to be out to avenge the death of his own son, and the formalized patterning of the drama extends to revealing his quarry to be the father (John Anderson) of Walker's more vicious side-kick (David Carradine). Mitchum's eventual confrontation with Anderson is particularly well managed, with the former circumventing an ambush by hiding on top of a stagecoach in a 'wooden horse' manoeuvre. There are echoes of Howard Hawks in Mitchum's humorous self-reliance and in the tutelary relationship in which Walker stands to him, while Angie Dickinson, as the saloon queen whom at the end Mitchum (literally) carries off, imports fitting memories of *Rio Bravo*. TP
1969/89 min/Talbot-Youngstein Prods – UA/*p* Max E. Youngstein/*d/s* Burt Kennedy/*c* Harry Stradling Jr./*m* Shelly Manne/*lp* Robert Mitchum, Angie Dickinson, Robert Walker, David Carradine, John Anderson, Jack Kelly

PART IV

A DICTIONARY OF WESTERN FILM-MAKERS

A

Acord, Art (1890-1931) · Actor. Acord had been an authentic cowpuncher, a champion bulldogger who could throw a steer in 24 seconds. He entered the movies in 1909 as a stuntman with Bison and Selig, and soon was acting, making films in winter when the rodeos shut down. In 1915 he starred in the Buck Parvin series, little satires on Western film-making. He served with distinction in World War I, and made Western features through the 20s. But all went sour when he began to drink heavily and became a notorious brawler. Relegated from Universal to minor companies, he was involved in bootlegging, went briefly to jail, and then to Mexico. He did odd jobs, gambled and died, in Chihuahua, from cyanide poisoning. Evidence points to suicide. JL

The Two Brothers/1910 · The Indian Massacre/The Invaders/Custer's Last Fight/ Heart of an Indian/1912 · The Squaw Man/ 1914 · Author! Author!/Buck Parvin and the Movies/Buck's Lady Friend/A Cattle Queen's Romance/The Cowboy's Sweetheart/Film Tempo/This Is the Life/Man-Afraid-of-His-Wardrobe/Buckshot John/When the Fiddler Came to Big Horn/1915 · The Extra Man and the Milk-Fed Lion/Curlew Carliss/With a Life at Stake/Sandy, Reformer/The Cactus Cyclone/North of the Rio/Margy of the Foothills/A Modern Knight/A Man's Friend/ The Return/Snow Stuff/Under Azure Skies/ Water Stuff/1916 · Headin' South/1918 · The Fighting Line/The Wild Westerner/1919 The Moon Riders/The Kid and the Cowboy/Out West/1920 · Winners of the West/The Call of the Blood/The Cowpuncher's Comeback/Fair Fighting/The Fightin' Actor/The Showdown/1921 · In the

Art Acord

Days of Buffalo Bill/Dead Game/The Gipsy Trail/The Ranger's Reward/Tracked Down/ Unmasked/1922 · The Oregon Trail/White Horseman/1923 · Fighting for Justice/Looped for Life/1924 · Pals/The Call of Courage/ Three in Exile/The Circus Cyclone/The Wild Girl/Roads to Hollywood/1925 · The Scrappin' Kid/The Silent Guardian/Rustlers' Ranch/Lazy Lightning/The Man from the West/The Terror/The Ridin' Rascal/Sky High Corral/Western Pluck/The Set-Up/1926 · Loco Luck/Set Free/Hard Fists/Spurs and Saddles/The Western Rover/1927 · Two Gun

O'Brien/His Last Battle/The Texas Battler/ 1928 · The White Outlaw/The Arizona Kid/ Bullets and Justice/An Oklahoma Cowboy/ Wyoming Tornado/Fighters of the Saddle/ Pursued/Flashing Spurs/1929

Acosta, Rodolfo (1920-74) · Actor. Acosta began in Mexican films, working several times with the distinguished director Emilio Fernandez. Then he obtained a part in John Ford's *The Fugitive* when Ford was shooting in Mexico, and inevitably hit the trail for Hollywood. Here his lot was usually to play heavies in Western or adventure movies, but he achieved one lead, as an honest editor embroiled with racketeers in *The Tijuana Story*, and usually made his small parts tell. Occasionally Acosta played Indians, 'the fearsome Silva in *Hondo* being a notable example. JL

Pancho Villa Returns/1950 · Horizons West/ 1952 · San Antone/City of Bad Men/Wings of the Hawk/Hondo/1953 · Passion/Drum Beat/1954 · The Littlest Outlaw/1955 · The Proud Ones/Bandido/1956 · Apache Warrior/Trooper Hook/1957 · From Hell to Texas/1958 · Flaming Star/Walk Like a Dragon/One-Eyed Jacks/1960 · Posse from Hell/The Second Time Around/El ultimo rebelde/1961 · How the West Was Won/ 1962 · Savage Sam/1963 · Rio Conchos/1964 · The Sons of Katie Elder/The Reward/1965 · Return of the Seven/1966 · Young Billy Young/1969 · Flap/1970 Television Have Gun, Will Travel/57 · Jefferson Drum/Cheyenne/58 · The Texan/ The Rebel/59 · Rawhide/60 · The Big Valley/Daniel Boone/65 · Iron Horse/66 · The High Chaparral/Stranger on the Run/67 · Bonanza/68 · The Outcasts/69 · Cade's County/71

Adams, Julie (b 1926) · Actress, aka Betty Adams, Julia Adams. One of the actresses most identified with the Western during the 50s, when she was a contract player at Universal, she bore some resemblance to Joanne Dru, not only in looks but in combining an air of practicality with hints of hauteur. Much at home in both wagon train and saloon, she was more usually seen in domestically-inclined roles. But if given the chance, as when playing the object of Robert Ryan's desire in *Horizons West*, she could command a provocative sensuality. TP
The Dalton Gang/1949 · *West of the Brazos/ Hostile Country/Colorado Ranger/Crooked River/Marshal of Heldorado/Fast on the Draw*/1950 · *Bend of the River/The Treasure of Lost Canyon*/1951 · *Horizons West/The Lawless Breed*/1952 · *Wings of the Hawk/ The Mississippi Gambler/The Man from the Alamo/The Stand at Apache River*/1953 · *Slim Carter*/1957 · *The Gunfight at Dodge City*/1958 · *The Last Movie*/1971 · *The Wild McCullochs*/1975
Television *Lash of the West*/53 · *Dick Powell's Zane Grey Theatre/Yancy Derringer*/ 58 · *Bronco/Maverick/The Alaskans*/59 · *Cheyenne/The Rifleman/Tate/Wrangler*/60 · *Bonanza/The Outlaws*/61 · *The Virginian/ The Big Valley*/66 · *The Trackers*/71

Akins, Claude (b 1918) · Actor. Stocky, with a rugged, lived-in face, he started out in Westerns usually as a member of an outlaw gang. His most memorable role is as the powerful rancher's brother held for murder by John Wayne in the siege of the jail in *Rio Bravo*. In the 60s he became a more sympathetic character and in recent years has switched to comedy roles in movies and especially television. TM
The Raid/Bitter Creek/1954 · *The Man with the Gun*/1955 · *Johnny Concho/The Burning Hills/The Lonely Man*/1956 · *Joe Dakota*/ 1957 · *Rio Bravo*/1958 · *Yellowstone Kelly/*

Comanche Station/1959 · *How the West Was Won*/1962 · *Black Gold*/1963 · *A Distant Trumpet*/1964 · *Ride Beyond Vengeance/Incident at Phantom Hill*/1965 · *Return of the Seven*/1966 · *Waterhole No. 3*/1967 · *The Great Bank Robbery*/1969 · *Sledge/Flap*/1970
Television *Gunsmoke*/55 · *Dick Powell's Zane Grey Theatre*/56 · *Wagon Train/Tales of Wells Fargo*/57 · *Bonanza*/59 · *The Outlaws*/60 · *Daniel Boone*/64 · *Branded/ Laredo/The Big Valley*/65 · *Lock, Stock and Barrel*/71

Aldrich, Robert (1918-83) · Director. Three Aldrich Westerns deserve prominent places in the history of the genre. Two are 'Indian Westerns', and while *Apache*, a key film of the 50s, is clearly pro-Indian, *Ulzana's Raid* produces a much more complex and controversial representation of the Indian, which goes beyond the stereotypes of noble savage and evil threat. *Vera Cruz* can be seen as an important precursor of later developments in the genre. Its Mexican setting and its amoral tone anticipate both the Peckinpah of *The Wild Bunch* and the hard, cynical world of the Italian Western of the 60s. TR
Apache/Vera Cruz/1954 · (p only) *The Ride Back*/1957 · *The Last Sunset*/1961 · *4 for Texas*/1963 · *Ulzana's Raid*/1972 · *The Frisco Kid*/1979
Television *Hotel de Paree*/59

Altman, Robert (b 1925) · Director. An American auteur whose unconventional career has undergone great critical and commercial fluctuations. In many of his films he has boldly transformed Hollywood genres to capture the absurdity and moral emptiness of American society. His two Westerns, *McCabe & Mrs. Miller* and *Buffalo Bill and the Indians*, subvert the genre's conventions by providing a narration with loose ends, scenes with overlapping sound and action,

and central figures who behave very differently from the traditional Western hero. Buffalo Bill is portrayed as an insecure, vain figure, who is purely a product of promotion and grandiose rhetoric. He is an empty shell, and for Altman an apt symbol of an America whose reality is lost in a mythology which it has itself begun to believe. Altman is an idiosyncratic and ambitious director whose Westerns can alternately provide luminous epiphanies into the heart of American culture, and in the next scene (this is particularly true of *Buffalo Bill and the Indians*) turn into a turgid, chaotic mess. LQ
McCabe & Mrs. Miller/1971 · *Buffalo Bill and the Indians or Sitting Bull's History Lesson*/1976
Television *U.S. Marshal*/58 · *Lawman/The Man from Blackhawk*/59 · *Sugarfoot/Bronco/ Maverick*/60 · *Bonanza*/64

Anderson, Broncho Billy (1882-1971) · Actor, aka Gilbert M. Anderson, real name Max Aronson. A trade advert in 1912 called him 'The World's Greatest Photoplay Star', a large but justifiable claim, for he was undoubtably the most prominent and prolific personality of the early Western. One of his earliest roles was as a passenger in *The Great Train Robbery*. In 1907 he formed the Essanay Co. with George K. Spoor. It was under the Essanay brand that he established the popular Broncho Billy series, beginning in 1910 with *Broncho Billy's Redemption*. The name Broncho Billy, taken from a Peter B. Kyne story, belonged to Anderson and not to any consistent screen characterization. Each film had a self-contained narrative, so that he might be an outlaw in one film, a good guy in the next, get killed in another, and reappear fit and healthy in the following film. His most typical role, if he can be said to have had one in a career that spanned some 300 films, was as the Good-Badman: beginning as an outlaw and ending the film as

Rodolfo Acosta

Julia Adams

Claude Akins

Robert Aldrich

a reformed, and conforming, citizen. His films are as utilitarian as his dowdy costumes, foregrounding the characters' psychological traits rather than, say, stunts, furious riding, or large-scale spectacle. PS

The Great Train Robbery/1903 · A Girl from Montana/His First Ride/1907 · The Bandit Makes Good/1908 · The Best Man Wins/ The Black Sheep/The Heart of a Cowboy/His Reformation/The Indian Trailer/Judgement/A Mexican's Gratitude/The Ranchman's Rival/ The Spanish Girl/A Tale of the West/A Western Maid/Naked Hands/1909 · Away Out West/The Badman's Christmas Gift/The Badman's Last Deed/The Bandit's Wife/The Bearded Bandit/The Cowboy and the Squaw/ The Cowboy's Mother-in-Law/A Cowboy's Vindication/The Cow Puncher's Ward/The Deputy's Love/The Desperado/The Dumb Half Breed's Defense/Patricia of the Plains/ The Tout's Remembrance/The Flower of the Ranch/The Forest Ranger/Broncho Billy's Redemption/The Girl on the Triple X/The Marked Trail/The Mexican's Faith/The Millionaire and the Ranch Girl/The Mistaken Bandit/An Outlaw's Sacrifice/The Silent Message/Pals of the Range/The Pony Express Rider/The Ranch Girl's Legacy/The Ranchmen's Feud/The Sheriff's Sacrifice/The Tenderfoot Messenger/Under Western Skies/ The Unknown Claim/Western Chivalry/A Westerner's Way/A Western Woman's Way/ 1910 · Across the Plains/The Badman's Downfall/The Badman's First Prayer/The Border Ranger/Broncho Bill's Last Spree/The Corporation and the Ranch Girl/The Girl of the West/The Last Round-Up/The Romance of Bar O/Carmenita, the Faithful/The Count and the Cowboys/The Cowboy Coward/The Faithful Indian/Broncho Billy's Adventure/ Broncho Billy's Christmas Dinner/A Gambler of the West/The Girl Back East/The Hidden Mine/The Stage Driver's Daughter/The Indian Maiden's Lesson/The Infant at Snakeville/The Lucky Card/On the Desert's

Broncho Billy Anderson in Broncho Billy's Oath

Edge/The Outlaw and the Child/The Puncher's New Love/The Sheriff/The Sheriff's Brother/The Sheriff's Chum/Spike Shannon's Last Fight/Strike at the Little Jonny Mine/A Thwarted Vengeance/The Tribe's Penalty/ The Two Reformations/1911 · Alkali Bests Broncho Billy/The Bandit's Child/Broncho Billy and the Bandits/Broncho Billy and the Girl/Broncho Billy and the Indian Maid/ Broncho Billy and the Maid/Broncho Billy and the School Mistress/A Child of the Purple Sage/The Dance at Silver Gulch/(d only) The Shotgun Ranchman/(d only) The Mother of the Ranch/(d only) Cutting California Redwoods/(d only) The Boss of the Katy Mine/(d only) The Prospector/(d only) The Sheriff's Luck/(d only) The Sheriff's Inheritance/The Dead Man's Claim/ The Deputy and the Girl/The Deputy's Love Affair/The Desert Sweethearts/The Foreman's Cousin/Broncho Billy for Sheriff/Broncho Billy Outwitted/Broncho Billy's Bible/Broncho Billy's Escapade/Broncho Billy's Gratitude/ Broncho Billy's Heart/Broncho Billy's Last Hold-Up/Broncho Billy's Love Affair/ Broncho Billy's Mexican Wife/Broncho Billy's Narrow Escape/Broncho Billy's Pal/ Broncho Billy's Promise/The Indian and the Child/An Indian's Friendship/An Indian Sunbeam/(d only) The Loafer's Mother/(d only) Love on Tough Luck Ranch/A Moonshiner's Heart/On El Monte Ranch/On the Cactus Trail/The Ranch Girl's Mistake/ The Ranch Girl's Trial/The Ranch Man's Trust/The Reward for Broncho Billy/A Road Agent's Love/The Sheepman's Escape/The

Smuggler's Daughter/A Story of Montana/ The Tenderfoot Foreman/The Tomboy on Bar Z/Under Mexican Skies/Western Hearts//A Western Legacy/A Wife of the Hills/A Woman of Arizona/1912 · Broncho Billy and the Express Rider/Broncho Billy and the Navajo Maid/Broncho Billy and the Outlaw's Mother/(d only) The Sheriff's Child/(d only) The Sheriff's Story/(d only)The Sheriff's Honeymoon/Broncho Billy and the Rustler's Child/Broncho Billy and the School Mam's Sweetheart/Broncho Billy and the Sheriff's Kid/Broncho Billy and the Squatter's Daughter/The Doctor's Duty/The Episode at Cloudy Canyon/The Accusation of Broncho Billy/Broncho Billy and the Step-Sisters/Broncho Billy and the Western Girls/ Broncho Billy Gets Square/Broncho Billy Reforms/Broncho Billy's Brother/Broncho Billy's Capture/Broncho Billy's Christmas Deed/Broncho Billy's Conscience/Broncho Billy's Elopement/Broncho Billy's First Arrest/ Broncho Billy's Gratefulness/Broncho Billy's Grit/Broncho Billy's Gun-Play/Broncho Billy's Last Deed/Broncho Billy's Mistake/Broncho Billy's Oath/Broncho Billy's Reason/Broncho Billy's Secret/Broncho Billy's Sister/Broncho Billy's Squareness/Broncho Billy's Strategy/ Broncho Billy's Ward/Broncho Billy's Way/The Influence of Broncho Billy/The Making of Broncho Billy/The Man in the Cabin/The Ranch Feud/The Redeemed Claim/The Redemption of Broncho Billy/The Struggle/The Tenderfoot Sheriff/The Three Gamblers/A Western Sister's Devotion/Why Broncho Billy Left Bear County/1913 ·

Robert Altman

Broncho Billy, a Friend in Need/Broncho Billy and the Bad Man/Broncho Billy and the Escaped Bandit/Broncho Billy and the Gambler/Broncho Billy and the Greaser/Broncho Billy and the Mine Shark/Broncho Billy and the Rattler/Broncho Billy and the Red Man/Broncho Billy and the Sheriff's Office/Broncho Billy and the Sheriff/Broncho Billy and the Settler's Daughter/Broncho Billy Butts In/Broncho Billy – Favorite/Broncho Billy – Gunman/Broncho Billy – Outlaw/Broncho Billy Puts One Over/Broncho Billy Rewarded/Broncho Billy's Christmas Spirit/Broncho Billy's Close Call/Broncho Billy's Cunning/Broncho Billy's Dad/Broncho Billy's Decision/Broncho Billy's Duty/Broncho Billy's Fatal Joke/Broncho Billy's Indian Romance/Broncho Billy's Jealousy/Broncho Billy's Judgement/Broncho Billy's Leap/Broncho Billy's Mission/Broncho Billy's Mother/Broncho Billy's Punishment/Broncho Billy's Scheme/Broncho Billy's Sermon/Broncho Billy's True Love/Broncho Billy's Wild Ride/Broncho Billy, the Vagabond/Broncho Billy Trapped/Broncho Billy Wins Out/The Good-for-Nothing/(d only) Red Riding Hood of the Hills/Broncho Billy – Guardian/Broncho Billy's Double Escape/The Calling of Jim Barton/The Interference of Broncho Billy/Snakeville's New Doctor/(sc, d only) Snakeville's Peace-Maker/The Squatter's Gal/The Strategy of Broncho Billy's Sweetheart/The Tell-Tale Hand/The Treachery of Broncho Billy's Pal/1914 · Andy of the Royal Mounted/The Bachelor's Baby/The Bachelor's Burglar/Broncho Billy Well Repaid/Broncho Billy and the Baby/Broncho Billy and the Card Sharp/Broncho Billy and the Claim Jumpers/Broncho Billy and the False Note/Broncho Billy and the Land Grabber/Broncho Billy and the Lumber King/Broncho Billy and the Parson/Broncho Billy and the Posse/Broncho Billy and the Sisters/The Burglar's Godfather/A Christmas Revenge/The Convict's Threat/The Escape of

Broncho Billy/The Face at the Curtain/Her Realization/Her Return/His Regeneration/His Wife's Secret/The Indian's Narrow Escape/Ingomar of the Hills/The Little Prospector/The Other Girl/The Outlaw's Awakening/Broncho Billy and the Revenue Agent/Suppressed Evidence/The Tie that Binds/Too Much Turkey/An Unexpected Romance/The Wealth of the Poor/The Western Way/When Love and Honor Called/Wine, Women and Song/Broncho Billy and the Vigilante/Broncho Billy Begins Life Anew/Broncho Billy Evens Matters/Broncho Billy Misled/Broncho Billy's Brother/Broncho Billy's Cowardly Brother/Broncho Billy's Greaser Deputy/Broncho Billy, Sheepman/Broncho Billy's Love Affair /Broncho Billy's Marriage/(a different film) Broncho Billy's Marriage/Broncho Billy's Mexican Wife/Broncho Billy's Parents/Broncho Billy's Protégé/Broncho Billy's Sentence/Broncho Billy Steps In/Broncho Billy's Teachings/Broncho Billy's Vengeance/Broncho Billy's Word of Honor/Broncho Billy Well Repaid/Broncho's Surrender/The Champion/1915 · The Book Agent's Romance/Her Lesson/The Man in Him/1916 · Humanity/1917 · Red Blood and Yellow/Shootin' Mad/The Son of a Gun/1918 · The Bounty Killer/1965

Armendariz, Pedro (1912-63) · This US-educated Mexican actor débuted in 1934 as a romantic lead in ranchero pictures and quickly achieved stardom. Best known in Mexico for the classic melodramas in rural settings directed by Emilio Fernandez, aka El Indio, co-starring Dolores del Rio, Armendariz was typecast in Hollywood as a fiery mustachioed Latin. His best work there was under Ford's direction, notably as one of the Three Godfathers. Returning to Mexico, he did Buñuel's El bruto (1952) and went on to a prolific international career that included work in France and in Italy. He shot himself in Los Angeles on learning he had terminal

cancer. PW
Las cuatro Milpas/Amapola del camino/Jalisca nunca pierde/La Adelita/1937 · El Indio/1938 · Con los dorados de Villa/El Charro negro/El Zorro de Jalisco/1939 · Las calaveras del terror/Flor silvestre/Maria Candelaria /1943 · Alma de bronce/Las abandonadas/El capitan Malacara/Bugambilia/1944 · Enamorada/1946 · Juan Charrasqueado/1947 · Fort Apache/3 Godfathers/En la hacienda de la Flor/1948 · Pancho Villa vuelve/The Torch/1949 · Border River/1953 · La escondida/1955 · El Zarco/Asi era Pancho Villa/1957 · Pancho Villa y la Valentina/Cuando viva Villa es la muerte/La cucaracha/1958 · Calibre .44/The Wonderful Country/1959 · La carcel de Cananca/1960 · La bandida/1962

Armstrong, R[obert] G[olden] (b 1920) · Actor. Armstrong's impressive portrayal of the fearsome bible-quoting Joshua Knudsen in Sam Peckinpah's Ride the High Country established a gruff and unsmiling persona which was to be used in many Westerns during the 60s and 70s. He became part of the Peckinpah stock company, appearing in three more films from the dominant Western director of the time, and he also worked with other significant genre specialists such as Hawks, Hathaway and the prolific R. G. Springsteen. TR
From Hell to Texas/1958 · No Name on the Bullet/1959 · Ten Who Dared/1960 · Ride the High Country/1962 · He Rides Tall/1963 · Major Dundee/1964 · El Dorado/1966 · The McMasters/1969 · The Ballad of Cable Hogue/1970 · J W Coop/1971 · The Great Northfield Minnesota Raid/1972 · Pat Garrett and Billy the Kid/Il mio nome è Nessuno/1973 · Boss Nigger/1974
Television Gunsmoke/55 · Wagon Train/57 · The Texan/The Californians/Jefferson Drum/The Rifleman/58 · Lawman/Wanted: Dead or Alive/Black Saddle/Bonanza/Elfego

Pedro Armendariz

R. G. Armstrong

James Arness

Jean Arthur

Gene Autry

Baca/59 · The Tall Man/Laramie/Rawhide/ The Westerner/Cheyenne/60 · The Life and Legend of Wyatt Earp/Bat Masterson/61 · The Wide Country/63 · The Big Valley/65 · The Guns of Will Sonnett/Custer/Cimarron Strip/Daniel Boone/67 · Lancer/68 · Here Come the Brides/69 · The High Chaparral/ 70 · Alias Smith and Jones/The Trackers/71 · Hec Ramsey/72 · The Legend of the Golden Gun/79 · Independence/87

Arness, James (b 1923) · Actor. Arness had played supporting roles, mainly in Westerns, for eight years before television made him a star. He stood all of six and a half feet and, unless one is playing a Thing from Another World (which Arness strikingly did), such height is hard to accommodate. He fitted effectively into *Wagon Master* as one of the evil Cleggs, but there was little else that mattered until John Wayne recommended him for television's *Gunsmoke*. With the small screen cutting him to size, Arness played Marshal Matt Dillon for twenty years. JL

The Man from Texas/1948 · Wagon Master/ Wyoming Mail/Sierra/1950 · Cavalry Scout/ 1951 · Horizons West/Hellgate/1952 · Hondo/Lone Hand/1953 · Many Rivers to Cross/1955 · The First Traveling Saleslady/ Gun the Man Down/1956

Television The Lone Ranger/50 · Gunsmoke/ 55 · The Macahans/76 · How the West Was Won/77 · The Alamo: 13 Days to Glory/87

Arthur, Jean (b 1908) · Actress, born Gladys Greene. Not until the middle 30s did Jean Arthur establish herself as one of the screen's great comediennes. Before that, she had been the ingenue in many silent Westerns, and she came back to the West in DeMille's *The Plainsman*, where she was a spirited Calamity Jane. Her last film, made in 1952 after some years back on the stage, was George Stevens' classic Western, *Shane*. She played a homesteader's wife who fell quietly in love with Alan Ladd's wandering hero; it was a performance of great gentleness and charm, and a marvellous way to end. JL

Biff Bang Buddy/Bringin' Home the Bacon/ Fast and Fearless/Thundering Romance/ Travelin' Fast/1924 · Drugstore Cowboy/The Fighting Smile/Hurricane Horseman/A Man of Nerve/Tearin' Loose/Thundering Through/ 1925 · Born to Battle/The Cowboy Cop/ Double Daring/The Fighting Cheat/Lightning Bill/Twisted Triggers/Under Fire/1926 · Stairs of Sand/1929 · The Plainsman/1936 · Arizona/1940 · Shane/1952

Television Gunsmoke/65

Autry, Gene (b 1907) · Actor. Autry was the first successful singing Western star. His lack of acting ability was countered by the fact that he always played himself: 'Gene Autry' was his only role. The traits of the screen character that he fashioned (the Autry Code) created a 'pure' cowboy, who was never the first to shoot or strike an adversary, and who never smoked or drank. In the contemporary settings of his films, the frontier has long since been settled, and crimes of violence have in the main given way to crimes of intrigue. Both he and his horse Champion were immensely popular in rural America, and with young audiences everywhere; Autry headed the *Motion Picture Herald* poll of top money-making Western stars from 1937 until he entered the army in 1942. JH

In Old Santa Fe/Mystery Mountain/1934 · The Phantom Empire/Tumbling Tumbleweeds/Melody Trail/The Sagebrush Troubadour/The Singing Vagabond/1935 · Red River Valley/Comin' Round the Mountain/The Singing Cowboy/Guns and Guitars/Oh, Susannah!/Ride, Ranger, Ride/ The Big Show/The Old Corral/1936 · Round-Up Time in Texas/Git Along, Little Dogies/Rootin' Tootin' Rhythm/Yodelin' Kid from Pine Ridge/Public Cowboy No. 1/Boots and Saddles/Springtime in the Rockies/1937 · The Old Barn Dance/Gold Mine in the Sky/Man from Music Mountain/Prairie Moon/Rhythm of the Saddle/Western

Jamboree/1938 · Home on the Prairie/ Mexicali Rose/Blue Montana Skies/ Mountain Rhythm/Colorado Sunset/In Old Monterey/Rovin' Tumbleweeds/South of the Border/1939 · Rancho Grande/Shooting High/Gaucho Serenade/Carolina Moon/Ride, Tenderfoot, Ride/Melody Ranch/1940 · Ridin' on a Rainbow/Back in the Saddle/ Meet Roy Rogers/The Singing Hill/Sunset in Wyoming/Under Fiesta Stars/Down Mexico Way/Sierra Sue/1941 · Cowboy Serenade/ Heart of the Rio Grande/Home in Wyomin'/ Stardust on the Sage/Call of the Canyon/ Bells of Capistrano/1942 · Sioux City Sue/ 1946 · Trail to San Antone/Twilight on the Rio Grande/Saddle Pals/Robin Hood of Texas/Hollywood Cowboys/The Last Round-Up/1947 · The Strawberry Roan/1948 · Loaded Pistols/The Big Sombrero/Riders of the Whistling Pines/Rim of the Canyon/The Cowboy and the Indians/Riders in the Sky/ 1949 · Sons of New Mexico/Mule Train/ Cow Town/Beyond the Purple Hills/Indian Territory/The Blazing Sun/Gene Autry and the Mounties/1950 · Texans Never Cry/ Whirlwind/Silver Canyon/Hills of Utah/ Valley of Fire/1951 · The Old West/Night Stage to Galveston/Apache Country/Barbed Wire/Wagon Team/Blue Canadian Rockies/ Winning of the West/1952 · On Top of Old Smoky/Goldtown Ghost Riders/Pack Train/ Saginaw Trail/Last of the Pony Riders/1953 · Hollywood Bronc Busters/1956 · Alias Jesse James/1959

Television The Gene Autry Show/50

B

Ballard, Lucien (b 1908) · Cinematographer. Born in Miami, Ballard became one of Hollywood's finest location photographers (though he began his career working predominantly in the studio at Paramount with Sternberg). His best work in the genre was for Sam Peckinpah, and to a lesser extent

Lucien Ballard

Budd Boetticher. His invaluable contribution to the Peckinpah canon can be usefully appraised by comparing his and John Coquillon's camerawork; whereas the latter's use of colour tends towards harsh and burnished tones (*Pat Garrett and Billy the Kid*), Ballard's tends towards warm autumnal ones (*Ride the High Country*). DR
Rio Grande/1938 · *The Thundering West/ Texas Stampede*/1939 · (co-c uncredited) *The Outlaw*/1940 · *Return of the Texan/ 1952* · *The Raid*/1954 · *White Feather*/1955 · *The Proud Ones/The King and Four Queens*/1956 · *Buchanan Rides Alone*/1958 · *Ride the High Country*/1962 · *The Sons of Katie Elder/Nevada Smith*/1965 · *An Eye for an Eye*/1966 · *Hour of the Gun/Will Penny*/1967 · *The Wild Bunch/True Grit/A Time for Dying*/1969 · *The Ballad of Cable Hogue*/1970 · *Junior Bonner*/1972 · *Breakheart Pass/From Noon till Three*/1975 Television *Elfego Baca*/58

Barboni, Enzo (b 1922) · Aka E. B. Clucher. After photographing several early Italian Westerns (including *Django*), Barboni directed the double-act of Mario Girotti ('Terence Hill') and Carlo Pedersoli ('Bud Spencer') in the 'Trinity' series of slapstick Westerns at Cinecittà. The double-act had first appeared in *Quattro dell'Ave Maria* (1968), which had enormous success in Europe. Trinity was the lazy but agile blue-eyed 'Northerner', while his brother Bambino ('don't *ever* call me Bambino') was the stout, slow-moving but tough 'Southerner'. Together, they were to become the Tom and Jerry of the Spaghetti Western – with a lot of noisy fistfights and not much bloodshed. *Continuavano a chiamarlo Trinità* made more money in Italy than any other Western before or since. CF
As photographer *Massacro al Grande Canyon*/1963 · *I crudeli/Django/Texas addio/The Bounty Killer*/1966 · *Rita nel west*/1967 · *Vivo per la tua morte/Un treno per Durango*/1968 · *Un esercito di 5 uomini/ 1969
As director *Ciak Mull, l'uomo della vendetta*/1969 · *Lo chiamavano Trinità*/1970 · (sc) *Continuavano a chiamarlo Trinità/ 1971* · *E poi lo chiamarono il magnifico*/ 1972

Barcroft, Roy (1902-69) · Actor, born Howard Ravenscroft. The young Barcroft worked briefly in many trades before reaching Los Angeles in the early 30s. His first film work was as an extra on Garbo's *Mata Hari*. Unimpressed, Barcroft spent six years away, and then, in 1938, began the thirty years that made his name synonymous with that of the B-Western heavy. Large, scowling and moustached, he came to inspire such love-hate that a book on Western players was dedicated to his memory. And at last, even he mellowed, and the Barcroft of his last films is almost a patriarch. JL
Heroes of the Hills/The Stranger from Arizona/The Frontiersman/1938 · *Silver on the Sage/Mexicali Rose/Riders of the Frontier/Renegade Trail*/1939 · *Rancho Grande/Hidden Gold/Bad Man from Red Butte/Yukon Flight/Stage to Chino/Ragtime Cowboy Joe/Trailin' Double Trouble*/1940 · *Pals of the Pecos/The Bandit Trail/Wide Open Town/Jesse James at Bay/Outlaws of the Cherokee Trail/The Masked Rider/West of Cimarron*/1941 · *Sunset on the Desert/ Romance on the Range/Stardust on the Sage/ Sunset Serenade/West of the Law/Pirates of the Prairie/Land of the Open Range/The Old Chisholm Trail*/1942 · *Hoppy Serves a Writ/ Cheyenne Roundup/Calling Wild Bill Elliott/ Carson City Cyclone/The Stranger from Pecos/Bordertown Gun Fighters/False Colors/ Wagon Tracks West/Riders of the Rio Grande*/1943 · *The Laramie Trail/Hidden Valley Outlaws/Code of the Prairie/Lights of Old Santa Fe/Stagecoach to Monterey/ Firebrands of Arizona/Sheriff of Sundown/ Cheyenne Wildcat/The Big Bonanza*/1944 · *The Bells of Rosarita/Sunset in El Dorado/ Dakota/Along the Navajo Trail/Colorado Pioneers/Corpus Christi Bandits/The Cherokee Flash/Lone Texas Ranger/Marshal of Laredo/The Topeka Terror/Trail of Kit Carson/Wagon Wheels Westward*/1945 · *Home on the Range/Alias Billy the Kid/Sun Valley Cyclone/My Pal Trigger/Stagecoach to Denver*/1946 · *Last Frontier Uprising/Oregon Trail Scouts/Son of Zorro/Vigilantes of Boomtown/Rustlers of Devil's Canyon/ Springtime in the Sierras/Wyoming/The Marshal of Cripple Creek/Along the Oregon Trail/The Wild Frontier/Bandits of Dark Canyon*/1947 · *The Bold Frontiersman/ Oklahoma Badlands/The Timber Trail/Eyes of Texas/Sons of Adventure/Grand Canyon Trail/Renegades of Sonora/Desperadoes of Dodge City/Marshal of Amarillo/Sundown in Santa Fe/The Far Frontier*/1948 · *Sheriff of Wichita/Prince of the Plains/Ghost of Zorro/Law of the Golden West/Frontier Investigator/South of Rio/Down Dakota Way/San Antone Ambush/Ranger of Cherokee Strip/Outcasts of the Trail/Powder River Rustlers/The Savage Horde/Pioneer Marshal*/1949 · *Gunmen of Abilene/Arizona Cowboy/The Vanishing Westerner/Rock Island Trail/Code of the Silver Sage/Salt Lake Raiders/Vigilante Hideout/Rustlers on Horseback/The Missourians/Under Mexicali Stars/North of the Great Divide*/1950 · *Wells Fargo Gunmaster/In Old Amarillo/Night Riders of Montana/The Dakota Kid/Rodeo King and the Senorita/Fort Dodge Stampede/ Arizona Manhunt/Utah Wagon Train/ Honeychile/Pals of the Golden West*/1951 · *Leadville Gunslinger/Oklahoma Annie/ Border Saddlemates/Wild Horse Ambush/ Black Hills Ambush/Thundering Caravans/ Old Oklahoma Plains/Ride the Man Down/ South Pacific Trail/Captive of Billy the Kid/*

Roy Barcroft

Lex Barker

Don Barry

Anne Baxter

Alfonso Bedoya

Montana Belle/1952 · The Marshal of
Cedar Rock/Down Laredo Way/Iron
Mountain Trail/Bandits of the West/Savage
Frontier/Old Overland Trail/El Paso
Stampede/Shadows of Tombstone/1953 · The
Desperado/Two Guns and a Badge/1954 ·
Man Without a Star/Oklahoma!/The
Spoilers/1955 · Gun Brothers/1956 · The
Domino Kid/Last Stagecoach West/1957 ·
Escort West/1958 · Six Black Horses/1962 ·
Billy the Kid vs. Dracula/1965 · Texas
Across the River/1966 · The Way West/1967
· Bandolero!/1968
Television The Life and Legend of Wyatt
Earp/55 · Fury/56 · Trackdown/Have Gun,
Will Travel/57 · The Rough Riders/58 ·
Wanted: Dead or Alive/Tales of Wells
Fargo/The Texan/The Deputy/59 ·
Gunsmoke/Laramie/61 · Empire/62 ·
Rawhide/65 · The Iron Horse/67

Barker, Lex (1919-73) · The athletic, bland
and blond New York-born actor took over
the Tarzan persona from Johnny Weiss-
muller in the late 40s. His prolific career
started in 1946 and culminated in European
adventure films, where he achieved a major
success as Karl May's Aryan Übermensch,
Old Shatterhand, in a series of Euro-
Westerns directed by Harald Reinl. His brief
moment of cinematic respectability came
when Fellini cast him in La dolce vita (1959).
Arlene Dahl and Lana Turner were among
his five wives. He died of a heart attack in
Hollywood. PW
Under the Tonto Rim/Unconquered/1947 ·
Return of the Bad Men/1948 · The Battles of
Chief Pontiac/Thunder Over the Plains/1952
· The Yellow Mountain/1954 · The Man
from Bitter Ridge/1955 · War Drums/1956 ·
The Deerslayer/1957 · Der Schatz im
Silbersee/1962 · Winnetou/1963 · Winnetou
II/1964 · Winnetou III/La ballada de Johnny
Ringo/1965 · Winnetou und das Halbblut
Apanatschi/1967 · Winnetou und
Shatterhand im Tal der Toten/1968

Barry, Don (1912-80) · Actor. A very tough
man indeed, with the physique to match his
footballing past, Don Barry made his first
Western mark in 1939, supporting John

Wayne and the Mesquiteers, and a year later
played the lead in the Red Ryder serial,
acquiring for himself the sobriquet of 'Red'
Barry. Then came series Westerns for
Republic, smaller parts in the 50s, and a
come-back in A. C. Lyles Westerns for
veterans. Not all of this was routine. He
played Jesse James twice and Billy the Kid
once, had a dual role in Two-Gun Sheriff as
good guy and bad, and even enlisted Presi-
dent McKinley's aid to sort out the Arizona
Terrors. JL
Wyoming Outlaw/Saga of Death Valley/
Days of Jesse James/1939 · Ghost Valley
Raiders/Adventures of Red Ryder/One Man's
Law/The Tulsa Kid/Frontier Vengeance/
Texas Terrors/1940 · Kansas Cyclone/The
Apache Kid/A Missouri Outlaw/Wyoming
Wildcat/Two-Gun Sheriff/The Phantom
Cowboy/Desert Bandit/Death Valley
Outlaws/1941 · Jesse James Jr./Stagecoach
Express/The Cyclone Kid/Arizona Terrors/
The Sombrero Kid/Outlaws of Pine Ridge/
1942 · The Sundown Kid/Carson City
Cyclone/Canyon City/Black Hills Express/
Fugitive from Sonora/Dead Man's Gulch/
The Man from the Rio Grande/Days of Old
Cheyenne/1943 · Outlaws of Santa Fe/
California Joe/Mojave Firebrand/1944 · Bells
of Rosarita/1945 · Out California Way/The
Plainsman and the Lady/1946 · Square
Dance Jubilee/Tough Assignment/The Dalton
Gang/Red Desert/1949 · Gunfire/Border
Rangers/Train to Tombstone/I Shot Billy the
Kid/1950 · (d) Jesse James' Women/
Untamed Heiress/1954 · The Twinkle in
God's Eye/1955 · Seven Men from Now/
1956 · Gun Duel in Durango/1957 · Born
Reckless/Warlock/1959 · Walk Like a
Dragon/1960 · Law of the Lawless/1963 ·
War Party/Fort Courageous/Convict Stage/
Town Tamer/1965 · Apache Uprising/
Alvarez Kelly/1966 · Fort Utah/Red
Tomahawk/Hostile Guns/The Shakiest Gun
in the West/1967 · Shalako/Bandolero!/1968
· Dirty Dingus Magee/Rio Lobo/The
Cockeyed Cowboys of Calico County/1970 ·
Junior Bonner/1972
Television Colt .45/58 · Lawman/Sugarfoot/
59 · Bat Masterson/Maverick/60 · Bronco/62
· Gunsmoke/63 · Bonanza/64 · The
Virginian/65 · Laredo/66 · Cimarron Strip/
68 · The Wild, Wild West/69 · Little House
on the Prairie/76

Baxter, Anne (1923-85) · Actress. In her
non-Western films Anne Baxter could be the
essence of calm: calmly devious in All About
Eve, calmly sincere in The Magnificent
Ambersons. But something about the West

seemed to transform the lady – into the
high-spirited youngster of Yellow Sky, the
dance-hall girl of The Spoilers (a role in which
she followed Dietrich), even the sharp-
shooting miss of A Ticket to Tomahawk.
Perhaps that was where her heart was: hear-
ing her tell the story of the Indian in
Ambersons one could well have thought so.
She would have made a wonderful Ford
heroine. JL
20 Mule Team/1940 · Smoky/1946 · Yellow
Sky/1948 · A Ticket to Tomahawk/1950 ·
The Outcasts of Poker Flat/1952 · The
Spoilers/1955 · Three Violent People/1956 ·
Cimarron/1960 · Las siete magnificas/1966 ·
Fools' Parade/1971
Television Wagon Train/58 · Dick Powell's
Zane Grey Theatre/Riverboat/59 · The Loner/
65 · Stranger on the Run/67 · The Virginian/
68 · The Big Valley/69

Bedoya, Alfonso (1904-57) · Actor. While
filming The Treasure of the Sierra Madre on
location in Mexico, John Huston met
Alfonso Bedoya and cast him for what was
to prove a key role in the film. As the
smiling, deadly bandit who is Humphrey
Bogart's nemesis, Bedoya exuded a bizarre
menace which precisely fitted the film's
allegory of self-destructive greed. Bedoya
stayed on in American movies, but not until
The Big Country did he appear in another
major Western. Before he met Huston, he
had made around 170 Mexican films, the
titles impossible to trace. JL
The Treasure of the Sierra Madre/1948 ·
Streets of Laredo/1949 · Man in the Saddle/
1951 · California Conquest/1952 · The
Stranger Wore a Gun/Border River/1953 ·
The Outcast/Ricochet Romance/Ten Wanted
Men/1954 · The Big Country/1958

Beery, Wallace (1885-1949) · Actor. In the
movies from 1913 until his death, Beery
began, astonishingly, as a female imperso-

Wallace Beery

nator. He moved into light comedy, and then into features, where until sound he was often the heavy for which his physique and face fitted him. Sound made him a star, and sympathetic. His Pat Garrett in Vidor's *Billy the Kid* was his first Western hero. Many others followed – gnarled old-timers with dubious pasts, and underneath the tough exterior often sentimental to a fault. Apart from *Viva Villa!* the films were mainly routine fare: he never had the luck to work with the great Western directors. JL
Sagebrush Trail/1919 · *The Last of the Mohicans*/*The Round-Up*/*The Mollycoddle*/1920 · *The Last Trail*/1921 · *The Northern Trail*/*I Am the Law*/*The Man from Hell's River*/*The Sagebrush Trail*/1922 · *Dynamite Smith*/1924 · *The Great Divide*/*The Pony Express*/*Coming Through*/1925 · *The Stairs of Sand*/1929 · *Billy the Kid*/1930 · *Viva Villa!*/1934 · *Bad Man of Brimstone*/1937 · *Stand Up and Fight*/1939 · *The Man from Dakota*/*20 Mule Team*/*Wyoming*/1940 · *The Bad Man*/1941 · *Jackass Mail*/1942 · *Barbary Coast Gent*/1944 · *Bad Bascomb*/1946 · *Big Jack*/1949

Bellah, James Warner (1899-1976) · Writer. Bellah's short stories about the life and times of the horse soldiers at Fort Starke (mostly published in the *Saturday Evening Post*) became the basis for John Ford's cavalry trilogy. Most of them, including 'Mission With No Record' (*Rio Grande*) and 'Massacre' (*Fort Apache*), were reprinted in the collection *Reveille* (Fawcett, 1962). His responsibility-under-pressure story, 'Rear Guard', became the basis of the Warners cavalry saga *The Command* and 'Captain Buffalo' (co-written with Willis Goldbeck, after the latter approached Bellah with an idea based on a Frederic Remington painting of Negro cavalrymen) became Ford's *Sergeant Rutledge*. One of Bellah's finest non-cavalry collaborations with Goldbeck, again for Ford, was *The Man Who Shot Liberty Valance*, based on a story by Dorothy M. Johnson. The Western/cavalry world of James Warner Bellah can be summed up in the closing narration from *She Wore a Yellow Ribbon*: 'So here they are. The dogfaced soldiers, the regulars, the fifty-cents-a-day professionals. Riding the outposts of a nation. From Fort Reno to Fort Apache, from Sheridan to Starke, they were all the same. Men in dirty-shirt blue and only a cold page in the history books to mark their passing. But wherever they rode and whatever they fought for, that place became the United States.' TV

(st only) Fort Apache/1948 · *(st only) She Wore a Yellow Ribbon*/1949 · *(st only) Rio Grande*/1950 · *(novel only) The Command*/1954 · *(co-st, co-sc) Sergeant Rutledge*/1960 · *(st) A Thunder of Drums*/*(co-sc) The Man Who Shot Liberty Valance*/1962 · *(st only) The Legend of Nigger Charley*/1972
Television *The Americans*/61 · *Temple Houston*/63

Bennett, Bruce (b 1906) · Actor. An Olympic Games shot-putter and world-record holder, Bennett entered movies in the mid-30s under his real name of Herman Brix. He starred in serials and played Tarzan in two modest ventures. Changing his name in 1940, he played supporting roles effectively in a wide variety of films (*Mildred Pierce*, *Dark Passage*), and was outstanding as the intrusive lone prospector in *The Treasure of the Sierra Madre*. After appearing in several minor Westerns, he retired to television in the early 60s. JL
(As Brix) The Lone Ranger/1938 · *(As Bennett) Blazing Six-Shooters*/*West of Abilene*/1940 · *Frontier Fury*/1943 · *Cheyenne*/1947 · *The Treasure of the Sierra Madre*/*Silver River*/*The Younger Brothers*/1948 · *The Great Missouri Raid*/1950 · *The Last Outpost*/1951 · *Robber's Roost*/*Hidden Guns*/1955 · *Daniel Boone, Trail Blazer*/*Three Violent People*/1956 · *Flaming Frontier*/1958
Television *The Texan*/58 · *Laramie*/60 · *Branded*/65 · *The Virginian*/67

Bernstein, Elmer (b 1922) · One of the most popular composers to come out of the 50s, Bernstein's scores for action movies created a unique and memorable sound. His start with Westerns was nothing spectacular but in 1959 his music for the television series *Riverboat* was the first signs of stirring things to come. The following year he was to compose the music for one of the classic Westerns, *The Magnificent Seven*. Following the success of the film Bernstein became one of the most prolific composers of the 60s and 70s. TM
The Battles of Chief Pontiac/1952 · *Drango*/*The Tin Star*/1957 · *Saddle the Wind*/1958 · *The Magnificent Seven*/1960 · *The Comancheros*/1961 · *Hud*/1962 · *The Hallelujah Trail*/1964 · *The Reward*/*The Sons of Katie Elder*/1965 · *Return of the Seven*/1966 · *The Scalphunters*/1967 · *Guns of the Magnificent Seven*/1968 · *True Grit*/1969 · *A Cannon for Cordoba*/1970 · *Big Jake*/1971 · *The Magnificent Seven Ride!*/1972 · *Cahill United States Marshal*/1973 · *The Trial of Billy Jack*/1974 · *From Noon till Three*/1975 · *The Shootist*/1976
Television *Riverboat*/59

Bettger, Lyle (b 1915) · Actor. Fair-haired, cold-eyed, Bettger is one of the great Western villains. He has excelled playing heartless characters, usually a rancher with a hatred of farmers or Indians, or the callous leader of an outlaw gang. His best remembered roles are that of Ike Clanton, the man who opposed Wyatt Earp in *Gunfight at the O.K. Corral*, and the powerful rancher who starts an Indian uprising in *The Lone Ranger*. TM
Denver and Rio Grande/1952 · *The Vanquished*/*The Great Sioux Uprising*/1953 · *Drums Across the River*/*Destry*/1954 · *The Lone Ranger*/*Showdown at Abilene*/*Gunfight at the O.K. Corral*/1956 · *Guns of the Timberland*/1959 · *Town Tamer*/*Johnny Reno*/*Nevada Smith*/1965 · *The Fastest Guitar Alive*/1966
Television *Death Valley Days*/52 · *Gunsmoke*/55 · *Tales of Wells Fargo*/*Dick Powell's Zane Grey Theatre*/56 · *Wagon Train*/57 · *The Rifleman*/58 · *Laramie*/*The Deputy*/*Bonanza*/*Rawhide*/*Law of the Plainsman*/59 · *Daniel Boone*/64 · *Cimarron Strip*/*Return of the Gunfighter*/67 · *The Men from Shiloh*/70

Bruce Bennett

Lyle Bettger

Bickford, Charles (1889-1967) · Actor. Bickford came from the stage to Hollywood with the introduction of sound, and ability combined with a rough handsomeness gave him immediate leads, even opposite Garbo in *Anna Christie*. *Hell's Heroes* of 1929 was a version of *Three Godfathers*, with Bickford in the lead. As he aged, he moved into character parts. Rugged, laconic, and still handsome, he was as effective for the law as against it. For over 30 years he made occasional Westerns: in his last, he was one of the hoodwinked gamblers in the delicious *A Big Hand for the Little Lady*. JL
Hell's Heroes/1929 · *River's End*/1930 · *The Squaw Man*/1931 · *Rose of the Rancho/The Plainsman*/1936 · *Thunder Trail/High, Wide and Handsome*/1937 · *Valley of Giants*/1938 · *Stand Up and Fight/Romance of the Redwoods*/1939 · *Queen of the Yukon*/1940 · *Riders of Death Valley*/1941 · *Duel in the Sun*/1946 · *Four Faces West*/1948 · *Branded*/1950 · *The Last Posse*/1953 · *The Big Country*/1958 · *The Unforgiven*/1959 · *A Big Hand for the Little Lady*/1966
Television *Wagon Train*/58 · *The Americans*/61 · *The Virginian*/62

Big Tree, Chief John (1865-1967) · Isaac Johnny John, as he really was, became the greatest of Indian actors. His career lasted from 1915 to 1950. When he was 84, in *She Wore a Yellow Ribbon*, he and John Wayne agreed they were too old for war, and Big Tree urged his friend to ride away to smoke and drink together. Earlier, he appeared quietly in Claudette Colbert's kitchen in *Drums Along the Mohawk*, and scared the wits out of that city girl, and in *Stagecoach*, at 73, he stunted alongside Yakima Canutt. And not until his 102nd year did Isaac Johnny John decide that it was a good day to die. JL
Author! Author!/The Cactus Blossom/1915 · *A Fight for Love*/1919 · *The Primitive Lover*/

1922 · *The Huntress*/1923 · *The Iron Horse*/1924 · *The Red Rider*/1925 · *The Desert's Toll/The Frontier Trail/Ranson's Folly/Winners of the Wilderness*/1926 · *Painted Ponies/The Frontiersman/Spoilers of the West*/1927 · *Wyoming*/1928 · *The Overland Telegraph/Sioux Blood*/1929 · *Red Fork Range*/1931 · *The Singing Vagabond*/1935 · *Hills of Old Wyoming*/1937 · *Stagecoach/Destry Rides Again/Susannah of the Mounties/Drums Along the Mohawk*/1939 · *Brigham Young – Frontiersman*/1940 · *Hudson's Bay/Western Union*/1941 · *Unconquered*/1947 · *She Wore a Yellow Ribbon*/1949 · *Devil's Doorway*/1950

Boehm, Sydney (b 1908) · Writer. Boehm's masterpiece is undoubtedly *The Big Heat*. Of the Westerns, Hugo Fregonese's brilliant Civil War drama *The Raid* and Raoul Walsh's cattle-driving epic *The Tall Men* (which Boehm co-scripted with Frank Nugent) show off the writer's tough, spare, economical style to best advantage. JP
(co-sc) *Branded*/1950 · *The Savage*/1952 · *The Siege at Red River*/1953 · *The Raid*/1954 · (co-sc) *The Tall Men*/1955 · (co-sc, p) *One Foot in Hell*/1960 · (co-sc) *Rough Night in Jericho*/1967

Boetticher, Budd [Oscar] (b 1916) · Director. Boetticher is the perfect example of the auteur: his Westerns gain immeasurably when viewed as a totality. This is especially true of the series with Randolph Scott, beginning with *Seven Men from Now*, most of which were produced by Harry Joe Brown and scripted by Burt Kennedy. Working in the tradition of the B-Western, with modest resources, Boetticher achieved works of great beauty, formally precise in structure and visually elegant, notably in their use of the distinctive landscape of the California Sierras. As the hero of these 'floating poker games' (as Andrew Sarris called them), Scott

tempers their innately pessimistic view of the world with quiet, stoical humour, as he pits his wits against such charming villains as Richard Boone in *The Tall T* and Claude Akins in *Comanche Station*. Boetticher had trained as a bullfighter and made several films about matadors. His Westerns are concerned exclusively with individual courage and self-reliance, showing none of Ford's interest in the values of the community or sense of historical tradition. Jim Kitses in his book *Horizons West*, the best description of Boetticher's work, calls his films 'small, glittering morality plays'. Yet characteristically, even overt statements of this morality emerge in stylishly laconic form: 'There are some things a man can't ride around.' EB
The Wolf Hunters/1949 · *The Cimarron Kid/Bronco Buster*/1951 · *Horizons West*/1952 · *Seminole/The Man from the Alamo/Wings of the Hawk*/1953 · *Seven Men from Now/The Tall T*/1956 · *Decision at Sundown*/1957 · *Buchanan Rides Alone/Westbound*/1958 · *Ride Lonesome/Comanche Station*/1959 · (sc) *A Time For Dying*/(st only) *Two Mules for Sister Sara*/1969
Television *Maverick*/57

Bond, Ward (1905-60) · Actor. Ward Bond's Western career began in the epic *The Big Trail* and his last film but one was the Hawks classic *Rio Bravo*. In between he established a gruff though sometimes genial persona in a prolific career ranging from Buck Jones Westerns to more prestigious pictures such as *Dodge City* and *Sante Fe Trail*. He became a prominent member of the John Ford stock company of actors and played key supporting roles in many of Ford's best known Westerns, notably *My Darling Clementine*, *Fort Apache*, *Wagon Master* and *The Searchers*. At the end of his career he had great success with the anchor role in *Wagon Train*. TR

Charles Bickford

Chief Big Tree

Budd Boetticher

Ward Bond

Richard Boone

Ernest Borgnine

William Boyd

The Big Trail/1930 · *White Eagle*/*Hello Trouble*/1932 · *The Fighting Code*/*Unknown Valley*/*The Sundown Rider*/1933 · *Frontier Marshal*/*The Fighting Ranger*/1934 · *The Crimson Trail*/*Fighting Shadows*/*Justice of the Range*/*Western Courage*/1935 · *The Cattle Thief*/*Avenging Waters*/1936 · *Gun Law*/*The Law West of Tombstone*/1938 · *Trouble in Sundown*/*The Oklahoma Kid*/*Dodge City*/*Return of the Cisco Kid*/*Drums Along the Mohawk*/*Frontier Marshal*/*The Cisco Kid and the Lady*/1939 · *Virginia City*/*Kit Carson*/*Sante Fe Trail*/*Buck Benny Rides Again*/1940 · *The Shepherd of the Hills*/1941 · *Wild Bill Hickok Rides*/*Sin Town*/1942 · *The Cowboy Commandos*/1943 · *Tall in the Saddle*/1944 · *Dakota*/1945 · *Canyon Passage*/*My Darling Clementine*/1946 · *Unconquered*/1947 · *Fort Apache*/*3 Godfathers*/1948 · *Singing Guns*/*Wagon Master*/*Only the Valiant*/1950 · *The Great Missouri Raid*/1951 · *Hellgate*/1952 · *The Moonlighter*/*Hondo*/*Gypsy Colt*/1953 · *Johnny Guitar*/1954 · *A Man Alone*/1955 · *The Searchers*/*Dakota Incident*/*Pillars of the Sky*/1956 · *The Halliday Brand*/1957 · *Rio Bravo*/1958 · *Alias Jesse James*/1959 Television *Wagon Train*/57

Boone, Richard (1921-81) · Actor. Burly and grizzled, ageless and taciturn, Richard Boone was one of the most striking of the Western's good-badmen. Boone was an actor filled with the weight of experience. It took a Western hero all his time to live with him, and perhaps only Randolph Scott, in Budd Boetticher's *The Tall T*, really managed it. In that finely judged film Boone's outlaw, who is a homesteader at heart, rightly takes his share of the viewer's sympathy. Boone created another memorable outlaw in *Hombre*; yet on the side of virtue, as with his Sam Houston in *The Alamo*, he could be equally impressive. From 1957 he became well known in the lead part in *Have Gun, Will Travel*. JL
Return of the Texan/*Way of a Gaucho*/1952 · *City of Bad Men*/*The Siege at Red River*/1953 · *The Raid*/*Ten Wanted Men*/1954 · *Man Without a Star*/*Robber's Roost*/1955 · *Star in the Dust*/*The Tall T*/1956 · *The Alamo*/1960 · *A Thunder of Drums*/1961 · *Rio Conchos*/1964 · *Hombre*/1966 · *Madron*/1970 · *Big Jake*/1971 · *Against a Crooked Sky*/1975 · *The Shootist*/*Diamante lobo*/1976 Television *Frontier*/56 · *Have Gun, Will Travel*/57 · *Cimarron Strip*/67 · *Hec Ramsey*/72

Borgnine, Ernest (b 1918) · Actor. As Bart

Lonergan in Nicholas Ray's *Johnny Guitar*, Ernest Borgnine utilizes to great effect the sadistic and menacing screen persona established in the army picture *From Here to Eternity*. Although he was to display a greater range in *Marty*, it is the villainous potential of his expressive face that has best suited the genre. TR
The Stranger Wore a Gun/1953 · *Johnny Guitar*/*The Bounty Hunter*/*Vera Cruz*/*Run for Cover*/*Bad Day at Black Rock*/1954 · *The Last Command*/1955 · *Jubal*/1956 · *The Badlanders*/1958 · *Chuka*/1967 · *Villa Rides*/1968 · *The Wild Bunch*/*Quei disperati che puzzano di sudore e di morte*/1969 · *Hannie Caulder*/1971 · *The Revengers*/1972 Television *Wagon Train*/*Dick Powell's Zane Grey Theatre*/57 · *Laramie*/59 · *Sam Hill: Who Killed the Mysterious Mr Foster?*/*The Trackers*/71 · *Little House on the Prairie*/74

Bowers, William (1916-87) · A former journalist, he began a prolific screenwriting career in 1942, and despite once claiming that he had never been near a horse, he worked quite often on Westerns. His scripts vary widely in tone and achievement, but include the beautifully modulated *The Law and Jake Wade*. His most distinct contribution to the genre, however, was in the vein of relaxed, semi-satirical comedy, as with *The Sheepman* and *Support Your Local Sheriff!* TP
(co-st) *The Wistful Widow of Wagon Gap*/1947 · (co-sc) *Black Bart*/(co-sc) *River Lady*/1948 · (co-st, co-sc) *The Gal Who Took the West*/1949 · (co-st, co-sc) *The Gunfighter*/1950 · (co-sc) *The Sheepman*/*The Law and Jake Wade*/1958 · (co-sc) *Alias Jesse James*/1959 · (co-sc) *Advance to the Rear*/1963 · (co-sc) *The Ride to Hangman's Tree*/1967 · (p, sc) *Support Your Local Sheriff!*/1968 Television *Sidekicks*/*The Gun and the Pulpit*/74 · *Kate Bliss and the Ticker Tape Kid*/78 · *The Wild Wild West Revisited*/79 · *More Wild Wild West*/80

Boyd, William (1895-1972) · A star in the 20s, Boyd's career had flagged in the early 30s until he took the title role in Paramount's *Hop-A-Long Cassidy* in 1935. From this moment Boyd played no other part. After this first outing, Boyd cleaned up the Hopalong character and eliminated the limp which had given him his name. Mounted on his white horse, Topper, Boyd's Hopalong cut a striking figure – blue-eyed with prematurely white hair, and garbed, somewhat against tradition, in black. The series, which featured Hopalong and his two accomplices in their endeavours to capture rather than kill the villains, popularized the 'trio Western'. So successful was the Hopalong formula that the series ran for fourteen years and sixty-six films, the last twelve of which Boyd produced himself. JH

The Last Frontier/1926 · *Jim the Conqueror*/1927 · *The Spoilers*/*The Storm*/1930 · *The Painted Desert*/1931 · *Carnival Boat*/1932 · *Hop-A-Long Cassidy*/*The Eagle's Brood*/*Bar 20 Rides Again*/1935 · *Call of the Prairie*/*Three on the Trail*/*Heart of the West*/*Hopalong Cassidy Returns*/*Trail Dust*/1936 · *Borderland*/*Hills of Old Wyoming*/*North of the Rio Grande*/*Rustler's Valley*/*Hopalong Rides Again*/*Texas Trail*/1937 · *Heart of Arizona*/*Bar 20 Justice*/*Pride of the West*/*In Old Mexico*/*The Frontiersman*/*Partners of the Plains*/*Cassidy of Bar 20*/1938 · *Sunset Trail*/*Range War*/*Law of the Pampas*/*Silver on the Sage*/*Renegade Trail*/1939 · *Santa Fe Marshal*/*The Showdown*/*Hidden Gold*/*Stagecoach War*/*Three Men from Texas*/1940 · *Doomed Caravan*/*In Old Colorado*/*Border Vigilantes*/*Pirates on Horseback*/*Wide Open Town*/*Outlaws of the Desert*/*Riders of the Timberline*/*Secrets of the Wasteland*/*Stick to Your Guns*/*Twilight on the Trail*/1941 · *Undercover Man*/*Lost Canyon*/*Border Patrol*/*The Leather Burners*/1942 · *Colt Comrades*/*Bar 20*/*Hoppy Serves a Writ*/*False Colors*/*Riders of the Deadline*/1943 · *Mystery Man*/*Forty Thieves*/*Texas Masquerade*/*Lumberjack*/1944 · *The Devil's Playground*/*Fool's Gold*/1946 · *Unexpected Guest*/*Dangerous Venture*/*Hoppy's Holiday*/*The Marauders*/*Silent Conflict*/1947 · *The Dead Don't Dream*/*Sinister Journey*/*Borrowed Trouble*/*False Paradise*/*Strange Gamble*/1948 Television *Hopalong Cassidy*/51

Brady, Scott (1924-85) · A one-time lumberjack and navy boxing champion, he was a prolific, though generally rather impassive, actor in an assortment of programmers,

usually playing the second-lead or 'other man'. He was at his most effective in roles vitalized by a degree of neurotic instability, notably the 'Dancing Kid' in *Johnny Guitar*. He proved sufficiently durable to appear in several of the A. C. Lyles Westerns of the 60s, and later still starred, more impassive than ever, in a gory exploitation Western, *Cain's Way*. TP

The Gal Who Took the West/1949 · *Kansas Raiders*/1950 · *Montana Belle*/*Bronco Buster*/1951 · *Untamed Frontier*/1952 · *A Perilous Journey*/1953 · *Johnny Guitar*/*The Law vs. Billy the Kid*/1954 · *The Vanishing American*/*Mohawk*/1955 · *The Maverick Queen*/1956 · *The Storm Rider*/*The Restless Breed*/*Ambush at Cimarron Pass*/*Blood Arrow*/1957 · *Stage to Thunder Rock*/*Black Spurs*/1964 · *Red Tomahawk*/1966 · *Fort Utah*/*Arizona Bushwhackers*/1967 · *The Gun Riders*/1969 · *Cain's Way*/1970 Television *Dick Powell's Zane Grey Theatre*/57 · *Shotgun Slade*/59 · *The Virginian*/68 · *Gunsmoke*/69 · *Lancer*/*The High Chaparral*/70 · *The Men from Shiloh*/71 · *The Last Ride of the Dalton Gang*/79

Brand, Neville (b 1921) · Actor. Brand started in army training films and was promoted as the fourth most decorated soldier of World War II. He worked himself into the position of one of Hollywood's heaviest villains. His hulking figure, fleshy, thick-set face and rasping voice made him ideally suited for mobster roles, a career topped by his performance as the loud-mouthed, cigar-chewing Capone in *The Untouchables*. In Westerns he was the black-clad villain who terrorized young Anthony Perkins in *The Tin Star*. His screen presence exudes a sense of physical power and ruthlessness, combined with near-psychotic unpredictability, providing memorable moments in many otherwise routine films. PW

Only the Valiant/1950 · *Red Mountain*/1951

· *The Man from the Alamo*/*The Charge at Feather River*/*Gun Fury*/1953 · *The Lone Gun*/1954 · *The Return of Jack Slade*/*Mohawk*/1955 · *Fury at Gunsight Pass*/*Gun Brothers*/*Love Me Tender*/*The Three Outlaws*/*The Lonely Man*/1956 · *The Tin Star*/1957 · *Badman's Country*/1958 · *The Last Sunset*/1961 · *The Desperados*/1968 · *Cahill United States Marshal*/*The Deadly Trackers*/1973 Television *The Texan*/58 · *Dick Powell's Zane Grey Theatre*/59 · *Rawhide*/*Bonanza*/60 · *Death Valley Days*/61 · *Destry*/*Wagon Train*/64 · *The Virginian*/*Gunsmoke*/*Laredo*/65 · *The Men from Shiloh*/70 · *Lock, Stock and Barrel*/*Alias Smith and Jones*/71 · *Hitched*/73 · *The Barbary Coast*/75 · *The Quest*/76 · *The Seekers*/79

Brando, Marlon (b 1924) · Actor. Always a commanding presence on the screen, Brando remains controversial for his semi-articulate, 'physical' performances – sometimes judged mannered or 'excessive'. Trained at The Actor's Studio, he quickly became the most celebrated 'method' actor in cinema. In his first three Westerns (including *One-Eyed Jacks*, which he directed), Brando plays brooding, rebellious loners struggling for self-expression. In these masochistic roles, he is abused, humiliated, seemingly defeated, until the force inherent in his powerful physique explodes in purifying violence. The crafty, sardonic side of his mature screen personality dominates *The Missouri Breaks*, where he plays the sadistic Lee Clayton with extravagant gusto. DG

Viva Zapata!/1952 · (d) *One-Eyed Jacks*/1960 · *The Appaloosa*/1966 · *The Missouri Breaks*/1976

Brennan, Walter (1894-1974) · Actor. Most moviegoers' persisting image of Brennan is that of the toothless old rummy of *To Have and Have Not*, asking passers-by whether

Scott Brady

Neville Brand

Marlon Brando

Walter Brennan

they was ever stung by a dead bee. There was far more to the man than that engaging characterization. From 1927 he worked in B-Westerns, branched out in the 30s as a versatile character man, appeared in 1932 in a major Western, *Law and Order*, on what would become the familiar theme of cleaning up Tombstone, was one of the Three Godfathers in the 1936 version, and then won three Oscars for Best Supporting Actor in five years – one of them for his portrayal of the ruthless Judge Roy Bean in *The Westerner*. And *Red River* and *Rio Bravo* were still to come. JL

Tearin' into Trouble/The Ridin' Rowdy/1927 · The Ballyhoo Buster/1928 · Smilin' Guns/ The Lariat Kid/The Long, Long Trail/1929 · Law and Order/Texas Cyclone/Two-Fisted Law/1932 · Man of Action/Fighting for Justice/Silent Men/1933 · Northern Frontier/ Land Beyond the Range/1935 · Three Godfathers/The Prescott Kid/1936 · Wild and Woolly/1937 · The Texans/The Cowboy and the Lady/1938 · Northwest Passage/The Westerner/1940 · Dakota/1945 · My Darling Clementine/1946 · Red River/1947 · Blood on the Moon/1948 · Brimstone/1949 · A Ticket to Tomahawk/Singing Guns/Curtain Call at Cactus Creek/The Showdown/1950 · Along the Great Divide/Best of the Badmen/1951 · Return of the Texan/1952 · Drums Across the River/Four Guns to the Border/Bad Day at Black Rock/The Far Country/1954 · Gunpoint/1955 · The Proud Ones/1956 · The Way to the Gold/1957 · Rio Bravo/1958 · Shoot Out at Big Sag/How the West Was Won/1962 · Support Your Local Sheriff!/ 1968 · Smoke in the Wind/1971 Television Dick Powell's Zane Grey Theatre/ 56 · The Guns of Will Sonnett/67 · The Over-the-Hill Gang/69 · The Over-the-Hill Gang Rides Again/The Young Country/70 · Alias Smith and Jones/71

Bridges, Lloyd (b 1913) · Actor. A physically imposing figure, tall and blond, he has a somewhat featureless aspect, which has tended to be exploited in characterizations displaying moral weakness. The most notable example in the genre is his role as Gary Cooper's disgruntled deputy in *High Noon*, and he played to somewhat similar effect as an unscrupulous cavalry officer in *Ride Out for Revenge*. More recently he has been a ubiquitous television performer, but has seldom gone West on the small screen. TP

The Royal Mounted Patrol/The Son of Davy Crockett/1941 · Riders of the Northland/ Pardon My Gun/North of the Rockies/West of Tombstone/1942 · Hail to the Rangers/ 1943 · Saddle Leather Law/1944 · The Medico of Painted Springs/1945 · Abilene Town/Canyon Passage/1946 · Ramrod/ Unconquered/1947 · Red Canyon/1948 · Calamity Jane and Sam Bass/1949 · Colt .45/1950 · Little Big Horn/1951 · High Noon/Last of the Comanches/1952 · The Tall Texan/City of Bad Men/1953 · Wichita/Apache Woman/1955 · Ride Out for Revenge/1957 Television Wagon Train/Dick Powell's Zane Grey Theatre/57 · The Great Adventure/64 · The Loner/65 · The Silent Gun/69 · How the West Was Won/77

Bronson, Charles (b 1921) · Actor, aka Charles Bushinski, Charles Buchinsky. Craggily built actor who achieved great box-office popularity in the late 60s, especially in Europe, on the strength of films like *C'era una volta il west*. He began in minor supporting roles, generally villainous, and on more than one occasion, perhaps because of his high cheekbones, was cast as an Indian (prime example, *Run of the Arrow*). In his later starring days, he played half-breeds in *Chato's Land* and *Valdez il mezzosangue*. Many of his roles have been on the one-dimensional side; one that made a positive virtue of the fact was the posturing villain of *4 for Texas*. TP

Riding Shotgun/1952 · Apache/Vera Cruz/ Drum Beat/1954 · Jubal/1956 · Run of the Arrow/Showdown at Boot Hill/1957 · The Magnificent Seven/1960 · A Thunder of Drums/1961 · 4 for Texas/1963 · La Bataille de San Sebastian/Villa Rides/C'era una volta il west/1968 · Soleil rouge/Chato's Land/ 1971 · Valdez, il mezzosangue/1973 · Breakheart Pass/From Noon till Three/1975 · The White Buffalo/1977 · Death Hunt/ 1981 Television The Roy Rogers Show/52 · Gunsmoke/56 · Have Gun, Will Travel/Colt .45/57 · Tales of Wells Fargo/Sugarfoot/58 · U.S. Marshal/Yancy Derringer/59 · Laramie/Riverboat/60 · Empire/62 · The Travels of Jaimie McPheeters/Redigo/63 · Bonanza/64 · The Big Valley/The Virginian/ Rawhide/65 · The Legend of Jesse James/66 · Dundee and the Culhane/67

Brown, Harry (1917-86) · The novelist and poet Harry Brown wrote largely of War and the West. He made his name with the novel *A Walk in the Sun*, based on his war service in Italy and filmed by Lewis Milestone. He collaborated on the scripts of four Westerns, but two others drawn from his novels were far more important. Val Lewton's last film, *Apache Drums*, came from Brown's *Stand at Spanish Boot*, while Hawks' marvellous *El Dorado* was based on Brown's *The Stars in Their Courses*. That film perfectly catches the sad, stoical tone of Brown's best writing. JL

(co-sc) Only the Valiant/(novel only) Apache Drums/1950 · (co-sc) Bugles in the Afternoon/1951 · (co-sc) Many Rivers to Cross/1955 · (co-sc) The Fiend Who Walked the West/1958 · (novel only) El Dorado/ 1966

Brown, Harry Joe (1892-1972) · Director, producer. Trained as a lawyer, Brown first made his mark in cinema as production manager for the short-lived Western star Fred Thomson, whose first two films he also directed in 1924. In 1926 he became associate producer on the Ken Maynard series at First National (later at Universal), a number of which he directed himself. Abandoning direction, he became a jack-of-all-trades producer during the 30s, first at RKO-Pathé, then Fox, returning to the Western as associate producer to Fritz Lang on *Western Union*. Struck by Randolph Scott's authoritative Western persona, Brown worked with the actor again on *The Desperadoes*, *The Gun-fighters* and *Coroner Creek*, and in 1948 set up a production company in partnership with him. The culmination of their efforts together was the very fine series starring Scott and directed by Budd Boetticher that ran from *Seven Men from Now* (the only one not produced by Brown) to *Comanche Station*. Although Brown worked almost exclusively within the B-Western, his output richly deserves the term 'superior'. TMi

(co-sc, c) The Fighting Smile/1925 · As director/associate producer: Galloping Gallagher/1924 · Moran of the Mounted/ 1926 · The Land Beyond the Law/Gun Gospel/The Wagon Show/1927 · Code of the Scarlet/1928 · The Lawless Legion/Señor Americano/The Royal Rider/The Wagon Master/Lucky Larkin/Parade of the West/ 1929 · The Fighting Legion/Mountain Justice/Song of the Caballero/Sons of the Saddle/1930 · As supervisor: The Red Raiders/Somewhere in Sonora/1927 · The Canyon of Adventure/The Glorious Trail/ The Phantom Trail/The Upland Rider/1928 · The California Mail/Cheyenne/1929 · As production manager: Señor Daredevil/The Unknown Cavalier/The Overland Stage/ 1926 · As producer: The Mask of Lopez/ The Dangerous Coward/The Fighting Sap/ North of Nevada/The Silent Stranger/1924 ·

(ass p) *Western Union*/1941 · *The Desperadoes*/1943 · *The Gunfighters*/1947 · *Coroner Creek*/*The Untamed Breed*/1948 · *The Walking Hills*/*The Doolins of Oklahoma*/1949 · *The Nevadan*/1950 · *Stage to Tucson*/*Santa Fe*/*Man in the Saddle*/1951 · *Hangman's Knot*/1952 · *The Last Posse*/*The Stranger Wore a Gun*/1953 · *Three Hours to Kill*/*Ten Wanted Men*/1954 · *A Lawless Street*/1955 · *7th Cavalry*/*The Guns of Fort Petticoat*/*The Tall T*/1956 · *Decision at Sundown*/1957 · *Buchanan Rides Alone*/1958 · *Ride Lonesome*/*Comanche Station*/1959 · *A Time for Killing*/1967

Brown, Johnny Mack (1904-74) · Actor. Brown was an athlete and a football player of some repute when he was signed by MGM in 1927. He was soon playing opposite some of Hollywood's leading ladies, including Garbo, Crawford, Marion Davies and Norma Shearer. An accomplished actor, he had appeared in over forty films (only eight Westerns), before starring in his first series Western, *Branded a Coward*, at Supreme in 1935. For a series star Brown had the unusual combination of athleticism and acting ability, which he brought to a wide range of roles at Supreme, Republic and Universal. In the 40s, at Monogram, he played in a long series of films as (Marshal) Nevada John McKenzie, with Raymond Hatton as side-kick. JH
The Bugle Call/1927 · *Montana Moon*/*Billy the Kid*/1930 · *The Great Meadow*/*Lasca of the Rio Grande*/1931 · *The Vanishing Frontier*/1932 · *Fighting with Kit Carson*/1933 · *Rustlers of Red Dog*/*Branded a Coward*/*Between Men*/*Courageous Avenger*/1935 · *Valley of the Lawless*/*The Desert Phantom*/*Rogue of the Range*/*Everyman's Law*/*The Crooked Trail*/*Under Cover Man*/*Lawless Land*/1936 · *Bar Z Bad Men*/*The Gambling Terror*/*Trail of Vengeance*/*Guns in the Dark*/*A Lawman Is Born*/*Wild West*

Days/*Boothill Brigade*/*Wells Fargo*/1937 · *Born to the West*/*Flaming Frontiers*/1938 · *The Oregon Trail*/*Desperate Trails*/*Oklahoma Frontier*/*Chip of the Flying U*/1939 · *West of Carson City*/*Riders of Pasco Basin*/*Bad Men from Red Butte*/*Son of Roaring Dan*/*Ragtime Cowboy Joe*/*Law and Order*/*Pony Post*/*Bury Me Not on the Lone Prairie*/1940 · *Boss of Bullion City*/*Law of the Range*/*Rawhide Rangers*/*The Man from Montana*/*The Masked Rider*/*Arizona Cyclone*/*Fighting Bill Fargo*/*Ride 'Em Cowboy*/1941 · *Stagecoach Buckaroo*/*The Silver Bullet*/*Boss of Hangtown Mesa*/*Deep in the Heart of Texas*/*Little Joe, the Wrangler*/*The Old Chisholm Trail*/*The Lone Star Trail*/1942 · *Tenting Tonight on the Old Camp Ground*/*The Ghost Rider*/*Cheyenne Roundup*/*Raiders of San Joaquin*/*The Stranger from Pecos*/*Six Gun Gospel*/*Outlaws of Stampede Pass*/*The Texas Kid*/1943 · *Raiders of the Border*/*Partners of the Trail*/*Law Men*/*Range Law*/*West of the Rio Grande*/*Land of the Outlaws*/*Law of the Valley*/*Ghost Guns*/1944 · *Navajo Trail*/*Gun Smoke*/*Stranger from Santa Fe*/*Flame of the West*/*Frontier Feud*/*Border Bandits*/1945 · *The Lost Trail*/*Drifting Along*/*The Haunted Mine*/*Under Arizona Skies*/*The Gentleman from Texas*/*Shadows on the Range*/*Trigger Fingers*/*Silver Range*/1946 · *Raiders of the South*/*Valley of Fear*/*Trailing Danger*/*Land of the Lawless*/*The Law Comes to Gunsight*/*Code of the Saddle*/*Flashing Guns*/*Prairie Express*/*Gun Talk*/1947 · *Overland Trails*/*Crossed Trails*/*Frontier Agent*/*Triggerman*/*Back Trail*/*The Fighting Ranger*/*The Sheriff of Medicine Bow*/*Gunning for Justice*/*Hidden Danger*/1948 · *Law of the West*/*Trails End*/*West of El Dorado*/*Range Justice*/*Stampede*/*Western Renegades*/1949 · *West of Wyoming*/*Over the Border*/*Six Gun Mesa*/*Law of the Panhandle*/*Outlaw Gold*/*Short Grass*/*Fence Riders*/1950 · *Colorado Ambush*/*Man from Sonora*/*Blazing Bullets*/*Montana Desperado*/

Oklahoma Justice/*Whistling Hills*/*Texas Lawmen*/1951 · *Texas City*/*The Man from the Black Hills*/*Dead Man's Trail*/*Canyon Ambush*/1952 · *The Marshal's Daughter*/1953 · *The Bounty Killer*/*Requiem for a Gunfighter*/*Apache Uprising*/1965 Television *Tales of Wells Fargo*/58

Brynner, Yul (1915-85)· Actor. The shaven-headed star who achieved celebrity in the musical *The King and I* on Broadway and in the subsequent film version might have seemed an unlikely recruit to the Western. But *The Magnificent Seven* provided his only out-and-out success away from the King of Siam. With his bald pate mainly concealed by a stetson, Brynner's combination of precise physical movement and slightly pedantic diction contrived to bring out the quizzical, contemplative aspect of an idealized gunslinger to distinctive effect. As if in macabre tribute to his prevailing impassivity, the gunfighters he played in *Westworld* and *Futureworld* turned out to be robots. TP
The Magnificent Seven/1960 · *Invitation to a Gunfighter*/1964 · *Return of the Seven*/1966 · *Villa Rides*/1968 · *Catlow*/*Indio Black sai che ti dico: sei un gran figlio di...*/1971 · *Westworld*/1973 · *Futureworld*/1976

Buchanan, Edgar (1903-79) · Actor. Another of the great Western old-timers, Edgar Buchanan spent thirty odd years in movies and made around 100 films, almost half of them Westerns. He could be benign and humorous, with his wheezy laugh and the worn features wrinkling with fun, or just slightly crooked; but even when his judge or sheriff carried a small taint of corruption, there was always a remnant of sympathy for the character. That kind of role was made for Buchanan or Brennan: when producers couldn't get one, they went for the other. JL
When the Daltons Rode/*Arizona*/1940 · *Texas*/1941 · *Tombstone, the Town too*

Lloyd Bridges

Charles Bronson

Johnny Mack Brown

Yul Brynner

Tough to Die/1942 · Buffalo Bill/1944 · Abilene Town/Renegades/The Sea of Grass/1946 · Coroner Creek/Adventures in Silverado/The Man from Colorado/The Untamed Breed/Red Canyon/1948 · The Walking Hills/1949 · Devil's Doorway/The Great Missouri Raid/Rawhide/1950 · Silver City/Cave of Outlaws/Flaming Feather/The Big Trees/1951 · Toughest Man in Arizona/Wild Stallion/Shane/1952 · Dawn at Socorro/Destry/1954 · Rage at Dawn/Wichita/The Lonesome Trail/1955 · Day of the Badman/The Sheepman/1958 · King of the Wild Stallions/1958 · Four Fast Guns/Cimarron/1960 · The Comancheros/1961 · Ride the High Country/1962 · McLintock!/1963 · The Rounders/1964 · The Man from Button Willow/Gunpoint/1965 · Welcome to Hard Times/1966

Television Hopalong Cassidy/51 · Broken Arrow/The Adventures of Judge Roy Bean/56 · Tales of Wells Fargo/57 · The Rifleman/The Californians/The Restless Gun/Maverick/The Adventures of Jim Bowie/58 · The Deputy/Lawman/Wanted: Dead or Alive/Trackdown/59 · Stagecoach West/The Outlaws/Bonanza/60 · The Tall Man/Klondike/Have Gun, Will Travel/61 · The Wide Country/Laramie/Gunsmoke/Stoney Burke/62 · The Over-the-Hill Gang/69 · The Over-the-Hill Gang Rides Again/70 · The Men from Shiloh/Cade's County/71 · Stoney Burke/72

Burnette, Smiley (1911-67) · Actor, aka Lester Burnette. Autry's almost ever-present side-kick at Republic, before Autry joined the war effort in 1942, he was later to provide comic relief for Roy Rogers and Charles Starrett, before rejoining Autry for the latter's final six Columbia pictures. A talented musician and composer, Burnette is best known as the Frog Millhouse character in the Autry films, where his chubby, dishevelled appearance, and voice alternating

between deep bass and high-pitched treble as he told his celebrated 'tall tales', provided the comic contrast to Autry. JH

In Old Santa Fe/Mystery Mountain/1934 · The Phantom Empire/Tumbling Tumbleweeds/Melody Trail/The Sagebrush Troubador/The Singing Vagabond/1935 · Red River Valley/Comin' Round the Mountain/The Singing Cowboy/Guns and Guitars/Oh, Susannah!/Ride, Ranger, Ride/The Big Show/The Old Corral/The Border Patrolman/1936 · Round-Up Time in Texas/Git Along Little Dogies/Rootin' Tootin' Rhythm/Yodelin' Kid from Pine Ridge/Public Cowboy No. 1/Boots and Saddles/Springtime in the Rockies/1937 · The Old Barn Dance/Gold Mine in the Sky/Man from Music Mountain/Prairie Moon/Rhythm of the Saddle/Western Jamboree/Under Western Stars/Billy the Kid Returns/1938 · Home on the Prairie/Mexicali Rose/Blue Montana Skies/Mountain Rhythm/Colorado Sunset/In Old Monterey/Rovin' Tumbleweeds/South of the Border/1939 · Rancho Grande/Gaucho Serenade/Carolina Moon/Ride, Tenderfoot, Ride/1940 · Ridin' on a Rainbow/Back in the Saddle/The Singing Hill/Sunset in Wyoming/Under Fiesta Stars/Down Mexico Way/Sierra Sue/1941 · Cowboy Serenade/Heart of the Rio Grande/Home in Wyomin'/Stardust on the Sage/Call of the Canyon/Bells of Capistrano/Heart of the Golden West/1942 · Idaho/Beyond the Last Frontier/King of the Cowboys/Silver Spurs/1943 · Beneath Western Skies/Call of the Rockies/The Laramie Trail/Code of the Prairie/Pride of the Plains/Bordertown Trail/Firebrands of Arizona/1944 · Roaring Rangers/Galloping Thunder/Frontier Gun Law/Two-Fisted Stranger/Heading West/Terror Trail/Gunning for Vengeance/The Desert Horseman/Landrush/The Fighting Frontiersman/1946 · The Lone Hand Texan/Prairie Raiders/Riders of the Lone Star/The Buckaroo from Powder River/West of Dodge City/Law of the

Canyon/The Stranger from Ponca City/The Last Days of Boot Hill/South of the Chisholm Trail/1947 · Whirlwind Raiders/Phantom Valley/Blazing Across the Pecos/El Dorado Pass/West of Sonora/Six Gun Law/Trail of Laredo/Quick on the Trigger/1948 · Desert Vigilante/Challenge of the Range/Horsemen of the Sierras/Bandits of El Dorado/The Blazing Trail/South of Death Valley/Laramie/Renegades of the Sage/1949 · Trail of the Rustlers/Outcasts of Black Mesa/Across the Badlands/Raiders of Tomahawk Creek/Texas Dynamo/Streets of Ghost Town/Lightning Guns/Frontier Outpost/1950 · Whirlwind/Fort Savage Raiders/Prairie Roundup/Bonanza Town/The Kid from Amarillo/Ridin' the Outlaw Trail/Snake River Desperadoes/Cyclone Fury/Pecos River/1951 · Junction City/Smoky Canyon/The Hawk of Wild River/The Rough Tough West/Laramie Mountains/The Kid from Broken Gun/1952 · On Top of Old Smoky/Winning of the West/Goldtown Ghost Riders/Saginaw Trail/Last of the Pony Riders/Pack Train/1953

Busch, Niven (b 1903) · The writer most associated with the advent of the supposed 'psychological Western' in the late 40s, as screenwriter of Pursued and author of the novels from which Duel in the Sun and The Furies derived. Busch himself denied any overt Freudian intent and said his aim was only to 'make the people real and give them three dimensions in terms of modern culture'. He went on to write and produce The Capture, which starred his then wife Teresa Wright, but his involvement with the cinema later seemed to wane. Apart from a contribution to the story of The Man from the Alamo, his 50s work is much more ordinary, with The Treasure of Pancho Villa particularly disappointing. TP

(co-sc) The Westerner/1940 · (co-st only) Belle Starr/1941 · Pursued/1947 · (novel

Edgar Buchanan

Smiley Burnette

Bruce Cabot

only) *Duel in the Sun*/1946 · (p) *The Capture*/(novel only) *The Furies*/1950 · (st, co-sc) *Distant Drums*/1951 · (st) *The Moonlighter*/(co-st only) *The Man from the Alamo*/1953 · *The Treasure of Pancho Villa*/1955

Buttolph, David (b 1902) · Composer. Buttolph reached Hollywood in the mid-30s. He had studied music in New York and Vienna, worked in night clubs in Vienna and Munich, and coached opera in Munich. He became music director at Fox and later at Warners, and from 1940 onwards composed scores for over 100 films. John Ford's *The Horse Soldiers* is an excellent example of his work. Buttolph weaves the lively and the sombre, marching music and Stan Jones' cavalry songs, into a pattern which illuminates but never intrudes. JL

As music director: *The Return of Frank James*/*The Mark of Zorro*/1940 · *Western Union*/1941 · As composer: *In Old California*/1942 · *Buffalo Bill*/1944 · *Colorado Territory*/*Montana*/1949 · *Return of the Frontiersman*/*The Redhead and the Cowboy*/1950 · *Along the Great Divide*/*Fort Worth*/*Lone Star*/*Carson City*/1951 · *The Man Behind the Gun*/*Thunder over the Plains*/*Riding Shotgun*/1952 · *The Bounty Hunter*/1954 · *The Burning Hills*/*The Lone Ranger*/1956 · *The Big Land*/1957 · *Westbound*/1958 · *The Horse Soldiers*/*Guns of the Timberland*/1959 · *The Man from Galveston*/1964

Television *Cheyenne*/56 · *Maverick*/57 · *Frontier Circus*/61

C

Cabot, Bruce (1904-72) · Actor. Cabot was tall, tough and very much a man of the people, successfully disguising in his screen roles the fact that he was descended from French aristocracy. Early in his forty-year career he could often be found on the side of right (notably so in *King Kong*, of course), but as time went on Cabot's nasty side usually prevailed. He was in good Westerns galore, but no masterpiece – typical of a career which never quite took off. JL

The Robin Hood of El Dorado/*The Last of the Mohicans*/1936 · *The Bad Man of Brimstone*/1937 · *Dodge City*/1939 · *Wild Bill Hickok Rides*/*Pierre of the Plains*/*Silver Queen*/1942 · *Smoky*/*Angel and the Badman*/1946 · *The Gunfighters*/1947 · *The Gallant Legion*/1948 · *Rock Island Trail*/*Fancy Pants*/1950 · *Best of the Badmen*/1951 · *Lost in Alaska*/1952 · *The Sheriff of Fractured Jaw*/1958 · *The Comancheros*/1961 · *McLintock!*/*Law of the Lawless*/1963 · *Black Spurs*/1964 · *Cat Ballou*/*Town Tamer*/1965 · *The War Wagon*/1967 · *The Undefeated*/1969 · *Chisum*/1970 · *Big Jake*/1971

Television *Bonanza*/64 · *Daniel Boone*/65

Calhoun, Rory (b 1922) · Tall, good-looking actor, best known for his Western roles although he has played in light comedy and drama. He got his movie break through a friendship with Alan Ladd, and his first starring role was in *Way of a Gaucho*. He then starred in a series of Westerns that made him one of the most popular Western stars of the mid-50s. Towards the end of the decade he began to produce some of his films, and he also co-wrote the Sterling Hayden Western *Shotgun*. In 1958 he starred in and co-produced the television Western series *The Texan*, which ran for two years. TM

Massacre River/*Sand*/1949 · *Rogue River*/*A Ticket to Tomahawk*/*Return of the Frontiersman*/1950 · *Way of a Gaucho*/1952 · *The Silver Whip*/*Powder River*/*Yellow Tomahawk*/1953 · *River of No Return*/*Dawn at Socorro*/*Four Guns to the Border*/1954 · *The Spoilers*/*The Treasure of Pancho Villa*/*Red Sundown*/(co-sc only) *Shotgun*/1955 ·

Raw Edge/1956 · *Utah Blaine*/(co-p) *Domino Kid*/*Ride Out for Revenge*/1957 · (co-p) *The Hired Gun*/(co-p) *Apache Territory*/*The Saga of Hemp Brown*/1958 · *The Gun Hawk*/1963 · *Young Fury*/*Black Spurs*/1964 · *El dedo en el gatillo* · *Apache Uprising*/1965 · *Mulefeathers*/1975 · *Kino the Padre on Horseback*/1977

Television *Death Valley Days*/52 · *Gunsmoke*/55 · *Dick Powell's Zane Grey Theatre*/56 · *Wagon Train*/57 · *The Texan*/58 · *Bonanza*/59 · *The Virginian*/62 · *Custer*/67 · *Lancer*/68 · *Alias Smith and Jones*/71 · *Hec Ramsey*/72

Calleia, Joseph (1897-1975) · Maltese by birth and originally an opera singer, Joseph Calleia became typecast by his swarthy complexion and heavy-lidded eyes in character roles as either Mexican bandit or Italianate hood. An actor of considerable range and subtlety, at his best as the monstrous Captain Quinlan's haplessly loyal sidekick in *Touch of Evil*, he usually managed to imbue his villains with a sardonic sense of humour that hinted at a Machiavellian malevolence. He earned one co-screenplay credit, with William Wellman, on *The Robin Hood of El Dorado* (1936). TMi

The Bad Man of Brimstone/1937 · *Wyoming*/*My Little Chickadee*/1940 · *Four Faces West*/1948 · *The Palomino*/*Branded*/1950 · *The Iron Mistress*/1952 · *The Littlest Outlaw*/1954 · *The Treasure of Pancho Villa*/1955 · *The Burning Hills*/1956 · *The Light in the Forest*/1958 · *The Alamo*/1960

Television *Have Gun, Will Travel*/58 · *Zorro*/59

Cameron, Rod (1912-83) · The Code of the West surely ordains that the hero should not divorce his wife and marry her mother, yet in 1960 Cameron, six foot four and very tough indeed, did precisely that. It was a striking episode in an otherwise straightfor-

Rory Calhoun

Joseph Calleia

Rod Cameron

Yakima Canutt

ward career, which led him from stunt double for Buck Jones to small parts at Paramount, and then on to leads in serials, B-Westerns, television series, and towards the end to the far-off pastures of German and Spanish Westerns. JL
North West Mounted Police/1940 · *The Parson of Panamint*/1941 · *Riding High*/*The Kansan*/1943 · *The Old Texas Trail*/*Boss of Boomtown*/*Trigger Trail*/*Riders of the Santa Fe*/*Beyond the Pecos*/*Renegades of the Rio Grande*/1944 · *Frontier Gal*/*Salome, Where She Danced*/1945 · *Pirates of Monterey*/1947 · *Belle Starr's Daughter*/*River Lady*/*Panhandle*/*The Plunderers*/1948 · *Brimstone*/*Stampede*/*Dakota Lil*/1949 · *Short Grass*/1950 · *Stage to Tucson*/*Cavalry Scout*/*Oh Susanna*/*Fort Osage*/1951 · *Wagons West*/*Woman of the North Country*/*Ride the Man Down*/1952 · *San Antone*/1953 · *Southwest Passage*/*Hell's Outpost*/1954 · *Santa Fe Passage*/1955 · *Yaqui Drums*/1956 · *The Gun Hawk*/1963 · *Las pistolas no discuten*/1964 · *The Bounty Killer*/*Requiem for a Gunfighter*/*Die letzten Zwei vom Rio Bravo*/1965 · *Winnetou und sein Freund Old Firehand*/1966 · *The Last Movie*/1971 · *Jessie's Girls*/1975

Television *Laramie*/59 · *Bonanza*/60 · *Tales of Wells Fargo*/62 · *Wagon Train*/64 · *The Iron Horse*/*Branded*/66 · *Hondo*/67 · *The Men from Shiloh*/70 · *Alias Smith and Jones*/72

Canutt, Yakima (1895–1986) · Stuntman par excellence, known best for his uncredited work on *Stagecoach* and as director of the chariot race in the 1959 *Ben Hur*. A champion rodeo rider before he entered the movies, he got his first starring role in *Ridin' Mad*. But it was in *The Devil Horse* that his reputation as a stuntman was formed. The stunts included a ninety-foot clifftop leap on horseback. Due to damaged vocal cords his days as a star ended with the advent of sound and he turned to stunt work full-time. The titles listed below include many on which Canutt worked as a stunt double and for which he received no on-screen credit. DR
Lightning Bryce/1919 · *The Heart of a Texan*/1922 · *The Forbidden Range*/1923 · *Branded a Bandit*/*The Desert Hawk*/*Ridin' Mad*/*Sell 'Em Cowboy*/*The Riddle Rider*/*The Days of '49*/1924 · *The Cactus Cure*/*The Human Tornado*/*Ridin' Comet*/*Romance and Rustlers*/*Scar Hanan*/*The Strange Rider*/*A Two-Fisted Sheriff*/*White Thunder*/*Wolves of the Road*/1925 · *Hellhound of the Plains*/*Desert Greed*/*The Devil Horse*/*The Fighting Stallion*/1926 · *Open Range*/*The Outlaw Breaker*/1927 · *The Vanishing West*/1928 · *Bad Men's Money*/*Captain Cowboy*/*Riders of a Storm*/*A Texan's Honor*/*(st, co-sc, co-p) The Three Outcasts*/1929 · *Bar L Ranch*/*Canyon Hawks*/*Firebrand Jordan*/*The Lonesome Trail*/*Ridin' Law*/*The Cheyenne Kid*/*The Texan*/1930 · *Battling with Buffalo Bill*/*The Vanishing Legion*/*Two-Fisted Justice*/*Hurricane Horseman*/*Pueblo Terror*/*The Lightning Warrior*/*Westward Bound*/1931 · *The Last of the Mohicans*/*The Last Frontier*/*Wyoming Whirlwind*/*Battling Buckaroo*/*Cheyenne Cyclone*/*Guns for Hire*/*Riders of the Golden Gulch*/*Texas Tornado*/*The Devil Horse*/*Law and Lawless*/1932 · *Via Pony Express*/*Fighting Texans*/*Sagebrush Trail*/*The Telegraph Trail*/*West of the Divide*/*Scarlet River*/*Fighting with Kit Carson*/*Wolf Dog*/1933 · *Riders of Destiny*/*Fighting Through*/*Blue Steel*/*Lawless Frontier*/*The Lucky Texan*/*Man from Hell*/*The Man from Utah*/*Randy Rides Alone*/*The Star Packer*/*Carrying the Mail*/*The Trail Beyond*/*Mystery Mountain*/*Outlaw Rule*/*Blazing Guns*/*Desert Man*/*Pals of the West*/1934 · *'Neath the Arizona Skies*/*Circle of Death*/*Cyclone of the Saddle*/*Pals of the Range*/*Branded a Coward*/*The Phantom*

Empire/*Rough Ridin' Rangers*/*The Dawn Rider*/*The Lawless Range*/*Paradise Canyon*/*Texas Terror*/*Westward Ho!*/1935 · *The Oregon Trail*/*The Lonely Trail*/*The Trail of the Lonesome Pine*/*The Lawless Nineties*/*The Big Show*/*Roarin' Lead*/*The Bold Caballero*/*The Vigilantes Are Coming*/*King of the Pecos*/*Wildcat Trooper*/*Winds of the Wasteland*/*Ghost Town Gold*/1936 · *Riders of the Dawn*/*Rootin' Tootin' Rhythm*/*Gunsmoke Ranch*/*Riders of the Whistling Skull*/*Come on Cowboys*/*Heart of the Rockies*/*Hit the Saddle*/*The Painted Stallion*/*Prairie Thunder*/*Range Defenders*/*Riders of the Rockies*/*Trouble in Texas*/*Zorro Rides Again*/1937 · *The Lone Ranger*/*Santa Fe Stampede*/*The Girl of the Golden West*/*Heroes of the Hills*/*Pals of the Saddle*/*Overland Stage Raiders*/1938 · *Man of Conquest*/*Zorro's Fighting Legion*/*The Lone Ranger Rides Again*/*Jesse James*/*Dodge City*/*The Night Riders*/*The Oregon Trail*/*Stagecoach*/*Wyoming Outlaw*/*Cowboys from Texas*/*Kansas Terrors*/1939 · *Virginia City*/*Shooting High*/*Deadwood Dick*/*Oklahoma Renegades*/*Prairie Schooners*/*Young Bill Hickok*/*Pioneers of the West*/*Ghost Valley Riders*/*Under Texas Skies*/*The Ranger and the Lady*/*(2nd unit d) Dark Command*/*Frontier Vengeance*/1940 · *Kansas Cyclone*/*White Eagle*/*Western Union*/*Bad Man of Deadwood*/*King of the Texas Rangers*/*Prairie Pioneers*/*Gauchos of Eldorado*/*(2nd unit d) They Died with their Boots On*/1941 · *Shadows on the Sage*/1942 · *King of the Cowboys*/*Santa Fe Scouts*/*Calling Wild Bill Elliott*/*Song of Texas*/*(2nd unit d) In Old Oklahoma*/1943 · *(2nd unit d) Zorro's Black Whip*/*Pride of the Plains*/*Hidden Valley Outlaws*/1944 · *(2nd unit d) The Topeka Terror*/*Sunset in El Dorado*/*(2nd unit d) Flame of the Barbary Coast*/*(d) Sheriff of Cimarron*/*(2nd unit d) Dakota*/1945 · *(2nd unit d) Sun Valley Cyclone*/*(2nd unit d) Under Nevada Skies*/*(2nd unit d) Angel and the Badman*/1946 · *(2nd unit d) Twilight on the Rio Grande*/*(2nd unit d) Northwest Outpost*/*(2nd unit d) Wyoming*/1947 · *(co-d) Dangers of the Canadian Mounted*/*(co-d) The Adventures of Frank and Jesse James*/*(d) Oklahoma Badlands*/*(d) Carson City Raiders*/*(d) Sons of Adventure*/1948 · *(2nd unit d) Red Stallion in the Rockies*/*(2nd unit d) Hellfire*/*(2nd unit d) The Doolins of Oklahoma*/1949 · *Rocky Mountain*/*(2nd unit d) The Great Missouri Raid*/*The Showdown*/*(2nd unit d) Devil's Doorway*/1950 · *(2nd unit d) Hangman's Knot*/*(2nd unit d) Last of the Comanches*/1952 · *(d) The Lawless Rider*/*(2nd unit d) The Far Horizons*/1954 ·

Harry Carey

(2nd unit d) Westward Ho the Wagons/1956 · (2nd unit d) Old Yeller/1957 · (2nd unit d) How the West Was Won/1962 · (2nd unit d) Cat Ballou/1965 · (2nd unit d) Blue/1968 · (2nd unit d) A Man Called Horse/(2nd unit d) Rio Lobo/1970 · (2nd unit d) Breakheart Pass/1975

Carey, Harry (1878-1947) · Carey started his film career at Biograph, becoming part of D. W. Griffith's stock company and appearing in a number of his one- and two-reel Westerns. Moving to Universal in 1915, he formed a close relationship with John Ford and starred in the latter's first Westerns, often playing the character 'Cheyenne Harry'. More craggy than handsome, Carey was an actor rather than an athlete, and this is reflected in the (Hart-like) roles he played at Universal and throughout the 20s. In the early 30s he was a Western serial and series star, but thereafter was mainly cast as a character actor. JH
In the Aisles of the Wild/Heredity/My Hero/A Feud in the Kentucky Hills/Three Friends/A Chance Deception/1912 · Broken Ways/The Abandoned Well/The Tenderfoot's Money/The Sheriff's Baby/The Wanderer/

The Ranchero's Revenge/Two Men of the Desert/(st) Gambler's Honor/The Stolen Treaty/1913 · The Battle at Elderbush Gulch/1914 · The Heart of a Bandit/The Sheriff's Dilemma/The Battle of Frenchman's Run/The Gambler's IOU/Judge Not, or The Woman of Mona Diggings/Just Jim/1915 · (sc) A Knight of the Range/Stampede in the Night/The Night Riders/The Passing of Hell's Crown/The Three Godfathers/The Conspiracy/The Devil's Own/(d) For the Love of a Girl/Guilty/The Committee on Credentials/(co-p) Love's Lariat/The Bad Man of Cheyenne/1916 · (st) The Outlaw and the Lady/The Fighting Gringo/The Almost Good Man/Blood Money/The Drifter/Goin' Straight/Hair-Trigger Burk/The Honor of an Outlaw/A 44-Caliber Mystery/The Golden Bullet/The Mysterious Outlaw/The Wrong Man/Six Shooter Justice/The Soul Herder/Cheyenne's Pal/Straight Shooting/The Texas Sphinx/The Secret Man/A Marked Man/Bucking Broadway/1917 · The Phantom Riders/Wild Women/Thieves Gold/The Scarlet Drop/Hell Bent/A Woman's Fool/Three Mounted Men/1918 · Roped/A Fight for Love/Bare Fists/Riders of Vengeance/The Outcasts of Poker Flat/The Ace of the Saddle/The Rider of the Law/A Gun Fightin' Gentleman/Marked Man/1919 · Overland Red/Bullet Proof/Blue Streak McCoy/Sundown Slim/(st) Hearts Up!/West Is West/1920 · 'If Only' Jim/The Freeze Out/The Wallop/Desperate Trails/The Fox/1921 · Man to Man/The Kick Back/Good Men and True/1922 · Canyon of the Fools/Crashin' Thru/Desert Driven/The Miracle Baby/1923 · The Night Hawk/The Lightning Rider/Tiger Thompson/The Man from Texas/The Flaming Forties/1924 · (st) Soft Shoes/Beyond the Border/Silent Sanderson/The Bad Lands/The Texas Trail/The Prairie Pirate/The Man from Red Gulch/1925 · Driftin' Thru/The Seventh Bandit/The Frontier Trail/Satan Town/1926 · Burning Bridges/The Border Patrol/1928 · The Trail of '98/1929 The Vanishing Legion/Cavalier of the West/Horsehoofs/The Hurricane Rider/1931 · Without Honors/Law and Order/Border Devils/The Last of the Mohicans/The Night Rider/The Devil Horse/1932 · The Thundering Herd/Sunset Pass/Man of the Forest/1933 · Wagon Trail/Rustler's Paradise/Powdersmoke Range/The Last of the Clintons/Wild Mustang/1935 · Aces Wild/Ghost Town/Sutter's Gold/The Last Outlaw/1936 · Border Cafe/1937 · The Law West of Tombstone/1938 · The Shepherd of the Hills/1941 · The Spoilers/1942 · Duel in the Sun/The Sea of Grass/1946 · Angel and the

Badman/Red River/1947

Carey, Harry, Jr. (b 1921) · Not at all like his father in looks, or in the prominence of his film roles. Nevertheless, he appeared in some of the finest Westerns of the late 40s and 50s, including most of John Ford's from *3 Godfathers* onward. His ginger hair and fair complexion gave him boyish looks, which were often exploited in his earliest roles such as the impetuous Brad in *The Searchers*. However, he was soon playing character parts, including, at a relatively young age, old-timers. JH
Pursued/Red River/1947 · Blood on the Moon/3 Godfathers/1948 · She Wore a Yellow Ribbon/Copper Canyon/1949 · Wagon Master/Rio Grande/1950 · Warpath/1951 · San Antone/1953 · The Outcast/Silver Lode/1954 · The Searchers/The Great Locomotive Chase/7th Cavalry/Gun the Man Down/1956 · From Hell to Texas/Rio Bravo/Escort West/1958 · Noose for a Gunman/Geronimo's Revenge/1960 · Two Rode Together/Gunfight at Sandoval/The Comancheros/1961 · Cheyenne Autumn/The Raiders/Taggart/1964 · Shenandoah/Billy the Kid vs. Dracula/1965 · Alvarez Kelly/The Rare Breed/1966 · The Way West/The Ballad of Josie/1967 · Bandolero!/1968 · The Undefeated/Death of a Gunfighter/Ride a Northbound Horse/1969 · Dirty Dingus Magee/One More Train to Rob/1970 · Continuavano a chiamarlo Trinità/Big Jake/Something Big/1971 · E poi lo chiamarono il magnifico/1972 · Cahill United States Marshal/1973 · Take a Hard Ride/1975 · The Long Riders/1980 · Endangered Species/1982 Television Have Gun, Will Travel/Broken Arrow/Texas John Slaughter/58 · Wagon Train/Gunsmoke/59 · Bonanza/Hotel de Paree/The Rifleman/The Tall Man/60 · Whispering Smith/Laramie/Tales of Wells Fargo/61 · Redigo/63 · Branded/65 · The Outcasts/69 · Little House on the Prairie/80

Harry Carey Jr.

Carradine, John (b 1906) · Actor. Known as John Peter Richmond prior to signing a contract with Fox in 1935, Carradine was for over half a century one of Hollywood's leading support players. Thin-lipped and with piercing eyes, he had a tall, gaunt frame ideally suited to the role of screen villain, with which he is so closely associated, particularly in the 30s (the vengeful farmer in *Ramona*; the treacherous Bob Ford in *Jesse James*; the evil Caldwell in *Drums Along the Mohawk*). In *Stagecoach* he played a gentlemanly Southern gambler, and later in his career he was often seen in very different roles from those of his early career, including a poignant performance as Joan Crawford's faithful servant, Old Tom, in *Johnny Guitar*. JH

To the Last Man/1933 · Ramona/Daniel Boone/White Fang/1936 · Jesse James/Drums Along the Mohawk/Frontier Marshal/Stagecoach/1939 · The Return of Frank James/Brigham Young – Frontiersman/1940 · Western Union/1941 · Northwest Rangers/1942 · Silver Spurs/1943 · Barbary Coast Gent/Alaska/1944 · Thunder Pass/Johnny Guitar/Stranger on Horseback/1954 · The Kentuckian/Hidden Guns/1955 · The True Story of Jesse James/Showdown at Boot Hill/1957 · The Proud Rebel/1958 · The Oregon Trail/1959 · The Man Who Shot Liberty Valance/1962 · Cheyenne Autumn/1964 · Billy the Kid vs. Dracula/1965 · The Good Guys and the Bad Guys/Cain's Way/The McMasters/Five Bloody Graves/1969 · The Gatling Gun/1971 · Hex/1973 · The Shootist/1976 · The White Buffalo/1977 · Zorro the Gay Blade/1981

Television The Adventures of Wild Bill Hickok/54 · Gunsmoke/55 · Cheyenne/57 · The Restless Gun/Wagon Train/Have Gun, Will Travel//58 · The Life and Legend of Wyatt Earp/The Rough Riders/Bat Masterson/The Rebel/Johnny Ringo/The Rifleman//59 · Overland Trail/Wanted:

John Carradine

Dead or Alive/60 · Maverick/Bonanza/61 · Branded/65 · The Legend of Jesse James/Laredo/66 · Hondo/67 · Daniel Boone/68 · The Big Valley/69 · The Cowboys/74 · The Seekers/79

Carson, Sunset (b 1925) · Actor. If there are cowboys in Heaven, they will look like Sunset Carson. He was six and a half feet tall, wavy-haired and impossibly handsome. His uniform was tailor-made and freshly laundered, his gun decorated, his expensive belt loaded with a dozen brightly burnished shells. But before the studios remodelled him, he had been a rodeo champion, and through the 40s he rode gallantly through some 20 minor Westerns. After that came two brief television series, and a return to the Wild West shows. (Note: Carson's *Rio Grande* of 1949 is not the John Ford film of a year later.) JL

Firebrands of Arizona/Code of the Prairie/Bordertown Trail/Call of the Rockies/Song of Nevada/1944 · Bandits of the Badlands/Bells of Rosarita/The Cherokee Flash/Oregon

Trail/Santa Fe Saddlemates/Rough Riders of Cheyenne/Sheriff of Cimarron/1945 · Alias Billy the Kid/Days of Buffalo Bill/Red River Renegades/Rio Grande Raiders/The El Paso Kid/1946 · Deadline/Fighting Mustang/Sunset Carson Rides Again/1948 · Rio Grande/1949 · Battling Marshal/Indian Territory/1950

Castle, Peggie (1927-73) · Actress. An attractive blonde with eyes variously described as 'green' or 'sad', Peggie Castle was a regular in 50s B-Westerns, sometimes as a virtuous heroine, but more satisfyingly as a glamorous saloon entertainer, a scrapper (in *Jesse James' Women* she takes part in a no-holds-barred set-to), or even a gunslinger (as in *Two Gun Lady*, where like many a Western hero she pursues the murderers of her parents). When her movie career ended, she became a saloon lady once again in television's *Lawman*. JL

Wagons West/1952 · Cow Country/Son of Belle Starr/The Yellow Tomahawk/1953 · Jesse James' Women/Southwest Passage/Overland Pacific/Tall Man Riding/1954 · Two Gun Lady/Oklahoma Woman/Quincannon, Frontier Scout/1956 · Hell's Crossroads/1957

Television Cheyenne/Dick Powell's Zane Grey Theatre/56 · Gunsmoke/57 · The Texan/The Restless Gun/58 · Lawman/59 · The Outlaws/60 · The Virginian/66

Chandler, Jeff (1918-61) · Actor. Chandler made a number of non-Westerns during his Hollywood career yet he is likely to remain closely identified with the genre in a quite specific way. His role as Cochise, the Apache chief in *Broken Arrow*, created a striking impression and he was to repeat it in *The Battle at Apache Pass* and in *Taza, Son of Cochise*. He played other Western characters, lawmen and cavalrymen for example, but it is as the famous Indian chief that his

Sunset Carson

Peggy Castle

Jeff Chandler

Lane Chandler

place in the history of the genre is guaranteed. TR
*Broken Arrow/Two Flags West/*1950 · *The Battle at Apache Pass/*1952 · *The Great Sioux Uprising/War Arrow/Taza, Son of Cochise/*1953 · *Foxfire/The Spoilers/*1955 · *Pillars of the Sky/*1956 · *Drango/Man in the Shadow/*1957 · *Thunder in the Sun/The Jayhawkers!/*1959 · *The Plunderers/*1960

Chandler, Lane (1899-1972) · Actor. The claim in a recent book on the Western that Lane Chandler once starred opposite Garbo is surprising – and wrong. He was in *The Single Standard*, but billed fifth. That was none the less a rare experience for a man who spent nearly 40 years on the plains. Chandler played leads in silent Westerns and in many B-films in the 30s, and still had a quarter-century as a supporting actor in him. His better films included Walsh's *Pursued* and Sirk's delightful *Take Me to Town*. JL
*The Vanishing American/*1925 · *Arizona Bound/The Last Outlaw/Open Range/*1927 · *Firebrand Jordan/Beyond the Law/*1930 · *The Reckless Rider/Riders of the Rio/Under Texas Skies/Hurricane Horseman/*1931 · *The Cheyenne Cyclone/Wyoming Whirlwind/Guns for Hire/Battling Buckaroo/Texas Tornado/*1932 · *Via Pony Express/War on the Range/Sagebrush Trail/*1933 · *Beyond the Law/The Lone Bandit/The Outlaw Tamer/*1934 · *The Lawless Nineties/Winds of the Wasteland/Idaho Kid/Stormy Trails/*1936 · *Law of the Ranger/Heroes of the Alamo/*1937 · *The Lone Ranger/Lawless Valley/Heart of Arizona/Two Gun Justice/Come On Rangers/*1938 · *Outpost of the Mounties/Oklahoma Frontier/North of the Yukon/Union Pacific/*1939 · *Man from Montreal/Pioneers of the West/North West Mounted Police/Deadwood Dick/Pony Post/*1940 · *Sundown Jim/*1942 · *Tenting Tonight on the Old Camp Ground/Riding High/Law of the Saddle/*1943 · *Silver City Kid/Trigger Law/Riders of the Santa Fe/Trigger Trail/Rustlers' Hideout/Sagebrush Heroes/*1944 · *Along Came Jones/*1945 · *Gunning for Vengeance/Two-Fisted Stranger/Duel in the Sun/Terror Trail/*1946 · *Pursued/The Vigilantes Return/*1947 · *Belle Starr's Daughter/Northwest Stampede/*1948 · *Montana/*1949 · *Outcasts of Black Mesa/*1950 · *Prairie Round Up/*1951 · *The Lion and the Horse/The Hawk of Wild River/Thunder Over the Plains/*1952 · *Take Me to Town/The Charge at Feather River/Border River/*1953 · *Tall Man Riding/*1954 · *The Indian Fighter/Shotgun/*1955 · *The Lone Ranger/*1956 · *Quantrill's Raiders/*1958 · *Noose for a Gun-*

Lee J. Cobb

*man/*1960 · *Requiem for a Gunfighter/*1965
Television *Cheyenne/The Adventures of Wild Bill Hickok/*56 · *The Life and Legend of Wyatt Earp/*57 · *Have Gun, Will Travel/*59 · *Gunsmoke/*64

Chase, Borden (1900-71) · Writer. One of the princes of the Western, responsible for writing most of *Red River* (although the ending is not his own and runs against the grain of the picture) and some of Mann's finest Westerns. His themes revolve around revenge, self-esteem, male friendship and rivalry, and the individual's need for a place in the community. Chase's scripts are not only action-packed but also historically very specific, and his great gift is in the placing of intense personal conflicts within precise social and historical contexts. Thanks to directors like Mann and Hawks his films combine the grandeur and nobility of classical tragedy with all that is best in the classical American style. JP
(co-sc) *Flame of Barbary Coast/*1945 · (st, co-sc) *Red River/*1947 · (st) *The Man from Colorado/*1948 · (co-sc) *Montana/*1949 · (co-sc) *Winchester '73/*1950 · (st) *Lone Star/Bend of the River/*1951 · (st) *Vera Cruz/(st) The Far Country/*1954 · (co-sc) *Man Without a Star/*1955 · *Backlash/*1956 · *Night Passage/*1957 · *Ride a Crooked Trail/*1958 · (co-st, co-sc) *Los Pistoleros de Casa Grande/*1964 · (co-sc) *A Man Called Gannon/*1968
Television *Bonanza/*59 · *Whispering Smith/*61 · *The Virginian/*63 · *Daniel Boone/*64 · *Laredo/*65

Clothier, William H. (b 1903) · Cinematographer. A newsreel cameraman and camera

assistant at Paramount, Clothier did some aerial work on *Wings* (1927), was camera operator on *Cimarron* (1931), worked on several features in Spain, and served with the Army Air Corps during World War II (shooting *Memphis Belle* for William Wyler in 1944). Required to qualify as a director of photography, he worked as camera assistant on Ford's *Fort Apache*, after which his career blossomed. Following his work on Sternberg's *Jet Pilot*, William Wellman (director of *Wings*) gave him his first Western chance on *Track of the Cat*, where his striking experiments in bleached-out colour and the sensuous sheen of his landscapes led to regular employment, not only with Wellman and Ford but with John Wayne (producer of *Track of the Cat*) and the Batjac Company. TMi
*Track of the Cat/*1954 · *Seven Men from Now/Gun the Man Down/*1956 · *Dragoon Wells Massacre/*1957 · *Fort Dobbs/Escort West/*1958 · *The Horse Soldiers/*1959 · *The Alamo/*1960 · *The Deadly Companions/The Comancheros/*1961 · *The Man Who Shot Liberty Valance/*1962 · *McLintock!/*1963 · *A Distant Trumpet/Cheyenne Autumn/*1964 · *Shenandoah/The Rare Breed/*1965 · *Stagecoach/*1966 · *The Way West/The War Wagon/Firecreek/*1967 · *Bandolero!/*1968 · *The Undefeated/*1969 · *The Cheyenne Social Club/Chisum/Rio Lobo/*1970 · *Big Jake/*1971 · *The Train Robbers/*1973

Cobb, Lee J. (1911-76) · Actor, born Leo Jacob. Although Lee Cobb had had a successful year or two with New York's Group Theatre, he began his Western career billed tenth in a Hopalong Cassidy movie. Far better things lay ahead. A weighty and deliberate actor, he gave perhaps his finest Western performance as the crazed outlaw Dock Tobin in Anthony Mann's *Man of the West*. And there was a moment elsewhere which Western addicts recall with undying affection. It came in Siegel's *Coogan's Bluff*, when Cobb's New York cop gazed wearily at Eastwood's naive Western lawman, and, humouring him all the way, agreed that 'a man's gotta do what a man's gotta do'. JL
*North of the Rio Grande/Rustler's Valley/*1937 · *Buckskin Frontier/*1943 · *The Fighter/*1952 · *The Tall Texan/*1953 · *Road to Denver/*1955 · *Man of the West/*1958 · *How the West Was Won/*1962 · *Coogan's Bluff/McKenna's Gold/*1968 · *Macho Callahan/Lawman/*1970 · *The Man Who Loved Cat Dancing/*1973
Television *Dick Powell's Zane Grey Theatre/*56 · *The Virginian/*62 · *Gunsmoke/*74

Coburn, James (b 1928) · Actor. Coburn made his début in Budd Boetticher's *Ride Lonesome*, became one of the Magnificent Seven and then played the key role of Sam Potts in Sam Peckinpah's *Major Dundee*. Although subsequently he was sidetracked into the spy movie, he managed to re-establish himself as a presence in the genre with splendid performances in Leone's *Giù la testa* and Peckinpah's *Pat Garrett and Billy the Kid*. In the latter film he played the legendary lawman who gunned down his erstwhile friend. TR
Ride Lonesome/Face of a Fugitive/1959 · *The Magnificent Seven*/1960 · *The Man from Galveston*/1963 · *Major Dundee*/1964 · *Waterhole No. 3*/1967 · *Giù la testa/The Honkers*/1971 · *Una ragione per vivere e una per morire*/1972 · *Pat Garrett and Billy the Kid*/1973 · *Bite the Bullet*/1975 · *The Last Hard Men*/1976
Television *Wagon Train/The Rifleman*/58 · *Wanted: Dead or Alive/The Rough Riders/ Bonanza/The Californians/Trackdown/Black Saddle/The Restless Gun/Johnny Ringo/The Life and Legend of Wyatt Earp*/59 · *Klondike/Bat Masterson/Tate/Dick Powell's Zane Grey Theatre/Bronco/Lawman/The Deputy/The Texan*//60 · *Laramie/The Tall Man/The Outlaws/Stagecoach West*/61 · *Stoney Burke*/63 · *Draw!*/84

Cody, Iron Eyes (b 1907) · Actor. A Cherokee, Cody was taken by his parents to Hollywood when a small child. His father worked as an adviser on Indian movies, and the boy played Indian children. His recent autobiography reveals that in 1912 he was in Griffith's *The Massacre*. His acting career continued through the 20s. By the 30s he was a technical adviser himself, and gradually playing larger parts, flourishing in the 50s when the Indian gained more serious treatment in films. He may be the only man to have played Sitting Bull *and* Crazy Horse. JL

The Massacre/1912 · *The Covered Wagon*/1923 · *North of 36/The Iron Horse*/1924 · *The Vanishing American*/1925 · *War Paint*/1926 · *Back to God's Country*/1927 · *Wolf Song*/1929 · *The Lightning Warrior*/1931 · *The Plainsman*/1936 · *Union Pacific/ Crashin' Thru*/1939 · *My Little Chickadee/ North West Mounted Police*/1940 · *Western Union*/1941 · *Ride 'Em Cowboy*/1942 · *Bowery Buckaroos/Unconquered*/1947 · *Blood on the Moon/Indian Agent/The Paleface*/1948 · *Sand/Massacre River*/1949 · *Comanche Territory/Broken Arrow/California Passage/Cherokee Uprising/Devil's Doorway/ Tomahawk*/1950 · *The Last Outpost/Red Mountain/Fort Defiance/Fort Osage/ Montana Belle*/1951 · *Son of Paleface/Night Raiders/The Big Sky/The Savage/The Half-Breed*/1952 · *The Tall Texan/Arrowhead/ The Yellow Tomahawk*/1953 · *Arrow in the Dust/Sitting Bull/Broken Lance*/1954 · *Comanche*/1955 · *Wild Dakotas/The Last Wagon/Westward Ho the Wagons/Gun for a Coward*/1956 · *Run of the Arrow/Gun Fever/* 1957 · *The Light in the Forest*/1958 · *Alias Jesse James*/1959 · *The Great Sioux Massacre/Nevada Smith*/1965 · *The Fastest Guitar Alive*/1966 · *El Condor/A Man Called Horse*/1970 · *Grayeagle*/1977
Television *The Adventures of Wild Bill Hickok/Davy Crockett*/54 · *The Life and Legend of Wyatt Earp*/57 · *The Adventures of Rin Tin Tin*/58 · *The Rebel*/61 · *Daniel Boone*/64 · *Branded*/65 · *Gunsmoke*/68 · *How the West Was Won*/78

Connors, Chuck (b 1921) · Actor. Connors, a former baseball player, entered films in the early 50s, first catching the eye as the Police Captain in *Pat and Mike*. His Western career was split between film and television, and on film his parts varied between fairly routine leads (the hard-bitten soldiers of *Tomahawk Trail* and *The Broken Sabre*) and more interesting character roles like that of Burl Ives'

depraved son in *The Big Country* or the title part in *Geronimo*. In *Support Your Local Gunfighter* he revealed an unsuspected comic sense. JL
Tomahawk Trail/1956 · *The Hired Gun/Old Yeller*/1957 · *The Big Country*/1958 · *Geronimo*/1962 · *The Broken Sabre/Ride Beyond Vengeance*/1965 · *Ammazzali tutti e torna solo*/1968 · *La spina dorsale del diavolo*/1970 · *Support Your Local Gunfighter/Pancho Villa*/1971
Television *Gunsmoke/Frontier*/56 · *Tales of Wells Fargo/Wagon Train*/57 · *The Adventures of Jim Bowie/Dick Powell's Zane Grey Theatre/The Rifleman*/58 · *Branded*/65 · *The Men from Shiloh*/71 · *Banjo Hackett: Roamin' Free*/76 · *Standing Tall*/78 · *Best of the West*/82

Cook, Elisha, Jr. (b 1906) · Actor. Of small stature, with shifty eyes, Cook specialized in losers. Appearing in numerous small roles from the mid-30s onwards, it was not until 1952 that he made his first Western appearance, in *Shane*, where with typical false bravado he falls victim to Jack Palance's gunslinger. Thereafter, he made regular brief appearances in Westerns, invariably playing small-time losers or luckless townsmen. JH
Shane/Thunder Over the Plains/1952 · *The Outlaw's Daughter/Drum Beat/Timberjack*/ 1954 · *The Indian Fighter*/1955 · *The Lonely Man*/1956 · *Day of the Outlaw*/1959 · *One-Eyed Jacks*/1960 · *Blood on the Arrow*/1964 · *Welcome to Hard Times*/1966 · *The Great Bank Robbery*/1969 · *El Condor*/1970 · *The Great Northfield Minnesota Raid*/1972 · *Pat Garrett and Billy the Kid* (scenes deleted from final release print, but shown in some television versions)/1973 · *Winterhawk*/1975 · *Tom Horn*/1980
Television *The Life and Legend of Wyatt Earp*/57 · *Gunsmoke/Trackdown/Bat Masterson*/58 · *Johnny Ringo/Rawhide*/59 · *Wagon Train/The Rebel*/60 · *Laramie/The*

James Coburn

Iron Eyes Cody

Chuck Connors

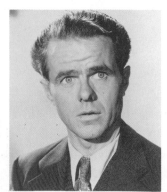

Elisha Cook Jr.

Deputy/61 · The Outlaws/62 · Temple Houston/63 · Destry/64 · The Wild, Wild West/65 · Bonanza/The Road West/66 · The Monroes/Cimarron Strip/67

Cooper, Gary (1901-61) · Actor. At Paramount in 1925, Frank Cooper (the 'Gary' came later) was a lanky kid from Montana, picking up a living as stunt rider and cowboy extra. Engaged by Henry King to ride in *The Winning of Barbara Worth*, he was promoted, when another actor failed to appear, to play the vital small role of Abe Lee. Already the Cooper sincerity stood out, and a career could begin. Stardom came three years later, with the title role in the most famous version of *The Virginian*. For 30 years Cooper's heroes, whether in the West or the city, were cut to the same pattern. They were quiet and thoughtful men, unassuming and gently humorous, and they wore their integrity without conceit. Though arguably not his best Western, *High Noon* won him an Academy Award. JL
The Thundering Herd/Wild Horse Mesa/The Lucky Horseshoe/The Vanishing American/Tricks/Lightnin' Wins/1925 · *The Enchanted Hill/The Winning of Barbara Worth*/1926 · *Arizona Bound/The Last Outlaw/Nevada*/1927 · *Wolf Song/The Virginian*/1929 · *The Texan/The Spoilers*/1930 · *Fighting Caravans/I Take This Woman*/1931 · *The Plainsman*/1936 · *The Cowboy and the Lady*/1938 · *The Westerner/North West Mounted Police*/1940 · *Along Came Jones/Saratoga Trunk*/1945 · *Unconquered*/1947 · *Dallas*/1950 · *Distant Drums*/1951 · *High Noon/Springfield Rifle*/1952 · *Garden of Evil/Vera Cruz*/1954 · *Friendly Persuasion*/1956 · *Man of the West*/1958 · *The Hanging Tree/Alias Jesse James/They Came to Cordura*/1959

Corbucci, Sergio (b 1927) · Director. Aka Stanley Corbett, Gordon Wilson Jr. Ex-film critic (in Rome) who trained as an assistant to Roberto Rossellini before becoming a director of popular Italian films in a variety of genres (sometimes with his brother Bruno). Usually based at Cinecittà, he directed 'peplums' such as *Romulus and Remus* and wrote comedies before specializing in Italian Westerns. His comic-strip style, with an emphasis on graphic visual clichés, then came into its own. Corbucci was the first Italian director of Westerns to use his real name, and in the late 60s moved on to 'political' Spaghettis. His films tend to chuck strong visual images in the direction of the audience, like an animator. CF
(co-sc) Minnesota Clay/(co-sc, co-d) Massacro al Grande Canyon/1964 · *(co-st, co-sc) Django/Navajo Joe/I crudeli/Johnny Oro*/1966 · *(co-sc) Il mercenario/(co-sc) Il grande silenzio/(co-st, co-sc, p) Gli specialisti*/1968 · *(st, co-sc) Vamos a matar, compañeros*/1970 · *(st, co-sc) La banda J & S – cronaca criminale del far west*/1973 · *(co-sc) Il bianco, il giallo, il nero*/1975

Cotten, Joseph (b 1905) · Actor. Cotten came to films in *Citizen Kane* after a successful career on the New York stage and in radio. Often typecast as a well-meaning, sophisticated loser, once in a while, as in *Duel in the Sun*, he played a part of more weight, though even then he didn't get the girl. More at home in thrillers (*The Third Man, Shadow of a Doubt*) than in the Western. JC
Duel in the Sun/1946 · *Two Flags West*/1950 · *Untamed Frontier*/1952 · *The Halliday Brand*/1957 · *The Last Sunset*/1961 · *The Great Sioux Massacre*/1965 · *Gli uomini dal passo pesante/I crudeli*/1966 · *Brighty of the Grand Canyon*/1967 · *Comanche blanco*/1968 · *Heaven's Gate*/1980
Television *Dick Powell's Zane Grey Theatre/58 · Wagon Train*/61 · *The Great*

Adventure/63 · Cimarron Strip/67 · The Virginian/The Men from Shiloh/Cutter's Trail/70

Crabbe, Buster (1908-83) · Actor, aka Larry Crabbe. Usually remembered as an Olympic swimming champion and/or from the *Flash Gordon* and *Buck Rogers* serials, he was also the star of over fifty Westerns. He started out playing bit roles in Randolph Scott Westerns at Paramount in 1933, and eventually got the title role in *Nevada*. He starred in several more Paramount Westerns before moving to PRC, where, between 1941 and 1946, he played the title role in the Billy the Kid/Billy Carson series thirty-six times. JH
Man of the Forest/To the Last Man/The Thundering Herd/1933 · *The Wanderer of the Wasteland/Nevada*/1935 · *Drift Fence/Desert Gold/The Arizona Raiders/Arizona Mahoney*/1936 · *Forlorn River*/1937 · *Colorado Sunset*/1939 · *Billy the Kid Wanted/Billy the Kid's Roundup*/1941 · *Billy the Kid Trapped/Billy the Kid's Smoking Guns/Law and Order/Mysterious Rider/Sheriff of Sage Valley*/1942 · *The Kid Rides Again/Fugitive of the Plains/The Renegade/Western Cyclone/Cattle Stampede/Blazing Frontier/Devil Riders/The Drifter*/1943 · *Thundering Gun Slingers/Frontier Outlaws/Valley of Vengeance/Fuzzy Settles Down/Rustlers' Hideout/Wild Horse Phantom/Oath of Vengeance*/1944 · *Gangster's Den/His Brother's Ghost/Shadows of Death/Border Badmen/Stagecoach Outlaws/Fighting Bill Carson/Lightning Raiders/Prairie Rustlers*/1945 · *Gentlemen with Guns/Ghost of Hidden Valley/Terrors on Horseback/Overland Raiders/Outlaws of the Plains/Prairie Badmen*/1946 · *The Last of the Redmen*/1947 · *Gun Brothers*/1956 · *The Lawless Eighties*/1957 · *Badman's Country*/1958 · *Gunfighters of Abilene*/1959 · *The Bounty Killer/Arizona Raiders*/1965 · *The Comeback Trail (unreleased)*/1971

Gary Cooper

Sergio Corbucci

Joseph Cotten

Buster Crabbe

Cruze, James (1884-1942) · Director. Cruze made only five Westerns, two of them marginal to the genre, but the first of them was the classic pioneer movie, *The Covered Wagon*. The sweep and vigour of this film, the realism and urgency of the fording of the river and the buffalo hunt, the superb use of landscape, combine to make it perhaps the first great Western. *The Pony Express* was a worthy successor. If Cruze's version of *Ruggles of Red Gap* survives, we may one day see Edward Everett Horton in the Laughton role, but unhappily several of Cruze's major silents are lost. JL
The Covered Wagon/Ruggles of Red Gap/ 1923 · *The Pony Express/*1925 · *Helldorado/* 1934 · *Sutter's Gold/*1936

Curtis, Ken (b 1916) · Actor. If you were the son of a cattle-rancher, attended Muddy Creek Grade School, had a pleasant singing voice, and were young in the 40s, you had to make the grade as a star of B-Westerns. Ken Curtis did, with a string of them for Columbia. He also appeared in several films, not separately credited, as a member of the Western singing group The Sons of the Pioneers. But ahead lay another career as a gifted character actor. Curtis married John Ford's daughter Barbara, and appeared in many Ford movies, most memorably as the engaging Charlie of *The Searchers*, whom Vera Miles so cruelly ditches in favour of the long-absent Jeffrey Hunter. JL
*Song of the Prairie/Rhythm Round-up/*1945 · *Singing on the Trail/Cowboy Blues/Lone Star Moonlight/Throw a Saddle on a Star/That Texas Jamboree/*1946 · *Over the Santa Fe Trail/*1947 · *Call of the Forest/Stallion Canyon/*1949 · *Rio Grande/*1950 · *Don Daredevil Rides Again/*1951 · *The Searchers/* 1956 · *The Missouri Traveler/The Young Land/*1957 · *Escort West/*1958 · *The Horse Soldiers/*1959 · *The Alamo/*1960 · *Two Rode Together/*1961 · *How the West Was Won/*

1962 · *Cheyenne Autumn/*1964 · *Pony Express Rider/*1976
Television *Gunsmoke/Have Gun, Will Travel/Rawhide/*59 · *Wagon Train/*60 · *California Gold Rush/*81

D

Dano, Royal (b 1922) · Dano was a supporting player who could make a small part the most memorable thing in a routine movie or an essential factor in a fine one. Not that this hard, dogged character was in many poor films – his first four Westerns were all masterpieces. In *The Red Badge of Courage* (only marginally a Western) Dano, then relatively new to cinema, created an extraordinary figure of the Tattered Man, lost, haunted but surviving, and in that vein he would continue, with four films for Anthony Mann and one for Nicholas Ray giving him a remarkable first decade. His later parts, less striking, were still impressively done. JL
*The Red Badge of Courage/Bend of the River/*1951 · *Johnny Guitar/The Far Country/*1954 · *Tribute to a Bad Man/*1955 · *Tension at Table Rock/Gun in his Hand/* 1956 · *Trooper Hook/*1957 · *Saddle the Wind/Man of the West/These Thousand Hills/*1958 · *Cimarron/*1960 · *Posse from Hell/*1961 · *Savage Sam/*1963 · *Gunpoint/* 1965 · *Welcome to Hard Times/*1966 · *Day of the Evil Gun/*1968 · *The Undefeated/ Death of a Gunfighter/*1969 · *The Great Northfield Minnesota Raid/The Culpepper Cattle Co./*1972 · *Cahill United States Marshal/*1973 · *The Outlaw Josey Wales/* 1976
Television *Death Valley Days/*52 · *Gunsmoke/*55 · *The Restless Gun/*57 · *The Rebel/Wanted: Dead or Alive/The Rifleman/* 59 · *Tate/Johnny Ringo/Tales of Wells Fargo/*60 · *Frontier Circus/Have Gun, Will Travel/Gunslinger/*61 · *Rawhide/The*

*Virginian/Bonanza/*62 · *Temple Houston/ Wagon Train/The Dakotas/*63 · *The Travels of Jaimie McPheeters/*64 · *The Legend of Jesse James/*65 · *The Iron Horse/The Big Valley/Daniel Boone/The Dangerous Days of Kiowa Jones/*66 · *Cimarron Strip/Hondo/The Guns of Will Sonnett/*67 · *The Outcasts/*68 · *Alias Smith and Jones/*71 · *How the West Was Won/The Quest/*76 · *Little House on the Prairie/*81

Darkfeather, Mona (n. d.) · Actress. In the early days of the Western the Indian was not always the savage menace that he would become in the 20s and later. Until around 1915 the hero or heroine might well be an Indian, and players like James Young Deer or Mona Darkfeather were among the early Western stars. Darkfeather was a beautiful Seminole girl who worked for the Bison, Selig and Kalem companies in her brief six-year career. That she achieved the ultimate accolade of the day – her name in the title – is a measure of her appeal. JL
The Hand of Fate/The Massacre of Santa Fe Trail/The Massacre of the Fourth Cavalry/A Red Man's Love/A Crucial Test/Big Rock's Last Stand/Trapper Bill, King of Scouts/A White Indian/When Uncle Sam Is Young/ Blackfoot's Conspiracy/At Old Fort Dearborn or Chicago in 1812/Darkfeather's Strategy/ 1912 · *A Dream of the Wild/A Forest Romance/An Indian Maid's Strategy/Juanita/ The Love of Men/The Oath of Conchita/The Return of Thunder Cloud's Spirit/The Spring in the Desert/Darkfeather's Sacrifice/An Apache Father's Vengeance/*1913 · *Defying the Chief/The Fate of a Squaw/The Fight of Deadwood Trail/The Fuse of Death/Gray Eagle's Last Stand/The Vengeance of Winona/The War Bonnet/The Cave of Death/The Call of the Tribe/The Bottled Spider/At the End of the Rope/The Redskins and the Renegades/The Gypsy Gambler/The Indian Agent/The Indian Suffragettes/*

James Cruze

Ken Curtis

Royal Dano

Delmer Daves

Yvonne De Carlo

Kidnapped by Indians/The Legend of the Amulet/The Vanishing Tribe/The Medicine Man's Vengeance/The Moonshiners/The Navajo Blanket/The New Medicine Man/Priest or Medicine Man?/Brought to Justice/The Coming of Lone Wolf/The Gambler's Reformation/Gray Eagle's Revenge/His Indian Nemesis/The Hopi Raiders/The Indian Ambuscade/Indian Blood/Indian Fate/An Indian's Honor/Lame Dog's Treachery/The Paleface Brave/Red Hawk's Sacrifice/The Squaw's Revenge/The Tigers of the Hills/1914 · Her College Experience/The Miser of Monterey/A Spanish Madonna/The Stolen Invention/The Western Border/1915 · None So Blind/The Seeds of Jealousy/The Circle of Death/1916 · The Crimson Arrow/The Hidden Danger/The Red Goddess/1917

Daves, Delmer (1904-77) · Director. Daves' Westerns have never received their proper due in America, and even his considerable Gallic reputation has never been unanimous. Best known for *Broken Arrow* (originally a Losey project and one of the first anti-racist Westerns) and the psychological drama *3:10 to Yuma*, Daves is in fact the author of an amazingly diverse oeuvre. It is as if he intended to create a vast tableau chronicling the evolution of the West, focusing not on glamorous, legendary figures and events but, rather, on more humble, modest and particularized dramas. His *mise en scène* is similarly varied, though its modest self-effacement has led to ill-considered charges of aesthetic paucity. Daves' very considerable strengths and virtues are best summed up by one French critic's description of him as 'the honest man of the Western'. JP
Broken Arrow/1950 · Return of the Texan/1952 · (st, sc, p) Drum Beat/1954 · (co-sc only) White Feather/1955 · (co-sc) Jubal/(co-sc) The Last Wagon/1956 · 3:10 to Yuma/1957 · Cowboy/The Badlanders/1958 · The Hanging Tree/1959

De Carlo, Yvonne (b 1922) · A performer more closely identified with Arabian Nights 'Easterns', she also graced a good many Westerns, mainly in the co-feature bracket, from the late 40s to the 60s. Her projection of elaborately made-up glamour, seen to particular effect in *Border River*, was complemented when occasion demanded by down-to-earth practicality (for example in *Shotgun*) and by an undercurrent of humour. The latter came to the fore when she graduated to the semi-character role of John Wayne's housekeeper in *McLintock!* TP
The Deerslayer/1943 · Frontier Gal/1945 · Black Bart/River Lady/1948 · Calamity Jane and Sam Bass/The Gal Who Took the West/1949 · Tomahawk/1950 · Silver City/1951 · The San Francisco Story/1952 · Border River/1953 · Passion/1954 · Shotgun/1955 · Raw Edge/1956 · McLintock!/Law of the Lawless/1963 · Hostile Guns/1967 · Arizona Bushwhackers/1967
Television Death Valley Days/52 · Bonanza/59 · The Virginian/63 · Custer/67 · The Mark of Zorro/74

Dehner, John (b 1915) · A disc-jockey and animator before taking up acting, he brought to a plethora of usually villainous supporting roles a laconic quality which could be inflected toward irony and even sensitivity, as well as toward hard-bitten intransigence. Most of his earlier appearances were in routine B-features, but he later had some more expansive opportunities, notably as one of Lee J. Cobb's gang in *Man of the West*. His most memorable Western role was as a sympathetic and authoritative Pat Garrett in *The Left Handed Gun*. TP
Out California Way/1946 · Vigilantes of Boom Town/1947 · Horsemen of the Sierras/Bandits of El Dorado/Riders of the Pony Express/1949 · Texas Dynamo/Dynamite Pass/1950 · Fort Savage Raiders/Al Jennings of Oklahoma/When the Redskins Rode/The

Texas Rangers/Hot Lead/1951 · Desert Passage/California Conquest/Junction City/Cripple Creek/1952 · Powder River/Gun Belt/(narrator) The Cowboy/1953 · Southwest Passage/Apache/Tall Man Riding/1954 · The Man from Bitter Ridge/Top Gun/1955 · A Day of Fury/The Fastest Gun Alive/Tension at Table Rock/1956 · Revolt at Fort Laramie/The Iron Sheriff/Trooper Hook/The Left Handed Gun/1957 · Apache Territory/Man of the West/1958 · Cast a Long Shadow/1959 · The Sign of Zorro/1960 · The Canadians/1961 · (narrator) The Hallelujah Trail/1964 · Support Your Local Gunfighter/1971 · Guardian of the Wilderness/1976
Television Gunsmoke/55 · Frontier/56 · Cheyenne/Have Gun, Will Travel/57 · Dick Powell's Zane Grey Theatre/The Restless Gun/Maverick/Zorro/58 · Black Saddle/Wanted: Dead or Alive/Tales of Wells Fargo/The Rifleman/Bat Masterson/The Alaskans/Wichita Town/The Law of the Plainsman/59 · Laramie/Rawhide/The Westerner/The Texan/The Rebel/Bonanza/60 · Stagecoach West/61 · Empire/Lawman/Bronco/62 · The Virginian/Stoney Burke/Temple Houston/63 · Branded/The Wild, Wild West/A Man Called Shenandoah/The Big Valley/65 · The Road West/66 · The Monroes/Winchester '73/67 · The Outcasts/Something for a Lonely Man/68 · The High Chaparral/69 · Honky Tonk/74 · The New Daughters of Joshua Cabe/76 · Young Maverick/79 · California Gold Rush/81

De Kova, Frank (1910-81) · Actor. A teacher and then stage actor in New York before going to Hollywood in 1951. In his Westerns he specialized in Mexicans and Indians, though most often playing the latter. In many ways better known for his regular television appearances, especially as the Indian chief White Eagle in F Troop. JH
Viva Zapata!/The Big Sky/Pony Soldier/1952 · Arrowhead/1953 · Passion/Drum Beat/They

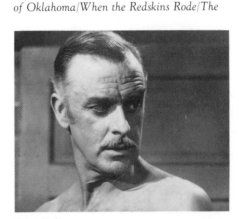

John Dehner

Frank De Kova

Cecil B. DeMille

Rode West/1954 · The Man from Laramie/
Strange Lady in Town/1955 · The Lone
Ranger/Pillars of the Sky/Reprisal!/The White
Squaw/1956 · Run of the Arrow/Ride Out
for Revenge/1957 · Cowboy/Apache
Territory/1958 · Day of the Outlaw/The
Jayhawkers!/1959 · (narrator) The Legend of
the Boy and the Eagle/1967 · The Wild
Country/1970 · Johnny Firecloud/1975
Television Gunsmoke/The Adventures of Rin
Tin Tin/57 · The Californians/The Restless
Gun/58 · The Alaskans/The Deputy/
Cheyenne/Black Saddle/59 · Hotel de Paree/
Lawman/Tales of Wells Fargo/The Rifleman/
The Tall Man/60 · The Gunslinger/
Maverick/61 · The Outlaws/Wagon Train/
62 · Laramie/The Dakotas/63 · Daniel
Boone/64 · F Troop/65 · The High
Chaparral/68 · Little House on the
Prairie/79

DeMille, Cecil B[lount] (1881-1959)
Director, producer, screenwriter, dema-
gogue. Although latterly identified with Biblical epics or risqué society comedies,
DeMille was an important figure in the early
history of the Western. In 1914 he co-
directed The Squaw Man, a six-reel epic that
was among the first films to be shot in
Hollywood, and later he remade it, twice.
The bulk of his Western output was produced before 1920, but he returned to the
genre in the sound era and made several
large-scale films that could be touted either
as saddle sagas or as epics of Americana.
None of these quite has the verve of Reap the
Wild Wind (1942), which in its use of John
Wayne, Raymond Massey and a lawman vs.
outlaws plot is almost a Western at sea, but
there is still much to enjoy in such overblown entertainments as The Plainsman or
Union Pacific. KN
(co-sc, co-p, co-d) The Squaw Man/(sc, p)
The Call of the North/(sc, p) The Virginian/
(sc, p) Rose of the Rancho/1914 · (sc, p) The
Girl of the Golden West/(p) The Warrens of
Virginia/(co-sc, p) Chimmie Fadden Out
West/(sc, p) The Trail of the Lonesome Pine/
1915 · (co-sc, p) Romance of the Redwoods/
1917 · The Squaw Man/1918 · (p) The
Squaw Man/1931 · (p) The Plainsman/1936
· (p) Union Pacific/1939 · (p) North West
Mounted Police/1940 · (p) Unconquered/
1947

Dern, Bruce (b 1936) · Actor. Blessed with
steely eyes and a toothy grin, Dern was
typecast early in his eclectic career into
playing a succession of nervy psychos and
losers. Even after meatier leading roles
started coming his way in the 70s, his
Western appearances remained in the realm
of villainy, though the amiable Jack Straw-
horn who is Posse's lesser evil and the
eponymous outlaw of Harry Tracy represent
somewhat more sympathetic characters than
that of the man who shot John Wayne in the
back in The Cowboys. PT
Waterhole No. 3/The War Wagon/Will

Penny/1967 · Hang 'Em High/1968 ·
Support Your Local Sheriff!/1969 · The
Cowboys/1971 · Posse/1975 · Harry Tracy/
1981
Television Stoney Burke/62 · Wagon Train/
63 · The Virginian/64 · Rawhide/Gunsmoke/
A Man Called Shenandoah/Laredo/65 · The
Big Valley/The Loner/Branded/66 ·
Bonanza/Lancer/68 · The High Chaparral/
70 · Sam Hill: Who Killed the Mysterious
Mr Foster?/71

de Toth, André (b 1910) · Director. Born
(Mihaly Endré Tóth Sásvrai) and educated
in Hungary where he learned his trade as
actor, editor, scenarist and assistant director, he was hired by Alexander Korda and
followed him to Hollywood in 1940. De
Toth's American films are often stylishly
directed and expertly edited genre pieces
with an eye (he had only one eye) for bizarre
details. Although sometimes pushing style
over the edge into flashiness as in the 3-D
House of Wax (1953), the bitter undertones
of a disillusioned romanticism give an extra
edge to his lyrical treatment of landscape. He
often worked with Randolph Scott, including on Carson City and Man in the Saddle, but
none of the films quite matched the actor's
work for Boetticher. However, the austere
Day of the Outlaw and the disturbingly
intense The Indian Fighter are superior contributions to the genre. PW
Ramrod/1947 · Man in the Saddle/Carson
City/1951 · Springfield Rifle/Last of the
Comanches/Thunder Over the Plains/Riding
Shotgun/1952 · The Stranger Wore a Gun/
1953 · The Bounty Hunter/1954 · The
Indian Fighter/1955 · Day of the Outlaw/
1959 · (p only) El Condor/1970
Television Maverick/Bronco/The Westerner/
60

Devine, Andy (1905-76) · Actor. A great
barrel of a man with the scratchy, high-

Bruce Dern

André de Toth

Andy Devine

pitched voice of a child. He played delightfully infectious comic characters, most memorably as Buck, the stage-driver in *Stagecoach*. After a few small parts he landed a contract with Universal in 1930, where he stayed for seventeen years. In 1947 he moved to Republic, where he was given his first continuing sidekick role, Cookie Bullfincher in a Roy Rogers series. The coda of his cowboy career was in the *Wild Bill Hickok* television series, in which for over a hundred episodes he could be heard yelping, 'Hey, Wild Bill, wait for me!' DR
Law and Order/Destry Rides Again/1932 · Stagecoach/1939 · Geronimo!/Buck Benny Rides Again/Man from Montreal/When the Daltons Rode/Trail of the Vigilantes/1940 · Men of the Timberland/The Kid from Kansas/Badlands of Dakota/Road Agent/ 1941 · North to the Klondike/Sin Town/1942 · Frontier Badmen/1943 · Frontier Gal/Frisco Sal/1945 · Canyon Passage/1946 · Michigan Kid/Bells of San Angelo/Springtime in the Sierras/The Marauders/The Vigilantes Return/On the Old Spanish Trail/The Fabulous Texan/1947 · The Gay Ranchero/ Old Los Angeles/Under California Stars/ Eyes of Texas/The Gallant Legion/Nighttime in Nevada/Grand Canyon Trail/1948 · The Far Frontier/The Last Bandit/1949 · Traveling Saleswoman/Never a Dull Moment/1950 · New Mexico/Slaughter Trail/The Red Badge of Courage/Montana Belle/1951 · Thunder Pass/1954 · Two Rode Together/1961 · The Man Who Shot Liberty Valance/How the West Was Won/1962 · The Ballad of Josie/1967 · Ride a Northbound Horse/1969
Television *The Adventures of Wild Bill Hickok/51 · Wagon Train/59 · The Rounders/66 · The Virginian/67 · Bonanza/ 68 · Gunsmoke/The Over-the-Hill Gang/69 · The Over-The-Hill Gang Rides Again/70 · The Men from Shiloh/71 · Alias Smith and Jones/72*

Dickinson, Angie (b 1931) · Actress. The blonde and long-legged Dickinson's sexual allure has been exploited throughout her career. In the 50s she had a succession of bit parts in minor Westerns, in which she often played that archetypal Western character, the whore with the heart of gold. She dubbed Sarita Montiel on *Run of the Arrow*. In 1958 she was finally given a role, as Feathers in Hawks' *Rio Bravo*, in which she was allowed to display intelligence and humour as well as sexuality. Similar roles were not forthcoming, and she has featured in few Westerns since, although she gave

notable performances in the comedy Westerns *Sam Whiskey* and *Young Billy Young*. JH
Tennessee's Partner/1954 · Man with the Gun/The Return of Jack Slade/Hidden Guns/ 1955 · Tension at Table Rock/Gun the Man Down/The Black Whip/1956 · Shoot-out at Medicine Bend/1957 · Rio Bravo/1958 · The Last Challenge/1967 · Sam Whiskey/Young Billy Young/1969 · Death Hunt/1981
Television *The Life and Legend of Wyatt Earp/Broken Arrow/56 · Gunsmoke/ Cheyenne/57 · The Restless Gun/Colt .45/ Tombstone Territory/Northwest Passage/58 · Wagon Train/59 · The Virginian/66 · Hec Ramsey/73*

Dierkes, John (1908-75) · Tall, gaunt, craggy-faced character actor, formerly an economist, who made his début in Orson Welles' *Macbeth* (1948) and left an indelible impression with his extraordinary death scene as the Tall Soldier in Huston's *The Red Badge of Courage* (1951). Few roles as memorable came his way subsequently, but he established himself as a reliable feature of the Western landscape, usually cast as a sternly upright, God-fearing citizen. TMi
Silver City/1951 · Shane/1952 · Gun Fury/A Perilous Journey/The Vanquished/The Moonlighter/1953 · The Desperado/Silver Lode/The Raid/Passion/Hell's Outpost/ Timberjack/1954 · The Vanishing American/ Road to Denver/1955 · Jubal/The Fastest Gun Alive/The Guns of Fort Petticoat/The Buckskin Lady/1956 · The Halliday Brand/ Duel at Apache Wells/Valerie/The Left Handed Gun/Blood Arrow/1957 · The Rawhide Trail/1958 · The Hanging Tree/ The Oregon Trail/1959 · The Alamo/One-Eyed Jacks/1960 · The Comancheros/1961
Television *Gunsmoke/56 · The Adventures of Rin Tin Tin/Wanted: Dead or Alive/58*

Dix, Richard (1894-1949) · Actor. Richard Dix's career in Westerns began at the top.

John Dierkes

Two years after entering films he played the lead in two Zane Grey movies directed by Victor Fleming for Paramount. That was in 1923, and Dix, a tough and sturdy character, remained a big name for a dozen years. He returned frequently to the Western, playing the pioneer Yancey Cravat in the epic *Cimarron* in 1930, and another major lead in the 1935 *The Arizonian*, which had a script by Dudley Nichols. In *Badlands of Dakota* Dix was Wild Bill Hickok, and in *Tombstone* he was Wyatt Earp – not bad roles for a man nearing the end of his career. JL
To the Last Man/The Call of the Canyon/ 1923 · The Vanishing American/1925 · The Gay Defender/1927 · Redskin/1929 · Cimarron/1930 · The Conquerors/1932 · West of the Pecos/The Arizonian/1935 · Yellow Dust/1936 · It Happened in Hollywood/1937 · Man of Conquest/1939 · Cherokee Strip/1940 · The Round Up/ Badlands of Dakota/1941 · Tombstone, the Town Too Tough to Die/American Empire/ 1942 · Buckskin Frontier/The Kansan/1943

Angie Dickinson

Richard Dix

Donlevy, Brian (1899-1972) · Actor. A powerfully built, dominating – and often domineering – presence on the screen, he was born in Ireland and after arriving in the US as a boy led a colourful life which included serving as a bugler in General Pershing's expedition against Pancho Villa. He moved into acting via the unlikely-seeming activity of modelling shirts, and created a strong impression in the late 30s, playing unregenerately nasty characters in several major Westerns of the time (though perhaps most famously in the Foreign Legion movie *Beau Geste*, 1939). He subsequently played leads in lesser films, sometimes in comedies or on the side of right, but it seems appropriate that he should have twice (in *Kansas Raiders* and *The Woman They Almost Lynched*) impersonated the notorious guerrilla Charles Quantrill. TP
Jamestown/1923 · *Jesse James*/*Union Pacific*/ *Destry Rides Again*/*Allegheny Uprising*/1939 · *When the Daltons Rode*/*Brigham Young – Frontiersman*/1940 · *Billy the Kid*/1941 · *The Great Man's Lady*/1942 · *The Virginian*/*Canyon Passage*/1946 · *Heaven Only Knows*/1947 · *A Southern Yankee*/ 1948 · *Kansas Raiders*/1950 · *Slaughter Trail*/1951 · *Ride the Man Down*/1952 · *The Woman They Almost Lynched*/1953 · *Escape from Red Rock*/1957 · *Cowboy*/1958 · *Waco*/1966 · *Hostile Guns*/*Arizona Bushwhackers*/1967
Television *Rawhide*/*Wagon Train*/*The Texan*/*Hotel De Paree*/59 · *Dick Powell's Zane Grey Theatre*/60

Douglas, Gordon (b 1909) · Director. Douglas' Westerns are among the best films of this prolific, variable, efficient and occasionally inspired director. *The Iron Mistress*, a biography of Jim Bowie, contains a knife fight in pitch darkness, *Yellowstone Kelly* is powerfully anti-racist and both this and the other two Clint Walker vehicles, *Fort Dobbs*

Kirk Douglas

and *Gold of the Seven Saints*, display considerable skill in the dramatic handling of landscape and décor. *The Fiend Who Walked the West* is an interesting remake of *Kiss of Death* but Douglas' undoubted masterpiece is the demented *Rio Conchos*, in which Douglas abandons his normal businesslike style of direction for something much more baroque. The arid setting, the crazy characters, the picaresque and violent action put one in mind of a Western Breughel, and all combine to produce a delirious climax of almost operatic proportions. JP
Girl Rush/1944 · *The Doolins of Oklahoma*/ 1949 · *The Nevadan*/*The Great Missouri Raid*/*Only the Valiant*/1950 · *The Iron Mistress*/1952 · *The Charge at Feather River*/ 1953 · *The Big Land*/1957 · *Fort Dobbs*/*The Fiend Who Walked the West*/1958 · *Yellowstone Kelly*/1959 · *Gold of the Seven Saints*/1961 · *Rio Conchos*/1964 · *Stagecoach*/1966 · *Chuka*/1967 · *Barquero*/ 1970
Television *Nevada Smith*/75

Douglas, Kirk (b 1916) · Actor. Kirk Douglas is most at home in the melodrama, with a performance style of barely contained emotional explosiveness and below-surface tension. However, he has appeared in many successful Westerns and both directed and acted in *Posse*. In *Man Without a Star* he becomes a symbol of the genre's 'freedom versus restraint' theme with his hatred of being fenced in, and in *Lonely Are the Brave* he becomes a symbol of the outdated Western hero when he is run down by an articulated truck. He also appeared as Doc Holliday in *Gunfight at the O.K. Corral*. TR
Along the Great Divide/*The Big Trees*/1951 · *The Big Sky*/1952 · *Man Without a Star*/ *The Indian Fighter*/1955 · *Gunfight at the O.K. Corral*/1956 · *Last Train from Gun Hill*/1958 · *The Last Sunset*/1961 · *Lonely Are the Brave*/1962 · *The Way West*/*The War Wagon*/1967 · *There Was a Crooked Man...*/*A Gunfight*/1970 · (d) *Posse*/1975 · *The Villain*/1979
Television *Draw!*/84

Dru, Joanne (b 1923) · Actress. All but her first three Westerns were little more than routine, but what a marvellous three those were. Joanne Dru was as pretty and spirited a Western heroine as one could wish, and in *Red River* she created a Hawksian woman as attuned to a man's world as Rosalind Russell or Jean Arthur had been before. After that, she was in the two most lyrical of John Ford's Westerns, a bright and comforting presence. Strangely, there was little else of note, but she had done enough. JL
Red River/1947 · *She Wore a Yellow Ribbon*/ 1949 · *Wagon Master*/*Vengeance Valley*/ 1950 · *Return of the Texan*/1952 · *Hannah Lee*/*The Siege at Red River*/1953 · *Southwest Passage*/1954 · *Drango*/1957 · *The Light in the Forest*/1958 · *The Wild and the Innocent*/ 1959
Television *Wagon Train*/57

Brian Donlevy

Joanne Dru

Dan Duryea

Allan Dwan

Clint Eastwood

Duryea, Dan (1907-68) · Actor. Although equally at home in the murky world of film noir, Duryea is an ideal Western villain. He usually plays the smiling gunman who will kill without qualms. He has sneered his way through a number of great Westerns; one of the best is *Silver Lode*, in which he plays the crooked sheriff who comes to town to kill John Payne and who with his smiling charm turns the entire town against Payne. Towards the end of his career he mellowed slightly into a more amiable character. TM
Along Came Jones/1945 · *Black Bart/River Lady*/1948 · *Winchester '73*/1950 · *Al Jennings of Oklahoma*/1951 · *Ride Clear of Diablo*/1953 · *Rails into Laramie/Silver Lode*/1954 · *The Marauders*/1955 · *Night Passage*/1957 · *Six Black Horses*/1961 · *He Rides Tall*/1963 · *Taggart*/1964 · *The Bounty Killer/Incident at Phantom Hill*/1965 · *Un fiume di dollari*/1966
Television *Dick Powell's Zane Grey Theatre*/56 · *Wagon Train*/57 · *Cimarron City/Texas John Slaughter/Rawhide*/58 · *Laramie/Riverboat/Bonanza*/59 · *Frontier Circus*/60 · *The Virginian/The Wide Country*/62 · *Daniel Boone*/64 · *The Loner*/65 · *Winchester '73*/67

Dwan, Allan (1885-1981) · Director. In the period 1911-13, at the American Film Company, Dwan made hundreds of films, often as writer/director/producer. The great majority of these films were split-reel Western comedies and one-reel Western dramas. D.W. Griffith was an acknowledged influence, and later Dwan worked under Griffith's supervision at Triangle, where he also established what was to be a long working

relationship with Douglas Fairbanks. In the 20s his only Western was (the part-talking) *Tide of Empire*. A director of mostly B-pictures in the 30s and thereafter, his first full sound Western, *Frontier Marshal*, was a well-made, if lowly budgeted, version of the Wyatt Earp story. His later Westerns fall into two broad categories: the comic/parodic and those (in the 50s) that display a period 'innocence'. JH
Bloodhounds of the North/1913 · *The Honor of the Mounted/Tragedy of Whispering Creek*/1914 · *The Love Route*/1915 · *The Good Bad Man/The Half-Breed/Manhattan Madness*/1916 · *Tide of Empire*/1929 · *Frontier Marshal*/1939 · *Trail of the Vigilantes*/1940 · *Northwest Outpost*/1947 · *Belle le Grand/Montana Belle*/1951 · *The Woman They Almost Lynched*/1953 · *Silver Lode/Passion/Cattle Queen of Montana/Tennessee's Partner*/1954 · *The Restless Breed*/1957

E

Eastwood, Clint (b 1930) · Tall, raw-boned actor who made his mark on television in the *Rawhide* series, then went on to acquire an international reputation as the laconically silent, supernaturally fast-drawing 'Man With No Name', in a trio of Spaghetti Westerns directed by Sergio Leone. Returning to Hollywood, he consolidated his status as heir appearent to John Wayne (though more in line of descent from Randolph Scott) in a trio of Westerns directed by Don Siegel, who also guided his first steps in the profitable and highly popular rogue cop series that began with *Dirty Harry* in 1971. Subsequently doubling as a director of considerable talent, Eastwood has alternated maddeningly between films that are purely commercial pot-boilers, and others that constitute an attempt to explore the elements of his success. *High Plains Drifter*, for example, can be seen as an exorcism of his twin debt to Siegel and Leone in an extension of their influence on him; while *The Outlaw Josey Wales* is the best of several mockingly critical appraisals of his own persona. TMI
The First Traveling Saleslady/1956 · *Ambush at Cimarron Pass*/1957 · *Per un pugno di dollari*/1964 · *Per qualche dollaro in più*/1965 · *Il buono, il brutto, il cattivo*/1966 · *Hang 'Em High/Coogan's Bluff*/1968 · *Paint Your Wagon/Two Mules for Sister Sara*/1969 · *The Beguiled*/1970 · *Joe Kidd/*(d) *High Plains Drifter*/1972 · (d) *The Outlaw Josey Wales*/1976 · (d) *Bronco Billy*/1980 · (d) *Pale Rider*/1985

Television *Wagon Train*/57 · *Maverick/Rawhide*/59

Elam, Jack (b 1916) · Actor. Dark-haired, gaunt, and with a sightless left eye, Elam portrayed an evil-looking villain in dozens of Westerns in the 50s and 60s. Invariably playing character roles, which were on occasion sadistic, his mere presence was enough to establish evil intent. He has also played comedy roles throughout his career and, increasingly as he has got older, roles which parody his villainous persona. Leone most successfully utilized these twin aspects of Elam in *C'era una volta il west*, in which the wordless Elam is tormented by a fly. JH
Trailin' West/The Sundowners/1949 · *A Ticket to Tomahawk/High Lonesome/Rawhide*/1950 · *The Bushwhackers*/1951 · *The Battle at Apache Pass/High Noon/Rancho Notorious/Montana Territory/Ride, Vaquero!*/1952 · *Gun Belt/The Moonlighter/Ride Clear of Diablo*/1953 · *Jubilee Trail/Vera Cruz/Cattle Queen of Montana/The Far Country*/1954 · *The Man from Laramie/Wichita/Man Without a Star*/1955 · *Jubal/Thunder over Arizona/Pardners/Gunfight at the O.K. Corral*/1956 · *Dragoon Wells Massacre/Night Passage*/1957 · *The Last Sunset/The Comancheros*/1961 · *4 for Texas/*1963 · *The Rare Breed*/1965 · *The Night of the Grizzly*/1966 · *The Last Challenge/The Way West/Firecreek*/1967 · *C'era una volta il west/Sonora/Support Your Local Sheriff!/*1968 · *Ride a Northbound Horse*/1969 · *Dirty Dingus Magee/Rio Lobo/The Wild Country/The Cockeyed Cowboys of Calico County*/1970 · *Support Your Local Gunfighter/Hannie Caulder/The Last Rebel*/1971 · *Pat Garrett and Billy the Kid*/1973 · *Pony Express Rider/Hawmps*/1976 · *Grayeagle*/1977 · *Hot Lead and Cold Feet*/1978 · *The Villain/The Apple Dumpling Gang Rides Again*/1979 · *Sacred Ground/*1982

Jack Elam

Television *Tales of Wells Fargo/Zorro/57 ·
The Texan/Bronco/The Restless Gun/The
Rifleman/Lawman/58 · Tombstone Territory/
Have Gun, Will Travel/59 · Cheyenne/
Sugarfoot/Klondike/Gunslinger/The
Americans/Bonanza/Laramie/The Rebel/61 ·
The Dakotas/Temple Houston/63 · Daniel
Boone/The Legend of Jesse James/65 ·
Gunsmoke/66 · The Wild, Wild West/The
Guns of Will Sonnett/Hondo/67 · Cimarron
Strip/The High Chaparral/68 · The
Outcasts/The Over-the-Hill Gang/Lancer/69
· The Virginian/70 · Alias Smith and Jones/
Nichols/The Daughters of Joshua Cabe/72 ·
Sidekicks/Shootout in a One-Dog Town/74 ·
The New Daughters of Joshua Cabe/76 ·
How the West Was Won/77 · Lacy and the
Mississippi Queen/78 · The Sacketts/79*

Elliott, Wild Bill (1903-65) · Actor, aka
Gordon Elliott, Bill Elliott. A bit-player in
dozens of Warners films in the early 30s, he
came to prominence as a Western star in the
Columbia serial *The Great Adventures of
Wild Bill Hickok*. As a Western series star at
Columbia and later Republic (where he was
billed as 'Wild Bill'), he portrayed a strong
yet compassionate hero. Unlike some of his
contemporaries his screen garb was rela-
tively restrained, although he did adopt the
gimmick of wearing his guns reversed in
their holsters. JH
*The Arizona Wildcat/1927 · The Valley of
Hunted Men/1928 · The Great Divide/1929
· Moonlight on the Prairie/Trailin' West/
Guns of the Pecos/1935 · Boots and Saddles/
Roll Along, Cowboy/1937 · The Great
Adventures of Wild Bill Hickok/In Early
Arizona/Frontiers of '49/1938 · Lone Star
Pioneers/The Law Comes to Texas/Taming of
the West/Overland with Kit Carson/1939 ·
The Return of Wild Bill/Pioneers of the
Frontier/The Man from Tumbleweeds/Prairie
Schooners/Beyond the Sacramento/The
Wildcat of Tucson/1940 · North from the*
*Lone Star/Across the Sierras/The Return of
Daniel Boone/The Son of Davy Crockett/
Hands Across the Rockies/King of Dodge
City/Roaring Frontiers/The Lone Star
Vigilantes/1941 · Bullets for Bandits/North
of the Rockies/The Devil's Trail/Prairie
Gunsmoke/Vengeance of the West/Valley of
Vanishing Men/1942 · Calling Wild Bill
Elliott/The Man from Thunder River/Wagon
Tracks West/Death Valley Manhunt/
Bordertown Gunfighters/Overland Mail
Robbery/Hidden Valley Outlaws/1943 ·
Mojave Firebrand/Tucson Raiders/Marshal
of Reno/The San Antonio Kid/Cheyenne
Wildcat/Vigilantes of Dodge City/Sheriff of
Las Vegas/1944 · Bells of Rosarita/Great
Stagecoach Robbery/Lone Texas Ranger/
Phantom of the Plains/Marshal of Laredo/
Colorado Pioneers/Wagon Wheels Westward/
1945 · California Gold Rush/Sheriff of
Redwood Valley/Sun Valley Cyclone/
Conquest of Cheyenne/In Old Sacramento/
The Plainsman and the Lady/1946 ·
Wyoming/The Fabulous Texan/1947 · Old
Los Angeles/The Gallant Legion/1948 ·
Hellfire/The Last Bandit/The Savage Horde/
1949 · The Showdown/1950 · The Longhorn/
Waco/Fargo/The Maverick/Kansas Territory/
Vigilante Terror/1952 · The Homesteaders/
Rebel City/Topeka/1953 · Bitter Creek/The
Forty-Niners/1954*

F

Farnsworth, Richard (b 1920) · Actor, aka
Dick Farnsworth. A stuntman for thirty
years, Farnsworth specialized in riding and
archery. He worked in an estimated 300
pictures, later in bit parts as stagecoach
drivers and unnamed cowboys. He was
approaching age sixty when he won acting
acclaim as the hired hand in *Comes a
Horseman*. With an understated manner,
soft voice, clear eyes, and broad, white
moustache he brings a quiet dignity to his
roles. His years generally relegate him to
supporting parts, though he perfectly suited
the lead in *The Grey Fox*, the gentlemanly
train robber Bill Miner. BA
*Stallion Road/Red River/1947 · The Tin
Star/1957 · Major Dundee/1964 · Cat
Ballou/Duel at Diablo/1965 · Texas Across
the River/1966 · Monte Walsh/1970 · The
Cowboys/1971 · Pocket Money/The Life and
Times of Judge Roy Bean/Ulzana's Raid/
1972 · The Duchess and the Dirtwater Fox/
1976 · Un Autre homme, une autre chance/
1977 · Comes a Horseman/1978 · Tom
Horn/1980 · The Legend of the Lone Ranger/
1981 · The Grey Fox/1983*
Television *Wanted: Dead or Alive/57 ·
Bonanza/59 · The High Chaparral/67 ·
Little House on the Prairie/74 · Wild Horses/
85*

Farnum, Dustin (1874-1929) · Actor,
brother of William Farnum, who also
appeared in Westerns. Dustin was brought
to Hollywood by Cecil B. DeMille, for the
Lasky Feature Play Co., to star in *The Squaw
Man*, in which he had appeared on
Broadway. The film was a considerable
success and DeMille quickly followed it
with the first screen adaptation of Owen
Wister's *The Virginian*, which Farnum had
also played on the stage. Leaving Lasky he
moved to Paramount, where he made a
number of society dramas. He signed with
Fox in the early 20s and returned to the
genre, making several prestigious Western
melodramas. PS
*The Squaw Man/The Virginian/1914 ·
Captain Courtesy/The Iron Strain/The
Gentleman from Indiana/1915 · Davy
Crockett/The Parson of Panamint/1916 · The
Light of the Western Stars/Durand of the
Bad Lands/North of '53/1917 · Man in the
Open/1919 · The Primal Law/The Call of
the North/1921 · Strange Idols/Iron to Gold/
The Trail of the Axe/While Justice Waits/*

Wild Bill Elliott

Richard Farnsworth

Dustin Farnum

1922 · *Bucking the Barrier/The Buster/The Grail/Kentucky Days/The Man Who Won/Three Who Paid/*1923 · *The Flaming Frontier/*1926

Ferguson, Frank (1899-1978) · Actor. A latecomer to Hollywood from Broadway in 1940, his slightly doleful expression and toothbrush moustache became a regular feature in Westerns of the 50s. Not always on the right side of the law, he almost invariably played a townsman of the professional or business classes – a newspaperman in *Fort Apache*, a preacher in *Rancho Notorious*, and in one of his most notable roles, the fair-minded but ultimately powerless marshal in *Johnny Guitar*. JH
*They Died with their Boots On/*1941 · *Canyon Passage/California/*1946 · *The Fabulous Texan/Rachel and the Stranger/*1947 · *Fort Apache/*1948 · *Under Mexicali Skies/The Furies/Frenchie/The Great Missouri Raid/*1950 · *Thunder in God's Country/Santa Fe/Warpath/The Cimarron Kid/Bend of the River/*1951 · *Rancho Notorious/Wagons West/Rodeo/Oklahoma Annie/Riding Shotgun/*1952 · *The Lone Hand/Star of Texas/The Marksman/The Woman They Almost Lynched/Powder River/Hannah Lee/Texas Badman/*1953 · *Johnny Guitar/The Outcast/Drum Beat/The Violent Men/*1954 · *A Lawless Street/Gun Point/Tribute to a Badman/*1955 · *The Phantom Stagecoach/The Iron Sheriff/Gun Duel in Durango/The Lawless Eighties/*1957 · *The Light in the Forest/Cole Younger, Gunfighter/Terror in a Texas Town/Man of the West/*1958 · *The Quick Gun/*1964 · *The Great Sioux Massacre/*1965
Television *My Friend Flicka/*56 · *Tales of Wells Fargo/Trackdown/*57 · *Tales of the Texas Rangers/The Restless Gun/Colt .45/*58 · *Maverick/The Texan/The Alaskans/Wichita Town/*59 · *Sugarfoot/Lawman/The Rifleman/Cheyenne/Klondike/*60 · *The Tall Man/The Life and Legend of Wyatt Earp/Have Gun, Will Travel/*61 · *The Macahans/*76

Fix, Paul (1902-83) · Actor. Short, wiry and hard-faced, Paul Fix spent fifty years as a character actor in Hollywood. He appeared in numerous crime films, usually as a villain, and in around sixty Westerns. Here he proved more versatile. His looks barred him from hero roles, but he could manage anything else required, ending, at the age of 75, as an ancient Indian chief in *Grayeagle*. One movie encyclopedia says that Fix played 'Both villains and good buys'. That says it beautifully, if by accident. For any producer, Paul Fix was a very good buy. JL
*The Avenger/The Fighting Sheriff/*1931 · *South of the Rio Grande/*1932 · *Fargo Express/Gun Law/Somewhere in Sonora/*1933 · *Rocky Rhodes/*1934 · *The Crimson Trail/The Desert Trail/The Eagle's Brood/His Fighting Blood/Bar 20 Rides Again/Valley of Wanted Men/*1935 · *Border Café/*1937 · *Heritage of the Desert/*1939 · *Triple Justice/Virginia City/The Fargo Kid/Trail of the Vigilantes/*1940 · *Down Mexico Way/A Missouri Outlaw/*1941 · *South of Santa Fe/*1942 · *In Old Oklahoma/*1943 · *Tall in the Saddle/*1944 · *Dakota/Flame of Barbary Coast/*1945 · *Red River/*1947 · *The Plunderers/*1948 · *Hellfire/Fighting Man of the Plains/The Fighting Kentuckian/*1949 · *California Passage/The Great Missouri Raid/*1950 · *Warpath/*1951 · *Denver and Rio Grande/Ride the Man Down/*1952 · *Star of Texas/Hondo/*1953 · *Johnny Guitar/*1954 · *Giant/Stagecoach to Fury/*1956 · *Man in the Shadow/*1957 · *Mail Order Bride/*1963 · *The Outrage/*1964 · *The Sons of Katie Elder/Shenandoah/Nevada Smith/Ride Beyond Vengeance/Incident at Phantom Hill/*1965 · *An Eye for an Eye/El Dorado/Welcome to Hard Times/*1966 · *The Ballad of Josie/*1967 · *Day of the Evil Gun/*1968 · *Young Billy Young/The Undefeated/*1969 · *Dirty Dingus Magee/*1970 · *Shoot Out/Something Big/*1971 · *Pat Garrett and Billy the Kid/Cahill United States Marshal/*1973 · *Grayeagle/*1977
Television *Gunsmoke/*56 · *The Rifleman/Bronco/Northwest Passage/Sugarfoot/Colt .45/The Texan/*58 · *Riverboat/Dick Powell's Zane Grey Theatre/Tales of Wells Fargo/*60 · *Wagon Train/*62 · *Have Gun, Will Travel/*63 · *The Travels of Jaimie McPheeters/*64 · *The Big Valley/*65 · *Daniel Boone/A Man Called Shenandoah/The Wild, Wild West/*66 · *Winchester '73/The Virginian/Bonanza/The Guns of Will Sonnett/*67 · *The High Chaparral/*68 · *Here Come the Brides/The Outcasts/*69 · *Alias Smith and Jones/*71 · *How the West Was Won/*77

Flippen, Jay C. (1898-1971) · Character actor with a background in vaudeville and minstrel shows, miscast but memorable as the loquaciously philosophical Sioux, outcast from his tribe, who becomes Rod Steiger's mentor in *Run of the Arrow*. Looking like a ruggedly authentic Westerner with his seamed features and measured movements, he was usually cast as a stern but kindly father figure. Continued acting after suffering a leg amputation following completion of *Cat Ballou*. TMI
*Winchester '73/Two Flags West/*1950 · *The Lady from Texas/Bend of the River/*1951 · *Woman of the North Country/*1952 · *Devil's Canyon/*1953 · *The Far Country/*1954 · *Man Without a Star/Oklahoma!/*1955 · *The King and Four Queens/7th Cavalry/*1956 · *The Halliday Brand/The Restless Breed/Night Passage/Run of the Arrow/The Deerslayer/Escape from Red Rock/*1957 · *From Hell to Texas/*1958 · *The Plunderers/*1960 · *How the West Was Won/*1962 · *Cat Ballou/*1965 · *Firecreek/*1967
Television *Wanted: Dead or Alive/*58 · *Johnny Ringo/*60 · *Stagecoach West/*61 ·

Frank Ferguson

Paul Fix

Jay C. Flippen

Gunsmoke/Bonanza/Elfego Baca/63 ·
Rawhide/64 · A Man Called Shenandoah/
The Virginian/66 · The Road West/67 · Sam
Hill: Who Killed the Mysterious Mr. Foster?/
71

Flynn, Errol (1909-59) · Actor. Despite his
aptitude for dashing roles, Flynn made comparatively few Westerns; possibly he was
just too much of a ladies' man to fit comfortably into the genre. Undoubtedly best
remembered for his portrayal of an heroic
but headstrong Custer in *They Died with their
Boots On*, he was also a spirited Wyatt
Earp-type figure in *Dodge City*. EB
Dodge City/1939 · *Virginia City*/*Santa Fe
Trail*/1940 · *They Died with their Boots
On*/1941 · *San Antonio*/1946 · *Silver River*/
1948 · *Montana*/1949 · *Rocky Mountain*/
1950

Fonda, Henry (1905-82) · Actor. Colin
McArthur has suggested that Henry Fonda
'emerged, in *My Darling Clementine*, as the
archetypal Western hero, possessed of
infinite control and gentleness.' Yet, some
23 years after his justly celebrated portrait of
Wyatt Earp in Ford's classic film, Fonda was
to play the coldest of cold-blooded villains
in Sergio Leone's *C'era una volta il west*.
These two performances represent the
extremes of the persona that Fonda constructed across a number of Western
appearances in his lengthy screen career. He
was an outlaw in *Jesse James*, progressed to
the martinet General Custer figure in Ford's
Fort Apache, and near the end was a cowboy
whose pal (James Stewart) inherits a brothel
in the comedy *The Cheyenne Social Club*. The
Wyatt Earp image sticks, however, probably
because it lines up more closely with Fonda's
most famous non-Western roles in films
such as *The Grapes of Wrath* and *Twelve
Angry Men*. TR
The Trail of the Lonesome Pine/1936 · *Jesse*

James/*Drums Along the Mohawk*/1939 · *The
Return of Frank James*/1940 · *Wild Geese
Calling*/1941 · *The Ox-Bow Incident*/1942 ·
My Darling Clementine/1946 · *Fort Apache*/
1948 · *The Tin Star*/1957 · *Warlock*/1959 ·
How the West Was Won/1962 · *The
Rounders*/1964 · *A Big Hand for the Little
Lady*/*Welcome to Hard Times*/1966 ·
Firecreek/1967 · *C'era una volta il west*/1968
· *There Was a Crooked Man...*/*The
Cheyenne Social Club*/1970 · *Il mio nome è
Nessuno*/1973
Television *The Deputy*/59 · *Stranger on the
Run*/67

Foran, Dick (1910-79) · Actor. Foran was
the second of the singing cowboys, his series
for Warner Bros. starting in 1935, a matter
of weeks after the first Gene Autry releases.
Fair-haired and burly, with a warm personality and a pleasant baritone voice, Foran
was a highly competent actor who played
leads and supporting roles in many types of
film. He was in one Western masterpiece,
John Ford's *Fort Apache*, playing Sergeant
Quincannon, the role later immortalized by
Victor McLaglen. In the 60s television
claimed him. JL
Moonlight on the Prairie/1935 · *Treachery
Rides the Range*/*Song of the Saddle*/*Trailin'
West*/*The California Mail*/1936 · *Guns of
the Pecos*/*Cherokee Strip*/*Land Beyond the
Law*/*Blazing Sixes*/*Empty Holsters*/*The
Devil's Saddle Legion*/*Prairie Thunder*/1937
· *Cowboy from Brooklyn*/*Heart of the North*/
1938 · *My Little Chickadee*/*Winners of the
West*/*Rangers of Fortune*/1940 · *Road Agent*/
Riders of Death Valley/1941 · *Ride 'Em
Cowboy*/1942 · *Fort Apache*/1948 · *El Paso*/
Deputy Marshal/*The Sunday Roundup*/1949
· *Al Jennings of Oklahoma*/1951 · *Treasure
of Ruby Hills*/1955 · *Sierra Stranger*/1957 ·
Taggart/1964 · *Brighty of the Grand
Canyon*/1967
Television *The Adventures of Wild Bill*

Hickok/55 · *Colt .45*/57 · *Maverick*/*Have
Gun, Will Travel*/*Trackdown*/58 · *Wanted:
Dead or Alive*/59 · *Yancy Derringer*/
Laramie/*The Deputy*/61 · *Lawman*/
Cheyenne/*The Rifleman*/62 · *Gunsmoke*/*The
Dakotas*/*The Great Adventure*/*Death Valley
Days*/63 · *The Virginian*/64 · *Rawhide*/65 ·
Daniel Boone/66 · *Bonanza*/68

Ford, Francis (1881-1953) · Actor. Generally given only a footnote in film histories
as the elder brother of John, in whose
Westerns he typically appeared as an amiable drunken trapper. He was, however, as
an actor and director, one of the most
prominent screen personalities of the 'teens,
participating in perhaps as many as 400 silent
films, the majority of which, prior to 1915,
had Western or Civil War subjects. His
most successful period in box-office terms
was at Universal, playing alongside Grace
Cunard in crime dramas and serials. By 1920
his star had waned and he ended the silent
period as a director of low-budget, mostly
Western, pictures. (Note: it is uncertain
which films Ford appeared in for Gaston
Méliès' New York Star Film Co., so all their
Westerns of 1910-1912 have been included.
Unless otherwise indicated, Ford appears in
all the films listed below.) PS
Cyclone Pete's Matrimony/*Branding the
Thief*/*The Debt Repaid*/*A Texas Joe*/*White
Doe's Lovers*/*The Return of Ta-Wa-Wa*/*The
Romance of Circle Ranch*/*In the Mission
Shadows*/*The Salt on the Bird's Tail*/*A
Plucky American Girl*/*Billy's Sister*/*Out for
Mischief*/*Uncle Jim*/*Under the Stars and
Bars*/*A Mountain Wife*/*His Sergeant's
Stripes*/*The Cowboys and the Bachelor*/*Pals*/
What Great Bear Learned/*Old Norris'
Gal*/*A Western Welcome*/*In the Tall Grass
Country*/1910 · *The Crimson Scars*/*Fire! Fire!
Fire!*/*The Owner of the L.L. Ranch*/
Changing Cooks/*How Mary Met the
Cowpunchers*/*Tony the Greaser*/*Billy and His*

Errol Flynn

Henry Fonda

Dick Foran

Pal/My Prairie Flower/In the Hot Lands/The Snake in the Grass/The School Marm of Coyote County/Sir Percy and the Punchers/The Warrant of Red Rube/The Faithful Heart/Jack Mason's Last Deal/The Reformation of Jack Robin/Mary's Stratagem/The Spring Roundup/The Immortal Alamo/The Honor of the Flag/The Great Heart of the West/Bessie's Ride/At the Gringo's Mine/Red Cloud's Secret/A Spanish Love Song/The Call of the Wilderness/The Hobo Cowboy/The Mission Waif/The Stolen Gray/Mexican As It Is Spoken/A Western Girl/The Better Man/The Mission Father/The Ranchman's Debt of Honor/Bar Z's New Cook/The Foreman's Courage/Cow Girl's Pranks/An Indian Martyr/Falsely Accused/Getting His Man/1911 · Roped In/The Outlaw and the Baby/Cowboy vs. the Tenderfoot/Dodging the Sheriff/Smilin' Bob/Melita's Rose/Seven Bars of Gold/The Sheriff's Daughter/Troubles of the XL Outfit/The Ghost of Sulfur Mountain/True Till Death/Finding the 'Last Chance' Mine/The Rustler's Daughter/Making Good/Ghosts at Circle X Ranch/The Cowboy Kid/The Man Inside/A Cowboy's Proposal/The String of Beads/The Will of Destiny/The Ranger's Girl/A Romance at Catalina/His Partner's Share/The Obsession/The Unworthy Son/A Western Coquette/Wrongly Accused/The Governor's Clemency/Linked By Fate/The Sheriff Pro-Tem/A Woodland Christian in California/An Indian Maid's Elopement/The Gambler's Heart/The Laugh on Dan/The Honor of the Tribe/War on the Plains/The Ranch Girl's Love/The Empty Water Keg/Tenderfoot's Revenge/Broncho Billy's Love Affair/Wild West Circus/The Deputy's Sweetheart/The Indian Massacre/The Battle of the Red Man/The Deserter/The Lieutenant's Last Fight/The Outcast/(d?) Memories of a Pioneer/A Soldier's Honor/(d?) His Punishment/(d?) On the Warpath/(d?) His Message/The Colonel's Peril/The Sheriff of Stony Butte/His Nemesis/The Restoration/Reconciled/The Sheriff's Mysterious Aide/The Last Resource/The Desert/The Gambler and the Girl/The Reformed Outlaw/The Garrison Triangle/(d?) The Bugle Call/The Buffalo Hunt/The Reckoning/(d) The Bandit's Gratitude/The White Lie/For the Honor of the Tribe/(d) The Fugitive/(d uncredited) A Frontier Child/The Penalty/Sundered Ties/(d) The Hidden Trail/(d) His Better Self/On the Firing Line/(d uncredited) For the Honor of the Seventh/(co-d) Custer's Last Fight/(d) An Indian Legend/The Sergeant's Boy/(d) The Sheriff's Adopted Child/(d) The Vengeance of Fate/(d) The Story of the Savage Modoc

Francis Ford (l.) with Alan Mowbray in Wagon Master

Mine/The Colonel's Ward/(d) How Shorty Kept His Word/On Secret Service/The Man They Scorned/When Lee Surrendered/Mary of the Mines/The Alter of Death/(d uncredited) The Civilian/(d) The Army Surgeon/(d) The Ball Player and the Bandit/(d uncredited) The Invaders/(d) His Squaw/(d) For the Cause/A Double Reward/Blood Will Tell/His Sense of Duty/The Dead Pays/(d) The Prospector's Daughter/(d uncredited) The Law of the West/Crisis/The Post Telegrapher/Blazing the Trail/1912 · An Indian's Gratitude/(d) The Favorite Son/From Dawn till Dark/The Black Masks/(d) The Burning Brand/The Great Sacrifice/In the Ranks/(d) The Paymaster's Son/A Bluegrass Romance/(d) The Little Turncoat/A Shadow of the Past/The Struggle/Wheels of Destiny/(d) Smilin' Dan/(d) The Sharpshooter/(d) Tell Tale Hat Band/The Barrier/The Lost Despatch/The Sergeant's Secret/Pride of the South/(d) A Frontier Wife/The Iconoclast/(d) Texas Kelly at Bay/Sheridan's Ride/(d) The Coward's Atonement/(d) His Brother/(d) The Battle of Bull Run/(d) The Light in the Window/(d) The Half-Breed Parson/Tap/The Darling of the Regiment/War/The Vengeance of the Skystone/(d) The Toll of War/(d) The Stars and Stripes Forever/(d) The Honor of the Regiment/(d) Wynona's Vengeance/(d) The White Vacquero/1913 · The Adventures of Shorty/The Ghost of Smiling Jim/(d) A War Time Reformation/(d) In the Fall of '64/1914 · (d) Three Bad Men and a Girl/(d) And They Called Him Hero/(d) The Curse of the Desert/1915 · (d) The Dumb Bandit/(d) The Unexpected/(d) The Bandit's Wager/1916 ·

(d) John Ermine of Yellowstone/(d) The Little Rebel's Sacrifice/The Rebel's Net/The Avenging Trail/1917 · (d, sc) The Craving/(d only) The Avenging Trail/1918 · (d only) Thunderbolt Jack/(d only) A Man's Country/(d only) A Man from Nowhere/(d) Flower of the Range/1920 · Action/(d only) Cyclone Bliss/(d) The Stampede/(d) I Am the Woman/1921 · (d?) Cross Roads/(d) So This Is Arizona/(d only) Angel Citizens/(d only) Trail's End/Another Man's Boots/(d) Thundering Hoofs/(d) Gold Grabbers/The Boss of Camp 4/1922 · Three Jumps Ahead/The Santa Fe Trail/1923 · (d only) Western Feuds/(d) A Rodeo Mixup/(d) Western Yesterdays/(sc, d) Lash of the Whip/(sc, d) Range Blood/(sc, d) In the Days of the Covered Wagon/(sc, d) Cupid's Rustlers/(sc, d) Midnight Shadows/(sc, d) The Cowboy Prince/The Measure of a Man/(sc, d) The Diamond Bandit/(d only) The Lash of Pinto Pete/1924 · The Sign of the Cactus/A Roaring Adventure/The Taming of the West/Scar Hanan/Ridin' Thunder/Soft Shoes/The Red Rider/1925 · Trooper 77/1926 · Men of Daring/The Devil's Saddle/The Heart of Maryland/(d only) Wolf's Trail/One Glorious Scrap/1927 · The Branded Sombrero/(d only) Call of the Heart/Four-Footed Ranger/1928 · The Lariat Kid/1929 · The Mounted Stranger/Song of the Caballero/Sons of the Saddle/The Indians Are Coming/1930 · Battling with Buffalo Bill/1931 · Heroes of the West/1932 · Clancy of the Mounted/Gordon of Ghost City/The Man from Monterey/Life in the Raw/Gun Justice/1933 · The Arizonian/1935 · The Texans/Stagecoach/Drums Along the

Mohawk/Bad Lands/1939 · Geronimo!/Viva Cisco Kid/Lucky Cisco Kid/1940 · Last of the Duanes/1941 · Outlaws of Pine Ridge/ The Ox-Bow Incident/King of the Mounties/ 1942 · San Antonio/1945 · California/My Darling Clementine/Renegades/1946 · Unconquered/Bandits of Dark Canyon/1947 · Timber Trail/Fort Apache/3 Godfathers/ Eyes of Texas/The Plunderers/The Far Frontier/1948 · She Wore a Yellow Ribbon/ Frontier Investigator/San Antone Ambush/ 1949 · Wagon Master/1950 · Toughest Man in Arizona/The Marshal's Daughter/1952

Ford, Glenn (b 1916) · Actor who became a leading man in films in the mid-40s, and is equally at home in drama, light comedy or Westerns. He has often played the loner unjustly accused, or the young cowboy who drifts into trouble. Though his performances usually have a hard edge, he can combine this with comedy, as in *The Sheepman*, where he plays a cowboy who arrives in the middle of cattle country with a herd of sheep. In 1971 he turned to television and starred in *Cade's County*, a modern Western series in which he played the town marshal. TM
Texas/Go West, Young Lady/1941 · The Desperadoes/1943 · The Man from Colorado/1948 · Lust for Gold/1949 · The Redhead and the Cowboy/1950 · The Man from the Alamo/1953 · The Violent Men/The Americano/1954 · Jubal/The Fastest Gun Alive/1956 · 3:10 to Yuma/ 1957 · Cowboy/The Sheepman/1958 · Cimarron/1960 · Advance to the Rear/1963 · The Rounders/1964 · The Last Challenge/A Time for Killing/1967 · Day of the Evil Gun/1968 · Heaven With a Gun/Smith/1969 · Santee/1972
Television Cade's County/71 · The Sacketts/ 79

Ford, John (1895-1973) · Director, born Sean Aloysius O'Feeney in Cape Elizabeth,

Glenn Ford

John Ford

Maine, the 13th child of Irish immigrants. At a meeting during the McCarthy era, called by Cecil B. DeMille to hound the supposedly 'pinko' Joseph Mankiewicz, Ford began his defence of Mankiewicz with the famous announcement: 'My name's John Ford. I make Westerns.' No other major director identified himself so closely with the genre, and in the public mind the association between Ford and the Western is so close that one seems to merge into the other.

To put things into perspective, Ford directed a mere 56 Westerns out of the many thousands made since 1903. And these Westerns represent less than half of the 125 films Ford directed in all (excluding non-fiction shorts and television shows). Ford would still be an important director without his Westerns – between *Three Bad Men* in 1926 and *Stagecoach* in 1939 Ford directed 32 films, not one a Western. And the Western would still be a rich and varied genre without his contribution.

So what specifically did Ford contribute? In the first place, a landscape. Ford was not the first director to shoot in Monument Valley, but his virtual appropriation of this location from the moment of *Stagecoach*, his first film there, gave his work a visual signature unmatched by any other director. No other place evokes, so unambiguously and resonantly, the West. And perhaps no other landscape in the cinema is so quintessentially American. Ford, more than any other director, defines what is American about the Western.

Ford's work encompasses virtually all the major themes which the Western has derived from the clash of savagery and civilization. In *The Iron Horse* he takes a positive view of the railroad's contribution to 'progress'. *My Darling Clementine* and *The Man Who Shot Liberty Valance* deal, in their different ways, with the establishment of law

and order. *Sergeant Rutledge*, *The Searchers* and *Two Rode Together* tackle the problem of racial difference. The so-called cavalry trilogy (*Fort Apache*, *She Wore a Yellow Ribbon* and *Rio Grande*) explores the tensions between public duty and personal affections which the tradition of military conquest attempts to suppress. *Drums Along the Mohawk* and *Wagon Master* express the urge towards the settlement of the land. *Cheyenne Autumn* is Ford's belated yet clearly heartfelt attempt to set the record straight on the dispossession of the Indians.

Counter-balancing Ford's oft-remarked emphasis on the values of the community, especially precious amid the anarchy and savagery of the frontier, is his fondness (sometimes explicitly Christian) for outcasts and misfits: the Magdalene (Claire Trevor) in *Stagecoach*, the outlaw heroes of *3 Godfathers*, mad old Mose Harper in *The Searchers*, and drunks *passim*.

Yet it is not the importance of his themes which makes Ford both a great director and the most pivotal figure in the genre. Ford's genius is his gift for combining the epic and the intimate in a single moment. Ford manages to invest personal emotion with historical significance, and anchor a mighty theme to a detail of individual character. In *The Searchers* Lars Jorgenson (John Qualen) gestures at the vastness of the landscape. Words fail him. 'Oh, Ethan, this country...' is all he can utter. The moment both captures the emotion pent up in an inarticulate man who is fighting against personal grief and despair, and eloquently communicates the fearsome grandeur of the West, its resistance to human domination. Perhaps the most famous of such moments comes in *My Darling Clementine* when Wyatt Earp (Henry Fonda) takes his 'lady fair' out on to the floor of the half-built church in Tombstone. As Earp waltzes awkwardly to the music it's both the epiphany of an intensely private

Sam Fuller

emotion and, with the emptiness of the desert in the background, a highly-charged symbol of the precariousness of all civilization.

Only two of all the Westerns which Ford made before *The Iron Horse* (*Straight Shooting* and *Just Pals*) are still known to exist, and we cannot be sure whether Ford's Universal shorts with Pete Morrison or the Cheyenne Harry series with Harry Carey decisively affected the progress of the genre. But in his later films Ford's special contribution is clear. He managed, in a way that no one else did, to unite the personal and the public, to combine the traditional Hollywood emphasis on individual character with a perspective on history which gave the Western dignity and a claim to serious attention. Uniquely, Ford drew both on the popular strengths of the dime novel and the tradition of serious historical enquiry represented by Frederick Jackson Turner. To realize how difficult this was, and how brilliantly Ford managed it, one has only to compare *The Iron Horse* with the contemporaneous *The Covered Wagon*. In *The Covered Wagon* the history is stiff, the individual characters banal. Ford humanizes history. EB

(act only) *Three Bad Men and a Girl*/1915 · (act only) *The Bandit's Wager*/1916 · (act, sc) *The Tornado*/(sc) *The Trail of Hate*/(act, sc) *The Scrapper*/*The Soul Herder*/(st) *Cheyenne's Pal*/*Straight Shooting*/*The Secret Man*/(st) *A Marked Man*/*Bucking Broadway*/1917 · *The Phantom Riders*/*Wild Women*/*Thieves' Gold*/(st) *The Scarlet Drop*/(co-sc) *Hell Bent*/*A Woman's Fool*/*Three Mounted Men*/1918 · *Roped*/*The Fighting Brothers*/*A Fight for Love*/*By Indian Post*/*The Rustlers*/*Bare Fists*/*Gun Law*/(co-st) *The Gun Packer*/(co-sc) *Riders of Vengeance*/(co-st) *The Last Outlaw*/*The Outcasts of Poker Flat*/*The Ace of the Saddle*/*The Rider of the Law*/(co-st) *A Gun Fightin' Gentleman*/1919 · *Marked Men*/*Just Pals*/*Hitchin' Posts*/(st only) *Under Sentence*/1920 · *The Freeze Out*/*The Wallop*/*Desperate Trails*/*Action*/*Sure Fire*/(co-sc) *The Big Punch*/1921 · (sc) *Three Jumps Ahead*/*North of Hudson Bay*/1923 · *The Iron Horse*/1924 · (co-sc) *Three Bad Men*/1926 · (co-st only) *The Last Outlaw*/1936 · *Stagecoach*/*Drums Along the Mohawk*/1939 · *My Darling Clementine*/1946 · (co-p) *Fort Apache*/(co-p) *3 Godfathers*/1948 · (co-p) *She Wore A Yellow Ribbon*/1949 · (co-p) *Wagon Master*/(co-p) *Rio Grande*/1950 · (2nd unit only) *Hondo*/1953 · *The Searchers*/1956 · *The Horse Soldiers*/1959 · *Sergeant Rutledge*/(2nd unit only) *The Alamo*/1960 · *Two Rode Together*/1961 · *The Man Who Shot Liberty Valance*/(co-d) *How the West Was Won* ('The Civil War')/1962 · *Cheyenne Autumn*/1964
Television *Wagon Train* ('The Colter Craven Story')/60

Frank Jr., Harriet See **Irving Ravetch**

Fuller, Samuel (b 1911) · Director. Sam Fuller's Westerns are oddly related to the generic mainsteam. Jacques Bontemps, the French critic, has suggested that the first three 'refused to follow the rules laid down by the genre' and *Forty Guns* was 'nothing but a sequence of incidents in which the central Western ethos is missing'. Psychological elements are prominent in *I Shot Jesse James*, whilst *The Baron of Arizona* blends the gothic with some familiar Western themes. However, his best Western, *Run of the Arrow*, seems less at odds with its generic contemporaries and can be seen as part of the 'Indian cycle' of the 50s. TR
(sc) *I Shot Jesse James*/1948 · (sc) *The Baron of Arizona*/1950 · (sc, p) *Run of the Arrow*/(sc, p) *Forty Guns*/1957 · (act only) *The Last Movie*/1971
Television *The Virginian*/62 · *The Iron Horse*/66

Furthman, Jules (1888-1960) · Writer. If Furthman's contribution to cinema has been distinctly under-rated it is because auteur critics have ignored him the better to sing the praises of Sternberg (for whom he wrote at least nine films) and Hawks (for whom he wrote five, including *Rio Bravo*). Even his early Westerns tend to fall under the mantle of Henry King (*When a Man Rides Alone*, *Where the West Begins*) and Ford (*North of Hudson Bay*). All of Furthman's most characteristic works revolve around a remote male enclave into which an energetic young woman comes to provoke first disruption but then eventual regeneration, a grid on to which *The Outlaw* fits almost as neatly as *Rio Bravo*. JP
(st only) *Mountain Justice*/1915 · *When a Man Rides Alone*/1918 · *Six Feet Four*/*Some Liar*/(st) *Brass Buttons*/*Where the West Begins*/1919 · (st) *The Man Who Dared*/(st) *The Valley of Tomorrow*/*The Texan*/*The Iron Rider*/1920 · *Singing River*/*The Last Trail*/*The Roof Tree*/1921 · *A California Romance*/*Gleam O'Dawn*/(st) *The Yellow Stain*/*The Love Gambler*/1922 · *North of Hudson Bay*/1923 · (st) *Call of the Mate*/1924 · (co-sc uncredited) *Northwest Passage*/*The Outlaw*/1940 · (co-sc) *Rio Bravo*/1958

Gable, Clark (1901-60) · Actor. A top star for many years, with enough magnetism to gain the sobriquet 'King of Hollywood', though his quizzical side tended to offset his more straightforwardly romantic persona. He played traditional go-getters in the pseudo-Westerns *Honky Tonk* and *Boom Town*, but in the 50s, his elderliness becoming evident, he contributed memorable studies in laconic masculine individualism to *Across the Wide Missouri*, *The King and Four Queens*, and especially *The Tall Men*, where his dispossessed trail boss may, a bit disconcertingly, 'dream small', but stands morally tall enough to win not only the heart of Jane Russell but even the reluctant admiration of bested villain Robert Ryan. His last movie characterization, in the modern Western *The Misfits*, intimated a yearning for heroic stature in a fashion clear-eyed enough to permit him to go out in splendour. TP
North Star/1925 · *The Painted Desert*/1931 · *The Call of the Wild*/1935 · *Boom Town*/1940 · *Honky Tonk*/1941 · *Across the Wide Missouri*/1950 · *Lone Star*/1951 · *The Tall Men*/1955 · *The King and Four Queens*/1956 · *The Misfits*/1961

Gamet, Kenneth (n. d.) · Writer. Gamet's screenplays include a number of effective Warner Bros. thrillers, but for ten years from 1948 he concentrated on the Western. These scripts, economical and assured, were in one respect remarkable. Eight of them were for Randolph Scott, and they did much to create the Scott character which Budd Boetticher would inherit. The self-contained, upright man, living only to put right his private world, is already there in Gamet's work on films like *Coroner Creek* and *The Stranger Wore a Gun*. JL
(co-sc) *Adventures in Silverado*/*Coroner*

Clark Gable

Creek/(add dial) Thunderhoof/1948 · (co-sc)
Canadian Pacific/The Doolins of Oklahoma/
The Savage Horde/1949 · Santa Fe/Man in
the Saddle/(co-sc) Indian Uprising/1951 ·
Last of the Comanches/1952 · The Stranger
Wore a Gun/(co-sc) The Last Posse/1953 ·
Hell's Outpost/Ten Wanted Men/1954 · A
Lawless Street/1955 · (co-sc) The Maverick
Queen/1956 · Domino Kid/The Lawless
Eighties/1957

Garner, James (b 1928) · Tall, handsome
actor with a flair for comedy, Garner is one
of the few superstars of television to become
a movie superstar, and then remain on top of
both media for almost 30 years. He started in
television with small appearances in
Cheyenne; this led to his starring role as
television's most famous gambler, Bret Maverick. Garner was an instant hit and stayed
with Maverick for three years. He then
starred in a number of feature Westerns,
some comedies and some drama. In 1971 he
returned to television to star in Nichols, and
1981 he reappeared in the role that made him
a star, in Bret Maverick. TM
Shoot-Out at Medicine Bend/1957 · Duel at
Diablo/1965 · Hour of the Gun/1967 ·
Support Your Local Sheriff!/1968 · Sledge/
1970 · Support Your Local Gunfighter/Skin
Game/1971 · One Little Indian/1973 · The
Castaway Cowboy/1974
Television Cheyenne/55 · Maverick/57 ·
Nichols/71 · The New Maverick/78 · Bret
Maverick/81

George, Chief Dan (1899-1981) · Actor. In
reality Chief Nawanath of the Burrard tribe
in British Columbia, George worked as a
stevedore and logger until 1947, when an
injury kept him from continuing such heavy
labour. As musicians, he and his family also
played rodeos and country fairs before he
came to public attention as Ol' Antoine in
the Canadian television series, Cariboo

Country (a role repeated when Disney bought
one of the stories for Smith), onstage in The
Ecstasy of Rita Joe, and on US television in
such shows as Bonanza and The High
Chaparral. He accepted only positive native
roles, and although his age and imposing
figure conferred iconic status, his roles also
involved ironic humour, particularly the
part that won him international recognition,
Old Lodge Skins in Little Big Man. BA
The Trap/1966 · Smith/1969 · Little Big
Man/1970 · Cancel My Reservation/Cold
Journey/1972 · Alien Thunder/1973 · The
Bears and I/1974 · The Outlaw Josey Wales/
Shadow of the Hawk/1976 · Spirit of the
Wind/1979
Television The High Chaparral/69 ·
Bonanza/71 · Cade's County/72 ·
Centennial/78

Gibson, Hoot (1892-1960) · Actor, aka Ed
Gibson. One of the biggest Western stars of
the 20s, a veteran of Wild West shows, and
the World's Champion Cowboy at the Pen-
dleton, Oregon Roundup in 1912. He got his
first real break in the movies working as a
stuntman, wrangler and double in many of
Harry Carey's Universal Westerns, and as a
supporting actor in Tom Mix and Pete
Morrison vehicles. He made a number of
silent Westerns with John Ford and later had
a small part in The Horse Soldiers. By mid-
1919 he was starring in his own series of
two-reelers, playing a good-natured, light-
hearted cowpoke. Gibson was the antithesis
of the puritan Hart or the stoic Carey, and
was less flamboyant than Mix. His films
emphasized comedy, in which he was often
the butt of the jokes. PS
The Two Brothers/1910 · Shotgun Jones/The
Man from the East/1914 · The Man from
Texas/Judge Not: or, the Woman of Mona
Diggins/The Ring of Destiny/1915 · A
Knight of the Range/The Night Riders/The
Passing of Hell's Crown/The Stampede in the

Hoot Gibson with Marian Nixon

Night/The Witch of the Dark House/1916 ·
The Voice on the Wire/A 44-Caliber
Mystery/The Golden Bullet/The Wrong
Man/Cheyenne's Pal/The Soul Herder/The
Texas Sphinx/The Secret Man/Straight
Shooting/A Marked Man/1917 · Play
Straight or Fight/The Midnight Flyer/The
Branded Man/Headin' South/1918 · The
Black Horse Bandit/His Buddy/The Fighting
Brothers/By Indian Post/Gun Law/The
Rustlers/Ace High/The Gun Packer/Kingdom
Come/The Fighting Heart/The Four-Bit
Man/The Jack of Hearts/The Crow/The Tell
Tale Wire/The Face in the Watch/The Lone
Hand/The Trail of the Holdup Man/The
Double Hold-Up/The Jay Bird/1919 · West
Is Best/Roarin' Dan/Marryin'/The Smiler/
Dawgone/The Brand Blotter/The Sheriff's
Oath/Hair Trigger Stuff/Runnin' Straight/
Held Up for the Makin'/The Rattler's Hiss/
The Texas Kid/Wolf Tracks/Masked/
Thieves' Clothes/The Broncho Kid/The
Fightin' Terror/The Shootin' Kid/The Smilin'
Kid/The Champion Liar/The Big Catch/A
Gamblin' Fool/The Grinning Granger/One
Law for All/Some Shooter/In Wrong Wright/
Cinder/Double Danger/The Two-Fisted
Lover/Tipped Off/Superstition/Fight It
Out/The Man with the Punch/The Trail of
the Hound/The Saddle King/Marryin'
Marion/A Pair of Twins/Harmony Ranch/
Winning a Home/The Stranger/Ransom/The
Teacher's Pet/The Shootin' Fool/A Nose in a
Book/1920 · The Driftin' Kid/Sweet Revenge/
Kickaroo/The Fighting Fury/Out of Luck/The
Cactus Kid/Who Was the Man?/Crossed

James Garner

Chief Dan George

Clues/Double Crossers/The Wild, Wild West/Bandits Beware/The Movie Trail/The Man Who Woke Up/Beating the Game/Too Tired Jones/The Winning Track/Action/Red Courage/Sure Fire/The Fire Eater/1921 · Headin' West/The Bearcat/Step On It!/Trimmed/The Loaded Door/The Galloping Kid/The Lone Hand/Ridin' Wild/Kindled Courage/1922 · The Gentleman from America/Dead Game/Shootin' for Love/Out of Luck/Blinky/The Ramblin' Kid/The Thrill Chaser/1923 · Hook and Ladder/Ride for Your Life/Forty-Horse Hawkins/Broadway or Bust/The Sawdust Trail/The Ridin' Kid from Powder River/The City of Stars/1924 · The Hurricane Kid/The Taming of the West/Let 'Er Buck/The Saddle Hawk/Spook Ranch/The Calgary Stampede/Roads to Hollywood/1925 · The Arizona Sweepstakes/Chip of the Flying U/The Phantom Bullet/The Man in the Saddle/The Shoot 'Em Up Kid/The Texas Streak/The Buckaroo Kid/The Flaming Frontier/The Silent Rider/1926 · The Denver Dude/Hey! Hey! Cowboy/The Prairie King/A Hero on Horseback/Painted Ponies/Galloping Fury/1927 · The Rawhide Kid/A Trick of Hearts/The Flying Cowboy/Wild West Show/Riding for Fame/Clearing the Trail/The Danger Rider/1928 · King of the Rodeo/Burning the Wind/Smilin' Guns/The Lariat Kid/The Winged Horseman/Points West/The Long Long Trail/Courtin' Wildcats/1929 · The Mounted Stranger/Trailin' Trouble/Roaring Ranch/Trigger Tricks/Spurs/The Concentratin' Kid/1930 · Clearing the Range/Wild Horse/Hard Hombre/1931 · The Local Bad Man/The Gay Buckaroo/Spirit of the West/A Man's Land/The Cowboy Counselor/The Boiling Point/1932 · The Dude Bandit/The Fighting Parson/Boots of Destiny/1933 · Sunset Range/Rainbow's End/Powdersmoke Range/Swifty/1935 · Lucky Terror/Feud of the West/The Riding Avenger/The Last Outlaw/Calvacade of the West/Frontier Justice/1936 · The Painted

Stallion/1937 · Wild Horse Stampede/The Law Rides Again/Blazing Guns/Death Valley Rangers/1943 · Arizona Whirlwind/Outlaw Trail/Sonora Stagecoach/The Utah Kid/Marked Trails/Trigger Law/Westward Bound/1944 · Flight to Nowhere/Hollywood Cowboys/1947 · The Marshal's Daughter/1953 · Hollywood Bronc Busters/1956 · The Horse Soldiers/1959

Glennon, Bert (1895-1967) · Cinematographer. Glennon was one of the first to experiment with mercury vapour lamps to improve lighting effects and was a favourite of Sternberg. His Western work includes some of Ford's most outstanding films, taking in the director's first colour venture *Drums Along the Mohawk* (one of both men's best-looking works), the high-contrast shadowplay of *Stagecoach* and the open-air lyricism of *Wagon Master*. *The Man from Galveston*, on which the TV series *Temple Houston* was based, was his last film. JP
Lightning Bryce/1919 · *Wild Horse Mesa*/1925 · (d only) *South of Santa Fe*/1932 · (add c uncredited) *Under the Pampas Moon*/1935 · *Stagecoach/Drums Along the Mohawk*/1939 · *They Died with their Boots On*/1941 · *San Antonio*/1946 · *Wagon Master/Rio Grande*/1950 · *The Big Trees*/1951 · *The Man Behind the Gun/Riding Shotgun/Thunder Over the Plains*/1952 · *The Moonlighter*/1953 · *Sergeant Rutledge*/1960 · *The Man from Galveston*/1963
Television *Disneyland*/55

Gordon, Leo (b 1922) · Actor. Mean is the word for this stalwart heavy, an authoritative performer able to lend an edge, frequently of the psychotic sort, to what have basically been stock supporting characters. A typical part was as one of the most recalcitrant of the 'guardhouse rats' under Randolph Scott's command in *7th Cavalry*; his largest Western role was as Quantrill in *Quantrill's Raiders*. He has also scripted several minor films, among them an offbeat Western, *Black Patch*. TP
Gun Fury/City of Bad Men/Hondo/1953 · *The Yellow Mountain/Ten Wanted Men/Tennessee's Partner*/1954 · *Seven Angry Men/Robber's Roost/Santa Fe Passage/Man with the Gun/Red Sundown*/1955 · *Great Day in the Morning/Johnny Concho/7th Cavalry*/1956 · *The Tall Stranger/Man in the Shadow/The Restless Breed*/(sc) *Black Patch*/1957 · *Quantrill's Raiders/Apache Territory/Ride a Crooked Trail*/(sc) *Escort West*/1958 · *The Jayhawkers!*/1959 · *Noose for a Gunman*/1960 · *McLintock!*/1963 ·

(co-sc only) *The Bounty Killer*/1965 · *Night of the Grizzly*/1966 · *Hostile Guns*/1967 · *Buckskin*/1968 · *Il mio nome è Nessuno*/1973
Television *The Adventures of Rin Tin Tin*/54 · *Gunsmoke/Broken Arrow*/56 · *Tombstone Territory/Maverick*/57 · *The Rough Riders/Bat Masterson/Tales of the Texas Rangers/Texas John Slaughter/The Rifleman*/58 · *Escort West/Bonanza/Bronco*/59 · *The Law of the Plainsman/The Outlaws/The Deputy*/60 · *Lawman/The Life and Legend of Wyatt Earp*/61 · *Cheyenne/The Virginian*/62 · *Laredo*/65 · *Pistols 'n' Petticoats*/66 · *The High Chaparral*/68 · *The Outcasts*/69 · *The Trackers*/71 · *Little House on the Prairie*/79

Grant, James Edward (1904-66) · Writer. Grant had been a Chicago newspaperman and a popular novelist before coming to Hollywood in the mid-30s. After working mainly in thrillers and comedy he turned with great success to Westerns in the 40s and provided many scripts for John Wayne (not all of them Westerns). Their tone, frequently jingoistic, suited the actor's philosophy; their simplicity and emphasis on action fitted his style. Grant also directed two films from his own scripts, *Angel and the Badman* and *Ring of Fear*. JL
Belle of the Yukon/1944 · (d) *Angel and the Badman*/1946 · (st only) *The Plunderers*/1948 · *Rock Island Trail/California Passage*/1950 · *Hondo*/1953 · (co-sc) *The Last Wagon/Three Violent People*/1956 · (st only) *The Proud Rebel*/(st, co-sc) *The Sheepman*/1958 · (ass p) *The Alamo*/1960 · (co-sc) *The Comancheros*/1961 · *McLintock!*/1963 · (co-st only) *Hostile Guns*/1967 · *Support Your Local Gunfighter*/1971

Griffith, D[avid] W[ark] (1875-1948) · Director. Alongside Ince and Broncho Billy, Griffith is often cited as a prime mover in the development of the early Western. How-

Leo Gordon

D. W. Griffith

ever, this undoubtedly has more to do with his status as the 'father of film art' than for any outstanding innovations within the genre. Nevertheless, the production values of the later Biograph films (1908-13) were matched only by Ince's Bison films in this period. Griffith was able to engage large casts and to employ them within a suitably convincing *mise en scène*. Staging-in-depth became something of a hallmark of his Westerns; as opposed, for example, to the relatively flat playing areas of the Broncho Billy films. Particularly noteworthy is his dextrous use of editing to build tension and suspense, such as the elaborate use of cross-cutting in *The Battle at Elderbush Gulch*. The narratives typically take the form of a love triangle, often highlighting the corrupting effects of alcohol. The settings range across the battlefields of the Civil War, mining camps, frontier towns, Indian villages, to both sides of the Mexican border; the characters tend to conform to the crude stereotypes of the period. PS

(act only) *Rescued from an Eagle's Nest*/ 1907 · (act only) *The Kentuckian/The Stage Rustler/The Redman and the Child/The Tavern Keeper's Daughter/The Greaser's Gauntlet/The Girl and the Outlaw/The Red Girl/The Vaquero's Vow/The Call of the Wild/The Ingrate/A Woman's Way/The Guerrilla*/1908 · *The Road to the Heart/The Eavesdropper/Mexican Sweethearts/The Renunciation/The Mended Lute/The Indian Runner's Romance/In Old Kentucky/Comata, the Sioux/Leather Stocking/The Redman's View/The Dancing Girl of Butte/The Honor of His Family/Fools of Fate/(co-sc) The Mountaineer's Honor*/1909 · *The Thread of Destiny/In Old California/A Romance of the Western Hills/The Gold Seekers/The Man/A Rich Revenge/Over Silent Paths/Unexpected Help/The Broken Doll/The Two Brothers/ Ramona/In the Border States/The House with the Closed Shutters/A Mohawk's Way/That Chink at Golden Gulch/The Fugitive/Rose O' Salem Town/The Twisted Trail/The Song of the Wildwood Flute/His Trust*/1910 · *Was He a Coward?/The Chief's Daughter/His Mother's Scarf/In the Days of '49/The Two Sides/His Trust Fulfilled/The Heart of a Savage/The Lonedale Operator/The White Rose of the Wilds/The Red Man and the Girl/The Indian Brothers/Fighting Blood/The Last Drop of Water/Swords and Hearts/The Squaw's Love/The Battle/A Tale of the Wilderness/Billy's Stratagem*/1911 · *Under Burning Skies/Iola's Promise/The Goddess of Sagebrush Gulch/The Female of the Species/ A Lodging for the Night/A Temporary*

Truce/The Girl and Her Trust/In the North Woods/(sc) A Feud in the Kentucky Hills/ Man's Lust for Gold/The Chief's Blanket/In the Aisles of the Wild/Heredity/A Pueblo Legend/Black Sheep/Friends/The Informer/ The Massacre/My Hero/Three Friends/1912 · *The Sheriff's Baby/A Misunderstood Boy/The Little Tease/Just Gold/The Yaqui Cur/The Ranchero's Revenge/During the Round-up/ Two Men of the Desert/The Battle at Elderbush Gulch*/1913 · *Scarlet Days*/1919 · *America*/1924

Gruber, Frank (1904-69) · Writer. An immensely prolific crime and Western novelist, Gruber went to Hollywood in 1942. In addition to the films made from his stories, he wrote many original screenplays. His Westerns often had an historical slant, and he did not enjoy the frequent studio tampering. His novel *Fort Starvation* had a macabre background of cannibalism: Borden Chase's script (*Backlash*) removed all that. Another story, set in New Mexico, was transferred to Oklahoma at the request of star Dale Robertson, who came from Oklahoma, and Gruber's Indian hogans and his gold-mines, neither a common sight in Oklahoma, duly appeared there too. JL

(novel only) *The Kansan*/1943 · (novel only) *The Oregon Trail*/1945 · (co-sc) *In Old Sacramento*/1946 · *Fighting Man of the Plains/(st only) Dakota Lil*/1949 · *The Cariboo Trail/(novel) The Great Missouri Raid*/1950 · (st only) *The Texas Rangers/ (novel) Warpath/Silver City/(co-sc) Flaming Feather*/1951 · *Denver and Rio Grande/ (novel only) Pony Express*/1952 · (st only) *Rage at Dawn*/1955 · (novel only) *Tension at Table Rock/(novel only) Backlash*/1956 · (novel only) *The Big Land*/1957 · (novel) *Town Tamer*/1965

Television *The Life and Legend of Wyatt Earp*/55 · *Tales of Wells Fargo*/57 · *The Texan*/58 · *Shotgun Slade*/59

H

Hale, Alan (1892-1950) · Bluff actor who played leads during the silent era, then after a brief spell as a director gravitated to character roles. Good-humoured even in villainy, he is probably best remembered as Errol Flynn's rumbustiously faithful sidekick in a string of films that started with *The Adventures of Robin Hood* in 1938 and included three Westerns: *Dodge City, Virginia City* and *Sante Fe Trail*. Although of Scottish descent, a bluster of Irish blarney was generally a feature of his rascally jovia-

lity, especially in his frequent appearances in Raoul Walsh movies. TMi

The Cowboy and the Lady/1911 · *Strongheart*/1914 · *The Americano*/1915 · *The Barbarian/The Fox*/1921 · *The Trap*/ 1922 · *Cameo Kirby/The Covered Wagon*/ 1923 · *Code of the Wilderness*/1924 · (d only) *Braveheart*/1925 · *Hearts and Fists*/ 1926 · *The Country Beyond/God's Country and the Woman*/1936 · *High, Wide and Handsome*/1937 · *Valley of the Giants*/1938 · *Dodge City*/1939 · *Virginia City/Santa Fe Trail*/1940 · *Pursued/Cheyenne*/1947 · *The Younger Brothers*/1948 · *South of St Louis/ Stars in My Crown*/1949 · *Colt .45*/1950

Hale, Monte (b 1921) · Actor. A native of San Angelo, Texas, he started his career singing at barn dances and rodeos. He made his movie début in 1944 and was picked by Republic to star in a series of B-Westerns. Although a star in his own right he was one of several actors groomed as a possible replacement for Roy Rogers. When the B-Western era ended Hale went on tour as a singing cowboy, appeared at rodeos and also did an occasional television guest appearance. TM

The Big Bonanza/1944 · *Bandits of the Badlands/Colorado Pioneers/Rough Riders of Cheyenne*/1945 · *Home on the Range/ California Gold Rush/Sun Valley Cyclone/ Man from Rainbow Valley/Out California Way*/1946 · *Last Frontier Uprising/Along the Oregon Trail/Under Colorado Skies*/1947 · *California Firebrand/Timber Trail/Son of God's Country*/1948 · *Prince of the Plains/ Law of the Golden West/Outcast of the Trail/South of Rio/San Antonio Ambush/ Ranger of the Cherokee Strip/Pioneer Marshal*/1949 · *The Vanishing Westerner/ The Old Frontier/The Missourians/The Trail of Robin Hood*/1950 · *Yukon Vengeance*/ 1954 · *Giant*/1956

Television *The Adventures of Wild Bill Hickok*/52 · *Gunsmoke*/55

Hart, William S[urrey] (1865-1946) · Actor. Known as 'The Good-Badman', Hart did for feature Westerns what Griffith had done for melodrama, taking existing elements of the film genre and bringing it to new levels of dramatic power, building his own stardom in the process to a rank equal to that of Chaplin and Fairbanks. Though born in the urban East, he seemed to embody, physically and temperamentally, one ideal of the Western hero, skilful, lean, taciturn, ruthless but honorable. Hart's version of the Westerner was actually the carefully-honed product of twenty years' stage work, backed in films by the well-organized resources of producer Thomas H. Ince. Hart made an immediate impression during his first season of work in two-reelers; moving to the new feature-length format utilized his acting and directorial skills with even greater impact. His films embody a romantic 'Truth of the West' but one solidly grounded in authentic locale and Western paraphernalia, strong plots with fundamentalist and populist colouring, crisp editing and restrained performance. Changing audience tastes forced his retirement in 1925; he continued his interest in Westerns by collaborating with his sister Mary Ellen Hart on children's books and novels. DK

His Hour of Manhood/Jim Cameron's Wife/ The Bargain/(d) The Passing of Two-Gun Hicks/(d) In the Sage Brush Country/1914 · (d) The Scourge of the Desert/(d) Mr 'Silent' Haskins/(d) The Sheriff's Streak of Yellow/ (d) The Grudge/(d) The Roughneck/On the Night Stage/(d) The Taking of Luke McVane/(d) The Man from Nowhere/(d) 'Bad Buck' of Santa Inez/(d) The Darkening Trail/(d) The Conversion of Frosty Blake/(d) Tools of Providence/(d) The Ruse/(d) Cash Parrish's Pal/(d) A Knight of the Trails/(d) Pinto Ben/(d) Keno Bates, Liar/(d) The Disciple/1915 · (d) Between Men/(co-d) Hell's Hinges/(d) The Aryan/(d) The Primal Lure/(d) The Apostle of Vengeance/The Captive God/(d) The Dawn Maker/(d) The Return of Draw Egan/(d) The Patriot/(d) The Devil's Double/1916 · (d) Truthful Tulliver/(d) The Gun Fighter/(d) The Square Deal Man/(d) The Desert Man/(d) Wolf Lowry/(d) The Cold Deck/(d) The Silent Man/(st) The Narrow Trail/1917 · (st, d) Wolves of the Rail/(d) Blue Blazes Rawden/ (d) The Tiger Man/(d) Selfish Yates/(d) Shark Monroe/(d) Riddle Gawne/(d) The Border Wireless/(d) Branding Broadway/1918 · (d) Breed of Men/(d) The Poppy Girl's

William S. Hart

Husband/(st, d) The Money Corral/(co-d) Square Deal Sanderson/Wagon Tracks/John Petticoats/1919 · (st, co-sc) The Toll Gate/ The Cradle of Courage/(st) The Testing Block/1920 · (st) O'Malley of the Mounted/ The Whistle/Three Word Brand/(st) White Oak/1921 · (st) Travelin' On/1922 · (st) Wild Bill Hickok/1923 · (st) Singer Jim McKee/1924 · Tumbleweeds/1925

Hathaway, Henry (1898-1985) · Director. Born as the Marquis Henri Leopold de Frennes in Sacramento from a long line of adventurers and actors, he started as a child actor in 1908 and graduated to direction in 1932 at Paramount, where he remade Zane Grey Westerns and numerous adventure pictures. After World War II he directed some semi-documentary thrillers for Louis de Rochemont and the intriguingly erotic *Niagara* (1953) with Marilyn Monroe. Prolific and always reliably professional, his work never achieved an overall coherence, incarnating instead the very model of the classic Hollywood studio director. Nevertheless, some darker neuroses erupt into the films with such regularity that 'manic moments' come to function as an authorial signature: Cagney's laughter at the end of *13 rue Madeleine* (1946), the child's panic in *Rawhide*, Widmark pushing the old lady down the stairs in *Kiss of Death* (1947). Such moments reveal something of what underpins the sentimental religiosity that pervades his action and adventure pictures and make him a far more interesting director than his reputation indicates. It was his friend John Wayne who received the Oscar for *True Grit*. PW

Heritage of the Desert/Wild Horse Mesa/ 1932 · Under the Tonto Rim/Sunset Pass/ Man of the Forest/To the Last Man/The Thundering Herd/1933 · The Last Round-Up/1934 · The Trail of the Lonesome Pine/Go West Young Man/1936 · Brigham Young – Frontiersman/1940 · Rawhide/1950 · Garden of Evil/1954 · From Hell to Texas/ 1958 · (p) North to Alaska/1960 · (co-d) How the West Was Won ('The Rivers', 'The Plains', 'The Outlaws')/1962 · (p) The Sons of Katie Elder/1965 · (p) Nevada Smith/1966 · 5 Card Stud/1968 · True Grit/ 1969 · Shoot Out/1971

Hawks, Howard (1897-1977) · Director. The Westerns Hawks directed fall into two categories: epics which deal with historical figures or events (*The Outlaw, Red River, The Big Sky*) and more intimate dramas which explore, through a theme and variation

Alan Hale

Monte Hale

Henry Hathaway

Howard Hawks

format, the permutational possibilities of certain plot and character configurations (*Rio Bravo*, *El Dorado*, *Rio Lobo*). Though the epic Westerns (excluding *The Outlaw*) address traditional generic concerns such as trailblazing, empire building and the creation of the frontier, Hawks' other Westerns tend to belie the notion of a generically 'Western' plot, taking their inspiration from other, non-Western sources. Even *Red River*, so traditional a Western that it is often mistakenly attributed to Ford, derives, in large part, from the sea epic *Mutiny on the Bounty*, while *The Big Sky* resembles *A Girl in Every Port*. Hawks is master of the non-Western Western, films which though iconographically, geographically and temporally Western, re-invent the traditional motifs and concerns of the classic Western to accommodate the desires, feelings, and behaviour of essentially *contemporary* characters. If one understands the Western as the site for the dramatization of the formation of America's evolving national identity, then a Hawks Western, though still concerned with issues of identity, explores those issues on a much more local level, tracing the responses of individual characters to the outside forces of history or to the immediate demands of their profession, rather than, as in Ford, revealing the essential equivalency between characters and national identity. JB
(d uncredited) *Viva Villa!*/1934 · (d uncredited) *The Outlaw*/1940 · (p) *Red River*/1947 · (p) *The Big Sky*/1952 · (p) *Rio Bravo*/1958 · (p) *El Dorado*/1966 · (p) *Rio Lobo*/1970

Hayes, George (1885-1969) · Actor. In most of Hayes' Westerns (he made almost 150) he was the hero's garrulous, gutsy, not very bright sidekick – a grey and toothless veteran who usually lived in his highly romanticized past. He rode with William Boyd's Hopalong Cassidy, supported Wild Bill Elliott and Rex Bell, Buck Jones and Hoot Gibson, and gently wound down listening to Roy Rogers sing. At first Hayes was plain George: the familiar sobriquet 'Gabby' came only when he joined Republic in 1938. JL
God's Country and the Man/*Nevada Buckaroo*/*Cavalier of the West*/*Rose of the Rio Grande*/1931 · *Border Devils*/*From Broadway to Cheyenne*/*Riders of the Desert*/*The Night Rider*/*Man from Hell's Edges*/*Klondike*/*Texas Buddies*/*Boiling Point*/*The Fighting Champ*/*Wild Horse Mesa*/1932 · *Sagebrush Trail*/*Trailing North*/*The Gallant Fool*/*The Ranger's Code*/*The Fugitive*/*Galloping Romeo*/*Crashing Broadway*/*Breed*

of the Border/*The Fighting Texans*/*Riders of Destiny*/1933 · *The Man from Utah*/*The Star Packer*/*Brand of Hate*/*In Old Santa Fe*/*Neath The Arizona Skies*/*West of the Divide*/*The Lucky Texan*/*Blue Steel*/*Randy Rides Alone*/*Lawless Frontier*/1934 · *Justice of the Range*/*Texas Terror*/*Smokey Smith*/*Tumbling Tumbleweeds*/*The Throwback*/*Rainbow Valley*/*Thunder Mountain*/*The Eagle's Brood*/*Hop-A-Long Cassidy*/*Bar 20 Rides Again*/*Swifty*/1935 · *Call of the Prairie*/*Three on the Trail*/*The Lawless Nineties*/*Heart of the West*/*The Texas Rangers*/*Hopalong Cassidy Returns*/*The Plainsman*/*Trail Dust*/1936 · *Borderland*/*Hills of Old Wyoming*/*North of the Rio Grande*/*Rustler's Valley*/*Hopalong Rides Again*/*Texas Trail*/1937 · *Gold Is Where You Find It*/*Heart of Arizona*/*Bar 20 Justice*/*Pride of the West*/*In Old Mexico*/*The Frontiersman*/1938 · *Sunset Trail*/*Man of Conquest*/*Let Freedom Ring*/*Southward Ho!*/*In Old Monterey*/*In Old Caliente*/*The Arizona Kid*/*Wall Street Cowboy*/*Saga of Death Valley*/*Days of Jesse James*/*Silver on the Sage*/*Renegade Trail*/1939 · *Wagons Westward*/*Dark Command*/*Young Buffalo Bill*/*The Carson City Kid*/*The Ranger and the Lady*/*Colorado*/*Young Bill Hickok*/*Melody Ranch*/*The Border Legion*/1940 · *Robin Hood of the Pecos*/*In Old Cheyenne*/*Sheriff of Tombstone*/*Nevada City*/*Jesse James at Bay*/*Red River Valley*/*Badman of Deadwood*/1941 · *South of Santa Fe*/*Sunset on the Desert*/*Man from Cheyenne*/*Romance on the Range*/*Sons of the Pioneers*/*Sunset Serenade*/*Heart of the Golden West*/*Ridin' Down the Canyon*/1942 · *Calling Wild Bill Elliott*/*Bordertown Gunfighters*/*Wagon Tracks West*/*Death Valley Manhunt*/*In Old Oklahoma*/1943 · *Tucson Raiders*/*Hidden Valley Outlaws*/*Marshal of Reno*/*Mojave Firebrand*/*Tall in the Saddle*/*Lights of Old Santa Fe*/*The Big Bonanza*/1944 · *Utah*/*Bells of Rosarita*/*The Man from Oklahoma*/

George Hayes

Sunset in El Dorado/*Don't Fence Me In*/*Along the Navajo Trail*/1945 · *Out California Way*/*Home in Oklahoma*/*Song of Arizona*/*Badman's Territory*/*Rainbow Over Texas*/*My Pal Trigger*/*Roll On Texas Moon*/*Under Nevada Skies*/*Helldorado*/1946 · *Trail Street*/*Bells of San Angelo*/*Wyoming*/1947 · *Albuquerque*/*The Untamed Breed*/*Return of the Bad Men*/1948 · *El Paso*/*Susanna Pass*/*The Golden Stallion*/1949 · *Bells of Coronado*/*Trigger Jr.*/*The Cariboo Trail*/*Twilight in the Sierras*/1950 · *South of Caliente*/*Pals of the Golden West*/1951
Television *The Gabby Hayes Show*/50

Heflin, Van (1910-71) · Actor. His ruggedly unactorish appearance, allied to a flexibility of technique, lent particular conviction to his playing of the Western-style common man in the persons of the farmers in *Shane* and *3:10 to Yuma*, and also contributed a down-to-earth sincerity to more conventional roles like the cavalry scout in *Tomahawk*. In a more obsessive vein, he was effective as the domineering father in *Gunman's Walk*, and in his last but one Western outing he was a grittily persuasive law officer in the remake of *Stagecoach*. TP
The Outcasts of Poker Flat/1937 · *Santa Fe Trail*/1940 · *Tap Roots*/1948 · *Tomahawk*/1950 · *Shane*/1952 · *Wings of the Hawk*/1953 · *The Raid*/1954 · *Count Three and Pray*/1955 · *3:10 to Yuma*/1957 · *Gunman's Walk*/1958 · *They Came to Cordura*/1959 · *Stagecoach*/1966 · *Ognuno per sè*/1968
Television *The Great Adventure*/63

Heston, Charlton (b 1923) · Actor. Charlton Heston is most closely identified with the epic genre and films such as *The Ten Commandments*. His screen persona blends the awesome qualities derived from portrayals of Moses, John the Baptist and Michelangelo with more conventional 'man of action' elements, and although Western heroes do require charismatic qualities which set them apart from ordinary folk, it may be that Heston is a shade too Olympian for the genre. However, of his fifty-odd films eleven are Westerns; at Paramount in the formative stage of his career he was cast as a white man reared by Indians, as the famous Indian scout, Al Sieber, and as Buffalo Bill Cody. His epic persona was matched more closely by the epic proportions of William Wyler's *The Big Country*, but his most substantial contribution to the genre probably lies in his roles as the eponymous heroes of *Major Dundee* and *Will Penny*. TR
The Savage/*Pony Express*/1952 · *Arrowhead*/

1953 · *The Far Horizons*/1954 · *Three Violent People*/1956 · *The Big Country*/1958 · *Major Dundee*/1964 · *Will Penny*/1967 · *The Call of the Wild*/1972 · *The Last Hard Men*/1976 · *The Mountain Men*/1979

Hibbs, Jesse (1906-85) · Director. Hibbs worked exclusively for Universal through the 1950s, usually with Audie Murphy as his lead character. His Western plots cover a wide spectrum of revenge, railroads, wild horses, gold, Apaches, outlaws, etc. His featured players have either continued the Western tradition (John Payne, Joel McCrea) or, as in the curious case of Murphy, developed their own unique footnote to the genre. Hibbs directed the fifth version of *The Spoilers* in 1955, which, like Universal's other delving into the vaults with the 1954 Audie Murphy-starring remake of *Destry*, is a strictly by-the-numbers affair. TV
Ride Clear of Diablo/1953 · *Rails into Laramie*/*Black Horse Canyon*/*The Yellow Mountain*/1954 · *The Spoilers*/1955 · *Walk the Proud Land*/1956 · *Ride a Crooked Trail*/1958
Television *Wagon Train*/58 · *Rawhide*/59 · *The Alaskans*/60 · *The Outlaws*/61 · *Laramie*/62 · *The Wild, Wild West*/*The Iron Horse*/66

Hillyer, Lambert (b 1889) · Director. The illustrious start he made to his career as a director and scriptwriter on some of W.S. Hart's most prestigious pictures was not continued into the sound era, when he worked almost exclusively as a series director, principally with Johnny Mack Brown and Buck Jones. His style was nearly always subordinate to the demands of his stars, which were usually set in a mould by the time he became involved with them. PS
(sc only) *The Desert Man*/(sc only) *Wolf Lowry*/*The Narrow Trail*/(sc only) *One Shot Ross*/1917 · (sc only) *The Money Corral*/*Wagon Tracks*/(sc, co-d) *Square Deal Sanderson*/*John Petticoats*/1919 · (sc) *Sand*/(co-sc) *The Toll Gate*/(sc) *The Cradle of Courage*/(sc) *The Testing Block*/1920 · (sc) *O'Malley of the Mounted*/(sc) *The Whistle*/*White Oak*/(sc) *Travelin' On*/(sc) *Three Word Brand*/*The Man from Lost River*/1921 · *Caught Bluffing*/1922 · *Eyes of the Forest*/(sc) *The Lone Star Ranger*/*Mile-a-Minute Romeo*/*The Spoilers*/1923 · *The Knockout*/1925 · *War Horse*/(co-d) *30 Below Zero*/1926 · *Chain Lightning*/*Hills of Peril*/1927 · *The Branded Sombrero*/1928 · *Beau Bandit*/1930 · *One Man Law*/*The Deadline*/1931 · *The Fighting Fool*/*South of the Rio Grande*/*Born to Trouble*/*White Eagle*/*Hello Trouble*/*The Forbidden Trail*/*The Sundown Rider*/*South of Sante Fe*/1932 · *The California Trail*/*Unknown Valley*/*The Fighting Code*/1933 · (sc) *The Man Trailer*/1934 · *The Durango Kid*/*The Wild Cat of Tucson*/*Beyond the Sacramento*/1940 · *The Medico of Painted Springs*/*The Pinto Kid*/*Thunder Over the Prairie*/*The Son of Davy Crockett*/*The Return of Daniel Boone*/*North from the Lone Star*/*The King of Dodge City*/*Roaring Frontiers*/*Hands Across the Rockies*/*Prairie Stranger*/*The Royal Mounted Patrol*/1941 · *The Devil's Trail*/*North of the Rockies*/*Prairie Gunsmoke*/*Vengeance of the West*/1942 · *Six Gun Gospel*/*Fighting Frontier*/*Stranger from Pecos*/*The Texas Kid*/1943 · *Partners of the Trail*/*Law Men*/*Range Law*/*West of the Rio Grande*/*Land of the Outlaws*/*Ghost Guns*/1944 · *Beyond the Pecos*/*Flame of the West*/*Frontier Feud*/*Stranger from Sante Fe*/*South of the Rio Grande*/*The Lost Trail*/1945 · *Border Bandits*/*Under Arizona Skies*/*The Gentleman from Texas*/*Shadows on the Range*/*Trigger Fingers*/*Silver Range*/1946 · *Raiders of the South*/*Valley of Fear*/*Trailing Danger*/*Land of the Lawless*/*The Law Comes to Gunsight*/*Flashing Guns*/*Prairie Express*/*Gun Talk*/1947 · *Song of the Drifter*/*Overland Trails*/*Oklahoma Blues*/*Crossed Trails*/*Partners of the Sunset*/*Frontier Agent*/*Range Renegades*/*The Fighting Ranger*/*Outlaw Brand*/*The Sheriff of Medicine Bow*/1948 · *Gun Runner*/*Gun Law Justice*/*Haunted Trails*/*Riders of the Dusk*/*Range Land*/*Trail's End*/1949

Hoch, Winton C. (1907-79) · Cinematographer. Graduated in physics from the California Institute of Technology, Hoch worked twenty years for Technicolor and freelanced as a cinematographer, first on Fitzpatrick travelogues, then on features. He never shot black-and-white, but used his expertise in filters and processing for expressive colour effects, in studio conditions and on location, using the accidents of nature. Among the most notable examples are the desert storms in *3 Godfathers* and *She Wore a Yellow Ribbon*. His technical perfectionism made for a fractious relationship with John Ford, though the two worked together on a total of five pictures. BA
Tap Roots/*3 Godfathers*/(live action only) *Melody Time*/1948 · *She Wore a Yellow Ribbon*/*The Sundowners*/1949 · *The Redhead from Wyoming*/1953 · *The Searchers*/1956 · *The Missouri Traveler*/(co-c) *The Young Land*/1957 · *Sergeants 3*/1961

Holden, William (1918-81) · Actor. Many of Holden's Western appearances were in routine, modestly budgeted films, but although he is not a major Western star, three of his performances merit attention. Most memorable is his role in Sam Peckinpah's *The Wild Bunch* as Pike Bishop, the psychologically complex leader of the doomed outlaw gang, displaced from both the space and time of the conventional world of the genre. Two lesser though still notable appearances are in John Ford's *The Horse Soldiers* as the cavalry troop's doctor and conscience, and in Blake Edwards' *Wild*

Van Heflin

Charlton Heston

Lambert Hillyer

William Holden

Jack Holt

Rovers, as an aging bank robber. TR
Arizona/1940 · *Texas*/1941 · *Rachel and the
Stranger*/1947 · *The Man from Colorado*/
1948 · *Streets of Laredo*/1949 · *Escape from
Fort Bravo*/1953 · *The Horse Soldiers*/1959 ·
Alvarez Kelly/1966 · *The Wild Bunch*/1969
· *Wild Rovers*/1971 · *The Revengers*/1972

Holt, Jack (1888-1951) · Actor. Mustachioed and with jutting jaw, Holt was
instantly recognizable. He started his movie
career in 1914 as a stuntman and extra, but
by 1916 was the star of Universal's twenty-
chapter Western serial *Liberty*. A top Western star in the 20s, he played the lead in many
of the quality Famous Players-Lasky/
Paramount Westerns derived from Zane
Grey novels. Holt continued to have star
billing in action melodramas at Columbia in
the 30s, but after war service he mainly
played support roles. He was the father of
Western star Tim Holt. JH
Salomy Jane/1914 · *What the River Foretold*/
The Power of Fascination/1915 · *The
Desperado*/*The Better Man*/*Liberty*/1916 ·
The Cost of Hatred/1917 · *A Desert
Wooing*/*The Squaw Man*/*Headin' South*/
1918 · *Kitty Kelly M.D.*/1919 · *The Call of
the North*/1921 · *North of the Rio Grande*/
While Satan Sleeps/1922 · *Wanderer of the
Wasteland*/*North of 36*/1924 · *The
Thundering Herd*/*The Light of Western
Stars*/*Wild Horse Mesa*/*The Ancient
Highway*/*The Enchanted Hill*/1925 · *Man of
the Forest*/*Born to the West*/*Forlorn River*/
1926 · *The Mysterious Rider*/1927 · *The

Vanishing Pioneer/*The Water Hole*/
Avalanche/1928 · *Sunset Pass*/1929 · *The
Border Legion*/1930 · *North of Nome*/1936 ·
Roaring Timber/1937 · *End of the Trail*/
1938 · *Northwest Rangers*/1942 · *My Pal
Trigger*/*Renegade Girl*/1946 · *The Wild
Frontier*/1947 · *The Arizona Ranger*/*The
Gallant Legion*/*The Strawberry Roan*/1948 ·
Loaded Pistols/*The Last Bandit*/*Brimstone*/
Red Desert/1949 · *The Daltons' Women*/
Return of the Frontiersman/*Trail of Robin
Hood*/*King of the Bullwhip*/*Across the Wide
Missouri*/1950

Holt, Tim (1918-73) · Actor. From 1941 to
1943 and 1948 to 1952 Holt was listed among
the top ten money-making Western film
stars in the *Motion Picture Herald*. He worked
almost exclusively for RKO, appearing as the
youthful-looking star in a long series of
B-Westerns, often with Richard Martin (as
Chito) providing the comic relief. His other
Western appearances include fine support-
ing roles in Ford's *Stagecoach* and *My Dar-
ling Clementine*. But he never really
capitalized on his excellent parts in *The
Magnificent Ambersons* (1942) and *The
Treasure of the Sierra Madre*. JH
The Vanishing Pioneer/1928 · *The Law
West of Tombstone*/*Gold Is Where You Find
It*/*The Renegade Ranger*/1938 · *Stagecoach*/
1939 · *The Fargo Kid*/*Wagon Train*/1940 ·
Dude Cowboy/*The Bandit Trail*/*Along the
Rio Grande*/*Robbers of the Range*/*Riding the
Wind*/*Six Gun Gold*/*Cyclone on Horseback*/
1941 · *Land of the Open Range*/*Come On
Danger*/*Thundering Hoofs*/*Bandit Ranger*/
Pirates of the Prairie/1942 · *The Avenging
Rider*/*Red River Robin Hood*/*Sagebrush Law*/
Fighting Frontier/1943 · *My Darling
Clementine*/1946 · *Thunder Mountain*/*Wild
Horse Mesa*/*Under the Tonto Rim*/1947 ·
The Treasure of the Sierra Madre/*The
Arizona Ranger*/*Guns of Hate*/*Western
Heritage*/*Indian Agent*/*Gun Smugglers*/1948 ·
The Stagecoach Kid/*Brothers in the Saddle*/
Rustlers/*Masked Raiders*/*The Mysterious
Desperado*/*Riders of the Range*/1949 ·
Dynamite Pass/*Storm over Wyoming*/*Rider
from Tucson*/*Border Treasure*/*Rio Grande
Patrol*/*Law of the Badlands*/1950 · *Saddle
Legion*/*Gunplay*/*Pistol Harvest*/*Overland
Telegraph*/*Hot Lead*/1951 · *Trail Guide*/
Target/*Road Agent*/*Desert Passage*/1952

Homeier, Skip (b 1930) · Actor, aka Skippy
Homeier, G. V. Homeier. Six foot, blue-
eyed, fair-haired actor who came to prominence in Westerns when he played the
young cowboy out to make a name for

himself by killing Gregory Peck in *The
Gunfighter*. In the Western roles that foll-
owed he sometimes played the troublesome
son of the local rancher, but more often was
cast as the adolescent gunman out to kill.
One of his best roles is as part of the outlaw
gang trying to take Nancy Gates away from
Randolph Scott in Boetticher's *Comanche
Station*. TM
Boys' Ranch/1946 · *The Gunfighter*/1950 ·
The Last Posse/1953 · *The Lone Gun*/*Dawn
at Socorro*/*Ten Wanted Men*/1954 · *Gun
Point*/*Road to Denver*/1955 · *Stranger at My
Door*/*Dakota Incident*/*The Burning Hills*/
Thunder Over Arizona/*The Tall T*/1956 ·
Day of the Bad Man/1957 · *Plunderers of
Painted Flats*/*Comanche Station*/1959 ·
Showdown/1963 · *Bullet for a Badman*/1964
· *Starbird and Sweet William*/1975
Television *Dick Powell's Zane Grey Theatre*/
56

Hopper, Dennis (b 1936) · Actor, born in
Dodge City, Kansas. Hopper's bony
features, intense eyes and edgy movements
made him a natural to play psychopathic
youngsters, embodying the menacingly
impulsive counterpart to James Dean's sensitively masochistic character in *Rebel Without a Cause* (1955) and *Giant* (1956). Hopper
enlivened some Westerns with performances on the edge of hysteria: in *From Hell to
Texas* he literally catches fire and becomes a
human torch. *Easy Rider* (1969) revealed him
as an accomplished director, a promise fully
fulfilled by his eccentric masterpieces *The
Last Movie* and the acidly self-critical *Out of
the Blue* (1980). Hopper imbues his films
with a nervous energy and cinematic literacy
equalled in Hollywood only by Scorsese. In
addition, his acute perception of cultural
and social disintegration testifies to a critical
intelligence rarely encountered in American
directors. PW
Giant/*Gunfight at the O.K. Corral*/1956 ·

Tim Holt

The Young Land/1957 · *From Hell to Texas*/1958 · *The Sons of Katie Elder*/1965 · *Hang 'Em High*/1968 · *True Grit*/1969 · (d) *The Last Movie*/1971 · *Kid Blue*/1973 · *Mad Dog*/1976
Television *Cheyenne*/56 · *Sugarfoot*/57 · *Dick Powell's Zane Grey Theatre*/*The Rifleman*/58 · *Wagon Train*/63 · *Bonanza*/*Gunsmoke*/64 · *The Legend of Jesse James*/66 · *The Big Valley*/*The Guns of Will Sonnett*/67 · *Wild Times*/80

Hotaling, Frank (1900-77) · Art director. Hotaling's career is a classic instance of being in the right place at the right time. An art director at Republic in the 40s, he worked on some 40 B-Westerns. Then in 1950 John Ford came to the studio for *Rio Grande*, employed Hotaling, and liked what he saw. Hotaling worked on four more Ford films, including *The Searchers*, on which he collaborated with James Basevi, and *The Horse Soldiers*, films as perfectly designed as any in the Ford canon. JL
Firebrands of Arizona/*Lights of Old Santa Fe*/*The Big Bonanza*/1944 · *Along the Navajo Trail*/*Colorado Pioneers*/*Rough Riders of Cheyenne*/*Santa Fe Saddlemates*/*Sunset in El Dorado*/*Wagon Wheels Westward*/1945 · *California Gold Rush*/*Home in Oklahoma*/1946 · *Wyoming*/*Twilight on the Rio Grande*/1947 · *The Gay Ranchero*/*The Bold Frontiersman*/*Under California Stars*/*The Timber Trail*/*Eyes of Texas*/*Grand Canyon Trail*/*Night Time in Nevada*/*Desperadoes of Dodge City*/*The Far Frontier*/*Sundown in Santa Fe*/*I Shot Jesse James*/1948 · *Rose of the Yukon*/*Death Valley Gunfighter*/*Frontier Investigator*/*Law of the Golden West*/*South of Rio*/*Down Dakota Way*/*San Antone Ambush*/*The Golden Stallion*/*Ranger of Cherokee Strip*/*Powder River Rustlers*/*Pioneer Marshal*/*Twilight in the Sierras*/*Bells of Coronado*/1949 · *Covered Wagon Raid*/*Sunset in the West*/*North of the Great Divide*/*Rio Grande*/1950 · *Rough Riders of Durango*/*Thunder in God's Country*/*Night Riders of Montana*/*Heart of the Rockies*/*Silver City Bonanza*/*Wells Fargo Gunmaster*/*In Old Amarillo*/*The Dakota Kid*/*Arizona Manhunt*/*Fort Dodge Stampede*/*Honeychile*/*South of Caliente*/*Pals of the Golden West*/1951 · *Colorado Sundown*/*Thundering Caravans*/*Old Oklahoma Plains*/*Desperadoes' Outpost*/*Toughest Man in Arizona*/*The Marshal of Cedar Rock*/1952 · *Shadows of Tombstone*/*Red River Shore*/1953 · *Carolina Cannonball*/1955 · (co-art d) *The Searchers*/1956 · *3:10 to Yuma*/1957 · *The Big Country*/1958 · *The Horse Soldiers*/1959 · *Sergeants 3*/1961

Hoxie, Jack (1890-1965) · Actor, aka Hart Hoxie, and brother of Western actor Al Hoxie. Apart from Hoot Gibson he was, with his horse Scout, Universal's biggest cowboy attraction in the 20s. His films relied heavily on fast-paced action and stunts rather than on personality for their appeal. Before moving to the Universal lot in 1923, he starred in a number of Westerns for Poverty Row independents such as Arrow and Sunset Pictures. He retired from the movies after a series of extremely low-budget sound Westerns for Majestic. PS
The Invaders/*Brought to Bay*/*The Battle at Fort Laramie*/*The Big Horn Massacre*/*The Tragedy of Big Eagle Mine*/*The Hold Up at Black Rock*/1913 · *The Operator at Black Rock*/1914 · *Three Godfathers*/*Nan of Music Mountain*/*The Vulture of Skull Mountain*/*The Man from Tiajuana*/*Blind Fury*/*Border Wolves*/*Buck Simmons, Puncher*/*The Fight for Paradise Valley*/*The Harvest of Gold*/*The Oil Field Plot*/*On the Brink of War*/*The Oil Plunderers*/*The Quarter Breed*/*The Son of Cain*/*The Stain of Chuckawalla*/*Tigers Unchained*/1916 · *The Secret of the Lost Valley*/*The Door in the Mountain*/*The Ghost

Jack Hoxie

of the Desert*/*The Skeleton Canyon Raid*/*The Trapping of Two-Bit Tuttle*/*The Tyrant of Chiricahua*/*The Vanished Line Rider*/1917 · *Blue Blazes Rawden*/1918 · *Told in the Hills*/*The Valley of the Giants*/*Lightning Bryce*/1919 · *Thunderbolt Jack*/*A Man from Nowhere*/1920 · *Broken Spur*/*Cupid's Brand*/*Cyclone Bliss*/*Dead or Alive*/*Devil Dog Dawson*/*Hills of Hate*/*The Sheriff of Hope Eternal*/*Sparks of Flint*/*The Double O*/1921 · *Back Fire*/*Barb Wire*/*The Crow's Nest*/*A Desert Bridegroom*/*The Marshal of Moneymint*/*The Desert's Crucible*/*Riders of the Law*/*Two Fisted Jefferson*/1922 · *Desert Rider*/*Don Quickshot of the Rio Grande*/*The Forbidden Trail*/*Galloping Thru*/*Men in the Raw*/*The Red Warning*/*Where Is This West?*/*Wolf's Tracks*/1923 · *The Back Trail*/*Daring Chances*/*Fighting Fury*/*The Galloping Ace*/*The Man From Wyoming*/*The Phantom Horseman*/*Ridgeway of Montana*/*The Western Wallop*/1924 · *Bustin' Thru*/*Don Dare Devil*/*Flying Hoofs*/*Hidden Loot*/*The Red Rider*/*Ridin' Thunder*/*A Roaring Adventure*/*The Sign of the Cactus*/*Two-Fisted Jones*/*The White Outlaw*/1925 · *The Border Sheriff*/*The Demon*/*The Fighting Peacemaker*/*The Last Frontier*/*Looking for Trouble*/*Red Hot Leather*/*A Six Shootin' Romance*/*The Wild Horse Stampede*/1926 · *The Fighting Three*/*Grinning Guns*/*Men of Daring*/*The Rambling Ranger*/*Rough and Ready*/*The Western Whirlwind*/*Heroes of the Wild*/1927 · *Gold*/1932 · *Gun Law*/*Law and Lawless*/*Outlaw Justice*/*Trouble Busters*/*Via Pony Express*/1933

Skip Homeier

Dennis Hopper

Hudson, Rock (1925-85) · Actor. From *Magnificent Obsession* (1954) onwards, Rock Hudson's screen image became closely identified with romantic comedies and melodramas. Prior to that, however, more than a third of his appearances had been in Westerns. He worked with leading genre specialists such as Anthony Mann (*Winchester '73*, *Bend of the River*), Budd Boetticher (*Horizons West*, *Seminole*) and Raoul Walsh (*The Lawless Breed*) in a variety of roles including plain Westerners, cavalry officers and Indians. Subsequent appearances in the genre were few but he had the central role of the Texas cattle baron in the contemporary Western *Giant*. TR

*Winchester '73/Tomahawk/*1950 · *Bend of the River/*1951 · *Horizons West/The Lawless Breed/*1952 · *Seminole/Taza, Son of Cochise/Gun Fury/Back to God's Country/*1953 · *Giant/*1956 · *The Last Sunset/*1961 · *The Undefeated/*1969 · *Showdown/*1972

Huffaker, Clair (b 1927) · Writer, formerly a boxer and sub-editor on *Time* and *Life*, and a prolific producer of almost pulp Westerns, many of which have been filmed, of original screenplays and television series scripts. Although his work is marred by a tendency towards adolescent machismo and lazy plotting, he has written the original novels and screenplays for several fine Westerns, including the uncharacteristic, serious *Flaming Star* and the rip-roaring, adventurous *The Comancheros* and *The War Wagon*. KN

(sc, novel) *Seven Ways from Sundown/*(co-sc, novel) *Flaming Star/*1960 · (novel) *Posse from Hell/*(co-sc [as 'Cecil Dan Hansen']) *The Second Time Around/*(co-sc) *The Comancheros/*1961 · (co-sc, novel) *Rio Conchos/*1964 · (novel) *The War Wagon/*1967 · (co-sc) *100 Rifles/*1968 · (novel) *Flap/*(co-sc) *La spina dorsale del diavolo/*1970 · *Valdez, il mezzosangue/*1973
Television *Rawhide/*59

Hull, Henry (1890-1977) · Actor. As a young man Henry Hull played leads in silent films. After a spell on stage, he returned in the mid-30s as a character player, and after a notable leading role in *The Werewolf of London* lent his solid, thoughtful presence to countless movies, including a number of Westerns. He had spent time, years before, as a mining engineering and prospector in Canada, and must have been comfortably at home in the open air. JL

*Jesse James/The Return of the Cisco Kid/*1939 · *The Return of Frank James/*1940 · *The Woman of the Town/*1943 · *El Paso/Colorado Territory/*1949 · *The Treasure of Lost Canyon/*1951 · *Thunder Over the Plains/*1952 · *The Last Posse/*1953 · *Kentucky Rifle/Man with the Gun/*1955 · *The Proud Rebel/*1958 · *The Oregon Trail/The Sheriff of Fractured Jaw/*1958
Television *Trackdown/*58 · *Wagon Train/The Restless Gun/*59 · *Bonanza/Laramie/Dick Powell's Zane Grey Theatre/*60 · *The Outlaws/*61 · *The Travels of Jaimie McPheeters/*63

Hunnicutt, Arthur (1911-79) · Actor. A tall, lean, bearded figure, with a distinctive 'country' voice, he was a stage actor before entering films in 1942. Many of his roles in the early 40s were as comic support in Charles Starrett's series of B-Westerns at Columbia. By 1950 he was a top character star, typically playing old-timers or backwoodsmen. For his role as the grizzled fur trapper in Hawks' *The Big Sky* he was nominated for an Oscar. JH

*Silver Queen/Riding Through Nevada/Pardon My Gun/*1942 · *Fighting Buckaroo/Frontier Fury/Law of the Northwest/Robin Hood of the Range/Hail to the Rangers/*1943 · *Riding West/*1944 · *Lust for Gold/Stars in My Crown/*1949 · *A Ticket to Tomahawk/The Furies/Two Flags West/Broken Arrow/*1950 · *Passage West/Sugarfoot/The Red*

*Badge of Courage/Distant Drums/*1951 · *The Big Sky/The Lusty Men/*1952 · *Devil's Canyon/*1953 · *The Last Command/*1955 · *The Tall T/*1956 · *Born Reckless/*1959 · *Cat Ballou/Apache Uprising/*1965 · *El Dorado/*1966 · *The Adventures of Bullwhip Griffin/*1967 · *Shoot-Out/*1971 · *The Spikes Gang/*1974 · *Winterhawk/*1975
Television *Bonanza/Black Saddle/Wanted: Dead or Alive/*59 · *The Man from Blackhawk/*60 · *The Great Adventure/*64 · *Laredo/*65 · *Daniel Boone/*66 · *The Outcasts/*69 · *Mrs. Sundance/*74

Hunter, Jeffrey (1926-69) · Actor. Blue-eyed and handsome, he had the physical attributes of a Western hero, hence it is somewhat surprising that he was often cast in ethnic roles: a young Indian in *White Feather*, a Mexican in *Joaquin Murrieta* and, in one of his most successful roles, the half-breed Martin Pawley in *The Searchers*. Ford also used Hunter as Lt Cantrell in *Sergeant Rutledge* and he appeared in another court-room role in *The Man from Galveston*. JH

*Three Young Texans/*1953 · *White Feather/Seven Angry Men/*1955 · *The Proud Ones/The Searchers/The Great Locomotive Chase/Gun for a Coward/*1956 · *The True Story of Jesse James/*1957 · *Sergeant Rutledge/*1960 · *The Man from Galveston/*1963 · *Joaquin Murrieta/*1964 · *Custer of the West/*1966 · *Joe! cercati un posto per morire/*1968
Television *Daniel Boone/*60 · *Andrew's Raiders/*61 · *Laramie/*62 · *Temple Houston/*63 · *Death Valley Days/*64 · *The Legend of Jesse James/*66 · *The Monroes/*67

Huston, John (1906-87) · Director. Somewhat surprisingly for a director and scriptwriter of Huston's stature and longevity he was involved in the production of relatively few Westerns compared to such as Ford and Walsh. Furthermore, amongst his credits as a director only the excellent and

Rock Hudson

Henry Hull

Arthur Hunnicutt

Jeffrey Hunter

highly self-reflexive *The Life and Times of Judge Roy Bean* and *The Unforgiven* can be said to be Westerns in the classic sense. *The Red Badge of Courage* is an adaptation of Stephen Crane's celebrated Civil War novel. Both *The Misfits* and *The Treasure of the Sierra Madre* have contemporary settings, and the latter is in any case marginal to the genre. PS

(act only) *Hell's Heroes*/1929 · (act only) *The Storm*/1930 · (co-sc only) *Law and Order*/1932 · (sc, act) *The Treasure of the Sierra Madre*/1948 · (sc) *The Red Badge of Courage*/1951 · *The Unforgiven*/1959 · *The Misfits*/1961 · (act only) *La spina dorsale del diavolo*/1970 · (act only) *Man in the Wilderness*/1971 · (act) *The Life and Times of Judge Roy Bean*/1972

Huston, Walter (1884-1950) · Actor. Huston's distinguished career in theatre and film included some notable Western portraits. In middle-age he played Trampas, that quintessential Western villain, in *The Virginian*, and in the 1932 classic *Law and Order* he was a thinly disguised Wyatt Earp, shifting easily a decade later to Doc Holliday in *The Outlaw*. Later still, in his son John's *The Treasure of the Sierra Madre*, he was the shrewd, garrulous, undaunted old prospector – a richly earned Oscar – and ended, in the year he died, with a moving study of an obsessed rancher in Anthony Mann's *The Furies*. JL

The Virginian/1929 · *The Bad Man*/1930 · *Law and Order*/1932 · *The Outlaw*/1940 · *Duel in the Sun*/1946 · *The Treasure of the Sierra Madre*/1948 · *The Furies*/1950

I

Ince, Thomas H. (1882-1924) · Producer. One of Hollywood's great self-promoters, commonly credited as the innovator of the studio system. In fact, he was just one of many, though perhaps the most adroit, at applying the techniques of assembly-line production to the film industry in the early 'teens. He first worked briefly for IMP and Biograph as an actor and director, before moving to California in 1911 to join Bison, part of the New York Motion Picture Co, which specialized in Westerns. Beginning as a jack of all trades he soon took overall control of production. Under his management Bison became the premier Western production company, due, in part, to the signing of The Miller Brothers 101 Ranch Wild West Show, which gave Bison access to large casts of extras, props and livestock. Whilst at Bison Ince placed William S. Hart under a personal contract which he held him to for most of his career. (Note: Ince worked in a number of capacities on close to eight hundred films. The following is a representative selection of his work, including all of the films he made with W. S. Hart, on which he generally served as production supervisor.) PS

Bar Z's New Cook/The Foreman's Courage/Little Dove's Romance/The New Cowboy/Cowgirl's Pranks/An Indian Martyr/Falsely Accused/Getting His Man/1911 · *An Indian Maid's Elopement/The Honor of the Tribe/The Ranch Girl's Love/A Tenderfoot's Revenge/Broncho Bill's Love Affair/The Wild West Circus/The Deputy's Sweetheart/War on the Plains/The Indian Massacre/The Battle of the Red Men/The Deserter/Blazing the Trail/Memories of a Pioneer/On the Warpath/The Reformed Outlaw/The Buffalo Hunt/For the Honor of the Seventh/Custer's Last Fight/The Sheriff's Adopted Child/When Lee Surrenders/The Invaders/His Squaw/The Law of the West*/1912 · *The Wheels of Destiny/The Pride of the South/A Frontier Wife/Texas Kelly at Bay/With Lee in Virginia/The Battle of Gettysburg/An Indian's Gratitude/The Drummer of the Eighth/A Cowtown Reformation/An Indian's Honor/The Claim Jumper/Days of '49*/1913 · *The Gringos/A Frontier Mother/His Hour of Manhood/Jim Cameron's Wife/The Sheriff of Bisbee/A Tale of the Northwest Mounted/The Desperado/The Bargain/The Passing of Two-Gun Hicks/In the Sage Brush Country/*1914 · *The Iron Strain/The Last of the Line/On the Night Stage/The Scourge of the Desert/The Gun Fighter/Mr 'Silent' Haskins/The Sheriff's Streak of Yellow/The Grudge/The Roughneck/The Taking of Luke McVane/The Man from Nowhere/'Bad Buck' of Santa Ynez/The Darkening Trail/The Conversion of Frosty Blake/Tools of Providence/The Ruse/Cash Parrish's Pal/A Knight of the Trails/Pinto Ben/Keno Bates, Liar/Shorty's Ranch/The Disciple*/1915 · *Between Men/Hell's Hinges/The Aryan/The Primal Lure/The Apostle of Vengeance/The Dawn Maker/The Return of Draw Egan/The Patriot/The Devil's Double*/1916 · *Truthful Tulliver/The Gun Fighter/The Square Deal Man/The Desert Man/Wolf Lowry/The Flame of the Yukon/The Cold Deck/The Silent Man/The Narrow Trail*/1917 · *Wolves of the Rail/Blue Blazes Rawden/The Tiger Man/Selfish Yates/Riddle Gawne/The Border Wireless/Branding Broadway/The Law of the North*/1918 · *The Sheriff's Son/The Lady of Red Butte/L'Apache/Breed of Men/The Poppy Girl's Husband/The Money Corral/Square Deal Sanderson/Wagon Tracks/John Petticoats*/1919 · *The Last Frontier*/1926

Ireland, John (b 1914) · Actor. The John Ireland Western character, whether he's playing good, bad or otherwise, is the man of the silent expression, all looks and laconic exchanges. But it's an urgent silence, a unique style which is performed to perfection in one of his earliest Western roles, as Cherry Valance in *Red River*. In the screenplay Ireland's character (who is killed off well before the end in the original Borden

John Huston

Walter Huston

Thomas Ince with William Eagleshirt

John Ireland

Chase novel) becomes something of a composite of the Thomas Dunson (Wayne) and Matthew Garth (Clift) characters, exercising the restraint lacking in one and supplying the force not fully developed in the other. In the film, when it comes to the final Abilene showdown for Dunson and Garth, Ireland's Cherry, calmly loading bullets into his gun, responds to Harry Carey's concerned 'You know that young man [Clift] isn't going to use his gun, don't you?' with a cold 'Yeah. But I haven't any such notion.' He then forces Wayne to draw with 'Mr Dunson! Mr Dunson, I'll say it just one more time....' Wayne spins around and shoots him. It was the end of the beginning of an excellent Western player. TV

My Darling Clementine/1946 · *Red River*/1947 · *A Southern Yankee*/*I Shot Jesse James*/1948 · *The Walking Hills*/*Roughshod*/*The Doolins of Oklahoma*/1949 · *The Return of Jesse James*/*Vengeance Valley*/1950 · *Little Big Horn*/*Red Mountain*/*The Bushwhackers*/1951 · (co-p, co-d) *Outlaw Territory*/1953 · *Southwest Passage*/1954 · *Gunslinger*/*Gunfight at the O.K. Corral*/1956 · *Fort Utah*/*Arizona Bushwhackers*/*Odio per odio*/*Fidarsi è bene, sparare è meglio*/1967 · *Villa Rides*/*Tutto per tutto*/*Corri, uomo, corri*/*Quanto costa morire*/1968

Dean Jagger

· *La sfida dei Mackenna*/1970 · *Kino, the Padre on Horseback*/1977 · (The following titles may be Westerns: *Una pistola per cento bare*/*T'ammazzo! Raccomandati a Dio*/1968 · *Zenabel*/1969 · *Dieci bianchi uccisi da un piccolo indiano*/1974 · *Quel pomeriggio maledetto*/1977)
Television *Dick Powell's Zane Grey Theatre*/56 · *Riverboat*/59 · *Rawhide*/62 · *Branded*/65 · *A Man Called Shenandoah*/*Gunsmoke*/66 · *The Iron Horse*/*Bonanza*/*Daniel Boone*/67 · *The Men from Shiloh*/70 · *The Quest*/76

J

Jagger, Dean (b 1903) · Actor. Though his film career began in 1929, Jagger became identified with the strong, sometimes ruthless patriarchs he played in the last decades of his career. With his craggy face, sharp eyes and bald dome he seemed comfortable outdoors, though many of the Westerns he appeared in were not particularly distinguished, with the notable exception of John Sturges' classic *Bad Day at Black Rock*. Jagger's alcoholic, self-hating sheriff is one of the most memorable performances in that superbly acted film. JC

Home on the Range/1934 · *The Wanderer of the Wasteland*/1935 · *Brigham Young – Frontiersman*/1940 · *Western Union*/1941 · *Valley of the Sun*/*The Omaha Trail*/1942 · *Alaska*/1944 · *Pursued*/1947 · *Sierra*/*Rawhide*/1950 · *Warpath*/1951 · *Denver and Rio Grande*/1952 · *Bad Day at Black Rock*/1954 · *Red Sundown*/1955 · *Forty Guns*/1957 · *The Proud Rebel*/1958 · *Firecreek*/1967 · *Day of the Evil Gun*/1968 · *Smith*/1969
Television *Dick Powell's Zane Grey Theatre*/57 · *Bonanza*/71 · *Alias Smith and Jones*/*The Hanged Man*/74

Johnson, Ben (b 1918) · Actor. After following his father into ranch and rodeo work he went to Hollywood where he worked as a wrangler and stuntman on *The Outlaw* and *Fort Apache* amongst others. He was given his first featured role in *3 Godfathers* and thereafter became a regular in Ford's stock company. His later appearances in Peckinpah and McLaglen Westerns helped foster their reputations as artistic heirs to Ford's vision of the West. However, his taciturn, good-humoured and dignified performances for Ford were not exploited by his later employers, who tended to cast him as an inarticulate villain or sidekick. PS

Badman's Territory/1946 · *3 Godfathers*/1948 · *She Wore a Yellow Ribbon*/1949 ·

Wagon Master/*Rio Grande*/1950 · *Fort Defiance*/1951 · *Wild Stallion*/*Shane*/1952 · *Rebel in Town*/1956 · *War Drums*/*Slim Carter*/1957 · *Fort Bowie*/1958 · *Ten Who Dared*/1960 · *One-Eyed Jacks*/*Tomboy and the Champ*/1961 · *Cheyenne Autumn*/*Major Dundee*/1964 · *The Rare Breed*/1965 · *Will Penny*/1967 · *Hang 'Em High*/1968 · *The Undefeated*/*The Wild Bunch*/*Ride a Northbound Horse*/1969 · *Chisum*/1970 · *Something Big*/1971 · *Junior Bonner*/1972 · *The Train Robbers*/*Kid Blue*/1973 · *Bite the Bullet*/*Breakheart Pass*/1975 · *Grayeagle*/1977
Television *Laramie*/*Have Gun, Will Travel*/60 · *Bonanza*/62 · *The Virginian*/*Gunsmoke*/63 · *The Monroes*/*Branded*/66 · *The Sacketts*/79 · *Wild Times*/80 · *Louis L'Amour's 'The Shadow Riders'*/82 · *Wild Horses*/85 · *Dream West*/86

Johnson, Chubby (1903-74) · Actor. One great part in one great film can immortalize a character actor. Mose in *The Searchers* did it for Hank Worden, and for Charles Randolph Johnson, credited as Chubby, Captain Mello in *Bend of the River* brought the same reward. Johnson played the greying, rough-voiced old-timer in some thirty Westerns. In Mann's film he captained a riverboat in Oregon, enjoyed the doubtful assistance of Stepin Fetchit as crew, and was for ever saying he should never have left the Mississippi – a performance that made a career. JL
Rocky Mountain/1950 · *Fort Worth*/*Fort Dodge Stampede*/*Night Riders of Montana*/*Wells Fargo Gunmaster*/*Westward the Women*/*Bend of the River*/1951 · *The Treasure of Lost Canyon*/*Last of the Comanches*/1952 · *Gunsmoke*/*Law and Order*/*Back to God's Country*/*Calamity Jane*/1953 · *Overland Pacific*/*Cattle Queen of Montana*/*The Far Country*/*Tennessee's Partner*/1954 · *Rage at Dawn*/*The Rawhide Years*/*Tribute to a Badman*/1955 · *The*

Ben Johnson

Fastest Gun Alive/The First Texan/The Young Guns/1956 · Drango/The True Story of Jesse James/Gunfire at Indian Gap/1957 · The Firebrand/1962 · The Adventures of Bullwhip Griffin/1967 · Support Your Local Sheriff!/1968 · Sam Whiskey/1969
Television The Adventures of Jim Bowie/57 · The Adventures of Rin Tin Tin/58 · Maverick/59 · Wanted: Dead or Alive/The Rifleman/60 · Gunsmoke/64 · The Big Valley/65

Jones, Buck (1889-1942) · Actor. Jones' own life had been little less adventurous than those of his Western heroes. He had been a cowboy with the 101 Wild West Show, a cavalry sergeant wounded in the Philippines, aviation mechanic, sheep herder and, in World War I, horse-breaker for the French government. From Western extra and stunt double for Mix and Hart, he was a star by 1920, and continued his workmanlike B-Westerns for over 20 years, with his own production company and occasional forays into direction. Fading at last by 1940, he joined Monogram for their Rough Riders series, on which he was still working when in December 1942 he died, with over 400 others, in a night-club fire in Boston, during a testimonial dinner in his honour. JL

Western Blood/True Blue/Riders of the Purple Sage/The Rainbow Trail/1918 · The Sheriff's Son/Wilderness Trail/1919 · Forbidden Trails/The Square Shooter/Firebrand Trevison/Sunset Sprague/Two Moons/1920 · The One-Man Trail/Get Your Man/Straight from the Shoulder/To a Finish/Bar Nothin'/Riding with Death/1921 · Pardon My Nerve!/Western Speed/Rough Shod/Trooper O'Neil/West of Chicago/The Fast Mail/Bells of San Juan/1922 · The Footlight Ranger/Snowdrift/Hell's Hole/1923 · The Vagabond Trail/The Circus Cowboy/Western Luck/Against All Odds/The Desert Outlaw/The Man Who Played Square/The Arizona Romeo/1924 · The Trail Rider/Gold and the Girl/Hearts and Spurs/Durand of the Bad Lands/Timber Wolf/The Desert's Price/1925 · The Cowboy and the Countess/The Fighting Buckaroo/A Man Four-Square/The Gentle Cyclone/The Flying Horseman/Desert Valley/30 Below Zero/1926 · Whispering Sage/Hills of Peril/Good as Gold/Chain Lightning/Black Jack/Blood Will Tell/The Branded Sombrero/1927 · The Lone Rider/Shadow Ranch/Men Without Law/The Dawn Trail/1930 · Border Law/Branded/The Range Feud/Desert Vengeance/The Avenger/The Texas Ranger/The Fighting Sheriff/Deadline/1931 · Ridin' for Justice/South of the Rio Grande/One Man Law/Hello Trouble/McKenna of the Mounted/White Eagle/Forbidden Trail/1932 · Treason/The California Trail/The Thrill Hunter/Unknown Valley/Gordon of Ghost City/The Fighting Code/The Sundown Rider/1933 · The Fighting Ranger/The Man Trailer/Rocky Rhodes/When a Man Sees Red/The Red Rider/1934 · The Crimson Trail/Stone of Silver Creek/The Roaring West/Border Brigands/Outlawed Guns/The Throwback/The Ivory-Handled Gun/1935 · The Boss Rider of Gun Creek/The Phantom Rider/Sunset of Power/Silver Spurs/(d) For the Service/The Cowboy and the Kid/Empty Saddles/Ride 'Em Cowboy/1936 · Sandflow/(co-d) Law for Tombstone/Left-Handed Law/Smoke Tree Range/(d) Black Aces/Hollywood Round-Up/Headin' East/Boss of Lonely Valley/Sudden Bill Dorn/1937 · The Overland Express/California Frontier/Law of the Texan/The Stranger from Arizona/1938 · Wagons Westward/1940 · Riders of Death Valley/White Eagle/Arizona Bound/The Gunman from Bodie/Forbidden Trails/1941 · Ghost Town Law/Down Texas Way/Riders of the West/West of the Law/Below the Border/Dawn on the Great Divide/1942

Jones, L. Q. (b 1927) · Actor, aka Justus E. McQueen. One of the finest supporting actors of the 60s and 70s and a regular member of Peckinpah's 'stock company', in whose films he invariably played a retarded, psychotic range-tramp, most memorably with Strother Martin in The Wild Bunch and The Ballad of Cable Hogue, where they appear as a pair of vulture-like brothers in filth and profanity. His c.v. claims he has appeared in over 500 television episodes, nearly 200 of which have been Westerns. PS
Buchanan Rides Alone/1958 · Warlock/1959 · Flaming Star/Cimarron/1960 · Ride the High Country/1962 · Showdown/1963 ·

Buck Jones

Major Dundee/Apache Rifles/1964 · Hang 'Em High/1968 · The Wild Bunch/The McMasters/1969 · The Ballad of Cable Hogue/1970 · The Hunting Party/1971 · Pat Garrett and Billy the Kid/1973 · Winterhawk/1975 · Timerider/1982 · Lone Wolf McQuade/1983
Television Cheyenne/55 · Black Saddle/59 · Two Faces West/Johnny Ringo/The Rebel/Klondike/60 · The Life and Legend of Wyatt Earp/Have Gun, Will Travel/The Americans/61 · Laramie/Lawman/The Virginian/62 · Wagon Train/Gunsmoke/Empire/63 · Rawhide/64 · Laredo/65 · A Man Called Shenandoah/The Big Valley/66 · Cimarron Strip/Hondo/67 · Lancer/69 · Cade's County/Alias Smith and Jones/71 · The Bravos/72 · Mrs. Sundance/74 · Banjo Hackett: Roamin' Free/76 · Standing Tall/78 · The Sacketts/How the West Was Won/79 · Wild Times/80

Chubby Johnson

L. Q. Jones

Victor Jory

Jory, Victor (1902-82) · Actor. Jory came to Hollywood after establishing himself as a stage actor, but his sharp, dark features soon caused him to be typed as the perfect Western villain. Though he was involved in some prestigious projects (Oberon in Reinhardt's *A Midsummer Night's Dream*, *Gone with the Wind*), the bulk of his Westerns were B-features. He was memorable as the mad Judge Roy Bean in Boetticher's *A Time for Dying*. JC

Smoky/1933 · *Dodge City*/*Man of Conquest*/ *Susannah of the Mounties*/1939 · *Cherokee Strip*/*Knights of the Range*/*The Light of Western Stars*/*River's End*/1940 · *Bad Men of Missouri*/*Border Vigilantes*/*Riders of the Timberline*/*Wide Open Town*/1941 · *Shut My Big Mouth*/*Tombstone, the Town Too Tough to Die*/*The Leather Burners*/1942 · *Bar 20*/*Buckskin Frontier*/*Colt Comrades*/ *Hoppy Serves a Writ*/*The Kansan*/1943 · *Canadian Pacific*/*Fighting Man of the Plains*/*South of St Louis*/1949 · *The Capture*/ *The Cariboo Trail*/1950 · *Cave of Outlaws*/ *Flaming Feather*/1951 · *Toughest Man in Arizona*/1952 · *The Man from the Alamo*/ *Devil's Canyon*/1953 · *Blackjack Ketchum, Desperado*/1956 · *Last Stagecoach West*/ 1957 · *Cheyenne Autumn*/1964 · (narration only) *McKenna's Gold*/*A Time for Dying*/

Katy Jurado

1969 · *Flap*/1970 · *Kino, the Padre on Horseback*/1977 · *The Mountain Men*/1979 Television *Wanted: Dead or Alive*/*Rawhide*/ 59 · *Empire*/62 · *The Wide Country*/*Temple Houston*/63 · *The Virginian*/*The Great Adventure*/64 · *Gunsmoke*/65 · *Bonanza*/*The Legend of Jesse James*/*The Iron Horse*/*The Loner*/*F Troop*/66 · *The Road West*/67 · *The High Chaparral*/68 · *Young Maverick*/80

Jurado, Katy (b 1927) · Actress. Katy Jurado began and ended her career in Mexican films. In between, she came to Hollywood on a journalistic assignment and stayed on, as an actress, for twenty years. Dark, fiery and sensuous, she played some leads and a few notable supporting roles, gaining an Oscar nomination for her study of the cattle baron's Indian wife in *Broken Lance*. Another memorable Jurado performance was as the heroine of *The Badlanders*, Delmer Daves' curious retelling of *The Asphalt Jungle* as a Western. JL

High Noon/1952 · *San Antone*/*Arrowhead*/ 1953 · *Broken Lance*/1954 · *Man from Del Rio*/1956 · *Dragoon Wells Massacre*/1957 · *The Badlanders*/1958 · *One-Eyed Jacks*/1960 · *Smoky*/1966 · *Pat Garrett and Billy the Kid*/1973

Television *The Rifleman*/59 · *Death Valley Days*/64 · *The Men from Shiloh*/70 · *Alias Smith and Jones*/72

K

Kane, Joseph (1897-1975) · One of the most prolific directors of series Westerns and an action director par excellence. He worked as an editor at Pathé and Paramount before becoming a house director at Republic in 1935, where he helped establish the careers of Autry and Rogers, amongst others. He was associate or co-producer on most of his films from 1939. After the collapse of Republic in 1958 he worked principally on television Westerns. PS

(co-d uncredited) *In Old Sante Fe*/1934 · *Tumbling Tumbleweeds*/*Melody Trail*/*The Sagebrush Troubadour*/1935 · *The Lawless Nineties*/*King of the Pecos*/*The Lonely Trail*/ *Guns and Guitars*/*Oh, Susannah!*/*Ride, Ranger, Ride*/*The Old Corral*/*Ghost Town Gold*/1936 · *Gunsmoke Ranch*/*Come On Cowboys*/*Heart of the Rockies*/*Round Up Time in Texas*/*Git Along, Little Dogies*/ *Yodelin' Kid from Pine Ridge*/*Public Cowboy No. 1*/*Boots and Saddles*/*Spring Time in the Rockies*/1937 · *The Old Barn Dance*/*Gold Mine in the Sky*/*Man from Music Mountain*/ *Under Western Stars*/*Billy the Kid Returns*/

Come On, Rangers!/*Shine On Harvest Moon*/1938 · *In Old Monterey*/*Rough Riders' Roundup*/*Frontier Pony Express*/*Southward Ho!*/*In Old Caliente*/*Wall Street Cowboy*/ *The Arizona Kid*/*Saga of Death Valley*/ *Days of Jesse James*/1939 · *Young Bill Hickok*/*Young Buffalo Bill*/*The Carson City Kid*/*The Ranger and the Lady*/*Colorado*/*The Border Legion*/(2nd unit only) *Dark Command*/1940 · *Robin Hood of the Pecos*/*In Old Cheyenne*/*Nevada City*/*Sheriff of Tombstone*/*Bad Man of Deadwood*/*Jesse James at Bay*/*Red River Valley*/*The Great Train Robbery*/1941 · *South of Sante Fe*/*Man from Cheyenne*/*Sunset on the Desert*/*Romance on the Range*/*Sons of the Pioneers*/*Sunset Serenade*/*Heart of the Golden West*/*Ridin' Down the Canyon*/1942 · *Idaho*/*King of the Cowboys*/*Silver Spurs*/(2nd unit only) *In Old Oklahoma*/*Song of Texas*/*Man from Music Mountain*/1943 · *Hands Across the Border*/ *The Cowboy and the Senorita*/*The Yellow Rose of Texas*/*Song of Nevada*/1944 · *Flame of Barbary Coast*/*Dakota*/1945 · *In Old Sacramento*/*The Plainsman and the Lady*/ 1946 · *Wyoming*/1947 · *The Gallant Legion*/ *Old Los Angeles*/*The Plunderers*/1948 · *Brimstone*/*The Last Bandit*/*The Savage Horde*/1949 · *Rock Island Trail*/*California Passage*/1950 · *Oh, Susanna*/1951 · *Ride the Man Down*/*Woman of the North Country*/ 1952 · *San Antone*/1953 · *Jubilee Trail*/ *Timberjack*/1954 · *Hell's Outpost*/*Road to Denver*/*The Vanishing American*/1955 · *The Maverick Queen*/*Thunder Over Arizona*/ 1956 · *Duel at Apache Wells*/*Spoilers of the Forest*/*Last Stagecoach West*/*The Lawless Eighties*/*Gunfire at Indian Gap*/1957 · (2nd unit only) *Shakiest Gun in the West*/1967 · *Smoke in the Wind*/1971

Television *Cheyenne*/57 · *Bonanza*/*Laramie*/ *Rawhide*/59

Kaye, Gordon (b 1916) · Producer. The Republic studio made 386 B-Westerns, and each of them needed an associate producer, seldom present on set or location, whose job was to see that the films were smoothly and economically turned out in a week or so. One such man was Gordon Kaye. An executive and not a film-maker, he shepherded 25 Westerns home before becoming the studio's secretary-treasurer. In 1955 he moved across to Universal, where he produced a number of rather more expensive Westerns. JL

The Wild Frontier/*Bandits of Dark Canyon*/ 1947 · *Oklahoma Badlands*/*The Bold Frontiersman*/*Carson City Raiders*/ *Desperadoes of Dodge City*/*Renegades of*

Sonora/Marshal of Amarillo/The Denver Kid/1948 · Sheriff of Wichita/Death Valley Gunfighter/Frontier Investigator/The Wyoming Bandit/Bandit King of Texas/ Navajo Trail Raiders/Powder River Rustlers/ 1949 · Gunmen of Abilene/Code of the Silver Sage/Salt Lake Raiders/Covered Wagon Raid/Vigilante Hideout/Frisco Tornado/ Rustlers on Horseback/1950 · Night Riders of Montana/Rough Riders of Durango/1951 · Quantez/Day of the Bad Man/1957 · The Saga of Hemp Brown/1958 · Hell Bent for Leather/1959 · Seven Ways from Sundown/ 1960 · Posse from Hell/Six Black Horses/ 1961 · Showdown/He Rides Tall/1963 · Bullet for a Badman/Taggart/1964 · Gunpoint/1965

Keene, Tom (1904-63) · Actor, aka George Duryea, Richard Powers. A stage actor who was brought to the movies by Cecil B. DeMille, he changed his name to Tom Keene when he was signed for a series of reasonably budgeted Westerns at RKO. After a series of 'historical' Westerns for Paramount (1936-7), he moved to Monogram (1937-42). Disillusioned with playing cowboys and Indians, he changed his name to Richard Powers in 1944 in the hope of being offered a greater diversity of roles. PS
Tide of Empire/In Old California/1929 · Beau Bandit/Pardon My Gun/The Dude Wrangler/1930 · The Sundown Trail/ Freighters of Destiny/1931 · Partners/The Saddle Buster/Ghost Valley/Beyond the Rockies/Come On Danger/Renegades of the West/1932 · Scarlet River/Son of the Border/ Cheyenne Kid/Crossfire/Sunset Pass/1933 · Drift Fence/The Glory Trail/Rebellion/Desert Gold/1936 · Battle of Greed/Old Louisiana/ Under Strange Flags/The Law Commands/ Drums of Destiny/Raw Timber/God's Country and the Man/Where Trails Divide/ Romance of the Rockies/1937 · Painted Trail/ 1938 · Wanderers of the West/Dynamite

Canyon/The Driftin' Kid/Ridin' the Sunset Trail/Lone Star Law Men/1942 · Western Mail/Arizona Roundup/Where Trails End/ 1943 · Lights of Old Santa Fe/1944 · Thunder Mountain/Under the Tonto Rim/ Wild Horse Mesa/1947 · Return of the Bad Men/Blood on the Moon/Indian Agent/ Western Heritage/1948 · Brothers in the Saddle/1949 · Storm Over Wyoming/ Desperados of the West/Trail of Robin Hood/ 1950 · Texans Never Cry/1951 · Once Upon a Horse/1958
Television *Sergeant Preston of the Yukon/55*

Keith, Brian (b 1921) · Actor. The son of character actor and writer Robert Keith, Brian presented a very different figure from his father. Robert was short, neat, very much under control, while Brian was burly, expansive and, in his early movies at least, prone to violence. In his early Western, *The Violent Men*, he holds his own comfortably with Stanwyck and Robinson. He played the lead in Peckinpah's television series *The Westerner*, and continued the association in *The Deadly Companions*. This gave him his finest role as Yellowleg, a Civil War survivor with scarred scalp and crippled arm, forever obsessed with revenge. A gallery of cattle barons, frontier old-timers and mountain men followed in due course. JL
Arrowhead/1953 · The Violent Men/1954 · Run of the Arrow/Hell Canyon Outlaws/ 1957 · Sierra Baron/Fort Dobbs/Villa!/1958 · Ten Who Dared/1960 · The Deadly Companions/1961 · Savage Sam/1963 · The Raiders/The Hallelujah Trail/1964 · Nevada Smith/The Rare Breed/1965 · Something Big/ Scandalous John/1971 · The Mountain Men/ 1979
Television *Dick Powell's Zane Grey Theatre/ Rawhide/Laramie/59 · The Westerner/60 · Frontier Circus/The Outlaws/61 · The Virginian/Wagon Train/63 · The Quest/76 · The Court Martial of George Armstrong*

Custer/77 · How the West Was Won/78 · The Chisholms/The Seekers/Centennial/79 · The Alamo: 13 Days to Glory/87

Kennedy, Arthur (b 1914) · Actor. Kennedy has played few lead roles in his career. Usually cast as a villain in Westerns, often as an embittered character of some psychological depth, particularly in the Anthony Mann films *Bend of the River* and *The Man from Laramie*. Even as the 'hero' in Lang's *Rancho Notorious*, he is a man who becomes unbalanced by his singular desire for revenge. JH
Bad Men of Missouri/They Died with their Boots On/1941 · Cheyenne/1947 · The Walking Hills /1949 · Red Mountain/Bend of the River/1951 · Rancho Notorious/The Lusty Men/1952 · The Naked Dawn/1954 · The Man from Laramie/The Rawhide Years/ 1955 · Cheyenne Autumn/Joaquin Murrieta/ 1964 · Nevada Smith/1965 · Escondido/1967 · Day of the Evil Gun/1968

Kennedy, Burt (b 1923) · Writer, director. The son of vaudeville performers, and a former radio and television writer, he provided the screenplays for several exemplary small-scale Westerns directed by Budd Boetticher in the latter 50s. These tightly constructed scripts show a delight in both formal organization and idiosyncrasy of language and humour, and these carried over into much of Kennedy's subsequent, and generally more expansive, work as a director. Many of his films have been humorous in disposition, either indirectly (*The War Wagon*) or overtly (*Support Your Local Sheriff!*); the one complete exception is the rather strenuously grim *Welcome to Hard Times*. Kennedy's movies are variable in overall quality, but even when the content is rather thin, there is still pictorial distinctiveness and a confident narrative rhythm. His keen response to the genre, as a genuine exponent rather than a mere *pasticheur*, comes through

Tom Keene

Brian Keith

Arthur Kennedy

Burt Kennedy

in his juggling of themes, notably that of an exemplary relationship between an older man and a younger one, as well as in his assured use of stars and featured players with long service in the movie West. TP
(act only) *The Man from the Alamo*/1953 · As writer only (st) *Seven Men from Now*/*Gun the Man Down*/*The Tall T*/1956 · (co-sc) *Fort Dobbs*/1958 · *Ride Lonesome*/*Yellowstone Kelly*/*Comanche Station*/1959 · *Six Black Horses*/1962 · As director: (sc) *The Canadians*/1961 · (sc) *Mail Order Bride*/1963 · (sc) *The Rounders*/1964 · *Return of the Seven*/(sc) *Welcome to Hard Times*/1966 · *The War Wagon*/1967 · *Support Your Local Sheriff!*/1968 · (sc) *Young Billy Young*/*The Good Guys and the Bad Guys*/1969 · (p) *Dirty Dingus Magee*/*La spina dorsale del diavolo*/1970 · *Support Your Local Gunfighter*/(co-sc) *Hannie Caulder*/1971 · (sc) *The Train Robbers*/1973
Television *Lawman*/*The Virginian*/62 · *The Rounders*/66 · *Shootout in a One-Dog Town*/*Sidekicks*/74 · *How the West Was Won*/76 · *Kate Bliss and the Ticker Tape Kid*/78 · *The Wild, Wild West Revisited*/79 · *More Wild, Wild West*/80 · *The Alamo: 13 Days to Glory*/87

Kennedy, George (b 1925) · Actor. Tall, burly character actor who played the brutish heavy in a number of action films. In middle age he graduated to more sympathetic roles, often with a humorous touch. JC
Lonely Are the Brave/1962 · *Shenandoah*/*The Sons of Katie Elder*/1965 · *The Ballad of Josie*/1967 · *Bandolero!*/*Guns of the Magnificent Seven*/1968 · *The Good Guys and the Bad Guys*/1969 · *Dirty Dingus Magee*/1970 · *Fools' Parade*/1971 · *Cahill United States Marshal*/1973
Television *The Alaskans*/*Colt .45*/*Cheyenne*/*Sugarfoot*/59 · *Gunsmoke*/*Have Gun, Will Travel*/*Riverboat*/60 · *Klondike*/*Bonanza*/*Bat Masterson*/*The Tall Man*/*Tales of Wells

Fargo/61 · *Rawhide*/62 · *The Travels of Jaimie McPheeters*/63 · *The Virginian*/64 · *Daniel Boone*/*A Man Called Shenandoah*/*Laredo*/*The Legend of Jesse James*/*The Big Valley*/65

King, Louis (1898-1962) · Director, aka Lewis King, L. H. King. His elder brother Henry, thirty years a contract director at Fox, made few Westerns, though two of them, *Jesse James* and *The Gunfighter*, were landmarks. By contrast, Louis King spent his entire career among the Bs, starting with William Fairbanks Westerns and a series featuring the child star Buzz Barton. He graduated to working with Buck Jones on his first sound series, then made two charming George O'Brien Westerns (*Life in the Raw*, *Robbers' Roost*) and a singing cowboy movie with Dick Foran (*Song of the Saddle*). A neat craftsman with a sure sense of pace, King did his best work in the late 30s with a fine string of thrillers and gangster movies for Paramount, notably *Hunted Men*, *Prison Farm* (both 1938) and *Persons in Hiding* (1939). Condemned by *Thunderhead, Son of Flicka* to latter-day Westerns about horses, he never really found his stride again, although *Powder River* is tautly directed. TMI
Peaceful Peters/*The Sheriff of Sun Dog*/1926 · *Spawn of the Desert*/*The Devil's Dooryard*/*The Law Rustlers*/*Sun Dog Trails*/*The Boy Rider*/*The Slingshot Kid*/1927 · *The Pinto Kid*/*The Little Buckaroo*/*The Bantam Cowboy*/*Young Whirlwind*/*Terror*/*Rough Ridin' Red*/*Orphan of the Sage*/*The Fightin' Redhead*/1928 · *The Vagabond Cub*/*The Freckled Rascal*/*The Little Savage*/*Pals of the Prairie*/1929 · *The Lone Rider*/*Men Without Law*/*Shadow Ranch*/1930 · *Desert Vengeance*/*The Fighting Sheriff*/*Border Law*/1931 · *Robbers' Roost*/1932 · *Life in the Raw*/1933 · *Song of the Saddle*/1936 · *Thunderhead, Son of Flicka*/1945 · *Smoky*/1946 · *Green Grass of Wyoming*/1948 · *Mrs

Mike/*Sand*/1949 · *Frenchie*/1950 · *The Lion and the Horse*/1952 · *Powder River*/1953 · *Massacre*/1956
Television *The Adventures of Wild Bill Hickok*/51

Kinski, Klaus (b 1926) · German actor who played in a number of Italian Westerns before becoming a star of art cinema for directors such as Werner Herzog. His cadaverous looks suited him for villainous roles, memorably in Corbucci's *Il grande silenzio*. CF
Der Letzte Ritt nach Santa Cruz/1963 · *Winnetou II*/1964 · *Per qualche dollaro in più*/1965 · *Quien sabe?*/1966 · *L'uomo, l'orgoglio, la vendetta*/1967 · *Ognuno per sè*/*Sartana*/*Il grande silenzio*/1968 · *Sono Sartana, il vostro becchino*/1969 · *Per una bara piena di dollari*/*Prega il morto e ammazza il vivo*/*Giù le mani ... carogna*/1970 · *Doppia taglia per Minnesota Stinky*/*Il ritorno di Clint il solitario*/1972 · *Un genio, due compari, un pollo*/1975

L

Ladd, Alan (1913-64) · Actor. Alan Ladd did not appear in that many Westerns during his 30-year Hollywood career, yet on the basis of a single role he has become closely identified with the genre. It was *Shane* which placed him with the handful of stars who incarnate the archetypal qualities of the Western hero. This may be partly due to the self-consciously mythological character of the film, with Shane dressed in light buckskins whilst his adversary is clad in black leather, but Ladd's gentle yet decisive performance and his sculpted features play their part in establishing the mythical dimensions of the picture. None of his subsequent Western appearances repeated this success, however, and his last screen role before his premature death in 1964 was, appropriately

George Kennedy

Klaus Kinski

Alan Ladd

Jack Lambert

enough, as a fading Western star in *The Carpetbaggers*. TR

In Old Missouri/The Light of Western Stars/
1940 · *Whispering Smith/*1949 · *Branded/*
1950 · *Red Mountain/*1951 · *The Iron Mistress/Shane/*1952 · *Saskatchewan/Drum Beat/*1954 · *The Big Land/*1957 · *The Proud Rebel/The Badlanders/*1958 · *Guns of the Timberland/*1959 · *One Foot in Hell/*1960

Lambert, Jack (b 1920) · Actor. That Jack Lambert obtained a degree at a Colorado college with a view to becoming a professor of English may be studio publicity. If true, his prospective students were well spared, for Lambert turned actor, and became one of the meanest Western villains to swagger into an unsuspecting town. The essence of the man is in a still from *Day of the Outlaw*. Glaring eyes, down-curled lip, gun under arm, gun hand at the ready – beside him, Burl Ives looks a kindly old uncle. JL
*The Harvey Girls/*1945 · *Abilene Town/The Plainsman and the Lady/*1946 · *The Vigilantes Return/*1947 · *Belle Starr's Daughter/River Lady/*1948 · *Brimstone/Big Jack/Stars in My Crown/Dakota Lil/Down Dakota Way/*1949 · *The Secret of Convict Lake/Bend of the River/Montana Belle/*1951 · *Vera Cruz/Run for Cover/*1954 · *Gun Point/*1955 · *Canyon River/Backlash/*1956 · *Day of the Outlaw/Alias Jesse James/*1959 · *How the West Was Won/*1962 · *4 for Texas/*1963
Television *The Adventures of Rin Tin Tin/*56 · *Lawman/Tales of Wells Fargo/*58 · *Riverboat/Colt .45/The Californians/The Texan/Bat Masterson/Gunsmoke/*59 · *Bonanza/Wagon Train/Have Gun, Will Travel/*60 · *The Virginian/*65 · *Daniel Boone/*66

Lancaster, Burt (b 1913) · Actor. After an early career as an acrobat, and war service, Lancaster appeared on the New York stage in 1946, and a year later was in films. In his second film, *The Killers*, his performance as the sadly resigned victim made him a star, and in doing so outlined the Lancaster character which would endure. He would be quiet-spoken, straightforward (even in the occasional foray into villainy), resolute, and a shade world-weary, but that formula could encompass a wide variety of creations. He ranged from the doomed Indian of *Apache* to Wyatt Earp in *Gunfight at the O.K. Corral*, from the patriarch of *The Unforgiven* to the Mexican sheriff of *Valdez Is Coming*, from the hard-bitten mercenary of *The Professionals* to the amiably dangerous adventurer of *Vera Cruz*. JL
*Vengeance Valley/*1950 · *Apache/Vera Cruz/*1954 · (d) *The Kentuckian/*1955 · *Gunfight at the O.K. Corral/*1956 · *The Unforgiven/*1959 · *The Hallelujah Trail/*1964 · *The Professionals/*1966 · *The Scalphunters/*1967 · *Valdez Is Coming/Lawman/*1970 · *Ulzana's Raid/*1972 · *Buffalo Bill and the Indians or Sitting Bull's History Lesson/*1976 · *Cattle Annie and Little Britches/*1980

Lane, Allan 'Rocky' (1901-73) · Actor. After starring in three Republic serials, Allan Lane was tried out as a series star in six films before replacing Bill Elliott as Fred Harmon's 'Red Ryder' character. Winning a loyal audience, he was promoted by the studio to his own series in 1947, given the 'Rocky' appellation and the requisite customized equine ('Black Jack'). He spent the next seven years turning out variable yet rarely dull movies, whose qualities were those of an earlier, rougher, non-musical age. Wearing work jeans and plain striped shirt, with a policy of hard-riding action and pell-mell punch-ups, Lane came over as a 'professional', like a cop or private eye doing investigative work. What makes the films work at their best is the taut unity of action, often wittily-knowing screenplays and Lane's authoritative, sometimes cynical modern persona, usually devoid of the sanctimoniousness of the conventional series hero. A far better actor than most of the cowboy stars, he brought conviction, honesty and sometimes a touch of sad wisdom to the oft-times feeble frolics he was participating in. CW
*King of the Royal Mounted/*1940 · *King of the Mounties/*1942 · *Daredevils of the West/*1943 · *Sheriff of Sundown/Silver City Kid/Stagecoach to Monterey/*1944 · *Corpus Christi Bandits/The Topeka Terror/Trail of Kit Carson/*1945 · *Out California Way/Santa Fe Uprising/Stagecoach to Denver/Vigilantes of Boom Town/*1946 · *Homesteaders of Paradise Valley/Oregon Trail Scouts/The Marshal of Cripple Creek/Rustlers of Devil's Canyon/Wild Frontier/Bandits of Dark Canyon/*1947 · *Bold Frontiersman/Carson City Raiders/Marshal of Amarillo/The Denver Kid/Desperadoes of Dodge City/Oklahoma Badlands/Renegades of Sonora/Sundown in Santa Fe/*1948 · *Powder River Rustlers/Sheriff of Wichita/The Wyoming Bandit/Bandit King of Texas/Death Valley Gunfighter/Frontier Investigator/Navajo Trail Raiders/*1949 · *Gunmen of Abilene/Trail of Robin Hood/Code of the Silver Sage/Covered Wagon Raid/Frisco Tornado/Rustlers on Horseback/Salt Lake Raiders/Vigilante Hideout/*1950 · *Night Riders of Montana/Desert of Lost Men/Fort Dodge Stampede/Rough Riders of Durango/Wells Fargo Gunmaster/*1951 · *Black Hills Ambush/Captive of Billy the Kid/Desperado's Outpost/Leadville Gunslinger/Thundering Caravans/*1952 · *Bandits of the West/Marshal of Cedar Rock/Savage Frontier/El Paso Stampede/*1953 · *The Saga of Hemp Brown/*1958

Lang, Charles B., Jr. (b 1902) · Cinematographer. Lang's work ranged from the visionary (*Death Takes a Holiday*) to the grimly realistic (*The Big Heat*), from the glitter of *Midnight* to the subdued browns and yellows of *The Man from Laramie*. But whatever the context, Lang said, he always tried 'not to let lighting become contrived to the point where a sense of realism is lost'. In some of his major Westerns plot and character may well have been contrived, but Lang always made their ambiance real. JL
*The Light of Western Stars/*1930 · *Buck Benny Rides Again/*1940 · (co-c) *The Shepherd of the Hills/*1941 · *Copper Canyon/*1949 · *Branded/*1950 · *Red Mountain/*1951 · *The Man from Laramie/*1955 · *Gunfight at*

Burt Lancaster

Allan Lane

the O.K. Corral/1956 · Last Train from Gun Hill/1958 · The Magnificent Seven/One-Eyed Jacks/1960 · (co-c) How the West Was Won ('The Rivers')/1962 · The Stalking Moon/1968

Lang, Fritz (1890-1976) · Director. The conventional optimism of the Western is, arguably, at odds with the sombre universe of Fritz Lang. In a Hollywood career dominated appropriately by the film noir and the thriller, Rancho Notorious, with its murder of the hero's fiancée and its femme fatale figure played by Marlene Dietrich, is closer to The Big Heat than to its generic contemporaries such as Shane. André Bazin, however, regarded Lang's earlier Westerns as significant contributions to the classic phase of the genre in the late 30s, though subsequent French critics were to see all Lang's genre work in terms of artistic subversion. TR
The Return of Frank James/1940 · Western Union/1941 · Rancho Notorious/1952

LaRue, Lash (b 1921) · Actor, aka Al LaRue. In his first Western role at PRC, LaRue, dressed all in black, played the role of a gunman. Subsequently, despite retaining the black outfit, he was always on the side of law and order. Of striking appearance, with more than a passing resemblance to Humphrey Bogart, his trademark was the bullwhip ('a gimmick thought up by publicity men,' he remarked). The gimmick was successful, and from 1946 until the end of his career it was a feature of his films. JH
Song of Old Wyoming/1945 · The Caravan Trail/Wild West/1946 · Border Feud/Cheyenne Takes Over/Return of the Lash/The Fighting Vigilantes/Ghost Town Renegades/Law of the Lash/Pioneer Justice/Stage to Mesa City/1947 · Dead Man's Gold/Frontier Revenge/Prairie Outlaws/1948 · Mark of the Lash/Outlaw Country/Son of a Bad Man/Son of Billy the Kid/1949 · The Daltons' Women/King of the Bullwhip/1950 · The Thundering Trail/The Vanishing Outpost/1951 · The Black Lash/The Frontier Phantom/1952 · Hard on the Trail/1971
Television Lash of the West/53 · The Life and Legend of Wyatt Earp/59

Lawton, Charles, Jr. (1904-65) · Cinematographer. Lawton began in the mid-20s as a camera assistant at First National. He moved up to camera operator at MGM and Paramount, and by 1937 was a cinematographer. He was adept enough at atmospheric black-and-white (The Lady from Shanghai), but unsurpassed in his appreciation of and feel-

ing for colour, especially when shooting in the open air. It was Lawton who photographed the changing landscapes of Two Rode Together, Lawton who lent visual magnificence to three great films of Boetticher. JL
The Untamed Breed/1948 · The Walking Hills/The Doolins of Oklahoma/1949 · The Nevadan/1950 · Santa Fe/Stage to Tucson/Man in the Saddle/1951 · Hangman's Knot/Last of the Comanches/1952 · They Rode West/1954 · Jubal/The Tall T/1956 · 3:10 to Yuma/1957 · Cowboy/Gunman's Walk/1958 · Ride Lonesome/Comanche Station/1959 · Two Rode Together/1961

LeMay, Alan (1899-1964) · A prolific Western novelist, a screenwriter, and on one occasion only a director, LeMay wrote the novel which lies behind John Ford's great Western, The Searchers. At the climax of that film, Wayne cradles Natalie Wood in his arms, all rancour gone, and takes her home. It was a different story with LeMay. His hero has mistaken an Indian girl for the lost Debbie, and she shoots him dead. People will argue for ever as to whether Ford's darkest work should have gone to that last dreadful extreme. John Huston's The Unforgiven, dealing with a similar racial theme, was also based on a LeMay novel. JL
(co-sc) North West Mounted Police/1940 · (novel only) Along Came Jones/1945 · (co-sc) San Antonio/1946 · The Gunfighters/(co-sc) Cheyenne/1947 · Tap Roots/1948 · (st) The Walking Hills/(p) Trailin' West/(p) The Sundowners/1949 · (d) High Lonesome/(st, co-sc) Rocky Mountain/1950 · The Vanishing American/1955 · (novel only) The Searchers/1956 · (novel only) The Unforgiven/1959
Television Cheyenne/55

Leone, Sergio (b 1929) · Director, aka Bob Robertson. Born in Naples, into a family deeply involved in Italian cinema (father a

Fritz Lang

director, mother an actress), Leone worked his apprenticeship with neo-realist directors before becoming an assistant on over 50 films (many of them American, such as Ben Hur, The Nun's Story and Helen of Troy). His first films as a director were 'peplums' (including The Colossus of Rhodes and the Italian version of Sodom and Gomorrah, made with Aldrich – with whom he did not get on). His first Western (the twenty-fifth Italian Western) revived a genre which was already dying, and used sets in Almeria which looked like a lived-in ghost town: his breakthrough was to redefine the Western within an authentically Italian cultural context, rather than trying to 'copy' American originals. Paradoxically, this led to international success; after his 'dollars' trilogy, Leone cut loose from the Cinecittà Western and made his masterpiece, C'era una volta il west, partly on American locations such as Monument Valley. The set for 'Flagstone' cost more than the whole of Per un pugno di dollari. 'They call me the father of the Spaghetti Western,' he says today. 'If so, how many sons of bitches have I spawned!' CF
(co-sc) Per un pugno di dollari/1964 · (co-st, co-sc) Per qualche dollaro in più/1965 · (co-st, co-sc) Il buono, il brutto, il cattivo/1966 · (co-st, co-sc) C'era una volta il west/1968 · (co-st, co-sc) Giù la testa/1971 · (st, supervised only) Il mio nome è Nessuno/1973 · (supervised only) Un genio, due compari, un pollo/1975

Lewis, Joseph H. (b 1907) · Director. Lewis began and ended his career in Westerns, though the end came not as sometimes thought with Terror in a Texas Town but on television, and indeed the 'One Killer on Ice' segment of Gunsmoke, along with 'Boots With My Father's Name' and 'Night of the Wolf' from The Big Valley, are as curious as anything in the Lewis canon. Like all Lewis' films, his Westerns have an overlay of decided weirdness, express a dark and melancholic vision of the world and overcome the intractability of much of their material by means of remarkable formal inventiveness. The moving camera of A Lawless Street, Sterling Hayden fighting a duel with a harpoon in Terror in a Texas Town, the melancholy of 7th Cavalry and the fascinating use of space in The Halliday Brand are all, in their different ways, unforgettable. JP
Courage of the West/The Singing Outlaw/1937 · Border Wolves/The Last Stand/1938 · Two-Fisted Rangers/1939 · Blazing Six Shooters/Texas Stagecoach/The Man from

Tumbleweeds/The Return of Wild Bill/1940 ·
Arizona Cyclone/1941 · The Silver Bullet/
The Boss of Hangtown Mesa/1942 · A
Lawless Street/1955 · 7th Cavalry/1956 ·
The Halliday Brand/1957 · Terror in a
Texas Town/1958
Television *The Rifleman/58 · Gunsmoke/64 ·*
Branded/The Big Valley/65 · A Man Called
Shenandoah/66

Lyles, A.C. (b 1918) · Producer. A publicity
representative with the Pine-Thomas organization from 1940, Lyles produced the first
dozen episodes of television's *Rawhide*
series, then set up his own production
company, eventually carving a small niche
for himself as a producer of B-Westerns.
Employing journeyman directors (usually
William F. Claxton, R. G. Springsteen or
Lesley Selander) and busy rather than inventive scripts, his productions relied largely on
the nostalgic charm of casts packed to the
brim with veteran character actors and over-
the-hill stars. TMi
Law of the Lawless/1963 · Stage to Thunder
Rock/Young Fury/Black Spurs/1964 · Town
Tamer/Johnny Reno/1965 · Apache
Uprising/Waco/Red Tomahawk/1966 · Fort
Utah/Hostile Guns/Arizona Bushwhackers/
1967 · Buckskin/1968
Television *Rawhide/59 · The Last Day/75*

M

McCoy, Horace (1897-1955) · Writer.
Tennessee-born McCoy wrote for Dallas
newspapers before moving to Hollywood to
start an acting career in 1931, a period he
documented in his most famous novel, *They*
Shoot Horses, Don't They? McCoy wrote
hard-boiled stories about Captain Jerry
Frost, an airborne Texas Ranger, for *Black*
Mask, and two of his earliest pictures, *Hold*
the Press and *Speed Wings*, cast cowboy hero
Tim McCoy (no relation) as a reporter and

aviator respectively. Writer McCoy turned
out scripts for several studios, though his
best was probably *The Lusty Men*, directed
by Nicholas Ray for RKO, which updated the
myths of the genre in a rodeo setting, with a
strong female lead and a strain of documentary authenticity. BA
(co-sc) Trail of the Lonesome Pine/1936 ·
(co-sc) Texas Rangers Ride Again/1940 ·
(co-sc) Texas/Wild Geese Calling/1941 ·
Valley of the Sun/1942 · (co-sc) The
Fabulous Texan/1947 · (co-sc) Bronco Buster/
(co-sc) Montana Belle/1951 · (co-sc) The
Lusty Men/1952 · Rage at Dawn/(co-sc)
Road to Denver/Texas Lady/1955
Television *Maverick/67*

McCoy, 'Colonel' Tim (1891-1978) · Actor.
'Gentleman Tim Madigan – All of him is
very polite' is the description on a 'Wanted'
poster of the character McCoy plays in *Aces*
and Eights – which well encapsulates the
overall McCoy persona: polite, correct,
true, morally just – somehow fearsomely so.
A flashing glance from his powerful eyes
would put you on the spot. He rarely needed
to use his guns or gallop off in a chase.
Coming into movies via the unique route of
being a government agent for Indian affairs
and serving as advisor on *The Covered*
Wagon (1923) and *The Vanishing American*
(1925), McCoy was something of a pedago-
gue compared to the likes of Hart (old-time
thespian) and Gibson, Mix and Maynard
(real life cowboys or circus performers). He
could ride and shoot well enough – but these
were never the attributes which distinguished him; instead a seriousness of purpose, a moral rectitude, animated even the
dumbest of movies he found himself in. His
career began on the highest possible note in a
series of MGM super-productions, whose
emphasis was on historical accuracy and
legitimate spectacle rather than formulaic
action, and effectively ended some sixteen

Tim McCoy

years later after a string of work for Poverty
Row studios like Puritan and Victory. Some
remarkable films resulted: *End of the Trail*, a
widely admired pro-Indian narrative over
which he reputedly had creative control, and
such fascinating and downbeat works as
Lightnin' Bill Carson and *Aces and Eights*,
which have much of the sombre quality of
Hart at his most remorseless. On minute
budgets, and at a time when flamboyant
singing cowboys were invading the range,
these two films especially eschew virtually
every marketable ingredient, concentrating
instead on miniature tragedies with the
McCoy character as helpless justicier whose
'rightness' and control over his own life is of
no value to the other people whose lives his
intersects. So persuasive, intriguing and singular are his talent and manifest thematic
concerns that one feels a complete archeo-
logical dig is required before his true nature
and value will be appreciated. He was one of
a rare breed – just how rare awaits complete
authentication. CW

Lash LaRue

Sergio Leone

Joseph H. Lewis

A. C. Lyles

Joel McCrea

The Thundering Herd/1925 · *War Paint*/
1926 · *Winners of the Wilderness*/*California*/
The Frontiersman/*Spoilers of the West*/1927 ·
The Law of the Range/*Wyoming*/*Riders of
the Dark*/*Beyond the Sierras*/1928 · *Morgan's
Last Raid*/*The Overland Telegraph*/*The
Desert Rider*/*A Night on the Range*/*Sioux
Blood*/1929 · *The Indians Are Coming*/1930
· *The One Way Trail*/*Shotgun Pass*/*The
Fighting Marshal*/1931 · *Daring Danger*/*End
of the Trail*/*The Riding Tornado*/*Texas
Cyclone*/*Two Fisted Law*/*Cornered*/*The
Fighting Fool*/*Fighting for Justice*/*The
Western Code*/1932 · *Man of Action*/*Rusty
Rides Alone*/*Silent Men*/*The Whirlwind*/
1933 · *Beyond the Law*/*The Prescott Kid*/*The
Westerner*/1934 · *Justice of the Range*/*Square
Shooter*/*Law Beyond the Range*/*The Outlaw
Deputy*/*The Revenge Rider*/*Riding Wild*/
Fighting Shadows/*The Man from Guntown*/
Bulldog Courage/1935 · *Lightnin' Bill
Carson*/*Aces and Eights*/*The Lion's Den*/
Roarin' Guns/*Border Caballero*/*Ghost Patrol*/
The Traitor/1936 · *Code of the Rangers*/*Two
Gun Justice*/*West of Rainbow's End*/*Phantom
Ranger*/*Outlaws' Paradise*/*Lightning Carson
Rides Again*/*Six-Gun Trail*/1938 · *Trigger*

Fingers/*Straight Shooter*/*Code of the Cactus*/
The Fighting Renegade/*Texas Wildcats*/1939
· *Frontier Crusader*/*Arizona Gang Busters*/
Gun Code/*Riders of Black Mountain*/*Texas
Renegades*/1940 · *Outlaws of the Rio
Grande*/*The Texas Marshal*/*Arizona Bound*/
Gunman from Bodie/*Forbidden Trails*/1941 ·
Below the Border/*Down Texas Way*/*Riders of
the West*/*Ghost Town Law*/*West of the Law*/
1942 · *Run of the Arrow*/1957 · *Requiem for
a Gunfighter*/1965
Television *The Tim McCoy Show*/53

McCrea, Joel (b 1905) · Actor. From small
parts in silent films McCrea reached stardom in the early 30s. For a while he moved
easily between thrillers, crazy comedy and
social drama, but he was tall, rugged and
physically ideal for outdoor action movies,
and from around 1946 seldom appeared
outside the Western. But he was always a
Western actor – never a cowboy star. He had
much in common with Randolph Scott.
Each had imposing presence, was slow of
speech and of manifest integrity, and each
had a way with a cutting line, yet in McCrea
there was a basic geniality which set him
apart. Fittingly, in *Ride the High Country*, two
great careers reached their climax together.
After that, two touching exercises in nostal-
gia completed McCrea's score. JL
The Silver Horde/1930 · *Scarlet River*/1933 ·
Wells Fargo/1937 · *Union Pacific*/1939 ·
Buffalo Bill/1944 · *The Virginian*/1946 ·
Ramrod/1947 · *Four Faces West*/1948 ·
South of St Louis/*Colorado Territory*/*Stars in
My Crown*/*The Outriders*/1949 · *Saddle
Tramp*/*Frenchie*/1950 · *Cattle Drive*/
Hollywood Story/1951 · *The San Francisco
Story*/1952 · *Lone Hand*/*Border River*/1953 ·
Black Horse Canyon/*Stranger on Horseback*/
1954 · *Wichita*/1955 · *The First Texan*/1956
· *The Oklahoman*/*Trooper Hook*/*Gunsight
Ridge*/*The Tall Stranger*/*Cattle Empire*/1957
· *Fort Massacre*/*The Gunfight at Dodge City*/

1958 · *Ride the High Country*/1962 · *Cry
Blood, Apache*/1970 · *Mustang Country*/
1976
Television *Wichita Town*/59 · *Wagon
Train*/65

MacDonald, Ian (b 1914) · No actor ever
had his entrance built up as long and as
carefully as Ian MacDonald in *High Noon*.
He played Frank Miller, the pathological
killer whose return the town awaits with
long-drawn-out anxiety, and when at last he
appeared, a dark, heavy man barely containing his violence, one saw just why they were
worried. The real MacDonald was rather
different. He had been a teacher in Montana;
then trained as an actor at the Pasadena
Playhouse. He played assorted villains,
gamblers, Indians (Geronimo in *Taza, Son of
Cochise*), and wrote the occasional script. JL
Secrets of the Wasteland/*They Died with
their Boots On*/1941 · *North of the Rockies*/
1942 · *Ramrod*/*Pursued*/1947 · *The Man
from Colorado*/1948 · *Montana*/1949 ·
Comanche Territory/*Colt .45*/1950 · *The
Texas Rangers*/*New Mexico*/*Thunder in
God's Country*/*Flaming Feather*/1951 · *High
Noon*/*The Savage*/*Toughest Man in
Arizona*/*Hiawatha*/1952 · *The Silver
Whip*/*A Perilous Journey*/*Taza, Son of
Cochise*/1953 · *Johnny Guitar*/*Apache*/
Timberjack/1954 · (co-sc) *The Lonesome
Trail*/(co-st, co-sc only) *The Silver Star*/1955
· *Stagecoach to Fury*/*Two Gun Lady*/1956 ·
Duel at Apache Wells/1957 · *Warlock*/
Money, Women and Guns/1959
Television *The Adventures of Rin Tin
Tin*/55 · *The Life and Legend of Wyatt
Earp*/57

MacDonald, Joseph P. (1906-68) · Cinematographer. A camera assistant in 1921,
MacDonald served a long apprenticeship
before his first film as director of photography in 1941. In the years of waiting he had

Ian MacDonald

John McIntire

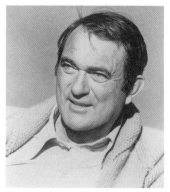

Andrew V. McLaglen

Victor McLaglen

learned well. In films like *The Dark Corner* he showed a mastery of urban realism, while he gave an airy freshness to *My Darling Clementine*. He photographed a dozen Westerns, from *Broken Lance* onwards working in colour, and in his last decade making some indifferent films look rather better than they merited. JL

My Darling Clementine/1946 · *Yellow Sky*/1948 · *Viva Zapata!*/1952 · *Broken Lance*/1954 · *The True Story of Jesse James*/1957 · *The Fiend Who Walked the West*/1958 · *Warlock*/1959 · *Rio Conchos/Invitation to a Gunfighter*/1964 · *The Reward*/1965 · *Alvarez Kelly*/1966 · *(co-c) McKenna's Gold*/1968

McGuane, Thomas (b 1939) · Writer. A successful novelist probably inspired to the screenwriter's trade by such close Montana friends and neighbours as Sam Peckinpah, Warren Oates and Peter Fonda, McGuane brings to a loose trilogy of late Westerns a distinctive absurdist sensibility and a relish for the quirky tang of both archaic and regional dialogue patterns. Each of these films presents imaginative permutations of three sets of stock characters – ranchers, rustlers and a hired regulator – though it is the colourful flesh on this structural skeleton which most marks McGuane's art. His only directorial credit, *92 in the Shade*, is outside the genre, but its Florida location and face-off dynamics combined to earn it the tag of 'Key Western'. PT

Rancho Deluxe/1974 · *The Missouri Breaks*/1976 · *(co-sc) Tom Horn*/1980

McIntire, John (b 1907) · Actor. McIntire's air of easy domination and his incisive speech bore witness to the stage actor and radio announcer he had been. He was tall, balding and wry of expression, and if in his Westerns he was occasionally villainous, one was always aware of a very pleasant man trying hard to be nasty. But more often he stood for virtue, as, notably, in television's *Wagon Train*, where he took over the lead from Ward Bond on the latter's death. JL

Black Bart/River Lady/Red Canyon/1948 · *Ambush*/1949 · *Saddle Tramp/Winchester '73*/1950 · *Westward the Women*/1951 · *Horizons West/The Lawless Breed*/1952 · *The Mississippi Gambler/War Arrow*/1953 · *Apache/Four Guns to the Border/The Yellow Mountain/The Far Country/Stranger on Horseback*/1954 · *The Kentuckian/The Spoilers*/1955 · *Backlash*/1956 · *The Tin Star*/1957 · *The Light in the Forest/The Gunfight at Dodge City*/1958 · *Seven Ways from Sundown/Flaming Star*/1960 · *Two Rode Together*/1961 · *Rough Night in Jericho*/1967 · *Rooster Cogburn*/1975 Television *Cimarron City/Wanted: Dead or Alive/Wagon Train/Wichita Town/Dick Powell's Zane Grey Theatre*/59 · *Laramie/The Overland Trail*/60 · *Bonanza/The Americans*/61 · *Daniel Boone*/65 · *A Man Called Shenandoah*/66 · *The Virginian/Dundee and the Culhane*/67 · *Dirty Sally*/74 · *The New Daughters of Joshua Cabe*/76 · *Young Maverick*/79

McLaglen, Andrew V. (b 1920) · Director. Son of actor Victor McLaglen, he is sometimes considered an heir to the Western tradition of John Ford. An assistant to Ford in the late 40s and early 50s, McLaglen was prolific in television, directing multiple episodes of several popular Western series. Among his films *McLintock!* is representative; it perpetuates the John Wayne persona and mixes broad levels of humour with traditional explorations of the genre. His later Westerns, however, follow patterns of violent anti-heroes and often have elements of self-parody. JD

Gun the Man Down/1956 · *McLintock!*/1963 · *Shenandoah/The Rare Breed*/1965 · *The Way West/The Ballad of Josie*/1967 · *Bandolero!*/1968 · *The Undefeated*/1969 · *Chisum/One More Train to Rob*/1970 · *(p) Something Big/Fools' Parade*/1971 · *Cahill United States Marshal*/1973 · *The Last Hard Men*/1976 Television *Gunsmoke/Have Gun, Will Travel*/56 · *Rawhide*/59 · *Gunslinger*/61 · *The Virginian*/64 · *Hec Ramsey*/74 · *Banjo Hackett: Roamin' Free*/76 · *Louis L'Amour's 'The Shadow Riders'*/82

McLaglen, Victor (1886-1959) · Actor. Arriving in Hollywood in the 20s after a few British films, McLaglen became a reliable character actor and occasional lead. From

Barton MacLane

silent days he worked often with John Ford, and near the end gave three glorious performances in the cavalry trilogy. In it, he was either Sergeant Mulcahy or Sergeant Quincannon, but always the same McLaglen – enormous, swaggering, crafty, but a child at heart, as witness the wonderful moment in *Yellow Ribbon* when Mildred Natwick marches him off to the brig, a picture of injured docility. JL

The Beloved Brute/1924 · *Winds of Chance/The Hunted Woman*/1925 · *Not Exactly Gentlemen*/1931 · *The Gay Caballero*/1932 · *Klondike Annie*/1936 · *Let Freedom Ring!*/1939 · *Michigan Kid*/1947 · *Fort Apache*/1948 · *She Wore a Yellow Ribbon*/1949 · *Rio Grande*/1950 · *Many Rivers to Cross*/1955 Television *Have Gun, Will Travel*/58 · *Rawhide*/59

MacLane, Barton (1902-69) · Actor. For many years MacLane was the Warner Bros. all-purpose heavy. He was slow-moving, thick-set and menacing, and did not give the impression of an intellectual. Yet before his long stint at the studios he had written and starred in a Broadway play (*Rendezvous*, 1932), an achievement which would have roused the suspicions of most of the characters he later played. His finest Western part was perhaps in *The Treasure of the Sierra Madre* – as the crooked contractor, he oozed false bonhomie from every pore. JL

Man of the Forest/To the Last Man/The Thundering Herd/The Lone Cowboy/1933 · *The Last Round-Up*/1934 · *God's Country and the Woman*/1936 · *Gold Is Where You Find It*/1938 · *Stand Up and Fight*/1939 · *Melody Ranch*/1940 · *Western Union*/1941 · *Song of Texas*/1943 · *Santa Fe Uprising*/1946 · *Cheyenne*/1947 · *The Treasure of the Sierra Madre/Relentless/The Dude Goes West/Silver River*/1948 · *Bandit Queen*/1950 · *Best of the Badmen/Drums in the Deep South/Bugles in the Afternoon*/1951 · *The Half-Breed*/1952 · *Jack Slade/Kansas Pacific/Cow Country*/1953 · *Rails into Laramie/Jubilee Trail/Hell's Outpost*/1954 · *Treasure of Ruby Hills/The Silver Star/Last of the Desperados*/1955 · *Backlash/The Naked Gun*/1956 · *Sierra Stranger/Naked in the Sun/Hell's Crossroads*/1957 · *Frontier Gun*/1958 · *Gunfighters of Abilene*/1959 · *Noose for a Gunman*/1960 · *Law of the Lawless*/1963 · *The Rounders*/1964 · *Town Tamer*/1965 · *Arizona Bushwhackers*/1967 · *Buckskin*/1968 Television *Cheyenne*/56 · *Black Saddle*/59 · *The Outlaws/The Overland Trail*/60 · · *Laramie*/62 · *Gunsmoke*/66 · *Hondo*/67

McNally, Stephen (b 1913) · Actor, aka Horace McNally. Of saturnine aspect and laconic manner, he tended to be cast as a villain, most notably as James Stewart's deep-dyed brother in *Winchester '73*, and strikingly nasty also in the lesser known *Devil's Canyon*. The undertone of neurosis in his screen personality lent depth to ostensibly sympathetic characters like the gambler in *Apache Drums*, and he could summon up some unexpected geniality for occasional semi-humorous roles, as in *The Man from Bitter Ridge*. TP

The Harvey Girls/1945 · *Winchester '73/Wyoming Mail/Apache Drums*/1950 · *Duel at Silver Creek*/1952 · *Devil's Canyon/The Stand at Apache River*/1953 · *The Man from Bitter Ridge/Tribute to a Bad Man*/1955 · *Hell's Crossroads*/1957 · *The Fiend Who Walked the West*/1958 · *Hell Bent for Leather*/1959 · *Requiem for a Gunfighter*/1965

Television *Dick Powell's Zane Grey Theatre*/56 · *Wagon Train/Texas John Slaughter/The Texan*/59 · *Riverboat/Laramie*/60 · *Rawhide*/61 · *The Virginian*/63 · *Branded*/65 · *The Iron Horse/The Big Valley*/66 · *Gunsmoke/The Guns of Will Sonnett*/67 · *The Men from Shiloh*/71

McQueen, Steve (1930-80) · Actor. After a series of roles in low-budget films and television, he gained stardom as a bounty hunter on *Wanted: Dead or Alive*, then became one of the most popular film personalities of the late 1960s and through the 70s. He specialized in roles involving the most gruelling physical action, taking pride in performing many of his own stunts. Despite a somewhat boyish appearance, he played tough, durable loners who 'never quit'. Persevering through seemingly impossible physical challenges, his dogged courage is opposed to the compromised and cynical values of society. His most relaxed role was that of the aging, but still rebellious, rodeo star in Peckinpah's *Junior Bonner*. DG

The Magnificent Seven/1960 · *Nevada Smith*/1965 · *Junior Bonner*/1972 · *Tom Horn*/1980

Television *Tales of Wells Fargo/Trackdown/Wanted: Dead or Alive*/58

Madison, Guy (b 1922) · Actor. Born Robert Mosely, the lanky, fair-haired actor incarnated boyishly charming, young officer types, often with a stubborn streak. His film career never took off but he achieved stardom in television as the lead in one of the first major Western series, *Wild Bill Hickok*. His comic sidekick was Andy Devine and the series ran for 113 episodes from 1951 to 1958. The two of them also played in the radio version of the series, which ran simultaneously. Madison ended his career in European Bond-imitations and guesting in Italian Westerns. PW

Massacre River/1949 · *Drums in the Deep South*/1951 · *The Charge at Feather River*/1953 · *The Command*/1954 · *The Last Frontier*/1955 · *The Beast of Hollow Mountain/Reprisal!*/1956 · *The Hard Man*/1957 · *Bullwhip*/1958 · *Shatterhand*/1964 · *Jennie Lees ha una nuova pistola*/1965 · *I cinque della vendetta*/1966 · *Il ritorno di Ringo/Sette Winchester per un massacro*/1967 · *I lunghi giorni dell'odio*/1968

Television *The Adventures of Wild Bill Hickok*/51 · *Wagon Train*/57 · *Dick Powell's Zane Grey Theatre*/61

Mahoney, Jock (b 1919) · Actor, aka Jacques J. O'Mahoney, Jock O'Mahoney, Jack Mahoney. When Jock started out in movies he wanted to be an actor, but with his first-class physique he ended up as a stunt double for several big stars. It was during this period that he met actor Charles Starrett and became his stunt double, and with his help started getting small acting parts. In 1951 his big break came when he was picked to star in a new action television Western series, *The Range Rider*. This led to several starring roles. TM

The Fighting Frontiersman/1946 · *The Stranger from Ponca City/South of the Chisholm Trail*/1947 · *Blazing Across the Pecos*/1948 · *Horsemen of the Sierras/Renegades of the Sage/Rim of the Canyon/The Doolins of Oklahoma/Bandits of Eldorado/The Blazing Trail/Frontier Marshal/Frontier Outpost*/1949 · *The Nevadan/Cow Town/Texas Dynamo/Punchy Cowpunchers/Lightning Guns/Cody of the Pony Express/Roar of the Iron Horse/The Kangaroo Kid*/1950 · *Santa Fe/The Texas Rangers/Pecos River*/1951 · *Smokey Canyon/The Hawk of Wild River/Junction City/The Rough Tough West/The Kid from Broken Gun/Laramie Mountains*/1952 · *Overland Pacific*/1954 · *A Day of Fury/Showdown at Abilene*/1956 · *Joe Dakota/Slim Carter*/1957 · *Last of the Fast Guns*/1958 · *Money, Women and Guns*/1959

Television *The Range Rider*/51 · *Wagon Train/Rawhide/Yancy Derringer*/57 · *Laramie*/59 · *Daniel Boone*/64

Malden, Karl (b 1914) · Actor, born Mladen Sekulovich. He made his first movie in 1940, but came to prominence with his supporting roles in Elia Kazan productions in the early 1950s. His rugged face and bulbous nose suited him for the role of heavy, though he never seemed entirely at home in period films. JC

The Gunfighter/1950 · *The Hanging Tree*/1959 · *One-Eyed Jacks*/1960 · *How the West Was Won*/1962 · *Cheyenne Autumn*/1964 · *Nevada Smith*/1965 · *The Adventures of Bullwhip Griffin*/1967 · *Blue*/1968 · *Wild Rovers*/1971

Malone, Dorothy (b 1925) · Actress. Her film career has two distinct periods. Spotted

Stephen McNally

Steve McQueen

Guy Madison

Jock Mahoney

by a talent scout in 1943 she was signed up by RKO, but soon moved to Warner Bros. However, despite her obvious talents as an actress her 'nice girl' roles brought little esteem. Likewise, her Western performances as romantic interest were no showcase for her real talents. In 1955 a change of image also saw a change of hair colour (from brunette to blonde), and her roles began to reflect this change – superb, both as a woman bent on revenge in *Warlock* and as the centre of sexual tension in *The Last Sunset*. JH
Two Guys from Texas/1948 · *South of St Louis*/*Colorado Territory*/1949 · *The Nevadan*/1950 · *Saddle Legion*/*The Bushwhackers*/1951 · *Law and Order*/*Jack Slade*/1953 · *The Lone Gun*/*Tall Man Riding*/1954 · *Five Guns West*/*Gun Point*/1955 · *Pillars of the Sky*/*Tension at Table Rock*/1956 · *Quantez*/1957 · *Warlock*/1959 · *The Last Sunset*/1961

Mann, Anthony (1906-67) · Director. The Westerns Mann made during the 50s, several of them starring James Stewart, make him by any reckoning one of the key directors of the genre. Mann began as a director of low-budget thrillers, and in a sense the protagonists of his Westerns are related to those of the film noir, in that they are frequently haunted by the past, and concomitantly the past is apt to catch up with them. The modernity of Mann's Westerns derives from the individualistic ethos of his central characters; yet while these figures show a determination in pursuing their goals which sometimes verges on the psychopathic, they are ultimately heroes, not anti-heroes, and show themselves ready to act for the common good (even if, as in *The Far Country*, it takes the death of a friend to provoke a change of demeanour).

Similarly, Mann is at heart a traditionalist, whose films show a love of sheer storytelling and tend to be constructed (the clearest example is *Winchester '73*) after an elaborately formal design; often this involves a physical quest or journey, the stages of which symbolically parallel the protagonists' progress toward self-knowledge. Many of his Westerns show a strongly physical response to landscape and topography, with *The Naked Spur* taking place entirely in exterior settings. Side by side with this, though, went a love, perhaps inherited from his background in the theatre, for complex staging of interior scenes (see especially *The Tin Star*). Mann was a consummate film-maker for whom the Western provided the ideal arena. TP
Devil's Doorway/*Winchester '73*/*The Furies*/1950 · *Bend of the River*/1951 · *The Naked Spur*/1952 · *The Far Country*/1954 · *The Man from Laramie*/*The Last Frontier*/1955 · *The Tin Star*/1957 · *Man of the West*/1958 · *Cimarron*/1960

Marin, Edwin L. (1899-1951) · Director. Marin, best known for the atmospheric films noirs *Johnny Angel*, *Nocturne* and *Race Street*, settled into the Western at the end of his career; indeed, *Fort Worth* was his last film. In his Westerns, many of which star Randolph Scott, the direction tends towards the anonymous and merely efficient; but notable are *Tall in the Saddle*, which is unusually energetic, and *Abilene Town*, a taut and pacey account of Randolph Scott cleaning up the famous town at the end of the Chisholm Trail. JP
Gold Rush Maisie/1940 · *Tall in the Saddle*/1944 · *Abilene Town*/1946 · *The Younger Brothers*/1948 · *Canadian Pacific*/*Fighting Man of the Plains*/1949 · *Colt .45*/*The Cariboo Trail*/*Sugarfoot*/*Raton Pass*/1950 · *Fort Worth*/1951

Marshall, George (1891-1975) · A notable director of comedy – Marshall worked with Laurel and Hardy and later Bob Hope – his comedy Westerns are his greatest contribution to the genre. He several times directed Tom Mix at Fox in the early 20s, but it was his first major sound Western, *Destry Rides Again*, for which he is most remembered. His other comedy Westerns include *Fancy Pants*, a remake of *Ruggles of Red Gap*, starring Bob Hope, and the Glenn Ford films *The Sheepman* and *Advance to the Rear*. JH
(co-st, co-sc, co-p only) *Love's Lariat*/1916 · (co-sc) *The Man from Montana*/(co-sc) *Border Wolves*/1917 · *Ruth of the Rockies*/*Prairie Trails*/1920 · *Hands Off*/(sc) *A Ridin' Romeo*/*After Your Own Heart*/1921 · *Haunted Valley*/*Don Quickshot of the Rio Grande*/*Where Is This West?*/*Men in the Raw*/1923 · *Wild Gold*/1934 · *Destry Rides Again*/1939 · *When the Daltons Rode*/1940 · *Texas*/1941 · *Valley of the Sun*/1942 · *Riding High*/1943 · *Fancy Pants*/*Never a Dull Moment*/1950 · *The Savage*/1952 · *Red Garters*/*Destry*/1954 · *The Second Greatest Sex*/1955 · *Pillars of the Sky*/*The Guns of Fort Petticoat*/1956 · *The Sheepman*/1958 · *How the West Was Won* ('The Railroad')/1962 · *Advance to the Rear*/1963
Television *Daniel Boone*/64 · *Cade's County*/71

Martin, Strother (1919-80) · A rotund character actor, Martin frequently played the villain's sidekick or a secondary heavy, for example one of Liberty Valance's henchmen. Grizzled and ragtag, Martin often invested even his bit parts with a manic edge. Sam Peckinpah memorably teamed him with L. Q. Jones as demented members of the band of hired cut-throats pursuing the Wild Bunch – few actors have kissed a gun barrel with such wild-eyed lust as Martin did – and as the treacherous partners Cable Hogue traps in a pit of rattlesnakes. Despite his few and unmemorable lead roles, Martin developed a cult following among young

Karl Malden

Dorothy Malone

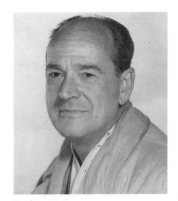
Anthony Mann

George Marshall

movie and television audiences. BA
Drum Beat/1954 · *The Black Whip*/*Johnny Concho*/1956 · *Copper Sky*/*Black Patch*/1957 · *Cowboy*/1958 · *The Horse Soldiers*/*The Wild and the Innocent*/1959 · *The Deadly Companions*/1961 · *The Man Who Shot Liberty Valance*/1962 · *McLintock!*/*Showdown*/1963 · *Invitation to a Gunfighter*/1964 · *Shenandoah*/*The Sons of Katie Elder*/*Nevada Smith*/1965 · *An Eye for an Eye*/1966 · *The Wild Bunch*/*True Grit*/*Butch Cassidy and the Sundance Kid*/1969 · *The Ballad of Cable Hogue*/1970 · *Fools' Parade*/*Hannie Caulder*/1971 · *Pocket Money*/1972 · *Rooster Cogburn*/1975 · *The Great Scout and Cathouse Thursday*/1976 · *The Villain*/1979 Television *Gunsmoke*/55 · *Have Gun, Will Travel*/57 · *Broken Arrow*/*Trackdown*/*Jefferson Drum*/58 · *The Rebel*/*The Texan*/*Black Saddle*/*Hotel de Paree*/59 · *The Dakotas*/63 · *Rawhide*/*Bonanza*/*The Virginian*/65 · *The Big Valley*/*A Man Called Shenandoah*/66 · *The Iron Horse*/*The Road West*/*The Guns of Will Sonnett*/67 · *Daniel Boone*/69 · *Nichols*/72

Marvin, Lee (1924-87) · Actor. Marvin's image as a psychotically violent heavy was established in non-starring roles in numerous action pictures during the 50s. Thrillers such as *The Big Heat* possibly served his image best but many of these early roles were in Westerns, with Boetticher's *Seven Men from Now* the most notable. The 60s saw this image capitalized upon in *The Man Who Shot Liberty Valance* with a near-symbolic version of generic villainy and in *Cat Ballou*, where his villain became a figure of fun. One of his finest yet gentlest performances, against his earlier image, is in *Monte Walsh*. TR
Duel at Silver Creek/*Hangman's Knot*/1952 · *Gun Fury*/*Seminole*/*The Stranger Wore a Gun*/1953 · *The Raid*/*Bad Day at Black Rock*/1954 · *Pillars of the Sky*/*Seven Men from Now*/1956 · *The Missouri Traveler*/

1957 · *The Comancheros*/1961 · *The Man Who Shot Liberty Valance*/1962 · *Cat Ballou*/1965 · *The Professionals*/1966 · *Paint Your Wagon*/1969 · *Monte Walsh*/1970 · *Pocket Money*/1972 · *The Spikes Gang*/1974 · *The Great Scout and Cathouse Thursday*/1976 · *Death Hunt*/1981
Television *Wagon Train*/60 · *The Americans*/61 · *Bonanza*/*The Virginian*/62

Maté, Rudolph (1898-1964) · Director. Born in Poland, trained in Hungary on Korda pictures, he became Karl Freund's assistant in Germany and reached the top of his profession as a cinematographer in France, shooting Dreyer's *La Passion de Jeanne d'Arc* (1928) and *Vampyr* (1932). He emigrated to Hollywood in 1935 where he worked with Hitchcock, René Clair and Lubitsch, as well as being responsible for the look of *Gilda* (1946). He started directing in 1947, making some respectable thrillers (*D.O.A.*, 1949; *Union Station*, 1950), many low budget action films and a few Westerns. The nervous energy animating *The Violent Men* and the atmospheric jungle-scapes of *The Far Horizons* show there was more to him than emerges in most of his surprisingly conventional directorial efforts. He ended his career making Italian adventure films. PW
Branded/1950 · *The Mississippi Gambler*/*The Siege at Red River*/1953 · *The Violent Men*/*The Far Horizons*/1954 · *The Rawhide Years*/1955 · *Three Violent People*/1956

Maynard, Ken (1895-1973) · Actor. Before embarking on a film career, Maynard had been a champion rodeo and circus trick rider. After signing for First National in 1926, he went on to become one of the most popular screen cowboys of the 20s and early 30s, invariably playing a role in which he was friendly, non-drinking and bashful in the presence of women. (Maynard's off-screen drinking was later to damage his career.)

Utilizing his riding talents, his films also gave a prominent role to his 'wonder horse' Tarzan. The films are also notable for their comic interludes, to which Tarzan often contributed. In the sound era his Westerns were the first to introduce musical interludes. JH
Brass Commandments/*The Man Who Won*/1923 · *Fighting Courage*/*The Demon Rider*/*$50,000 Reward*/*North Star*/1925 · *The Grey Vulture*/*The Haunted Range*/*The Range Fighter*/*Señor Daredevil*/*The Unknown Cavalier*/1926 · *The Overland Stage*/*Somewhere in Sonora*/*Land Beyond the Law*/*The Devil's Saddle*/*The Red Raiders*/*Gun Gospel*/1927 · *The Wagon Show*/*The Canyon of Adventure*/*The Upland Rider*/*Code of the Scarlet*/*The Glorious Trail*/*The Phantom City*/1928 · *Cheyenne*/*The Lawless Legion*/*The Royal Rider*/*California Mail*/*The Wagon Master*/*Senor Americano*/1929 · *Parade of the West*/*Lucky Larkin*/*Voice of Hollywood No. 9*/*The Fighting Legion*/*Mountain Justice*/*Song of the Caballero*/*Sons of the Saddle*/*Fighting Thru, or California in 1878*/1930 · *The Two Gun Man*/*Alias the Bad Man*/*The Arizona Terror*/*Range Law*/*Branded Men*/*The Pocatello Kid*/1931 · *The Sunset Trail*/*Texas Gunfighter*/*Hell Fire Austin*/*Whistlin' Dan*/*Dynamite Ranch*/*Come On, Tarzan*/*Between Fighting Men*/*Tombstone Canyon*/1932 · *Drum Taps*/*The Phantom Thunderbolt*/*The Lone Avenger*/*King of the Arena*/(d) *The Fiddlin' Buckaroo*/*The Trail Drive*/*Strawberry Roan*/*Fargo Express*/*Gun Justice*/1933 · *Wheels of Destiny*/*Honor of the Range*/(st) *Smoking Guns*/*In Old Santa Fe*/*Mystery Mountain*/1934 · (st) *Western Frontier*/*Western Courage*/*Lawless Riders*/(st) *Heir to Trouble*/1935 · *The Cattle Thief*/*Avenging Waters*/*Heroes of the Range*/*The Fugitive Sheriff*/1936 · *Boots of Destiny*/*Trailing Trouble*/1937 · *Whirlwind Horseman*/*Six Shootin' Sheriff*/1938 · *Flaming Lead*/1939 · *Death*

Strother Martin

Lee Marvin

Rudolph Maté

Ken Maynard

Virginia Mayo

Rides the Range/Phantom Rancher/Lightning Strikes West/1940 · Wild Horse Stampede/ The Law Rides Again/Blazing Guns/Death Valley Rangers/1943 · Harmony Trail/ Westward Bound/Arizona Whirlwind/1944

Mayo, Virginia (b 1920) · Actress. Best known for her comedy roles alongside Bob Hope and Danny Kaye, she brought a fresh-faced domestic sexuality to her characterizations. In her best films, for Walsh and Tourneur, this would be fully exploited by presenting her initially as an assertive individual who later gives up her independence. This is often symbolized by her change from contoured and tight-fitting pants into more 'feminine' apparel, as in *Along the Great Divide* and *Great Day in the Morning*. PS
Colorado Territory/1949 · Along the Great Divide/1951 · The Iron Mistress/1952 · Devil's Canyon/1953 · Great Day in the Morning/1955 · The Proud Ones/1956 · The Big Land/The Tall Stranger/1957 · Fort

Dobbs/Westbound/1958 · Young Fury/1964 · Fort Utah/1967
Television *Wagon Train/58*

Meyer, Emile (1903-87) · Actor. Throughout the 50s Meyer was one of Hollywood's finest character players. Middle-aged, tall and heavily built, quiet-voiced and serious, he played villains effectively, first making his mark as the unscrupulous rancher of *Shane*, but was never typecast as a bad man. On the other side were his sheriff in Jacques Tourneur's *Stranger on Horseback*, a timorous man who finds strength in the end, and another finely played lawman in *Gun the Man Down*. And outside Westerns, there was the priest of *Paths of Glory*. JL
Cattle Queen/1950 · Shane/1952 · Silver Lode/Drums Across the River/Stranger on Horseback/1954 · White Feather/The Tall Men/Man with the Gun/1955 · The Maverick Queen/Raw Edge/Gun the Man Down/1956 · Badlands of Montana/1957 · The Fiend Who Walked the West/Good Day for a Hanging/King of the Wild Stallions/ 1958 · Young Jesse James/1960 · Taggart/ 1964 · Hostile Guns/A Time for Killing/ 1967
Television *Dick Powell's Zane Grey Theatre/ 57 · Colt .45/58 · Bat Masterson/59 · Wichita Town/60 · The Legend of Jesse James/66*

Miles, Vera (b 1930) · Ordinarily pretty actress, whose down-to-earth practicality and toughness made her ideally suited to the role of frontier woman in Westerns. Her best genre roles were for John Ford: as Laurie, Jeffrey Hunter's frustrated love interest in *The Searchers*, memorably uncoy when confronted with her boyfriend's nudity in the bath scene; and as Hallie, who goes from illiterate waitress to senator's wife in *The Man Who Shot Liberty Valance*. Never quite

glamorous or strong enough to get Barbara Stanwyck-type lady cattle baron roles, Miles tends to play heroines who are defined almost exclusively by their relationships with strong cowboy heroes. KN
The Charge at Feather River/1953 · Wichita/ 1955 · The Searchers/1956 · The Man Who Shot Liberty Valance/1962 · The Wild Country/1970 · Molly and Lawless John/ 1972 · One Little Indian/1973 · The Castaway Cowboy/1974
Television *Rawhide/Wagon Train/Riverboat/ 59 · Dick Powell's Zane Grey Theatre/ Laramie/60 · Frontier Circus/61 · The Virginian/63 · Bonanza/66 · Gunsmoke/The Men from Shiloh/70 · Alias Smith and Jones/71 · How the West Was Won/78*

Mitchell, Thomas (1895-1962) · For many years one of Hollywood's top character actors, Mitchell had a richly enjoyable repertoire of sympathetic and deeply felt roles. His Western types tended towards the worldly wise, drink-sodden, garrulous and Irish-tinged, the best example of which is the alcoholic doctor in *Stagecoach*, for which he won an Academy Award as best supporting actor. In *The Outlaw* he played Pat Garrett, bringing a good deal of complexity to the role, and is also one of the local notables who abandon Gary Cooper at the last moment in *High Noon*. JP
Stagecoach/1939 · The Outlaw/1940 · Buffalo Bill/1944 · The Romance of Rosy Ridge/1947 · Silver River/1948 · High Noon/ 1952 · Tumbleweed/1953 · Destry/1954
Television *Dick Powell's Zane Grey Theatre/ 58 · Laramie/59 · Stagecoach West/61*

Mitchum, Robert (b 1917) · Actor. Although he is not closely identified with the genre in the way that Wayne and Fonda are, about a quarter of Mitchum's films are in fact Westerns. He began his film career in 1943 as villain to William Boyd's Hopalong

Emile Meyer

Vera Miles

Thomas Mitchell

Robert Mitchum

Tom Mix in Destry Rides Again

Cassidy series and subsequently worked with prominent genre specialists such as Howard Hawks, Henry Hathaway and Burt Kennedy. His screen persona took shape in a number of film noirs in the late 40s and early 50s but it was adaptable enough to make him a credible Western hero during the same period in *Blood on the Moon*, *The Lusty Men* and *River of No Return*. Two of his most notable Western performances are as the memory-haunted orphan from *Pursued*, that most noir of Westerns, and his replay of Dean Martin's drunken deputy from *Rio Bravo*, in Hawks' *El Dorado*. TR
Hoppy Serves a Writ/The Leather Burners/ Border Patrol/Colt Comrades/Beyond the Last Frontier/Bar 20/The Lone Star Trail/False Colors/Riders of the Deadline/1943 · Girl Rush/Nevada/1944 · West of the Pecos/1945 · Pursued/1947 · Blood on the Moon/1948 · The Red Pony/1949 · The Lusty Men/1952 · River of No Return/Track of the Cat/1954 · Man with the Gun/1955 · Bandido/1956 · The Wonderful Country/1959 · El Dorado/ 1966 · The Way West/1967 · Villa Rides/5 Card Stud/1968 · Young Billy Young/The Good Guys and the Bad Guys/1969

Mix, Tom (1880-1940) · Actor. Considered by many Western aficionados to be the greatest cowboy star of all time, Mix established the formula for the sexless, flirt and run Western which later stars, such as Autry and Rogers, were to draw upon. In the early Selig one- and two-reelers his dress conformed to the crude clothing worn by Hart and Broncho Billy. But with his move to Fox in 1917 he soon adopted the flamboyant costume of the dude or rodeo star. In complete contrast to Hart, his films at Fox emphasized daredevil stunting, furious breakneck riding on his horse Tony, and action for action's sake. By 1920 he had overtaken Hart as the most popular screen cowboy, a position that remained unchallenged until the advent of sound. In 1986 the 7th annual Tom Mix festival was held in Dubois, Pennsylvania, his home state. PS
Ranch Life in the Great Southwest/On the Little Big Horn or Custer's Last Stand/1909 · The Range Riders/An Indian Wife's Devotion/The Long Trail/The Millionaire Cowboy/The Trimming of Paradise Gulch/ Pride of the Range/1910 · Kit Carson's Wooing/In the Days of Gold/In Old

California When the Gringos Came/A Romance of the Rio Grande/The Schoolmaster of Mariposa/Western Hearts/ The Telltale Knife/Back to the Primitive/ Captain Kate/The Man from the East/1911 · Outlaw Reward/A Reconstructed Rebel/ 1912 · How It Happened/The Range Law/ Juggling with Fate/The Sheriff of Yawapai County/The Lifetimer/Pauline Cushman, the Federal Spy/A Prisoner of Cabanas/The Shotgun Man and the Stage Driver/His Father's Deputy/The Noisy Six/Religion and Gun Practice/The Wordless Message/The Law and the Outlaw/The Marshal's Capture/Songs of Truce/Sallie's Sure Shot/ Bud Doble Comes Back/Made a Coward/The Taming of Texas Pete/An Apache's Gratitude/The Stolen Moccasins/The Good Indian/Tobias Wants Out/Saved by the Pony Express/The Sheriff and the Rustler/A Muddle in Horse Thieves/A Child of the Prairie/The Escape of Jim Dolan/Local Color/1913 · The Little Sister/Shotgun Jones/ Me an' Bill/The Leopard's Foundling/In Defiance of the Law/His Fight/Wiggs Takes the Rest Cure/The Wilderness Mail/When the Cook Fell Ill/Etienne of the Glad Heart/ The Reveler/The White Mouse/Chip of the Flying U/To Be Called For/The Fifth Man/ Jim/The Lonesome Trail/The Livid Flame/ Four Minutes Late/The Real Thing in Cowboys/Hearts and Masks/The Moving Picture Cowboy/The Way of the Redman/The Mexican/The Going of the White Swan/ Jimmy Hayes and Muriel/Garrison's Finish/ Why the Sheriff Is a Bachelor/The Losing Fight/The Ranger's Romance/If I Were Young Again/Out of Petticoat Lane/The Sheriff's Reward/The Scapegoat/Your Girl and Mine/In the Days of the Thundering Herd/The Rival Stage Lines/Saved by a Watch/The Soul Mate/The Man from the East/Wade Brent Pays/Cactus Jake, Heartbreaker/Buffalo Hunting/The Lure of the Windigo/The Flower of Faith/A Militant School Ma'am/The Sheep Runners/1914 · Harold's Bad Man/Cactus Jim's Shopgirl/ The Grizzly Gulch Chariot Race/Heart's Desire/Forked Trails/Roping a Bride/Bill Haywood, Producer/Hearts of the Jungle/Slim Higgins/The Man from Texas/The Stagecoach Driver and the Girl/The Puny Soul of Peter Rand/Sagebrush Tom/The Outlaw's Bride/Jack's Pals/(d) The Legal Light/Ma's Girls/Getting a Start in Life/Mrs Murphy's Cooks/The Conversion of Smiling Tom/The Face at the Window/An Arizona Wooing/A Matrimonial Boomerang/Pals in Blue/Saved by Her Horse/The Heart of the Sheriff/With the Aid of the Law/The Parson

Who Fled West/The Foreman of Bar Z Ranch/The Child, the Dog and the Villain/The Taking of Mustang Pete/The Gold Dust and the Squaw/A Lucky Deal/Never Again/How Weary Went Wooing/The Auction Sale of Run-Down Ranch/The Range Girl and the Cowboy/Her Slight Mistake/The Girl and the Mail Bag/The Brave Deserve the Fair/The Stagecoach Guard/The Race for a Gold Mine/The Foreman's Choice/Athletic Ambitions/The Tenderfoot's Triumph/(d) The Chef at Circle G/The Impersonation of Tom/Bad Man Bobbs/On the Eagle Trail/ 1915 · The Desert Calls its Own/A Mix-Up in Movies/Making Good/The Passing of Pete/Trilby's Love Disaster/A Five-Thousand-Dollar Elopement/Along the Border/Too Many Chefs/The Man Within/The Sheriff's Duty/(sc, d) Crooked Trails/Going West to Make Good/The Cowpuncher's Peril/Taking a Chance/The Girl of Gold Gulch/Some Duel/Legal Advice/Shooting Up the Movies/ (sc, d) Local Color on the A-1 Ranch/An Angelic Attitude/A Western Masquerade/A Bear of a Story/Roping a Sweetheart/Tom's Strategy/The Taming of Grouchy Bill/The Pony Express Rider/A Corner in Water/The Raiders/The Canby Hill Outlaws/A Mistake in Rustlers/An Eventful Evening/The Way of the Redman/A Close Call/Tom's Sacrifice/ When Cupid Slipped/The Sheriff's Blunder/ Mistakes Will Happen/Twisted Trails/The Golden Thought/Starring in Western Stuff/In the Days of Daring/The Resurrection of Dan Packard/1916 · The Saddle Girth/The Luck that Jealousy Brought/The Heart of Texas Ryan/The Rustler's Vindication/Delayed in Transit/Hearts and Saddles/A Roman Cowboy/Six Cylinder Love/A Soft Tenderfoot/Durand of the Badlands/Tom and Jerry Mix/1917 · Cupid's Roundup/Six Shooter Andy/Western Blood/Ace High/ Who's Your Father?/Mr Logan, U.S.A./ Fame and Fortune/1918 · Treat 'Em Rough/ Hell-Roarin' Reform/Fighting for Gold/The Coming of the Law/The Wilderness Trail/ Rough-Riding Romance/The Speed Maniac/ The Feud/1919 · The Cyclone/The Daredevil/Desert Love/The Terror/Three Gold Coins/The Untamed/The Texan/Prairie Trails/The Road Demon/1920 · Hands Off/A Ridin' Romeo/Big Town Round-Up/ After Your Own Heart/The Night Horsemen/ The Rough Diamond/Trailin'/1921 · Sky High/Chasing the Moon/Up and Going/The Fighting Streak/For Big Stakes/Just Tony/Do and Dare/Arabia/Catch My Smoke/1922 · Romance Land/Three Jumps Ahead/Stepping Fast/Soft-Boiled/The Lone Star Ranger/Mile-A-Minute Romeo/North of Hudson Bay/Eyes

of the Forest/1923 · The Foreman of Bar Z Ranch/A Golden Thought/The Trouble Shooter/The Heart Buster/The Last of the Duanes/Oh, You Tony/Teeth/The Deadwood Coach/1924 · Riders of the Purple Sage/The Rainbow Trail/Law and the Outlaw/The Lucky Horseshoe/The Everlasting Whisper/ The Best Bad Man/1925 · The Yankee Senor/My Own Pal/Tony Runs Wild/Hard-Boiled/No Man's Gold/The Great K & A Train Robbery/The Canyon of Light/1926 · The Last Trail/The Broncho Twister/Outlaws of Red River/The Circus Ace/Tumbling River/Silver Valley/The Arizona Wildcat/ 1927 · Daredevil's Reward/A Horseman of the Plains/Hello Cheyenne/Painted Post/Son of the Golden West/King Cowboy/1928 · Outlawed/The Drifter/The Big Diamond Robbery/1929 · Rider of Death Valley/Texas Bad Man/Destry Rides Again/My Pal, the King/The Fourth Horseman/Hidden Gold/ Flaming Guns/1932 · Terror Trail/Rustler's Roundup/1933 · The Miracle Rider/1935

Montgomery, George (b 1916) · Handsome leading man of the 40s and 50s whose break in movies began when he was offered work as a stuntman. This led to small parts in several Gene Autry films. One of his first co-starring roles was in the Lone Ranger serial, where he played one of five masked Rangers. Further small parts in Roy Rogers and Gene Autry movies followed. His first starring role in a Western was in 1941 in The Cowboy and the Blonde. After World War II Montgomery resumed his movie career and throughout the 50s played the lead in a number of action Westerns. In 1958 he starred in and produced the television series Cimarron City. TM

The Singing Vagabond/1935 · Springtime in the Rockies/1937 · The Lone Ranger/Gold Mine in the Sky/Billy the Kid Returns/1938 · Rough Riders Roundup/Frontier Pony Express/ Man of Conquest/Wall Street Cowboy/The

Cisco Kid and the Lady/1939 · The Cowboy and the Blonde/Last of the Duanes/Riders of the Purple Sage/1941 · Ten Gentlemen from West Point/1942 · Belle Starr's Daughter/ 1948 · Dakota Lil/1949 · Davy Crockett, Indian Scout/The Iroquois Trail/1950 · The Texas Rangers/Indian Uprising/1951 · Cripple Creek/The Pathfinder/Jack McCall Desperado/1952 · Gunbelt/Fort Ti/1953 · Battle of Rogue River/The Lone Gun/ Masterson of Kansas/Seminole Uprising/ 1954 · Robber's Roost/1955 · Canyon River/ 1956 · Last of the Bad Men/Gun Duel in Durango/Pawnee/Black Patch/The Toughest Gun in Tombstone/1957 · Man from God's Country/Badman's Country/King of the Wild Stallions/1958 · Hostile Guns/1967
Television Wagon Train/57 · Cimarron City/58 · Alias Smith and Jones/71

Moore, Clayton (b 1914) · In his early career he switched from hero to villain and back. He was rarely the star; usually well down in the cast, he occasionally had a starring role in serials. It was not until 1949 with the coming of television that he found the role he was made for, when he put on the black mask and became the Lone Ranger. This was one of the earliest television Westerns and became an instant hit; even today to millions of people the Lone Ranger will always be Clayton Moore. TM

Kit Carson/1940 · Outlaws of Pine Ridge/ 1942 · Jesse James Rides Again/Along the Oregon Trail/1947 · Marshal of Amarillo/ Adventures of Frank and Jesse James/The Gay Amigo/1948 · The Far Frontier/1949 · Sheriff of Wichita/Frontier Investigator/ Masked Raiders/Bandits of Eldorado/The Cowboy and the Indians/Riders of the Whistling Pines/South of Death Valley/Ghost of Zorro/Frontier Marshal/1949 · Sons of New Mexico/1950 · Cyclone Fury/1951 · Son of Geronimo/Night Stage to Galveston/The Hawk of Wild River/Buffalo Bill in

George Montgomery

Clayton Moore

Tomahawk Territory/Desert Passage/
Montana Territory/Barbed Wire/Captive of
Billy the Kid/1952 · Kansas Pacific/Down
Laredo Way/1953 · Gunfighters of the
Northwest/The Black Dakotas/1954 · The
Lone Ranger/1956 · The Lone Ranger and
the Lost City of Gold/1958
Television The Lone Ranger/49

Morgan, Henry (b 1915) · Actor, born
Harry Bratsberg, sometimes billed as Harry
Morgan. Stage-trained character player,
usually seen as a top-hatted townie, either a
mayor or an ineffectual sheriff, and particularly adept at the type of comedy perfected
by Burt Kennedy in his James Garner Westerns. Often on television, most famously in
M*A*S*H*, he was a regular on the short-
lived Hec Ramsey series, thanks to an association with that show's star that went back to
The Richard Boone Show. KN
The Ox-Bow Incident/The Omaha Trail/
1942 · Yellow Sky/1948 · The Showdown/
1950 · Belle Le Grand/Bend of the River/
1951 · High Noon/Toughest Man in
Arizona/Apache War Smoke/1952 · Arena/
1953 · The Far Country/The Forty-Niners/
1954 · Backlash/1956 · Cimarron/1960 ·
How the West Was Won/1962 · Support
Your Local Sheriff!/1968 · Support Your
Local Gunfighter/Scandalous John/1971 ·
Jeremiah Johnson/1972 · The Apple
Dumpling Gang/1974 · The Shootist/1976 ·
The Apple Dumpling Gang Rides Again/
1979
Television Have Gun, Will Travel/58 · The
Virginian/63 · Gunsmoke/70 · Hec Ramsey/
72 · Sidekicks/74 · Kate Bliss and the Ticker
Tape Kid/78 · The Wild, Wild West
Revisited/79 · More Wild, Wild West/80

Morricone, Ennio (b 1928) · Composer, aka
Dan Savio, Leo Nichols. Closely associated
with the Italian Westerns of Sergio Leone,
Morricone has often worked with Bruno

Nicolai, who has conducted many of his
scores. Just as the Spaghetti Western frequently parodies the themes and situations
of the Hollywood Western, bringing conventions into the foreground, so Morricone's scores, with their lush operatic
melodies combined with unusual instru-
ments such as the jew's harp and effects such
as whistling, send up the emotionalism of
traditional Hollywood film scoring. CF
Duello nel Texas/1963 · Le pistole non
discutono/Per un pugno di dollari/1964 · Per
qualche dollaro in più/Una pistola per
Ringo/Il ritorno di Ringo/Cento mila dollari
per Ringo/1965 · Sette pistole per i Mac
Gregor/(supervised only) Quien sabe?/Il
buono, il brutto, il cattivo/Un fiume di
dollari/(co-m) La resa dei conti/Navajo Joe/I
crudeli/(co-m) Per pochi dollari ancora/Sette
donne per i Mac Gregor/1966 · Faccia a
faccia/Da uomo a uomo/1967 · C'era una
volta il west/E per tetto un cielo di stelle/Il
grande silenzio/(co-m) Il mercenario/Corri,
uomo, corri/1968 · Un esercito di 5 uomini/
1969 · Vamos a matar, compañeros/1970 ·
Giù la testa/1971 · La banda J & S –
cronaca criminale del far west/1972 · Il mio
nome è Nessuno/1973 · Un genio, due
compari, un pollo/1975 · Occhio alla penna/
1981
Television The Men from Shiloh/70

Morrison, Pete (1891-1973) Actor. Pete
Morrison was born in Colorado, and in
1908 was working on the railroad there when
Francis Boggs' Selig company arrived on
location. Morrison was enlisted as an extra.
Next year, Billy Anderson took the boy on,
and he went to Hollywood as extra and stunt
man. Handsome, well-built and a fine rider,
he was starring by 1918, and had a great
period in the 20s playing leads in Universal's
Blue Streak Westerns. He faded in the 30s,
by now middle-aged and somewhat portly. JL
On the Warpath/On the Border/1909 · The

Call of the West/The Little Doctor of the
Foothills/1910 · Rattlesnakes and
Gunpowder/Cattle Thief's Brand/The Smoke
of the Forty-Five/1911 · The Range Detective/
The New Cowpuncher/1912 · Curlew
Corliss/1916 · Fighting Back/1917 · Keith of
the Border/1918 · A Western Wooing/
Kingdom Come/The Captive Bride/The Jaws
of Justice/Neck and Noose/The Rustlers/To
the Tune of Bullets/Gun Magic/Dynamite/
The Fighting Brothers/The Fighting Heart/
The Fighting Sheriff/The Flip of a Coin/The
Four-Gun Bandit/The Hidden Badge/His
Buddy/By Indian Post/Even Money/Gun
Law/Ace High/The Gun Packer/At the Point
of a Gun/The Best Bad Man/The Black
Horse Bandit/1919 · West Is West/1920 ·
Headin' North/Crossing Trails/1921 · Duty
First/Daring Danger/The Better Man Wins/
West Is East/1922 · Making Good/Smilin'
On/Western Blood/Ghost City/1923 · The
Bull Tosser/The Little Savage/Black Gold/
False Trails/Pioneer's Gold/Buckin' the West/
Pot Luck Pards/Rainbow Rangers/1924 · One
Shot Ranger/Range Buzzards/Always Ridin'
to Win/Cowboy Grit/The Empty Saddle/The
Ghost Rider/The Mystery of Lost Ranch/A
Ropin' Ridin' Fool/Santa Fe Pete/Stampede
Thunder/Triple Action/West of Arizona/
1925 · Blue Blazes/Bucking the Truth/
Chasing Trouble/The Desperate Game/The
Escape/1926 · The Three Outcasts/Courtin'
Wildcats/1929 · The Big Trail/Beyond the
Rio Grande/Phantom of the Desert/Spurs/
Trails of Peril/Trailin' Trouble/Ridin' Law/
1930 · Westward Bound/1931 · Rider of
Death Valley/1932 · Five Bad Men/1935

Murphy, Audie (1924-71) · Actor. There are
two widely known facts about Audie
Murphy. Firstly, he was America's most
decorated soldier in World War II and,
secondly, he is the B-Western star of the
post-war period. Occasional appearances
outside of the genre include To Hell and

Henry Morgan

Pete Morrison

Audie Murphy

J. Carrol Naish

Back, in which he played himself as war hero, but the majority of his film career was spent in the saddle. He first came to attention as Billy the Kid in *The Kid from Texas*, and his version of the famous outlaw remained definitive until later more complex portrayals by Paul Newman and Kris Kristofferson. His last role was as Jesse James in Budd Boetticher's *A Time for Dying*, the title of which anticipated the star's premature death in a plane crash in 1971. TR

Texas, Brooklyn and Heaven/1948 · *The Kid from Texas*/1949 · *Sierra*/*Kansas Raiders*/1950 · *The Red Badge of Courage*/*The Cimarron Kid*/1951 · *The Duel at Silver Creek*/1952 · *Gunsmoke*/*Column South*/*Tumbleweed*/*Ride Clear of Diablo*/1953 · *Drums Across the River*/*Destry*/1954 · *Walk the Proud Land*/(co-p) *The Guns of Fort Petticoat*/1956 · *Night Passage*/1957 · *Ride a Crooked Trail*/1958 · *No Name on the Bullet*/*The Wild and the Innocent*/*Cast a Long Shadow*/*Hell Bent for Leather*/*The Unforgiven*/1959 · *Seven Ways from Sundown*/1960 · *Posse from Hell*/*Six Black Horses*/1961 · *Showdown*/*Gunfight at Comanche Creek*/1963 · *The Quick Gun*/*Bullet for a Badman*/*Apache Rifles*/1964 · *Arizona Raiders*/*Gunpoint*/1965 · *The Texican*/*Forty Guns to Apache Pass*/1966 · (p) *A Time for Dying*/1969
Television *Whispering Smith*/61

N

Naish, J. Carrol (1900-73) · Actor. An Irish-American who had knocked about the world and acquired experience of many peoples and languages, Naish put the knowledge to good use in his acting career. He played characters (usually but not invariably unscrupulous) of countless nationalities and in countless dialects. He was a convincing Indian (Sitting Bull in *Annie Get Your Gun*, and again in *Sitting Bull* itself), Italian or Mexican (passim), or even Chinese (Charlie Chan on television) or, perhaps with a shade of reluctance, plain American (Phil Sheridan in *Rio Grande*). JL

Gun Smoke/1931 · *The Last Trail*/1933 · *Under the Pampas Moon*/1935 · *The Robin Hood of El Dorado*/1936 · *Border Cafe*/*Thunder Trail*/1937 · *Jackass Mail*/1942 · *Bad Bascomb*/1946 · *The Kissing Bandit*/1948 · *Canadian Pacific*/1949 · *Annie Get Your Gun*/*Rio Grande*/*Across the Wide Missouri*/1950 · *Mark of the Renegade*/1951 · *Denver and Rio Grande*/*Woman of the North Country*/*Ride the Man Down*/1952 · *Saskatchewan*/*Sitting Bull*/1954 · *Rage at

Dawn*/*The Last Command*/1955 · *Rebel in Town*/*Yaqui Drums*/1956
Television *Wanted: Dead or Alive*/*Cimarron City*/*The Texan*/58 · *The Restless Gun*/*Wagon Train*/59 · *Bonanza*/68 · *Cutter's Trail*/70

Nazarro, Ray (1902-86) · Director. Speed was the keyword with Nazarro. His Westerns, all of the second-feature variety, were noted for their rapid, almost non-stop, action, and the pace at which Nazarro turned them out must have made his employers, until the mid-50s Columbia, contented men. In 14 years Nazarro made close on 70 movies, with Charles Starrett's Durango Kid series perhaps the best. In 1958 he took five years off – no vacation better earned – and then ended his career in Europe. JL

Outlaws of the Rockies/*Song of the Prairie*/*Texas Panhandle*/1945 · *The Desert Horseman*/*Galloping Thunder*/*Roaring Rangers*/*Throw a Saddle on a Star*/*Gunning for Vengeance*/*That Texas Jamboree*/*Two-Fisted Stranger*/*Heading West*/*Singing on the Trail*/*Terror Trail*/*Lone Star Moonlight*/*Cowboy Blues*/1946 · *The Lone Hand Texan*/*Over the Santa Fe Trail*/*West of Dodge City*/*Law of the Canyon*/*Buckaroo from Powder River*/*The Last Days of Boot Hill*/1947 · *Song of Idaho*/*Six Gun Law*/*West of Sonora*/*Trail to Laredo*/*Phantom Valley*/*Blazing Across the Pecos*/*El Dorado Pass*/*Singing Spurs*/*Smoky Mountain Melody*/*Quick on the Trigger*/1948 · *Bandits of El Dorado*/*Home in San Antone*/*The Blazing Trail*/*Laramie*/*Challenge of the Range*/*South of Death Valley*/*Renegades of the Sage*/1949 · *Frontier Outpost*/*The Palomino*/*Outcasts of Black Mesa*/*Texas Dynamo*/*Hoedown*/*Trail of the Rustlers*/*Streets of Ghost Town*/1950 · *Al Jennings of Oklahoma*/*Fort Savage Raiders*/*Cyclone Fury*/*The Kid from Amarillo*/*Indian Uprising*/1951 · *Montana Territory*/*Cripple Creek*/*Junction City*/*Laramie Mountains*/*The Rough, Tough West*/1952 · *Kansas Pacific*/*Gun Belt*/1953 · *The Black Dakotas*/*Southwest Passage*/*The Lone Gun*/1954 · *Top Gun*/1955 · *The White Squaw*/1956 · *The Phantom Stagecoach*/*The Domino Kid*/*The Hired Gun*/1957 · *Return to Warbow*/*Apache Territory*/1958 · *Arrivederci Cowboy*/1967
Television *Fury*/*Buffalo Bill Jr.*/55

Newman, Alfred (1901-70) · Composer, long one of Hollywood's leading purveyors of lush, romantic, actionful scores, also a conductor and music director. He won 9 Academy Awards, worked on over 200

movies, and possessed the archetypal boring name that inspired *MAD Magazine*'s Alfred E. Neuman. His best Western work was on epics of American history like *Drums Along the Mohawk* and *How the West Was Won*, but a long association with 20th Century-Fox and director Henry King led him to provide the uncharacteristically sparse score for *The Gunfighter*. KN

(md) *The Call of the Wild*/1935 · (md) *The Gay Desperado*/*Ramona*/1936 · *The Cowboy and the Lady*/1938 · *Drums Along the Mohawk*/1939 · *Brigham Young – Frontiersman*/*The Mark of Zorro*/(co-m uncredited) *The Westerner*/1940 · *Belle Starr*/*Hudson's Bay*/1941 · *My Friend Flicka*/1943 · (md) *Fury at Furnace Creek*/*Yellow Sky*/1948 · (md) *Two Flags West*/*The Gunfighter*/1950 · (md) *Viva Zapata!*/1952 · (co-m) *How the West Was Won*/1962 · *Nevada Smith*/1965 · *Firecreek*/1967

Newman, Paul (b 1925) · Trained at the Actor's Studio, he became a major film star after a brief apprenticeship in theatre and television drama. The young Newman brings to his Westerns the image of a shrewd, unprincipled man on-the-make, displaying a slick and manipulative charm; *Hud* epitomizes the role. From *Butch Cassidy* onwards, his performances are relaxed, underplayed, often comic. The 'revisionist' Westerns *Roy Bean* and *Buffalo Bill* debunk legends while returning a mature but playful Newman to his earlier persona of enterprising hustler. His most ambitious role may be that of the Mexican bandit in *The Outrage* – a remake of Kurosawa's *Rashomon*; but his most intense performance remains that of the brooding and explosive Billy the Kid in Arthur Penn's *The Left Handed Gun* – the first feature Western for each, though they had first collaborated on the television version, *The Death of Billy the Kid*. DG
The Left Handed Gun/1957 · *Hud*/1962 ·

Paul Newman

The Outrage/1964 · *Hombre*/1966 · *Butch Cassidy and the Sundance Kid*/1969 · *Pocket Money/The Life and Times of Judge Roy Bean*/1972 · *Buffalo Bill and the Indians or Sitting Bull's History Lesson*/1976

Nichols, Dudley (1895-1960) · Writer. A journalist in New York in the 20s, Nichols became one of Hollywood's most respected scenarists in the 30s and 40s. He produced screenplays for Ford, Hawks, Lang, Clair and Renoir, adapted for the screen works by Hemingway, Graham Greene and Eugene O'Neill, and directed three films. His first major Western was *Stagecoach*, the only Western of the fourteen screenplays he wrote for John Ford. Despite its success, it was not until the 50s that Nichols wrote another. In the 50s he was less active as a scriptwriter, though it is notable that of his last eight films, six were Westerns. DR
Robbers' Roost/1932 · (st) *The Arizonian*/1935 · *Stagecoach*/1939 · (st) *Rawhide*/1950 · *Return of the Texan/The Big Sky*/1952 · *The Tin Star*/1957 · *The Hangman*/1959 · (co-sc) *Heller in Pink Tights*/1960
Television (st only) *The Deputy*/59

Nugent, Frank S. (1908-66) · Writer. As a *New York Times* reporter and critic, Nugent had praised John Ford's films and appreciated, for example, the terse dialogue and sweeping canvas of *Stagecoach*, 'a motion picture that sings a song of camera.' He got the opportunity to meet Ford when Darryl Zanuck brought Nugent to 20th Century-Fox as a script doctor in 1940. Of Irish descent, Nugent shared Ford's mythic attachment to immigrant experience and the romanticism that expressed itself in Westerns. As a scriptwriter, he became Ford's favourite 'body and fender man', and his scripts exemplified the verbal economy and encouraged the visual breadth that characterized the director's finest work. BA

Fort Apache/(co-sc) *3 Godfathers*/1948 · (co-sc) *She Wore a Yellow Ribbon*/1949 · (co-st, co-sc) *Wagon Master*/(co-st only) *Two Flags West*/1950 · (co-sc) *They Rode West*/1954 · (co-sc) *The Tall Men*/1955 · *The Searchers*/1956 · *Gunman's Walk*/1958 · *Two Rode Together*/1961 · (co-sc) *Incident at Phantom Hill*/1965
Television *Empire*/62

O

Oates, Warren (1928-82) · Actor. Towards the end of Peckinpah's *Ride the High Country*, Warren Oates as one of the infamous Hammond brothers fires his pistol in frustration at some nearby chickens. This memorable image of aimless violence defined a near-psychotic persona for Oates and one that he was to carry into many of his Western roles. His most substantial contributions to the genre in the cinema were as a member of Peckinpah's stock Western company in the above film, in *Major Dundee* and in *The Wild Bunch*. His television credits (some also involving Peckinpah) constitute a roll call of the major Western series. TR
Yellowstone Kelly/1959 · *Ride the High Country*/1962 · *Mail Order Bride*/1963 · *Major Dundee/The Rounders*/1964 · *Return of the Seven/The Shooting/Welcome to Hard Times*/1966 · *Smith/The Wild Bunch*/1969 · *Barquero/There Was a Crooked Man...*/1970 · *The Hired Hand*/1971 · *Kid Blue*/1973 · *China 9 Liberty 37*/1978
Television *Wanted: Dead or Alive/Gunsmoke/The Rifleman*/58 · *Trackdown/Tombstone Territory/Black Saddle/Bat Masterson/Buckskin/The Rough Riders/The Adventures of Rin Tin Tin*/59 · *Johnny Ringo/Tate/Sugarfoot/Bronco/Lawman/The Westerner/Have Gun, Will Travel/Wrangler*/60 · *Laramie/Stagecoach West*/61 · *Stoney Burke/Bonanza*/62 · *The Travels of Jaimie McPheeters/Rawhide/The Virginian*/63 ·

George O'Brien

Branded/A Man Called Shenandoah/65 · *Shane/The Big Valley/The Monroes*/66 · *Dundee and the Culhane/The Iron Horse/Cimarron Strip*/67 · *Something for a Lonely Man*/68 · *Lancer*/69 · *True Grit*/78

O'Brien, Edmond (1915-85) · A versatile actor, seen to best advantage in offbeat roles, he had a fleshy, somewhat bulbous, appearance, rendering him less than charismatic when he essayed a few conventional Western leads in 50s programmers. Later, however, he contributed three relishably scenery-chewing character roles – the elbow-lifting, Shakespeare-spouting editor of *The Man Who Shot Liberty Valance*; the crazed ex-Confederate colonel in *Rio Conchos*; and, almost unrecognizably bewhiskered, the oldest member of *The Wild Bunch*. TP
The Redhead and the Cowboy/1950 · *Warpath/Silver City*/1951 · *Denver and Rio Grande*/1952 · *Cow Country*/1953 · *The Big Land*/1957 · *The Man Who Shot Liberty*

Warren Oates

Edmond O'Brien

Maureen O'Hara

Jack Palance

Valance/1962 · Rio Conchos/1964 · The
Wild Bunch/1969
Television Dick Powell's Zane Grey Theatre/
57 · Laramie/59 · The Virginian/67 · The
Intruders/70 · The High Chaparral/71 ·
Cade's County/72

O'Brien, George (1899-1985) · Actor. Roles
in John Ford's The Iron Horse and Cheyenne
Autumn mark the beginning and end points
of O'Brien's movie career. In between he
established a long working relationship with
director David Howard, first at Fox and then
at RKO, where his athleticism and muscular
physique well suited him for the action
movies he starred in. Unlike many of the
Western series stars he was a very adaptable
actor, capable of portraying a range of
character types – including the gently
humorous in such films as The Cowboy
Millionaire and Whispering Smith Speaks. His
career was interrupted by two lengthy
periods in the Navy (1939-45, 1953-60). JH
The Iron Horse/1924 · Rustling for Cupid/
Three Bad Men/1926 · The Lone Star
Ranger/Rough Romance/Last of the Duanes/
1930 · Fair Warning/A Holy Terror/Riders
of the Purple Sage/1931 · The Rainbow
Trail/The Gay Caballero/Mystery Ranch/The
Golden West/Robbers' Roost/1932 · Smoke
Lightning/Life in the Raw/The Last Trail/
1933 · Frontier Marshal/The Dude Ranger/
1934 · When a Man's a Man/The Cowboy
Millionaire/Thunder Mountain/Whispering
Smith Speaks/1935 · O'Malley of the
Mounted/The Border Patrolman/Daniel
Boone/1936 · Hollywood Cowboy/Park
Avenue Logger/1937 · Gun Law/Border
G-Man/The Painted Desert/The Renegade
Ranger/Lawless Valley/1938 · The Arizona
Legion/Trouble in Sundown/Racketeers of the
Range/Timber Stampede/The Fighting
Gringo/The Marshal of Mesa City/1939 ·
Legion of the Lawless/Bullet Code/Prairie
Law/Stage to Chino/Triple Justice/1940 ·
Fort Apache/1948 · She Wore a Yellow
Ribbon/1949 · Gold Raiders/1951 · Cheyenne
Autumn/1964

O'Hara, Maureen (b 1920) · Actress, born
Maureen Fitzsimons. This Irish redhead, in
films from the late 30s, grew from sweet
ingenue to spitfire. At her best in roles which
required her to be 'spunky', she was several
times teamed with John Wayne in Westerns,
though her best work with him was in John
Ford's Irish drama The Quiet Man. JC
Buffalo Bill/1944 · Comanche Territory/Rio
Grande/1950 · The Redhead from Wyoming/
War Arrow/1953 · The Deadly Companions/

1961 · McLintock!/1963 · The Rare Breed/
1965 · Big Jake/1971

P

Palance, Jack (b 1919) · Actor, aka Walter
Jack Palance. Tall, gaunt and hatchet-faced
(partly as a result of plastic surgery after a
wartime injury), he proved a natural for
menacing heavies, and achieved rapid fame
with his playing of the murderous, soft-
spoken hired gun in Shane. Shortly afterwards, he brought a fearsome sense of barely
contained violence to Charlton Heston's
Indian adversary in Arrowhead. He has subsequently played a fairly wide range of roles,
sometimes of a sympathetic and reflective
kind, and gave effective low-key performances as former gunfighters trying to adapt to a
peaceful life in The Lonely Man and Monte
Walsh. TP
Shane/1952 · Arrowhead/1953 · The Lonely
Man/1956 · The Professionals/1966 · Il
mercenario/The Desperados/1968 · The
McMasters/1969 · Monte Walsh/Vamos a
matar, compañeros/1970 · Si può fare,
amigo/Chato's Land/1971 · Te Deum/1972 ·
Diamante lobo/1976 · Welcome to Blood
City/1977
Television Dick Powell's Zane Grey Theatre/
56 · The Godchild/74 · The Hatfields and
the McCoys/75 · The Last Ride of the
Dalton Gang/79

Parker, Fess (b 1926) · Actor. Fresh-faced
and handsome, and every boy's old-
fashioned hero, Parker played a few minor
roles in the early 50s before achieving fame
as television's Davy Crockett in a series later
re-edited as two cinema films. Later still,
Parker was another television incarnation of
an American folk-hero, this time as Daniel
Boone. That series too had a cinema release,
but one point should be noted – although
Parker was in the 1956 Boone movie, he was

not Boone that time (Bruce Bennett was). JL
Untamed Frontier/Springfield Rifle/Thunder
Over the Plains/1952 · Take Me to Town/
1953 · Daniel Boone, Trail Blazer/The Great
Locomotive Chase/Westward Ho the
Wagons!/1956 · Old Yeller/1957 · The
Hangman/Alias Jesse James/The
Jayhawkers!/1959 · Smoky/1966
Television Annie Oakley/Davy Crockett/54 ·
Andrew's Raiders/61 · Daniel Boone/Destry/
64

Pate, Michael (b 1920) · Wide-mouthed,
swarthy character player, often seen as
treacherous Indian or bar-room troublemaker. The highlight of his career out west is
probably Curse of the Undead, in which he
plays Drake Robey, a black-clad vampire
gunslinger who used to be a conquistador
and wins all his shoot-outs because he can
only be killed by a bullet containing a sliver
of the True Cross. Recently, Pate has returned to his native Australia and concentrated
on directing and producing. KN
Hondo/1953 · A Lawless Street/1955 · 7th
Cavalry/The Oklahoman/Reprisal!/1956 ·
The Tall Stranger/1957 · Westbound/1958 ·
Curse of the Undead/1959 · Walk Like a
Dragon/1960 · The Canadians/Sergeants
3/1961 · California/1962 · McLintock!/
Advance to the Rear/1963 · Major Dundee/
1964 · The Great Sioux Massacre/1965 ·
Mosby's Marauders/1966
Television Broken Arrow/56 · Gunsmoke/
Have Gun, Will Travel/57 · Wagon Train/
The Texan/Zorro/58 · Black Saddle/Wanted:
Dead or Alive/The Adventures of Rin Tin
Tin/Rawhide/The Rifleman/Dick Powell's
Zane Grey Theatre/59 · Tales of Wells
Fargo/The Law of the Plainsman/Wichita
Town/Bronco/Zorro/The Tall Man/60 ·
Lawman/Maverick/Frontier Circus/61 · The
Virginian/63 · Temple Houston/64 ·
Branded/Daniel Boone/66 · Return of the
Gunfighter/Hondo/67

Fess Parker

Michael Pate

Payne, John (b 1912) · Actor. An attractive leading man, Payne started out his film career in the early 40s in musical comedies – he usually played a song and dance man or romantic crooner. At the beginning of the 50s he switched to Westerns and although he made only a handful they were all classy action movies. He usually played the loner with a shady past. In the late 50s he switched to television and produced and starred in *The Restless Gun*. TM

Badlands/1939 · *El Paso*/1949 · *The Eagle and the Hawk*/1950 · *Passage West*/1951 · *The Vanquished*/1953 · *Silver Lode/Rails into Laramie/Tennessee's Partner*/1954 · *Santa Fe Passage/Road to Denver*/1955 · *Rebel in Town*/1956

Television *Gunsmoke*/55 · *Dick Powell's Zane Grey Theatre*/56 · *The Restless Gun*/57 · *Cade's County*/71

Peck, Gregory (b 1916) · A star whose fashion-plate looks as a young man may have risked obscuring his range and capacity as an actor. The flamboyant anti-hero of *Duel in the Sun* makes a startling contrast with the doomed protagonist of *The Gunfighter*, where Peck's banked-down playing was supplemented by an unflattering moustache with which studio head Darryl Zanuck was reputedly not at all pleased. Later, another sharp contrast can be seen between the driven avenger of *The Bravados* and the modest self-assurance of *The Big Country's* hero, while the gambler of *How the West Was Won* draws on Peck's skill in ironic light comedy. His most recent Western lead, in *Billy Two Hats*, was a bizarre character role as a Scots-born bank robber. TP

Duel in the Sun/1946 · *Yellow Sky*/1948 · *The Gunfighter/Only the Valiant*/1950 · *The Bravados/(co-p) The Big Country*/1958 · *How the West Was Won*/1962 · *The Stalking Moon/McKenna's Gold*/1968 · *Shoot Out*/1971 · *Billy Two Hats*/1973

Peckinpah, Sam (1926-84) · Perhaps the most brilliant talent to emerge from the forcing-house of the television Western in the 50s. Of all the great directors of the Western, Peckinpah is the most self-conscious, the most aware of working in a tradition. In his very first feature, *The Deadly Companions*, there is a scene in which some Indians who have captured a stagecoach re-enact their deed as a kind of game. This playfulness with Western icons emerges again in his next feature, *Ride the High Country*, the most perfectly formed of all his films. Gil Westrum (Randolph Scott, brilliantly cast) has fallen on hard times and is now reduced to scratching a living in a fairground side-show. Wearing a Buffalo Bill-type beard and wig, he appears as the Oregon Kid, a shoddy caricature of a Western hero. Peckinpah's masterpiece *Major Dundee*, though flawed by studio interference, is in constant dialogue with Ford's cavalry Westerns. Peckinpah's desire to reflect upon the Western and not merely to repeat it drove him in his later films to confront head-on the violence which lies at the heart of the genre. The graphic depiction in *The Wild Bunch* of wholesale slaughter in slow motion, defended by Peckinpah as prophylactic realism, earned him notoriety. At the time it was also seen as the result of Italian influence, though in truth the despair at the centre of Peckinpah's later work is a world away from Sergio Leone's cynicism. Whereas the Italian Western tends towards farce, Peckinpah's films, even those such as *The Ballad of Cable Hogue* in which a certain serenity is achieved, all tend towards tragedy. EB

The Deadly Companions/1961 · *Ride the High Country*/1962 · (co-sc) *Major Dundee*/1964 · (co-sc only) *The Glory Guys*/1965 · (co-sc only) *Villa Rides*/1968 · (co-sc) *The Wild Bunch*/1969 · (p) *The Ballad of Cable Hogue*/1970 · *Junior Bonner*/1972 · *Pat Garrett and Billy the Kid*/1973

Television *Gunsmoke*/55 · *Broken Arrow*/56 · *Have Gun, Will Travel/Tales of Wells Fargo*/57 · *Trackdown/Tombstone Territory/Man Without a Gun/Dick Powell's Zane Grey Theatre/The Rifleman*/58 · *Klondike/The Westerner*/60 · *Pony Express*/61

Pickens, Slim (1919-83) · Actor. A big hulk of a man in his later years, whose lack of a chin is made up for by his ample girth. His film career began at Republic playing the comic sidekick in a Rex Allen series. The character he developed there, a kind-hearted, garrulous and none too bright cowpoke, generally remained with him throughout his working life, and was used to great effect in his most famous role as Major King Kong in Kubrick's *Dr Strangelove*, and in his self-mocking, scene-stealing performance in *Blazing Saddles*. DR

Rocky Mountain/1950 · *Colorado Sundown/The Last Musketeer/Border Saddle Mates/Old Oklahoma Plains/South Pacific Trail*/1952 · *Iron Mountain Trail/Down Laredo Way/Old Overland Trail/Shadows of Tombstone/Red River Shore*/1953 · *The Boy from Oklahoma/The Outcast/The Phantom Stallion*/1954 · *Santa Fe Passage/The Last Command*/1955 · *Stranger at My Door/The Great Locomotive Chase/Gun Brothers*/1956 · *Gunsight Ridge*/1957 · *The Sheepman/Tonka/Escort West*/1958 · *Stampede at Bitter Creek*/1959 · *One-Eyed Jacks*/1960 · *A Thunder of Drums*/1961 · *Savage Sam*/1963 · *Major Dundee*/1964 · *The Glory Guys*/1965 · *Stagecoach/An Eye for an Eye*/1966 · *Rough Night in Jericho/Will Penny*/1967 · *The Ballad of Cable Hogue/La spina dorsale del diavolo*/1970 · *The Honkers/The Cowboys*/1971 · *Pat Garrett and Billy the Kid*/1973 · *The Apple Dumpling Gang/Blazing Saddles/Rancho DeLuxe*/1974 · *Hawmps*/1976 · *The White Buffalo*/1977 · *Shadow of Chikara*/1978 · *Tom Horn*/1980

John Payne

Gregory Peck

Sam Peckinpah

Slim Pickens

Television *The Lone Ranger*/56 · *The Saga of Andy Burnett*/57 · *Wagon Train*/ *Maverick*/58 · *The Swamp Fox*/59 · *Overland Trail*/*Riverboat*/*The Westerner*/60 · *The Outlaws*/*The Americans*/61 · *The Tall Man*/62 · *Bonanza*/*The Travels of Jaimie McPheeters*/*The Virginian*/*The Wide Country*/63 · *Gunsmoke*/*Rawhide*/64 · *Daniel Boone*/*The Legend of Jesse James*/66 · *Custer*/67 · *Cimarron Strip*/*The Outcasts*/68 · *Desperate Mission*/69 · *Alias Smith and Jones*/*The Men from Shiloh*/*The Devil and Miss Sarah*/*Sam Hill: Who Killed the Mysterious Mr Foster?*/71 · *Hitched*/73 · *The Gun and the Pulpit*/*Kung Fu*/74 · *Banjo Hackett: Roamin' Free*/76 · *How the West Was Won*/78 · *The Sacketts*/79 · *Best of the West*/81

Power, Tyrone (1913-58) · Actor. He shared the dark, fashion-plate good looks of Robert Taylor, and in the late 30s was to Fox movies very much what the latter was to MGM, a bankable romantic lead to be cast at random in comedies, dramas and action movies. Most of his earlier parts were routine, though in subsequent years he showed some adventurousness in extending his range. He was sympathetic, if slightly stolid, in the title role of *Jesse James* and as the scout in *Brigham Young – Frontiersman*. But his 'double' role in *The Mark of Zorro*, the ostensible fop who has a secret life as a masked avenger, effectively juxtaposed his capacities of physical presence and humorous poise. His post-war Westerns were not among his more rewarding later roles. TP
Northern Frontier/1935 · *Jesse James*/1939 · *Brigham Young – Frontiersman*/*The Mark of Zorro*/1940 · *Rawhide*/1950 · *Pony Soldier*/1952 · *The Mississippi Gambler*/1953

Preston, Robert (1918-87) · Actor. Preston waited in the wings for twenty years until the Broadway production of *The Music Man*

made him a star, but his work in those years was varied and consistently interesting. His Western roles included characters as far apart as the weakling of *North West Mounted Police* and the violent Wichita Kid of *The Sundowners*, the disciplinarian colonel of *The Last Frontier* and the shy sheriff of *Face to Face*, and best of all, McQueen's sad, drunken father in *Junior Bonner*. JL
Union Pacific/1939 · *North West Mounted Police*/1940 · *The Lady from Cheyenne*/1941 · *Blood on the Moon*/1948 · *Whispering Smith*/*The Sundowners*/1949 · *My Brother the Outlaw*/*Best of the Badmen*/1951 · episode of *Face to Face* ('The Bride Comes to Yellow Sky')/1952 · *The Last Frontier*/1955 · *How the West Was Won*/1962 · *Junior Bonner*/1972
Television *The Chisholms*/79 · *September Gun*/83

Pyle, Denver (b 1920) · Actor. Fair hair and blue eyes do not normally mark a man out for villainy, but Pyle did more than his share in that line, frequently crossing the paths of Roy Rogers or Gene Autry. Behind all those mean men, however, was an under-used and superbly gifted comedian. Watch Pyle in *The Rounders* as Glenn Ford tries to unload a malevolent horse on him; Pyle is touched by the gift, half-suspects he is being had, just can't quite make out whether to be delighted or on guard, and expresses it all with looks and barely a word. JL
Where the North Begins/1947 · *The Man from Colorado*/*Marshal of Amarillo*/*Red Canyon*/1948 · *Hellfire*/1949 · *The Old Frontier*/*Dynamite Pass*/1950 · *Hills of Utah*/*Rough Riders of Durango*/1951 · *Canyon Ambush*/*Man from the Black Hills*/*Fargo*/ *Desert Passage*/*The Maverick*/*Oklahoma Annie*/1952 · *Vigilante Terror*/*Goldtown Ghost Raiders*/*Topeka*/*Rebel City*/*Texas Bad Man*/*Ride Clear of Diablo*/1953 · *The Forty-Niners*/*Johnny Guitar*/*Run for Cover*/*Ten

Wanted Men*/1954 · *Rage at Dawn*/*Top Gun*/*The Naked Hills*/1955 · *7th Cavalry*/ *Yaqui Drums*/*The Lonely Man*/1956 · *Gun Duel in Durango*/*Domino Kid*/*The Left Handed Gun*/1957 · *Fort Massacre*/*Good Day for a Hanging*/*King of the Wild Stallions*/1958 · *Cast a Long Shadow*/*The Horse Soldiers*/1959 · *The Alamo*/1960 · *The Man Who Shot Liberty Valance*/*Geronimo*/ 1962 · *Mail Order Bride*/1963 · *The Rounders*/1964 · *Shenandoah*/*Gunpoint*/1965 · *Incident at Phantom Hill*/*Welcome to Hard Times*/1966 · *Bandolero!*/*5 Card Stud*/1968 · *Something Big*/1971 · *Cahill United States Marshal*/1973 · *Winterhawk*/1975 · *Hawmps*/*Buffalo Bill and the Indians or Sitting Bull's History Lesson*/*Spirit of the Wild*/*Guardian of the Wilderness*/1976
Television *The Roy Rogers Show*/52 · *Wild Bill Hickok*/54 · *The Life and Legend of Wyatt Earp*/*Fury*/55 · *The Lone Ranger*/56 · *The Adventures of Jim Bowie*/*Gunsmoke*/*The Restless Gun*/*Tales of Wells Fargo*/*The Californians*/57 · *Broken Arrow*/*Jefferson Drum*/*Tales of the Texas Rangers*/58 · *Bat Masterson*/*The Texan*/*The Deputy*/*Lawman*/ *The Rifleman*/*Have Gun, Will Travel*/59 · *Two Faces West*/*Overland Trail*/*The Tall Man*/*Stagecoach West*/*Hotel de Paree*/*The Man from Blackhawk*/60 · *The Rifleman*/ *Cheyenne*/*Bonanza*/*Empire*/*Maverick*/*Bronco*/ 61 · *Rawhide*/*Temple Houston*/*Laramie*/63 · *The High Chaparral*/*Hondo*/*Cimarron Strip*/ 67 · *The Guns of Will Sonnett*/68 · *Here Come the Brides*/70 · *Hitched*/73 · *Sidekicks*/ 74 · *The Life and Times of Grizzly Adams*/ 77 · *How the West Was Won*/79

Q

Quinn, Anthony (b 1915) · Actor. A dark and powerful Irish-Mexican, Quinn played many small roles, often as a Mexican, a Spaniard or an Indian (including Crazy Horse), before his career suddenly took off

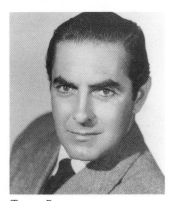

Tyrone Power

Robert Preston

Denver Pyle

Anthony Quinn

in the 50s. He often went over the top, carried away by his own rhetoric, but when held in check could be extremely effective. Notable Western parts included the leading citizen plagued by a delinquent son in *Last Train from Gun Hill*, the club-footed gunman of *Warlock*, and the idealistic if frequently drunken Indian of Carol Reed's unjustly maligned *Flap*. His last Western saw him quiet at last, as a deaf-mute in the Italian *Los amigos*. JL

The Plainsman/1936 · *Union Pacific*/1939 · *Texas Rangers Ride Again*/1940 · *They Died with their Boots On*/1941 · *The Ox-Bow Incident*/1942 · *Buffalo Bill*/1944 · *California*/1946 · *Viva Zapata!*/*Ride, Vaquero!*/1952 · *Seminole*/1953 · *Seven Cities of Gold*/1955 · *Man from Del Rio*/1956 · *The Ride Back*/1957 · *Last Train from Gun Hill*/1958 · *Warlock*/1959 · *Heller in Pink Tights*/1960 · *La Bataille de San Sebastian*/1968 · *Flap*/1970 · *Los amigos*/1972

R

Ravetch, Irving (b 1915) · Irving Ravetch and Harriet Frank Jr. met at a course for young writers at MGM. They married, and formed a highly successful writing team which functioned for some 25 years. Ravetch and Frank were noted for a series of adaptations from the novels of William Faulkner, and for films of social conscience like *Conrack* and *Norma Rae*. All the Westerns below, except the first three, by Ravetch alone, were Ravetch-Frank collaborations. Frank co-scripted *Silver River*/1948 without Ravetch. Their masterpiece, *Hombre*, has in it something of the controlled passion of Faulkner. JL

The Outriders/1949 · *Vengeance Valley*/1950 · (st) *The Lone Hand*/1953 · (co-st only) *Ten Wanted Men*/(co-st) *Run for Cover*/1954 · (co-sc, co-p) *Hud*/1962 · (co-sc,

co-p) *Hombre*/1966 · (co-sc) *The Cowboys*/1971 · (co-sc) *The Spikes Gang*/1974

Ray, Nicholas (1911-79) · Director of four fine Westerns and rightly judged by Andrew Sarris to be an auteur just the Far Side of Paradise. *Johnny Guitar* is a limit case of the genre, a rococo melodrama out west with Scott Brady expressing his potency by pillaging a bank vault and Mercedes McCambridge repressing hers in attempting to punish him. The rhetorics of Western and Melodrama clash extravagantly. *The True Story of Jesse James* vindicates the studio system which frustrated Ray's desire to make a modernist theatrical performance and gave us instead one of the best CinemaScope Westerns and the finest Jesse James film. RC

The Lusty Men/1952 · *Johnny Guitar*/*Run for Cover*/1954 · *The True Story of Jesse James*/1957

Reagan, Ronald (b 1911) · Actor. It was somehow typical of Ronald Reagan's movie career that even when he got to play a major figure like General Custer in *Santa Fe Trail*, it wasn't the lead part, Reagan having to play second fiddle to Errol Flynn as Jeb Stuart. His 'nice guy' image, which was to prove so profitable in politics, appeared to hinder his credibility as a Western leading man. The talent for villainy he displayed late in his career in *The Killers* (1964) was never tapped in the Western. As a result Reagan's film performances alone would scarcely justify the cartoon image of the 'cowboy' President. In fact Reagan's public profile as a Westerner was in large part based on the four years he spent dressed in Western clothes as on-screen announcer and advertising pitchman for *Death Valley Days*, the long-running television series sponsored by the US Borax Corporation. EB

Cowboy From Brooklyn/1938 · *Santa Fe*

Trail/1940 · *The Bad Man*/1941 · *The Last Outpost*/1951 · *Law and Order*/1953 · *Cattle Queen of Montana*/*Tennessee's Partner*/1954
Television *Dick Powell's Zane Grey Theatre*/61 · *Wagon Train*/63 · *Death Valley Days*/64

Redford, Robert (b 1936) · Actor. Handsome if limited leading man who has made a number of commercially successful genre films, usually teamed with a stronger actor. The Paul Newman-Redford combination made the pleasant *Butch Cassidy and the Sundance Kid* a big hit, overshadowing the more interesting, offbeat work of Abraham Polanski, *Tell Them Willie Boy Is Here*, made the same year. JC

Tell Them Willie Boy Is Here/*Butch Cassidy and the Sundance Kid*/1969 · *Jeremiah Johnson*/1972 · *The Electric Horseman*/1979
Television *The Deputy*/*Tate*/60 · *The Americans*/*Whispering Smith*/61 · *The Virginian*/63

Reinl, Harald (1908-86) · Director. Born in Bad Ischl as Karl Reiner, he started film work as a ski champion in Arnold Fanck's mountain movies. He worked closely with the Nazi propagandist Riefenstahl on her *Tiefland* (1940-44) and her influence dominated his own feature debut, *Bergkristall* (1949). A skilful artisan with a predilection for cloying – and occasionally morbid – romanticism, he was able to deliver a Hollywood-style professionalism while recycling many aspects of pre-war fascist culture, including the sentimental rural nationalism of *Heimat* films. He developed into post-war Germany's most prominent mainstream director, responsible for accomplished examples of whichever genre did well at the box office. He launched the acting career of his wife, Karin Dor, and relaunched the ex-Tarzan Lex Barker in

Nicholas Ray

Ronald Reagan

Robert Redford

Duncan Renaldo

Europe. Most successful of all were his 60s adaptations of the turn of the century novelist Karl May's popular stories about an Aryan Übermensch called Old Shatterhand and his faithful noble savage sidekick Winnetou, the Apache chief. Reinl was stabbed to death by his last wife. PW
Der Schatz im Silbersee/1962 · *Winnetou I*/1963 · *Winnetou II*/1964 · *Der letzte Mohikaner*/*Winnetou III*/1965 · *Winnetou und Shatterhand im Tal der Toten*/1968 · *Der Schrei der schwarzen Wölfe*/1972 · *Die blutigen Geier von Alaska*/1973

Renaldo, Duncan (1904-80) · Actor, a one-time contract player with Republic who specialized in romantic Latin American characters. He had a short stint as one of the Three Mesquiteers playing a new character, Rico, who replaced John Wayne's Stony Brooke in the series. He is best remembered for his starring performances in the long-running television series, *The Cisco Kid*, a role he had played in eight films for Monogram and United Artists. PS
Pals of the Prairie/1929 · *Rebellion*/1936 · *The Painted Stallion*/*Zorro Rides Again*/1937 · *Rose of the Rio Grande*/1938 · *Kansas Terrors*/*The Lone Ranger Rides Again*/*South of the Border*/*Rough Riders' Roundup*/*Cowboys from Texas*/1939 · *Pioneers of the West*/*Covered Wagon Days*/*Heroes of the Saddle*/*Oklahoma Renegades*/*Rocky Mountain Rangers*/*Gaucho Serenade*/1940 · *Gauchos of Eldorado*/*Down Mexico Way*/*King of the Texas Rangers*/*Outlaws of the Desert*/1941 · *King of the Mounties*/1942 · *Border Patrol*/1943 · *The San Antonio Kid*/*Hands Across the Border*/*Sheriff of Sundown*/1944 · *The Cisco Kid Returns*/*In Old New Mexico*/*South of the Rio Grande*/1945 · *The Bells of San Fernando*/*The Valiant Hombre*/*The Gay Amigo*/1948 · *The Daring Caballero*/*Satan's Cradle*/1949 · *The Girl from San Lorenzo*/1950
Television *The Cisco Kid*/51

Rennahan, Ray (1896-1980) · Raymond Rennahan was one of the earliest specialists in colour photography. In 1921 he joined the Boston Technicolor group, and a year later, although not the credited cameraman, he was the expert responsible for a sensational Technicolor feature, *The Toll of the Sea*. Through the 20s he contributed colour sequences to a variety of movies, and then, with the increasing use of colour, became a cinematographer in his own right. In the 40s and 50s Rennahan concentrated on Westerns. None save *Duel in the Sun* was a prestige

picture, but many of them looked splendid – the three for director Joseph Lewis superbly so. JL
Blood Test/1923 · (co-c) *Wanderer of the Wasteland*/1924 · (co-c) *Redskin*/1929 · (co-c) *Under a Texas Moon*/1930 · (co-c) *Drums Along the Mohawk*/(co-c) *Dodge City*/1939 · (co-c) *Belle Starr*/1941 · *Belle of the Yukon*/1944 · *California*/(co-c) *Duel in the Sun*/1946 · *Unconquered*/1947 · *The Paleface*/1948 · *Whispering Smith*/*Streets of Laredo*/1949 · *The Great Missouri Raid*/1950 · *Warpath*/*Silver City*/*Flaming Feather*/1951 · *Denver and Rio Grande*/*Pony Express*/1952 · *Arrowhead*/1953 · *Stranger on Horseback*/1954 · *A Lawless Street*/*Texas Lady*/*Rage at Dawn*/1955 · *7th Cavalry*/*The Guns of Fort Petticoat*/1956 · *The Halliday Brand*/1957 · *Terror in a Texas Town*/1958
Television *Riverboat*/59

Ritter, Tex (1907-74) · Actor. After a dynamic start, with a series of rugged, rough-hewn and immensely enjoyable movies, Ritter was the first serious rival to Gene Autry. Baby-faced, cream-puffed at first sight, he in fact had more hard edges and authentic conviction than first appearance suggested. But by 1941 Ritter found himself in films like *The Pioneers*, with its shamelessly gargantuan use of stock footage, and subsequently co-starring with progressively less prestigious partners (Bill Elliott, Johnny Mack Brown, Dave O'Brien). By 1946 his on-screen career was effectively over – but as a recording artist and theme-song champ (*High Noon*) Ritter remains an Old Master of country music. CW
Song of the Gringo/*Headin' for the Rio Grande*/1936 · *Arizona Days*/*The Mystery of the Hooded Horsemen*/*Trouble in Texas*/*Tex Rides with the Boy Scouts*/*Riders of the Rockies*/*Sing Cowboy Sing*/*Hittin' the Trail*/1937 · *Frontier Town*/*Rollin' Plains*/*Utah Trail*/*The Man from Texas*/*Song of the*

Buckaroo/*Where the Buffalo Roam*/*Starlight Over Texas*/1938 · *Down the Wyoming Trail*/*Riders of the Frontier*/*Rollin' Westward*/*Sundown on the Prairie*/*Westbound Stage*/1939 · *Arizona Frontier*/*Cowboy from Sundown*/*The Golden Trail*/*Pals of the Silver Sage*/*Take Me Back to Oklahoma*/*Rainbow Over the Range*/*Rhythm of the Rio Grande*/*Roll Wagons Roll*/*Rolling Home to Texas*/1940 · *The Pioneers*/*Riding the Cherokee Trail*/*King of Dodge City*/*Roaring Frontiers*/1941 · *Vengeance of the West*/*Bullets for Bandits*/*The Devil's Trail*/*Lone Star Vigilantes*/*North of the Rockies*/*Prairie Gunsmoke*/*Deep in the Heart of Texas*/*Little Joe the Wrangler*/*The Old Chisholm Trail*/1942 · *Raiders of San Joaquin*/*Cheyenne Roundup*/*Frontier Badman*/*The Lone Star Trail*/*Arizona Trail*/1943 · *Tenting Tonight on the Old Camp Ground*/*Cowboy Canteen*/*Marshal of Gunsmoke*/*Oklahoma Raiders*/*Dead or Alive*/*Gangsters of the Frontier*/*The Whispering Skull*/1944 · *Enemy of the Law*/*Flaming Bullets*/*Frontier Fugitives*/*Marked for Murder*/*Three in the Saddle*/1945 · (song only) *High Noon*/1952 · (song only) *The Marshal's Daughter*/1953 · (song only) *Wichita*/*Apache Ambush*/1955 · (song only) *Trooper Hook*/1957
Television *Dick Powell's Zane Grey Theatre*/58 · *The Rebel*/61

Robards, Jason, Jr. (b 1920) · Actor, son of silent film actor Jason Robards Sr. He came to film after becoming identified on stage with the works of Eugene O'Neill. With the exception of a few adaptations of stage plays and a memorable role in *All the President's Men* he hasn't had the best of luck with films. But he has played character roles in some notable Westerns. JC
A Big Hand for the Little Lady/1966 · *Hour of the Gun*/1967 · *C'era una volta il west*/1968 · *The Ballad of Cable Hogue*/1970 ·

Tex Ritter

Jason Robards Jr.

Roy Rogers

Pat Garrett and Billy the Kid/1973 · Comes a Horseman/1978 · The Legend of the Lone Ranger/1981

Robertson, Dale (b 1923) · Actor. A native of Oklahoma, he had several unsuccessful attempts to break into movies until he was spotted by producer Nat Holt, who gave him a small part in *Fighting Man of the Plains*. This led to a contract with Fox and a number of Westerns in the mid-50s. By 1956 the television Western was almost at the peak of its popularity when Robertson appeared in a half-hour anthology series. This led to the role he will best be remembered for – that of special investigator Jim Hardie in *Tales of Wells Fargo*. In 1966 he returned to television as Ben Calhoun, a gambler who wins a railroad in *The Iron Horse*. TM
Fighting Man of the Plains/1949 · The Cariboo Trail/Two Flags West/1950 · Return of the Texan/The Outcasts of Poker Flat/1952 · The Silver Whip/Devil's Canyon/City of Bad Men/1953 · Sitting Bull/The Gambler from Natchez/1954 · A Day of Fury/Dakota Incident/1956 · Hell Canyon Outlaws/1957 · Law of the Lawless/1963 · Blood on the Arrow/(p, voice-over) The Man From Button Willow/1964
Television *Tales of Wells Fargo/57 ·*

Scalplock/The Iron Horse/66 · Death Valley Days/69 · The Last Ride of the Dalton Gang/79

Rogers, Roy (b 1912) · Actor. Born Leonard Slye, he had his first success as singer Dick Weston, performing with his group The Sons of the Pioneers. When Gene Autry left Republic in 1942, Roy Rogers, as he had then become, was promoted by the studio as 'King of the Cowboys' and for twelve consecutive years he became the number one box-office Western star. Initially appearing with his horse Trigger in actioners, usually set in the Old West, by the early 40s his films had become structured around musical routines, and the settings had become modern, with Rogers garishly outfitted. When William Witney became Rogers' regular director in 1946, action was again stressed at the expense of music, and Rogers, now more simply attired, often featured in bloody fistfights. JH
Tumbling Tumbleweeds/The Gallant Defender/1935 · The Mysterious Avenger/ Rhythm on the Range/The Big Show/The Old Corral/1936 · The Old Wyoming Trail/Wild Horse Rodeo/1937 · The Old Barn Dance/ Under Western Stars/Billy the Kid Returns/ Come On Rangers/Shine On Harvest Moon/ 1938 · Rough Riders Round-Up/Frontier Pony Express/Southward Ho!/In Old Caliente/ Wall Street Cowboy/The Arizona Kid/Saga of Death Valley/Days of Jesse James/1939 · Young Buffalo Bill/Dark Command/The Carson City Kid/The Ranger and the Lady/ Colorado/Young Bill Hickok/The Border Legion/1940 · Robin Hood of the Pecos/In Old Cheyenne/Arkansas Judge/Sheriff of Tombstone/Nevada City/Bad Man of Deadwood/Jesse James at Bay/Red River Valley/1941 · The Man from Cheyenne/ South of Sante Fe/Sunset on the Desert/ Romance on the Range/Sons of the Pioneers/ Sunset Serenade/Heart of the Golden West/

Ridin' Down the Canyon/1942 · Idaho/King of the Cowboys/Song of Texas/Silver Spurs/ Man from Music Mountain/Hands Across the Border/1943 · Cowboy and the Senorita/ The Yellow Rose of Texas/Song of Nevada/ San Fernando Valley/Lights of Old Santa Fe/1944 · Utah/Bells of Rosarita/Man from Oklahoma/Sunset in El Dorado/Don't Fence Me In/Along the Navajo Trail/1945 · Song of Arizona/Rainbow Over Texas/My Pal Trigger/Under Nevada Skies/Roll On Texas Moon/Home in Oklahoma/Out California Way/Helldorado/1946 · Apache Rose/Bells of San Angelo/Springtime in the Sierras/On the Old Spanish Trail/1947 · The Gay Ranchero/Under California Skies/Eyes of Texas/Melody Time/Night Time in Nevada/ Grand Canyon Trail/The Far Frontier/1948 · Susanna Pass/Down Dakota Way/The Golden Stallion/1949 · Bells of Coronado/ Twilight in the Sierras/Trigger Jr./Sunset in the West/North of the Great Divide/Trail of Robin Hood/1950 · Spoilers of the Plains/ Heart of the Rockies/In Old Amarillo/South of Caliente/Pals of the Golden West/1951 · Son of Paleface/1952 · Alias Jesse James/ 1959 · Mackintosh and T. J./1975
Television *The Roy Rogers Show/51*

Roland, Gilbert (b 1905) · Actor, born in Mexico as Luis Antonio Damaso de Alonso. Curly-haired, mustachioed leading man who began his career in the silent era. He showed great durability, still playing lead roles in the 1950s. He was the dashing caballero in several films, but specialized as a pirate and as a Mexican in Westerns. JC
Rose of the Golden West/1927 · Men of the North/1930 · Thunder Trail/1937 · Rangers of Fortune/1940 · The Gay Cavalier/South of Monterey/Beauty and the Bandit/1946 · Riding the California Trail/Robin Hood of Monterey/King of the Bandits/Pirates of Monterey/1947 · The Dude Goes West/1948 · The Torch/1949 · The Furies/1950 · Mark

Dale Robertson

Gilbert Roland

Ruth Roman

Robert Ryan

of the Renegade/1951 · *Apache War Smoke*/1952 · *The Treasure of Pancho Villa*/1955 · *Bandido*/*Three Violent People*/1956 · *The Last of the Fast Guns*/1958 · *The Wild and the Innocent*/*Guns of the Timberland*/1959 · *Cheyenne Autumn*/1964 · *The Reward*/1965 · *Vado l'ammazzo e torno*/1967 · *Ognuno per sè*/*Anche nel west, c'era una volta Dio*/*Quella sporca storia del west*/*Sonora*/1968 · *Barbarosa*/1982
Television *Wagon Train*/58 · *Zorro*/60 · *Frontier Circus*/62 · *Gunsmoke*/63 · *Death Valley Days*/*Bonanza*/65 · *The High Chaparral*/71 · *The Mark of Zorro*/74 · *The Sacketts*/79

Roman, Ruth (b 1923) · She began her career on the stage and became a leading Hollywood actress in the mid-40s. Her raven hair, voluptuous figure and exuberant personality made her a natural for the part of determined, strong-willed, earth-mother figures who run the saloon or dance-hall, talk loud but love quietly, and end up sacrificing themselves for the hero, as in *The Far Country* and *Great Day in the Morning*. PS
White Stallion/1947 · *Belle Starr's Daughter*/1948 · *Barricade*/1949 · *Colt .45*/*Dallas*/1950 · *The Far Country*/1954 · *Great Day in the Morning*/1955 · *Rebel in Town*/1956
Television *Bonanza*/59 · *Gunsmoke*/*The Outcasts*/69 · *The Men from Shiloh*/71 · *Hec Ramsey*/73 · *The Sacketts*/79

Rosenberg, Aaron (1912-79) · Producer. After working for several years as an assistant director (including a stint with the Randolph Scott-Harry Joe Brown unit at Columbia) Rosenberg became an associate producer at Universal and graduated to fully-fledged producer status there in 1949 with *Johnny Stool Pigeon*. His main claim to fame is the batch of Westerns he produced for the company during 1950-7, including several Anthony Manns, two interesting Boettichers and *Backlash*, from John Sturges' best period. He was lured to MGM on the broken promise of handling *How the West Was Won* and in 1964 entered television in partnership with Fess Parker to make the *Daniel Boone* series. JP
Winchester '73/1950 · *Cattle Drive*/*Bend of the River*/1951 · *Gunsmoke*/*The Man from the Alamo*/*Wings of the Hawk*/1953 · *Saskatchewan*/*The Far Country*/1954 · *Man Without a Star*/1955 · *Backlash*/*Walk the Proud Land*/1956 · *Night Passage*/1957 · *The Badlanders*/1958 · *The Reward*/1965 · *Smoky*/1966
Television *Daniel Boone*/64

Ryan, Robert (1909-73) · Actor. Trained for the theatre, to which he intermittently returned, he is perhaps best known for his convincing portrayals of malevolent and bigoted thugs in crime films and thrillers, notably in *Crossfire* and *Odds Against Tomorrow*. The black, brooding intensity of his performances with their suggestion of inner torment and uncertainty, particularly in *The Wild Bunch*, gives his characterizations a sense of ambiguity and disquiet that is rarely seen in the Western outside the James Stewart/Anthony Mann films. Indeed, one of Ryan's best performances was as Stewart's taunting and divisive captive in *The Naked Spur*. PS
North West Mounted Police/*Texas Rangers Ride Again*/1940 · *Trail Street*/1947 · *Return of the Bad Men*/1948 · *Best of the Badmen*/1951 · *Horizons West*/*The Naked Spur*/1952 · *Bad Day at Black Rock*/1954 · *The Tall Men*/1955 · *The Proud Ones*/1956 · *Day of the Outlaw*/1959 · *The Canadians*/1961 · *The Professionals*/*Custer of the West*/1966 · *The Hour of the Gun*/*Escondido*/1967 · *The Wild Bunch*/1969 · *Lawman*/1970
Television *Dick Powell's Zane Grey Theatre*/56 · *Wagon Train*/62

Sais, Marin (1890-1971) · Actress. Marin Sais made her first Western in 1911; she finished in 1949 by appearing in all four of Eagle-Lion's short-lived Red Ryder series. She had retired briefly in the 30s, but that record still makes her the most enduring lady in the whole Western saga. In her early days she was queen of two series, *The Girl from Frisco* and *The American Girl*. She married cowboy star Jack Hoxie and supported him in pictures through the 20s (most uncomfortably at times, for *Behind Two Guns* had her hypnotized and stuffed into the boot of a stagecoach), and after their divorce she rode on alone. JL
How Texas Got Left/1911 · *The Tenderfoot's Troubles*/*Days of '49*/*Death Valley Scotty's Mine*/1912 · *The Struggle*/*The Invaders*/*On the Brink of Ruin*/*The Attack at Rocky Pass*/*The Big Horn Massacre*/*The California Oil Crooks*/1913 · *The Death Sign of High Noon*/*The Barrier of Ignorance*/*The Bond Eternal*/1914 · *When Thieves Fall Out*/*The Dream Seekers*/*The Tragedy of Bear Mountain*/*The Accomplice*/*The Straight and Narrow Path*/*The Wolf's Prey*/*The Secret Well*/*Ham Among the Redskins*/1915 · *The Fighting Heiress*/*The Turquoise Mine Company*/*The Oil Field Plot*/*Tigers*

Marin Sais (with Jack Hoxie)

Unchained/*The Ore Plunderers*/*The Treasure of Cibola*/*The Gun Runners*/*A Battle in the Dark*/*The Web of Guilt*/*The Reformation of Dog Hole*/*The Yellow Hand*/*The Harvest of Gold*/*The Son of Cain*/*The Witch of the Dark House*/*The Mystery of the Brass Bound Chest*/*The Fight for Paradise Valley*/*Border Wolves*/*The Poisoned Dart*/*The Stain of Chuckawalla*/*On the Brink of War*/1916 · *The Fake Prophet*/*The Resurrection of Gold Bar*/*The Homesteaders' Feud*/*Wolf of Los Alamos*/*The Dominion of Fernandez*/*The Black Rider of Tasajara*/*The Phantom Mine*/*The Fate of Juan Garcia*/*Lost Legion of the Border*/*The Vulture of Skull Mountain*/*The Tyrant of Chiricahua*/*The Secret of the Lost Valley*/*The Trapping of Two-Bit Tuttle*/*The Vanished Line Rider*/*The Man Hunt at San Remo*/*The Skeleton Canyon Raid*/*The Door in the Mountain*/*Sage Brush Law*/*The Pot of Gold*/*The Man from Tiajuana*/*The Golden Eagle Trail*/*The Ghost of the Desert*/1917 · *His Birthright*/1918 · *Bonds of Honor*/*The Gray Wolf's Ghost*/1919 · *Wolf Tracks*/*Thunderbolt Jack*/*The Golden Hope*/1920 · *The Broken Spur*/*Dead or Alive*/*The Sheriff of Hope Eternal*/1921 · (co-st) *Barb Wire*/*Riders of the Law*/1922 · *Good Men and Bad*/1923 · *Behind Two Guns*/*The Measure of a Man*/1924 · *The Red Rider*/*A Roaring Adventure*/1925 · *The Wild Horse Stampede*/1926 · *The Fighting Three*/*Men of Daring*/*Rough and Ready*/1927 · *A Son of the Desert*/1928 · *Pioneer Trail*/*Phantom Gold*/1938 · *Wild Horse Range*/*Deadwood Dick*/1940 · *Sierra Sue*/*Saddlemates*/*Two Gun Sheriff*/1941 · *Frontier Outlaws*/*Oath of Vengeance*/1944 · *Border Badmen*/*Lightning Raiders*/1945 · *Terrors on Horseback*/1946 · *Ride, Ryder, Ride!*/*Roll, Thunder, Roll!*/*The Cowboy and the Prizefighter*/*The Fighting Redhead*/1949

Sampson, Will (1935-87) · A full-blooded Creek Indian actor, Sampson came to

prominence as Chief Bromden in *One Flew Over the Cuckoo's Nest*. He became Hollywood's token Indian, importing a Western touch to films as resolutely out-of-genre as *Insignificance* and *Poltergeist II*. A few genuine Westerns like *The Outlaw Josey Wales* and *Buffalo Bill and the Indians* have used his dignity and humour very well. On television, he was associated with several documentaries on Native Americans. KN
The Outlaw Josey Wales/Buffalo Bill and the Indians or Sitting Bull's History Lesson/1976 · The White Buffalo/1977 · Fish Hawk/1978 Television *Standing Tall/78 · Born to the Wind/79 · The Mystic Warrior/84*

Scott, Randolph (1903-87) · Actor. 1945 must have felt strange to Randolph Scott; it was the only year between 1932 and 1959 that he didn't make a Western. Of all the major stars whose name is associated with the Western, Scott most closely identified with it. He was born (George Randolph Scott) in Virginia and raised in North Carolina, where his father was a textile engineer. When after leaving college he decided to try an acting career, his father wrote to the only man he knew in show business, Howard Hughes. When Scott arrived in Hollywood, he got work as an extra in a couple of films, including Victor Fleming's version of *The Virginian*. His six feet, two inch build and stylish good looks eventually persuaded Paramount to try him out in *Heritage of the Desert*, one of their series of Zane Grey Westerns. It was a success and Scott had found his niche. Several other Zane Grey Westerns followed. In the 30s and early 40s he displayed his considerable gifts for light comedy in films such as *Follow the Fleet* (with Fred Astaire and Ginger Rogers) and *My Favorite Wife* (with Cary Grant and Irene Dunne). But from 1947 he made nothing but Westerns.

In his earlier Westerns, as befits his Southern origins, the Scott persona is debonair, easy-going, graceful, though with the necessary hint of steel. As he matures into his fifties his roles change. Increasingly Scott becomes the man who has seen it all, who has suffered pain, loss and hardship, and who has now achieved (but at what cost?) a stoic calm proof against vicissitude. Such is the personality he projects in the great series of Westerns he made for the company he formed in 1950 with Harry Joe Brown, a series culminating in the masterpieces directed by Budd Boetticher from 1956. Scott's last role, in Sam Peckinpah's *Ride the High Country*, is a cunning piece of casting. In the character of Gil Westrum, Scott's earlier persona of debonair charm has become a parody of itself, used to mask the pain of a man who has found stoicism pays no bills. EB
The Virginian/1929 · Heritage of the Desert/ Wild Horse Mesa/1932 · Man of the Forest/ To the Last Man/Sunset Pass/The Thundering Herd/1933 · The Last Round-Up/Wagon Wheels/Home on the Range/1934 · The Rocky Mountain Mystery/1935 · The Last of the Mohicans/1936 · High, Wide and Handsome/1937 · The Texans/1938 · Jesse James/Susannah of the Mounties/ Frontier Marshal/1939 · Virginia City/When the Daltons Rode/1940 · Western Union/ Belle Starr/1941 · The Spoilers/1942 · The Desperadoes/1943 · Belle of the Yukon/1944 · Abilene Town/Badman's Territory/1946 · Trail Street/Gunfighters/1947 · Albuquerque/ Coroner Creek/Return of the Bad Men/1948 · Canadian Pacific/The Walking Hills/The Doolins of Oklahoma/Fighting Man of the Plains/1949 · The Nevadan/Colt .45/The Cariboo Trail/1950 · Sugarfoot/Santa Fe/Fort Worth/Man in the Saddle/Carson City/1951 · Hangman's Knot/The Man Behind the Gun/Thunder Over the Plains/Riding Shotgun/1952 · The Stranger Wore a Gun/ 1953 · The Bounty Hunter/Ten Wanted Men/Tall Man Riding/1954 · Rage at

Dawn/A Lawless Street/1955 · Seven Men from Now/7th Cavalry/The Tall T/1956 · Shoot-Out at Medicine Bend/Decision at Sundown/1957 · Buchanan Rides Alone/ Westbound/1958 · Ride Lonesome/Comanche Station/1959 · Ride the High Country/1962

Selander, Lesley (1900-79) · Director. His prolific credits testify to the fact that he was a highly proficient and professional director of, almost exclusively, series Westerns. Beginning on Buck Jones oaters at Universal, he then moved to Paramount, where he worked on numerous Hopalong Cassidy pictures as well as on their Zane Grey series. In 1944 he moved to Republic, where he directed, amongst others, Tim Holt. During the 50s he directed some forty episodes of *Laramie*. PS
The Boss Rider of Gun Creek/Ride 'Em Cowboy/Empty Saddles/Sandflow/1936 · Left-Handed Law/The Barrier/Hopalong Rides Again/Smoke Tree Range/1937 · Bar 20 Justice/Heart of Arizona/Cassidy of Bar 20/The Frontiersman/The Mysterious Rider/ Partners of the Plains/Pride of the West/1938 · Heritage of the Desert/Sunset Trail/Range War/Renegade Trail/Silver on the Sage/1939 · Cherokee Strip/Hidden Gold/Knights of the Range/The Light of Western Stars/Three Men from Texas/Santa Fe Marshal/ Stagecoach War/1940 · Riders of the Timberline/Stick to Your Guns/The Round Up/Wide Open Town/Doomed Caravan/ Pirates on Horseback/1941 · Undercover Man/Thundering Hoofs/Bandit Ranger/Lost Canyon/Border Patrol/1942 · Buckskin Frontier/Red River Robin Hood/Bar 20/Colt Comrades/Riders of the Deadline/1943 · Forty Thieves/Sheriff of Las Vegas/Sheriff of Sundown/Stagecoach to Monterey/ Lumberjack/Bordertown Trail/Call of the Rockies/Cheyenne Wildcat/Firebrands of Arizona/1944 · Trail of Kit Carson/Phantom of the Plains/Great Stagecoach Robbery/1945

Will Sampson

Lesley Selander

Nell Shipman

Don Siegel

Randolph Scott

· *Out California Way*/1946 · *Last Frontier Uprising*/*Robin Hood of Texas*/*The Red Stallion*/*Saddle Pals*/1947 · *Belle Starr's Daughter*/*Guns of Hate*/*Panhandle*/*Indian Agent*/1948 · *Brothers in the Saddle*/*Rustlers*/*Stampede*/*Masked Raiders*/*The Mysterious Desperado*/*Dakota Lil*/1949 · *Riders of the Range*/*Rio Grande Patrol*/*The Kangaroo Kid*/*Rider from Tucson*/*Storm over Wyoming*/*Short Grass*/1950 · *Pistol Harvest*/*Law of the Badlands*/*Gunplay*/*Overland Telegraph*/*Saddle Legion*/*Cavalry Scout*/*Fort Osage*/1951 · *Desert Passage*/*The Raiders*/*Road Agent*/*Trail Guide*/*Riders of Vengeance*/1952 · *Cow Country*/*War Paint*/*The Yellow Tomahawk*/1953 · *Arrow in the Dust*/*Tall Man Riding*/1954 · *Shotgun*/*Fort Yuma*/*The Broken Star*/1955 · *Quincannon, Frontier Scout*/*Outlaw's Son*/*Tomahawk Trail*/1956 · *Revolt at Fort Laramie*/1957 · *The Lone Ranger and the Lost City of Gold*/1958 · *Town Tamer*/*War Party*/*Convict Stage*/*Fort Courageous*/1965 · *The Texican*/1966 · *Fort Utah*/1967 · *Arizona Bushwhackers*/1967 Television *Fury*/55 · *Laramie*/59 · *The Tall Man*/60 · *Frontier Circus*/61

Sherman, George (b 1908) · Director. At the age of 15, Sherman was an assistant director at First National, moving on to Sennett and later still to Republic, where in 1937 he began a directorial career of some 35 years. In the early 40s Sherman made some effective thrillers, but the bulk of his work was in the Western, where he used the modest resources which he could command like the craftsman he was. Bigger budgets came later, but the little early movies had more zest –

and, just once, Louise Brooks. JL
(*co-d uncredited*) *Hollywood Cowboy*/*Wild Horse Rodeo*/1937 · *The Purple Vigilantes*/*Outlaws of Sonora*/*Riders of the Black Hills*/*Heroes of the Hills*/*Pals of the Saddle*/*Overland Stage Raiders*/*Rhythm of the Saddle*/*Santa Fe Stampede*/*Red River Range*/1938 · *Mexicali Rose*/*The Night Riders*/*Three Texas Steers*/*Wyoming Outlaw*/*Colorado Sunset*/*New Frontier*/*Cowboys from Texas*/*Kansas Terrors*/*Rovin' Tumbleweeds*/*South of the Border*/(*co-st only*) *In Old Monterey*/1939 · (*p*) *Ghost Valley Raiders*/(*p*) *One Man's Law*/(*p*) *The Tulsa Kid*/(*p*) *Texas Terrors*/*Covered Wagon Days*/*Rocky Mountain Rangers*/*Under Texas Skies*/*The Trail Blazers*/*Lone Star Raiders*/(*p only*) *Frontier Vengeance*/1940 · (*p*) *Wyoming Wildcat*/(*p*) *The Phantom Cowboy*/(*p*) *Two-Gun Sheriff*/(*p*) *Desert Bandit*/(*p*) *Kansas Cyclone*/(*p*) *Death Valley Outlaws*/(*p*) *The Apache Kid*/(*p*) *A Missouri Outlaw*/1941 · *Arizona Terrors*/*Stagecoach Express*/*Jesse James Jr.*/*Cyclone Kid*/*The Sombrero Kid*/1942 · *Renegades*/1946 · *The Last of the Red Men*/1947 · *Relentless*/*Black Bart*/*Red Canyon*/1948 · (*st*) *Calamity Jane and Sam Bass*/*River Lady*/1949 · *Comanche Territory*/*Tomahawk*/1950 · *The Battle at Apache Pass*/1952 · *Lone Hand*/*War Arrow*/*Border River*/1953 · *Dawn at Socorro*/1954 · *Chief Crazy Horse*/*Count Three and Pray*/*The Treasure of Pancho Villa*/*Comanche*/1955 · *Reprisal!*/1956 · *The Hard Man*/1957 · *The Last of the Fast Guns*/(*p*) *Ten Days to Tulara*/1958 · *Hell Bent for Leather*/1959 · (*p only*) *The Comancheros*/1961 · *Joaquin Murrieta*/1964 · *Smoky*/(*p*) *Daniel Boone – Frontier Trail Rider*/1966 · *Big Jake*/1971 Television *Rawhide*/59 · *Daniel Boone*/64

Shipman, Nell (1892-1970) · Actress. One of the most fascinating figures on the margin of the Western, Nell Shipman was writer, producer, director and star. Her first successes were with Vitagraph, but soon she struck out on her own with spectacular films set usually in the Northwest and filmed in such places as Spokane, Priest Lake in Idaho and Calgary, this last making her one of the pioneers of the Canadian film industry. She was a fine horsewoman and at home with animals, her studio including a zoo whose inmates featured in the films. By the end of the silents, the big studios had left her behind, but she had done enough. For *The Girl from God's Country* she had produced, co-directed, written story and screenplay, and played three parts. *Variety*, churlishly, thought she should have stuck to acting, but

that was not Nell's way. JL
God's Country and the Woman/1916 · *The Home Trail*/*A Gentleman's Agreement*/*The Girl from Beyond*/*Cavanaugh of the Forest Rangers*/*Baree, Son of Kazan*/1918 · *The Trials of Texas Thompson*/(*sc, co-p*) *Back to God's Country*/1919 · *The Trail of the Arrow*/*The Trail of the North Wind*/1920 · (*st, sc, p, co-d*) *The Girl from God's Country*/1921 · (*st, p*) *The Grub Stake*/1923 · *The Tamiami Trail*/1925 · (*st, sc, co-d*) *The Golden Yukon*/1927

Shumate, Harold (b 1893) · Writer. For nearly 30 years Shumate worked in Hollywood, providing numerous stories and screenplays, mainly for Westerns. That long stint began in 1924, but earlier still, when John Ford was still Jack, he had made *Hitchin' Posts* from a Shumate story. A Westerner himself, born in Texas, Shumate was something of an all-round man, scripting, adapting, writing dialogue, producing, and even, if the credits of Art Acord's *The Call of Courage* are right, having a crack at photography. Is he with us yet, at 94, still dreaming the Western dream? JL
(*st only*) *Hitchin' Posts*/1920 · (*st*) *The Outlaw's Daughter*/(*st, c*) *The Call of Courage*/1925 · *West of Broadway*/1926 · *Whispering Sage*/*Outlaws of Red River*/*Black Jack*/(*st only*) *The Circus Ace*/1927 · (*st, co-sc, p*) *The River Woman*/1928 · (*st only*) *South of the Rio Grande*/(*st*) *Ridin' for Justice*/(*co-sc*) *Heritage of the Desert*/(*co-sc*) *Wild Horse Mesa*/1932 · (*st*) *Scarlet River*/(*co-sc*) *Son of the Border*/(*co-sc*) *Man of the Forest*/(*st only*) *Cross Fire*/1933 · *Beyond the Law*/*The Westerner*/(*co-sc*) *Home on the Range*/1934 · (*st*) *Square Shooter*/1935 · *End of the Trail*/(*st*) *Dodge City Trail*/1936 · (*co-st only*) *Man of Conquest*/*Konga, the Wild Stallion*/1939 · *When the Daltons Rode*/(*st*) *Trail of the Vigilantes*/1940 · (*co-sc*) *Romance of the Rio Grande*/*The Round Up*/(*co-sc*) *The Parson of Panamint*/(*co-sc*) *Under Fiesta Stars*/(*st only*) *The Badlands of Dakota*/(*co-sc*) *Ride 'Em Cowboy*/1941 · (*st, co-sc*) *Men of Texas*/1942 · *The Kansan*/1943 · *Abilene Town*/(*st only*) *Renegades*/1946 · (*co-sc*) *Blood on the Moon*/1948 · *Saddle Tramp*/1950 · (*st only*) *The Lady from Texas*/(*st, co-sc*) *Little Big Horn*/1951 · (*co-sc*) *The Half-Breed*/1952

Siegel, Don (b 1912) · Director. The characteristic Siegel hero is a distinct loner, sometimes an outcast even, and this is as true of his Westerns as of his better-known crime films. In *Flaming Star* (originally written for

Brando) Presley plays a half-caste victim of racial prejudice; *Coogan's Bluff* features Eastwood (in his first Siegel film) as an Arizona deputy at odds with contemporary New York; Sheriff Richard Widmark is rejected by his own townspeople in *Death of a Gunfighter* (finished by Siegel, but started by Robert Totten); drifter Eastwood teams up with prostitute MacLaine in *Two Mules for Sister Sara*; *The Beguiled* finds a wounded Eastwood stranded in a ladies' seminary in the Civil War; and in *The Shootist* Wayne plays a decidedly out-of-time gunfighter. In spite of their differing styles, the former gothic, the latter spare and bleak, these last two films are among Siegel's very finest works. JP

Duel at Silver Creek/1952 · *Flaming Star*/1960 · *Coogan's Bluff*/1968 · (co-d) *Death of a Gunfighter*/*Two Mules for Sister Sara*/1969 · *The Beguiled*/1970 · *The Shootist*/1976 Television *Frontier*/55 · (co-sc only) *The Man from Blackhawk*/59 · *Destry*/64 · *The Legend of Jesse James*/66 · *Stranger on the Run*/67

Silverheels, Jay (1919-80) · Actor. That name sounds so romantic that it is sad to record that he was really Harold J. Smith. But names can mean very little, and Smith's father was in fact a Mohawk chief. The son had been in films for only a few years when in 1949 television gave him the part which made him famous, that of Tonto, loyal companion of the Lone Ranger in the long-running series and in the movies drawn from it. He also played Geronimo twice – in *Broken Arrow* and *Walk the Proud Land*. JL

The Prairie/1947 · *Fury at Furnace Creek*/*Singing Spurs*/*Yellow Sky*/1948 · *Sand*/*Lust for Gold*/*Laramie*/*Trail of the Yukon*/*The Cowboy and the Indians*/1949 · *Broken Arrow*/1950 · *Red Mountain*/1951 · *The Battle at Apache Pass*/*Brave Warrior*/*The Pathfinder*/*Jack McCall Desperado*/1952 ·

The Nebraskan/*War Arrow*/1953 · *Saskatchewan*/*Four Guns to the Border*/*The Black Dakotas*/*Drums Across the River*/*Masterson of Kansas*/1954 · *The Vanishing American*/1955 · *The Lone Ranger*/*Walk the Proud Land*/1956 · *The Lone Ranger and the Lost City of Gold*/1958 · *Alias Jesse James*/1959 · *Indian Paint*/1965 · *True Grit*/*Smith*/1969 · *Santee*/1972 · *The Man Who Loved Cat Dancing*/*One Little Indian*/1973 Television *The Lone Ranger*/49 · *Wanted: Dead or Alive*/59 · *Branded*/65 · *Pistols 'n' Petticoats*/66 · *The Virginian*/68 · *Cade's County*/71

Simpson, Russell (1880-1959) · Back in 1921 the *New York Times* called Simpson 'as sincere an actor as there is on the screen'. For the next 38 years that was to remain true. Simpson was the essence of gentle yet firm integrity, and he seemed ageless. The man in *Blue Jeans* (1917) is the same man as Pa Joad in 1939, looking perhaps a couple of years younger. John Ford recognized the actor's worth, and gave him many a memorable role, notably as the preacher in *My Darling Clementine* who has 'read the good book through from cover to cover and back again' and 'ain't nary found one word agin' dancin'.' JL

The Girl of the Golden West/1915 · *Salt of the Earth*/*The Barrier*/1917 · *Desert Gold*/*The Border Legion*/*The Brand*/1919 · *The Branding Iron*/1920 · *Shadows of Conscience*/*Snowblind*/1921 · *Across the Dead-Line*/*Fools of Fortune*/1922 · *The Girl of the Golden West*/*Hearts Aflame*/*The Huntress*/*The Virginian*/1923 · *Beauty and the Bad Man*/*The Splendid Road*/1925 · *Rustling for Cupid*/1926 · *The Frontiersman*/*The Heart of the Yukon*/*God's Great Wilderness*/1927 · *The Trail of '98*/1929 · *Billy the Kid*/*The Lone Star Ranger*/1930 · *The Great Meadow*/*Ridin' for Justice*/1931 · *Law and Order*/*The Riding Tornado*/*Hello Trouble*/

1932 · *Frontier Marshal*/1934 · *West of the Pecos*/1935 · *Ramona*/1936 · *Yodelin' Kid from Pine Ridge*/1937 · *Valley of the Giants*/*Heart of the North*/*Gold Is Where You Find It*/1938 · *Dodge City*/*Western Caravans*/*Desperate Trails*/*Drums Along the Mohawk*/1939 · *Virginia City*/*Geronimo!*/*Brigham Young – Frontiersman*/*Three Faces West*/*Santa Fe Trail*/1940 · *Last of the Duanes*/*Bad Men of Missouri*/*Lone Star Ranger*/1941 · *Wild Bill Hickok Rides*/*Shut My Big Mouth*/*The Spoilers*/*Border Patrol*/1942 · *The Woman of the Town*/1943 · *Texas Masquerade*/1944 · *The Big Bonanza*/*Along Came Jones*/1945 · *Bad Bascomb*/*My Darling Clementine*/*California Gold Rush*/1946 · *The Romance of Rosy Ridge*/*Bowery Buckaroos*/*The Fabulous Texan*/1947 · *Albuquerque*/*Coroner Creek*/*Tap Roots*/*Sundown in Santa Fe*/1948 · *The Gal Who Took the West*/*The Beautiful Blonde from Bashful Bend*/1949 · *Wagon Master*/*Saddle Tramp*/*Call of the Klondike*/*Across the Wide Missouri*/1950 · *Lone Star*/1951 · *Broken Lance*/*Seven Brides for Seven Brothers*/1954 · *The Last Command*/*The Tall Men*/1955 · *The Brass Legend*/*Friendly Persuasion*/*The Lonely Man*/1956 · *The Tin Star*/1957 · *The Horse Soldiers*/1959 Television *Wagon Train*/57 · *The Texan*/59

Springsteen, R. G. (b 1904) · Director, some credits as Robert Springsteen. After lengthy service as an assistant director he began directing at Republic, where between 1945 and 1957 he made over fifty films, mainly Westerns. His first directing credits were on the 'Red Ryder' features, in all being responsible for fourteen of the twenty-three films. After the demise of Republic, Springsteen directed a number of low-budget Westerns for the producer A.C. Lyles, though with the possible exception of *Johnny Reno* of little note. JH

Marshal of Laredo/*Colorado Pioneers*/*Wagon*

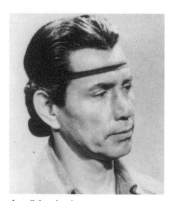

Jay Silverheels

Russell Simpson

R. G. Springsteen

Harry Dean Stanton

Wheels Westward/1945 · *California Gold Rush*/*Stagecoach to Denver*/*Sheriff of Redwood Valley*/*Home on the Range*/*Sun Valley Cyclone*/*Man from Rainbow Valley*/*Conquest of Cheyenne*/*Santa Fe Uprising*/1946 · *Vigilantes of Boomtown*/*Oregon Trail Scouts*/*Homesteaders of Paradise Valley*/*Rustlers of Devil's Canyon*/*Marshal of Cripple Creek*/*Along the Oregon Trail*/*Under Colorado Skies*/1947 · *Sundown in Santa Fe*/*Renegades of Sonora*/*Son of God's Country*/1948 · *Sheriff of Wichita*/*Death Valley Gunfighters*/*Hellfire*/*Navajo Trail Raiders*/1949 · *Singing Guns*/*The Arizona Cowboy*/*Hills of Oklahoma*/*Covered Wagon Raid*/*Frisco Tornado*/1950 · *Honeychile*/1951 · *Oklahoma Annie*/*Toughest Man in Arizona*/1952 · *A Perilous Journey*/1953 · *Cole Younger, Gunfighter*/*King of the Wild Stallions*/1958 · *Showdown*/1963 · *He Rides Tall*/*Bullet for a Badman*/*Taggart*/*Black Spurs*/1964 · *Apache Uprising*/*Johnny Reno*/1965 · *Waco*/*Red Tomahawk*/1966 · *Hostile Guns*/1967
Television *Gunsmoke*/59 · *Rawhide*/*Riverboat*/*Trackdown*/*Wagon Train*/60 · *Bonanza*/*Laredo*/65

Stallings, Laurence (1894-1968) · Writer. Trained in the military, Stallings was decorated as a hero for a World War I incident that also necessitated the amputation of a leg. His writing both demonstrates a fascination with combat and denounces war, for example in the play he co-wrote with Maxwell Anderson, *What Price Glory?*, and in his first film script, *The Big Parade*. His film writing was at its best with strong collaborators, in particular King Vidor and John Ford. He invested scripts with strong dramatic structure and evocative scenes that underline the principal themes, such as the testimonial presentation of the watch and Nathan Brittles's graveside conversation with his wife in *She Wore a Yellow Ribbon*. BA

Barbara Stanwyck

(co-sc) *Billy the Kid*/1930 · *The Man from Dakota*/(co-sc) *Northwest Passage*/1940 · *Salome, Where She Danced*/1945 · (co-sc) *3 Godfathers*/1948 · (co-sc) *She Wore a Yellow Ribbon*/1949

Stanton, Harry Dean (b 1926) · Actor. Perhaps only entering the wider public consciousness when he walked out of the Fordian desert-scape at the beginning of *Paris, Texas*, one of latter-day Hollywood's most adventurous and dependable character actors has a remarkably lengthy filmography, opening with bit-part credits in a pair of Western programmers from Lesley Selander. He played cavalry sergeants in each of the late 60s movies below; while of his more substantial supporting roles in the 70s, his rustler in *The Missouri Breaks* remains most memorable for his severe haircut and his shocking demise. PT
Tomahawk Trail/1956 · *Revolt at Fort Laramie*/1957 · *The Proud Rebel*/1958 · *How the West Was Won*/1962 · *Ride in the Whirlwind*/1966 · *A Time for Killing*/1967 · *Day of the Evil Gun*/1968 · *Count Your Bullets*/1972 · *Pat Garrett and Billy the Kid*/1973 · *Zandy's Bride*/*Rancho DeLuxe*/1974 · *The Missouri Breaks*/1976
Television *The Adventures of Rin Tin Tin*/*The Texan*/*Gunsmoke*/58 · *Have Gun, Will Travel*/*Bat Masterson*/*The Rifleman*/59 · *The Tall Man*/*Johnny Ringo*/60 · *Cheyenne*/61 · *The Virginian*/62 · *Empire*/63 · *The Dangerous Days of Kiowa Jones*/66 · *Cimarron Strip*/*The Wild, Wild West*/*The Guns of Will Sonnett*/67 · *The High Chaparral*/68 · *The Young Maverick*/79

Stanwyck, Barbara (b 1907) · One of the great Hollywood actresses, virtually without peer in the portrayal of tough, fearsome, women of the West. She typically plays a wisecracking, cynical and aggressive woman, demanding respect and eliciting fear from her male counterparts. However, her characters always pay the price for this assault on the patriarchal order, either with their life (*The Maverick Queen*), or neutralized into merely one half of a couple in the final reel (*Forty Guns*). The theme song from the latter film which describes her as 'a high-riding woman with a whip' catches the essence of the Stanwyck Western persona. She starred in her own Western television series *The Big Valley* 1965-9. In 1973 she was admitted to the National Cowboy Hall of Fame. PS
Mexicali Rose/1930 · *Annie Oakley*/1935 · *Union Pacific*/1939 · *The Great Man's Lady*/1942 · *California*/1946 · *The Furies*/

Charles Starrett

1950 · *The Moonlighter*/1953 · *Cattle Queen of Montana*/*The Violent Men*/1954 · *The Maverick Queen*/1956 · *Trooper Hook*/*Forty Guns*/1957
Television *Dick Powell's Zane Grey Theatre*/58 · *Wagon Train*/61 · *Rawhide*/62 · *The Big Valley*/65

Starrett, Charles (1903-86) · Actor. Starrett started his movie career in the early 30s playing leading roles in romantic films. It was only after he appeared in the adventure movie *The Mask of Fu Manchu* that his career took a different direction. It started with a switch from Paramount to Columbia, whom he talked into letting him make a series of Westerns. In the next five years he starred in over thirty films, and in 1940 he starred in the first of a series that would make him one of the most popular of the Western stars of the 40s and 50s, as the mysterious black-clad avenger, the Durango Kid. TM
Return of Casey Jones/1933 · *Gallant Defender*/*Undercover Men*/1935 · *The Mysterious Avenger*/*Secret Patrol*/*Code of the Range*/*The Cowboy Star*/*Stampede*/*Dodge City Trail*/1936 · *Westbound Mail*/*Trapped*/*Two Gun Law*/*Two Fisted Sheriff*/*One Man Justice*/*The Old Wyoming Trail*/*Outlaws of the Prairie*/1937 · *Cattle Raiders*/*Call of the Rockies*/*Law of the Plains*/*West of Cheyenne*/*South of Arizona*/*The Colorado Trail*/*West of Santa Fe*/*Rio Grande*/*The Thundering West*/1938 · *Texas Stampede*/*Spoilers of the Range*/*Western Caravans*/*The Man from Sundown*/*North of the Yukon*/*Raiders of the Black River*/*Outpost of the Mounties*/*The Stranger from Texas*/1939 · *Two Fisted Ranger*/*Bullets for Rustlers*/*Blazing Six Shooters*/*Texas Stagecoach*/*The Durango Kid*/*West of Abilene*/*Thundering Frontier*/1940 · *The Pinto Kid*/*Outlaws of the Panhandle*/*The Medico of Painted Springs*/*Thunder Over the Prairie*/*Prairie Strangers*/*The Royal Mounted Patrol*/*Riders of the*

Badlands/1941 · West of Tombstone/Lawless Plainsmen/Down Rio Grande Way/Riders of the Northland/Bad Men of the Hills/Overland to Deadwood/Riding Through Nevada/Pardon My Gun/1942 · The Fighting Buckaroo/Law of the Northwest/Frontier Fury/Robin Hood of the Range/Hail to the Rangers/Cowboy in the Clouds/1943 · Cowboy Canteen/Sundown Valley/Riding West/Cowboy from Lonesome River/Cyclone Prairie Rangers/Saddle Leather Law/1944 · Return of the Durango Kid/Rough Ridin' Justice/Rustlers of the Badlands/Blazing the Western Trail/Outlaws of the Rockies/Lawless Empire/1945 · Texas Panhandle/Frontier Gunlaw/Roaring Rangers/Gunning for Vengeance/Galloping Thunder/Two Fisted Stranger/The Desert Horseman/Heading West/Landrush/Terror Trail/The Fighting Frontiersman/1946 · South of the Chisholm Trail/The Lone Hand Texan/West of Dodge City/Law of the Canyon/Prairie Raiders/The Stranger from Ponca City/Riders of the Lone Star/Buckaroo from Powder River/Last Days of Boot Hill/1947 · Six Gun Law/Phantom Valley/West of Sonora/Whirlwind Raiders/Blazing Across the Pecos/Trail to Laredo/El Dorado Pass/Quick on the Trigger/1948 · Challenge of the Range/Laramie/The Blazing Trail/South of Death Valley/Bandits of El Dorado/Desert Vigilante/Horseman of the Sierras/Renegades of the Sage/1949 · Trail of the Rustlers/Outcasts of Black Mesa/Texas Dynamo/Streets of Ghost Town/Across the Badlands/Raiders of Tomahawk Creek/Lightning Guns/Frontier Outpost/1950 · Prairie Roundup/Ridin' the Outlaw Trail/Fort Savage Raiders/Snake River Desperadoes/Bonanza Town/Cyclone Fury/The Kid from Amarillo/Pecos River/1951 · Smoky Canyon/The Hawk of Wild River/Laramie Mountains/The Rough Tough West/Junction City/The Kid from Broken Gun/1952

Steele, Bob (b 1906) · Actor, aka Bob Bradbury Jr. Cheerful, two-fisted star of series Westerns during the 30s who did his own stunting, and who had made his début as a juvenile in two-reelers directed by his father Robert North Bradbury, a Western specialist. Edged out by the rise of the singing cowboy towards the end of the decade, he turned to character roles (notably as Curly, vindictive tormentor of the half-witted Lennie in *Of Mice and Men*, 1939) before recapturing his popularity in three further series during the 40s (*Billy the Kid, The Three Mesquiteers* and *The Trail Blazers*). After that, with his grin transformed into a

sneer, he trod a morose path through the West in supporting villain roles, only occasionally (as in *Hang 'Em High*, where he is the only member of the lynching party to counsel leniency) being allowed out of the rut. The author of two Western novels published in the 30s, Steele latterly toured in circuses and rodeos, and appeared regularly on television in the *F Troop* series. TMI *The Border Sheriff/Davy Crockett at the Fall of the Alamo/1926 · Sitting Bull at the Spirit Lake Massacre/The Mojave Kid/The Bandit's Son/1927 · Driftin' Sands/The Riding Renegade/Breed of the Sunsets/Man in the Rough/The Trail of Courage/Headin' for Danger/1928 · The Amazing Vagabond/The Invaders/The Cowboy and the Outlaw/A Texas Cowboy/1929 · Breezy Bill/Hunted Men/The Man from Nowhere/Near the Rainbow's End/The Oklahoma Sheriff/Oklahoma Cyclone/The Land of Missing Men/Headin' North/1930 · The Ridin' Fool/Sunrise Trail/Nevada Buckaroo/Near the Trail's End/1931 · Law of the West/South of Santa Fe/Riders of the Desert/The Man from Hell's Edges/Texas Buddies/Hidden Valley/The Fighting Champ/Son of Oklahoma/Young Blood/1932 · Breed of the Border/The California Trail/Trailing North/The Gallant Fool/Ranger's Code/Galloping Romeo/1933 · Brand of Hate/A Demon for Trouble/1934 · Kid Courageous/No Man's Range/Big Calibre/Rider of the Law/Alias John Law/Powdersmoke Range/Western Justice/Smokey Smith/Tombstone Terror/Trail of Terror/1935 · Sundown Saunders/The Kid Ranger/Cavalry/Brand of the Outlaws/Last of the Warrens/The Law Rides/1936 · Gun Lords of Stirrup Basin/Arizona Gunfighter/Border Phantom/Doomed at Sundown/The Red Rope/Ridin' the Lone Trail/The Trusted Outlaw/The Gun Ranger/The Colorado Kid/Lightnin' Crandall/Thunder in the Desert/1937 · Desert Patrol/Paroled to Die/Durango Valley Raiders/The Feud Makers/1938 · Smoky Trail/El Diablo Rides/Riders of the Sage/Feud of the Range/The Pal from Texas/Mesquite Buckaroo/1939 · The Carson City Kid/Billy the Kid in Texas/Billy the Kid Outlawed/Billy the Kid's Gun Justice/Wild Horse Valley/Pinto Canyon/The Trail Blazers/Under Texas Skies/Lone Star Raiders/1940 · Billy the Kid in Santa Fe/Billy the Kid's Fighting Pals/Billy the Kid's Range War/The Great Train Robbery/Saddlemates/Gangs of Sonora/Outlaws of Cherokee Trail/Gauchos of El Dorado/Pals of the Pecos/Prairie Pioneers/1941 · West of Cimarron/Code of the Outlaw/The Phantom Plainsmen/Shadows of the Sage/Raiders of*

the Range/Valley of Hunted Men/Westward Ho/1942 · The Blocked Trail/Thundering Trails/Santa Fe Scouts/Riders of the Rio Grande/Death Valley Rangers/1943 · Arizona Whirlwind/Sonora Stagecoach/Westward Bound/The Utah Kid/Marked Trails/Outlaw Trail/Trigger Law/1944 · The Navajo Kid/Northwest Trail/Wildfire/1945 · The Sheriff of Redwood Valley/Thunder Town/Six Gun Man/Rio Grande Raiders/Ambush Trail/1946 · Bandits of Dark Canyon/Cheyenne/Twilight on the Rio Grande/1947 · South of St. Louis/The Savage Horde/1949 · Silver Canyon/Cattle Drive/Fort Worth/Bugles in the Afternoon/1951 · Rose of Cimarron/The Lion and the Horse/1952 · Savage Frontier/San Antone/Column South/1953 · The Outcast/Drums Across the River/1954 · The Spoilers/Last of the Desperados/1955 · Pardners/Gun for a Coward/1956 · Duel at Apache Wells/The Parson and the Outlaw/Decision at Sundown/1957 · Once Upon a Horse/Rio Bravo/1958 · Hell Bent for Leather/1959 · The Comancheros/Six Black Horses/1961 · The Wild Westerners/1962 · McLintock!/He Rides Tall/1963 · Bullet for a Badman/Taggart/(uncredited) Cheyenne Autumn/(uncredited) Major Dundee/1964 · The Bounty Killer/Town Tamer/Requiem for a Gunfighter/Shenandoah/1965 · Hang 'Em High/1968 · The Great Bank Robbery/1969 · Rio Lobo/1970 · Skin Game/Something Big/1971
Television *Gunsmoke/Cheyenne/The Life and Legend of Wyatt Earp/55 · Have Gun, Will Travel/The Californians/Tales of Wells Fargo/58 · The Rebel/Rawhide/59 · F Troop/65*

Steiner, Max (1888-1971) · Composer. Steiner worked on over 200 films, mostly for RKO and Warner Bros., and is best known for the species of dark romanticism found in his work on *King Kong, Gone With the Wind*

Bob Steele

and *The Treasure of the Sierra Madre*. Austrian by birth, he worked on many archetypally American movies, drawing on traditional material for such masterpieces of scoring as *Dodge City*, *They Died with their Boots On* and *The Searchers*. He was particularly associated with the films of Michael Curtiz, Walsh and Ford, and received three Oscars, which wasn't enough. KN
Cimarron/1930 · *The Conquerors*/1932 · *The Cheyenne Kid*/1933 · *West of the Pecos*/1935 · *God's Country and the Woman*/1936 · *Gold Is Where You Find It*/1938 · *Dodge City*/*The Oklahoma Kid*/1939 · *Virginia City*/*Santa Fe Trail*/1940 · *They Died with their Boots On*/1941 · *Saratoga Trunk*/1945 · *San Antonio*/1946 · *Cheyenne*/*Pursued*/1947 · *Silver River*/*The Treasure of the Sierra Madre*/1948 · *South of St Louis*/1949 · *Dallas*/*Rocky Mountain*/*Raton Pass*/1950 · *Sugarfoot*/*Distant Drums*/1951 · *Springfield Rifle*/*The Lion and the Horse*/*The Iron Mistress*/1952 · *The Charge at Feather River*/*The Boy from Oklahoma*/1953 · *The Violent Men*/1954 · *The Last Command*/1955 · *The Searchers*/*Bandido*/1956 · *Fort Dobbs*/1958 · *The Hanging Tree*/1959 · *A Distant Trumpet*/1964
Television *The Virginian*/62

Stewart, James (b 1908) · Actor. Stewart's work with Anthony Mann and John Ford ensures him a permanent place in the history of the Western. His range extends from the gentle self-assurance of a traditional Western hero such as Henry Fonda to the hysteria and neurotic violence more usually associated with such leading 'heavies' as Lee Marvin and Warren Oates. This is especially evident in Mann's films, with the gentle side prominent in *Bend of the River* and the hysteria breaking out in *The Naked Spur*. Stewart's work with Ford belongs to the director's self-reflective and somewhat cynical period, crystallized in Stewart's par-

odies of Fonda's Wyatt Earp-style heroics in *Two Rode Together* and *Cheyenne Autumn*. Perhaps his greatest Western performance is in *The Man Who Shot Liberty Valance*, as the idealistic lawyer whose belated recognition of the pragmatics of frontier life ensures his success as tamer of the wilderness. TR
Destry Rides Again/1939 · *Winchester '73*/*Broken Arrow*/1950 · *Bend of the River*/1951 · *The Naked Spur*/1952 · *The Far Country*/1954 · *The Man from Laramie*/1955 · *Night Passage*/1957 · *Two Rode Together*/1961 · *The Man Who Shot Liberty Valance*/*How the West Was Won*/1962 · *Cheyenne Autumn*/1964 · *Shenandoah*/*The Rare Breed*/1965 · *Firecreek*/1967 · *Bandolero!*/1968 · *The Cheyenne Social Club*/1970 · *Fools' Parade*/1971 · *The Shootist*/1976

Strode, Woody (b 1914) · Strode's career as a supporting actor took an upturn when he was given the central role in *Sergeant Rutledge*, John Ford's tale of black cavalrymen. He was also cast by Ford as an Indian (*Two Rode Together*) and as Tom Doniphon's black retainer in *The Man Who Shot Liberty Valance*. His status as a minor icon of the genre was consolidated when he appeared as one of the gunmen in the opening sequence of *C'era una volta il west*. TR
The Gambler from Natchez/1954 · *Sergeant Rutledge*/1960 · *Two Rode Together*/1961 · *The Man Who Shot Liberty Valance*/1962 · *The Professionals*/1966 · *Shalako*/*C'era una volta il west*/1968 · *La collina degli stivali*/1969 · *La spina dorsale del diavolo*/1970 · *The Last Rebel*/1971 · *The Revengers*/1972 · *The Gatling Gun*/1973 · *Winterhawk*/*Keoma*/1976 · *Lust in the Dust*/1984
Television *The Man from Blackhawk*/60 · *Rawhide*/61 · *Daniel Boone*/66 · *The Quest*/76

Sturges, John (b 1911) · Director. Sturges' reputation, especially in France (in America

he is largely ignored), has fluctuated wildly over the years. At first spoken of in the same breath as Daves and Mann, he has now been relegated to the critical back lot. In truth Sturges is no auteur, but at his best he is at least as efficient and impressive a *metteur en scène* as Gordon Douglas. His strengths are a lively yet precise direction of actors, his judicious and imaginative use of space and colour and his ability to handle large-scale action sequences (witness the Indian attacks in *Fort Bravo* and *Jake Wade*, the showdown in *O.K. Corral* and the final battle in *The Magnificent Seven*). On the debit side the impressively made *Last Train from Gun Hill* is just too close for comfort to *3:10 to Yuma*, *Sergeants 3* is a dreadful remake of *Gunga Din* as a Western comedy, and *The Hallelujah Trail* an elephantine would-be parody. Yet when Sturges returned to form with the excellent *Hour of the Gun*, a cynical and bitter continuation of the Wyatt Earp story after the O.K. Corral, nobody noticed. JP
The Walking Hills/1949 · *Escape from Fort Bravo*/1953 · *Bad Day at Black Rock*/1954 · *Backlash*/*Gunfight at the O.K. Corral*/1956 · *The Law and Jake Wade*/*Last Train from Gun Hill*/1958 · *The Magnificent Seven*/1960 · *Sergeants 3*/1962 · *The Hallelujah Trail*/1964 · *Hour of the Gun*/1967 · *Joe Kidd*/1972 · *Valdez, il mezzosangue*/1973

Sullivan, Barry (b 1912) · Actor. With somewhat narrow features, frequently accompanied by a pencil moustache, he was a dependable, slightly colourless, presence during the 40s and 50s. His two best Western roles were opposite Barbara Stanwyck: in *The Maverick Queen* the ambiguity of his screen persona (he sometimes played villains) lent substance to his playing of a Pinkerton man masquerading as an outlaw, while he brought a somewhat unaccustomed vigour to the town-taming lawman of *Forty Guns*. In the 60s he achieved the feat of top

James Stewart

Woody Strode

John Sturges

Barry Sullivan

Robert Taylor

billing amid a plethora of other stalwarts in two A.C. Lyles Westerns. TP

The Woman of the Town/1943 · *Bad Men of Tombstone*/*The Outriders*/1949 · *Texas Lady*/1955 · *The Maverick Queen*/1956 · *Dragoon Wells Massacre*/*Forty Guns*/1957 · *Seven Ways from Sundown*/1960 · *Stage to Thunder Rock*/1964 · *Buckskin*/1968 · *Tell Them Willie Boy Is Here*/1969 · *Pat Garrett and Billy the Kid*/1973 · *Take a Hard Ride*/1975

Television *Dick Powell's Zane Grey Theatre*/58 · *Bonanza*/59 · *The Tall Man*/60 · *Wagon Train*/62 · *The Great Adventure*/*The Virginian*/63 · *The Loner*/65 · *The Road West*/66 · *The High Chaparral*/70 · *Yuma*/71 · *Kung Fu*/72 · *Little House on the Prairie*/79

Sullivan, C. Gardner (1879-1965) · Writer. After years as a journalist, Sullivan sent his first film story to Thomas Ince in 1912. Ince accepted it, hired Sullivan, and a career that would include almost 400 scripts began. Ince was the first producer to insist that scripts contained details of camera set-ups, angles and other technical data, and thus Sullivan as his leading writer became a pioneer of a new art form – the scenario. He had a hand in the classic *Civilization*, his scripts moulded the character played by William S. Hart, and far ahead, in the 40s, he would still be writing major Westerns for DeMille. JL

(st) *Custer's Last Fight*/*The Invaders*/1912 · *Days of '49*/1913 · (co-st, co-sc) *The Passing of Two-Gun Hicks*/(co-st, co-sc) *In the Sage Brush Country*/1914 · (co-st, co-sc) *On the Night Stage*/*The Iron Strain*/(co-st, co-sc) *Mr 'Silent' Haskins*/(co-st, co-sc) *The Grudge*/(co-st, co-sc) *The Roughneck*/(st) *The Man from Nowhere*/(st) *The Darkening Trail*/(co-st, co-sc) *Tools of Providence*/*The Man from Oregon*/(st) *Between Men*/*The Last of the Line*/1915 · (st) *Hell's Hinges*/*Lieutenant Danny*/(st) *The Aryan*/(st) *The Dawn*

Maker/(st) *The Return of Draw Egan*/1916 · (co-sc) *Carmen of the Klondyke*/(st) *Selfish Yates*/(st) *Shark Monroe*/*The Border Wireless*/(st) *Branding Broadway*/1918 · *The Poppy Girl's Husband*/(st) *John Petticoats*/(st) *Wagon Tracks*/1919 · (st) *Dynamite Smith*/1924 · *Tumbleweeds*/1925 · (st only) *The Bugle Call*/(supervised) *White Gold*/1927 · (co-sc) *Union Pacific*/1939 · (co-st, co-sc) *North West Mounted Police*/(st only) *Kit Carson*/1940 · (st only) *Jackass Mail*/1942

T

Taylor, Robert (1911-69) · For an actor who was promoted to stardom as a matinée idol, Taylor subsequently proved an admirably tough and uncompromising movie Westerner, though it is true that apart from *Stand Up and Fight* and the anodyne *Billy the Kid*, the Westerns he made came after his popularity had peaked. To cite only three striking later performances, he was particularly hardbitten as the scout in *Westward the Women*, brought a laconic brand of stoicism to the lawman whose past catches up with him in *The Law and Jake Wade*, and made a persuasive job of the psychotic villain in *The Last Hunt*. TP

Stand Up and Fight/1939 · *Billy the Kid*/1941 · *Ambush*/1949 · *Devil's Doorway*/1950 · *Westward the Women*/1951 · *Ride, Vaquero!*/1952 · *Many Rivers to Cross*/*The Last Hunt*/1955 · *Saddle the Wind*/*The Law and Jake Wade*/1958 · *The Hangman*/1959 · *Cattle King*/1963 · *Johnny Tiger*/*Pampa salvaje*/1966

Television *Death Valley Days*/66 · *Return of the Gunfighter*/*Hondo*/67

Teal, Ray (1902-76) · Actor. Ray Teal made his film début in a Gene Autry Western in 1938, and played character roles for over 30 years. In his youth he had played the saxophone, and had his own show touring the South, but there was seldom anything as innocuous as that in the parts he portrayed. He was large, heavy, moustached and menacing, and always with a touch of slyness – the quintessential crooked sheriff. He played good men too, but they were never quite as credible. JL

Western Jamboree/1938 · *Cherokee Strip*/*Prairie Schooners*/*Pony Post*/*Adventures of Red Ryder*/*Northwest Passage*/1940 · *They Died with their Boots On*/*Honky Tonk*/*Outlaws of the Panhandle*/1941 · *Wild Bill Hickok Rides*/*Northwest Rangers*/*Apache Trail*/1942 · *Barbary Coast Gent*/1944 · *Along Came Jones*/*The Harvey Girls*/1945 ·

Canyon Passage/1946 · *Unconquered*/*Michigan Kid*/*Ramrod*/1947 · *The Man from Colorado*/1948 · *Whispering Smith*/*Streets of Laredo*/*Ambush*/*The Kid from Texas*/1949 · *Davy Crockett, Indian Scout*/*Winchester '73*/*The Redhead and the Cowboy*/*The Great Missouri Raid*/1950 · *Fort Worth*/*Along the Great Divide*/*The Secret of Convict Lake*/*Distant Drums*/*Flaming Feather*/*Montana Belle*/*The Wild North*/1951 · *The Lion and the Horse*/*Hangman's Knot*/*Cattle Town*/1952 · *The Last Posse*/1953 · *The Command*/*Run for Cover*/1954 · *Rage at Dawn*/*The Indian Fighter*/*Apache Ambush*/*The Man from Bitter Ridge*/1955 · *The Burning Hills*/*The Young Guns*/*The Guns of Fort Petticoat*/1956 · *Utah Blaine*/*The Phantom Stagecoach*/*The Oklahoman*/*The Tall Stranger*/*Decision at Sundown*/1957 · *Gunman's Walk*/*Saddle the Wind*/1958 · *One-Eyed Jacks*/1960 · *Posse from Hell*/1961 · *Cattle King*/1963 · *Bullet for a Badman*/*Taggart*/1964 · *Chisum*/1970

Television *Frontier*/*Cheyenne*/55 · *Broken Arrow*/56 · *Maverick*/57 · *The Restless Gun*/*The Texan*/*Trackdown*/*Wanted: Dead or Alive*/58 · *Bonanza*/*Bronco*/*Bat Masterson*/*The Alaskans*/*Laramie*/59 · *Colt .45*/*Klondike*/60 · *Lawman*/61 · *The Monroes*/66

Tessari, Duccio (b 1926) · Director. In the early 1950s he made documentary films in Genoa, before working as assistant and scriptwriter on some of the best 'peplums' such as *Hercules Conquers Atlantis*. His Italian Western scripts, including *Sette pistole per i Mac Gregor*, are notable for their sense of humour: he also, uncredited, helped to write *Per un pugno di dollari*. He directed spy films and the parody classical 'epic' *Sons of Thunder*, before making the two 'Ringo' films back to back with the same production crews and leading players. These Westerns contain 'commentaries' on Ford, Hawks and Walsh and, according to Tessari, 'challenge the worst forms of Hollywood cliché'. They are well-constructed, carefully written and surprisingly sophisticated. Later, he parodied the 'political' Spaghettis in a wild variation on the theme of *Two Mules for Sister Sara*. CF

(co-sc only) *Per un pugno di dollari*/1964 · (sc) *Una pistola per Ringo*/(co-sc) *Il ritorno di Ringo*/1965 · (co-sc only) *Sette pistole per i Mac Gregor*/1966 · (co-sc only) *Un treno per Durango*/1967 · (co-sc) *Vivi o preferibilmente morti*/1969 · (co-sc) *Viva la muerte ... tua!*/1972 · (co-sc) *Zorro*/1975

Television *Tex e il signore degli abissi*/85

Thomson, Fred (1890-1928) · Actor. Fred Thomson's Westerns cry out for revival. The only ordained minister to abandon the church for the prairie, Thomson married the famous screenwriter Frances Marion, began (sometimes as a villain) in his wife's movies, and then, of a sudden, became a Western hero second only, in the 20s, to Tom Mix. His movies were (naturally) strong on uplift, action-filled, and had superb photography and stunt work, performed by Thomson himself. They could also be engagingly droll. In *The Sunset Legion* Thomson played dual roles of good man and bad: when he was the baddie, his horse, Silver King, wore a specially tailored suit of black cloth. He died of pneumonia at the height of his success. JL
Galloping Gallagher/The Dangerous Coward/The Fighting Sap/The Mask of Lopez/North of Nevada/The Silent Stranger/ Thundering Hoofs/1924 · *All Around Frying Pan/The Bandit's Baby/Ridin' the Wind/ That Devil Quemado/The Wild Bull's Lair*/ 1925 · *Hands Across the Border/Lone Hand Saunders/A Regular Scout/The Tough Guy/The Two-Gun Man*/1926 · *Arizona Nights/Don Mike/Jesse James/Silver Comes Through*/1927 · *The Pioneer Scout/The Sunset Legion/Kit Carson*/1928

Thundercloud, Chief (1889-1955) · Chief Thundercloud, as the Indian actor Victor Daniels was credited, was part-Cherokee, and not, strictly speaking, a chief. After years of stunting and playing bits, he was Tonto in Lone Ranger serials, had a lead in *King of the Stallions*, and then, remarkably for an Indian actor, became a series hero when he replaced Ken Maynard in Monogram's Trail Blazers movies. Thundercloud was also a radio actor and singer, and had gone the round of rodeos in his youth. JL
The Big Trail/1930 · *Rustler's Paradise/The*

Singing Vagabond/1935 · *Ride, Ranger, Ride/Ramona/The Plainsman/For the Service/* 1936 · *Wild West Days/Renfrew of the Royal Mounted*/1937 · *The Lone Ranger/Flaming Frontiers/The Great Adventures of Wild Bill Hickok*/1938 · *Union Pacific/The Lone Ranger Rides Again*/1939 · *Geronimo!/Young Buffalo Bill/Wyoming/North West Mounted Police/Murder on the Yukon*/1940 · *Hudson's Bay/Western Union/Silver Stallion*/1941 · *Shut My Big Mouth/King of the Stallions/* 1942 · *Daredevils of the West*/1943 · *Black Arrow/Buffalo Bill/Sonora Stagecoach/ Outlaw Trail*/1944 · *The Phantom Rider/* 1945 · *Romance of the West/Badman's Territory/Renegade Girl*/1946 · *Unconquered/* 1947 · *Blazing Across the Pecos/Call of the Forest*/1949 · *Ambush/Indian Territory/Colt .45/A Ticket to Tomahawk/Davy Crockett, Indian Scout/I Killed Geronimo*/1950 · *Santa Fe*/1951 · *Buffalo Bill in Tomahawk Territory/The Half-Breed*/1952

Tiomkin, Dimitri (1899-1979) · A prolific composer of film music who went to the USA from Russia via Berlin and Paris. Through his friendship with Frank Capra he was introduced to indigenous folk and country music, an influence which is evident in nearly all his Westerns, and in particular *The Alamo*. For *Duel in the Sun*, the music was suitably rhetorical and melodramatic. But of more interest is his work for *High Noon* and *Gunfight at the O.K. Corral*, in which the entire scores are based (unconventionally) on single themes. For Hawks' epic *Red River* the main theme is for full choral orchestra, whereas in *Rio Bravo* Tiomkin returns to a simple folk song as the theme music. DR
The Westerner/1940 · *Duel in the Sun*/1946 · *Red River*/1947 · *The Dude Goes West/* 1948 · *Canadian Pacific/Dakota Lil*/1949 · *Drums in the Deep South/Bugles in the Afternoon*/1951 · *High Noon/The Big Sky/* 1952 · *The Command*/1954 · *Strange Lady*

in Town/1955 · *Tension at Table Rock/ Friendly Persuasion/Giant/Gunfight at the O.K. Corral*/1956 · *Night Passage/The Young Land*/1957 · *Rio Bravo*/1958 · *Last Train from Gun Hill*/1958 · *The Unforgiven*/1959 · *The Alamo*/1960 · *(theme song only) The Last Sunset*/1961 · *The War Wagon*/1967 · *McKenna's Gold*/1968
Television *Rawhide/Hotel de Paree*/59 · *Gunslinger*/61

Tourneur, Jacques (1904-77) · Director. The son of the great Maurice Tourneur, the ten-year-old Jacques accompanied his father to Hollywood, where he grew up in the film world. After a brief return to France where he edited his father's films and directed four light comedies, Jacques became an American director in 1939. At RKO he made some hauntingly poetic low-budget pictures with the producer Val Lewton (*Cat People*, 1942, and *I Walked with a Zombie*, 1943) as well as the doom-laden, magnificently directed *Out of the Past* (1947). Tourneur was one of the few masterful cinéastes whose films far outstripped the interest of whatever script he was given, conjuring up complex networks of meaning through a sophisticated interaction of framing, lighting, *mise en scène* and camerawork. His best efforts manage to dramatize in their visual texture the very processes of fantasy and psychological repression at work below a storyline's surface, giving the film an emotional intensity rarely equalled in Hollywood. Unfortunately, his subtle approach marginalized his work and his career stalled. He ended up working in television and directing potboilers in Europe. PW
Canyon Passage/1946 · *Stars in My Crown/* 1949 · *Way of a Gaucho*/1952 · *Stranger on Horseback*/1954 · *Wichita/Great Day in the Morning*/1955
Television *Northwest Passage*/58 · *Bonanza/ The Californians*/59 · *The Alaskans*/60

Ray Teal

Fred Thomson

Chief Thundercloud

Dimitri Tiomkin

Claire Trevor

Forrest Tucker

Tom Tyler

Trevor, Claire (b 1909) · Actress. Trevor began her film career with B-Westerns for Fox. Six years later, as Dallas in *Stagecoach*, she was to create one of the classic Western heroines, and in her later roles that character's essence remained. Entertainer, bargirl, saloon-keeper, they had seen bad days and would see more, but they had good sense, and gaiety, and the spirit to endure. Outside Westerns, Trevor's range was very wide; within them, that one character sufficed, and Trevor played her gloriously. JL
Life in the Raw/The Last Trail/1933 · *Wild Gold*/1934 · *Valley of the Giants*/1938 · *Stagecoach/Allegheny Uprising*/1939 · *Dark Command*/1940 · *Honky Tonk/Texas*/1941 · *The Desperadoes/The Woman of the Town*/1943 · *Best of the Badmen*/1951 · *The Stranger Wore a Gun*/1953 · *Man Without a Star*/1955
Television *Wagon Train*/59

Trotti, Lamar (1900-52) · Writer. A former journalist, Trotti had by the mid-30s become one of Fox's leading scenarists, and by the 40s was acting as producer also. He wrote three films for John Ford. Dudley Nichols collaborated on *Steamboat Round the Bend*, and Sonya Levien on *Drums Along the Mohawk*, but the magnificent *Young Mr Lincoln* was a solo effort. So also was Trotti's script for one of the greatest of all Westerns, *The Ox-Bow Incident*. For a Western, this film has a deal of talk, but what talk it is – alert, colourful, and vivid with feeling for character. JL
(co-sc) *The Country Beyond*/1936 · (co-sc) *Drums Along the Mohawk*/1939 · *Brigham Young – Frontiersman*/1940 · *Hudson's Bay/Belle Starr*/1941 · (p) *The Ox-Bow Incident*/1942 · (p) *Yellow Sky*/1948

Tucker, Forrest (1919-86) · Six feet four, blond, blue-eyed, rugged-looking actor of Swedish and English descent, his big break came when he was spotted by Samuel Goldwyn and given a small part in *The Westerner*. After his war service, when he did a small hitch in the 3rd Cavalry, he starred in a number of Westerns from the mid-40s until the late 50s. In 1965 he starred in the comedy Western television series *F Troop*, and in 1973 he returned in a similar show, *Dusty's Trail*. TM
The Westerner/1940 · *The Renegades*/1946 · *Gunfighters*/1947 · *Coroner Creek/The Plunderers/Two Guys from Texas/Adventures in Silverado*/1948 · *The Last Bandit/Brimstone/Hellfire*/1949 · *Rock Island Trail/The Nevadan/California Passage*/1950 · Oh,

Susanna/Warpath/Flaming Feather/Bugles in the Afternoon/Montana Belle/1951 · Ride the Man Down/Pony Express/1952 · San Antone/1953 · Jubilee Trail/1954 · Rage at Dawn/The Vanishing American/1955 · Stagecoach to Fury/Three Violent People/The Quiet Gun/1956 · The Deerslayer/1957 · Fort Massacre/Gunsmoke in Tucson/1958 · Chisum/1970
Television *Death Valley Days*/55 · *Gunsmoke*/57 · *Wagon Train*/61 · *Whispering Smith*/62 · *The Virginian/The Wide Country*/64 · *Daniel Boone*/65 · *F Troop/Hondo*/67 · *Lock, Stock and Barrel/Alias Smith and Jones/Cade's County*/71 · *Dusty's Trail*/73 · *Little House on the Prairie*/74 · *The Incredible Rocky Mountain Race*/77 · *The Rebels*/79

Tyler, Tom (1903-54) · A granite-faced star of series Westerns who had the physique of a bodybuilder. Best remembered now for his portrayal of the nervous Luke Plummer, one of Wayne's adversaries in *Stagecoach*. He appeared in series Westerns for, amongst others, FBO, Monogram, Republic, and in a number of serials at Mascot and Universal. While at Republic he made thirteen appearances as Stony Brooke in their Three Mesquiteers series. PS
Leatherstocking/1924 · *Let's Go Gallagher/Wyoming Wildcat*/1925 · *The Cowboy Musketeer/Born to Battle/Wild to Go/The Masquerade Bandit/The Arizona Streak/Red Hot Hoofs/Out of the West*/1926 · *The Cowboy Cop/Lightning Lariats/The Sonora Kid/Splitting the Breeze/Cyclone of the Range/Tom's Gang/Tom and His Pals/The Cherokee Kid/The Desert Pirate/The Flying U Ranch*/1927 · *When the Law Rides/Phantom of the Range/The Texas Tornado/Terror Mountain/The Tyrant of Red Gulch/The Avenging Rider*/1928 · *Trail of the Horse Thieves/Idaho Red/Gun Law/Pride of the Pawnee/Law of the Plains/The Man from Nevada/The Lone Horseman/The Phantom Rider/'Neath the Western Skies*/1929 · *Pioneer of the West/The Canyon of Missing Men/Call of the Desert/Phantom of the West*/1930 · *West of Cheyenne/Rose of the Rio Grande/A Rider of the Plains/God's Country and the Man/Battling with Buffalo Bill/Galloping Thru/The Man from Death Valley*/1931 · *Two Fisted Justice/Vanishing Men/Single-Handed Sanders/The Tenderfoot/The Man from New Mexico/Partners of the Trail/Honor of the Mounted/The Forty Niners*/1932 · *When a Man Rides Alone/Deadwood Pass/War on the Range/Clancy of the Mounted*/1933 · *Tracy Rides/Mystery*

Ranch/*The Fighting Hero/The Unconquered Bandit/The Silver Bullet/Terror of the Plains/* 1934 · *Ridin' Thru/Rio Rattler/Coyote Trails/ The Laramie Kid/The Silent Code/Born to Battle/Silent Valley/Powdersmoke Range/* 1935 · *Fast Bullets/Santa Fe Bound/Ridin' On/Roamin' Wild/Pinto Rustlers/Trigger Tom/The Last Outlaw/Rip Roarin' Buckaroo/*1936 · *Phantom of the Range/ Cheyenne Rides Again/Feud of the Trail/ Mystery Range/Brothers of the West/Lost Ranch/Orphan of the Pecos/*1937 · *The Law West of Tombstone/*1938 · *Stagecoach/Drums Along the Mohawk/The Night Riders/ Frontier Marshal/*1939 · *The Westerner/The Light of Western Stars/Cherokee Strip/*1940 · *Outlaws of the Cherokee Trail/Gauchos of Eldorado/West of Cimarron/Texas Rangers Ride Again/Border Vigilantes/*1941 · *Code of the Outlaw/Raiders of the Range/Westward Ho/The Phantom Plainsmen/Shadows on the Sage/The Valley of Hunted Men/Valley of the Sun/*1942 · *Thundering Trails/The Blocked Trail/Santa Fe Scouts/Wagon Tracks West/Riders of the Rio Grande/*1943 · *Boss of Boomtown/Sing Me a Song of Texas/*1944 · *San Antonio/Badman's Territory/*1946 · *Cheyenne/Red River/*1947 · *The Dude Goes West/Return of the Bad Men/Blood on the Moon/*1948 · *The Younger Brothers/I Shot Jesse James/*1948 · *Lust for Gold/She Wore a Yellow Ribbon/Square Dance Jubilee/Riders of the Range/Hellfire/Masked Raiders/*1949 · *The Great Missouri Raid/The Daltons' Women/Trail of Robin Hood/*1950 · *Best of the Badmen/Crooked River/Rio Grande Patrol/Marshal of Heldorado/Fast on the Draw/Hostile Country/West of the Brazos/ Colorado Ranger/*1951 · *Road Agent/*1952 · *Cow Country/*1953

V

Van Cleef, Lee (b 1925) · Actor. Though he played many small parts, generally as a villain, in thrillers and Westerns (an early role was as one of the three gunmen waiting for the mid-day train in *High Noon*), he was all but forgotten until Sergio Leone placed him firmly on the Western map as Eastwood's antagonist in *Per qualche dollaro in più* and *Il buono, il brutto, il cattivo*. Since then his hooked, hawk-like nose, snake eyes and tight, sunken features have become synonymous with the Spaghetti Western. DR
*The Showdown/*1950 · *Untamed Frontier/ High Noon/The Lawless Breed/*1952 · *Arena/Tumbleweed/Jack Slade/The Nebraskan/The Yellow Tomahawk/*1953 · *Arrow in the Dust/Dawn at Socorro/The Desperado/Rails into Laramie/Ten Wanted Men/*1954 · *A Man Alone/Man Without a Star/The Kentuckian/Treasure of Ruby Hills/ Road to Denver/The Vanishing American/ Tribute to a Bad Man/Red Sundown/*1955 · *Pardners/Backlash/The Quiet Gun/Gunfight at the O.K. Corral/The Last Stagecoach West/The Lonely Man/*1956 · *Joe Dakota/ Gun Battle at Monterey/The Tin Star/ Raiders of Old California/The Badge of Marshal Brennan/Day of the Bad Man/*1957 · *The Bravados/*1958 · *Ride Lonesome/*1959 · *Posse from Hell/*1961 · *How the West Was Won/The Man Who Shot Liberty Valance/* 1962 · *Per qualche dollaro in più/*1965 · *Il buono, il brutto, il cattivo/*1966 · *La resa dei conti/Da uomo a uomo/Al di là della legge/I giorni dell'ira/*1967 · *Ehi, amico ... c'è Sabata, hai chiuso!/*1969 · *Barquero/El Condor/*1970 · *Captain Apache/Bad Man's River/E tornato Sabata ... hai chiuso un' altra volta/*1971 · *The Magnificent Seven Ride!/*1972 · *Il grande duello/*1973 · *Blood Money/*1974 · *Take a Hard Ride/*1975 · *Diamante lobo/*1976 · *Kid Vengeance/*1977 Television *The Lone Ranger/*52 · *Tales of Wells Fargo/Trackdown/*57 · *Colt .45/ Wagon Train/Lawman/Zorro/*58 · *Yancy Derringer/The Rifleman/Tombstone Territory/ The Law of the Plainsman/Wanted: Dead or Alive/*59 · *Hotel de Paree/The Alaskans/The Deputy/Gunsmoke/Laramie/Bonanza/Black Saddle/*60 · *Stagecoach West/Maverick/ Bronco/*61 · *Cheyenne/Have Gun, Will Travel/*62 · *The Dakotas/*63 · *Destry/ Rawhide/*64 · *Branded/*65 · *Laredo/*66

Vidor, King (1894-1982) · Director. Vidor's Westerns make a major contribution to the genre. Although the last five have their roots in the historical West, Vidor's populist politics mostly take back seat to the boldness of his visual conceptions (the canyons of New Mexico in *Billy the Kid*, the sunsets and red rocks of *Duel in the Sun*), and the sheer intensity of emotions wound up to a frenzy. Indeed, frenzy is hardly adequate to describe his masterwork, *Duel in the Sun*; Andrew Sarris has rightly called it delirious. EB
*The Sky Pilot/*1921 · *Billy the Kid/*1930 · *The Texas Rangers/*1936 · *Northwest Passage/*1940 · *Duel in the Sun/*1946 · *Man Without a Star/*1955

W

Wales, Wally (1895-1980) · Actor, aka Hal Taliaferro, Floyd Taliaferro. A minor cowboy star and character actor of many years standing who performed alongside virtually every Western series star. His ranching background helped him get numerous bit parts in Westerns during the 'teens. In 1925 he got his first starring role at Action Pictures, where Jean Arthur was often his co-star. In the early sound period he alternated between starring, featured and minor roles. His last headlining film was made in 1934. In 1936 he changed his name to Hal Taliaferro and concentrated on playing heavies. PS
*Western Hearts/Crossing Trails/*1921 · *The Kingfisher's Roost/Travelin' On/*1922 · *Tearin' Loose/Hurricane Horseman/*

Lee Van Cleef

King Vidor

Wally Wales

391

Galloping On/1925 · *Roaring Rider/The Fighting Cheat/Vanishing Hoofs/Riding Rivals/Double Daring/Twisted Triggers/Ace of Action*/1926 · *The Cyclone Cowboy/Tearin' into Trouble/The Meddlin' Stranger/Skedaddle Gold/White Pebbles/Soda Water Cowboy/The Desert of the Lost*/1927 · *Desperate Courage/Saddle Mates/The Flying Buckaroo*/1928 · *Overland Bound*/1929 · *Bar L Ranch/Canyon Hawks/Trails of Peril/Breed of the West*/1930 · *Red Fork Range/Westward Bound/Hell's Valley/So This Is Arizona/Riders of the Cactus/Flying Lariats*/1931 · *Law and Lawless*/1932 · *Deadwood Pass/The Fighting Texans/The Trail Drive/Sagebrush Trail*/1933 · *Potluck Pards/Wheels of Destiny/Nevada Cyclone/Honor of the Range/Smoking Guns/The Fighting Rookie/Fighting Through/The Law of the Wild/The Oil Raider/Mystery Mountain/Arizona Cyclone/Carrying the Mail/Desert Man/The Lone Bandit/The Lone Rider/Pals of the West/The Sundown Trail/The Way of the West/West of the Law*/1934 · *Rustlers of Red Dog/Unconquered Bandit/Six Gun Justice/The Phantom Empire/Range Warfare/The Cowboy and the Bandit/The Silver Bullet/The Laramie Kid/The Vanishing Riders/Powdersmoke Range/Lawless Riders/Swifty/Heir to Trouble/Danger Trails/Fighting Caballero/Five Bad Men/Gun Play/The Miracle Rider/The Pecos Kid/Silent Valley/Trigger Tom/Western Racketeers*/1935 · *Lucky Terror/The Phantom Rider/Avenging Waters/Heroes of the Range/The Traitor/Ambush Valley/Law and Lead/The Unknown Ranger/Rio Grande Ranger/Hair-Trigger Casey*/1936 · *The Gun Ranger/Law of the Ranger/Rootin' Tootin' Rhythm/The Painted Stallion/One Man Justice/The Ranger Steps In/Heart of the Rockies/The Trigger Trio*/1937 · *The Lone Ranger/Stagecoach Days/The Great Adventures of Wild Bill Hickok/Pioneer Trail/South of Arizona/Phantom Gold/Black Bandit/West of*

Santa Fe/Guilty Trail/Prairie Justice/Rio Grande/1938 · *The Thundering West/Frontiers of '49/North of the Yukon/Man of Conquest/Western Caravans/Riders of the Frontier/Overland with Kit Carson/Outpost of the Mounties/Saga of Death Valley/The Stranger from Texas*/1939 · *Bullets for Rustlers/Pioneers of the West/Dark Command/Colorado/Young Bill Hickok/Texas Terrors/The Border Legion/Two Fisted Rangers/The Carson City Kid/Cherokee Strip/Adventures of Red Ryder*/1940 · *The Great Train Robbery/Border Vigilantes/Sheriff of Tombstone/Law of the Range/Under Fiesta Stars/Bad Man of Deadwood/Riders of the Timberline/Roaring Frontiers/Jesse James at Bay/Red River Valley/Along the Rio Grande/In Old Cheyenne*/1941 · *Bullets for Bandits/Romance on the Range/Tombstone, the Town Too Tough to Die/Sons of the Pioneers/King of the Mounties/Little Joe the Wrangler/American Empire/Ridin' Down the Canyon*/1942 · *Song of Texas/The Woman of the Town/Man from Music Mountain/Idaho/Hoppy Serves a Writ/The Leather Burners/Silver Spurs/Cowboy in the Clouds*/1943 · *Lumberjack/The Cowboy and the Senorita/Forty Thieves/Yellow Rose of Texas/Vigilantes of Dodge City/Zorro's Black Whip*/1944 · *Utah/Springtime in Texas*/1945 · *San Antonio/The Phantom Rider/Duel in the Sun/In Old Sacramento/Heading West/The Plainsman and the Lady*/1946 · *Ramrod/West of Sonora/The Gallant Legion/Red River/Brimstone*/1947 · *Blood on the Moon*/1948 · *The Savage Horde*/1949 · *Colt .45/California Passage*/1950 · *Junction City*/1952

Walker, Clint (b 1927) · Actor. Big (six foot six) Walker was working as a deputy sheriff in Las Vegas when actor Van Johnson spotted him and suggested he try acting. He moved to Hollywood, and in 1955 his big break came when he was cast as Cheyenne

Bodie in one of the first of the adult television Westerns, *Cheyenne*. The series was extremely popular and although Walker was constantly in dispute with Warner Bros. it ran eight years. TM
Fort Dobbs/1958 · *Yellowstone Kelly*/1959 · *Gold of the Seven Saints*/1961 · *Night of the Grizzly*/1966 · *More Dead Than Alive*/1968 · *Sam Whiskey/The Great Bank Robbery*/1969 · *Pancho Villa*/1971 · *Baker's Hawk*/1976 · *The White Buffalo*/1977
Television *Cheyenne*/55 · *Maverick*/60 · *Yuma*/71 · *Hardcase/The Bounty Man*/72 · *Centennial*/78

Walsh, Raoul (1887-1981) · Director. Walsh's Westerns are more varied than his reputation as a director of straightforward adventure films would suggest. *The Big Trail* is an epic in the tradition of *The Covered Wagon*, and *They Died with their Boots On* a heroic version of the Custer story which nevertheless, in its portrayal of Custer's descent into drunkenness at a low point in his career, does not avoid the darker side of the legend. There are several small-scale but intense portraits of revenge or outlawry (*Along the Great Divide*, *The Lawless Breed*). *The Tall Men* is memorable for its handling of the love affair between Clark Gable and Jane Russell. More varied still are the baroquely Freudian *Pursued* and the broadly farcical *The Sheriff of Fractured Jaw*. Walsh's last Western, *A Distant Trumpet*, is a cavalry picture somewhat in the manner of John Ford; except that in none of his Westerns does Walsh seem at all interested in the traditional *themes* of the genre. Unlike Ford, his Westerns are, as Peter Lloyd has said, resolutely narratives of individual characters, dispassionately observed, carrying no weight of cultural symbolism or historical abstraction. It's no surprise, then, that Walsh was untroubled by the commission to make *Colorado Territory* as a Western version of his gangster classic *High Sierra*. EB
(act, sc, co-d) *The Life of General Villa/The Fatal Black Bean*/(act only) *Sierra Jim's Reformation*/1914 · *The Death Dice*/(act) *The Greaser/A Bad Man and Others*/1915 · (sc, p) *Blue Blood and Red*/1916 · (sc) *Betrayed*/(sc) *The Conqueror*/1917 · *Serenade*/1921 · (co-d) *In Old Arizona*/1929 · *The Big Trail*/1930 · *Wild Girl*/1932 · *Dark Command*/1940 · *They Died with their Boots On*/1941 · (2nd unit) *San Antonio*/1946 · *Pursued/Cheyenne*/1947 · *Silver River*/1948 · *Colorado Territory*/1949 · *Along the Great Divide/Distant Drums*/1951 · *The Lawless Breed*/1952 · *Gun Fury*/1953 ·

Clint Walker   *Raoul Walsh*

John Wayne

Saskatchewan/1954 · The Tall Men/1955 ·
The King and Four Queens/1956 · The
Sheriff of Fractured Jaw/1958 · A Distant
Trumpet/1964

Warren, Charles Marquis (b 1917) · Director (also writer and producer) who has
specialized in the Western. One of his first
published novels, Only the Valiant, based on
his Saturday Evening Post short story, became
a 1951 Warners feature with Gregory Peck.
Warren is part traditional-historical
romanticist, part Western military adventurer. The former expresses itself through
films like Pony Express and Arrowhead (with
Charlton Heston leading both the ponies
and the arrows); the latter is an extension of
his cavalry novels Valley of the Shadow and
Only the Valiant, but with a central Civil
War element or theme: Trooper Hook, Ride a
Violent Mile. However, it is Hellgate, Trooper
Hook and Seven Angry Men, all with their
problems of people seeking some form of
moral if not legal justice, that remain as the
more memorable dramas in Warren's filmography. For over ten years he was a significant force in the television Western, creating
a popular landscape for the frontier professional (with law enforcement, the cattle-
drive, large-scale ranching, the railroad). His
Rawhide series gained him a Western Heritage Award. TV
(co-sc only) Streets of Laredo/1949 · (sc
only) The Redhead and the Cowboy/(novel
only) Only the Valiant/1950 · (sc only) Oh,
Susanna/(sc) Little Big Horn/1951 · (co-sc

only) Springfield Rifle/(co-sc only) Woman
of the North Country/(co-sc, p) Hellgate/(sc
only) Pony Express/1952 · (sc) Arrowhead/
1953 · Seven Angry Men/1955 · Tension at
Table Rock/The Black Whip/1956 · (co-sc)
Trooper Hook/(p) Copper Sky/(p) Ride a
Violent Mile/Cattle Empire/(st, p) Blood
Arrow/1957 · (co-sc only) Day of the Evil
Gun/1968 · (sc, p) Charro!/1969
Television Gunsmoke/55 · Rawhide/59 ·
Gunslinger/61 · The Virginian/62 · The Iron
Horse/66

Wayne, John (1907-1979) · An American
icon and a powerful symbol of post-war
American masculinity, whose contribution
to the genre, particularly in some of Ford's
and Hawks' classic Westerns, is almost
inestimable. Born Marion Michael Morrison in Iowa, he later moved to California
and won a football scholarship. After a
handful of small parts Wayne got his first
starring role in Raoul Walsh's epic The Big
Trail. The film flopped at the box-office and
for the rest of the 30s Wayne was confined to
leading roles in a long run of series Westerns, most notably for Republic in their
Three Mesquiteers series. His success as the
Ringo Kid in John Ford's Stagecoach in 1939
gave his career a new lease of life, and from
1950 to 1965 he was the number one male
box-office star in America. In nearly ninety
screen appearances as a cowboy Wayne only
bit the dust on four occasions; most memorably, perhaps, as the aging gunfighter
stricken with cancer in The Shootist. It was a

brave part to play in view of Wayne's own
battle with cancer and, appropriately, it was
his last. PS
Rough Romance/The Big Trail/1930 · The
Range Feud/1931 · Texas Cyclone/Two-
Fisted Law/Ride Him Cowboy/The Big
Stampede/1932 · Haunted Gold/The
Telegraph Trail/Somewhere in Sonora/The
Man from Monterey/Sagebush Trail/West of
the Divide/1933 · Riders of Destiny/The
Lucky Texan/Blue Steel/The Man from
Utah/Randy Rides Alone/The Star Packer/
The Trail Beyond/1934 · The Lawless
Frontier/Neath the Arizona Skies/Texas
Terror/Rainbow Valley/The Desert Trail/The
Dawn Rider/Paradise Canyon/Westward
Ho/The New Frontier/Lawless Range/1935 ·
The Oregon Trail/The Lawless Nineties/
King of the Pecos/Winds of the Wasteland/
The Lonely Trail/1936 · Born to the West/
Pals of the Saddle/Overland Stage Raiders/
Santa Fe Stampede/Red River Range/1938 ·
The Night Riders/Three Texas Steers/
Stagecoach/Wyoming Outlaw/New Frontier/
Allegheny Uprising/1939 · Dark Command/
Three Faces West/(uncredited stunt double
only) Melody Ranch/1940 · The Shepherd of
the Hills/1941 · The Spoilers/In Old
California/1942 · The Lady Takes a
Chance/In Old Oklahoma/1943 · Tall in the
Saddle/1944 · Flame of the Barbary Coast/
Dakota/1945 · (p) Angel and the Badman/
1946 · Red River/1947 · Fort Apache/3
Godfathers/1948 · The Fighting Kentuckian/
She Wore a Yellow Ribbon/1949 · Rio
Grande/1950 · (p) Hondo/1953 · (co-p only)
Track of the Cat/1954 · The Searchers/(co-p
only) Seven Men from Now/1956 · Rio
Bravo/1958 · The Horse Soldiers/1959 · (d,
p) The Alamo/North to Alaska/1960 · The
Comancheros/1961 · The Man Who Shot
Liberty Valance/How the West Was Won/
1962 · McLintock!/1963 · The Sons of Katie
Elder/1965 · El Dorado/1966 · The War
Wagon/1967 · True Grit/The Undefeated/
1969 · Chisum/Rio Lobo/1970 · Big Jake/
The Cowboys/1971 · The Train Robbers/
Cahill United States Marshal/1973 · Rooster
Cogburn/1975 · The Shootist/1976
Television Gunsmoke/55 · Wagon Train/60

Weaver, Dennis (b 1924) · Actor. Weaver's
most memorable performances (the motel
clerk in Touch of Evil, the tormented driver
in Duel), have been outside the Western, but
he served a hard apprenticeship in the genre,
with supporting roles in thirteen Westerns
in three years. Weary of this, he quit Universal in search of variety, but ironically it
was another Western chore, nine years in

Gunsmoke as Matt Dillon's drawling, limping deputy, which made him into a familiar name. Then, with *Kentucky Jones*, he at last played a lead. JL

*The Raiders/Horizons West/The Lawless Breed/*1952 · *The Mississippi Gambler/Law and Order/Column South/The Nebraskan/ The Redhead from Wyoming/The Man from the Alamo/War Arrow/*1953 · *Ten Wanted Men/*1954 · *Seven Angry Men/Chief Crazy Horse/*1955 · *Duel at Diablo/*1965 · *Sledge/* 1970

Television *Gunsmoke/*55 · *The Virginian/*70 · *Female Artillery/*73 · *Ishi: the Last of his Tribe/Centennial/*78

Webb, James R. (1909-74) · Writer. A prolific author of short stories and novelettes, James Webb first worked for the cinema in 1941, when he wrote scripts for three Roy Rogers movies and the story for a fourth. His later work was more demanding, including as it did one of the first and best pro-Indian films of the 50s in *Apache*, the lively *Vera Cruz* and the work for which he won his Academy Award, *How the West Was Won*. His feeling for the Indians was there again in his last Western script, for John Ford's epic *Cheyenne Autumn*. JL

*(st) Nevada City/(st) Badman of Deadwood/ (st only) Sheriff of Tombstone/Jesse James at Bay/*1941 · *South of Santa Fe/*1942 · *(co-sc) South of St. Louis/(co-sc) Montana/*1949 · *(co-sc) Raton Pass/*1950 · *(co-sc) The Big Trees/*1951 · *The Iron Mistress/*1952 · *(st) The Charge at Feather River/*1953 · *Apache/ (co-sc) Vera Cruz/*1954 · *(co-sc) The Big Country/*1958 · *(st) How the West Was Won/*1962 · *Cheyenne Autumn/*1964

Wellman, William A. (1896-1975) · Director. After a turbulent youth spent partly as a pilot in World War I, he entered the film business in 1919 as an actor and stunt man, becoming director in 1923. Compulsively

living up to his image of 'Wild Bill', both on and off the set, he achieved many outstanding movies in a wide variety of genres, ranging from the flying epic *Wings* (1927) to brutal gangster stories (*The Public Enemy*, 1931); from hard-edged social concern films (*Beggars of Life*, 1928, *Wild Boys of the Road*, 1933) to the stylized and over-praised Western *The Ox-Bow Incident*; from semi-documentary war films to exuberantly cynical comedies (*Nothing Sacred*, 1937; *Roxie Hart*, 1942). Wellman's films never seemed to achieve as coherent a vision as Ford or Hawks. His critical reputation has fluctuated, possibly because of the unsettling undercurrents of homosexuality that haunt his images of virility. His positive female characters tend to get masculinized and his male ones cope with their homoerotic drives through playful but often suggestive ribaldry, ostentatious displays of toughness and sudden explosions of violence towards women. In this way, his work allows the usually repressed aspects of classic Hollywood masculinity to shimmer through to the surface, giving the films a neurotic edge rather than a moral cohesion, making them more complex in the process. In this respect, Wellman's work is richer than that of his chief heir, Peckinpah. PW

*The Man Who Won/*1923 · *Not a Drum Was Heard/The Circus Cowboy/*1924 · *The Boob/*1926 · *The Conquerors/*1932 · *Stingaree/*1934 · *The Call of the Wild/*1935 · *(co-sc) The Robin Hood of El Dorado/*1936 · *(p) The Great Man's Lady/The Ox-Bow Incident/*1942 · *Buffalo Bill/*1944 · *Yellow Sky/*1948 · *Across the Wide Missouri/*1950 *Westward the Women/*1951 · *Track of the Cat/*1954

Widmark, Richard (b 1914) · Actor. His screen début as a laughing psychopath in *Kiss of Death* led to him being typecast as a villain in his early Western appearances such

Robert Wilke

as *Yellow Sky*. But eventually his blue eyes came to signal not the ice-cold killer but the man of transparent integrity, albeit with an underlying steely determination. Possibly the key film in this transformation is *The Last Wagon*, where he starts out bad and ends up redeemed. His most engaging performance is in *Two Rode Together*, playing an impoverished army officer as foil to James Stewart's cynically venal sheriff. EB

*Yellow Sky/*1948 · *Garden of Evil/Broken Lance/*1954 · *Backlash/The Last Wagon/* 1956 · *The Law and Jake Wade/*1958 · *Warlock/*1959 · *The Alamo/*1960 · *Two Rode Together/*1961 · *How the West Was Won/*1962 · *Cheyenne Autumn/*1964 · *Alvarez Kelly/*1966 · *The Way West/*1967 · *Death of a Gunfighter/*1969 · *When the Legends Die/Alleluja e Sartana, figli di ... Dio/Trinità e Sartana, figli di ... /*1972 Television *The Last Day/*75 · *Mr. Horn/*79

Wilke, Robert J. (b 1911) · Actor, aka Bob Wilke, Robert Wilkie. Tall, raw-looking actor with a cruel smile, originally a stuntman. After long labours in the dusty vineyard of the B-feature and series Western he rose to some memorable bit parts in bigger pictures, usually as a bullying villain. He has one of his best scenes in *The Magnificent Seven*, when James Coburn gets him with a knife. EB

Come On Rangers!/Under Western Stars/ 1938 · *Rough Riders' Roundup/In Old Monterey/*1939 · *The Adventures of Red Ryder/King of the Royal Mounted/*1940 · *California Joe/*1943 · *San Antonio Kid/Call of the Rockies/Sheriff of Las Vegas/Beneath Western Skies/The Cowboy and the Senorita/ Yellow Rose of Texas/Marshal of Reno/ Bordertown Trail/Cheyenne Wildcat/ Vigilantes of Dodge City/Sheriff of Sundown/* 1944 · *Sunset in El Dorado/Trail of Kit Carson/The Topeka Terror/Sheriff of Cimarron/Santa Fe Saddlemates/Rough*

Dennis Weaver

Richard Widmark

Riders of Cheyenne/Corpus Christi Bandits/ Trail of the Badlands/The Man from Oklahoma/Bandits of the Badlands/1945 · Roaring Rangers/Out California Way/The Phantom Rider/The El Paso Kid/King of the Forest Rangers/1946 · Michigan Kid/West of Dodge City/Law of the Canyon/The Vigilantes Return/Last Days of Boot Hill/ 1947 · River Lady/Carson City Raiders/Six-Gun Law/West of Sonora/Trail to Laredo/ 1948 · The Wyoming Bandit/Laramie/1949 · Outcast of Black Mesa/Mule Train/Beyond the Purple Hills/Across the Badlands/Frontier Outpost/1950 · Gunplay/Saddle Legion/Best of the Badmen/Pistol Harvest/Cyclone Fury/ Hot Lead/Overland Telegraph/1951 · Road Agent/High Noon/Cattle Town/Hellgate/ Fargo/Laramie Mountains/The Maverick/ Wyoming Roundup/1952 · Cow Country/ Powder River/Arrowhead/War Paint/1953 · The Lone Gun/Two Guns and a Badge/The Far Country/1954 · Shotgun/Strange Lady in Town/Smoke Signal/Wichita/The Rawhide Years/1955 · The Lone Ranger/Backlash/Raw Edge/Canyon River/Gun the Man Down/ 1956 · Night Passage/1957 · Return to Warbow/Man of the West/1958 · The Magnificent Seven/1960 · The Long Rope/ 1961 · The Gun Hawk/1963 · The Hallelujah Trail/1964 · Smoky/1966 · The Cheyenne Social Club/A Gunfight/1970 · Santee/1972

Television *The Roy Rogers Show/53 · Cheyenne/56 · The Adventures of Jim Bowie/ Tombstone Territory/57 · Zorro/Colt .45/ Gunsmoke/Lawman/58 · Bat Masterson/The Texan/The Deputy/Wanted: Dead or Alive/ The Rifleman/Have Gun, Will Travel/The Law of the Plainsman/59 · Bonanza/ Laramie/Tales of Wells Fargo/The Tall Man/Texas John Slaughter/60 · Frontier Circus/The Americans/Rawhide/61 · Maverick/62 · The Virginian/64 · The Legend of Jesse James/65 · Daniel Boone/66 · Cimarron Strip/The Guns of Will Sonnett/ The Wild, Wild West/The Monroes/67 · Lancer/68 · Desperate Mission/69 · The Quest/76 · How the West Was Won/78*

Williams, Guinn (1899-1962) · Actor. Williams came from the rodeo circuit to Hollywood in 1919. He was a friend of Will Rogers, who nicknamed him 'Big Boy' (as which he was often credited) and gave him his first parts. Through the 20s he played leads in many very minor Westerns, and had his own series in the 30s, thereafter moving over to supporting roles. Large and chunky, slow of speech and with a wry grin, he now became the hero's none-too-bright friend,

and at odd times a likeable villain. He once said, tongue in cheek perhaps, that he hated every one of his movies, that he would glance at the script and bluff it out, for all he lived for was to drink and play polo. JL
Cupid, the Cowpuncher/1920 · (st) The Jack Rider/(st) The Vengeance Trail/Western Firebrands/1921 · Across the Border/The Cowboy King/Rounding Up the Law/Blaze Away/The Freshie/Trail of Hate/1922 · Cyclone Jones/End of the Rope/$1000 Reward/Riders at Night/1923 · The Avenger/ The Eagle's Claw/1924 · Bad Man from Bodie/Big Stunt/Courage of Wolfheart/Fangs of Wolfheart/(st) Red Blood and Blue/Riders of the Sand Storm/Rose of the Desert/Sporting West/Whistling Jim/Wolfheart's Revenge/ Black Cyclone/1925 · The Desert's Toll/1926 · Lightning/1927 · The Bad Man/1930 · The Great Meadow/1931 · Heritage of the Desert/1932 · Man of the Forest/1933 · Thunder Over Texas/Cowboy Holiday/1934 · Gun Play/Big Boy Rides Again/Powdersmoke Range/Law of the 45s/1935 · End of the Trail/North of Nome/The Vigilantes Are Coming/1936 · The Bad Man of Brimstone/ 1937 · Dodge City/Bad Lands/1939 · Virginia City/Santa Fe Trail/Wagons Westward/1940 · Billy the Kid/Riders of Death Valley/1941 · Silver Queen/American Empire/1942 · The Desperadoes/Buckskin Frontier/1943 · Hands Across the Border/ Belle of the Yukon/Swing in the Saddle/ Nevada/The Cowboy and the Senorita/ Cowboy Canteen/1944 · Song of the Prairie/ Sing Me a Song of Texas/Rhythm Round-Up/ 1945 · That Texas Jamboree/Cowboy Blues/ Singing on the Trail/Throw a Saddle on a Star/Singin' in the Corn/1946 · King of the Wild Horses/1947 · Station West/1948 · Bad Men of Tombstone/Brimstone/1949 · Hoedown/Rocky Mountain/1950 · Al Jennings of Oklahoma/Man in the Saddle/ 1951 · Springfield Rifle/Hangman's Knot/ 1952 · Southwest Passage/The Outlaw's

Daughter/The Outcast/Massacre Canyon/ 1954 · Hidden Guns/1955 · The Man from Del Rio/1956 · The Hired Gun/1957 · The Alamo/1960 · The Comancheros/1961
Television *The Adventures of Wild Bill Hickok/55 · My Friend Flicka/56 · Cheyenne/Gunsmoke/57 · Tales of Wells Fargo/The Adventures of Rin Tin Tin/58 · The Restless Gun/59*

Wills, Chill (1903-78) · Gravel-voiced character actor, whose first Western appearances were as a singer (Chill Wills and the Avalon Boys). Mainly in comedy parts, he was occasionally villainous, memorably as Turk in Peckinpah's *The Deadly Companions*. EB
Bar 20 Rides Again/1935 · Call of the Prairie/Way Out West/1936 · Lawless Valley/1938 · Arizona Legion/Trouble in Sundown/Racketeers of the Range/Timber Stampede/Allegheny Uprising/1939 · The Westerner/1940 · Western Union/The Bad Man/Billy the Kid/Belle Starr/Honky Tonk/ 1941 · The Omaha Trail/Apache Trail/1942 · Barbary Coast Gent/1944 · The Harvey Girls/1945 · Northwest Stampede/Loaded Pistols/Red Canyon/1948 · The Sundowners/ 1949 · Rock Island Trail/High Lonesome/Rio Grande/1950 · Oh, Susanna/Cattle Drive/ Bronco Buster/1951 · Ride the Man Down/ 1952 · The Man from the Alamo/ Tumbleweed/1953 · Hell's Outpost/ Timberjack/1954 · Kentucky Rifle/Giant/Gun for a Coward/1956 · Gun Glory/1957 · From Hell to Texas/1958 · The Sad Horse/1959 · The Alamo/1960 · Gold of the Seven Saints/ The Deadly Companions/1961 · Young Guns of Texas/1962 · McLintock!/1963 · The Rounders/1964 · Guns of a Stranger/Pat Garrett and Billy the Kid/1973
Television *Wagon Train/58 · Trackdown/ The Texan/59 · Frontier Circus/61 · Gunsmoke/62 · Rawhide/64 · The Rounders/ 66 · The Over-the-Hill Gang/69 · The Over-the-Hill Gang Rides Again/70 · The Men*

Guinn Williams

Chill Wills

from Shiloh/The Virginian/71 · Alias Smith and Jones/72 · Hec Ramsey/74

Windsor, Marie (b 1922) · Actress. An expert horserider, as demonstrated in many of her Western roles, and one of the few leading ladies who could be as tough as the men. Frequently seen as a dance-hall girl or saloon-keeper, she mellowed nicely in some later Burt Kennedy comedy Westerns. EB
The Romance of Rosy Ridge/1947 · The Kissing Bandit/1948 · The Beautiful Blonde from Bashful Bend/Hellfire/The Fighting Kentuckian/Dakota Lil/1949 · The Showdown/Frenchie/1950 · Little Big Horn/1951 · Outlaw Women/1952 · The Tall Texan/1953 · The Bounty Hunter/1954 · The Silver Star/1955 · Two Gun Lady/1956 · The Parson and the Outlaw/Day of the Bad Man/1957 · Mail Order Bride/1963 · The Good Guys and the Bad Guys/1969 · One More Train to Rob/1970 · Support Your Local Gunfighter/1971 · Cahill United States Marshal/1973 · Hearts of the West/1975 Television Cheyenne/The Californians/ Maverick/57 · Yancy Derringer/Bat Masterson/58 · Rawhide/The Deputy/The Alaskans/59 · The Rebel/60 · The Life and Legend of Wyatt Earp/Bronco/Whispering Smith/61 · Lawman/62 · Destry/64 · Branded/The Legend of Jesse James/ Bonanza/65 · Wild Women/70 · Gunsmoke/ 71 · Alias Smith and Jones/Hec Ramsey/72

Witney, William N. (b 1910) · Director. 'I made you mean once, I can do it again,' hisses villainess Nana Bryant to the once-killer alsatian she trained, now gentled by star Roy Rogers in *Eyes of Texas* – and given half a chance, making 'mean' movies out of unpromising premises was Witney's forte. (Elsewhere in *Eyes of Texas* the pack of four killer-dogs chase poor old Francis Ford, dragging him off his horse and killing him; a henchman is half-strangled and thrown in the cellar where the dogs are in order to dispose of him; there are beatings-up and a brutal fight with a whip; and chief villain Roy Barcroft is set on fire during the climactic gundown!) And when he couldn't make 'em mean, Witney's best films are at least majestically exhilarating – like such serials as *The Lone Ranger* and *Zorro's Fighting Legion* – with a penchant for wild tracking shots and a predilection for geometrically constructed action. While this is plainly relished, Witney was honest enough to show its consequences. His heroes win, most often – but in so doing they suffer broken arms, bloody noses and bullet holes. If not for his serials (mostly co-directed with John English), or his series Westerns with Rex Allen and Roy Rogers, he should have an honourable place in the pantheon for his only really major movies, *The Outcast* and *Santa Fe Passage*. CW
(co-d) The Painted Stallion/The Trigger Trio/ 1937 · (co-d) Zorro Rides Again/(co-d) The Lone Ranger/1938 · (co-d) Zorro's Fighting Legion/(co-d) The Lone Ranger Rides Again/ 1939 · (co-d) King of the Royal Mounted/ (co-d) Adventures of Red Ryder/Heroes of the Saddle/1940 · King of the Mounties/Outlaws of Pine Ridge/(co-d) King of the Texas Rangers/1941 · Roll on Texas Moon/Home in Oklahoma/Helldorado/1946 · Apache Rose/ Bells of San Angelo/Springtime in the Sierras/On the Old Spanish Trail/1947 · The Gay Ranchero/Under California Stars/ Eyes of Texas/Nighttime in Nevada/Grand Canyon Trail/1948 · The Far Frontier/ Susanna Pass/Down Dakota Way/The Golden Stallion/1949 · Bells of Coronado/ Twilight in the Sierras/Trigger, Jr./Sunset in the West/North of the Great Divide/Trail of Robin Hood/1950 · Spoilers of the Plains/ Heart of the Rockies/In Old Amarillo/South of Caliente/Pals of the Golden West/1951 · Colorado Sundown/The Last Musketeer/Iron Mountain Trail/Border Saddlemates/Old Oklahoma Plains/South Pacific Trail/1952 · Old Overland Trail/Down Laredo Way/ Shadows of Tombstone/1953 · The Outcast/ 1954 · Santa Fe Passage/1955 · Stranger at My Door/1956 · The Long Rope/1961 · Apache Rifles/1964 · Arizona Raiders/1965 · Forty Guns to Apache Pass/1966 Television Stories of the Century/54 · Frontier Doctor/57 · Zorro/58 · The Tall Man/60 · Riverboat/Frontier Circus/Wagon Train/61 · Bonanza/The Virginian/Tales of Wells Fargo/62 · Laramie/63 · Daniel Boone/64 · Branded/The Wild, Wild West/65 · Laredo/66 · Hondo/67 · The High Chaparral/68 · The Cowboys/73

Worden, Hank (b 1901) · Actor. Tall and thin, and often typecast as a half-wit, he has nevertheless played his part in an impressive list of Westerns. A member of Ford's stock company, he appeared in half a dozen of his Westerns, usually cast as comic relief, although he did play one of the malevolent Cleggs in *Wagon Master*. In his most memorable role, as the simpleton Mose Harper in *The Searchers*, Worden imbues the character with a moving combination of pathos and comedy. JH
The Plainsman/Ghost Town Gold/1936 · Sing, Cowboy, Sing/Hittin' the Trail/1937 · Frontier Town/Tex Rides with the Boy Scouts/ The Singing Outlaw/Rollin' Plains/Stranger from Arizona/Ghost Town Riders/1938 · Sundown on the Prairie/Timber Stampede/ Rollin' Westward/1939 · Northwest Passage/ Brigham Young – Frontiersman/Viva Cisco Kid/Ride, Tenderfoot, Ride/Rollin' Home to Texas/The Range Busters/Gaucho Serenade/ 1940 · Border Vigilantes/Robbers of the Range/1941 · Riding the Wind/1942 · Tenting Tonight on the Old Camp Ground/ Black Market Rustlers/1943 · Lawless Breed/ Duel in the Sun/Angel and the Badman/ 1946 · The Sea of Grass/Prairie Express/Red River/1947 · Tap Roots/Fort Apache/Yellow Sky/3 Godfathers/Red Canyon/1948 · The Fighting Kentuckian/Hellfire/Streets of Laredo/1949 · Wagon Master/1950 · Sugarfoot/1951 · Sky Full of Moon/The Big Sky/Woman of the North Country/Apache War Smoke/1952 · The Outcast/1954 · Road to Denver/The Vanishing American/The Indian Fighter/1955 · The Searchers/The Quiet Gun/The Buckskin Lady/1956 · Spoilers of the Forest/Dragoon Wells Massacre/Forty Guns/1957 · Bullwhip/The Toughest Gun in Tombstone/1958 · The Horse Soldiers/1959 · The Alamo/Sergeant Rutledge/One-Eyed Jacks/1960 · McLintock!/ 1963 · True Grit/1969 · Chisum/Rio Lobo/ Zachariah/1970 · Big Jake/1971 · Cahill

Marie Windsor

Hank Worden

United States Marshal/1973
Television *The Lone Ranger*/52 · *Davy Crockett*/54 · *Sheriff of Cochise*/56 · *The Adventures of Jim Bowie*/*Tales of Wells Fargo*/57 · *Cheyenne*/*Rawhide*/59 · *Bonanza*/*Wagon Train*/60 · *The Travels of Jaimie McPheeters*/63 · *The Rounders*/66 · *The Iron Horse*/*Daniel Boone*/67 · *The Outcasts*/*Lancer*/68 · *The Virginian*/69 · *Black Noon*/72

Wright, Will (1891-1962) · Actor. Whenever in the late 40s or the 50s a script called for a crabbed, mean, utterly unlikeable old man, Will Wright was there to fill the gap. He had been a journalist, and worked on the legitimate and vaudeville stages, before making his first film in 1936. He was much in demand for thrillers and Westerns, and though seldom a major villain, portrayed in his time a whole gallery of conniving storekeepers, crooked financiers, dubious sheriffs and shifty-eyed no-goods. JL
Silver on the Sage/1939 · *Honky Tonk*/1941 · *Shut My Big Mouth*/1942 · *In Old Oklahoma*/*Saddles and Sagebrush*/1943 · *Salome, Where She Danced*/*Gun Smoke*/1945 · *California*/1946 · *Along the Oregon Trail*/1947 · *Relentless*/*Green Grass of Wyoming*/*Black Eagle*/1948 · *Whispering Smith*/*Lust for Gold*/*Big Jack*/*Brimstone*/*Mrs Mike*/*The Savage Horde*/1949 · *A Ticket to Tomahawk*/*Dallas*/*Sunset in the West*/1950 · *Vengeance Valley*/1951 · *The Last Posse*/1953 · *Johnny Guitar*/*River of No Return*/*The Raid*/1954 · *The Tall Men*/*The Kentuckian*/1955 · *The Iron Sheriff*/*The Missouri Traveler*/1957 · *Quantrill's Raiders*/*Gunman's Walk*/1958 · *Alias Jesse James*/1959 · *The Deadly Companions*/1961
Television *Fury*/55 · *Sugarfoot*/57 · *Trackdown*/*Maverick*/*The Restless Gun*/*The Adventures of Rin Tin Tin*/58 · *The Rough Riders*/*Tales of Wells Fargo*/59 · *Lawman*/*Bat Masterson*/61

Will Wright

Yordan, Philip (b 1913) · Writer. Yordan is best known for his work (Western and otherwise) with Mann and Ray, especially *The Man from Laramie* which he co-wrote, and *Johnny Guitar*, though *Broken Lance* (Dmytryk), *The Fiend Who Walked the West* (Douglas) and *Day of the Outlaw* (de Toth) are also noteworthy. Yordan was decidedly anti-McCarthyite and may have assisted some blacklisted writers by providing a cover for them. Certainly *Johnny Guitar* is itself an anti-McCarthy parable. Of his Westerns Yordan has said 'I detest a certain type of modern would-be "hero", people who are obsessed only by getting their daily bread. I have tried to react against this petty bourgeois mentality and attempted to discover again the purity of the heroes of classical tragedy. I have always wanted to re-create a tragic mythology, giving a large role to destiny, solitude, nobility. At the same time I've tried to join this type of hero to typically American characters, the characters of popular fiction.' JP
(co-sc) *Bad Men of Tombstone*/1948 · (co-sc) *Drums in the Deep South*/1951 · (st only) *Broken Lance*/*Johnny Guitar*/1954 · (co-sc) *The Man from Laramie*/(co-sc) *The Last Frontier*/1955 · *The Bravados*/(co-sc) *The Fiend Who Walked the West*/1958 · *Day of the Outlaw*/1959 · (p only) *Custer of the West*/1966 · (co-sc, co-p) *Captain Apache*/(co-sc) *E continuavano a fregarsi il milione di dollari*/1971

Young, Victor (1900-56) · Composer, mostly associated with high-budgeted Paramount gloss. His Western scores include several stirring, lyrical accompaniments to DeMille blockbusters, some delirious strings to go with *The Outlaw*, and the melodious mythicism of *Shane*. He scored the successful comedy *Paleface*, but Jay Livingstone and Ray Evans wrote that film's Oscar-awarded hit 'Buttons and Bows'. KN
Klondike Annie/1936 · *Wells Fargo*/1937 · *Range War*/*Heritage of the Desert*/*The Llano Kid*/*Man of Conquest*/1939 · *Arizona*/*Three Faces West*/(co-m) *Buck Benny Rides Again*/*Knights of the Range*/*The Light of Western Stars*/*Three Men from Texas*/*North West Mounted Police*/*Dark Command*/*The Outlaw*/1940 · *Silver Queen*/1942 · *Buckskin Frontier*/1943 · *California*/1946 · *Unconquered*/1947 · *The Paleface*/1948 · *Streets of Laredo*/1949 · *Rio Grande*/1950 · *Belle Le Grand*/*Honeychile*/1951 · *Shane*/1952 · *A Perilous Journey*/1953 · *Johnny*

Guitar/*Jubilee Trail*/*Drum Beat*/*Timberjack*/1954 · *A Man Alone*/*The Tall Men*/1955 · *The Maverick Queen*/1956 · *Run of the Arrow*/1957

Yowlachie, Chief (1891-1966) · Actor. Daniel Simmons, known to the movies as Chief Yowlachie, left his reservation at 21, and by the mid-20s was in Hollywood, an actor and adviser on Indian matters. Yowlachie could be fierce or stoical, but also very funny, as in the railroad scene from *Ella Cinders* (not a Western), forcing a cigar of friendship on a reluctant Colleen Moore, or when winning Walter Brennan's teeth in *Red River*. In the 30s a singing career as bass-baritone took him from the movies, and into the White House to sing for Hoover and Roosevelt. In 1940 he returned, for another 20 years. JL
Wanderer of the Wasteland/1924 · *Tonio, Son of the Sierras*/1925 · *Hands Up!*/*Moran of the Mounted*/*Forlorn River*/*War Paint*/1926 · *The Red Raiders*/*Sitting Bull at the Spirit Lake Massacre*/1927 · *The Glorious Trail*/1928 · *Hawk of the Hills*/*Tiger Rose*/*The Invaders*/1929 · *The Girl of the Golden West*/*The Santa Fe Trail*/1930 · *North West Mounted Police*/*Winners of the West*/1940 · *White Eagle*/*Ride 'Em Cowboy*/1941 · *King of the Stallions*/1942 · *Canyon Passage*/*Wild West*/1946 · *Bowery Buckaroos*/*Red River*/1947 · *Yellow Sky*/*The Paleface*/*The Dude Goes West*/*Prairie Outlaws*/1948 · *El Paso*/*Mrs Mike*/*The Cowboy and the Indians*/*Canadian Pacific*/1949 · *A Ticket to Tomahawk*/*Winchester '73*/*Annie Get Your Gun*/*Cherokee Uprising*/*Indian Territory*/1950 · *Warpath*/1951 · *Buffalo Bill in Tomahawk Territory*/*Son of Geronimo*/*The Pathfinder*/1952 · *Rose Marie*/*Gunfighters of the Northwest*/1954 · *Heller in Pink Tights*/1960
Television *The Adventures of Rin Tin Tin*/56 · *The Tall Man*/61

Chief Yowlachie

*Jack Lord in
Stoney Burke*

THIS LISTING of television Westerns, though comprehensive within its own terms, does not claim to be complete, because it is restricted to episodic series (such as *Gunsmoke*), mini-series (such as *Centennial*), Western anthologies (such as *Dick Powell's Zane Grey Theatre*) and made-for-TV movies (such as *Shootout in a One-Dog Town*). Anthology series which included merely the occasional Western episode are not listed. For instance, the drama anthology series *20th Century-Fox Hour* (1955-7) remade several Fox features for television, including *The Ox-Bow Incident* (as 'The Lynch Mob'), *The Gunfighter* (as 'End of the Gun') and *Two Flags West* (as 'The Still Trumpet'). These are not included below. Walt Disney's television Westerns *are* listed, on the other hand, since though part of an anthology such early mini-series as *Elfego Baca* and *The Saga of Andy Burnett* were pretty much self-contained within the anthology format, as well as enjoying a separate theatrical release in Europe. Other television Westerns not included are animation series, documentaries, shorter pilots (try-out films intended to launch a series) and 'back-door' pilot episodes in anthologies. Finally, in the early 1950s there were several American local TV stations transmitting afternoon Western shows, usually put out live. These have proved too elusive for research.

Though the longer Western pilots (90 mins and over) have been listed, other pilots and made-for-TV films are difficult to locate and document accurately. Thus while reports in the trade press may list such tantalizing pilot titles as *Vera Cruz* and *Apache* (from Burt Lancaster's company) and *The Jayhawkers* (with a script by Edmund North, with Jack Arnold to direct), it is doubtful whether any of these ever existed as a completed film.

Similar doubts may arise over announcements of forthcoming series. For example, in 1954 S & S Films were listed as producing a series entitled *Royal Canadian Mounted Police*, to appear in 26 half-hour episodes with Lloyd Bridges starring. (This is not to be confused with the later, Canadian-produced *R.C.M.P.* featuring Gilles Pelletier.) Again, in the issue of *Hollywood Reporter* for 11 December 1959 a half-page advertisement announces, 'Completed! The first of 39 Eastman Color segments of *The Legend of Billy the Kid*', available from Sanrok Productions. But have these series ever been seen? Because of such uncertainties caution has been exercised in compiling the following list. TV

PART V

TELEVISION WESTERNS
Compiled by
Tise Vahimagi

A

Action in the Afternoon · This early 50s Western was shot in· Philadelphia, using local station WCAU-TV's studio and standing outdoor set (a remarkable reconstruction of a frontier town, called Huberle, Montana, set in the 1890s). It featured a half-hour episode Monday to Friday every week, with each week completing a chapter or story, and went out live. The five-afternoons-a-week format assisted the serial cliffhanger effect. The hero, Jack Valentine, was also a guitar-strumming crooner who entertained during non-action saloon sequences.
1953-4/b & w/tx live x 25 min/WCAU-TV/p Charles Vanda/lp Jack Valentine, Mary Elaine Watts, Barry Cassell

The Adventures of Champion · A boy and his horse-opera, set in the Southwest of the 1880s. Opening and closing with a catchy theme song, this series featured a wild stallion who befriends a 12-year-old boy, Ricky, and his dog, named Rebel.
1955-6/b & w/26 ep x 26 min/Flying A Prods/p Louis Gray/lp Barry Curtis, Jim Bannon

The Adventures of Jim Bowie · Set in the 1830s, and based on *Tempered Blade* by Monte Barrett, this series follows the dashing adventures of the knife-wielding pioneer from New Orleans to Texas. Downplaying the visual use of the legendary knife, many stories deal with mystery and psychological conflict.
1956-8/b & w/78 ep x 26 min/Jim Bowie Enterprises/exec p Louis F. Edelman/lp Scott Forbes, Robert Cornthwaite, Peter Hanson

The Adventures of Judge Roy Bean · Edgar Buchanan, in the title role, was the 'law west of the Pecos' in Langtry, Texas during the 1870s. Routine juvenile Western series of the mid-1950s; the Roy Bean character was depicted as a strong enforcer of frontier justice.
1955-6/b & w: colour/39 ep x 26 min/Quintet Prods/p Russell Hayden/lp Edgar Buchanan, Jack Beutel, Jackie Loughery

The Adventures of Kit Carson · Based on the exploits of Frémont's famed scout, this series falls into the hero-and-sidekick pattern of the early 1950s Westerns (*Cisco Kid*, *Lone Ranger*, *Wild Bill Hickok*) but here, at least, a little bit of Southern Californian history is injected into the storylines.
1952-5/b & w/104 ep x 26 min/Revue Prods/p Leon Fromkess/lp Bill Williams, Don Diamond

The Adventures of Rin Tin Tin · The *Lassie* format in the Old West as a young boy and his dog share the exploits of the 101st Cavalry at Fort Apache during the 1880s. For a youthful audience, the series mixed rugged action with pleasant comedy. In 1958 a feature film was released, *The Challenge of Rin Tin Tin*, comprising three episodes from the series ('Farewell to Fort Apache'; 'The White Wolf'; 'The Return of Rin Tin Tin'). New colour wrap-arounds were later shot for the syndication market. ·
1954-9/b & w/164 ep x 26 min/Screen Gems/p Herbert B. Leonard/lp Lee Aaker, James Brown, Joe Sawyer

The Adventures of Wild Bill Hickok Hard-riding, gun-toting incidents in the life of US Marshal James Butler Hickok, with Guy Madison as the buckskin-clad hero and Andy Devine as his sidekick, Jingles. 16 'features', edited from episodes, were released between 1952 and 1955: *Behind Southern Lines*; *Trail of the Arrow* aka *Arrow in the Dust/The Frontier Trail*; *The Ghost of Crossbones Canyon*; *The Yellow-Haired Kid*; *Six-Gun Decision*; *Secret of Outlaw Flats*; *Border City Rustlers*; *Two Gun Marshal*; *Marshals in Disguise*; *Trouble on the Trail*; *The Two-Gun Teacher*; *Outlaw's Son*; *Timber Country Trouble*; *The Titled Tenderfoot*; *The Match-Making Marshal* and *Phantom Trails*. A radio version of the show using the same players ran at the same time.
1951-8/b & w: colour/113 ep x 26 min/William Broidy Prods/p William F. Broidy, Wesley Barry/lp Guy Madison, Andy Devine

The Alamo: 13 Days to Glory · Dramatic reconstruction of the 13-day military action between Colonel William Travis' militia and volunteers and the massed Mexican army under General Santa Anna, with a teleplay based on Lon Tinkle's book *Thirteen Days to Glory: The Siege of the Alamo* (published in 1958 and from which the 1960 John Wayne film was also adapted). Just about all the historical characters are present: Travis (Alec Baldwin), Jim Bowie (James Arness), Davy Crockett (Brian Keith), Sam Houston (Lorne Greene) and Santa Anna (Raul Julia).
1987/tx '180 min'/Briggle, Hennessy, Carrothers Prods – The Finnegan Co/p Bill and Pat Finnegan, Sheldon Pinchuk/d Burt Kennedy/s Clyde Ware, Norman McLeon Morrill/c John Elsenbach/lp James Arness, Brian Keith, Alec Baldwin, David Ogden Stiers, Jim Metzler, Lorne Greene, Raul Julia

The Alaskans · Adventure-comedy set in Alaska during the gold rush days of 1889. Formula Western antics from the Warners' TV stable of the time, with the relatively fresh small-screen locale of Skagway.
1959-60/b & w/36 ep x 52 min/WB-TV/exec p William T. Orr/lp Roger Moore, Jeff York, Ray Danton, Dorothy Provine

Alias Smith and Jones · Pilot and series in which Hannibal Heyes and 'Kid' Curry, under their respective aliases, are inept robbers trying to stay out of trouble in order to earn an amnesty from the governor. Though the pilot had too many overtones of *Butch Cassidy and the Sundance Kid*, impressive photography, roguish humour and interesting voice-over dialogue exchanges in the series helped a little in an already yellowing format.
Pilot/1971/90 min/U/p Glen A. Larson/d Gene Levitt/s Matthew Howard, Glen A. Larson/c John Morley Stephens/lp Peter Duel, Ben Murphy, Forrest Tucker, Susan Saint James, James Drury
Series/1971-3/49 ep x 52 min/U-TV – Public Arts/cr Glen A. Larson/lp Peter Duel, Ben Murphy, Roger Davis

The Americans · A mixture of fiction and fact, this Civil War series goes to great pains to ensure historical accuracy as it tells of two brothers fighting on opposing sides during the conflict. The series was based on a story by James Warner Bellah.
1961/b & w/17 ep x 52 min/NBC-TV/exec p Frank Telford/lp Darryl Hickman, Dick Davalos

Andrews' Raiders (1961). See **Walt Disney Presents**

Annie Oakley · As played by Gail Davis, Annie Oakley has discarded her historic role as Wild West show performer and become a female law-enforcer with her sheriff uncle and young brother. Routine ridin' & shootin' adventures aimed at the junior league.
1953-8/b & w/80 ep x 26 min/Flying A Prods/p Louis Gray/lp Gail Davis, Brad Johnson, Jimmy Hawkins

The Awakening Land · Wonderfully photographed by Michel Hugo, this mini-series production (based on a trilogy of novels by Conrad Richter) tells the haunting story of the life, from teenager to grandmother, of a nineteenth-century Ohio pioneer. Authentic-sounding dialogue and excellent acting enhance a superb series.
1978/300 min/Bensen-Kuhn-Sagal Prods – WB/p Robert E. Relyea/d Boris Sagal/s James Lee Barrett, Liam O'Brien/c Michel Hugo/lp Elizabeth Montgomery, Hal Holbrook, Jane Seymour, Steven Keats

B

Banjo Hackett: Roamin' Free · Quest for a stolen horse in the Old West of the 1880s as an itinerant horse trader and his young nephew search through a series of adventures in this undemanding yarn. Pilot for an unmade series.
1976/100 min/Bruce Lansbury Prods – COL/p Bruce Lansbury/d Andrew V. McLaglen/s Ken Trevey/c Al Francis/lp Don Meredith, Ike Eisenmann, Jennifer Warren, Chuck Connors

The Barbary Coast · Series about an undercover agent (William Shatner) and his casino-owning gambling partner trying to clean up the San Francisco Bay area in the 1870s. The excellent studio sets (recreating foggy waterfronts and glittering gambling halls) suited perfectly the gaudy atmosphere of this easygoing series. Doug McClure took over as the gambler, played by Dennis Cole in the pilot.
Pilot/1975/98 min/PAR/p Douglas Heyes/d Bill Bixby/s Douglas Heyes/c Robert B. Hauser/lp William Shatner, Dennis Cole, Charles Aidman, Michael Ansara, Neville Brand
Series/1975-6/13 ep x 52 min/Francy Prod – PAR-TV/exec p Cy Chermak/lp William Shatner, Doug McClure

The Bastard · First of the lengthy John Jakes Bicentennial mini-series focusing on the illegitimate French son (Andrew Stevens) of an English nobleman as he moves from eighteenth-century Europe to pre-Revolutionary Boston. Once on colonial shores he meets a string of historic figures, including Benjamin Franklin, Paul Revere and Lafayette. His adventures continue in *The Rebels* and *The Seekers*, both 1979.
1978/200 min/U/p Joe Byrne/d Lee H. Katzin/s Guerdon Trueblood/c Michel Hugo/lp Andrew Stevens, Tom Bosley, Kim Cattrall, Buddy Ebsen

Bat Masterson · The law-enforcing adventures of William Bartley Masterson as portrayed in dapper fashion by Gene Barry. The series was a notch above the other action Westerns from the Ziv-TV factory.
1959-61/b & w/108 ep x 26 min/Ziv-TV – UA-TV/p Frank Pittman, Andy White/lp Gene Barry

Belle Starr · The story of female outlaw Belle Starr, played by Elizabeth Montgomery. The mother of a son and daughter, Belle divides her time between Cole Younger and train-robbing with the Dalton gang. Although she finally gets her comeuppance in 1889, James Lee Barrett's script wanders between 1880s 'reality' and 1980s banality.
1980/97 min/Unlimited Prods – Hanna-Barbera Prods/p Doug Chapin/d John A. Alonzo/s James Lee Barrett/c John A. Alonzo/lp Elizabeth Montgomery, Cliff Potts, Michael Cavanaugh, Jesse Vint, Alan Vint

Best of the West · Comedy Western series spoofing the 'serious' Western. The setting is a small frontier town in 1865; the series regulars are Sheriff Sam Best, a Civil War veteran from Philadelphia who has romantic ideas about the West, his prissy Southern belle wife, their city-bred kid, and a cart-load of caricatured townsfolk: the drunken doctor, the tough-talking frontier gal, the devious saloon-keeper, etc.
1981/22 ep x 25 min/Weinberger-Daniels Prods – PAR-TV/cr Earl Pomerantz/lp Joel Higgins, Carlene Watkins, Meeno Peluce, Leonard Frey

The Big Valley · The San Joaquin Valley, California in the 1870s was the setting for this wide-open-spaces family saga of wealthy ranching folk. Barbara Stanwyck headed the cast as Victoria Barkley, a strong-willed matriarch who sometimes had difficulty with her offspring, which included an illegitimate son, Heath, played by young Lee Majors. *The Big Valley* embraced moral and psychological themes with some excellent teleplays; the Joseph H. Lewis-directed 'Boots With My Father's Name' and 'Night of The Wolf' are two above-average episodes.
1965-9/112 ep x 52 min/Four Star Prods/cr A. I. Bezzerides, Louis F. Edelman/lp Barbara Stanwyck, Richard Long, Peter Breck, Lee Majors, Linda Evans

Black Noon · Witchcraft in a western town as young minister Roy Thinnes and his wife arrive and spark off a series of supernatural happenings. Yvette Mimieux plays a *Bell, Book and Candle* Kim Novak-type, while expressionless Henry Silva comes across as a sort of gunfighter from Hell.
1971/73 min/Fenady Associates – Screen

Dan Blocker, Lorne Greene in Bonanza

Gems/*p* Andrew J. Fenady/*d* Bernard Kowalski/*s* Andrew J. Fenady/*c* Keith Smith/*lp* Roy Thinnes, Lyn Loring, Yvette Mimieux, Ray Milland, Henry Silva

Black Saddle · Post-Civil War New Mexico is the setting for a wandering ex-gunfighter turned lawyer who moves from one troubled town to the next, with a US Marshal following his trail. Naturally, when law books failed to resolve a situation the gunfighter would strap on his guns....
1959-60/b & w/44 ep x 26 min/Four Star-Halmac – Zane Grey Prods/*cr* Hal Hudson, John McGreevey/*lp* Peter Breck, Russell Johnson, Anna Lisa

Bonanza · The first hour-long Western filmed in colour premiered in 1959 to lukewarm reviews but went on to run on NBC for 14 years, coming pretty close to *Gunsmoke's* longest-running (networked) record. A sprawling family saga along the lines of *The Big Valley*, *Lancer* and *The High Chaparral*, this series was based near Virginia City, Nevada during the early 1860s at a vast timber and ranching spread called 'The Ponderosa'. Widower Ben Cartwright was the head of the clan which consisted of young son Little Joe, middle brother Hoss and eldest son Adam. There was also a Chinese cook and, at different periods, various drifters and ranch-hands were taken into the family fold. The majority of stories

revolved around guest characters, exploring all levels of social misfits and misunderstood vagabonds. Historical characters who drifted through 'The Ponderosa' included Samuel Langhorne Clemens, Henry T. P. Comstock, and Cochise. Two 1966 episodes ('Ride the Wind' Pts I & II) were edited into a theatrical feature and released in 1967 under the original episode title. Directors Robert Altman and William Witney worked on several episodes, as did Borden Chase and Elliott Arnold.
1959-73/430 ep x 52 min/NBC-TV Prods/*cr* David Dortort/*lp* Lorne Greene, Michael Landon, Dan Blocker, Pernell Roberts, Victor Sen Yung

Boots and Saddles · Subtitled 'The Story of the 5th Cavalry', this series tells of the life and times of US cavalrymen during the 1870s. Routine stories involving local bad men and Indians on the warpath are at times made interesting by good action sequences and photography of Utah locations.
1957/b & w/39 ep x 26 min/California National Prods/*p* George Cahan, Robert Stillman/*lp* Jack Pickard, Patrick McVey, John Alderson

Born to the Wind · A dramatized anthropological study of a band of plains Indians living in the wilderness during the 1820s when the first contact with the white man was made. The only Native American Indian in the cast appears to be Will Sampson, the rest being mostly Spanish-American players.
1979/4 ep x 45 min/Edgar Scherick Assoc. – WB-TV/*p* I. C. Rapoport/*lp* Will Sampson, Henry Darrow, James Cromwell, A. Martinez, Dehl Berti

The Bounty Man · Clichéd Western drama about a bounty hunter taking his man in, accompanied by a woman and pursued by villains also interested in the reward. The bounty hunter falls for the woman, the captive gets killed, the villains get the body, the bounty hunter and woman ride off into the fade-out.
1972/74 min/ABC Circle Films/*p* Aaron Spelling, Leonard Goldberg/*d* John Llewellyn Moxey/*s* Jim Byrnes/*c* Ralph Woolsey/*lp* Clint Walker, Richard Basehart, John Ericson, Margot Kidder

Branded · Unjustly accused of cowardice and court-martialled out of the army, Chuck Connors wanders the West with a broken sabre. Set in the 1880s, the stories dealt more with psychological situations than routine

Chuck Connors in Branded

gunplay. A feature was edited together from a three-part episode ('The Mission') and released in Europe as *Broken Sabre* in 1965.
1965-6/b & w: colour/48 ep x 26 min/ Goodson-Todman Prods/*cr* Larry Cohen/ *lp* Chuck Connors

Brave Eagle · This is a sort of *Broken Arrow* for youngsters, featuring Keith Larsen as an Indian chief. The show clearly delineated between the good and the bad Indian, as well as observing the role of the white 'pioneers'.
1955-6/b & w/26 ep x 26 min/Frontier Prods/*p* Jack Lacey/*lp* Keith Larsen, Kenna Numkena, Bert Wheeler, Kim Winona

The Bravos · Big budget TV-movie about conflict with the Indians at a run-down fort in the days following the Civil War. Killing, revenge and rescue are the main story points. L. Q. Jones and Bo Svenson emerge as the most interesting and colourful characters.
1972/100 min/U/*p* Norman Lloyd/*d* Ted Post/*s* Christopher Knopf, Ted Post/*c* Enzo Martinelli/*lp* George Peppard, Pernell Roberts, Belinda Montgomery, L. Q. Jones, Bo Svenson

Bret Maverick · James Garner tried for a successful revival of his earlier *Maverick* character and managed to bring it off for a while. The series was produced by almost the same creative personnel (and regular player Stuart Margolin) who helped make a success of Garner's *Rockford Files* private eye show a few years earlier. Garner was the delightfully devious Bret Maverick once again, now settling down to a supposedly easy life in a frontier town called Sweetwater, Arizona.

1981-2/17 ep x 52 min/Cherokee Prods – WB-TV/*p* Meta Rosenberg/*lp* James Garner, Darleen Carr, Ed Bruce, Stuart Margolin

Bridger · The story of Jim Bridger in the Pacific Northwest of 1830 is related with only a slight nudge toward history and a large shove into Western mythology. Location photography in the Sierra Madre mountains by Bud Thackery is a plus point.

1976/100 min/U/*p* David Lowell Rich/*d* David Lowell Rich/*s* Merwin Gerard/*c* Bud Thackery/*lp* James Wainwright, Ben Murphy, Dirk Blocker, Sally Field

Broken Arrow · Based, like the 1950 feature film *Broken Arrow*, on Elliott Arnold's novel *Blood Brother*, this series tells of the partnership (and conflict) between mail rider and Indian agent Tom Jeffords and Cochise, chief of the Apaches in the 1870s. The anthology series *20th Century-Fox Hour* remade *Broken Arrow* in 1956 with Ricardo Montalban, John Lupton and Rita Moreno, with direction by Robert Stevenson. It was this which acted as the series' pilot.

1956-8/b & w/72 ep x 26 min/FOX-TV/*p* Mel Epstein/*lp* John Lupton, Michael Ansara, Tom Fadden

Bronco · The exploits of an ex-Confederate Army captain made up this Warner Bros. series, which ran alongside the studio's other two television Westerns of the time, *Cheyenne* and *Sugarfoot*. In fact the character only came into his own series (after running as a rotating part of *The Cheyenne Show*) through Warners' dispute with Clint Walker, when the *Cheyenne* actor walked out and the studio needed a replacement series quickly. However, the Bronco Layne character remains indistinguishable from other itinerant do-gooders of the period.

1958-62/b & w/68 ep x 52 min/WB-TV/*exec p* William T. Orr/*lp* Ty Hardin

Buckskin · Stories relating the life and times of a Montana frontier town during the 1800s, as seen through the eyes of a young boy growing up.

1958-9/b & w/39 ep x 26 min/Betford Prods – Revue/*cr* Harold Swanton/*lp* Tommy Nolan, Sallie Brophy, Michael Road

Buffalo Bill Jr. · Dick Jones as a two-fisted 'teenager' who is also handy with his guns in this juvenile series set in the Texas of the 1890s. Young Bill Jr. and his kid sister Calamity are orphans adopted by kindly old Judge Wiley and the stories recount the scrapes the youngsters get into.

1955/b & w/42 ep x 26 min/Flying A Prods/*p* Louis Gray/*lp* Dick Jones, Nancy Gilbert, Harry Cheshire

---

C

Cade's County · Southwest police series in the form of a contemporary Western. Glenn Ford is Sheriff Sam Cade, whose jurisdiction takes in everything from modern Apache Indian affairs to combatting organized crime. Three 'developed for television' movies emerged from the series: *Marshal of Madrid* (from episodes 'Gun for Billy' and 'Criss Cross'), *Sam Cade* (from 'Homecoming' and 'The Fake') and *Slay Ride* (from 'Slay Ride' Pts I & II).

1971-2/24 ep x 52 min/FOX-TV/*p* Charles Larson/*lp* Glenn Ford, Edgar Buchanan, Peter Ford, Sandra Ego

Calamity Jane · Jane Alexander's performance as the legendary Calamity Jane presents her as an intense, no-nonsense frontier woman. The teleplay by Suzanne Clauser is said to be based on letters written by Jane to her daughter Jean (from a historically unverified 'marriage' to Wild Bill Hickok).

1984/100 min/CBS Entertainment/*p* Herbert Hirschman, Jane Alexander/*d* James Goldstone/*s* Suzanne Clauser/*c* Terry K. Meade/*lp* Jane Alexander, Frederic Forrest, Ken Kercheval

California Gold Rush · Author Bret Harte travels west during the 1840s and personally 'experiences' the events in the stories 'The Luck of Roaring Camp' and 'The Outcasts of Poker Flat'.

1981/100 min/Schick Sunn Classics – Taft International Pictures/*p* James L. Conway/*d* Jack B. Hively/*s* Roy London, Tom Chapman/*c* Stephen W. Gray/*lp* John Dehner, Henry Jones, Gene Evans, Ken Curtis

The Californians · 1850s San Francisco during the gold rush era, with lawlessness as the order of the day. A straightforward baddies and good guys action-drama, as a group of vigilantes attempt to clean up the town.

1957-9/b & w/69 ep x 26 min/Californian

Film Enterprises/*exec p* Louis F. Edelman/ *lp* Adam Kennedy, Sean McClory, Nan Leslie

The Call of the Wild · Jack London's 1903 adventure classic set during the Klondike gold rush is told, like the original, from the dog's point of view (with Marvin Miller's voice-over commenting on the dog's thoughts and feelings). John Beck trudges the frozen path previously worn by Clark Gable (in 1935) and Charlton Heston (in 1972) but it is the dog, Buck, who is given the lead in James Dickey's script.

1976/100 min/Charles Fries Prods/*p* Malcolm Stuart/*d* Jerry Jameson/*s* James Dickey/*c* Matthew F. Leonetti/*lp* John Beck, Bernard Fresson, John McLiam, Donald Moffat, Michael Pataki

The Capture of Grizzly Adams · A sequel to the 1976 feature *The Life and Times of Grizzly Adams* and its short-run TV series, with the innocent fugitive Adams finally coming down from his mountain hideout to the town from which he was forced to flee.

1982/100 min/Schick Sunn Classics – Taft International Pictures/*p* James L. Conway/ *d* Don Kessler/*s* Arthur Heinemann/*c* Paul Hipp/*lp* Dan Haggerty, Kim Darby, Noah Beery, Keenan Wynn

Casey Jones · The famous locomotive engineer is immortalized in this action-before-character series, with Alan Hale Jr. in the title role. The stories deal with Casey's adventures running the legendary Cannonball Express of the Illinois Central.

1957-8/b & w/32 ep x 26 min/Screen Gems – Briskin Prods/*p* Harold Greene/*lp* Alan Hale Jr., Bobby Clark, Dub Taylor

Centennial · Marathon mini-series based on marathon novel by James Michener about the West from the late 1700s to the 20th century. The story is told in twelve chapters, beginning with a French-Canadian trader, moving through the Indian Wars and Texas cattle-drives to the growth of big business and its battles with conservationists. One of the more spirited and eventful chapters was 'The Longhorns', about a Texas cattle-drive through hostile terrain, and the lives of the cowboys, led by Dennis Weaver's excellent R. J. Poteet character.

1978-9/26½ hours/U/*p* Malcolm R. Harding, Howard P. Alston, Alex Beaton, George E. Crosby/*d* Virgil W. Vogel, Paul Krasny, Harry Falk, Bernard McEveety/*s* John Wilder, Jerry Ziegman, Charles

Larson/c Duke Callaghan, Ronald Browne, Jacques R. Marquette, Charles W. Short/lp Robert Conrad, Richard Chamberlain, Raymond Burr, Dennis Weaver, Barbara Carrera, David Janssen, Brian Keith

Charlie Cobb: Nice Night for a Hanging · Pilot for projected series about an 1870s private detective in the West, this introduced Charlie Cobb (Clu Gulager), a roguish character hired to deliver the long-lost daughter of a California rancher back to her father.
1977/100 min/U/p Peter S. Fischer/d Richard Michaels/s Peter S. Fischer/c Andrew Jackson/lp Clu Gulager, Ralph Bellamy, Blair Brown, Christopher Connelly

Cheyenne · Perhaps the Western series most responsible for the small-screen stampede of the late 50s, *Cheyenne* (along with *Wyatt Earp* and *Gunsmoke*) stressed character development above shooting, riding and other Western accomplishments. The Clint Walker character was an adventurer with a strong sense of honour and justice who drifted around the West. The series initially went out under the umbrella title *Warner Bros. Presents*. Warners took the *Cheyenne* title from their 1947 feature film, which was later renamed *The Wyoming Kid*. Nine 'features' edited from *Cheyenne* episodes were released to European cinemas between 1956 and 1958: *Julesberg*; *The Storm Riders*; *The Outlander*; *Decision*; *Argonauts*; *West of the River*; *Mountain Fortress*; *Johnny Bravo*; *Last Train West*.
1955-63/b & w/107 ep x 52 min/WB-TV/exec p William T. Orr/lp Clint Walker, L.Q. Jones

The Cheyenne Show · This was an ABC-TV umbrella title for three rotating Warners Western series: *Cheyenne*, *Bronco* and *Sugarfoot*. *Cheyenne* started out as part of the *Warner Bros. Presents* series during 1955-6. *The Cheyenne Show* alternated *Sugarfoot* and *Bronco* during 1958-9, then rotated all three series during 1960-2.

The Chisholms · The story of a family who pull out of Virginia and set a course for California during the 1840s, experiencing the usual problems and perils of similar family groups in other TV productions. A six-hour mini-series paved the way for a short-lived episodic series with some new characters.
Mini-series/1979/300 min/Alan Landsburg

Prods/p Paul Freeman/d Mel Stuart/s Evan Hunter/c Jacques R. Marquette/lp Robert Preston, Rosemary Harris, Ben Murphy, Brian Kerwin, Jimmy Van Patten
Series/1980/12 ep x 52 min: 1 ep x 100 min/Alan Landsburg Prods/cr David Dortort/lp Robert Preston, Rosemary Harris, Ben Murphy, Brett Cullen

Cimarron City · Narrated in a flashback fashion by star George Montgomery, the series was about a growing town in Oklahoma. Montgomery played a peace-loving rancher who becomes mayor and aids the townsfolk during the city's boom days of the 1890s.
1958-9/b & w/26 ep x 52 min/Mont Prods – Revue – NBC-TV/p Felix Jackson/lp George Montgomery, Audrey Totter, John Smith, Stuart Randall

Cimarron Strip · This was television's third '90-minute' Western and focused on US Marshal Jim Crown as he policed the border region between Kansas and Indian Territory. Located in Cimarron City, Marshal Crown experienced pretty much the same frontier problems as Matt Dillon in *Gunsmoke*. Excellent colour photography by Harry Stradling Jr. and fine theme music from Maurice Jarre.
1967-8/23 ep x 74 min/CBS-TV/exec p Philip Leacock/lp Stuart Whitman, Percy Herbert, Randy Boone, Jill Townsend

The Cisco Kid · O. Henry's hero, the 'Robin Hood of the West', galloped around the New Mexico Territory of the 1890s with his sidekick Pancho, his horse Diablo and an outsize sense of justice. The series has the distinction of being the first television Western shot in colour, though it was initially transmitted in black and white.
1951-6/b & w: colour/156 ep x 26 min/Ziv-TV/lp Duncan Renaldo, Leo Carillo

Cliffhangers: The Secret Empire · *Secret Empire* was a twenty-minute chapter in a short-run series which also featured two other 'cliffhanging' chapters from other genres. *Secret Empire* was a Western based on the 1935 Mascot serial *The Phantom Empire*, which starred Gene Autry. Set in the 1880s, it serialized the adventures of Marshal Jim Donner as he fought the Phantom Riders and some Flash Gordon-style aliens who lived in a secret underground city.
1979/13 ep x 52 min/U-TV/cr Kenneth Johnson/lp Geoffrey Scott, Tiger Williams, Carlene Watkins, Peter Breck

Leo Carrillo, Duncan Renaldo in The Cisco Kid

Colt .45 · This was Warners' fourth TV Western series and featured an Army intelligence agent, Christopher Colt, who masquerades as a gun salesman demonstrating the new .45 handgun. Later, with the addition of a Sam Colt Jr. character, the series was also known (in syndication markets) as *Colt Cousins*. The 1950 Columbia film *Colt .45* was later renamed *Thundercloud*.
1957-60/b & w/67 ep x 26 min/WB-TV/cr Roy Huggins/lp Wayde Preston, Donald May

The Court-Martial of George Armstrong Custer · A speculation on what might have happened had Custer lived, with Brian Keith's defence lawyer battling it out with Ken Howard's prosecutor. Basically a courtroom drama; the verdict is acquittal, the suggestion being that the military would have given him the Congressional Medal of Honor in exchange for his resignation.
1977/100 min/Norman Rosemont Prods – WB/p Norman Rosemont/d Glenn Jordan/s John Gay/c (video) Jim Kilgore, John Field/lp Brian Keith, Ken Howard, Stephen Elliott, J.D. Cannon, James Olson, Blythe Danner

Jack Elam, Larry Ward, Chad Everett in The Dakotas

Cowboy G-Men · Exploits and adventures of two undercover Government agents in 1880s California who pose as cowhand and wrangler.
1954-5/b & w: colour/39 ep x 25 min/ Telemount – Mutual Prods/p Henry Donovan/lp Russell Hayden, Jackie Coogan

The Cowboys · Taking almost everything except the violence from the 1972 John Wayne film, this series features the kids hired by Wayne's widow to help run the ranch after her husband's death.
1974/13 ep x 26 min/WB-TV/p David Dortort/lp Moses Gunn, Diana Douglas, Jim Davis, A. Martinez, Robert Carradine, Sean Kelly, Kerry Maclane, Clint Howard

Custer · Set in the period 1868 to 1875, this deals with the adventures of George Armstrong Custer as he patrols Kansas with his 7th Cavalry. Brigadier General Terry, Captain Miles Keogh and, of course, Crazy Horse were among the regular historic characters. A 'feature' developed from the series, *Legend of Custer* (1968, directors Sam Wanamaker, Norman Foster), was made available for television.
1967/b & w: colour/17 ep x 52 min/FOX-TV/cr Samuel A. Peeples, David Weisbart/ lp Wayne Maunder, Slim Pickens, Peter Palmer, Michael Dante

Cutter's Trail · Set around Sante Fe in 1873, this is a part revenge, part self-redemption yarn about a US Marshal who goes across the border in search of the violent gang who turned his town over. After the initial shootout, where he's wounded and aided by a small Mexican boy and his mother, the Marshal returns for the climactic gunfight.
1970/100 min/CBS Studio Center/p John Mantley/d Vincent McEveety/s Paul Savage/c Richard Batcheller/lp John Gavin, Manuel Padilla Jr., Marisan Pavan, Beverly Garland, Joseph Cotten

——————— D ———————

The Dakotas · A team of four lawmen, a US Marshal and his three deputies, patrol the Dakota territory. Characterization and moral conflict supplied most of the action, although the Jack Elam character tended to be quicker with his gun than his reasoning.
1963/b & w/19 ep x 52 min/WB-TV/exec p William T. Orr/lp Larry Ward, Jack Elam, Chad Everett, Mike Greene

The Dangerous Days of Kiowa Jones · Robert Horton attempted to develop another Western series character with this MGM pilot about a drifter who is assigned by a dying sheriff to take two prisoners to Fort Smith for execution. The prisoners are by far the most interesting characters: Sal Mineo as a coward-killer and Nehemiah Persoff as a gypsy accused of murdering his wife.
1966/100 min/MGM/p Max E. Youngstein, David Karr/d Alex March/s Frank Fenton, Robert W. Thompson/c Ellsworth Fredricks/lp Robert Horton, Diane Baker, Sal Mineo, Nehemiah Persoff, Gary Merrill, Harry Dean Stanton

Daniel Boone (1960-1). See **Walt Disney Presents**

Daniel Boone · Fess Parker continued his coonskin cap tradition from *Davy Crockett* with this colourful Fox series set during colonial and revolutionary days. Top production values made the series an across-the-board success. The series opened with George Marshall directing a Borden Chase script. In 1966 a two-part episode ('The High Cumberland') was edited into a feature and released in Europe as *Daniel Boone – Frontier Trail Rider* (directed by George Sherman).
1964-70/b & w: colour/165 ep x 52 min/ Arcola – Fesspar – FOX-TV/exec p Aaron Rosenberg/lp Fess Parker, Albert Salmi, Ed Ames, Patricia Blair

The Daughters of Joshua Cabe · Buddy Ebsen is a landowner who is facing eviction from his land at the time of the first Homestead Act. He hopes his three daughters can help file claim to the land, but they've moved back east, so he goes to St Louis and finds three unlikely women to play the parts: a prostitute, a pickpocket and an ex-convict.
1972/74 min/Spelling-Goldberg Prods/p Richard E. Lyons/d Philip Leacock/s Paul Savage/c Arch R. Dalzell/lp Buddy Ebsen, Karen Valentine, Lesley Warren, Sandra Dee, Don Stroud

The Daughters of Joshua Cabe Return · Cabe and his three hired 'daughters' are back in an adventure full of army deserters, kidnappers and various double-dealers.
1975/74 min/Spelling-Goldberg Prods/p Richard E. Lyons/d David Lowell Rich/s Kathleen Hite/c Tim Southcott/lp Dan Dailey, Dub Taylor, Ronne Troup, Christina Hart, Brooke Adams

Davy Crockett (1954-5). See **Disneyland**

Death Valley Days · Long-running Western anthology based on the 1930s radio series which tells the stories of early pioneers in the Southwest. The series was a showcase for many emerging young players during the 1950s and was hosted in turn by Stanley Andrews, Ronald Reagan, Robert Taylor and Dale Robertson.
1952-72/b & w: colour/532 ep x 26 min/ Flying A Prods – McGowan Prods – Filmaster Prods – Madison Prods/exec p Armand Schaefer, Dorrel McGowan, Robert W. Stabler

The Deerslayer · Further adventures of Steve Forrest's Hawkeye (first seen in *Last of the Mohicans*) as he and Chingachgook get involved in kidnappings, rescues and conflict with the Hurons. Filmed on location in Utah, the movie is like a colourful matinee serial but with more dialogue.
1978/74 min/Schick Sunn Classics/p Bill Conford/d Dick Friendenberg/s S.S. Schweitzer/c Paul Hipp/lp Steve Forrest, Ned Romero, John Anderson

The Deputy · Henry Fonda's debut as a regular character in a TV series was something of a cheat. Fonda stars as Chief Marshal Simon Fry of Silver City, Arizona during the 1880s, assisted by his young deputy Clay McCord (Allen Case). But for most of the time Marshal Fry was out of town on business and thus out of the stories; hence the title. Fonda acted as narrator for all the episodes.
1959-61/b & w/76 ep x 26 min/Top Gun Prods/cr Roland Kibbee, Norman Lear/lp Henry Fonda, Allen Case, Wallace Ford

Henry Fonda in The Deputy

Desperado · Pilot for a possible series with a plot line that retreads Westerns of the 1950s. The hero rides into a town run by bad guys, gets involved with a landowner and his daughter, gets framed for the landowner's death but gets off the hook, which, of course, leads to the inevitable shoot-out.
1987/tx '120 min'/Walter Mirisch Prods – Charles E. Sellier – U/p Charles E. Sellier Jr./d Virgil W. Vogel/s Elmore Leonard/c Dick Bush/lp Alex McArthur, Lise Cutter, David Warner, Yaphet Kotto, Robert Vaughn

Desperate Mission · California in the 1840s is the backdrop for this Western concerning the 'Zorro'-like adventures of Ricardo Montalban as the Mexican-American Murieta and a weird bunch of characters trekking across the Southwest. Released theatrically in Europe as *Joaquin Murieta*, the film was shot on location in Durango, Mexico and Southern California.
1969/98 min/FOX/p David Silver/d Earl Bellamy/s Jack Guss, Richard Collins/c Jorge Stahl/lp Ricardo Montalban, Slim Pickens, Rosey Grier, Earl Holliman

Desperate Women · Western comedy-drama which weaves a one-note story about an ex-gunslinger sheriff teaming up with three female convicts in the desert and overcoming various human and natural hazards. Filmed in Mexico.
1978/100 min/Lorimar Prods/p Robert Stambler/d Earl Bellamy/s Jack B. Sowards/c Jorge Stahl/lp Susan Saint James, Dan Haggerty, Ronee Blakley, Ann Dusenberry

Destry · From Max Brand's 1930 novel and through three film versions comes this short-lived TV series featuring John Gavin as young Harrison Destry, an offbeat, humorous character in search of the men who once framed him for embezzlement. Despite the photography by Lionel Lindon and contribution by director Don Siegel the series failed to bring freshness to the old story.
1964/b & w/13 ep x 52 min/U-TV/p Frank Telford, Howard Brown/lp John Gavin

The Devil and Miss Sarah · A homesteading couple find themselves escorting an outlaw after the marshal whose prisoner he was dies from bullet wounds. The twist is that the outlaw, Gene Barry, is believed to have some sort of Satanic powers. Filmed in southern Utah, the movie is an offbeat mixture of Western actioner and ESP thriller.
1971/73 min/U/p Stan Shpetner/d Michael Caffey/s Calvin Clements/c Harry Wolf/lp Gene Barry, James Drury, Janice Rule, Charles McGraw, Slim Pickens

Dick Powell's Zane Grey Theatre · Initially based on stories by Zane Grey, this Western anthology series presented some engrossing frontier drama and fine character studies. Hosted by Dick Powell, who featured in many of the early episodes, and produced under his Four Star aegis, the series included some excellent performances from players like Robert Ryan, Ernest Borgnine, Jack Palance, Walter Brennan, Jack Lemmon and Sterling Hayden. 'The Sharpshooter' (for *The Rifleman*) and 'Trouble at Tres Cruces' (for *The Westerner*) were two episodes in the anthology that launched series of their own.
1956-61/b & w/147 ep x 26 min/Four Star – Zane Grey – Pamric Prods/p Hal Hudson/host Dick Powell

Dirty Sally · The character of the feisty old eccentric Dirty Sally Fergus was first introduced in 'Pike', a two-part episode of *Gunsmoke* in 1971. Here she is revived, with reluctant partner and former gunslinger Cyrus Pike, on their way by wagon to California. Both Jeanette Nolan and Dack Rambo carried over their parts from the *Gunsmoke* segments, but their characters weren't strong enough to sustain a series.
1974/13 ep x 25 min/CBS-TV/p Leonard Katzman/lp Jeanette Nolan, Dack Rambo

Disneyland · The Walt Disney studios were the first major film company to enter into TV production, premiering via the ABC-TV network in 1954 with the *Disneyland* nature-drama-animation-history in rotation anthology. One of these sub-divisions was called *Frontierland*, which introduced a mini-series (already planned for release to theatres) about the legendary life and adventures of frontiersman Davy Crockett. The first three episodes ('Davy Crockett, Indian Fighter', 'Davy Crockett Goes to Congress' and 'Davy Crockett at the Alamo', 1954-5) told the story of Crockett from his Indian-fighting days through his spell in politics to his final stand at the Alamo. These three episodes were re-edited into the feature *Davy Crockett, King of the Wild Frontier*, directed by Norman Foster and released in 1955. The character suddenly became so popular that Disney was forced to revive him and film two further adventures dipping back into his early days: 'Davy Crockett and the Keelboat Race' and 'Davy Crockett and the River Pirates' (both 1955). These became the feature *Davy Crockett and the River Pirates* (1955). *The Saga of Andy Burnett* (see below) was also shown as a part of *Disneyland*.
Davy Crockett/1954-5/5 ep x 52 min/Walt Disney Prods/p Walt Disney/lp Fess Parker, Buddy Ebsen

Donner Pass: The Road to Survival · The events leading up to the well-documented experiences of the unfortunate Donner party settlers, who found themselves stranded in the Sierras during winter and were forced to survive by cannibalism. In avoiding cheap sensationalism the film is perhaps too restrained to do its drama justice.
1978/100 min/Schick Sunn Classics/p James Simmons/d James L. Conway/s S.S. Schweitzer/c Henning Schellerup/lp Robert Fuller, Andrew Prine, Michael Callan, Diane McBain

Draw! · Spoof gunfighter Western which makes fun of the genre as well as allowing Kirk Douglas' aging outlaw and James Coburn's over-the-hill lawman to parody their past Western roles.
1984/94 min/Astral Film Prods – Bryna Company/p Ronald I. Cohen/d Steven Hilliard Stern/s Stanley Mann/c Laszlo George/lp Kirk Douglas, James Coburn, Alexandra Bastedo, Graham Jarvis

Dream West · Historical incidents in the life of John Charles Frémont as he leads an expedition to map the Oregon Trail, crosses paths with Kit Carson (Rip Torn), treks across the wintry Rockies, and meets President Lincoln. Although a romantic dream of the Old West rather than a dip into true history, *Dream West* is an exciting mini-series with some fine visual moments and a well-crafted teleplay.

1986/tx '420 min'/Schick Sunn Classics/p Hunt Lowry/d Dick Lowry/s Evan Hunter/c Jack Wallner, Bob Baldwin/lp Richard Chamberlain, Alice Krige, F. Murray Abraham, Ben Johnson, Rip Torn

Dundee and The Culhane · The West in the 1880s as British lawyer John Mills and his young law partner, Sean Garrison, attempt to uphold justice inside and outside the courtrooms of California. The series failed to emulate the polemics of *The Defenders* 'out west', repeatedly resorting to open Western violence.

1967/17 ep x 52 min/Filmways TV Prods/cr Sam Rolfe/lp John Mills, Sean Garrison

Dusty's Trail · Short-lived comedy Western about an inept wagon train headed west, with Bob Denver doing his *Gilligan's Island* routine and the rest of the cast performing similar character roles.

1973/26 ep x 25 min/Metromedia Prods Corp/p Elroy Schwartz/lp Bob Denver, Forrest Tucker, Ivor Francis

E

Elfego Baca · Running as part of the *Walt Disney Presents* anthology series, *Elfego Baca* is reputedly based on a real-life lawman who defended the down-trodden Mexican people in New Mexico territory in 1884. Legend has it that he held off 80 men for 33 hours while trapped alone in a mud hut, which earned him the nickname El Gato (the cat). The Disney version was all fistfights and flying lead, adapting the Disney TV approach to the then-popular stream of 'adult Westerns'. Two Elfego Baca features were released theatrically (from re-edited episodes) as *The Nine Lives of Elfego Baca* (1959, directed by Norman Foster) and *Six-Gun Law* (1962, directed by Christian Nyby).

1958-60/10 ep x 52 min/Walt Disney Prods/p James Pratt/lp Robert Loggia

Empire · The colossal Garret ranch located near Santa Fe, New Mexico is the background for this contemporary Western. The central figures are a widowed matriarch, her two offspring and the ranch foreman, Jim Redigo, played by Richard Egan. Frank Nugent wrote the initial teleplay (with photography by Joseph Biroc), which lavishly introduced the series' format of a large outdoor operation, from horse-breeding to oil-rigging. This premiere episode ('The Day the Empire Stood Still') was expanded and released theatrically in 1965 as *This Rugged Land* (directed by Arthur Hiller). When the series wrapped up Egan's Jim Redigo character went on for one more season in his own series, *Redigo*.

1962-4/32 ep x 52 min/Screen Gems – Wilrich Prods/cr Kathleen Hite/lp Richard Egan, Terry Moore, Anne Seymour, Ryan O'Neal, Charles Bronson

Evil Roy Slade · Comedy Western about an outlaw with a mean reputation trying various ways to reform for the love of a young schoolteacher. Originally produced as a half-hour comedy pilot called *Sheriff Who?* which failed to trigger a series, this is a longer version still hoping for a series to develop.

1972/100 min/U/p Garry Marshall, Jerry Belson/d Jerry Paris/s Garry Marshall/c Sam Leavitt/lp John Astin, Mickey Rooney, Dick Shawn, Henry Gibson

F

Father Murphy · 'Heartwarming' series from the Michael Landon *Little House on the Prairie* stable, set in the gold-mining Dakota territory of the 1870s. Merlin Olsen and Katherine Cannon play a dedicated couple who run a frontier school and orphanage for the children of deceased prospectors. The prospectors' diggings and surrounding scenery were beautifully photographed by Haskell B. Boggs.

1981-2/55 ep x 52 min/Michael Landon Prods/p Kent McCray/lp Merlin Olsen, Timothy Gibbs, Katherine Cannon, Charles Tyner

Female Artillery · Would-be comedy-drama Western about an outlaw forced to join up with a wagon-load of tough women stranded in the wilderness. The outlaw is pursued by a bandit gang for a large sum of money, which also sparks the interest of the women. The final battle sees the outlaw and women take on the bandits at an abandoned fort. A slow ride through familiar territory.

1973/73 min/U/p Winston Miller/d Marvin Chomsky/s Bud Freeman/c Enzo A. Martinelli/lp Dennis Weaver, Ida Lupino, Sally Ann Howes, Linda Evans

Frontier · Unromantic, average Western anthology series depicting stories of pioneering and told in an adult fashion without the usual 'adult' violence. Director Don Siegel contributed.

1955-6/b & w/30 ep x 26 min/Tomoda Prods/exec p Worthington Miner/narr Walter Coy

Frontier Circus · Stories of a travelling circus in the Southwest during the late 1800s, combining traditional circus adventure with wagon train action. Veteran director William Witney contributed.

1961-2/b & w/26 ep x 52 min/Calliope Prods/cr Samuel A. Peeples/m David Buttolph, Jeff Alexander/lp Chill Wills, John Derek, Richard Jaeckel

Frontier Doctor · Stories about Bill Baxter, a doctor struggling to bring medical assistance to the pioneers of late 1890s Arizona, with veteran B-Western cowboy actor Rex Allen. Appropriately, veteran director William Witney contributed to the series, which was also shown as *Man of the West* and *Unarmed.*

1956-7/b & w/39 ep x 26 min/REP – Studio City TV Prods/p Edward J. White/lp Rex Allen

F Troop · A sort of Bilko in the Old West was the format of this Warners comedy series, with a scheming cavalry sergeant and his sidekick operating out of a dilapidated fort in the post-Civil War West. Comedian Larry Storch as a gold-bricking corporal supplied most of the humour.

1965-7/b & w: colour/65 ep x 26 min/WB-TV/cr Richard M. Bluel/lp Ken Berry, Forrest Tucker, Larry Storch, Melody Patterson, Frank De Kova, Bob Steele

Fury · A contemporary Western about a young boy growing into manhood while living on a ranch and his adventures with a black stallion called Fury. Obviously aimed at the junior audience, the stories frequently alerted youngsters to the facts about outdoor life and supposedly inspired them to a healthy attitude toward society.

1955-9/b & w/114 ep x 26 min/TPA/exec p Leon Fromkess/lp Peter Graves, Bobby Diamond, William Fawcett

G

The Gabby Hayes Show · There appear to be two formats under the Gabby Hayes heading; the earlier, 1950-4 series featured live dramatizations of early Americana (such as the Seminole uprising in the Everglades), while the 1956 show simply used excerpts from old Buster Crabbe, Hoot Gibson, Lash LaRue and Tex Ritter movies. Both formats, however, had Gabby opening and closing

Forrest Tucker, Melody Patterson, Ken Berry, Larry Storch in F Troop

the episodes with one of his 'tall tales'.
1950-4/b & w/live tx x 25 min · 1956/b & w/live tx x 25 min/*p* Martin Stone, Vincent J. Donehue, Joe Clair, Roger Muir/*host* Gabby Hayes

The Gambler · Developed from a song made famous by country crooner Kenny Rogers, *The Gambler* stars Rogers as a veteran poker ace helping the son he never knew he had against the villainous antics of Clu Gulager. Most of the film takes place on board an El Paso to Yuma train. Also known as *Kenny Rogers as The Gambler*.
1980/95 min/Kragen and Company/*p* Jim Byrnes/*d* Dick Lowry/*s* Jim Byrnes/*c* Joseph Biroc/*lp* Kenny Rogers, Christine Belford, Bruce Boxleitner, Harold Gould, Clu Gulager

The Gene Autry Show · If Gene Autry was not already a millionaire through his feature films, the runaway success of his TV series would have made him one. The format was just the same: Autry was defender of justice, with no official title or function, sidekick Buttram was the comic relief and Champion was his smarter-than-average horse. Autry's appeal faded when the 'adult Western' came in during the mid-50s.
1950-6/b & w: colour/86 ep x 26 min/ Flying A Prods/*p* Armand Schaefer/*lp* Gene Autry, Pat Buttram, Gail Davis

The Godchild · Television reworking of the oft-filmed Peter B. Kyne *Saturday Evening Post* story, the best known version being John Ford's 3 *Godfathers*/1948. Jack Palance, José Perez and Ed Lauter are three prisoners on the run from the Army who adopt a baby they find in the desert.
1974/74 min/MGM/*p* Richard Collins/*d* John Badham/*s* Ron Bishop/*c* Stevan Larner/*lp* Jack Palance, Jack Warden,

Keith Carradine, Ed Lauter, José Perez

Go West, Young Girl · Another ill-suited duo blundering about the West forms the storyline for this comedy Western. Female journalist from eastern newspaper and pioneer-spirited girl team up to investigate if rumours about Billy the Kid still being alive are true.
1978/74 min/Bennett-Katleman Prods – COL/*p* George Yanok/*d* Alan J. Levi/*s* George Yanok/*c* Gerald Perry Finnerman/ *lp* Karen Valentine, Sandra Will, Stuart Whitman, Richard Jaeckel

The Gray Ghost · Fact-based series concerning Confederate cavalry officer John Singleton Mosby and his Rangers during the Civil War. The series deals with the South from a sympathetic point of view though it treats both sides of the conflict with respect.
1957-8/b & w/39 ep x 26 min/Lindsley Parsons Prods/*p* Lindsley Parsons/*lp* Tod Andrews, Phil Chambers

The Great Adventure · This series dramatized American historical events, primarily during the 1800s. The anthology was supported by a stirring score from Richard Rodgers. Among the historical figures spotlighted were Sitting Bull, James Butler Hickok and Sam Houston.
1963-5/b & w/26 ep x 52 min/CBS-TV/*p* Bert Granet/*narr* Van Heflin, Russell Johnson

The Gun and the Pulpit · Former child evangelist Marjoe Gortner plays a gunfighter who is forced to disguise himself as a preacher in order to avoid a posse and then rides into a frontier town where the townsfolk take him for the real thing. Gortner slides in and out of his dual personality, mostly to humorous effect, until finally faced with Geoffrey Lewis's superbly-played professional gunslinger. A TV-movie pilot intended to launch a series.
1974/74 min/Danny Thomas Prods/*p* Paul Maslansky/*d* Daniel Petrie/*s* William Bowers/*c* Richard C. Glouner/*lp* Marjoe Gortner, Slim Pickens, David Huddleston, Geoffrey Lewis

Gun Shy · This spin-off from *The Apple Dumpling Gang* movies reverts to sitcom practice in its juvenile-market theme of a gambler (now played by Barry Van Dyke) taking care of a couple of kids and getting involved in horse racing capers. The standard two comic bad guys are played by Tim

Thomerson and Geoffrey Lewis.
1983/6 ep x 25 min/Walt Disney Prods/*p* Eric Cohen/*lp* Barry Van Dyke, Tim Thomerson, Keith Mitchell, Bridgette Anderson, Henry Jones, Geoffrey Lewis

Gunslinger · Stories about an undercover troubleshooter for the post-Civil War US Army, mostly set in New Mexico. Tony Young plays the part with expressionless determination.
1961/b & w/12 ep x 52 min/CBS-TV/*exec p* Charles Marquis Warren/*lp* Tony Young, Preston Foster

Gunsmoke · This famous Western series with the longest-running episodic format in history (20 years) started life as a radio show with actor William Conrad in the part of Marshal Matt Dillon. When CBS decided to develop the TV series they asked John Wayne to star as Matt Dillon but Wayne turned them down, suggesting James Arness for the role instead. Wayne, however, introduced the show when it premiered on CBS-TV on the night of 10 September 1955. *Gunsmoke* had its setting in Dodge City, Kansas during the 1880s and featured four main running characters: Matt Dillon, Doc Adams, Longbranch Saloon owner Kitty Russell, and Deputy Chester Goode (later replaced by Festus Haggen). *Gunsmoke*, for the most part, did not concern itself with Western history or even Western mythology, but merely presented self-contained Western adventures within an action-drama format. The 'serious' approach of *Gunsmoke* (along with *The Life and Legend of Wyatt Earp*) can be said to be directly responsible for the 1950s rush into TV Westerns. The half-hour series was shown in Britain under the title of *Gun Law*; it was also syndicated as *Marshal Dillon* while the hour-long episodes were still running.
1955-75/b & w: colour/233 ep x 26 min: 402 ep x 52 min/Filmaster Prods – CBS-TV – Arness & Company/*p* Charles Marquis Warren, Norman Macdonnell, Philip Leacock, John Mantley/*lp* James Arness, Milburn Stone, Amanda Blake, Dennis Weaver, Ken Curtis, Burt Reynolds, Glenn Strange

The Guns of Will Sonnett · Walter Brennan is a rough-hewn former cavalry scout, Will Sonnett, searching the West for his notorious gunfighter son. On his quest he takes with him his grandson, the gunfighter's offspring. Jason Evers as the gunfighter rarely turned up in the stories, which were

Richard Boone in Have Gun, Will Travel

centred on the theme of family loyalty.
1967-9/52 ep x 26 min/Thomas-Spelling
Prods/p Aaron Spelling/lp Walter
Brennan, Norman (Dack) Rambo

H

The Hanged Man · A Western with a
supernatural twist with Steve Forrest as a
gunman who is hanged and pronounced
dead, but miraculously survives and goes on
to become a mystical adventurer – like a
benevolent cousin of Yul Brynner's gunfighter in *Westworld*.
1974/74 min/Fenady Associates – Bing
Crosby Prods/p Andrew J. Fenady/d
Michael Caffey/s Ken Trevey/c Keith C.
Smith/lp Steve Forrest, Cameron Mitchell,
Sharon Acker, Dean Jagger, Will Geer

Hardcase · Clint Walker pursues his
runaway wife who has taken off with a
Mexican revolutionary. The movie shifts in
and out of gear too often to sustain interest,
with doses of traditional gunplay followed
by slow-moving dialogue scenes.
1972/74 min/Hanna-Barbera Prods/p
Matthew Rapf/d John Llewellyn Moxey/s
Harold Jack Bloom, Sam H. Rolfe/c
Rosalio Solano/lp Clint Walker, Stefanie
Powers, Pedro Armendariz Jr., Alex
Karras

The Hatfields and the McCoys · Legendary
family feud of the 1880s rekindled here for
the small screen. Jack Palance and Steve
Forrest head this slow-moving story of petty
and violent mountain folk. Clyde Ware

(notable as a writer with the *Gunsmoke*
series) appears to have lost direction here.
Also known as *Story of the Hatfields and the
McCoys*.
1975/74 min/Charles Fries Prods/p George
Edwards/d/s Clyde Ware/c Fred H.
Jackman/lp Jack Palance, Steve Forrest,
Richard Hatch, Karen Lamm, James
Keach

Have Gun, Will Travel · Richard Boone's
Paladin character was a sort of gun-for-hire
with a difference. Between assignments he
would enjoy a gentlemanly life of culture in
his hotel base in San Francisco, but when
called out on assignment he would garb
himself in ominous black and set off to
straighten out the bad guys. Boone's almost
satanic presence along with 'adult' stories
and characterizations made the series a fast-
paced, demanding Western drama, a quality
production in sharp contrast to contemporary cowpoke shows. Andrew V. McLaglen directed several episodes.
1957-63/b & w/156 ep x 26 min/Filmaster
Prods/cr Herb Meadow, Sam Rolfe/lp
Richard Boone, Kam Tong, Lisa Lu

Hawkeye and The Last of the Mohicans ·
The James Fenimore Cooper novel was the
basis of this Canadian-produced series featuring the adventures of Nat Cutler (aka
Hawkeye) and his Indian companion
Chingachgook as they battle hostile Hurons
in New York State in the 1750s. Aimed
mainly at the moppet market, the series hit
its target with plenty of outdoor action and
one-note plots.
    Four edited-from-episodes TV movies
were developed from the series: *The Long
Rifle and the Tomahawk*; *The Pathfinder and
the Mohican*; *The Redmen and the Renegades*
and *Along the Mohawk Trail*.
1956-7/b & w/39 ep x 26 min/CBC –
Normandie Prods/p Sigmund Neufeld/lp
John Hart, Lon Chaney Jr.

Hec Ramsey · Richard Boone is a deputy
chief of police in a growing Western town in
1901 who is fascinated by the new crime-
solving methods of ballistics, finger-printing
and microscope tests. Another series success
for Richard Boone, supported by some very
literate teleplays.
1972-4/9 ep x 74 min: 1 ep x 100
min/U-TV – Mark VII Prod/p Doug
Benton/lp Richard Boone, Rick Lenz

Here Come the Brides · The theme here,
part comedy, part adventure, is something

of 100 brides for 100 brothers. The head of
an 1870s Seattle logging camp organizes a
boatload of single women to come out west
as prospective brides for his crew of lumberjacks. The premiere/pilot episode was written by N. Richard Nash, with several
elements from his play *Rainmaker* creeping
into the opening story.
1968-70/52 ep x 52 min/COL-TV/cr Alan
Marcus/lp Robert Brown, Bobby
Sherman, David Soul, Joan Blondell,
Bridget Hanley, Bo Svenson

The High Chaparral · Empire-building in
Arizona in the 1870s was the main theme
behind *The High Chaparral*, featuring the Big
John Cannon family (his brother, his Mexican wife, his young son from a previous
marriage, his wife's brother and various
ranch-hands) as they face the human and
natural hazards coming out of the desert.
Created by David Dortort, following his
huge success with *Bonanza*, *The High
Chaparral* related pleasing, often poetic stories concerning the precarious relationship
between the white man and the Apache, as
well as dealing with the politically unstable
understanding with the Mexicans and the
occasional nomadic character. In a welcome
change from the norm, the representation of
the Apache Indian was effected with care and
dignity.
1967-71/98 ep x 52 min/NBC-TV – Xanadu
Prods/cr David Dortort/lp Leif Erickson,
Cameron Mitchell, Mark Slade, Henry
Darrow, Linda Cristal, Don Collier

**High Noon, Part II: The Return of Will
Kane** · Retired lawman Will Kane steps in to
protect a man hounded by a corrupt
marshal. Lee Majors takes on the original

John Hart, Lon Chaney Jr. in Hawkeye and
the Last of the Mohicans

Gary Cooper role in this TV movie which claims to pick up where the Fred Zinnemann film left off, but fails to explain why.
1980/100 min/Charles Fries Prods/p Edward J. Montagne/d Jerry Jameson/s Elmore Leonard/c Harry J. May/lp Lee Majors, David Carradine, J.A. Preston, Michael Pataki, Katherine Cannon

Hitched · A cliché-scattered but amusing small-screen Western version of something like *It's a Mad Mad Mad Mad World*, as a young couple on their way to California in 1886 get separated and on their journeys meet a host of outrageous and delightful Western caricatures.
1973/73 min/U/p Richard Alan Simmons/d Boris Sagal/s Richard Alan Simmons/c Gerald Perry Finnerman/lp Sally Field, Tim Matheson, Neville Brand, Slim Pickens, Denver Pyle

Hondo · Spawned by the 1953 Warners feature based on the story by Louis L'Amour, this Western adventure series set Ralph Taeger in John Wayne's buckskins as a cavalry scout in Arizona in the 1870s, though the hero was not as cynical and mercenary as in the Wayne version. The series' feature-length pilot (guest starring Robert Taylor) was released to theatres in Europe as *Hondo and the Apaches*.
1967/17 ep x 52 min/MGM-TV – Batjac Prods - Fenady Assoc/p Andrew Fenady/lp Ralph Taeger, Kathie Brown, Buddy Foster, Noah Beery Jr.

Honky Tonk · A flimsy reworking of the 1941 Jack Conway movie, this is set in Cascade, Nevada during a gold strike in the 1880s. Richard Crenna plays a con man who views the gold-mining territory as a prime grazing ground for his double-dealing talents.
1974/74 min/MGM/p Hugh Benson/d Don Taylor/s Douglas Heyes/c Joseph Biroc/lp Richard Crenna, Stella Stevens, Will Geer, Margot Kidder

Hopalong Cassidy · After a series of 66 theatrical features in the saddle as Hopalong Cassidy between 1935 and 1948, William Boyd turned to television and re-ran edited versions of his movies on NBC in the late 1940s. Then in 1951 he produced a series of Hopalong Cassidy episodes specially made for TV, with Edgar Buchanan as his sidekick Red Connors, on the same chasing-rustlers-and-outlaws level as the features.
1951-2/b & w/52 ep x 26 min/William

Boyd Prods/p William Boyd/lp William Boyd, Edgar Buchanan

Hotel de Paree · Set in and around Georgetown, Colorado during the 1870s, the stories revolve around fast gun Sundance as he takes care of the fancy Hotel de Paree and its attractive female owner, Monique. The series opened with a top-rate production force, including photography by Joseph Biroc, a score by Dimitri Tiomkin and direction by Robert Aldrich.
1959-60/b & w/33 ep x 26 min/CBS-TV/p William Self/lp Earl Holliman, Judi Meredith, Jeanette Nolan, Strother Martin

Houston: The Legend of Texas · Biography of Sam Houston spanning the period 1829 to 1836, with the Alamo as a dramatic chaser. Set in flashback format as Houston (Sam Elliott) reflects from the besieged Alamo fortress on the previous seven years: his life with the Cherokee, his diplomatic huddle with old friend President Andrew Jackson, his meeting with Jim Bowie (Michael Beck), and the American Texans' break with Mexico heating up to boiling point.
1986/tx '180 min'/J.D. Feigelson Prod Inc – Taft Entertainment Television Inc/p Frank Q. Dobbs/d Peter Levin/s John Binder/c Frank Watts/lp Sam Elliott, Claudia Christian, Devon Ericson, Michael C. Gwynne, Ned Romero

How the West Was Won · See **The Macahans**

Hudson's Bay · Adventures of the fur trappers set around the Hudson's Bay region during the early 1800s. Created and directed by Sidney Furie, it was not too distant in style and content from the other Canadian-produced northwoods series, *Tomahawk*.
1959/b & w/39 ep x 25 min/North Star/cr Sidney J. Furie/lp Barry Nelson, George Tobias

Buddy Foster, Ralph Taeger in Hondo

I

I Married Wyatt Earp · Based on the memoirs of singer Josephine Marcus, who married the famous lawman, the film tells in flashback how Earp and Sheriff John Behan vied for her affections. The high point, of course, is the celebrated Gunfight at the O.K. Corral, with Mrs Wyatt Earp relating how it 'really' happened.
1983/100 min/Osmond Television Prods – Comworld Prods/p Richard E. Lyons/d Michael O'Herlihy/s I. C. Rapoport/c John C. Flinn III/lp Marie Osmond, Bruce Boxleitner, John Bennett Perry

The Incredible Rocky Mountain Race · Played strictly for thrills and fun, this was the colourful story of a race between rivals Mark Twain and Mike Fink from St Joseph, Missouri to California in 1861.
1977/100 min/Schick Sunn Classics/p Robert Stabler/d James L. Conway/s Tom Chapman, David O'Malley/c Henning Schellerup/lp Christopher Connelly, Forrest Tucker, Larry Storch

Independence · A pleasant return to the traditional, well-crafted Western, about a no-nonsense sheriff whose town is under threat from marauders. With Michael Kozoll, co-creator of *Hill Street Blues*, as a consultant, the movie uses the multiple

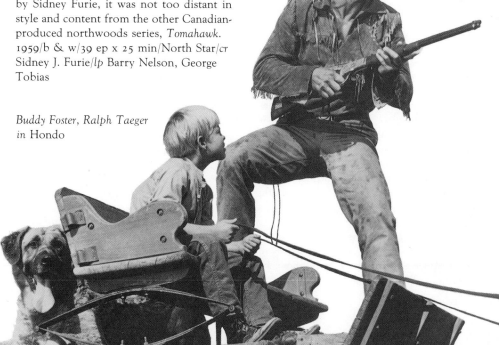

character structure and gritty realism popularized by that show.
1987/tx '120 min'/Schick Sunn Classics/p Joseph B. Wallenstein/d John Patterson/s Gordon Dawson/c John Coquillon/lp John Bennett Perry, Isabella Hofmann, Sandy McPeak, Anthony Zerbe, R.G. Armstrong

The Intruders · A psychological Western about a spineless township preparing for an onslaught from the combined forces of the James gang and the Youngers. Reminiscent of *High Noon*, with a civil rights theme as half-breed John Saxon becomes the town's saviour.
1970/95 min/U/p James Duff McAdams/d William A. Graham/s Dean Reisner/c Ray Flin/lp Don Murray, Anne Francis, Edmond O'Brien, John Saxon

The Invasion of Johnson County · Disappointing account of the greed, violence and injustice of the Johnson County War, reduced to a circus of TV Western types and conventional gunplay.
1976/100 min/Roy Huggins Prods – U/p Roy Huggins/d Jerry Jameson/s Nicholas E. Baehr/c Rexford Metz/lp Bill Bixby, Bo Hopkins, John Hillerman

The Iron Horse · The made-for-TV movie *Scalplock* acted as the pilot for this action-adventure series about the men involved in the construction of a railroad on the frontier in the 1870s. All the Western building-a-railway hazards and problems were evident, providing plenty of action under the executive eye of Charles Marquis Warren. Director Sam Fuller also contributed to the series' first season.
1966-8/47 ep x 52 min/Screen Gems/cr Stephen Kandel, James Goldstone/exec p Charles Marquis Warren/lp Dale Robertson, Gary Collins, Bob Random

Ishi, The Last of his Tribe · Splendid factual account of the last surviving member of the Yahi Indian tribe, discovered by an anthropologist in a small California town in 1911. We learn, via flashback, how the Yahi tribe dwindled over the years until only Ishi remained as a witness to history. Screenwriter Dalton Trumbo died while adapting Theodora Kroeber's book (she was the anthropologist's wife) and his son Christopher completed the script.
1978/150 min/An Edward and Mildred Lewis Prod/p James F. Sommers/d Robert Ellis Miller/s Dalton and Christopher Trumbo/c Woody Omens/lp Dennis

James Whitmore, Ned Romero in I Will Fight No More Forever

Weaver, Eloy Phil Casados, Devon Ericson, Geno Silva, Joseph Running Fox

I Will Fight No More Forever · A film about Chief Joseph's attempt to lead his people to freedom in Canada toward the end of the bitter Nez Percé Indian War of the late 1870s. A sensitive story, largely expressed through the fine characterizations of Chief Joseph (Ned Romero) and General Otis Howard (James Whitmore). The production received Emmy Awards for writing and editing (by Robert K. Lambert).
1975/74 min/David Wolper Prods/p Stan Margulies/d Richard T. Heffron/s Jeb Rosebrook, Theodore Strauss/c Jorge Stahl/lp James Whitmore, Ned Romero, Sam Elliott, John Kauffman

J

Jack London's Tales of the Klondike · Stories of gold prospectors and other adventurers as they tramp across the frozen wastes of northwest Canada during the Klondike gold rush of the 1890s. A rather tame series trying to boost its teleplays with an international cast: Neil Munro, Cherie Lunghi, John Candy, Doug McGrath, Eva Gabor, Tom Butler, etc.
1980/7 ep x 52 min/Norfolk Communications – CBC – Primetime TV/p William I. MacAdam/narr Orson Welles

Jefferson Drum · Routine stories of a two-fisted newspaperman trying to keep a lid on the violence and corruption in a lawless mining town in the 1850s.
1958-9/b & w/26 ep x 26 min/Goodson-Todman Prods – Screen Gems/p Matthew Rapf/lp Jeff Richards, Cyril Delavanti

Johnny Ringo · A series featuring three young leads in traditional Western roles

usually portrayed (during the late 50s) by more mature players. Don Durant has the title role, supposedly based on the real-life gunfighter-turned-law enforcer.
1959-60/b & w/38 ep x 26 min/Four Star – Pamaron – Zane Grey Prods/cr Aaron Spelling/lp Don Durant, Karen Sharpe, Mark Goddard

K

Kate Bliss and The Ticker Tape Kid · Light-hearted Western about a lady detective despatched out West to investigate a case of rustling. The players appear to have fun with their characters and the comic situations.
1978/100 min/Aaron Spelling Prods/p Richard E. Lyons/d Burt Kennedy/s William Bowers, John Zodorow/c Lamar Boren/lp Suzanne Pleshette, Don Meredith, Harry Morgan, Tony Randall

Kenny Rogers as 'The Gambler' – The Adventure Continues · Kenny Rogers somehow managed to keep Westerns alive on TV during the early 80s (his 1980 *The Gambler* received a surprisingly high audience rating), but this one strains the back-by-popular-demand concept. Outlaws kidnap Rogers' son and he spends the mini-series pursuing them, collecting various unwanted frontier characters along the trail.
1983/200 min/Lion Share Prods/p Dick Lowry, Ken Kragen/d Dick Lowry/s Jim Byrnes/c James Pergola/lp Kenny Rogers, Bruce Boxleitner, Linda Evans

Klondike · Tales of gold rush fever in Skagway, Alaska during the 1890s, with the setting and the main plot of this short-run series based on Pierre Berton's *The Klondike Fever*. Ralph Taeger's good guy was often at odds with James Coburn's not-so-nice guy, with Mari Blanchard's hotel owner hovering somewhere between them. Sam Peckinpah contributed scripts.
1960-1/b & w/18 ep x 26 min/UA-TV/p William Conrad/lp Ralph Taeger, James Coburn, Mari Blanchard, Joi Lansing

Kung Fu · The concept of transferring the science and philosophy of ancient China to the early West sounds better than it sometimes proved. Kwai Chang Caine was a hunted Shaolin monk pursued across the West by Chinese assassins and American bounty hunters (for the self-defence killing of a Chinese royal) while searching for a long-lost half-brother. Nevertheless, cryptic

dialogue, superb colour photography by Fred Koenecamp and the stylized use of slow-motion action sequences made this a wonderfully offbeat Western.
Pilot/1972/75 min/WB/p/d Jerry Thorpe/s Ed Spielman, Howard Friedlander/c Richard Rawlings/lp David Carradine, Barry Sullivan, Albert Salmi, Wayne Maunder, Benson Fong, Philip Ahn
Series/1972-5/62 ep x 52 min/WB-TV/p Jerry Thorpe/lp David Carradine, Keye Luke

Kung Fu: The Movie · David Carradine's Shaolin monk returns to seek out his grown-up son while dodging the assassins of an evil Manchu sent over from China to California.
1986/100 min/A Lou Step Prod – WB/p Skip Ward/d Richard Lang/s Durrell Royce Crays/c Robert Seaman/lp David Carradine, Martin Landau, Brandon Lee

L

Lacy and The Mississippi Queen · Failed pilot-TV movie involving two sisters, one a headstrong frontier-smart gal, the other a sophisticated domestic type, who set out to avenge their father's murder in the kind of Wild West where Jack Elam is an Indian scout named Willie Red Fire.
1978/74 min/Lawrence Gordon Prod – PAR/p Lew Gallo/d Robert Butler/s Kathy Donnell, Madeline DiMaggio-Wagner/c Ted Voigtlander/lp Kathleen Lloyd, Debra Feuer, Edward Andrews, Jack Elam

Lancer · Another ranching family saga, set in much the same male-orientated mould as *Bonanza* and located in the very same 1870s San Joaquin Valley as *The Big Valley*. Rugged Murdoch Lancer runs a cattle ranch and is joined by his two sons, Mexican-style outlaw Johnny and dandy Easterner Scott, when the ranch is in danger from land pirates. An otherwise formula family Western except for James Stacy's stylish bandit character.
1968-70/51 ep x 52 min/FOX-TV/cr Sam Peeples/lp James Stacy, Wayne Maunder, Andrew Duggan, Elizabeth Baur, Paul Brinegar

Laramie · The main location of this series is a relay station in Wyoming in the 1870s. John Smith as the station owner and Robert Fuller as a saddle tramp hired to help were the series' main characters; Hoagy Carmichael and, in turn, Spring Byington filled the role of housekeeper, while Bobby Crawford

Jr. and later Dennis Holmes appeared as the juvenile member of this Western 'family'.
1959-63/b & w: colour/124 ep x 52 min/ Revue Prods/p John Champion, Robert Pirosh/lp John Smith, Robert Fuller, Hoagy Carmichael, Bobby Crawford Jr., Dennis Holmes, Spring Byington

Laredo · A Western adventure with a nice line in black humour featuring the exploits of three Texas Rangers as they tackle their various missions with a less-than-serious intent. The action was expertly staged, with some fine and exciting combat scenes. *The Virginian* series provided the springboard for *Laredo* in an early 1965 episode ('We've Lost a Train'), which introduced the three Ranger characters and also provided the 'feature' *Backtrack* (scripted by Borden Chase; shown in 1969). There was also a 1968 *Laredo* 'feature', *Three Guns for Texas*, comprised of the episodes 'Yahoo', 'Jinx' and 'No Bugles, One Drum'.
1965-7/56 ep x 52 min/U-TV – NBC-TV/p Frederick Shorr, Richard Irving/lp Neville Brand, Peter Brown, William Smith, Philip Carey

Lash of the West · Originally produced under the title of *Tales of Famous Outlaws*, this was pretty much in the same format as the Gabby Hayes shows of the mid-1950s. LaRue would introduce a story about his 'grandfather' in the Old West, then feed in an extract from one of his own 1940s B-Westerns.
1953/b & w/13 ep x 15 min/Western Adventure Prods/host Lash LaRue

The Last Day · The events of the last day of the Dalton gang as they strike the bank in Coffeyville, Kansas. Retired gunman Richard Widmark is forced to defend the town as the gang enter. Produced by A. C. Lyles in a pseudo-documentary style with Harry Morgan supplying the narration.
1975/98 min/PAR/p A.C. Lyles/d Vincent McEveety/s Jim Byrnes, Steve Fisher/c Robert B. Hauser/lp Richard Widmark, Christopher Connelly, Robert Conrad, Gene Evans, Richard Jaeckel

The Last Days of Frank and Jesse James · Set in the time before Bob Ford shoots Jesse, when the James brothers are living respectably under assumed names. Johnny Cash and Kris Kristofferson fit the parts quite adequately and even give a psychological edge to their relationship.
1986/100 min/Joseph Cates Prods/p Phillip

Cates/d William A. Graham/s William Stratton/c Tony Imi/lp Johnny Cash, Kris Kristofferson, Ed Bruce, Gail Youngs, Willie Nelson

Last of the Mohicans · Filmed in the Scottish Highlands, this adventurous British serial is faithful to the Fenimore Cooper novel. Lots of lush scenery and glimmering lakes; the makeup department made mini-masterpieces of some of the Huron extras. Available for American TV in 13 ep x 26 min format.
1971/8 ep x 45 min/BBC-TV/p John McRae/ lp Kenneth Ives, John Abineri, Richard Warwick, Philip Madoc

Last of the Mohicans · TV-movie remake of Fenimore Cooper's novel about a frontier scout, Hawkeye, and his Indian companions who escort a British party through hostile territory at the time of the French and Indian Wars. Steve Forrest and Ned Romero repeated their Hawkeye and Chingachgook roles in the follow-up, *The Deerslayer*.
1977/100 min/Schick Sunn Classics/p Robert Stabler/d James L. Conway/s Stephen Lord/c Henning Schellerup/lp Steve Forrest, Ned Romero, Andrew Prine, Don Shanks

The Last Ride of the Dalton Gang · Structured as a flashback which reaches from 1934 to 1867, the film depicts the outlaw Daltons as heroes in an environment where progress is evil and a gang of backwater hicks with murder and robbery on their minds can appear merely as a group of misunderstood youths. A bizarre view of Western outlaw history.
1979/150 min/Dan Curtis Prods/p Joseph Stern/d Dan Curtis/s Earl W. Wallace/c Frank Stanley/lp Cliff Potts, Randy Quaid, Larry Wilcox, Sharon Farrell, Jack Palance, Dale Robertson

Lawman · In the breed of Warners 'adult' Westerns, this is a direct-hit actioner with little time given to the psychology behind the action. The characterization is strong and the production above average; and John Russell is a hard-bitten, shoot-to-kill lawman.
1958-62/b & w/156 ep x 26 min/WB-TV/ exec p William T. Orr/lp John Russell, Peter Brown, Peggy Castle, Dan Sheridan

Law of the Land · Pilot for a potential series called *The Deputies*. The plot served to establish the main lawmen characters while investigating Jack the Ripper-like prostitute slayings in the early days of Denver, Colorado. Jim Davis is the marshal and Cal Bellini, Nicholas Hammond, Charles Martin Smith and Glenn Corbett (later Don Johnson) are his youthful deputies. The format is reminiscent of Warners' series *The Dakotas*.

1976/100 min/Quinn Martin Prods/*p* John Wilder/*d* Virgil W. Vogel/*s* John Wilder, Sam Rolfe/*c* William Spencer/*lp* Jim Davis, Don Johnson, Cal Bellini, Nicholas Hammond, Barbara Parkins

Law of the Plainsman · This series evolved from the Michael Ansara character in *The Rifleman* in 1959. Originally called *Tales of the Plainsman*, the stories draw on the exploits of Buckhart, an Apache Indian who is also a deputy US Marshal. Ansara, who could never quite shake off being typecast as an Indian, played the Harvard-educated lawman with style and authority. The setting is New Mexico in the 1880s.

1959-60/b & w/30 ep x 26 min/Four Star–Cardiff Prods/*p* Peter Packer/*lp* Michael Ansara, Dayton Lummis, Gina Gillespie

The Legend of Jesse James · This short-lived series presented the celebrated outlaw as a teenager with a tendency to get into trouble. Nevertheless, the character was projected as a series hero, with more than a promise of violence.

1965-6/b & w/26 ep x 26 min/FOX-TV/*p* Don Siegel/*lp* Christopher Jones, Allen Case, John Milford, Robert Wilke

The Legend of the Golden Gun · A young man bent on revenge against Quantrill for the murder of his family is taken under his wing by a legendary retired gunfighter. After schooling in the ways of a Western hero, the young man continues his quest, meeting General Custer and Buffalo Bill along the way. Originally called *The Shiny Western*, it was a pilot that failed to inspire a series.

1979/100 min/Bennett-Katleman Prods – COL/*p* B.W. Sandefur, Dan Cohan/*d* Alan J. Levi/*s* James D. Parriott/*c* Gerald Perry Finnerman/*lp* Jeffrey Osterhage, Carl Franklin, Hal Holbrook, Keir Dullea

The Legend of Walks Far Woman · The life story of a Pikuni Blackfoot Indian woman, starting out in 1875 as she survives the wilderness, white traders and Sioux Indians, finally taking up with the latter. Raquel Welch portrays the Indian woman with the fire of a Sioux suffragette. Excellent

colour photography uses the lush Montana locations to full effect.

1982/122 min/Roger Gimbel Prods – Raquel Welch Prods Inc – Lee Levinson' Prods – EMI Television/*p* Lee Levinson, William S. Gilmore/*d* Mel Damski/*s* Evan Hunter/*c* Gayne Rescher/*lp* Raquel Welch, Bradford Dillman, George Clutsei

The Life and Legend of Wyatt Earp · Based on Stuart N. Lake's biography of the famous lawman. Scriptwriter Frederick Hazlitt Brennan fashioned one of TV's Western legends with this long-running series, which was structured more like a continuing serial than an episodic show, Hugh O'Brian's Earp became Marshal of Ellsworth, Kansas in the opening episode, then some 35 stories later moved to Dodge City and remained there for 114 stories. Eventually he drifted over to Tombstone, Arizona, where he kept the peace until the climactic five-part episode ('Gunfight at the O.K. Corral') saw the historic shoot-out between the Earp brothers and the Clanton gang which closed the six-year series. Among the historical characters turning up were Bat Masterson, Ned Buntline, Doc Holliday and Curly Bill Brocius.

1955-61/b & w/226 ep x 26 min/Wyatt Earp Enterprises – Desilu/*exec p* Louis F. Edelman/*lp* Hugh O'Brian, Mason Alan Dinehart III, Denver Pyle, Gloria Talbot, Douglas Fowley, Lloyd Corrigan, Trevor Bardette, Lash LaRue, Steve Brodie

The Life and Times of Grizzly Adams · The rugged wilderness of the late 1880s is the background for this story of a fur trapper who is hiding in the mountains for a crime he did not commit. The series, aimed directly at a 'primetime family audience', came off as little more than Disney's *Bear Country* with actors.

1977-8/37 ep x 52 min: 2 ep x 74 min/ Schick Sunn Classics/*cr* Charles E. Sellier Jr./*lp* Dan Haggerty, Denver Pyle, Don Shanks

Little House: A New Beginning · In 1982 Michael Landon's Charles Ingalls character left the *Little House on the Prairie* series, bidding farewell to his daughter, Laura, and her husband and selling his farm to a couple of new arrivals. A new schoolteacher and a couple of other characters also joined the show and life continued as eventfully as before in 1870s Minnesota.

1982-3/22 ep x 52 min/NBC-TV – Ed Friendly Prod/*p* Kent McCray/*lp* Melissa

Gilbert, Dean Butler, Stan Ivor

Little House: Bless All the Dear Children · Christmas with the Walnut Grove folk involves the temporary kidnapping of a Wilder family toddler as well as several traditional Yuletide yarns.

1984/96 min/NBC-TV – Ed Friendly Prods/*p* Kent McCray/*d* Victor French/*s* Chris Abbott-Fish/*c* Haskell B. Boggs/*lp* Melissa Gilbert, Dean Butler, Victor French, Patricia Pearcy, Joel Graves

Little House on the Prairie · Domestic Western series based on the books by Laura Ingalls Wilder about the life of her family in southwestern Minnesota during the 1870s. Structured in the same fashion as the pioneering family-on-the-move drama (*The Chisholms*, etc), *Little House* tells of the Ingalls family after they have moved from Kansas to Minnesota. Michael Landon was the power behind the series and the many episodes he wrote and directed are among the finest episodic stories ever aired for this type of drama. After the Landon character left the series in 1982 the title was switched to *Little House: A New Beginning*.

Pilot/1974/96 min/NBC Prods/*p/d* Michael Landon/*s* Blanche Hanalis/*c* Ted Voigtlander/*lp* Michael Landon, Karen Grassle, Melissa Gilbert, Melissa Sue Anderson, Victor French

Series/1974-82/216 ep x 52 min/NBC-TV – Ed Friendly Prods/*p* John Hawkins, Winston Miller, B.W. Sandefur, William F. Claxton/*lp* Michael Landon, Melissa Gilbert, Melissa Sue Anderson, Lindsay and Sidney Green Bush

Little House: The Last Farewell · The final curtain at Walnut Grove as the citizens of this small community literally blow up the town to prevent a property tycoon from taking over. Last of three TV movies produced after the series ended.

1984/96 min/Ed Friendly Prods – NBC Prods/*p* Kent McCray/*d/s* Michael Landon/*c* Ted Voigtlander/*lp* Michael Landon, Karen Grassle, Melissa Gilbert, Dean Butler, Richard Bull

The Little House Years · A *Little House* series special which presents flashbacks from the early years of the Ingalls family at Walnut Grove via their reminiscences as they gather for a holiday dinner.

1979/150 min/Ed Friendly Prods – NBC-TV/*p* Ed Friendly/*d/s* Michael Landon [various *d* & *s* on flashback sequences]/*lp*

Michael Landon, Karen Grassle, Melissa Gilbert, Melissa Sue Anderson

Lock, Stock and Barrel · A breezy Western in which a runaway couple are pursued by the girl's father and brothers as they trek toward Oregon in the hope of setting up a new life. During their journey they meet various scallywags and desperados, none of whom are really so bad as they seem. There was a sequel, *Hitched*, in 1973.
1971/96 min/U/p Richard Alan Simmons/d Jerry Thorpe/s Richard Alan Simmons/c Russell Metty, Harry J. May/lp Tim Matheson, Belinda Montgomery, Claude Akins, Jack Albertson

The Loner · Lloyd Bridges is an ex-Union cavalry captain wandering through the turbulent post-Civil War West in search of a meaning to his life. Expertly scripted stories by Rod Serling involved flashbacks, dream sequences, slow motion and optical diffusion.
1965-6/b & w/26 ep x 26 min/Greenway Prods – FOX-TV – Interlaken Prods/cr Rod Serling/lp Lloyd Bridges

The Lone Ranger · A radio hit since 1933, the *Lone Ranger* series premiered on television in 1949 and ran with remarkable success on ABC for eight years. Opening with the 'William Tell' Overture and a hearty 'Hi-yo, Silver' the stories told of an ex-Texas Ranger and his faithful Mohawk Indian partner, Tonto, as they rode the West fighting for the underdog and vanquishing villains in true B-Western fashion. Basically juvenile viewing, since the Lone Ranger never shot to kill and spoke only the most perfect English, which at times clashed ridiculously with Tonto's 'kemo sabe' utterings. Clayton Moore and Jay Silverheels also appeared in two features: *The Lone Ranger* (1956) and *The Lone Ranger and The Lost City of Gold* (1958). 13 edited-from-episodes TV movies were developed from this series, all running at 75 min: *Champions of Justice*; *Count the Clues*; *Justice of the West*; *The Lawless*; *Masquerade*; *More Than Magic*; *Not Above Suspicion*; *One Mask Too Many*; *The Search*; *Tale of Gold*; *Trackers*; *The Truth*; *Vengeance Vow*
1949-57/b & w: colour/221 ep x 26 min/ Apex – Jack Chertok – Clayton Moore – Jack Wrather Corp/cr George W. Trendle, Fran Striker/lp Clayton Moore, John Hart, Jay Silverheels

Louis L'Amour's 'The Shadow Riders' · A back-by-popular-demand movie from the same team as produced *The Sacketts*, also based on L'Amour novels. *The Shadow Riders* tells of two brothers who, after fighting on opposite sides in the Civil War, reunite to rescue members of their family from a band of renegade Confederates.
1982/100 min/Pegasus Group Ltd – COL/p Dennis Durney, Verne Nobles/d Andrew V. McLaglen/s Jim Byrnes/c Jack Whitman/lp Tom Selleck, Sam Elliott, Ben Johnson, Geoffrey Lewis

M

The Macahans · Filmed on the vast Utah plains, this series pilot features the epic journey of a family as they trek toward California at the outbreak of the Civil War. James Arness returned to the TV Western as a rugged mountain man. The format and characters became the basis for the mini-series *How the West Was Won*.
Pilot/1976/124 min/Albert S. Ruddy Prod – MGM/p Jim Byrnes/d Bernard McEveety/s Jim Byrnes/c Edward R. Plante/lp James Arness, Eva Marie Saint, Richard Kiley, Bruce Boxleitner, Kathryn Holcomb
Series (titled **How the West Was Won**)/ 1978/2 ep x 150 min: 4 ep x 52 min/John Mantley Prods – MGM-TV/p John G. Stephens/lp James Arness, Fionnula Flanagan, Bruce Boxleitner, Kathryn Holcomb

Mackenzie's Raiders · The real-life exploits of Indian fighter Colonel Ranald S. Mackenzie (based on *The Mackenzie Raid* by Colonel Red Reeder) are the premise of this 1870s period Texas actioner, with Richard Carlson's Mackenzie leading a small group of 4th Cavalry raiders against marauding Indians and Mexican bandits across the Rio Grande border.
1958-9/b & w/39 ep x 26 min/Ziv-TV – UA-TV/p Elliott Lewis/lp Richard Carlson, Morris Ankrum, Brett King, Jim Bridges

A Man Called Shenandoah · The itinerant hero here is an amnesiac as the result of a bullet wound. Somewhat like the characters in *Branded* and *The Loner*, Horton's character wanders the West searching for his true identity.
1965-6/b & w/34 ep x 26 min/MGM-TV/p Vincent Fennelly/lp Robert Horton

The Man from Blackhawk · The title character is a special insurance investigator for the Blackhawk Insurance Company in the late 1800s. Resorting to his fists (rather than a gun) when trouble looms, he travels around uncovering fraudulent claims and investigating dubious policies.
1959-60/b & w/37 ep x 26 min/Screen Gems – Stuart-Oliver Prods/p Herb Meadow/lp Robert Rockwell

Man Without a Gun · The unarmed title character is a fearless newspaper editor in the lawless Dakota Territory of the 1880s. Rex Reason played the role in a routine fashion.
1957-9/b & w/52 ep x 26 min/FOX-TV – NTA/p Alan A. Armer, Mel Epstein/lp Rex Reason, Mort Mills

The Mark of Zorro · The Don Diego/Zorro story with Frank Langella as the hero, a campy, comic-strip blend of Republic serials and *The Cisco Kid*. Reportedly, the production changed directors midway through.
1974/74 min/FOX/p Robert C. Thompson, Rodrick Paul/d Don McDougall/s Brian Taggert/c Jack Woolf/lp Frank Langella, Ricardo Montalban, Gilbert Roland, Yvonne De Carlo, Louise Sorel

Mark Twain's America · Four-part anthology series dramatizing moments in the lives of famous Americans. The Will Rogers episode deals with young Will's problems with Indians in his Oklahoma hometown while he's trying to audition for Buffalo Bill's Wild West Show. The other episodes in the series feature Lincoln, Edison and the Wright Brothers; Walker Edmonston appears as Mark Twain in the opening and closing scenes of the show.
1979-80/4 ep x 52 min/Schick Sunn Classics – NBC-TV/cr Charles E. Sellier Jr., James L. Conway/host Walker Edmonston

The Marshal of Gunsight Pass · Creaky Western series from the early, live days of television, featuring the traditional singing cowboys and usual economical studio settings of the B-Western. Russell Hayden was the marshal, later replaced by Eddie Dean.
1950/b & w/tx 'live' x 25 min/ABC-TV/lp Russell Hayden, Eddie Dean, Roscoe Ates, Jane Adrian

Maverick · *Maverick* remains one of the small-screen Western's classics. It turned the late 1950s TV Western on its head with a lively series that could be enjoyed on various levels. The central character, Bret Maverick (later joined by brother Bart), was a devious, cowardly card-sharp who drifted from one

James Garner in Maverick

David Carradine, Enrique Lucero
in Mr. Horn

dubious adventure to the next, exploiting easy situations and vanishing when faced with potentially violent ones. The main credit for this rather unique show must go to producer Roy Huggins and star James Garner, who seemed to share a mischievous sense of humour. Noted Western director Budd Boetticher handled *Maverick*'s opening three episodes. In 1979 Warners returned with *Young Maverick*, a short-run series featuring Bret's nephew, and in 1981 Garner's Cherokee Prods produced a season of *Bret Maverick* which continued the adventures of the popular character.
1957-62/b & w/124 ep x 52 min/WB-TV/cr Roy Huggins/lp James Garner, Jack Kelly, Diane Brewster, Roger Moore, Robert Colbert

The Men from Shiloh · The 1970 off-season renovation of *The Virginian* into *The Men from Shiloh* was a peculiar one. Possibly a keeping-up-with-the-times idea, the only points that appeared to remain the same were the Shiloh Ranch and James Drury's 'Virginian' character. Doug McClure of course was still there, but now brandishing an Old West handlebar moustache, as was new regular Lee Majors (draped like a gunfighter from an Italian Western). The new series introduced Stewart Granger's Colonel MacKenzie as a retired British officer and new owner of the ranch. A dirty, rugged look (again, in tune with the then-fashionable Spaghettis) had come over the Shiloh people, but the one great addition was the use of an excellent title credit sequence (in silhouette against red, not unlike the early Leone 'Dollars' films) with a lashing Ennio Morricone score.
1970-1/24 ep x 90 min/U-TV/p Glen A. Larson/m Ennio Morricone/lp Stewart Granger, Lee Majors, Doug McClure, James Drury

Mr. Horn · Produced a couple of years before Steve McQueen's *Tom Horn*, this William Goldman-scripted television tale of the legendary adventurer and stock detective leaves out more than it tells. The story was originally intended as a Robert Redford vehicle.
1979/200 min/Lorimar Prods/p Robert L. Jacks/d Jack Starrett/s William Goldman/c Jorge Stahl Jr./lp David Carradine, Richard Widmark, Karen Black, Richard Masur, Jack Starrett

Mrs. Sundance · Elizabeth Montgomery plays Etta Place in the days after the death of

Butch and Sundance, now living on her memories and her wits.
1974/90 min/FOX-TV/p Stan Hough/d Marvin J. Chomsky/s Christopher Knopf/c Michel Hugo/lp Elizabeth Montgomery, Robert Foxworth, L.Q. Jones, Arthur Hunnicutt

The Monroes · The adventures of five orphaned children struggling to maintain a homestead in Wyoming in the 1870s. Displaying some fine colour photography, the series was filmed in the Jackson Hole region of Grand Teton National Park.
1966-7/26 ep x 52 min/Qualis Prods – FOX-TV/exec p Fred Brogger/lp Michael Anderson Jr., Barbara Hershey, Keith Schultz, Kevin Schultz, Ben Johnson

More Wild Wild West · Second return to the 1960s *Wild Wild West* series and agents James T. West and Artemus Gordon (again played by Robert Conrad and Ross Martin). This time they battle with Jonathan Winters' outrageous megalomaniac. All the old gimmicks are back (invisibility gadgets, etc) in a recycling of the matinee serials.
1980/100 min/CBS Entertainment/p Robert L. Jacks/d Burt Kennedy/s Tony Kayden, William Bowers/c Charles G. Arnold/lp Robert Conrad, Ross Martin, Jonathan Winters, Harry Morgan

My Friend Flicka · Colourful outdoor drama aimed at children and based on Mary O'Hara's story and the 1943 Fox movie. The series, a standard boy-and-his-horse adventure, just about passes as a Western by way of its turn-of-the-century period and Montana ranch setting. A sugar-coated cousin of the *Fury* and *Champion* family of juvenile adventure.
1956-8/b & w: colour/39 ep x 26 min/FOX-TV/p Sam White, Peter Packer/lp Gene Evans, Anita Louise, Johnny Washbrook

The Mystic Warrior · The life of an individual Indian, a member of the Mahato band of the Oglala Lakota Tribe in the early 1800s, based on Ruth Beebe Hill's novel *Hanta Yo* and 'other material'. The production was the subject of controversy in 1980 when Native American pressure groups questioned the original novel's anthropological accuracy.
1984/240 min/David Wolper-Stan Margulies Prods – WB/p Paul Freeman/d Richard T. Heffron/s Jeb Rosebrook/c Stevan Larner/lp Robert Beltran, Devon Ericson, Rion Hunter, Victoria Racimo, Nick Ramos, Will Sampson

N

Nevada Smith · Television translation of the characters from Harold Robbins' *The Carpetbaggers* and the 1966 Steve McQueen film. Cliff Potts plays the title character, now involved in shipping explosives across Utah in the late 1800s. Not so much a remake, more a remodelling of the original characters for small-screen consumption.
1975/74 min/MGM-TV – Rackin-Hayes Prods/*p* John Michael Hayes, Martin Rackin/*d* Gordon Douglas/*s* John Michael Hayes, Martin Rackin/*c* Gabriel Torres/*lp* Cliff Potts, Lorne Greene, Adam West

The New Daughters of Joshua Cabe · Cabe's 'Wild West Angels' return when old Joshua is falsely imprisoned and set to hang. Here in this third outing John McIntire steps into Dan Dailey's boots, originally worn by Buddy Ebsen.
1976/74 min/Spelling-Goldberg Prods/*p* Paul Savage/*d* Bruce Bilson/*s* Paul Savage/*c* Dennis Dalzell/*lp* John McIntire, Jack Elam, Jeanette Nolan, Liberty Williams

The New Land · Loosely follows the theme and setting of the two Jan Troell Swedish films (*The Emigrants* and *The New Land*), about settlers in the West. Superior stories and beautiful colour photography support the high standards of this well-produced series.
1974/6 ep x 52 min/WB-TV/*p* William Blinn/*lp* Scott Thomas, Bonnie Bedelia, Kurt Russell, Todd Lookinland

The New Maverick · Both James Garner and Jack Kelly guest-starred in this pilot, which introduced a new generation Maverick to the mythology. Young Ben Maverick (son of Cousin Beau, who was played briefly in the original by Roger Moore) maintains the Maverick tradition of sly and crafty manoeuvres and the following year launched a series of his own adventures, *Young Maverick*.
1978/100 min/Cherokee Prods – WB/*p* Bob Foster/*d* Hy Averback/*s* Juanita Bartlett/*c* Andrew Jackson/*lp* James Garner, Charles Frank, Jack Kelly, Susan Blanchard

Nichols · One part *Maverick*, one part *Support Your Local Sheriff!* and one part the delightful James Garner, this is an amusing Western series. Garner starts off, reluctantly, as the cowardly sheriff of an unruly Arizona town, and when at the end of the series he is shot stone-cold dead by one of the bad guys, his twin brother (played by Garner of course) rides into town to avenge his death. The series is set in 1915, as motor cars join the horse traffic in the street.
1971-2/26 ep x 52 min/Cherokee Prods – WB-TV/*cr* Frank R. Pierson/*lp* James Garner, Margot Kidder, Neva Patterson, Stuart Margolin

The Night Rider · Pilot-TV movie about a fop-by-day, Night Rider-by-night character who moves from New Orleans to Virginia City to avenge his family. Swordplay and gunplay, but the format failed to excite enough interest for a series to evolve.
1979/78 min/Stephen J. Cannell Prods – U/*p* J. Rickley Dumm/*d* Hy Averback/*s* Stephen J. Cannell/*c* Steven Poster/*lp* David Selby, Percy Rodriguez, Kim Cattrall, George Grizzard, Anna Lee

No Man's Land · Pilot about a strong-willed woman who assumes her dead sheriff husband's role as the protector of a little frontier town, with the aid of her three daughters. Intended as an action drama with humour, the movie fails to find its way and becomes a sort of sitcom out West.
1984/120 min/Jadda Prods – WB/*p* Rod Holcomb, Christopher Nelson/*d* Rod Holcomb/*s* Juanita Bartlett/*c* Ted Voigtlander/*lp* Stella Stevens, Terri Garber, Melissa Michaelsen, Donna Dixon

Northwest Passage · Based on Kenneth Roberts' novel (and the 1940 MGM film), this well-produced series set its sights firmly on action with little time wasted on dialogue. Actual pursuit of the Northwest Passage takes second place to the Rangers' commando tactics during the French and Indian wars. Three European-release features were edited from the series, directed by Jacques Tourneur and George waGGner (*Fury River*, 1958; *Frontier Rangers*, 1959; *Mission of Danger*, 1959). Impressive colour photography by Harkness Smith.
1958-9/26 ep x 26 min/MGM-TV/*p* Adrian Samish/*lp* Keith Larsen, Buddy Ebsen, Don Burnett, Philip Tongue

O

The Oregon Trail · Sentimental saga of a pioneering family heading west along the Oregon Trail in the 1840s, led by solid farmer-widower Rod Taylor.
Pilot/1976/100 min/U/*p* Michael Gleason/*d* Boris Sagal/*s* Michael Gleason/*c* Jack Woolfe/*lp* Rod Taylor, Blair Brown, David Huddleston, Douglas V. Fowley
Series/1977/13 x 52 min/U-TV – NBC-TV/*p* Carl Vitale/*lp* Rod Taylor, Andrew Stevens, Tony Becker, Gina Marie Smika

Orphan Train · Majestically photographed in Savannah, Georgia and near Hill City, South Dakota, *Orphan Train* is based on Dorothea G. Petrie's story about how the Children's Rescue Mission transported New York orphans by train to homes in the Midwest in 1854. With the usual hazards en route, though the film overplays its heartwarming moments.
1979/135 min/Roger Gimbel Prods – EMI-TV/*p* Dorothea G. Petrie/*d* William A. Graham/*s* Millard Lampell/*c* Terry K. Meade/*lp* Jill Eikenberry, Kevin Dobson, Linda Manz, Graham Fletcher-Cook, Melissa Michaelson

The Outcasts · Adventure drama following the less-than-honourable exploits of an ex-Virginia aristocrat turned gunman and a quick-witted one-time slave. The stories sustained a racial theme as the bounty-hunting partnership of the two heroes is torn by antagonism. The series was supplemented with a lavish Morricone-like score by Hugo Montenegro.
1968-9/26 ep x 52 min/Screen Gems/*cr* Leon Tokatyan, Ben Brady/*lp* Don Murray, Otis Young

Outlaws · Utilizing the old 'what if...?' story premise; through time travel, a bunch of 1899 cowpokes get whipped through to the 20th century where, after several amusing clashes with modern-day life, they set up a detective agency.
1986-7/13 ep x 52 min: premiere ep x '120 min'/U-TV/*exec p* Nicholas Corea/*lp* Rod Taylor, William Lucking, Richard Roundtree, Charles Napier

The Outlaws · Starting off as a series that traced the origin and eventual extinction of Western badmen, and for the most part related from their point of view, the stories soon dissolved into routine hero-lawmen dramas. Oklahoma in the 1890s was the backdrop for the series.
1960-2/b & w: colour/12 ep x 52 min/NBC-TV Prods/*exec p* Frank Telford/*lp* Barton MacLane, Don Collier, Jock Gaynor, Bruce Yarnell, Slim Pickens

The Overland Trail · The story of pushing a stagecoach route from Missouri through to

the Pacific coast is told in a rather tired, old-fashioned cowboys-and-Indians fashion.
1960/b & w/17 ep x 52 min/Stage Coach Prods/p Samuel A. Peeples/lp William Bendix, Doug McClure

The Over the Hill Gang · With its illustrious line-up of veteran Western performers (reminiscent of the A. C. Lyles actioners) this mediocre comedy-Western attempts to echo the style of *Support Your Local Sheriff!*. Ex-Texas Ranger Pat O'Brien recalls his former buddies to help clean up a nest of badmen who are terrorizing his son-in-law, Rick Nelson.
1969/74 min/Thomas-Spelling Prods/p Aaron Spelling, Shelly Hull/d Jean Yarbrough/s Jameson Brewer/c Henry Cronjager/lp Pat O'Brien, Walter Brennan, Chill Wills, Edgar Buchanan, Gypsy Rose Lee, Andy Devine, Jack Elam

The Over the Hill Gang Rides Again · A sequel to the above, this doesn't ring any changes. Fred Astaire (in place of the original's Pat O'Brien), playing a town drunk who's rehabilitated and made marshal, re-assembles the Gang to out-smart another bunch of badmen.
1970/74 min/Thomas-Spelling Prods/p Shelly Hull/d George McCowan/s Richard Carr/c Fleet Southcott III/lp Walter Brennan, Fred Astaire, Edgar Buchanan, Andy Devine, Chill Wills

P

Peter Lundy and The Medicine Hat Stallion · Based on the novel *San Domingo – The Medicine Hat Stallion* by Marguerite Henry, this is a compelling tale of a young man's passage into manhood via his experiences as a Pony Express rider carrying mail from Nebraska to the Pacific coast. It received an Emmy nomination for Outstanding Children's Special.
1977/100 min/Ed Friendly Prods/p Ed Friendly/d Michael O'Herlihy/s Jack Turley/c Robert L. Morrison/lp Leif Garrett, Milo O'Shea, Bibi Besch, John Quade

Pioneer Woman · Joanna Pettet and her two children fight to survive in the harshness of Wyoming in 1867 after her husband has been killed in a freak accident. Focusing on the woman's point of view (and underlining this via voice-over narration) the story avoids typical Western action scenes in order to emphasize a domestic side. With its

careful introduction of characters and settings, the film was a pilot for a projected series.
1973/74 min/Filmways/p Edward S. Feldman, Robert M. Rosenbloom/d Buzz Kulik/s Suzanne Clauser/c Charles F. Wheeler/lp Joanna Pettet, William Shatner, David Janssen, Lance LeGault

Pistols 'n' Petticoats · Comedy Western series set in the town of Wretched, Colorado during the 1870s. The stories concern a hillbilly-type family of rascals who could stand up to any Western renegade or outlaw who was foolish enough to cross their path. The result was a noisy blend of *Beverly Hillbillies* and the Dogpatch characters from *Li'l Abner*. Feature actress Ann Sheridan lent some dignity to the rough-and-tumble proceedings.
1966-7/b & w: colour/26 ep x 26 min/U-TV/p Joe Connelly/lp Ann Sheridan, Douglas Fowley, Ruth McDevitt

Pony Express · Set in the 1860s, about the men who established the Pony Express from St Joseph, Missouri to Sacramento. Weaving fact with fiction and action, the series dealt intelligently and thoughtfully with characters and events, and produced some exciting moments from pioneer history.
1959-60/b & w/39 ep x 26 min/California National Prods/p Tom McKnight/lp Grant Sullivan, Bill Cord, Don Dorell

Q

The Quest · This story of two brothers in search of their sister, captured long ago by the Cheyenne, runs close to Alan LeMay's *The Searchers*. The difference here is that one of the brothers (Kurt Russell) has been at one time also a captive of the Cheyenne and grown up with their traditions and customs. The other brother (Tim Matheson) is an educated city boy with little experience of frontier folk and Indians. An adult fable on the understanding of different cultures, *The Quest* was a beautifully photographed, often violent drama that rose above the customary Western adventure.
Pilot/1976/100 min/David Gerber Prods – COL/p Christopher Morgan/d Lee H. Katzin/s Tracy Keenan Wynn/c Robert L. Morrison/lp Tim Matheson, Kurt Russell, Brian Keith, Keenan Wynn, Will Hutchins, Neville Brand
Series/1976/15 ep x 52 min/David Gerber Prods – COL-TV/cr Tracy Keenan Wynn/lp Kurt Russell, Tim Matheson

The Quick and the Dead · Louis L'Amour Western, adapted by James Lee Barrett, with Sam Elliott in the saddle again as a gunslinger who protects Tom Conti's covered wagon family from a band of bad guys. The setting is Wyoming in 1876.
1987/'95' min/Joseph Cates Prod/p Phillip Cates/d Robert Day/s James Lee Barrett/c Dick Bush/lp Sam Elliott, Tom Conti, Kate Capshaw, Kenny Morrison

R

The Range Rider · Heralded by the 'Home on the Range' theme and featuring former stuntman Jock Mahoney as another frontier fighter for truth and justice, *The Range Rider* was a popular early 50s Western actioner with plenty of destructive fights and saddle tricks (shooting from under a galloping horse's neck, for instance). The series, like other Gene Autry productions, was mostly shot around the Flying A Ranch.
1951-2/b & w/76 ep x 26 min/Flying A Prods/lp Jock Mahoney, Dick Jones

Rango · The misadventures of a bumbling Texas Ranger who more often shattered the peace than kept it. A comedy vehicle for star Tim Conway, not unlike the spy-com *Get Smart*, with the inept 'hero' forever frustrating his superior but somehow managing to come through with results in the end.
1967/17 ep x 26 min/Thomas-Spelling Prods/p Aaron Spelling/lp Tim Conway, Guy Marks, Norman Alden

Ransom for Alice! · Almost comic-strip in its *Barbary Coast*-like adventures of two undercover deputy marshals investigating a white slavery ring in 1890s Seattle. Gil Gerard and Yvette Mimieux are law officers, adopting disguises and battling Tongs. Doubtless intended to spark off a series.
1977/74 min/U/p Franklin Barton/d David Lowell Rich/s Jim Byrnes/c Jacques R. Marquette/lp Gil Gerard, Yvette Mimieux, Charles Napier, Gene Barry

Rawhide · Set in the 1860s, this long-running series featured the lives of the men who worked on the great cattle-drives from Texas to Kansas. Created by Charles Marquis Warren and based on material from an 1866 diary by drover George Duffield, the series was something like a small-screen version of *Red River* but with an assortment of 'guest' characters. Warren had directed the film *Cattle Empire* before turning to *Rawhide* and originally planned to call the

Clint Eastwood in Rawhide

series *Cattle Drive*. Directors on the show included Andrew V. McLaglen and Tay Garnett; teleplays were contributed by Elliott Arnold and Clair Huffaker.
1959-66/b & w/217 ep x 52 min/CBS-TV/cr Charles Marquis Warren/m Dimitri Tiomkin/lp Eric Fleming, Clint Eastwood, Sheb Wooley, Paul Brinegar

The Rebel · Nick Adams plays another post-Civil War drifter, this time called Johnny Yuma. His travels take him from town to town where, with his angry-young-man attitude, he often confronts social and moral issues. Cinematography by Ernest Laszlo.
1959-61/b & w/76 ep x 26 min/Goodson-Todman Prods – Celestial Prods – Fen-Ker-Ada Prods/p Andrew J. Fenady/lp Nick Adams

The Rebels · Second instalment of the adventures of young Philip Kent, first seen in *The Bastard*, during the War of Independence, this one concerned with an attempt to assassinate George Washington. *The Seekers* later completed the 'Kent Chronicles' trilogy. Based on the novel *The Rebels* by John Jakes.
1979/200 min/U/p Gian R. Grimaldi, Hannah L. Shearer/d Russ Mayberry/s Robert A. Cinader, Sean Baine/c Frank Thackery/lp Andrew Stevens, Don Johnson, Doug McClure, Jim Backus, Richard Basehart

Redigo · In its last season the series *Empire*

changed its title to *Redigo*. Richard Egan's title role is based on his foreman character from the original series but he now operates from a spread of his own. The stories centred around the problems faced by modern-day ranching: for horse, read helicopter.
1963/b & w/15 ep x 26 min/Screen Gems – Wilrich Prods/p Andy White/lp Richard Egan, Roger Davis, Rudy Solari

The Restless Gun · Relying more on character clashes and mature reasoning than on gunplay and physical action, this John Payne series moves its hero through the post-Civil War Southwest from one unavoidable conflict to the next. The series stemmed from a pilot episode shown as part of *Schlitz Playhouse of Stars* in early 1957.
1957-9/b & w/77 ep x 26 min/Window Glen Prods/exec p John Payne/lp John Payne

Return of the Gunfighter · Early made-for-TV movie, from a story by Burt Kennedy and Robert Buckner, about an aging gunfighter who takes up the gun again to avenge the murder of two old friends. Black-garbed Robert Taylor goes through the time-honoured paces in a part he's no stranger to (e.g. *The Law and Jake Wade*).
1967/98 min/MGM/p Frank King, Maurice King/d James Neilson/s Robert Buckner/c Ellsworth Fredricks/lp Robert Taylor, Ana Martin, Chad Everett, Mort Mills, Lyle Bettger

The Rifleman · This series started life as a 1958 episode of *Dick Powell's Zane Grey Theatre* entitled 'The Sharpshooter', scripted by Sam Peckinpah and featuring Chuck Connors. Stories deal with homesteader Lucas McCain and his young son trying to eke out a peaceful existence in North Fork, New Mexico. The series owes its title to Connors' effectiveness with a modified Winchester that operates with the fire power of a machine gun. Michael Ansara's Indian marshal turned up in the series prior to launching *Law of the Plainsman*.
1958-63/b & w/168 ep x 26 min/Four Star – Sussex Prods/cr Sam Peckinpah/lp Chuck Connors, Johnny Crawford, Paul Fix

Riverboat · The focal point is a riverboat trading along the Mississippi and Ohio rivers during the 1840s. A grand-scale production with an excellent *Magnificent Seven*-like score by Elmer Bernstein, colour photo-

graphy by Ray Rennahan, at least for the initial/pilot episode, and big-name guest stars as well as some quite intriguing stories. Burt Reynolds was the paddleboat's pilot for most of the series' first season.
1959-61/b & w; colour/44 ep x 52 min/Meladre Company Prods/p Jules Bricken/lp Darren McGavin, Burt Reynolds, William D. Gordon, Noah Beery Jr.

The Road West · The story of a family group as they travel west and try to establish a new home in turbulent Kansas during the 1860s. The traditional problems of homesteading supplied most of the action for the stories. The opening two-part episode ('This Savage Land', a violent actioner with George C. Scott) was released as a feature to European cinemas.
1966-7/26 ep x 52 min/U-TV/exec p Norman MacDonnell/lp Barry Sullivan, Andrew Prine, Brenda Scott, Kelly Corcoran, Glenn Corbett

The Rough Riders · Reconstruction-period adventures of three Civil War veterans, two of the Union Army and one of the Confederacy, who search for a new life out West. Standard Ziv-TV package-factory Western of the late 1950s; Rod Serling's *The Loner* would follow the same path some six years later, but with its psychological boundaries clearly mapped.
1958-9/b & w/39 ep x 26 min/Ziv-TV/p Maurice Unger/lp Kent Taylor, Jan Merlin, Peter Whitney

The Rounders · The misadventures of two carefree young cowboys in contemporary Texas, based on the novel by Max Evans and the 1964 MGM feature film, with Chill Wills holding over his con-artist role from the movie. Ron Hayes and Patrick Wayne aren't Glenn Ford and Henry Fonda but at least Burt Kennedy (who wrote and directed the original film) directed the series' premiere episode.
1966-7/17 ep x 26 min/MGM-TV/p Ed Adamson/lp Ron Hayes, Patrick Wayne, Chill Wills

The Roy Rogers Show · Long-running contemporary children's Western series starring the warbling cowpoke himself, aided by wife Dale Evans, sidekick Pat Brady, horse Trigger and dog Bullet.
1952-7/b & w/100 ep x 26 min/Roy Rogers Prods – Frontier Prods/p Jack Lacet/lp Roy Rogers, Dale Evans, Pat Brady

S

The Sacketts · Based on two Louis L'Amour novels (*The Daybreakers* and *Sackett*) about three brothers and their adventures in post-Civil War New Mexico. A well-produced Western that manages to sustain its intertwining narrative for its lengthy running-time.
1979/200 min/Douglas Netter – MB Scott Prods – Shalako Enterprises Inc/p Douglas Netter, Jim Byrnes/d Robert Totten/s Jim Byrnes/c Jack A. Whitman Jr./lp Sam Elliott, Tom Selleck, Jeff Osterhage, Glenn Ford, Ben Johnson, Gilbert Roland

The Saga of Andy Burnett · Six-part mini-series transmitted as a part of the *Disneyland* anthology series during the show's fourth season. Based on the novel by Stewart Edward White, it told the story of a young man, Andy Burnett (Jerome Courtland), who joins a party of mountain men on their way to see the Mexican governor of New Mexico in the hope of opening friendly trade with St Louis. Typically, there was plenty of en route action in the form of Indians and bandits. The series was transmitted in black and white but is very likely to have been produced in colour.
1957-8/tx b & w/6 ep x 52 min/Walt Disney Prods/exec p Walt Disney/lp Jerome Courtland, Jeff York, Slim Pickens, Andrew Duggan

Sam Hill: Who Killed the Mysterious Mr Foster? · A Western murder mystery as well as a pilot show about two characters, played by Ernest Borgnine and Bruce Dern, running for sheriff in a small town during the 1870s; the one who first solves the murder of the preacher gets elected to the post. Scripted by the 'Ellery Queen' of television, Richard Levinson and William Link. Also shown as *Who Killed the Mysterious Mr Foster?*
1971/100 min/U/p Jo Swerling Jr./d Fielder Cook/s Richard Levinson, William Link/c Gene Polito/lp Ernest Borgnine, Stephen Hudis, Judy Geeson, Will Geer, Bruce Dern

Sara · A young Philadelphia schoolteacher moves to Independence, Colorado in the 1870s and fights against the school board and the traditional 'schoolmarm' image in order to help the townsfolk and their kids. Cinematographer Russell Metty brought the studio-produced show a certain outdoor freshness.
1976/13 ep x 52 min/U-TV/p Richard Collins/lp Brenda Vaccaro, Bert Kramer, Albert Stratton

Saturday Roundup · Kermit Maynard was the cowboy star of this early Western anthology series based on the stories of James Oliver Curwood. The series was produced on film and went out in a primetime slot during the between-season summer months.
1951/b & w/13 ep x 52 min/NBC-TV/lp Kermit Maynard

Scalplock · Pilot for *The Iron Horse* series (1966-8) which sets up the situation of Dale Robertson's gambler winning the Scalplock & Defiance Railroad and then trying to maintain the line despite crooked opposition.
1966/100 min/COL-TV/p Herbert Hirschman/d James Goldstone/s Steven Kandel/c Fred Gately/lp Dale Robertson, Robert Random, Diana Hyland, Sandra Smith

The Seekers · Set in colonial and revolutionary days, this was the third mini-series based on historical novels by John Jakes. The convoluted story chronicles two generations of a Boston family and spans half the continent, with the more interesting parts taking place as the story progresses to the Midwest frontier. *The Bastard* and *The Rebels* were the first two segments of the trilogy.
1979/200 min/U/p Gian R. Grimaldi, Hannah L. Shearer/d Sidney Hayers/s Steve Hayes/c Vincent A. Martinelli/lp Randolph Mantooth, Edie Adams, Neville Brand, Delta Burke, John Carradine

September Gun · Photographed on Arizona locations, this concerns the efforts of a determined nun to transport a group of Apache orphans from New Mexico to Colorado with the aid of an aging gunfighter, played with relish by Robert Preston. A predictable format but some colourful characters and moments.
1983/100 min/Brademan-Self Prods – QM Prods/p Bill Brademan, Ed Self/d Don Taylor/s William Norton/c Gerald Perry Finnerman/lp Robert Preston, Patty Duke Astin, Geoffrey Lewis, Sally Kellerman

Sergeant Preston of the Yukon · Juvenile action series set in the Klondike at the turn of the century, featuring a Northwest Mounted Police officer and his dog patrolling the frozen gold rush territory. Despite cliché elements, outdoor photography by Gilbert Warrenton adds up to an impressive production for this kind of fare.
1955-8/b & w: colour/78 ep x 26 min/Charles E. Skinner Prods/pr Charles E. Skinner/lp Richard Simmons

Shane · Based on George Stevens' 1953 classic feature, this conventional series retells basically the same tale of Wyoming settlers in conflict with the local ranchers. David Carradine emerged as the true star of the series with his deadpan, slowburn technique, exterminating the bad guys with the most direct and violent means.
1966/17 ep x 52 min/Titus Prods – ABC-TV/exec p Herbert Brodkin/lp David Carradine, Jill Ireland, Tom Tully

The Sheriff of Cochise · A modern-day Western set in Arizona, which moves in the middle ground somewhere between *Gunsmoke* and *Highway Patrol*. John Bromfield's sheriff performs the traditional law-enforcer role with steely authority, whether he's tracking the bad guys on horse or wheels. After two years Bromfield was promoted from the Sheriff's division of Cochise County to a new series called *U.S. Marshal*.
1956-8/b & w/78 ep x 26 min/Desilu/p Mort Briskin/lp John Bromfield, Stan Jones

Shootout in a One-Dog Town · Action-packed Western drama produced in the style of the 1950s big-screen gunmen-in-town actioners. A determined gang of outlaws tries to bust into a small-town bank which contains $200,000. Richard Crenna is the lone but equally determined figure who stands between the gang and the loot.
1974/74 min/Hanna-Barbera Prods/p Richard E. Lyons/d Burt Kennedy/s Dick Nelson, Larry Cohen/c Robert B. Hauser/lp Richard Crenna, Stefanie Powers, Jack Elam, Richard Egan, Dub Taylor, Gene Evans

Shotgun Slade · Scott Brady is the title character, a freelance Western detective armed with a customized shotgun. Less sophisticated than *Have Gun, Will Travel* but played along similar gun-for-hire lines.
1959-61/b & w/78 ep x 26 min/Shotgun Prod Company – Revue/p/cr Frank Gruber/lp Scott Brady

Sidekicks · A pilot, unfortunately unsuccessful, based on the superb 1971 Western *Skin Game*, from the story by Richard Alan Simmons. Larry Hagman takes the James

Garner role as the con man and Lou Gossett recreates his part as the college-educated 'slave', running their scam of selling Gossett as a slave then making off with the money. The duo get mistaken for a couple of dangerous criminals and become involved in a bank heist organised by Jack Elam and his gang.
1974/75 min/wb/p/d Burt Kennedy/s William Bowers/c Robert B. Hauser/lp Larry Hagman, Lou Gossett, Blythe Danner, Jack Elam, Harry Morgan

The Silent Gun · Lloyd Bridges is a gunman who nearly guns down a small girl – except that his gun is empty. This becomes the turning point of his life as he vows never to load his weapon again. After that his reputation, and that of his young partner, John Beck, leads the way when they protect a family of settlers from the town bullies.
1969/74 min/par/p Bruce Lansbury/d Michael Caffey/s Clyde Ware/c Howard R. Schwartz/lp Lloyd Bridges, John Beck, Ed Begley, Edd Byrnes, Pernell Roberts

Sky King · Kirby Grant was Sky King, a California rancher with a difference. He was a former World War II navy flyer who flew – rather than rode – over the territory, maintaining law and order in modern style. He looked like a traditional tv Western cowboy and wore a six-gun but the stories (though they did at times deal with local Navajo Indian matters) mixed modern problems with conventional Western adventure.
1951-6/b & w/72 ep x 26 min/McGowan Prods/p Clark Paylow/lp Kirby Grant, Gloria Winters, Ron Haggerty

Something for a Lonely Man · Dan Blocker, taking time off from his role as Hoss in *Bonanza*, stars as a shy blacksmith who has built up a small town in anticipation of the railroad but is now an outcast because the rail line has stopped short of the settlement. However, when a steam engine is accidentally left nearby Blocker and girl-next-door Susan Clark set about retrieving it and finally restore the community's respect. Blocker and Clark have some sensitive moments but the rest of the movie loses steam very fast.
1968/98 min/u/p Richard E. Lyons/d Don Taylor/s John Fante, Frank Fenton/c Benjamin H. Kline/lp Dan Blocker, Susan Clark, John Dehner, Warren Oates

Stagecoach · Second remake of the John Ford original, following the first in 1966. This tv version carries a heavy passenger-load of celebrity players who have jettisoned all the character and drama that made the original a landmark.
1986/100 min/Raymond Katz Prods – Heritage Entertainment/p Hal W. Polaire, Jack Thompson/d Ted Post/s James Lee Barrett/c Gary Graver/lp Johnny Cash, Willie Nelson, Kris Kristofferson, Waylon Jennings, Elizabeth Ashley

Stagecoach West · About a team of drivers who run the stagecoach lines between Missouri and California, and the people, places and problems they encounter en route.
1960-1/b & w/38 ep x 52 min/Four Star – Hildegarde Enterprises/p Vincent Fennelly/lp Wayne Rogers, Robert Bray, Richard Eyer

Standing Tall · Independent cattle rancher vs. land baron makes up the meat of this Western, with a sub-plot of a half-breed Indian and racial hatred. Stately-paced plot is enhanced by wide-open Oregon exteriors.
1978/100 min/Quinn-Martin Prods – nbc-tv/p Marty Katz/d Harvey Hart/s Franklin Thompson/c Steve Larner/lp Robert Forster, Linda Evans, Chuck Connors, Will Sampson, L.Q. Jones

Steve Donovan, Western Marshal · An elusive Western series to research. Some reports state that it was set in Wyoming during the 1870s, others say it was about the Texas Rangers. Whatever it really was, it featured the adventures of a us Marshal and his deputy, Rusty Lee, and was produced by the man who (during this period) also held the producer's reins on the *Lone Ranger* series. Also known as *Western Marshal*.
1953-5/b & w/39 ep x 26 min/Vi-Bar Prods – Jack Chertok Prods/p Jack Chertok/lp Douglas Kennedy, Eddy Waller

Stoney Burke · The sadly short-lived story of a young rodeo rider who wants to become world champion. Writer-producer-director Leslie Stevens was behind this project and, although it featured some powerful stories (filmed on location), it failed to build on its dramatic ingredients.
1962-3/b & w/32 ep x 52 min/Daystar Prods – ua-tv/cr Leslie Stevens/lp Jack Lord, Robert Dowdell, Bruce Dern, Warren Oates

Stories of the Century · Jim Davis played a railroad detective, Matt Clark, whose investigations (based on official newspaper files and records) traced the exploits of famous desperados of the time. The series made its mark by introducing little-known facts into the stories, such as Geronimo's last days on a reservation and Billy the Kid's New York background. The show is also known as *Legend of the West* and (in some syndication markets) as *The Fast Guns*. In 1954 Republic released a feature version combining two episodes ('Quantrill and his Raiders' and 'Belle Starr') as *Stories of the Century No. 1*, running for 59 minutes and directed by William Witney. Three other similar theatrical versions were planned, consisting of two episodes each, but there is no record of these ever being released.
1954-5/b & w/39 ep x 25 min/rep – Studio City tv/p Ed White/lp Jim Davis, Mary Castle, Kristine Miller

Stranger on the Run · Scripted from a story by Reginald Rose, this film introduced Henry Fonda and Anne Baxter to the made-for-tv movie in a powerful 'chase' story. Fonda is a grizzled drifter wrongly accused of murder in New Mexico and pursued by a posse of deputized gunmen who purposely prolong the game of death. Anne Baxter plays a widow with whom Fonda seeks shelter. Siegel and Thackery make excellent use of exterior zooms and long-shots, complemented by effective low-angle lighting and interiors.
1967/97 min/u/p Richard E. Lyons/d Donald Siegel/s Dean Reisner/c Bud Thackery/lp Henry Fonda, Anne Baxter, Michael Parks, Dan Duryea, Sal Mineo

Sugarfoot · Not unlike Max Brand's Destry character in his dislike for gunplay, the main character is a genial plainsman who is studying law via a correspondence course. The plot here is derived from a *Saturday Evening Post* story by Michael Fessier (originally filmed by Michael Curtiz for Warners in 1953 as *The Boy from Oklahoma*); the opening episode of the series ('Brannigan's Boots') virtually retells the movie story. In some overseas markets the series was known as *Tenderfoot*. Also, because of the tv series, the 1951 Randolph Scott film *Sugarfoot* was retitled *Swirl of Glory*.
1957-61/b & w/69 ep x 52 min/wb-tv/exec p William T. Orr/lp Will Hutchins

The Swamp Fox · A delightfully offbeat representation of American history by Disney. Set in South Carolina in 1780, the series depicts the guerrilla adventures of Revolutionary War hero General Francis

Marion as he strikes and harasses the British forces around the Carolina swamps. Limited-run series (shown as a part of *Walt Disney Presents*) which used some excellent 'swampland' colour photography by Philip Lathrop and suitably exciting music by William Lava. Transmitted in black and white.

1959-61/8 ep x 52 min/Walt Disney Prods/p James Pratt/lp Leslie Nielsen, John Sutton, Robert Douglas, Henry Daniell, Slim Pickens, Tim Considine

T

Tales of the Texas Rangers · The exploits of the famous Texas Rangers, with Willard Parker and Harry Lauter as the two regular series characters. The stories leap back and forth in time from the Old West right up to the 1950s. The TV series was based on an early 50s radio show in which Joel McCrea had played one of the Rangers.

1955-9/b & w/52 ep x 26 min/Screen Gems/p Colbert Clark/lp Willard Parker, Harry Lauter

Tales of Wells Fargo · Developing from half-hour tales to hour-long colour stories, this series revolves around special agent Jim Hardie, a trouble-shooter for the stage lines run by the Wells, Fargo company. Dale Robertson's Hardie was a solid, tight-lipped type who often proved himself deadly with his left-handed gun. Originated by Frank Gruber, the series derived from a 1956 segment of *Schlitz Playhouse of Stars* titled 'A Tale of Wells Fargo'. There is also an edited-for-TV (from episodes) 'feature' called *Gunfight in Black Horse Canyon*, dating

Dale Robertson in Tales of Wells Fargo

from 1961 and featuring George Kennedy and Ellen Burstyn (although Burstyn must have been Ellen McRae in those days).

1957-62/b & w: colour/167 ep x 26 min: 34 ep x 52 min/Overland Prods – Revue – Juggernaut Inc/cr Frank Gruber/lp Dale Robertson, Jack Ging, William Demarest

The Tall Man · New Mexico in the 1870s is the setting for this series about the fictionalized partnership of lawman Pat Garrett and the doomed William H. Bonney, aka Billy the Kid.

1960-2/b & w/75 ep x 26 min/MCA-TV/cr Samuel A. Peeples/lp Clu Gulager, Barry Sullivan

Tate · Rugged-looking David McLean, as the title character, is a wandering gunfighter and a casualty of the Civil War, his left arm and hand encased in black leather. Unable to find solid work he reluctantly takes up the role of a gun-for-hire whenever the situation arises.

1960/b & w/13 ep x 26 min/RonCom Prods/cr Harry Julian Fink/lp David McLean

Temple Houston · The dramatic frontier life of circuit court lawyer Temple Houston, son of the Texas hero Sam Houston, provides the setting and stories. Jeffrey Hunter's Temple Houston may not accurately resemble the historical character but Jack Elam as a travelling US Marshal more than makes up for it in authentic 'ruggedness'. The 57-minute pilot film, *The Man from Galveston*, was released theatrically in January 1964. James Warner Bellah was one of the writers on the series.

1963-4/b & w/26 ep x 52 min/WB-TV/exec p Jack Webb/lp Jeffrey Hunter, Jack Elam

Testimony of Two Men · Complex family drama weaving a Western soap-opera story over the latter part of the 19th century. More a costume drama than a period actioner (although it begins in the middle of the Civil War), the mini-series is based on the sprawling novel by Taylor Caldwell.

1977/300 min/U/p Jack Laird/d Larry Yust, Leo Penn/s James M. Miller, Jennifer Miller, William Hanley/c Isidore Mankofsky/lp David Birney, Barbara Parkins, Steve Forrest, Ralph Bellamy

The Texan · Based on Bill Longley's life as a cowhand, rancher and gunfighter in 1870s Texas. Co-producer Rory Calhoun portrays the title character as a gunfighting drifter

effecting mood largely through icy facial expressions. The premiere episode was taken from a story by Frank Gruber.

1958-60/b & w/78 ep x 26 min/Rorvic – Desilu/p Rory Calhoun, Vic Orsatti/lp Rory Calhoun

Texas John Slaughter · Another based-on-real-life-character mini-series from the *Walt Disney Presents* anthology, this time featuring a part-time Texas Ranger (played by Tom Tryon) who galloped like the wind and fought like fury across the American Southwest. Five features were edited from the series and released theatrically as *Texas John Slaughter* (1958; director Harry Keller), *Stampede at Bitter Creek* (1959; director Harry Keller), *Gunfight at Sandoval* (1961; director Harry Keller), *A Holster Full of Law* (1961; director James Neilson) and *Geronimo's Revenge* (1962; directors James Neilson, Harry Keller).

1958-61/17 ep x 52 min/Walt Disney Prods/p James Pratt/lp Tom Tryon

Tex e il signore degli abissi · Rare Italian made-for-TV Western featuring Giuliano Gemma as the buckskin-clad hero Tex Willer (based on the long-running Italian comic-book series) who takes on a *Wild Wild West*-like team of heavies, including a crazed scientist-cum-witch-doctor, some offbeat Yaqui Indians and a weird collection of phosphorescent volcanic stones. William Berger turns up as Kit Carson.

1985/103 min/RAI-Rete 3 – Cinecittà/exec p Enzo Porcelli/d Duccio Tessari/s Gianfranco Clerici, Marcello Coscia, Duccio Tessari, Giorgio Bonelli/c Pietro Morbidelli/lp Giuliano Gemma, Carlo Mucari, William Berger, Isabel Russinova

This Is the West That Was · Executive producer Roy Huggins tried for another *Alias Smith and Jones* (right down to narration by Roger Davis) with this pilot movie about the lighthearted adventures of Wild Bill Hickok, Calamity Jane and Buffalo Bill. This was the comedy Western series that wasn't.

1974/78 min/Public Arts Prods – U/p Jo Swerling Jr./d Fielder Cook/s Sam H. Rolfe/c Earl Rath/lp Ben Murphy, Kim Darby, Jane Alexander, Anthony Franciosa

The Tim McCoy Show · This early 1950s series was a minor comeback for Colonel Tim McCoy. Produced for the afternoon children's audience, it had McCoy inter-

*Charles Bronson, Kurt Russell
in The Travels of Jaimie McPheeters*

preting Indian lore and ran extracts from his old feature films in a semi-educational style.
1953/b & w/39 ep x 15 min/Mercury International Pictures/*p* Virgil E. Ellsworth/*host* Tim McCoy

Tomahawk · The story of Pierre Radisson, the early French-Canadian explorer who blazed a path through the wilderness of the Canadian Northwest. The series featured plenty of conflict with the Indian tribes and supplied, for its time, exciting outdoor adventure for the younger audience.
1957-8/b & w/26 ep x 26 min/CBC/*d* Pierre Gauvreau/*lp* Jacques Godin, Rene Caron, Percy Rodriquez, Julien Besette

Tombstone Territory · Tombstone, Arizona was the 'town too tough to die' in this series based on the files of Arizona's oldest weekly newspaper, *The Tombstone Epitaph*. Pat Conway as Sheriff Clay Hollister kept things in order in traditional Wyatt Earp fashion.
1957-9/b & w/91 ep x 26 min/Ziv-TV/*p* Andy White, Frank Pittman/*lp* Pat Conway, Richard Eastham, Gil Rankin

Trackdown · Based on cases from the files of the Texas Rangers, with Robert Culp as Ranger Hoby Gilman; the series features his exploits across the Southwest during the 1870s. Steve McQueen's Josh Randall character appeared in a 1958 episode ('The Bounty Hunter'), which led to the series *Wanted: Dead or Alive*. *Trackdown* itself sprang from a May 1957 episode ('Badge of Honor') in *Dick Powell's Zane Grey Theatre*.
1957-9/b & w/71 ep x 26 min/Four Star/*p* Vincent M. Fennelly/*lp* Robert Culp

The Trackers · A curious combination in casting sees Ernest Borgnine as a father whose daughter has been taken by the Indians and Sammy Davis Jr. as the unlikely

tracker he hires to rescue her. Predictable conflict is offset by the easygoing performances, laced with humour.
1971/73 min/Aaron Spelling Prods/*p* Aaron Spelling, Sammy Davis Jr./*d* Earl Bellamy/*s* Gerald Gaiser/*c* Tim Southcott/*lp* Sammy Davis Jr., Ernest Borgnine, Julie Adams, Connie Kreski, Jim Davis

The Travels of Jaimie McPheeters · MGM-TV's Western Odyssey, based on the 1958 Pulitzer Prize-winning novel by Robert Lewis Taylor, tells the exciting and colourful story of Doc McPheeters and his young son, Jaimie, as they journey west with a wagon train bound for California during the 1849 gold rush. Top quality MGM production was enhanced by Leigh Harline's music. A 'feature' was released to cinemas in Europe as *Guns of Diablo*, taken from 'The Day of Reckoning' episode with additional footage.
1963-4/b & w/26 ep x 52 min/MGM-TV/*p* Robert Sparks, Don Ingalls, Boris Ingster/*lp* Dan O'Herlihy, Kurt Russell, James Westerfield, Charles Bronson

True Grit · Reworking of the 1969 John Wayne/Henry Hathaway Western with Warren Oates donning Wayne's eyepatch and Lisa Pelikan playing the Kim Darby character. Unlike the feature movie, this version, intended to launch a series, is set in Wyoming in 1881, though it was actually shot outside Canon City, Colorado.
1978/100 min/PAR/*p* Sandor Stern/*d* Richard T. Heffron/*s* Sandor Stern/*c* Stevan Larner/*lp* Warren Oates, Lisa Pelikan, Lee Meriwether, Jeff Osterhage

26 Men · This series is based on authentic stories of the Arizona Rangers at the turn of the century. The title refers to the company of men (restricted by law to twenty-six) under the command of Captain Tom Rynning. Photography by Ken Peach and John Nickolaus used actual Arizona locations.
1957-9/b & w/78 ep x 26 min/Russell Hayden Prods/*p* Russell Hayden/*lp* Tris Coffin, Kelo Henderson

Two Faces West · Standard, by-the-numbers Western series, but one with a technical gimmick: Charles Bateman plays twin brothers, one a gentlemanly doctor, the other a quick-tempered, gun-happy cowboy. Despite using the split-screen technique to effect the 'twin' scenes, fast draws and showdowns were the main action ingredients of this show.
1960-1/b & w/39 ep x 26 min/Screen

*Gary Clarke, James Drury, Doug McClure
in The Virginian*

Gems/*p* Matthew Rapf/*lp* Charles Bateman, June Blaire, Francis De Sales

U

Union Pacific · Action-adventure series dramatizing the building of the railroad across hostile territory in the 1860s. Problems with outlaws and Indian attacks were just part of the responsibilities of construction boss Jeff Morrow.
1958/b & w/39 ep x 26 min/California National Prods/*p* George M. Cahan/*lp* Jeff Morrow, Judd Pratt, Susan Cummings

U.S. Marshal · Former *Sheriff of Cochise*, John Bromfield, now a U.S. Marshal, continues pursuing Arizona criminals in modern, station-wagon method of law enforcement. Exterior photography by Lucien Andriot took good advantage of the scenic Arizona locale. The series was based on the files of the sheriff of Cochise County. Robert Altman contributed from the director's chair.
1958-60/b & w/78 ep x 26 min/Desilu/*p* Mort Briskin/*lp* John Bromfield

V

The Virginian · Developed from Owen Wister's classic novel and set in Wyoming in the 1890s, *The Virginian* was TV's first ninety-minute colour Western series. The stories revolve around the inhabitants of the vast Shiloh Ranch, run by three successive owners over the eight-year period. James Drury played The Virginian, the 'mysterious' ranch foreman, while Doug McClure's Trampas, Gary Clarke and Clu Gulager, among others, made up the ranch-hands. The series was offered from an early pilot ('The Virginian') shown in 1958 as a segment of the *Decision* anthology but the final format didn't develop until some four years

Ward Bond in Wagon Train

Steve McQueen in Wanted: Dead or Alive

Brian Keith in The Westerner

later. Four features were released theatrically in Europe during 1962, composed of re-edited episodes: *The Brazen Bell*, *Bull of the West*, *The Devil's Children* and *The Final Hour*. The series premiered with a splendid music score by Max Steiner. In 1970 the format was 'updated' for one more season, under the new title of *The Men from Shiloh*. 1962-70/208 ep x 90 min/Revue Prods – NBC-TV/*exec p* Roy Huggins, Frank Price, Norman Macdonnell/*lp* Lee J. Cobb, James Drury, Doug McClure, Gary Clarke, Pippa Scott, Roberta Shore, Randy Boone, Clu Gulager, Charles Bickford, John McIntire

Wagon Train · Television's great odyssey of the West, setting its course out of St Joseph, Missouri to trek across the Great Plains and the Rocky Mountains toward California in the days following the Civil War. Inspired somewhat by John Ford's *Wagon Master*, the series in its early years was led by Ward Bond as wagonmaster Major Adams, with John McIntire taking over after Bond's death in 1961. Robert Horton's Flint McCullough was the trail scout for the first five years. The series embraced every form of conflict on the trail, natural and human, and excelled with its careful observation of character development and, quite often,

regression; two of the more colourful and intriguing episodes presented were Dorothy M. Johnston's 'A Man Called Horse' (1958) and the John Ford-directed 'The Colter Craven Story' (1960), the latter with John Wayne in a cameo as General Sherman. One of the most popular shows of the period, it went from black and white to colour in the early 60s and in one season expanded from hour-length episodes to ninety-minute stories. Re-runs of the series were sometimes known as *Major Adams* and *Major Adams, Trailmaster*.
1957-65/b & w: colour/252 ep x 52 min: 32 ep x 90 min/Revue Prods/*p* Howard Christie/*lp* Ward Bond, Robert Horton, Terry Wilson, Frank McGrath, John McIntire, Robert Fuller

Walt Disney Presents · When in 1958 *Disneyland* decided to broaden its television audience by overlapping into the adult primetime slot, it changed its title to the less juvenile *Walt Disney Presents* (it later became *Walt Disney's Wonderful World of Color*, then *Walt Disney*). In the early 1960s, when TV Westerns were still stampeding across the night-time schedules, Disney produced three Western mini-series under its *Presents* banner. The first was the four-part *Zorro*, continuing Don Diego de la Vega's masked adventures from the 1957-9 half-hour series. Next came *Daniel Boone*, a four-part show

which told the story of young Boone and a band of men who are lured across the Cumberland Gap by tales about the fertile lands of Kentucky. Following *Boone* in May of 1961 was a two-part mini-series called *Andrews' Raiders* (comprised of 'The Secret Mission' and 'Escape to Nowhere'), which related the exploits of a Union spy, 'James J. Andrews', who led his volunteers behind Rebel lines to smash the South's communications. Both *Elfego Baca* and *Texas John Slaughter* were originally shown under the *Walt Disney Presents* aegis. *Zorro* and *Andrews' Raiders* were transmitted in black and white but are very likely to have been produced in colour; *Daniel Boone* was filmed in colour.
Zorro/1960-1/tx b & w/4 ep x 52 min/Walt Disney Prods/*exec p* Walt Disney/*lp* Guy Williams, Gilbert Roland, Rita Moreno, Annette Funicello, Ricardo Montalban
Daniel Boone/1960-1/4 ep x 52 min/Walt Disney Prods/*exec p* Walt Disney/*lp* Dewey Martin, Mala Powers, Terry Thompson, Richard Banke, Kevin Corcoran
Andrews' Raiders/1961/tx b & w/2 ep x 52 min/Walt Disney Prods/*exec p* Walt Disney/*lp* Fess Parker, Jeffrey Hunter, Kenneth Tobey

Wanted: Dead or Alive · A fast-paced, action-filled and at times quite violent series

featuring Steve McQueen as Josh Randall, a professional bounty hunter who uses a sawn-off rifle as a high velocity handgun. The character came from a story in the *Trackdown* series and launched the career of McQueen in his capable loner image.
1958-61/b & w/94 ep x 26 min/Four Star – Malcolm Enterprises – CBS-TV/*p* John Robinson/*lp* Steve McQueen

Wanted: The Sundance Woman · Katharine Ross reappears as fugitive Etta Place in the post-Butch and Sundance days, with a one-man 'superposse' on her trail. In a switch from her character in the 1969 feature, Etta now comes across like Belle Starr in a 1940s B-Western, and at one point she even has a sexual skirmish with Pancho Villa. The movie is also known as *Mrs Sundance Rides Again*.
1976/100 min/FOX/*p* Ron Preissman/*d* Lee Philips/*s* Richard Fielder/*c* Terry K. Meade/*lp* Katharine Ross, Steve Forrest, Stella Stevens, Michael Constantine

The Westerner · Sam Peckinpah's gift to the TV Western genre, *The Westerner* was the story of Dave Blasingame, a working cowman travelling the Southwest of the 1890s. Not so much a Western 'actioner' with gratuitous gunplay, more a complex character study, set against a 'real' Western landscape of hardship and humour, courage and commonsense. An expertly crafted poetic drama. *The Westerner* developed from a *Dick Powell's Zane Grey Theatre* segment called 'Trouble at Tres Cruces' (1959), written and directed by Peckinpah. In addition, a *Westerner* episode entitled 'Line Camp' was the basis for the 1968 feature *Will Penny*, both directed by Tom Gries.
1960/b & w/13 ep x 26 min/Four Star – Winchester Prods/*cr* Sam Peckinpah/*lp* Brian Keith

Whispering Smith · Produced in 1959 but not shown until three years later, this series about an 1870s Denver, Colorado criminologist features Audie Murphy as Tom 'Whispering' Smith; apparently not connected with the 1948 Paramount Western or the novels of Frank Spearman. This series was one of the examples cited during the campaign against television violence in the early 1960s. Borden Chase was story consultant.
1961/b & w/25 ep x 26 min/Whispering Smith Company – NBC-TV – Revue/*p* Herb Coleman/*lp* Audie Murphy, Guy Mitchell, Sam Buffington

Wichita Town · Joel McCrea's debut in a TV series was as marshal of this Kansas trail head town in the 1870s, aided by his deputy (and real-life son) Jody. Stories relate how he and the Wichita townspeople deal with cowboys letting off steam at trail's end.
1959-60/b & w/26 ep x 26 min/Mirisch TV Enterprises – Mirisch-McCrea Prods – Four Star/*p* Walter Mirisch, Joel McCrea/*lp* Joel McCrea, Jody McCrea, Carlos Romero

The Wide Country · Contemporary Western series based on the itinerant life of a rodeo champ and his younger brother as they follow the gruelling rodeo circuit. The series' pilot ('Second Chance') premiered as an episode of the anthology *Alcoa Premiere* in early 1962.
1962-3/b & w/28 ep x 52 min/Gemini Prods/*p* Frank Telford/*lp* Earl Holliman, Andrew Prine

Wild and Wooly · Aaron Spelling Productions with yet another potential series pilot, concerning the *Charlie's Angels*-like efforts of a group of fetching young women setting out to foil the planned assassination of Teddy Roosevelt in 1903.
1978/100 min/Aaron Spelling Prods/*p* Earl W. Wallace/*d* Philip Leacock/*s* Earl W. Wallace/*c* Jack Swain/*lp* Chris Delisle, Susan Bigelow, Elyssa Davalos, Doug McClure

Wild Horses · Simple yet engrossing tale of an ex-cowboy living a domestic life in Texas who decides to take off for Wyoming for a wild mustang round-up. Kenny Rogers plays the ex-cowpoke and the setting carefully evokes a gritty, rugged feeling of the true West.
1985/100 min/Wild Horses Prods – Telepictures Prods/*p* Hunt Lowry/*d* Dick Lowry/*s* Roderick Taylor, Daniel Vining/*c* Keith Wagstaff/*lp* Kenny Rogers, Pam Dawber, Ben Johnson, David Andrews

Wildside · Action series about a group of undercover roughriders who, when not appearing as ordinary citizens in Wildside County, are out rounding up the evil elements in the territory. A winning combination of *The A-Team* and *Wild Wild West*.
1985/6 ep x 52 min/Touchstone Prods – Walt Disney Prods/*cr* Tom Greene/*lp* William Smith, J. Eddie Peck, Howard E. Rollins Jr., John di Aquino, Terry Funk

Wild Times · Heavy-handed story of a

sharpshooter whose frontier adventures are recounted by a dime novelist, ultimately building the character into a Wild West show 'hero'. Sam Elliott plays the sharpshooter and Pat Hingle is the Ned Buntline-like pulp scribe.
1980/200 min/Metromedia Producers Corp – Rattlesnake Prods/*p* Les Sheldon/*d* Richard Compton/*s* Don Balluck/*c* John C. Flinn III/*lp* Sam Elliott, Ben Johnson, Bruce Boxleitner, Pat Hingle

The Wild Wild West · Fittingly, this James Bond-inspired Western series was filmed on the site where the Republic serials were once produced (CBS Studio Center). Stories feature the post-Civil War espionage escapades of two government agents as they combat bizarre comic-book villains and pseudo-scientific plots on behalf of President Ulysses S. Grant.
1965-70/104 ep x 52 min/CBS-TV/*cr* Michael Garrison/*lp* Robert Conrad, Ross Martin

The Wild Wild West Revisited · The format of the late 1960s series repeated in an entertaining pilot attempting to resurrect its way-out escapism. Once more world domination is the villain's aim, and as usual our now over-the-hill agent heroes thwart the dastardly plot. Played more obviously for laughs than the original series.
1979/100 min/CBS Entertainment/*p* Robert L. Jacks/*d* Burt Kennedy/*s* William Bowers/*c* Robert B. Hauser/*lp* Robert Conrad, Ross Martin, Paul Williams, Harry Morgan, René Auberjonois

Wild Women · Based on Vincent Forte's *The Trailmakers*, about a group of Army engineers during the 1840s setting out to draw plans of the border area prior to war with Mexico. Hugh O'Brian as the mission leader disguises his soldiers and recruits a colourful batch of women prisoners to act as their 'wives'. Beautiful location photography, fine performances from Marilyn Maxwell and Anne Francis, and adequate direction from Don Taylor add interest to a *Dirty Dozen*-like story.
1970/74 min/Aaron Spelling Prods/*p* Lou Morheim/*d* Don Taylor/*s* Lou Morheim, Richard Carr/*c* Fleet Southcott/*lp* Hugh O'Brian, Anne Francis, Marilyn Maxwell, Marie Windsor

The Wild Women of Chastity Gulch · With the menfolk off to the Civil War, the female inhabitants of a small town (split into groups

of prim 'n' propers and saloon sluts) have to face a renegade horde of Union soldiers who have more than just watering their horses on their minds.
1982/100 min/Aaron Spelling Prods/p Shelly Hull/d Philip Leacock/s Earl W. Wallace/c Richard Rawlings/lp Priscilla Barnes, Lee Horsley, Howard Duff, Pamela Bellwood

Winchester '73 · Remake of the 1950 Anthony Mann classic, with Tom Tryon in the James Stewart role tracking down his brother and the one-of-a-thousand Winchester rifle. John Saxon (in the original Stephen McNally part) plays with an embittered cunning, while Duryea (in a different role this time) comes across sympathetically as their cousin. Bud Thackery's Technicolor photography is one of the high notes.
1967/97 min/p Richard E. Lyons/d Herschel Daugherty/s Stephen Kandel, Richard L. Adams/c Bud Thackery/lp Tom Tryon, John Saxon, Dan Duryea, John Drew Barrymore

The Wrangler · This stock series about a roving cowboy has the distinction of being the first TV Western made on video-tape. Shooting with Marconi cameras, the producers used an electronic device (Paramount's then-new TVola) for the editing; the TVola made possible frame by frame editing of video-tape, which had previously been a problem for such non-studio productions.
1960/b & w/6 ep (transmitted) x 26 min/ Hollis Prods/p Paul Harrison/lp Jason Evers

Y

Yancy Derringer · New Orleans-based Western set in the years following the Civil War with Jock Mahoney as a Southern gentleman-gambler-adventurer travelling the river paddleboats. Action rather than characterization was the keynote.
1958-9/b & w/34 ep x 26 min/Derringer Prods – Sharpe & Lewis Prods/cr Richard Sale, Mary Loos/lp Jock Mahoney, X. Brands, Kevin Hagen, Julie Adams

The Young Country · A lightweight Western with a humorous *Maverick* streak running through it, notably in the character of Roger Davis' gambler-adventurer. Roy Huggins (who originally created *Maverick*) returns here with a similar format: the charming hero is smart if not devious,

gun-shy but not too cowardly, and the various Western characters who roam in and out of his affairs are really not as black-hearted as they seem.
1970/90 min/Public Arts Prod – u/p/d/s Roy Huggins/c Vilis Lapenieks/lp Walter Brennan, Joan Hackett, Wally Cox, Peter Duel, Roger Davis

Young Dan'l Boone · The early career of woodsman Daniel Boone as he explores the Kentucky wilderness. Not much on character, the series was an action trailblazer with an authentic look and some fine location photography.
1977/8 ep x 52 min/FOX-TV – Frankel Prods/p Jimmy Sangster/lp Rick Moses, Devon Ericson, John Joseph Thomas, Ji-Tu Cumbuka

Young Maverick · A youthful update and hoped-for rejuvenation of the Warners series from 1957-62 (*Bret Maverick* in 1981 attempted a direct revival). Here the young Ben Maverick attempts to rekindle the unique spark that made the old show such a hit but by the very attempt to be easygoing and casual the series succeeded in snuffing itself out.
1979-80/13 ep x 52 min/WB-TV/p Chuck Bowman/lp Charles Frank, Susan Blanchard, John Dehner

Young Pioneers · The homespun hardships of a young couple starting a fresh life in the newly opened Dakota Territory of the 1870s. The producers were undoubtedly hoping for a successful prairie-opera similar to Landon's *Little House* dramas.
Pilot/1976/96 min/ABC Circle Film/p Ed Friendly/d Michael O'Herlihy/s Blanche Hanalis/c Robert L. Morrison/lp Roger Kern, Linda Purl, Robert Hays, Shelly Juttner
Series/1978/4 ep x 52 min/Lorimar Prods – Amanda Prods/p Robert L. Jacks/lp Linda Purl, Roger Kern, Robert Hayes, Robert Donner

Young Pioneers' Christmas · Follow-up to *Young Pioneers*, still battling with the rugged land. Their grief after the death of their infant son and the problems of an encroaching railroad are put aside in order to make arrangements for the festive season.
1976/96 min/ABC Circle Film/p Ed Friendly/d Michael O'Herlihy/s Blanche Hanalis/c Robert L. Morrison/lp Roger Kern, Linda Purl, Robert Hays, Kay Kimler

The Young Rebels · Set in Chester, Pennsylvania in 1777, this series features a group of young Americans during the Revolutionary War who organize the Yankee Doodle Society, a resistance outfit fighting the British behind their lines.
1970-1/15 ep x 52 min/COL-TV/cr Peter Gayle/lp Rick Ely, Lou Gossett, Alex Henteloff, Hilarie Thompson

Yuma · Another Aaron Spelling Productions pilot, with Clint Walker as a u.s. Marshal cleaning up the lawless Yuma of the late 1800s. The film opens like *Rio Bravo*, with Walker jailing a bad guy and then waiting for the man's family to come into town to settle the score. The slow-moving story takes in sub-plots involving corrupt Army officials and hostile Indians before arriving at a cop-out payoff.
1971/90 min/Aaron Spelling Prods/p Aaron Spelling/d Ted Post/s Charles Wallace/c John Morley Stephens/lp Clint Walker, Barry Sullivan, Kathryn Hays, Edgar Buchanan

Z

Zorro · An admirable small-screen presentation of the famous Zorro adventure. Walt Disney's handsome series, however, came closer to their stock Western productions (*Texas John Slaughter* and *Elfego Baca*) than to the swashbuckling cinema versions. The setting is of course the Pueblo de Los Angeles of early Spanish California but the action form is typically Western, with thundering horses, rousing chases and plenty of outdoor energy. Two theatrical features were edited from first-season episodes and released in 1958: *Zorro the Avenger* (director Charles Barton) and *The Sign of Zorro* (directors Lewis Foster, Norman Foster).
1957-9/b & w/70 ep x 26 min/Walt Disney Prods/exec p Walt Disney/lp Guy Williams, Gene Sheldon, Britt Lomond

Zorro (1960-1). See **Walt Disney Presents**

Zorro and Son · Comedy version of the old Disney series with Henry Darrow as an aging and not so nimble Don Diego who brings his son back from Spain to continue the Zorro adventures. Of course, the street-wise son (played by Paul Regina) doesn't much take to masks and capes but nevertheless assumes the role.
1983/5 ep x 25 min/Walt Disney Prods/p Kevin Corcoran/lp Henry Darrow, Paul Regina, Bill Dana, Gregory Sierra

CHART AND TABLES

| 1910 | 1920 | 1930 | 1940 | 1950 | 1960 | 1970 | 1980 |

G.M. Anderson ★★★★★★★★★★★
1908–18

Dustin Farnum ★★★★★★★★★★★★★★
1913–26

W.S. Hart ★★★★★★★★★★★★
1914–25

Tom Mix ★★★★★★★★★★★★★★★★★★★
1917–35

Jack Holt ★★★★★★★★★★★★★★★★★★★★★★★★★
1916–40

Harry Carey ★★★★★★★★★★★★★★★★★★★★★★★★★
1917–41

Art Acord ★★★★★★★★★★
1920–29

Hoot Gibson ★★★★★★★★★★★★★★★★★★★★★★★★★★
1919–44

Buck Jones ★★★★★★★★★★★★★★★★★★★★★★★★
1919–42

Fred Thomson ★★★★★
1924–8

Tim McCoy ★★★★★★★★★★★★★★★★★
1926–42

Ken Maynard ★★★★★★★★★★★★★★★★★★★★★
1924–44

George O'Brien ★★★★★★★★★★★★★★★★★
1924–40

John Wayne ★★
1930–76

William Boyd ★★★★★★★★★★★★★★
1935–48

Johnny Mack Brown ★★★★★★★★★★★★★★★★★★★★★★★★
1930–53

Gary Cooper ★★★★★★★★★★★★★★★★★★★★★★★★★★★★★★★★★
1926–59

Randolph Scott ★★★★★★★★★★★★★★★★★★★★★★★★★★★★★
1932–62

Charles Starrett ★★★★★★★★★★★★★★★★★★
1935–52

Bill Elliott ★★★★★★★★★★★★★★★★★
1938–54

Joel McCrea ★★★★★★★★★★★★★★★★★★★★★★★★★★
1937–62

Gene Autry ★★★★★★★★★★★★★★★★★★★
1935–53

Roy Rogers ★★★★★★★★★★★★★★
1938–51

Audie Murphy ★★★★★★★★★★★★★★★★★★
1950–67

Clint Eastwood ★★★★★★★★★★★★★★★★★★★★★★★★★★★★★
1964–

Career spans of 25 Western stars

Table 1

1921	102
1922	145
1923	98
1924	173
1925	227
1926	199
1927	145
1928	141
1929	92
1930	79
1931	85
1932	108
1933	65
1934	76
1935	145
1936	135
1937	135
1938	112
1939	123
1940	143
1941	130
1942	120
1943	103
1944	95
1945	80
1946	98
1947	95
1948	108
1949	97
1950	130
1951	109
1952	108
1953	92
1954	69
1955	68
1956	83
1957	70
1958	54
1959	39
1960	28
1961	22
1962	15
1963	11
1964	21
1965	22
1966	20
1967	20
1968	16
1969	20
1970	22
1971	24
1972	25
1973	16
1974	13
1975	20
1976	26
1977	7

Production of Westerns 1921-77

Table 2

	COL	*FOX	MGM	PAR	RKO	UA	U	†WB
1926	1/15	19/47	5/42	6/65	–	1-8	32/57	0/32
1927	0/25	14/50	5/48	9/72	–	0/12	30/64	1/43
1928	0/32	9/49	5/47	8/69	–	1/15	25/59	1/40
1929	0/22	3/53	5/49	5/61	0/12	0/18	17/49	7/87
1930	5/29	4/48	5/47	5/63	3/32	0/15	14/40	6/76
1931	11/31	5/48	2/46	6/61	4/33	0/13	2/23	0/54
1932	16/29	4/40	1/39	2/55	8/46	0/14	9/30	3/55
1933	10/32	5/50	0/42	6/59	4/48	1/16	9/37	3/55
1934	4/43	2/52	1/43	4/53	1/46	0/20	6/44	0/58
1935	13/49	3/52	1/47	8/58	3/40	1/19	9/37	2/49
1936	15/52	4/57	3/45	12/72	5/39	2/17	9/28	4/56
1937	15/52	6/61	2/51	12/64	5/53	0/25	9/37	8/68
1938	19/54	3/56	1/46	10/50	10/43	1/16	11/46	3/52
1939	14/52	5/59	3/49	8/57	8/49	1/19	7/49	2/53
1940	17/51	8/49	4/49	10/50	7/53	2/20	10/55	2/43
1941	17/61	8/50	3/52	12/50	7/46	0/15	10/58	2/51
1942	19/59	2/51	5/44	1/37	7/39	4/15	11/60	2/35
1943	11/47	2/33	0/33	0/27	5/50	9/18	7/58	0/20
1944	11/56	1/26	2/30	0/36	5/33	5/20	10/53	0/19
1945	12/38	0/27	2/29	0/23	3/32	0/18	8/50	1/19
1946	17/51	1/32	1/26	2/19	2/34	3/19	6/37	0/22
1947	17/49	0/27	0/26	1/27	5/40	7/22	4/19	2/20
1948	20/39	2/45	1/26	2/27	9/30	8/22	1/22	1/21
1949	18/52	1/31	1/34	2/22	9/36	4/21	3/25	3/27
1950	19/59	6/32	5/38	6/24	7/32	3/17	7/29	5/28
1951	19/63	2/39	5/41	6/25	8/38	2/23	6/33	6/27
1952	18/48	5/37	2/41	3/21	9/32	3/22	8/34	7/26
1953	17/47	3/39	2/37	5/25	1/24	6/33	14/33	6/29
1954	10/35	8/29	2/23	1/16	3/15	9/34	11/27	6/20
1955	9/38	2/29	2/24	2/17	5/14	8/28	8/31	2/21
1956	9/40	8/32	2/26	2/17	3/20	12/42	10/30	5/24
1957	7/46	10/50	2/28	3/19	1/10	14/53	4/30	2/26
1958	5/38	12/42	4/29	0/24	–	8/41	7/27	3/24
1959	7/36	7/34	3/24	4/17	–	8/35	3/11	5/19
1960	1/35	7/49	1/19	1/24	–	6/29	2/12	3/17
1961	1/28	5/35	1/24	1/13	–	5/34	2/11	1/16
1962	1/30	2/25	3/28	1/17	–	3/31	3/12	0/16
1963	0/19	1/18	2/30	1/14	–	1/22	1/11	1/15
1964	1/19	2/18	4/31	2/20	–	1/20	3/17	3/15
1965	4/29	4/26	2/30	4/22	–	2/17	2/21	1/15
1966	2/29	2/21	2/20	6/20	–	3/20	6/23	1/12
1967	2/22	1/19	4/25	5/31	–	6/24	4/15	0/21

Production of Westerns/Total Features by Studio 1926-67

* Becomes 20th Century-Fox in 1936
† Figures include First National after it combined with Warner Bros. in 1932.

Table 3

	1941	1942	1943	1944	1945
Majors					
COL	17	19	11	11	12
FOX	8	2	2	1	–
MGM	3	5	–	2	2
PAR	12	1	–	–	–
RKO	7	7	5	5	3
UA	–	4	9	5	–
U	10	11	7	10	8
WB	2	2	–	–	1
Total Westerns	59	51	34	34	26
Total features	383	340	286	273	236
Westerns as a percentage of majors' total features	15%	15%	12%	12%	11%
Majors' Westerns as a percentage of all Westerns	45%	43%	33%	36%	33%
Independents					
Republic	33	31	28	27	23
Monogram	19	17	15	17	13
PRC	13	19	19	17	14
Others	2	–	2	2	2
Total Westerns	67	67	64	63	52
Total features	124	142	118	139	122
Westerns as a percentage of independents' total features	54%	47%	54%	45%	43%
Independents' Westerns as a percentage of all Westerns	55%	57%	67%	64%	67%

Production of Westerns by Major and Independent Studios 1941-5

Table 4

	Total Features	Total Westerns	Westerns as percentage	Total Westerns Majors	Independents
1926	700 approx	199	28	64	135
1927	678	145	21	59	86
1928	641	141	22	49	92
1929	562	92	16	37	55
1930	509	79	16	44	35
1931	501	85	17	29	56
1932	489	108	22	44	64
1933	507	65	13	39	26
1934	480	76	16	17	59
1935	525	145	28	39	106
1936	522	135	26	56	79
1937	538	135	25	57	78
1938	455	122	27	57	55
1939	483	123	25	57	66
1940	477	143	30	73	70
1941	492	130	27	62	68
1942	488	120	25	53	67
1943	397	103	26	39	64
1944	401	95	24	32	63
1945	350	80	23	28	52
1946	378	98	26	35	63
1947	369	95	26	34	61
1948	366	108	30	49	59
1949	356	97	27	34	63
1950	383	130	34	61	69
1951	391	109	28	57	52
1952	324	108	33	60	48
1953	344	92	27	51	41
1954	253	69	27	40	29
1955	254	68	27	40	28
1956	272	83	31	55	28
1957	300	70	23	53	17
1958	241	54	22	38	16
1959	187	39	21	35	4
1960	154	28	18	22	6
1961	131	22	17	19	3
1962	147	15	10	10	5
1963	121	11	9	6	5
1964	141	21	15	17	4
1965	153	22	14	18	4
1966	156	20	13	18	2
1967	178	20	11	19	1

Westerns as a Proportion of all Features Produced 1926-67

In 1988 members of the British Film Institute were invited to take part in a poll to select the ten best Westerns of all time. The Members' Ten Best, in order of preference, were: 1. *High Noon* 2. *The Searchers* 3. *Stagecoach* 4. *Shane* 5. *Red River* 6. *The Wild Bunch* 7 = . *C'era una volta il west* (Once Upon A Time in the West): *The Outlaw Josey Wales*: *Rio Bravo* 10. *Ride the High Country* (Guns in the Afternoon)

Table 5

	1930	1931	1932	1933	1934	1935	1936	1937	1938	1939	1940	1941
COL												
All Films	29	31	29	32	43	49	52	52	54	52	51	61
All Westerns	5	11	16	10	4	13	15	15	19	14	17	17
'A' Westerns	–	–	–	–	–	–	–	–	–	–	1	1
*FOX												
All films	48	48	40	50	52	52	57	61	56	59	49	50
All Westerns	4	5	4	5	2	3	4	6	3	5	8	8
'A' Westerns	2	1	–	–	–	1	1	–	–	3	3	2
MGM												
All films	47	46	39	42	43	47	45	51	46	49	49	52
All Westerns	5	2	1	–	1	1	3	2	1	3	4	3
'A' Westerns	2	1	–	–	–	1	3	1	1	2	2	2
PAR												
All films	63	61	55	59	53	58	72	64	50	57	50	50
All Westerns	5	6	2	6	4	8	12	12	10	8	10	12
'A' Westerns	2	2	–	–	–	1	2	2	1	1	2	2
RKO												
All films	32	33	46	48	46	40	39	53	43	49	53	46
All Westerns	3	4	8	4	1	3	5	5	10	8	7	7
'A' Westerns	–	1	1	–	–	1	–	–	–	–	–	–
UA												
All films	15	13	14	16	20	19	17	25	16	19	20	15
All Westerns	–	–	–	1	–	1	2	–	1	1	2	–
'A' Westerns	–	–	–	1	–	–	–	–	–	–	2	–
U												
All films	40	23	30	37	44	37	28	37	46	49	55	58
All Westerns	14	2	9	9	6	9	9	9	11	7	10	10
'A' Westerns	1	–	1	–	–	–	1	–	–	1	1	1
†WB												
All films	76	54	55	55	58	49	56	68	52	53	43	51
All Westerns	6	–	3	3	–	2	4	8	3	2	2	2
'A' Westerns	2	–	–	–	–	–	–	–	2	2	2	1
Totals												
All films	350	309	308	339	359	351	366	411	363	387	370	383
All Westerns	42	30	43	38	18	40	54	57	58	48	60	59
'A' Westerns	9	5	2	1	–	4	7	3	4	9	13	9

Major Hollywood Studios' Production of 'A' and 'B' Westerns 1930-41.

Table 6

1949	1
1950	3
1951	8
1952	10
1953	13
1954	17
1955	23
1956	22
1957	32
1958	40
1959	48
1960	46
1961	36
1962	19
1963	17
1964	11
1965	15
1966	19
1967	20
1968	13
1969	12
1970	11
1971	9
1972	7
1973	6
1974	7
1975	4
1976	4
1977	4
1978	3
1979	3
1980	3
1981	3
1982	3
1983	3
1984	0
1985	1
1986	1
1987	1

Western Television Series on the Air 1949-87

The data in Tables 1-5 has been derived from Les Adams and Buck Rainey, *Shoot Em Ups*; *The American Film Institute Catalog of Motion Pictures Produced in the United States: Feature Films, 1921-30*; Phil Hardy, *The Western*; and *Film Daily Year Book*.

* Becomes 20th Century-Fox in 1936
† Figures include First National after it combined with Warner Bros. in 1932

BIBLIOGRAPHY

1. CINEMA AND TELEVISION

This bibliography lists books only. Articles are listed in Jack Nachbar's *Western Films: An Annotated Critical Bibliography* and elsewhere. Books on individual film-makers are omitted.

a) REFERENCE

Les Adams and Buck Rainey, *Shoot Em Ups* (New Rochelle, N.Y.: Arlington House, 1978). Credits, fuller than in Hardy, for all American sound Westerns, but no comment or plot summaries.

Ernest N. Corneau, *The Hall of Fame of Western Stars* (North Quincy, Mass.: Christopher Publishing House, 1969). Short biographies with incomplete filmographies and no dates.

Allen Eyles, *The Western* (London: Tantivy Press, rev. ed. 1975). Pioneering work of filmography, with credits and brief career description for 400 Western film-makers.

Brian Garfield, *Western Films* (New York: Rawson Associates, 1982). Brief, not very interesting comments on a selection of Westerns, with credits.

Phil Hardy, *The Western* (London: Aurum Press, 1983). Perceptive commentaries on 1,800 Westerns of the sound period, with credits. Several useful appendices, including box-office league table, Top Ten Money-Making Stars Poll and brief credits for all other sound Westerns. Indispensable.

Joe Hembus, *Western-Lexicon* (Munich: Hanser Verlag, 1976). Thorough reference guide in German to 1,272 Western films.

Joe Hembus, *Western Geschichte 1540-1894* (Munich: Wilhelm Heyne Verlag, 1979) Interweaves information on the history and mythology of the West (in German) with filmographies.

Kalton C. Lahue, *Winners of the West: The Sagebrush Heroes of the Silent Screen* (New York: A. S. Barnes, 1970). Unreliable and inadequate profiles of thirty-eight early Western stars.

Kalton C. Lahue, *Riders of the Range* (New York: Castle Books, 1973). Companion to above, on stars of sound Westerns, but this time the profiles even lack filmographies.

Arthur F. McClure and Ken D. Jones, *Heroes, Heavies and Sagebrush* (New York: A. S. Barnes, 1972). Career sketches of B-Western performers, with unreliable filmographies.

Jack Nachbar, *Western Films: An Annotated Critical Bibliography* (New York: Garland Publishing, 1975). Very useful guide to writing about the Western, which should be updated.

Michael R. Pitts, *Western Movies* (Jefferson, N. C.: McFarland & Co., 1986). Caption reviews and brief credits for 4,200 Westerns with US video availability information and index of film-makers.

Buck Rainey, *Saddle Aces of the Cinema* (New York: A. S. Barnes, 1980). Appreciations of fifteen early Western stars with good filmographies.

b) HISTORY AND CRITICISM

Henri Agel, *Le Western* (Paris: Lettres Modernes, 1969). Collection of essays in French on general aspects of the Western and on directors such as Hawks, Ford and Delmer Daves.

Georges-Albert Astre and Albert-Patrick Hoarau, *Univers du Western* (Paris: Editions Seghers, 1973). Interesting attempt to plot the history and imaginative sources of the Western against the history of the genre.

Alan G. Barbour, *The Thrill of It All* (New York: Collier Books, 1971). Lots of pictures and a slight text on the B-Western.

Michael Barson, 'The TV Western' in Brian G. Rose (ed.), *TV Genres* (Westport, Conn.: Greenwood Press, 1985). A useful survey.

Gretchen M. Bataille and Charles L. P. Silet, *The Pretend Indians: Images of Native Americans in the Movies* (Ames: Iowa State University Press, 1980). Collection of essays, mostly stronger on rhetoric and generalizations than on new ideas or information.

André Bazin, *What Is Cinema?* vol. II, trans. Hugh Gray (Berkeley: University of California Press, 1971). Contains Bazin's two key essays, 'The Western, or the American Film *par excellence*' and 'The Evolution of the Western'.

Raymond Bellour (ed.), *Le Western* (Paris: Union Général d'Editions, 1966). Critical appraisals of directors and actors, preceded by a collection of fifty lively and original short essays on such motifs as the horse, fistfights, cemeteries and lynching. One of the inspirations of the present volume.

Ralph Brauer, with Donna Brauer, *The Horse, the Gun and the Piece of Property: Changing Images of the TV Western* (Bowling Green, Ohio: Bowling Green University Popular Press, 1975). Chatty outline of the TV Western.

Kevin Brownlow, *The War, the West and the Wilderness* (London: Secker and Warburg, 1979). Full of valuable information, much elicited from participants, about the making of early Westerns.

Jenni Calder, *There Must Be a Lone Ranger* (London: Hamish Hamilton, 1974). Intermittently interesting but not always well-informed attempt to analyze the Western myth.

John Cawelti, *The Six-Gun Mystique* (Bowling Green, Ohio: Bowling Green University Popular Press, 1971). Short but highly stimulating essay attempting to define the essence of the genre.

John Cawelti, *Adventure, Mystery and Romance* (Chicago: University of Chicago Press, 1976). Includes a long essay on the Western in the context of a book about popular fictional genres, including detective stories and melodramas.

Walter C. Clapham, *Western Movies* (London: Octopus Books, 1974). A general history, thin.

Gianni di Claudio, *Il Cinema Western* (Rome: Libreria Universitaria Editrice, 1986). Basic history with a preface by Sergio Leone.

William K. Everson, *A Pictorial History of the Western Film* (Secaucus, N.J.: Citadel Press, 1969). The text is brief and concentrates on the B-Western. Lots of good pictures.

George N. Fenin and William K. Everson, *The Western from Silents to the Seventies* (New York: Penguin, 1973). Still the only full-scale history in English; increasingly showing its age. Gets less interested in films the further they get away from W. S. Hart.

Charles Ford, *Histoire du Western* (Paris: Albin Michel, 1976). Solid history by reputable French historian, strongest on silents and B-Westerns.

Christopher Frayling, *Spaghetti Westerns: Cowboys and Europeans from Karl May to Sergio Leone* (London: Routledge and Kegan Paul, 1981). The definitive study of the Italian Western.

Philip French, *Westerns* (London: Secker and Warburg, rev. ed. 1977). Well-written and knowledgeable series of essays on topics such as the Western's relation to American politics, the treatment of Indians, and violence; runs out of steam towards the end.

Ralph Friar and Natasha Friar, *The Only Good Indian ... The Hollywood Gospel* (New York: Drama Book Specialists, 1972). Impassioned attack on Hollywood's distortion of Native American history. Suffers from having only one point to make, though has useful lists at the back.

Barry Keith Grant (ed.) *Film Genre Reader* (Austin: University of Texas Press, 1986). Many of the articles in this collection about genre in the cinema bear directly on the Western.

Michael Hanisch, *Western: Die Entwicklung eines Filmgenres* (Leipzig: Henschelverlag Kunst & Gesellschaft, 1984). Well-illustrated general history from East Germany.

Charles W. Harris and Buck Rainey, *The Cowboy: Six-shooters, Songs and Sex* (Norman: University of Oklahoma Press, 1976). Collection of essays on such topics as porno Westerns, dude ranches and cowboy music.

Michael Hilger, *The American Indian in Film* (Metuchen, N.J.: Scarecrow Press, 1986). Adds nothing critically, but some useful lists.

James Horwitz, *They Went Thataway* (New York: E. P. Dutton, 1976). Nostalgic look at Western heroes such as Hopalong Cassidy and interviews with actors like Tim McCoy.

Jay Hyams, *The Life and Times of the Western Movie* (Bromley, Kent: Columbus Books, 1983). General over-view of Western film history, adequate but not adding anything.

Donald H. Kirkley, *A Descriptive Study of the Network Television Western during the seasons 1955-6 – 1962-3* (New York: Arno Press, 1979). Useful attempt to categorize plots, motifs, character types, etc.

Jim Kitses, *Horizons West* (London: Thames and Hudson, 1969). Still the best piece of sustained criticism on the Western generally and on a trio of directors: Mann, Boetticher and Peckinpah.

John H. Lenihan, *Showdown: Confronting Modern America in the Western* (Urbana: University of Illinois Press, 1980). An attempt to read the Western as a commentary on American politics and ideology. Despite occasional insights, damagingly reductionist.

Jean-Louis Leutrat, *L'Alliance brisée* (Lyon: Presses Universitaires de Lyon, 1985). Virtually the only work to deal adequately with the Western during the 1920s. Urgently in need of translation.

Jean-Louis Leutrat, *Le Western* (Paris: Armand Colin, 1973). Short but lively work of genre analysis, full of ideas.

Archie P. McDonald (ed.), *Shooting Stars* (Bloomington: Indiana University Press, 1987). Disappointingly thin collection of essays on major Western stars.

J. Fred MacDonald, *Who Shot the Sheriff: the Rise and Fall of the Television Western* (New York: Praeger, 1987). Brief history of Westerns on the networks. Useful material about the industry, ratings, etc.

Frank Manchel, *Cameras West* (Englewood Cliffs, N.J.: Prentice-Hall, 1971). Insubstantial general history.

Leonard Matthews, *History of Western Movies* (New York: Crescent Books, 1984). Picture book with brief text.

Richard A. Maynard (ed.), *The American West on Film: Myth and Reality* (Rochelle Park, N.J.: Hayden Book Company, Inc., 1974). A brief anthology of writing about Western history and film, produced for educational use.

William R. Meyer, *The Making of the Great Westerns* (New Rochelle, N.Y.: Arlington House, 1979). Contains useful information about the production of some well-known Westerns.

Don Miller, *Hollywood Corral* (New York: Popular Library, 1976). As good a guide as any to the series and B-Westerns.

Lee O. Miller, *The Great Cowboy Stars of Movies and Television* (New Rochelle, N.Y.: Arlington House, 1979). Yet another combination of biography, critical appreciation and filmography. More thorough than most.

Jack Nachbar (ed.), *Focus on the Western* (Englewood Cliffs, N.J.: Prentice-Hall, 1974). Useful collection of reprinted critical essays.

James Robert Parish, *Great Western Stars* (New York: Ace Books, 1976). Brief, not always reliable biographies of around 25 stars, with adequate filmographies.

James Robert Parish and Michael R. Pitts, *The Great Western Pictures* (Metuchen, N.J.: Scarecrow Press, 1976). Brief credits, plots and production information for around 300 films, redundant since the publication of Hardy.

Michael Parkinson and Clyde Jeavons, *A Pictorial History of Westerns* (London: Hamlyn, 1972). Just what it claims to be.

Rita Parks, *The Western Hero in Film and Television* (Ann Arbor: UMI Research Press, 1982). Covers theory and history of the Western in both film and TV in 150 pages; written by a nun.

William T. Pilkington and Don Graham (eds.), *Western Movies* (Albuquerque: University of New Mexico Press, 1979). Critical essays on a dozen well-known Westerns.

Jean-Louis Rieupeyrout, *La Grande aventure du Western* (Paris: Editions du Cerf, 1964). General history of the Western, grounding its cinematic evolution in the history of the American West. Unfortunately, never translated.

David Rothel, *The Singing Cowboys* (New York: A. S. Barnes, 1978). Appreciations of major and minor stars with thorough filmographies.

David Rothel, *Those Great Cowboy Sidekicks* (Metuchen, N.J. Scarecrow Press, 1984). Detailed filmographies and biographies on sidekick superstars such as Gabby Hayes and Smiley Burnette, and lots of others.

Wayne Michael Sarf, *God Bless You, Buffalo Bill* (East Brunswick, N.J.: Associated Universities Presses, 1983). Relentlessly jokey attempt to tell reality behind Hollywood versions of Western history.

Jon Tuska, *The Filming of the West* (Garden City, N.Y.: Doubleday & Co., 1976). Mainly a production history, based on a hundred key films. Contains a great deal of indispensable information.

Jon Tuska, *The American West in Film* (Westport, Conn.: Greenwood Press, 1985). Argumentative, occasionally perverse general account, much of it concerned with the gap between the reality of history and the fictional treatment of Billy the Kid, Jesse James, etc.

Robert Warshow, *The Immediate Experience* (Garden City, N.Y.: Anchor Books, 1964). Contains Warshow's influential essay 'Movie Chronicle: The Westerner'.

Will Wright, *Six Guns and Society* (Berkeley: University of California Press, 1975). Bold attempt at a structural study of the plots of popular Westerns, relating them to changes in American society.

2. HISTORY OF THE WEST

This is a vast subject. A comprehensive list of books would be out of place here; instead, a selection is offered of those most likely to be of service to students of the Western.

a) REFERENCE

Howard R. Lamar (ed.), *The Reader's Encyclopedia of the American West* (New York: Thomas Y. Cromwell Company, 1977). Thorough, reliable and comprehensive work of reference.

Michael P. Malone (ed.), *Historians and the American West* (Lincoln: University of Nebraska Press, 1983). Useful up-to-date guide to the historical literature by a score of experts.

Jon Tuska and Vicki Piekarski, *The Frontier Experience: A Reader's Guide to the Life and Literature of the American West* (Jefferson, N.C.: McFarland, 1984). Valuable annotated bibliography of western history, fiction and cinema, but too opinionated to inspire complete confidence, and marred by an obsessive idea that Westerns are better the more historically accurate they are.

b) GENERAL HISTORY

Ray Allen Billington, *Westward Expansion: A History of the American Frontier* (New York: Macmillan, 1982). Now in its fifth edition, this is still the most detailed general history.

Robert V. Hine, *The American West: An Interpretive History* (Boston: Little, Brown, 1973). Contains chapters on churches, schools and popular culture, as well as economic and social history.

Frederick Jackson Turner, *The Frontier in American History* (New York: Holt, Rinehart and Winston, 1962). Collection of the essays in which Turner advanced his famous 'Frontier Thesis'.

Walter Prescott Webb, *The Great Plains* (Waltham, Mass.: Ginn, 1931). Highly influential description of the plains as a unique environment determining its own distinctive culture.

c) SPECIAL TOPICS

Agriculture. Gilbert C. Fite, *The Farmers' Frontier 1865-1900* (New York: Holt, Rinehart and Winston, 1966). Reliable synthesis of the progress of agriculture throughout the West.

Everett Dick, *The Sod-House Frontier 1854-1890* (New York: Appleton-Century, 1937). Social history of agriculture on the plains.

Army. Robert Utley, *Frontiersmen in Blue: The United States Army and the Indian 1848-1865* (New York: Macmillan, 1967).

Robert Utley, *Frontier Regulars: The United States Army and the Indian 1866–1891* (New York: Macmillan, 1973). Thorough accounts of the Indian wars, though very much taking the army's side.

Billy the Kid. Stephen Tatum, *Inventing Billy the Kid: Visions of the Outlaw in America, 1881-1981* (Albuquerque: University of New Mexico Press, 1982). A model study of the Kid and the relationship between Western reality and imagination.

Blacks. W. Sherman Savage, *Blacks in the West* (Westport, Conn.: Greenwood Press, 1976). Useful short history.

Buffalo Bill. Don Russell, *The Lives and Legends of Buffalo Bill* (Norman: University of Oklahoma Press, 1960). The standard biography.

Canada. Douglas Hill, *The Opening of the Canadian West* (New York: John Day Company, 1967). Very readable account of another frontier.

Cowboys. Robert Dykstra, *The Cattle Towns* (New York: Knopf, 1968). Detailed history of Dodge City and other cow towns, dispelling many myths.

Joe B. Frantz and Julian E. Choate, *The American Cowboy: The Myth and the Reality* (Norman: University of Oklahoma Press, 1955). Now a little out-of-date, but still a useful account.

William W. Savage, *Cowboy Life: Reconstructing an American Myth* (Norman: University of Oklahoma Press, 1975). Well-chosen anthology of early writings about cowboys. Good illustrations.

William W. Savage, *The Cowboy Hero: His Image in American History and Culture* (Norman: University of Oklahoma Press, 1979). Stimulating account of how the image of the cowboy is central to much American popular culture.

Lonn Taylor and Ingrid Marr, *The American Cowboy* (Washington: Library of Congress, 1983). Catalogue of an exhibition organized by the Library of Congress; contains wonderful illustrations and much useful historical information.

Custer. Evan S. Connell, *Son of the Morning Star* (New York: Harper and Row, 1984). The most recent, most detailed and best written account of Custer's life and death.

Emigrants. John D. Unruh Jr, *The Plains Across: The Overland Emigrants and the Trans-Mississippi West 1840-60* (Urbana: University of Illinois Press, 1979). Superlative account of emigrants on the Overland Trail.

Europeans. Ray Allen Billington, *Land of Savagery, Land of Promise: The European Image of the American Frontier in the Nineteenth Century* (New York: W. W. Norton, 1980). Mainly a study of popular European fiction about the West.

Exploration. William H. Goetzmann, *Exploration and Empire: The Explorer and the Scientist in the Winning of the American West* (New York: Knopf, 1966). Panoramic study of nineteenth-century exploration.

Indians/Native Americans. Robert Berkhofer Jr., *The White Man's Indian* (New York: Vintage Books, 1979). A history of the stereotypes of the Indian constructed by whites.

Richard Drinnon, *Facing West: The Metaphysics of Indian-hating and Empire-building* (New York: New American Library, 1980). Argues that America's policy towards its Indians has been driven by the same forces that have shaped its aggressive foreign policy.

Peter Matthiessen, *Indian Country* (London: Fontana, 1986). Brilliant and angry exposé of the plight of Indians in contemporary America.

Wilcomb E. Washburn, *The Indian in America* (New York: Harper and Row, 1975). Good, straightforward general history.

Jesse James. William A. Settle, *Jesse James Was His Name* (Columbia: University of Missouri Press, 1966). Definitive account of the West's definitive outlaw.

Law and order; Violence. Wayne Gard, *Frontier Justice* (Norman: University of Oklahoma Press, 1949). General history of the administration of justice, with chapters on such topics as vigilantism, the Texas Rangers, the Johnson County War. Reliable.

W. Eugene Hollon, *Frontier Violence: Another Look* (New York: Oxford University Press, 1974). A valuable corrective to first impressions, finding that while the violence of cow towns was exaggerated, other violence such as that towards racial minorities has been ignored.

Bill O'Neal, *Encyclopedia of Western Gunfighters* (Norman: University of Oklahoma Press, 1979). Very useful compilation of biographies of several score of gunfighters.

Joseph. G. Rosa, *The Gunfighter: Man or Myth* (Norman: University of Oklahoma Press, 1969). One of the best of many books attempting to tell the truth about Western gunfighters.

Richard Slotkin, *Regeneration Through Violence: The Mythology of the American Frontier 1600-1860* (Middletown: Wesleyan University Press, 1973). Brilliant history of the role of the frontier in the American imagination.

Helena Huntingdon Smith, *The War on Powder River* (New York: McGraw-Hill, 1966). The standard work on the Johnson County War.

Kent Ladd Steckmesser, *The Western Hero in History and Legend* (Norman: University of Oklahoma Press, 1965). Sifts fact from fiction in the biographies of Billy the Kid, Wild Bill Hickok, Kit Carson and General Custer.

Mexico. John Womack Jr., *Zapata and the Mexican Revolution* (New York: Alfred A. Knopf, 1969). Well-written account of the events which make most impact on those Westerns set in Mexico.

Mining. J. S. Holliday, *The World Rushed In: The California Gold Rush Experience* (New York: Simon and Schuster, 1981). Brilliant description of the gold rush, based in part on a contemporary diary.

Rodman W. Paul, *Mining Frontiers of the Far West 1848-1880* (New York: Holt, Rinehart and Winston, 1963). Probably the best single volume on a large topic.

Mountain men. Bernard DeVoto, *Across the Wide Missouri* (Boston: Houghton Mifflin, 1947). Attractively written account of western fur trappers in the 1830s.

Dale L. Morgan, *Jedediah Smith and the Opening of the West* (Indianapolis: Bobbs-Merrill, 1953). A biography of the greatest of the mountain men and a major contribution to the history of the West.

Railroads. Robert G. Athearn, *Union Pacific Country* (Chicago: Rand McNally, 1971). Scholarly history of the UP railroad which takes a very positive view of its role in western expansion.

Dee Brown, *Hear That Lonesome Whistle Blow – Railroads in the West* (New York: Holt, Rinehart, 1977). Popularly written but informative history of western railroads.

Transportation. Oscar O. Winther, *The Transportation Frontier 1865-1890* (New York: Holt, Rinehart and Winston, 1964). Useful synthesis of information on wagon trails, stagecoach lines and railroads.

Wild Bill Hickok. Joseph G. Rosa, *They Called Him Wild Bill* (Norman: University of Oklahoma Press, 1964). The standard biography, a model of painstaking research.

Women. Sandra L. Myers, *Westering Women and the Frontier Experience 1800-1915* (Albuquerque: University of New Mexico Press, 1982). One of the best of several books belatedly recording women's contribution to the history of the West.

Miscellaneous. Leo Marx, *The Machine in the Garden: Technology and the Pastoral Ideal in America* (New York: Oxford University Press, 1967). Stimulating essay on a topic which has many implications for the study of the Western.

3. CULTURAL HISTORY

a) REFERENCE

Peggy & Harold Samuels, *The Illustrated Biographical Encyclopedia of Artists of the American West* (Garden City, N.Y.: Doubleday, 1976). The standard reference work on painters.

Jon Tuska and Vicki Piekarski (eds.), *Encyclopedia of Frontier and Western Fiction* (New York: McGraw-Hill, 1983). Useful and reliable guide to Western fiction of the 19th and 20th centuries.

James Vinson (ed.), *Twentieth-Century Western Writers* (London: Macmillan, 1982). Much larger than the volume above, with many more writers, though not always authoritative.

b) CRITICISM AND HISTORY

Christine Bold, *Selling the Wild West: Popular Western Fiction 1860-1960* (Bloomington: Indiana University Press, 1987). Invaluable account of formula novelists from Owen Wister to Louis L'Amour and after; especially good on Zane Grey and Max Brand.

James K. Folsom (ed.), *The Western: A Collection of Critical Essays* (Englewood Cliffs, N.J.: Prentice-Hall, 1979). Interesting though patchy assembly of writing on Western fiction.

William H. Goetzmann and William N. Goetzmann, *The West of the Imagination* (New York: W. W. Norton, 1986). Published as the companion to a PBS television series, a well-written history of the image of the West as produced by painters and photographers.

Daryl Jones, *The Dime Novel Western* (Bowling Green, Ohio: Bowling Green University Popular Press, 1978). Informative account of a key influence on the Western film.

Henry Nash Smith, *Virgin Land* (Cambridge, Mass.: Harvard University Press, 1950). Seminal account of what the West represented in the American imagination of the 19th century. A powerful influence on Jim Kitses and others writing about the Western in the 1960s.

Robert Taft, *Photography and the American Scene* (New York: Dover, 1964). Social history of American photography in the 19th century, with much detailed information about photography in the West.

ACKNOWLEDGMENTS

The following are gratefully acknowledged for permission to reproduce pictures: The Library of Congress (pp. 102, 104, 106, 109, 162, 173, 189, 201, 218); National Archives and Records Administration (pp. 56, 65, 85, 91, 130, 200); The New York Public Library at Lincoln Center (pp. 79, 239); The National Portrait Gallery, Smithsonian Institution (pp. 57, 104); Smithsonian Institution National Anthropological Archives (pp. 61, 164, 205, 209, 244); National Park Service (p. 223); The Beinecke Rare Book and Manuscript Library, Yale University Library (p. 207); Instituto Nacional de Antropologia y Historia, Mexico (pp. 153, 180, 232, 246); Courtesy of the Buffalo Bill Historical Center, Cody, WY (pp. 75, 92, 95, 113, 207, 217, 227, 239, 240); Public Archives Canada (p. 155, C-7866); Museum of the City of New York (pp. 56, 87, 190); Metropolitan Museum of Art, New York (pp. 67, 216); Wadsworth Atheneum, Hartford (Joseph Szaszfal, photog.) (p. 79); Museum of New Mexico (p. 81); State Historical Society of Missouri, Columbia (pp. 162, 245); Pinkerton's Inc. (pp. 83, 202); The Huntington Library, San Marino, California (p. 190); California State Library (p. 85); AGS Collection, University of Wisconsin-Milwaukee Library (p. 237); Washington University Gallery of Art, St. Louis (p. 71);

The Denver Public Library, Western History Department (pp. 116, 126, 127, 147, 150, 161, 197, 220, 223); The Bancroft Library (p. 198); Amon Carter Museum, Fort Worth (pp. 59, 62, 160); American Heritage Center, University of Wyoming, Laramie, Wyoming (pp. 76, 240); Kansas State Historical Society (pp. 74, 107, 111, 196); Montana Historical Society (pp. 145, 230); The Taft Museum, Cincinnati, Ohio (p. 122); Royal Ontario Museum, Toronto (p. 164); Nebraska State Historical Society (p. 68); The New York Historical Society (p. 129); Mrs Martha Hyer Wallis (p. 211); The Whyte Museum of the Canadian Rockies (p. 77); The Oakland Museum (pp. 201, 207); Museum of Modern Art Film Stills Archive (pp. 41, 97, 151, 157, 178, 240, 244, 292, 294); Harvard College Library (p. 214); Joslyn Art Museum, Omaha, Nebraska (p. 192); Western History Collections, University of Oklahoma (pp. 66, 69, 129, 167); Frederic Remington Art Museum, Ogdensburg, New York (p. 214); Library of the University of Exeter (pp. 105, 155, 170); Will Rogers Memorial, Claremore, Oklahoma (p. 213); Oklahoma Historical Society (p. 223); Arizona Historical Society (pp. 114, 149).

COLOUR PLATES: 1, 8: Architect of the Capitol; 2: Enron Art Foundation, Joslyn Art Museum, Omaha, Nebraska; 3: (C-426) Picture Division, Public Archives Canada, Ottawa; 4, 15, 20: The Thomas Gilcrease Institute of American History and Art, Tulsa, Oklahoma; 5: Wadsworth Atheneum, Hartford; 6, 7: Museum of the City of New York; 9: University of Michigan Museum of Art; 10: The Butler Institute of American Art, Youngstown, Ohio; 11: The Metropolitan Museum of Art, Rogers Fund, 1907; 12: National Museum of American Art, Smithsonian Institution; 13: Metropolitan Museum of Art; 14, 17, 21: Amon Carter Museum, Fort Worth; 16: Courtesy of the Buffalo Bill Historical Center, Cody, WY; 18: Courtesy of Museum of Western Art, Denver, Colorado; 19: Sterling and Francine Clark Art Institute, Williamstown, Massachusetts; 22: The Rockwell Museum, Corning, New York.
FILM STILLS courtesy of Allied Artists; Avco-Embassy; Cinerama; Columbia; Dino De Laurentiis; George Eastman House; ITC; Lippert; Mercury Pictures; MGM; Museum of Modern Art; National Film Archive Stills Collection; National General; Paramount; Rank; Republic; RKO; Tigon-British; 20th Century-Fox; United Artists; Universal; Vagabond; Warner Bros.

ALTERNATIVE TITLES

This list gives the original titles (in italics) of films also known under another name.

Aces High: *Il quattro dell' Ave Maria*
Among Vultures: *Unter Geiern*
Another Man, Another Chance: *Un Autre homme, une autre chance*
Antonio-das-Mortes: *O dragao da maldade contra o santo guerreiro*
Apache Gold: *Winnetou*
The Apaches' Last Battle: *Shatterhand*
The Avenger: *Texas addio*
Beyond the Law: *Al di là della legge*
The Big and the Bad: *Si pùo fare, amigo*
Big Deal at Dodge City: *A Big Hand for the Little Lady*
The Big Gundown: *La resa dei conti*
The Bounty Hunters: *Indio Black, sai che ti dico: sei un gran figlio di . . .*
Buffalo Bill, Hero of the Far West: *Buffalo Bill, l'eroe del west*
A Bullet for the General: *Quien sabe?*
Cactus Jack: *The Villain*
Canyon Pass: *Raton Pass*
Compañeros: *Vamos a matar, compañeros!*
Company of Cowards: *Advance to the Rear*
The Con Men: *Te Deum*
Dan Candy's Law: *Alien Thunder*
Day of Anger: *I giorni dell'ira*
Dead or Alive: *Escondido*
Deaf Smith and Johnny Ears: *Los amigos*
Death Rides a Horse: *Da uomo a uomo*
The Deserter: *La spina dorsale del diavolo*

The Desperado Trail: *Winnetou III*
Duck, You Sucker: *Giù la testa*
The Dynamite Man from Glory Jail: *Fools' Parade*
Face to Face: *Faccia a faccia*
A Fistful of Dollars: *Per un pugno di dollari*
A Fistful of Dynamite: *Giù la testa*
Five Giants from Texas: *I cinque della vendetta*
The Five Man Army: *Un esercito di 5 uomini*
For a Few Dollars More: *Per qualche dollaro in più*
The Good, the Bad and the Ugly: *Il buono, il brutto, il cattivo*
Gringo: *Duello nel Texas*
Gunfight at Red Sands: *Duello nel Texas*
Guns in the Afternoon: *Ride the High Country*
Hate for Hate: *Odio per odio*
The Hellbenders: *I crudeli*
The Hills Run Red: *Un fiume di dollari*
Hollywood Cowboy: *Hearts of the West*
The James Brothers: *The True Story of Jesse James*
Kill Them All and Come Back Alone: *Ammazzali tutti e torna solo*
Killer on a Horse: *Welcome to Hard Times*
Last of the Renegades: *Winnetou II*
The Last Rebel: *El ultimo rebelde*
The Last Tomahawk: *Der letzte Mohikaner*
The Last Warrior: *Flap*
A Man Called Sledge: *Sledge*
Man Hunt: *From Hell to Texas*
The Man Who Killed Billy the Kid: *El hombre que matao Billy el niño*
Murrieta: *Joaquin Murrieta*
My Name Is Nobody: *Il mio nome è Nessuno*
The New Land: *Nybyggarna*
Old Shatterhand: *Shatterhand*

Once Upon a Time in the West: *C'era una volta il west*
A Pistol for Ringo: *Una pistola per Ringo*
The Pistolero of Red River: *The Last Challenge*
Pistols Don't Say No: *La pistola non discutono*
A Professional Gun: *Il mercenario*
A Reason to Live, a Reason to Die: *Una ragione per vivere e una per morire*
Red Sun: *Soleil rouge*
The Return of Ringo: *Il ritorno di Ringo*
Return of Sabata: *E tornato Sabata . . . hai chiuso un'altra volta*
Revenge at El Paso: *Il quattro dell' Ave Maria*
Sabata: *Ehi, amico . . . c'è Sabata, hai chiuso!*
Savage Pampas: *Pampa salvaje*
Seven Guns for the MacGregors: *Sette pistole per i Mac Gregor*
Southwest to Sonora: *The Appaloosa*
They Call Me Trinity: *Lo chiamavano Trinità*
Thunder at the Border: *Winnetou und sein Freund Old Firehand*
Train to Durango: *Un treno per Durango*
The Tramplers: *Gli uomini dal passo pesante*
The Treasure of Silver Lake: *Der Schatz im Silbersee*
Trinity Is Still My Name: *Continuavano a chiamarlo Trinità*
The Valdez Horses: *Valdez il mezzosangue*
Valdez the Halfbreed: *Valdez il mezzosangue*
Vendetta: *Joaquin Murrieta*
Vengeance Is Mine: *Quei disperati che puzzano di sudore e di morte*
War of the Wildcats: *In Old Oklahoma*
Where the River Bends: *Bend of the River*
The White Man: *The Squaw Man*
Winnetou the Warrior: *Winnetou*

THE END